FINANCIAL TIMES

HANDBOOK OF MANAGEMENT

THIRD EDITION

In an increasingly competitive world, we believe it's quality of thinking that will give you the edge – an idea that opens new doors, a technique that solves a problem, or an insight that simply makes sense of it all. The more you know, the smarter and faster you can go.

That's why we work with the best minds in business and finance to bring cutting-edge thinking and best learning practice to a global market.

Under a range of leading imprints, including *Financial Times Prentice Hall*, we create world-class print publications and electronic products bringing our readers knowledge, skills and understanding which can be applied whether studying or at work.

To find out more about Pearson Education publications, or tell us about the books you'd like to find, you can visit us at
www.pearsoned.co.uk

FINANCIAL TIMES
HANDBOOK OF MANAGEMENT

THIRD EDITION

Edited by
Stuart Crainer and Des Dearlove

PEARSON EDUCATION LIMITED

Edinburgh Gate
Harlow CM20 2JE
Tel: +44 (0)1279 623623
Fax: +44 (0)1279 431059

First published in Great Britain in 1995
Second edition published in 2001
This edition published 2004

© Longman Group UK Limited 1995
© Pearson Education Limited 2000, 2004

ISBN 0 273 67584 2

British Library Cataloguing in Publication Data
A CIP catalogue record for this book can be obtained from the British Library

Library of Congress Cataloging-in-Publication Data
Financial times handbook of management / [editors], Stuart Crainer and Des Dearlove.—
3rd ed.
    p. cm.
  Includes bibliographical references and index.
  ISBN 0-273-67584-2 (alk. paper)
   1. Industrial management—Handbooks, manuals, etc. 2. Management—Handbooks, manuals, etc. I. Title: Handbook of management. II. Crainer, Stuart. III. Dearlove, Des. IV. Financial times (London, England)

HD38.15.F56 2004
658—dc22   2004040072

All rights reserved; no part of this publication may be reproduced, stored
in a retrieval system, or transmitted in any form or by any means, electronic,
mechanical, photocopying, recording, or otherwise without either the prior
written permission of the Publishers or a licence permitting restricted copying
in the United Kingdom issued by the Copyright Licensing Agency Ltd,
90 Tottenham Court Road, London W1T 4LP. This book may not be lent,
resold, hired out or otherwise disposed of by way of trade in any form
of binding or cover other than that in which it is published, without the
prior consent of the Publishers.

All trademarks used herein are the property of their respective owners.
The use of any trademark in this text does not vest in the author or
publisher any trademark ownership rights in such trademarks, nor does
the use of such trademarks imply any affiliation with or endorsement of
this book by such owners.

10 9 8 7 6 5 4 3 2 1

Typeset by 30
Printed and bound in Great Britain by Biddles Ltd, Guildford & King's Lynn

The Publishers' policy is to use paper manufactured from sustainable forests.

For Ro & Sara

Contents

Foreword	xv
Preface	xix
Acknowledgements	xx
Publisher's Acknowledgements	xxi

ONE: The state of the art

Management in the 21st century — 1

The rise of management: Stuart Crainer and Des Dearlove	5
The age of the individual: Jonas Ridderstråle and Kjell Nordström	15
The new knowledge landscape: Leif Edvinsson	19
A message to Garcia: Thomas L. Brown	24

Essentials: — 30
Peter Drucker; Henri Fayol; Adam Smith; Frederick W. Taylor

TWO: Foundations of management

1. Strategy and competition — 39

Strategy and control: John Kay	41
What is strategy and how do you know if you have one?: Costas Markides	48
Trajectory Management: Paul Strebel and Anne-Valérie Ohlsson	57
Making mergers and acquisitions work: Roger Pudney	63

Star Trek strategy: Peter Brews   71
Strategy and structure redux: Jorge Nascimento Rodrigues   86
Interview: C.K. Prahalad   91
Strategy in the knowledge economy: W. Chan Kim and Renée Mauborgne   96

Essentials: *100*

Igor Ansoff; balanced scorecard; Boston Matrix; Game Theory; Gary Hamel; Bruce Henderson; Henry Mintzberg; Richard Pascale; Michael Porter; scenario planning; Seven S framework; strategic inflection point; Sun Tzu

2. Globalization   117

Can globalization be fixed?: Deborah Doane   118
Strategies for China: Jonathan Story   127
Great global managers: Karl Moore   141
Transnational corporations: international citizens or new sovereigns?:
Dennis A. Rondinelli   147
Interview: Yves Doz and José Santos   160

Essentials: *164*

Geert Hofstede; Akio Morita; Kenichi Ohmae transnational corporations; Fons Trompenaars

3. Managing human resources   173

What managers do: David W. Birchall   175
Leading the democratic enterprise: Lynda Gratton   193
Succeeding at succession: Des Dearlove and Steve Coomber   204
Commentary: When employees attack   210
The management of humor and the humor of management:
David L. Collinson   212
Recruiting, selecting, and compensating board members:
Charles H. King and Caroline W. Nahas   217
Non-coercive thinking: Henri J. Ruff   221

Essentials: *225*

broadbanding; downsizing; empowerment; Mary Parker Follett; Frederick Herzberg; interim management; Jaques Elliott; Rosabeth Moss Kanter; the Managerial Grid; Maslow's Hierarchy of Needs; Elton Mayo; David Packard; Tom Peters; psychological contract; Edgar Schein; succession planning; Theories X and Y (and Z); 360-degree feedback

4. Operations and service   247

The laws of logistics and supply chain management:
Alan Braithwaite and Richard Wilding   249
Performance measurement: the new crisis: Andy Neely   260
Design to be different: Kjell Nordström and Jonas Ridderstråle   266
Outsourcing HR: Stephen Coomber   276
Interview: Andrew Kakabadse   278
Project management as value creation: Sebastian Nokes   281
The quality revolution: Stuart Crainer and Des Dearlove   290
Understanding the sources and drivers of supply chain risk: Helen Peck   300

Essentials: *309*
benchmarking; channel management; crisis management; W. Edwards Deming; Henry Ford; Joseph Juran; just-in-time (JIT); kaizen (quality circles); lean production; outsourcing; reengineering; supply chain management; time-based competition; total quality management

5. Marketing   326

Challenging the mental models of marketing: Yoram (Jerry) Wind   327
Marketing with a hard edge: Peter Fisk   336
Interview: Philip Kotler   350
Designing the market-facing organization: Sam Hill,
David Newkirk and Jong Chow   354
Understanding brand potential: Watts Wacker   362
Global marketing: H. David Hennessey   366
Capturing growth through lifetime customer value:
Sandra Vandermerwe   371
Interview: Chris Zook   383
Eleven misconceptions about customer relationship management:
Peter C. Verhoef and Fred Langerak   387
Seven of the best: Tony Cram   401
Connecting brand equity, brand economics, and brand value:
David Haigh   408
Corporate religion: Jesper Kunde   420

Essentials: *423*
affiliate marketing; Four Ps of marketing; Philip Kotler; Ted Levitt; permission marketing; relationship marketing

6. Finance   432

Better pricing processes for higher profits: Hermann Simon,
Stephan A. Butscher and Karl-Heinz Sebastian   433

Forecasting financials: Mark Whittington and Ken Bates	441
Commentary: The rise of the Chief Risk Officer	452
Financial literacy: understanding the numbers: Romesh Vaitilingam	455
The real Warren Buffett: James O'Loughlin	458
Marketing: the trouble with finance: Tim Ambler	465
Earnings – its role in assessing performance and value: Mike Cahill	479
Fools, gold, and greed: Gerry Griffin and Ciaran Parker	490

Essentials: *495*
activity-based costing; discounted cash flow; shareholder value

7. Organization 501

The secrets of success: Stuart Crainer and Des Dearlove	502
The new boy network: Georgina Peters	505
The integrated organization: Fons Trompenaars and Peter Wooliams	513
Commentary: Piling on the pounds	519
Organizational democracy and organizational politics: David Butcher and Martin Clarke	521
Capitalizing in on corporate competencies: Jonas Ridderstråle	531
Towards a networked economy: Seven management lessons from Microsoft: Jamie Anderson and Robin Wood	547
Commentary: What companies do wrong	555
Interview: Charles Handy	558

Essentials: *561*
adhocracy; agility; Chester Barnard; core competencies; Harold Geneen; Charles Handy; matrix model; shamrock organization; the virtual organization; Max Weber

8. Ideas, information, and knowledge 574

Open innovation: Henry Chesbrough	575
The 21st-century CIO: Mark Polansky with Tarun Inuganti and Simon Wiggins	581
Whose ideas are they anyway?: Stuart Crainer and Des Dearlove	587
The strategic potential of a firm's knowledge portfolio: David Birchall and George Tovstiga	594
Segmenting and destroying knowledge: Kevin C. Desouza	601
Interview: Sumantra Ghoshal	604
Securing information: governance issues: Jean-Noël Ezingeard and David Birchall	608

Essentials: 615
disintermediation; dynamic pricing; e-commerce; incubator; intellectual capital; intellectual property; knowledge management; Alvin Toffler

9. Entrepreneurship 625

The entrepreneur: Stuart Crainer and Des Dearlove	626
Commentary: Pitching and catching	631
Interview: Liam Black	633
Social entrepreneurship: The emerging landscape: Alex Nicholls	636
Commentary: The best of the fringe	644
Interview: Jeff Skoll	647
Where do good ideas come from?: John W. Mullins	650
Making corporate venturing work: Julian Birkinshaw	654

10. Ethics 658

Do principles count?: Eleanor R.E. O'Higgins	659
War and the corporation: Eric W. Orts	667
Commentary: Is corporate responsibility worth it?	677
Wanted: Boardroom coach: Susan Bloch	679
Commentary: Profiting from corporate philanthropy	687
Pathways to commitment: Values-driven performance: Matthew May	689
The changing role of business: Lance Moir	694
Interview: Robert A.G. Monks	699

THREE: Management skills

1. Managing globally 705

Doing business the American way: Allyson Stewart-Allen	706
Commentary: The art of Swedish leadership	714
Global account management: H. David Hennessey	716
Interview: John Micklethwait and Adrian Wooldridge	721
Interview: Fons Trompenaars	724
Commentary: Things to do in airports	728
Commentary: Traveling light	730

2. Leading 733

Leadership for the future: Des Dearlove	734
Commentary: What do CEOs really do?	738

Interview: Paul C. Reilly	741
Leadership roles and role models: Randall P. White and Phil Hodgson	745
The mantle of authority: Rob Goffee and Gareth Jones	755
Commentary: Wrinkles and the leader	761
Leading the way: Robert P. Gandossy and Marc Effron	763
Interview: Michael Critelli	773
Value leadership: The principles driving corporate value: Peter S. Cohan	777
Welcome to the real world – eight essential perspectives for the new top leader: Phil Hodgson	784
If Colin Powell had commanded Enron: The hidden foundation of leadership: Oren Harari and Lynn Brewer	790
Interview: Warren Bennis	801

Essentials: *805*
Warren Bennis; employability; the Peter Principle; Robert Townsend

3. Managing change   811

The reality of transformation: Tony Eccles	812
Commentary: Tipping over the edge	819
Interview: James Champy	821
When two companies become one: Andreas Hinterhuber	824
The myths of change management: Michael Jarrett	834
Interview: Rosabeth Moss Kanter	846

4. Communicating   850

Creating Strategic Dialog: Dan Yankelovich and Steve Rosell	851
The write stuff: Stuart Crainer and Des Dearlove	856
Commentary: Silence can be golden	864
Communicating in the age of consent: Mark Stuart	866
Commentary: We're blogging it	877

5. Managing yourself and your career   879

Who are you?: Georgina Peters	880
Commentary: Who gets training?	892
Generational Shift™: Bruce Tulgan	894
Interview: Alan Briskin	903
Personal agility: Elizabeth Weldon	905
Commentary: Beware burnout	910

Essentials:	*916*
Dale Carnegie; Niccolo Machiavelli	

6. Making it happen — 919

H.O.T. Management™: Bruce Tulgan	920
Decision making: risk and escalation: Helga Drummond	929
Measuring and managing the right things: Mike Kennerley and Andy Neely	938
Valuing the business – the use of enterprise value: Mike Cahill	945
Making projects fly: Stephen Carver	953
The rise and fall of the COO: Stuart Crainer and Des Dearlove	959
Commentary: Garageland	965
Essentials:	*968*
Decision theory	

7. Developing and learning — 971

Executive coaching: Laurence S. Lyons	972
Improving on success: Marshall Goldsmith	983
So you think you want to be coached?: Mick Cope	994
Training and development – new approaches for changing needs: David Birchall and Matty Smith	1005
Commentary: Mentoring	1012
Essentials:	*1019*
action learning; Chris Argyris; the learning organization; Kurt Lewin; thought leadership	

FOUR: Resources

50 great management decisions	1029
80 books all managers should read	1036
50 concepts all managers should be familiar with	1041
Six classic cases: Julian Birkinshaw	1044
Contributors	1053
Top lists	1068
Index	1075

Foreword

Michael Skapinker
Management Editor, Financial Times

In the opening chapter of this book, Stuart Crainer and Des Dearlove say that management began as soon as civilisation did. Advice and ideas on how to manage – which this book sets out to provide – began soon after that. The first recorded management adviser that I have been able to locate was Joseph, wearer of the coat of many colours, in the Book of Genesis.

Having acquired a reputation as a reliable interpreter of dreams during a spell in an Egyptian prison, Joseph found himself summoned to Pharaoh's palace. Pharaoh asked Joseph to tell him the meaning of two dreams. In the first, seven plump cows emerged from the river and began to graze in a meadow. They were followed by seven thin and scrawny cows, which ate the fat ones. In the second dream, seven thin ears of corn devoured seven fat ones. What did Joseph make of all this?

Easy, he said. Egypt would enjoy seven years of plenty, followed by seven years of famine. What Pharaoh needed to do was to look for a man "discreet and wise" to organize the storing of enough food during the good years to see Egypt through the bad. Pharaoh asked his servants if they could think of any discreet and wise men who could fit the bill. But before they had time to reply, his eyes alighted on Joseph. 'There is none so discreet and wise as thou art," he said, appointing him to implement his own plan. This made Joseph not only the first management consultant in recorded history, but the first to convert his consulting expertise into a top-level management position, along with the attendant perks, including a company car just a notch below the chairman's – or the "second chariot", as Genesis called it. As for the servants who failed to come up with a short-list of alternative discreet and wise men before Pharaoh settled on Joseph: they missed their opportunity to become humankind's first executive search consultants.

Pharaoh's dreams were a puzzle to him and did not give Joseph much to go on. Managers in later centuries would find themselves with little more hard data on which to base their decisions. This is why managers have always found their jobs so difficult: existing conditions are always subject to many interpretations and the future is desperately uncertain.

Or, as a senior executive of one of Britain's most illustrious organizations said to me when I was appointed the Financial Times's Management Editor in 2000: "Your job exists for the same reason that business books and business schools and management consultants exist: no one has a clue how to manage."

That senior executive resigned his post soon afterwards, deeply frustrated by his inability to persuade the organization, its managers and employees of the need to change. But his "no one has a clue" lament was not true. There have been many successful managers over the years: the sophisticated and generally smooth-running societies of the developed, democratic world would have been impossible without them. But within those societies are many management failures too: any list of the top 50 companies contains few names that were there 50 years before.

What my senior executive friend was right about was that there are few enduring truths in management. Conglomerates, for example, were once the rage; their benefit was their supposed ability to ensure that cyclical weakness in one business was balanced by strength in another. But this gave way to the next idea, which was that companies should focus on what they did best, leaving it to investors to decide how to allocate their money to balance their risk. Conglomerates were out of fashion – except that some of the most admired companies in the world today, including General Electric and Berkshire Hathaway, are multi-business conglomerates.

The same change in fashion occurred in the management of people. Frederick Taylor and Henry Ford had an instrumental approach to employees: they could be measured, managed and used in the same way as machines could (except that, even then, Ford understood that if you paid your workers enough they could afford to buy your cars). The development of service and research-based businesses, along with more sophisticated manufacturing enterprises, meant that companies had to rely more on the knowledge, intuition and initiative of their staff, leading to the growth of the human resourced movement and the late-twentieth century management cliché: "our most important asset is our people". That, in turn, was succeeded by the view that those very important people were just too expensive, resulting in the "downsizings" of the 1990s and the outsourcing and "offshoring" of subsequent years.

But if there are few enduring truths in management, there are enduring questions. Indeed, the same ones come up again and again. Shall we make it ourselves or pay others to do so? Shall we concentrate on a discrete customer niche or cut our prices to appeal to a broader market? And shall we bark at our employees to force them to do what we want or shall we treat them as adults who can be relied on to do their best?

There are some who believe that people can be trained to answer these questions before they embark on a career in management. Business schools that offer MBA degrees to young would-be managers set out to do just that. And many of these

MBA graduates go on to great managerial success. Business schools have grown rapidly over the past few decades. Students would not continue to register for their courses if they were not getting something out of it. The research carried out for the *Financial Times's* ranking of business schools, finds that MBA graduates, particularly those from the top schools, earn two to three times what they did before they went to business school. Others, however, scoff at the idea that inexperienced youngsters can be taught to manage in a classroom.

Henry Mintzberg, the renowned management writer and professor at McGill University in Canada, has, for decades, argued that management education works best when it is offered to experienced managers who already know what questions they need answered. Professor Mintzberg's interest in managers and what they do began when, as a child, he puzzled over what his father, the head of a small manufacturing company, did all day. He pursued the question as a doctoral student at the Massachusetts Institute of Technology, observing five managers closely as they went about their work. He discovered that, far from planning, organizing, co-ordinating, commanding and controlling – which is what Henri Fayol, the French mining engineer and management theorist, said they did – managers rushed around from one task to another. In *The Nature of Managerial Work*, the book that Professor Mintzberg based on his doctoral research, he said that what characterized managerial work was "brevity, variety and fragmentation".

Professor Mintzberg argued this had implications for the way managers learnt. Classroom-based lectures were of only limited utility. It was far better for experienced managers to come together and, aided by a facilitator, discuss their experiences and problems, and learn from one another. If there were issues that particularly troubled them, they could explore those with someone who had already found an answer.

This handbook cannot answer every managerial question – because it is only when managers come across a particular problem or confront a particular dilemma that they know what questions to ask. But there are plenty of ideas here, much history and discussion of best practice – whether on how to deal with customers, manage in China or set up a remuneration system for the board.

Management education and reading works best when someone, troubled by a problem at work, comes across an account by someone else and says: "That's it. That's what I need to do." Or perhaps, someone will read something and say: "Ah, so that is what we did." It was only when, some years ago, I began reading Michael Porter's work on clusters that I understood how the *Financial Times* had become so successful internationally, gaining more readers abroad than it had in its home market, the UK.

Professor Porter said these local clusters of businesses – ceramic tile manufacturers in Italy, for example – competed fiercely against each other, developing a pool of local talent and suppliers, building on their strengths and honing their skills. When these businesses ventured abroad, they were that much stronger and more innovative than the competitors they came across. It reminded me of the way that FT journalists have to make their way in London, the most competitive newspaper market in the world, where 10 daily newspapers compete for readers' attention. Miss a story, and the newsdesk will wake you at home at midnight asking why one of the other papers has something you do not. This sort of competitive pressure certainly made the FT sharper when we began to publish outside the UK – and reading Professor Porter's account of clusters helped me understand how we had got where we were, and set me thinking about what we should do next.

If this handbook sets you thinking about your managerial future – and your past – or simply gives you some ideas or insights you did not have before, it will have done its work.

Preface

We first edited the *Financial Times Handbook of Management* in 1995. At that time compiling a book of some 400,000 words with contributions from around the world was a time-consuming and complex task. Letters were written. Copy was faxed. Reams of paper made their way across the Atlantic and back again.

By the time we worked on the second edition in 1999, the world had changed. E-mail ruled. Ideas and words moved effortlessly and instantly through cyberspace. At the height of the dot-com boom the *Handbook* had new sections covering issues which had been unimagined only a few years previously.

As our experience proves, the world of business and management never stands still. Today's dominant force is tomorrow's sideshow. Fashions and best practice change. The third edition of the *Handbook* is, we hope, a creature of our times, reflecting what matters to managers in organizations in the first decade of the new century. It is the state of the art of management and, as such, is a statement of what preoccupies and concerns managers in organizations.

In addition to capturing the state of management thinking, the *Handbook* aims to help managers do their jobs more effectively. There is a far greater emphasis in this edition on the practicalities of managing. There is an entirely new section on skills. (Indeed, 90 percent of the contents are brand new.) Management is a unique practical and intellectual challenge and this is reflected in the range of issues it now embraces.

We hope that this edition of the *Financial Times Handbook of Management* helps you to think about how you manage in new ways.

Stuart Crainer and Des Dearlove, February 2004

Acknowledgements

While putting together this edition of the *Handbook* has generated less paper, it has still colonized large tranches of cyberspace. We are grateful to Stephen Coomber for his assiduous work in managing the flow of communications with contributors. Georgina Peters added her usual editorial va-va-voom.

Once again we would like to acknowledge Mark Allin who came up with the idea of the *Handbook*. The last two editions have been completed under the publishing guidance of Richard Stagg, a true ideas enthusiast.

Thanks are due to London Business School for permission to use versions of articles which have previously appeared in *Business Strategy Review*.

Most importantly we would like to thank all of the contributors to this and previous editions of the *Handbook*.

Publisher's Acknowledgements

We are grateful to the following for permission to reproduce copyright material:

"Creative Accounting" and "The Executive Commandments" from *THE BOTTOM LINE: A BOOK OF BUSINESS BALLADS* by B. Ramsbottom published by Century. Used by permission of The Random House Group Limited. Figure 1.2 (Part 2) from *Trajectory Management: Leading a Business Over Time*, Figure 10.2, Chapter 10, (Strebel, P., 2003) © John Wiley & Sons Limited. Reproduced with permission; Figures 1.4 and 1.5 (Part 2) from The Ashridge Strategic Management/R.Pudney (The Ashridge Journal, Summer 2003) © 2003, Ashridge (Bonar Law Memorial) Trust; Figures 5.1 and 5.2 (Part 2) from Hard-edged marketing. Published by The Chartered Institute of Marketing 2003. Reproduced with kind permission; Figure 5.7 (Part 2) copyright © 2001, by The Regents of the University of California. Reprinted from the *California Management Review*, Vol. 43, No. 4. By permission of The Regents; Figure 5.8 (Part 2) from Decision Support Systems, Vol 32, Verhoef, P.C. and Donkers, B., 'Predicting customer value: an application in the insurance industry', pp. 189–199, © (2001), with permission from Elsevier; Figures 5.12, 5.13, 5.14, 5.15, 5.16, 5.17, 5.18, 5.19 and 5.20 (Part 2) reproduced from "An Introduction to Brand Equity – How to understand and appreciate brand value and economic impact of brand investment", *Interactive Marketing*, Vol 5 No 1 (Haigh D., 2004) ©Henry Stewart Publications. Figure 10.2 (Part 2) from *The Civil Corporation: The New Economy Of Corporate Citizenship*, Earthscan, (Zadek, S., 2003); Table 3.2 (Part 2) reprinted from *Research in Organizational Behavior*, Vol 17, Creed, W.E.D., Miles R., "Organizational forms and managerial Philosophies: A Descriptive and Analytical Review", pp 333–379, © (1995), with permission from Elsevier; Figure 3.3 (Part 2), source: Pharma Strategy Consulting, reproduced with permission; Figure 7.2 (Part 3) from "Seven Management Lessons from Microsoft", *Business Strategy Review*, Vol 13, Issue 3, pp 28–33 (Anderson J., Wood R., 2002).

In some instances we have been unable to trace the owners of copyright material, and we would appreciate any information that would enable us to do so.

PART ONE

The state of the art

Management in the 21st century

"We know so much more today about workplaces, about marketplaces, and about human beings; yet, given today's tough economic climate, many managers are making huge leaps backwards. They are clamping down, acting reactionary, barking orders. Fear is driving managers to be 'old school' in their behaviors."

Meg Wheatley

"Management means, in the last analysis, the substitution of thought for brawn and muscle, of knowledge for folklore and superstition, and of co-operation for force."

Peter Drucker

"If you ask managers what they do, they will most likely tell you that they plan, organize, co-ordinate and control. Then watch what they do. Don't be surprised if you can't relate what you see to those four words."

Henry Mintzberg

"Management will remain a basic and dominant institution perhaps as long as Western civilization itself survives."

Peter Drucker

"To manage is to forecast and plan, to organize, to command, to co-ordinate and to control."

Henri Fayol

"Management is tasks. Management is discipline. But management is also people. Every achievement of management is the achievement of a manager. Every failure is the failure of a manager. People manage, rather than forces or facts. The vision, dedication and integrity of managers determine whether there is management or mismanagement."

Peter Drucker

"The art of management is to promote people without making them managers."

Bill Gates

"The function which distinguishes the manager above all others is his educational one. The one contribution he is uniquely expected to make is to give others vision and ability to perform. It is vision and more responsibility that, in the last analysis, define the manager."

Peter Drucker

The rise of management

STUART CRAINER AND DES DEARLOVE

[Management has always existed, but the way it is practiced has changed fundamentally. While being by no means clear, the new first principles embrace learning and values, as well as the idea of corporate mortality.]

So long as there has been civilization, management has been practiced. As Peter Drucker points out in his masterly celebration of the art, *Management: Tasks, Responsibilities, Practices*, management is an ancient discipline that has been conducted and considered throughout history.[1] The builders of the great monuments of the past, from the pyramids to the Great Wall of China, were involved in undertakings that demanded management if they were to succeed. The military leaders whose names litter history were similarly concerned with managing the people and the resources at their disposal to achieve clear objectives. Great religious leaders were also managers. (Indeed, there is a business book entitled *The Leadership Wisdom of Jesus*.)

Although management has always been a fundamental activity, the recognition and study of management as a discipline and profession constitute a thoroughly modern phenomenon. While huge professional and educational edifices were built around the legal and medical professions, management remained largely unacknowledged. Only in the 20th century did management come of age, gaining both respectability and credence.

Even now, the study of management is still in a fledgling state. While business schools like to give the impression of age-old permanence and wisdom, their lineage is relatively short. Indeed, by the standards of universities – especially in Europe – business schools scarcely register on the chronometer. (Oxford University is hundreds of years old; its business school is only now getting off the ground.)

Invented in the United States, the origins of the business school as we know it can be traced to the Wharton School at the University of Pennsylvania which was founded in 1881. The Wharton approach to business was numerical. Its bedrock was finance, and it was the management of money that was drummed into students from the earliest days. Other schools soon followed. These institutions grew out of a desire to train and educate future generations in management techniques and practices, an aspiration often supported by generous donations from industrialists.

Toward the end of the 19th century this desire led to the creation of a number of specialized departments and schools attached to leading US universities. For the first time commercial practices, and the philosophies that underpinned them, were elevated to the same sort of level as other academic disciplines. They have been unlikely and often uncomfortable bedfellows ever since.

The origins of the MBA, the best known business school qualification, date back to this period. Founded in 1900, the Tuck School at Dartmouth claims to have had the first graduate program in management. Although not technically an MBA, Tuck offered the first graduate degree in 1900. Originally it was a "three, two" program, with three years" study at undergraduate level at Dartmouth followed by two years at Tuck.

Postgraduate entry courses followed. Harvard Business School claims to have been the first business school to require a university degree for entry to its management program. Founded in 1908, the school awarded its first Masters degree in the discipline in 1910.

The idea of business education quickly took off. Management education has been one of the great success stories of the last century. Over 100,000 MBA graduates now emerge blinking into the sunlight every year. Yet, for all the MBAs in the boardroom, management remains as open to constant redefinition as ever. The universal science is an irritatingly ill-defined one. It eludes simple clarification. "Managing is like holding a dove in your hand. Squeeze too tight, you kill it. Open your hand too much, you let it go," baseball coach and player Tommy Lasorda once reflected.

Even now, there is little consensus as to what makes a manager, who is a manager, or what management involves. The more people you ask, the more confused you are liable to become. Traveling from country to country you quickly uncover differences in attitude and perception. In France, managers are usually referred to as *cadres*, a term founded on social class and education rather than managerial expertise or corporate standing. In Germany, engineers rather than managers run businesses. "In the UK managers are very proud to be managers; in Sweden they are apologetic; and in Germany, managers see themselves as highly qualified specialists," says leading management thinker Henry Mintzberg.[2] German managers emphasize their technical knowledge and competence. They believe that this, rather than an elevated position in the corporate hierarchy, invests them with authority. In contrast, UK managers emphasize their executive rather than their technical skills. In an age of global business and internationalization, such fundamental differences in outlook and practice provide enormous challenges for the organizations of the future and those who manage them.

In the past, a preoccupation with status and hierarchy enabled managers to explain away some of the inconsistencies. Grand-sounding titles hid a multitude of confusion. Unable to provide a concise answer when asked what they did, managers preferred to explain who they were in the organizational hierarchy. With hierarchies stripped away in many organizations, managers are now forced to confront the exact nature of their role and the new first principles of management.

Learning first and last

"It is no longer sufficient to have one person learning for the organization, a Ford or a Sloan or a Watson. It's just not possible any longer to 'figure it out' from the top, and have everybody else following the orders of the 'grand strategist.' The organizations that will truly excel in the future will be the organizations that discover how to tap people's commitment and capacity to learn at all levels in an organization," says Peter Senge of the Massachusetts Institute of Technology.[3]

Management is uniquely placed as a profession: it is driven by ideas. The emerging professional and practical agenda is not so much set by practitioners as by business schools, consulting firms, and an array of gurus. But these sources are not universally liked or even trusted. That there is skepticism about a great many of today's managerial ideas cannot be doubted. Managerial thinking is tainted with ever greater hyperbole. And some of its ideas can be seen as driven by the media as much as by the research interests of academics or the needs of business.

Depending on your perspective, this situation can be attributed to the substantial financial rewards available for those who sweep the globe with the next bright idea, or seen as a sign of ever-increasing desperation among managers to find ways to make sense of the business world. Alternatively, and more positively, you can regard the merry-go-round of ideas as an indication of just how vital effective management is to the economies and people of the world.

Although there is clearly cynicism on the part of executives who receive a deluge of material on how best to run their businesses, if you read through the stream of management books you can detect some degree of consensus. No book is now complete without a fresh interpretation of how Michael Dell reinvented the supply chain or how Jack Welch galvanized General Electric (GE). Toyota's production methods and Nokia's miraculous reinvention are similarly looked at with increasingly predictable wonderment. At least when IBM was the premier corporate model you knew where you stood. Now we have Nokia which reinvented itself as a mobile phone manufacturer after decades as an obscure Finnish conglomerate; GE, which appears to have been reinvented through the drive and imagination of a single individual (and one who has, against all the prevailing wisdom, spent decades with a single employer); Dell, which cuts out the intermediaries while other e-businesses insert them; and Toyota, which manages to remain elusive, always one step ahead.

Managers yearn for clear, unequivocal messages, but that is no longer what they receive. They are deluged in reports and books on creating the global organization, at the same time as they are still asking what that means. When it comes to the huge international corporations detailed in case study after case study, our knowledge is extensive but highly fragmented. There is a feeling that these companies possess something, but no one can quite encapsulate the entire message. There is no one great management book – though Peter Drucker has come pretty close to providing it. What one commentator pompously labeled "the over-arching meta-narrative" is usually notable by its absence. Management continues to defy the theorists who would like to guide it into a corner and nail it down. It continues to escape. It carries on slipping through our fingers.

As a consequence, managers are on a continual quest for new ideas, new interpretations, and new corporate cures. Inevitably, they consume a fair number of placebos along the way. Yet it is this quest for knowledge that marks management apart as a discipline. Fifty-year-old lawyers can afford to sit back and contemplate their bedrock of knowledge knowing that updating it will be an occasional chore; managers have no such luxury. If 50-year-old managers look back and contemplate their knowledge, they will quickly find they are out of a job. Management demands change and continuing development. There is no hiding place. Updating knowledge is an ever-present necessity.

Management, therefore, has become increasingly committed to the entire concept of learning. Albert Vicere and Robert Fulmer, two business professors from Penn State, have calculated that businesses worldwide spend more than $100 billion on training their employees every year. Dauntingly, they also estimate that over half of this is wasted as much is carried out with no objective. The global executive education market has been calculated to be worth in excess of $12 billion. Business schools are believed to account for approximately one-quarter of the total – about $3 billion.

If you add on all the many millions spent on management and business education at degree level, the figures become even more impressive.

The profusion of training and development is driven by a realization that companies must become "learning organizations" if they are to survive and prosper. "Any company that aspires to succeed ... must first resolve a basic dilemma: success in the marketplace increasingly depends on learning, yet most people don't know how to learn. What's more, those members of the organization that many assume to be the best at learning are, in fact, not very good at it," noted Harvard Business School's Chris Argyris in a typically far-sighted 1991 *Harvard Business Review* article.[4]

The trouble, in practice, is that the learning organization is often regarded as an instant solution; yet another fad to be implemented. Earnest attempts to turn it into reality have often floundered. Even so, Peter Senge argues that the interest in the concept of the learning organization is proof that institutions and people are ready for major change: "Our traditional ways of managing and governing are breaking down. The demise of General Motors and IBM has one thing in common with the crisis in America's schools and 'gridlock' in Washington – a wake-up call that the world we live in presents unprecedented challenges for which our institutions are ill prepared."[5]

Values maketh the manager

The quest for ideas and the rise of learning as an important ingredient of organizational life are only part of the changing face of management. Another aspect is the growing importance of values in both management thinking and practice. The issue of personal and corporate values is clearly related to that of motivation and loyalty.

If you believed everything you read in the business press, the business world would be entirely populated by jargon-speaking free agents, flitting from project to project, from one interesting assignment to the next. According to the fashionable pundits, corporate loyalty is dead. Today's employees are loyal to no one but themselves.

Perhaps, for some, working life really is like that. Meanwhile, back in reality, many millions of people continue to work in much the same way, for much the same hours, as they have done for decades.

The champions of free agency suggest that remaining with the same organization for 10, 15, maybe 20 years is mutually unsatisfactory. The employee becomes jaded, comfortable, and complacent, hardly good news for any organization. The bright and ambitious new arrival is surely preferable to the cynical long-term resident with an eye on retirement and a gift for corporate maneuvering.

The flip side of this is that an organization populated by people whose loyalty is at best fleeting and at worst elsewhere is hardly likely to take the world by storm. Indeed, it is more likely to be riven with political intrigue, uncertainty, and insecurity. Short-term employees have eyes only for the short term; free agents are set on their individual freedom and success rather than team goals. "Mercenaries tend to move on and not become marines. Can you build a company with a mercenary force?" asks the late Sumantra Ghoshal of London Business School, co-author of *The Individualized Corporation*.

Luckily, perhaps, the talk of an army of mercenaries appears overblown. Research by Incomes Data Services found that in 1993, 36 percent of men had been with the same employer for 10 years or more. This was at the peak of downsizing mania. Interestingly, and surprisingly given the hysterical talk of the emerging promiscuous workforce, the equivalent figure for 1968 was only 37.7 percent.

More research from Business Strategies forecast that 79.2 percent of all employees would be in full-time permanent jobs in 2005 – compared with 83.9 percent in 1986. The revolution has been postponed.

For better or worse, people stick around. Even after downsizing, the flurry of demographic time bombs, and talk of Generation X, working life retains a strong element of security. It may be unfashionable to spend 30 years working for a single employer, but many people still do. Some undoubtedly do so because they have limited opportunities elsewhere, limited ambition, or limited abilities. These are facts of life generally ignored by the free-agent propagandists.

But many actively choose to stay. They find their work and working environment stimulating, rewarding, or enjoyable. Indeed, some of the corporate titans of our age are devoted company loyalists. Perhaps the best known is GE's former CEO Jack Welch. Feted far and wide as the very model of the modern CEO, Welch spent over 40 years with one employer. No one suggests that his loyalty was misplaced. His successor, Jeff Immelt, can point to similar one-company dedication.

With decades of corporate service, such people may appear to some as a throwback to a more naïve, even simplistic age. It was never meant to be like that. In the 1970s pundits envisaged the leisure age; in the 1980s they talked of flexible working, a world of teleworkers. Well, the technology now exists and teleworking remains a decidedly minority pursuit. "The failure of teleworking to really catch on, despite the availability of the technology, demonstrates that some sort of a physical relationship is important to people at work. People want to feel part of a team and of something much bigger. They want to be connected," says Gerry Griffin, author of *The Power Game*.

Corporate loyalty is engendered by the fact that conventional working life still holds a remarkable attraction. Its immediacy makes business sense. In business, being there remains crucial. The psychological dynamics mean that conversations in corridors or over coffee actually move the business forward. Managers make an impact, make a difference, and get results by talking to people, walking around, and listening to others. They need to be there and for their people to be there. The reality is that people are loyal to the environment where they spend every day, and to their colleagues.

While the traditional attractions of office life remain, it is true that companies no longer have an aura of permanence. They change with accelerating regularity. The profusion of joint ventures, mergers, and acquisitions means that people's roles now change more frequently. In the past, people might have filled two or three roles in 15 years with a company. Now, they are likely to change positions every three years or so. This, perhaps perversely, can actually encourage them to stay. If you want a fast-moving, stimulating, constantly changing environment, why move when it is happening all around you and you're a player in making it work? If you stay with a company for 10 years or more, change will inevitably happen. You either develop your own skills and move forward with the organization, or you leave.

This is not to say that the corporate man of the 1950s and 1960s is alive and well. Blind loyalty is undoubtedly dead – and corporate man is now as likely to be corporate woman. Today's employees are more questioning and demanding. They are loyal but confident enough to air their concerns, grievances, and aspirations. If they were customers, we would call them sophisticated. (It is perhaps significant that we tend not to.) People are now more likely to question the action behind the corporate rhetoric. As a result, the human resources (HR) and internal communications functions are much more important. Indeed, internal communications has emerged as an industry in its own right, reflecting the need for companies to create communication channels to their own people.

Central to the demanding nature of today's employees is the notion of values. In the past and put simply, loyalty was bought. Job security, gradual progression up the hierarchy, and a decent salary were offered by the employer. In return, the employee offered unwavering loyalty and a hard day's work. Now, values determine loyalty. "Every organization needs values, but a lean organization needs them even more," GE's Jack Welch says. "When you strip away the support systems of staffs and layers, people have to change their habits and expectations, or else the stress will just overwhelm them."

In the post-Enron age, values matter. A report produced by consultants Blessing/White, "Heart and Soul," studied the impact of corporate and individual values on business. "Values have two critical roles: a company that articulates its values enables potential recruits to apply a degree of self-selection. Values also provide a framework to match individual career goals with the organization's objectives," it observed.

The challenge for organizations is that values are more complex than mere money. Values cannot be simplistically condensed into a mission statement or neatly printed on an embossed card. In the past there was a belief in one set of values. Now, in more sophisticated companies, there is an awareness that the uniqueness of the firm comes from multiple values and cultures. Previously, people's needs were interpreted as being homogenous. Now, there are flexible benefits and working arrangements and recognition that people are motivated by different things. Money and power don't work for everyone.

With values becoming an increasingly important aspect of loyalty and motivation, it is little wonder that companies are paying them more attention. Indeed, in the modern world, companies are crucial in identifying and developing the values that shape society. In the past, value systems were created by the church and the state. Corporations are the great institutions of our current age and, in a secular world, they create the belief systems, the values into which people may – or may not – buy. The choice is ours.

"Companies increasingly resemble tribes," says Jonas Ridderstråle of the Stockholm School of Economics. "Companies have to find people who share their values. Recruiting is now about finding people with the right attitude, then training them in appropriate and useful skills – rather than the reverse. We can no longer believe in the idea of bringing in smart people and brainwashing them at training camps into believing what is right."

Clearly, for the better executives there is a choice. They work for companies that are in accord with their own value systems. If they don't want to work for a polluter, they will not. After all, people want to hold their heads up when they are with their peers. They don't want an embarrassed silence when they announce who they work for.

If a company gives real meaning to people's work, as well as the freedom and resources to pursue their ideas, then it's a good place to be. Values are the new route to developing loyalty among employees. Loyalty is not dead, it simply must be earned and, increasingly, earned in different ways.

Corporate mortality

Implicit in all this is the notion that companies and individuals who fail to learn or identify appealing values will cease to exist. In the disposable society, companies and executives are more disposable than ever before.

This has led to a variety of lines of inquiry. First, there are those who argue that corporate mortality is a healthy thing. Over 10 years, Andrew Campbell of the UK's Ashridge Strategic Management Centre and his co-researchers exhaustively examined the role of corporate parents. (Cynthia Montgomery and David Collins at Harvard Business School and C.K. Prahalad and Yves Doz of France's INSEAD have also pursued this line of research.) "Parent companies are competing with each other for the right to parent businesses," says Campbell. "They need to offer parenting advantage for their existence to be justified. And parenting advantage can only come from doing things differently from other parents. Corporate parents, therefore, must offer unique and specialist skills and knowledge."

The trouble is that the rise of the professional general manager encourages corporate parents, and corporate managers, to be alike rather than different. "The manager is a hero in the Western world, but an impostor," says Campbell. "The concept of management has proved a huge distraction. The management side of running a company is trivial compared to the importance of being commercial or entrepreneurial, or having a particular specialist skill. Any organization needs to have people with the skills relevant to its business rather than concentrating on turning the marketing director into a rounded general manager."

Indeed, Campbell goes on to suggest that we have become preoccupied with creating immortal organizations rather than those that work in the present. "Why do we want organizations to thrive for ever?" he asks. "On average organizations survive for less time than the working life of an individual. They become dysfunctional and, at that point, they should be killed off. What is encouraging is that, first through management buy-outs and now through demergers, we are becoming more adept at bringing an end to corporate lives which have run their course and creating new organizations in their place."

The second line of inquiry is to examine what leads to corporate longevity. The most notable works in this field are Arie de Geus's *The Living Company*, Jim Collins' and Jerry Porras' *Built to Last* and Collins' solo work *Good to Great*.

Central to these books is the idea that the corporation is an important institution that needs to live for capitalist society to thrive. The trouble is that though companies may be legal entities, they are disturbingly mortal. "The natural average lifespan of a corporation should be as long as two or three centuries," writes de Geus, noting a few prospering relics such as the Sumitomo Group and the Scandinavian company Stora. But the reality is that companies do not head off into the Florida sunset to play bingo. They usually die young.

De Geus quotes a Dutch survey of corporate life expectancy in Japan and Europe that arrived at 12.5 years as the average life expectancy of all firms. "The average life expectancy of a multinational corporation – Fortune 500 or its equivalent – is between 40 and 50 years," says de Geus, noting that one-third of 1970's Fortune 500 had disappeared by 1983. He attributes such endemic failure to the focus of managers on profits and the bottom line rather than the human community making up their organization.

In an attempt to get to the bottom of this mystery, de Geus and a number of his colleagues at the Shell oil company carried out some research to identify the characteristics of corporate longevity. As you would expect, the onus is on keeping excitement to a minimum. The average human centurion advocates a life of abstinence, caution and moderation, and so it is with companies. The Royal Dutch/Shell team identified four key characteristics. The long-lived were "sensitive to their environment"; "cohesive, with a strong sense of identity"; "tolerant"; and "conservative in financing." (These conclusions are echoed in Porras' and Collins' equally thought-provoking *Built to Last*, which almost serves as a companion volume to de Geus' book.)

Key to de Geus' entire argument is that there is more to companies – and to longevity – than mere money making. "The dichotomy between profits and longevity is false," he says. His logic is impeccably straightforward. Capital is no longer king; the skills, capabilities, and knowledge of people are. The corollary from this is that "a successful company is one that can learn effectively." Learning is tomorrow's capital. In de Geus' eyes, learning means being prepared to accept continuous change.

Here, de Geus provides the new deal: contemporary corporate man or woman must understand that the corporation will, and must, change and it can change only if its community of people changes also. Individuals must change and the way they change is through learning. As a result, de Geus believes that senior executives must dedicate a great deal of time nurturing their people. He recalls spending around a quarter of his time on the development and placement of people. Jack Welch claimed to spend half of his time on such issues.

According to de Geus, all corporate activities are grounded in two hypotheses: "The company is a living being; and the decisions for action made by this living being result from a learning process." With its faith in learning, *The Living Company* represents a careful and powerful riposte to the corporate nihilism which dominated the 1990s.

From certainty to chaos

If the sanctity of corporate life is now open to debate, it is just another sign that while management thinking once provided a healthy diet of answers, it now produces confusion and yet more questions. The debate about outsourcing, for example, is expanding from the simple cost benefits to contemplation of its repercussions for the nature of the company – boundaryless and more abstract than ever before, it is difficult to determine where, why, and how the actual organization begins and ends.

Increasingly, attention is focussing on the nature of the questions rather than the pithiness of the answers. Indeed, many would argue that there are no longer any answers. Here, managers find themselves in the uncomfortable and discomfiting world of chaos and complexity theory. There is much talk of fractals and cognitive dissonance; uncertainty and ambiguity are the new realities. Organizational metaphors have metamorphosed. The organization was once talked of in mechanical terms. Now it is variously described through natural and scientific metaphors as an ameba or a random pattern.

Is such theory mere metaphorical color or is it practically useful? Reaching a definitive conclusion on this is impossible – although, theorists suggest, that is just the sort of thing that managers will have to become used to. "Complexity theory is intriguing. Going beyond the metaphor is the trouble," observes Richard Pascale.

Others insist that complexity is not simply a metaphor. Ralph Stacey, author of *Complexity and Creativity*, comments: "Complexity is an effective metaphor and practically useful. Everything's a metaphor. It's not possible to make sense of anything apart from through a paradigm. It is a different way of making sense of human systems and so it is more important than another recipe or technique. Some people are quite hostile because acceptance of complexity undermines their way of thinking. To others it is a release."

Systems thinking, the idea that all the activities in an organization are interlinked, fits comfortably with other popular notions of global networks and transnational organizations. It all seems to fit in some way, it's just that we don't have a master plan to reassemble it in the right way.

Where this leaves aspiring or practicing managers is a matter of lively conjecture. They are, according to different commentators, either fearful of the uncertainty now surrounding them or upbeat, set on making themselves indispensable in the managerial marketplace. In reality, there is no stereotypical situation or attitude. Instead, there is a bewildering array of options, tools, techniques, new and old ideas. Either/or questions have become either/and. The freewheeling pragmatism offered by some offers all the answers and yet none at all. There is a thin line between order and chaos and this line is likely to become ever more blurred and indistinct in the years to come.

RESOURCES

Crainer, Stuart, *The Management Century*, Jossey Bass, 2000.
Crainer, Stuart and Dearlove, Des, *Gravy Training*, Jossey Bass, 1999.
Drucker, Peter, *Management: Tasks, Responsibilities, Practices*, Heinemann, 1974.

The age of the individual

JONAS RIDDERSTRÅLE AND KJELL NORDSTRÖM

[This is the age of the individual. This provides a wide range of challenges for organizations, markets and for those blessed – or cursed – with the freedom to choose.]

On October 31, 1517, individualism as we know it was born. Martin Luther nailed his 95 theses to the door of the Wittenberg Palace All Saints' Church. The event signaled the beginning of the Protestant Reformation that was so fundamental to the development of capitalism. Rather than relying on the church to interpret the Bible, Luther gave this right to single human beings. He re-invented Christianity.

Some 500 years later, capitalism is re-inventing itself. People are now free to interpret just about any piece of information as they see fit. The arrival of such illuminated individuals will mean to our societies and organizations what Protestantism once meant to the Catholic Church. "Homo faber" – man as his own maker – is here to stay.

The Scandinavian subsidiary of a large US multinational corporation received an e-mail from headquarters. Despite the harsh winter, one of the company's top people was to honor them with a short visit. Attached was a list of requirements. The visiting American wanted a hotel room with white wallpaper. She also required white roses, lilies, tablecloths, curtains, candles, and sofas. In the white room she expected to have a CD player with a collection of Latin and R&B artists as well as a VCR. To drink, she requested mineral water (Evian exclusively) and Snapples (lemon, raspberry, and ice-tea). In addition, she needed a make-up table, plenty of fruit – but only mango, papaya, green grapes (without seeds), honey-melon, and water-melon. Finally, she would just love to have some chocolate-chip cookies, brownies, and vanilla ice cream.

Who could request such things? The demanding hotel guest was none other than J.Lo – Jennifer Lopez, latino-R&B-pop diva/movie starlet extraordinaire.

Now, consider this: what would you do if the head of R&D, the best sales person, the top designer, or someone else with an absolutely unique talent at your company sent a similar list? Perhaps they already do. In the future, some of them most certainly will. If not, there is a clear risk that you have recruited the wrong people.

Companies are getting the message. The top-of-the-line Volkswagen Phaeton comes with individualized climate zones. The driver may be in the desert while the passengers are in Patagonia. You decide. Unit-linked savings enable us to be our own personal investment managers. Soon, we may have "personalized medicine" where each patient will receive individualized treatment based on genetically determined drug responses.[6] At Spanish conglomerate Mondragon individual employees have a say in everything from how work is conducted to the selection of the CEO.[7] Today, everything is individualized. An open world requires open systems and an open architecture. Work against openness at your own peril.

You choose

We have come a long way in a short time. Not that long ago, our lives were largely shaped by chance. Now, for more and more people throughout the Western world, and increasingly elsewhere, lives are instead shaped by choice. This process can begin before you are born. There used to be one way of getting pregnant. Today, there are almost 20 – three of which do not require the presence of a man. Later in life, you can choose to move to London, Laos, or LA. You can choose to have a hair transplant. You can be red and curly this week, and have garlands of dreadlocks the next. You can choose the way you look through a myriad different nips and tucks. You can choose to work for Sun, Siebel, Siemens, or which ever company you prefer.

As futurist and social critic Watts Wacker puts it, you have the freedom to know, go, do, and be whoever you want to be. Individual choice is the holy grail of market forces. Demand is merely a reflection of millions and millions of individual decisions. And belief in market forces is the most powerful faith of our times. Choices that once converged in the age of collectivism are now diverging. Consumption has become an act of confession. "I shop therefore I am," says American artist Barbara Kruger. In fact, identity is no longer linked to production, but to consumption. The right to be, the right to choose, and the right to consume are central to our very being. We have the opportunity to invent meaning for ourselves. Preferences are also increasingly personal. The compromise is on the verge of extinction. Average customers or normal colleagues are now on the list of endangered species. From freedom follows fragmentation.

Skills, thrills, and greenbacks

But even in a world of choice, money talks; indeed money shouts more loudly than ever. In reality, cash still shapes our lives. We have freed money from the physical fetters of the past. Before you have finished reading this sentence, enormous sums will have traveled the world from one country to another. In the boardrooms of Big Business Inc. or the investment banks of the City of London and Wall Street there is little room for sentimentality over the death of distance. Capitalists do not make pilgrimages to the grave of geography. Instead, they cheerfully dance around its tomb.

Choice can be bought either by old-fashioned cash or through the possession of the right skills. Our lives are increasingly shaped by competence, or by the absence of competence.

To understand the power of competent individuals, consider Microsoft. The company went public in 1986. During the first day, the stock started trading at $21 and closed at $28. If you had held on to that original share for 15 years, adjusted for splits, it would have been worth $10,000. It would be a bit like buying a mountain bike and later trading it in for a BMW Z4 sports car. Henry Ford once shared some of his wealth by instituting the $5 per day salary. Bill Gates used stock options.

Having no education can be an economic death sentence, while a unique talent grants you a global passport. As the renowned sociologist Manuel Castells puts it: "Elites are cosmopolitan – people are local."[8] We used to have aristocrats, then bureaucrats. Now, as noted by *Economist* journalists John Micklethwait and Adrian Woolridge, we have *cosmocrats* – the new elite possessing either cash, competence, or both.

Capitalism karaoke style

Collectivism in all its many forms and manifestations – political communism, homogeneous national cultures, and monolithic organizations – is being challenged. It was challenged in the Eastern Bloc and the Wall came down. It is challenged in Japan, causing deflation and a recession. It was challenged at IBM and the company almost went bust before it changed. After the collapse of communism and the rise and fall of dot-communism, the dominant *ism* left on earth is individualism. People and organizations in the industrialized world simply have far greater choice than ever before. They know their rights.

Capital and competences may be the entry requirements to this new world of opportunity and liberty, but not even access to these resources guarantees success. There is a final choice. The ultimate choice is one of deciding whether to use your freedom to copy someone else or to create your own future. Unfortunately, it appears as if rather than trying to become a first class version of themselves, too many companies and individuals settle for being second rate copies of someone else.

Business schools, benchmarking, and international transfer of best practices have pushed us into the age of karaoke capitalism where pale copies of the real thing are aplenty. Minimalist architects are all studying Mies Van der Rohe. General Motors watches Toyota. Europe and Asia are looking toward the US. Think about it. Formally speaking, a karaoke bar is nothing more and nothing less than a place for institutionalized imitation. Here's the problem. Merely imitating someone else will never ever make you truly successful.

Applying for membership in the look-alike club certainly reduces uncertainty, but it also effectively eliminates any chance of making history. It's a bit like treating creative impotence with Prozac when you need Viagra to really score big. We admire the likes of Dell and Dylan, Microsoft and Madonna for their ability to innovate and then continuously re-invent themselves.

Successful corporations and people create monopolies in time or space. They identify imperfections – cracks in the wall of karaoke competition – and exploit them. To thrive, as individuals and in business, we need to dare to be different. True entrepreneurs accept no imitations – no limitations.

RESOURCES

Nordström, Kjell and Ridderstråle, Jonas, *Funky Business*, FT Prentice Hall, 2000.
Nordström, Kjell and Ridderstråle, Jonas, *Karaoke Capitalism*, FT Prentice Hall, 2004.

www.funkybusiness.com
www.karaokecapitalism.com

The new knowledge landscape

LEIF EDVINSSON

> We now live in the intangible economy. Knowledge economics is the new reality. In a technically and intellectually based economy, the rules of economics are being challenged and changed. Understanding of the new commercial realities requires radical new insights from radical new economists.

The law of diminishing returns has been turned on its head to produce the law of increasing returns. This means that under certain circumstances companies can quickly come totally to dominate a market. Such is the power of increasing returns that the power of market forces appears negated. The invisible hand of market forces is "a little bit arthritic," notes the Santa Fé Institute's Brian Arthur.

"The physical world is characterized by diminishing returns," observes Stanford's Paul Romer. "Diminishing returns are a result of the scarcity of physical objects. One of the most important differences between objects and ideas ... is that ideas are not scarce and the process of discovery in the realm of ideas does not suffer from diminishing returns."

We are now dealing with the economics of the exponential potential of "knowledge recipes."

Underpinning these arguments is a move away from solutions and foolproof models to questions and frameworks. "Economics has always taken a shortcut and said 'assume there is a problem and assume that we can arrive at a solution,'" says Arthur. "Now, I would say 'assume there's a situation, how do players cognitively deal with it?' In other words, what frameworks do they wheel up to understand the situation?"

Making sense of the situation is the critical first step. Assuming there is an economic model that will spit out a solution is a sure route to diminishing returns.

Of course, new insights do not constitute new economics. In fact, many of the basics remain unchanged. The fundamentals of demand and supply have not altered, nor for that matter has the imperative for businesses to make money. What can be said is that economics now has to be understood in a different perspective.

You can put things in context by looking back to the early days of the factory, the railroad, the automobile and, especially, the harnessing of electricity. If you do so, a lot of what seems new about the Internet starts to look familiar. The true commercial revolution took place in Western Europe 500 or so years ago. As a complete break with the past, it paved the way for subsequent technology-led revolutions. It was built on one of the key realizations of the age. Summed up by the economist Adam Smith in his book *The Wealth of Nations* in 1776, it asserted that the true wealth of a nation is measured not by how much gold it possesses but by what it can produce.

Smith crowned productivity king and it has reigned supreme ever since. This laid the foundation for a series of technology-related revolutions, of which the Internet is only the most recent.

Productivity was best achieved and improved through the advancement of technology and the division of labor. This system of maximizing productivity through technology and demarcation provided the basis for the management theorists of the early 20th century, such as Frederick Taylor, champion of scientific management, and practitioners such as Henry Ford. They translated the economic rigor of Smith's thinking into practices in the workplace. They did so in ways, and to a scale, that Smith could never have imagined.

If productivity was the goal, efficient processes were the means of achieving it. Companies continue to pursue efficiency through leanness and therefore, they hope, productive, organizational structures. As any dieter will tell you, the quest for leanness is often a tortured one. Indeed, leanness pretty soon leads to the corporate equivalent of anorexia – organizations emptied of people, experience, meaning, and value in all its manifestations.

Productivity still matters. It is just that our understanding of productivity and how to achieve it has changed and will continue to change. "Adam Smith realized that the factory model would stupefy people. The knowledge era creates opportunities that *smartify* people in exciting and unexpected ways," says Charles Savage of Knowledge Era Enterprises.

What is changing is the way we understand what is being supplied and what is in demand. Labor may be mental but it is still divided and has to migrate. This in turn changes the way we price goods and services as well as the entire notion of value and the dynamics of value.

The power of intangibles

At the heart of knowledge economics is the entire notion of intangible value, the role of intangible assets in value creation, and the exponential multiplier effect of knowledge recipes. In the knowledge economy, what has a value today may be different to what had a value yesterday or will have tomorrow.

The fact is that the nature of competitive advantage has shifted from the physical to the intangible, the visible to the invisible, the seen to the unseen.

In Sweden, only 22 percent of people employed in industry can now be categorized as blue-collar workers. Of these, perhaps half could be described as knowledge workers of some sort – they are qualified engineers or supervisors. In a high-tech modern factory, a cutting-machine supervisor is essentially a knowledge worker.

In the US, services have increased steadily as a share of measured total output in the economy, from 22 percent of gross domestic product (GDP) in 1950 to about 39 percent of GDP in 1999. Intangibles such as skills or professional knowledge, organizational capabilities, reputational capital, mailing lists, or other collections of data tend to be important factors in the provision of many services. In the US, investment in intangibles passed that in tangibles in 1992.

Microsoft, for example, has very little in the way of physical plant and equipment. Indeed, at one time, Microsoft had only $1.6 billion in property, plant, and equipment but a market capitalization heading toward $400 billion. The great corporation of our times is an illusion – albeit a lucrative one. "Given that no company can establish a monopoly on brains, how do you keep the people that make it work? There are no tangible assets to divest. There is intellectual property and that's about it – and a building," attorney Lloyd Cutler commented on the proposed break-up of Microsoft.

Intangible assets can account for 90 percent of a company's value. According to Andrew Mayo, in his book *The Human Value of the Enterprise*, in late 2000 a total of 74 percent of BP's value was accounted for by intangible assets. For 3M the figure was 82 percent.

A number of individuals and organizations have been wrestling with the challenges and potential of intangibles. In 2000 the European Community launched a study of "policy trends in intangible assets" in seven member states and set up a European "high level expert group" (HLEG) under the leadership of Clark Eustace to examine the subject. The HLEG took intangibles to be "non-material factors that contribute to enterprise performance in the production of goods or the provision of services, or that are expected to generate future economic benefits to the entities or individuals that control their deployment."

HLEG went on to conclude: "Even when we can visualize them, their intrinsic characteristics make intangibles difficult to track. Because we cannot see them, touch them or weigh them, we cannot measure them directly and have to rely on proxy or indirect measures of their impact. In both macro and business economics, their existence is revealed indirectly by incremental economic performance that is not accounted for by the conventional key indicators."

But however they are defined, there is no doubt that the power of intangibles is growing. The Brookings Research Institute found that in 1962, 62 percent of a company's value was represented by its physical capital. By 1992 that percentage had declined to 38 percent. It is still falling. Other research cited by the University of Calgary's Mitchell Williams showed that on average, in 1995, over 75 percent of the value of companies from the health care and personal services industries was attributed to their intellectual capital.

Research by Professor Baruch Lev in the US has found that in 1929 approximately 70 percent of US investments went into tangible goods and 30 percent into intangibles.

By 1990 this pattern was inverted and today the dominant investment is in intangibles such as research and development (R&D), education and competencies, IT software and the Internet.

This applies to a large number of countries. On average, more than 10 percent of GDP in OECD countries is calculated to go into intangibles. For countries such as Sweden this input is estimated to be more than 20 percent of GDP. Since 1992 more than $200 billion has been invested in intangibles in the US every year. Indeed, one estimate put US investment in intangibles in 2000 at a staggering $1,000 billion.

Knowledge traders

Take the concept of knowledge economics to its purest essence and you find yourself trading in knowledge.

There has always been a market for knowledge. The publishing industry is based on it. But today the Internet is making the distribution of knowledge ever easier. The days when the publisher decided what got published are over. Today anyone with a PC and a modem can talk to the world. This is reducing the friction in the knowledge economy as well as transaction value. The Internet spawns new possibilities. We all have knowledge but until now we had no way to trade it except through our jobs. The enterprise was the arena for trading knowledge under the umbrella label of employment.

Think of the possibilities. Everyone has knowledge in whatever industry he or she works. For example, say you are a computer dealer. Over the years you have compiled a list of the 10 lowest-price places to buy wholesale computer equipment. You can sell your knowledge to newer, younger computer dealers who have no way to track down this knowledge without losing thousands of dollars finding out the hard way. Why not?

The future lies in "knowledge exchange" as much as in "knowledge sharing." The future lies in the use of markets within, as well as outside, organizations to facilitate intellectual capital development. "There is much value in [developing] market mechanisms which create more efficient markets for knowledge," contends Larry Prusak of the Institute of Knowledge Management. "These markets enable 'buyers and sellers' of knowledge to exchange their goods at a 'market-derived' price."

Auctions for thought recipes will be the third generation of exchanges – the first were the raw material exchanges, which began life hundreds of years ago; second came the financial exchanges, which arose 100 years ago.

Bryan Davis, a knowledge management expert, believes that knowledge markets and exchanges are a new trillion-dollar market space in the making. "We are now witnessing the explosion and formation of a new galaxy, an economy fired by brainpower. This is about connections and contexts – expanding synapses in the 'global brain,'" he says.

And it gets better. Knowledge is a renewable resource. Better yet, it actually increases with use. Paul Romer has sagely suggested that knowledge has the distinct advantage of being the only asset that grows with use. Knowledge does not wear itself out; it grows and grows as surely as a benevolent virus.

So what does this mean? Well, it opens up exciting new vistas.

In 2000 Datamonitor, a global market analysis firm, projected that Internet "information exchanges" would generate transaction revenues of $6 billion annually by the year 2005, facilitating over $50 billion worth of online purchases.[9] The Datamonitor study also projected that knowledge management and exchange over the Internet would "create a new Internet sector with $30 billion in market capitalizations." Already there are sites such as Fatbrain.com, Xpertsite.com, Exp.com, and ExpertCentral.com where knowledge is the primary currency. There have also been early knowledge exchange prototypes, including IQ-port from NatWest and KnowNet from PDVS/the University of Valencia, Venezuela.

Auctions make up over 20 percent of the top e-commerce sites on the web. Forrester Research rated online auctions as one of the top three emerging B2B e-commerce models and also predicted this market would grow dramatically over the next few years.

The value of knowledge can be subject to a number of variables, such as time and the credibility of the seller. Certain knowledge, such as computer programming hints, might have a very limited shelf-life. Insight on how to set up an Internet business in China might be worth a fortune on one day and nothing the next, depending on changes in government policy. The dynamic pricing capability of an online auction is perfectly suited to knowledge markets – since valuations are free to fluctuate.

RESOURCES

Baruch, Lev, 'Seeing is believing,' *CFO Magazine*, February 1999.
Bontis, Nick, 'An explorative study that develops measures and models,' *Management Decision*, 36, 2, 1998.
Davenport, Thomas and Prusak, Lawrence, *Working Knowledge*, Harvard Business School Press, 1998.
Edvinsson, Leif, *Corporate Longitude*, FT Prentice Hall, 2002.
Kurtzman, Joel, 'An interview with W. Brian Arthur,' *Strategy & Business*, Second Quarter 1998; 'An interview with Paul Romer,' *Strategy & Business*, First Quarter 1997.
Mayo, Andrew, *The Human Value of Enterprise*, Nicholas Brealey, 2001.
Pine, Joseph and Gilmore, James, *The Experience Economy*, Harvard Business School Press, 1999.
Skyrme, David, *Capitalizing on Knowledge*, Butterworth Heinemann, 2001.
The Intangible Economy: Impact and Policy Issues, Report of the European High Level Expert Group on the Intangible Economy, 2000.
Wallman, Steven and Blair, Margaret, *Unseen Wealth*, Brookings Institute, 2001.

www.corporatelongitude.com

A message to Garcia

THOMAS L. BROWN

[The obscure writings of a 19th-century writer shed important light on the state of management in the first decade of a new millennium.]

I first saw it in 1976. It was a small booklet, just a few inches wide and deep, the size that slips easily into a breast pocket. It was given to people like me, who had a connection (no matter how loose) to the aerospace world. At that time, I worked full-time in management development for Honeywell Aerospace. The pale-blue booklet, *A Message To Garcia* by Elbert Hubbard, was passed along to me with this imprint on the front cover: "Space Shuttle Main Engine Controller Program."

The manager who had the idea of acquiring this booklet had a perverse sense of management history. The thoughts of Elbert Hubbard? Warmed up and re-served to managers and workers in 1976? For people involved in launching the Space Shuttle?

I wondered who exactly ordered thousands of copies of an almost 100-year-old pamphlet. Who in the world signed off on *this* corporate requisition?

"Life is just one damned thing after another"

Elbert Hubbard lived from 1856 to 1915. When writing, he also liked to use the Latin name "Fra Elbertus." With his roots in Bloomington, Illinois, from a family of modest means, he deferred his dreams of being a writer and became a businessman instead, selling soap for a relative's manufacturing business. He sold his interest in the hugely prosperous venture in 1893. Hubbard was the genesis for the Roycrofters, a type of artisans' community that was located near Buffalo, New York; this idea presumably came to Hubbard after he met the icon of the English Arts & Crafts movement, William Morris. At the age of 40, he enrolled in college, quitting after a year. He died in the torpedoing of the *Lusitania*; his body was never retrieved from the Irish Sea. As a writer, he lives on as he was eminently quotable:

Life is just one damned thing after another.

Genius may have its limitations, but stupidity is not thus handicapped.

One machine can do the work of 50 ordinary men. No machine can do the work of one extraordinary man.

The greatest mistake you can make in life is to be continually fearing you will make one.

These witticisms were penned years before Peter Drucker shook hands with his first editor. And Hubbard's name *still* brings up some 40,000 hits on Google. Not bad for a business philosopher whose main life contribution remains, for many of us, *A Message To Garcia*. But what a work it was.

Though it first appeared in a monthly magazine, *The Philistine*, the article was quickly reprinted as a standalone publication. As a small booklet, it filled fewer than 20 pages. Depending on the version, it comes in under 1,500 words. Hubbard himself, in a sort of preface, called it a "literary trifle." He says he wrote it in an hour, after supper, on February 22, 1899. That same year, Elgar wrote his "Enigma Variations." The Philippines demanded independence from the United States. Oscar Wilde provoked much laughter with *The Importance Of Being Earnest*. A scientist named Ernest Rutherford was delving into the mysteries of alpha and beta rays in radioactive atoms. And the first magnetic recording of sound occurred.

But it was not arts or sciences that stirred Hubbard to write his well-read booklet; it was war – and management. Hubbard, at the opening of his tract, reveals that US President William McKinley, enmeshed in a war with Spain, needed someone to help him "communicate quickly with the leader of the Insurgents … somewhere in the mountain fastnesses of Cuba – no one knew where." The man picked for the job was a "fellow by the name of Rowan." And US Army Colonel Andrew Rowan did deliver the message. Yet it was how Rowan accepted his mission that caught Hubbard's attention. As Hubbard understood it, the messenger accepted the job without pushing back. He didn't ask questions, or challenge the wisdom of the assignment. He didn't hesitate. He didn't delay. He moved. As fast as he could. In a matter of three weeks, Rowan "traversed a hostile country on foot" and completed the assignment. And though Hubbard was not directly involved, that feat, the completion of a tough assignment without demurral and with unyielding fortitude, swept Hubbard into a one-hour writing frenzy that culminated in *A Message To Garcia*.

In his writing, Hubbard used a pen with a bold – make that *blunt* – point. The whole message in his most famous work could be reduced to a few brusque sentences. There is no question that Hubbard was writing from an imperious point of view. He seemed to hold little sympathy for the "downtrodden denizens of the sweatshop." One writer says the tract proves that Hubbard was "the darling poster boy of the world's economic royalists." As a whole, though, the book has endured because it is a memorable call for taking action, accepting responsibility, doing the job that needs to be done and doing it now. This excerpt from Hubbard's booklet just about says it all: "The point I wish to make is this: McKinley gave Rowan a letter to be delivered to Garcia; Rowan took the letter and did not ask, 'Where is he at?' By the Eternal! there is a man whose form should be cast in deathless bronze and the statue placed in every college of the land. It is not book-learning young men need, nor instruction about this and that, but a stiffening of the vertebrae which will cause them to be loyal to a trust, to act promptly, concentrate their energies: do the thing – 'Carry a message to Garcia.'"

How many copies of the essay have been sold or read? No one knows. It's easy to find a free copy on the Internet. But Hubbard wasn't blessed to be born in an electronic world. Ideas then were communicated principally by printing presses. Thus Hubbard became, for his time, Drucker and Tom Peters and James Champy – and 25 other gurus you are welcome to name – all rolled into one man, one essay. Hubbard estimated 40 million copies of *A Message To Garcia* had been printed in all written languages, "a larger circulation than any other literary venture has ever attained during the lifetime of the author, in all history." He said this in 1913.

"If you want work well done, select a busy man – the other has no time"

This is the 21st century. Hubbard's thinking is but a relic in our times, a curiosity, a throwback to a time when managers could jeer at unmotivated workers who failed to snap-to when omniscient managers needed work done promptly, quickly, and without any mouthing off. But what's wrong with this assertion? After more business books, articles, magazines, CDs, videos, classes, lectures, case studies, and dissertations than even Hubbard himself would have imagined, where are we?

The magazine *Across The Board* started its 2004 publishing year with a cover story that asked "Will We All Be Unemployed?" The "we" in that question is aimed at managers. Managing editor Matthew Budman says: "With knowledge-worker jobs heading overseas along with manufacturing and service jobs, managers are worried, too – and should be."

F. John Reh, the well-read and influential guide to management news on *http://management.about.com*, began his 2004 reporting with a telling piece that centered on a purported speech by the CEO of General Electric. Per Reh: "CEO Jeff Immelt reportedly told GE's Global Leaders Management Meeting earlier this month that 'the era of professional management is dead.' He continued, 'the worst thing you can be called is a professional manager.' GE has not responded to my attempts to verify the accuracy of this quote, but it doesn't matter. Whether or not Immelt said it, the issue needs to be addressed. Is the era of professional management dead?"

And in reporting on the elite World Economic Forum in Davos, Switzerland (a first-of-the-year bellwether for the profession of managing business and the world), Mark Landler in *The New York Times* reported on the widespread failure of the attempt to make the Davos conference more attendee-friendly. Ties were to be abandoned under a new dress-down rule, with a penalty exacted against any top exec wearing a cravat. An infraction, he reported, triggered a fine of five Swiss francs to be given to charity. "The francs piled up in the collection box. Casual Fridays, it turns out, don't go down well with the kind of people who hang out at the Trilateral Commission ... The trouble is, the world in 2004 is anything but normal. At a time of uncertain economic prospects, political tumult and persistent dangers of a terrorist attack, the businesspeople and public officials who came to this year's conference were hardly in a mood to let down their hair."

What's going on? Most workplaces today are beehive busy, but the state of mind of their managers seems badgered and beleaguered. Things are getting done. People are busy. But the state of management thinking seems as bankrupt as an Enron spin-off business. There are fewer management books being published. Magazines and websites that report on new trends in management thinking are sparse. The "profession" of management consulting and speaking is in a slump. Peter Drucker is now considerably more than 90 years old, and recently shared that he thought his best management ideas captured in *The Practice of Management* (1955)[10] had been implemented by few, if any, corporations. Finding a "Corporate Camelot" that provides reliable high-quality products or services, with an intelligent, upbeat, can-do workforce, and with a savvy management team that generates solid profits, legally, year after year without desecrating the environment or ties to their home community – well, searching for such a company is much like searching for the Holy Grail.

"Men are punished by their sins, not for them"

Were Elbert Hubbard writing today, I suspect he might want to send a different message. It would not be a message from managers but *to* them. It would not be a poke at uninspired, under-motivated workers; it would, instead, be a left jab and right hook at managers who have missed the fundamental point of managing and leading. And Hubbard's 21st-century missive would have at least three major points:

- *Managers have lost their mission.* In times past, the presumed chain of corporate management was built on a logic of knowledge-at-the-top driving labor-at-the-bottom. Thus, the informed manager became a figure of authority because he or she knew what needed to be done and how. The mission of managers was to mobilize the uninformed. As the head would steer the hands, managers would guide the workforce.

    But in an age where, yes, a formal education does not necessarily connote any inherent wisdom (what does a newly minted MBA really know?), we have, in many cases, workers more aware of how business is done, how technology operates, how to traverse organizational mountains, and how to invest one's wages prudently in the stock market.

Managers are operating in most firms on a license that has expired. If most managers would inspect their credentials for leading, they might notice that their use-by date passed many years ago. The mission of most management teams is foggy at best, needs to be seriously honed if not rewritten entirely, and is ripe for some revolutionary twists. Managers don't make decisions; they exist only to make sure that good decisions are made by everyone, everywhere in the business, with or without the manager present.

■ *Managers have confused making money with building a business.* The argument in too many management meetings is how to meet profit quotas. The daily drill of tracking one's business health on or in relation to the Hang Seng or Nikkei indices, the FTSE 100, or the Dow Jones Industrial Average usually begets some moaning about the constant need to meet some stock analyst's expectations. And thus the business, using this monetary pair of glasses, becomes only a profit-making enterprise. Or, at least, it devolves to being principally a profit-making machine.

But soaring sales do not always translate into solid profits. And economic gain bought at the price of unhappy customers, cowed workers, a hostile community, or a guilty conscience is idiocy. A healthy business fits into the worldscape in exactly the same way a healthy government or church fits. It is the uniting of people to create a capacity for contribution. The purpose of a company may simply be to provide a basic commodity or service; it, of course, can be much more. But whether one's business is about making napkins or making spaceship modules, the business is what you make or provide and whom you serve. The profits are never the business. To miss that point is to move one's corporate purpose perilously closer to the same *raison d'être* as the Mafia. Don't go there.

■ *To lead, a manager must never stay present-tense.* So many people in management aspire to be a leader that many now use the words interchangeably. Someone overseeing the flipping of hamburgers in a fast-food chain can find any number of gurus who argue that such responsibility – making sure that the people making burgers make them well – is akin to leadership. In reality, unless that manager discovers a whole new way of making, serving, or selling burgers, that kind of managing is merely the maintenance of a well-established status quo. One should not demean that kind of managing, but to elevate it to a higher level is madness, whether it's tied to cows or not.

Management evolves into leadership only when a hunger for discovery fuels an appetite for innovation, and that in turn fires up a commitment to true innovation. It's a Thomas Watson transforming punchcard counting into the dawn of computers; it's a Taiichi Ohno figuring out how to embed an appreciation for quality into the mass production of Toyota vehicles. It's a

Ray Kroc taking a hamburger stand and expanding it into a global concept, fast food defined by golden arches.

Taking the status quo and just keeping it clicking along is not leadership. To speak eloquently using only present-tense verbs makes for pretty speech, but it is not the language of leadership.

> **"The secret of success is this: there is no secret of success"**

Were Elbert Hubbard writing today, he would undoubtedly focus his energies on shaking managers by the lapels and waking them up to the harsh reality that management by formula, by guru, by textbook, or by corporate hero worship is no guarantee for success. And that is not cause for sadness or distress. Success is always an if.

That is the only reality, the only measurement, that a manager can cling to. And that is why managers today must focus more – much more – on how decisions are made by people up, down, and all around the organization. They must focus more – much more – on profits as a gross (and often inaccurate) indicator of how well their business is performing. They must focus on how to cut a path into the future as effectively as that young messenger Rowan did in the Cuban jungles for President McKinley.

A Message To Garcia was aimed at the workers of Hubbard's time. "My heart goes out to the man,' says Hubbard at the end of his brief work, 'who does his work when the 'boss' is away, as well as when he is at home. And the man who, when given a letter for Garcia, quietly takes the missive, without asking any idiotic questions, and with no lurking intention of chucking it into the nearest sewer, or of doing aught else but deliver it, never gets 'laid off,' nor has to go on a strike for higher wages."

Sage words for 1899? Many thought they were. Some do, even now. But to my mind, Hubbard would be more distressed today at the slouch and sag in the manager's demeanor – the executive who holds command but does not stir respect, who speaks with authority but without any confidence, who attends endless meetings, reads (and generates) endless e-mails, flies here and flitters there, making the gears of large organizations mesh by the sheer oiliness of their secondhand interpretations of what top management is trying to do or what customers "really want."

Success is always an if.

Managers must engrave those words into their minds and hearts in order for the profession of management to grow in this harsh new century, fraught with perils, gleaming with possibilities. What a manager can do to maximize the number of good-for-the-business decisions and thereby renew the corporate lifespan by a decade or two is precisely why management has always existed. We in management cannot forget that. And we have. That's a message worth heeding.

Pass it on.

Essentials

MANAGEMENT IN THE 21ST CENTURY

Drucker, Peter

Far-sighted and always opinionated, Peter Drucker was born in Austria in 1909 where his father, Adolph, was the chief economist in the Austrian civil service. Drucker worked as a journalist in London, before moving to America in 1937. His first book, *Concept of the Corporation* (1946), was a groundbreaking examination of the intricate internal working of General Motors. His books have emerged regularly ever since and now total 29. Along the way he has coined phrases and championed concepts, many of which have become accepted facts of managerial life.

The coping stones of Drucker's work are two equally huge and brilliant books: *The Practice of Management* (1954) and *Management: Tasks, Responsibilities, Practices* (1973). Both are encyclopedic in their scope and fulsome in their historical perspectives. More than any other volumes, they encapsulate the essence of management thinking and practice.

Drucker's book production has been supplemented by a somewhat low-key career as an academic and sometime consultant. He was Professor of Philosophy and Politics at Bennington College in Vermont from 1942 until 1949 and then became a Professor of Management at New York University in 1950 – "The first person anywhere in the world to have such a title and to teach such a subject," he proudly recalls. Since 1971, Drucker has been a Professor at Claremont Graduate School in California. He also lectures in oriental art, has an abiding passion for Jane Austen, and has written two novels (less successful than his management books).

Drucker's greatest achievement lies in identifying management as a timeless, human discipline. It was used to build the Great Wall of China, to erect the Pyramids, to cross the oceans for the first time, to run armies. "Management is tasks. Management is discipline. But management is also people," he wrote. "Every achievement of management is the achievement of a manager. Every failure is the failure of a manager. People manage, rather than *forces* or *facts*. The vision, dedication and integrity of managers determine whether there is management or mismanagement."

Drucker's first attempt at creating the managerial bible was *The Practice of Management*; he largely succeeded. The book is a masterly exposition of the first principles of management. In one of the most quoted and memorable paragraphs in management literature, Drucker gets to the heart of the meaning of business life: "There is only one valid definition of business purpose: to create a customer. Markets are not created by God, nature or economic forces, but by businessmen. The want they satisfy may have been felt by the customer before he was offered the means of satisfying it. It may indeed, like the want of food in a famine, have dominated the customer's life and filled all his waking moments. But it was a theoretical want before; only when the action of businessmen makes it an effective demand is there a customer, a market."

Drucker also provided an evocatively simple insight into the nature and *raison d'être* of organizations: "Organization is not an end in itself, but a means to an end of business performance and business results. Organization structure is an indispensable means, and the wrong structure will seriously impair business performance and may even destroy it ... The first question in discussing organization structure must be: What is our business and what should it be? Organization structure must be designed so as to make possible the attainment of the objectives of the business for five, ten, fifteen years hence." With its examinations of GM, Ford, and others, Drucker's audience and world view in *The Practice of Management* are resolutely those of the large corporation.

In *The Practice of Management* and the equally enormous *Management: Tasks, Responsibilities, Practices* in 1973, Drucker established five basics of the managerial role: to set objectives; to organize; to motivate and communicate; to measure; and to develop people. "The function which distinguishes the manager above all others is his educational one," he wrote. "The one contribution he is uniquely expected to make is to give others vision and ability to perform. It is vision and moral responsibility that, in the last analysis, define the manager."

Drucker identified "seven new tasks" for the manager of the future. Given that these were laid down over 40 years ago, their prescience is astounding. Drucker wrote that tomorrow's managers must do the following:

1. Manage by objectives.
2. Take more risks and for a longer period ahead.
3. Be able to make strategic decisions.
4. Be able to build an integrated team, each member of which is capable of managing and of measuring his own performance and results in relation to the common objectives.
5. Be able to communicate information fast and clearly.
6. Traditionally a manager has been expected to know one or more functions. This will no longer be enough. The manager of the future must be able to see the business as a whole and to integrate his function with it.
7. Traditionally a manager has been expected to know a few products or one industry. This, too, will no longer be enough.

Recent years have seen Drucker maintain his remarkable work rate. In particular, his energies have been focussed on non-profit organizations. His ability to return to first principles and question the fundamentals remains undimmed. In the new millennium, Drucker remains worth listening to.

Fayol, Henri

Europe has produced precious few original management thinkers. It is surprising, therefore, that the achievements and insights of the Frenchman Henri Fayol (1841–1925) are granted so little recognition.

Fayol was educated in Lyon, France and at the National School of Mines in St Etienne. He spent his entire working career with the French mining company Commentry-Fourchamboult-Décazeville, and was its managing director between 1888 and 1918.

Fayol was important for two reasons. First, he placed management at center stage. Frederick Taylor's Scientific Management emasculated the working man, but still treated managers as stopwatch-holding supervisors. Fayol emerged from a similar background in heavy industry. His conclusions, however, were that management was critical and universal. "Management plays a very important part in the government of undertakings; of all undertakings, large or small, industrial, commercial, political, religious or any other," he wrote. It was not until 1954, and Drucker's *The Practice of Management*, that anyone else made such a bold pronouncement in management's favor.

Fayol's second contribution was to ponder the question of how best a company could be organized. In doing so, he took a far broader perspective than anyone else had previously done. He concluded: "All activities to which industrial undertakings give rise can be divided into the following six groups." The six functions he identified were technical activities; commercial activities; financial activities; security activities; accounting activities; and managerial activities.

Such functional separations have dominated the way companies were managed throughout the 20th century. It may be fashionable to talk of an end to functional mindsets and of free-flowing organizations, but Fayol's functional model largely holds.

In many respects, Henri Fayol was the first *management* thinker. While others concentrated on the worker and the mechanics of performance, he focussed on the role of management and the essential skills required of managers.

Smith, Adam

Born in Kirkcaldy, Scotland, Adam Smith (1723–90) entered the University of Glasgow at the age of 14. Strongly influenced by the university's professor of moral philosophy, Smith went to Balliol College, Oxford in 1740 and began to concentrate on moral philosophy. He returned to Scotland in 1746 and later joined Glasgow University as a professor of logic and then of moral philosophy.

Smith's writing career began in the 1750s and he published his *Theory of Moral Sentiments* in 1759. After leaving the university in 1763, Smith spent time in France, where he met leading thinkers, including Voltaire. There is some evidence to suggest that Smith's *Inquiry into the Nature and Causes of the Wealth of Nations* was begun in Toulouse. The bulk of it, however, was written on Smith's return to Scotland. In 1773, he moved to London, bringing his manuscript with him. When it was published in 1776, *The Wealth of Nations* was instantly successful and influential. Prime Minister Lord North's budget in 1777 and 1778 was influenced by Smith.

Smith returned to Scotland, where he worked as a tax collector and oversaw the destruction of most of his papers before his death in 1790 after a long illness.

Smith's undoubted classic is his book *Inquiry into the Nature and Causes of the Wealth of Nations*. For a book that is more than 200 years old, a great deal of it has a surprisingly modern ring. *The Wealth of Nations* is often viewed as a right wing-manifesto, a gloriously logical exposition of the beauty of market forces. This is only partly true. There is more to *The Wealth of Nations* than a statement of free market *über alles*. Exploration should not be mistaken for advocacy. *The Wealth of Nations* is a broad-ranging exploration of commercial and economic first principles. Indeed, Smith is often given credit for the founding of economics as a coherent discipline.

For those unversed in economics, *The Wealth of Nations* remains a useful starting point. Smith lays out the basics with precision. For example, regarding supply and demand, he explains: "The quantity of every commodity which human industry can either purchase or produce naturally regulates itself in every country according to the effectual demand." On the rudiments of career management, he points out: "Every individual is continually exerting himself to find out the most advantageous employment for whatever capital he can command."

Key to the text is Smith's argument that the value of a particular good or service is determined by the costs of production. If something is expensive to produce, then its value is similarly high. "What is bought with money or with goods is purchased by labor, as much as what we acquire by the toil of our own body ... They contain the value of a certain quantity of labor which we exchange for what is supposed at the time to contain the value of an equal quantity," writes Smith.

Smith's logic is remorseless. "The real price of everything, what everything really costs to the man who wants to acquire it, is the toil and trouble of acquiring it," he says. "What everything is really worth to the man who has acquired it, and who wants to dispose of it or exchange it for something else, is the toil and trouble of which it can save himself, and which it can impose on other people."

It is possible to put a spin on many of Smith's ideas. Agendas can be constructed around them. This is to do them a disservice. *The Wealth of Nations* was the first comprehensive exploration of the foundations, workings, and machinations of a free-market economy. It was an intellectual triumph, not a manifesto.

Taylor, Frederick W.

Frederick Taylor (1856–1917) had a profound effect on the working world of the 20th century and was a man of amazing versatility and brilliance. The inventor of what was known as Scientific Management, Taylor was the guru of mass production, the champion of measurement and control.

The son of an affluent family in Philadelphia, Taylor was an engineer and a prolific inventor. At the core of his view of the business world was his theory of how working life could be made more productive and efficient. This was painfully simple. Taylor was the first and purest believer in command and control. In his 1911 book, *The Principles of Scientific Management*, Taylor laid out his route to improved performance.

Taylor's "science" (which he described as "75 percent science and 25 percent common sense") came from the minute examination of individual workers" tasks. Having identified every single movement and action involved in performing a task, Taylor believed he could determine the optimum time required to complete it. Armed with this information, a manager could decide whether a worker was doing the job well.

The origins of Scientific Management lay in Taylor's observations of his fellow workers at the Midvale Steel Company. He noticed that they engaged in what was then called "soldiering." Instead of working as hard and as fast as they could, they deliberately slowed down. They had no incentive to go faster or to be more productive. It was in their interest, Taylor said, to keep "their employers ignorant of how fast work can be done."

Taylor regarded the humble employee as a robotic automaton. Motivation came in the form of piece work. Employees had to be told the optimum way to do a job and then they had to do it. "Each employee should receive every day clear-cut, definite instructions as to just what he is to do and how he is to do it, and these instructions should be exactly carried out, whether they are right or wrong," Taylor advised.

Taylorism was one of the first serious attempts to create a science of management. It elevated the role of managers and negated the role of workers. Armed with their scientifically gathered information, managers dictated terms. The decisions of foremen – based on experience and intuition – were no longer considered to be important.

The man most associated with the application of Scientific Management was Henry Ford, who used it as a basis for his model for mass production. But Taylor's thinking had a profound impact throughout the world. While his theories are now largely disregarded, his fingerprints can be seen on much of the management literature produced in the 20th century.

REFERENCES

1. Drucker, Peter, *Management: Tasks. Responsibilities, Practices*, Heinemann, London, 1974.
2. Author interview.
3. Senge, Peter, *The Fifth Discipline*, Doubleday, New York, 1990.
4. Argyris, Chris, "Teaching smart people how to learn," *Harvard Business Review*, May–June 1991.
5. Senge, Peter, "A growing wave of interest and openness," Applewood Internet site, 1997.
6. Meyerson, M., "Human genetic variation and disease," *The Lancet*, Vol. 362: 259, July 26, 2003.
7. *Fortune*, January 20, 2003.
8. For a deeper analysis see *The Power of Identity*, *The Rise of the Network Society*, and *End of Millennium* by Manuel Castells.
9. P2P eCommerce Information Exchanges, Datamonitor, 2000.
10. Drucker, Peter, *The Practice of Management*, Heinemann, 1955.

PART TWO

Foundations of management

CHAPTER 1

Strategy and competition

"Strategy is discovering and inventing, which makes strategy subversive, and the strategist a rule-breaker, or revolutionary."

Gary Hamel

"The real challenge in crafting strategy lies in detecting the subtle discontinuities that may undermine a business in the future. And for that there is no technique, no program, just a sharp mind in touch with the situation."

Henry Mintzberg

"The Japanese approach to strategic thinking is basically creative, intuitive, non-linear, and so seen by most Westerners as irrational. Phenomena and events in the real world do not always fit a linear model. Hence the most reliable means of dissecting a situation into its constituent parts and reassembling them in the desired pattern is not a step-by-step methodology, such as systems analysis. True strategic thinking thus contrasts sharply with the conventional mechanical systems approach based on linear thinking, or even using strategic framework, which some scholars have developed."

Kenichi Ohmae

"True competitiveness must be built around something we all know exists but which is seldom discussed in the business world: emotions and imagination."

Jonas Ridderstråle

"Unless structure follows strategy, inefficiency results."

Alfred Chandler

"There are several changes in strategy that largely relate to changes in the clarity and dynamism of markets. First, strategy has become simpler. In the kinds of markets that we saw in the 1990s and see today, there is too much fluctuation and ambiguity to make complicated strategies sensible. Simple strategies provide coherence while retaining flexibility to adjust. Second, it has become more organizational. Strategy depends a lot more on organizational processes of change – the ability to change is a key aspect of strategy. And, third, strategy has become more time related – not in the sense of speed but in the sense of rhythm as a central aspect of strategy.

"The key consequences for strategy formulation are: one, a delegation of responsibility for setting strategy to business unit teams; two, a change of responsibilities among corporate executives to center on organizing the internal and external boundaries of the corporation rather than on business strategy; three, a shift from an emphasis on analysis to one on recognizing patterns in the marketplace through intense reliance on information and the intuition that comes from this information; four, an increased importance for conflict management as smart people are likely to disagree; and finally, an increased need to be able to manage in a longer time frame – working in real time, short-term and long-term time frames."

Kathleen Eisenhardt

Strategy and control

JOHN KAY

[Business strategy has come a long way since the idea first came to prominence during the 1960s. This article traces its historical development and considers how a resource-based view shapes modern strategic thinking.]

It is the early 1960s. Robert Macnamara, recruited from US car maker Ford to run the Department of Defense, is managing the first stages of the Vietnam War on computers in the Pentagon. John Kenneth Galbraith, detesting the world Macnamara represents, writes of the New Industrial State, in which giant mechanistic corporations run our lives.

The Soviet Union is ahead in the space race, and while most of the West loathes the Russian empire, they do not dispute the claims made for its economic success. Every newly independent colonial territory looks forward to the realization of its development plan. British Prime Minister Harold Wilson talks of the white heat of the technological revolution; George Brown gives Britain its first, and only, national plan.

It is in this environment that the idea of business strategy is created. The early texts are by Igor Ansoff and Ken Andrews. Its principal journal is called *Long Range Planning*. It is founded on an illusion of rationality and the possibilities of control.

It is a world that will soon fall apart. Macnamara will be transferred to the World Bank, but history will note the failure of each of his careers – CEO, Secretary of State, international statesman. Half a million hippies will gather at Woodstock to celebrate the demise of the New Industrial State. And – although few people saw it then – the Soviet Union is on an unstoppable path from totalitarianism to disintegration.

Yet the delusion of control has continued to define the subject of business strategy. In the heady 1960s, no major firm was without its strategic plan. Few are without one today, although few devote the resources to it that they once did. The plans contain numbers, neither targets nor forecasts, which purport to describe the evolution of the company's affairs over the next five years.

But planning and strategy are no longer conflated. The delusion of control has changed its form if not its nature. What matters are vision and mission. Charismatic CEOs can transcend the boundaries of the firm. Their achievements, and those of the companies they inspired, could be restricted only by the limitations of their executive imagination.

However, companies are not restrained only by imagination. They are limited by their own capabilities, by technology, by competition, and by the demands of their customers. So visionary strategy has been succeeded by an era in which the cliché "formulation is easy, it is implementation that's the problem" holds sway. If strategizing consists of having visions, it is obvious that formulation is easy and implementation the problem: all substantive issues of strategy have been redefined as issues of implementation.

As organizations stubbornly fail to conform to the visions of their senior executives, we should not be surprised that organizational transformation has become one of the most popular branches of consultancy.

Or perhaps the CEO's vision is of the external environment rather than of the internal capabilities of the firm. The future belongs to those who see it first, or most clearly. Nevertheless, it is not just that forecasting is hard – although that difficulty should not be underestimated. Even if you do see the future correctly, its timing is hard to predict and its implications are uncertain.

US telecoms carrier AT&T understood that the convergence of telecommunications and computing would transform not only the company's own markets but much of business life. This was a perceptive vision, not widely shared. But the company failed to see – how could it have? – that the Internet was the specific vehicle through which the vision would be realized, or that its merger with US business machines manufacturer NCR was an irrelevant and inappropriate response. While there are many examples – take General Motors or International Business Machines – of companies that suffered from failing to see the future even after it had arrived, there are almost none of companies building sustainable competitive advantages from superior forecasting abilities.

Thoughtful strategy, then, is not about crystal balls, or grand designs and visions. The attempt to formulate these at the level of national economies is now seen to have been at best risible and at worst disastrous – as with Soviet economic planning, Mao's Cultural Revolution, or the improvement strategies of almost all developing countries. What has been true of states is true also in companies. No one has, or could hope to have, the knowledge necessary to construct these transformational plans. Nor – however totalitarian the structures they introduce, in governments or corporations – does anyone truly enjoy the power to implement them.

The subject of strategy

Business strategy is concerned with the match between the internal capabilities of the company and its external environment. Although there is much disagreement of substance among those who write about strategy, most agree that this is the issue.

The methods of strategy, and its central questions, follow from that definition. The methods require analysis of the characteristics of the company and the industries and markets in which it operates. The questions are twofold. What are the origins and characteristics of the successful fit between characteristics and environment: why do companies succeed? And how can companies and their managers make that fit more effective: how will companies succeed?

I once thought that these core questions of strategy – the positive question of understanding the processes through which effective strategies had been arrived at, the normative question of what effective strategy should be – were quite separate. I now believe that they are barely worth distinguishing, and that the conventional emphasis on the vision is a product of the illusion of control.

Strategy is not planning, visioning, or forecasting – all remnants of the belief that one can control the future by superior insight and superior will. The modern subject of business strategy is a set of analytic techniques for understanding better, and so influencing, a company's position in its actual and potential marketplace.

Evolving modern theory

Strategy, as I have defined it, is a subject of application rather than a discipline – rather as, say, geriatrics is to underlying disciplines of pharmacology or cell biology – and the obvious underpinning disciplines for strategy are economics and organizational sociology. Still, this is not how the subject developed in practice.

When the content of strategy was first set out 30 years ago, industrial economics was dominated by the structure–conduct–performance paradigm, which emphasized how market structure – the number of competitors and the degree of rivalry between them – was the principal influence on a company's behavior. Market structure was determined partly by external conditions of supply and demand, and partly (unless antitrust agencies intervened) by the attempts of firms to influence the intensity of competition.

This was a view of markets aimed at public policy, not business policy. It was correctly seen as having little relevance to the basic issues of business strategy. The neglect of the internal characteristics of companies is obvious and explicit. While some of the strategic tools developed by consultants in the 1970s – such as the experience curve and the portfolio matrix – might advantageously have had an economic basis, in practice microeconomic theory was largely ignored.

Not until 1980, with the publication of Michael Porter's *Competitive Strategy*, did economists attempt to recapture the field of strategy. But this was ultimately to prove a false move. Porter's work, essentially a translation of the structure–conduct–performance paradigm into language more appropriate for a business audience, suffered from the limitations of the material on which it was based. His "five forces" and value chain are usefully descriptive of industry structure, but shed no light on the central strategic issue: why different firms, facing the same environment, perform differently.

Much of the organizational sociology of the 1960s addressed strategic issues. Chandler's magisterial *Strategy and Structure*, or the empirical work of Tom Burns and G.M. Stalker, addressed directly the relationships between organizational form and the technological and market environment. But academic sociology was largely captured by people hostile to the very concept of capitalist organization. The subject drifted into abstraction, and further away from the day-to-day concerns of those in business.

More recent insights into the nature of organizations have come either from economics or from the accumulated practical wisdom of which Charles Handy and Henry Mintzberg are, in different ways, effective exponents. Porter's attention ultimately reverted to the public policy concerns of his former mentors in the Harvard economics department, as in *The Competitive Advantage of Nations*.

Strategy today – rents and capabilities

At about the same time as Porter first wrote about strategy, the *Strategic Management Journal*, today the leading journal in the field, was established. The currently dominant view of strategy – resource-based theory – has been principally set out in its pages. It also has an economic base, but has found its inspiration in different places and further back in history. It draws on the Ricardian approach to the determination of economic rent, and the view of the firm as a collection of capabilities described by Edith Penrose and George Richardson.

Economic rent is what firms earn over and above the cost of the capital employed in their business. The terminology is unfortunate. It is used because the central framework was set out by David Ricardo in the early part of the 19th century, when agriculture was the dominant form of economic activity. Economic rent has been variously called economic profit, super-normal profit and excess profit – terms that lack appeal for modern businesspeople. Most recently Stern Stewart, a consultancy, has had some success marketing the concept under the term "economic value added." The problem here is that value added – the value added that is taxed – means something different. Nor does my own attempt to call it "added value" help. Perhaps economic rent is best. The title doesn't matter; the concept does.

The objective of a firm is to increase its economic rent rather than its profit as such. A firm that increases its profits but not its economic rent – as through investments or acquisitions that yield less than the cost of capital – destroys value.

In a contestable market – one in which entry by new firms is relatively early and exit by failing firms is relatively quick – firms that are only just successful enough to survive will earn the industry cost of capital on the replacement cost of their assets. Economic rent is the measure of the competitive advantage that effective established firms enjoy, and competitive advantage is the only means by which companies in contestable markets can earn economic rents.

The opportunity for companies to sustain these competitive advantages is determined by their capabilities. A company's capabilities are of many kinds. For the purposes of strategy, the key distinction is between distinctive and reproducible capabilities.

Distinctive capabilities are those characteristics of a firm that cannot be replicated by competitors, or can be replicated only with great difficulty, even after these competitors realize the benefits they yield for the originating company. Distinctive capabilities can be of many kinds. Government licenses, statutory monopolies, or effective patents and copyrights are particularly stark examples. But equally powerful idiosyncratic characteristics have been built by companies in competitive markets. These include strong brands, patterns of supplier or customer relationships, and skills, knowledge, and routines that are embedded in teams.

Reproducible capabilities can be bought or created by any firm with reasonable management skills, diligence, and financial resources. Most technical capabilities are of this kind. Marketing capabilities are sometimes distinctive, sometimes reproducible.

The importance of the distinction for strategy is this: only distinctive capabilities can be the basis of sustainable competitive advantage. Collections of reproducible capabilities can and will be established by others and therefore cannot generate rents in a competitive or contestable market.

Matching capabilities to markets

So the strategist must first look inward. The strategist must identify the distinctive capabilities of the organization and seek to surround these with a collection of reproducible capabilities, or complementary assets, that enable the firm to sell its distinctive capabilities in the market in which it operates.

While this is easier said than done, it defines a structure in which the processes of strategy formulation and its implementation are bound together. The resource-based view of strategy – emphasizing rent creation through distinctive capabilities – has found its most widely accepted popularization in the core competencies approach of C.K. Prahalad and Gary Hamel. But that application has been made problematic by the absence of sharp criteria for distinguishing core and other competencies, which allows the wishful thinking characteristic of vision- and mission-based strategizing. Core competencies become pretty much what the senior management of the corporation wants them to be.

The perspective of economic rent – which forces the question "Why can't competitors do that?" into every discussion – cuts through much of this haziness. Characteristics such as size, strategic vision, market share, and market positioning – all commonly seen as sources of competitive advantage, but all ultimately reproducible by firms with competitive advantages of their own – can be seen clearly as the result, rather than the origin, of competitive advantage.

Strategic analysis then turns outward, to identify those markets in which the company's capabilities can yield competitive advantage. The emphasis here is again on distinctive capabilities, since only these can be a source of economic rent, but distinctive capabilities need to be supported by an appropriate set of complementary reproducible capabilities.

Markets have product geographic dimensions, and different capabilities each have their own implications for the boundaries of the appropriate market. Reputations and brands are typically effective in relation to a specific customer group, and may be valuable in selling other related products to that group. Innovation-based competitive advantages will typically have a narrower product focus, but may transcend national boundaries in ways that reputations cannot. Distinctive capabilities may dictate market position as well as market choice. Those based on supplier relationships may be most appropriately deployed at the top of the market, while the effectiveness of brands is defined by the customer group that identifies with the brand.

Since distinctive capabilities are at the heart of competitive advantage, every firm asks how it can create distinctive capabilities. Yet the question contains an inherent contradiction: if irreproducible characteristics could be created, they would cease to be irreproducible. What is truly irreproducible has three primary sources: market structure that limits entry; firm history that by its very nature requires extended time to replicate; tacitness in relationships – routines and behavior of "uncertain imitability" – that cannot be replicated because no one, not even the participants themselves, fully comprehends their nature.

So companies would do well to begin by looking at the distinctive capabilities they have rather than at those they would like to have. And established, successful companies will not usually enjoy that position if they do not enjoy some distinctive capability. Again, it is easy to overestimate the effect of conscious design in the development of firms and market structures.

The evolution of capabilities and environment

Strategy, with its emphasis on the fit between characteristics and environment, links naturally to an evolutionary perspective on organization. Processes that provide favorable feedback for characteristics that are well adapted to their environment – and these include both biological evolution and competitive market economies – produce organisms, or companies, that have capabilities matched to their requirements.

Recent understanding of evolutionary processes emphasizes how little intentionality is required to produce that result. Successful companies are not necessarily there because (except with hindsight) anyone had superior insight in organizational design or strategic fit. Rather, there were many different views of the firm capabilities a particular activity required; and it was the market, rather than the visionary executive, that chose the most effective match. Distinctive capabilities were established rather than designed.

This view is supported by detached business history. In his book *The Awakening Giant*, Andrew Pettigrew's description of ICI shows an organization whose path was largely fixed – both for good and for bad – by its own past. The scope and opportunity for effective management strategic choice – both for good and for bad – were necessarily limited by the past. This is not to be pessimistic about the potential for strategic direction or the ability of executives to make important differences, but to reiterate the absurdity and irrelevance of using the blank sheet of paper approach to corporate strategy.

New paradigm

The resource-based view of strategy has a coherence and integrative role that places it well ahead of other mechanisms of strategic decision making. I have little doubt that for the foreseeable future, major contributions to ways of strategic thinking will either form part of that framework or represent development of it. To use the most overworked and abused term in the study of management, after 30 years or so, the subject of strategy is genuinely acquiring what can be described as a paradigm.

RESOURCES

Andrews, Kenneth, *The Concept of Corporate Strategy*, Irwin, 1965.
Ansoff, H. Igor, *Corporate Strategy*, McGraw Hill, 1965.
Barney, J., 'Firm resources and sustained competitive advantage,' *Journal of Management*, 17, 1991.
Burns, Tom and Stalker, G.M., *The Management of Innovation*, Tavistock Publications, 1961.
Chandler, Alfred, *Strategy and Structure*, MIT Press, Cambridge, 1962.
Handy, Charles, *Understanding Organizations*, Penguin, 1976.
Kay, John, *The Business of Economics*, Oxford University Press, 1996.
Mintzberg, Henry, *The Structuring of Organizations*, Prentice Hall, 1979.
Montgomery, C.A., 'Of diamonds and rust,' in C.A Montgomery (ed.), *Resource Based and Evolutionary Theories of the Firm*, Kluwes, 1995.
Penrose, E., *The Theory of the Growth of the Firm*, Oxford University Press, 1959.
Pettigrew, Andrew, *The Awakening Giant*, Blackwell, 1985.
Porter, Michael, *Competitive Strategy*, Free Press, 1980.
Porter, Michael, *The Competitive Advantage of Nations*, Free Press, 1990.
Scherer, F.M., *Industrial Market Structure and Economic Performance*, Houghton Mifflin, 1970.

What is strategy and how do you know if you have one?

COSTAS MARKIDES

[Strategy bewilders and confuses at every turn. This led *The Economist* to claim that: "Nobody really knows what strategy is." The chasm at the heart of our knowledge of strategy requires a return to fundamentals.]

What is strategy, *really*? Despite the obvious importance of a superior strategy to the success of an organization and despite decades of academic research on the subject, there is little agreement among academics as to what strategy really is. From notions of strategy as positioning to strategy as visioning, several possible definitions are fighting for legitimacy. Lack of an acceptable definition has opened up the field to an invasion of sexy slogans and terms, all of which add to the confusion and state of unease.

Not that the confusion is restricted to academics! If asked, most practicing executives would define strategy as "how one could achieve their company's objectives." Although this definition is technically correct, it is so general that it is practically meaningless. One can put almost everything under the "how" umbrella to make this definition a motherhood statement.

Needless to say, this state of affairs is unfortunate. Perhaps nothing highlights better the sad (comical?) state of affairs surrounding strategy than the following. In November 1996, the most prominent strategy academic, Michael Porter of Harvard, published a *Harvard Business Review* article grandly entitled: "What is strategy?"[1] This was followed only a few months later by another famous academic, Gary Hamel of London Business School, with an equally impressively titled article: "The search for strategy."[2] That after 40 years of academic research on the subject, two of the most prominent academics in the field felt the need to go out of their way and start searching for strategy goes to show how much confusion we have managed to create regarding such a crucial business decision.

Although part of the confusion is undoubtedly self-inflicted, a major portion of it also stems from an honest lack of understanding about the content of strategy. I would like to propose a view of strategy which is based on my research on companies that have strategically innovated in their industries. These are companies which not only developed strategies which were fundamentally different from the strategies of their competitors but whose strategies also turned out to be tremendously successful.

Based on my research on these successful strategists, I would like to propose that there are certain simple but fundamental principles underlying every successful strategy. When one goes beyond the visible differences among strategies and probes deeper into their roots, one cannot fail to notice that all successful strategies share the same underlying principles or building blocks. Thus, the building blocks of the successful Microsoft strategy are the same as the building blocks of the strategy which propelled Sears to industry leadership 100 years ago. My argument is that by understanding what these building blocks are, a company can use them to develop its own successful strategy.

The building blocks of strategy

Strategy must decide on a few parameters.

In today's uncertain and ever-changing environment, strategy is all about making some very difficult decisions on a *few* parameters. It is absolutely essential that the firm decides on these parameters because they become the boundaries within which people are given the freedom and the autonomy to operate and try things out. They also define the company's *strategic position* in its industry. Without clear decisions on these parameters, the company will drift like a rudderless ship on the open seas.

What are these parameters? A company has to decide on three main issues: *who* will be its targeted customers and who it will *not* target; *what* products or services it will offer its chosen customers and what it will *not* offer them; and *how* it will go about achieving all this – what activities it will perform and what activities it will not perform.

These are not easy decisions to make and each question has many possible answers, all of them *ex ante* possible and logical. As a result, these kinds of decisions will unavoidably be preceded with debates, disagreements, politicking, and indecision. Yet, at the end of the day, a firm cannot be everything to everybody, so clear and explicit decisions must be made. These choices may turn out to be wrong, but that is not an excuse for not deciding.

It is essential that the organization makes clear and explicit choices on these three dimensions because the choices made become the parameters within which people are allowed to operate with autonomy. Without these clear parameters, the end result can be chaos. Seen in another way, it would be foolish and dangerous to allow people to take initiatives without some clear parameters guiding their actions.

Not only must the company make clear choices on these parameters, it must also attempt to make choices which are different from the choices its competitors have made. A company will be successful if it chooses a *distinctive* (i.e. different from competitors') strategic position. Sure, it may be impossible to come up with answers which are 100 percent different from the answers of our competitors, but the ambition should be to create as much differentiation as possible.

Given the importance of coming up with clear answers to these three issues, the question is, who comes up with possible answers to these questions; who decides what to do out of the many possibilities; and how long do the decisions remain unchanged?

Who comes up with ideas?

Given the right organizational context, strategic ideas (on who to target, what to sell and how to do it) can come from anybody, anywhere, any time. They may emerge through trial and error, or because somebody has a "gut feeling" or because somebody "got lucky" and stumbled across a good idea. They may even emerge out of a formal strategic planning session! However dismissive we can be of the modern corporation's formal planning process, the possibility still exists that some good ideas can come out of such a process. No matter how the ideas are conceived, it is unlikely that they will be perfect from the start. The firm must therefore be willing and ready to modify or change its strategic ideas as it receives feedback from the market.

In general, there are numerous tactics at our disposal to enhance creativity at the idea-generation stage. Let me list just a few of them:

- Encourage everybody in the organization to question the firm's implicit assumptions and beliefs (i.e. the firm's sacred cows) as to who our customers really are, what we are really offering to the customer, and how we do these things. Encourage also a fundamental questioning of the firm's accepted answer to the question: "What business are we in?"

- To facilitate this questioning, create a positive crisis. If done correctly, this will galvanize the organization into active thinking. If done incorrectly, this will demoralize everybody and create confusion and disillusionment throughout the organization.

- Develop processes in the organization to collect and utilize ideas from everybody – employees, customers, distributors, etc. At Lan & Spar Bank, every employee is asked to contribute ideas through a strategy workbook; at Schlumberger, they have the internal venturing unit; at Bank One, they have a specific customer center where all customers are encouraged to phone and express their complaints; at my local supermarket, they have a customer suggestion box. Different organizations have come up with different tactics, but the idea is the same: allow everybody to contribute ideas and make it

easy for them to communicate their ideas to the decision makers in the organization.
- Create variety in the thinking that takes place in a formal planning process. This can be achieved not only by using a diverse team of people but also by utilizing as many thinking approaches as possible.
- Institutionalize a culture of innovation. The organization must create the organizational environment (i.e. culture/structure/incentives/people) which promotes and supports innovative behaviors.

This is not an exhaustive list of tactics that could be used to increase creativity in strategy making. The principle, though, remains the same: at this stage of crafting an innovative strategy, the goal must be to generate as many strategic ideas as possible so that we have the luxury of choosing.

Who decides?

Even though anybody in the organization can come up with new strategic ideas (and everybody *should* be encouraged to do so), it is the responsibility of top management to make the final choices. There have been many calls lately to make the process of strategy development "democratic" and "flexible" – to bring everybody in the organization into the process. The thinking here is that the odds of conceiving truly innovative ideas are increased if thousands of people rather than just five or ten senior managers put their minds to work. And this much is true. But the job of choosing the ideas that the firm will actually pursue must be left to top management. Otherwise, the result is chaos, confusion, and ultimately a demotivated workforce. After all is said and done, it is the leaders of the organization, not every single employee, who must choose which ideas will be pursued.

Choosing is difficult. At the time nobody knows for sure whether a particular idea will work, nor does anybody know whether the choices made are really the most appropriate ones. One could reduce the uncertainty at this stage by either evaluating each idea in a rigorous way or by experimenting with the idea in a limited way to see whether it works or not. However, it is crucial to understand that uncertainty can be reduced but not limited. No matter how much experimentation we carry out and no matter how much thinking goes into it, the time will come when the firm must decide one way or another. Choices have to be made and these choices may turn out to be wrong. However, lack of certainty is no excuse for indecision.

Not only must the firm choose what to do, it must also make it clear what it will *not* do. The worst strategic mistake possible is to choose something but also keep our options open by doing other things as well. Imagine an organization where the CEO proclaims: "Our strategy is crystal clear: we will do ABC" and at the same time the employees of this organization see the firm doing ABC as well as XYZ. In their eyes, this means one of two things: either there is not really a strategy or top management is totally confused. Either way, the organization is left demoralized and confidence in senior management is shattered. Organizations which say one thing and then do another are those that have failed to make clear choices about what they will do and what they will not do with their strategy.

The difficult choices made by Canon in attacking Xerox highlight the importance of choosing in an explicit way what to do and what not to do. At the time of the attack, Xerox had a lock on the copier market by following a well-defined and successful strategy, the main elements of which were as follows. Having segmented the market by volume, Xerox decided to go after the corporate reproduction market by concentrating on copiers designed for high-speed, high-volume needs. This inevitably defined Xerox's customers as big corporations, which in turn determined its distribution method: the direct sales force. At the same time, Xerox decided to lease rather than sell its machines, a strategic choice that had worked well in the company's earlier battles with 3M.

Xerox's strategy proved to be so successful that several new competitors, among them IBM and Kodak, tried to enter this market, basically by adopting the same or similar strategies. Canon, on the other hand, chose to play the game differently. Having determined in the early 1960s to diversify out of cameras and into copiers, Canon segmented the market by end-user and decided to target small and medium-sized businesses while also producing PC copiers for the individual. At the same time, Canon decided to sell its machines through a dealer network rather than lease them, and while Xerox emphasized the speed of its machines, Canon elected to concentrate on quality and price as its differentiating features. Cutting the story short, where IBM's and Kodak's assault on the copier market failed, Canon's succeeded: within 20 years of attacking Xerox, Canon emerged as the market leader in volume terms.

There are many reasons behind the success of Canon. Notice, however, that just like Xerox did 20 years before it, Canon also created for itself *a distinctive strategic position* in the industry, a position that was different from Xerox's position: whereas Xerox targeted big corporations as its customers, Canon went after small companies and individuals; while Xerox emphasized the speed of its machines, Canon focussed on quality and price; and whereas Xerox used a direct sales force to lease its machines, Canon used its dealer network to sell its copiers. Rather than try to beat Xerox at its own game, Canon triumphed by creating its own unique strategic position.

As in the case of Xerox, these were *not* the only choices available to Canon and undoubtedly serious debates and disagreements must have taken place within Canon as to whether these were the right choices to pursue. Yet choices were made and a clear strategy with sharp and well-defined boundaries was put in place. As in the case of Xerox, Canon was successful because it chose a unique and well-defined strategic position in the industry – one with distinctive customers, products, and activities.

Strategy must put all our choices together to create a reinforcing mosaic

Choosing what to do and what not to do is certainly an important element of strategy. However, strategy is much more than this. Strategy is all about *combining* these choices into *a system* that creates the requisite *fit* between what the environment needs and what the company does. It is the combining of the firm's choices into a well-balanced system that is important, not the individual choices.[3]

The importance of conceptualizing the company *as a combination of activities* cannot be overemphasized. From this perspective, a firm is a complex system of interrelated and interdependent activities, each affecting each other: decisions and actions in one part of the business affect other parts, directly or indirectly. This means that unless we take a holistic, big-picture approach in designing the activities of our company, our efforts will backfire: even if each individual activity is optimally crafted, the whole may still suffer unless we take interdependencies into consideration. The numerous local optima almost always undermine the global optimum.

The problem is that human beings can never really comprehend all the complexity embedded in our companies. We therefore tend to focus on one or two aspects of the system and try to optimize these subsystems independently. By doing so, we ignore the interdependencies in the system and we are therefore making matters worse. Since it takes time for the effect of our actions to show up, we do not even see that we are the source of our problems. When the long-term effects of our short-sighted actions hit home, we blame other people, and especially outside forces, for our problems (we had no forecasts; demand is unpredictable; the economy is not growing; and so on).

In designing the company's system of activities, managers must bear four principles in mind. First, the individual activities we choose to do must be the ones that are demanded by the market. Second, the activities we decide to perform must fit with each other. Third, activities must not only fit but must also be in *balance* with each other. Finally, it is important to keep in mind that the collection of these activities will form an interrelated system. Not only should we pay particular attention to the interrelationships in this system, we should also be aware that the *structure* of this system will drive behavior in it. What our people do in the firm is conditioned by this underlying structure. Therefore, if we want to change behavior, we will have to change the structure of the system.

Strategy must achieve fit without losing flexibility

Creating the right fit between what the market needs and what the firm does can backfire if the environment changes and the firm does not respond accordingly. We are all familiar with the story of the frog: when a frog is put in a pot of boiling water, it jumps out; when, instead, the same frog is put in a pot of cold water and the water is slowly brought to the boil, the frog stays in the pot and boils to death. In the same manner, if our company does not react to the constant changes taking place in its environment, it will find itself boiled to death.

This implies that a company needs to create the requisite fit with its current environment while remaining flexible enough to respond to (or even create) changes in this environment. But what does it mean when we say that a firm *must remain flexible*? The way I use the term here, I imply three things: a firm must first be able to identify, early enough, changes in its environment; it must then have the cultural readiness to embrace change and respond to it; and it must have the requisite skills and competencies to compete in whatever environment emerges after the change. Thus, flexibility has a cultural element to it (i.e. being willing to change) as well as a competence element to it (i.e. being able to change).

Strategy needs to be supported by the appropriate organizational environment

Any strategy, however brilliant, needs to be implemented properly if it is to deliver the desired results. However, implementation does not take place in a vacuum. It takes place within an *organizational environment* which we, as managers, create. It is this organizational environment which produces the behavior that we observe in companies. Therefore, to secure the desired strategic behavior by employees, the firm must first create the appropriate environment – that is, the environment that promotes and supports its chosen strategy.

By environment, I mean four elements: the organization's culture, its incentives, its structure, and its people.[4] A company that wants to put into action a certain strategy must first ask the question: "What kind of culture, incentives, structure and people do we need to implement the strategy?" In other words, to create a superior strategy, a company must think beyond customers, products, and activities. It must also decide what underlying environment to create and how exactly to create it so as to facilitate the implementation of its strategy.

However, deciding on what kind of culture, structure, incentives, and people to have is not enough. The challenge for strategy is to develop these four elements of organizational environment and then put them together so that on the one hand they support and complement each other, while on the other hand they collectively support and promote the chosen strategy. As was the case with the activities which I described above, this is the real challenge for strategy: not only to create the *correct individual parts*, but to combine them to create a strong and reinforcing system.[5]

Achieving internal and external fit will bring only short-term success. Inevitably, fit will create contentment, overconfidence and inertia. Therefore, while a company aims to achieve fit, it must also create enough slack in the system so that, as the firm grows or as the external environment changes, the organizational environment can remain flexible and responsive.

Finally, if business conditions oblige a strategic change of direction, the internal context of the organization must change with it. This is extremely difficult. Not only do we need to change the individual pieces that make up the organizational environment, we must also put them together to form an overall organizational environment that will again fit with the new strategy.

No strategy remains unique for ever

There is no question that success stems from the exploitation of a distinctive or unique strategic position. Unfortunately, no position will remain unique or attractive for ever. Not only do attractive positions get imitated by aggressive competitors, but – and perhaps more importantly – new strategic positions keep emerging all the time. A new strategic position is simply a new viable Who-What-How combination – perhaps a new customer segment (a new Who), or a new value proposition (a new What), or a new way of distributing or manufacturing the product (a new How). Over time, these new positions may grow to challenge the attractiveness of our own position.

You see this happening in industry after industry: once formidable companies that built their success on what seemed to be unassailable strategic positions find themselves humbled by relatively unknown companies which base their attacks on creating and exploiting new strategic positions in the industry.[6]

New strategic positions – that is, new Who-What-How combinations – emerge all around us all the time. As industries change, new strategic positions emerge to challenge existing positions for supremacy. Changing industry conditions, changing customer needs or preferences, countermoves by competitors, and a company's own evolving competencies give rise to new opportunities and the potential for new ways of playing the game. Unless a company continuously questions its accepted norms and behaviors, it will never discover what else has become available. It will miss these new combinations and other, more agile players will jump in and exploit the gaps left behind.

Therefore, a company must never settle for what it has. While fighting it out in its current position, it must continuously search for new positions to colonize and new opportunities to take advantage of. Simple as this may sound, it contrasts sharply with the way most competitors compete in their industries: most of them take the established rules of the game as given and spend all their time trying to become *better* than each other in their existing positions, usually through cost or differentiation strategies. Little or no emphasis is placed on becoming *different* from competitors. This is evidenced from the fact that the majority of companies which strategically innovate by breaking the rules of the game tend to be small niche players or new market entrants. It is indeed rare to find a strategic innovator who is also an established industry big player – a fact which hints at the difficulties of risking the sure thing for something uncertain.[7]

There are many reasons why established companies find it hard to become strategic innovators. Compared with new entrants or niche players, leaders are weighed down by *structural* and *cultural* inertia, internal politics, complacency, fear of cannibalizing existing products, fear of destroying existing competencies, satisfaction with the status quo, and a general lack of incentives to abandon a certain present for an uncertain future. In addition, since there are fewer industry leaders than potential new entrants, the chances that the innovator will emerge from the ranks of the leaders is unavoidably small.

Despite such obstacles, established companies cannot afford not to strategically innovate. As already pointed out, dramatic shifts in company fortunes can take place only if a company succeeds in not only playing its game better than its rivals but also designing and playing a different game from its competitors. Strategic innovation has the potential to take third-rate companies and elevate them to industry leadership status; and it can take established industry leaders and destroy them in a short period of time. Even if the established players do not want to strategically innovate (for fear of destroying their existing profitable positions), somebody else will. Established players might as well pre-empt that.

The culture that established players must develop is that *strategies are not cast in concrete*. A company needs to remain flexible and ready to adjust its strategy if the feedback from the market is not favorable. More importantly, a company needs to continuously question the way it operates in its current position while still fighting it out in its current position against existing competitors.

Continuously questioning one's accepted strategic position serves two vital purposes. First, it allows a company to identify early enough whether its current position in the business is losing its attractiveness to others (and so decide what to do about it).[8] Second and more importantly, it gives the company the opportunity to proactively explore the emerging terrain and hopefully be the first to discover new and attractive strategic positions to take advantage of. This is no guarantee: questioning one's accepted answers will not automatically lead to new unexploited goldmines. But even a remote possibility of discovering something new will never come up if the questions are never asked.

RESOURCES

Ansoff, H.I., *Implanting Strategic Management*, Prentice Hall, 1984 (2nd edition, 1990).

Markides, Costas, *Diversification, Refocussing and Economic Performance*, MIT Press, 1995.

Markides, Costas, *All the Right Moves*, Harvard Business School Press, 1999.

Markides, Costas, and Geroski, Paul A., *Fast Second*, Jossey Bass, 2004.

Mintzberg, Henry, *The Rise and Fall of Strategic Planning*, Prentice Hall, 1994.

Trajectory Management

PAUL STREBEL AND ANNE-VALÉRIE OHLSSON

[There is no magic recipe for corporate success. Instead managers must select the right business drivers for the conditions in which their business is operating.]

Winning repeatedly over an extended period calls for differing approaches to exploit differing conditions. Timeless best practice, following the one true approach, is not enough. The business and its environment are continually changing; best practice has to be adapted to the conditions. The key to success is capitalizing on the uniqueness of a business and its changing opportunities. This calls for the right managerial practice – adopting the right drivers to adapt to and shape the conditions facing a business over time.

A business usually contains a variety of business models, organizational, leadership, and governance approaches. These are influenced by economic, socio-cultural, psychological, and political forces, which have their own separate dynamics and are not co-ordinated. At any point in time, to avoid confusion and pursue a direction, leaders have to emphasize a particular business model, organizational mode, leadership style, and governance role, for decision making and resource allocation. These dominant approaches are what we call the business drivers.

The business drivers have to fit both the external and internal conditions (as illustrated in Figure 1.1). Management has to develop a driving business model that not only exploits and shapes value-creating opportunities but also builds on the distinctive capabilities of the business. It has to install a driving mode of organization that not only deals with the complexity of the business environment but also reflects the available resources. It has to acquire a driving leadership style that not only takes account of the urgency to change in support of value creation but also works with the readiness of employees. It has to ensure that the driving governance role of the board not only deals with the externalities (non-market issues) that shape the agendas of the business stakeholders and shareholders but also complements its own power and effectiveness.

The internal conditions reflect the way the business has developed in the past. History shapes managerial effectiveness, the openness of employees to change, the available resources, and distinctive capabilities. The external conditions reflect the business environment, which is continually changing, so that management has to always have an eye on the future.

58   Strategy and competition

Internal conditions
Distinctive capabilities
Resources
Employee readiness
Managerial effectiveness

Business drivers
Dominant business model
Dominant organizational mode
Dominant leadership style
Dominant governance role

External conditions
Opportunities
Environment complexity
Change urgency
Externalities (non-market forces)

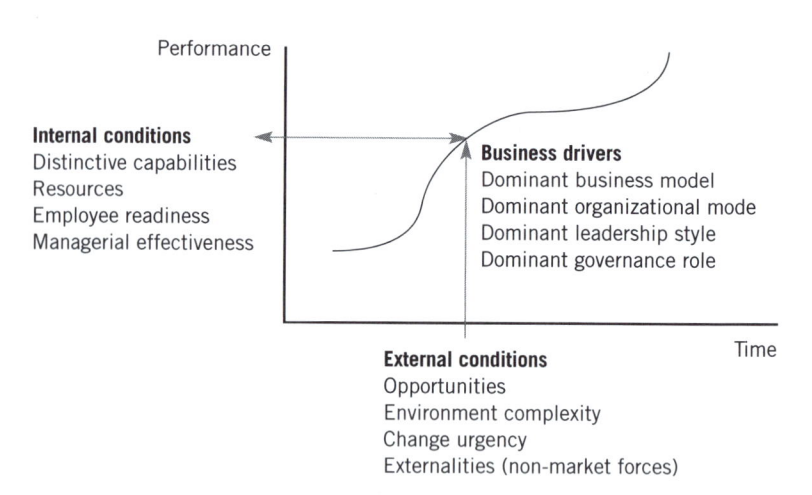

Figure 1.1: *Business drivers and conditions*

Over time, business performance, conditions, and the drivers, trace out a sequence or path, which is the *trajectory* of the business. Managing the trajectory of a business is about periodically switching the drivers. It's about matching differing drivers with differing conditions. It's about anticipating how the conditions might change and shaping the conditions to support new drivers, in order to win repeatedly over time.

We shall illustrate the main guidelines for successful trajectory management by referring to the well-known and extensively discussed story of Jack Welch's leadership of GE over two decades from 1981 to 2001. We can understand more easily why Welch was successful by thinking in terms of trajectory management.

Periodically realigning internal and external momentum

To take advantage of changing conditions, the business drivers have to be switched from time to time. First, Welch switched business drivers in response to pressure from the financial markets when he took over. Then, in the late 1980s and early 1990s, GE took advantage of international acquisition opportunities during the European and Japanese downturns. In the early 1990s, to increase margins, Welch extended the acquisition drive to include services. In the mid-1990s, he responded to the challenge of organizational integration created by the multiple acquisitions with the drive for process efficiency based on the Six Sigma program, while in the late 1990s, he used the e-business boom to re-energize the company.

These switches in the drivers Welch used to lead GE are summarized in Figure 1.2, which highlights the shifts in business model emphasis between product market innovation and value chain efficiency.

Figure 1.2

Y-axis: Product market innovation
X-axis: Value-chain efficiency

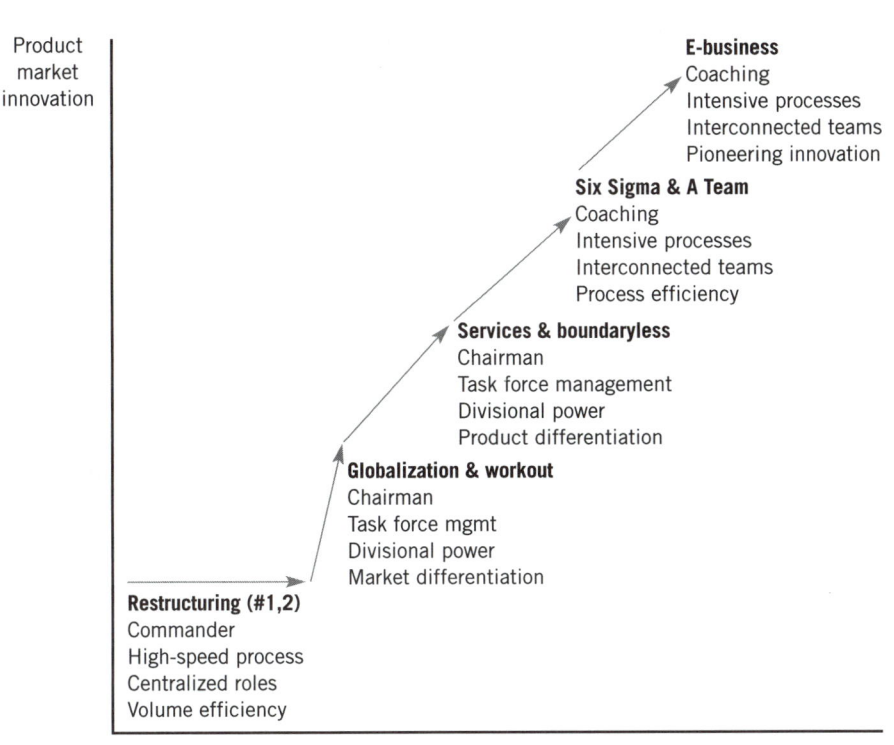

Restructuring (#1,2)
Commander
High-speed process
Centralized roles
Volume efficiency

Globalization & workout
Chairman
Task force mgmt
Divisional power
Market differentiation

Services & boundaryless
Chairman
Task force management
Divisional power
Product differentiation

Six Sigma & A Team
Coaching
Intensive processes
Interconnected teams
Process efficiency

E-business
Coaching
Intensive processes
Interconnected teams
Pioneering innovation

Figure 1.2: *Welch's switches in trajectory drivers*

As the GE example illustrates, trajectory management requires companies to develop a number of managerial competencies. These include the ability to do the following.

Develop an anticipatory organization to look ahead

Sensing new conditions early enough to turn them into opportunities is essential for the shaping of a successful trajectory. Welch gradually developed GE into an anticipatory organization that was energized, future-oriented, always learning, and continually acquiring new capabilities. To energize his people, Welch used open dialog, feedback meetings, brainstorming, and task forces to test and stretch them. To instil a future orientation, GE's strategy playbook for the business heads was structured around current market trends, competitor activities, and a three-year competitive scenario. To develop a "boundaryless" organization that is always learning, externally and internally, GE spread process-driven learning throughout the organization with the Six Sigma program. To get new capabilities, Welch made the acquisition of smaller companies, followed by a disciplined integration process, the basis for a highly effective way of continually acquiring talent and skills.

Look back and build on the existing business momentum

The new drivers have to build on the existing internal conditions, in terms of distinctive capabilities, available resources, employee readiness, and the effectiveness of management. If not, the business and company becomes unhinged from the past and risks falling apart, as happened to GE's European competitor, ABB, when it tried to switch drivers under Goran Lindahl and then Jörgen Centerman in the late 1990s and early 2000s. If the internal conditions do not support the desired drivers, a transformation process is needed to build a bridge from the existing conditions to those desired for the future. Welch was very aware of where GE was in the development of its internal capabilities and made sure that each new set of business drivers built on what went before. After restructuring around the number one or two position domestically, he went global, then he added services; to integrate the business portfolio, he emphasized Six Sigma; and finally he added e-business to enhance the processes even further.

Use contingency thinking to look sideways and match drivers with conditions

Surveying Welch's two decades at the helm, the differences between his approaches in successive periods can be expressed in terms of a gap between the existing business drivers and the right behavior for the emerging conditions in the following period. Figure 1.3 illustrates one such gap that emerged during the transition between the third and fourth phases of Welch's leadership in the mid-1990s. The actual behaviors emphasized by Welch in the mid-1990s are represented by the + signs, while the right behaviors that fit the newly emerging conditions of the later 1990s are depicted by the * signs.

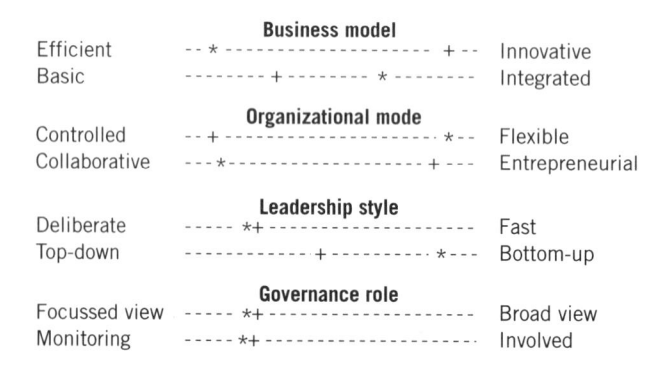

```
                     Business model
    Efficient   --*-----------------+--    Innovative
    Basic       --------+--------*--------  Integrated
                   Organizational mode
    Controlled   --+--------------------*--  Flexible
    Collaborative ---*-----------------+---  Entrepreneurial
                     Leadership style
    Deliberate   -----*+------------------  Fast
    Top-down     ------------+----------*--- Bottom-up
                     Governance role
    Focussed view -----*+------------------  Broad view
    Monitoring   -----*+-------------------  Involved
```

Figure 1.3: *Profile gap between actual (+) and right (*) driving behaviors emphasized by Welch in the mid-1990s*

The managerial behaviors that Welch emphasized in the later 1990s were consistent with those required to deal with the emerging conditions. In terms of the driving business model, an employee survey in the mid-1990s highlighted the need to integrate GE's many acquisitions. This called for a switch in the driving business model toward greater efficiency and integration, reducing the existing emphasis on product-market innovation. In terms of the organizational mode, the complexity of GE's business processes called for a more flexible rather than controlled organization. The increasing pressure on resources also made collaboration a more important overall priority than entrepreneurship. In terms of leadership, the openness of GE's employees to more efficiency, as shown in the survey, meant that an even more bottom-up leadership style, rather than top-down, was possible. GE's performance also provided the time for continuing a deliberate approach. Little information is available on the dominant governance behaviors of GE's board. However, given Welch's experience and track record, it is safe to assume that the board was reduced to a monitoring role focussed on financial performance.

Make sure the drivers are aligned vertically

The dominant leadership style and organizational mode have to complement the driving business model. Welch did not change the driving business model without putting complementary organizational and leadership drivers in place: streamlining around number one or two was accompanied by radical simplification of the planning process and organizational structure, with careful attention to the leadership succession pipeline; globalization was accompanied by organizational workouts to sensitize management to the frontline and a leadership emphasis on speed and simplicity to improve communication and build self-confidence; services were accompanied by the introduction of boundaryless learning with a leadership emphasis on stretch; and the process efficiency drive was supported by Six Sigma-based continual improvement, complemented by edge, energy, and execution on the leadership side.

Anchor the new drivers in the organization

Putting new drivers and conditions in place takes time; changing the drivers too frequently is counterproductive because there are limits to the change people and organizations can absorb without becoming dysfunctional, or being totally replaced. It takes time for the political forces behind governance, the psychological forces involved in leadership, and the cultural forces in the organization to be realigned with a new business model. Over the course of two decades, Welch shifted business drivers only five times. He is on record as saying that he began getting tired of hearing himself repeat the same message over and over again, until he realized that was his job. He insisted on making each switch in drivers stick, sustaining the new trajectory and exploiting it to the full over several years.

In sum, if Welch had not reinvented his leadership priorities and altered the business drivers periodically, in sync with both the external and internal conditions, he could not have achieved the levels of performance that GE enjoyed during his tenure. Doing so calls for a supporting organization that anticipates the future, as well as sensitivity to the speed with which new internal conditions can be shaped. The business drivers can be changed only periodically, because even with good learning skills it takes time and disciplined persistence to reshape a trajectory. Business leaders have to do what is right for longer-term value creation: select only a very limited number of new driver configurations and see the change in driving behaviors and conditions through to completion.

RESOURCES

Mintzberg, Henry, *The Strategy Process: Concepts, Contexts, Cases* (with J.B. Quinn), 2nd Edition, Prentice Hall, 1991.

Moore, J.I., *Writers on Strategy and Strategic Management*, Penguin, 1992.

Ohmae, Kenichi, *The Mind of the Strategist*, McGraw Hill, 1982.

Strebel, Paul, *Trajectory Management: Leading a Business over Time*, Wiley, 2003.

www.trajectorymanagement.com

Making mergers and acquisitions work

ROGER PUDNEY

[Mergers and acquisitions are a huge global business. But, for many companies, making them work remains as mysterious as ever.]

A variety of studies on the success rates of mergers and acquisitions (M&As) seem to converge around the conclusion that roughly 20 percent destroy value, 50 percent have a neutral impact, and 30 percent add value. A *Business Week* survey of large mergers concluded that 61 percent of buyers destroyed their own shareholders' wealth as a result of the deal and that, a year after the deals were made, their average return was 25 percent below that of their industry peers. Another study by KPMG concluded that 83 percent of mergers did not actually add any value at all.

Yet some organizations beat these odds substantially and have an M&A track record closer to 80–90 percent success (meaning that significant added value was created). These include companies such as General Electric, which has made 400 acquisitions in the past 20 years; Cisco Systems, which made 42 acquisitions in six years (and which announced three deals in the first quarter of 2003); and companies such as the Danish company ISS (the world's largest cleaning services company), which has made over 200 acquisitions in just four years.

So, what is it that drives companies toward a notoriously risky activity? Typical reasons include economies of scale, achieving global reach, sheer survival through creating critical mass, acquisition of core competencies and technologies, filling in gaps in the product or geographic portfolio, and getting access to scarce talent. These tend to be the rational reasons quoted, but the reasons can equate to growth for its own sake, empire building, and, as *Business Week* observed "'top executives' egomania which fostered bulking up on size and earnings seemingly without strategic thought or value."

In addition, many argue that true mergers are very rare and that the term is normally applied to hidden acquisitions. Many regard the mergers of HP and Compaq and Daimler and Chrysler as acquisitions by HP and Daimler Benz. One distinguished chairman of several major companies bans the use of the word "merger" in any of his organizations on the grounds that there is no such thing. To quote the CEO of an acquired US company in the defense industry: "Before the merger we were told we were an equal partner. After six months we felt like a junior partner. Now, a year later we feel like slaves."

Why do M&As fail?

The main reasons can be summarized as: lack of clarity on the strategic reasons for making the transaction and the desired outcomes (often leading to overpayment); excessive involvement in a deal-making state of mind; overestimating cost savings and synergies; an inadequate overall integration process; and failure to manage the softer factors in the integration process (particularly cultural issues and the retention of key people). When AT&T bought NCR in the 1990s for $7.5 billion, poor management of these factors (particularly the strategic analysis and lack of an integration plan) meant a $3.5 billion write-off before NCR was spun off as an independent company again.

Figure 1.4 shows a typical series of 11 stages which contains three major causes of failure. First, and in many cases, the acquisition is treated as a deal and has no real strategic objective. There is no robust assessment of its potential against strategic goals and no use of search criteria (or these are then adapted to fit). Successful companies acquire organizations or merge with other organizations which fit their strategy.

The second area of potential disaster is integration (stage 10). Many organizations leave discussion of this until the deal is signed. But the earlier you start to plan the integration process, the greater your chances of success. Indeed, an approach adopted by companies like Electrolux simulates integration at something like stage four for a number of candidates (not just for the most likely candidate) because this acts as a very good screening device. Naturally, this process sometimes raises significant issues which cause the potential acquirer to walk away. This can be a valuable outcome.

The third issue is lack of a good performance review process (stage 11). Many companies focus only on the cost savings promised to the outside world and not on the creation of real future added value in their marketplace.

Historically, most due diligence (stage seven) is focussed on financial, legal, manufacturing, and operational type issues. It tends to underestimate critical softer questions such as: what kind of organization is this, what values does it have, what is its culture, and how does that differ from the acquiring organization?

Successful integration involves:

- planning the process;
- managing cultural differences;
- managing the major stakeholders;
- managing communications issues;
- an implementation plan.

Making mergers and acquisitions work 65

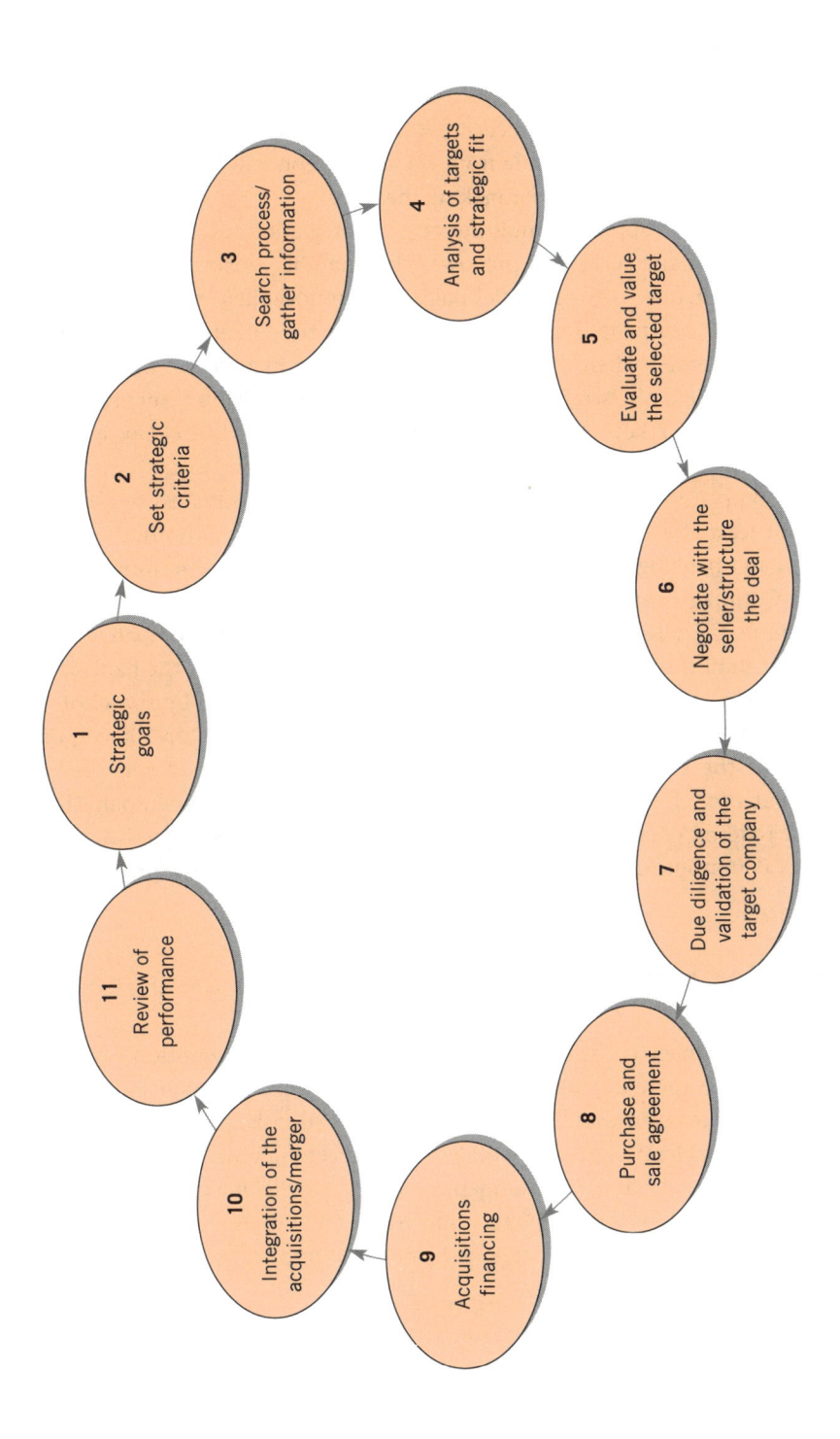

1. Strategic goals
2. Set strategic criteria
3. Search process/gather information
4. Analysis of targets and strategic fit
5. Evaluate and value the selected target
6. Negotiate with the seller/structure the deal
7. Due diligence and validation of the target company
8. Purchase and sale agreement
9. Acquisitions financing
10. Integration of the acquisitions/merger
11. Review of performance

Figure 1.4: *The mergers and acquisitions process (The Ashridge Journal, Summer 2003, © Ashridge (Bonar Law Memorial) Trust)*

Plan ahead

Primarily, the answer is a speedy process that is planned early and is driven by acute awareness of where the added value from the acquisition will be found. This links back to a tight, coherent strategy for making the deal.

The acquirer should appoint a multi-functional integration team as early as possible (ideally during the screening process). This may be constrained by issues of confidentiality but, once the companies publicly announce their intention to merge, they should draft key people from the acquiree into the integration team. This is obviously much easier when the acquiror's preparation includes an assessment of who the key people are. Cisco Systems typically has its integration team visiting and talking to groups of key people in the target company on the day after the announcement.

The HP/Compaq integration has been managed with real awareness of the classic pitfalls (not least as a result of studying successful integrations in other industries such as oil and banking). Joint co-chairmen of the integration team (one from HP, one from Compaq) were appointed before the deal became public in September 2001. To quote Carly Fiorina, the chief executive of the combined company: "We've had our first draft integration plans done since before we called in the bankers." In May 2002, immediately after the deal was (narrowly) approved by shareholders, rationalization of the two product ranges was announced and the top 100 corporate customers of the combined company were visited by senior salespeople with detailed plans for the future business relationship. Overall, the company had a three-year roadmap ready at that point and, by the end of 2002, the integration team was 1,000 people in total, with 1.3 million hours invested in the process.

Achieving cultural integration

An inability to manage cultural differences is one of the most significant causes of failure. Essentially, these are differences in what the companies value and regard as important in their businesses. The fundamental question is whether these differences are manageable. As early as possible in the screening process successful M&A companies find ways to describe and map these differences. One approach is simply to ask those from the potential acquisition to describe their culture and what is important to them and to reciprocate with the same information. The process has several key objectives:

- to map the differences between the two organizations;
- to identify which differences are potentially damaging to the success of the acquisition;

- to decide what the future joint culture will be, taking the preferred elements from both existing cultures to create a hybrid approach. Some of these differences, if manageable, can create real added value in the new combination.

Once the cultural integration agenda becomes clear, joint task groups should develop the detailed integration plans, including joint team building and other opportunities to learn about each other. In the integration between BP and Amoco, one BP general manager, speaking in the second year of the joint company said: "It takes time to get real integration and it only comes when the people know each other both personally and as business colleagues."

Stakeholder management

Irrespective of the size of the companies involved, key stakeholder groups include employees in the target company, employees in the acquiring company, key customers, key suppliers, and local government/local communities and local media. For larger acquisitions, central governments and national/international media may also be important.

The key process of managing this potential minefield is stakeholder mapping. This involves a number of simple techniques which identify key subgroups or individuals within a stakeholder group and categorizes them by, for example, attitude to the acquisition and the influence they can have on a successful outcome. This provides a blueprint for the priorities in the integration.

Often, acquiring companies underestimate the amount of anxiety among their own key people, who may see the acquired company's personnel and competences as a threat. As a director of Electrolux said: "We tend to treat the losers well and forget the people who will be building the future of the business." These key individuals can represent a substantial part of the future value of the acquisition, particularly when the company is small or medium-sized and entrepreneurial. Retention is key.

How can this best be achieved? First, and as soon as confidentiality permits, by rapid approaches to the individuals to assure them of their future role. Glaxo's hostile (but successful) acquisition of Wellcome in the pharmaceutical industry is an example of how to do this. Within 24 hours of the bid announcement every senior Wellcome manager who had been identified as crucial in the merged company had a face-to-face conversation with a senior Glaxo manager. One basic principle is to give the key individuals a role in shaping the future structure and strategy of the combined company.

As well as reassurance, money can help. Some companies have a rule of thumb which pays 50 percent of salary as a bonus to retain selected key employees for the first year – HP's bill for this is reported as $500 million.

In smaller companies, one of the unsung attractions is the opportunity to be exposed to more sophisticated management development. For example, ISS gives acquired managers in some countries the opportunity to go through 360° feedback processes and assessment centers.

Unless this retention process is managed well and early, key people may leave. As the CEO of a major US service company put it: "Our assets wear shoes" and, naturally, competitors tend to circle looking to poach the living intellectual capital.

Managing communications issues

Acquisitions involve substantial emotions, ranging from fear, denial, and anger through to delight. Without conscious communications, management, anxieties and rumors can proliferate.

There are two keys: fast and timely communications, and good and constant awareness of the state of mind of key players in the companies and key external stakeholders.

Figure 1.5 shows a simple model of the key sequence of communications to be followed immediately the transaction has been publicly announced (and while due diligence is still being carried out). First, explain to key stakeholder groups, notably both sets of employees, key customers, and the financial analysts/media, the exact reasons for the acquisition, the benefits which it will provide short and long term, and the broad timetable for implementation. Later in the process, as the joint integration teams have better information and have their own meetings with key players in the two companies, the communication process can move to the details of integration.

A key factor in the speed and smoothness of the integration is to provide a series of forums where staff and customers can express their anxieties and contribute suggestions. These need to answer, as far as possible, a very basic question in the minds of all stakeholders: "What's in it for me?"

Companies with high success rates check frequently what messages have actually been received and reactions to them. Useful feedback processes include questionnaires, video conferences with senior management (in global companies), help lines

Figure 1.5: *Triangle of acquisition success* (*The Ashridge Journal*, Summer 2003, © Ashridge (Bonar Law Memorial) Trust)

or, most powerfully, face-to-face interviews/focus groups with employers, customers, distributors, and suppliers. The importance of feedback is that many senior managers who have been involved with seeking, discussing, and planning the acquisition can often forget that key stakeholders actually know a lot less about the acquisition. Failure to manage uncertainty can be a prime killer of value.

If the reasons behind the deal are not well communicated, this can compromise the rest of the communication. We witnessed an example of this in the defense industry where a company made an acquisition to provide it with complementary skills to apply to major defense projects. Eight years after the consolidation of the two business units into one division, the collaboration was still poor. One of the key reasons emerged at a workshop when it became clear that middle management still needed to ask the question "exactly why did we come together in the first place?" The explanation of the rationale (which was strategically faultless) was a major catalyst for improvement in the quality of the future collaboration. It should, of course, have taken place eight years earlier.

One important communication channel is e-mail. IT integration in an acquisition is notoriously difficult, but a key to success is to select one e-mail system very quickly and impose conformity. For example, when the South African mining company Billiton merged with the Australian company BHP, a merged e-mail system for all 60,000 employees was actually ready for operation when the deal was completed, despite substantial differences in the two legacy systems.

The appropriate methods of communication depend on the individual situation. But research during the Astra-Zeneca merger showed that face-to-face communication was particularly important. In general, high visibility of senior management is important during the first few months after the deal is announced.

Making it happen

Successful M&A companies have early and comprehensive implementation plans, often structured as 100 Day Plans (starting with the public announcement of the deal). This is particularly important as a way of keeping momentum and a sense of urgency. There is often a tendency for companies to relax once the deal is signed, but this is precisely the point at which speed of implementation becomes crucial. Successful M&A companies stress the importance of quick wins as a way of demonstrating that the new combination is already producing added value.

The integration plan should be jointly developed as far as possible and should include:

- an early outline of the new structure (without names if necessary);
- clear dates for major decisions (integration of sales forces, appointments to roles at various levels, product portfolio decisions);

- rapid definition of key systems and policies, for example finance (top priority) IT, HR, and legal;
- a major section on stakeholder management;
- within this, strong focus on customers. Cisco calls this "customer advocacy," a process which makes sure that the interests of the customers have high priority before and after closing;
- key issues being managed by joint task forces with tight reporting deadlines – days or weeks rather than months.

The plan must be tightly monitored and reviewed against strategic objectives, performance against milestones, performance on cost savings, added value from synergies, and, crucially, on the softer factors, such as management of cultural issues, and levels of motivation and morale.

This kind of approach will avoid having to echo the comment of one CEO who summarized his company's experience as: "Buying companies is fun but integrating them is hell."

RESOURCES

Askenas, R. and Francis, S., Integration managers: special leaders for special times. *Harvard Business Review*, November/December, 2000.

Carey, D., Lessons from master acquirers: a CEO roundtable on making mergers succeed, *Harvard Business Review*, May/June, 2000.

Connor, M., M & A risk management. *Journal of Business Strategy*, January/February, 2001.

Donohue, K. *How to ruin a merger: five people management pitfalls to avoid.* Harvard Management Update, September, 2001.

Feldman, M. and Spratt, M., *Five Frogs on a Log*, John Wiley, 2001.

Habeck, M., Kroger, F. and Tram, M., *After the Merger*, FT Prentice Hall, 2000.

KPMG Survey, *World Class Transactions*, 2001.

Krell, E., Merging corporate cultures, *Training*, May, 2001.

Massmilian, D., Notes from the M&A Trenches, *Journal of Business Strategy*, January/February, 2001.

Mergers, H. D., Why Most Big Deals Don't Pay Off, *Business Week*, October 14, 2002.

Schuler, R. and Jackson, S. HR issues and activities in mergers and acquisitions, *European Management Journal*, Vol. 19, No. 3, 2001.

Star Trek strategy

PETER BREWS

> Strategic plans often contain generic or motherhood and apple pie statements accompanied by outcome-based "stretch" goals that are not strategy but measure whether or not good strategy has been implemented. "Star Trek strategy" underscores how strategy must be evaluated: as a work of creative fiction sending firms boldly where none has gone before.

Perhaps you are a CEO or business unit manager leading a group of people who have worked together for a long time. Until recently results were as expected but performance is now slipping and the way ahead is unclear. You face the hardest challenge of all: developing a strategy to arrest the decline.

In your predicament you have consulted a legion of strategy experts, who suggest a variety of approaches. Develop a formal, specific plan, say some. Shoot the formal planners and plan incrementally, counter others. Consider your industry structure and exploit generic strategies, advises a third. Refine your "strategic intent" and leverage core competencies, offers a fourth group. By now you are thoroughly confused – understandably so.

A review of your existing strategy documents is equally unhelpful. You find a mission statement that could apply to all your competitors: to be market leader in the quality delivery of xyz services to ABC consumers worldwide. Carefully crafted over months of intensive debate, the statement is accompanied by other "stretch" goals and desired firm attributes: to be the employer of choice in your industry; to have 1 million customers by 2008 (you currently have 670,000); to cut service delivery costs by 20 percent over the next financial year; to achieve above-average returns for stockholders. A set of desired "values" completes the document: innovation, teamwork, and customer focus are all highly valued, important, and vital but now, you discover, quite unhelpful when real strategy is needed.

Sadly, you are not alone. Often, what is done in the name of strategy misses the mark. The causes of this are twofold. First, the essence of strategy is misunderstood and considerable time and effort are devoted to developing ideas that at best are motherhood and apple pie statements supported by high-level outcome goals. Second, few appreciate how our current stock of knowledge about strategy assists in developing true strategy.

Star Trek strategy

What first comes to mind when you hear the words "strategy" or "strategy formation"? In my experience, most executives associate strategy with plans or planning – the process of setting goals and objectives and specifying the means to achieve those goals. Though valid and insightful, these conceptualizations focus on the processes used to form strategy rather than the substance of strategy itself. Neither do they differentiate "good" from "bad" strategy. To determine such differences, the quality of the ideas embodied in a plan must be evaluated.

A well-known line from a popular television series helped me develop a filter to conduct this evaluation. The *raison d'être* of strategy is to ensure that an organization "boldly goes where none has gone before."

The critical test for any real strategic idea is whether it describes an ambitious, imaginative yet feasible foray into a new quadrant of the competitive universe. Does it describe the characteristics of this new universe in clear and unambiguous terms, detailing the nature of the goods or services the firm intends to offer? If not, it may be an interesting idea but it is not real strategy.

At its core, good strategy is abstract, not yet existing in the annals of human experience. If, as is destined in the voyages of the starship *Enterprise*, no one has travelled to the quadrant of the universe about to be visited, the sector waits to be discovered (or, for our purposes, created or invented). In star trekking, creative imagination and the ability to develop a compelling abstract idea are essential. I often employ my "You have got to be kidding" test to evaluate the degree of abstraction of an idea. If after initial exposure to a proposal your reaction is "YHGTBK!" the idea may be on the right track.

Regrettably, most managers are more comfortable with tangible reality than creative fiction and the world of star trekking. When confronted with an idea that is even remotely strategic, the idea is immediately dismissed. For star trekking, tolerance or even a welcoming of abstraction is key. Star Trek strategy also captures the pioneering quality of strategy. Similar to the experiences of real-life pioneers, adversity and failure are likely. When evaluating a firm's strategic activities I always inquire how often failure is encountered. If the answer is seldom or never, I become concerned. Not experiencing some failure in the execution of strategy is worrisome: either the firm is exceedingly lucky and/or very smart (unlikely), or the "strategic" ideas being implemented are not strategic at all (more likely). Instead, the firm's concept of strategy is fundamentally flawed.

Firms that expect perfect execution and are quick to punish failure are unlikely to do much star trekking. If the message is "go boldly but go perfectly" after the first voyager has been chastized for failing, the message will be out – don't go boldly since a penalty follows failure.

Rather than punishing failure the intent must be to learn quickly from failure so that an alternative viable path is established. A cherished value for many years at

Honda Motor Company, arguably Japan's most innovative and creative car company, is that success is 99 percent failure. While hopefully the failure percentage in successful star trekking is not quite as high, trying then failing, then learning and trying again is an inescapable element of star trekking. This does not mean that failure is OK or to be encouraged. Failure should be avoided or minimized as much as possible. Unfortunately, given the nature of true strategy, failure is likely, indeed almost inescapable.

"Star trekking by business pioneers," below, presents five examples of true star trek strategy. Three have been successfully implemented and the last two are currently moving from creative fiction to profitable business reality.

Boldly going: Star trekking by business pioneers

Wal-Mart stores

Despite conventional wisdom that held full-line discount stores required populations of 100,000 or more to be sustainable, Sam Walton set out to build a discount store chain to serve small southwestern towns. The idea was to offer the same or a wider range of products at prices as good as or better than those offered by existing metropolitan-based, high-volume discount stores.

Canon's personal copier

Seeking to break Xerox's photocopying dominance, Canon's top management asked a cross-functional team of engineers to design and build a value-for-money, low-volume desk-top copier, 50 percent cheaper than conventional copiers, 10 times as reliable, and maintenance free. Three years later the smallest, lightest copier ever built was introduced, creating a new market niche and outselling Xerox in units sold. This revolutionized the copier industry and established Canon as a leading supplier of electronic office products.

Cementos Mexicanos" ready-mix concrete on demand

Cementos Mexicanos (CEMEX), the third largest cement company in the world, is revolutionizing the delivery of ready-mix concrete in congested third-world cities through the combination of advanced modeling based on chaos theory and the use of GPS (global positioning satellite) locators to co-ordinate large city-wide fleets of trucks. Preloaded trucks fulfill orders on demand, arriving within 10 minutes of the promised time – down from the three-hour window previously considered feasible – and eliminating the need to place orders 24 hours in advance. In the launch test market, CEMEX promoted its concrete delivery capability with miniature pizza boxes poking fun at a local pizza franchise that delivered pizza less efficiently. In these markets, CEMEX now offers an on-time guarantee and a 5 percent rebate on orders more than 20 minutes late.

> **Boldly going: Star trekking by business pioneers (continued)**
>
> **Caterpillar's just before failure (JBF) technology**
>
> Supported by the firm's global information system and legendary parts supply capability, Caterpillar is imbedding microchips in machines to identify key component breakdown before failure occurs. The impending failure will be automatically signaled from the machine via satellite to the local dealer, who will then schedule replacement at a convenient time to avoid downtime. Simultaneously, if not on hand, an electronic search for the nearest replacement part is commenced and the closest part is located and dispatched to the dealer. The JBF technology should vastly decrease downtime and considerably enhance Caterpillar's already excellent customer service.
>
> **Siemens Medical Solutions" digital hospitals**
>
> Siemens Medical Solutions, a division of Germany's Siemens AG, is pioneering the development of all digital, fully automated hospitals. Combining the expertise of several Siemens operating companies, the new facilities are expected to be significantly more efficient and safer than existing hospitals. Patients will wear wireless "wellness monitors" that signal problems as they arise, providing their exact location to enable immediate response. Administrators, physicians, and other health care providers will navigate electronic patient records, vital signs, images, test results, and enter medical orders and treatment information virtually. Process simplification and network-based IT should reduce medication cycles from around ten steps to four, cutting down medication errors and costs. Drug interactions will be automatically highlighted, averting errors that cost tens of thousands of lives a year in the US alone. Naturally – though the Siemens software will be compatible with competitor equipment – installations will mostly carry the Siemens brand. But the sale is not based on the quality of the hardware, where differentiation is difficult. Siemens is betting that integrated health care solutions will enable it to dominate competitors.

Each example tangibly reflects the essence of star trekking, and passes my YHGTBK test. The range of examples shows that star trekking occurs at many levels: firm, product, or function/technology. Though not apparent from the examples, individuals can star trek too, regardless of organizational position or status. "Grand" strategy differs only in scope, resource requirement, and impact. Strategically efficient firms encourage all employees to star trek within the purview of their individual responsibilities – strategy in these firms is the sum of both "grand" and "individual" boldly going.

The examples also illustrate that strategy is uncomplicated at the core. Voluminous plans of mind-numbing detail that cannot be reduced to accessible, exciting creative ideas are often more bureaucratic "busy" work than cogent strategic ideas. Does your strategy represent a compelling and accessible reconceptualization of your firm's business or operations, or a revolutionary product idea, or an inventive use of technology that will break the boundaries of the known competitive universe and offer unrivaled value to customers? Good strategy is usually a combination of all these. If drafted in such terms, your ideas are on track. If not, scrap them and start again.

Strategy formation synopsis

Though Star Trek strategy captures the essence of strategy, it masks the complexity of the strategy process. Most good strategic ideas appear obvious once implemented, but transforming ideas from creative conception to profitable reality is complex. This complexity is reflected in the strategy schools of thought that have surfaced since the field emerged as an independent academic discipline in the 1950s. These schools are summarized below.

Back to the future: a synopsis of strategy schools of thought

Strategy as SWOT (1950s–60s)

Strategy was first presented as the matching of firm Strengths and Weaknesses with environmental Opportunities and Threats. The essence of strategy was conceived as the development of products or services around (internal) firm strengths that matched (external) competitive conditions. The CEO/top management was responsible for strategy formation and the model assumed that firm strengths and weaknesses could be objectively identified and assessed and that external opportunities or threats existed independently of the firm in the competitive cosmos, ripe for plucking or neutralization by smart strategists. The best strategies were stated in simple, explicit terms, suitable for implementation once formed.

(Readers wishing to learn about Strategy as SWOT should read Kenneth R. Andrews" classic *The Concept of Corporate Strategy*, Dow Jones-Irwin, 1971.)

Strategy as Formal Planning (1960s–70s)

Building upon the ideas of Strategy as SWOT, Strategy as Formal Planning detailed the planning activities necessary in strategy formation. The school

Back to the future: a synopsis of strategy schools of thought (continued)

conceptualized strategy formation as a formal, conscious, elaborate planning process, composed into a number of distinct rational steps. Starting with a statement of firm mission and key strategic objectives, the process cascaded into detailed programs and action plans, and budgets and operating plans of ever-increasing specificity. Once developed, this plan bound the firm into a tightly coupled system of hierarchically controlled plans and programs that monitored, evaluated, controlled, and rewarded behavior and performance.

This ends/means conceptualization of strategy assumed strategy could be modeled before the fact and reduced to detailed, time-limited statements of objectives, programs and action plans. Similar to Strategy as SWOT, the external environment was assumed to be analyzable and predictable, and either top management or staff planners were considered responsible for the development of the plan.

(Igor Ansoff's work *Corporate Strategy: An Analytical Approach to Business Policy for Growth and Expansion*, McGraw Hill, 1965, exemplifies the early thinking of the Planning School.)

Strategy as Positioning (1980s)

Strategy as Positioning considered industry structure the key independent variable in strategic analysis, and suggested good firm performance resulted from an industry structure/firm strategy fit. Strategists identified attractive industries, then selected one of three "generic" strategies (low cost, differentiation, focus) that fitted the industry structure. Porter's Five Forces Model (arguably the most famous framework in strategy) provided a template to determine the degree of attractiveness of an industry. Industry attractiveness was presented as a function of five forces: buyer power; supplier power; threat of substitutes; threat of new entrants; and intensity of rivalry among incumbents. Powerful firms reside in industries with low buyer and supplier power, lack of substitutes, few new entrants due to high barriers to entry, and low intensity of rivalry among incumbents. Profits in such industries would be high.

Strategy as Positioning complemented both Strategy as SWOT and Strategy as Planning by presenting a technique that permitted a more rigorous analysis of one key segment of the external environment – the industry.

(Michael E. Porter's *Competitive Strategy: Techniques for Analyzing Industries and Competitors*, Free Press, 1980, sets out the initial thinking of Strategy as Positioning.)

Strategy as Learning (late 1970s–80s)

Arising mostly in reaction to the perceived excesses and limitations of Strategy as Formal Planning, Strategy as Learning viewed strategy formation as a process of trial and error learning, and not formal planning. Rather than being deliberate and conscious (as suggested by formal planners), strategies typically emerge over time as organizations learn from their successes and failures. In turbulent, complex, fast-changing contexts, predetermination, formality, and objective analysis were suggested as insufficient, even dysfunctional. Instead of emerging full blown and complete from the planning process, strategies start as broad intentions that are crafted over time through incremental learning into appropriate firm behaviors and policy. Strategy formation is more about incremental learning than the production of detailed specific plans.

(For perspectives on the Learning School, see J.B. Quinn, "Strategic change: logical incrementalism," *Sloan Management Review*, 20 (1), 1978, 7–21, or Henry Mintzberg's "Crafting strategy", *Harvard Business Review*, July–August 1987, 66–75.)

Strategy as Stretch and Leverage (late 1980s–present)

Similar to Strategy as Learning, Strategy as Stretch and Leverage emerged to counterbalance an earlier school. Restoring firms to the center of strategic analysis (in contrast to the industry-level orientation in Strategy as Positioning), Strategy as Stretch and Leverage holds strategy is about achieving seemingly unattainable "stretch" goals through the leverage of firm strategic resources (also referred to as core capabilities, core competencies, or, more generally, strategic resources). Firms are conceptualized as bundles of resources (now referred to as the resource-based view of the firm), a few of which are strategic, that is, unique, valuable, and hard to copy resources that when embodied in products and services present offerings competitors cannot match. The "Stretch" element requires the setting of ambitious, enduring goals far beyond current capabilities that rally firm members and force new and innovative uses of existing or to-be-developed strategic resources. Rather than being about fit within a given industry structure, strategy disrupts and creates "misfit" as innovative goods or services that competitors cannot replicate are created and voraciously consumed.

(For insights into Strategy as Stretch and Leverage, see Gary Hamel and C.K. Prahalad, *Competing for the Future*, Harvard Business School Press, 1994. The resource-based view of the firm is covered in "Competing on resources – Strategy in the 1990s" by D.J. Collis and C.A. Montgomery, *Harvard Business Review*, July–August 1995, 118–128.)

Our understanding of strategy has expanded impressively over the years. Strategy as SWOT usefully specified the overall strategy problem but in practice often produced listings of strengths, weaknesses, opportunities, and threats without a coherent connection of strengths to opportunities or threats. Strategy simply appeared once the SWOT analysis was completed. Today we know that strategy formation extends beyond SWOT analysis. We now appreciate that strengths have little value unless idiosyncratic and hard to copy and unless they attract and retain customers when embodied in products or services – in other words, unless they are strategic resources.

Opportunities and threats were also initially conceptualized as independent of the firm, awaiting either harvesting or neutralizing. Today we understand that firms create opportunities and threats (one firm's opportunity is another's threat) through good strategy, and that firm actions significantly influence competitive environments.

As initially depicted in Strategy as SWOT or Strategy as Planning, strategically smart firms do not attempt to predict or forecast the paths of powerful and capricious external environments – they create the environment by offering superior products or services that less capable competitors cannot match. Futures wait to be created, not predicted or forecast. One outcome of good strategy is it skews an environment toward dominant competitors and away from weaker ones.

In addition, the summary shows that the deepening of our understanding of strategy has progressed sometimes sequentially and sometimes in pendulum swings. Planning followed SWOT and suggested a range of processes that both complemented and added to the contribution of the earlier school, while Strategy as Positioning added techniques that deepened our understanding of industry – a vital part of the external environment.

In contrast, the Learning School surfaced in counterpoint to the perceived excesses of the Planning School. For years strategists were advised to plan formally, specifically, and in detail, only to be urged by the Learning School to abandon formal planning as dysfunctional – formal planning introduced rigidity and bureaucracy, making organizations inflexible and resistant to change.

To some Learning School adherents the term "strategic planning" became an oxymoron. Similar to the Learning School's appearance, Strategy as Stretch and Leverage also emerged partially in reaction to the dominance of Strategy as Positioning. To some supporters of Strategy as Stretch and Leverage, the Positioning School ignored the idiosyncratic and firm-specific nature of strategy (grounded at the firm level) in favor of higher-level aggregate "industry" constructs.

Given these controversies, can these divergent threads be woven into a tapestry that captures the complexity and challenges of strategy formation? Though the answer to this question is certainly yes, the integration must be done with care.

Star Trek strategy, and the strategy schools of thought

Star Trek strategy is Strategy as Stretch but with amendment

Star Trek strategy captures the essence of strategy. And though Strategy as Stretch approximates this, it does so often imprecisely. Proponents of "stretch" advise organizations to set enduring, ambitious, "winning" goals that go beyond current resources and capture the imagination and motivate. Though these definitional terms fall within the boundaries of star trekking, flawed enactment of the concept has accompanied the broad descriptions.

For example, an early exemplification set stretch goals in exhortations such as "Encircle Caterpillar" or "Beat Benz." Though such war cries motivate, they provide little guidance as exemplified in Star Trek strategy. It would be like Sam Walton setting out to "Beat K Mart" rather than accomplishing the goal described on page 73. Beating K Mart does not describe Wal-Mart's strategy – it records the outcome of Wal-Mart's powerful strategy in discount retailing.

Others depict stretch goals in more specific but equally unhelpful outcome-based terms, such as doubling sales in two years or increasing returns to 20 percent by 2009. These also fail to make the grade. Often imposed from on high for budgeting, control, or shock therapy purposes, these are not real Star Trek goals.

First, they focus attention wrongly. Rather than promoting debate on the cogency of a creative idea, discussion degenerates into the fine-tuning of outcomes to four decimal points: why a doubling (and not a 75 percent increase) in sales? Second, such goals are often arbitrarily imposed and demotivate, in the extreme representing an abuse of power. Third, defining strategy in outcome terms provides no means to evaluate intermediate progress – it does not develop beacons indicating where an organization intends boldly going or how it intends getting there. In short, performance-based outcome goals are not strategy. They establish the means to measure whether good (or bad) strategy has been implemented after the fact.

If your stretch goals are written in terms of doubling sales, becoming number one in your market, or increasing market share by 10 percent over the next three years, start again. Important strategic questions are not whether or by how much market share is to be increased, but how – with which offerings, in which market, using which resources? Though outcomes, before, during, and after the fact, are a part of setting and evaluating strategy, these can be estimated only once the creative core itself is specified.

Neither do qualitative statements specifying generalized desirable firm attributes qualify. These include mission statements such as "we will be the best in class company in the xxx industry, filled with empowered, motivated people doing great things." Not only is this statement outcome based – with the attendant weaknesses of outcome-based goals outlined above – it is also generic and potentially applicable to any organization in almost any industry.

Star trekking is anything but "generic." The idea of a generic strategy is in itself oxymoronic. Further, though warm and fuzzy motherhood and apple pie statements can motivate and are unlikely to do damage, they must not be confused with real strategy. Star Trek goals are creative, tangible, abstract ideas specified in product market terms that clearly describe a firm's competitive intentions: we will build this house on that hill with these unique and innovative characteristics that once constructed will attract customers from near and far with great return to all. Competitors, naturally, will be unable to match.

Before boldly going, know where others have boldly gone before: Strategy as Positioning

Gathering knowledge of competitor positions is advisable before embarkation on any Star Trek journey. Avoiding going boldly where other competitors already are requires such insights. However, similar to Strategy as Stretch, the prescriptions of the Positioning School should be applied with caution.

The concept of "average" industry attractiveness suffers from the deficiency of many aggregate statements: with one hand in the refrigerator and the other on the hob, on average you're OK. In practice, an industry may be attractive to one competitor but unattractive to others. Since attractiveness may differ according to who is asking, average statements of attractiveness in isolation are really unhelpful. Why has Toyota done so well while GM has struggled? Or why did Cisco Systems do so well in the internetworking business while Bay Networks fell by the wayside? Analysis per key competitor rather than per industry reveals these "positional" differences. Specifying competitor differences is key to understanding positioning in an industry.

Another reason for caution relates to the application of industry analysis. Industry analysis maps where key competitors have gone and where they are; if really comprehensive, where competitors intend going may be included. Strategy was often expected to appear magically upon completion of this analysis. This expectation is misplaced. Industry analysis does not create strategy but provides information vital to the strategy development that hopefully will follow. But this is creative and not analytical work.

Neither do "generic" strategies help much in determining where firms should boldly go. Terms such as low cost, focus, or differentiation cannot capture the substance of good strategy – star trekking defies reduction to such "generic" terms or descriptions.

Star trekking requires a route map: Strategy as Planning

Travelers embarking on a journey into the unknown are better off with a map. Plans should record where a firm intends boldly going and how it intends getting there. A healthy planning process allows the testing and refinement of fictional ideas, hopefully reducing the likelihood of failure and minimizing the costs of learning once translation from fictional intent to non-fictional reality begins. Plans also guide implementation – strategic control and learning can be achieved only by comparing actual outcomes against original Star Trek intentions.

The intensive and often bitter Planning School/Learning School debate on the pluses and minuses of formal planning has identified many elements of planning that must be avoided. However, one regrettable result of the Learning School's assault on formal planning has been the conclusion that the remedy for bad planning is no planning. In fact, the remedy for bad planning is good planning. Though many of the Learning School's criticisms of formal planning are insightful, there is a vital role for "good" planning in the strategy process.

For example, we now recognize that good planning requires formulation and that implementation should be neither separate nor performed separately – thinkers cannot be detached from doers. Those charged with creating the future must have a significant say in its conceptual design.

In this regard, I recommend two simple rules: never formulate a plan you are unlikely to implement, nor implement a plan you did not help formulate. Failing to observe either rule misaligns incentives, becoming most apparent when difficulties surface. Detached formulators attribute failure to poor execution while detached implementers blame flawed formulation. And while the planners and doers squabble, competitors advance. Moreover, it is astonishing how motivated people are to implement their own ideas and how demotivated they become when implementing the ideas of others.

Finally, more responsible formulation is likely when formulators know they will be required to implement the ideas they suggest.

We have also learned that good planning is a team-based line activity and not the bailiwick of isolated staff planners or senior managers. A key top management responsibility is ensuring that the appropriate people from the appropriate levels with the appropriate knowledge, background, and resources are entrusted to create and implement a firm's future.

Since formulation cannot be detached from implementation and since successful star trekking typically takes time, the core of the team should remain until implementation is achieved or the idea is abandoned. Teams comprising mostly or exclusively executives close to retirement may be unable to see the plan through to completion, often necessitating disruptive and costly hand-overs. At worst, ideas may be implemented to ensure good performance until retirement and stock options have been exercised.

But this does not mean that executives close to retirement should not be part of a strategy team. Though not the core, they certainly can mentor and advise as the team struggles to develop and implement its strategic ideas. And we also now know that implementation is complete only once a new prototype is up and operating after being tested with customers and shown to be viable.

Finally, today we recognize good strategic planning is essentially a future-oriented, creative process not to be confused with more precise though equally important activities such as the maintenance of ongoing operational efficiency.

Downsizing, rightsizing, restructuring, or cost cutting reflect the quest for operational efficiency. Operationally inefficient firms must cure the disease they are likely to die from first – no sense in boldly going when current costs are too high and the firm is bleeding to death. However, this operational "managing of the farm" is different from "betting the farm," which involves strategic efficiency and star trekking. But both are necessary – while some are entrusted to bet the farm, others must manage the farm to keep it operationally intact.

To reduce the probability of failure (star trekking is risky) have equipment that provides advantage and defense in the sector of the universe you intend entering: Strategy as Leverage

Strategy as Leverage points out that in addition to bold and innovative ideas, strategy is also about possessing unique resources that permit the transformation of creative fiction into sustainable fact despite competitor endeavors to prevent this.

I am often asked whether it is the innovative ideas or the leverage of unique resources that really counts. After all, star trekking can be achieved with freely available resources (Strategy as Stretch but without Leverage). Answering this question is easy: a valuable innovation offered with freely available resources is likely to be copied and the returns quickly traded away. Competitors may also force prices below levels that permit the innovator's pioneering costs to be recouped. Sustainable star trekking thus requires both creative ideas and unique resources. Execution through unique resources prevents competitor replication of the idea.

Applying the resource-based view does have challenges, however. Strategists view firms differently from customers and if they are any good they hide strategic resources to mask the true nature of their firm's competitiveness. I find likening firms to icebergs a helpful metaphor. The 90 percent of an iceberg below the water represents the strategic resources strategists see while the 10 percent above the water is the goods or services customers enjoy.

To customers, Nike sells shoes and clothing. To CEO Phillip Knight, athletic shoe design and brand management is a better "under the water" strategic description of Nike's business. To Wal-Mart shoppers the firm is a discount retailer but to Wal-Mart strategists the firm is in the IT/logistics management business displayed in the superior cross-docking, inventory replenishment, and transport management systems operated by the firm. Since these resources enable Wal-Mart to stock shelves at prices competitors cannot match, they define the firm's true nature of business and competitive substance.

Philip Morris's understanding of multi-purchase consumer marketing (developed over years of building strong cigarette brands) was the strategic resource the firm leveraged to acquire Miller Beer and enter the food business. CEMEX changed the ready-mix concrete business in developing country cities into an IT-based transport services business, leaving competitors with the daunting task of reconceptualizing their resource base to avoid being driven out of business. Siemens is changing the core of its medical business from the manufacture of medical systems to the provision of health care solutions that integrate the systems with other workflow processes in hospitals. This reflects a shift in resources to workflow management and integrated software development.

Resource-based analysis thus often requires getting hands around clouds, a process with considerable uncertainty and imprecision. Hidden layers of the strategic onion must be continually peeled back in the hope that the true layer of competitiveness is finally revealed. And there is no sure way to verify that your conceptualization of what is going on under the water is correct, especially when confronted by a carefully guarded competitor resource base.

A final concern regarding resource-based analysis relates to which comes first: innovative ideas or strategic resources? Examples of either sequence abound, as do combinations of both. Walton's vision for Wal-Mart preceded the logistics, inventory replenishment, and cross-docking capabilities that turned the vision into reality. Alternatively, Philip Morris" entry into the beer industry relied upon a pre-existing strategic resource developed in another context. Here resources preceded the idea.

Canon's personal copier illustrates an innovative idea achieved with both existing and new strategic resources. The desktop personal copier was built on the company's existing strategic knowledge in optics, fine chemicals, electronics, and precision mechanics but needed the development of new copier technology to circumvent Xerox's patents. Siemens' evolution to medical solutions was conceived in the mid-1990s but an acquisition in the late 1990s, provided some of the resources needed to digitize workflow processes in health care.

However, though the relationship between innovative ideas and strategic resources is messy and circular, which comes first does have important consequences. Attaining innovative ideas with yet-to-be-created strategic resources is probably more risky than ideas achieved through the application of existing strategic resources. It is more than likely that innovative ideas implemented with new resources will take longer and cost more than those relying on existing strategic resources.

All things being equal, such Star Trek ventures should produce greater returns than those applying existing resources to new arenas. A portfolio approach may be optimal – some Star Trek goals relying on resources yet to be created together with some ideas requiring the application of both existing and new strategic resources balanced by innovative ideas implemented out of existing strategic resources.

Once your journey into the unknown begins, mistakes and surprises will happen: Strategy as Learning

The Learning School's greatest contribution is the distinction between intended and realized strategy. Even the best-laid plans are intentions that may never be realized. Plans supported by the most cogent industry analysis and containing the most creative ideas remain fictional theories of action until implementation starts. Usually, as implementation proceeds, setbacks are encountered and learning takes place. What was thought feasible turns out to be impossible – the environment shifts, a competitor responds unexpectedly, or customer rejection gets in the way.

Stated differently, good strategy includes both before-the-fact planning and during-the-fact adjustment/recalibration as implementation proceeds. Neither formal planning nor incrementalism alone adequately describes the complexity of the strategy process. Recognizing that implementation is fundamentally a learning process avoids many of the dysfunctional planning processes the Learning School warns about – rigidity, inflexibility, and the fallacy of considering plans a perfect predetermination of the future.

What we do and do not know about strategy

The essence of strategy is the creation of a tangible but abstract description of a firm's bold intentions followed by a voyage of invention that turns these intentions into profitable reality.

Albert Einstein once said that imagination is more important than knowledge. Star Trek strategy endorses this – the bright spark of true strategy flows from this most important and unique of human capabilities. However, a gloss on Einstein's statement is necessary. Successful star trekking is unlikely to emerge from isolated creativity conceived in a vacuum or the uncontrolled experiments of scientists randomly tinkering in a laboratory.

Instead, successful star trekking requires creative but intelligent imagination informed by Positioning, shaped and refined by Planning, resourced through Leverage, and implemented while Learning. Imagination based on and supported by knowledge is the strategists" domain.

Five decades of investigation and experience have considerably enhanced our understanding of strategy and the strategy process. We now appreciate that strategy formation is multi-dimensional and complex. The strategy school currently in vogue holds that strategic success is contingent upon the ownership and application of idiosyncratic, hard-to-copy, valuable strategic resources. Though essential, this emphasizes only one dimension of the strategy puzzle. The other dimensions must neither be ignored nor forgotten; a sophisticated and balanced application of all is required.

However, if intelligent creativity is the Holy Grail of strategy, many questions remain. Though an understanding of Positioning, Planning, Stretch, Leverage, and Learning may increase the probability of strategic creativity, it is unclear whether organizations (or humans) can learn or be taught to be more creative.

How to develop and control creativity is another key question. Employing monthly budgets or short-term financial performance measures to shape and control abstract and hard-to-model creative ideas will probably hinder more than help. Since star trekking is typically longer term with uncertain payoffs, rewarding on the basis of short-term financial targets may kill creativity before it starts. Our current level of knowledge permits us to conclude only that we should be intelligently creative in strategy and incorporate appropriately the portfolio of capabilities that make up good strategy process. Hopefully, in 50 years' time our understanding will have expanded significantly, allowing many to boldly go where they first imagined they would be, to the benefit of us all.

RESOURCES

Andrews, Kenneth, *The Concept of Corporate Strategy*, Homewood, IL: Irwin, 1965.

Brews, Peter and Hunt, M.A., 'Learning to plan and planning to learn: resolving the planning school/learning school debate,' *Strategic Management Journal*, 20, 1999.

Burns, Tom and Stalker, G.M., *The Management of Innovation*, Tavistock Publications, 1961.

Hamel, Gary and Prahalad, C.K., *Competing for the Future*, Harvard University Press, 1994.

Hamel, Gary and Heene, Aimé (eds), *Competence-Based Competition*. John Wiley, 1995.

Hamel, Gary, *Leading the Revolution*, Harvard Business School Press, 2000.

Mintzberg, Henry, 'Crafting strategy,' *Harvard Business Review*, July–August 1987.

Mintzberg, Henry, *The Structuring of Organizations*, Prentice Hall, 1979.

Penrose, E., *The Theory of the Growth of the Firm*, Oxford University Press, 1959.

Porter, Michael, *Competitive Strategy*, Free Press, 1980.

Porter, Michael, *The Competitive Advantage of Nations*, Free Press, 1990.

Porter, Michael, *Competitive Advantage*, Free Press, 1985.

Porter, Michael, *Can Japan Compete?* (with Hirotaka Takeuchi and Mariko Sakakibara), Perseus, 2000.

Scherer, F.M., *Industrial Market Structure and Economic Performance*, Houghton Mifflin, 1970.

This article previously appeared in *Business Strategy Review*, Volume 14, Issue 3, Autumn 2003.

Strategy and structure redux

JORGE NASCIMENTO RODRIGUES

[*Alfred Chandler's seminal book* Strategy and Structure *was written over 40 years ago, yet it remains one of the most influential books in its field.*]

The Pulitzer Prize-winning business historian Alfred duPont Chandler Jr, now in his eighties, brought strategy into the modern age and championed the multi-divisional organizational form. After graduating from Harvard, he served in the US Navy before becoming, somewhat unusually, a historian at MIT in 1950. He has been Straus Professor of Business History at Harvard since 1971.

Chandler's hugely detailed research into the development of US companies between 1850 and 1920 has formed the cornerstone of much of his work. Chandler observed that organizational structures in companies such as DuPont, Sears Roebuck, General Motors, and Standard Oil were driven by the changing demands and pressures of the marketplace. He concluded that the market-driven proliferation of product lines led to a shift from a functional, monolithic organizational form to a more loosely coupled divisional structure.

Chandler was highly influential in the trend toward decentralization among large organizations during the 1960s and 1970s. In *Strategy and Structure*, Chandler praised Alfred Sloan's decentralization of General Motors in the 1920s. He argued that the chief advantage of the multi-divisional organization was that "it clearly removed the executives responsible for the destiny of the entire enterprise from the more routine operational responsibilities and so gave them the time, information, and even psychological commitment for long-term planning and appraisal."

Strategy and structure: the chicken and the egg

While the multi-divisional form has largely fallen out of favor, another of Chandler's theories continues to raise the blood pressure of those who care about such things. Chandler argued that strategy came before structure. Having developed the best possible strategy, companies could then determine the most appropriate organizational structure to achieve it. In the early 1960s, this was speedily accepted as a fact of life.

More recently, Chandler's premise has been regularly questioned. In a perfect world, critics say, companies would hatch perfect strategies and then create neat structures and organizational maps. Reality, however, is a mess in which strategy and structure mix madly.

Contemporary strategist Gary Hamel provides a more positive perspective on Chandler's insights. "Those who dispute Chandler's thesis that structure follows strategy miss the point," he argues. "Of course, strategy and structure are inextricably intertwined. Chandler's point was that new challenges give rise to new structures. The challenges of size and complexity, coupled with advances in communications and techniques of management control, produced divisionalization and decentralization. These same forces, several generations on, are now driving us toward new structural solutions – the federated organization, the multi-company coalition, and the virtual company. Few historians are prescient. Chandler was."

Strategy and Structure also contributed to the professionalization of management. Chandler traces the historical development of what he labels "the managerial revolution" fueled by the rise of oil-based energy, the development of the steel, chemical, and engineering industries, and a dramatic rise in the scale of production and the size of companies. Increases in scale, Chandler observes, led to business owners having to recruit a new breed of professional manager.

Chandler believes that the roles of the salaried manager and technician are vital, and talks of the "visible hand" of management co-ordinating the flow of product to customers more efficiently than Adam Smith's "invisible hand" of the market (see Chandler's 1977 book, *The Visible Hand*).

"*The Visible Hand* summarized and recast a half-century of scholarship in business history. It shifted the focus from the morality of individual business leaders to the effectiveness of different kinds of organizational forms – of which the most important was the industrial corporation (or what Chandler called the 'modern business enterprise'). In so doing, it gave the modern corporation a kind of moral legitimacy that altered the ways historians and economists wrote about the modern US economy," explains Richard R. John of the University of Illinois. "Chandler has always linked technological innovation with the modern business enterprise. Not everyone has agreed with him here but this is a consistent theme in his work. He has, in particular, encouraged a great deal of scholarship on industrial research and has recently been working on two high-tech fields: electronics and chemicals."

The logical progression from this is that organizations and their managements require a planned economy rather than a capitalist free-for-all dominated by the unpredictable whims of market forces. In the more sedate times in which *Strategy and Structure* was written, the lure of the visible hand proved highly persuasive.

"What is interesting is that 40 years after Chandler's seminal work in strategy, history is once again becoming a central feature in the analysis of strategy," says Christopher McKenna of Oxford's Said Business School and author of *The World's Newest Profession: Management Consulting in the 20th Century*. "In particularizing the analysis of strategy away from generic strategies and simple mnemonics, strategists, alongside historians, are once again demonstrating the important differences between strategy and economics. Chandler's work, in this way, is not simply the *alpha*, the starting point, but also the *omega*, the finishing point, in the growth of strategy as a subject."

Alfred Chandler speaks

What prompted you to write *Strategy and Structure*?

The decision to write *Strategy and Structure* came in 1954 when I was invited to create and teach a course at the Naval War College in Newport, Rhode Island on "the basis of national strategy." William Rietzal, who was at the college in another capacity, had become interested in the post-Second World War changes in military organizational structures, particularly those that came with the creation of the post-war Department of Defense. I was then developing my interest in the evolution of modern business structures. So we agreed that each of us would write a book on our respective intellectual concerns. Rietzal never completed his book. Mine came out in 1962.

Do you think strategy continues to determine structure?

Of course strategy continues to determine structure. This is the theme of a recently published book by Robert Burgelman, *Strategy is Destiny* (2002), that tells the evolution of Intel's strategy and its supporting structure.

Would it be fair to say that the visible hand of management and the rise of the managerial class have had a more profound influence on the high-tech sectors of the economy than on traditional sectors?

That is correct. The management structures whose evolution are described in *Strategy and Structure* were primarily adopted by enterprises in increasingly capital and knowledge-intensive industries, as pointed out in its concluding chapter. This is because the new multi-divisional structure permitted the commercializing of new technologies producing products for different markets. For example, chemical companies were from the 1920s on producing a variety of chemicals, fibers, film, finishes, plastics, explosives, and other things. The structure thus permitted them to lower their unit costs through the economies of scope as well as scale.

What's the difference between the entrepreneurs talked of by Schumpeter and the managerial class you talk about in *The Visible Hand*?

Schumpeter's entrepreneurs were the creators of a new product usually based on a new technology. The managers referred to in *The Visible Hand* were those that created the organization essential to capture the economies of scale and scope. For example, Henry Ford was the entrepreneur who invented the modern automobile industry with his mass-produced Model T. Alfred Sloan was the classic manager who built the essential management structure to benefit from the economies of scale and scope. In 1921, when Sloan took charge of General Motors, GM's share of the US market was 13 percent; Ford's was 56 percent. In 1927, after Sloan had completed and fully introduced the multi-divisional operating management structure, Ford's share was 9 percent and GM's 44 percent. Ford had little choice but to adjust to GM's strategy and structure.

So if Sloan's work at GM in the 1920s pioneered the divisional form of organization, are there any similarly instructive modern inspirations?

Yes, there is an excellent comparable comparison. Andy Grove's Intel as told by Burgelman's *Strategy is Destiny*.

How do you view strategy in relation to the advent of the new economy?

The new economy is primarily based on more than just the new technology but rather a major technological revolution based on electronic communications. The concept of strategy does not change. Strategy remains destiny but the strategies of individual enterprises have to be redefined in order to take advantage of the new electronic technology.

Events such as the collapse of Enron have brought the managerial class into disrepute. Are we approaching the end of the rule of the managerial class and their cohorts in the fields of management consulting and auditing?

I consider Enron's managers, as well as those in the accounting firms, as part of the managerial class. I assume that the latter will continue to provide consulting and accounting services, although they may have to operate within different enterprises if Congress passes a law separating consulting from auditing businesses.

RESOURCES

Books by Chandler:

Strategy and Structure: Chapters in the History of the Industrial Enterprise, MIT Press, Boston, 1962.

The Visible Hand: The Managerial Revolution in American Business, Harvard University Press, Cambridge, 1977.

Precursors of Modern Management: An Original Anthology, Ayer Publishing, 1980.

Railroads: Pioneers in Modern Management – An Original Anthology, Ayer Publishing, 1980.

The Philosophy of Management (editor with Oliver Sheldon), Ayer Publishing, 1980.

Managerial Innovation at General Motors: An Original Anthology (editor), Arno Press, 1980.

Managerial Hierarchies: Comparative Perspectives on the Rise of the Modern Industrial Enterprise (editor with Herman Deams), Harvard University Press, Cambridge, 1980.

Giant Enterprise, Ayer Publishing, 1980.

Application of Modern Systematic Management: An Original Anthology (editor), Ayer Publishing, 1980.

The Coming of Managerial Capitalism: A Casebook on the History of American Economic Institutions (editor with Richard S. Tedlow), Richard D. Irwin, 1985.

Scale and Scope: The Dynamics of Industrial Capitalism, Harvard University Press, 1990.

Management: Past and Present: A Casebook on the History of American Business (editor with Richard S. Tedlow and Thomas K. McGraw), South-Western College Publishing, 1995.

Big Business and the Wealth of Nations (editor with Franco Amatori and Takashi Hikino), Cambridge University Press, 1997.

The Dynamic Firm: The Role of Technology, Strategy, Organization and Regions (editor with Peter Hagstrom and Orjan Solvell), Oxford University Press, 1998.

A Nation Transformed by Information: How Information has Shaped the United States from Colonial Times to the Present (editor with James W. Cortada), Oxford University Press, 2000.

Inventing the Electronic Century: The Epic Story of the Consumer Electronics and Computer Science Industries, Free Press, 2001.

Related reading:

Burgelman, Robert, *Strategy is Destiny*, Simon & Schuster, 2002.

www.lib.uwo.ca/business/chandler.html

'Interview': C.K. Prahalad

The renowned corporate strategist and co-author of Competing for the Future *talks about his theory of co-creation, expounded in* The Future of Competition: Co-Creating Unique Value with Customers.

Competing for the Future *was first published in the mid-1990s and had a major impact on the way corporations think about strategy. How has your view of the world changed since then?*

Competing for the Future was a very firm-centric view of the world. We were still focussed on the firm. We were also very product and service centric. Think about what has happened since then. *Competing for the Future* was written before ubiquitous connectivity became common. Whether it is the PC or wireless, the book was pre-connectivity. Also the business world was not as well developed in terms of convergence of technologies and industries. That process was just starting.

Today there is convergence of a wide variety of industries and technologies: between pharmaceuticals, personal care and fashion, information technology, retailing and banking, and increasingly now even telecoms. So the fundamental change is the convergence of technologies – today it is not at all clear what is a phone, a digital camera, and a computer; it's all rolled into one. Not only is this happening in digital industries but in food, in personal care products, and in the automotive industry. This is new.

What else has changed in the intervening period?

In the last 10 years, following the *Competing for the Future* book, several other forces have changed the way we think and live. One is tremendous deregulation. Consider what is happening to wireless around the world. It's going crazy. Today there are more wireless phones than landlines. Ten years ago wireless was just a blip on the radar.

A second force is the increasing role of emerging markets today. China and India are driving wireless and the development of wireless devices as much as the developed world. Actually, I would argue that poor people have driven wireless more toward success than rich people. We have fundamentally new business models, like prepaid cards, where I don't have to own a home in order to get a telephone. I can be poor and still get access to a telephone.

What impact do you think these changes have had on the relationship between corporation and consumer?

Deregulation, emerging markets, new forms of globalization, convergence of technologies and industries, and ubiquitous connectivity, these have changed many aspects of business. They have changed the nature of consumers. Today you have consumers who are informed, networked, active, and global. As a consumer, I don't have to leave home in order to be globally connected and active.

They have also changed the nature of companies. Today firms can fragment their value chain in ways that they could not have done before. Not just the physical products, but the intellectual part of my company – the business processes, management processes, including research and development, engineering – all that can be fragmented. Some of it can be in India, some of it can be in the UK and the United States.

Combine digital technology and the telecommunications revolution, and the nature of consumer-to-consumer and consumer-to-company interactions, the nature of business becomes very different. It changes the very basis of all transactions – the interaction between the consumer and the company. The consumer is interacting differently with the firm, and not only that, consumers are interacting differently among themselves.

Could you give an example of how these interactions have changed?

There is a medication called Lotronex. It's used by people with irritable bowel syndrome. After about 250,000 people had taken the medication, various side effects became apparent. So the FDA suggested they withdraw the medication. But soon the people who were taking the medication organized themselves and appealed to the FDA, saying "we understand there are risks but we are willing to take the risks because the alternative is even worse for us."

So you find an activist consumer community emerging which is challenging the FDA, and the FDA has reinstated the medicine. Now the medication is available for a very selective subset of people. The doctors, the pharmacy, the company, GlaxoSmithKline in this case, the patients, and the FDA have all come together and agreed on the risks, how to make those risks explicit, and how to make sure that the medication is given under a fair level of supervision, higher than it used to be before. All the parties understand what the implications are. It is an intelligent way of taking risks. Let us reflect on what has happened here. The consumers, the patients, have created the ability for GlaxoSmithKline to remarket the product and create value for themselves. So have the patients. They are creating value for themselves. This is a "win–win" for both, an excellent example of co-creation of value, where the consumer is actively engaged.

Co-creation of value is a major theme of the new book. What exactly does this mean?

We are moving to a new form of value creation, when value is not created by the firm and exchanged with customer, but when value is co-created by the consumers and the company. So the first question is: how do you go from a unilateral view of value creation by the company to co-creation of value by consumers?

Co-creation of value is a very different thing from being consumer oriented. This is not about the firm targeting consumers and being more sensitive to them. It is about enabling consumers to be equal problem solvers, so that collectively they create value, and collectively they extract value; so that the consumer is helping the company to create value and also taking value away by extracting value through either explicit or implicit bargains. So, the first big idea is the concept of co-creation of value. It's no longer just unilateral creation of value by the firm to be exchanged with customers.

The second big idea is that it is no longer all about the product but it is about the experience. The product becomes the artifact around which an experience is created. If you think about Lotronex, the experience is about feeling well, and having a good relationship with the community of people who suffer from the same problem. So it is the experience that is of value, in addition to the medication. Medication is clearly the carrier, but the value is in the experience.

Thirdly, individuals do matter. Consumer communities, and the interaction with the consumers among themselves, and between the consumer communities and the company, are of great importance in thinking about value creation. So if you think about the transition we've made, we have moved away from a firm and product-centric view of value creation to an experience-centric view of co-creation of value. It's a huge distinction: from looking at consumers as targets, to looking at consumers as co-creators of value; looking at consumer networks, which are autonomously involved, with or without the sanction of the company, as an integral part of how we create value.

How significant is that shift?

My sense is that *Competing for the Future* was a clear conceptual and managerial break from the previous view of how to create value. Co-creation is an equally fundamental break from a firm-centric view.

What co-creation is saying, what the *Future of Competition* book is saying, is, because of the changes that have taken place during the last decade, we can no longer be firm-centric. We have to be experience-centric, and co-creation centric. That I think is a big change.

Earlier you touched on the influence of emerging markets. How does this process of co-creation roll out to the developing world, or does it just pass them by?

That's a very interesting question. The most interesting thing for me is that we cannot deal with the markets of the poor, or the bottom of the pyramid, without a view of co-creation. Because the poor are very value conscious. The poor cannot afford to take risks with their purchases. By definition, they are going to be a lot more concerned about their experiences with products. There is a lot more word-of-mouth, and a lot more community-based activism in making buying decisions.

So actually co-creation is more natural not among the rich but at the bottom of the pyramid, because the rich in developing and developed countries behave alike. So when they buy something the attitude is: "if we don't like it, it is no big deal, it won't break the bank." On the other hand, if you're very poor you can't afford to take that attitude. You have one shot at buying something, you'd better make sure that it is absolutely what you want, and therefore, by definition, they do a lot more networking and word-of-mouth discussion before they make any choices.

While we are on the subject of emerging economies, you have in the past spoken about the huge potential of the Indian economy. Do you foresee a major change in the economic world order?

A good question. I think three forces are changing the world order. One is the co-creation of value we have just been talking about. Second is the importance of the "bottom of the pyramid" markets. There are 5 billion people at the bottom of the pyramid. They have been below the radar screen of large companies, or not on the radar screen at all. But now they are asserting themselves. If you look at the number of television sets, the number of radios, and wireless devices that are being consumed by them, it is quite phenomenal. You suddenly find the Chinese poor, the Indian poor, and the Brazilian poor are changing the basic dynamics of industries worldwide.

The third thing I think is usually reported, unfortunately, as outsourcing, whether it's call-centers, or research and development, or engineering, or IT. What I think is happening is a new willingness of companies to fragment their value chains in search of speed, low cost, and quality. Improved quality is one discussion that we don't see so much of in the press, as all outsourcing is seen as primarily leveraging the asymmetry of wage rates in India and China, for example, compared to those in the UK and the United States. Yes, that's part of it. But the quality levels are far superior in IT, for example, in terms of what can be done in India, compared to a lot of companies here in the UK or the US.

And then of course there is access to a huge talent pool which I think as a manager you have the obligation to access.

So if you take these three – willingness to access talent pool and quality for speed and revenues and cost reduction worldwide; the emergence of "bottom of the pyramid" markets as agents of growth and change in the global economy; and co-creation, where active consumers become a resource for companies and become equal problem solvers to create new business opportunities – these three forces will collectively change the world economic order.

So do you see, as a corollary, a diminishing of the relative competitive position of the United States?

I think that would be premature. The United States is a funny place. They complain a lot but they also change very rapidly. For example, when manufacturing started moving out of the United States in the 1980s we had the same complaints and calls for protectionism to stop the import of Japanese cars and television sets. It was popular at the time to go and smash television sets in front of the Capitol building. So we went through that. Then people understand. This transition is inevitable and we have to do something. Now nobody is complaining about manufacturing jobs being lost as much, instead it's about high-end jobs going to India, and high-end jobs going to other places.

I think there is an immediate reaction, and I think that America is inventive enough to build new business opportunities, and new kinds of businesses. The leverage is the inventiveness of the community. Because after complaining and saying it is unfair, Americans are clever enough to realize that they are the ones pushing for globalization and their agenda is working. The only surprise is that they didn't think that if globalization worked they would also get hurt. And now globalization is working. Americans are hurting a little bit. But we have to move on. We cannot stop these forces.

Interview by Des Dearlove

Strategy in the knowledge economy

W. CHAN KIM AND RENÉE MAUBORGNE

[*Strategy in the knowledge economy must be more than just beating the competition.*]

At the heart of most strategic thinking is competition. Yet strategy driven by competition usually has three unintended effects:

- imitative, not innovative, approaches to the market;
- companies act reactively;
- a company's understanding of emerging mass markets and changing customer demands become hazy.

The reason is that when asked to build competitive advantage, most managers look at what their competitors are doing and then seek to do it better. In other words, their strategic thinking regresses toward the competition. As a result companies often achieve no more than an incremental improvement on what the competition is doing – imitation not innovation.

Over the last decade we have looked at companies that have recorded high levels of growth and profits compared with their competitors. The strategies they have followed are what we call "value innovation." This is fundamentally different from adding layers of competitive advantage or trying to outperform competitors. Value innovation focusses on the simultaneous pursuit of radically superior value and lower costs.

Starbucks, Virgin Atlantic Airways, Bloomberg, Home Depot, and others are examples of companies that have succeeded by focussing their innovative efforts on buyer value and lower costs.

Value innovation places an equal emphasis on both value and innovation. Value with no innovation stresses improving the net benefit to the customer or value creation. Innovation with no value can be too technology driven. Value innovation grounds innovation in buyer value. While innovation itself may be random, value innovation is not. It deliberately seeks a leap in buyer value at lower cost.

There are five key ways in which value innovation differs from conventional strategic logic:

1. While many companies may allow industry conditions to dictate what is possible, probable, and profitable, companies that value innovate see their

industries as inherently malleable and challenge the inevitability of industry conditions.
2. While the orthodox strategy may be to focus on outpacing the competition, companies that value innovate aim to dominate the market by introducing a major advance in buyer value.
3. Traditionally, companies focus on customer segmentation, customization, and retention. But companies that value innovate seek key value commodities that will allow them to capture the mass market even if they have to lose some customers.
4. Most companies start by more fully exploiting their existing key assets and capabilities, but while companies that value innovate do the same they are not constrained by them. They are willing to tear down and rebuild if necessary.
5. Conventional companies concentrate on improving traditional industry products and services. Companies that value innovate think in terms of a total customer solution, even if this means going outside traditional industry boundaries.

Thus value innovation differs from traditional strategy in both the height of its ambitions and the breadth of the way it defines customers. It does not focus on incremental improvements and it identifies its target market not merely as its own, or its competitors'', customers. Companies may often look to their customers for inspiration but the best ideas come from listening to competitors" customers and people who are not even, as yet, in your market.

For example, in 1991 US golf club manufacturer Callaway Golf launched the "Big Bertha" club. The product soon dominated the market, taking an increased market share and, more importantly, growing the total market. The reason is that in a highly competitive market Callaway did not focus on the competition. Rivals had fiercely benchmarked each other, resulting in very similar clubs with over-sophisticated enhancements. Callaway looked at why in the "country club" market, more people played tennis than golf. The answer was that small club heads made hitting a golf ball difficult. "Big Bertha's large club head made it easier and more fun, attracting both existing and new players.

Callaway Golf did not look at how it might beat other gold club manufacturers by offering an improved solution to the traditional goal – how to hit a golf ball further. Instead it looked at offering a solution to a customer problem – how to hit a golf ball more easily. By redefining the problem in this way Callaway grew the market by attracting customers who previously had not wished to play golf.

Companies that value innovate seek to create new and superior value. A conventional focus on retaining and better satisfying existing customers promotes a fear of challenging the status quo. Value innovators monitor existing customers but also pursue non-customers.

The conventional strategic objective is to gain a competitive advantage by offering improvements against industry benchmarks. But this type of benchmarking works against the value innovation process. Value innovation changes industries. For example, Bloomberg's value innovation leapfrogged existing market leaders to redefine an industry. Reuters and Dow Jones" Telerate were providing online stock price data. Bloomberg offered smart terminals capable of data analysis that allowed traders and analysts to make decisions more quickly and accurately.

Note, though, that while value innovation is the essence of strategy in the knowledge economy, it is not enough on its own. Any strategy that attracts customers will soon be copied. Value innovators therefore also need to deploy the tactics that traditionally preserve the first mover's advantage, and often these will be incremental improvements to the original value innovation. In this respect, value innovation produces a punctuated equilibrium – major change followed by periods of refinement and consolidation.

When they find superior value, companies that value innovate, deploy capabilities that exist both within and outside their companies to exploit it. They frequently have a network of partners that provide complementary assets and capabilities. For example, SMH, creator of the Swatch, had no expertise in the mass watch market, in plastics mounding, or even in design. It did have an idea of superior value – the wristwatch as a fashion accessory – plus the insight to create, buy, or borrow the expertise needed to produce it.

Quantum leaps in value almost always involve major changes in behavior and working practices. These will not be achieved without people willingly co-operating in the strategy process and making their skills and experience available to a company.

The importance of fair process

The key to gaining this willing co-operation is the idea of "fairness." Exercising "fair process" – fairness in the process of making and executing decisions – is a powerful way to recognize people's intellectual and emotional worth. Fair process promotes trust and commitment whereas treatment perceived as unfair makes people hoard their ideas and drag their feet. Fair process involves three basis principles:

- engagement – involving people in decisions that affect them by seeking their ideas and allowing them to challenge the ideas and assumptions of others;
- explanation – everyone involved or affected should understand the reasons for decisions and why their ideas were accepted or rejected;
- establishing clear expectations – people must know what the objectives are, how their performance will be judged, and who is responsible for what.

Fair process and value innovation create a positively reinforcing cycle. Fair process in strategy making exercises a positive effect on value innovation. Success in value innovation in turn strengthens the group and increases people's belief in the process, thus perpetuating the collaborative and creative models that are the basis of value innovation.

Most companies strive to deliver fair outcomes but do not distinguish this from fair process. Fair outcomes ensure that individuals receive the resources they need or material rewards in exchange for co-operation. But to induce knowledge creation and voluntary co-operation between individuals companies must go beyond fair outcomes to fair process.

Fair process is not about political or distributive justice. It is about procedural justice. It's not about participation and consensus. It is about being even-handed, consistent, and open to challenge.

Fair process is often not easy for managers. It forces them to be candid and to explain themselves. Just rewards are important, but people are not concerned only with what's best for them. If people feel respected and think that decision-making processes are fair, they will accept decisions they don't benefit from. Fair process creates an objective, meritocratic culture based on a belief in the intellectual and emotional worth of all employees.

People possessing knowledge are the key resource of companies that follow value innovation strategies. But this resource is increasingly independent and mobile. To capture it, companies must meet expectations of both fair outcome and fair process.

RESOURCES

Kim, W. Chan and Mauborgne, Renée, *Value Innovation: The Strategic Logic of High Growth*. Harvard Business Review, January–February 1977.

www.insead.edu/kim
www.insead.edu/mauborgne

Essentials

STRATEGY AND COMPETITION

Ansoff, Igor

Igor Ansoff (1918–2002) was one of the key figures in the formulation of a clear concept of strategic management. Ansoff was born in Vladivostok, the son of an American father and a Russian mother. In 1936, the Ansoff family moved to New York. Igor Ansoff trained as an engineer and mathematician. He worked for the RAND Corporation, and then the Lockheed Corporation where he was a vice-president.

In 1963 he left industry for academia, joining Carnegie-Mellon's Graduate School of Business Administration. He joined the San Diego-based US International University in 1983, where he became Distinguished Professor of Strategic Management.

Ansoff's first – and most important – book was *Corporate Strategy*, in which he sought to make sense of the broader implications of what he had learned at Lockheed. He believed that there was "a practical method for strategic decision making within a business firm" that could be made accessible to all.

Ansoff's work struck a chord. Until then, strategic planning had been a barely understood, *ad hoc* concept. It was practiced, while the theory lay largely unexplored. The result was a rational model by which strategic and planning decisions could be made. The model concentrated on corporate expansion and diversification rather than strategic planning as a whole. From this emerged the Ansoff Model of Strategic Planning, an intricate and somewhat daunting sequence of decisions.

Central to this was the reassuringly simple concept of gap analysis: see where you are; identify where you wish to be; and identify tasks that will take you there. Ansoff can also lay claim to introducing the word "synergy" into the management vocabulary. He explained it with uncharacteristic brevity as "2 + 2 = 5." In addition, he examined "corporate advantage" long before Michael Porter cornered the field 20 years later.

To the contemporary observer, Ansoff's work can appear excessively analytical and highly prescriptive. In an era where corporate change is increasingly recognized as a fact of life, thinkers argue that solutions are ever more elusive. Ansoff's model was better suited to a world of answers than one beset by turbulence and uncertainty.

Balanced scorecard

The balanced scorecard is a strategic management and measurement system that links strategic objectives to comprehensive indicators. It recognizes that companies have a tendency to fixate on a few measurements that blinker their assessment of how the business is performing overall. The balanced scorecard focusses management attention on a range of key performance indicators to provide an overall view.

The concept was originally put forward by David Norton, co-founder of the consulting company Renaissance Solutions, and Robert Kaplan, the Marvin Bower Professor of Leadership Development at Harvard Business School. It is explored in their book *The Balanced Scorecard: Translating strategy into action* (1996).

Kaplan and Norton compared running a company to flying a plane. The pilot who relies on a single dial is unlikely to be safe. Pilots must utilize all the information contained in their cockpit. "The complexity of managing an organization today requires that managers be able to view performance in several areas simultaneously," said Kaplan and Norton. "Moreover, by forcing senior managers to consider all the important operational measures together, the balanced scorecard can let them see whether improvement in one area may be achieved at the expense of another."

In many ways, it is simple common sense. Balance is clearly preferable to imbalance. Kaplan and Norton suggested that four elements need to be balanced.

- First is the customer perspective. Companies must ask how they are perceived by customers.
- The second element is "internal perspective." Companies must ask what it is at which they must excel.
- Third is the "innovation and learning perspective." Companies must ask whether they can continue to improve and create value.
- Finally there is the financial perspective. Companies must ask how they look to shareholders.

According to Kaplan and Norton, by focussing energies, attention, and measures on all four of these dimensions, companies become driven by their mission rather than by short-term financial performance. Crucial to achieving this is applying measures to company strategy. Instead of being beyond measurement, the balanced scorecard argues that strategy must be central to any process of measurement – "a good balanced scorecard should tell the story of your strategy."

Boston Matrix

So influential was the Boston Matrix that a whole generation of senior managers grew up with cows, dogs, stars, and question marks as a way to classify their businesses. The Boston Matrix became an icon in an era of strategic planning.

Until the 1960s, models were the impenetrable domain of economists. The man largely credited for bringing business models into the mainstream was an Australian, Bruce Henderson (1915–92), founder of the Boston Consulting Group (BCG).

Sometimes called the "dog star" matrix for obvious reasons, the Boston Matrix epitomized a generic view of strategic decision making. It is, in fact, a simple two-by-two matrix (a format popular with management consultants ever since) that measures market growth and relative market share for all the businesses in the company's portfolio (see Figure 1.6). Each business can be placed on the matrix and classified accordingly.

The hypothesis of the Boston Matrix is that companies with higher market share in faster-growing industries are more profitable. The further to the left a business is on the Boston Matrix, the stronger the company should be. (The matrix can be applied to individual products or entire businesses.)

Refinements have been added along the way. On its original matrix, BCG superimposed a theory of cash management that included a hierarchy of uses of cash, numbered from one to four in their order of priority. This identified the top priority as cash cows, characterized by high market share and low growth. Investment in cash cows is easily justified, as they are dull, safe, and highly profitable. Next in line are the stars (high growth; high market share), although their investment requirements are likely to be significant. More problematic is the third category, question marks (problem children, or wildcats in some versions) where there is high growth and low share. Any investment in them is risky. The final category is the

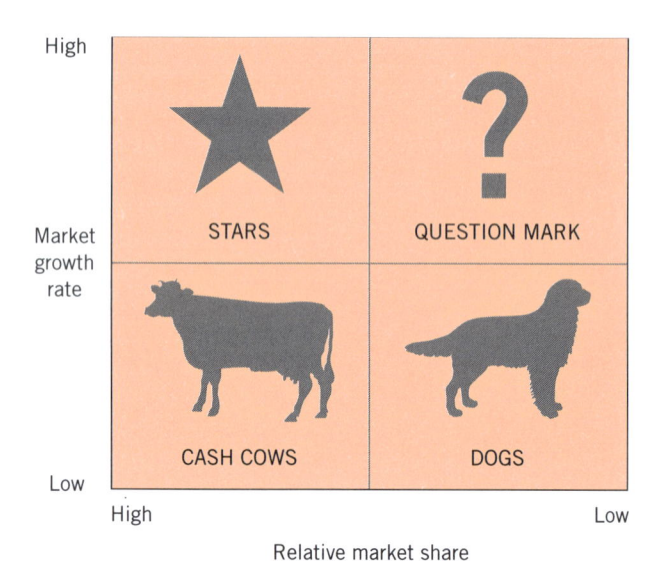

Figure 1.6: *The Boston Matrix*

aptly titled dogs, where low market share is allied to low growth. Dogs should not be approached.

The Boston Matrix proved a highly popular innovation. From a business point of view, it had the characteristics of any great model: it was accessible, simple, and useful. However, it was also limiting. Measuring corporate performance against two parameters is straightforward but potentially dangerous if these are the only two parameters against which performance is measured. A product of its time, the matrix offered a blinkered view of a world where growth and profitability were all that counted.

As a business tool, however, the Boston Matrix had a significant and long-term impact. Of equal significance was its influence on the management consulting industry. It spawned a host of imitators. Today, no consultant's report is complete without a matrix of some sort. More importantly, BCG could be said to have introduced the first off-the-shelf consulting product (although it wouldn't see it that way). Companies required the big idea. They wanted to see how they fared on the matrix and how it could shape their strategies. The consulting firm product was born.

Previously, consultants had gone in to client companies to solve specific business problems. The success of the Boston Matrix marked a change in approach. As well as problem solving, consultancy became concerned with passing on the latest ideas, the frameworks, models, and matrices that were in vogue. Problem solvers became peddlers of big ideas. This opened up huge new vistas for the management consultancy profession, which it has been assiduously – and profitably – chasing ever since.

Game Theory

Game Theory is based on the premise that no matter what the game, no matter what the circumstances, there is a strategy that will enable you to succeed.

Game Theory was conceived not in the classroom or in the boardroom but in the casino. In the 1930s, when he was a student at Princeton and Harvard, John Von Neumann was an attentive spectator at poker games. Von Neumann was a mathematical genius rather than a gambler and the result was Game Theory, a unique mathematical insight into the possibilities and probabilities of human behavior.

Game Theory has developed its own Zen-like language of dilemmas and riddles. The most famous of these is the Prisoner's Dilemma. Invented by Princeton University's Albert Tucker in 1950, the Prisoner's Dilemma is an imaginary scenario. Two prisoners are accused of the same crime. During interrogation in different cells they are each told that if one confesses and the other does not, the confessor will be released while the other will serve a long prison sentence. If neither confesses, both will be dispatched to prison for a short sentence, and if both confess they will both receive an intermediate sentence.

Working through the possibilities, the prisoners conclude that the best decision is to confess. As both reach the same decision, they receive an intermediate sentence.

The Prisoner's Dilemma has a fundamental flaw: Game Theory is rational; reality is not. Companies that have expressed an interest in Game Theory tend to be from tightly regulated industries, such as power generation, where there is limited competition or cartels (such as OPEC in the oil industry). With a limited number of players, playing by accepted rules, and behaving in a rational way, Game Theory can make sense of what the best competitive moves may be.

Broader interest in Game Theory was reignited in 1994 when the Nobel Prize for economics was awarded to three renowned thinkers: John Nash, John Harsanyi, and Reinhard Selten. In particular, the precociously brilliant Nash is the creator of Nash's Equilibrium: the point when no player can improve their position by changing strategy. Players in a game will change their strategies until they reach equilibrium.

In one classic example, an industry includes two competing companies. Each determines the price of its product. If both were to set high prices, they would maximize their profits. Similarly, if both set their prices at lower levels, they would remain profitable. The trouble comes when they choose different price levels. If one sets a high price and the other a low price, the company with the low price makes far more money. The optimal solution is for both to have high prices. The trouble is if one company has a high price, the other will undercut it and vice versa. Eventually, both companies end up with low prices and lesser profits.

The key lesson from this and other scenarios explored by Game Theory is simply that the interactions of companies and other organizations are interdependent. If a company decides to make an investment it should consider how others – whether they be competitors, customers, or suppliers – will react.

Game Theory is best seen as a way of considering the future, a tool to get people to think. As a rationalist's guide to business paradoxes, it can be a useful business weapon. Instead of seeking out strategies driven by win–lose scenarios, companies begin to explore the merits of other strategies that may be win–win, with mutual benefits for themselves, their customers, their suppliers, and even their competitors.

Hamel, Gary

Gary Hamel (born 1954) has established himself at the vanguard of contemporary thinking on strategy. Hard hitting, opinionated, and rigorously rational, Hamel summarizes the challenge of the 1990s in a typically earthy phrase, as "separating the shit from the shinola, the hype from the reality, and the timeless from the transient."

As well as being visiting professor of strategic and international management at London Business School, California-based Hamel is a consultant to major companies and chairman of Strategos, a worldwide strategic consulting company. His reputation has burgeoned as a result of a series of acclaimed articles in the *Harvard Business Review* as well as the popularity of the bestselling *Competing for the Future*, co-written with C.K. Prahalad. Along the way, Hamel has created a new vocabulary for strategy that includes strategic intent, strategic architecture, industry foresight (rather than vision), and core competencies.

The need for new perspectives on strategy is forcefully put by Hamel: "We like to believe we can break strategy down to Five Forces or Seven Ss. But you can't. Strategy is extraordinarily emotional and demanding. It is not a ritual or a once-a-year exercise, though that is what it has become. We have set the bar too low." As a result, managers are bogged down in the nitty-gritty of the present, spending less than 3 percent of their time looking to the future.[9]

Hamel's argument is that complacency and cynicism are endemic. "Dilbert is the bestselling business book of all time. It is cynical about management. Never has there been so much cynicism." It is only by challenging convention that change will happen. "Taking risks, breaking the rules, and being a maverick have always been important, but today they are more crucial than ever. We live in a discontinuous world – one where digitalization, deregulation, and globalization are profoundly reshaping the industrial landscape," he says.[10]

Hamel argues that there are three kinds of companies. First are "the real makers," companies such as British Airways and Xerox. They are the aristocracy: well-managed, consistent high achievers. Second, says Hamel, are the takers, "peasants who only keep what the Lord doesn't want." This group typically has around 15 percent market share, such as Kodak in the copier business or Avis in car rentals.

Third are the breakers, industrial revolutionaries. These are companies that Hamel believes are creating the new wealth, and include the likes of Starbucks in the coffee business. "Companies should be asking themselves, who is going to capture the new wealth in your industry?" he says.

When Hamel talks of change, he is not considering tinkering at the edges. "The primary agenda is to be the architect of industry transformation, not simply corporate transformation," he says. Companies that view change as an internal matter are liable to be left behind. Instead, they need to look outside of their industry boundaries. Hamel calculates that if you want to see the future coming, 80 percent of the learning will take place outside company boundaries. This is not something companies are very good at.

Many will continue to ignore Hamel's call for a revolution. "There is a lot of talk about creating shareholders' wealth. It is not a hard thing to do. Just find a 60-year-old CEO and set a 65-year-old retirement age and then guarantee a salary based on the share price growing." The trouble is that it is here, at the stock-option-packed top of the organization, that change needs to begin. "What we need is not visionaries but activists. We need antidotes to Dilbert," Hamel proclaims.

Henderson, Bruce

While managers may rely on experience to predict how their business will respond to their actions, strategists and economists rely on their models, which are amalgams of many different experiences.

The man who brought business models into the mainstream was the Australian Bruce Henderson (1915–92). Henderson was an engineer who worked as a strategic planner for General Electric. He then joined the management consultancy Arthur D. Little before leaving in 1963 to set up his own consultancy, the Boston Consulting Group.

BCG is regarded by some as the first pure strategy consultancy. It quickly became a great success. Within five years, BCG was in the top group of consulting firms, where it has largely remained. It has been called "the most idea-driven major consultancy in the world."

The first model Henderson discovered – or rediscovered in this case – was something of an antique. In the 1920s, an obscure company called Curtiss Aircraft came up with the concept of the "learning curve," which also became known as the "experience curve." This posited that unit costs declined as cumulative production increased because of the acquisition of experience. The idea had been applied solely to manufacturing. Henderson applied it to strategy rather than production and found that it still worked and provided a useful, practical tool.

The model for which Henderson and BCG are best known is the Growth/Share Matrix. This measures market growth and relative market share for all the businesses in a particular firm. The hypothesis of this particular framework is that companies with higher market share and growth are more profitable.

BCG then superimposed on the matrix a theory of cash management that included a hierarchy of uses of cash, numbered from 1 to 4 in their order of priority. Richard Koch comments in his *Financial Times Guide to Strategy:* "Bruce weaved it all together in a coherent philosophy of business that highlighted more clearly than ever before the compelling importance of market leadership, a low cost position, selectivity in business, and looking at cash flows."[11]

Mintzberg, Henry

Henry Mintzberg (born 1939) is one of the most interesting of management thinkers. Eschewing the guru seminar trail, he forges a unique intellectual path and is a great debunker of received wisdom. He is cheerfully quotable – "Great organizations, once created, don't need great leaders"; "Delayering can be defined as the process by which people who barely know what's going on get rid of those who do."

Mintzberg is Professor of Management at McGill University, Montreal and Professor of Organization at INSEAD in Fontainebleau, France. His first book, *The Nature of Managerial Work*, examined how managers worked. Not surprisingly, managers did not do what they liked to think they did. Mintzberg found that instead of spending time contemplating the long term, managers were slaves to the moment, moving from task to task with every move dogged by another diversion, another call. The median time spent on any one issue was a mere nine minutes.

From his observations, Mintzberg identified the manager's "work roles" as:

Interpersonal roles
Figurehead: representing the organization/unit to outsiders
Leader: motivating subordinates, unifying effort
Liaiser: maintaining lateral contacts

Informational roles
Monitor: of information flows
Disseminator: of information to subordinates
Spokesman: transmission of information to outsiders

Decisional roles
Entrepreneur: initiator and designer of change
Disturbance handler: handling non-routine events
Resource allocator: deciding who gets what and who will do what
Negotiator: negotiating.

Mintzberg's work on strategy has been highly influential. In particular, he has long been a critic of formulae and analysis-driven strategic planning. He defines planning as "a formalized system for codifying, elaborating, and operationalizing the strategies which companies already have."

Mintzberg identifies three central pitfalls to today's strategy planning practices. The first is the assumption that discontinuities can be predicated. Forecasting techniques are limited by the fact that they tend to assume that the future will resemble the past.

The second is that planners are detached from the reality of the organization. Planners have traditionally been obsessed with gathering hard data on their industry, markets, and competitors. Soft data – networks of contacts, talking with customers, suppliers and employees, using intuition, and using the grapevine – have all but been ignored. To gain real understanding of an organization's competitive situation soft data needs to be dynamically integrated into the planning process. Mintzberg writes: "While hard data may inform the intellect, it is largely soft data that generate wisdom. They may be difficult to 'analyze,' but they are indispensable for synthesis – the key to strategy making."

The third and final flaw identified by Mintzberg is the assumption that strategy making can be formalized. The left side of the brain has dominated strategy formulation with its emphasis on logic and analysis. Alternatives which do not fit into the pre-determined structure are ignored. The right side of the brain needs to become part of the process with its emphasis on intuition and creativity. "Planning by its very nature," concludes Mintzberg, "defines and preserves categories. Creativity, by its very nature, creates categories or rearranges established ones. This is why strategic planning can neither provide creativity, nor deal with it when it emerges by other means."

By championing the role of creativity in strategy creation and in providing carefully researched rebuttals of formulaic approaches to management, Mintzberg has provided new insights into strategy. "The real challenge in crafting strategy lies in detecting the subtle discontinuities that may undermine a business in the future," he says. "And for that there is no technique, no program, just a sharp mind in touch with the situation."

Pascale, Richard

Richard Pascale (born 1938) first came to the attention of a large audience with the advent of the Seven S framework, one of the most renowned and debated management tools of the 1980s. The framework emerged from a series of meetings during June 1978 between Pascale, Anthony Athos, then of Harvard Business School, and the McKinsey consultants Tom Peters and Robert Waterman, who were already involved in the research that was to form the basis of *In Search of Excellence*. The Seven Ss (strategy, structure, skills, staff, shared values, systems, and style) are a kind of *aide mémoire*, a useful memory jogger of what concerns organizations.

From Pascale's perspective, the Seven Ss presented a way into comparisons between US and Japanese management. Pascale and Athos concluded that the Japanese succeeded largely because of the attention they gave to the soft Ss – style, shared values, skills, and staff. In contrast, the West remained preoccupied with the hard Ss of strategy, structure, and systems. These conclusions formed the bedrock of *The Art of Japanese Management* (1981), one of the first business bestsellers.

Pascale was a member of the faculty at Stanford's Graduate School of Business for 20 years. He has since worked as an independent consultant and is the author of *Managing on the Edge* (1990).

In addition to the Seven S framework, Pascale's work is significant for a number of reasons. First, he was among the first researchers to provide original insights into Japanese approaches to business and management. The second influential area was vision, which he and Athos championed. Today, corporate visions are a fact of life, although many fail to match the Japanese practice mapped out by Pascale and Athos in which visions are dynamic, vivifying *modus operandi* rather than pallid or generic statements of corporate intent.

The third element of Pascale's work is in the related areas of corporate mortality and corporate transformation. In the late 1980s and 1990s, Pascale drew attention to the fragile foundations on which our grand corporate assumptions are made. *Managing on the Edge* begins with the line "Nothing fails like success." "Great strengths are inevitably the root of weakness," Pascale argued, pausing only to point out that from the Fortune 500 of 1985, 143 had departed five years later.

To overcome inertia and survive in a turbulent climate requires a constant commitment to what Pascale labels "corporate transformation." Incorporating employees fully into the principal business challenges facing the company is the first "intervention" required if companies are to thrive. The second is to lead the organization in a way that sharpens and maintains incorporation and "constructive stress." Finally, Pascale advocates instilling mental disciplines that will make people behave differently and then help them sustain their new behavior. In the latter element, Pascale cites the work of the United States Army, in which a strong culture allows minds and behavior to be changed through rigorous and carefully thought-through training.[12]

In his recent work (see 2001's *Surfing the Edge of Chaos*), Pascale has coined the term "agility" to describe the combination of skills and thinking required of the organizations of the future. Pascale and his co-researchers believe that there are "four indicators that tell us a great deal about how an organization is likely to perform and adapt." These are power (whether employees think they can have any influence on the course of events); identity (to what extent individuals identify with the organization as a whole, rather than with a narrow group); contention (whether conflict is brought out into the open and used as a learning tool); and learning (how the organization deals with new ideas).[13]

The trouble is that these four elements, under normal circumstances, tend to coagulate and the organization eventually stagnates. Pascale says this can be avoided only if an organization pursues seven disciplines of agility, which range from the self-explanatory "accountability in action" to the more elusive and painful "course of relentless discomfort."

Pascale's vision of the future is a troubling one. To survive, companies must continually move on, using the agility engendered by their individuals and culture to ask questions, discuss the undiscussible, and shake things up. Case studies of this in practice are few and far between.

Porter, Michael

If Peter Drucker is the intellectual giant of management thinking and Tom Peters its most charismatic populist, Michael Porter (born 1947) is perhaps the thinker with the greatest influence.

Porter is precociously talented and intellectually persuasive. He could have pursued a career as a professional golfer but chose instead to take a Harvard MBA. While completing his PhD at Harvard, Porter was influenced by the economist Richard Caves, who became his mentor. He joined the Harvard faculty at the age of 26, one of the youngest tenured professors in the school's history.

Porter has served as a counselor on competitive strategy to many leading US and international companies and plays an active role in economic policy with the US Congress and business groups, as well as acting as an adviser to foreign governments. Porter has also exerted a huge local influence on the state of Massachusetts.

In his 1980 book *Competitive Strategy: Techniques for Analyzing Industries and Competitors*, Porter developed the model still regarded as essential reading for strategy makers and MBA students the world over. His timing was impeccable. Publication of his model coincided with a wholesale rethink of Western business principles. In the 1970s, corporate America had watched in horror as Japanese companies stole market share in industry after industry. Initially, US companies put Japanese competitiveness down to cheap labor, but by the end of the decade it was dawning on them that something more fundamental was occurring. Porter encouraged a complete re-evaluation of the nature of competitiveness and changed the way companies thought about strategy for ever.

Porter's genius has lain in producing brilliantly researched and cogent models of competitiveness at a corporate, industry-wide, and national level. He took an industrial economics framework – the structure-conduct-performance (SCP) paradigm – and translated it into the context of business strategy. From this emerged his best-known model: the Five Forces framework.

In his 1980 book Porter wrote: "In any industry, whether it is domestic or international or produces a product or a service, the rules of competition are embodied in five competitive forces." These five competitive forces are as follows:

- *The entry of new competitors.* New competitors necessitate some competitive response that will inevitably use some of your resources, thus reducing profits.
- *The threat of substitutes.* If there are viable alternatives to your product or service in the marketplace, the prices you can charge will be limited.
- *The bargaining power of buyers.* If customers have bargaining power they will use it. This will reduce profit margins and, as a result, affect profitability.
- *The bargaining power of suppliers.* Given power over you, suppliers will increase their prices and adversely affect your profitability.
- *The rivalry among the existing competitors.* Competition leads to the need to invest in marketing, R&D, or price reductions that will reduce your profits.

The five forces, he asserted, shape the competitive landscape. Initially, they were passively interpreted as valid statements of the facts of competitive life. But by laying them bare, Porter provided a framework for companies to understand and challenge the competitive markets in which they operate. For strategy makers, the five forces represented levers on which any strategy must act if it is to have an impact on a company's competitive position. "The collective strength of these five competitive forces determines the ability of firms in an industry to earn, on average, rates of return on investment in excess of the cost of capital. The strength of the five forces varies from industry to industry, and can change as an industry evolves," Porter observed.

A late addition to his book was the concept of generic strategies. Porter argued that there were three "generic strategies," "viable approaches to dealing with ... competitive forces." Strategy, in Porter's eyes, was a matter of *how* to compete. The first of Porter's generic strategies was differentiation, competing on the basis of value added to customers (quality, service, differentiation) so that customers will pay a premium to cover higher costs. The second was cost-based leadership, offering products or services at the lowest cost. Quality and service are not unimportant, but cost reduction provides focus to the organization. Focus was the third generic strategy. Companies with a clear strategy outperform those whose strategy is unclear or those that attempt to achieve both differentiation and cost leadership. "Sometimes the firm can successfully pursue more than one approach as its primary target, though this is rarely possible," Porter said. "Effectively implementing any of these generic strategies usually requires total commitment, and organizational arrangements are diluted if there's more than one primary target."

If a company failed to focus on any of the three generic strategies, it was liable to encounter problems. "The firm failing to develop its strategy in at least one of the three directions – a firm that is *stuck in the middle* – is in an extremely poor strategic situation," Porter wrote. "The firm lacks the market share, capital investment, and resolve to play the low-cost game, the industry-wide differentiation necessary to obviate the need for a low-cost position, or the focus to create differentiation or low cost in a more limited sphere. The firm stuck in the middle is almost guaranteed low profitability. It either loses the high-volume customers who demand low prices or must bid away its profits to get this business away from low-cost firms. Yet it also loses high-margin businesses – the cream – to the firms who are focussed on high-margin targets or have achieved differentiation overall. The firm stuck in the middle also probably suffers from a blurred corporate culture and a conflicting set of organizational arrangements and motivation system."

When *Competitive Strategy* was published in 1980, Porter's generic strategies offered a rational and straightforward method of companies extricating themselves from strategic confusion. The reassurance proved short-lived. Less than a decade later, companies were having to compete on all fronts. They had to be differentiated, through improved service or speedier development, and be cost leaders, cheaper than their competitors.

Porter's 1990 book *The Competitive Advantage of Nations* must be ranked as one of the most ambitious books of our time. At its heart was a radical new perspective of the role and *raison d'être* of nations. His research encompassed 10 countries: the UK, Denmark, Italy, Japan, Korea, Singapore, Sweden, Switzerland, the US, and Germany (then West Germany). Porter has since extended his study to include Japan,

India, Canada, New Zealand, Portugal, and the state of Massachusetts.

Porter sought to examine what makes a nation's firms and industries competitive in global markets and what propels a whole nation's economy to advance. "Why are firms based in a particular nation able to create and sustain competitive advantage against the world's best competitors in a particular field? And why is one nation often the home for so many of an industry's world leaders?" he asked. "Why is tiny Switzerland the home base for international leaders in pharmaceuticals, chocolate, and trading? Why are leaders in heavy trucks and mining equipment based in Sweden?"

Porter identified a central paradox: companies have become globalized and more international in their scope and aspirations than ever before. This, on the surface at least, would appear to suggest that the nation has lost its role in the international success of its firms. "Companies, at first glance, seem to have transcended countries. Yet what I have learned in this study contradicts this conclusion," said Porter. "While globalization of competition might appear to make the nation less important, instead it seems to make it more so. With fewer impediments to trade to shelter uncompetitive domestic firms and industries, the home nation takes on growing significance because it is the source of the skills and technology that underpin competitive advantage."

Scenario planning

Scenario planning involves testing business strategies against a series of alternative futures. The technique was invented in the 1940s by Herman Kahn, the famous futurist from the Rand Corporation and the Hudson Institute. The term scenario – meaning a detailed outline for the plot of a future film – was borrowed from Hollywood by Kahn's friend, screenwriter and novelist Leo Rosten.

Kahn was best known for his scenarios about nuclear war and for his trademark phrase, "thinking the unthinkable." Other early pioneers of scenario thinking also tended to look at the macro level: the future of mankind, for example, or the economy of an entire region.

Although only now coming into wider use, scenario planning has been practiced in one form or another in the business world since the early 1960s. It was first used by a far-sighted team of planners at the oil company Royal Dutch Shell. They began to build on Kahn's work, developing their own version of the scenario approach as a possible answer to two questions: "How do we look up to 20 to 30 years ahead?" and "How can we get people to discuss the 'unthinkable' together?" Using the technique, they foresaw the energy crises of 1973 and 1979, the growth of energy conservation, the evolution of the global environmental movement, and even the break-up of the Soviet Union, years before these events happened.

What Shell realized, however, was that managers need these grand scenarios to be translated into something more recognizable. To have practical use in business, the story has to be focussed on a particular audience or issue. Learning to focus scenarios on a specific business purpose was part of the company's contribution to the practice.

In the 1990s, a string of books – including *The Art of the Long View* by futurist Peter Schwartz, *The Living Company* by former Shell manager Arie de Geus, and *The Age of Heretics* by Art Kleiner, who interviewed Shell managers – drew attention to scenario planning, placing it firmly on the management agenda. It is no coincidence, of course, that the technique came to the fore at a time when so many seemingly unassailable companies were wrong-footed by changes in their trading environments.

Although sometimes confused with disaster planning or contingency planning – which deals with how a company should respond when things go wrong – scenario planning is a way to identify both threats and opportunities that flow from decisions. According to Clem Sunter, chairman of the Anglo American Chairman's Fund and former head of scenario planning at the London-based mining conglomerate: "Scenarios are to organizations what radar is to a pilot. They help us look for the first signs of changes that can profoundly affect how we work, and make us think about our responses."

Seven S framework

The Seven S framework is no more than a simple distillation of the key elements that make up an organization's personality. Developed around 1980 by two business school academics, Anthony Athos and Richard Pascale, and a group of consultants at McKinsey and Company, including Tom Peters and Robert Waterman, it provides a useful checklist for thinking about what makes a business tick. It advocates examination in seven basic areas, all beginning with S: strategy, structure, systems, style, skills, staff, and superordinate goals.

The Seven S model was neatly alliterative, accessible, understandable, and with its logo (later named "the happy atom") highly marketable. Managers seemed to like it. This was a business theory to fit all occasions encapsulated on a single page.

Pascale and Athos introduced the Seven S model to a mass audience in *The Art of Japanese Management*, published in 1981. Peters and Waterman also featured the framework in *In Search of Excellence* a year later (despite the fact that Tom Peters initially thought the framework "corny").

The attraction of the Seven Ss is that they are memorable and simple. The framework is a model of how organizations achieve success. Inevitably, a model that simplifies something as complex as organizational behavior is open to abuse, misinterpretation, and criticism. The Seven S framework has suffered more than its fair share. (Contrast this with the generally positive response still reserved for Michael Porter's five forces model of competitiveness, which simplifies something equally as complex but does so in a far more analytical and academic way.)

Today, when Japanese companies have fallen off their pedestal and the cult of "excellence" started by Peters and Waterman seems to have finally run its course, it is easy to forget how influential the ideas behind them were. For the first time, the Seven S framework enabled meaningful comparisons between companies from completely different sectors, national cultures, and histories. As a way to cover the basics, it remains a useful concept.

No one ever ran a business with a framework. The Seven Ss are a helpful summation of the main issues bedeviling managerial life. But they are practically beneficial only as a memory jogger, a structure around which to build, or as a filter to determine key issues. They are not, never could be, and were never intended to be set in stone.

Like the Boston Matrix, the Seven S framework belongs to an era that is gone. The simple truths it uncovered are no longer considered worthy of our attention. But as a milestone in the evolution of management theory, it still has much to tell us.

Strategic inflection point

The strategic inflection point is a term associated with Andy Grove, chairman of the microprocessor company Intel and one of the best-known figures in the computer industry. Strategic inflection points, he says, occur when a company's competitive position goes through a transition. It is the point at which the organization must alter the path it is on, adapting itself to the new situation, or it risks going into decline. It is concerned with how companies recognize and adapt to "paradigm changes."

"During a strategic inflection point the way a business operates, the very structure and concept of the business, undergoes a change," Grove writes. But the irony is that at that point itself nothing much happens. "That subtle point is like the eye of a hurricane. There is no wind at the eye of the hurricane, but when it moves the wind hits you again. That is what happens in the middle of the transformation from one business model to another. The irony is that, even though these are the most cataclysmic changes that a business can undertake, more often than not those changes are missed."

Grove was so enamored of the term that "Strategic Inflection Points" was the original title of his 1996 book, until the publishers rejected it in favor of the more memorable *Only the Paranoid Survive*.

In the real world, the need to spot paradigm changes is most acute for high-tech companies such as Intel. Indeed, it was IBM's original failure to spot the switch from mainframe to personal computers that allowed Intel and Microsoft to create their dominant market positions. Both companies have inculcated their cultures with the lesson.

Grove explicitly recognizes that the pace of change in the modern business world is such that entire markets and industries can change almost overnight. This places an increasing burden on strategy makers and involves the ability to discard current assumptions to shape the future of the industry – before someone else does. Grove calls this "10x change," and it can either undermine the business model or create tremendous new growth opportunities.

The trouble with traditional strategic planning approaches is that they tend to extrapolate the past to create a view of the future. As a result, they often preserve, rather than challenge, industry assumptions. Traditional planning processes tend to analyze external factors individually, therefore missing the power that is unleashed when trends converge. The concept of strategic inflection points recognizes this phenomenon and gives it a name.

Sun Tzu

The link between the military and business worlds has existed since time immemorial. Its starting point, as far as it is possible to discern, is Sun Tzu's *The Art of War*, written 2,500 years ago.

The authorship of *The Art of War* remains clouded in mystery. It may have been written by Sun Wu, a military general who was alive around 500 BC. His book is reputed to have led to a meeting with King Ho-lü of Wu. Sun Wu, not having a flipchart available, argued his case for military discipline by decapitating two of the king's concubines. This proved his point admirably.

The book returned to grace business bookshelves in the 1980s. The attraction of the military analogy is that it is clear who your enemy is. When your enemy is evident, the world appears clearer whether you are a military general or a managing director. Sun Tzu is an aggressive counterpoint to the confusion of mere theory. After all, among his advice was the following: "Deploy forces to defend the strategic points; exercise vigilance in preparation, do not be indolent. Deeply investigate the true situation, secretly await their laxity. Wait until they leave their strongholds, then seize what they love."

Managers lapped up such brazen brutality. Yet *The Art of War* is more sophisticated than that. Why destroy when you can win by stealth and cunning? "If you are near the enemy, make him believe you are far from him. If you are far from the enemy, make him believe you are near," wrote the master. "To subdue the enemy's forces without fighting is the summit of skill. The best approach is to attack the other side's strategy; next best is to attack his alliances; next best is to attack his soldiers; the worst is to attack cities."

While the imagery of warfare continues to exert influence over managers, it appears to be on the wane. Contemporary business metaphors are as likely to emerge from biology and the environment as from the traditional sources of engineering and warfare.

REFERENCES

1. Porter, Michael, 'What is strategy?' *Harvard Business Review*, November–December 1996, pp. 61–78.
2. Hamel, Gary, 'The Search for Strategy,' London Business School working paper, 1997.
3. The idea that the firm is a complex system of *interrelationships* and that it should be viewed and managed as such is one of the founding principles of 'system dynamics' as developed by MIT's Jay W. Forrester. A powerful and managerial exposition of system dynamics and systems thinking principles can be found in Peter Senge: *The Fifth Discipline*, New York: Doubleday, 1990. See also David E. Meen and Mark Keough: 'Creating the learning organization: an interview with Peter Senge,' in *The McKinsey Quarterly Anthologies: Business Dynamics*, 1997, pp. 79–93; and 'The CEO as organization designer: an interview with Professor Jay W. Forrester,' *The McKinsey Quarterly*, 1992, No. 2, pp. 3–30.
4. What I call here 'environment' is what is widely known as the 7S framework developed by McKinsey and Company: style, strategy, structure, systems, skills, staff, and superordinate goals.
5. This point is made forcefully and in much more detail in David Nadler and Michael Tushman: *Competing by Design: The Power of Organizational Architecture*, New York: Oxford University Press, 1997.
6. For additional details, see Markides, C., 'Strategic innovation,' *Sloan Management Review*, Vol. 38, No. 3, Spring 1997, pp. 9–23.
7. Markides, C., 'Strategic innovation in established companies,' *Sloan Management Review*, Vol. 39, No. 3, Spring 1998, pp. 31–42.
8. If this happens, value will migrate from one strategic position to another; see the excellent study by Adrian J. Slywotzky: *Value Migration: How to Think Several Moves Ahead of the Competition*, Boston: HBS Press, 1996.
9. International Management Symposium, London Business School, November 11, 1997.
10. Hamel, Gary, 'Killer strategies that makes shareholders rich,' *Fortune*, June 23, 1997.
11. Koch, Richard, *Financial Times Guide to Strategy*, FT Pitman, London, 1995.
12. Pascale, Richard, Millemann, Mark and Gioja, Linda, "Changing the way we change,' *Harvard Business Review*, November–December, 1997.
13. Golzen, Godfrey, 'The next big idea,' *Human Resources*, March–April, 1997.

CHAPTER 2

Globalization

"No leader can hope to guide an enterprise into the future without understanding the commercial, political and social impact of the global economy."

Kenichi Ohmae

"We must ensure that the global market is embedded in broadly shared values and practices that reflect global social needs, and that all the world's people share the benefits of globalization."

Kofi Annan

"From the suites of Davos to the streets of Seattle, there is a growing consensus that globalization must now be reshaped to reflect values broader than simply the freedom of capital."

John J. Sweeney

"Globalization has altered the economic frameworks of both developed and developing nations in ways that are difficult to fully comprehend. Nonetheless, the largely unregulated global markets do clear and, with rare exceptions, appear to move effortlessly from one state of equilibrium to another. It is as though an international version of Adam Smith's 'invisible hand' is at work."

Alan Greenspan

Can globalization be fixed?

DEBORAH DOANE

[Anti-globalization protesters have been out in force challenging the rise of multinational corporations. The march of globalization may be inexorable but its direction and objectives could yet be – and may need to be – changed.]

It has become almost a truism that corporations are the bogeymen of globalization, stomping over the world like a herd of elephants. Intellectuals condemn them; governments quiver respectfully in their presence; and young protesters give up their holidays to throw bricks through their windows.

But the truth is more complex. In many ways the great corporations, as well as governments, are caught in a complicated tangle of relationships that hold them captive as much as the rest of us. The real truth is that nobody's in control. Globalization has left us with a vacuum in which we lack the systems to manage the challenges so well defined by the anti-globalization movement but so poorly prescribed for.

If that's true, what can we do about it? At an individual level probably not enough. But collectively – either as business or government – there are some modest steps forward that could have considerable impact and may just generate enough momentum for us to turn the corner. The challenge is to find the political will needed to take the first steps.

Winners and losers

Economic globalization has brought with it flows of goods and services across borders on an unprecedented scale. Multinational corporations (MNCs) are the primary vehicles for much of this activity, with international trade now worth an estimated US$7 trillion a year. This level of trade has resulted in a heightened sense of awareness that all is not well with the world.

Corporate power has been the primary target of anti-globalization protesters. Corporate executives now face ever-increasing pressure to manage the impacts of their behavior on society and the environment. And demands aren't coming from civil society alone; investors now regularly require companies to manage social and environmental risk through a variety of means.

The terrorist acts of September 11, 2001 acted as a further catalyst for business to consider how their actions might impact on wider society. Shortly after the attacks, an article in the *Financial Times* reported on a forum at Harvard Business School. Students, it seems, were discussing how corporate social responsibility could help bridge the gap between have and have-not nations and mitigate future risks of terrorism. The debate and the arena of the debate is widening.

Advocates of globalization and market-driven economies argue that the current system has brought more wealth creation than at any other time in history. And on the surface it is true: in 2000, global economic output reached a staggering US$43.6 trillion – over eight times higher than the level achieved in 1950. Much of this has resulted in change for the better. We now have longer life expectancy, reduced infant mortality, and higher levels of literacy than ever before. Development economists refer to this as a "rising tide lifts all boats" effect.

At the same time, there are some clear winners and losers in the game. In Latin America, one of the stars of the free-market movement, the number of people living in poverty has actually risen by over 5 million, while much of the new wealth generated in the region has been financed by unsustainable levels of debt.

But globalization *per se* is not really the problem. The problem is how globalization has been managed or, rather, not been managed. Anti-globalization groups should not be simply dismissed as anarchists – most are simply trying to articulate what they see as a deep malaise with the current state of play between market and society.

The fallout from globalization can be summed up under three key themes:

- *Poverty and an increasing gap between rich and poor:* the UN estimates that 800 million people in the world remain chronically malnourished while millions in the developing world continue to die from easily preventable diseases, often contracted due to lack of clean water and/or basic sanitation. Concerning the rich/poor gap, in 2000 the top 200 billionaires had a combined wealth of $1,135 billion while the total income of 582 million people in all developing countries was only $146 billion – less than 13 percent of the top 200. In Western economies, the share of GDP going to employees in the form of wages or other compensation has actually fallen over the past three decades; while the number of people living on less than US$1 per day has increased by almost one-third in places like sub-Saharan Africa.

    Poverty and the gap between rich and poor manifest themselves in several ways: unemployment, crime, and low participation in democratic processes; low economic growth; corruption and bribery; large movements of population that can destabilize nation states; and, most worryingly, an increase in global terrorism.

Poverty represents a particular challenge for business. On the one hand, companies looking to increase their profit margins can actively seek out workforces in countries willing to accept lower wages. On the other hand, over the long run, poverty creates a gap in the market – poor people, by definition, have low purchasing power.

- *Environmental vulnerability:* the threats of global environmental change are said by some to be the defining issue of the new millennium. Climate change is fueled by our dependence on fossil fuels and our increased consumption of non-renewable resources. Small island states, such as Tuvalu, which have seen unprecedented increases of flooding in recent years, are staging plans to close down when the floods become unbearable. Larger states, such as Bangladesh, could see the permanent displacement of 20 million people, with tens of millions more at risk in the Philippines, Cambodia, Thailand, and China.

  The UN Environment Program's financial services initiative, a partnership of private sector groups and the UN, estimates that the additional cost of natural disasters driven by climate change could run to over $300 billion a year. And that's a conservative estimate. The reality could be much worse. Re-insurance giant Munich Re has estimated that if we continue our current level of fossil fuel usage, by 2065 the economic costs of climate-related natural disasters could well exceed total world economic output.

- *Economic and political instability:* the last decade has brought more and more countries into the global economy, with restrictions on international capital flows gradually being lifted. Global investors are now able to shift funds from one country to another with relative ease. The foreign exchange market is the world's largest financial market, with $1.5 trillion changing hands on the global currency market each day.

  Currency speculation is profitable, providing banks and investors with multi-million dollar profits. However, as much as 80 percent of these are speculative, with a round-trip maturity of seven days or less. And the problem is that their impact on developing economies can be devastating. In emerging markets, the direct costs of large swings in the flow of international capital can exceed 10 percent of GDP.

  As a consequence of this, political stability is at risk. Choices that should be properly made by governments and democratic processes are now being forcibly made by markets, including level of budget deficits, the mix between private and public provision of services, and interest rates. When markets don't deliver the goods, such as in Argentina, political unrest can lead to near breakdown of the state.

Trade and ethics: prescription or placebo?

The argument favored by the mainstream development community is that foreign investment will bring job creation, much-needed capital, and technology transfer. This process leads, it is argued, to higher incomes among the middle classes, enabling them to buy more goods and services and thus spurring greater levels of employment and eventually income growth in other parts of the economy. The result? Reduced poverty, economic success, and wealth creation. So the theory goes.

Does FDI work?

Standard models of economic development assume that poor countries will grow only through increasing trade and foreign investment. The theory is that investment flows from the capital-rich north to the capital-poor south provide increasing returns for northern investors while making financial resources available where they are most needed. But for the poorest of developing countries, foreign investment is actually in decline. Of all foreign direct investment (FDI) into developing countries, only 1.4 percent is captured by the least developed countries, down from 3.5 percent in the 1980s.

Declines in investment are generally coupled with increases in foreign borrowing. This results in any benefits from FDI being stripped away through debt-servicing payments – effectively working as a vacuum cleaner. In Argentina, total capital flight has been estimated at $130 billion – almost equal to the country's total public debt of $150 billion, defaulted on in December 2001.

Equally important is the extent to which resources generated from FDI remain circulating within the local economy. For those countries that saw dramatic growth in incomes between 1960 and 1995, domestic investment was almost entirely financed from domestic savings from about 1970 onwards. FDI can work only if it has strong linkages with domestically owned firms with a view to strengthening local competitiveness and capacity, rather than extracting resources and labor.

But the primary problem is that the bulk of poorer countries have little to offer that is not vulnerable to the whims of the market. Peruvian economist Oscar Ugarteche argues that Africa and Latin America have essentially become "store-room continents" for the north, with their primary resources being commodities such as coffee or sugar, cheap labor, or raw minerals. Most developing countries lack a diversified economy, so when one area suffers a cold, the whole country comes down with the flu. Falls in commodity prices can have devastating effects on commodity-dependent countries, and most commodity prices for things like coffee or sugar, are in a state of terminal decline, due to a combination of overproduction and unreasonable production subsidies in the developed world.

Of course, there is a case to be made for bringing countries up the "value chain" – producing higher-value goods rather than just raw materials. But trade barriers in the north continue to prevent developing countries from climbing up the value chain. Cocoa-rich countries like Ghana are still unable to manufacture and export chocolate into Europe due to escalating trade barriers, rendering manufacturing virtually unfeasible.

Corporate social responsibility

So is the new wave of corporate social responsibility (CSR) the solution to our woes? CSR has attempted to fill some gaps where states have failed by injecting a market-driven voluntary requirement for companies to consider their social and environmental impacts alongside their financial bottom-line. Prescriptions for CSR include signing up to global codes of conduct, such as the UN Global Compact; adopting ISO-type standards for the environment or labor standards monitoring, such as ISO14001 and SA8000; or issuing "triple bottom-line" reports on environmental and social performance.

CSR practices are now rewarded by the investment industry, such as the London Stock Exchange's ethical index, FTSE4Good, or the Association of British Insurers, which have issued CSR guidelines for companies. The view is that companies which manage social and environmental issues will mitigate risk and perform better financially than those which do not. While this assessment is largely accurate vis-à-vis financial risk, relevant risk for a company does not necessarily equate to risk for a country or individual stakeholders. Although there are some success stories, much of CSR has been more about PR than anything deeper. A recent report from the charity Christian Aid finds that many of the leading companies espousing CSR credentials, from Shell to British American Tobacco, are doing little more than masking their real impacts on communities. As an ex-BP consultant observed about stakeholder dialog, a common tool of the CSR practitioner, is "a very subtle and intelligent management technique to evade criticism."

CSR is limited for a number of reasons. First, there are so many competing codes and standards emerging from the public sector, business consultancies, and society generally. Consequently, there is now considerable confusion as business struggles to define exactly what society's expectations are. Some codes are more demanding than others while many contain levels of information that would seem to go well beyond the core business. This means that companies tend to adopt practices only where there is an immediate risk to the brand. Nike faced a risk to its reputation as a result of allegedly poor labor practices in its supply chain and so has had to adopt a comprehensive approach to monitoring working conditions. Hanson plc, on the other hand, might recognize the need to manage its environmental impacts (as it does) but would be unlikely to face pressure from consumers on labor standards as it is not a household brand name.

A further limiting factor is the lack of enforcement mechanisms. The UN Global Compact gives companies its seal of approval by simply asking them to submit an annual report on how they have implemented the code. The OECD Guidelines on Multinational Enterprise, supported by all OECD countries and one of the strongest of the global codes, provides for a National Contact Point that facilitates challenges to corporate behavior but goes no further. Neither offer any sanction for misbehavior. Voluntary codes rely entirely on business to uphold them, making them effectively police, judge, and jury. Self-regulation by industry, as the Enron/ Andersen affair demonstrates, has some very unreliable outcomes.

The main problem, though, is that there is a lack of incentives for business to be responsible for social and environmental issues to the level that would be necessary to overturn the downsides of globalization. Nowhere is this more striking than when we look at businesses that have yet to adopt CSR programs but continue to do very well.

Corporation or state: who is to blame?

Until recently, the anti-globalization movement has largely focussed on corporate power as the target for what's wrong with the world. Naomi Klein's immensely successful book *No Logo* struck out against global brands and excessive corporate power as being the primary contributor to poverty and exclusion. Corporate power is an obvious target. Of the world's 100 largest economies, 51 are corporations. The total revenue of Mitsubishi, for example, exceeds the GDP of South Korea, while CitiGroup's revenue exceeds the total output of India. Indeed, the combined revenues of GM and Ford exceed the combined GDP for all sub-Saharan Africa.

But corporations do not have the power of states, either to make or enforce laws. Nor do they negotiate global economic treaties – the rules of the World Trade Organization (WTO) are set by states, not by companies. Corporations, one might argue, are simply playing a game whose rules have long been established.

Increasingly, non-governmental organizations point the finger at governments. Governments have a distinct responsibility to provide an adequate framework not only to protect citizens" rights but also to ensure that basic needs are met. In a market-based system, government must ensure that those who are excluded from the market have a leg-up and that sufficient information is available to allow citizens to make effective decisions. When things go awry, a government's responsibility is to protect citizens and consumers from harm. The environment, health, or education are all public goods issues requiring government intervention. Yet business is being asked to take a leading role in managing these issues without any enforced guidelines and certainly without legal boundaries.

Globalization holds governments captive by making it virtually impossible for single nation states to have any influence since they cannot enforce regimes beyond their borders. The introduction of extra-territorial legislation has yet to become mainstream practice by northern governments and the nature of globalization means that borders themselves are somewhat elusive.

The rules of global trade, established through the WTO, are the closest we have to global governance, as the powers of the UN are quite limited. But WTO rules limit rather than increase the power of states. At the national or regional level, states that sign onto the WTO, the backbone of globalization, are generally forced to ensure that any form of regulation does not limit "competitive advantage."

Of course, business is by no means absolved. Through corporate lobbying capacity, the state role is also now contained to promoting safe investment climates and reducing any burden on business to do more than simply generate wealth. Any regulation that would enforce business social responsibility is shunned for fear that business itself will pack up and move somewhere else.

In summary, no one is really holding the reins. Business has no incentives to behave differently, beyond protecting reputations, due to the short-term demands of the market and the need to protect shareholder value. At the same time, where society demands businesses consider their wider social and environmental impacts, they are offered no leadership from governments. Individual governments, on the other hand, are prevented from taking sufficient action because globalization has removed their traditional levers of control.

A new perspective

The challenges of globalization – from poverty to climate change – will not be solved easily. They require fundamental institutional change at the global level. The system of governance that we've inherited is not capable of managing the global common good.

But blaming everyone else is not going to solve things, either. The problems will continue to spin out of control unless, collectively, we decide to put aside self-interest and do something about it. And it means measuring what is important on a smaller, local scale. Simple trade-offs between environment and economic growth is fundamentally flawed – we cannot live without the atmosphere.

What follows are three "solutions" that see us measure and value things differently, and reverse incentives on actions that can cause undue harm. They are intentionally modest, though, and only the first step in what should be a major overhaul of the international system.

- *Internalizing externalities and measuring impacts:* business and consumers should ultimately be required to pay for the full cost of social and environmental impacts. Current subsidies on things like fuel result in perverse incentives for business not to economize or find sustainable alternatives. The first step is to adopt a framework for measuring social and environmental impacts. The recently launched Global Reporting Initiative (GRI) provides a basis for starting to do just that. But the GRI remains entirely voluntary. This means that while businesses can start to measure their impacts, unless all companies are doing it the practice can be highly uncompetitive. It ultimately requires government leadership to make the necessary structural change to require mandatory reporting and accounting in order to level the playing field for all.

- *Mobilizing local investment:* foreign investment in and of itself cannot guarantee positive impacts on development and the well-being of communities. Alongside controlling capital flows, companies and governments need to measure where money goes once it enters the local economy. The New Economics Foundation has developed a tool that enables us to measure the quality of investment in terms of its economic multiplier effect – seeing how much it generates locally before profits are returned. Ultimately, countries should be able to reject any foreign investment that does not have a minimum multiplier effect.

  Local multipliers are easily generated, for example having multinationals do as much procurement locally as possible. Greater impacts would be seen when companies increase the number of products that are manufactured closer to the source of materials. This would quickly move countries up the value chain and away from the storeroom.

- *Tobin tax:* the idea of a tax on currency transactions, first put forward by the late Nobel-prize winning economist James Tobin in the 1970s, is receiving renewed attention. Supporters have come from some G8 finance ministers, including in France, the UK and Canada. Even the International Monetary Fund (IMF), traditionally a proponent of full liberalization, has cautiously endorsed some limited reliance on taxes on selected international finance transactions.

  A Tobin tax would involve levying a small tax on foreign currency exchange transactions that would act as a major disincentive to short-term transactions. When Canada's *National Post* newspaper published an April Fool's Day news item in 2002 reporting that the Canadian finance minister was resigning to raise ducks, the Canadian dollar took a nose-dive. But the dollar came back and it ultimately had little impact on the Canadian economy. However, a similar run in a middle-income or developing country can have devastating effects – the Mexican Peso crisis in 1994, in part due to policy failure, led to herd-like behavior on the currency markets, resulting in a severe recession.

Moving forward

Relying on business to drive social change is not only a naive ideal, it is like relying on hounds to support a ban on fox hunting: it is not in their immediate interest to do so. Governments, though, have also abdicated their responsibility. And financial markets have become a beast with no mechanism of control, holding the rest of us to ransom.

Globalization has brought with it great wealth, but also a wealth of problems. We've opened the proverbial Pandora's box and there's no going back. But we cannot continue on our current trajectory either. Otherwise, we all lose.

The solutions presented here are only three modest steps that could be taken, although admittedly the Tobin tax is probably more ambitious (though certainly not impossible). There are more and bigger solutions out there, such as that from Aubrey Meyer, director of the Global Commons Institute, who suggests "contraction and convergence," providing each person with an equal share of the atmosphere. A global competition policy that would inhibit the ability of multinationals to dominate emerging markets is also in much demand, yet scant little attention is paid to such a need.

Most importantly, rather than hurling stones and accusations, each party in the game must recognize that the other has a relevant role to play. An all-private or all-public solution to tackling global problems is not the way forward. And without global protesters, we would all be ignorant about what is really going on. Just as there is a case to be made for private provision of some public services, there is also a "business case" to be made for relevant regulation.

In recent years, there has been a new awareness of the reality of the dark sides of globalization – awareness hopefully also brings forward the political will and practical solutions to take us out of the mess we're in.

RESOURCES

Bartlett, Christopher A. and Ghoshal, Sumantra, *Managing Across Borders: The Transnational Solution*, Harvard Business School Press, 1989.

Hertz, Noreena, *The Silent Takeover*, Arrow, 2002.

Klein, Naomi, *No Logo*, Flamingo, 2001.

Litvin, Daniel, *Empires of Profit: Commerce, Conquest and Corporate Responsibilty*, Texere, 2003.

Ohmae, Kenichi, *Triad Power: The Coming Shape of Global Competition*, Free Press, 1985.

Ohmae, Kenichi, *The Global Stage*, FT Prentice Hall, 2004.

Pettifor, Ann, *Real World Economic Outlook*, Palgrave Macmillan, 2003.

Stiglitz, Joseph, *Globalization and its Discontents*, Penguin, 2003.

World Commission on the Social Dimension of Globalization, *A Fair Globalization: Creating opportunities for all*, ILO, 2004.

Yip, George S., *Total Global Strategy: Managing for Worldwide Competitive Advantage*, Prentice Hall, 1992.

www.newconomics.org

This article previously appeared in *Business Strategy Review*, Volume 13, Issue 2, Summer 2002.

Strategies for China

JONATHAN STORY

[How can we make corporate strategy for a country as complex and multifaceted as China? By understanding China's transformation process, its business system, and what both imply for corporate operations.]

Business, markets, and politics dance for ever together anywhere in the world, and particularly so in China.[1] This huge and ancient country of 1.3 billion people is undergoing a deep transformation with four distinct, related, and synchronous features – from command to market, from a rural to an urban society, from autarky to interdependence, and from membership in the communist system to participation in the global polity.

China's transformation is the stuff of corporate strategy, particularly so as it has become the favorite destination for inward investment – in 2002 ahead of the US. Indeed, China is a central player in the "new diplomacy," where corporations scour the world for new markets and production platforms, and enter bargains with states on a bilateral basis.[2]

If we start with a definition of corporate strategy as shaped in part by the top team's view of what constitutes right policy, our top team has to consider the details of corporate activities in China in terms of the transformation both of China's political economy and of its business system.[3]

The first requirement is to become familiar with the recent history of China. A central task of corporate strategy is to read the transition right, particularly as it affects the business system whose elements penetrate to the heart of corporate operations in China.

The key political detonator for change from command economy toward a more market-driven system was the initial consolidation of Deng's position in 1978, and the ideological sleight of hand which defined Mao's leaps toward socialism as "premature."[4] The main impetus to economic growth, alongside the open door policy and the September 1984 settlement with the UK on Hong Kong, came from agricultural reforms and the easing of constraints on communal enterprises. Market-oriented measures were then extended to the state-owned enterprises (SOEs) in 1984 with "dual-track" market liberalization allowing the co-existence of two market prices, one for the liberalized market and the other for output still falling under the plan. Output rose sharply, but so did inflation. With corruption increasingly visible, demands for more thorough-going reforms culminated in the movement for democratization, Premier Zhao Ziyang's efforts to prevent confrontation, and finally the brutal crackdown on the students demonstrating in Tiananmen Square in June 1989.

After three anxious years, China's leadership adopted a new policy framework at the 14th Party Congress in November 1993. The aim was "to establish a nation-wide integrated and open market system ... to transform the government's functions in economic management and establish a sound macroeconomic system which chiefly relies on indirect means to ensure the healthy development of the national economy."[5] This policy direction was confirmed in the leadership's response to the East Asian financial crash in 1997–98, and the subsequent successful bid to enter the WTO in 2002. This incorporated global norms into Chinese legislation and practice.

This brief account may be stylized as an assumption of a China moving down a path toward a Chinese "economic society" – a term yet to be defined. The model is presented in Figure 2.1. On the outer vertical are some of the larger questions which our

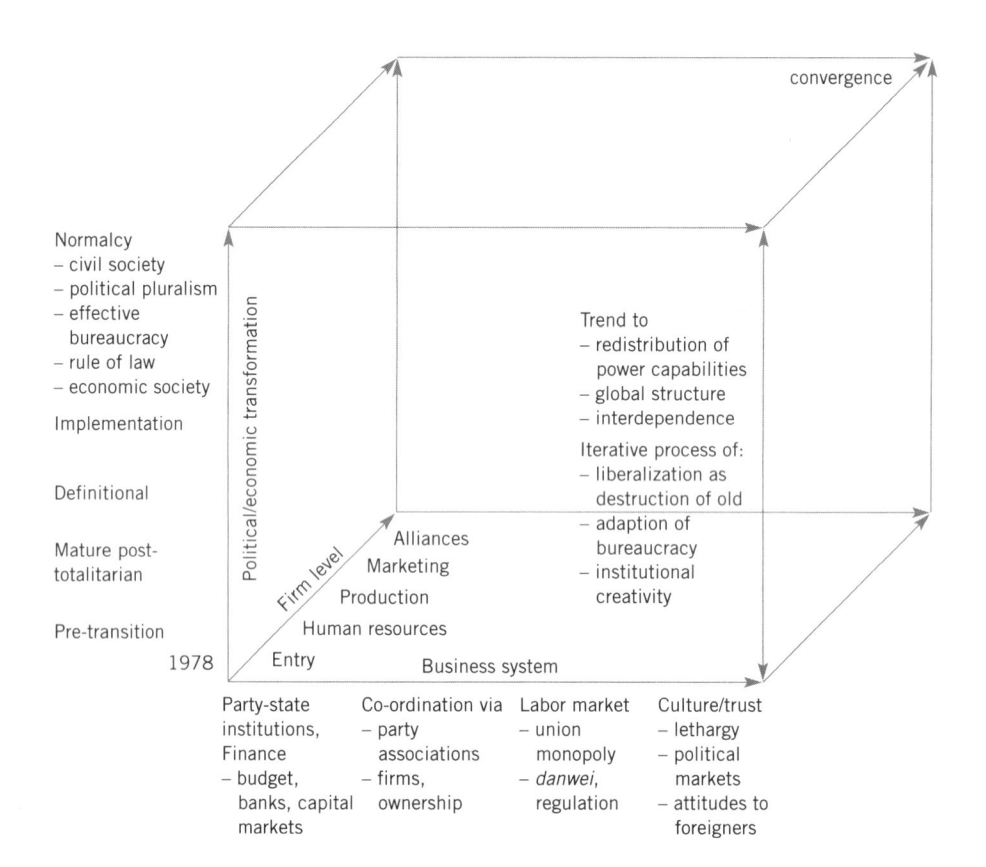

Figure 2.1: *FDI and the transformation of China's business system*

top managerial team should be asking themselves: What is happening worldwide in terms of the on-going redistribution of capabilities between the major powers? How is this affecting the global structure? How is China incorporated into the global, interdependent economy? Not least, how is the transition proceeding in China?

The vertical axis traces the political and economic transition, merged for brevity.[6] China, the conclusion will run, has experienced policy changes short of redefining its key political norms. It is still in a pre-transitional phase in terms of political evolution, described by political scientists as "mature post-totalitarian."[7] The horizontal axis depicts the key features of the business system, the subject of the next section. The base of the cube traces different features of corporate activities.

The vertical or diagonal in the cube also draws a time path, starting in 1978, and moves toward some time in the future. This point in the future we shall label convergence. This is located on the upper right angle of the cube because the way the story of one possible future is going to be told is biassed toward demonstrating that the process of transformation from a command economy leads to convergence of Chinese norms, rules, and institutions on those of the developed world. The flaws in this functionalist story are self-evident: all participants have to be agreed on how to interpret market signals, on the procedures to follow, and on the ultimate objectives. This is a very bold assumption to make. At each one of the decision points along the path, people have a quiver full of choices, which they select for a host of reasons related to their understanding of their own situation, their desires, their loves, and their hates. Real participants are made of blood, prejudice, and passion, by contrast to the bloodless calculating machines in our stylized story. But a stylized story of China's trajectory has an advantage: it highlights what has not been, or cannot be done, to achieve it, as well as isolating the major challenges which lie ahead. In effect, the institutions into which China is likely eventually to settle cannot be anything other than "Chinese-style." China will always remain divergent.[8]

The pre-transition phase

First comes the pre-transition phase, where the incumbent power is unable to resolve a growing list of problems. In China's case, these are easy to list: widening income gaps, party-state corruption, a ballooning on non-performing bank loans, rising unemployment in the cities, the revival of religious activities, or the shrinkage of the party-state's monopoly powers, as China's natural pluralism bursts into view. In the language of regime change, two contending coalitions form, initially led by hardliners in the regime against any change, and softliners who argue the case for a dialog with moderate opponents.[9] They deploy exclusive symbols and appeal to different mobilized factions within, or outside of the regime. In the case of China, the regime – from 1978 to Deng's death, and the watershed years of 1997–98 – fashioned policy through mutual trade-offs between two broad and constantly changing coalitions of conservatives and reformers.

China's condition is one which political scientists call "mature post-totalitarian" rule, where party members settle down to enjoy their privileges, with less fear of a knock at the door at dead of night. Party rule transforms into a vast political market for preference. In brief, the party-state has not challenged its foundational norms.

China's population acquiesces for the moment because of a widespread sense of acute fear for the consequences of social chaos. Ninety-three percent prefer to live in an orderly society than in a freer society that is prone to disruption.[10] Yet the regime implicitly recognizes that the status quo is tenable only to the extent that the party-state develops a more sophisticated political system. Hence, Jiang Zemin's adaptation of party policy as representing "three forces" essential for China's development: advanced productive forces, advanced cultural forces, and the fundamental interests of the largest number of citizens.

This broadening definition of what the party-state represents has not yet broken with its foundational norms. It is, after all, the party-state which does the representing. If the regime were to go public and admit that it is changing its foundational norms, it would be launched on political transition, *one* destination of which would be a consolidated Chinese democracy, located up the vertical path labeled "normalcy."

Clearly, the present degree of economic society achieved under a party dictatorship is restricted, either in terms of civil society, of the rule of law, of political legitimacy, or of bureaucratic viability. China's party-state has to continue to move toward laying the institutional foundations of a constitutional order if a market economy is to be consolidated. At issue is not if but when the leadership takes the plunge. The regime's preference is clear enough as to the when: later, rather than sooner. The chosen method is pragmatism.

The hour of decision

The hour of decision strikes as we move from the pre-transition phase and a new leadership takes over. One such moment came in 1997–98, when a caravan of forces converged. Paramount leader Deng Xiaoping died in February 1997, at the age of 92, Hong Kong returned to the mainland, Taiwan made a bid for WTO membership, and the Clinton administration adopted a policy of "engagement" with China. In addition, there was a notable deterioration in China's geo-strategic environment, as India, Pakistan, and then North Korea challenged nuclear non-proliferation policy. Then came the Asian financial crash. In September, the CCP's 15th Party Congress declared state-owned enterprise reform a priority and, in November 1997, financial market reform was launched at a National Affairs Conference, attended by most of China's high-ranking officials. In March 1998, Premier Li Peng, who had openly opposed WTO accession talks, was replaced by Zhu Rongji, the former mayor of Shanghai. The new premier pushed for accelerated changes in state-corporate relations, and vigorously championed China's WTO entry.

The definitional and implementational phases

The definitional phase comes when leaders start to distance themselves from previous policy paradigms, or go as far as to introduce new policy norms. In China, this took the form of the leadership's enthusiasm for WTO entry, while tolerating no threat to party hegemony. Without any doubt, the Asian financial crash was a central motive. It was not just that China's export markets were directly affected by the downturn in Asia Pacific's growth. The worry was that China's business system, like its richer neighbors, was geared to expansion of output rather than to adapting the business system to consumer demands. Adapting it challenged the leadership's determination to keep control over the "commanding heights" of the economy. WTO membership was the battering ram of the reformers to accelerate domestic changes.[11] The implication was clear enough: economic reform required a retreat of the party-state as presently constituted, while not relinquishing control over key levers of power.[12]

China's business system

The term "national business system" was coined by Richard Whitley to describe specific patterns of economic co-ordination and control in market economies.[13] Let us define a business system as composed of four prime components. One is how the party-state's institutions have dealt with business risk; another is the tight link between China's financial system and state-owned enterprises; the third is the party-state's provision of a safety net for urban workers; and the fourth the level of trust in workforce and society toward public officials.

Party-state institutions" changing approach to business risk

In China, the approach to business risk has obviously changed since the initial reforms of 1978. In the 1998 package, the State Council, China's equivalent of the Council of Ministers, encouraged enterprises in key industries to consolidate in key groups, continuing a policy begun in 1994, when the Ministry of Foreign Trade and Industry (MOFTEC) urged the formation of "national champions" in preparation for China's entry to the WTO. The party-state remains the ultimate owner of state assets, but reform's prime ally is the tremendous competitive pressure running through the markets. The link between ownership and market, as Professor Lu Feng of Qinghua University argues, has involved the re-assertion of managerial authority over operations.[14] Maoist worker committees have been relegated to a thoroughly subordinate position.

More discretion for managers means separating government functions from enterprise operations, and the elaboration of corporate law to provide a framework for companies becoming either limited liability or joint stock companies. The separation has been prompted by government policy to implement a hard budget constraint following the serious inflationary binge of 1993, while local governments have withdrawn from *danwei*, the old communist corporate-based social security system. This has created major social problems in China's rustbelt, in the northern provinces of Liaoning, Heilongjiang, and Jilin, which totaled over half of all state enterprises. In essence, the party-state has decided against socialist insurance for non-viable enterprises. The hidden text is that enterprises must adapt or die.

The CCP is "The Party of Public Finances"

The second key element to condition China's corporate reforms is the central role of the CCP. The party-state still rules supreme over the financial system, including banks, insurance, and securities markets. This creates major conflicts of interest. The party-state owns corporate assets – indeed it is the *Gongchan Dang*, "The Party of Public Assets." Yet it also regulates the markets. The China Securities and Regulatory Commission (CSRC), for instance, has powers to prevent insider trading. But most of the 1,000 enterprises listed on the two markets in Shanghai and Shenzen are state enterprises. Listing is decided by a highly politicized quota process, where new issues have been kept firmly in the communist party family: 99 percent of investment decisions on the Shanghai stock exchange, and decisions relating to key personnel and their remuneration, are taken by the communist party committee in the firm, in agreement with the local government.[15] In these firms, the state, in the form of many different organizations, keeps 60–70 percent of "red chip" shares, as the shares are appropriately called. The benefit is that diversified ownership facilitates mergers and acquisitions, as government organizations can exchange shares after negotiations. Also, the SOEs can raise capital on privileged terms.

But the downside is that so many party-state organizations holding shares, and with competing interests, can make for a very messy corporate strategy. It also makes for a messy regulatory stance: there is a glaring contradiction between the government's efforts to crack down on fraud in the financial markets, and its use of the media to talk China's 60 million or so frequent share buyers into buying dubious SOE stock. Continued administrative intervention in the securities markets is not the best way to promote them as a reliable, long-term source of capital.

The party-state turns away from the old social contract

The third key element to condition China's corporate reforms is the party-state's gradual abandonment of its key constituency, the urban working class. In the mid-1990s, up to 80 percent of the active urban workforce was employed by SOEs, either central or local government owned. Local governments tended to protect their own workforces, but such initiatives perpetuated China's fragmentation into local labor markets, and provided a constant rationale for beggar-my-neighbor protectionist policies to safeguard local jobs. They also ensured that the 1986 bankruptcy law remained a dead letter, as local governments preferred to merge enterprises rather than put them out of business.

The result was that an estimated 90 percent of all Chinese banking system loans went to SOEs, which left only 10 percent for the commercial sector of the economy.[16] The position could not be sustained. What to do? The party-state faced a harsh choice: the leadership had either to revert to financing SOE requirements through the printing press, or to sacrifice their prime constituency of urban labor on an altar of industrial adjustment. It chose an anti-inflation policy at the cost or rising rural and urban unemployment – a "floating population" of unemployed in the rural areas is estimated as high as 120–175 million. Furthermore, the one-child policy was changing China's age profile: while 6 percent of the population were elderly in 1998, 11 percent of a larger population would be over 65 by the 2020s. This spelt an explosion in pension obligations, prompting the party-state to fudge on its commitments.

In 1999, the party-state decided to bring private business in from the cold. The National People's Congress (NPC) voted an amendment to the constitution recognizing the contribution of private enterprise to the country's development. With 15 million new entrants to the job market per annum through to 2020, plus restructuring in state owned enterprises (SOEs), town-village enterprises (TVEs), and in agriculture, unleashing private enterprise on China is the only way forward, short of an explosion of unemployment and violence in the countryside and cities. Private enterprise created new jobs at the rate of +29 percent per annum from 1990 to 2000.[17]

Public opinion and the party-state

The fourth element to condition China's corporate reforms is the level of trust in workforce and society toward public officials. The evidence suggests that the general public in mainland China has rather low expectations about government. The public may complain, and even blame officials for wrongdoing, but people do not withdraw their support.[18] There is a stock of lethargy on which the regime can draw as it proceeds on its way.

The regime is clearly aware that corruption is a gangrene, from which it could perish. According to the US State Department record, the campaign against corruption, which began in earnest in 1996, yielded by 2000 a crop of 1,292 bent judges; 494 officers during that year, 54 of whom were criminally responsible for malfeasance; 17,931 government officials guilty of corruption or of accepting bribes; during 2000, 1,450 court employees were punished for misconduct. Overall, 2,000 people have been executed as part of the campaign.[19]

The danger is not so much the blurred line between its anti-corruption campaign and obscure battles for power within the party-state; it is simply that official corruption and organized crime converge to keep the gravy train running as long as possible, at the public's expense.[20] The communist honey-pot is too tasty for the sake of its guardians.

China's business system and corporate transformation

To recap, our top team has to consider the details of corporate activities in China in terms of the transformation both of China's political economy and of its business system. We have argued that China is still in a pre-transitional phase in terms of political evolution, and that the present degree of economic society achieved under a party dictatorship is clearly restricted, in terms of civil society, the rule of law, political legitimacy, or bureaucratic viability. China's party state has to continue to move toward laying the institutional foundations of a constitutional order, if a market economy is to be consolidated.

In terms of the business system, the process of marketization is messy. The party-state is caught in a vortex of change, but there is no going back. With WTO entry, China's internal agenda is to implement its commitments as best it can. What this spells for foreign businesses seeking entry to, or already operating in China, we can examine by following the firm level at the base of our cube, in terms of market entry, human resource management, and production, marketing in China, and corporate alliances.

Corporate capabilities and market entry

In the early 1980s, multinationals treated China much like other developing countries as a place to sell old products or as a location for the manufacture and distribution of old technologies. Because they knew little about the country, they often proceeded tentatively. The party-state behaved no differently. Public ownership was to be protected, but with sufficient incentives provided for a successful absorption by local firms of Western technologies and know-how. The interaction of evolving public policy, as depicted above, and a collective corporate learning process about how to operate in China are illustrated in Figure 2.2. The horizontal axis traces the widening of options, from setting up a rep office in Hong Kong, to

Strategies for China   **135**

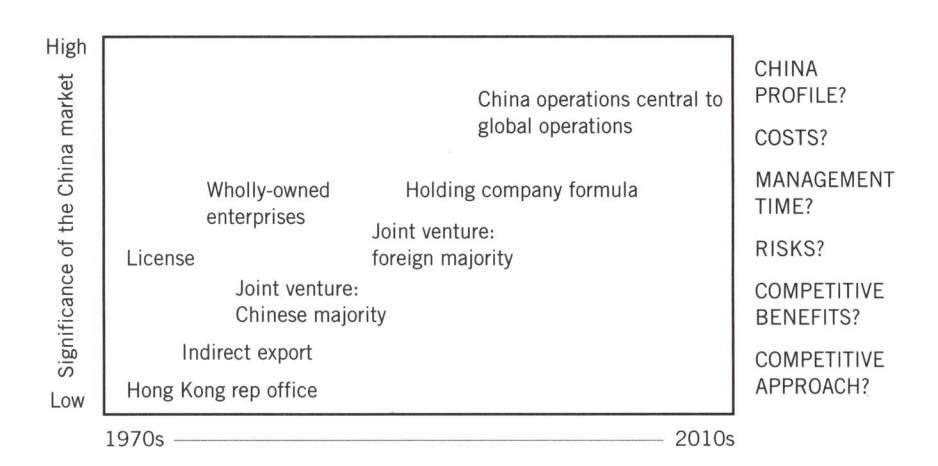

Figure 2.2: *Evolution of entry mode to China's markets*

[Figure shows a chart with vertical axis "Significance of the China market" (Low to High) and horizontal axis from 1970s to 2010s. Entry modes plotted: Hong Kong rep office, Indirect export, License, Joint venture: Chinese majority, Wholly-owned enterprises, Joint venture: foreign majority, Holding company formula, China operations central to global operations. On right side: CHINA PROFILE?, COSTS?, MANAGEMENT TIME?, RISKS?, COMPETITIVE BENEFITS?, COMPETITIVE APPROACH?]

Beijing's allowance of full foreign ownership in 1986, through to 1993 when the holding company formula received official sanction, while the vertical axis traces the prospective significance of the China market to the corporation's top management team.

On the right-hand horizontal planes is the basic question: what is the risk of doing business in China? We don't know much about the country, so perhaps we should find out first. Definitely, we don't know ahead of time what the costs of operating there will be. All we can do is to make a guess of the expected benefits. Those are going to hinge very much on how we enter the country. So what approach should we adopt?

How to enter the China market is related to two further factors: the expected significance of the China market to global operations, and the corporation's expected corporate bargaining power with the government.[21]

Given the many layers of Chinese government, the wide diversity of conditions in China, and the distinct features of different market segments, there is no single formula which emerges but rather a host of details which are specific to particular operations. Even so, a few general rules of thumb hold: both corporations and public officials are engaged in a learning process about how to enter the China market. In the future, foreign corporations can choose from a range of options on how to enter the China market, whereas 20 years ago they would have had to proceed sequentially and slowly.

Then there is a list of practical advice: be clear about your own objectives and those of your Chinese partners; don't tailor your strategy to government demands; control is best exercised by a majority stake, but failing that considerable influence can be exerted by exploiting the leverage derived from the provision of know-how, technology, etc.; being in there for the long term does not mean running a loss-making operation indefinitely; develop good antennae to help you learn about China's changing environment; remember the government in China is not a monolith, and relations have to be cultivated at all levels of the state.[22] Not least, remember that the best partner, as the Chinese saying goes, is one who shares the same dreams but not the same bed.

Market entry and party-state discretionary powers

Party-state institutions remain recognizably the same, but their content in terms of financial and legal instruments has changed considerably. Nonetheless, managers in foreign corporations cannot take institutions for granted. Private firms have only recently received constitutional recognition as contributing to the country's development, and the legal system is still in the early stages. With no history of rule of law, the absence of commercial ground rules gives public officials extensive discretionary powers. They can stop a firm selling its products, close it off to procurement, and issue a decree against it.

The lesson is clear: on China's way to the market, the mixture of unclear rules and official discretion gives plenty of incentives for public officials and their private counterparts to indulge in opportunistic behavior. How to acquire and use *guanxi* (literally translated as relationships, or connections, but in reality a more complex interconnection of contacts) will remain a key skill for a long time yet.

The process of transformation is making – and will make – China a more complex place to operate. Many markets are closed or restricted. Private enterprises, for instance, are not allowed into 30 sectors, and up to 17 further product lines in other industries. These include banking, railways, telecommunications, and wholesaling, all sectors where SOEs and their ministries have privileged positions. Private businesses, especially, lack access to stable sources of outside finance and they are very vulnerable to fees being imposed by bureaucracies hungry for funds.

And therein lies a central problem. Does the CCP want Chinese companies to emerge over the next few years, regardless of their ownership, or is the CCP concerned only to promote the enterprises still under its patronage? There are two trade associations for private enterprises. Both are under CCP surveillance. The party faces a clear choice: promote China or defend its privileges. As the country continues to marketize, the two are no longer identical.

Management of human resources

China is not a cheap labor country. Foreign firms operating JVs generally pay between 20 and 50 percent more than local firms, while non-wage costs vary widely across regions. Many other features of the labor market conspire to drive up total labor costs. Western firms have to select employees with an ability to anticipate problems, and who are ready to speak out and to act.[23] They also have to be sure not to confuse foreign language skills with local market knowledge.[24] Then, once they have hired people, companies have to invest in training, and to recognize thereby that they make their employees attractive to other companies. In addition, workplace relationships are on the radar screens of Western social auditors, as Nike and Reebok discovered when conditions among their sub-contractors in China, Indonesia, and Vietnam became headline news in the US. Many corporations have instituted voluntary standards programs designed to record their own performance, and satisfy shareholders.

The All China Federation of Trade Unions (ACFTU) is the party-state's monopoly union. As long as the ACFTU operated in SOEs, where party officials dominated all significant functions, it could not seriously claim to represent employees" interests. This changes when an SOE enters a joint venture with a foreign corporation, giving notably greater influence over corporate policy to union officials.

Consider, for instance, the case of Lafarge, the French cement maker and multinational. It made a JV with an SOE mining company, located at Huaibei, one hour's drive north of Beijing. Lafarge inherited a demoralized workforce. Management had been top-down, over-manning was rife, discipline was absent, and severance promises had been broken. Yet within four years, Lafarge management had turned the situation around, boosted productivity manyfold, and received the ACFTU's coveted "dual love" award, distributed that year to 88 other firms out of 50,000 candidates. Among other contributing factors to this success was Lafarge's upgrading of health and security measures, the introduction of severe but fair discipline, and a clear commitment to employee development and training. Above all, management successfully enlisted the support of the trade union, which could act more autonomously now that it was not subordinate to management and party. The lesson is that ACFTU members have an incentive to promote JVs and wholly-owned foreign enterprises.

Management of production

Once a viable operation has been set up, running day-to-day business takes over. In essence, this entails managing the technology transfer process, where the Chinese partners want the best fast but the foreign investor prefers a gradual build-up of local capabilities. Over time, foreign investors have acquired a body of practical experience related to raising productivity. Lessons may be classified under three broad headings. One, which we have in part dealt with, is how to go about the task of developing a skilled and motivated labor force, increasingly capable of taking on complex tasks.

A second cluster relates to the process of setting up a local supply chain, where the investor's prime concern is to ensure quality and to protect the brand name. Massive foreign investment in the 1990s in a full complement of supporting industries greatly altered the situation for companies relying on fast delivery. The build-up from importing assembled kits through to as near as 100 percent local content entails patience – it took Shanghai Volkswagen about a decade: establishing standards, bringing in home country suppliers, choosing appropriate locations, and keeping a close eye on transport problems. President Sam Lo of Tai Sun Plastic Novelties, which makes toys for J.C. Penney and Carrefour in Guandong, says, "You make a call, and tomorrow the parts are in your factory."[25]

A third cluster is protecting intellectual property rights (IPR), in a country which is one of the world's champion infringers. Acer, the personal computer corporation originating in Taiwan, has moved an increasing amount of its production and some of its research functions to the mainland, and to Shanghai in particular. Its software codes, though, are sourced in Taiwan. Not least, there is the perennial problem of anticipating demand. A rule of thumb may be of value here: if you have to choose between volume sales and profits, go for profits.

Marketing

China is not yet one integrated market. Local authorities are protective of their own producers. So the temptation for foreign businesses is often to congregate in the large cities where per capita incomes are reasonably high. Even here, it is worth remembering that per capita incomes are far below Western norms, and out in the countryside, where 900 million people live, they are sometimes at the level of the lowest in Africa. Getting products to this vast population is not easy.

Take the case of distribution networks, which the state began to marketize in the early 1990s. The sector was opened up to JVs, and rules about advertising were eased. Carrefour, the French retail giant, seized the opportunity to build up China's second biggest retail chain in five years. By 2000, Carrefour could boast 28 outlets in 15 cities and nearly a $1 billion turnover. Key to its success is simple, large stores offering a large variety of products and low prices. The stores move goods fast, cut tough deals with suppliers, carry minimal stocks, and cater to local tastes.

Corporate integration in China and into the global business system

A common problem for multinationals in China is integration of the business units which have been negotiated across the length and breadth of the country at different moments in the past. In the 1990s, foreign investors followed the example set by Johnson & Johnson, the US pharmaceutical corporation, which decided to launch its oral care, baby and female hygiene products under the wholly-owned foreign enterprise formula.[26] The formula allowed for greater control over operations, quicker expansion, less time spent on arduous negotiations with public officials and managers, and more protection over patents. Motorola, along with Nokia and Ericsson, a major force in China's huge cell-phone market, went even further and created a hybrid wholly-owned and JV operation. Motorola ran the integrated circuits and cell-phone operation itself, but entered JVs for marketing and sales. It thereby gave local partners a stake in the business and managed to develop countrywide. The risk for a wholly-owned operation in China is to be a self-sufficient island, cut off from *guanxi* and at risk of not winning contracts and placing orders.

Another way to consolidate is through the holding company formula, opened up by government measures to allow companies to register as joint-stock companies. Foreign companies have been able to convert JVs and wholly-owned operations into holding companies on the say-so of MOFTEC, and after demonstrating three years of profitable activities. Over 100 Western corporations have taken advantage of the opportunity. In fact, it served both Western corporations and Beijing's top brass: the multinationals could overcome local particularisms in which their JVs were embedded by giving them a minority stake in the success of a countrywide and more efficiently run group. It served Beijing by accelerating the diffusion of technologies and management know-how around the country.[27] China is learning to hitch multinational corporate strategies to its own industrial purposes.

Franchising is another formula that is helping companies to expand their market reach. Franchise owners grant rights to franchisees to use their trademarks. In China, the appeal of this formula is to small, family businesses. It was used by Beijing's Quanjude, a well-known roast duck restaurant, to establish over 60 restaurants across China. KFC, the US fast food chain, used a special franchising formula to develop nearly 450 outlets, first on the east coast and then in the poorer, inland provinces where families liked to go for weekend quality lunches at affordable prices. Affordable prices were helped by centralization of KFC's supply system. One of the secrets of Ericsson in taking the lead from Motorola and Nokia in the cell-phone business was to build up a franchising network among provincial telecom authorities. This enabled the Swedish giant to fasten its hold on China's richest regions. Countrywide reach is achieved best by giving the locals a major stake in success.

The take-away

Barring a massive breakdown, we are in the very early stages of China's incorporation into the global business system. Over the past 25 years, the party-state has presided over a remarkable, multi-dimensional transformation of the country and its economy. Politically, it is still recognizably the same, but all around it and much within the party-state has changed. In terms of economic policy, Chinese government norms are those outlined in the 1993 economic strategy, and confirmed and elaborated by the commitments undertaken on entry to the WTO. China's business system is thus in constant evolution: what it was in the 1980s is no longer what it is in the first decade of the new millennium.

Indeed, it is reasonable to argue that China's diversity in effect makes for many variations of its business system from the highly developed provinces of the eastern coastline to the rustbelt provinces of the north, and the economically isolated provinces of the west. What this spells for firm strategy in China now rhythms differently to conditions 10 or 15 years ago, and those which corporations are likely to confront a decade or two hence. If China is to make its way through to building efficient and effective institutions to sustain a modern market economy, deeply integrated with the rest of the world, it will have to be "China-style." So following the close interaction between the transformation of the political economy of China, and the evolution of its business system, will continue to lie at the heart of our team's corporate strategy in China. Politics, markets, and business dance together everywhere, particularly in China.

RESOURCES

Linz, Juan and Stepan, Alfred, *Problems of Democratic Transition and Consolidation: Southern Europe, South America and Post-Communist Europe*, Johns Hopkins University Press, 1996.

Prahalad, C.K. and Doz, Yves L., *The Multi-National Mission: Balancing Local Demands and Global Vision*, Free Press, 1987.

Stopford, John and Strange, Susan, *Rival States, Rival Firms: Competition for World Market Shares*, Cambridge University Press, 1991.

Story, Jonathan, *China: The Race to Market*, FT Prentice Hall, 2003.

Story, Jonathan, *The Frontiers of Fortune*, FT Prentice Hall, 1999.

Whitley, Richard, *Divergent Capitalisms: The Social Structuring and Change of Business Systems*, Oxford University Press, 1999.

Great global managers

KARL MOORE

> As globalization continues apace, the role of global executives becomes increasingly important. Most global managers are recruited from the major economic powers but there are signs that this is changing.

Of the many pressing questions that CEOs of global multinationals face, one remains constant: where will I find the next generation of global managers? Traditionally, multinationals have recruited most of their top executives from their home countries. This is especially true in the head offices of firms based in major power countries such as the United States, Japan, France, the United Kingdom, and Germany. But this approach is changing. Companies recognize that it produces too narrow a pool of candidates and can have a demotivating impact on foreign high-potential employees who view their careers as limited by their nationality. Why bother striving to become an executive at Toyota if one is a gaijin and not Japanese? As firms evolve from nationally centric to multinational to truly transnational, they must adopt new solutions.

Since the early 1990s, I have both studied and consulted with a number of multinationals based in North America, the European Union, and Japan, including Nokia, Volvo, Hewlett-Packard, Accenture, IBM, Pfizer, and Hitachi. Recently, my McGill University colleague Henry Mintzberg and I have been discussing an observation we have both made about top global firms: certain countries seem to produce more good global managers than their size would warrant; they punch above their weight in their output of global managers. This suggests an important component to incorporate into CEOs' search for the next generation of global managers.

Small and medium-sized nations

The list of countries includes those generally thought of as the most global in terms of their involvement in world trade and investment: Canada, Switzerland, Belgium, Singapore, Norway, Sweden, the Netherlands, Denmark, Australia, and Finland. Most are in northern Europe; one is in North America; two are on the Pacific Rim.

These 10 countries are quite diverse. What do they have in common? To begin with, none of the 10 is a major power. Singapore is an island off the tip of Malaysia; Norway has but 3 million people. Canada has a population and gross national product (GNP) only one-tenth that of the United States; Australia, one-twentieth.

Why do these countries produce great global managers? Let me first turn to an underlying question: what does it take to be a great global manager?

Research suggests a number of characteristics, the most important being the ability to understand, empathize, and work with multiple cultures. A multinational company investing around the world will face clients and customers from cultures totally different from that of the home country. For example, business in Latin America is based very much on relationships of personal trust: one gets to know a Mexican or Argentinian boss before one presents them with a formal contract. In France, one deals directly with the powerful patron at the top. In Germany, on the other hand, written rules and procedures are all-important: a foreign manager seeking to speak to a German CEO will immediately be directed to the appropriate department head. In contrast to Germany's strict written rules, the Japanese operate on strict unwritten rules, known as *kata*. Job security is considered in America to produce a mediocre employee, but in Japan, the lack of job security will do the same. The French admire intellectual prowess, the Americans short-term success; Australians are often wary of both.

The old model of multinationals styled after how the British ran their empire, in which each country manager was sovereign and little was shared between subsidiaries, is a sound approach in a limited set of industries. For most, however, regional if not global integration and synergies are paramount. In such industries, managers will spend a considerable amount of their careers in foreign countries and will need to manage and co-ordinate with people who have different views of the world than their own. That brings us back to our list of 10 countries: what sets apart these countries and their citizens?

The 10 are all mid-range economic powers that must constantly take note of what the big powers are thinking. Managers in the United States, Japan, Germany, France, Britain, Russia, China, India, or any other economic or military power can all too easily begin to interpret the world from their own points of view. Having lived in the United States for six years and the United Kingdom for five, I recognize that both Americans and Britons see the world primarily from their own viewpoints.

In the vast US economy, the world's most important, a company can grow to a considerable size without ever leaving American soil. Dominant countries become dominant because of their very success, and their achievements ought to be admired and applauded. There is a downside, however, to such size and success: it can cause managers of big firms in big countries to become complacent and begin to think that, for instance, the American shareholder is the only one that matters or that the Japanese *keiretsu* system, a network of affiliated companies, is the only way to do business. When the global economy hits what Andy Grove of Intel calls a 10X Crisis – a major tectonic shift – such complacency can be dangerous.

Cultural tension

Middle-economy countries such as Canada or Finland, and the firms that they host, face the everyday reality that they are not the most dominant or important. The United Nations recently ranked Norway as the nicest place to live, with Canada a close second, but neither can claim to be one of the great powerhouse economies of the world. Citizens of these middle countries often experience a tension between their own and a dominant foreign culture. Belgian Walloons are influenced by France, Belgian Flemings by Holland and Germany. Norwegians are influenced by Denmark, the Swiss by Germany, France, and Italy. The Canadian beaver always looks over his shoulder to ponder whether the American eagle is healthy or angry. What Ottawa thinks or does economically is usually less important to a Canadian than what Washington, London, Brussels, or New York thinks. Most countries in Europe have cultures that go back for centuries. Citizens have little doubt of their identity. Nor do Americans. But in the middle countries, people grow up with a different experience. They are caught between their own culture and those nearby.

Canada provides a good example. English Canadians grow up with their own Canadian culture but are often just as well versed in American culture. They know almost as much about US politics as they do about their own. They watch American television as much as Canadian television and listen to NPR as well as CBC. Canadians must always be aware of what their cousins to the south are about. To make things even more complex, English Canadians must consider what French Canadians think and what their views are. Canadians must think as North Americans but also as Canadians. French Canadians must think as North Americans, members of a global French cultural community, as Canadians, and as Quebeçois.

Americans can indulge in talk of economic nationalism, a luxury that Canadians can no longer afford, if they ever could – Canada is simply too dependent on the giant US economy. The Dutch have to learn German, English, and French in addition to Dutch in order to trade with their dominant neighbors to the east, west, and south. In these bicultural countries, children grow up differently than children do in their dominant neighboring countries. Practically from birth, they are aware of the other reality: Swiss children whose neighbors speak French, German, or Italian; Singaporeans who hear Chinese and English side by side. The vast majority of Montrealers in the midst of a day at work or on the school playground switch numerous times between the two languages. They grow up in a duality that provides an excellent preparation for life as a global manager.

It is interesting to consider the Nordic countries. Finnish and other Nordic managers cannot afford to focus on just their neck of the woods – it is simply too unimportant. Nokia chairman and CEO Jorma Ollila is an outstanding example of the new breed of Nordic global manager. He holds several advanced degrees, some from Helsinki universities and a Master's from the London School of Economics. He realizes that a strong focus on Finland for a Nokia employee makes no sense: three out of every five Nokia employees now work outside of Finland, and one out of every three outside of Europe. Contrast this with Wal-Mart, the world's largest retailer but almost exclusively a North American business, with only 9.6 percent of its stores being outside of the NAFTA region. In terms of revenue, only 16.3 percent of Wal-Mart's revenue is international, and again, most of this is in North America. The vast majority of Wal-Mart managers don't need to worry about global business. Nokia, Volvo, Alcan, and Bombardier, however, must be vitally concerned about markets outside their home countries – they have no alternative.

Managers in medium-sized countries must by nature entertain two views of the world. They have to. If Nokia intends to set up its GSM cell-phone technology in the European Union, Russia, and China, its executives had better know German, Russian, and Chinese. It is the ability to be all things to all countries based upon cultural experience that gives many executives from medium-sized countries the skills to be great global managers.

When working on global teams or in other countries, the ability to think outside your own culture and see an issue through the eyes of another is critical to success. From a marketing point of view, empathizing with your customer's culture is paramount. Finns and Canadians do this naturally, not because they are better people but because it comes to them naturally as citizens of a multicultural environment.

Embracing diversity

Where does that leave other, more dominant countries, like the United States, Germany, and Japan? Even these cannot afford to ignore the lessons of globalization. California, crucible for so much of the American future, as usual leads the way. The growing integration of the United States and Latin America is creating not only a California but a Texas, a Florida, and even a New York that is increasingly bicultural. The State Department has come to tolerate, if not fully embrace, the concept of dual citizenship, and acceptance of multiple citizenship is a strong barometer of globalization. As the United States continues to accept a more multicultural country, at least in some regions, US managers will also develop this duality of mind. Many will be of Hispanic heritage.

I recently spent a couple of weeks teaching an executive program in Los Angeles. I had lived in L.A. for six years in the 1970s and it was eye-opening to see the differences between then and now. In the 1970s, Spanish was often seen as a second-class language stereotypically spoken by the maid or the gardener. In my MBA class at the University of Southern California, there was no discussion about learning Spanish or, indeed, any other language – English was sufficient. Today, Spanish is tremendously important in Southern California. Many signs are bilingual, and there are numerous Spanish radio and television stations. And no wonder: they are targetting a very attractive potential market. Hispanics are the region's largest ethnic group. With a population of close to 6 million, if Hispanic Los Angeles were its own city, it would be the nation's sixth-largest city.

In Canada, it is unthinkable that a prime minister does not speak both English and French. Prime-ministerial hopefuls often signal their early interest by spending time in Quebec taking French-immersion programs. George W. Bush speaks fluent Spanish (more or less): how could a serious Texan politician do otherwise? Has Bush, unlikely as it may seem, set a language standard for future presidents? Will the United States ever again elect a president who is not bilingual? But while the nation is changing quite significantly, the US still has a long way to catch up, for in being truly global, companies like Nokia and Bombardier are light-years ahead of most of those in big countries.

Other big economies, like those of Germany, the United Kingdom, France, and Japan, lag considerably behind the United States. Having taught for five years in the United Kingdom and spent considerable time as a visiting professor in France, I know firsthand that although English has become the *de facto lingua franca*, the language skills of the vast majority of people in these countries are not at the level of the citizens of our 10 nations. And it's not just language – the British and the French lack a truly multicultural view that allows a bridge of understanding to be easily built between managers and their peers, employees, and customers.

This is a gap that one finds in Europe's bigger countries. But the true laggard of the major economies is Japan. It is one of the world's leading nations, but diversity in Japan is very low. Trying to find someone who speaks any language other than Japanese in Tokyo, let alone other parts of Japan, stands in marked contrast to my experience in the Netherlands, Finland, or Sweden. This is a considerable challenge for Japan, which ranks as the world's number two country for the number of Fortune 500 multinationals. Traditionally, only natives can scale the heights within Japanese companies, which dramatically reduces the interest of ambitious young foreigners, cutting off Japanese multinationals from a critical source of new ideas and making it difficult for them to truly understand foreign markets and develop a cadre of global managers. Japan must change to maintain its premier ranking in the table of global multinationals.

When CEOs of global firms look for their next generation of global managers, they should focus on the middle-economy countries I've named. The home countries of multinationals will continue to provide the bulk of global managers, but wise firms are widening the pool. It is a strength of Canada, Finland, the Netherlands, and others that their citizens learn from the cradle to take into account other perspectives. We may not always agree, but we must listen and respect.

RESOURCES

Adler, Nancy J., *From Boston to Beijing: Managing with a Worldview*, Thomson Learning, 2000.

Green, Stephen, Hassen, Fred, Immelt, Jeffery, Marks, Michael, and Meiland, Daniel, 'In Search of Global Leaders,' *Harvard Business Review*, Vol. 81, Issue 8, August 2003.

Gregersen, Hal, Morrison, Allen, and Black, Stewart, 'Developing Leaders for the Global Frontier,' *Sloan Management Review*, Vol. 40, Issue 1, 1998, p. 21.

Marquardt, Michael and Berger, Nancy, *Global Leaders for the 21st Century*, State University of New York Press, 2000.

Pound, Richard and Moore, Karl, 'Building Better Executive Leaders,' *Strategy + Business*, Spring, 2004.

Transnational corporations: international citizens or new sovereigns?

DENNIS A. RONDINELLI

> Transnational corporations are increasingly involved in private foreign aid, self-regulation, and private certification of business practices, even shaping public policy. The question is: is this a sign of corporate citizenship and social responsibility or is it a threat to democratic decision making and national sovereignty?

The growth of transnational corporations (TNCs) is increasing their influence around the world. Together and individually they work with international agencies and non-governmental organizations (NGOs) to define policy issues and even intervene on their own account to solve social problems. Within and across industries they develop, put in place, and police self-regulatory codes. They also help to shape regulatory policies or administrative decisions by governments and international organizations on key business issues.

Increasingly they are sources of charitable giving to poorer countries and deprived groups via direct corporate contributions and executives" personal and family foundations. They endeavor to influence public opinion through socially targeted advertising campaigns and use their wealth to affect the way governments deal with social, economic, and environmental problems.

In both advanced economies and developing countries the privatization of a wide range of what had previously been thought of as public goods and services – such as telecommunications, transport, health, education, utilities, job training and vocational education, and even safety and security – has moved decision making about resource allocation, terms of service provision, service coverage, and pricing from the public sector to the private sector.

This increasing public influence on both business and public policy wielded by giant corporations around the world raises questions. Are they acting solely in their own interests (to the detriment of unorganized and poorer groups)? And do their public roles distort or pre-empt the legitimate regulatory functions of sovereign national governments?

Indeed, debate about "globalization" has increasingly focussed on whether the growing public roles of TNCs reflect a new and stronger sense of corporate citizenship or are an attempt to expand their political influence in ways that weaken the sovereign powers of national governments.

We can define "corporate citizenship" as those activities that ensure compliance with laws and regulations, maintain ethical behavior, contribute to social and economic welfare, and generate profits that provide a fair return to investors. In this sense, "citizenship" not only imposes responsibilities and obligations on corporations but also confers the right to influence policy decisions.

In international law, sovereign states have the right to regulate their territory and citizens without external pressure or intervention. But globalization has blurred the concept of national citizenship, generating new concepts of "transnational" or "post-national" citizenship. Transnational citizenship implies that fundamental human rights transcend national boundaries in a world in which the responsibilities and privileges of citizenship are quickly becoming denationalized.

The expansion of international trade and investment, the spread of telecommunications and transport technology, and the growth of international commerce have given TNCs the ability to operate beyond the constraints of any one nation's laws and regulations in ways that can be both beneficial and detrimental to host countries. In a globalizing economy, TNCs, NGOs, international organizations, and other non-state institutions have all achieved greater power and influence, some would argue at the expense of national sovereignty. The ability of TNCs to create separate legal entities to shield shareholders from liability in different countries around the world, their location in multiple legal jurisdictions, and the political reluctance of some governments to enforce laws against large investors and employers all tend to weaken conventional concepts of national sovereignty.

The economic power of TNCs is undisputed. By 2000, the 60,000 transnational corporations identified by the United Nations Conference on Trade and Development had more than 800,000 international affiliates. The foreign affiliates of TNCs employ more than 45 million people and together constitute a powerful economic influence. Their foreign direct investment is in excess of $1.3 trillion. By virtue of their sales alone, TNCs rival the financial resources of all but the largest states. ExxonMobil's total annual sales exceed the gross national product of 104 countries. The annual sales worldwide of General Electric, General Motors, Ford, Toyota, and Wal-Mart are each larger than the gross national product of nearly 100 countries. Indeed, the combined revenues of the 10 largest international companies exceed the GNP of all except eight countries in the world.

Unsurprisingly, the economic power of TNCs has attracted attention. But a less visible, though nonetheless significant, aspect of globalization is the rapidly expanding roles that these corporations and their executives and industry associations have assumed in social, economic, and environmental policy – areas that had in the past been the primary or exclusive responsibilities of governments.

Although many critics of globalization and of TNCs view this with foreboding, the growing public role of the private sector should not be surprising. Even the most hardened critics of globalization argue that TNCs making billions of dollars in countries around the world have responsibilities as corporate citizens to contribute to the social and economic well-being of people living in places where they do business. This is especially so in developing countries where governments lack the resources to address crucial economic and social problems.

Often, and perhaps ironically, the TNCs' strongest critics – NGOs – have been the driving force in cajoling corporations into exercising greater social responsibility. NGOs identify the negative social, economic, and environmental impacts of TNCs' operations and pressure companies to use some of their wealth to address complex international problems. As a result, TNC executives may feel compelled to pursue corporate citizenship in order for their firms to profit.

The public face of the private sector

TNCs, business and industry associations, corporate foundations, and wealthy business executives are playing stronger international public roles in at least three significant ways. First, they are supplanting or supplementing government and multilateral foreign aid programs through philanthropy. Second, they are involved in international standard setting and voluntary participation in self-regulation and private certification arrangements on social, human rights, and environmental issues. Third, they play a key role in framing and shaping international policies both inside and outside of the conventional processes of government decision making.

Private foreign aid

Over the past 25 years TNCs have become major providers of private foreign aid. TNCs, first through private capital flows and later by philanthropic contributions both directly and through international organizations, began in the 1980s to fill the void left by the dwindling official development assistance from national governments and international aid agencies. By 1991 private capital investment exceeded official development assistance as the primary source of financial transfers from richer to poorer countries. A decade later, private flows of capital accounted for 87 percent of the nearly $296 billion transferred from richer to poorer countries while official development assistance comprised less than 13 percent.

Although the full amount of private charitable contributions for social, economic, and political development is not known, all indications are that it is significant. TNCs, business associations, corporate foundations, and corporate executives are now providing financial assistance to developing countries in areas that a few decades ago were exclusively the preserve of government and multilateral aid agencies.

Perhaps the most dramatic example of private foreign aid was Ted Turner's $1 billion gift to the UN for social and health programs and his offer of $35 million in personal contributions to meet the gap caused by the US's decision in 2000 to reduce its financial support for the international organization. But other corporate foundations and wealthy business leaders have, perhaps more quietly, far exceeded Turner's philanthropic gesture. The Foundation Center reported that by 1999 corporate foundation philanthropy in the US alone had grown to nearly $3 billion. Corporations contribute directly even larger amounts of money and in-kind goods and services to organizations in their home and host countries and to developing nations.

TNCs – mostly based in the US and Western Europe but increasingly in the more prosperous countries of Asia and Latin America as well – are seeking to solve health, education, and environmental problems, work with international organizations and activist groups to address human rights issues, and partner with community organizations to alleviate poverty.

The Finnish telecommunications corporation Nokia, for example, launched a three-year $11 million campaign with the International Youth Foundation and its own employee volunteers to help children with learning difficulties in South Africa, China, Mexico, Brazil, the UK, and Germany. Unilever invests more than $45 million a year through charitable gifts and assistance to social investment projects and disaster relief in communities around the world.

The personal philanthropic foundations of wealthy corporate executives such as Bill Gates and George Soros are also playing influential roles in private foreign aid. The Bill and Melinda Gates Foundation contribution of $50 million was matched by the Merck Corporation's contribution of antiretroviral medicines and services to develop and manage an HIV program in Botswana. Since the early 1990s Soros" Open Society Institute has financed 30 national foundations in emerging economies to promote "open society."

Self-regulation and certification

In addition to private foreign aid, corporations and industry associations address corruption, human rights, and social and environmental issues through voluntary international standard setting, self-regulation, and private certification. The private sector plays an expanded role in monitoring social behaviors via membership of UN international advisory committees and specialized organizations, and working with NGOs to set criteria for human rights, labor conditions, environmental protection, and certifying corporate social or environmental practices. In the past, these were often regulated by governments.

Levi Strauss, Texas Instruments, Unocal, Johnson & Johnson, and hundreds of other TNCs engage in self-regulation by adopting corporate codes of conduct. Others, such as international chemical companies, adopt industry standards like the

Responsible Care® program. In the field of environmental management, a growing number of TNCs voluntarily submit their environmental management systems for private certification by external auditors and registrars using the International Organization for Standardization's ISO-14000 series guidelines.

By late 2001 almost 32,000 organizations worldwide had their internally developed environmental management systems certified by ISO-14001 standards. In Europe, nearly 4,000 companies have voluntarily registered them under European Eco-Management and Audit Scheme guidelines. Thousands more companies are adopting major components of voluntary international standards for environmental management without formally certifying them.

As part of the UN "Global Compact," TNCs and business organizations have agreed to develop and support appropriate policies and practices on human rights, labor, and the environment. Adherents develop standards for and pledge to uphold freedom of association and the right to collective bargaining, the elimination of employment discrimination and all forms of forced and compulsory labor, and abolition of child labor. Member corporations also support pollution prevention measures, undertake initiatives to promote environmental protection, and encourage the development and diffusion of environmentally friendly technologies.

TNCs within the same industry are developing their own voluntary regulatory standards or working with government agencies and international organizations to do so. For example, in 2001 seven international energy and mining companies – Royal Dutch/Shell Group, BP-Amoco, Texaco, Conoco, Chevron, Freeport-McMoRan Copper & Gold, and Rio Tinto – agreed to a set of voluntary human rights agreements designed to prevent abuses linked to energy and mining operations in developing countries. The standards were developed by the companies and a group of NGOs – including Human Rights Watch, International Alert, Lawyers Committee for Human Rights, Fund for Peace, Council on Economic Priorities, Business for Social Responsibility, the Prince of Wales Business Leaders Forum, and the International Chemical, Energy, Mine, and General Workers Unions – and backed by the US and UK governments.

Framing and influencing international public policies

Beyond developing and participating in agreements on voluntary standards of behavior and self-regulation, TNCs also influence international policy dialogs prior to national governments and international organizations enacting laws and regulations, or attempt to influence the pace and direction of decisions by governments and international organizations. Corporations and industry groups increasingly use social advertising to make issues that they favor or oppose more visible, shape public opinion, influence key policy makers, and help set the agenda on policy proposals affecting their industry.

Lobbying governments is, of course, nothing new for corporations. More than 3,000 trade associations are located in the Washington DC area, employing about

100,000 people. More than 10,000 lobbyists, many from major corporations, are assigned to influence the governing institutions of the EU in Brussels. TNCs are, directly or indirectly, seeking to shape policies or avert government regulation on a wider range of international issues through their industry associations and international chambers of commerce and as members of business-oriented non-profit interest groups.

TNCs increasingly take part in government trade negotiations, in the development of bilateral and multilateral trade relationships and in international forums on policy questions. Unilever, for example, helped organize the Second World Water Forum at The Hague in 2000 and led the business panel. It also provided information on technology and policy alternatives for increasing access to water in poor countries. Chief executives of TNCs based in Mexico, the US, UK, Germany, Sweden, Nigeria, and Japan joined with government ministers of finance and development to form an Investment Advisory Council to the UN to propose foreign aid programs for Africa at the international conference on foreign assistance in Monterrey, Mexico, in 2001.

Leaders of private corporations and industry associations attend World Trade Organization meetings to influence the outcome of negotiations and to offset the influence of NGOs and special interest groups, which also lobby national delegations. TNCs play an increasingly important role in influencing the outcome of WTO trade disputes, sometimes in ways that are at odds with the goals of member states.

Corporate representatives have participated heavily in activities to influence government decisions on global warming. For more than a decade, the American Chemistry Council, the National Association of Manufacturers, the US Chamber of Commerce, and representatives of international petroleum, electric utility, railroad, iron and steel, and mining companies used the Global Climate Coalition to lobby US and European governments to oppose the Kyoto Protocol, a global treaty to reduce greenhouse gas emissions. The coalition was disbanded once the Bush Administration announced that the US would not implement the protocol.

Seven major corporations joined with an NGO, Environmental Defense, in proposing flexible emissions trading mechanisms at The Hague meetings to negotiate an international treaty on global warming that would amend the Kyoto Protocol. More than 30 corporations worked with Environmental Defense, the Nature Conservancy, and the Pew Center for Global Climate Change to develop a set of emissions trading agreements acceptable to both the corporations and some environmental groups.

The TNC effect

The private sector's growing international influence raises complex questions about whether TNCs engage in corporate citizenship in order to make public policy more effective or simply to weaken, displace, or circumscribe the regulations of sovereign governments. The complexity and diversity of TNCs' public roles and differences in their motivations provide no easy answers.

For example, what seems like good citizenship by TNCs in assisting poor countries and poor groups within richer countries to address economic, social, and environmental issues and in voluntarily regulating their own behavior to protect human rights can also be interpreted as strategic positioning to enhance their commercial interests. TNCs" public influence can be considered beneficial or harmful, but in either case it raises serious questions for many about national sovereignty, democratic governance, and the proper means of protecting the "public interest."

Beneficial impacts

TNCs – as contributors of private foreign aid, as international standard setters and self-regulators, and as shapers of international policies – can and do play beneficial roles as corporate citizens.

First, the financial resources and business expertise that TNCs bring to these efforts can significantly leverage the financial and human resources of governments, international organizations, and NGOs in addressing important policy problems. Advocates of corporate citizenship argue that TNCs can be strong sources of funding and potentially valuable allies for NGOs and governments seeking to solve many environmental and social problems.

UN Secretary-General Kofi Annan hailed the private sector's participation in the Investment Advisory Council as a public-private partnership that can bring sorely needed foreign investment to Africa and said that the foreign aid programs that it generates "can play an important role in advancing Africa's development." The partnership of the Bill and Melinda Gates Foundation, Merck Corporation, and the government of Botswana was essential to tackle HIV and other health problems in a country where nearly 30 percent of the adult population is HIV-positive.

Since 1985 Rotary International, working with Coca-Cola and other major corporations, has raised more than $400 million to promote polio immunization around the world, working with the World Health Organization (WHO), UNICEF, the US Center for Disease Control, and foreign aid programs of the US, UK, Japan, and Denmark. Johnson & Johnson's assistance for health care facilities in Mexico, Zimbabwe, Singapore, China, and the Philippines, as well as in other countries where the company has manufacturing plants or sales offices, extends the ability of NGOs and government agencies to meet health needs and respond to disasters.

Second, these activities also respond to the growing demands of NGOs and activist groups (which are often critical of globalization) that TNCs return to society a portion of the profits they earn from using the natural, human, and other resources of the countries in which they operate. TNCs now substantially supplement NGO and government assistance to poor groups and communities, especially in developing countries. Moreover, TNCs' involvement in community and social projects offers a model for local businesses. A survey of more than 1,750 companies in Brazil by IPEA, a respected think-tank, found that 67 percent were involved in some type of social project.

Third, TNC involvement in development activities often enables and empowers community and social groups to solve problems they might not otherwise be able to tackle without additional resources. The growing influence of TNCs on the social and environmental practices of their joint-venture partners, affiliates, licensees, suppliers, vendors, contractors, and customers can be more powerful in changing behavior, or at least in setting standards, than actions of either governments or NGOs. At the same time, participation in self-regulation, codes of ethical behavior, or external certification of their business practices forces TNCs to pay attention to all aspects of corporate social responsibility.

Fourth, the use of private resources by corporations and NGOs can often address problems faster, and sometimes more efficiently and effectively, than government programs. Johnson & Johnson responds quickly to disaster relief needs in many countries through its network of production and distribution facilities. The Soros-sponsored Open Society Institute in Hungary funded an extensive local government and public service reform project because it could provide information and assistance faster than the national government or international aid agencies.

Fifth, corporate participation in international standard setting creates voluntary guidelines for social responsibility in the private sector that often cannot be easily imposed by governments. TNCs can often mitigate some social problems by offering solutions that go beyond the limits of national political constraints or by attacking issues that governments might not wish to address. Media exposure and the willingness of large corporations and private foundations to use their resources to supplement international health organization campaigns have forced governments in Africa to recognize the seriousness of the HIV-AIDS problem and become involved in public health prevention, screening, and treatment programs.

Sixth, TNCs can often act in concert to improve their behavior more expeditiously than governments or international organizations can negotiate and implement formal regulations. The slow pace of WTO negotiations over global labor standards and continuing complaints by human rights groups led clothing manufacturers in Bangladesh, the Philippines, and Cambodia voluntarily to adopt International Labour Organization principles and to arrange for third-party inspection of their factories and company practices.

Seventh, corporate participation also brings managerial expertise and perspectives to social problem solving not normally found in government. Governments often take a purely regulatory view of complex problems that force corporations to judicially challenge, or seek loopholes in, unrealistic laws. The private sector sometimes brings a different if not broader perspective, generates information that is not available to government, and proposes solutions that may be more viable for implementation.

Lastly, corporate philanthropy and social initiatives and the privatization of "public services" save poor governments money that can be used to solve problems with which the private sector may not be able to assist. Observing the Coca-Cola and Rotary International Partnership on polio immunization in India, Gro Harlem Brundtland, Director-General of the WHO, pointed out that "by reducing the burden of disease, we reduce cost and increase productivity. The polio eradication campaign is a clear example; when we succeed, direct saving alone will be $1.5 billion per year worldwide."

The dangers of corporate influence

Although corporate participation in international development has potential and actual benefits, critics contend that TNCs' roles in private foreign aid and in international standard setting and policy making also hold dangers.

First, skepticism concerning the motivations of TNCs and private organizations in pursuing corporate citizenship and political influence arises from the fact that corporations benefit financially and competitively from these activities. The NGO Business for Social Responsibility points out that global community involvement by TNCs can help them expand in new markets, retain valued employees, enhance their images, attain brand recognition, and gain access to a broader and more skilled labor force. Critics argue that expansion of corporate citizenship movements allows TNCs to shift liability and risk by focussing on voluntary codes of conduct, plea agreements, and civil and administrative actions in place of criminal indictments, thereby undermining criminal law and – when pursued internationally – national sovereignty.

Second, when corporations become the dominant sources of funding for social programs or influential forces in standard setting, the issues and solutions selected may be heavily biased toward the interests of sponsoring organizations. Corporations such as Nokia and Johnson & Johnson, no matter how well intentioned, are most likely to focus their resources on problems related to their businesses and to ignore others that do not fall within the scope of their commercial interests. Strong corporate influence on social programs and public policies can lead to selective or limited intervention in ways that may not address the underlying causes of problems.

Third, much of the private sector's participation in voluntary codes of conduct is not closely monitored and often the standards are not enforceable by signatories or third parties. Because of allegations that the medical, accounting, and legal professions have done such a poor job of enforcing voluntary ethical codes for their members, public interest groups often question the efficacy of similar self-policing by TNCs. In response to the energy and mining company agreement on human rights protection, a mining watchdog group, Project Underground, expressed the view of many other NGOs in arguing that "with no way to hold companies accountable, you can rest assured that we will only see business as usual."

Fourth, when corporations act in "quasi-governmental" or political roles they may bias rule making and standard setting toward narrow interests rather than a broader "public interest." TNCs clearly are not accountable to the public, may not represent the clientele they seek to assist, and may not involve or consult stakeholders in their activities.

Heavy corporate participation in international development and policy making may pre-empt or constrain the search for broad solutions and focus on those that corporations are willing to support. The services they finance may not be accessible to people who need them most. Reliance on corporate funding may lead governments to ignore problems or address them only superficially when TNCs and NGOs become involved. The unwillingness or inability of governments in some developing countries to address issues of worker mistreatment by TNCs has led NGO and human rights groups such as the Worker Rights Consortium, the Fair Labor Association, and Social Accountability International to demand the right to carry out audits and inspections of factories to ensure the safety and well-being of employees.

Fifth, some critics argue that growing corporate involvement in foreign aid, social policies, and quasi-regulatory activities undermines the sovereign functions of national governments or at least displaces legitimate government regulatory responsibilities. The International Council on Human Rights Policy, a strong critic of relying on voluntary corporate codes and self-regulation, contends that "the concept of the sovereignty of states ... should not be replaced by a new corporate sovereignty, which is unrestricted or unaccountable." It notes that voluntary approaches are "soft law" standards that cannot be enforced and that do not impose legal obligations on companies to comply with human rights principles.

Self-regulation commits TNCs that do abide by voluntary agreements to practices and costs that may put them at a competitive disadvantage with companies that do not make the same commitments. And under voluntary codes of self-regulation, and in the absence of strong national laws, victims may have no legal redress for grievances.

Sixth, critics also complain that the growing international influence of TNCs opens the way for legitimizing policy making outside conventional government processes. And if it does take place with government agreement it may be done in such secrecy that the public is not informed. One of the leading observers of the new trends in corporate citizenship, Simon Zadek, calls growing TNC and NGO involvement in international policies "the new civil governance." This new system of governance, Zadek argues, requires acceptance of systems of partial and temporary rules with participation and oversight by diverse organizations and institutions with complex and sometimes unstable bases of legitimacy that are unaccountable to popular electorates.

Seventh, because they are pursued outside of government supervision, corporate self-regulation and private foreign aid often lack transparency, credibility, and legitimacy. Skeptics claim, for example, that Nokia's international assistance program for children with learning difficulties is at the same time a subtle way for the Finnish telecommunications company to strengthen its market position among younger people and develop brand identity with a new generation of customers.

Similarly, WHO severely criticized the voluntary ban against marketing tobacco to children adopted by three of the biggest tobacco TNCs in the US, UK and Japan as self-serving, deceptive, and ineffective in implementation. WHO charged the tobacco companies with merely trying to derail or delay government bans on all tobacco advertising on radio and television. "We have seen no evidence that tobacco companies are capable of self-regulation," argued WHO chief Brundtland, "and we need to be alert to any new attempts to persuade us that this new effort will succeed."

Counteracting corporate influence

The growing economic influence of TNCs almost assures continued expansion of the public role of the private sector in international policy. For that reason many NGOs continue to pressure them into even stronger programs of social responsibility. Some international organizations seek incentives to support corporate assistance programs or requirements that they openly report their social responsibility activities.

France, for example, recently enacted new requirements that mandate all French corporations to issue reports on the sustainability of their environmental and social performance and to document their activities in protecting human rights, to identify local impacts of their operations and their dialogs with stakeholders, and to explain their human resources, community relations, and labor standards policies.

The Commission of the European Communities argues that EU policies should encourage corporate social responsibility and help establish a framework for ensuring that corporations integrate into their business operations social and environmental activities.The Global Reporting Initiative (GRI), a joint permanent institution launched by the UN Environmental Program and the Coalition for Environmentally Responsible Economies (CERES), seeks to convince corporations to put environmental and social sustainability reporting on an equivalent level with financial reporting. More than 100 TNCs use GRI guidelines for corporate disclosure, reporting, and transparency.

Other organizations, such as the International Council on Human Rights Policy (ICHRP), contend that the enactment and implementation of strong regulations by national governments and the development of international laws that impose legal responsibilities and accountability on TNCs are essential to maintain state sovereignty and to rein in the potential abuses of corporate power. ICHRP contends that although voluntary agreements and international laws are not effective substitutes for national regulations in maintaining sovereign control, international laws "can help harmonize rules at a time of weak national regulation. They can act as a common reference point for national law, setting benchmarks, drawing attention to core minimum requirements, and establishing clearly what is not permissible."

A strong international legal system can encourage new national legislation and help national governments strengthen existing laws. International laws can create countervailing forces that motivate TNCs to comply with minimum social, economic, and environmental standards and enhance NGOs' ability to continue pressuring TNCs to go beyond regulatory compliance through voluntary means.

Given the long gestation period and the inevitable political compromises that mark the birth of international laws and agreements, informal as well as formal countervailing forces – more effective systems of checks and balances – are needed to address continuing concerns about TNCs' motives.

A stronger system of countervailing forces would require governments to more closely monitor TNCs' business practices in their countries, industry associations to take a stronger role in promoting voluntary agreements and codes of conduct, NGOs to monitor abuses and participate more actively in certifying regulatory compliance, and international institutions to develop processes through which disputes can be settled and grievances can be redressed. Many elements of such a system are slowly beginning to emerge.

But countervailing powers that encourage and at the same time check the potentially adverse consequences of increasing TNC participation in international policy making require better knowledge of the scope, magnitude, and impacts of TNCs' public roles. NGOs are pressing firms to issue social responsibility reports, and several have established Internet clearinghouses by which the reports can be accessed. The growth of social investment funds composed of shares in companies that are screened by indicators of social responsibility also provide visibility and financial rewards to TNCs that develop reputations for good corporate citizenship. By 2001, more than $2.3 trillion had been invested in professionally managed social funds in the US.

Greater transparency may assuage some concerns about the power of TNCs to undermine national governments' sovereign functions. Other than what the public learns from their press releases and the annual social responsibility reports of corporations and the complaints of NGOs and special interest groups, however, little is generally known about why and how corporations are assuming stronger public roles. Little attention has been given to how corporations and corporate foundations decide which roles to play and how to carry them out.

The impacts of private foreign aid in addressing critical social and economic needs have not been widely monitored or assessed and the efficacy of self-regulation and voluntary codes of conduct are only beginning to be examined. The legitimacy of TNC influence on national and international public policy making is still under scrutiny because corporations have not always made their activities fully transparent.

Clearly, the expanding international public role of the private sector has both potential benefits and potential dangers. As responsible corporations, TNCs must give priority to serving customers and generating a fair return for shareholders. Promoting social reform will never be the primary mission of most TNCs. But they are increasingly asked to be good corporate citizens and they will continue to enter or be drawn into public roles as providers of private foreign aid, as self-regulators, and as influential political forces in shaping national and international policies. They are sources of enormous wealth and power, some of which can be put to effective use in preventing and alleviating social ills. But that wealth and power can also be used in ways that undermine the ability and willingness of governments to protect the common interest.

A more effective system of countervailing forces – allowing governments, NGOs, and TNCs to apply checks and balances that reduce the potential of any of the major participants in the global economy abusing their power or shirking their legitimate social responsibilities – depends on a better understanding of the types of public roles that TNCs are playing and the scope and magnitude of their impacts.

RESOURCES

Carroll, A.B., 'The Four Faces of Corporate Citizenship,' *Business and Society Review*, Nos 100–101: 1–7, 1998.

Dunning, John H. (ed), *Governments, Globalization and International Business*, Oxford University Press, 1997.

Gereffi, Gary, Garcia-Johnson, Ronie, and Sasser, Erica, 'The NGO-industrial complex,' *Foreign Policy*, (1): 56–65, July–August, 2000.

Haufler, Virginia A., 'Public Role for the Private Sector: Industry Self-Regulation in a Global Economy,' Washington, D.C.: Carnegie Endowment for International Peace, 2001.

Klodoner, Eric, 'Transnational corporations: impediments or catalysts of social development?' Occasional Paper No. 5, Geneva, Switzerland: United Nations Research Institute for Social Development, 1994.

Korten, David, *When Corporations Rule the World*, Kumarian Press, 1996.

Krasner, Stephen D., *Sovereignty: Organized Hypocrisy*, Princeton University Press, 1999.

Rondinelli, Dennis A., 'Privatization, governance and public management: the challenges ahead,' *Business & the Contemporary World*, Vol. 10, No. 1 (1998): 149–170.

Rondinelli, Dennis A., 'Sovereignty On Line: Challenges of Transnational Corporations and Information Technology in Asia,' in John D. Montgomery and Nathan Glazer (eds), *Sovereignty Under Challenge: How Governments Respond*, New Brunswick, N.J.: Transaction Books, 2002.

Vernon, Raymond, *Sovereignty at Bay: The Multinational Spread of US Enterprises*, Basic Books, 1971.

Zadek, Simon, *The Civil Corporation: The New Economy of Corporate Citizenship*, Earthscan, 2001.

'Interview': Yves Doz and José Santos

The INSEAD professors talk about their concept of the *metanational* company.

Why did you choose the word metanational and what is special about the companies it describes?

We chose the prefix "meta" in the sense of "beyond." Metanationals do not have countries or nation-states as a fundamental dimension. To the metanational, globalization is not about taking home-country know-how to other national markets around the globe. It is about efficiently fishing for knowledge in a global pool, harnessing that knowledge for innovation, and then harvesting its value for its stakeholders.

What's the difference with the "born global" firms studied by Finnish scholars, such as Erkko Autio, which include companies like Nokia?

It is a different classification. Concepts such as "born global" (or "global start-ups") are used in reference to firms that become international in a very short period of time – say, achieving one third or more of their sales in foreign markets after just one year of operations. However, a "born global" may be a traditional multinational or a metanational.

Which is the main target of your message: global born start-ups or incumbent multinationals?

The main target is the traditional multinational companies. We present a roadmap for the multinationals to change. Not trying to force-fit an existing multinational organization and its people into a metanational mold. That would be a wrong way that could undermine its operational excellence and could imperil the company's very survival. We suggest a way out.

What's wrong with the step-by-step internationalization process which worked in the 1970s and 1980s?

There is nothing wrong with it, as long as you can find all you need to achieve global competitive advantage in your home country (that is, if you have a "diamond" in your backyard). Indeed, businesses such as consumer electronics or semiconductors did become global in the 1970s and 1980s with traditional multinationals leading the way. But the empirical evidence shows that as globalization intensifies and technology continues to reduce the cost of distance, the probability of succeeding with a traditional internationalization strategy is getting lower by the day.

Is the metanational phenomenon restricted to companies in high-tech industries?

We found examples in many different industries, including cosmetics, music, and food, as well as in biotech, software, and semiconductors. What matters is the knowledge-intensity of the product, service, or solution. "High-tech" industries are usually very high in knowledge-intensity and therefore it will be more likely to observe metanationals there.

Your research is very Europe-focussed. Is this coincidence or is there another reason?

There is surely a tendency for academics to study the reality closer to them. Management researchers in the US, for example, will tend to look at American firms. The size of the domestic market in the US is such that most companies don't even reach national scale, let alone international – so why be "born global" there? (However, note that there were references to global start-ups made in the US in the early 1990s.) And it is not only size: the American economy is of such scope and competitiveness that it was the home base of so many traditional multinationals that gained world scale in many industries, so why be metanational? As we observed when looking at companies from Asia, Europe, and the US, the companies that were somewhat metanational were those that had been "born in the wrong place," as we say.

Can you give some examples of European metanationals?

STMicroelectronics, for example, a company with French-Italian state origin, is a very good example of a metanational. But there are other examples, such as Nokia, Polygram, Business Objects, or Logitech – and Airbus, of course.

Is being cosmopolitan an important psychological ingredient for metanational managers and entrepreneurs?

Surely. One of the attributes that we observed in all the metanational companies that we studied was that the top managers were cosmopolitan: they had been around the world and knew it well. They had a network of acquaintances in several countries. They were at ease in different cultures. In most cases, that attribute had been developed during a managerial career in a traditional multinational company (for example, all but four of the top 16 executives at STMicroelectronics had been managers at companies such as Motorola, Texas Instruments, National Semiconductors, or Toshiba). In other cases, metanational entrepreneurs had studied abroad for a while (for example, the Swiss and Italian founders of Logitech met when studying at Stanford, Palo Alto).

Did the rise of the new economy in the late 1990s help the emergence of metanationals?

The Internet and GSM are part of the technological evolution that is continuously reducing the cost of distance, in this case for information. In this sense, they participate in the creation of the conditions for the emergence of metanationals. In what refers to the bull market of the 1990s, the generalized optimism surely helped the financing of some metanational start-ups. These metanational start-ups are riskier than traditional ones, given the nature of the challenge and the managerial and organizational capabilities required.

Is being born in the wrong place – distant from Silicon Valley and the main industrial districts of the world – critical for metanational strategies?

It was certainly critical for the metanational pioneers that we have identified in our research. In essence, necessity was the mother of invention. When Shiseido wants to become a global player in cosmetics or Nokia aspires at being a leader in mobile phones, it is clear that Japan and Finland are not the right places to be. However, there is nothing in our current theoretical model that prevents a metanational strategy from any origin. And what seems evident now is that very few "right places" remain out there: even Silicon Valley is no longer enough for Intel.

Michael Porter and others have identified clusters of specialized companies in areas such as Silicon Valley. They note that being inside a cluster can be a major advantage in knowledge-intensive industries. Are clusters relevant for these metanational strategies?

Clusters were and will continue to be relevant. But, as you say, the views of clusters as self-contained and integral will most likely lock companies in the typical projection mode of traditional multinationals. Some limitations of an integral cluster have been overcome by locating different activities in different clusters and moving products or components around the world. But the conventional wisdom remains that the knowledge-intense activities (namely, innovation activities such as R&D or new product development) should be done in the home cluster. What the metanational does is to innovate by bridging various clusters, by bringing together knowledge that is dispersed around the world.

What has changed in the competitive advantage theory?

It is now clear that scale is not the source of competitive advantage in almost all industries. There is a much better understanding of the dynamics of competition, as well as the realization that more important than some "position" in the market is the quality of the resources owned by the firm. The key source of sustainable competitive advantage is valuable, firm-specific tacit knowledge.

North American companies are usually conservative in their internationalization strategies. Are new economy stars like Yahoo! and Amazon the same?

Yes, absolutely. Both cases are good examples of traditional multinational companies, only much faster in their internationalization than their elder cousins such as Ford or McDonald's (and they seem to have been unable to learn from the experience of such companies as they moved abroad). But both Yahoo! and Amazon are essentially American creations for the American market, a representation of the high level of development of information technologies in the US. The case of Amazon is remarkable: after only one month of operations, it had exported to 45 different countries (I believe that this is a world record that will be very hard to beat). But it took the company several years to even begin to realize the potential of such foreign markets, and it did so in the most conventional of ways: sequentially, country by country, starting with a subsidiary in the UK. What's "new"?

Some of them are creating centers of excellence in Europe, trying to mobilize their European knowledge.

I don't like the label *center of excellence*. It could give the idea that only there, in one or some places, we can find excellence. As we mention in our book (*From Global to Multinational: How Companies Win in the Knowledge Economy*), knowledge is dispersed globally, is increasingly scattered around the world, is fragmented. So, the real challenge is to build a network of excellence, connecting globally dispersed knowledge. Connectivity is the key word. We must access multiple sources of new knowledge, probably from outside the multinational's current network of subsidiaries.

The so-called global federalism of ABB and the multi-localism of Unilever are valid approaches?

Yes, in what concerns what we call the "operations plane," the locus for strategies to exploit and leverage the value of innovations worldwide. In another way, these are strategies to optimize the capture of value by a multinational company, but not the creation of value. The logic of "operations" is efficiency, flexibility, and financial discipline. Those approaches are valid if they perform well in these three dimensions. Let me note that "global federalism" and "multi-localism" are not alternatives to a metanational approach. Metanational is the alternative to projecting from a home country.

But you reverse the famous glocalization theory of Percy Barnevik?

We say that the real challenge is think local and act global, not think global and act local. We have to learn from the periphery and then *meld* the local innovations. We must act like a vacuum cleaner and then meld the various knowledge.

How does this differ from the "transnational" concept of Bartlett and Ghoshal?

We are in the same tradition. We think, however, that they put the right questions but give the wrong answer. We put more substance in the global learning problem and we separate clearly the new metanational capabilities, the new skill sets, from the operational field, where the transnational concept works.

Interview by Jorge Nascimento Rodrigues

Essentials

GLOBALIZATION

Hofstede, Geert

According to *The Economist*, Geert Hofstede (born 1928) "more or less invented [cultural diversity] as a management subject." Few would deny that this is the case. The Dutch academic has exerted considerable influence over thinking on the human and cultural implications of globalization.

Hofstede trained as a mechanical engineer before becoming a psychologist. He spent time working in factories as a foreman and plant manager; was chief psychologist on the international staff of IBM; and joined IMEDE, the Swiss business school, in 1971. He is now Emeritus Professor of Organizational Anthropology and International Management at the University of Limburg in Maastricht.

In Hofstede's hands, culture becomes the crux of business. He defines it as "the collective programming of the mind which distinguishes the members of one group or category of people from another." Hofstede's conclusions are based on huge amounts of research. His seminal work on cross-cultural management, *Culture's Consequences*, involved over 100,000 surveys in more than 60 countries. The sheer size of Hofstede's research base leads to perennial questions about how manageable and useful it can be.

Each society faces some similar problems, but solutions differ from one society to another. Hofstede identified five basic characteristics distinguishing national cultures. These dimensions are:

- *power distance* – the extent to which the less powerful members of institutions and organizations expect and accept that power is unequally distributed;
- *individualism* – in some societies the ties between individuals are loose, while in others there is greater collectivism and strong cohesive groups;
- *masculinity* – how distinct are social gender roles?;
- *uncertainty avoidance* – the extent to which society members feel threatened by uncertain or unknown situations;
- *long-term orientation* – the extent to which a society exhibits a pragmatic, future-oriented perspective.

Morita, Akio

Akio Morita (1921–1999) was the co-founder of Sony and the best known of the new wave of Japanese businessmen who rose to prominence in the West in the 1980s.

Trained as a physicist and scientist, he founded a company with Masaru Ibuka (1908–97) immediately after the end of the Second World War. In 1957, the company produced a pocket-sized radio and a year later renamed itself Sony (*sonus* is Latin for sound). In 1960, it produced the first transistor TV in the world.

Increasingly, the world was Sony's market. Its combination of smaller and smaller products at the leading edge of technology proved irresistible. In 1961, Sony Corporation of America was the first Japanese company to be listed on Wall Street and, in 1989, Sony bought Columbia Pictures, so that by 1991 it had more foreigners than Japanese on its 135,000 payroll.

Morita and Sony's story parallels the rebirth of Japan as an industrial power. When Sony was first attempting to make inroads into Western markets, Japanese products were sneered at as being of the lowest quality. Surmounting that obstacle was a substantial business achievement.

Morita and Sony's gift was to invent new markets. Describing what he called Sony's "pioneer spirit," Morita said: "Sony is a pioneer and never intends to follow others. Through progress, Sony wants to serve the whole world. It shall be always a seeker of the unknown."

While companies such as Matsushita were inspired followers, Sony set a cracking pace with product after product, innovation after innovation. It brought the world the handheld video camera, the first home video recorder, and the floppy disk. The blemishes on its record were the Betamax video format, which it failed to license, and color television systems. Its most famous success was the brainchild of Morita, the Walkman. The evolution of this now ubiquitous product is the stuff of corporate legend.

Ohmae, Kenichi

There is no doubting Kenichi Ohmae's (born 1943) credentials as a modern Renaissance man. He is a graduate of Waseda University, the Tokyo Institute of Technology, and has a PhD in nuclear engineering from Massachusetts Institute of Technology. He is also a talented flautist and sometime adviser to the former Japanese Prime Minister Nakasone. Ohmae joined McKinsey in 1972, becoming managing director of its Tokyo office. McKinsey Americanized him as "Ken," but the ambitions of his thinking remained resolutely global.

Ohmae's work is important for two reasons. First, he revealed the truth behind Japanese strategy making to an expectant Western audience. Second, he has explored the ramifications of globalization more extensively than virtually any other thinker.

Ohmae's first contribution was to explode simplistic Western myths about Japanese management. Forget company songs and lifetime employment, there was more to Japanese management. Most notably, there was the Japanese art of strategic thinking. This, said Ohmae, is "basically creative and intuitive and rational" – although none of these characteristics were evident in the usual Western stereotype of Japanese management.

Ohmae pointed out that unlike large US corporations, Japanese businesses tend not to have large strategic planning staffs. Instead, they often have a single, naturally talented strategist with "an idiosyncratic mode of thinking in which company, customers, and competition merge in a dynamic interaction out of which a comprehensive set of objectives and plans for action eventually crystallizes."

Ohmae also noted that the customer was at the heart of the Japanese approach to strategy and key to corporate values. "In the construction of any business strategy, three main players must be taken into account: the corporation itself, the customer, and the competition. Each of these 'strategic three Cs' is a living entity with its own interests and objectives. We shall call them, collectively, the 'strategic triangle,'" he said. "Seen in the context of the strategic triangle, the job of the strategist is to achieve superior performance, relative to competition, in the key factors for success of the business. At the same time, the strategist must be sure that his strategy properly matches the strengths of the corporation with the needs of a clearly defined market. Positive matching of the needs and objectives of the two parties involved is required for a lasting good relationship; without it, the corporation's long-term viability may be at stake."

The central thrust of Ohmae's arguments was that strategy as epitomized by the Japanese approach is irrational and non-linear. (Previously, the Japanese had been feted in the West for the brilliance of their rationality and the far-sighted remorselessness of their thinking.) "Phenomena and events in the real world do not always fit a linear model. Hence the most reliable means of dissecting a situation into its constituent parts and reassembling them in the desired pattern is not a step-by-step methodology such as systems analysis. Rather, it is that ultimate non-linear thinking tool, the human brain. True strategic thinking thus contrasts sharply with the conventional mechanical systems approach based on linear thinking. But it also contrasts with the approach that stakes everything on intuition, reaching conclusions without any real breakdown or analysis."

Ohmae went on to suggest that an effective business strategy "is one by which a company can gain significant ground on its competitors at an acceptable costs to itself." This can be achieved in four ways: by focussing on the key factors for success (KFSs); by building on relative superiority; through pursuing aggressive initiatives; through utilizing strategic degrees of freedom. By this, Ohmae means that the company can focus on innovation in areas that are "untouched by competitors."

The second area that Ohmae has greatly influenced is globalization. In

Triad Power (1985), he suggested that the route to global competitiveness is to establish a presence in each area of the Triad (United States, Japan and the Pacific, Europe). Also, companies must utilize the three Cs of commitment, creativity, and competitiveness.

To Ohmae, countries are mere governmental creations. In the Interlinked Economy (also made up of the Triad), consumers are not driven to purchase through nationalistic sentiments, no matter what politicians suggest or say. "The essence of business strategy is offering better value to customers than the competition, in the most cost-effective and sustainable way," Ohmae writes. "But today, thousands of competitors from every corner of the world are able to serve customers well. To develop effective strategy, we as leaders have to understand what's happening in the rest of the world, and reshape our organization to respond accordingly. No leader can hope to guide an enterprise into the future without understanding the commercial, political and social impact of the global economy."[28]

He suggests that corporate leaders should concentrate on building networks. "We have to learn to share, sort, and synthesize information, rather than simply direct the work of others. We have to rethink our basic approach to decision making, risk taking, and organizational strategy. And we have to create meaning and uphold values in flatter, more disciplined enterprises," Ohmae concludes. "We will, it seems, have to forget the past in order to create the future."

Transnational corporations

The transnational corporation is a concept developed by Harvard Business School's Christopher Bartlett and Sumantra Ghoshal (1948–2004). (Ghoshal joined London Business School in 1994 and was formerly Professor of Business Policy at INSEAD and a visiting professor at MIT's Sloan School.) At the heart of Ghoshal and Bartlett's work during the late 1980s and early 1990s is the demise of the divisionalized corporation, as exemplified by Alfred Sloan's General Motors.

Their work on globalization and organizational forms came to prominence with the book *Managing Across Borders* (1989), which was one of the boldest and most accurate pronouncements of the arrival of a new era of worldwide competition and truly global organizations.

Bartlett and Ghoshal, unlike others, suggest that new, revitalizing organizational forms can emerge and are emerging. Crucial to this is the recognition that multinational corporations from different regions of the world have their own management heritages, each with a distinctive source of competitive advantage.

The first multinational form identified by Bartlett and Ghoshal is the *multinational* or multidomestic firm. Its strength lies in a high degree of local responsiveness. It is a decentralized federation of local firms (such as Unilever or Philips), linked together by a web of personal controls (expatriates from the home country firm who occupy key positions abroad).

The second is the *global* firm, typified by US corporations such as Ford early in the 20th century and Japanese enterprises such as Matsushita. Its strengths are scale efficiencies and cost advantages. Global-scale facilities, often centralized in the home country, produce standardized products, while overseas operations are considered as delivery pipelines to tap into global market opportunities. There is tight control of strategic decisions, resources, and information by the global hub.

The *international* firm is the third type. Its competitive strength is its ability to transfer knowledge and expertise to overseas environments that are less advanced. It is a co-ordinated federation of local firms, controlled by sophisticated management systems and corporate staffs. The attitude of the parent company tends to be parochial, fostered by the superior know-how at the center.

Bartlett and Ghoshal argue that global competition is now forcing many of these firms to shift to a fourth model, which they call the *transnational*. This firm has to combine local responsiveness with global efficiency and the ability to transfer know-how – better, cheaper, and faster.

The transnational firm is a network of specialized or differentiated units, with attention paid to managing integrative linkages between local firms as well as with the center. The subsidiary becomes a distinctive asset rather than simply an arm of the parent company. Manufacturing and technology development are located wherever it makes sense, but there is an explicit focus on leveraging local know-how in order to exploit worldwide opportunities.

Ghoshal and Bartlett conclude that, in the flux of global businesses, traditional solutions are no longer applicable. They point to the difficulties in managing growth through acquisitions and the dangerously high level of diversity in businesses that have acquired companies indiscriminately in the quest for growth. They have also declared obsolete the assumption of independence among different businesses, technologies, and geographic markets that is central to the design of most divisionalized corporations. Such independence, they say, actively works against the prime need: integration and the creation of "a coherent system for value delivery."

Today's reality, as described by Ghoshal, is harsh: "You cannot manage third-generation strategies through second-generation organizations with first-generation managers," he observed.[29] "Third-generation strategies are sophisticated and multi-dimensional. The real problem lies in managers themselves. Managers are driven by an earlier model. The real challenge is how to develop and maintain managers to operate in the new type of organization."

While *Managing Across Borders* was concerned with bridging the gap between strategies and organizations, the sequel, *The Individualized Corporation* (1997), moved from the elegance of strategy to the messiness of humanity. In it, Bartlett and Ghoshal examine the factors that are likely to be crucial to the success of the organizational forms of the future.

One of the phenomena they examine is the illusion of success that surrounds some organizations. "Satisfactory underperformance is a far greater problem than a crisis," Ghoshal said, pointing to the example of Westinghouse, which is now one-seventh the size of GE in revenue terms. "Over 20 years, three generations of top management have presided over the massive decline of a top US corporation," he adds. "Yet 80 percent of the time the company was thought to be doing well."

The explanation he gave for this delusion of grandeur is that few companies have an ability for self-renewal. "You cannot renew a company without revitalizing its people." And Ghoshal argued that revitalizing people is fundamentally about changing people. The trouble is that adults don't change their basic attitudes unless they encounter personal tragedy. Things that happen at work rarely make such an impact. If organizations are to revitalize people, they must change the context of what they create around people. "Companies that succeed are driven by internal ambition. Stock price doesn't drive them. Ambition and values drive them. You have to create tension between reality and aspirations," he said. "We intellectualize a lot in management. But if you walk into a factory or a unit, within the first 15 minutes you get a smell of the place."

As vague and elusive as "smell" sounds, Ghoshal – no touchy-feely idealist – believed that it can be nurtured. "Smell can be created and maintained – look at 3M. Ultimately the job of the manager is to get ordinary people to create extraordinary results."

To do so requires a paradoxical combination of what Ghoshal labeled "stretch" and "discipline." These factors do not render obsolete attention to strategy, structure, and systems. Businesses can still be run by strict attention to this blessed corporate trinity. These were, in Ghoshal's eyes, the legacy of the corporate engineer, Alfred Sloan, and the meat and drink of business school programs. They are necessary, but he added a warning: "Sloan created a new management doctrine. Sloan's doctrine has been wonderful but the problem is that it inevitably ends up creating downtown Calcutta in summer."

Trompenaars, Fons

Dutch consultant and author Fons Trompenaars (born 1952) takes as his subject the universal one of cultural diversity: How do we think? How do we behave in certain situations? How does that affect the way we manage businesses? And what are the skills essential to managing globally?

"Basic to understanding other cultures is the awareness that culture is a series of rules and methods that a society has evolved to deal with the recurring problems it faces," says Trompenaars. "They have become so basic that, like breathing, we no longer think about how we approach or resolve them. Every country and every organization faces dilemmas in relationships with people; dilemmas in relationship to time; and dilemmas in relations between people and the natural environment. Culture is the way in which people resolve dilemmas emerging from universal problems."

Brought up by a Dutch father and a French mother, Trompenaars studied at top American business school Wharton. He spent three years with Shell, finishing up working on a culture change project. He then worked part-time for the company before founding the Center for International Business Studies. He now develops his research and ideas further through the Trompenaars-Hampden-Turner Group.

Trompenaars' book, *Riding the Waves of Culture*, was published in 1993. Now in his mid-forties, he has a troubled relationship with the American business world, which tends to regard his work as concerned with diversity, racial and sexual, rather than different cultures. Undeterred, Trompenaars remains dismissive of the American (or any other) managerial model. "It is my belief that you can never understand other cultures. I started wondering if any of the American management techniques I was brainwashed with in eight years of the best business education money could buy would apply in the Netherlands, where I came from, or indeed in the rest of the world." The answer he provides is simply that they do not.

To the ethereal world of culture, Trompenaars has brought enthusiastic vigor. His books are based around exhaustive and meticulous research. At the heart of this research is a relatively simple proposition: the only positive route forward for individuals, organizations, communities, and societies is through reconciliation. "Our hypothesis is that those societies that can reconcile better are better at creating wealth. More successful companies are those which reconcile more effectively," says Trompenaars. The rich don't get even; they get on with each other.

The wide range of fundamental differences in how different cultures perceive the world provides a daunting array of potential pitfalls. "We need a certain amount of humility and a sense of humor to discover cultures other than our own; a readiness to enter a room in the dark and stumble over unfamiliar furniture until the pain in our shins reminds us of where things are," says Trompenaars. Most managers, it seems, are more intent on protecting their shins than blundering through darkened rooms.

Honing in on the dramatic success of the East Asian "tiger economies" is Trompenaars' 1997 book *Mastering the Infinite Game* (written with long-term collaborator, Charles Hampden-Turner of Cambridge's Judge Institute of Management Studies). Not surprisingly, Trompenaars and Hampden-Turner identify fundamental differences in Western and Eastern values. The West believes in rule by laws (universalism), while the East believes in unique and exceptional circumstances (particularist); winning is opposed by negotiating consensus; success is good opposes the belief that the good should succeed.

The differences between West and East have been much debated and there is little to disagree about in Trompenaars and Hampden-Turner's list. But that is not their argument. Instead, this remains the same: reconciling different values is key to success – and it is something Eastern cultures have proved marvelously adept at achieving. While the East settles the difference, the West remains obsessed with splitting the difference. This is a cultural imponderable that is enough to make even Fons Trompenaars despair.

REFERENCES

1. I develop the arguments in my book, *The Frontiers of Fortune*, FT Prentice Hall, 1999.
2. Stopford, John and Strange, Susan, *Rival States, Rival Firms: Competition for World Market Shares*, Cambridge University Press, 1991.
3. The classic statement is Prahalad, C.K. and Doz, Yves L., *The Multi-National Mission: Balancing Local Demands and Global Vision*, The Free Press, 1987.
4. See Qian, Yingyi, "The Process of China's Market Transition (1978–98): The Evolutionary, Historical and Comparative Perspectives (1978–98), June 9–11, 1999; also "Understanding China's reform: Looking Beyond Neoclassical Explanations," Ma, Shu-Yun, in *World Politics*, 52 (July 2000), pp. 586–603.
5. Decision of the CCP Central Committee on Some Issues Concerning the Establishment of a Socialist Market Economic Structure. Adopted November 14, 1993. *Beijing Review*, Nov. 22–28, 1993.
6. The political and economic policy transitions are separated out in my book, *China: The Race to Market*, FT Prentice Hall, London, 2003.
7. Linz, Juan and Stepan, Alfred, *Problems of Democratic Transition and Consolidation: Southern Europe, South America and Post-Communist Europe*, Baltimore: The Johns Hopkins University Press, 1996.
8. See Richard Whitley's discussion on why capitalisms remain divergent, *Divergent Capitalisms: The Social Structuring and Change of Business Systems*, Oxford University Press, 1999.
9. Donnell, G.O. and Schmitter, P., *Transitions From Authoritarian Rule: Tentative Conclusions*, Johns Hopkins University Press, 1986.
10. Chen, Jie, Zhong, Yang, and Hillard, Jan William, *The Level and Sources of Popular Support for China's Current Political Regime*, Communist and Post-Communist Studies, Vol. 30, No. 1, pp. 45–64.
11. See Yongtu, Long, "On the Question of Economic Globalization," *The Chinese Economy*, Vol. 33, No. 1, January–February, pp. 53–76.
12. Yongtu, Long, "On the Question of Our Joining the World Trade Organization." *The Chinese Economy*, Vol. 33, No. 1, p. 28, January–February 2000.
13. Whitley, Richard, *Divergent Capitalisms: The Social Structuring and Change of Business Systems*, Oxford University Press, 1999.
14. Lu, Feng, *State, Market, and Enterprise: The Transformation of Chinese State Industry*, Unpublished PhD dissertation, Columbia University, 1999.
15. *Financial Times*, November 5, 2000.
16. Moody's Investors Service, *Banking System Outlook China, The Start of a Long March*, August 1999.
17. See Gregory, Neil, Stoyan, Tenev, and Dileep, Wagle, *China's Emerging Private Enterprises: Prospects for the New Century*, International Finance Corporation, 2000.
18. Shi, Tinjin, 'Cultural Values and Political Trust', *Comparative Politics*, July 2001, 33(4), pp. 401–419.
19. Country Reports on Human Rights Practices, 2001 http://www.state.gov/g/drl/rls/hrrpt/2001/ March 4, 2002, US State Department.

20 Ding, X. L. 'The quasi criminalization of a business sector in China,' *Crime, Law and Social Change*, 35: 177–201, 2001.
21 See Björkman, Ingmar and Osland, Gregory O., 'Multinational Corporations in China: Responding to Government Pressures,' *Long Range Planning*, Vol. 31, No. 3, pp. 436–445, 1998.
22 Child, John and Yan, Yanni, 'Investment and Control on International JVs: The Case of China,' *Journal of World Business*, Vol. 34, No. 1, pp. 3–15.
23 See Weldon, Elizabeth and Vanhonacker, Wilfried, 'Operating a Foreign-Invested Enterprise in China: Challenges for Managers and Management Researchers,' *Journal of World Business*, 34(1), 1999.
24 See my case, and accompanying documentary on Spanish companies' experience in China, 'Conquistadores in China,' INSEAD, 2003.
25 Quoted in *Business Week*, October 22, 2001.
26 On the wholly-owned formula, see Wilfried Vanhonacker, 'Entering China: an Unconventional Approach,' *Harvard Business Review*, March-April 1997.
27 Björkman, Ingmar and Lu, Yuan, 'A Corporate Perspective on the Management of HR in China,' *Journal of World Business*, 34 (1), pp. 16–25, 1999.
28 Ohmae, Kenichi, 'Strategy in a world without borders,' *Leader to Leader*, Winter 1998.
29 International Management Symposium, *London Business School*, 11 November, 1997.

– CHAPTER 3 –

Managing human resources

"Retain the best people one at a time, one day at a time, on the basis of an on-going negotiation with each individual on their own unique terms."

Bruce Tulgan

"Companies tend to die early because their leaders and executives concentrate on production and profit, and forget that the corporation is an institution – that it is a community of human beings that should be in business to survive, and not to die after a while."

Arie de Geus

"How come when I want a pair of hands I get a human being as well."

Henry Ford

"The micro-division of labor has fostered a basic distrust of human beings. People weren't allowed to put the whole puzzle together. Instead they were given small parts because companies feared what people would do if they knew and saw the whole puzzle. Human assets shouldn't be misused. Brains are becoming the core of organizations – other activities can be contracted out."

Charles Handy

"Amazing things happen when you make people feel they are valued as individuals, when you dignify their suggestions and their ideas, when you show your respect for them by allowing them to exercise their own wisdom and judgement and discretion."

Herb Kelleher

"Your most precious possession is not your financial assets. Your most precious possession is the people you have working there, and what they carry around in their heads, and their ability to work together."

Robert Reich

What managers do

DAVID W. BIRCHALL

[What is the job of management? How do – and should – managers spend their days?]

Throughout the 20th century researchers and observers were eager to know more about what managers actually do. There is an assumption that if we can establish what particularly successful managers do, we can then encourage and train others to emulate this behavior and also be more effective as managers. Even now, in the 21st century, solutions to the managerial imponderables are difficult to find – despite decades of intensive research and observation.

In fact, the legacy of early management thinkers remains deeply embedded in many of our organizations and managerial practices. For all its high technology and modernity, management today owes much to the work of people at the end of the 19th century. Their classical studies of management were based more on observation and reflection than research. Frederick Taylor (1856–1917) was one of the first to write about management, advocating what was then termed a "scientific approach."

Early management theory

Taylor's book *Principles of Scientific Management* was published in 1911.[1] Its contribution to management thinking and practice has to be put in the context of the industrial times in which he lived. Much of the labor entering the newly established factories was untrained and unused to any form of industrial work. Taylor advocated the subdivision of work into simple jobs. Management could then devote its energies to understanding how best to do the primary tasks: the scientific selection and training of the workers, motivating them to perform in accordance with management's principles, and planning and controlling the productive activity. Taylor's pioneering work focussed on the level of supervisor and foreman rather than more senior levels of management.

Recognized as the "father of work study," Taylor's principles have been widely adopted and, even now, are still applied in many organizations involved in mass production or mass processing of paper work.

Frenchman Henri Fayol (1841–1925) took another approach. In *Industrial and General Administration* (1916),[2] Fayol enunciated five elements (together with 15 principles) of administrative management: planning, organizing, co-ordinating, commanding, and controlling. These elements have been widely disseminated to generations of managers and formed the basis of later writings. In 1937 Luther Gulick modified the list to include staffing, reporting, and budgeting.[3] And in a 1931 study of the state, the Roman Catholic Church, the military, and industry, Mooney and Reiley advocated four main principles:[4]

1. the co-ordination principle, which directed attention to the unity of action toward a common purpose;
2. the scalar principle, which defined the hierarchical flow of authority and the definite assignment of duties to subunits of an organization;
3. the functional principle, which stressed the need for specialization of duties;
4. the staff principle, which answered the need for advice and ideas by line executives.

As with Taylor, these ideas very much reflected the times in which the writers lived and worked. Dominant in their thinking was a strong expectation of respect for authority among the management classes, a lack of training and development for the workforce, the influence of a bureaucratic model of organization, and the relatively inward-looking nature of the managerial role.

Generally operating in a suppliers' market, organizations were not under great pressure to change other than to improve profitability for shareholders by carefully planned productivity improvement. Labor was in plentiful supply and there was little government intervention regulating the employment contract, allowing employers to hire and fire at will.

As a result, it would be easy for today's managers to dismiss these theories. Taylor in particular has been routinely castigated for many years. The world of paper-pushing bureaucracy and harsh manual labor is far removed from modern reality. But although the context has changed, many of the ideas of scientific management remain in place. Taylorism lives on in highly functionalized organizations intent on relentless supervision rather than empowerment.

Since these writers, there has tended to be greater emphasis on the human aspects of the managerial role and on leading rather than commanding. For example, American political scientist Mary Parker Follett (1868–1933) believed that in a democratic society the primary task of management is to create a situation where people readily contribute of their own accord. She repeatedly emphasized the need for managers to learn from their own experience by systematically observing, recording, and relating to the overall situation. She saw the manager as responsible for integrating the contributions of specialisms such as marketing, production, cost accountancy, and industrial relations so that they contributed effectively for the benefit of all.

In 1953 Louis Allen was sponsored by the National Industrial Conference Board in the US to investigate what management methods were most effective, which new management techniques had proved most effective, and what companies should do to manage more effectively. This was the managerial equivalent of seeking the Holy Grail.

Allen continued the original research over a 15-year period and in his 1973 book *Professional Management* put forward four functions of management based on a belief that managers think and act rationally: planning, organizing, leading, and controlling.[5] He broke these functions down into 19 management activities:

1. **Planning function** – forecasting, developing objectives, programming, scheduling, budgeting, developing procedures, and developing policies.
2. **Organizing function** – developing organization structure, delegating, developing relationships.
3. **Leading function** – decision making, communicating, motivating, selecting and developing people.
4. **Controlling function** – developing performance standards, measuring, evaluating, and correcting performance.

These and similar ideas about the nature of managerial work have been influential on later researchers, but more importantly on those actually managing organizations. However, these formulations of management work are not without their critics.

Generally, they are seen as focussing on a rational view of organization that tends to omit the human and political side. Also, in the main, they lack support from empirical studies. They attempt to produce a general theory of management work while disregarding the diversity of such work in different types of organization and in different functions, such as marketing, production, or finance. They are based on observations of a particular society that is greatly different from many of those in which we now live. Probably most importantly, they focus on what it was believed managers *should* do rather than what they *actually* do, and they fail to give any priority to the various roles or to relate them to superior performance.

Despite these limitations, the propositions may still have some validity in certain types of organization, though interpretation of meaning and translation into action is probably much different from that intended by the original authors.

Empirical studies

In recent years, studies have rigorously attempted to research what managers actually do by undertaking empirical work. Just as the early writings of management theorists have inherent weaknesses, so do these later studies. Nevertheless, several research approaches have merit.

Many studies have relied on questionnaires asking managers about their work and the emphasis placed on various activities. Others have requested that managers complete diaries detailing their activities or used direct observation with the researcher present throughout the manager's working day. These observation studies have employed a variety of approaches: activity sampling, critical incident, sequence of episodes, unstructured and structured observations.

The model, explicit or implicit, always limits questionnaire studies. So if the investigator were influenced by classical management theory, the survey questions would reflect this theory. Diaries, while useful in giving an impression of the work carried out, suffer from the unreliability of managers when recording activities and the difficulties of then classifying their records.

Observational studies are usually confined to a small sample that cannot claim to be representative of management generally. In the case of observation, it is not always possible to see what a manager is doing because so much activity is cerebral, and it is particularly difficult to interpret the purpose of much of the observed activity.

Many of these studies have contributed more to our understanding of the characteristics of managerial work than to the actual content of the manager's job. They have revealed that much management time is spent with other people. In 1964 an early study of this type reported that 20 percent of managers' time was spent with superiors, 33 percent with peers, and 50 percent with subordinates. Fifty percent of the activities were planning or programing, 20 percent were dealing with technical matters, and 10 percent with personnel administration.[6]

Probably the most influential and widely cited observational study is that of five chief executives in the US undertaken by Henry Mintzberg. In *The Nature of Managerial Work*, published in 1973, Mintzberg claimed:

1. There is a similarity in managerial work whether carried out by the company president, the health service administrator, or the general foreman. He categorized it into 10 basic roles and six sets of work characteristics.

2. While differences exist arising from functional or hierarchical level, the job can largely be described according to common roles and characteristics.

3. The managerial job is made up of regular and programmed duties as well as non-programmed activities.

4. The manager is both a generalist and a specialist.

5. The manager is reliant on information, particularly that which has been verbally received.

6. Work activities are characterized by brevity, variety, and fragmentation.

7. Management work is more an art than a science, reliant on intuitive and non-explicit processes.

8. Management work is increasingly complex.[7]

Mintzberg's model of managerial work identified three overall categories and specific roles within each:

1. Interpersonal category.
    a. The figurehead role where the manager performs symbolic duties as head of the organization.
    b. The leader role where the manager establishes the work atmosphere and motivates subordinates to achieve organizational goals.
    c. the liaison role where the manager develops and maintains webs of contacts outside the organization.
2. Informational category.
    a. The monitor role where the manager collects all types of information relevant and useful to the organization.
    b. The disseminator role where the manager transmits information from the outside to members in the organization.
    c. The spokesman role where the manager transmits information from inside the organization to outsiders.
3. Decisional category.
    a. The entrepreneur role where the manager initiates controlled change in their organization to adapt to the changing environment.
    b. The disturbance handler role where the manager deals with unexpected changes.
    c. The resource allocator role where the manager makes decisions on the use of organizational resources.
    d. The negotiator role where the manager deals with other organizations and individuals.

While it proved highly influential, this research is also not without its critics. Later researchers have experienced difficulties in categorizing their observations according to the Mintzberg framework. A focus on individual activities is also criticized as likely to lead to failure to understand the big picture. Other descriptors are seen as equally valid: later in the 1970s researchers carried out a factor analysis of data collected against the Mintzberg framework and derived six factors:

1. Managing the organizational environment and its resources;
2. Organizing and co-ordinating;
3. Information handling;
4. Providing for growth and development;
5. Motivation and conflict handling;
6. Strategic problem solving.[8]

This research went on to study managerial effectiveness in two organizations. It reported that the managerial behavior resulting in effectiveness varied between the two organizations, suggesting that the context in which managers are working will determine the work activities required for success.

While much of this early research has been influential in how managers view their role within the context of organization design, it is based on observation of organizations that were operating in an environment much removed from the situation now facing many businesses. Numerous studies were undertaken in the US at a time when it was the most powerful manufacturing nation. The threat of Japanese manufacture and service industry had not dawned on the average American. Customer focus, total quality management, just-in-time, distributed computing, empowerment, key organizational competencies, partnership sourcing, and continuous change and improvement were not yet articulated as concepts. Strategy formulation was still the exclusive domain of executive management and execution the province of middle management. Much of the research was based on observing the way managers function in their world, rather than looking at changes taking place and how they might affect the way management might be carried out in the future.

Management work in the modern organization

Over 700 managers, in a variety of organizations and at all levels of management, were surveyed at the Singapore Institute of Management at the beginning of the 1990s. From factor analysis, five "mega-components" of management work were identified:

1. goal setting and review;
2. creating a conducive working environment;
3. managing quality;
4. relating to and managing the external environment;
5. managing performance.[9]

The strongest contributing factor to the mega-components was "managing organizational climate," which focussed on encouraging and supporting employee involvement and contribution. The second most dominant was "organizational work control," which combined with mega-component number five and dealt with the importance of policies and procedures in ensuring the smooth functioning of the work organization. The strategic aspects of the work are reflected in analysis of the external environment and goal setting and review.

Clearly, there are differences in management practices in Singapore compared with Western management. However, the expressions used to describe the components reflect the current management agenda, including quality and performance management, and the underlying factors bear a similarity to those identified by earlier researchers such as Mintzberg.

How do managers do what they do?

Clearly, understanding what managers do is important when trying to understand how organizations function and how one might go about training managers to achieve high performance levels. However, these various studies tell us little about the attributes needed for superior performance. More recent research has focussed on the key competencies required for superior managerial job performance.

The roots of much of this work can be traced back to the extensive work done by Richard Boyatzis for the American Management Association.[10] This study, published in 1982, involved over 2,000 managers who held 41 different jobs in 12 different public and private organizations. The researchers set out to develop a generic model of managerial competencies applicable in different contexts and organization types.

Boyatzis defined job competency as an underlying characteristic of a person that results in effective and/or superior performance. The underlying characteristic may be a motive, trait, skill, aspect of one's self-image, or a social role, but it is manifest in an observable skill. The resulting model comprises 12 competencies in six clusters (see Table 3.1).

Table 3.1: *A competence framework*

Cluster	Competency	Threshold competency
Goal and action management	■ *concern with impact* ■ *diagnostic use of concepts* ■ *efficiency orientation* ■ *proactivity*	
Leadership	■ *conceptualization* ■ self-confidence ■ use of oral presentations	■ logical thought
Human resource	■ *managing group process* ■ use of socialized power	■ accurate self-assessment ■ positive regard
Directing subordinates		■ *developing others* ■ spontaneity ■ use of unilateral power
Focus on others	■ *perceptual objectivity* ■ self-control (trait) ■ stamina and adaptability (trait)	
Specialized knowledge		■ specialized knowledge

Note: Italics for the most relevant to executive levels of management; self-control is a competency for entry-level jobs only

Work investigating the competencies of successful senior managers carried out by the Northern Regional Management Centre for the Management Charter Initiative

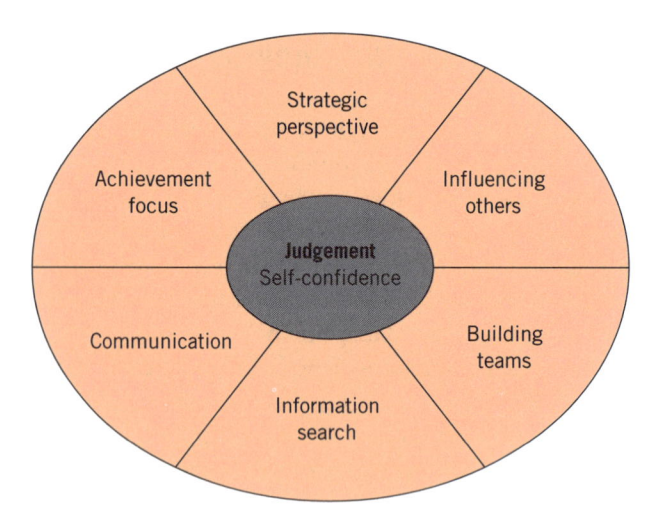

Figure 3.1: *Personal competencies*

in the UK developed the personal competence model shown in Figure 3.1. Each competence is made up of key behaviors demonstrated by managers through a process of "behavioral event interviewing," a technique used earlier by Boyatzis. In their report to the MCI, the researchers emphasized that one particular competence may be dominant in any one particular situation or event, but that it will usually be supported by other competencies. They also point out that effective managers will be those who use judgement to apply the appropriate competence at the right time.

Competence in itself does not result in high performance. The theory of motivation evinced by Porter and Lawler in their 1968 book *Managerial Attitudes and Performance*[11] suggests that performance will result only where the person has opportunities to perform and the motivation to do so in addition to the skills (or competencies) required by the job. In addition, if the goals for the task are not clear, the combination of motivation, opportunities, and competencies will still not result in high performance levels.

Rosemary Stewart in *Managers and their Jobs* found that managers with the same job requirements will use their time and energies differently.[12] Given each person's unique combination of competencies, knowledge and understanding, and aspirations, it is not surprising that managers operate differently in seeking to achieve the same organizational goals. Each will accommodate to the job as well as modify the job to suit themselves.

The benefit of competence models is as much to assist managers in self-assessment and the identification of development needs as in recruitment and allocation of managers to organizational roles.

The research available gives some idea of the work carried out by managers as well as the personal competencies required for effective performance at senior levels. Yet it has become clear that there is no one best theory of management work and managerial competencies. Applied to any one organization, the models inevitably appear deficient. In attempting to develop a universal theory, the investigators have had to compromise and overlook industry or organization-specific requirements.

Additionally, much of the research is based on current practice and may well not reflect what managers will be doing, nor how they will be doing it, in the future.

So managerial philosophies can be seen to vary over time. Our starting point was the philosophy based on the scientific model, widely attributed to Taylor, that assumed workers to have low skills, not to be trusted, and wanting to minimize their contribution while maximizing pay. The resulting management policies are summarised in Table 3.2. This model is based on a contract with labor – the transaction – and the need to ensure compliance. The Human Relations philosophy puts the worker more central to the organization but is also based on an assumption of limited worker capability. Creed and Miles (1995) suggest that the human resources school argues that most organizational members share not only managers' needs to belong and be recognized but also their desires for achievement. This view reflects the shift in the nature of work from highly repetitive and simplified assembly or office work to the more knowledge-based with its higher demands placed on workers as well as the move to greater use of information and communications technology to distribute work and workers. Managers in this model are seeking to work in partnership with their staff with implied higher levels of trust. While the management functions identified earlier still have to be undertaken tasks are being more widely distributed. In consequence further changes are taking place in the roles managers perform and the way in which managers are expected to carry out those roles.

Table 3.2: *Changing philosophies of management and their interpretation*

	Traditional Model	**Humans Relations Model**	**Human Resources Model**
Assumptions	Most people have an inherent dislike of work.	People like feeling useful and important.	People want to be involved in determining goals that are meaningful.
	Workers are more motivated through their pay packet than the nature of what they do to earn it.	People want to belong and be personally recognized.	Most people have creative powers beyond their current job's demands, are capable of greater self-management and self-control.
		Money is less important as a motivator than the sense of belonging.	

Table 3.2: *Changing philosophies of management and their interpretation (continued)*

	Traditional Model	**Humans Relations Model**	**Human Resources Model**
Policies	The manager's basic job is to closely supervise the workforce.	The manager should focus on making workers feel useful and important.	The manager should create a climate where staff can use their own and the team's full potential.
	The overall activity should be broken down into simple, easy-to-learn tasks.	Regular communications with subordinates.	Encouragement of staff to accept new challenges and develop new competencies.
	Detailed processes and procedures, based on best practice, should be strictly enforcedly by management.	Staff should be allowed a degree of self-control on routine matters.	Staff should be encouraged to participate in the overall activity.
Expectations	People will tolerate work if the pay is fair and the manager is decent.	Involvement in routine decision making will satisfy staff needs.	Increasing staff influence, self-direction, and self-control will result in greater efficiency.
	Simple tasks and close monitoring will result in satisfactory output.	Staff will be generally compliant if these needs are met.	Overall satisfaction will also improve.

Source: Developed from Creed and Miles (1995)

The changing world of organizations and its impact on management

The last few years have probably seen changes in the organization and management of work as dramatic as at any period since the emergence of the large corporate entity. Depending on the background of the commentator, the explanations for radical change will differ. There is no doubt that factors such as global competition, the convergence of information and communications technology, and the emergence of the digital economy, recession in most Western economies in the 1990s, the emergence of customer power, and changing political philosophy have all contributed to the changes.

As a consequence, it is clear that much of the work undertaken by middle management no longer requires the considerable number of layers of management that has for so long been a feature of the large organization. In part this results from a recognition that front-line employees, with proper training and support, as well as the support of powerful IT systems, may be capable of dealing directly with the customer and responding on behalf of the organization to the specific needs of that customer.

If one accepts that there is much unrecognized talent at the point of contact with the customer and that empowerment is an appropriate strategy, it follows that there is less need for immediate supervision. The employee dealing directly with the customer now takes the queries and decisions previously taken by the supervisor. So a task that used to take up a great deal of management time in hierarchical structures is now possible with minimal intervention.

The impact of modern technology on lower and middle managers can be compared to the effects of the introduction of automated production processes on shopfloor workers. In both cases, a large proportion of the workforce was no longer required.

Many organizations, when in the process of empowering their front-line staff, have reassessed the role of first-line management. Rather than the traditional supervisory role of allocating work, determining how it should be done, and ensuring progress, the first-line manager in many organizations has become a facilitator. The manager has more of a support role, assisting staff in meeting customer needs, training and developing staff, and counseling them.

Another change affecting management has come about because the complexity of the design of many products and services is increasing, pressures are growing to compress the time from concept to market, and in many industries the costs of developing new products are proving beyond the capability of any one organization. Companies that were previously in competition are having to combine resources in order to share the costs and risks of new product development. In many cases, duplication of effort in the various organizations has been eliminated, with resulting reductions in employee and management numbers.

Companies previously adopted a policy of vertical integration to control the production processes through to market, but many are now changing their approach to one of specialization in areas within their supply chains where the potential for added value is greatest. Each organization will then form new relationships with suppliers and customers in order to protect its position and develop a strategic advantage through its unique supply network or constellation.

Concentration on core activities has led organizations to divest those parts not seen as central to their strategy or have them undertaken by other companies. This reduction in size has resulted in a need for fewer managers, particularly in support functions. Then, as these support functions have themselves been reviewed and deemed no longer central to the strategy, they in turn have been outsourced.

Work previously undertaken in functional departments has become too complex and specialized for organizations to carry the numbers of technical specialists needed to deal with the business problems encountered. So there is a strong move toward the use of consultants, whether legal, marketing, or management. The use of external consultants may well be more cost effective than retaining in-house staff. In addition, it allows companies to choose the most appropriate skills available, with the prospect of appointing someone whose knowledge base is up to date through exposure to the way similar problems have been tackled in a variety of situations and organizations. This broad exposure can have additional benefits in making sure that the organization does not take an insular view. This again reduces the need for managers, particularly in functional departments.

Much of an organization's work is now carried out in projects. Some industries, such as construction, have for many years used subcontracting as the basis of project sourcing. Other sectors have been slower to adopt this approach but now it is widespread. Projects may be managed internally and sourced from a range of outside providers, or outside contractors may be appointed to manage the total project on a turnkey basis. Again, this policy enables the organization to utilize the most suitable resources rather than retaining internal staff with less specialized expertise to do the work.

By concentrating on a focussed core activity and keeping employment levels to a minimum, the organization is able to manage its lower number of direct employees more effectively. Given the greater dependence on this group of key personnel – sometimes called "gold-collar" employees – they are likely to be well rewarded and well trained. If this is not the case, they are likely to see the alternative of being a contract employee as financially rather more attractive and no more risky than being directly employed.

Companies are seeking ways of maintaining commitment and contribution without any guarantee to employees of a job for life. With no long-term security, employee expectations of immediate rewards are higher than would have been the case in the large bureaucracy of the 1970s and 1980s with its "job for life" policy and generous pension provisions.

There remains a shortage of first-class personnel in many professional areas, including management. Numerous managers who have left the umbrella and safety of the large corporation have found that their new lifestyle has not left them disadvantaged, financially or otherwise. Their example serves to unsettle the corporate man or woman who is committed to the organization but realizes that the company has dispensed with the services of a large number of their colleagues.

In addition, as business becomes more global, the economics of sourcing activities change. Certain types of work can easily be transferred to areas where labor costs are significantly lower or for political reasons. The economics of production may be distorted by tax breaks and other financial incentives. With companies increasingly thinking on a global scale, they also need their managers to have a range of new skills and aspirations. Some will not be able to adjust, and others will have to make way for managers from other national backgrounds in order to achieve the organization's desire to become truly international.

As organizations attempt to become more customer facing, they depend more and more on having excellent front-line staff who can offer high levels of customer service and provide information about changing customer needs and the impact of competition in the marketplace. Partly as a result of this change, the role of senior executives is also changing. They need to involve people at all levels to ensure that they remain in touch. They also have to win the commitment of staff to the organization's mission and strategy. More emphasis is being put on a manager's ability to gather views from a wide range of stakeholders and integrate them into a shared vision, mission, and strategy. There is also an emphasis on the strategic leadership role, translating strategy into action, and developing strong core values. Just as the focus at lower levels of management has moved more to counseling, senior executives are having to pay much more attention to the development of their successors. It is also important for them to help create a learning culture and a learning organization.

Probably the greatest contributory factor to the reduction of management in organizations is the realization that managers are a highly expensive resource – the more senior, the greater the cost. Many organizations have recognized that they can have greater control over their costs if they employ consultants as and when necessary to carry out special assignments previously undertaken by in-house management, without the on-going expensive overhead of the employee. In a fast-changing world, flexible employment contracts are attractive to employers for work that is non-standard and not a core activity.

We are seeing the realization of what Charles Handy calls the "shamrock organization."[13] This comprises a central core with a lean organization, supported by a network of suppliers for non-core activities and a network or peripheral staff brought in to carry out specialist and project-based activity.

New roles for a new era

Despite all these changes, the general principles of management espoused by the early thinkers still seem remarkably robust. However, three vital differences are apparent in how work is undertaken.

First, management is no longer the sole prerogative of an elite group called "managers." The functions of management are being much more widely shared within an enterprise. Second, while goals and a clear sense of direction remain fundamental, who decides and agrees those goals and the strategies for their implementation are very different from those in earlier times. Third, organizations still need leadership and direction, but the style of approach required is changing as organizations become much more open and responsive to customer needs.

Nevertheless, there is still a need for management and a role for managers. They are likely to fall into two broad categories:

1. Those managing within the smaller corporate structure or in organizations servicing the corporate. Some of the latter companies will have been created specifically for the purpose, and in seeking to widen the base of their business they will probably be highly entrepreneurial.
2. Independent or networked managers providing specific services to both of the other groups.

Those managers wishing to stay within the larger corporate structure will have to be prepared for continual change, at both the organizational and personal level. In order to remain useful to the organization, they will have to adapt quickly to the business's changing needs. The more successful managers will be those who anticipate the direction of changes and prepare themselves for new roles and ways of working. Organizations will have to be prepared to invest more resources in the development of key managers, but those managers will also have to be more proactive in demanding and using opportunities for personal development.

Much of that development may well come through non-conventional methods such as distance learning, mentored on-the-job learning, secondments, and project assignments. Distance learning will become available "on-tap" for many more managers at a time and place to suit their personal needs. Consequently, more development will be delivered on a "just-in-time" basis, when managers are confronted by a particular problem. Managers will also put emphasis on gaining qualifications to demonstrate their competence and on ensuring their marketability outside the organization, so the qualifications deemed important will reflect capability rather than academic achievement.

Rewards will have to be commensurate with risks. Since increasing length of service makes alternative employment more difficult to obtain, companies may have to pay a premium to retain the people they want.

Managers will have to develop new frameworks to guide their actions in a rapidly changing business environment. For example, the emphasis on core activities and outsourcing requires managers to exercise rather different skills to those required in the effective management of direct employees. Managing contractors and contract staff in new-style partnership arrangements demands a non-adversarial framework or conceptual model. Getting the best out of these suppliers depends on more subtle approaches to relationship building and management, as well as high-level commercial skills. Managers will have to be capable of developing these new models, internalizing them, and adjusting their behavior appropriately.

Many managers will find themselves managing people who spend much of their time outside the office. Employers will accept more flexible ways of working for managers and their staff and be concerned more with work outputs than the management of the input. Such work arrangements are based on trust, performance measurement, and individual appraisal. Managers will have to adjust their ways of both thinking and working in order to make these new arrangements work.

Those managers in the peripheral workforce will have to spend considerable time networking. This will no longer necessarily be playing the internal political games of a large organization to promote their own career but to maintain a number of contacts to generate consultancy assignments. So they may well have to develop networking skills as well as competence in marketing and sales.

Delayering and the introduction of budgetary responsibility even for junior managers have resulted in considerable levels of responsibility at a relatively young age and with relatively limited experience. More far-sighted companies are investing considerable resources in training new entrants to cope with these new demands.

It is important for new entrants to get a breadth of experience at an early stage, probably by transferring laterally between functions or product divisions. By doing this they can prepare themselves for more senior levels or alternatively for a career as a consultant. Traditionally, the latter has been used as a path to senior positions in organizations and it may well prove the ideal route for aspiring executives.

The nature of many consultancy assignments will be political. A consultant needs to be able to enter an organization and quickly assess the sources of power and influence and how they might affect the outcome of the assignment. The skills required may well be different to those that led to a reasonably successful career in a large organization.

Some consultants will spend part of their time as interim managers, standing in before replacements are found for those who leave or to cover for illness. Others will specialize in turnarounds, spending relatively short periods in any one business. The consultant may be called on to carry out specific investigative work, although many organizations are equally concerned about implementation. In such cases the assignment may include the development of a strategy for implementation and then a contribution to the process, for example through running training and development programs. Again, the skills needed to design and deliver a development program are outside the range of experience of most corporate managers.

It is obvious from this discussion that independent managers will have to devote a large amount of time to updating and self-development. This will be achieved partly through experience on assignments of different types and in varying contexts. It will also require a concerted effort to read widely in order to maintain understanding of broad business developments as well as of the specialist areas of expertise being offered to clients. Research skills will be important to keep adding value for clients. The choice of clients will also be important to the consultant, as the key to future success will be an impressive client list along with personal recommendations resulting from high-quality delivery.

The new generation of manager: the all-rounder

One thing is certain about the new style of manager – they will be much more competent in a broader range of activities. They will possess a broad understanding of business principles and a range of competencies, some of which will be at a high level.

There will be a particular requirement to understand how technology can be applied to move the business forward, as well as to have personal competence in the use of technology to aid managerial effectiveness. It will be less important for the manager to have computer literacy skills than competence in recognizing how IT can assist in the management process and then deploying it effectively.

So how will IT change the way managers work? We have already seen the widespread adoption of tools such as spreadsheets. However, in many ways the spreadsheet is fairly unsophisticated. Expert systems will be used increasingly in executive decision making, which will create problems for those who have difficulty understanding not only the opportunities that expert systems offer but also their limitations.

Managers will make more use of international data sources in decision making. For the consultant with a particular expertise, electronic networks will enable services to be sold and provided globally. Networks such as the Internet also enable managers to keep in touch with the latest thinking in their area of expertise, something vital to the success of the independent consultant but also the corporate manager who wants to keep ahead of the demands of their job and build their reputation and career.

Probably the fastest-growing application at present is groupware. Using electronic networks, this has been designed to enable teams of people to work more effectively, particularly where time and distance separate them. It can facilitate the operation of distributed teams and virtual organizations, whether for a specific project or for an on-going business venture. The potential is considerable, although the barriers to making its application effective are equally significant.

Electronic communication is a new art form and managers currently have a clear preference for face-to-face meetings rather than remote communication. This is largely because they can pick up cues from body language and other non-verbal signals. They also use these opportunities to pick up other information peripheral to the meeting, but vital to their role and position in the company. Electronic meetings preclude much of this information.

Managers without this source of information often feel naked and politically exposed. The reality is that the technology is here to stay and managers will have to adjust. If they need other kinds of information they will have to find new ways of obtaining them. It may well be the case, however, that managers will have more time to concentrate on their main purpose – establishing goals and managing complex organizations to achieve them.

Possibly the greatest potential lies in releasing the organization's creative capabilities. The traditional bureaucracy did not welcome creativity. Ted Levitt, in a classic 1963 article in the *Harvard Business Review*, wrote: "One of the collateral purposes of an organization is to be inhospitable to a great and constant flow of ideas and creativity ... The organization exists to restrict and channel the range of individual actions and behavior into a predictable and knowable routine. Without organization there would be chaos and decay. Organization exists in order to create that amount and kind of inflexibility that is necessary to get the most pressingly intended job done efficiently and on time."[14]

Many companies are still working to this model. However, those that are moving toward being customer focussed are endeavoring to harness the creativity of all stakeholders, including all employees as well as those in interfacing organizations such as customers and suppliers. Managers have a key role to play in this process by fostering an innovative climate and encouraging risk taking.

The companies that will be successful in the new millennium are those that innovate in order to get ahead of their competitors. They will be innovating in a number of areas, including:

- challenging existing business assumptions to identify the customers and products/services they most want to have;
- identifying and developing new methods of delivery, e.g. e-commerce;
- product/service improvement;
- new products and services;
- identifying, attracting, and looking after external and internal customers more effectively by building stronger customer relationships;
- doing whatever they can to increase efficiency and/or reduce costs.

Research at Henley Management College in the UK has led to the formulation of eight working hypotheses that form the basis of critical success factors leading to the innovative organization:[15]

- situational empowerment;
- remuneration systems that reward trial and error;
- clear understanding of customers' needs and external changes, well articulated within the organization;
- a mixture of training for innovation and change as well as specific skills, both "hard" and "soft";
- top executives' internal focus of control should be such that executives are convinced of their own ability to influence their situation;
- an innovation fund that at least matches competitors';
- explicit targets for innovation;
- high-quality managers.

Executive management has to create a vision of where it wants the organization to go and then agree an appropriate strategy for getting there. For many this will lead to a streamlining of the organization to increase its focus and long-term profitability. Middle management, in particular, will be a continuing target for change. Some organizations may well have already introduced the type of changes in the way management is undertaken that are identified above, but many have still to follow.

The primary stimulus will be corporations rather than governments or individuals themselves. These corporations will be responding to market pressures, reacting to global competition, and seeking ways of doing what they can best do, but doing it much better.

RESOURCES

Boyatzis, Richard E., *The Competent Manager: a model for effective performance*, John Wiley, 1982.

Creed, W.E.D. and Miles, R., 'Organizational Forms and Managerial Philosophies: A Descriptive and Analytical Review,' Research in *Organizational Behavior*, 17, 333–79, 1995.

Handy, Charles, *The Future of Work*, Blackwell, 1984.

Mintzberg, Henry, *The Nature of Managerial Work*, Prentice Hall, 1973.

Schwartz, Peter, *The Art of the Long View*, Doubleday, 1991.

Leading the democratic enterprise

LYNDA GRATTON

[Over the last decade the forces of globalization, competition, and ever more demanding customers have made many companies flatter, less hierarchical, more fluid, and more virtual. This provides us with fertile ground on which to create a more democratic way of working. Democratic enterprises require leaders to take on radically new roles.]

Leaders are faced with day-to-day decisions that subtly shape the context and processes of organizations. At the same time, they are called on to create and articulate a sense of the longer-term purpose and goals of their company. In making these day-to-day decisions and in articulating their view of the future they are inevitably making constant reference to their own assumptions and their theory of the firm. In particular, they are influenced by their personal beliefs about the nature of people and personal philosophies about the nature of the competitive environment. These are based on past experiences, biases, and personal views. Leaders may be operating a philosophy at a purely personal and tactical level, not amenable to others. But whether they choose or are able to articulate these personal theories, they exist as a coherent set of beliefs.

The first role of the leader in the democratic enterprise is to create and communicate a philosophy that embraces the notion of individual autonomy. They do this primarily by engaging those around them in a conversation and debate about the company that has both intellectual rigor and insight.

Champion of individual autonomy

The relationship BP Amoco (BP) CEO John Browne seeks to create between the individual and the organization is reflected and made apparent in a myriad subtle ways. In the democratic enterprise, the autonomous individual becomes so through a process of creating intellectual, emotional, and social capital within a learning frame of self-reflection, awareness, model building, and choice. The way in which Browne relates with his senior team sends subtle messages within the company about the role of intellectual curiosity, the importance of conversation, and the means of engagement.

Browne and his colleagues were described by the *Financial Times* as "an unusually active and well-financed university faculty – earnest, morally engaged and careful of other's sensibilities." As Browne comments: "This company is founded on a deep belief in intellectual rigor ... Rigor implies that you understand the assumptions you have made – assumptions about the state of the world, of what you can do and how your competitors will interact with it, and how the policy of the world will or will not allow you to do something."

Browne's appetite for knowledge is insatiable and he himself is a creator of knowledge, building a model of the role of the CEO and of the structure and aspirations of BP that he articulates. By engaging in conversation and knowledge creation on his own behalf he sends a clear signal about the appropriateness of these activities. At the same time this striving toward individual autonomy is something he reinforces in the way the senior team works together.

This is how he describes his relationship with deputy CEO Rodney Chase: "Rodney and I have worked together since 1984, and we have worked close up the ranks and it is a very close relationship. You would think that we would be so familiar with each other that we would know the way each other think but it is actually the reverse. We challenge each other very hard, in a very appropriate way, but it is the purpose of the relationship to get a better result, and we do that. And that, in turn, encourages others to do that."

The intellectual curiosity he displays legitimizes intellectual curiosity in others – curiosity both about themselves and about the corporate community. What Browne and his team have done at BP is to elevate the importance of intellectual discovery and the creation of self-awareness and autonomy.

Taking the lead in mentoring and coaching

This legitimization of rational and emotional conversations and support of reflection creates an environment in which individual autonomy can flourish. For Rajat Gupta, managing director of consulting firm McKinsey, this relentless building of human capital is tied closely to the individual's attitude to their self-development: "If you are an industry leader, you are there for three to five years: this is not a lifelong position. I do not have a discussion with the head of the London office about this. It is an obligation for industry leaders to give leadership opportunity to other people."

The same is true at financial services group Goldman Sachs, where choices and support for mentoring and development are seen to be crucial to the culture of the firm and are assigned importance from the very top of the organization. The leadership history of Goldman Sachs, from the days of Marcus Goldman and Sam Sachs, has demonstrated a clear belief in the need for the leaders of the firm to actively engage in supporting each one of their talented employees to become the best they could be.

Stephen Friedman, co-leader in the period 1990–94, says: "Our success is directly related to six things – people and culture, culture and people, people and culture."

Across the history of Goldman Sachs, the actions of the senior team continuously reinforce the relentless building of human capital. This is demonstrated most clearly by the way in which the leaders of the firm choose to spend their time, perhaps their most valuable commodity. Each one of the leaders of Goldman Sachs spends an enormous proportion of their time in supporting, evaluating, and coaching other members of the firm.

Their dedication to this is far beyond that associated with other leaders in the financial sector. Every year each vice-president will participate in a series of in-depth performance and coaching conversations and from these conversations prepare performance review documents for between 50 and 60 people. They will take part in between 15 and 30 conversations with prospective new hires. They will be members of the "cross-ruffing" teams (responsible for the selection of partner managing directors) for up to eight people. At each step of the creation of human capital the time involvement is substantial. Members of the cross-ruffing teams speak with the colleagues of those nominated, prepare a detailed report on the nominee, then participate in the various meetings at which selection decisions are made.

Successive leaders at Sony have also actively and publicly engaged in building human capital. Founder Masaru Ibuka initiated *Sony juku* in which 20 middle managers, typically in their mid-30s, worked closely with him. In small taskforces they identified an organizational challenge and worked with him to develop a set of organizational actions. From this beginning successive leaders have given their time and energy to supporting the development of others.

At BP each member of the executive typically coaches and mentors up to 10 group vice-presidents. Chase, deputy CEO of BP, describes it this way: "I gossip with them about what is really going on within the inner cabinet; I share confidences; I tell them about my discussions with John Browne. I build trust with them. I agree with them what their weaknesses are and agree to work with them. You have to take the time to engage them with examples that will make them broader and wiser. To develop their sense of responsibility for the firm; who they are developing. The greatest pleasure I get is the development of talent."

By engaging in a deep conversation about strengths and weaknesses Chase is supporting the creation of self-awareness and understanding. And by engaging in this way, Chase and the executive team are ensuring that this "talking partner" becomes a model for relationships and conversations across the corporation. In turn, the group vice-presidents coach the business unit heads, as they in turn coach their executive teams.

Supporter of choice and variety

Autonomous individuals are crucial to the Democratic Enterprise but this is only part of what is required. These autonomous individuals need the possibility of exercising choice in order to become the best they can be and, by doing so, to build the potential of the whole organization.

Leaders play a crucial role in supporting choice and variety. Alternatively, they can play a crucial role in blocking them. Letting go, trusting order to emerge from chaos, can be tough for leaders more familiar with command and control. In pioneering companies the leadership teams played a number of distinct roles in facilitating choice and variety. Leaders actively supported widening variety and enabling people to exercise choices. Next, they pioneered the technology and mind-set of an information-rich environment to enable people to understand the basis on which choice could be made. And finally, in some cases, they were active role models in constructing lives of choice.

Widening the latitude of discretion

The day-to-day behavior of leaders sends out pervasive messages across an organization about what is valued. Leaders in pioneering companies supported choice and variety in many subtle ways. Perhaps most importantly they sent out clear messages that people were free to choose. They did this by encouraging people to take roles and responsibilities that were far from their current capability and by maximizing the latitude of discretion within which people worked.

Gupta speaks for many of these leaders when he says: "Each associate at McKinsey must have the freedom to follow their own passions, to have the opportunity to have multiple careers within a career. In McKinsey … everyone needs to learn how to say yes to opportunities which expand their competencies and knowledge."

Pioneering technology and information

The technology that supports the delivery of employee choice is built from employee portals and significant investments in software. At a time when much IT spending has been directed at distribution and systems integration, employee portal investments are often seen as second order. Not so in many pioneering companies where the leadership team personally championed the resources required to speedily embed the technology.

David Reid, deputy chairman of Tesco, ensured his team developed some of the most sophisticated technologies to support consumer insight and choice. As he comments: "We spend a lot of time trying to understand customers. We take that understanding and translate it into detailed plans to add value for customers. We value data-mining skills so strongly that the company we engaged to do the analytical work is now a subsidiary of Tesco."

The executive board was then concerned that it knew more about Tesco's customers than it did about its employees. That was the impetus to creating the technologies, methodologies, and resources that supported the employee insight unit. This investment enabled the technologies and data mining developed for customer insight to be leveraged to learn more about employees and was the basis for groundbreaking employee profiling work.

At BP Browne's support came through a technological platform capable of unifying the different heritage companies of the group. From the end of 1999 he insisted the company put substantial resources behind stitching together the 275 human resource intranet systems it had developed and inherited. As Dave Latin, who managed the project, commented: "Following the mergers we saw this as an opportunity to simplify. What got the board excited was the aspiration that e-HR could touch each of the 100,000 employees and cause a shift in behavior." Browne's championing of the company intranet enabled a much deeper sharing of information and the creation of choice and variety.

These technological platforms have no impact on the creation of the Democratic Enterprise unless they are the conduit that enables meaningful information to be shared. In many of these companies the leadership team plays an active role in the technology of meaningful information.

Rodney Chase comments: "One of the most pressing reasons to create a dialog… has been the rise of connectivity within the space in which BP operates. There are people who by dint of communications, flexibility, and immediacy have the capacity to find things out and transmit the information instantaneously … It is palpable, it is very real, and it is expressed with great frequency. For a global institution we are very nimble. How does it happen? I have no idea. It is some combination of informal word of mouth … informal networks based on career friendships or based on professional groupings, or based on clubs on the intranet. If you've got an important message that needs to get out in the firm it will happen in 24 hours. And you can be certain that every thinker in the organization will have heard about it and will be thinking about it. It means that the forces of inertia have been largely swept away."

Constructing lives of choice

Employees look to their leaders for guidance on how they themselves should behave. Leaders who ignore the diverse needs of members of their team or who reinforce "presenteeism" are a significant barrier to the creation of the Democratic Enterprise. Pioneering leaders supported choice and variety in many subtle ways: by what they said and by their actions. Many have actively demonstrated conscious choice in the ways in which they have configured their roles or in the breadth of projects and jobs with which they have been involved. A few have become role models for location or time choice.

As one of the senior team at BP reflects: "About 12 months ago I came to the realization that something had to give. The only possibility was to leave the organization. Following the BP brand launch, I said to myself, there is another possibility – I can work fewer hours and it will be OK for me to do so. And that is what I am doing. Twelve months ago if you had asked if that was possible, I would have said absolutely not."

The same is true of a small number of managers at BT where location choice and job sharing have been pioneered by members of the senior team. These tend to be highly idiosyncratic choices rather than main stream. But, by doing so, the members of the team are showing that variety is tolerated and in some cases actually celebrated.

Architect of shared purpose

Perhaps more than any other aspect of the creation of the Democratic Enterprise, it is in the creation of a shared destiny that the role of the leadership team is most vital. Without this, independent people simply go their own way. It is this sense of purpose and of shared destiny that stops employees from exploiting the choices they have by building and leveraging their own asset base at the expense of the performance of the organization.

It is the leader's capacity to instil purpose that stops each employee behaving as an autonomous asset maximizer, working individually with no collective responsibility. In the bureaucratic principles on which many contemporary organizations were built, providing employees with limited freedom of choice minimized the potential for the exploitative individual. With democracy and enhanced choice the leader plays a key role as the integrator, the force operating against random drift.

In the leaders of pioneering companies there is a subtle balance between the "hard" of clearly articulated business goals, and the "soft" of strong relationship ties based on trust and respect. The leaders acted as forces of integration by the "soft" of purpose, trust, and relationships, and the "hard" of performance management.

The soft integrators

Many of the leaders used a sense of shared purpose, of common good, to act as an integrating force. John Thornton, president and co-chief co-ordinating officer of

Goldman Sachs says: "I believe that anyone with any depth and any talent has to ask the question, 'what am I doing with my life?' The purpose of my life is to use my talent for some larger and better purpose. I believe that some form of that sentiment is what motivates most highly talented people."

These "soft" integrators were also created through the manner in which the leaders of these companies built trust across individuals and teams and the manner in which they shared power. For Sony CEO Nobuyuki Idei it was his absolute clarity of the goals of the business that created the space in which experimentation could take place. Idei's was a vision of the digital universe: "We have to shift our thinking toward developing, along with the PC and software industries, what in effect are audio/visual-orientated computers and components and the software to play on them. If we can do this, I believe Sony can become the master of the digital universe."

The rigors of such "line of sight" thinking are the performance bonds that tie employees together in a sense of common purpose. But leaders can also create shared destiny by forging relationship ties. The assumption is that individuals are more likely to create choices which are mutually beneficial rather than exploitative when they like and trust their colleagues. Trust is built over time through co-operative and collaborative behaviors and with practices and procedures that are fair and just.

The leader plays a key role in reinforcing relationship ties by being seen to build deep, discursive relationships with their colleagues. Cultures of trust arise when employees are treated with respect and in a just and fair way. Certainly, with regard to justice and fairness, employees are sensitive to the procedures that frame the resource allocation of choice, as indeed they are sensitive to outcomes.

However, at the heart of perceptions of justice and fairness is not the "what" but the "how." Those who lead transformation are aware that the hard wiring of technology and goal setting sets the context; but that's not enough. Negotiating choices one at a time is troublesome. What matter most are the day-to-day experiences of employees. Are they treated as individuals with dignity? Are their choices respected? Leaders play a crucial role in setting this context. They profoundly understand that fair decision making and strong bonds of friendship can bridge the differences in interests and values between employees.

In pioneering companies the leadership team played a key role in building relationships and trust. At BP the relationships between the members of the senior team acted as a model for others. At Goldman Sachs relationships within the organization are one of the key "soft" integrators that hold the company together. Much of the lengthy selection of young associates and partner managing directors is aimed at ensuring only relationship-oriented people get to join the company and then to progress within it.

As vice-chairman Bob Steel comments: "We work collaboratively better than anyone else does. We are collaborative, secure people who are comfortable being collaborative. We enjoy affiliation and being part of the team. Even as children in a sandbox we would have wanted to build a road together."

The hard integrators

A common sense of purpose is a crucial leadership capability. At the same time, leaders drive the articulation of the business goals. The leaders of these companies created a sense of shared destiny by unambiguously and rigorously articulating the short-term and longer-term goals of the business. In each of these pioneering companies the leadership team drives the goals of the business with absolute clarity.

At BP, Browne and his team periodically review the performance of each of the business unit managers and agree on the next targets. According to Chase: "The actual performance contract is relatively simple, a few financial goals – profit before tax, cash flow, investment, return on invested capital – I have never seen more than four. Then there are two or three high-level non-financial targets. Once the contract is decided, people are free to achieve them in whatever way they find appropriate."

Browne, Chase, and the executive team meet each business unit leader quarterly to review progress and agree goals. By building a shared sense of purpose they create a "line of sight" in which every employee understands exactly what is expected of him or her. Moreover, these performance expectations are articulated primarily as outcomes, so while the "what" is clearly articulated, there is space around the "how." These broad business goals set the parameters and create the frame within which choices can be made. These performance contracts clearly and unambiguously articulate the accountabilities and obligations of every employee as a member of the corporation.

The same is true at McKinsey, where there is a clear alignment of accountabilities and obligations. Between 1996 and 1997 Gupta initiated a strategic review of the firm that looked at how to continue to recruit and retain the most talented people. From this came a clearer articulation of what he terms "self governance": "We would be a client service firm and nothing else; that we would demonstrate true commitment to our people; and that we would remain a partnership."

The HR role

The leadership role is crucial in the championing of individual autonomy, in the support of choice and variety, and in the creation of a shared sense of destiny. At the heart of the Democratic Enterprise is a subtle and articulated belief about people and assumptions about their behavior and development.

This focus on the human side of the enterprise places a particularly key role in the hands of the human resource function. In each pioneering company the members of the HR function played key roles as business champions and employee advocates. More specially, they developed the techniques and processes to create insight about employees; they built trials and experiments that enabled them to create variety and test the benefits in a relatively low-risk environment; and they began the process of structuring the HR function around choice.

Creator of employee insight

The capacity of leaders to make realistic and accurate judgements about people requires depth and breadth of information. The leadership teams need to understand what motivates individuals and build a picture of their capacity to exercise choice and the most appropriate choices for them. The creation of this information lies within the domain of the HR function.

Major interventions undertaken by Tesco and BT began with the HR team presenting insights about present and future employees to the executive committee. At BT, successive employee surveys showed that people increasingly felt under stress, that their work and life were out of balance, and, as a result, many would not take more responsibility. When the HR team presented this to BT's executive committee it created an opportunity for the executive team to have realistic and sensible discussions about the engagement of employees and the factors, such as stress and work imbalance, denuding this engagement. Moreover, when the HR team went on to commission a study about the future of work it became clear that these issues would increase rather than decrease.

At Tesco, access to reliable and timely information about employees gave the senior team the opportunity to have a realistic conversation about employees. What emerged from initial employee surveys was an understanding that the axis of the company had tipped toward the needs and aspirations of customers without a similar appreciation of the needs and aspirations of employees.

This was one of the key drivers behind the creation of the employee insight unit. In their presentations to the Tesco board, the unit used statistical modeling and data-warehousing capabilities to present a complex and comprehensive view of employees. The sophistication and depth of this data enabled Tesco to make hard choices about where resources could most usefully be deployed.

In both of these companies employee insight was created using highly sophisticated employee survey analysis techniques, through focus groups, and the use of data warehousing to integrate data on 360-degree feedback with leaver data and performance measures. Clearly the capacity to create such a depth of employee insight is crucial to steering the course of the Democratic Enterprise.

Builder of trials and experiments

When we consider the history of choice in pioneering companies, many began one or even two decades ago as specific projects or trials. The BT location and time flexibility trials began in the 1980s; the BP open internal labor market began at about the same time.

Such trials serve a number of important functions. Perhaps most importantly they allow experimentation to take place at the periphery of the organization. This creates the variety that is so important to the evolution of self-organization. Through trials and experiments, the HR and leadership teams are in a stronger position to make accurate evaluations and to take a bet on what will work best.

For the HR team at BT, the development of location and time flexibility that was so important to them at the beginning of the new century began 10 years earlier as a series of discrete trials. These trials enabled the team to monitor the problems as they emerged and to take "before" and "after" measures of key variables such as performance, commitment, and satisfaction with work-life balance. As a result the team understood that technology could be a major problem and were able to specify the commitment in technological development imperative if these trials were rolled out.

The clear measure of outcomes also enabled the team to write a detailed brief about the potential business savings and the costs of location and time flexibility. The results of these trials formed the basis of the business case to show the impact on employee engagement and output by building greater choice and variety.

Structuring around choice

Academics Joseph Pine, Don Peppers, and Martha Rogers argue in their analysis of mass customization that there are two paramount roles in the process of customization: that of customer manager and that of capability manager. The role of the customer manager is to profile, understand, and act as the champion for specific groups of customer. The role of the capability manager is to manage the product options and choice of the consumer. By doing so they are more able to take a detailed view of the needs of the marketplace and to ensure that the voice of various customer groups is not drowned out. Increasingly consumer-oriented companies are adopting this model to structure their resources.

Apply these roles to the creation of choice and variety, and the role of the customer manager becomes that of *employee manager*. This role oversees the relationship with the employee, is responsible for the portfolio of employees with similar needs, and also for understanding the performance equation for each employee.

To do this, employee managers must know the preferences of employees and be able to help them articulate their needs. They serve as the gatekeepers for all communication to and from each employee. At the moment the only employee groups to have discrete representation in most HR functions are the small percentage of employees who are deemed to be high potential. Building from experience in the marketing function, these foci of attention should be on other employee groups: young parents who want to balance life and work and older people who are still committed and excited by their work. At Tesco there are five categories from which discrete employee management roles could be created. These managers champion the employee group they represent and ensure their needs are heard.

In addition, companies need *capability managers*, each of whom executes a distinct process for fulfilling each customer's requirements. The head of each capability ensures that appropriate capacity exits and that the process can be executed reliably and efficiently.

Employee managers must know what capability managers can provide and must take the lead in determining when new capabilities may be required to meet employee needs. For their part, capability managers must know what employees require and be able to figure out how to create it.

RESOURCES

Gratton, Lynda, *The Democratic Enterprise*, FT Prentice Hall, 2003.
Gratton, Lynda, *Living Strategy*, FT Prentice Hall, 2000.
Kanter, Rosabeth Moss, *Men and Women of the Corporation*, Basic Books, 1977.
Kanter, Rosabeth Moss, *World Class: Thriving Locally in the Global Economy*, Simon & Schuster, 1995.

Succeeding at succession

DES DEARLOVE AND STEVE COOMBER

[Despite the growing attention on succession planning, very few organizations manage a successful transition from one leader to another. Why do so many companies drop the CEO baton?]

An often under-appreciated task of any corporate leader is to ensure a smooth transition for his or her successor. A fumbled succession can damage staff morale and organizational performance. The early departure of a replacement can also prove costly in severance pay and tarnished reputation. Yet despite increasing attention on the issue, companies still struggle to get succession planning right.

Richard Thoman lasted just over a year as CEO of Xerox, taking the tiller in April 1999 and relinquishing it in May 2000. (During his brief watch, the market capitalization of Xerox fell by around $1,000 million – 45 percent.) Other recent short-lived successions include Robert Nakasone who became CEO of Toys R Us in 1998, and left just 18 months later; Gregory Wolf who lasted less than two years as CEO of Humana; and M. Douglas Ivester, who took charge at Coca-Cola in October 1997 and was shown the door in February 2000.

Warren Bennis of the University of Southern California believes that the growing number of CEO failures is directly linked to poor CEO succession planning. Professor Bennis acknowledges that other factors including shareholder impatience may be contributing to CEO failures, but believes the root of the problem lies with how boards appoint successors. "I am certain that it's the selection process that's at fault, not the lack of forgiveness of the shareholders," he says. "Boards that go into rhapsodic overtures about leadership never really define what they mean by that word, nor do they pay enough attention to the human factor."

The human factor

Human factors appear to be the nub of the problem. Most bungled successions can be traced to five all-too-human failings. First, boards frequently fail to define or adhere to an objective set of selection criteria, allowing themselves to be swayed by force of personality. M. Douglas Ivester, for instance, was ousted from the CEO job at Coca-Cola in 2000 after a series of misjudgements. Professor Bennis surmises that the aura of his predecessor, Roberto Goizueta, dazzled the board into doing only a cursory vetting of his nominated successor. "Did the board really take a serious look at his capacity to work with people, to thoroughly examine his relationship with his peers and direct reports? I doubt it," says Bennis.

The second factor is what may be called the Thatcher phenomenon. The leader just doesn't know when to call it a day. Many incumbent leaders are reluctant to give up the reins of power, either hanging on too long or trying to foist like-minded successors onto their boards. "There is a benefit to having an orderly succession process and not staying until the board of directors forces you to leave," says Michael Critelli, CEO of mail and document management company Pitney Bowes. "Beyond a certain length of time you get to believe that you can't be replaced so it is best to leave when you are still on top and still fresh."

The third obstacle to a successful succession is that all too often the process is overtaken by events. Short-term concerns are frequently allowed to dictate the succession timetable, with the decision driven by external pressures rather than the needs of the organization. Fourth, boards have a tendency to appoint a safe replacement, rather than someone who will question their own role. In selecting someone who will give them an easy ride they put their own interests above those of the organization. Finally, many organizations don't look beyond the most visible senior management candidates, and therefore fail to identify potential leaders from the next generation of leaders.

Add to this the usual heady mix of executive egos, organizational politics, and greed and you have a recipe for trouble. What works in one situation can backfire badly in another.

William Byham, president and CEO of Pittsburgh-based HR consultancy Development Dimensions International, which specializes in leadership selection, believes the problems with succession planning are deeply embedded in many organizations. "In traditional succession management, senior managers spend an inordinate amount of time considering and naming potential replacements for themselves and their subordinates. Labels such as 'ready now' or 'ready in two years' are often applied. These systems are often very expensive, forms driven, bureaucratic, and out of touch with organizational strategy. Most importantly, the majority are inaccurate – fewer than 30 percent of senior positions are filled by these hand-picked back-ups."

The right way

Some companies seem to have mastered the art of succession. For companies like GE, for example, succession planning comes naturally. It is viewed as part and parcel of executive leadership. Jack Welch's handover at GE was in many ways an exemplary succession – though not without hitches. GE prides itself on the bench strength of its executive pool. The CEO job was always going to go to an internal candidate. Welch's retirement was meticulously planned and minutely observed, with media speculation focussing on three internal front-runners. In November 2000, Welch finally ended the agony by naming Jeffrey Immelt, the former head of GE's medical systems, as his replacement. Welch stepped down as CEO in September 2001.

Given his phenomenal success it would have been easy for Welch to stay on as CEO. But he was wise to the temptation. Asked whether he thought retirement at 65 was outmoded, Welch replied: "If I had been in this job six years, seven years, it would be totally outmoded. I feel great. I have more ideas than I ever had. But I've been here 20 years and an organization needs vitality. And while we've created a lot of vitality below it, this next change will create a lot more vitality because I'll go and some people will leave. We'll get filled in. It will create another fertilization of the company. So 20 years is why I'm leaving, not because I'm 65."

Others also benefitted from GE's rigorous succession planning. Robert Nardelli, former head of GE Power Systems, who had been passed over for the top job at GE, was appointed CEO of Home Depot, succeeding the company's co-founder Arthur Blank. This highlights an important aspect of the succession conundrum: different stages in a company's development seem to require different styles of leader. Nardelli was deemed wrong for GE, but right for Home Depot as it seeks to move out of the shadow of its founders. Bernard Marcus, Home Depot's chairman, explained that his appointment was a result of a 10-year evaluation process. In the end, the top half dozen Home Depot executives came to acknowledge that they were not quite ready to fill the founders' shoes. Nardelli was seen as someone who would allow the in-house talent to mature.

Homegrown talent

The merit of internal versus external candidates is a topic of on-going debate in CEO succession. The only area of consensus is that, again, different circumstances suggest different solutions. A company humming with self-confidence is more likely to favor an insider, while an organization in crisis, or seeking to widen its executive gene pool, is more likely to look elsewhere.

Research by the headhunter Spencer Stuart indicates that internal CEO appointments are still more common, but external appointments are increasing. Bringing in a CEO from outside can be spectacularly successful. The much quoted example is Louis Gerstner, who turned IBM around in the 1990s. But the temptation to import outside expertise and wisdom, while increasingly strong, can also backfire.

The computer company Apple is a case in point. After its first flush of success it brought in John Sculley from Pepsi to enable it to make the next leap forward. Sculley then usurped Apple CEO and co-founder Steve Jobs. Sculley was himself deposed in 1993 after a disastrous period that saw Apple's market share plummet from 20 percent to just 8 percent. Two CEOs later, Apple's market share had fallen to 4 percent and the CEO at the time Gil Amelio invited Steve Jobs to help. Soon after, Amelio departed. Jobs remains as CEO, and Apple is now making steady progress.

Gurnek Bains, managing director of the UK-based business psychology consultancy YSC, has researched the issue of internal and external successions. "We have talked to search companies, analyzed the literature, and drawn on our own database of CEOs," he says. "Our conclusion is that high-performing companies grow their own talent. People who head up high-performing businesses really know the business inside out and tend to have been there for a long time. In contrast, a high proportion of unsuccessful CEOs have been transplanted from one company to another."

The message is that success in one place cannot be easily replicated in another. "Success is rooted in context," concludes Dr Bains. "So, highly successful executives with one organization often find it difficult to repeat the success elsewhere."

It's a message Southwest Airlines took on board when it was planning the succession of Herb Kelleher, the company's colorful and long-standing president. Kelleher stood down in June 2001. He was succeeded by a homegrown leadership double act. Colleen Barrett, a 30-year Southwest stalwart and formerly EVP-customers and corporate secretary, became president and chief operating officer, with vice-chairman James Parker, the company's former VP-general counsel, taking on the CEO mantle. Kelleher remained as chairman.

Barrett, credited with being the architect of Southwest's customer-focussed culture, concentrates on the day-to-day running of the airline. She has worked with Kelleher since 1967, and she has broad experience in all aspects of the business. Parker, who joined Southwest in 1986 (and has worked personally with Kelleher since 1979), concentrates on the financial and legislative aspects, and provides the company's public face.

Kelleher is not an easy act to follow, a point Parker acknowledges. "Comparing me to Herb is like comparing a 40-watt light bulb to the sun," he has quipped. Changing a light bulb is relatively easy, but with successful CEO successions it is illumination that really counts.

Passing the CEO baton: The Westfield Group

Westfield Group is a private financial services company with a 150-year history. It started life in 1851 as the Ohio Farmers Mutual Fire Insurance Company. Today, it employs 2,300 staff, with 20,000 independent insurance agencies. Cary Blair recently celebrated 41 years with the organization. Now 63, Blair has been CEO for over a decade and has been planning his succession for the past four years.

"Part of good board governance is making good plans and identifying candidates for succession," he says. "I've been CEO for 11 years and that's long enough. It's a stressful job but getting the board involved with the succession process is not an easy task either. First of all the CEO has got to get him or herself mentally prepared, but then you've got to engage your board in it."

Westfield has followed a structured process that began with the identification of a competency model for the next CEO. The process was facilitated by an outside consultant, corporate and executive performance expert Dr Mark Otto, who worked with the board and the senior management team to develop a formal competency framework.

Cary Blair explains: "We asked ourselves what the next CEO in this changing business environment should be like. What sorts of skills or competencies should he or she have? Even though you know you're not going to get all of these competencies in one candidate, nevertheless you should be able to identify what you want. "We got into skills sets and we got into innate qualities that you can't train for. We talked about language skills – should the next CEO in a global society have multiple language capability? We talked about the global mindset and those sorts of things."

As well as skills set, the process identified some innate qualities that could not be trained, including leadership style. "If you think about a leader who identifies with external or internal stakeholders, we wanted a CEO to have probably a little bit more external stakeholder focus than internal. We even talked about the spouses and their role in the organization. We thought we needed a corporate cheerleader in the organization, someone to meet the press and be constantly involved with big customers. That's all style of leadership, that's not education or basic skills sets," says Blair.

Another important issue Westfield considered was the need for a balanced team at the top. If someone with an operational background was to be CEO, they would require a close relationship with someone with a strong financial background, and vice versa.

Passing the CEO baton: The Westfield Group (continued)

Westfield's new CEO was named at the beginning of 2003. "It's been about a four-year process," says Cary Blair. "We've used board retreats – full-day sessions two or three times a year – that talk about key issues including succession, and assess the candidates' skills and what sort of progress are they making. I've been very careful to talk to the candidates about their pluses and minuses. They are very aware of the process. I talk to them at least once a month about the issues. That's a sit-down discussion. And they may be involved in some scenario planning and visioning exercises, so we see how they are doing there. That's good practice, because the toughest thing about the CEO role is visioning. It is probably the number one skill I would require in a good CEO."

RESOURCES

Beeson, J., 'Succession planning,' *Across the Board*, Vol. 37, No. 2, February 2000.

Dyck, B., Mauws, M., Starke, F.A., and Mischke, G.A., 'Passing the Baton: the Importance of Sequence, Timing Technique and Communication in Executive Succession,' *Journal of Business Venturing* (USA), Vol. 17, No. 2, March 2002.

Greengard, Samuel, 'Why Succession Planning Can't Wait,' *Workforce* (USA), Vol. 80, No. 12, December 2001.

Lorsch, Jay and Khurana, Rakesh, 'Changing leaders: The Board's role in CEO succession,' *Harvard Business Review*, January 1999.

Rothwell, William, *Effective Succession Planning: Ensuring Leadership Continuity and Building Talent From Within*, AMACOM, 2000.

www.tcm.com/trdev/dutchsp.htm
www.workforce.com/section/00/feature/22/97/54/

Commentary

When employees attack

Workplace violence is a significant and growing problem in business. We've all seen the shocking headlines. In August 2003 a disgruntled ex-employee gunned down and killed six people at an auto parts warehouse in Chicago. In July 2003, an employee at a Lockheed Martin plant in Meridian, Mississippi, shot 14 co-workers, killing six. The list goes on.

Media coverage of workplace shootings barely scratches the surface of workplace violence. It is not just violence perpetrated by employees; the violence can come from co-workers or from people external to the organization. Definitions of workplace violence vary. The US Occupational Safety and Health Administration (OSHA) defines workplace violence as violence or the threat of violence against workers. Not just physical violence but also verbal assaults. OSHA estimates that 2 million Americans are the victims of workplace violence each year.

Hard data on workplace violence is unavailable for many countries. What evidence there is suggests that it is a global phenomenon. In the UK the Trades Union Congress puts the number of employees attacked in the workplace at 1.3 million a year. *Violence at Work*, published in 2002 by the Finnish Institute of Occupational Health, reported that 78 percent of workers in South Africa had experienced bullying at work. It also reported a high incidence of workplace bullying in Japan.

One reason suggested for the prevalence of workplace violence is a causal relationship between rising stress levels and violence at work. An economic downturn, increased layoffs, increased workloads, longer working hours, tougher deadlines, and increased competition – are all factors that add to stress levels. "Worried at Work: Mood and Mindset in the American Workplace" a 2003 survey by CIGNA Behavioral Health, revealed that 44 percent of those surveyed thought their job was more stressful than the previous year. Research from Kenan-Flagler business school in North Carolina reported in 2000 that 12 percent of people had left jobs to avoid unpleasant people at work, and 45 percent were considering leaving.

The good news is that there are several steps companies can take to reduce violence in the workplace. If violence is usually the result of severe stress, then detecting the behavioral changes leading up to the outburst of violence, and eliminating the causes of stress in the workplace, can reduce the violence itself. Employee screening, training, workplace analysis, and hazard prevention are some of the tools companies can employ to help minimize the problem.

Employee screening may be constrained by legal considerations but companies may still ask questions covering matters such as an applicant's prior violent behavior. Psychological and behavioral profiling are useful. A detailed analysis of the workplace and working environment may reveal areas that need improving. The effects of the working environment on the employee are not always obvious. A study by Cornell University in 2002, "Stress and Open Office Noise," reported that employees exposed to constant low-level office noise such as the hum of photocopiers, computers, and lighting had increased levels of stress hormones compared with workers in a quiet office.

Besides the obvious physical and psychological effects violence in the workplace has upon employees, there are wider implications for corporations, not least the potential cost in lawsuits and compensation as well as the negative effects on employee morale, adverse publicity, and detrimental impact on productivity. The Workplace Violence Research Institute estimates the cost to US business to be in excess of $36 billion. Make no mistake: whether it is verbal abuse, desk rage, or homicide, violence in the workplace is bad for business.

The management of humor and the humor of management

DAVID L. COLLINSON

> There is growing interest in the corporate construction of workplace humor and its underlying functionalist assumptions. But the meaning and consequences of humor can often be much more ambiguous and problematic than is frequently appreciated.

A burgeoning literature now exists that analyzes what managers and leaders do. Typically, leadership and management are viewed as highly rational processes, concerned with "serious" workplace issues like strategy, decision making, and the effective exercise of power and control. In this rather somber context humor, joking, and laughter would seem to be inappropriate and out of place. Jocularity appears frivolous and unproductive, typically viewed as leisure and pleasure rather than work and toil.

Throughout the ages leaders and managers have frequently tried to retain a somber demeanor for themselves and a serious organizational climate for subordinates. In their concern with social control, they have sometimes viewed jocularity as uncivilized or dangerous and have sought its censorship through exhortation or legal imposition, or both.

In contemporary organizations there has been a growth of interest in humor as a tool for increasing employee motivation. Leaders and managers have identified a positive connection between employee humor, laughter, and productivity. There is a growing belief in the value of jocularity as a medium for communicating sometimes quite serious messages. Management training programs frequently utilize humor in conveying their messages. Selectors increasingly evaluate job-seekers for their sense of humor. Similarly, research suggests that in practice it is managers and leaders who most frequently use humor. Joking is often the prerogative of those in authority, and leaders can use humorous situations to facilitate their exercise of power and control. Conversely, in the presence of superiors, subordinates tend either to refrain from joking or to make their humor non-threatening.

In the United States a significant number of so-called "humor consultants" encourage managers and leaders to recognize the workplace benefits of laughter and frivolity. Writers and consultants have promoted the view that leaders should use humor to solve problems, exercise discipline, and defuse tense situations. They suggest that jocularity can foster divergent thinking, creative problem solving, and a willingness to take risks, while also humanizing the hierarchy by making leaders more approachable, making difficult messages more agreeable, and providing a discreet way of sanctioning deviant behavior. Equally, writers have argued that humor can revitalize corporate cultures and build momentum for organizational change.

Management writers like Insead's Jean-Louis Barsoux recommend that leaders and managers encourage subordinates' oppositional humor, no matter how critical this may be. They subscribe to a "safety-valve" theory of humor that views employees' oppositional joking as a way of "letting off steam" without threatening the status quo. From this perspective, a humorous managerial response to employee satire affirms leaders' power because it implies that those in authority are strong enough to tolerate criticism. This view interprets employee resistance in a similar way to that of the dissenting voice of the court jester. Able to speak the unspeakable, the jester's nonconformist clowning reduced hostility and social tension. The jester's very existence implicitly affirmed the ruler's tolerance. Similarly, others contend that those employees who take on the role of "organizational fool" and operate as a questioning truthsayer are able to moderate leaders' tendencies toward narcissism and hubris. The fool's humor is more easily accepted because it is articulated through a self- deprecating kind of teasing.

This view of subordinate humor as a conservative safety valve that inverts the usual power/status hierarchy was also evident in the medieval culture of the carnival. By temporarily inverting prevailing hierarchical relationships, the carnivalesque culture of laughter could be seen as a subversive satirizing of authority by those in subordinate positions. Yet its temporary nature had the broader effect of reinforcing the status quo. A present-day example of this temporary inversion is the office Christmas party where subordinates can take the opportunity to lampoon their seniors.

A number of corporate leaders have deliberately tried to generate a carnivalesque culture within their organizations. In the US, Southwest Airlines actively rewards employees who use humor at work. In the UK the National Health Service created a Laughter Clinic in 1991, and professional comedians act as jesters to the sick and elderly. It is also increasingly common for managers to encourage employees to wear silly hats or pajamas on special "dress-down days." Typically, these "fun days" are organized toward the end of the working week to improve productivity when motivation might otherwise be flagging and absenteeism increasing.

Timing

But why humor? And why now? While job insecurity and workplace stress would seem to make the corporate manufacture of laughter superficial and irrelevant, managers may be attracted to claims that humor can raise employee morale, create a sense of community, and improve both productivity and customer satisfaction.

Certainly, a number of studies suggest that laughter may have positive medicinal effects. Research suggests that laughter can reduce stress and pain, lower blood pressure, and massage the heart, lungs, and other vital organs. It has been argued that laughter enhances respiration and circulation while lowering the pulse-rate and increasing oxygen flow to the muscle tissue. Equally, studies suggest that it can boost the auto-immune system by triggering the release of the antibody, immunoglobin A; a chemical that identifies viruses, bacteria, and potentially cancerous cells, enabling white blood cells to destroy them.

This growing managerial interest in humor also appears to be compatible with the typical dynamics found in many, if not most, workplace cultures. Organizations constitute fertile sites for the emergence of laughter and jocularity. Inconsistencies, paradoxes, and contradictions in workplace practices can be ideal source material for irony, satire, and sarcasm. Humor is indeed a pervasive feature of organizational life, being present virtually everywhere that people congregate to earn a living. Joking dynamics have been recorded in a great variety of organizations, from slaughter houses and betting shops to breweries, and in a large number of occupations from accountancy and banking to selling. Manual work is the most frequently cited setting for humor. Subordinates often deploy humor as a "survival strategy" in coping with deskilled work, high-pressure incentive schemes, and physically dangerous tasks. Far from being austere, impersonal, and somber bureaucracies (as much organization, management, and leadership theory would have us believe), workplaces are frequently characterized by extensive joking relationships.

The *fun*ctionalist legacy

Perhaps the most influential perspective within humor studies is that of the social anthropologist A.R. Radcliffe-Brown whose functionalist approach crucially informs the current interest in the motivational value of humor. Radcliffe-Brown argued that joking relations in tribal societies were vital to social order because they reduced tension and conflict, particularly between those individuals who have competing interests but who must also co-operate to accomplish certain tasks. In his view, the joking relationship was a "peculiar combination of friendliness and antagonism ... the relationship is one of permitted disrespect." Radcliffe-Brown found that teasing was especially likely between a husband and his wife's brothers and sisters. This sham conflict of permitted disrespect was an important means of sustaining social stability.

As a theory, functionalism has been criticized for its preoccupation with the regulated nature of social life and its alignment with the interests of the powerful.

Radcliffe-Brown's research was based on a specific kind of tribal kinship relationship. Attempts to transpose his findings to quite different empirical settings may be too great a stretch for the original research. In contemporary Western organizations joking relations are often characterized by much more aggressive teasing that can lead to dysfunctional feuds.

In practice, manufactured joking relations are likely to be much more ambiguous and potentially more destabilizing than management writers, humor consultants, and functionalist theorists recognize. The classic case of leadership humor backfiring is that of Gerald Ratner, the head of the family-owned UK jewelry chain Ratners, which he had established over a 20-year period. In 1991 Ratner's was the largest jewelry chain in the world, with 2,500 outlets, a stock market value of £650 million, and a profit in 1990 of £120 million. Gerald Ratner was the managing director, earning £600,000 a year. However, in an Institute of Directors speech to 6,000 businesspeople at the Albert Hall, Ratner joked that some of the products sold in his jewelry stores were "total crap." Heavily criticized by the tabloid press, Ratner was forced to resign in 1992, and eventually the company had to be sold off.

Leadership and management humor may also encourage subordinate resistance. For example, employees may refuse to respond to leaders' humor. In my study of a UK engineering factory, shop stewards refused to engage in the informal, joking relations encouraged by the new US senior managers. Employees can also resist by rejecting the artificiality of manufactured happiness and the corporate smile that is central to customer care. For example, airline attendants may engage in "surface acting" by smiling "less broadly with a quick release and no sparkle in their eyes." Insurance salespeople may resist managerially prescribed standard jokes because customers dislike their insincerity. Hence, in seeking to manufacture humor, leaders may actually suppress it.

Research also suggests, however, that leaders can become the objects of followers' irony and sarcasm. Much contemporary joking at work may constitute a satirical debunking of the pretensions of those in positions of power and authority.

There is a long tradition of lampooning religious leaders, monarchs, and politicians through popular satire and cartoons. Wit has been used as a weapon in various countries, particularly where groups are oppressed within authoritarian regimes. The satirical debunking of leaders is also a common feature of more liberal societies where, historically, the adult cartoon has been influential in providing humorous social comment and critique.

Humor can be extremely damaging when it is the vehicle for expressing prejudices or when it is used as a form of harassment. For example, before and during the Second World War, the Nazis used anti-Semitic cartoons portraying Jews as either manipulative capitalists or subversive Communists. Similarly, numerous studies describe how men managers use sexual innuendo, "off-color" jokes and patronizing flattery in everyday interactions with female employees. In a number of recent cases employees' Internet use has also involved potentially offensive sexual joking and this has resulted in dismissals. Sexual joking can have negative consequences in customer relations too. There are a growing number of anti-discrimination lawsuits claiming that sexual joking in the workplace is a form of sexual harassment. Research suggests that some managers prefer to turn a blind eye to such oppressive humor, but their failure to intervene may result in negative publicity and costly court cases for the organization.

Humor in the workplace can be a highly positive and creative feature of organizational life, enhancing dialog, communication, and teamworking. But it can backfire. In particular, managers' attempts to manufacture humor may generate employee resistance or offer an opportunity to express pent-up resentment. Equally, oppressive forms of joking, whether perpetrated by managers or subordinates, can result in lawsuits. Hence, while it might generate stability and a sense of belonging, workplace humor can have highly disruptive effects. In seeking to construct "a fun workplace," leaders' and managers' joking practices may inadvertently have the opposite effect.

RESOURCES

Ackroyd, S. and Thompson, P., *Organizational misbehavior*. London: Sage, 1999.

Adams, S., *The Dilbert principle*, Boxtree, 1996.

Avolio, B.J., Howell, J.M., and Sosik, J.J. 'A funny thing happened on the way to the bottom line: Humor as a moderator of leadership style effects.' *Academy of Management Journal*, 42 (2), 219–227, 1999.

Barsoux, J.-L., *Funny business: Humor, management and business culture*, Cassell, 1993.

Collinson, D.L. 'Managing humor,' *Journal of Management Studies*, 39 (2), 269–288, 2002.

Collinson, D.L., 'Engineering humor: Masculinity, joking and conflict in shop floor relations.' *Organization Studies*, 9 (2), 181–199, 1988.

Collinson, D.L., *Managing the shopfloor: Subjectivity, masculinity and workplace culture*, Walter de Gruyter, 1992.

Hochschild, A., *The Managed Heart*, University of California Press, 1983.

Kets de Vries, M.F.R., 'The organizational fool: Balancing a leader's hubris.' *Human Relations*, 43 (8), 751–770, 1990.

Powell, C. and Paton, G.E., *Humor in Society: Resistance and Control*, Macmillan, 1988.

Priest, R.F. and Swain, J.E., 'Humor and its implications for leadership effectiveness.' *Humor*, 15 (2), 169–190, 2002.

Radcliffe-Brown, A.R., *Structure and Function in Primitive Society*, Free Press, 1965.

Recruiting, selecting, and compensating board members

CHARLES H. KING AND CAROLINE W. NAHAS

[Changing expectations of corporate boards – not to mention stricter regulation and greater media attention – means that recruiting, selecting, and compensating board members is now an important part of the corporate agenda. As in all aspects of corporate life, successful board recruitment hinges on maintaining realistic expectations.]

The first few years of the 21st century brought nothing but turbulence to corporate boardrooms. Maddening volatility in the markets, a sharp decline in investor confidence, intense scrutiny of financial reporting practices, and many high-profile corporate collapses laid the groundwork for reform. For both better and worse, in the United States, Sarbanes-Oxley emerged and the forms and functions of corporate boards will never be the same.

Change was clearly overdue in one area, board recruitment. Historically, the search for new directors was led by the chairman/CEO, who often acted as the critical first screener. He or she would identify a few "good" candidates, meet with a limited number, and pick personally acceptable options; then let a board committee make the final decision. While there was nothing inherently wrong with that streamlined approach, it certainly didn't communicate independence and objectivity, nor did it look like the board had done a full and proper job.

In recent years, many boards have become far better at candidate identification and selection. Still, they tend to make three important miscalculations: underestimating the degree of difficulty of the task; ignoring the limited supply of, and great demand for, top talent; and over-estimating the attractiveness of the opportunity.

Finding a winning team

If assembled properly, a board of directors is the best bargain in modern business because it represents a cadre of expert consultants to management, with a level of talent and experience the company could never hire on a *per diem* basis. The right directors can make a huge difference in a company's performance, but getting a winning team requires a disciplined approach.

How do boards find the A-list talent they need for sound corporate governance? Ideally, recruitment is led by a strong, organized nominating committee, which has the full faith and backing of the chairman, CEO, and other key directors. The committee also needs a common commitment to board balance and to finding the best people through a thorough, transparent process. Great recruiting happens only when people are personally engaged and passionate about the work. Anyone involved in a search must be fully prepared and able to answer any question about the company, a director's role, board dynamics, and expectations.

The first step is to define the characteristics required in a good director for this specific board. That requires a clear-eyed review of company needs from many standpoints. Where is the business going in the short and long term? What are the most pertinent performance objectives? What types of people already serve on the board? That data is overlaid on the current directors, producing a human gap analysis and a profile of the ideal candidate(s). A simple matrix reveals, for example, the voids in CEO or operating experience, industry or functional expertise, or diversity/gender representation.

With a well-defined director specification in place, the corporation must cast the widest net possible to find true "impact players." Previously, board recruitment relied too heavily on the personal networks of the current board and senior executives. Today, a database of thousands of names is the standard starting point and that must be augmented by original sourcing of good prospects. Candidate identification is an incredibly research-intensive process, with lots of blocking and tackling involved. One common pitfall to avoid is star shopping – compiling a list of marquee names, without really knowing the individuals, their specific skills, and personal styles. In most cases, 120 days is a reasonable length of time for a search, with 90 days clearly falling in the category of fast track. The timeline varies for many reasons, but the biggest problem is calendar crowding. Often, busy executives have extensive scheduling conflicts.

A solid slate of candidates can be assembled within 30 days, but then the nominating committee must thoroughly review the list, discuss and prioritize it, and conduct interviews. Because of the ferocious competition for "A+" and "A" leaders, the greatest difficulty in any director search is simply attracting their attention. Facing greater demands from their own companies and a heightened level of accountability in board service, quality people are not inclined to take on any additional responsibilities – unless there is a huge upside potential for themselves or their businesses.

Many companies envision a board comprised of brilliant sitting CEOs from non-competitors. Given the current business landscape, that is not only unlikely but unwise. To achieve a balanced and effective board, consider taking a "tapestry" approach that integrates sitting chief executive officers with recently retired CEOs, international operating executives, presidents of large and complex divisions, people with functional expertise, partners retired from major public accounting firms, association or nonprofit executives, business-savvy academics, and/or senior consultants.

It is important to look for proven leaders who have effectively addressed the kinds of issues and opportunities the corporation is facing. Good candidates must have a well-developed appreciation of group dynamics and a reasoned point of view that can be expressed forcefully, but not abrasively. And, for the foreseeable future, financial acumen is a very desirable quality. To secure one top-drawer director, the nominating committee will need to consider 15–20 qualified candidates. Contacting and evaluating candidates must be done systematically because every top person requires a precisely tailored approach. The initial point of contact can range from the recruiter to the chair of the nominating committee to a board member acquainted with the prospect. Face-to-face meetings with board members are an essential part of learning more about the person and of sharing company strategy and board expectations.

No matter how persuasive the candidate or how sterling his or her pedigree, the best approach is to trust but verify. Reference checking is a crucial and time-consuming part of the exercise, often done best by a third party who can pose delicate questions without seeming to snoop. Some of the more reliable information sources are directors or executives with whom the candidate serves elsewhere. Does he or she understand the business, take the role of director seriously, ask good questions, offer relevant insight, do a fair share of work, not hold a grudge, listen to peers, and in general make the organization better?

The most devastating consequence of choosing poorly is the least obvious. A bad selection represents a wasted opportunity to add someone of genuine value. Since most boards do not have term limits, the company must assume it will live with a director for a very long time. Clearly unproductive board members aren't allowed to languish any more, but it is not easy to replace one. That can have a negative effect on group dynamics and distract the board from more pressing matters. There is no magic formula for compensating directors, but there is a fundamental principle. It has to be fair – both to the person contributing valuable time and to the corporation. A-list people don't serve on boards for the money. They usually want three things out of their involvement: to make a valuable contribution, learn something useful, and associate with other interesting people. If a candidate's first question is some form of "what's the comp package?," you probably want to look elsewhere.

In general, excessive board compensation is a thing of the past. Companies striving for fairness and balance usually arrive at around 50 percent cash and 50 percent stock, so directors benefit from strong corporate performance but not excessively. It is not uncommon, however, for directors in critical, time-intensive roles such as audit committee chair to be compensated more than their peers.

If a company conducts its own director search, it can be difficult to maintain a truly independent process, or the appearance of one. However, if the corporation uses an executive search firm, the result will be only as good as the consultant leading the search.

Boards that do their own recruitment must clearly acknowledge the limits of their reach and research. Recently, a client engaged us after trying and failing on a crucial search. The company wanted an African-American with a PhD in thermal chemistry who was not an academic – a microscopic needle in a field of haystacks.

An outside firm creates a useful buffer between the company and the candidates. Professional recruiters can manage candidate expectations, so the organization won't alienate the unsuccessful candidates. With, say, five finalists for one position, no one wants to lose – and this caliber of person isn't used to coming in second. Also, search professionals can help a board realistically assess its current situation, do a thorough needs analysis, and share best practices of other high-performance boards.

Attractive candidates have a shelf life, so a company must be prepared to move quickly after completing its due diligence. On the flip side, persistence can pay off. In one instance, the perfect candidate was not interested at first, but the executive recruiter, chairman, and CEO maintained contact over the next two years. A relationship of trust developed and finally the board secured exactly what it needed.

RESOURCES

Coulson-Thomas, Colin, *Creating Excellence in the Boardroom*, McGraw Hill, 1993.

Non-coercive thinking

HENRI J. RUFF

[*In many political and business situations logic is used not to make better decisions but to coerce opponents into accepting a particular point of view. Other methods of decision making may exclude fewer people and consequently prove more productive.*]

Rational thought is one of the cornerstones of modern management. Yet, in an increasingly diverse business world, logic can be used to bully others into accepting a particular view of the world. Global business and politics require us to find new ways to foster dialog without alienating others.

Our obsession with logic dates back to the Ancient Greeks. Since Socrates' day our cerebral grasp of everything surrounding us, and our efforts to persuade others of our own interpretation or understanding, has been a process of rational thought. Rational argument in search of objectivity relies on the ability to dismiss the opposing case by means of an unrelenting series of incisive questions. Coercion is a legacy of Socratic thought.

Robert Nozick (1938–2002) has probably done more than anyone else to draw attention to the characteristically coercive nature of rational thinking. Nozick was one of the most creative philosophical voices among the chorus who defend personal freedom and the virtues of the marketplace. A graduate of Princeton, Nozick became a full professor at Harvard at the early age of 30. He made a particularly significant contribution in the field of theories of rational choice in *The Nature of Rationality* (1993), and objectivity in *Invariances: the structure of the objective world* (2001). But perhaps the greatest lesson managers and students of organizational behavior can learn from him is his non-coercive approach.

As Nozick puts it, traditionally philosophical argument is an attempt to get someone to believe something. A successful argument compels or propels someone to that belief. The speed and elegance of that journey constitutes the strength of the argument. This strength underscores the coercion required to influence, persuade, or cajole someone to accept the argument whether or not they want to believe it.

This coercion also rests on a scheme of penalties. Anyone not prepared to accept the position that the force of logic drives them to, runs the risk of being labeled irrational. This aspect of coercion plays upon our emotions for its effects. It ostracizes irrationals, banishing them to the nether-world of the uncomprehending. They become outcasts unless they recant. Rationality is an unforgiving deity.

Freedom of choice

Against this background, Nozick's starting point is to wonder whether it would not be better if arguments left individuals with their dignity intact. This might come about in a number of ways. The root of it, however, lies in the personal freedom to choose, or at least some semblance of choice. If people perceive themselves as having some choice about which arguments they are prepared to accept, they are likely to do so mainly on the basis of their own values and beliefs. In this way they are left with a sense of not having been coerced.

Whether addressing the board of directors, or the layers of the executive, or their consultant advisers, Nozick points to a "road less traveled." Practitioners following this road in business and public service stand to benefit from the disarming eloquence of non-coercive logic in striving for objectivity, excavating root causes, exploring cogent options, and avoiding flawed decisions.

To an extent this already happens in practice. For example, the currently fashionable "menu" approach may have come from the restaurant world, but it can now be found wherever decisions are made. For example, consider the recent but growing trend toward "off shoring" call-centers, often to countries such as India.

The coercive approach would be to make, justify, and explain such a decision to offshore on the basis of the singular logic of cost effectiveness. Objections and objectors would be handled in a dismissive way, emphasizing the inevitability of the trend, and the absence of any viable alternatives. Conversely, the non-coercive approach would be to explore and debate among stakeholders a menu of options and their respective consequences. The aim would be to arrive at a consensus decision, justifying the decision on the basis of a majority view. The non-coercive voice explains and expresses that consensus decision differently and selectively according to the various stakeholders being addressed.

There are many situations in business where non-coercion could usefully be put into practice. Conflict-resolution can be based on non-coercive systems such as mediation or arbitration, rather than the adversarial approach which characterizes the courtroom or the battlefield. Likewise, in the learning world, the Didactic – lecturing – and Socratic – questions and answers – approaches are giving way to the Facilitative – independent learning – approach.

In Facilitative, or Reflective, learning greater understanding is achieved in a non-coercive way by whetting the student's "appetite" rather than the "force-feeding" or "spoon feeding" which characterizes the coercive Didactic and Socratic approaches respectively. Likewise, scenario analysis, and its simpler form of "brainstorming," rests upon a non-linear scheme of exploring the likely, the unlikely, and the unthinkable as a means of mapping possible and plural futures. This is in contrast to coercive historical trend analysis whereby the singular future bears many of the hallmarks left by past imprints.

The non-coercive way does not rely on the force of jealous logic. Instead, it relies on individual acceptance and ultimately mutual agreement. Freedom to accept the argument that accords with one's own values and beliefs is a pre-requisite for the proper functioning of the non-coercive approach. That freedom to choose what is acceptable in an argument may be hard-fought. Alternatively, it may be benignly bestowed upon us by those in a position to do so.

If that freedom has to be hard-fought, then a degree of belligerence is common to both the coercive and non-coercive approach alike. Similarly, the non-coercive approach to argument may be as manipulative as the coercive approach. Regardless of how freedom is achieved, it is clear that even the semblance of that freedom is seductive. Like temptation, seduction is as manipulative as it is difficult to resist.

Forced to think again

The non-coercive approach is not intended to rescue the feeble or faint-hearted, who are less than able to stand up to combative argument. Nozick, himself, was an original thinker. His work was stylish and robust. From his graduate days at Princeton he earned a reputation as "the visiting professor's ordeal." Yet in his writing as much as his lectures, the tone of quiet confidence that comes with the non-coercive style was pervasive. This empowered him to lay bare the gaps or weaknesses even in his own argument, and to offer an open invitation to others to bridge the gaps, and correct the weaknesses. The non-coercive approach is inviting whereas the coercive approach is dismissive.

Nozick is not without his critics, though their focus rests on his first and best known book, *Anarchy, State and Utopia* (1974) rather than his championing of the non-coercive approach. Broadly, his critics form along two flanks, one philosophical and the other political. The former argue that much of his theorizing on freedom, which also underpins the non-coercive approach, rests on fairly restrictive assumptions. The effect of this is to make his analysis only remotely useful to practitioners. The second flank, somewhat misguidedly, regards his philosophy as right-wing.

He grew up in Brooklyn as a socialist and a member of the radical left as a student. It had been arguments with people of the right that encouraged him "to take libertarianism seriously enough to refute it." He also chided self-serving conservatives who were highly selective in extolling the virtues of his work. For example, the emphasis on personal freedom provided philosophical support for the policies of Ronald Reagan and Margaret Thatcher. Similarly, there was resonance with the right-wing when

Nozick equated taxation to forced labor. Yet they would baulk at some of Nozick's other arguments in favor of legalizing hard drugs and prostitution.

Consistent with the tenor of Nozick's thesis, he is not out to convince us of the virtues of the non-coercive approach. As Nozick says, "My thoughts do not aim for your assent – just place them alongside your own for a while." Its real value lies in promoting an intellectually mature approach by a process of reflection. Nozick regards this process of reflection like an on-going journey. As a fellow traveler, Nozick would encourage us to have more ideas as the journey progresses. These ideas will be our own, not his, nor anyone else's.

Nozick's approach appears both disarming and charming at the same time. If you are *not* convinced of the virtues of the non-coercive approach, Nozick would no doubt have been delighted. No compulsion, no coercion.

RESOURCES

Nozick, Robert, *The Nature of Rationality*, Princeton University Press, 1993.
Wolff, Jonathan, *Robert Nozick: Property, Justice and the Minimal State*, Stanford University Press, 1991.

Essentials

MANAGING HUMAN RESOURCES

Broadbanding

Popular in the 1990s, broadbanding was seen as an antidote to the demise of regular promotions and salary increments associated with the traditional career ladder. It involves a compression of the traditional hierarchy of pay grades into a fewer, wider bands, which provide a more flexible and less hierarchy-driven reward system.

Broadbanding originated in the US and was heavily influenced by the pioneering efforts of the General Electric Corporation. It became more established outside GE in the late 1980s as a result of the move to flatter management structures. Indeed, many argue that the switch to broadbanding is a necessary step to support a delayered organization, as a failure to tackle pay will otherwise demotivate employees who have fewer opportunities for promotion.

If there appears to be no reward for their efforts, there is a risk that people will feel disinclined to develop, expand, and innovate. Broadbanding is supposed to mitigate this problem. It allows employees to enjoy salary increases without being promoted to a more senior position. So, for example, a pay increase could result from a sideways move or from developing new skills in their existing job. By focussing attention on career development, continuous improvement, and role flexibility, broadbanding encourages a less rigid interpretation of career progression and provides a sense of direction and achievement. It can also be used to highlight the skills and competencies the organization identifies as important to its future.

Multinationals such as Glaxo Wellcome, IBM, and British Petroleum have already introduced broadbanding pay systems and other employers seem likely to follow suit.

Downsizing

Downsizing is the *bête noire* of management thinking. It reached its height during the recession of the early 1990s. It advocated a wholesale reduction in staffing levels as the key to greater efficiency and improved financial performance. Originally intended as the antidote to the growing bureaucracy within large US organizations, downsizing became a flag of convenience for many organizations looking to boost profits by cutting headcount.

Downsizing was a natural extension of the prevailing ideology of the time. In the 1980s market forces were elevated to the status of elemental forces. Downsizing was pursued with such vigor and disregard for the human cost that its victims and survivors alike came to regard it as little more than a cynical exercise. In many cases where companies downsized, corporate income rose significantly while conditions for many working families continued to stagnate or decline. At the heart of the downsizing movement was the assumption that the sole purpose of companies was to increase the wealth of shareholders.

Downsizing was in keeping with other changes taking place in the business world in the late 1980s and early 1990s. Probably the most significant is the trend toward *delayering*. Much of the restructuring over recent years has involved cutting out layers of middle management "fat" to create "lean" management structures. American economist Robert Topel estimates that in the US alone, more than 12.2 million white-collar workers lost their jobs between 1989 and 1991 and another 3 million since then.

Public anger at seemingly unnecessary corporate blood letting led to downsizing being reinvented in the more politically correct guise of "rightsizing." No one was fooled. Much of the damage, anyway, has already been done. Many companies have lost some of their most experienced middle managers, whom some commentators believe contain the "corporate memory." An optimistic view of the downsizing binge would be that it may have been a painful but necessary step toward the re-evaluation of the fundamental purpose of business in society.

Empowerment

Empowerment is one of the most overused (and misused) words to enter the business lexicon in recent years. As the term suggests, it is all about empowering workers – providing them with additional power. Logically, that means the power to make decisions and pursue the best interests of the organization.

In theory, empowerment is all about the removal of constraints preventing an individual from doing their job as effectively as possible. The idea is to cascade power – especially discretionary decision-making power – down through the organization, so that the people performing tasks have greater control over the way they are performed. Worthy as that aspiration may be, often it fails to translate into practice.

The origins of the empowerment movement date back to the 1920s and the work of Mary Parker Follett, the forgotten prophet of modern management theory. Follett criticized hierarchical organizations; she detested the "command and control" leadership style, favoring instead more "integrated" democratic forms of management. She thought that front-line employee knowledge should be incorporated into decision making.

The work of Follett has found a modern-day echo in that of another woman, Rosabeth Moss Kanter, who has championed empowerment in recent years. *Change Masters*, the book that helped establish Kanter's reputation, also helped establish the concept of empowerment and greater employee participation on the corporate agenda. "By empowering others, a leader does not decrease his power, instead he may increase it – especially if the whole organization performs better," Kanter observed in 1997.[16]

But early signals of the empowerment revolution came from Japan. In 1979, Konosuke Matsushita of Matsushita Corporation gave a presentation to a group of American and European managers. Describing the commercial battle ahead, he quietly explained: "We are going to win and the industrial West is going to lose. There's nothing you can do about it, because the reasons for your failure are within yourselves. Your firms are built on the Taylor model: even worse, so are your heads. With your bosses doing the thinking while the workers wield the screwdrivers, you're convinced deep down that this is the right way to run a business."

His point was that when a Japanese organization of 100,000 employees was in competition with a Western one of the same size, the Japanese firm would win because it utilized and empowered the brainpower of all 100,000 people, whereas the Western company used only the brains of the 20,000 or so people called managers.

The message was clear – but it took several years and a great deal of painful learning before its implications dawned on Western companies. With typical gusto they seized on empowerment as the answer to all corporate woes. But what they didn't realize was that it is a lot easier said than done. For one thing, simply telling people they are empowered to make decisions does not mean they have the necessary support to do so. Decisions require resources (money, staff, etc.), authority, and information. In many cases, companies that talked about empowerment failed to provide these or to consider the implications for training and rewarding their newly empowered workforces.

But there is another problem. In organizations where operational decisions have previously been made by middle managers and supervisors, it is unrealistic to expect them to give up that power overnight or for employees lower down to be ready to accept it.

In addition, the downsizing bandwagon saw many companies stripping out layers of middle managers – the very people who were supposed to cascade decision making under empowerment. Not surprisingly, many empowerment initiatives were simply stopped in their tracks by middle managers who had no desire to give up their power at a time when they already felt threatened by redundancy.

In other cases, the wholesale removal of middle management meant that the transfer of skills required to make empowerment successful simply didn't happen. In the most extreme cases, this created a decision-making vacuum at the heart of the organization, with no one prepared to pick up difficult issues.

Those organizations that have made empowerment work have discovered that it requires a fundamental re-evaluation of the role of managers within the organization – as facilitator, coach, and mentor, rather than decision maker, boss, and police officer.

Follett, Mary Parker

American political scientist Mary Parker Follett (1868–1933) was ahead of her time. She was discussing issues such as teamworking and responsibility (now reborn as empowerment) in the first decades of the 20th century. Follett was a female, liberal humanist in an era dominated by reactionary males intent on mechanizing the world of business.

Born in Quincy, Massachusetts, Mary Parker Follett attended Thayer Academy and the Society for the Collegiate Instruction of Women in Cambridge, Massachusetts (now part of Harvard University). She also studied at Newnham College, Cambridge in the UK and in Paris, France.

The simple thrust of Follett's thinking was that people were central to any business activity – or indeed, to any other activity. She said: "I do not think that we have psychological and ethical and economic problems. We have human problems, with psychological, ethical, and economical aspects, and as many others as you like."

In particular, Follett explored conflict. She pointed out three ways of dealing with confrontation: domination, compromise, or integration. The latter, she concluded, is the only positive way forward. This can be achieved by first "uncovering" the real conflict and then taking "the demands of both sides and breaking them up into their constituent parts." "Our outlook is narrowed, our activity is restricted, our chances of business success largely diminished when our thinking is constrained within the limits of what has been called an either-or situation. We should never allow ourselves to be bullied by an 'either-or.' There is often the possibility of something better than either of two given alternatives," Follett wrote.

Follett advocated giving greater responsibility to people, at a time when the mechanical might of mass production was at its height. She was also an early advocate of management training and that leadership could be taught. Her work was largely neglected in the West, although not in Japan, which even boasts a Follett Society.[17]

Herzberg, Frederick

It is astonishing how little time is spent by management researchers actually talking to people in real situations. The strategist Henry Mintzberg is a notable exception to this, as is Frederick Herzberg (born 1923). In the late 1950s, as part of their research, the clinical psychologist Herzberg and his colleagues asked 203 Pittsburgh engineers and accountants about their jobs and what pleased and displeased them.

This approach was hardly original, but Herzberg's conclusions were. He separated the motivational elements of work into two categories – those serving people's animal needs (hygiene factors), and those meeting uniquely human needs (motivation factors).

Hygiene factors – also labeled maintenance factors – were determined as including supervision, interpersonal relations, physical working conditions, salary, company policies and administrative practices, benefits, and job security. "When these factors deteriorate to a level below that which the employee considers acceptable, then job dissatisfaction ensues," observed Herzberg. Hygiene alone is insufficient to provide the "motivation to work." Indeed, Herzberg argued that the factors that provide satisfaction are quite different from those leading to dissatisfaction.

True motivation, said Herzberg, comes from achievement, personal development, job satisfaction, and recognition. The aim should be to motivate people through the job itself rather than through rewards or pressure.

After the success of his 1956 book *The Motivation to Work*, there was a hiatus until Herzberg returned to the fray with an influential article in the *Harvard Business Review* in 1968. The article, "One more time: how do you motivate employees?," has sold over 1 million copies in reprints, making it the *Review*'s most popular article ever. The article introduced the helpful motivational acronym KITA (kick in the ass) and argued: "If you have someone on a job, use him. If you can't use him get rid of him." Herzberg said that KITA came in three categories: negative physical, negative psychological, and positive. The latter was the preferred method for genuine motivation.

Herzberg's work has had a considerable effect on the rewards and remuneration packages offered by corporations. Increasingly, there is a trend toward "cafeteria" benefits in which people can choose from a range of options. In effect, they can select the elements they recognize as providing their motivation to work. Similarly, the current emphasis on self-development, career management, and self-managed learning can be seen as having evolved from Herzberg's insights.

Interim management

It is hard to pinpoint exactly when the first interim manager emerged, but most commentators agree that the practice started in the Netherlands in the mid to late 1970s.[18] At that time, it was seen as a way to get around the strict Dutch labor laws, which meant that companies taking on full-time managers incurred substantial additional fixed costs. The opportunity to take on executives on a temporary basis was therefore seen as an ideal way to add additional executive resource without the negative effects.

Since then, the practice has spread to other countries. Interim management is seen as one solution to corporate crises and other managerial resourcing issues. It entails hiring highly qualified, highly experienced freelance executives and dropping them into a business dilemma, with a specific brief and a limited length of time to implement it.

Such appointments can actually reassure investors. In September 1996, for example, PepsiCo Inc. appointed Karl von der Heyden to be chief financial officer (CFO) and vice-chairman for a year. A former chief of RJR Nabisco, his main role at Pepsi was to help chart strategy in the wake of a string of operational problems that had plagued the company and to find a "world-class" CFO to succeed him. Wall Street clearly approved of the idea: when the announcement was made Pepsi shares promptly jumped 50 cents to $29.50.

Today, the use of interim managers – also known variously as "transition managers," "flexi-executives," "impact managers," "portfolio executives," and "Handymen" (after management guru Charles Handy, who was one of the first to advocate flexible working patterns) – is establishing itself as a key strategic resource for companies.

In her 1998 book *Strike a New Career Deal*, Carole Pemberton explains the rise of interim management as follows: "An organization seeks help because there are major projects where it does not have sufficient in-house expertise, but where once the change has been introduced, the job can be managed internally. They [the top management team] know that they are getting an individual who has not only done the job before but will probably have done it for a far larger enterprise."

Scenarios where an interim manager might be considered could include any of the following:

- implementation of systems, particularly new or updated high-tech installations;
- helping companies to take advantage of expansion or new opportunities;
- an underperforming company, one in dire need of reorganization, preparing a subsidiary for sale;
- the sudden or unexpected departure or illness of a senior executive.

The wider strategic significance of the interim management concept is becoming apparent. It is very much in tune with other employment trends. According to *Fortune* magazine, for example, one in four Americans is now a member of the contingent workforce, people who are hired for specific purposes on a part-time basis.

There is little doubt that interim management is a timely addition to the corporate resourcing armory. Interim managers are ideally matched to the changing business environment that companies now face.

Jaques, Elliott

The Canadian-born psychologist Elliott Jaques (1917–2003) plowed an idiosyncratic furrow throughout his career. His work was based on exhaustive research and was generally ignored by the mass managerial market.

Jaques is best known for his involvement in an extensive study of industrial democracy in practice at the UK's Glacier Metal Company between 1948 and 1965. Glacier introduced a number of highly progressive changes in working practices. A works council was set up and no change of company policy was allowed unless all members of the works council agreed. "Clocking on," the traditional means of recording whether someone had turned up for work, was abolished.

The emphasis was on granting people responsibility and understanding the dynamics of group working. "I'm completely convinced of the necessity of encouraging everybody to accept the maximum amount of personal responsibility, and allowing them to have a say in every problem in which they can help," said Jaques.[19] The Glacier research led to Jaques' 1951 book, *The Changing Culture of a Factory*.

Later, in *The General Theory of Bureaucracy* (1976), Jaques presented his theory of the value of work. This was ornate, but aimed to clarify something Jaques had observed during his research: "The manifest picture of bureaucratic organization is a confusing one. There appears to be no rhyme or reason for the structures that are developed, in number of levels, in titling, or even in the meaning to be attached to the manager-subordinate linkage."

His solution was labeled the *time span of discretion* which contended that levels of management should be based on how long it was before their decisions could be checked, and that people should be paid in accordance with that time. This meant that managers were measured by the long-term impact of their decisions.

Kanter, Rosabeth Moss

Born in 1943, Rosabeth Moss Kanter has a perspective that is resolutely humane. For someone who tends to the utopian, however, she is a diligent and persuasive commentator on industrial reality.

Now Class of 1960 Professor of Business Administration at Harvard Business School, Rosabeth Moss Kanter began her career as a sociologist before her transformation into international business guru. Her first book, *Men and Women of the Corporation* (1977), looked at the innermost workings of an organization. It was a premature epitaph for company man and corporate America before downsizing and technology hit home.

Kanter has mapped out the potential for a more people-based corporate world, driven by smaller, or at least less monolithic, organizations. She introduced the concept of the post-entrepreneurial firm, which manages to combine the traditional strengths of a large organization with the flexible speed of a smaller organization.

Key to this is the idea of innovation. This has been a recurrent theme of Kanter's since her first really successful book, *Change Masters*, subtitled "Innovation and entrepreneurship in the American corporation." In the book she defines change masters as "those people and organizations adept at the art of anticipating the need for, and of leading, productive change." At the opposite end to the change masters are the "change resisters," intent on reining in innovation.

Change is fundamentally concerned with innovation (or "newstreams" in Kanter-speak). The key to developing and sustaining innovation is, says Kanter, an "integrative" rather than a "segmentalist" approach. (This has distinct echoes of the theories of that other female management theorist, Mary Parker Follett, whose work Kanter admires.) American woes are firmly placed at the door of "the quiet suffocation of the entrepreneurial spirit in segmentalist companies."

Kanter was partly responsible for the rise in interest – if not in practice – of empowerment. "The degree to which the opportunity to use power effectively is granted to or withheld from individuals is one operative difference between those companies which stagnate and those which innovate," she says.

The Managerial Grid

The Managerial Grid was invented by Dr Robert R. Blake and the late Dr Jane Mouton. First published in 1964, it seeks to identify an individual's management style.

Crude as it is, the Grid helps people who are not conversant in psychology to see themselves and those they work with more clearly, to understand their interactions, and to identify the sources of resistance and conflicts. It arose out of Blake's experience working as a consultant with Esso (Exxon), where he observed the effects of different managers' personalities in a traditional corporate environment. The Managerial Grid was a way of characterizing managers in terms of their orientation toward employees (people skills) and production (task skills). This became a three-dimensional model with the addition of motivation as a third axis.

With the Managerial Grid, concern for production is represented on a 1 to 9 scale on the x axis (horizontal axis). Concern for people is represented on a 1 to 9 scale on the y axis (vertical axis). So a score of 1 on the x axis and 9 on the y axis would be designated by the co-ordinates 1,9, and indicates someone with a low concern for people and a high concern for task completion. The Managerial Grid argues strongly for a 9,9 management style. The team-builder approach in most cases, it is argued, will result in superior performance.

Motivation is the third dimension, running from negative (motivated by fear) to positive (motivated by desire). This is indicated by a + or – sign. According to Blake: "The negative motivations are driven by fear, the positive ones by desire. The 9,1 corner, for instance, is down to the lower right – very high on concern for production, little or no concern for people. At that corner, 9,1+ illustrates the desire for control and mastery. At the same corner, 9,1– represents a fear of failure. These two work together. If I need control I rely to the most limited degree possible on you, because you're liable to screw up and the failure will reflect on me."

What the third dimension does is clarify the emotional driver underlying the grid style. So, for example, 1,9+ describes a "people pleaser" who cares little for production, and operates wholly from a desire to be loved. On the other hand, 9,1– describes a whip cracker who cares little about people, and operates in fear of something going wrong.

More sophisticated analysis using the Grid also takes account of the reaction of subordinates. Blake and Mouton identified additional management styles that combine various Grid positions. The "paternalist" style combines the whip cracking (1,9) and the people pleasing (9,1), depending on the response of the subordinate. A subordinate who co-operates, for example, is rewarded with a "people-pleasing" relationship; one who doesn't is subjected to the whip. The "opportunist" manager, on the other hand, is a chameleon, taking on whatever Grid style seems appropriate for the interaction of the moment, never revealing their true feelings.

Mouton died in 1987, but Blake, along with various co-authors, has explored the Grid and its uses in a steady stream of work. Probably the most useful for executives who want to explore the usefulness of the Grid idea is his 1991 book *Leadership Dilemmas – Grid Solutions* (written with Anne Adams McCanse).

Maslow's Hierarchy of Needs

One of the best-known theories explaining the actions of people is that of behavioral psychologist Abraham Maslow (1908–70). In his book *Motivation and Personality*, published in 1954, Maslow hypothesized that people are motivated by an ascending scale of needs. When low-level needs are satisfied, individuals are no longer motivated by them. As each level of needs is met, individuals progress to higher-level motivators. Maslow's Hierarchy of Needs has been used ever since to underpin a variety of people management techniques, especially approaches to motivation.

Maslow asserted that people are not merely controlled by mechanical forces (the stimuli and reinforcement forces of behaviorism) or unconscious instinctive impulses as asserted by psychoanalysis, but should be understood in terms of human potential. He believed that people strive to reach the highest levels of their capabilities. Maslow called the people who were at the top "self-actualizing."

Maslow created a hierarchical theory of needs. The animal or physical needs were placed at the bottom, and the human needs at the top. This hierarchical theory is often represented as a pyramid, with the base occupied by people who are not focussed on values because they are concerned with the more primal needs of physical survival. Each level of the pyramid is dependent on the previous level. For example, a person does not feel the second need until the demands of the first have been satisfied.

There are five basic levels in Maslow's Hierarchy of Needs:

- *Physiological needs.* These needs are biological: oxygen, food, water, and a relatively constant body temperature. These needs are the strongest because if deprived of them, the person would die.

- *Safety needs.* Except in times of emergency or periods of disorganization in the social structure (such as widespread rioting), adults do not experience their security needs. Children, however, often display signs of insecurity and their need to be safe.
- *Love, affection and belongingness needs.* People have needs to escape feelings of loneliness and alienation and give (and receive) love, affection, and the sense of belonging.
- *Esteem needs.* People need a stable, firmly based, high level of self-respect and respect from others in order to feel satisfied, self-confident, and valuable. If these needs are not met, the person feels inferior, weak, helpless, and worthless.
- *Self-actualization needs.* Maslow describes self-actualization as an on-going process. Self-actualizing people are devoted, and work at something, some calling or vocation.

This, Maslow said, explained why a musician must make music, an artist must paint, and a poet must write. If these needs are not met, the person feels restless, on edge, tense, and lacking something. Lower needs may also produce a restless feeling, but the cause is easier to identify. If a person is hungry, unsafe, not loved or accepted, or lacking self-esteem, the cause is apparent. But it is not always clear what a person wants when there is a need for self-actualization.

Maslow believed that the only reason people would not move through the scale of needs to self-actualization is because of the hindrances placed in their way by society, including their employer. Work can be a hindrance or can promote personal growth. Maslow indicated that an improved educational process could take some of the steps listed below to promote personal growth:

- Teach people to be authentic; to be aware of their inner selves and to hear their inner-feeling voices.
- Teach people to transcend their own cultural conditioning, and become world citizens.
- Help people discover their vocation in life, their calling, fate, or destiny. This is especially focussed on finding the right career and the right mate.
- Teach people that life is precious, that there is joy to be experienced in life, and if people are open to seeing the good and joyous in all kinds of situations, it makes life worth living.

Maslow's work can be regarded as utopian, but it was undoubtedly a powerful argument for more inclusive and humane thinking to be applied in the workplace.

Mayo, Elton

The Australian Elton Mayo (1880–1949) had an interestingly diverse career, although he remains best known – if known at all – for his contribution to the famous Hawthorne experiments into motivation.

The Hawthorne Studies were carried out at Western Electric's Chicago plant between 1927 and 1932. Their significance lay not so much in their results and discoveries, although these were clearly important, but in the statement they made – that whatever the dictates of mass production and Scientific Management, people and their motivation were critical to the success of any business; and in their legacy – the Human Relations school of thinkers which emerged in the 1940s and 1950s.

Mayo's belief that the humanity needed to be restored to the workplace struck a chord at a time when the dehumanizing side of mass production was beginning to be more fully appreciated. "So long as commerce specializes in business methods which take no account of human nature and social motives, so long may we expect strikes and sabotage to be the ordinary accompaniment of industry," Mayo noted. He championed the case for teamworking and for improved communications between management and workforce. The Hawthorne research revealed informal organizations between groups as a potentially powerful force that companies could utilize or ignore.

Mayo's work and that of his fellow Hawthorne researchers redressed the balance in management theorizing. The scientific bias of earlier researchers was put into a new perspective. Mayo's work served as a foundation for all who followed on the humanist side of the divide.

Packard, David

David Packard (1912–96) was one half of the partnership that created one of the business and management benchmarks of the last century. In 1937, with a mere $538 and a rented garage in Palo Alto, California, Bill Hewlett and David Packard created one of the most successful corporations in the world. "We thought we would have a job for ourselves. That's all we thought about in the beginning," said Packard. "We hadn't the slightest idea of building a big company." That garage was the birthplace of Silicon Valley.

Hewlett and Packard's legacy lies in the culture of the company they created and the management style they used to run it, the HP way. From the very start, Hewlett-Packard worked to a few fundamental principles. It did not believe in long-term borrowing to secure the expansion of the business. Its recipe for growth was simply that its products needed to be leaders in their markets. It got on with the job.

The company believed that people could be trusted and should always be treated with respect and dignity. "We both felt fundamentally that people want to do a good job. They just need guidelines on how to do it," said Packard.

HP believed that management should be available and involved – Managing By Wandering About was the motto. Indeed, rather than the administrative suggestions of management, Packard preferred to talk of leadership. If there was conflict, it had to be tackled through communication and consensus rather than confrontation.

While all about were turning into conglomerates, Hewlett and Packard kept their heads down and continued with their methods. When their divisions grew too big – and by that they meant around 1,500 people – they split them up to ensure that they didn't spiral out of control.

They kept it simple. Nice guys built a nice company. Their values worked to save the company when times were hard. During the 1970s recession, Hewlett-Packard staff took a 10 percent pay cut and worked 10 percent fewer hours. Commitment to people clearly fostered commitment to the company.

Packard retired as chairman in 1993. On his death in 1996, the company had 100,000 employees in 120 countries with revenues of $31 billion.

Peters, Tom

In 1982, Thomas J. Peters and Robert H. Waterman's *In Search of Excellence* was published. This marked a watershed in business book publishing. Since then, the market has exploded into a multi-million pound global extravaganza. And, in parallel, the management guru industry has burgeoned.

Tom Peters (born 1942) was born and brought up near Baltimore. He studied engineering at Cornell University and served in Vietnam. He also worked for the drug enforcement agency in Washington. Peters has an MBA and PhD from Stanford, where he encountered a number of influential figures, including Gene Webb and Harold Leavitt. After Stanford he joined the consultancy firm McKinsey & Company. He left the firm (prior to the publication of *In Search of Excellence*) to work independently.

Tom Peters was both a beneficiary and the instigator of the boom in business books and the rise of the guru business. He was, in effect, the first management guru. While his predecessors were doughty, low-profile academics, Peters was high profile and media friendly. A business sprung up around him. First there were the books, then the videos, the consultancy, and the conferences. The medium threatened to engulf the message.

Peters' critics suggest that while he may have raised awareness, he has done so in a superficial way. He has pandered to the masses. Although his messages are often hard hitting, they are overly adorned with empty phrase making – "yesterday's behemoths are out of step with tomorrow's madcap marketplace" – and with insufficient attention to the details of implementation.

Over the years, the message has been radically overhauled. Peters' ideas have been refined, popularized, and, in many cases, entirely changed. What he celebrates today is liable to be dismissed in his next book. His critics suggest that Peters vacillates as readily as he pontificates.

In Search of Excellence celebrated big companies. Its selection of 43 "excellent" organizations featured such names as IBM, General Electric, Procter & Gamble, Johnson & Johnson, and Exxon. The book presented, on the surface at least, the bright side of an American crisis. The Japanese were seemingly taking over the industrial world, unemployment was rising, depression was a reality, and the prospects for the future looked bleak. The management world was ready for good news and Peters and Waterman provided it.

For such a trail-blazing book, *In Search of Excellence* is, in retrospect at least, surprisingly uncontroversial. Peters and Waterman admitted that what they had to say was not particularly original. But they also had the insight to observe that the ideas they were espousing had been generally left behind, ignored, or overlooked by management theorists.

Peters and Waterman's conclusions were distilled down into eight crucial characteristics. These have largely stood the test of time:

- a bias for action;
- close to the customer;
- autonomy and entrepreneurship;
- productivity through people;
- hands-on values driven;
- stick to the knitting;
- simple form, lean staff;
- simultaneous loose-tight properties.

Two years after *In Search of Excellence* was published, US magazine covered its front page with a single headline: "Oops!" It then went on to reveal that the companies featured in *In Search of Excellence* were anything but excellent. The article claimed that about a quarter of the "excellent" companies were struggling. The single and undeniable fact that the excellent companies of 1982 were no longer all excellent two years later has continued to haunt Peters. "We started to get beaten up. When the magazine ran the *Oops* story it was a bad week," says Peters. "I was certain the phone would stop ringing. I wouldn't disagree that I had been on the road too much and in that respect it was a great wake-up call."

Peters' next two books carried on in much the same vein. *A Passion for Excellence* (1985) emphasized the need for leadership. Co-written with Nancy Austin, it was hugely successful but added little in the way of ideas. His next book, *Thriving on Chaos* (1987), was an answer to the big question: How could you become excellent?

Thriving on Chaos opened with the bravado proclamation: "There are no excellent companies." This is probably the most quoted single line from Peters' work – either used as proof of his inconsistency, as evidence that he learned from his mistakes, or as a damning indictment of his propensity to write in slogans. *Thriving on Chaos* was a lengthy riposte to all those critics who suggested that Peters' theories could not be turned into reality. Each chapter ended with a short list of suggested action points. "*Thriving on Chaos* was the final, engineering-like, tidying up," says Peters. "It was organized in a hyper-organized engineering fashion."

The major change in Peters' thinking occurred at the beginning of the 1990s. In effect, he dismissed the past and heralded in a brave new world of small units, freewheeling project-based structures, hierarchy-free teams in constant communication. Big was no longer beautiful and corporate structure, previously ignored by Peters, was predominant.

Peters did not mean structure in the traditional hierarchical and functional sense. Indeed, his exemplars of the new organizational structure were notable for their apparent lack of structure. And herein lay his point. Companies such as CNN, ABB, and Body Shop thrived through having highly flexible structures able to change to meet the business needs of the moment. Free flowing, impossible to pin down, unchartable, simple yet complex, these were the paradoxical structures of the future. "Tomorrow's effective organization will be conjured up anew each day," Peters pronounced.

Key to the new corporate structures envisaged by Peters were networks with customers, with suppliers, and, indeed, with anyone else who could help the business deliver. "Old ideas about size must be scuttled. 'New big,' which can be very big indeed, is 'network big.' That is, size measured by market power, say, is a function of the firm's extended family of fleeting and semi-permanent cohorts, not so much a matter of what it owns and directly controls," he wrote.

Examining his output, Peters is engagingly candid. "My books could be by different authors. I have no patience with consistency so regard it as a good thing. I consider inconsistency as a compliment."

To Peters the moment is all important. If what he sees and what he thinks run totally counter to what he has previously argued, it is simply proof that circumstances have changed. (Not for nothing did Peters name his boat *The Cromwell*, inspired by Oliver Cromwell's comment, "No one rises so high as he who knows not whither he is going.")

Indeed, what distinguishes Peters – and partly explains his success – is that he is not shackled to a particular perspective. While Michael Porter covers competitiveness and Rosabeth Moss Kanter human resources, Peters stalks restlessly from one issue to another. He has also proved remarkably adept at picking up ideas at exactly the right time. He has moved with the flow of ideas, but has always managed to be ahead of the tide.

If there is a consistent strand through his work, Peters believes it is "a bias for action." Forget the theorizing, get on with the job. This is a message that leads academics to shake their heads at its simplicity. With managers, however, it appears to strike a chord.

Psychological contract

During the stable 1950s and 1960s, the careers enjoyed by corporate executives were built on an implicit understanding and mutual trust. Influenced by their parents' hardships in the 1930s to value job security, and by their parents' military service in the Second World War to be obedient to those above, the term "organization man" or "corporate man" was invented for this generation.

Implicit to such careers was the understanding that loyalty and solid performance brought job security. This was mutually beneficial. The executive gained a respectable income and a high degree of security. The company gained loyal, hard-working executives. This unspoken pact became known as the psychological contract. The originator of the phrase was the social psychologist Ed Schein of MIT. Schein's interest in the employee–employer relationship developed during the late 1950s. He noted the similarities between the brainwashing of prisoners of war that he had witnessed during the Korean War and the corporate indoctrination carried out by the likes of GE and IBM.

As Schein's link with brainwashing suggests, there was more to the psychological contract than a cozy mutually beneficial deal. It raised a number of issues. First, the psychological contract was built around loyalty. While loyalty is a positive quality, it can easily become blind. What if the corporate strategy is wrong or the company is engaged in unlawful or immoral acts?

The second issue was perspectives. With careers neatly mapped out, executives were not encouraged to look over their corporate parapets to seek out broader viewpoints. The corporation became a self-contained and self-perpetuating world supported by a complex array of checks, systems, and hierarchies.

Clearly, such an environment was hardly conducive to the fostering of dynamic risk takers. The reality was that the psychological contract placed a premium on loyalty rather than ability, and allowed a great many poor performers to seek out corporate havens. It was also significant that the psychological contract was regarded as the preserve of management. Lower down the hierarchy, people were hired and fired with abandon.

The rash of downsizing in the 1980s and 1990s marked the end of the psychological contract that had existed for decades. Expectations have now changed on both sides. Employers no longer wish to make commitments – even implicit ones – to long-term employment. The emphasis is on flexibility. On the other side, employees are keen to develop their skills and take charge of their own careers. Employability is the height of corporate fashion.

The new reality of corporate life means that the traditional psychological contract between employer and employee is unlikely to return. But in any employment deal, each side carries expectations, aspirations, and an understanding of the expectations and aspirations of the other side. The challenge is for both sides to make the new psychological contract an explicit arrangement.

Schein, Edgar

Social psychologist Ed Schein (born 1928) has eschewed a high media profile during a lengthy academic career. Yet his work has exerted a steadily growing influence on management theory, particularly over the last 20 years. His thinking on corporate cultures and careers has proved highly important.

Schein joined MIT in 1956 and initially worked under the influence of Douglas McGregor. He has remained there ever since.

Schein noted the similarities between the brainwashing of prisoners of war and the corporate indoctrination carried out by the likes of GE at its Crotonville training base and IBM at Sands Point. "There were enormous similarities between the brainwashing of the POWs and the executives I encountered at MIT," says Schein. "I didn't see brainwashing as bad. What were bad were the values of the Communists. If we don't like the values, we don't approve of brainwashing." From this work came Schein's 1961 book, *Coercive Persuasion*.

The ability of strong values to influence groups of people is a strand that has continued throughout Schein's work. As he points out, recent trends, such as the learning organization (championed by his MIT colleague Peter Senge), are derivatives of brainwashing – "Organizational learning is a new version of coercive persuasion," he says.

The dynamics of groups and Schein's knowledge of brainwashing led to a developing interest in corporate culture, a term Schein is widely credited with inventing. His work on corporate culture culminated in the 1985 book *Organizational Culture and Leadership*. He describes culture as "a pattern of basic assumptions – invented, discovered, or developed by a given group as it learns to cope with its problems of external adaptation and internal integration – that has worked well enough to be considered valid and, therefore, to be taught to new members as the correct way to perceive, think, and feel in relation to those problems."

These basic assumptions, says Schein, can be categorized along five dimensions:

- Humanity's relationship to nature – while some companies regard themselves as masters of their own destiny, others are submissive, willing to accept the domination of their external environment.

- The nature of reality and truth – organizations and managers adopt a wide variety of methods to reach what becomes accepted as the organizational "truth," through debate, dictatorship, or simple acceptance that if something achieves the objective it is right.

- The nature of people – organizations differ in their views of human nature. Some follow McGregor's Theory X and work on the principle that people will not do the job if they can avoid it. Others regard people in a more positive light and attempt to enable them to fulfill their potential for the benefit of both sides.

- The nature of human activity – the West has traditionally emphasized tasks and their completion rather than the more philosophical side of work. Achievement is all. Schein suggests an alternative approach – "being-in-becoming" – emphasizing self-fulfillment and development.

- The nature of human relationships – organizations make a variety of assumptions about how people interact with each other. Some facilitate social interaction, while others regard it as an unnecessary distraction.

These five categories are not mutually exclusive, but are in a constant state of development and flux. Culture does not stand still.

Key to the creation and development of corporate culture are the values embraced by the organization. Schein acknowledges that a single person can shape these values and, as a result, an entire corporate culture. He identifies three stages in the development of a corporate culture: birth and early growth, organizational mid-life, and organizational maturity.

More recently, Schein's work on culture has identified three cultures of management that he labels "the key to organizational learning in the 21st century." The three cultures are the operator culture ("an internal culture based on operational success"); the engineering culture (created by "the designers and technocrats who drive the core technologies of the organization"); and the executive culture, formed by executive management, the CEO, and immediate subordinates. Success is related to how well the three cultures are aligned. It is a precarious balance, easily disturbed. For example, when executives move from one industry to another, cultures are often pushed out of alignment.

Another focus of Schein's attentions in recent years has been the subject of careers. He originated key phrases such as the psychological contract – the unspoken bond between employee and employer – and career anchors. Schein proposed that when mature we have a single "career anchor," the underlying career value that we could not surrender. "Over the last 25 years, because of dual careers and social changes, the emphasis of careers has shifted," he says. "The career is no longer overarching. It is probably healthy because it makes people more independent. Lifestyle has become the increasingly important career anchor."

Succession planning

Succession planning is all about having able understudies in place to step into key positions when they become vacant. Although it is often associated with senior management roles, it is a key issue running right through an organization.

In recent years, it has become increasingly evident that the transfer of power from one leader to the next can have a major impact not just on morale and business performance but also on a company's share price.

Until very recently, most companies of any size created succession plans for senior posts, and development plans for key individuals in order to ensure that there was a ready supply of individuals prepared for the top jobs in the future. Usually, this involved accelerated or "fast-track" programs for so-called high flyers – graduates and other high-potential recruits. How appropriate the whole concept of succession planning is in leaner corporate structures is unclear, however. The problem with traditional succession planning – and fast tracking in particular – is that it creates an expectation of upward progression, even though in today's leaner management structures there are far fewer rungs on the corporate ladder. It also fails to take account of non-managerial roles – in particular, knowledge workers in creative roles, who may be vital to the future of the business. The question here is how you retain a brilliant research scientist or software designer who has no desire for promotion.

In effect, then, traditional fast tracking and succession planning are likely to be less effective ways of retaining talent in the future. More flexible approaches will be required, customized to suit employees, their families, and the changing skills mix of the organization.

In recent years, there has also been considerable debate about the best way to handle the transfer of power from one CEO to the next. Certain organizations pride themselves on promoting from within and have a long history of grooming insiders for the top jobs. The best scenario, they believe, is a seamless succession, where the baton is passed from one executive to the next with virtually no interruption to the momentum and style of the business.

Other companies prefer a different succession strategy. Rather than anoint a new CEO in advance, they prefer a Darwinian approach, aiming to create a strong, highly motivated cadre of senior management from which the new CEO will "emerge" when the time is right. Cometh the hour, cometh the man (or woman).

But the "succession of the fittest" approach also has some drawbacks. It encourages political intrigue, as senior managers jockey for power to the detriment of the business. A homegrown CEO isn't always the answer, especially when a company is in trouble. Sometimes a new broom is required. There is also a school of thought that says regular injections of new blood are necessary to add diversity to the corporate gene pool. Either way, the solution is to bring in an outsider.

An external appointment at the top, on the other hand, can drive a coach and horses through the succession plan lower down, especially if the incoming leader brings their own team with them or slashes the management development budget. Such a short-sighted approach can leave holes in the succession plan further down the road, dooming it to failure.

Perhaps the thorniest succession issue of all involves a small group of business leaders – Bill Gates and Richard Branson among them – who are genuinely irreplaceable. These people play such a dominant role in the company that they come to be viewed as inseparable from it. The difficulty then becomes, what happens to the business when they go?

The current trend appears to be that many organizations are actively reinstating succession planning. How appropriate such plans are to the needs of "high flyers," to other employees, and to the organizations themselves is questionable.

Theories X and Y (and Z)

Even though he died over 40 years ago, Douglas McGregor (1906–64) remains one of the most influential and most quoted thinkers in human relations (what was known in the 1940s and 1950s as behavioral science research). His work influenced and inspired the work of thinkers as diverse as Rosabeth Moss Kanter, Warren Bennis, and Robert Waterman. Most notably, McGregor is renowned for his motivational models, Theories X and Y.

These were the centerpiece of McGregor's 1960 classic, *The Human Side of Enterprise*. Theory X was traditional carrot-and-stick thinking built on "the assumption of the mediocrity of the masses." This assumed that workers were inherently lazy, needed to be supervised and motivated, and regarded work as a necessary evil to provide money. The premises of Theory X, wrote McGregor, were "(1) that the average human has an inherent dislike of work and will avoid it if he can, (2) that people, therefore, need to be coerced, controlled, directed, and threatened with punishment to get them to put forward adequate effort toward the organization's ends, and (3) that the typical human prefers to be directed, wants to avoid responsibility, has relatively little ambition, and wants security above all."

McGregor lamented that Theory X "materially influences managerial strategy in a wide sector of American industry," and observed, "if there is a single assumption that pervades conventional organizational theory it is that authority is the central, indispensable means of managerial control."

The other extreme was described by McGregor as Theory Y, based on the principle that people want and need to work. If this was the case, then organizations had to develop the individual's commitment to their objectives, and then to liberate their abilities on behalf of those objectives. McGregor described the assumptions behind Theory Y: "(1) that the expenditure of physical and mental effort in work is as natural as in play or rest – the typical human doesn't inherently dislike work; (2) external control and threat of punishment are not the only means for bringing about effort toward a company's ends; (3) commitment to objectives is a function of the rewards associated with their achievement – the most important of such rewards is the satisfaction of ego and can be the direct product of effort directed toward an organization's purposes; (4) the average human being learns, under the right conditions, not only to accept but to seek responsibility; and (5) the capacity to exercise a relatively high degree of imagination, ingenuity, and creativity in the solution of organizational problems is widely, not narrowly, distributed in the population."

Theories X and Y were not simplistic stereotypes. McGregor was realistic: "It is no more possible to create an organization today which will be a full, effective application of this theory than it was to build an atomic power plant in 1945. There are many formidable obstacles to overcome."

The common complaint against McGregor's Theories X and Y is that they are mutually exclusive, two incompatible ends of an endless spectrum. To counter this, before he died in 1964, McGregor was developing Theory Z, a theory synthesizing the organizational and personal imperatives. The concept of Theory Z was later seized on by William Ouchi. In his book of the same name, he analyzed Japanese working methods. Here, he found fertile ground for many of the ideas McGregor was proposing for Theory Z: lifetime employment, concern for employees including their social life, informal control, decisions made by consensus, slow promotion, excellent transmittal of information from top to bottom and bottom to top with the help of middle management, commitment to the firm, and high concern for quality.

360-degree feedback

The annual appraisal was once a bureaucratic chore to be completed as speedily as possible. Every year, at an appointed hour, a manager sat in an office with his or her boss. The manager's performance over the previous year was discussed and dissected. The manager emerged from the room and headed back to his or her desk, until the next year. The traditional form of appraisal may linger on in some companies; in a fast-growing number, however, the annual ritual has been reinvented.

Appraisal's *raison d'être* is straightforward: to improve an individual's – and, therefore, an organization's – performance. To do so, the appraisal has to be responsive to individual needs and be available to individuals throughout the organization. As a result, the modern appraisal tends to be flexible, continuous, revolves around feedback, involves many more people than one manager and a boss, and seeks to minimize bureaucracy.

Appraisal is now seen in the broader-ranging context of "performance management." This means that it must embrace issues such as personal development and career planning, in addition to simple analysis of how well the individual has performed over the last year. Extending the range of this approach is the increasingly fashionable concept of 360-degree feedback. This involves a manager's peers, subordinates, bosses, and even customers airing their views on the manager's performance, usually by way of a questionnaire.

The attraction of 360-degree feedback is that it gives a more complete picture of an individual's performance. Different groups see the person in a variety of circumstances and can, as a result, give a broader perspective than that of a single boss. This, of course, relies on a high degree of openness and trust, as well as perception.

To ensure that comments are made as honestly as possible, without fear of sanction, anonymity is the almost universal rule. Inevitably, however, the truth can become clouded by prejudice and politics. People can be incredibly sycophantic or completely negative. Perceptions and the objectivity of the data can also be affected by prejudices and other influential factors.

An additional danger is that if managers are to be judged by subordinates, their motivation will be to be liked. Good management isn't necessarily about being liked, so there is the risk of management by popularity. Perhaps more significant is that, for traditional managers, 360-degree feedback can be a highly disturbing experience. Managers are not renowned for their willingness to contemplate their weaknesses. Counseling and support are often necessary if the experience is to be a positive one.

More mundanely, actually running 360-degree feedback programs is demanding and time consuming, which means it is common for companies to bring in consultants to run their programs effectively. It also means that 360-degree feedback largely remains the preserve of a small number of senior managers. The logistics of expanding the concept to others in the organization are usually not persuasive.

REFERENCES

1. Taylor, Frederick W., *Principles of Scientific Management*, Harper, 1911.
2. Fayol, Henri, *Industrial and General Administration*, Pitman, 1916.
3. Gulick, Luther H. and Urwick, Lyndall F. (eds), 'Notes on the theory of organizations' in *Papers on the Science of Administration*, Columbia University Press, 1937.
4. Mooney, J.D. and Reiley, A.C., *Onward Industry: The Principles of Organizations and Their Significance to Modern Industry*, Harper, 1931.
5. Allen, L.A., *Professional Management: New Concepts and Proven Practices*, McGraw Hill, Maidenhead, 1973.
6. Kelly, J., 'The study of executive behavior by activity sampling,' *Human Relations*, 17, 1964.
7. Mintzberg, Henry, *The Nature of Managerial Work*, Prentice Hall, 1973.
8. Morse, J.J. and Wagner, F.R., 'Measuring the process of managerial effectiveness,' *Academy of Management Journal*, 21, 1978.
9. Tan, J.H., 'Management work in Singapore: developing a factor model,' Henley Management College/Brunel University, 1994.
10. Boyatzis, Richard E., *The Competent Manager: A Model for Effective Performance*, John Wiley, New York, 1982.
11. Porter, L.W. and Lawler, E.E., *Managerial Attitudes and Performance*, Irwin Dorsey, 1968.
12. Stewart, Rosemary, *Managers and their Jobs: A Study of the Similarities and the Differences in the Way Managers Spend Their Time*, Macmillan, 1967.
13. Handy, Charles, *The Age of Unreason*, Business Books, 1989.
14. Levitt, Ted, 'Creativity is not enough,' *Harvard Business Review*, Vol. 41, 1963.
15. Birchall, D.W., Swords, S., Brown, M. and Swords, D.F., *Growth and Innovation*, Henley Management College, 1993.
16. Griffith, Victoria, 'It's a People Thing,' *Financial Times*, July 24, 1997.
17. Graham, Pauline (ed.), *Mary Parker Follett: Prophet of Management*, Harvard Business School Press, 1994.
18. In his 1992 book *Interim Management*, Godfrey Golzen puts the actual year that interim management started at 1978.
19. 'Here comes the boss,' BBC Radio Four, 1 August, 1997.

– CHAPTER 4 –

Operations and service

"If you can't describe what you are doing as a process, you don't know what you're doing."

W. Edwards Deming

"I believe that the current economy isn't a high-tech economy, nor an Internet economy, nor an m-commerce economy but, instead, a customer economy."

Patricia Seybold

"Reducing the cost of quality is in fact an opportunity to increase profits without raising sales, buying new equipment, or hiring new people."

Philip Crosby

"Superior service is doing whatever it takes to satisfy your customers, your co-workers, your boss. It is providing quality products and services and learning as much as you can about the products and services you provide. It is going out of your way to ensure that the people you work with, and for, have positive experiences when doing business with you."

John Tschohl

"Quality in a product or service is not what the supplier puts in. It is what the customer gets out and is willing to pay for. A product is not quality because it is hard to make and costs a lot of money, as manufacturers typically believe. This is incompetence. Customers pay only for what is of use to them and gives them value. Nothing else constitutes quality."

Peter Drucker

"Continuous improvement is better than delayed perfection."

Mark Twain

"Quality is our best assurance of customer allegiance, our strongest defense against foreign competition, and the only path to sustained growth and earnings."

Jack Welch

The laws of logistics and supply chain management

ALAN BRAITHWAITE AND RICHARD WILDING

[Companies increasingly compete not on the basis of product and services but on the strength of their supply chains. Seven laws enable companies to unlock the value that resides in their logistics.]

Supply chain and logistics are two of the last frontiers of business improvement. Traditionally we have leveraged efficient manufacturing, modern marketing, customer relationship management, strategic procurement, and efficient transportation. Now we are told that the new horizon is to look to the total end-to-end system of satisfying customers' requirement at a price they are prepared to pay and which generates a satisfactory return to the corporation.

It has been recognized that the performance and characteristics of the end-to-end chain can be tuned and optimized for dramatic improvement. In the future, it is said, companies will increasingly compete on the basis of their total supply chains. The challenge is to understand the guiding "laws" regulating the complex system that is the supply chain and how these can be turned into specific business actions to generate sustained value.

The supply chain and logistics concept

There are countless definitions of supply chain and logistics. These range from the very simple, "the management of inventory at rest or in motion," through to the more involved definitions used by the Institute of Logistics and Transportation (ILT) in the UK and by the Council of Logistics Management (CLM) in the US:

- ILT: "The total sequence of business processes, within a single or multiple enterprise environment, that enables customer demand for a product or service to be satisfied."
- CLM: "Supply chain management is the systemic, strategic co-ordination of the traditional business functions and the tactics across these business

functions within a particular company and across businesses within the supply chain for the purposes of improving the long-term performance of the individual companies and the supply chain as a whole."

The word logistics has a long history in commerce, but supply chain management (SCM) is a more recent addition to the business lexicon. SCM was first documented in the 1980s. It was used to imply an inter-organizational, rather than an intra-organizational, perspective. However, the definitions of both the Institute of Logistics and the CLM imply an end-to-end approach.

Today, SCM and logistics have become broadly interchangeable in their everyday usage. There is, however, no consistent view of what SCM really is or should be.

Recent writing suggests that supply chain management goes further than the standard definitions and that it transcends firms, functions, and business processes. This makes SCM more than just logistics and positions it as a complete business integration framework covering all functions and operating over extended networks. In this context, supply chain management is a process orientation to managing business in an integrated way that transcends the boundaries of firms and functions, leading to co-operation, through-chain business process synchronization, effective ranging, and new product introduction, as well managing the entire physical logistics agenda.

The mechanism by which the complex network of entities (that together comprise the supply chain) works is through shared information and closely aligned processes.

Experience of applying supply chain management (even partially across a business) is that improved visibility and synchronization leads to some or all of:

- improved customer service experience;
- reduced inventories;
- lower operating costs; and
- improved use of fixed assets.

The implication is that this supply chain potential can transform a company in terms of its profitability. The leverage through the combination of many small (albeit radical in their conception) improvements in the economic structure of a company can be remarkable.

The big idea behind SCM

The big idea that sits behind the supply chain concept is a move from function to process. The principle is that effectiveness of the chain is enhanced dramatically by optimizing across functions and through the whole chain compared with the accumulation of optimized functions.

Striking a balance between functional excellence and the total business view is a crucial dimension of SCM; breaking down the barriers between functions to improve supply chain integration is not a substitute for functional excellence. Companies need to be both retaining and improving their competence in all the functions in the supply chain.

The idea that the supply chain environment conforms to some immutable physical laws is attractive since it implies that the characteristics of complex supply chains are predictable. With predictability comes the potential to make focussed improvements in complex networks and realize the associated market and financial benefits.

The Seven Laws of Logistics

In 1999, the first version of the Laws of Logistics was published and, arising from these, a set of diagnostic and organizational prescriptions for making supply chain improvements. Over the past few years we have identified additional laws and updated the originals.

The Seven Laws are:

1. The law of supply chain volatility: unmanageable volatility will be caused back through the chain, creating cost and service failure, unless information is synchronized and time is compressed across the supply chain.

2. The law of lowest total cost: attempts to manage functions to their lowest individual cost will result in higher total cost and insert performance risk and volatility in the chain, unless costs are known and balanced across the chain.

3. The law of logistical variety and complexity: complexity is introduced exponentially to the supply chain by the addition of new lines, customers, and channels; cost and service will spiral out of control – unless the true "cost of variety" is understood and the supply chain designed to accommodate it.

4. The law of speed, quality, and accuracy: attempts to reduce cost by increasing batch sizes and lead times and trading off service goals invariably result in higher costs; doing things faster and better is almost always cheaper and less volatile.

5. The law of organizational difficulty: the way that we organize ourselves inside the company and with our customers and suppliers is based on functional rather than supply chain thinking, contributing to long lead times, poor visibility, sub-optimal costs, excessive inventory, and poor service – unless we give our managers cost and performance visibility and set balanced measures for them, linked to their rewards.

6. The law of supply chain asymmetry: the commercial interests and strategic priorities between entities in the supply chain are never symmetrical and

working to share mutual interest is an unreal proposition – defining trading or functional relationships to work to co-operative self-interest is the objective.

7. The law of counter intuition: the normal human response to the uncertainty represented by complex supply chain networks is to delay in an attempt to increase accuracy, reduce risk, and avoid blame whereas the right action is to make faster, more frequent, and smaller decisions – effective supply chain management is counter intuitive.

Below we discuss these Seven Laws in more detail.

1. The law of supply chain volatility

"Unmanageable volatility will be caused back through the chain, creating cost and service failure, unless information is synchronized and time is compressed across the supply chain."

The characteristics of supply chain volatility are that without visibility and synchronization through the supply chain the experience of demand at suppliers can be unmanageable. This is due to the various supply chain rules or oblivious practice applied by each function and trading entity in the chain in its dealing with its adjacent functions. These are expressed in terms of lead times and order, batch, and shipment sizes in relation to actual demand. The distortions experienced through the chain as a result generally lead to the simultaneous condition of customer service failure and excess stocks across the range.

Many companies observe that they are maintaining excess capacity to deal with this volatility, which is uneconomic; the commercial option is to force even more inventory and consequential risk onto customers or suppliers. The implications of the law of volatility are that failure is generally self-inflicted and the usual scapegoats of forecast error and supply unreliability are only part of the problem; indeed demand signals that have been created through asynchronous behaviors become unforecastable and suppliers are bound to fail. The oscilloscope diagram that is most commonly used to describe this phenomenon is reproduced in Figure 4.1.

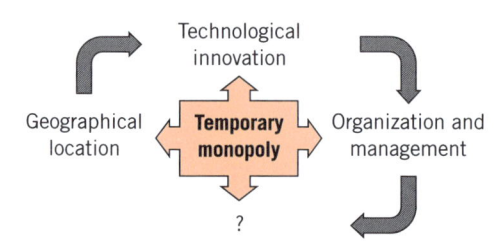

Figure 4.1: *The evolution of sources of competitive advantages*

There are five ways of reducing volatility. In order of effectiveness these are:

- removal of distributor layer in model;
- integration of information flow;
- reduction of time delays;
- improvement of pipeline inventory policy;
- tuning existing ordering parameters.

2. The law of lowest total cost

"Attempts to manage functions to their lowest individual cost will result in higher total cost and insert performance risk and volatility in the chain, unless costs are known and balanced across the chain."

The effect of optimizing functional cost can be to prevent the achievement of the most cost-effective end-to-end supply chain. Not only that, but it will also most likely insert undesirable volatility. For example, the cost of inventory holding and storage may be driven up by freight or batch quantities at a greater rate than these functions save through internal economies of scale; or the cost reduction from installing the fastest and most cost-effective manufacturing equipment may create scheduling and operating constraints that drive up costs elsewhere in the chain. Individually targetted and budgeted functions based on what it cost last year and making functional savings will lead those functions toward inter-functional conflict and budgetary shocks as the actual costs move out of line when the business changes.

The implications of the law of lowest total cost are that traditional functional and general ledger methods of business and operational planning will never lead to "breakthrough" thinking in supply chain redesign and, indeed, are a cause of organizational problems.

The prescription requires that the corporation measure the end-to-end cost-to-serve, at least internally but preferably looking inside both its customers' and suppliers' operations, to enable a fundamental re-balancing across the business on a holistic basis to achieve the lowest total cost.

The law of lowest total cost links closely to that of volatility since the causes of cross-functional dynamics are the process rules that are set to lower the functional costs. These rules and hence the drivers of cost are different for every business and depend on the physical characteristics of the product, the profile of customer demand, the nature of the manufacturing processes (e.g. capital intensiveness, capacity utilization, changeover times), the supply chain network from source to customer, and the sources of supply.

3. The law of logistical variety and complexity

"Complexity is introduced exponentially to the supply chain by the addition of new lines, customers, and channels; cost and service will spiral out of control unless the true 'cost of variety' is understood and the supply chain designed to accommodate it."

Volatility and total cost are significantly impacted by the variety in the chain. Variety drives complexity, creating internal conflicts between customers, manufacturing, marketing, and distribution. So, complexity is represented by the product range, the customer profile, the supplier base, and the sourcing and network routing structure. According to Pareto's Law or the 80:20 rule, it is the universal maxim that 80 percent of the activity (profit, sales, movements) is derived from just 20 percent of the products and customers. The supply chain implications of Pareto's Law are less commonly understood and are illustrated in Figure 4.2.

This shows that the difference between the fast movers or the bigger customers and slow movers or the smaller customers is a factor of 100 times or more in the physical throughput that they create. Furthermore, high-volume sales to large customers are intrinsically less volatile than those of smaller lines to minor customers. Yet it costs nearly the same to take a large order as it does a small one and proportionately more to deliver a small order as it does a large one. Inside the supply chain, the effect of batch size for both manufacturing and its suppliers can be to position months of stock with a single buying or manufacturing event – leading to risks of obsolescence and high costs of finance and storage. The mixture of variety in a company's chain is a powerful driver of both volatility and cost, which has given us the term cost-of-variety.

The implications of the law of logistical variety and complexity are that the seemingly straightforward task of adding a new product or customer can impact the effectiveness of the chain to a much greater extent than the straight percentage increase of the addition. Since the additions are usually in the middle or the tail of the Pareto curve, they give the organization the challenge of dealing with more of the least cost-effective part of its activities and this may further compromise the ability to handle the real profit drivers effectively.

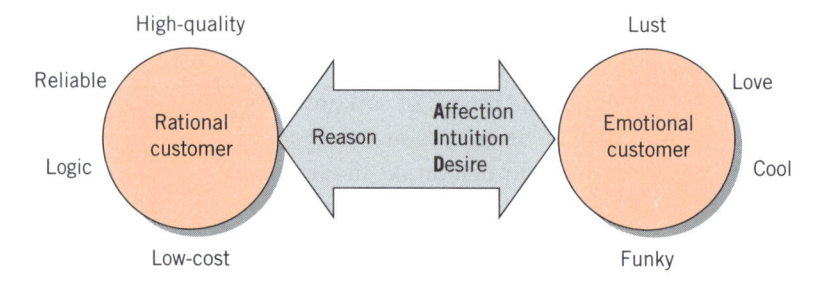

Figure 4.2: *A new logic for providing meaning*

4. The law of speed, quality and accuracy

"Attempts to reduce cost by increasing batch sizes and lead times and trading off service goals invariably result in higher costs; doing things faster and better is almost always cheaper and less volatile."

The first three laws point to the core themes of doing things faster and in a more synchronized way through the chain from a background where the total chain cost is known along with its drivers. This understanding, aligned to the effects of variety, points to the need for segmented design and actions based on the characteristics of customers and products. However, organizations have been conditioned through years of mass-production thinking to the idea that there is a trade-off between speed and quality.

The law of speed, quality, and accuracy states that these trade-offs are largely an illusion; smaller batches on shorter lead times with 100 percent right first time should cost no more and can easily cost less. The meteoric rise of Japanese manufacturing in the 1970s, 1980s, and early 1990s was significantly attributable to W. Edwards Deming and T. Ohno, who identified that waste in every step of the manufacturing operation could be eliminated to give massive reductions in cost and big increases in flexibility – delivering greater variety with higher levels of quality. The bottom line of this attack on waste was that Japanese auto makers were able to offer greater choice at lower cost and with a lower model breakeven.

These ideas have been described as "lean thinking" but the criticism of this approach has been that it is tightly bounded by the manufacturing function. The idea of agility has been introduced to institute the ability of the firm to respond to demand volatility that was otherwise dealt with by high finished goods inventories and the risk of obsolescence and higher total system costs.

The implications of these conclusions on speed, quality, and accuracy for supply chain design are profound. The established ideas of trade-off need to be challenged and overwritten. The motor industry that was the home of lean thinking is now talking about the three-day car made to order and achieving this at no extra cost where the stock of finished cars was two months.

The prescription is simple: look for any potential way to cut lead time and batch size and start from the premise that it will not cost more. From the first four laws, we have a framework that provides a new way of designing and running supply chains. The end-to-end supply chain that connects and synchronizes the elements of the business can deliver better service with lower cost, reduced assets and hence less organizational pain.

The final three laws deal with the organizational pain and the human dimension of supply chain management. It is becoming increasingly evident that behavioral and organizational issues are the key to unlocking competitive advantage and achieving alignment.

5. The law of organizational difficulty

"The way that we organize ourselves inside the company and with our customers and suppliers is based on functional rather than supply chain thinking, contributing to long lead times, poor visibility, sub-optimal costs, excessive inventory, and poor service – unless we give our managers cost and performance visibility and set balanced measures for them linked to their rewards."

The law of organizational difficulty states that supply chain change is and will be difficult. The implication is that we had better organize to recognize and deal with this. The alternatives are at best passive resistance and at worst active sabotage. The reasons are that we are creatures of our education and experience, which has traditionally been functional and vocational. The ideas of "rebalancing the chain" and of "no cost to achieving speed, quality, and accuracy" strike at the heart of our personal value sets; the new supply chain perspectives challenge the beliefs and training that people have spent years accumulating.

The implications are that we are inviting people who have spent years perfecting functional excellence that they need to add a new perspective. It is always difficult to tell people that they need to change their perspective and expect an immediately favorable response! We have to give people time and space and the opportunity to experience the new model to win them over.

Although the law of organizational difficulty tells us that people and organization can be a great barrier to supply chain change, we must also recognize that the benefits of improving the supply chain will not fall equally across the participants in the chain. Indeed the benefit model will be quite different for suppliers, internal functions, and customers respectively. The idea of partnership and collaboration has been widely proposed as a sinecure for supply chain improvement; the expectation is that benefits will be somehow shared. From our observations and experience this is naive and largely a fiction, which leads us to the law of supply chain asymmetry.

6. The law of supply chain asymmetry

"The commercial interests and strategic priorities between entities in the supply chain are never symmetrical and working to share mutual interest is an unreal proposition – defining trading or functional relationships to work to co-operative self-interest is the objective."

The law of supply chain asymmetry says that relationships are never symmetrical between functions and parties in the supply chain. Look at what Wal-Mart managed to persuade its suppliers to do. The Wal-Mart model has been to progressively build its position by offering suppliers the potential for huge volume; in return it asks them to price on an ex-factory basis, cut their margin, and deliver responsively to a small number of distribution centers. Their supply chains are more synchronized and they cost less, so that both the supplier and Wal-Mart save. This enables the goods to be sold for less to the consumer with reasonably high levels of availability. The customer proposition is unassailable and has swept all before it to create the world's largest business.

The implications for those that did not join the "movement" have been savage. Competitors such as K-Mart have passed into Chapter 11 bankruptcy, while others have lost share and had to reinvent themselves with a different consumer proposition. Suppliers have seen themselves become increasingly dependent on Wal-Mart and at the same time suffering higher cost-to-serve for the remainder of their channel after it has been stripped of the Wal-Mart volume. The benefits are tangible for both Wal-Mart and its suppliers, but it is a two-edged sword for the suppliers. The one thing it is not is a cosy or balanced relationship in which they "look out" for the interests of each other.

The implications are clear: take on the challenge of supply chain alignment from the twin perspectives of relative power and identify the benefits you intend to keep: holding front of mind the principle of asymmetry.

7. The law of counter intuition

"The normal human response to the uncertainty represented by complex supply chain networks is to delay in an attempt to increase accuracy, reduce risk, and avoid blame whereas the right action is to make faster, more frequent, and smaller decisions – effective supply chain management is counter intuitive."

Management guru Warren Bennis once wrote on leadership: "If in doubt, do something." By implication, almost anything would do and the principle behind this maxim was that the effect of the change would give additional information on the real state of affairs. He clearly saw that rapid action would be a competitive advantage and this is a key principle of control theory where many measurements and rapid adjustments are the key to retaining control of the complex system. But the human response to uncertainty is to delay; we tend to hang fire to see what is going to happen in the hope that we can get a better fix on the most effective action. The same is true in supply chain management where we delay to try to improve the forecast, or secure a more accurate schedule, or increase the predictability of a whole host of factors. The reasons are simple: we are educated to strive for greater accuracy and to avoid the blame when things go wrong. Thus our instincts are counter productive.

Unlocking value in the supply chain

The implications for business management arising from supply chain and logistics thinking are profound. The potential exists to initiate radical changes in the way that organizations have traditionally operated to secure step changes in performance. However, to realize these gains, managers in the area of logistics and the supply chain must recognize they are working in an environment characterized by both industrial and people dynamics: with complex performance-balances to strike, commercially and functionally. They need a broadly based framework of understanding and skills to grasp and resolve the complex issues and make change happen.

We believe that supply chain and logistics performance is predictable and can be described through laws, which can be applied to the specific circumstances of the corporation. By recognizing each of these laws when undertaking supply chain re-design and change projects, practitioners and academics can be guided in both unlocking value and reducing the chance of failure.

RESOURCES

Ballou, Ronald H., *Business Logistics Management*, Prentice Hall, 1992.

Bowersox, Donald J. and Closs, David J., *Logistical Management*, McGraw-Hill, 1996.

Braithwaite, Alan, 'The Laws of Logistics,' Preceding of advanced logistic workshop, Cranfield School of Management, Cranfield UK, November 11, 1999.

Christopher, Martin and Peck, Helen, *Marketing Logistics*, Butterworth Heinemann, 2003.

Cooper, Martha C., Lambert, Douglas M., and Pagh, Janus D., 'Supply Chain Management: More Than A New Name for Logistics,' *The International Journal of Logistics Management*, Vol. 8, No. 1, 1997.

Forrester, Jay, *Industrial Dynamics*, MIT Press, 1961.

Hines, P.A., *Creating World Class Suppliers*. FT Pitman, 1994.

Hines, P.A., Lamming, R.C., Jones, D.T., Cousins, P.D., and Rich, N., *Value Stream Management*. FT Prentice Hall, 2000.

Jarillo, J.C., *Strategic Networks: Creating the Borderless Organization*, Butterworth Heinemann, 1993.

Lamming, Richard, *Beyond Partnership: Strategies for Innovation and Lean Supply*, Prentice Hall, 1993.

Macbeth, D.K. and Ferguson, Neil, *Partnership Sourcing: An Integrated Supply Chain Approach*, FT Pitman, 1994.

Wilding, Richard D., 'The Supply Chain Complexity Triangle: Uncertainty Generation in the Supply Chain,' *International Journal of Physical Distribution and Logistics Management*, MCB University Press, Vol. 28, No. 8, pp. 599–616, 1998.

Wilding, Richard D., 'Cost-to-Serve: An Alternative to ABC?' *Supply Chain Excellence – The Management Today Report on Supply Chain Strategies for Competitive Advantage*, *Management Today*, Haymarket Business Publications, pp. 6–11, May, 1999.

Womack, J.P., Jones, D.T., and Roos, D., *The Machine that Changed the World*, Maxwell Macmillan, 1990.

Performance measurement: the new crisis

ANDY NEELY

['What gets measured gets done' has become a management cliché. Yet despite the growing recognition that it is critical to business success, does performance measurement face a new crisis?]

Management's obsession with measurement appears to grow unbounded. Data from Gartner, the Connecticut-based research organization, suggests that over 70 percent of large US firms had adopted the balanced scorecard by the end of 2001. The Enron scandal has provoked a flurry of debate about corporate reporting, disclosure, and the use of creative accounting practices to smooth income and earnings statements. There has been a storm of related activity in the consulting community. PwC has launched its Value Reporting initiative.[1] CGE&Y continues to work on the Measures that Matter.[2] Accenture and the Center for Business Performance at Cranfield School of Management have produced research on the planning and budgeting revolution.[3]

The software industry is also playing a significant role in driving the measurement agenda forward. There are now in excess of 50 vendors worldwide that offer performance reporting solutions.[4] Some of these so-called solutions are little more than glorified spreadsheets, while others enable executives to access immense amounts of data. Note the use of the word data rather than information or insight. The problem with many of the software reporting packages on the market today is that all they offer is data. They do not provide information. They do not provide insight. Instead they provide access to so much data that executives can end up drowning.

Drowning in data

The theme of drowning in data lies at the heart of what we believe is the new measurement crisis. When commentators, such as Bob Kaplan and H. Thomas Johnson, began criticizing the measurement systems used by most firms in the 1980s, the thrust of their argument was, quite simply, that the wrong things were being measured.[5] Today the problem is not that the wrong things are being measured, but that too much is being measured. Executives appear to be obsessed with quantification. They want everything described in numerical terms – customer satisfaction, customer loyalty, customer profitability, brand value, employee satisfaction, supplier performance, health and safety, efficiency, productivity, innovation, new product development, and so on. The list of things that would be nice to measure, in even a moderately sized business, is endless. And the result, in many cases, is that organizations fall into the trap of simply trying to measure too much.

This situation is becoming so serious that some executives are starting to question what value they are getting from their organization's measurement systems. These questions become even more frantic when the executives concerned think about how much their organization's measurement systems cost them to run. Research by the Hackett Group, for example, found that the average company devotes a mean of 25,000 person days to planning and measuring performance per $1 billion of sales. Research, completed by members of the Center for Business Performance at Cranfield School of Management, found that Ford spent 0.7 percent of sales – $1.2 billion – annually on budgeting alone.[6] These sums are clearly significant, but somewhat surprisingly it seems that the vast majority of executives have no real idea how much they are spending on measurement. Everyone knows they are spending a lot, but no one knows how much.

Of course, just because you spend a lot on something does not mean that it is not worthwhile. The current spend on measurement does not mean that organizations should stop or trim back their measurement initiatives. But it does mean that they should think carefully about how they can best utilize their measurement systems to ensure that they deliver maximum value. It is to this issue – how to make measurement pay – that we will now turn our attention.

Making measurement pay

If you review recent writing and efforts in the field of performance measurement it becomes clear that significant effort has been devoted to improving measurement methodologies. People have sought and developed new methods of measuring financial performance – activity-based costing, activity-based management, economic profit, free cash flow analysis, and shareholder value analysis – and new frameworks to balance financial and non-financial measures – the balanced scorecard and the performance prism.

Research has focussed on how to design and implement such methodologies and frameworks. How do you decide which measures to use? How do you access the necessary data? How do you measure the softer dimensions of performance, such as intangible assets and/or intellectual capital? How do you overcome the social, political, and cultural barriers associated with performance measurement? How do you align measures with strategy? How do you ensure measures encourage appropriate behaviors? Clearly these topics are important, but as we enhance our understanding of them we need to broaden the agenda and ask explicitly: how do we make measurement pay?

More specifically, we should:

1. *Think in terms of performance planning, not performance reviews.* In most organizations measurement forms the basis of performance reviews, which are historic or backward looking in nature and – either implicitly or explicitly – designed to put people on the defensive. I recently had the opportunity to evaluate a performance review presentation that someone in a large oil major had put together for the next board meeting. The presentation, which consisted of over 20 slides, was scheduled to take half an hour, but basically said "everything in my area is fine." Having reviewed the slides I asked the simple question: "If everything is fine, then why can't you stand up, say everything is fine, and then sit down again? That way you'll only spend 30 seconds on this subject and the meeting can finish half an hour early, or alternatively the spare time can be devoted to a topic that needs it." The response was one of horror. "We can't possibly do that … we never do that."

   Why? Why is it that in performance reviews people spend most of their time justifying why performance is as it is? They come to the review armed to teeth with excuses that explain *why they are where they are*. "We are only at 70 percent of our target because our suppliers let us down, or our customers have not yet confirmed their orders, or our competitors have introduced a new product." Such discussions, which focus on *why we are where we are*, are irrelevant, or at least relatively unimportant in comparison to those discussions that focus on *how we are going to get to where we want to be*. But discussions about *how we are going to get to where we want to be* are not performance reviews, they are performance planning sessions. They require executive teams to understand the reasons why performance is as it is and then focus on how they are going to make progress. Excuses become irrelevant. What matters in performance planning sessions is how we are going to deliver.

2. *Ask for answers not for data*. Why do people get sucked into performance reviews rather than performance planning sessions? A significant reason is that far too often the meetings themselves are structured as performance reviews. Far too often we simply present raw performance data to executives and expect them to analyze it there and then. You would never conduct a scientific experiment that way. You never make a presentation to an audience without first analyzing the data and understanding the messages it contains.

Yet far too often in performance reviews we do. We give people figures on profitability by customer segment. We give them figures on absenteeism levels. We give them figures on productivity. But nobody in advance has been through the data and extracted the insights from it. David Coles, former managing director of DHL UK, used an excellent phrase to describe this in a recent presentation: "numerical crosswords." He explained to the audience how his board used to spend all of their time at performance reviews trying to join up the pieces of the numerical jigsaw that they were presented with. Individual directors would be looking at performance reports trying to draw spurious correlations between different events to offer explanations for unusual observations.

When they realized this was what they were doing, DHL UK decided to change the structure of their board meetings and define specific questions that they wanted answered beforehand. They now ask their performance analysts to come to the board meeting armed not with raw data, not with excuses, but instead with presentations which address questions of fundamental concern to the board – e.g. are we going to hit budget this year, how are our customers feeling, how are our employees feeling? The analysts' role at the board meeting is to present their answers to the questions. The board's role is to probe the quality of the analysis and once they are comfortable with it, decide what they are going to do to move performance in the desired direction. In changing the structure of their board meetings the board of DHL UK has been able to eliminate the defensive behaviors associated with performance reviews and encourage the creative dialog associated with performance planning.

3. *Build the capability of performance analysts.* In adopting this new structure and format DHL recognized that they had to upgrade the skills of their performance analysts. But at least DHL had performance analysts. Many organizations do not and in these cases they need to appoint them. These performance analysts need not only to be able to manipulate performance data but also to interpret it and present it in a way that engages and provides insight to others. Research being undertaken in the Center for Business Performance at Cranfield School of Management in the UK into this issue has resulted in the development of a concept we call the Performance Planning Value Chain, which effectively encapsulates a systematic process for extracting insights from performance data. The analogy underpinning the Performance Planning Value Chain is that of a journalist. If you think about what a journalist does when presenting a story, he or she is very careful to identify the "hook," or headline, that will capture the readers' attention and then flesh out the detail in the small print. Rarely do we do this with performance reports. Rarely do we ask our performance analysts to tell us the

headline. In fact, rarely do we ask our performance analysts really to analyze data. Instead we expect them to spend all of their time pulling, collecting, and collating data.

This issue becomes even more important when the focus of measurement is shifted to systems, not functions. The reality of organizations, as every executive knows, is that they consist of complex interdependencies. Marketing relies on operations. Operations relies on human resources. Human resources relies on finance, etc. Yet when it comes to measurement we often ignore these interdependencies. Marketing looks at the marketing and customer satisfaction data. Human resources looks at the people data. Operations looks at the operational data, etc.

The obsession with measurement has effectively spawned a new function – the measurement function. We have functionalized measurement, just as we have functionalized everything else in organizations. This is dangerous. If there is a downturn in employee satisfaction, everyone assumes this will have an adverse impact on customer service. If the operation becomes too inefficient, everyone knows this will impact the financial results. The reality of organizations is that the activities being undertaken in different parts of them interact and we have to recognize this interaction if we are to get the most from our measurement data. Rather than operating in functional silos we need to use our measurement data to understand the big picture, the big story of what is happening inside the organization. And this requires us to equip performance analysts with the skills needed to cope with understanding this complexity.

The way forward

To date in the field of performance measurement has focussed on two specific issues: designing measurement systems, and implementing measurement systems.

The first stream of work is concerned with making choices about what to measure, how to measure it, what frameworks to use, etc. The second stream of work is concerned with overcoming the political, social, and cultural barriers associated with measurement, as well as the technical ones. These two streams of work are clearly important, for unless they are addressed, it is impossible to develop and implement a robust measurement system. But I believe that we now know how to address these issues. You can hire consultants and attend courses designed to help you through these minefields. The problem is that measurement is worth nothing unless it is acted upon – unless we move into the world of managing through measurement. And this, for me, is the emerging measurement agenda. What tools and techniques can we use to better manage through measurement? How can we extract insights from data? How can we communicate these insights? How can we make sure measurement influences action, which in turn delivers results? It is work in these areas that I believe we will see the academic and practitioner community focussing on as the field of performance measurement enters a new and more mature age.

RESOURCES

Brown, S.E., *Manufacturing the Future – Strategic Resonance and Enlightened Manufacturing*, FT Prentice Hall, 2000.

Dimancescu, D., Hines, P.A., and Rich, N., *The Lean Enterprise: Designing and Managing Strategic Processes for Customer-Winning Performance*. AMACOM, 1997.

Johnson, H.T. and Kaplan, R.S., *Relevance Lost – The Rise and Fall of Management Accounting*, Harvard Business School Press, MA, 1987.

Kaplan, Robert S. and Norton, David P., *The Balanced Scorecard*, Harvard Business School, 1996.

Neely, A.D., Bourne, M., Jarrar, Y., Kennerley, M., Marr, B., Schiuma, G., Walters, A.H., Sutcliff, M., Heyns, H., Reilly, S., and Smythe, S. *Delivering Value Through Strategic Planning and Budgeting*, Accenture and Cranfield School of Management, 2001.

www.valuereporting.com

Design to be different

KJELL NORDSTRÖM AND JONAS RIDDERSTRÅLE

[*In the quest for differentiation, companies are increasingly embracing design as a competitive weapon. Yet espousing the virtues of design is one thing; inculcating design into a corporate culture quite another.*]

We live in a surplus society. This is the age of more – more fun, more fear, more freedom, more responsibilities, more products, more services, more competition, more opportunities. We have entered an age of abundance. The competition for our attention is intensive and intensifying. Yet, *more* quite often simply means more of the same. Products have become increasingly homogenous. In 1996, the annual survey of the car industry, produced by JD Power, concluded: "There are no bad cars any longer, because they are all good." In our age of techno-economic parity, there are few raw materials, technologies, and insights that are available to people in the West that are not also available to people in Bangalore, Warsaw, Santiago, and Manila. From a strict price/performance view, it no longer really matters what microwave, stereo, or vacuum cleaner you buy. Sameness rules.

With markets becoming increasingly global and efficient, most organizations have access to the same input goods. Success depends on our ability to combine and recombine things into something that is desirable. In the corporate equivalent of a blind tasting, the companies which emerge victorious will be those which have, as Stanford's Paul Romer puts it, the most potent, alluring, and attractive recipes. Increasing competitive pressure means that companies incapable of serving the flavor of the future may well be facing their Last Supper.

Different ways to differentiate

In the morass of sameness, differentiation is vital. Successful companies add unique value to a specific group of customers. They are different, offer different things in different ways to different people. Companies seek to be different because it is the route to the corporate Holy Grail of a temporary monopoly.

Once, difference was based on location – being closest to the mine, forest, or whatever. However, the development of international markets for raw materials eventually preempted these advantages. By the beginning of the 20th century, difference was based on technological innovation. In certain industries, such as the software industry where increasing returns and lock-ins are powerful forces, this still largely holds true. But for most companies the reality is, and has been, that products are rapidly imitated and patents sold or acquired in global markets.

When technological innovations became open to all-comers, companies pursued differentiation elsewhere. We entered the organizational age. Progressively, throughout the latter half of the 20th century, organizational innovations gave rise to new temporary monopolies. Through their adoption of an array of organizational innovations, companies differentiated themselves – albeit briefly. Just-in-time, reengineering, ISO 9000, kanban, outsourcing, downsizing, lean production, and many more were seized upon. In the quest for difference, companies pursued management fads and fashions with increasing zeal. They refocussed, leveraged their competencies in all imaginable directions, reengineered and restructured in the belief that this was the recipe for future success. These initiatives are laudable and useful, but have now become standard; necessary but not sufficient for securing success. They are available through the international market for expert advice and can potentially become the property of any organization.

The result is that, for most firms, competitiveness can no longer be based solely on a superior location, technological innovation, or a new way of structuring the organization. Any advantages these factors might provide are likely to be extremely short-lived. Traditional competitive strategies will get you nowhere. Momentarily you may be one step ahead, but the others will soon catch up.

Entering the emotional economy

If being good is no longer enough, there has to be a better way, a more original route to differentiation. There is. Look at the Finnish company Nokia which has come from almost nowhere to become the leading maker of mobile phones in the world. Nokia does not possess groundbreaking technology which its competitors cannot get hold of. Nor has its CEO, Jorma Olilla, stumbled upon a management book yet to be translated from Finnish. It is true that Nokia has world-class, top-of-the-line technology, and that it pioneers organizational solutions. It is also the case that Nokia seeks out the best IT solutions that money can buy and works with the best suppliers in the world, rather than the closest. All this is necessary. There is no choice. But it is not sufficient because Ericsson, Philips, Motorola, Sony, Siemens, and many more companies are doing the same things.

Nokia, and other such firms, succeed because they have realized that the new economics are emotional rather than rational. True competitiveness must be built around something we all know exists but which is seldom discussed in the business world: emotions and imagination.

The new quest for differentiation requires that companies develop sensational strategies which embrace the emotions and capture the attention of consumers. Strategies never used to target emotions; they now must. Instead of running faster, companies must play a different game. "People take technology for granted these days. What they want are warm, friendly products – something to seduce them," says the designer Phillipe Starck.

As Mr Starck's comments suggest, attracting the emotional customer and colleague is not a question of superior price or performance. Again, this is necessary but not sufficient. Ethics and aesthetics, feelings and fantasy, have little to do with logic, but everything to do with affection, intuition, and desire. Sushi is nothing more and nothing less than cold, dead fish, but that is not the way you convince people to buy it.

Design is the synthesis of these elements. Design is about truth, love, and beauty and, increasingly, about whether a business has a sensational strategy or the same strategy as everyone else. "Design is not done with rules, but with intuition. Intuition never lies," says leading British designer Jasper Morrison. To some this is frivolous indulgence, a world away from the realities of the bottom line. To them, design is mere decoration rather than pure meaning. "People have an enormous need for art and poetry that industry does not yet understand," argues Alberto Alessi, CEO of the eponymous company. The public's appetite for art and poetry enables Alessi to charge $80 for a toilet brush.

The companies which accept Alessi's viewpoint are cutting a swathe through the competition. Furniture retailer IKEA proclaims its vision of "good design, good function, and good quality." The US airline JetBlue announces that its priorities are "simplicity, friendly people, technology, design, and entertainment." "Customers really respond to products that involve new thinking and connect with their souls," says Ron Jonson, former vice-president of Target, the low-cost retailer with close to 1,000 stores which works with renowned designers such as Michael Graves and Phillipe Starck. Nokia built art and poetry into its 8810 mobile phone which resembles a Zippo lighter. Add some art and poetry to a computer and you get Apple's iMac. Apple claims that around one-third of the people who have bought an iMac did not previously own a computer. Apple's Steve Jobs was asked what distinguishes the company's new Mac OS X operating system. He replied: "We made the buttons on the screen look so good you'll want to lick them." He did not utter a single word about megahertz and gigabytes. Such companies understand that although economies of scale and skill still matter, the new game is one of economies of soul.

Design is an increasingly rich source of differentiation. "We won't make things cheaper than the Far Eastern nations, but we can make things better through design and innovation,' says British designer Sir Terence Conran. Robert Hayes of Harvard Business School echoes similar ideas by claiming: "Fifteen years ago companies competed on price. Now it's quality. Tomorrow it's design." A good price/performance relationship is necessary but no longer sufficient. Getting that stuff right buys you a ticket to sit close to the ring, but it will not win the fight.

There is some reassurance for those who insist on old certainties. Even traditional industrial firms admit that emotion and imagination are the way forward. Just listen to one of the head designers at Ford: "In the past we tended to focus inwardly, looking for functional efficiency. Now the mindshift is to more outwardly focussed, emotional satisfaction for the consumer."

Inevitably, some companies have been exploiting emotional economics and the power of design for many years. Look, for example, at Sony. "At Sony we assume that all our competitors' products will have the same technology, price, performance, and features. Design is the only thing that differentiates one product from another in the marketplace," says Norio Ogha, Sony CEO.

Infinite innovation

If design is to be a crucial determinant of competitive advantage, the rules of the game need to be changed. Historically, the competitive game focussed on finite dimensions. The new game is infinite. There is no limit to how beautiful, attractive, or gorgeous a product can be. The permutations are endless.

Finite dimensions have the attraction of being objectively measurable and clear. As a result, it is easy for consumers to evaluate the performance of different competitors. Finite strategies combined with the Internet mean that comparison shopping becomes a picnic for the well-informed customer. By focussing on these finite aspects of the offering, companies enable the customer to become even more of a demanding dictator.

Design, on the other hand, is subjective. It evokes opinions. We love and loathe different things. People differ. So designs must differ. Not everyone likes the pristine expanses of marble and giant-sized revolving doors of London's St Martin's Lane Hotel (designed by Starck). Some may even be appalled. Not all people like the design of Helmut Lang's clothes or Alessi's kettles.

Design strikes at the emotions. It seduces. In an excess economy, it is better to be something for someone rather than nothing to everyone. Differentiation cannot lie in eliciting the same response from everyone. In an emotional economy, it is better to thoroughly annoy 90 percent of the people while capturing the attention and interest of the other 10 percent, than to be merely acceptable to all of them. In the age of affection, mediocrity, average, and almost won't do. People want amazing things, spectacular things.

In a broader sense, design is even more important. In essence, according to Chris Bangle, head of design at BMW, design is meaning. So, if a company is not design-driven it is by definition meaningless.

Table 4.1: *The transition from rational to emotional competition*

Dimension	From	To
Strategy	Competitive	Sensational
Goal	Being one step ahead	Playing a different game
Implementation	Finite dimensions	Infinite dimensions
View of customer	Objective – rational	Subjective – emotional
Provider of meaning	Everything to everyone	Something to someone

Embracing emotions everywhere

The fear and the attraction of design lie in its infinite possibilities. Design is a fact of life (though not always appreciated) and all embracing. Design concerns all aspects of the organization, from branding to how we deal with customers and colleagues – the office architecture, the stores, packaging, sales people, etc. Design touches all aspects of business life. Companies must, as a result, optimize the emotional experiences they create and offer.

Look at the evolution of retail stores. Until recently, we designed, built, manned, organized, and decorated stores to sell things in them. In an economy where sales almost always equaled physical presence this was reasonable and sound. Now, with the advent of the mobile Internet, people will soon be able to bring their own cash register in the phone to the store, have a look at the product, then search the web to find the best deal.

Companies must, in response, add esthetics and entertainment to the retailing experience – fusing function with fun. All customer offerings contain an esthetical element. We should, perhaps, think of them as pieces of art. The corollary of this is that we should look to museums and galleries for our inspirations. Rubbermaid has sent groups to the British Museum – they reportedly emerged with inspirations for new kitchen products. Visit MoMa in New York and learn something about the shop of the future. "The store entrance should be almost stage-like, creating a sensation similar to when you descend into an amazing restaurant. At the same time, it had to have the luxury of a sleek modern residence, so you feel completely enveloped and relaxed," says Tom Ford on the new Gucci store. Bill Sofield, the architect behind the project, adds: "Because so much of Gucci's image is built around architecture, be it advertising or the clothes, it allowed us to create a new design vocabulary with the stores that speaks to a global consumer."

Many balk at such notions. They regard design as superficial, driven by the vicissitudes of fashion. On one level this is, indeed, the case. Business is increasingly fashion-driven. The CEO of one of Europe's largest stainless steel companies recently asked us: "So you think we should enter the fashion business?" The reality is, we told him, you already are in that industry – you just don't know it yet. In fact all companies are, regardless of whether they make stainless steel, sneakers, or suits. Today, there is fashion in everything – the beautiful train, the trendy wrench, and the stylish lawn-mower. Recently, one of us visited a computer games manufacturer in Silicon Valley where games are developed and launched in winter and summer collections. The only fashion victims are those who fail to keep pace.

The reality is that fashion is simply another word for constant improvement. We suspect that few executives would have a problem with constant improvement.

How to make design work for you

So, how do we unleash the potential for emotional competitiveness and corporate imagination? At many companies, the preferred approach for handling increased organizational complexity has been to add yet another box to the organizational chart. Setting up a department for emotions and imagination will not work. By making design a big thing for a select few, the others stop caring. Instead, the critical components and true sources of competitive advantage must be turned into a small thing for all people in the organization. Emotions and imagination cannot be neatly compartmentalized. They are a philosophy, an attitude, a frame of mind, and must concern everyone and everything, go on everywhere and non-stop.

If design touches everything, making design work for an organization involves reevaluating everything the organization does.

1. Build an organizational tribe

Design is personal and demands a much more personalized company. Oscar Wilde was right when he noted that "consistency is the last refuge of the unimaginative." A design-driven company that competes on feelings and fantasy must thrive on variation, difference, and diversity. Yet most of us live and work in organizations built by and for 6.5 percent of the population – middle-aged white males. Tom Peters, a long-term advocate of the importance of design, noted that women make 65 percent of all car-buying decisions in the US. Yet a mere 7 percent of all car sales people are women, men design virtually all cars, and men dominate the managerial echelons of car companies. This is not only a question of equality, it is a question of quality of decisions and customer offerings.

Variation can lapse into chaos if it is not grounded in solid and articulated values. Design-driven companies require strong cultures. Indeed, these firms resemble organizational tribes. (Or, as someone once said of Nike: "It is like a cult – but it's a nice cult.") In a tribe people get energy from one another. The Zulus have a word for it: "ubuntu" (short for *unmunta ngumuntu nagabuntu*). This can be translated as a person is a person because of other persons. Or as Jung put it: "I need we to be fully I."

There is a lot of mystification surrounding the subject of values. In reality, the simplest way to get people to share your values is to recruit people who already do. Southwest Airlines hires attitudes rather than aptitudes. The logic is that you can make positive people into good pilots, but turning great pilots with attitude problems into charming servers of customers is close to impossible. Consequently, smart companies recruit people with the right attitude, then train them in the necessary skills, rather than the reverse. Lenin was right. Find the revolutionaries. Do not try to change people.

2. Extend the tribe biographically

The world of yesterday was geographically structured, and so were its tribes. The new tribes – whether they are Hell's Angels, computer nerds, or Amnesty International – are biographically structured. They are global tribes of people who feel they have something in common, no matter where they were born.

Since design is subjective, success is about targetting such global biographical tribes – core customers. It doesn't matter what kind of tribe, where it's based or how large it is. What does matter is that the targetted tribe has a common bond – values and attitudes – with your organizational tribe.

"We're all listening to the same music, watching the same movies, drinking the same vodka at exactly the same time, and now we have stores that will convey the same unified message around the world," says Gucci's Tom Ford. And Gucci is not alone. Violent drug barons create tribes. Miguel Caballero is the Armani of the armored apparel world. His company sells customized and fashionable bullet-proof vests. It has targeted a specific tribe. Its home base is Columbia where demand is great.

Pilgrims create tribes. Futurist Watts Wacker tells the story of how every year, 75,000 Chevrolet Suburban vans are sold in Saudi Arabia. The explanation for this sales phenomenon is that the pilgrims who visit Mecca are allowed to enter the city only in a vehicle with specific measurements. The only car that fits the specifications happens to be the Chevrolet Suburban.

The female population remain – astonishingly and somewhat depressingly – the most obvious and largely unexploited tribe. Prior to 1994 when Nokia launched the 2110 – the first mobile phone with rounded-off corners and a large display – all mobile phones came in one color. The 2110 came in a variety of colors and was targetted at women. It was a huge success.

The Norwegian furniture manufacturer Stokke has built an international reputation for its innovative designs. Among its most successful products is the Tripp Trapp, a wooden chair for babies and children. Designed by Peter Opsvik, the height and the depth of the Tripp Trapp are adjustable so that the chair can grow with the child. The Tripp Trapp does not look like a conventional children's chair.

One of the reasons Stokke has succeeded with the Tripp Trapp and its other unusual looking designs is a keen awareness of its tribes. The target audience for the

Tripp Trapp is essentially new parents who want the best for their children. So Stokke gives Tripp Trapps to children's nurseries and kindergartens where parents can see the chairs being used and abused. At times, Stokke has had to take on an educational role. In France, Tripp Trapps failed and then failed again. The problem was that the French had got out of the habit of eating *en famille*. They had no need for a children's chair. Stokke responded in a number of ways. First, it targetted French people who had worked outside the country and returned. It reasoned that they were more likely to have picked up the international habit of eating together. Second, the company sought out publicity opportunities based on the chair's unusual design. It also emphasized the "newness" of the product as the French have a predilection for anything new.

Stokke's other products – ergonomically designed furniture – attract a different tribe. These can basically be categorized as "free agents," freelance professionals. The company sometimes refers to them as "people who buy Apple Macs." The trouble with this tribe is that it is disparate, with a wide range of ages, occupations, and needs. Stokke's approach is to let the tribe come to them. Having decided that face-to-face interaction was important, it established Stokke Centers in major cities. These Centers host regular parties for specific groups such as physiotherapists and musicians to introduce them to the company's products. From being a small, local company with 40 employees in the mid-1980s, Stokke has expanded to become an international organization with 500 people.

3. Identify and involve individuals

Within a tribe there must be room for personalization and individual differences. "A product that matters needs to say something about the person who owns it," argues Barry Shepard, co-founder of the design consultancy SHR which helped develop the Volkswagen Beetle. Customers, confused by the array of products and services on offer, are looking to companies for help in expressing their individuality. They want products that in certain respects are as unique as their own fingerprints. Companies must, as a result, deal with micro markets of single individuals and extreme diversity.

Companies must customize – then customize still further. 3M's Post-it notes now come in 18 colors, 27 sizes, 56 shapes, and 20 fragrances. All in all, more than half a million combinations are available. Truck-maker Scania created modularized trucks which allow customers to build their personal truck – cafeteria style. Barbie now comes complete with 15,000 combinations. The management thinkers were right: mass customization is child's play. Change the outfit, the eyes, the color, the hairdo, the clothes, the name – but don't even think about the legs. All for $40.

In a fragmenting world, niches are becoming ever smaller. Increasing individualization combined with changes in technologies and values mean that micro markets have overtaken mass markets. The next step is one-to-one design, one-to-one manufacturing, one-to-one marketing, one-to-one everything, one customer–one solution.

We are entering a one-to-one society. In an age of abundance where sameness rules, people cry out for limited-edition products that make them stand out.

The relationship between the producer and the consumer is blurring. Recent developments in computer aided design (CAD) and computer aided manufacturing (CAM) open up many new opportunities. Companies can move from standardized to personalized; from mass production to flexible production and, now, mass customization. With fewer tools we can produce more and better quality models. "We used to wish we had the technology to do things ... Now technology is giving us things we don't even know how to use,' says Ian Schrager, owner of Schrager Hotels.

4. Replace the rational with the emotional

Regardless of tribal belonging or individual preferences, there are basically four ways in which you can communicate with people: you appeal either to their reason, affection, intuition, or desire. Every time we communicate with someone we use a mix of these elements. The critical question for companies is whether they are using a potent mix. In an age of abundance and information overload, where attention is a scarce resource, are they really getting through?

Most managers are expert in communicating through reason. Reasoning is what the typical manager is rewarded for and trained in. The problem is that success depends less and less on our reasoning skills. The only way to create real profit is to attract the emotional rather than the rational consumer. If you try reasoning you will have to deal with the purely economic rationality of the demanding customer. This inevitably results in zero profits as you will compete globally with an infinite number of other similar firms.

Noel Tichy of the University of Michigan says: "The best way to get people to venture into unknown terrain is to make it desirable by taking them there in their imagination." The emphasis needs increasingly to be on affection, intuition, and desire.

A good case in point is Harley-Davidson. The company and the customer offering are not for everyone. You have to share certain traits with the other members of the Harley tribe. The company is not just selling a motorcycle; it is selling American nostalgia. The arguments for buying a Harley have little to do with rational reasoning – price, performance, etc. – and everything to do with affection, intuition, and desire. CEO Richard Teerling says: "There's a high degree of emotion that drives our success. We symbolize the feelings of freedom and independence that people really want in this stressful world."

By inviting its consumer tribe to join the organizational tribe, Harley-Davidson has dramatically extended its community. It uses parties to initiate new members. Storytelling around the campfire keeps messages moving throughout the tribe. Closing ceremonies and continuous reinforcement are also part of the deal. What Harley-Davidson and other companies have realized is that a tribe targeting another tribe does not merely have to produce value – the customers also want values.

Value and values are inextricably linked. Raymond Loewe, the father of industrial design who provided mankind with such quintessential things as the Lucky Strike cigarette pack and the Greyhound bus, once said: "The most beautiful curve is a raising sales graph." Beauty remains in the eye of the beholder. Companies must amaze, daze, and seduce their customers. They must design to be different – or die.

RESOURCES

Nordström, Kjell and Riddestråle, Jonas, *Funky Business*, FT.com, 1999.
Nordström, Kjell and Riddestråle, Jonas, *Karaoke Capitalism*, FT Prentice Hall, 2004.

Outsourcing HR

STEPHEN COOMBER

[Companies increasingly outsource the management of their most important asset of all: their people.]

In September 2003, the consumer products giant Procter & Gamble announced a $400 million outsourcing contract with outsourcing provider IBM Global Services. At first glance it might seem like just another of many large IT outsourcing deals struck in recent years, but this is a deal with a difference. Procter & Gamble is outsourcing key HR functions such as benefits administration, travel and expense management, and compensation planning. It is part of a growing trend to outsource HR business processes.

Today outsourcing is about far more than just transferring data processing or data storage to a third-party supplier. Business processes in particular are being targetted. In fact, Business Power Outsourcing (BPO) is now the fastest growing segment of the outsourcing industry. Much of that growth is reflected in an increase in HR outsourcing (HRO). The HR function is now the most outsourced business process. Industry analyst Gartner Inc. predicted worldwide HR BPO revenue would reach $51 billion in 2004, while International Data Corporation (IDC) predicted a global market for outsourced HR services in excess of £60 billion by 2007.

"The attention that needs to be given to staff, employees, and managers in any organization will require rethinking of HR systems and procedures and of management," says Cranfield School of Management's Professor Andrew Kakabadse, co-author of *Smart Sourcing*. "Hence, the growth areas in outsourcing in the next few years are likely to be IT and HR."

Early HR outsourcing was about outsourcing distinct elements of the HR function such as payroll and employee benefits administration. The aim was to allow the HR department to focus on more strategic issues. The same logic still drives many HR outsourcing deals. "If the HR director spends all day worrying about why Sally hasn't been paid," says Mary-Sue Rogers, global HR Consulting leader for IBM Business Consulting Services, and lead partner in the P&G outsourcing deal, "they can't help the CEO orchestrate cultural change with employees in a new acquisition."

In the US, HR outsourcing is now big business. In 2000, for example, Bank of America signed a deal with the California-based outsourcing company Exult worth $1.1 billion. Deals of that magnitude have yet to hit the UK.

Many UK-based companies have so-called carve-out HR outsourcing arrangements – for example, outsourcing payroll administration to third-party providers. RebusUK (formerly Peterborough Software), for example, has been involved in the field of HR provision business for over 30 years. Today it provides payroll and similar HR services to a client list that includes companies such as Sainsbury, EasyJet, Powergen, IKEA, and Aventis. Other leading players include global outsourcing operations such as Hewitt Bacon & Woodrow and IBM Global Services.

But as HR outsourcing matures and both clients and providers become more sophisticated, so HR outsourcing has expanded to become a full-service or end-to-end outsourcing solution, including training, hiring and firing, drafting employee handbooks, and even regulation compliance. "Different processes are at different stages of maturity," says Julia Bailey, BPO Business Development Director at business consultants Cap Gemini. "The outsourcing of payroll processes is mature whilst the outsourcing of other HR processes is increasingly being seen as a real opportunity for niche providers."

In full-service HR outsourcing, the US is some way ahead of the UK. In the US, it is often undertaken by a professional employer organization (PEO). These companies assume the responsibility for the administration of the entire HR function of the client company. The PEO becomes a co-employer with all the legal responsibilities. According to the US-based National Association for Professional Employer Organizations, 2–3 million Americans are co-employed in a PEO arrangement. There are 800 PEO companies and the industry is growing at 20 percent year-on-year.

Kevin Barrow is joint managing partner of Tarlo Lyons, a London law firm that specializes in outsourcing issues. According to Barrow, some aspects of HRO by specialist suppliers are well advanced, especially payroll and recruitment. In the UK and Europe, however, the concept of full-service HR outsourcing has been slower to take off. Barrow points to three limiting factors: a smaller and fragmented European market, less sophisticated customers, and cultural resistance.

That may be about to change. "Some major corporates will move from shared services to full HRO," says Barrow. US outsourcing service providers are now targetting the UK market. For example, Convergys, a provider of outsourced employee care, has established a "center of excellence" in Guildford, Surrey. In the US, such centers have allowed the company to streamline HR processes, automating up to 80 percent of the HR process that it handles for a client. "HR business process outsourcing is where business integration, organizational strategy, and the changing role of HR meet," says Convergys' Paul Turner. "It is this evolution that is behind the explosive growth in HR BPO."

US experience suggests the potential benefits of successful HR outsourcing are considerable. New York-based Prudential Financial is one of the largest financial services companies in the US. It recently streamlined its in-house HR department by outsourcing a swathe of HR services, including payroll, benefits administration, training administration, and recruitment up to middle management. The outsourcing deal had a major impact on the bottom line – a $25 million reduction in HR-related expenditure over a period of a year.

With cost savings of that magnitude on the table, HR outsourcing will be moving up the agenda in the world's boardrooms.

Interview 9: Andrew Kakabadse

Andrew Kakabadse, Professor of International Management Development at Cranfield School of Management and author of *Smart Sourcing: International Best Practice*, talks about the future of outsourcing.

What do you envisage the state of outsourcing to be circa 2008?

The likelihood is that outsourcing over the next 5–6 years will evolve from single outsource contracts to a much more Japanese model of the horizontal *keiretsu*. In effect, what this means is a much more integrated supply chain with the parent company whereby the relationship is above and beyond just single contracts and issues such as costs. The emphasis will be to focus on what it means to promote value added in the marketplace and how to differentiate the whole supply chain from other competitive supply chains. Hence, in summary, I see outsourcing migrating from outsourcing to integrated *keiretsu* like supply chains in competition with other comparable supply chains.

How is the business case for outsourcing changing?

The business case for outsourcing is growing stronger and stronger for the following reasons:

- *The challenge of differentiation.* A critical issue that so many senior managers have to face is, how is their organization differentiated from competitors? On the basis that both shareholders and customers may find it difficult to truly understand what is the unique value-adding contribution of any one enterprise when compared against another, it does become important for each organization to focus on its areas of strength and pass on responsibility for other more peripheral activities to those organizations that are really more capable and more effective in those areas.
- *Innovative management.* Most organizations today are actually pretty efficient and quite effective. The reason for this is that most top directors have introduced critical reforms and improvements ranging from downsizing, right-sizing, team development, quality improvement/quality circles, leadership development, more effective and efficient cascading patterns of communication, as well as reasonably well thought through mergers and acquisitions. Hence, if competitors have introduced similar improvements, what really differentiates one organization from the other?

One critical differentiator is the moral, motivation, and pro-active nature of the people in the organization. The second is the quality of outsourcing and the quality of outsourced relationships. Both quality of people and the quality of managing outsource relationships can make a 2 percent difference in terms of differentiation, but that 2 percent difference can make a 20 percent difference in terms of enterprise performance. Thus, in summary, what else can any enterprise do to show that it is different, better, more effective than its competitors when virtually all other organizations have introduced the same innovations and reforms? The answer is to have a much more competently managed supply chain.

What do you think will be the key areas of growth in outsourcing?

The evidence we have is that continuous innovation in IT will mean ever greater IT outsourcing. Further, the attention that needs to be given to staff, employees, and managers in any organization will require rethinking of HR systems and procedures and of management development. Hence, the growth areas are likely to be IT and HR. From there on in, anything can be outsourced. So the situation is unpredictable. What may be seen as a core and critical function or process within any organization may be viewed within a 24–36-month period as being less critical and more a candidate for outsourcing. Thus, the highly effective parent organization will be one that is flexible in terms of what is outsourced (or for that matter insourced) according to market demands, shareholder demands, and market dynamism and volatility. Do not be surprised to find that all sorts of different views will emerge as to what will be key areas of growth in terms of outsourcing largely because it is difficult to predict how market dynamics will affect any single enterprise.

Has the practice of outsourcing peaked?

No. But the practice of outsourcing simply for economies of scale and cost reduction has peaked. Thus the value that can be gained from outsourcing is likely to vary contract by contract and organization by organization.

Outsourcing will have to address not only cost and economy of scale issues but also quality improvement, employee enhancement, and brand effectiveness issues. On this basis, an organization managing multiple outsourcing contracts in the most effective way is going to be the key to differentiate it from its competitors; thus the horizontal *keiretsu* conclusion that is highlighted above. When will outsourcing peak in reality? I do not know.

Taking Japan as an example, despite its economic and social problems, still the most proficient, global, and effective organizations have maintained their horizontal *keiretsu* supply chain philosophy. What they may change is any one individual supplier within that supply chain but not the *keiretsu* practice itself. A rather depressing thought is that outsourcing the way we know it today and the way it is likely to evolve in the future is likely to change only if there is some sort of crisis in terms of world politics, such as war. Otherwise the future that I foresee is that there any too many goods and services chasing too few customers, i.e. supply exceeds demand and, continual improvement is the only way to differentiate and no single organization can provide a total service – thus the *keiretsu* concept.

Interview by Des Dearlove

Project management as value creation

SEBASTIAN NOKES

[Most of the new value created by companies occurs through projects. Project management should be viewed as the major source of value rather than a cost.]

Projects are the management mechanism by which all change happens. Think about it. Every activity in an organization is either a continuing operation, which is to say more of what was done before, or a project, which is to say something new.

New things can happen without projects but only if they happen by accident or by evolution and gradual change. In other words, change that does not occur through projects is unplanned. Since accidents and natural change produce a very slow rate of change, in the modern, competitive environment, to all practical ends, it is only projects that deliver change.

In corporate finance, for example, each deal is a project; each acquisition is a project. In the legal world, each case or opinion is a project. In the wider business world, all change initiatives are projects. Projects are vital to any organization. Indeed, it is estimated that they account for 25 percent of the economy – and almost all the growth in the economy.

Yet despite its obvious importance, project management is the Cinderella of management subjects. Rather like IT in the 1970s, it remains the exclusive province of specialists, some might even say nerds. In the past, senior management tended to regard project management as something for new recruits and middle management to cut their teeth on, but of no significance in strategic decisions. Happily, this is now changing. The biggest projects are corporate takeovers. The fact is that most of these destroy value. One of the main reasons is poor execution of project management. For this and other reasons, senior management's attitude to project management is shifting.

Project management is now seen in many companies as a core skill that all senior management must have, just as senior managers must have some minimum competence in finance. This represents an important change. Ten years ago few corporations monitored the performance of their projects in a centralized way, and few senior managers had project management experience. This meant that the corporation had little idea of whether its investment in projects was efficient and effective in supporting corporate strategy. It also meant that senior managers were likely to be good project sponsors only by chance. This is also now changing.

In the past five years an increasing number of companies have begun setting up mechanisms to monitor the performance of their portfolio of projects, to propagate best practice, and to increase the project delivery capability of the organization. The UK government's Prime Minister's Delivery Unit is just one high-profile example of this trend, which shows that it is not limited to the private sector. Also in the last five years an increasing number of senior managers have been learning about project management, not because they are managing projects but because they are sponsoring projects or sitting on project steering committees and want to have a better grasp of the subject.

What is a project?

As the quotes below illustrate, definitions of a project vary:

- "Any piece of work requiring more than five man-days to complete" – *an international bank*
- "A project is a temporary endeavor undertaken to create a unique product or service. Projects are a means to respond to those requests that cannot be addressed within the organization's normal operational limits" – *PMI® PMBOK®*
- "A unique process, consisting of a set of co-ordinated activities, with a specific start and finish, pursuing a specific goal with constraints on time, cost, and resources." – *ISO 8402*
- "A management environment that is created for the purpose of delivering one or more business products according to a specified business case" – *PRINCE2®*

The term "program" is sometimes used synonymously with "project." A more common usage of the word "program" is to describe a set of related projects. Program management is related but distinct from project management. One of the chief differences is that whereas the aim of the project is always to deliver the end result, the aim of the program may be to deliver only some fraction of the projects within it, depending on the changing economic circumstances.

For example, the revenue increase program may have a project to deal with a sunny summer and a project to deal with a rainy summer. One will be killed when the state of the summer is known.

The rest of this article covers two things:

- how to do project management; and
- how to improve the project management capability of an organization.

These are related endeavors, the first applying at the level of the individual manager, the second at the level of the organization.

How to manage projects

Three kinds of knowledge are necessary to run projects:

- general management knowledge;
- subject matter knowledge; and
- project management knowledge.

This article covers only the last of these, but the effective project manager must understand the difference between these three kinds of knowledge. Subject matter knowledge is specific to the kind of projects being done. A research project in pharmacology requires a research pharmacologist and their skills, and building a tunnel requires civil engineering skills. In a sense project management is a branch of general management, but whether one agrees with this statement is of no interest here. The point is that there is a discipline called project management which applies generally to most projects, in all industries, most of the time.

The structure of a project will depend to a significant extent on the structure of the organization from which it comes. Organizations which are in effect little more than a collection of projects will spawn projects with quite different characteristics and structures from organizations in which projects are rare. This is important because managers who have seen projects working well in one environment should not assume that the same approach will work in another, or risk high project failure rates.

There are seven key sets of people in a project:

- stakeholders
- steering group (or project board)
- sponsor
- project manager
- customer
- subject matter experts
- project staff.

The stakeholders are all those on whom the project will have an effect. The steering group is the group of managers who collectively have oversight of the project. They delegate to the sponsor the day-to-day role of directing the project. The project manager manages the project on behalf of the steering group on a day-to-day basis, and keeps the sponsor informed of all significant issues. The customer is the beneficiary of the project. Project staff report to the project manager and perform the work of the project. Subject matter experts (SMEs) are individuals with specialist knowledge to be made available to the project. In addition to these seven, there may also be a project office (or program office) to provide administrative support to the project. The following shows a typical project structure.

The life cycle of a project

Projects go through a lifecycle, which can be broken into six stages:
1. conceiving
2. initiating
3. planning
4. executing
5. controlling
6. closing.

1. Conceiving

Conceiving is the informal, very first formulation of a project. Projects do not arrive neatly packaged and labeled as projects. Projects arise from an often vague and nebulous cloud of good ideas. There is much work to be done between having the good idea and seeing any action, let alone a result. Projects are usually the mechanism by which ideas are turned into tangible action, and the first stage in this long chain of events we call "conceiving." It is often ignored or missed out entirely in project management thinking, but there are good reasons to understand what the conceiving phase of a project is about and it may be valuable to formalize this in your organization's particular approach to project management.

The conceiving phase of project management requires answers to the following questions:

- How do we generate new ideas?
- How do we identify projects?
- How do we assess ideas for projects?
- How are new ideas communicated?

2. Initiating

Initiation is the formal selection of a project. In this stage the who, what, why, where, how, when of the project is first sketched out. Deciding the answers to these questions is an iterative process; the main planning work happens in the next stage.

Before initiation the project may have been nothing more than an idea, but by the end of the initiation stage the project is a project (or potential project) and is defined in sufficient detail to be such.

The key output of the initiation stage is a project initiation document (PID). This document serves three purposes. Putting it together forces you to think through the project in sufficient detail to form a reliable judgement of it and to communicate it to colleagues professionally. Second, it collects together all the vital information about the project in one place. Third, it shows the business benefit of the project – perhaps not in detail but it answers the question "has this idea got legs?"

There are a number of templates available for project initiation documents, including the PMI PMBOK and PRINCE2 methodologies. At the minimum, a project initiation document should have the following headings and need be only one or two pages long in total for a small project:

- What?
  - A brief description of the project, including:
  - What customer or internal problem does it resolve or what needs does it meet?
  - What is the overall deliverable?
  - What is the business benefit, in dollars?
  - How much investment is required?
- How?
  - How will the project be executed? The point of this section is to give the reader a sense of the approach to the project and its feasibility.
  - How will the project's deliverables be designed, delivered, marketed, and supported? How do we compete in the skills and expertise required if the project is not within our core competencies?
- Who?
  - Who will need to be involved in this project and who can affect its success other than those involved?
  - Who will be vital to the success of this project on the inside? Our people, regulators, suppliers, partners?
  - Who on the outside will affect the success of this project? Who are our relevant competitors? What are they doing that indicates that this project is a good idea for us?
- Where?
  - Where does this program fit in our business strategy?
  - Where is the market?
- When?
  - Give the key time factors and constraints, are there any key dates? When? (For example, year 2000 preparations had to be completed by 31/12/99 at the latest.) When can we start the project?
  - When are key resources available/unavailable?

- Why?
  - Why are we doing the project? Generally the reasons are one of the following, but expand on the reason so that there is a compelling answer to the "why?" question:
  - regulatory/mandatory/health and safety;
  - strategic imperative;
  - revenue-generation opportunity;
  - cost-reduction opportunity;
  - risk reduction.

The initiation phase ends when management has approved and signed off the PID. This then becomes the mandate and budget authorization, or preliminary authorization, for the project.

For large or complex projects the sign-off may be limited to a pre-project or exploratory project, in which further research and design of the project is carried out to enable a more considered decision to be made. (Breaking down the approval of projects into phases like this is known in UK government circles as the Stage-Gate approach, and is cited by the Ministry of Defence as being the main reason for recent improvement in the performance of major projects.)

3. Planning

The planning phase takes the PID and works it up into a proper project plan. Note that a project plan is not the chart produced by project management software. Such charts are useful but are only a very small part of a project plan. In a small project of 10 man-days or so of effort, the project plan may be little different from the PID. But in larger projects, say 30 days or more of effort, a more detailed plan will be required, and in 1,000-day projects the planning stage is in a sense a project in itself.

A good project plan will do three things. First, it will tell project workers what they should do, when, how they should do it, and to what quality. No further analysis of what needs to be done or how to do it beyond the plan should be required, although of course verbal explanation of the contents of the plan should be expected. Second, it will tell the project manager what they should do to manage the plan and make it all happen, and – which is really part of the same thing – it should have all reasonably foreseeable "what ifs" identified and contingency planned. Third, the plan is a communication tool. A large or complex project will have many stakeholders (see below) and managing their expectations is a vital task for the project manager. A good project plan is an invaluable communications tool.

Planning a project is hard work but is not normally intellectually difficult. The most important part of planning is the work breakdown structure (WBS). Work breakdown, as its name implies, is simply a breakdown of all the work that must be done in the project. At its most basic, a WBS is nothing more than a list of tasks – of every single task to be done in the project. On a project of any size the list should be hierarchical, with headings and subheadings. How many levels of subheadings to have depends on the size and complexity of the task, but as a rule of thumb three levels of subheading are enough for most projects, and six levels should be enough for all but the largest and most complex projects.

The first cut of a work breakdown for designing a new product might look like this:

- Research product market space.
- Identify possible new products.
- Select best new product.

If you tell someone to "research product market space" you will be lucky if they know what to do, and even luckier if they do what you expect them to do. This means you need another level of detail, to answer the question "what do we mean by this?"

- Research product market space.
    - Obtain from management a list of markets to be researched.
    - Obtain a list of products to be considered in this project:
        - our existing products;
        - our competitor's existing products.
    - Identify which existing products are a threat to our future profitability.
    - Obtain existing information on the market space.
    - Obtain direction on what market space to target.
    - Research and validate target market space.
- Identify possible new products.
- Select best new product.

So now under the first heading, we have another two levels of detail, and a much better idea of what to do. In a work breakdown keep adding detail until you are confident that there is enough for someone to be able to start work and deliver what you expect. How much detail this requires will always be a matter of management judgement. Depending on the kind of staff in your organization, a line at the lowest level of detail in the WBS should occupy between a day and a week of time for the person or team doing the work.

Before starting a WBS there are two prerequisites, a project charter (or terms of reference) and a scope statement. The project charter is a one-paragraph statement of the aim and rationale of the project, linking it into the strategy of the organization. This should be approved by all the project's stakeholders and signed off by the project's sponsor (see below). The statement of scope is a list of things that are definitely included in the project and other things which are definitely not included in the project. For example, if a project is started to reengineer the way that tax is deducted from payroll, the scope statement would state whether National Insurance contributions are in or out of scope.

Alongside the WBS it is often necessary to have a WBS dictionary. This document defines what is meant by key terms in the WBS. Each dictionary entry is a what/how/who/where/when/why. It states what work is to be done and what the outputs or deliverables of the work will be; how the work is to be done in terms of tools and techniques to be used; by whom it is to be done, perhaps in terms of qualifications, experience, job title, business unit; where the work is to be done; when the work is to start and finish, either in terms of hard calendar dates or in terms of dependencies; and why the work is to be done, in terms of how it fits into the overall project.

The project charter, scope statement, WBS, and WBS dictionary together are the basis for creating whatever other parts of the plan are necessary. These may include:

- dependencies between activities;
- duration of activities;
- sequence of activities;
- quality plan;
- cost estimate and project budget;
- project organization chart;
- staffing plan;
- risk management plan and risk register;
- issue management plan and issue register;
- change management plan and change register;
- quality assurance plan;
- communications needs assessment and plan;
- procurement plan.

When completed the project plan should be signed off by the sponsor and key stakeholders.

4. Executing

This is the phase where the actual work gets done. Because there is a solid project plan the management of the execution stage is management by exception. The project manager monitors execution of the work and focusses only on areas where there is deviation from the plan. Deviation from the plan is to be expected because even the best plan will need to change once in contact with reality. However, if the planning was good then the changes will be manageable.

In this phase three other vital activities occur. Most important is communication – tell stakeholders what is happening and continue to manage their expectations. Second, develop the team both in their individual skills required for the project and as a whole. Good teamwork makes for successful projects. Third, manage the quality of the deliverable. Following the plan is one thing, but it is a separate task to monitor that what the project is producing meets the quality standards defined and agreed in the project plan.

5. Controlling

Management by exception means replanning work to take account of the inevitable changes and surprises during execution. This is logically a separate activity from executing the work, and fits in a stage we call "controlling." In practice the executing and controlling stages run in parallel, but experience shows that it is valuable for management to think of the two as different things. The heart of the controlling stage is change control. Changes to the plan may be required for a number of reasons, including changes in the economic situation, changes in the organization, risks crystallizing, user requirement changing, tools or techniques that were included in the plan being found to be inadequate to the task, and so on. The wrong way to deal with the need for change is to just make the change and not tell anyone. Proper change control means understanding why a change is necessary, making the change in the best possible way, anticipating and preparing for all the ramifications of the change, and ensuring that any extra costs or risks are signed off.

There should be a formal change control mechanism, including a body appointed for the purpose of approving changes.

6. Closing

When the project is finished it should be closed in a controlled way. This is to ensure that assets used by the project are returned to their proper owners, that lessons learned are captured, staff records are updated, and risks are closed out. If the project had budget codes and general ledger codes assigned to it, these should be closed out.

RESOURCES

Belbin, Meredith, *The Coming Shape of Organization*, Butterworth Heinemann, 1996.

Nokes, Sebastian, *The Definitive Guide to Project Management*, FT Prentice Hall, 2nd Edition, 2004.

The quality revolution

STUART CRAINER AND DES DEARLOVE

[Japan may be the nation most closely associated with TQM and the quality revolution but the founding fathers of the quality movement were American: W. Edwards Deming and Joseph Juran.]

In 1924, a physicist called Walter Shewhart (1891–1967) came up with the idea of a production control chart. A year later, he joined Western Electric as an engineer and found that the desire for exactitude found in theory was inevitably disappointed in practice. Shewhart's response was to develop a statistical approach to quality that emphasized the stability of production and supply, and applied the standards of the end user to the producer. Basically, Shewhart argued that minimal variation in production and maximum human co-operation were the most productive routes forward.

During the Second World War, the US War Department, anxious to enhance productivity as much as possible, brought in Western Electric's Bell Telephone Laboratories to promote its quality control methods. The armaments industry was given a crash course in Shewhart-style quality. Its impact was generally seen as positive. Indeed, Lord Cherwell, wartime scientific adviser to Winston Churchill, said that the Shewhart quality philosophy was the single most significant US contribution to the whole Allied war effort.

Such steps forward seemed to suggest that the Allied victors had the industrial world at their feet. Wartime had been a proving ground for modern management and manufacturing. It had emerged triumphant, able to produce reliable goods quickly in huge quantities.

In the immediate post-war years, however, the pursuit of more became the driving economic force. Shewhart was largely forgotten in the rush to get on with business life. Quality initiatives like those at Western Electric disappeared – from the US at least. Meanwhile, the scale and speed of the revival of the countries defeated and devastated by the war were startling. The destruction was enormous, beyond parallel, at individual, national, and corporate levels. In Germany, the huge Siemens corporation was all but destroyed. By 1945, only about 400 of the 24,000 machine tools originally installed were still operative in the company's Berlin plants. After only 14 days of occupation, the Allied powers allowed work to resume and, by the end of 1945, around 14,000 workers were employed at Siemens' Berlin plants, cleaning up and making a bizarre collection of products, including bicycle tires, coal shovels, cooking pots, and coal-fired stoves.

On September 2, 1945 the Japanese surrendered on board the USS *Missouri*. However, the Japanese had begun planning their future before their final defeat. (As had German industrialists. "Group directorates" were already established in southern and western Germany by Siemens in the final months of the war. These directorates were later able to start the reconstruction work independently of the head office in Berlin.) In the summer of 1945, Japanese ministers met secretly to discuss the future revival of their country. The aim, according to Foreign Minister Shigeru Yoshida, was to ensure that "we could indeed rebuild Imperial Japan out of this way of defeat ... science will be advanced, business will become strong with the introduction of American capital, and in the end our Imperial country will be able to fulfill its true potential. If that is so, it is not so bad to be defeated in this war." This combination of pragmatism, optimism, planning, and blind faith was characteristic of the rebuilding of the country.

The Japanese were greatly helped by General MacArthur's commitment to rebuilding the country. He wanted to rebuild not through re-establishing the old elite but through elevating the middle ranks to take charge. One of the immediate post-war objectives was to set up a Japanese radio receiver industry so that the occupying powers could communicate directly to the people. The team of engineers charged with helping Japan's radio industry included a number who had worked at Western Electric and were, as a result, aware of the concept of quality control.

The approach of the American team of engineers in post-war Japan was greatly influenced by Shewhart's work. The team included Homer Sarasohn, W.S. Magil, Frank Polkinghorn, and Charles Protzman. Magil used Shewhart's quality control theories at the Nippon Electric Company in 1946 and lectured on the subject while in Japan.

Then Sarasohn and Protzman were supported by MacArthur in their idea of establishing a management training program to ensure that their approaches reached as many people in industry as possible. During 1949–50, Sarasohn and Protzman organized a series of eight-week courses on industrial management to which only top executives in the Japanese communications industry were invited. The students included Matsushita Electric's Masaharu Matsushita, Mitsubishi Electric's Takeo Kato, Fujitsu's Hanzou Omi, Sumitomo Electric's Bunzaemon Inoue, and Sony's founders Akio Morita and Masaru Ibuka.

Another post-war initiative was the creation (in August 1946) of Japan's Federation of Economic Organizations (FEO). This sounds like a glorified talking shop; it wasn't. FEO became one of the mainsprings of Japanese economic renewal, with over 750 large corporations and 100 major national trade associations. It was the power behind the revival of Japan Inc. and announced its main purpose as "to maintain close contact with all sectors of the business community for the purpose of adjusting and harmonizing conflicting views and interests of the various businesses and industries represented in its huge membership. It is the front office of the business community and is in effect a partner of the government." FEO's first president was Ichiro Ishikawa, a successful industrialist, who was also president of the Japan Union of Scientists and Engineers (JUSE), Japan's most important quality control organization, founded in 1946.

Quality control was, therefore, well under way to becoming established in Japan very soon after the end of the war. Its impetus was to become irreversible.

The next move forward came when Ishikawa invited a Census Bureau statistician called W. Edwards Deming (1900–93) to give a lecture to Tokyo's Industry Club in July 1950. Deming had first visited Japan in 1947 to aid in the development of what was to become the 1951 census. His message was different to the usual quality control theory in that he emphasized the deficiencies of management. If quality was to happen it had to be led by management. The new generation had to seize the day.

As Ishikawa had sent out the invitations, the lecture was well attended, including 21 company presidents (some have suggested there were up to 45 in attendance). "I did not just talk about quality. I explained to management their responsibilities," Deming recalled. "Management of Japan went into action, knowing something about their responsibilities and learning more about their responsibilities."[7]

Deming eventually delivered a series of lectures. He asked for no fee, but JUSE sold reprints. The money raised through reprint sales was used to create the Deming Application Prize. This award for outstanding total quality programs was first awarded in 1951 to Koji Kobayashi.

Over the next three decades, Japanese business put Deming's theories – and those of other quality gurus – into impressive practice. The West did not. Then, in 1979, NBC was fishing around for subjects for a documentary. The basic idea was for a program on the decline of American business. Executive producer Reuven Frank had began with the far from populist working title of "What to do about America's falling productivity?," which had metamorphosed into "What ever happened to good old Yankee ingenuity?" Neither seemed likely to set the world alight. Then it was suggested to Frank that he send someone along to see an elderly NYU academic who lived in Washington DC.

Clare Crawford-Mason was working on the project with Frank and was assigned to pay the mysterious old man a visit. Later she recalled: "I called the man's office and set up an appointment. It wasn't difficult; his schedule was open. I recall postponing the first meeting. I was directed to go to the side of a residential house and come down the basement steps. I did. I knocked on the cellar door and walked into a two-room, below-ground office, filled with books and papers and overflowing desks and a blackboard covered with mathematical formulas." She found "the old gentleman ... pleasant, courtly and vehement."[8]

The man was W. Edwards Deming. To the outside observer, Deming matched the stereotype of the academic eccentric. He eschewed luxury and wrote the date of purchase on his eggs with felt-tip pen. (Later, when he was wealthy, Deming continued to drive a 1969 Lincoln Continental and to use public transport.) His staff comprised a single assistant – Cecilia "Ceil" Kilian, who eventually worked with him for 39 years – and he worked six days a week for 12 hours.

Deming told the NBC team that he had played a central part in the renaissance of the Japanese economy in the post-war years. This was news to virtually everyone in the Western world. Deming was unheard of, an obscure statistician. But he was persuasive and impressive. The facts checked out. He was well known and honored in Japan. An NBC program evolved from that mysterious first meeting. It was broadcast on June 26, 1980 with its final title: "If Japan can, why can't we?"

The NBC program was a seminal moment in the development of Western management theory and practice. It was also a late and long-delayed recognition of W. Edwards Deming. (There was some irony in the fact that, at that point, Deming didn't own a television and had watched it only once to see the 1969 moon landing.) He gave American businesspeople a lecture in the quality basics. "Inspection does not build quality, the quality is already made before you inspect it. It's far better to make it right in the first place," he intoned. "Statistical methods help you to make it right in the first place so that you don't need to test it. You don't get ahead by making product and then separating the good from the bad, because it's wasteful. It wastes time of men, who are paid wages; it wastes time of machines, if there are machines; it wastes materials.'

After the program, NBC was inundated with phone calls. The executives of the Fortune 500 woke up in front of their TV sets. The program's message was simple but stark. "It was the first time anyone had said that if America did not improve its productivity our children would be the first generation of Americans who could not expect to live better than their parents," says Clare Crawford-Mason.[9]

The early 1980s provided wake-up calls aplenty. Bad news stalked every corner. Western industry was, by common consensus, held to be on its knees. The oil-crisis of the mid-1970s was the portent of a period of navel examination, self-analysis. Businesspeople contemplated their poor-performing companies and their under-productive workforces with bemusement. By the beginning of the 1980s, Western industrialists were willing to hold their hands up and admit, "We've screwed up." They would also have quickly moved on to blaming irresponsible unions and greedy sheiks for this sad situation before desperately professing that they had little clue about what to do next.

The death knell of post-war industrial optimism and unquestioning faith in the mighty corporation was sounding. Only the profoundly deaf carried on regardless – and there were many who chose to ignore the signals.

There was no shortage of obituary notices. A few days after the Deming TV program, two Harvard Business School academics, Robert Hayes and Bill Abernathy, had their article "Managing our way to economic decline" published in the July/August 1980 issue of the *Harvard Business Review*. It proved grim and highly influential reading.

Hayes and Abernathy had wrestled with the demons of decline and emerged dismayed. "Our experience suggests that, to an unprecedented degree, success in most industries today requires an organizational commitment to compete in the marketplace on technological grounds – that is, to compete over the long run by offering superior products," they wrote. (It is astounding in retrospect that such commercial facts of life needed restating.) "Yet, guided by what they took to be the newest and best principles of management, American managers have increasingly directed their attention elsewhere. These new principles, despite their sophistication and widespread usefulness, encourage a preference for (1) analytic detachment rather than the insight that comes from 'hands on' experience and (2) short-term cost reduction rather than long-term development of technological competitiveness. It is this new managerial gospel, we feel, that has played a major role in undermining the vigor of American industry."[10]

Hayes and Abernathy went on to champion customer orientation as a vital ingredient in reversing the apparently irreversible trend. Their message was that management was the problem. Forget about union militancy, forget about foreign competition, look upstairs to the boardroom.

An article buried in the *Harvard Business Review* does not usually excite or ignite debate; this one did. Hayes and Abernathy announced that the Western corporate post-war dream was approaching its final hours. People asked: what next?

Turning Japanese

One answer was to take Deming's advice and look to the East. This was a new experience. The ability – not to mention the arrogance and torpor – to ignore the rise of Japan was truly astonishing. The emergence of Japanese competitors had been generously signaled by the media.

As early as 1964, *Fortune* noted: "American manufacturers of radios, television sets, and other consumer electronic equipment have been repeatedly confounded by the agile competitiveness of Japan's Sony Corp. A small company even by Japanese standards – its sales last year amounted to $77 million – Sony has astutely used its limited capital to concentrate on a few unusually designed products beamed to a great extent at export markets, particularly the US."[11] In the very same article, it was noted that the Sony founder Akio Morita had been based in New York rather than Tokyo since 1963. The other founder of the company, Masaru Ibuka, visited the US in 1952; by 1958 Sony's export sales totaled $2.6 billion.[12]

The *Fortune* article went on to cite a 1960s survey that had asked American radio dealers whether they had ever handled Japanese radios. Most dealers said no. The next question asked whether they had ever handled Sony radios. The majority said yes.[13] *Fortune* concluded that Sony's "well-made products are usually priced a notch or so above competitive US-made equipment and well above the normal run of imports from Japan."[14]

The warnings were ignored. Suddenly, however, the appetite for knowledge was enormous. A succession of books examined the secrets behind the perceived success of Japan.[15]

William Ouchi's 1981 *Theory Z* venerated Japan's employment and managerial practices. Theory Z was the natural development of McGregor's Theories Y and X. Richard Pascale and Anthony Athos also published the bestselling *The Art of Japanese Management*. This played a crucial role in the discovery of Japanese management techniques, as Pascale and Athos considered how a country the same size as Montana could be outstripping the American industrial juggernaut. "In 1980, Japan's GNP was third highest in the world and, if we extrapolate current trends, it would be number one by the year 2000," they warned.[16]

Harsh home truths lurked on every page of *The Art of Japanese Management*. "If anything, the extent of Japanese superiority over the United States in industrial competitiveness is underestimated," wrote Pascale and Athos, observing that "a major reason for the superiority of the Japanese is their managerial skill." In its comparisons of US and Japanese companies, *The Art of Japanese Management* provided rare insights into the truth behind the mythology of Japanese management and the inadequacy of much Western practice.

Among the key components of Japanese management identified by Pascale and Athos was that of vision, something they found to be notably lacking in the West. "Our problem today is that the tools are there but our 'vision' is limited. A great many American managers are influenced by beliefs, assumptions, and perceptions about management that unduly constrain them," they commented. The book, they said, was "not an assault on the existing tools of management, but upon the Western vision of management which circumscribes our effectiveness."[17]

Adding his voice to the argument was Japanese consultant Kenichi Ohmae. Ohmae did much to reveal the truth behind Japanese strategy making to an expectant Western audience. He demonstrated that the Japanese were human after all; at the time, Western managers were beginning to wonder.

Ohmae explored – and largely exploded – simplistic Western myths about Japanese management. Forget company songs and lifetime employment, there was more to Japanese management than that. Most notably, there was the Japanese art of strategic thinking. This, said Ohmae, is "basically creative and intuitive and rational." Japanese companies weren't mired in endless analysis or pointless hierarchies. "Most Japanese companies don't even have a reasonable organization chart," Ohmae told Peters and Waterman, authors of *In Search of Excellence*. "Nobody knows how Honda is organized, except that it uses lots of project teams and is quite flexible ... Innovation typically occurs at the interface, requiring multiple disciplines. Thus, the flexible Japanese organization has now, especially, become an asset."[18]

Ohmae's *The Mind of the Strategist* reached America in 1982. It had been published in Japan in 1975, though at that time there was no interest in the West in how Japan did anything. Ohmae pointed out that unlike large US corporations, Japanese businesses tend not to have large strategic planning staffs. Instead, they often have a single, naturally talented strategist with "an idiosyncratic mode of thinking in which company, customers, and competition merge in a dynamic interaction out of which a comprehensive set of objectives and plans for action eventually crystallizes."

Ohmae also noted that the customer was at the heart of the Japanese approach to strategy and key to corporate values. "In the construction of any business strategy, three main players must be taken into account: the corporation itself, the customer, and the competition. Each of these 'strategic three Cs' is a living entity with its own interests and objectives. We shall call them, collectively, the 'strategic triangle,' Ohmae wrote. "Seen in the context of the strategic triangle, the job of the strategist is to achieve superior performance, relative to competition, in the key factors for success of the business. At the same time, the strategist must be sure that his strategy properly matches the strengths of the corporation with the needs of a clearly defined market. Positive matching of the needs and objectives of the two parties involved is required for a lasting good relationship; without it, the corporation's long-term viability may be at stake."

The central thrust of Ohmae's arguments was that strategy as epitomized by the Japanese approach is irrational and non-linear. (Previously, the Japanese had been feted in the West for the brilliance of their rationality and the far-sighted remorselessness of their thinking.) "Phenomena and events in the real world do not always fit a linear model," wrote Ohmae. "Hence the most reliable means of dissecting a situation into its constituent parts and reassembling them in the desired pattern is not a step-by-step methodology such as systems analysis. Rather, it is that ultimate non-linear thinking tool, the human brain. True strategic thinking thus contrasts sharply with the conventional mechanical systems approach based on linear thinking. But it also contrasts with the approach that stakes everything on intuition, reaching conclusions without any real breakdown or analysis."

Unfortunately, faith in the linear model remained strong. (Managers had been ignoring Henry Mintzberg's similar exhortations to increase the level of creativity in strategy formulation for years.) Western managers weren't ready for the ultimate non-linear thinking tool, they wanted something to measure, something to do, something to get hold of.

The quality gospel

They found it in the notion of "quality." Western managers grabbed hold of quality with the enthusiasm of the truly desperate. "I think people here expect miracles.

American management thinks that they can just copy from Japan. But they don't know what to copy," Deming said on the famous NBC broadcast. He became the great deliverer, the aging sage from Sioux City, Iowa, the miracle worker.

Deming's impact was huge. Ignored for the previous five decades – though celebrated in Japan – Deming made up for lost time. In 1991, US News & World Report identified nine people or events that had changed the world. The Apostle Paul was the first; W. Edwards Deming was the most recent.

Deming's message remained remarkably similar to that delivered in Japan in 1950. First, management was responsible for the mess. "Failure of management to plan for the future and to foresee problems have brought about waste of manpower, of materials, and of machine-time, all of which raise the manufacturer's cost and price that the purchaser must pay. The consumer is not always willing to subsidize this waste. The inevitable result is loss of market," he wrote.[19] Quality must be led from the top. Exhortations to work harder do not lead to quality.

Second, the customer was king, emperor, CEO, and dictator. Or, as Deming phrased it, "the consumer is the most important part of the production line." Quality is defined by the customer. Third, the old Shewhart mantra: understand and reduce variation in every process. The process, not the product, is the thing (by the time the inspector has a product in his hands, it is too late). Four, never stop and apply quality to everything. Change and improvement affect and must involve everyone in the organization (as well as suppliers) and must be continuous and all-encompassing. Five, train people. Deming's faith in the willingness of people to do a good job was undimmed by his seven decades on earth.

Deming's call to arms was most powerfully put in his well-known Fourteen Points:

1. Create constancy of purpose for improvement of product and service.
2. Adopt the new philosophy.
3. Cease dependence on inspection to achieve quality.
4. End the practice of awarding business on the basis of price tag alone. Instead, minimize total cost by working with a single supplier.
5. Improve constantly and forever every process for planning, production, and service.
6. Institute training on the job.
7. Adopt and institute leadership.
8. Drive out fear.
9. Break down barriers between staff areas.
10. Eliminate slogans, exhortations, and targets for the workforce.
11. Eliminate numerical quotas for the workforce and numerical goals for management.
12. Remove barriers that rob people of pride of workmanship. Eliminate the annual rating or merit system.

13. Institute a vigorous program of education and self-improvement for everyone.
14. Put everybody in the company to work to accomplish the transformation.

For some, Deming's Fourteen Points became the commandments of the quality movement. In his efforts to move quality off the factory floor and on to the desk of every single executive, Deming recreated it as a philosophy of business and, for some, of life. "Unfortunately, a system of totality insists, by definition, that it will solve everything," noted one obituary of Deming.[20]

Deming did not have a monopoly on quality. A procession of other quality gurus emerged from the shadows with varying degrees of credibility. The career of the most notable, Joseph Juran (born 1904), bore a resemblance to Deming's. Trained as an electrical engineer, Juran worked for Western Electric in the 1920s and then for AT&T. In 1953, he made his first visit to Japan at the invitation of the Japanese Federation of Economic Associations and the Japanese Union of Scientists and Engineers. For two months, Juran observed Japanese practices and trained managers and engineers in what he called "managing for quality."

Juran's weighty *Quality Control Handbook* was published in 1951. He was later awarded the Second Class Order of the Sacred Treasure by the Emperor of Japan – the highest honor for a non-Japanese citizen – for "the development of quality control in Japan and the facilitation of US and Japanese friendship."

Juran argued that there was a blessed quality trinity of planning, control, and improvement. In keeping with the desire for simplification and checklists, he produced his "Quality Planning Road Map," which advocated nine steps to quality nirvana:

1. Identify who are the customers.
2. Determine the needs of those customers.
3. Translate those needs into our language.
4. Develop a product that can respond to those needs.
5. Optimize the product features so as to meet our needs as well as customer needs.
6. Develop a process which is able to produce the product.
7. Optimize the process.
8. Prove that the process can produce the product under operating conditions.
9. Transfer the process to operations.

Such neat prescriptions helped the quality gospel spread throughout the world. Deming and Juran criss-crossed time zones with the enthusiasm of rock stars whose breakthrough album has just topped the *Billboard* chart. The quality concept – though not necessarily the practice – carried all before it. Deming Associations appeared in France, the UK, and other countries. Total Quality Management Institutes were launched, though without Deming's blessing as he didn't like the phrase.

Deming, Juran, and the other quality gurus went out of their way to stress that miracles simply did not happen. Their audience continued to believe in miracles. "Solving problems, big problems and little problems, will not halt the decline of American industry, nor will expansion in use of computers, gadgets, and robotic machinery," wrote Deming. "Benefits from massive expansion of new machinery also constitute a vain hope. Massive immediate expansion in the teaching of statistical methods to production workers is not the answer either, nor wholesale flashes of quality control circles. All these activities make their contribution, but they only prolong the life of the patient, they can not halt the decline."[21]

The key to halting the decline lay in changes in management. Deming's audience, however, preferred to introduce quality circles and to publish quality newsletters.

Some companies did embrace the quality gospel with genuine vigor and commitment. The Nashua Corporation was the first US company to adopt Deming's quality management principles. Other well-known converts included the Ford Motor Company and Florida Power & Light (the first US winner of The Deming Prize and advised by Asaka Tetsuichi). Ford initially turned to Japanese quality guru Ishikawa Kaoru for guidance but found his lectures too complex and, anyway, its management was tired of having Japan's virtues thrust down its throat at every opportunity. It then turned to Deming, acknowledging that he was opinionated and abrasive but reassuringly American.

Others embraced the idea and then failed to reap the expected dividends. Typical of this group was Kodak, which introduced a company-wide quality campaign in the early 1980s. Its "corporate policy quality statement" committed Kodak "to be world leader in the quality of its products and services. We will judge this quality by how well we anticipate and satisfy customer needs."[22] Kodak seemed to do everything prescribed: employees were trained in statistical techniques, annual worldwide quality conferences were held, top managers were actively involved, and so on. None of this got the company very far. In 1991, Kodak announced a $1.6 billion restructuring of the company and contemplated whether stronger medicine would do the trick.

Quality opened Western eyes; but it did not necessarily open their minds.

RESOURCES

Deming, W. Edwards, *Out of the Crisis*, Mercury, 1986.
Juran, Joseph, *Managerial Breakthrough*, McGraw Hill, 1964.
Juran, Joseph, *Juran on Planning for Quality*, Free Press, 1988.
Pascale, Richard and Athos, Anthony, *The Art of Japanese Management*, Simon & Schuster, 1981.
Peters, Tom and Waterman, Robert, *In Search of Excellence*, Harper & Row, 1982.

Understanding the sources and drivers of supply chain risk

HELEN PECK

[Globalization means that supply chain management is increasingly important. Despite this there is little research on the risks involved.]

Supply chain risk is still a relatively unexplored area of management research, though one that's time has come. In the UK, the economic impact of two events focussed the minds of policy makers on the need to understand more about the vulnerabilities of the nation's supply networks. The first was the impact of fuel protests in 2000, followed by the outbreak of foot-and-mouth disease in the nation's livestock herds just a few months later. The terrorist attacks of 9/11 made supply chain vulnerability a global issue.

Of course, supply chain risk did not emerge with the new millennium, though the threat of "Y2K" related disruptions did draw attention to aspects of it. For some time there had been growing unease among practitioners who suspected that supply chains were becoming more brittle. Fingers were pointed at a number of trends in supply chain management and business strategy. These included the application of lean manufacturing and just-in-time logistics, outsourcing, global sourcing and supply, together with the centralization of production and distribution. Nevertheless, little research had hitherto been undertaken to see whether the "usual suspects" were actually guilty. UK government-funded research by Cranfield,[23, 24] did just that. It investigated the sources and drivers of risk in eight sectors of industry.

What do we mean by supply chain risk?

The term "supply chain" can be interpreted in many ways, here it refers to "the network of organizations that are involved, through upstream and downstream linkages, in the different processes and activities that produce value in the form of products and services in the hands of the ultimate consumer.[25] It is a broad-based definition that embraces products, processes, organizations, and networks. "Risk" is another term that has many meanings, but it is used here in the sense that it relates to the vulnerability of supply chain networks, meaning "at risk," i.e. likely to be lost or damaged.

What the research uncovered was a picture of supply chains – sets of processes, information, and workflows – passing within and between messy, complex, dynamic interacting networks that link organizations, industries, and economies. Complex systems theory gives some pointers to academics on how we might improve our understanding of the dynamics of these networks.

Conventional approaches to supply chain management and indeed corporate risk management have failed to keep pace with the reality of networked global supply chains. It is a shortcoming that has latterly attracted the attention of leading international insurers. The insurance industry has well-honed actuarial techniques, developed over centuries, for assessing the direct risks to persons and property. These traditional methods assess the probability of an event – a known risk – occurring (usually based on broad historical data), combined with the impact of the event, should it occur. With the growth of new types of policies – notably for business interruption – insurers have become aware that the risks they are required to assess may be invisible to or beyond the control of their client firms. They may be "knowable," i.e. detectable if enough effort is spent searching for them, but beyond that there are often other consequential risks which remain undetectable and unquantifiable. Moreover, consequential risks have no definitive solutions because they are by their very nature unknown before they emerge.

Within supply chains, consequential risks often emerge as unintended side effects of well-meaning actions – such as outsourcing or off-shoring – which produce unanticipated or unpredictable outcomes. Research, notably in defense,[26, 27] has already highlighted the problems of consequential risks within supply chains. In fact US Defense Secretary Donald Rumsfeld famously referred to these "unknowable unknowns" when discussing problems faced by coalition forces during the 2003 invasion of Iraq. While few supply chain managers must mount missions as hazardous as armed invasions, it should be recognized that there may be useful lessons to be learned from that experience, notably, the dangers of decision making based on incomplete information and flawed assumptions.

The next point to consider is that even if business interruption insurance is available and affordable, it is unlikely ever to cover the full costs of the resulting supply chain failures. It is therefore incumbent upon supply chain managers and corporate risk specialists to take what action they can to understand the sources and drivers of these risks. The task is complex, but not hopeless. The framework put forward in this article provides a starting point.

A multi-level framework

To understand the dynamics of supply chain risk it is essential to consider the sources and drivers of risk at each of the levels of analysis suggested by the definition of supply chains put forward earlier, i.e. in terms of the products or process, organizations, and networks. All are set within a wider social and natural environment. The drivers of supply chain risk within each of these levels are inextricably linked, but for the purpose of clarity they are dealt with separately here.

- Level 1 – process, product, or value stream.
- Level 2 – asset and infrastructure dependencies.
- Level 3 – organizations and inter-organizational networks.
- Level 4 – the wider social and natural environment.

Level 1 – process, product, or value stream

At Level 1 the emphasis is on *what is being carried* in the supply chain, on workflow or flows of goods, and accompanying information. It is a view of the supply chain that is in keeping with prevailing process engineering-based perspectives. Such views see the supply chain as the contents of a linear "pipeline" flowing through and between organizations in the network (see Figure 4.3). It is a perspective that underpins integrated demand-driven "lean" or "agile" supply chain management concepts. Goals tend to revolve around the efficient, value-based, management of individual workflows – "value streams" – and their accompanying information.

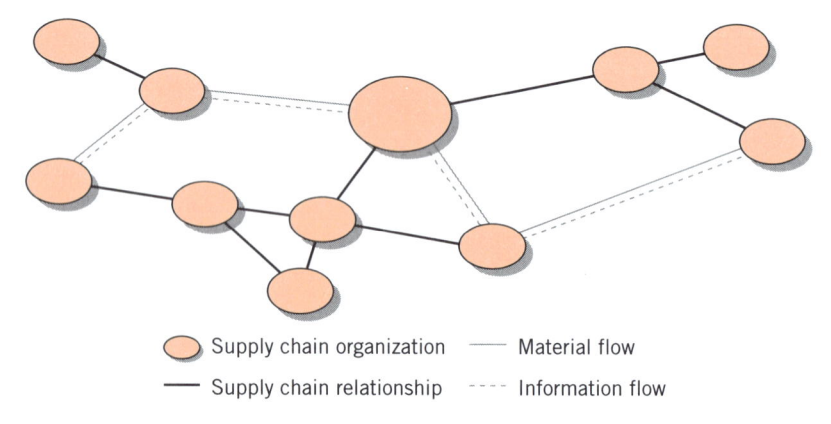

Figure 4.3: *Supply chains as processes within networks*

Source: Peck, H., 'Supply Chain Vulnerability: Levels in a Landscape,' *Proceedings of Defence and Material Support*, London, 2003.

From this process-orientated perspective, supply chain risks are principally the financial or commercial risks arising from poor quality, sub-optimal supply chain performance, demand volatility, and shifting marketplace requirements. Risk management is therefore about improving efficiency – often by removing uncertainty of process outcomes or deviations from plans – and about becoming more responsive to customer demand. The principles of visibility, velocity, and control are central to risk management here. Better visibility of demand reduces forecasting risk and allows the progress of orders, payments, and finished goods to be monitored within the system. Better monitoring opens the way for more effective control and greater velocity. If the goods and information flow are traveling faster through the system, inventory holding costs and the risk of obsolescence are both reduced, better asset utilization brings them down even further. Technology is a great facilitator here, allowing risk reduction through the "substitution of information for inventory."

The availability of credible and reliable information is absolutely central, and is in turn dependent on the willingness of the parties to share demand and monitoring data. This requires a high level of trust and co-operation between adjacent organizations. In short, it is an approach that aspires to a seamless flow of information and materials, facilitated by all supply chain partners thinking and acting as one.

In many ways Level 1 of the framework presents a supply chain management ideal. It also reflects an engineer's view of the world. It is one that has provided many useful diagnostic tools, as well as technological "solutions" which continue to be of value to supply chain management. However, complex systems theorists would call this a "hard" or "closed" systems perspective. When this view is combined with an "open" or "soft" systems view, we see how a range of other factors – including social and natural forces – can intervene to disrupt the harmony of our well-managed, perfectly balanced supply chains. Those forces are introduced through the other three levels of the framework.

Level 2 – asset and infrastructure dependencies

Level 2 represents supply chains in terms of assets needed to make or carry the goods and information flows in Level 1. It also looks at infrastructure dependencies. At this level, the nodes in Figure 4.3 become fixed commercial assets – sites or facilities (e.g. fields, factories, distribution centers, retail outlets). The facilities may house ICT assets (hardware or service centers). These nodes are themselves connected through the nodes and links of national and international communications infrastructure (e.g. cables, radio masts, and satellites) and through the links and nodes of the transportation/distribution infrastructure. The links are pipelines, grids, roads, rail, waterways, shipping lanes, and flight paths, the nodes can be rail terminus/stations, ports, or airports. The broken dotted lines in Figure 4.3 can now be viewed as the mobile transportation assets (trucks, trains, boats, and planes) that ply the links in transportation networks.

At Level 2 the resilience of the network should be assessed in terms of the implications of the loss of links, nodes, and other essential operating assets – including people. Maintaining them is likely to be the responsibility of functional managers in manufacturing operations, IT, logistics, and personnel. It is also the territory of business continuity planning or disaster recovery specialists.

The threat of Y2K did much to raise awareness of business continuity issues in terms of IT dependencies. Loss of site (e.g. through fire or flood), loss of skills as well as product or service-related health and safety scares (with implications for reverse logistics) may also fall within the business continuity remit. Any of these scenarios could disrupt supply chain operations. Nevertheless, research suggests that organizations continue to undertake business continuity planning and corporate risk management on a single-firm or even single-site basis.[28, 29] Consequently many may fail to take account of transportation risks and the interdependencies between organizations and infrastructure.

Transportation failures are a significant source of risk, whether through damage, loss, or delay. All can have a significant impact on service levels, with the first two also causing discrepancies in demand and stock availability data. The choice of transport mode will automatically determine immediate transportation risks and infrastructure dependencies. Unfortunately, as with everything else in this networked world, elements of infrastructure are interconnected. The point was illustrated in 2003 when Heathrow Airport ground to a halt after a localized power failure knocked out British Airways' baggage-handling system, preventing security screening and thereby the departure of numerous flights.

Transport capabilities and infrastructure dependencies are also frequently overlooked when organizations outsource or relocate activities to developing countries in pursuit of low-cost labor. However, these are not the only "own goals" organizations inflict upon themselves and their supply chain neighbors. Site consolidations are notoriously disruptive, as are "routine" ICT upgrades. Careful contingency planning for the moves could avert the worst effects of both, but so often this does not occur.

Level 3 – organizations and inter-organizational networks

Level 3 of the framework steps back further to view supply chains as inter-organizational networks. It moves supply chain vulnerability up to the level of business strategy. Here the nodes in Figure 4.3 revert to being the organizations – commercial and public sector – that own or manage the assets and infrastructure, through which the products and information flow. The links become trading relationships, particularly the power dependencies between organizations.

The principles of integrated approaches to supply chain management (as set out in Level 1) rely on the premise that strong organizations will not seek to abuse their position of power vis-à-vis weaker ones. Additionally, that information *and risk* will be shared selflessly for the good of all. Unfortunately examples abound of powerful customers using contractual means to push risk associated with inventory management, technology, or new product development back up the chain to weaker suppliers who are less able to shoulder the burden.

Where dominant organizations have the power, capabilities, and the will to manage their supply chains in an open and collaborative way, we have seen the emergence of extended enterprises. Establishing and monitoring such close cooperative partnering relationships is resource-intensive. Consequently, large sophisticated customers have reduced the number of direct suppliers, often opting for single sourcing (usually by product line) as the lowest-cost way to develop, manage, and monitor the supplier base. The downside of this is that it has given rise to one of the most widely recognized sources of supply chain risk – disruptions caused by the failure of a single-source supplier.

Suppliers may of course choose to improve their own strategic position vis-à-vis competitors, customers or their own suppliers through mergers, acquisitions, or strategic alliances. These high level consolidations – increasingly operating on a global scale – can change the balance of power in customer-supplier relationships overnight. They can leave customers with fewer switching options. They can also herald the post-merger removal of "excess" capacity and instability at Level 2. The leaning down of consolidated networks will likely improve the suppliers' margins, but it will also make the supply chains more vulnerable to Level 2 failures and possibly reduce their ability to cope with unexpected surges in demand.

Similarly, customers may require intra- and inter-organizational production and distribution networks to be redesigned simply to enable cost savings to be made in their own operations. The move to factory gate pricing in the grocery industry is one example of a customer-determined reconfiguration. The danger here is that by optimizing the system for their own interests, customers can unwittingly strip out vital volume from existing suppliers' networks, undermining their viability.

Unlike many of the scenarios above, strategic outsourcing is likely to be an elective reconfiguration, determined by the organizations concerned. Loss of visibility and control are the most obvious risks. Throughout the 1990s the literature on outsourcing was dominated by the core competence concept, encouraging organizations to focus on their core value-adding activities. High on the list of non-strategic activities ripe for divestment or outsourcing have been the provision of transport and ICT services. While these may not be seen as core activities for the organizations concerned, they are the backbone of integrated supply chain management.

Level 4 – the wider social and natural environment

The fourth and final level in the framework is the wider macroeconomic and natural environment, within which organizations do business, assets and infrastructure are positioned, supply chains pass, and value streams flow.

Here the factors for consideration are the political, economic, social, and technological elements of the operating environment (encompassing regulatory and legal issues). There are also natural phenomena – geological, meteorological, and pathological – to be considered. All can affect a supply chain at each of the previous three levels of the framework. The sources of risks emanating at Level 4 are likely to be beyond the direct control of supply chain managers. Nevertheless the susceptibility of the networks to each can often be assessed in advance, thus enabling informed decisions to be made regarding the merits of risk avoidance or mitigation strategies.

Socio-political disruptions, e.g. protests, strikes, or regulatory changes, rarely happen without warning, so routine scanning of industry and general news services should be able to identify threats of this kind. The industrial action that affected the US West Coast Ports in 2002 had been publicized in advance, but many organizations failed to heed the warnings.

In terms of geo-politics, the consolidation of the European Union, the collapse of the former Soviet Union, together with the gradual emergence of China after years of isolationism, have had a profound effect on international trade, opening the way for truly global sourcing and supply. Businesses have redesigned their supply chains accordingly. However, the prospect of war in the Middle East in 2003 raised uncertainty over oil prices and some uncomfortable questions about the future cost-effectiveness of global supply chains. Moreover, contemporary patterns of purchasing and procurement policies have been established on the premise of low inflation and macroeconomic stability. If these practices were to be applied in situations of high inflation or economic volatility it could result in more bankruptcies and swift shifts in customer–supplier power-dependencies.

Some of the implications of technological developments have already been addressed indirectly in this piece. Others include the emergence of new technologies (such as e-business) which redefine supply chains and business models, or new product technologies which radically change demand patterns for established products.

Moving on finally to the forces of nature, there are numerous well-documented examples of how natural phenomena such as earthquakes, hurricanes, floods, etc. have disrupted JIT supply chains. Meteorological and geological susceptibilities are also identifiable, though exactly when and where disruptive events will occur is less predictable. Pathological phenomena are perhaps the most difficult of all to predict, and potentially the most disruptive because they are mobile. Threats of this kind, whether foot-and-mouth, SARS, or the man-made computer viruses that mimic them, highlight how consolidated seamless distributions systems can become victims of their own success. Pathological hazards hitch a ride with the "goods" and information flows (highlighted at Level 1 of the framework) and bring down the system from within.

The foot-and-mouth outbreak of 2001 illustrates this point. The UK's livestock rearing industry has gone through the same process of vertical disaggregation and specialization as almost every other business sector, simultaneously moving from a local to a regional and international industry. Bovine spongiform encephalopathy (BSE) had previously surfaced as a threat to public health and to the livestock and meat processing industries, so new regulations had been introduced. Better visibility (British cattle became traceable) and tighter process controls in slaughterhouses were introduced to manage this known risk. The measures added cost into the slaughtering process, which together with retail-driven demands for tighter quality controls led to a consolidation of the livestock supply chain networks. Unfortunately the measures introduced to manage a known risk (BSE) unwittingly increased the vulnerability of the system to another risk – foot-and-mouth. The disease was not totally unknown in the UK, but it is an infrequent visitor. Once infected sheep entered the newly consolidated network, the speed and efficiency of the distribution system spread the disease more rapidly than anyone had imagined possible.

The case for slack

If we accept the notion of supply chains as inter-organizational networks, embedded within an environment characterized by many uncontrollable forces, then we must also accept that complexity and limited managerial control are facts of life for supply chain managers. Nevertheless managers are contractually, morally, and legally obliged to identify, manage, or mitigate risks which pose a threat to organizational health and supply chain continuity. It is therefore important for both business strategists and the supply chain managers charged with tactical and operational supply chain management to recognize that threats come in many guises. In taking action to reduce known risks – be they deemed to be corporate or supply chain – managers are likely to be changing the risk profile for that organization and for others in the network. This in turn highlights a second major finding from research undertaken by Cranfield: that few organizations have integrated supply chain management specialists in their boardrooms. Unfortunately this means that the supply chain implications – and consequential risks – of strategic decisions are often not recognized until serious problems emerge.

Effective supply chain risk management actually embraces elements of supply chain management, corporate risk management, and business continuity planning. There are public policy dimensions too. In the UK and elsewhere, governments are increasingly looking to the private sector to reduce costs and deliver efficiency improvements in the management of national infrastructure and public services. In doing so they are introducing new commercial pressures, often without an explicit understanding of the likely impact on network resilience. Even when there is a recognition, they and their private sector counterparts may choose to accept the risks as they see them. On balance the perceived benefits of the proposed changes may outweigh the potential costs of managing or mitigating the effects of a disruption if and when it occurs. Informed judgements can of course be made only for known or knowable risks, not hitherto totally unrecognizable ones. Hence the need for greater understanding of the way consequential problems can emerge at any or all of the levels identified in this article. Related to this is the case for the rehabilitation of slack.

Under "lean" thinking slack has become "waste," but when supply chains are viewed as complex open systems, not simply engineered processes, extant theory supports the case for the rehabilitation of slack. Slack in the system, though suboptimal in a "steady state" environment, is essential if complex systems (i.e. inter-organizational supply chains) are to remain effective in dynamic and evolving environments. In the uncertain times we live in, that means slack, together with awareness and constant vigilance, are necessities if supply chains are to become and remain truly resilient.

RESOURCES

Christopher, Martin, *Logistics and Supply Chain Management*, FT Pitman, 1998.

Essentials

OPERATIONS AND SERVICE

Benchmarking

Benchmarking became a buzzword of the 1980s and 1990s (although it actually relies on techniques developed by the quality movement). It involves the detailed study of productivity, quality, and value in different departments and activities in relation to performance elsewhere.

The principle behind benchmarking is very simple. If you want to improve a particular aspect of your organization or the service it provides, find someone else who is good at the activity and use them as a benchmark to raise your own standards. In effect, it's a way of pulling performance up by the bootstraps.

There are three different techniques that can be used in benchmarking:

1. *Best Demonstrated Practice* (BDP), a technique used successfully for the last 15 years, is the comparison of performance by units within one firm. For example, the sales per square foot of a retail outlet in one location can be compared with the same statistic for a store in another, within the same chain. BDP usually throws up large variances, some of which can be explained by lack of comparability, but much of which is due to superior techniques or simply greater efficiency at one site. That site can then be used as a challenge to lever up all other sites' performance.

2. *Relative Cost Position* (RCP) analysis looks at each element of the cost structure (e.g. manufacturing labor) per dollar of sales in firm X compared to the same thing in competitor Y. Good RCP analysis is hard to do but very valuable, as much for its insight into competitors' strategies as for cost reduction.

3. *Best Related Practice* is like BDP, but takes the comparisons into related (usually not competing) firms, where direct comparisons can often be made by co-operation between firms to collect and compare data.

Companies that take benchmarking seriously, like the Xerox Corporation, have a web of benchmarking partners both within the organization and outside across a wide spectrum of activities. So, for example, a manufacturing company might benchmark its transport and delivery performance against other business units it owns and against a transportation specialist such as one of the courier companies. The same company might also benchmark its accounting systems against a financial services company, and so on.

Channel management

Channel management recognizes that companies no longer compete just on the quality of their products and services. The channels they create to reach customers differentiate their offerings and play an increasingly important role in their competitive positioning. In recent years, a number of companies have utilized effective channel management to secure competitive advantage and add value to their business performance. The most obvious example is the use of the Internet to create a new channel serving a growing segment of customers who prefer to shop online.

Steven Wheeler and Evan Hirsh, two consultants at Booz-Allen Hamilton and the authors of *Channel Champions*, define the term as follows: "Channels are how and where you purchase a product (or service) and how and where you use the product." A channel, then, they note "is the essence of how customers and the product interact. It is a business' route to its customer and a business' on-going relationship with its customer."

Channel management, Hirsh and Wheeler argue, is a systematic means of reaching and taking care of your customers wherever they are and however they like to be reached. It is about identifying the most important customers to the business. It is how you consummate the relationship with customers. It is how you communicate with customers. It is how you create and capture value from the product after the initial sale.

They use the simple example of grocery shopping. Some customers will always prefer the traditional channel, visiting their local grocery store or, more likely, supermarket. But others will welcome the introduction of a home shopping service, via telephone, cable service, or the Internet. For both groups of customers, the product – i.e. the groceries – is the same; only the channels change. But it is the channel that imbues the relationship with additional value.

Channel management, then, is not a narrow discipline. It is not merely distribution or logistics, although these are obviously important. Instead, it is a way of thinking. Channel management is a way of making new connections with customers to exploit new commercial opportunities. Think channels, say its supporters, and you should be thinking strategy. Effective channel management offers the chance to reinvent not just your business but also the industry you are in. In a nutshell, Amazon.com became the biggest book retailer in the world simply by offering book buyers a new channel – via the Internet.

Crisis management

Crises are a fact of corporate life. In recent years, this realization has fueled the creation of a whole field of specialized advisers and crisis management specialists.

In corporate terms, a crisis is a major, unpredictable event with a potentially negative impact on the company's employees, products, services, financial situation, or reputation. It is a decisive moment. The American Institute for Crisis Management (ICM) defines a crisis as "a significant business disruption which stimulates extensive news media coverage. The resulting public scrutiny will affect the organization's normal operations and also could have a political, legal, financial and governmental impact on its business."

Crises are caused by a multitude of events and factors. Some are pure acts of nature – storms destroying a factory – or the result of mechanical malfunctions, such as when metal fatigue causes an airplane to crash. More avoidable are crises precipitated by human error or management. Indeed, the ICM calculates that 62 percent of business crises can be traced back to management and 23 percent to employees.

Companies increasingly accept that crises, in whatever form, are inevitable. While there is a variety of theories and opinions on how best to manage a crisis, some fundamentals are common. First, accurate information is essential. Any attempt to conceal relevant facts and to manipulate the situation ultimately backfires and increases the damage to the company. Perrier's management maintained that its mineral water did not contain any toxic element in spite of persuasive evidence to the contrary. When it finally admitted the failure, the damage to Perrier's public image was already done. Honesty is the best policy – even if there is nothing to report.

Second, the company must react quickly as possible. In 1989, Exxon CEO Lawrence Rawl waited two weeks before paying a visit to the scene of the *Exxon Valdez* oil spill. This sent a clear message about where mass pollution figured on his priorities. For all the media clamor, actions speak louder than words.

Third, the response must come from the top. Texaco CEO Peter Bijur took control of the company's reaction to a potentially damaging lawsuit. British Midland's Sir Michael Bishop was the company's spokesman after the M1 air crash. The level of response is an indication of the importance that management places on the problem.

The fourth fundamental is a long-term perspective. The long-term goodwill the company enjoys from its customers should be kept in mind when considering the short-term costs of corrective measures. Immediately withdrawing all your products from supermarket shelves if there is a suggestion of contamination sends a clear signal that you are taking the problem seriously and are intent on sorting it out.

Fifth, predicting problems requires a coherent strategy. Companies need to be prepared for a crisis. Bombs do explode; planes do crash; products do go wrong; boats do sink; and people sometimes make disastrous mistakes. Companies need to review and rehearse options in advance. Systems need to be in place. Most large organizations now have crisis management plans covering a variety of eventualities.

Deming, W. Edwards

W. Edwards Deming (1900–93) has a unique place among management theorists. He had an impact on industrial history in a way that others only dream of.

Deming was born in Iowa and spent his childhood in Wyoming. He trained as an electrical engineer at the University of Wyoming and then received a PhD in mathematical physics from Yale in 1928. He worked as a civil servant in Washington at the Department of Agriculture. While working at the Department he invited the statistician Walter Shewhart to give a lecture. This proved an inspiration. In 1939, Deming became head statistician and mathematician for the US census. During the Second World War he championed the use of statistics to improve the quality of US production and, in 1945, joined the faculty of New York University as a Professor of Statistics.

Deming visited Japan for the first time in 1947 at the invitation of General MacArthur. He was to play a key role in the rebuilding of Japanese industry. In 1950, he gave a series of lectures to Japanese industrialists on "quality control." "I told them that Japanese industry could develop in a short time. I told them they could invade the markets of the world – and have manufacturers screaming for protection in five years. I was, in 1950, the only man in Japan who believed that," Deming later recalled.

In fact, Deming was probably the *only* man in the world to believe that Japanese industry could be revived. But, helped by him, revive it did in a quite miraculous way. During the 1950s, Deming and the other American standard bearer of quality, Joseph Juran, conducted seminars and courses throughout Japan. The message – and the practice – spread.

The Japanese were highly receptive to Deming's message. The country was desperate and willing to try anything. But, much more importantly, Deming's message of teamwork and shared responsibility struck a chord with Japanese culture.

Deming's message was that organizations needed to "manage for quality." To do so required a focus on the customer: "Don't just make it and try to sell it. But redesign it and then again bring the process under control ... with ever-increasing quality ... The consumer is the most important part of the production line." At the time such pronouncements would have been greeted with disdain in the West, where production lines ran at full speed with little thought of who would buy the products.

Instead of the quick fix, Deming called for dedication and hard work. His message was never tainted by hype or frivolity. "Quality is not something you install like a new carpet or a set of bookshelves. You implant it. Quality is something you work at. It is a learning process," he said. Also difficult for the West to swallow was Deming's argument that responsibility for quality must be taken by senior managers as well as those on the factory floor. Only with senior management commitment could belief in and implementation of quality cascade down through the organization. Quality, in Deming's eyes, was not the preserve of the few but the responsibility of all.

These exhortations were backed by the use of statistical methods of quality control. These enabled business plans to be expanded to include clear quality goals.

While the Japanese transformed their economy and world perceptions of the quality of their products, Western managers flitted from one fad to the next. Deming was completely ignored. Discovery came in 1980 when NBC featured a TV program on the emergence of Japan as an industrial power. Suddenly, Western managers were seeking out every morsel of information they could find. By 1984, there were over 3,000 quality circles in American companies and many thousands of others appearing throughout the Western world.

Although Deming was in his eighties by the time he was feted in the West, he dedicated the rest of his life to preaching his quality gospel. His message was distilled down to his famed Fourteen Points.

Toyota is the living exemplar of Deming's theories. As working examples go, it remains impressive. Gary Hamel has pointed out that its Western competitors have simply followed what Toyota has done for the last 40 years. If Western car manufacturers had listened to W. Edwards Deming, the roles might have been reversed. If Western industry as a whole had listened, who knows what might have happened.

Ford, Henry

The standard view of Henry Ford (1863-1947) is that he was the first exponent of mass production. While this is true, there was a great deal more to the career, personality, and achievements of the car maker.

Ford built his first car in 1896. He quickly became convinced of the commercial potential and started his own company in 1903. In 1908, Ford's Model T was born. Through innovative use of new mass production techniques, between 1908 and 1927 Ford produced 15 million Model Ts.

Henry Ford did not develop mass production because he blindly believed in the most advanced production methods. Ford believed in mass production because it meant he could make cars that people could afford. And this, with staggering success, is what he achieved.

Ford's commitment to lowering prices cannot be doubted. Between 1908 and 1916 he reduced prices by 58 percent, at a time when demand was such that he could easily have raised prices.

Ford's was a triumph of marketing as much as of production methods. He realized that the mass car market existed – it just remained for him to provide the products the market wanted. Model Ts were black, straightforward, and affordable. The corollary of this was to prove Ford's nemesis. Having given the market what it wanted, he presumed that more of the same was also what it required. When other manufacturers added extras, Ford kept it simple and dramatically lost ground. The company's reliance on the Model T nearly drove it to self-destruction.

In the same way that Ford didn't believe in Models Ts in different colors with fins and extras, he didn't believe in management. Production, in the Ford Company's huge plant, was based around strict functional divides – demarcations. Ford believed in people getting on with their jobs and not raising their heads above functional parapets. He didn't want engineers talking to salespeople, or people making decisions without his say-so.

The methods used by Ford were grim and unforgiving. "How come when I want a pair of hands I get a human being as well?" he complained. Ford will never be celebrated for his humanity or people management skills. Among his many innovations was a single human one: Ford introduced the $5 wage for his workers, which, at the time, was around twice the average for the industry. Skeptics suggest that the only reason he did this was so his workers could buy Model Ts of their own.

Juran, Joseph

Trained as an electrical engineer, Joseph M. Juran (born 1904) worked for Western Electric in the 1920s and then AT&T. His weighty *Quality Control Handbook* was published in 1951. In 1953, he made his first visit to Japan. For two months Juran observed Japanese practices and trained managers and engineers in what he called "managing for quality."

For the next quarter of a century, the Romanian-born Juran continued to give seminars on the subject of quality throughout the world. Western companies continued to assume that the Japanese were low quality imitators. Then, at the beginning of the 1980s, the world woke up to quality. From being peripheral, Juran and his Juran Institute found themselves near the epicenter of an explosion of interest.

Juran's quality philosophy is built around a quality trilogy: quality planning, quality management, and quality implementation. "In broad terms, quality planning consists of developing the products and processes required to meet the customers' needs." While Juran is critical of W. Edwards Deming as being overly reliant on statistics, his own approach is based on the forbiddingly entitled Company-Wide Quality Management (CWQM) which aims to create a means of disseminating quality to all.

Where Juran is innovative is in his belief that there is more to quality than specification and rigorous testing for defects. The human side of quality is regarded as critical. He was an early exponent of what has come to be known as empowerment; for him, quality has to be the goal of each employee, individually and in teams, through self-supervision.

Juran's message – most accessibly encapsulated in his book *Planning for Quality* – is that quality is nothing new. If quality is so elemental and elementary, why had it become ignored in the West? Juran's unwillingness to gild his straightforward message is attractive to some but has made the communication of his ideas less successful than he would have liked.

Just-in-time (JIT)

Just-in-time or *Kanban* is an approach to inventory management based on the efficient delivery of components to the production line at the time they are required. A management technique associated with the Japanese economic miracle after the Second World War, it is one of a range of quality approaches introduced by, among others, the Toyota Motor Corporation and the Kawasaki Heavy Industries Group, and is an essential part of the lean production process.

The goal of Kanban was zero inventory. It aimed at a system whereby components for final assembly should arrive just when they were needed, reducing inventory carrying costs. Early production management emphasized ordering materials in economic lot sizes, but the JIT model utilized computer technology to emphasize timing rather than the amount of inventory.

Since the 1980s, international competition and lessons from Japanese practice have encouraged the adoption of just-in-time methods and quality management methods throughout the Western world. Technological advances have also had a significant impact on inventory management.

New mechanical and automated equipment has made stock movement more efficient, with better use of warehousing and major improvements in distribution and logistics management. In particular, IT-based stock control systems with bar coding are integrated with other systems to give better control over order assembly, stock availability, and monitoring.

By creating a system that pulls in parts as and when they are needed, JIT dramatically reduces the amount of capital tied up in inventory laying idle, thereby increasing efficiency and reducing costs. Under JIT, the company must manage the overall supply chain efficiently and effectively. Reducing levels of stock in manufacturing is seen as both an internal and external matter, involving relationships between workers at different stages in the production process and relationships with external suppliers.

JIT, however, is not an easy concept to apply. In the past, a number of Western companies attempted to introduce it in isolation from other total quality techniques, without understanding the wider implications, and without instigating the necessary changes in production management.

The human aspects of quality management are sometimes overlooked. Quality management systems that emphasize a "right first time" philosophy also promote the "empowerment" of employees via team development, quality circles, and training. In particular, plant maintenance improvements to reduce downtime and secure better reliability of machinery are integral to the successful application of JIT. This is coupled with improved "housekeeping," to maintain clean, tidy, orderly facilities. Typically, this is part of a "team or cells" discipline, with staff making a vital contribution to the overall efficiency of the approach.

In recent years, many firms have implemented ISO 9000 systems to define quality standards, processes, and control systems with documentation of action taken to ensure quality. Introduction of such systems involves close examination of existing production, operational, and support processes (including inventory standards and flows). Standards and systems are improved as a consequence.

If change is piecemeal and management attention wanes, then JIT is unlikely to produce the desired improvements. An integrated perspective is needed, with coherent strategic direction to secure improvements in productivity/effectiveness at each operational level, so that the whole supply chain has a competitive edge. JIT is only as good as the weakest link in the production chain.

Kaizen (quality circles)

As much a social system as an industrial process, Kaizen is at the heart of the quality philosophy, and involves the use of quality circles – small teams of workers who analyze and make suggestions for improving their own work tasks. In his book *Kaizen*, translated into English in the early 1980s, Masaaki Imai describes the continuous improvement concepts that underpin the quality approach.

The American quality pioneer W. Edwards Deming is credited with introducing the continuous improvement philosophy into Japan. Deming's work inspired small, problem-solving teams of workers, supervisors, and experts (later called quality circles), with the aim of improving the efficiency and quality of work. The idea was developed by Japanese companies, notably Toyota, and quality circles were instrumental in the Japanese economic miracle.

While many Western concepts are based on the notion of a step-change improvement, Kaizen is precisely the opposite. The word literally means "gradual progress" or "incremental change." Through continuous gradual improvements, Kaizen aims to achieve continual evolutionary rather than revolutionary change – hence the term continuous improvement.

Kaizen consciousness is based on a group of shared values rooted in the Japanese culture. These include self-realization, recognition of diverse abilities, and mutual trust. These values lead to a strong belief that individual workers are the experts at their jobs and therefore know better than anyone else how to analyze and improve their work. Integral to the system is an understanding that managers will consider and where possible support workers' efforts to improve work processes.

Interestingly, the pendulum may now be swinging back toward the Western style of thinking and the notion of a "leap forward." The pace of change means that many of the high-tech companies that have emerged in recent years take a much more revolutionary approach to innovation, favoring "discontinuous change" over "incremental improvement."

Quality circles are not a panacea for quality improvement but, given the right top management commitment, employee motivation, and resourcing, they can support continuous quality improvement at shopfloor level.

Lean production

Lean production is a catch-all term to describe a combination of techniques used to help companies attain low-cost status (e.g. just-in-time and total quality management).

Although it is a relatively new term, the genesis of lean production goes back much further. Its origins lie in Japan in the years after the Second World War, specifically with the development of the Toyota Motor Company. In the beginning – in 1918 – the company was called the Toyoda Spinning & Weaving Co. In the 1930s, the development of automatic looms convinced the company that its future lay elsewhere. Kiichiro Toyoda, the founder's son, had studied engineering and visited the US and Europe. He decided that the future lay in car making and changed the company's name to Toyota in 1936. In the aftermath of the Second World War, Toyoda announced his company's intention to "catch up with America in three years. Otherwise, the automobile industry of Japan will not survive." Within 12 years, the company began its assault on the American automobile industry.

Toyota's initial foray into the US proved unsuccessful. Its Crown model was designed for the Japanese market and was ill suited to American freeways. A willingness to adapt and sheer tenacity meant that despite its initial disappointment, in the 1960s the company managed to establish itself in the US. By 1975, it had replaced Volkswagen as the US's number one auto importer. Along the way, the company acquired an unrivaled reputation for build quality and reliability. Toyota is now the third biggest car maker in the world (behind GM and Ford). It sells 5 million vehicles a year (1.3 million in North America, 2 million in Japan, and 0.5 million in Europe).

How the company achieved its remarkable aim is the story of lean production. Visitors to the Toyota headquarters building in Japan can still find three portraits. One is of the company's founder; the next of the company's current president; and the final one is a portrait of the American quality guru, W. Edwards Deming. Deming was the inspiration and the original source of the techniques that gave rise to the lean production concept.

Toyota has become synonymous with lean production. Through the diligent application of Total Quality Management techniques, it progressed to what became labeled lean production, or the Toyota Production System.

Lean production was based on three simple principles. The first was just-in-time production. There is no point in producing cars, or anything else, in blind anticipation of someone buying them. Production has to be closely tied to the market's requirements. Second, responsibility for quality rests with everyone and any quality defects need to be rectified as soon as they are identified. The third, more elusive, concept was the "value stream." Instead of the company being viewed as a series of unrelated products and processes, it should be seen as a continuous and uniform whole, a stream including suppliers as well as customers.

Outsourcing

Outsourcing involves an organization passing the provision of a service or execution of a task, previously undertaken in-house, to a third party to perform on its behalf.[30] It arises from the recognition that no company can excel at everything. Activities involving competencies that are not central to what the business does may be best left to those who specialize in them.

What has made outsourcing a hot topic is its application to information technology. Mary Lacity and Leslie Willcocks, two academics at Oxford University, link this to a decision taken by Eastman Kodak in 1989 to turn over the bulk of its IT operations to three outsourcing partners.[31] In so doing, it ignited the fashion for outsourcing and other Fortune 500 companies followed suit. In the UK, similar outsourcing deals followed, involving companies such as British Petroleum, British Aerospace, and British Home Stores, and central government departments including the Inland Revenue and the Department of Social Security.

Outsourcing, however, is another simple concept that is hard to apply in practice. Striking the right balance between who gets the projected benefits – in particular, how cost savings are divided between the company and the vendor of the outsourced IT services – requires careful consideration (all too often the bulk of the savings go in profits to the vendor or supplier of the outsourced services, as, for example, do the intellectual property rights from developing new technology).

Outsourcing is no longer being applied just to IT. In the past, for instance, many administrative activities were seen as part and parcel of running the business. It simply didn't occur to companies to outsource areas such as payroll, delivery of finished goods, and secretarial services. That has now changed as it has become fashionable for companies to focus on their core activities – those providing competitive advantage.

In recent years, however, companies and commentators have begun to question the benefits of outsourcing. In a 1998 article, David Bryce and Michael Useem, two academics from the University of Pennsylvania's Wharton School, one of America's most influential business schools, examined the outsourcing experience and evaluated its consequences.[32] They concluded that while outsourcing is not the cure to all known corporate ills, it is an extremely useful and value-creating business tool. "Outsourcing will never be a silver bullet nor a turnaround engine, but the evidence to date indicates that it is one of contemporary management's more promising new tools."

Reengineering

Reengineering (or business process reengineering, as it is often called) was brought to the fore by James Champy, co-founder of the consultancy company CSC Index, and Michael Hammer, an electrical engineer and former computer science professor at MIT. The roots of the idea lay in the research carried out by MIT from 1984 to 1989 on "management in the 1990s."

Champy and Hammer's book, *Reengineering the Corporation*, was a bestseller that produced a plethora of reengineering programs, the creation of many consulting companies, and a deluge of books promoting alternative approaches to reengineering. (Thanks to the popularity of reengineering, CSC also became one of the largest consulting firms in the world.)

The fundamental idea behind reengineering is that organizations need to identify their key processes and make them as lean and efficient as possible. Peripheral processes (and, therefore, peripheral people) need to be discarded. "Don't automate; obliterate," Hammer proclaimed.

In their book, Hammer and Champy set out what they described as a "manifesto for business revolution." Far from revolutionary, however, some commentators have observed that reengineering was simply a logical next step from scientific management (Taylorism), industrial engineering, and business process improvement (total quality management). What reengineering had going for it, however, was that it fitted the needs of companies looking for a reason to continue the attack on bureaucracy and complacency, and with them the traditional hierarchical decision-making structures.

Champy and Hammer eschewed the phrase "business process reengineering," regarding it as too limiting. In their view, the scope and scale of reengineering went far beyond simply altering and refining processes. True reengineering was all embracing, a recipe for a corporate revolution.

To start the revolution, it was suggested that companies equip themselves with a blank piece of paper and map out their processes. This was undoubtedly a useful exercise. It encouraged companies to consider exactly what their core activities were, and what processes were in place, and needed to be in place, to deliver these efficiently. It also encouraged them to move beyond strict functional demarcations to freer-flowing corporate forms governed by key processes rather than fiefdoms. Having come up with a neatly engineered map of how their business should operate, companies could then attempt to translate the paper theory into concrete reality.

The concept was simple; actually turning it into reality has proved immensely more difficult than its proponents suggested. The first problem was that the blank piece of paper ignored the years, often decades, of cultural evolution that led to an organization doing something in a certain way. Such preconceptions and often justifiable habits were not easily discarded. Functional fiefdoms may be inefficient, but they are difficult to break down.

The second problem was that reengineering appeared inhumane. In some cases, people were treated appallingly in the name of reengineering. As the name suggests, it owed more to visions of the corporation as a machine than a human, or humane, system. The human side of reengineering has proved its greatest stumbling block. To reengineering purists, people were objects who handle processes. Depersonalization was the route to efficiency. (Here, the echoes of Taylor's management by dictatorship are most obvious.)

Reengineering became a synonym for redundancy and downsizing. The gurus and consultants could not be entirely blamed for this. Often, companies that claimed to be reengineering – and there were plenty – were simply engaging in cost cutting under the convenient guise of the fashionable theory. Downsizing appeared more publicly palatable if it was presented as implementing a leading-edge concept.

The third obstacle was that corporations are not natural nor even willing revolutionaries. Instead of casting the reengineering net widely, they tended to reengineer the most readily accessible process and then leave it at that.

Related to this – and the subject of Champy's sequel, *Reengineering Management* – reengineering usually failed to impinge on management. Not surprisingly, managers were all too willing to impose the rigors of a process-based view of the business on others, but often unwilling to inflict it on themselves. Champy suggested three key areas: managerial roles, managerial styles, and managerial systems. In retrospect, the mistake of reengineering was not to tackle reengineering management first.

Supply chain management

Traditionally, the nitty-gritty of moving raw materials and products around was regarded as the truly dull side of business. Companies knew that products had to be transported, stored, and distributed, but it hardly set their pulses racing. Competitiveness had little to do with whether raw materials arrived on Tuesday or Friday.

Today, the logistics of moving things around has become an exact science supply chain management. This is, at its simplest, logistics with added strategy (and a plethora of acronyms). It has been defined by Bernard La Londe of Ohio State University as "the delivery of enhanced customer and economic value through synchronized management of the flow of physical goods and associated information from sourcing through consumption."

Supply chain management has emerged as being of critical importance to the modern organization for a number of reasons. First, the balance of power has shifted. In the past, manufacturers dictated terms to retailers. Now, it is retailers who call the tune with sophisticated systems designed so they get what they want when they want it. Companies such as Wal-Mart now store terabytes of information on customers. Manufacturers have to deliver to their increasingly demanding specifications.

Second, time is an increasingly important factor in overall corporate competitiveness. Speed is of the essence, whether it be in terms of product development, production, or distribution. Late deliveries close down production lines or lead to disappointed customers all too willing to look elsewhere.

The third factor is the expansion of information technology. This allows companies to manage the flow of goods, materials, thoughts, and information in ways never previously imagined. IT enables each element of the supply chain – whether it be the manufacturer, retailer, or end consumer – to know the situation of the others. For example, if a supermarket runs out of a particular product line, technology enables this to be automatically reordered.

The final factor bolstering the standing of supply chain management is globalization. Truly global businesses require global supply chains. The right raw materials have to arrive in the obscurest of corporate outposts at the right time in the right amount. For major multinational companies, global supply chain management is a highly complex challenge, but one critical to their competitiveness.

Time-based competition

Despite the fact that its underlying logic has been accepted for decades, time-based competition became a management fashion in the early 1990s, largely due to the work of the Boston Consulting Group (BCG). Its chief proponents were two BCG consultants, George Stalk and Thomas Hout. Their book, *Competing Against Time*, calls on companies to seek to compress time at every stage in every process. "Time is the secret weapon of business because advantages in response time lever up all other differences that are basic to overall competitive advantage," they write. "Providing the most value for the lowest cost in the least amount of time is the new pattern for corporate success."

They point to Honda's triumph in the 1980s in its lengthy battle with Yamaha. Honda produced 60 new motorbikes in a year and once managed 113 new models in 18 months. Its speed of development far outstripped Yamaha's and Honda emerged triumphant.

Time-based competition contends that organizations should be structured in the most time-efficient way. The rationale is that processes and systems that are needlessly time consuming have a direct impact on competitiveness. Being slow costs you money. Unfortunately, traditional hierarchical organizations are not built with speed in mind. One calculation estimated that over 95 percent of the time products spend in an organization is wasted. Lengthy inventories as well as periods on hold during production cost money.

Stalk and Hout suggest that managers should focus on accomplishing three key tasks. First, they need to "make the value-delivery systems of the company two to three times more flexible and faster than the value-delivery systems of competitors." Second, management needs to "determine how its customers value variety and responsiveness, focus on those customers with the greatest sensitivity, and price accordingly."

Finally, managers must "have a strategy for surprising its competitors with the company's time-based advantage."

In general, the logic of time-based competition remains hard to dispute. Fast is undoubtedly good, and being faster than competitors is clearly a route to competitiveness. However, as with many other such ideas, there is the suspicion that this is simply restating the first principles of business. Frederick Taylor's Scientific Management was also based on minimizing time to maximize efficiency and, therefore, profitability.

"Time waste differs from material waste in that there can be no salvage," noted Henry Ford, who had one eye on the clock and the other on costs. In this and many other ways, Ford was ahead of his time.

Total quality management

The quality movement is associated with the Japanese economic renaissance after the Second World War. Total quality management (TQM) is an approach based on the use of quality concepts developed in Japan (see also just-in-time and Kaizen). By the late 1970s, the diligent application of these techniques by Japanese manufacturing companies had enabled them to overtake many Western manufacturers. Ironically, however, the quality movement was originally inspired by American ideas.

Under TQM, the use of sophisticated statistical production control ensures that quality is built into production, removing the need to check quality later. The aim of TQM is to minimize waste and reworking by achieving "zero defects" in the production process. TQM is not a single magic bullet, but rather an approach that integrates a group of concepts. These include many of those associated with lean production, such as just-in-time [see page 315] and Kaizen [see page 316]. Although process driven, TQM is underpinned by a management philosophy that advocates continuous improvement and a "right first time" approach to manufacturing.

It was largely due to the application of TQM among a highly disciplined workforce that in the space of just 25 years, Japanese companies were able to catch up with and outperform their rivals in America and Europe. One of the first American companies to heed the warning was the Xerox Corporation. While other parts of corporate America clung to the notion that the Japanese success story was based not on superior process management but on cheap labor costs, Xerox took a long, hard look. It quickly realized that there was more to the superior Japanese performance than the US wanted to admit. Xerox was one of the first American companies to embrace the new Japanese management techniques that had inflicted the damage.

The company became an enthusiastic convert to the quality movement and set about introducing the "right first time" philosophy into everything it did. In 1983, "Leadership Through Quality," the Xerox total quality process, was unveiled. Important lessons had been learned.

As interest in the quality movement grew, others began to write and consult on how Western companies could adopt the approach. The best known of these Western thinkers were Joseph Juran and Philip Crosby. In time, a number of Japanese quality gurus also became better known in the West, including Genichi Taguchi, Taiichi Ohno, and Shiego Shingo.

By the 1980s, TQM had become a byword for efficiency and success throughout the business world. Indeed, such was the impact of TQM that by the end of the decade it was almost possible to divide the world's top manufacturing companies into two categories: those that had introduced TQM and those that were just about to. Reinforcing the trend was the widespread adoption of quality accreditation. International ISO 9000 standards created a global quality benchmark (although some companies complained that the bureaucracy the documentation procedures created actually undermined the improvements in competitiveness).

TQM is no quick fix. It requires a fundamental shift in thinking and production techniques. Companies that have successfully implemented TQM confirm that it requires a culture change at all levels – and that can take many years to achieve.

REFERENCES

1. See *http://www.valuereporting.com*.
2. Anon, 'Measures that Matter: An Outside-in Perspective on Shareholder Recognition,' Ernst and Young, UK Study 2000.
3. Neely, A.D., Bourne, M., Jarrar, Y., Kennerley, M., Marr, B., Schiuma, G., Walters, A.H., Sutcliff, M., Heyns, H., Reilly, S., and Smythe, S., *Delivering Value Through Strategic Planning and Budgeting*, Accenture and Cranfield School of Management, 2001.
4. Marr, B. and Neely, A.D., *'Balanced Scorecard Software Report,'* Gartner, Stamford, CT, 2001.
5. Johnson, H.T. and Kaplan, R.S., *Relevance Lost – The Rise and Fall of Management Accounting*, Harvard Business School Press, 1987.
6. Neely *et al.*, op. cit.
7. Deming, W. Edwards, Speech, Tokyo, Japan, November, 1985.
8. Crawford-Mason, Clare, 'The discovery of the prophet of quality,' *SPC INK* (newsletter published by Statistical Process Controls Inc, Knoxville TN), Fall, 1992.
9. Ibid.
10. Hayes, Robert and Abernathy, William, 'Managing our way to economic decline,' *Harvard Business Review*, July/August 1980
11. 'Around the globe,' *Fortune*, July, 1964.
12. Ibid.
13. Ibid.
14. Ibid.
15. American companies had, to be fair, taken an interest in how the Japanese had managed to rebuild their economy. Shortly before Deming's TV appearance, teams from Ford and Pontiac visited Japan to see how Japanese car makers organized themselves. They found nothing different.
16. Pascale, Richard and Athos, Anthony, *The Art of Japanese Management*, Simon & Schuster, 1981.
17. Ibid.
18. Peters, Tom and Waterman, Robert, *In Search of Excellence*, Harper & Row, 1982.
19. Deming, W. Edwards, *Out of the Crisis*, Mercury, 1986.
20. Reed, Christopher, 'A prophet in his own country,' *The Observer*, January 9, 1994.
21. Deming, W. Edwards, *Out of the Crisis*, Mercury, 1986.
22. Kodak Annual Report 1984.
23. Christopher, M. *et al.*, *Supply Chain Vulnerability*, Final Report on behalf of DTLR, DTi and Home Office, Cranfield University, 2002.
24. Peck *et al.*, *Supply Chain Resilience*, Final Report on behalf of the Department for Transport, Cranfield University, 2003.
25. Christopher, M., *Logistics and Supply Chain Management*, Pitman Publishing, 1998.
26. Demchak, C. (1996), 'Tailored precision armies in fully networked battlespace: high reliability organizational dilemmas in the information age.' *Journal of Contingencies and Crisis Management*, Vol. 4, No. 2, pp. 93–103.

27. Haywood, M. and Peck, H. (2003), 'Improving the management of supply chain vulnerability in UK aerospace manufacturing,' in One World? One View of OM? Euroma-POMS Conference, pp. 121–130.
28. Peck, H. and Jüttner, U. (2002), 'Risk management in the supply chain,' *Logistics and Transport Focus*, Vol. 4. No. 11, December, pp. 17–22.
29. Starr, R., Newfrock, J., and Delurey, M. (2003), 'Enterprise resilience: managing risk in the networked economy,' Booz, Allen and Hamilton Inc, *Strategy and Business*, Issue 30, No. 30.
30. Reilly, P. and Tamkin, P., 'Outsourcing: A Flexible Option for the Future?,' Institute for Employment Studies, 1996.
31. Lacity, Mary and Willcocks, Leslie, 'Best Practice in Information Technology Sourcing,' Oxford Executive Research Briefings, Templeton College, Oxford University, 1996.
32. Bryce, David and Useem, Michael, 'The impact of corporate outsourcing on company value', *European Management Journal*, Vol. 16, No. 6, December 1998.

CHAPTER 5

Marketing

"Changes in the market environment can quickly alter prices and technologies, but close relationships can last a lifetime."

Regis McKenna

"Business has only two basic functions: marketing and innovation. Marketing and innovation produce results. All the rest are costs."

Peter Drucker

"Marketing is too important to be left to the marketing department."

David Packard

"Marketing strategy is a series of integrated actions leading to a sustainable competitive advantage."

John Sculley

"Any damn fool can put on a deal, but it takes genius, faith, and perseverance to create a brand."

David Ogilvy

"Marketing battles are fought inside the mind. Inside your own mind and inside the mind of your prospects, every day of the week. A terrain that is tricky and difficult to understand."

Al Ries

Challenging the mental models of marketing

YORAM (JERRY) WIND

[Mental models allow us to make sense of the world rapidly and efficiently.[1] They aid in the progress and application of disciplines such as marketing by facilitating understanding and action. But, if we allow them to, these models can also become traps.]

The marketing discipline is defined by a set of mental models that gives marketers distinctive perspectives on business challenges and solutions. These mental models, however, also have limits which need to be recognized and challenged to respond to shifts in the environment and to develop more creative solutions to business problems. This article examines some of the limits of the mental models of marketing and considers ways to expand our thinking about marketing to increase its creativity and value.

Why models matter

Breaking through the current mental model has tremendous power. The four-minute mile was an unthinkable barrier until British runner Roger Bannister ran the mile in 3 minutes 59.4 seconds on an Oxford track in 1954.[2] Two months later, another runner also broke this magical threshold that had previously seemed beyond human achievement. Within three years, 16 runners had turned in times of less than four minutes for the mile. Had there been some breakthrough in human evolution that allowed this achievement? No. The runners were the same. They had simply changed their mental model and this opened up the possibilities for new achievements.

In marketing, the well-known 4Ps (product, price, place, promotion) have offered a useful framework to help boil down a complex set of marketing challenges into a few core decisions. But there is a lot more to marketing today than the 4Ps. What does "product" mean when customers can customize their offerings? What does "price" mean when eBay is selling through auctions and Ryanair is giving airline seats away for free? What does "place" mean in an online world? How does "promotion" work in a world of buzz, communities, and interactive communications? In addition to expanding our view of each "P," the overall framework of the 4Ps is itself too narrow. It does not include segmentation and positioning, other stakeholders, and the deeper implications of marketing perspectives across the organization. Our mental models tend to lock us into the past, so that we solve new problems in the same old way.

This reliance on mental models is a particular problem when the world is changing rapidly. Marketing is currently in a state of flux. We see the emergence of many new channels; new technologies that allow for more personal interaction; the emergence of real-time organizations; increased concern about privacy; a decline in consumer confidence and trust; empowerment of the consumer; increased dependency of individuals on Google, BlackBerry, and other life-changing technologies; and a redefinition of the roles of buyers and sellers. These and other changes are transforming the context for marketing decisions. Our old mental models may need to be modified or replaced in this environment.

Yet mental models are very hard to change, even when we become aware that they need to be. They persist long after their relevance has faded. Like the application of the term "horseless carriage" to the early automobiles or "information superhighway" to the early Internet, new innovations are placed in the context of the existing model. These relics of past thinking may seem harmless at first, but they limit the way we can think originally about these innovations.

Another challenge in changing our mental models lies in the difficulty of recognizing them for what they are. For the most part, we are not aware of these filters that are affecting our view of reality. We think the world we see is the real world. Yet neuroscience pioneer Walter Freeman[3] and others have shown that the neural activity from sensory stimuli disappears in the brain's cortex. We use these stimuli to evoke an internal model that we then accept as reality. In effect, we screen out what doesn't fit with our mental models. There are obvious advantages to not having to process every bit of sensory data that floods over us, but there are also obvious disadvantages to ignoring a good part of the world. We are, in effect, seeing magic tricks every day but accepting them as reality.

What are the mental models in marketing that hold us back? How can we rethink them? It is only by recognizing the limitations of our current marketing mental models that we can reconsider them to develop more relevant and effective marketing strategies.

Challenging marketing mental models

How can the current marketing mental models be challenged to create new opportunities for action and create value for the organization and its stakeholders? The following section illustrates some of the opportunities to think differently about marketing. These shifts in mindset can open new opportunities to increase the effectiveness and value of marketing. Consider a few examples:

- *Beyond focussing on consumers to concern with all stakeholders.* One of the overriding concerns of early marketing practice was to get the organization to look beyond its own products, services, and internal operations to understand the consumer. Instead of selling the current inventory of the company, marketing focussed on understanding consumer needs and meeting them. But this view is now too narrow. The company's progress depends not only on creating customers but also on effectively managing a complex web of other stakeholders, including investors, regulators, employees, partners, and communities. For example, Ryanair realized it could offer zero-price tickets on its airline flights by having destination governments and businesses subsidize the flight to promote commerce and tourism. To take a more negative example, Monsanto had a well-thought-out marketing strategy for genetically modified foods, but didn't recognize the impact of protests by non-customers such as environmental activists and governments, as well as farmers in its supply chain, that derailed its progress.

    The same tools that marketing has developed to gain better insights into customers can also be applied to understanding the evolving needs of other stakeholders, but this is rarely done in practice.

    Do you have real insights into the evolving needs, objectives, and behaviors of your customers, their clients, and other key stakeholders?

- *Combining mass markets with segments of one.* Traditional marketing is built around mass production for mass markets, and this is an enduring part of the marketing mindset even as the world has changed. New technologies allow for greater customization and personalization of products and services. To take advantage of these changes, however, we also need to change the way we think about marketing to focus on segments of one (or, in B2B markets, customer account strategies instead of fragmented business strategies). The diverse options need to be presented in a way that doesn't overwhelm customers. Recognizing that customers don't always want to invest the time and attention for customization, companies often need to offer the options for both off-the-shelf solutions and customization.

    Do you have the right segments for your markets? Are you using customization and personalization to create segments of one?

- *Empowering consumers by augmenting answers with choice tools.* Marketers have traditionally tried to convince consumers to buy their product, laying out the arguments for purchase. But today, people want to make their own decisions and they have the tools to do so. Instead of laying out selling points, marketers need to look for ways to put tools into the hands of customers.

Customers use a variety of tools, including search engines (google.com), comparison engines (bizrate.com), customer evaluation engines (Zagat.com), or expert evaluation engines (consumerreport.com) to make decisions. Amazon.com, for example, provides a very robust platform for other customers to share their reviews and opinions about specific books or other products. By giving more power to consumers, organizations can move from a focus on customer relationship management (CRM), where the company is in charge of the relationship, to customer-managed relationships (CMR), where customers are given the tools to manage their own relationship with the company.

In addition to choice tools, technology gives consumers more control over the television and advertising content they see. As *American Demographics* points out in a cover story, "Whatever – whenever video devices have put the fate of the TV programming and distribution business in the hand of the viewer. Meet Tinseltown's and Madison Avenue's new boss: You."[4] This empowerment requires a rethinking of entertainment, advertising, and marketing strategies.

Are your offerings capitalizing on the increased empowerment of the consumer? Are you giving consumers access to the tools and information they need to make rational choices among products and services based on any criteria that are important to them? Are your CRM efforts augmented with a customer-managed relationship platform?

- *Expanding from viewing marketing as a function to marketing as a philosophy for creating value and an engine of growth.* Companies are increasingly aware that marketing is too important to leave to the marketing department. Marketing is essential to driving growth, and creating, delivering, and enhancing value. In too many organizations, marketing still does not play a central role in developing the business and corporate strategy. But as companies have fewer opportunities for growth through acquisitions or to increase profits through greater efficiencies, they are turning increasingly to the insights of marketing to identify new opportunities for growth. So marketing insights need to be engaged in developing strategy. Objectives should be market driven (such as increasing lifetime value of the customer), focus on stretch goals, and consider ways to capture not only the achievements but also the lost opportunities in the market. Marketing perspectives need to be diffused throughout the organization. Some companies have disbanded their central marketing functions to achieve this goal but others use the chief marketing officer (CMO) to champion marketing throughout their organizations.

Every decision has a marketing component, so there should be marketing expertise throughout the organization.

Is your business strategy focussed on growth opportunities and centered on specific segments of your customers, prospects, and customer's clients and the benefits and solutions they seek? Are your vision, values, objectives, and value proposition, business, and revenue models consistent with the creation, delivery, and enhancement of value to your customers, their clients, and other key stakeholders?

- *Building brands around consumer solutions.* While branding and brand equity are increasingly critical aspects of corporate strategy today, we need to take a broader view of brands. Pharmaceutical companies, for example, have traditionally promoted separate brands for the treatment of specific illnesses. Yet individual patients may have multiple illnesses that cut across brands. A diabetes patient may also need to be concerned about obesity or high cholesterol. Instead of purchasing a different brand for each problem, this patient may much rather have a solution that incorporates a variety of brands to address the different treatment needs. Today, this kind of work is left to (usually unbranded) doctors, who look across the available solutions to tailor one that meets the customer's needs. But there are opportunities in pharmaceuticals and other industries for companies to look beyond their narrow brand definitions to develop broader and more creative solutions to customers needs.

   Do you have effective branding strategies that reinforce your positioning and create brand equity? Are your brands built around customer solutions?

- *Developing offerings that combine benefits with experience.* Marketing has traditionally focussed on encouraging customers to engage in a transaction with the company to purchase a product or service, with an offering based on rational benefits and features rather than emotions. Consumers can now get comparative information on any number of features and benefits (and sort them based on their own criteria), and competitors replicate important innovations and advantages more quickly. Much of marketing has been concerned with designing and marketing products or services, but the offering cannot just focus on the product or service itself; it also needs to focus on the overall experience. Starbucks doesn't get several dollars for a cup of coffee based on the beans alone. It also offers the experience of what it calls a "third place" (in addition to work and home), with comfortable café environment, music, and even wireless Internet connections.

   Positioning cannot be based only on features and benefits alone but also needs an emotional link. Nike, for example, has achieved this by adding an aspirational emotion to the once near-commodity product of athletic shoes.

   Are your product and service offerings and experience and their associated positioning addressing the evolving needs and wants of your customers and their clients? And are they capitalizing on the opportunities created by new technologies and changing business environment?

- *Combining supplier-set pricing with consumer-led value pricing.* New pricing models and technologies have changed pricing strategies. Instead of these prices being set by the seller, they are determined by an interaction between the seller and the customer. Traditional fixed prices have given way to auction models such as eBay or name-your-own-price systems such as Priceline. Given the complexity of modern consumers, however, companies often offer multiple pricing strategies. For example, eBay offers a "buy it now" feature on many of its auctions so customers who want to pay a fixed price can avoid the auction process. Priceline has similarly added a more traditional purchase option in addition to its innovative consumer-initiated pricing system.

New pricing models create opportunities to rethink revenue models, and, in turn, business models. For example, while traditional record companies were using legal strong-arm tactics to enforce their existing model of selling high-priced CDs' protected intellectual property, Apple launched the very successful iTunes with 99-cent songs that can be copied and transferred to a variety of formats (including its own iPod players). Pay-per-song pricing changed the business model.

Are you offering innovative pricing and revenue models? Are you capitalizing on the lessons from Costco, Priceline, eBay, Apple, Ryan Air, and other companies with innovative revenue models?

- *Combining advertising and sales force with the buzz of customer communities.* Marketing has traditionally been carried out through advertising, and, in B2B markets, by a dedicated sales force to make the case to potential customers. Word of mouth always existed but it usually was seen as happy accident that added to the formal marketing efforts such as the sales force and advertising. Now, however, companies are rethinking this assumption and beginning to view customer communities as an active part of the sales effort. Instead of a relatively small sales force, Procter & Gamble has created a "stealth sales force" of 280,000 teenagers who spread buzz about new products.[5] This changes the way companies look at their sales force, approach word of mouth, and involve customers in their marketing.

While many companies are so set in their commitment to advertising that their question is *how much* to spend on advertising next year, the fundamental question is whether to advertise at all. Costco, for example, has built a very profitable retail business based on a warehouse model and membership fees, without advertising. It instead relies upon the buzz of customers who discover great products in its stores.

Have you moved beyond major reliance on national television to innovative integrated and interactive communication (such as creating buzz, creative product placement, edutainment)?

- *Joining separate channels to create convergence.* Marketing has traditionally seen the pathways to customers as different "channels." Some marketers used retail stores, others direct mail, and management often tries to avoid "channel conflicts." But customers see their interactions with the company as a whole. Customers want to be able to "call, click, or visit," and have a seamless interaction with the company regardless of channel.[6] They want to buy a product online and return it in the store. They want to order on the phone and check the status online. This integration of channels represents a shift in the way that customers interact with companies, and requires a change in the models and systems that companies use to respond to this demand. Webvan failed as an online grocery retailer because it staked itself to one channel only, while UK retailer Tesco has been very successful with its online business because it was integrated into its existing bricks-and-mortar channel and branding.

Are you capitalizing on innovations in distribution (Costco, Starbucks, and Home Depot), converging channels to meet the needs to "call, click, or visit," and the advances in integrated global supply networks?

- *Augmenting instinct with dashboards and rigorous metrics.* While marketing has traditionally been guided by gut and creativity as much as by research and formal metrics, this is changing. There is better information available, from scanners and databases, so the impact of marketing can be gauged. Companies are also building sophisticated dashboards to link changes in marketing initiatives on the ground with performance measures that guide the progress of the organization. Dashboards can be combined with advanced data-mining and marketing science tools to help managers make better decisions on an on-going basis and drive the business based on market-driven objectives.

    This focus on more rigorous metrics, which was identified as one of the top priorities for research of the Marketing Science Institute, helps bridge the organizational gaps between marketing and finance and other business functions. These metrics also increase the effectiveness of marketing initiatives and demonstrate their value to the organization. Companies are also changing their structure, processes, and incentives to build and reward a strong marketing focus throughout the organization. These innovations highlight the need for innovation, and they are raising the accountability and visibility of marketing, and changing the way it is approached.

    Are your marketing and business decisions assisted by a dashboard that in turn is linked to customer and client databases with associated data-mining and marketing science analytics? Do you know the ROI of your marketing initiatives?

- *Combining long-term planning and discrete tests with adaptive experimentation to improve results.* In a changing environment, it is rare that people can come up with the optimal strategy right away and for all time. Marketing has always used test markets and pilots to demonstrate the value of a new campaign or strategy before rolling it out on a broad scale. But in an environment that places a premium on learning, experimentation needs to be on-going and more open ended. For example, David Ogilvy used to test advertising approaches that he expected to fail. This was in addition to the ones he expected to succeed (which also sometimes failed). By creating these broader experiments, he was able to test not only the ads but also his *model* for evaluating advertising, and learn about new approaches that might work. When these approaches unexpectedly succeeded, they would generally suggest new directions for this thinking.

We cannot be satisfied with marketing response rates for successful direct mail and Internet advertising of less than 1 percent. This means that 99 percent of the effort of these campaigns is wasted. What other part of the business would accept this level of inefficiency? There is clearly a need for continued adaptive experimentation and truly innovative new directions.

Do you engage in continuous adaptive experimentation and other initiatives to increase the effectiveness of your marketing activities?

■ *Building bridges and transforming the organizational culture, structure, processes, and competencies.* In most organizations, marketing, finance, operations, and other functional areas are separate worlds. By bridging these silos, organizations can capitalize on the strengths and insights of specific disciplines while developing more effective solutions to business challenges by considering them in a more holistic fashion. To become more market driven, companies need to think about organizing not just by products and brands but based on the market. To make marketing a more integral part of organizational decision making and strategy, companies need to rethink their approaches to culture, structure, processes, competencies, technology, incentives, and other aspects of the organizational architecture.

Is your organization structured around customers (markets and accounts as SBUs)? Are the value-creation processes customer driven? Do you have processes and culture to bridge the various organizational silos? Are marketing competencies employed effectively by all parts of the organization?

It is important to recognize that these shifts in mindset are not *from* one way of looking at the world *to* another perspective but rather to expand thinking to embrace both views. The focus should be on *convergence* rather than revolution and divergence. In challenging and changing our mental models, we need to avoid the extremes of black-and-white, either-or thinking. We need to look at the value of the old model and create a portfolio of approaches to choose the most useful one in a given situation. The more models we have in our portfolio, the more we can see paradigm shifts as a "two-way street."

It is also important to take an integrative approach to addressing the issues highlighted above. These are not piecemeal changes, but should be approached as part of an overall focus on changing the organizational mindset. The temptation in organizations is to break things down into component parts. Even within marketing, specific questions such as new product development, pricing, and advertising are considered separately. While a detailed focus is important, we need to cultivate the practice of zooming in on the details and then zooming out to be sure we haven't lost sight of the bigger context.

Conclusions: gorillas in our midst?

Why is challenging our mental models so important? If we are trapped in our models, we can become so locked in and focussed that we fail to even see the world changing around us. One of the most graphic illustrations of this phenomenon and its results is an experiment conducted at Harvard University. Researchers Daniel Simons and Christopher Chabris asked subjects to view a videotape of a basketball game between players in white and black shirts and to count how many times the white-shirted players passed the ball.[7] More than half of the subjects were so engrossed in focussing on the white shirts that they failed to see a person in a black gorilla costume walk through the center of the scene, pound his chest, and move off to the side. The study demonstrated that we are able to overlook an entire gorilla that is smack in the center of our field of vision. After reflecting on this study, one has to ask: what gorillas are moving through our company's field of vision that we are unable to see because we are so focussed on the task at hand? How is our current mental model blocking our ability to see these gorillas, and will they ultimately eat our lunch?

The suggestions in this chapter are not a revolutionary manifesto, however. While many fads have emerged that have sought to overthrow traditional marketing, these interesting innovations such as guerilla marketing or viral marketing are best seen as additional tools that can be added to the marketing arsenal rather than a wholesale revolution. We should be careful not to lose sight of the strengths of marketing. The discipline of marketing has developed tremendous depth and rigor over the past few decades, thanks to the intense focus in this area. There have been enormous advances in marketing research and modeling. Marketing has the needed concepts and tools to make major contributions to corporate growth and performance. The problem has been that these concepts and tools are not widely used.

The limitations of the marketing mindset highlighted in this article are meant to encourage more companies to build on this foundation to challenge their current mental models, enhance their creativity and innovation, engage in adaptive experimentation, and broaden their thinking. This broadening occurs in two ways: to expand their thinking about marketing itself, and to apply marketing perspectives more broadly throughout the organization. By moving in these directions, we can broaden the usefulness, relevance, and impact of marketing.

Marketing with a hard edge

PETER FISK

[*The importance of marketing is widely acknowledged yet acceptance of its value to business has not been accompanied by enhancements to the influence, status and reputation of marketing and marketers. How can marketing address this paradox?*]

Though fundamental to business and broader economic success – and recognized as such – in most large companies the influence, status, and reputation of marketing and marketers is limited. This paradox lies at the heart of modern marketing thinking and practice.

Nowhere is this more evident than in the boardroom where marketing remains woefully under-represented. In 2003, for example, only 20 companies in the FTSE 100 had someone with a marketing background on their board of directors.[8] Just five companies in the FTSE 100 have dedicated marketing directors on their main boards.[9] Of the top 20 companies in the *Fortune 500*, only one, General Electric, has a Chief Marketing Officer.[10]

Under represented and denied a voice, marketing remains on the periphery of strategic decision making. Marketers are limited in their ability to contribute to the future direction and strategy of their organizations and to influence priorities.

Marketing's low status is also evident in how it is viewed by senior managers. In a survey among companies from *The Times* 1000, fewer than 57 percent of finance directors believed investment in marketing was necessary for long-term corporate growth; 27 percent thought marketing investment to be only a short-term tactical measure; and 32 percent said marketing was the first budget they would cut in hard times.[11]

Driving future success

So, how can marketing drive business success in the future? How can marketing shake off the legacy of the past to connect more directly and constructively with the CEO agenda?

The answer lies in hard-edged marketing, the disciplined process of marketing decision making based on what really drives success. It is supported by the application of robust business metrics to marketing activities to create demonstrably superior value for all stakeholders.[12] The result: optimal marketing-driven strategy, decisions, and performance.

Central to hard-edged marketing is the realization that marketing must undergo a fundamental change in attitude and direction. It must overcome the long-standing obstacles to achieving influence at board level and persuade the business world of its strategic importance. It must embrace metrics to connect with opinion formers and decision makers who often attach more importance to the language of finance than what they perceive as the ethereal world of creatives.

"Marketing has too often been treated as a department, one that essentially carries out marketing communications and promotions. Marketing, properly conceived, is a strategic function and should be the driver of company strategy," says the doyen of marketing thinkers, Philip Kotler.[13]

Marketing must satisfy the needs of, and create value for, customers and shareholders – and for other stakeholders – to drive a virtuous circle of wealth creation. "There is no conflict whatsoever between being customer-driven and shareholder-driven," observes Don Peppers, co-author of *One-to-One Future*.[14]

This needs to be built on an appreciation that different stakeholders have different perceptions of value. Shareholder value, for example, is the perception of the economic benefit through the eyes of shareholders. For customers, value is the perceived worth of the proposition to them. And, for employees, value is the perceived worth of their efforts relative to the rewards. But, in reality, these different perspectives on value center on how economic benefits are distributed rather than the actual creation of value.

Economists talk about "consumer's surplus" and "producer's surplus" (also known as economic profit) to describe how much of the economic value is captured by customers and by the company respectively. (Similarly, "employees' surplus," or "labor surplus," can be used to describe how much economic value goes to the workforce.)

How economic value is distributed is a function of price, labor costs and shareholder returns (via dividends and capital gains on share price). But unless economic benefit is created there is nothing to distribute.

In this article the perception of economic benefit is referred to as economic value.

Creating economic value

Economic value is based on the idea that an activity should create a surplus. In other words, outputs should have a perceived value in excess of the monetary inputs, or costs. The first priority of any economic activity must be to create economic benefits, which in turn translate into economic value.

The creation of economic value, and the capturing of that value, is central to hard-edged marketing. It is only by generating a producer surplus (economic profit) that companies can remain in business. All activities can be assessed on this basis. In this way it is possible to determine whether a marketing activity creates or destroys value.

Understood and practiced in this way, hard-edged marketing will enable marketers to shape and drive the value agenda. It will allow marketers to:

- make the right decisions faster;
- identify the best sources of long-term value;
- find ways to create exceptional value for both shareholders and customers;
- focus resources and creativity on what matters;
- make an unarguable case for investment in marketing;
- be more influential and credible in the boardroom;
- drive business decision making and direction.

Hard-edged marketing is not a panacea. Magic bullets have a tendency to backfire. Rather, it is a way of practicing and thinking about marketing. At its heart is the recognition that marketing does not exist in a creative or a commercial vacuum. Marketing activities must be directly linked to organizational goals. As such, the impact of marketing activities should be judged against the organization's key performance indicators.

This does not mean donning the marketing equivalent of a straitjacket. Marketing performance measures need also to be flexible enough to cope with changes in organizational priorities. The marketing agenda – and metrics – should mirror and support the evolving CEO agenda.

Hard-edged marketing recognizes that much of the value of modern businesses resides in intangible assets, such as brands, intellectual property, and relationships. The challenge is to find ways to make the intangible tangible. In other words: to quantify brands, intellectual property, relationships. Hard-edged marketing allows marketers to get a grip on what really matters to business today.

The case for hard-edged marketing is summed up by Sir John Browne of BP Amoco. "We have more than 10 million interactions with customers every day; and more than 100,000 staff in more than 100 countries. Every action and every activity is an act of marketing," says Sir John. "We defined marketing as the art of driving the creation of value through the development of relationships with both customers and with those whose decisions influence and shape the environment in which we work."[15]

Why hard-edged marketing?

Hard-edged marketing enables marketers to demonstrate their contribution to the business, to justify their budgets, and to focus investment on those marketing activities that offer the best returns. Crucially, it also enables them to eliminate unprofitable marketing activities. At present, many marketing activities are pursued as an act of faith. Often, the return on the investment is unquantified and elusive. In large part this is because marketers fail to apply business discipline to what they do.

Consider brands. There is growing evidence that a relatively small number of brands deliver the vast majority of returns. It has been estimated, for example, that 20 percent of packaged goods brands account for 80 percent of all sales and an even greater proportion of profits.[16]

By applying more rigorous analysis of their brand portfolios, some brand-led companies have dramatically reduced the number of brands they invest in. Unilever, for example, is committed to reducing its brands portfolio from 1,600 in 2000 to 400 by 2004. As of August 2003, it had already disposed of about 1,000 brands.

Consider advertising. Despite growing concerns about its effectiveness, the money spent on TV advertising continues to soar. Investment on traditional TV advertising in the US continues to rise even as audiences fall. In June 2002, for example, the major American television networks received a record $8 billion in upfront advertising revenues – this was up $1 billion on 2001. Yet, over the same period their audience share against cable TV fell from 41 percent to 37 percent.[17]

Or look at Customer Relationship Management (CRM). Huge amounts of money have been invested in CRM and loyalty programs, often with little attempt to quantify the benefits. In 2000, for example, the top 16 European retailers spent in excess of $1 billion on loyalty programs. Yet the correlation between customer loyalty and profitability is often weak or non-existent.[18]

Such statistics confirm prejudices that marketing is a fuzzy discipline – an inexact art rather than a rigorous science. The debate about the deficiencies of marketing practice is unfortunately a long-running one.

Hard-edged marketing addresses these challenges in three ways:

First, by interpreting value broadly. Historically, marketing has focussed on value for customers almost to the exclusion of all else. Even today many marketers have a limited interest in or understanding of broader business issues such as shareholder value.

Second, by hard wiring marketing into the business and its financial reporting, using metrics to quantify, as much as possible, marketing's contribution to the business. In the past limited efforts were made to measure the return on marketing activities or to connect marketing with business goals.

Third, by operating at board level. As stated before, marketing has been seen as a lower status function. This is still largely the case. Marketers are seen as lacking in commercial, strategic and especially financial skills. As a result, marketers do not speak the language of the boardroom. They need to learn – in order to communicate and influence.

Broad interpretation of value

The concept of value is central to hard-edged marketing. But value is not easily defined. As discussed earlier, different stakeholders hold different notions of value.

All stakeholders matter.[19] Hard-edged marketing must embrace all stakeholders, while realizing that the balance has shifted toward the relationship with shareholders. Marketers must recognize that business performance is increasingly judged on creating long-term shareholder value. The important point to note here is that the focus is on long-term shareholder value rather than simply a rise in short-term share price.

The idea that businesses should be managed for shareholder value alone has received some criticism. Evidence suggests that where only one indicator is used to evaluate performance, it tends to subvert its original purpose. The problem is familiar to economists, who have noted that whenever a macro economic indicator is taken as the mainstay of policy – whether it be a monetary target (measure of money supply), inflation, or some other lever – its predictive qualities often desert it. The challenge is therefore to find a balanced way of capturing and then maximizing economic value.

Marketers need to understand that creating economic value is an end in itself. Unless marketing activities create – or at least contribute to – an economic surplus they will not be sustainable in the long term. At the same time, marketers must also recognize that companies are ultimately measured on shareholder value, and the only sustainable way to increase shareholder value is by creating value for all stakeholders.

This is a dynamic system – a value exchange between multiple parties. The dynamic must be managed to achieve the optimal balance of outcomes. A sustainable position requires that customers as well as the producer enjoy a surplus. Otherwise, customers will buy from firms that they perceive give them more value. So, if the value pendulum swings too far toward shareholders – i.e. by appropriating all the economic value – the company is likely to lose customers and its most talented employees.

The only sustainable way to grow shareholder value is to do more for customers and employees and other stakeholders.

It is a mistake to view shareholder value in isolation from other stakeholders. Rather, think of an eco-system, where all stakeholder groups are interdependent.

Without customers there is no business. Without employees there is no business. Without shareholders there is no business. The task of management is to allocate both the resources and the economic surplus generated – via dividends, wages, and price promotions.

The best way to increase customer and employee value is to increase the total economic value, of which they are a proportion. The best way to influence how that value is distributed is to gain a voice in the boardroom.

Figure 5.1 area

Shareholder Value

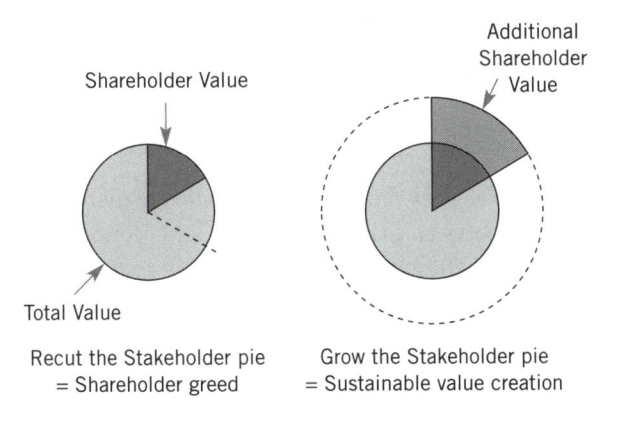

Total Value

Recut the Stakeholder pie
= Shareholder greed

Additional Shareholder Value

Grow the Stakeholder pie
= Sustainable value creation

Figure 5.1: *Value allocation*

Measuring what's key

To speak the language of CEOs, marketers must demonstrate a connection between marketing expenditure and contribution to the bottom line. In the past this has not always been the case. Marketers have often regarded their activities as beyond measurement. Unfortunately, in the language of senior management this translates into a lack of accountability.

There remains a lingering suspicion that marketers are simply not measurement-oriented. Cranfield's Robert Shaw and marketing author Laura Mazur suggest that non-marketer dissatisfaction with marketing is partly due to a perception that measurement is not taken seriously by marketers. "Marketing executives themselves have shown a marked reluctance to take on 'support' roles, preferring the glamor of big-budget advertising over developing corporate marketing measures," they note. Moreover: "Marketing is rarely involved in measurement development, and consequently the finance department is left alone to do the job as best it can."[20]

Some confusion also comes from a lack of clarity about what is meant by "metrics." A metric is a performance measure that top management should review. In other words, a measure that matters to the whole business. Shaw and Mazur's statement that metrics should be limited to performance measures which are "high level, necessary, sufficient, unambiguous, and, ideally, predictive" is broadly acceptable as a basis for definition.

Hard-edged marketing is not about producing measures for their own sake – as has tended to happen in the past. Rather, it is about identifying key areas for measurement – those which have a direct and demonstrable impact on corporate performance – and developing appropriate metrics. It involves a clear understanding of which measures are the key value drivers. Hard-edged marketing is about measuring the few things that really matter.

A disciplined approach to the development of these new marketing metrics is essential.

The popularity of market share illustrates the challenge marketers face if they are to make the connection between marketing metrics and economic value. In an organization that equates marketing performance with the acquisition of market share there may be a disconnect between marketing activity and the value that activity creates.

The price reduction reduces the margin on the product. The end result could be an increase in market share but an overall decline in economic value. A small operating profit generated by a product which has required significant capital investment in the manufacturing processes or facilities required to produce it may, in economic terms, destroy value. What the marketing function considers a success has in fact resulted in the destruction of value. Hard-edged marketing recognizes that not all growth is good growth. And, indeed, it is entirely possible to create value without growth – such as by focussing on a highly profitable niche as Porsche has done in the auto market where it has far from the highest sales while creating far more overall economic value than its competitors.

Consider brands. The importance of a particular brand to a company may be intuitively obvious. The intangible nature of this intellectual property, however, makes it difficult to reflect in the balance sheet. Attempts to attach a financial valuation to brands and other intangibles are making some inroads. Yet it has taken many years to devise appropriate accounting methods and to have such methods accepted as general practice.

Even today, the valuation of intangible marketing assets, such as brands, remains a contentious issue. The challenge for marketers is to find hard measures for evaluating the economic value that resides in brands, and to do so with reference to a metric that matters to those in the boardroom. For example, linking brand equity to future cash flow is more likely to attract the attention of CEOs and analysts.

However, the pursuit of financial rigor should not be at the expense of creativity. The danger of spending too much time on spreadsheets at the expense of customer insights, or on evading radical ideas because they are more risky, must be avoided. At present much creative energy is dissipated. Hard-edged marketing supports creativity by focussing creative effort on where it is most needed. In fact, by directing creativity at the areas and challenges that add most value to the business, hard-edged marketing sparks even more creative solutions.

As Don E. Schultz of Northwestern University observes: "Maybe we've been focussing on the wrong people. Maybe what we need are more results-oriented creative directors and fewer after-the-fact measurement analysts, fewer statistical algorithms, all based on more upfront commitments to what is supposed to happen on the other end. Today, for most marketing communications programs, the creatives present the messages and pictures. The media people offer up where and in what media forms the materials will appear. The promotional people develop incentives and offers. The public relations people present the stories and press releases that will go out. Meanwhile, the rest of the marketing and communications team cheers them on. The client approves all the work and off we go – everyone to do his own thing with nary a result even suggested."[21]

The acid test of economic value

The challenge for hard-edged marketing is to determine whether a marketing activity creates or destroys economic value for the company. This requires marketers to evaluate whether activities create an economic profit (a surplus for the producer).

One approach is to use metrics that enable activities to be assessed in terms of the shareholder value they create. The attraction of shareholder value is that once an allowance has been made for the cost of capital, it allows a company to run a rule over its activities and determine which are profitable, and which are not. To allow shareholder value to be quantified throughout the organization a number of specific metrics have been devised to measure EP (economic profit).

This value-based approach can be applied to every aspect of marketing – from products to markets, medium to channel – finally allowing it to demonstrate an easily understood contribution to shareholder value creation. This approach involves applying existing shareholder value metrics to the marketing activities of the firm. This can provide new insights.

In practice, one difficulty with the shareholder value approach has been the narrowness of its application and definition. An unerring focus on shareholder value, without consideration for other stakeholders, can lead to unwanted results. At Enron, for example, the company's poor structure enabled greed and short-term value to take priority over creating sustainable long-term value. In the aftermath the concept of shareholder value received a mauling at the hands of business commentators. However, a long-term approach offers benefits, in terms of an absolute focus on what invariably matters most to CEOs.

Hard-edged marketing relies on using metrics for determining the overall economic outcome of a given marketing activity. It will not be possible to evaluate every single activity in this way, but with the development of appropriate metrics the aggregate effect of an advertising campaign, for example, could potentially be evaluated.

The key to the boardroom

If marketing is to influence strategy it must be championed at board level. At the moment, many marketers are held back by a lack of financial training. This training shortfall, however, can easily be remedied – through capability development and working more closely with financial colleagues. What is more difficult to change is the mindset of many marketers. The key to the boardroom lies with a willingness and ability to see the world from the board's perspective. This requires a new attitude.

The professional bodies, marketing consultancies and training companies are making strides toward equipping marketers with much needed measurement and evaluation skills. But there is still a gap between theory and practice, and more needs to be done to help marketers translate evaluation techniques into practical applicable tools.

Making hard-edged marketing happen

Theory only gets you so far. Making hard-edged marketing a reality requires hard work on the part of the marketing profession. The benefits are worth the toil.

Several well known companies have adopted a value-based approach with varying degrees of success. Cadbury Schweppes is an example of how shareholder value metrics applied to marketing activities can revitalize a company.

Its Managing for Value program, introduced in 1997 by CEO John Sunderland, was built around what Sunderland called a "whole business" approach to value-based management. Marketing strategy was led from the top, and all initiatives were geared toward increasing long-term shareholder return. He set out the apparently ambitious aim of doubling shareholder value in four years and to grow earnings by 10 percent every year. He achieved 84 percent by 2001.

Not all companies have fared so well with the concept. Some have abandoned this approach entirely. AT&T for example adopted value-based management in 1992 and abandoned it in 2000.[22] Others have wholeheartedly embraced the approach and are still struggling with it. Siemens, for example, adopted value-based management in 1998 – in 2003 after shedding 34,000 jobs over two years it is still struggling to reach profitability targets in its 13 main divisions – with deadlines shifted back a year for five divisions.[23]

Success requires hard work. As David Haigh, chief executive of Brand Finance, observes: "We need to acknowledge the difficulty of doing this stuff. One of the problems is that sometimes companies want simple answers when none exists. There is no silver bullet. We must also be careful not to say this is an impossible task so we shouldn't bother. The important point is that we don't let the desire for perfection drive out the good. Financial measures are never perfect. The issue is that marketers have engaged in a meaningful debate, among themselves and with other parts of the business including the board, and come up with the very best measures available."[24]

Making hard-edged marketing a reality requires that marketers:

- rethink objectives and priorities;
- focus on the best source of value;
- engage with new metrics;
- develop new skills;
- become pivotal in the organizational structure and more influential in driving business strategy and management.

Re-think objectives and priorities

If it is to work, hard-edged marketing involves a fundamental reshaping of objectives and priorities. The way the organization thinks and behaves must change. Hard-edged marketing requires culture change. Underestimating the nature and extent of the culture change explains the failure of many value-based management initiatives.

Those that succeed re-think everything. Consider Diageo, formed by the mega merger of Guinness and Grand Metropolitan. It has transformed its business by re-focussing on its premium drinks brands. Driving this is the quest for value creation. Back in 2000, Diageo was a lumbering giant with a portfolio of household name brands. The shift in focus began under chief executive John McGrath, and has continued under his successor Paul Walsh.

The decision was taken to focus on a number of "global priority brands." Initially there were nine, but this was later reduced to eight: Guinness, Johnnie Walker, Baileys, Smirnoff, J&B, Cuervo, Tanqueray and Malibu. At the time the decision was taken the priority brands accounted for almost 60 percent of group sales – but some 80 percent of operating profits. Other brands were put on warning: either they turned around their performance so they were creating value rather than destroying it, or they faced being dropped. At least 15 brands that were initially not creating value have subsequently been revitalized by Diageo's marketers.

On its journey of transformation Diageo has demonstrated its resolve by jettisoning a number of famous brands, including Pillsbury (sold in 2001) and Burger King (sold in 2002 – for a substantial loss). The results of Diageo's hard-edged approach are gilt-edged: economic profit up $160 million to $880 million; dividend up 8 percent; $1.4 billion returned to shareholders; operating profits up 14 percent; operating profit up 11 percent in North America and 15 percent in the UK.

Focus on the best source of value

Hard-edged marketing facilitates better, and faster, decision making on marketing activities. It enables marketers to identify where investment will add the most value. At the same time, it also enables marketers to understand which activities, even though they generate an operating profit, actually destroy value.

When Brian Pitman became chief executive of Lloyds Bank (now Lloyds TSB) in 1983, one of his first acts was to convince the board and subsequently the management team that they should decide on a single performance measurement to assess performance. This measure would drive all decision making within the company.

After some discussion, return on equity (ROE) was selected as the key metric. It was on this criterion that Pitman signaled he would judge the company's performance. The point here, however, is not what measure was selected – it might easily have been another financial metric – but rather how Pitman inculcated the selected measurement within the bank. "We not only established ROE as the key measure of financial performance but also set the demanding target of every business achieving a return that exceeded its cost of equity," he notes in an article in the *Harvard Business Review*.[25] "ROE was reported in the management accounts, initially with separate figures for domestic and internal operations and ultimately on a country by country basis. It was also used in determining executive compensation; before then managers' raises had been linked to inflation. The cry 'Improve ROE' could be heard all round the organization."

Pitman also set what Jim Collins and Jerry Porras, authors of *Built to Last*, call "Big Hairy Audacious Goals."[26] These goals were consistent with the overall objective and

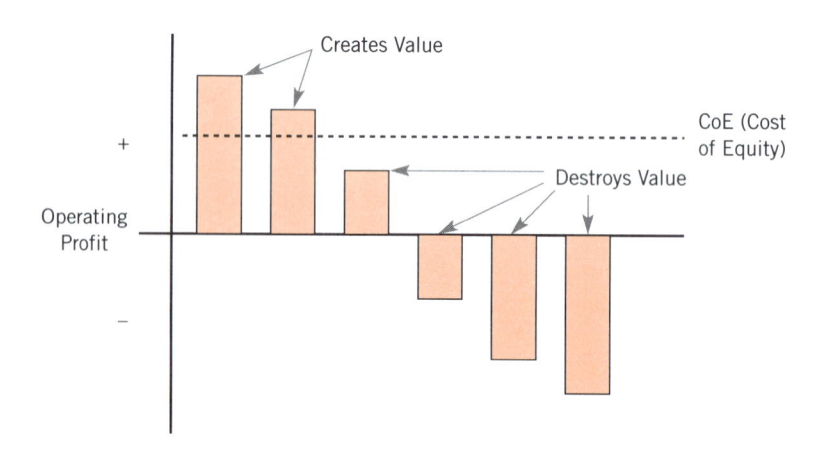

Figure 5.2: *Value creation and value destruction*

act as drivers toward that objective. So, for example, he set a goal to double the market value of the company every three years. This in turn was linked to bonuses. Initially this target was met with some resistance. Pitman insisted that he wanted only people on his team who were committed to the company objective.

"For people to be truly committed to a strategy of shareholder value creation," says Pitman, "they have to believe in it. They have to believe, for example, that profitability is more important than growth, which, pursued for its own sake, usually destroys value. They have to believe in the importance of focussing on those businesses with profit potential and getting rid of the others. If they adopt such convictions – and don't simply pay the service to them – it will change the way they run their operations."

Between 1983 and 2001, when Pitman retired, Lloyds' market capitalization rose 40-fold – from £1 billion to £40 billion. Compound return to shareholders during that period allowing for reinvestment of dividends rose to 26 percent annually.

Engage with robust metrics

It is important that the metrics selected are robust. According to Michael Perla, a senior consultant at a CRM software company, metrics should be:[27]

- *reliable:* capable of consistent application throughout the organization;
- *valid:* the metric should do the job it is meant to – i.e. it should measure what it is intended to measure;
- *responsive:* can the metric be used in real time? Is there latency between a movement in the underlying observed data and the resultant change signified by the metric?;
- *economic:* the costs of collecting, measuring, and analyzing the data should not outweigh the benefits;
- *clear:* metrics should be easily understood. A metric that is complex and difficult to explain or understand will be of little value to stakeholders.

To these, add some further criteria:

- *balanced:* financial metrics are not the only yardstick marketers should measure their business by. The balanced scorecard approach, introduced by Robert Kaplan and David Norton, presents a means of broadening measurement beyond financial metrics to include measures geared toward the customer, employees, training, knowledge transfer, and other criteria;
- *not overly financial or analytical:* marketers must also remember not to get carried away with the financials. While talking the language of the boardroom is helpful, obsessive analysis is not. Hard-edged marketers are able

to do both. The emphasis is on selecting and communicating a few key metrics, rather than trying to measure anything and everything.

- Finally, *the link to economic value should be clear:* marketers should start with the stated business objective set out by the board – shareholder value metric, for example – and work backwards to the appropriate marketing metrics – and not the other way round.

Develop new skills

Hard-edged marketing requires marketers to learn new skills. Marketers need to foster new attitudes, competencies, and characteristics. The implication of this is that what is needed now is a major rethinking of marketing capabilities.

When it introduced value-based management, for example, Dow Chemical retrained 75 percent of its nearly 40,000 employees. Its marketing people focussed on supply demand and pricing analysis and how that linked to economic profit as well as receiving basic training on how to calculate economic value.[28]

Diageo estimates it has invested £35 million over four years in developing skills and capabilities related to the Diageo Way of Brand Building. Over 6,000 people have been through five days of interactive training. "If we just increase the efficiency or effectiveness of our marketing programs by only 5 percent a year, the payback is virtually instantaneous," says Rob Malcolm, president of global marketing sales and innovation.[29]

Hard-edged marketers require new skills. These include:

- *finance:* marketers must be able to measure and communicate progress, in particular by connecting improved performance with business results and economic value-added by marketing activities;

- *communication:* marketers must be able to engage with people. People still matter. "Managing for value is 20 percent about the numbers and 80 percent about the people ... because people create value," observes John Sunderland of Cadbury Schweppes. Marketers must, therefore, build a value-based business case for the development of high performance marketers, engaging the support of leaders across the business. "Marketing is about expressing real purpose in a way which huge numbers of people, who are not familiar with the detail, can understand instantly. Marketing is about showing people what a company is trying to do," says Sir John Browne of BP Amoco;[30]

- *strategy:* marketers must understand the business priorities and explore what marketing needs to do to address them effectively in a way that creates significant value. They must be able to focus – and to enable others to focus. At IBM executives with strategic marketing skills are labeled "Big M" types. In contrast "small m" types remain trapped in narrowly defined silos. One estimate of the number of people equipped to be strategic marketers in the United States puts the population as low as 50 people;[31]

- *leadership:* marketers must address the roles and responsibilities of marketing leaders, understanding the value they add through direction and facilitation, coaching and control. At Cadbury Schweppes the company set out to create a cadre of senior managers who were totally dedicated to value-based management – and had the requisite leadership skills. In all, 50 percent of the top 150 managers either left the company or were assigned to new positions;[32]

- *creativity:* hard-edged marketing might seem contradictory to creativity. On the contrary, it enables marketers to focus their creativity in the right places and often sparks far more innovative solutions which create value for customers and the business;

- *open thinking:* marketers must act as catalysts by building their mental agility, thinking in more open and innovative ways – and stimulating others to do so. In doing so they create a context built around a framework for people, process, and infrastructure development that is issue-driven and action-driving;

- *open practice:* marketers must collaborate. They need to work with specialist collaborators to make urgent projects happen, and to accelerate new solutions to market. Unfortunately, many marketing departments are still not aligned with business reality, where consumers don't exist in media specific silos.

For many marketers this is a daunting list. The number of marketers who possess these skills is small. For more to join their ranks requires that marketers break free from functional shackles. By doing so they will become pivotal in the organizational structure – and more influential in driving business strategy and management.

RESOURCES

Doyle, Peter, *Value-Based Marketing*, John Wiley and Sons, 2000.
Kotler, Philip, *Marketing Management: Analysis, Planning and Control* (8th edition), Prentice Hall, 1994.
Kunde, Jesper, *Corporate Religion*, FT Prentice Hall, 2000.
Levitt, Ted, *Innovation in Marketing*, McGraw Hill, 1962.
Levitt, Ted, *The Marketing Mode*, McGraw Hill, 1969.
Levitt, Ted, *The Marketing Imagination*, Free Press, 1983.
Levitt, Ted, *Thinking About Management*, Free Press, 1991.
Peppers, Don and Rogers, Martha, *The One-to-One Field Book*, Capstone, 1999.
Rappaport, Alfred, *Creating Shareholder Value*, Free Press, 1998.

'Interview': Philip Kotler

The world's leading marketing expert, Philip Kotler, S.C. Johnson and Son Distinguished Professor of International Marketing at the J. L. Kellogg Graduate School of Management, Northwestern University, talks about why marketing isn't high enough up the boardroom agenda, what place social responsibility has in marketing, and other topical marketing issues.

There is a lot of debate at present about how to move marketing higher up the boardroom agenda. What are your thoughts on this?

Marketing is poorly understood by business leaders and the public. Business leaders largely view marketing as a promotion function. In too many companies, marketers have become 1P marketers, the 1P being promotion. Their responsibility and control of the other 3Ps, product, price, and place (distribution) has weakened and is handled more actively by others. One factor is that many CEOs view marketing as the marketing budget, which is largely spent on promotion. Persons in other departments work actively on the other Ps: product (R&D), price (finance), and distribution (the sales force).

Where is the unified vision that starts with defining target markets and their needs and carries this all the way to preparing integrated solutions? My view is that marketing must become the driver of business strategy. Businesses that grasp the true role and potential of marketing will use it as the driver of their business strategy, and not simply as a tactical complement. Not only that, but marketing must also gain a seat on the board, which is too rarely found. Today top management consists largely of people versed in accounting, finance, and law.

That said, marketing cannot be resurrected overnight. In the first place, too many marketers have become so specialized that they don't think in terms of the company's big picture. Marketers typically lack financial and strategic skills. This can be made up by training more marketers in financial and strategic skills. In the second place, marketers won't get more respect until they learn how to deliver more ROI accountability for their expenditures. CEOs want and deserve better metrics for measuring marketing's ROI.

Is CRM living up to its promise?

Customer relationship management (CRM) remains one of the most promising new marketing developments in recent years. CRM can be tremendously effective when it is used right. The more a company knows about its customers and prospects, the more effectively it can compete.

However, the performance of CRM investments in recent years has been poor, with somewhere between 40 and 60 percent of companies reporting disappointing results. Too often CRM is imported as a technology before the company has adopted a genuine customer culture. Adding technology to an old organization only makes it a more expensive old organization.

So the challenge is to know when CRM is appropriate and how to implement it successfully. CRM makes the most sense in data-rich industries such as banking, credit cards, insurance, and telecommunications. It makes the least sense in mass consumer markets selling low price goods. Coca-Cola is not going to benefit by accumulating the names of its 2 billion consumers of Coke.

In deciding whether to invest in an expensive CRM system, consider what the Royal Bank of Canada did. They asked the vendor, the Siebel Company, for four estimates:

1. What will the system cost?
2. How long will it be before the system will be operationally ready?
3. In how many months will the incremental sales above baseline cover the initial system investment?
4. What is the long-run ROI that we will get from this system?

I like the following quotes about CRM. Steve Silver, the highly respected marketing consultant, says: "CRM is not a software package. It's not a database. It's not a call center or a website. It's not a loyalty program, a customer service program, a customer acquisition program, or a win-back program. CRM is an entire philosophy." And Edmund Thompson of the Gartner Group says: "A CRM program is typically 45 percent dependent on the right executive leadership, 40 percent on project management implementation, and 15 percent on technology." These comments sound right to me.

What kind of impact are the Internet and other advances in communications technology having on marketing?

In the business-to-business area, the Internet is revolutionizing business practice and efficiency. Companies have much more information on suppliers and their prices; there is more reliance on auctions and requests for proposals; and many more transactions are taking place over the net.

Other technologies are also finding growing use, among them database marketing and CRM, sales automation, marketing automation, marketing processes dashboards, smart cards, wireless marketing, and others.

My guess is, however, that the average US or European company is only using about 10 percent of the Internet's potential. Most companies think that their Internet potential is achieved when they open up a company website. I would, however, ask the company the following questions: Do you use the Internet to test new product and marketing concepts using online focus groups and consumer panels?

Have you assigned someone to research competitors' strategies, tactics, and resources using the Internet's rich information highway? Do you use the Internet to train and communicate with your employees, dealers, and suppliers? Do you use your website to recruit new employees? Do you distribute coupons and samples through the Internet? Do you monitor chat room discussions to learn how people talk about products, companies, and brands related to your business? I suspect that most companies would not be able to answer yes to many of these questions.

The economist Milton Friedman famously said: "There is one and only one social responsibility of business – to use its resources and engage in activities designed to increase its profits." What are your thoughts on the social responsibility of marketing?

In the 1970s, I began to distinguish between business marketing, non-profit marketing, social marketing, and societal marketing. We know what *business marketing* is. *Non-profit marketing* describes the work of non-profit organizations to attract clients and funds to support social and cultural services such as aid to the needy, museum, and theatrical performances, public health initiatives, and so on. I formulated *social marketing* as a discipline for trying to influence healthy behavior (e.g. healthy eating, daily exercise) and discourage unhealthy behavior (smoking, using hard drugs). *Societal marketing* focusses on the impact that marketing practices have on the well-being of society. In this case, I said that companies should distinguish between satisfying a person's needs, weighing the impact on the person's well-being, and the impact on the public's well-being. Thus smoking a cigarette meets the person's need, but hurts his health, and increases the public's health costs.

At the present time, Nancy Lee and I are researching a book on Corporate Social Responsibility. We are attempting to help companies answer the following questions: Are we giving anything back to society? How much should we give back? What social initiatives would create the most good for the company and the social cause? How can we measure the impact of our contributions?

We have contacted 40 companies that have exhibited high social responsibility – among them Avon, Kraft, Levi Strauss, Body Shop, Ben & Jerry's, and Procter & Gamble. Their approaches differ and shed light on the variety of ways that a company can contribute to the social good. A company can sponsor a major social cause, or do volunteer work in the community, or give philanthropic gifts, or establish highly ethical business practices. We are learning how they chose their social initiative, what benefits they expected, and what benefits they received. Our aim is to produce a framework that companies can use to determine what kind of social "caring" to give, at what level, and with what expected results on their own business performance and on social welfare.

Let's look at marketing in the future. What do you think the biggest challenges facing marketing are?

I would list the following challenges.

Getting better financial measures of the impact of marketing programs. Marketing has been lax in developing marketing metrics to show what particular marketing expenditures have achieved. CEOs are no longer satisfied with communication measures of how much awareness, knowledge, or preference has been created by marketing programs. They want to know how much sales, profit, and shareholder value has been created. One step in the right direction is at Coca-Cola where its marketers must estimate – before and after a campaign – the financial impacts of their programs even if it is guesswork. At least this will produce a financial mindset in Coca-Cola's marketers.

Developing more integrated information about important customers. Customers come in contact with a company at various touchpoints: by e-mail, snail mail, phone, in-person, and so on. Yet if these touchpoints are not recorded, the company won't have a 360-degree view of a prospect or customer and therefore is handicapped in developing sound offers or communications with the customer.

Getting marketing to be the company's designer and driver of market strategy. Too much marketing today is 1P marketing, namely, marketing dealing only with promotion, whereas other departments determine the product, the price, and the place. I remember a major European airline where the Vice President of Marketing confessed that he doesn't manage the price or the product conditions (food, staff, décor) or the flight schedules but only the advertising and sales force. How can marketing be effective if the 4Ps are not under unified planning and control?

Facing lower cost/higher quality competitors. As China develops economically, firms will face a repeat of the Japanese threat which consisted of competing with Japanese companies able to offer better products at lower costs. This will force more companies to shift production to China and change the face of industry and employment at home.

Coping with the increasing power and demands of mega-distributors. Mega-retailers such as Wal-Mart, Costco, Toys R Us, Office Depot, and others are commanding a larger share of the retail marketplace. Many supermarket chains are creating store brands that are equal in quality to national brands and lower in price, thus forcing down manufacturers' margins. National brand companies feel more than ever at the mercy of mega-retailers and are desperately searching for defense and offense strategies.

Who would you say have been the greatest marketing thinkers and practitioners in business?

My nominations would include: Walt Disney of Disney Enterprises; Ray Kroc of McDonald's; Roberto Goizueta of Coca-Cola; Howard Schultz of Starbucks; Ingvar Kamprad of IKEA; Sam Walton of Wal-Mart; Richard Branson of Virgin; Jeff Bezos of Amazon; Fred Smith of FedEx; Anita Roddick of The Body Shop; and Nicolas Hayek of Swatch watches.

Designing the market-facing organization

SAM HILL, DAVID NEWKIRK AND JONG CHOW

[Restructuring as a market-facing organization is one way for a company to stimulate organic growth. How should companies go about making the transition?]

All journeys start with a single step. All business strategies start with reorganization. Reorganizing often remains the most flexible, quickest, and least costly means to affect change available to the CEO.

Companies looking for strategies to generate significant organic growth are increasingly turning to one particular type of structure: the market-facing organization. Market-facing organizations are particularly well-suited for driving innovation and delivering revenue. By focussing top management on specific segments with distinct needs, they typically create new opportunities to deliver greater value more cost effectively.

However, they are difficult to design, install, and operate, as they often fragment the traditional responsibilities for marketing, manufacturing, and control. This chapter is intended as a primer for those considering adopting market-facing organizations.

Background

While every company's organization is unique, each tends to be built around one of six basic skeletons: geographic, SBU (strategic business unit), product, functional, brand, or market-facing. Organization skeletons, or models, get their names from the titles and responsibilities of the executives in the first level of the structure. For example, a geographic organization is one in which the direct reports to the CEO (or equivalent) have full P&L responsibility for a geographic region, e.g. Vice President of Europe.

This does not mean that there are not functional elements to a geographic organization or people responsible for products in an SBU organization. Every organization, regardless of structure, has people at some level responsible for locations, territories, products, functions, customers, and brands. What differs is the primary focus of senior management and how responsibilities are allocated. This is easier to illustrate than it is to describe. For example, in a geographic organization, the manager of European sales would report to the Vice President of Europe, and the manager of North American sales would report to the Vice President of North America, with a focus on regional success. In a functional organization, the manager for European sales and the manager for North American sales would both report to the same person, the Vice President of worldwide sales, typically with a greater focus on common approaches and tools.

To complete the descriptions of the basic models, in an SBU organization structure the managers reporting to the CEOs are themselves mini-CEOs, each with his or her own sales force, marketing, manufacturing operations, distribution, staff functions, etc. Product organizations are in essence modified SBU organizations, maintaining sales and marketing but drawing on central operating and support functions reporting to the CEO, either directly or through an executive in charge of shared services. For example, in a product organization the line executive would likely have marketing and research and development under him or her, but would seldom have human resources or finance. Sales, manufacturing, and logistics can be either shared or dedicated, depending on the degree of commonality across products.

Functional organizations are those where the direct reports of the CEO are responsible for functional areas, such as marketing and sales. Brand management organizations, prototyped by Unilever and popularized by Procter & Gamble, are a variant of functional organization, designed to capture much of the value of an SBU structure. The marketing department is organized into smaller units each responsible for the marketing of a particular set of trademarked products, with similar products grouped into needs-focussed categories (say toothpaste, mouthwash, and toothbrushes combined into oral care). What makes it unique (and powerful) is that brand managers notionally have P&L responsibility, while the category managers balance portfolio coverage and build customer insight. (This P&L responsibility is, in practical terms, more of a watching brief than anything else, since brand managers do not have direct control over other functional areas like manufacturing, and must rely on negotiation and persuasion to effect decisions.)

Let's analyze the pros and cons of each.

- Geographic structures are good for entering new markets for recruiting talent, and for tactical delivery of day-to-day results. Their drawback is that they encourage the creation of fiefdoms. They fragment resources (research, manufacturing, marketing) making it hard to realize economies of scale. Typically, each market develops its own processes, which can lead to a severe case of the not-invented-here syndrome and create significant barriers to systems deployment. As markets converge and companies pursue global technology platforms, geographic models are declining in popularity. Even the most staunch defenders of the geographic P&L (ABB, Unilever, HSBC) are moderating their approach with increasingly strong product and functional leads.

- SBU organizations, typified by GE, are superb for managing companies with very diversified operations and do a very good job of grooming potential CEOs. They accommodate radically different capabilities and cultures easily because each unit is autonomous. However, SBU organizations often have high levels of conflict between the units, even to the point of competing for the same acquisitions or markets. They seldom achieve maximum efficiency, since functions, such as accounts payable and benefits administration, are duplicated in each business unit. To deal with these issues, many SBU-focussed companies are creating key-account management to limit conflict and using shared services (internal or external) to capture scale, both of which move the SBU model toward more of a product organization.
- Product-focussed organizational structures are useful for driving technical innovation. They are not so good at responding to market needs, developing non-technical expertise, or realizing customer synergies across product lines. Product organizations, by definition, employ shared resource units.
- Functional organizations develop and deploy deep expertise effectively. They also provide the best way to realize economies of scale, particularly in back office areas. However, they are seldom responsive to changing market conditions, and organizational silos can slow or even paralyze decision making. Only companies with a single product, service, or brand can operate effectively in a strongly functional model.
- Brand organizations generate a high level of focussed marketing activity and groom middle management talent. However, they tend to result in superficial innovation and a lack of underlying product-based differentiation. They also under-leverage customer relationships across brands – particularly critical in businesses with strong distribution channels. In late 2003, Kraft replaced its CEO because of the failure of its brand management organization to generate and implement significant new growth platforms.
- Market-facing organizations are superb at responding to customer needs and thus at accessing major new sources of growth. By focussing on market segments, they excel at spotting new trends, finding underserved areas, and creating out-of-the-box product/service ideas. Well executed, they can match the services delivered (and their costs) to the value perceived by each segment – tailoring the business to its markets. Market-facing organizations can also go a long way toward clearing up the internal conflict and competition created by years of acquisitions folded into SBU structures. However, market-facing organizations are complex to design, implement, and manage, requiring new skills and behavior from the managers involved.

Having said all this, very few companies actually employ organization structures that are purely functional or purely geographic or purely anything. In practice, each company creates a hybrid to fit its market, the unique characteristics of its businesses and the skills of its executives. Every organization employs some variation from the pure. They adopt processes, systems, and operating practices to offset the weaknesses of their core structure. For example, one of our clients operates an almost pure functional organization, with vice presidents of sales, marketing, operations, human resources, information technology, etc. However, the vice president of new business has three small standalone companies reporting to her. Our client has made this exception both to meet the needs of the companies – they are recent acquisitions that might well get lost if disassembled and incorporated into the various functional areas – and to groom the young executive for a future role. Every organization employs some variation from the pure.

Not only that, but many modern organizations are so large and complex that they employ a set of virtual organization overlays to ensure co-operation between units. There are two common "integrative mechanisms." The first is the use of project teams (or task forces), where a manager may be formally in one part of the organization, but is expected for some portion of his or her time to operate on a team comprised of managers drawn from other parts of the company. Unlike formal organization structures, project teams are temporary and have a very limited set of responsibilities.

The second is *matricing*, where various parts of the organization have joint responsibility for certain costs or revenues. Aerospace companies invented matrix management to bring together distinct functional disciplines (aerodynamics, structural engineering, control design, testing) in a single project team. They are now common wherever distinct capabilities need to be brought together in a market. For example, in Citibank, both the regional head and the head of the product organization are responsible for revenues and profit performance. The net result of all this modifying is to create organization models that are never pure but are always highly customized hybrids.

Designing the market-facing organization

The critical first step in designing the market-facing organization is to agree on the definition of the market. A market segment should be an identifiable group with distinct needs – identifiable so the organization can address them effectively, with distinct needs to allow the tailoring of services and offerings. While this might appear to be relatively straightforward, it only appears thus for those who have not attempted it. For companies who use distributors, retailers, or resellers, it is first necessary to decide whether or not the key segments are these channel partners or whether the critical "customer" segments are the end-user. In an ideal world, the answer would most often be the end-users, because meeting their needs in new ways drives product or service innovation, and intermediaries such as resellers are seldom effective at identifying those unmet needs and relaying them back to the manufacturer. However, in many markets, the channels themselves have distinct service needs, offering equally powerful opportunities for service differentiation and innovation.

For example, one of our clients provides medical texts. The end-users of these are physicians. However, physicians rarely buy books themselves. For the most part books are bought by hospital libraries, medical schools, and pharmaceutical companies (as gifts). Therefore, the ideal might be to organize around different physician specialties. In practical terms, the appropriate market-facing organization must be designed around the intermediaries that actually write the checks and their distinct buying behaviors, e.g. libraries and medical schools. The differing needs of channels explain why soft drink bottlers organize sales and marketing around grocery stores, impulse outlets (petrol stations), restaurants/bars, and vending machines.

The next question becomes which segmentation to use. The objective is to group sales, marketing, and innovation around customers with similar sets of needs. There are several options.

For companies with a few large accounts, it is often easiest just to dispense with market segmentation altogether and assign different accounts to different organizational units. For example, an aluminum casting foundry in Ohio has four clients, and is accordingly organized into four units. In the UK, where four large grocers account for most sales, many suppliers serve each through dedicated sales, marketing, and logistics teams.

Alternatively, it is possible to organize around standard industry segments. For example, banks often organize into high-level market-facing units around individuals (retail), corporate, mid-market, and small business. Industrial companies often organize their market facing units around SIC code classifications – for example, one division might serve aerospace, another automotive, and another telecommunications. There are any number of standard segmentations available: demographics, size, company structure (e.g. private versus public), etc. The advantage of these types of segmentations is that they are straightforward and intuitively appealing. The weakness is that within a standard segment are often customers with very different sets of needs. For example, a boutique investment bank may technically be a small business, but have the same sophisticated needs as a Citibank or HSBC.

The most powerful option is often some form of custom segmentation. In both consumer and industrial markets, customers can be grouped by demographics (their characteristics: size, wealth, locations) and psychographics (their buying behavior: knowledge/self-confidence; willingness to "bundle," brand sensitivity). The demographics typically shape the "what" of the offer, while psychographics should influence the "how" of selling it.

For example, 3M, the Minneapolis-based adhesives and industrial products company, has defined its business into five units: industrial; transportation, graphics, and safety; health care; consumer and office; and electronics and communications. In other words, 3M is saying that consumers and offices belong in the same segment because they have similar needs, use similar products, can be reached through similar channels, buy in similar ways, etc.

The strength of a custom segmentation is it is possible to tailor the organization exactly to meet the needs of the business. Banks have long targetted customers by life stage and wealth, tailoring offers to meet distinct needs and demographics. The sophisticated now target risk preference and other psychographics as well. An industrial client segmented its market by its customers' own manufacturing focus (quality, efficiency, flexibility) and their buying process (detailed "bid-to-spec" versus co-design), driving changes in both the product offering, the selling cycle, and organizational skills.

The challenge is that it is much harder to analyze and track custom segments, e.g. there is no off-the-shelf industry report that defines the size and composition of the transportation, graphics, and safety market, and it is impossible to tell from the outside whether a customer is a "specifier" or an "outsourcer." Therefore, in general, custom segmentations work best for the very large and very small companies, and are more challenging for mid-sized companies.

It is also possible to combine these approaches. For example, a mid-Western software company has four divisions: the insurance industry, banking, specialist credit, and named accounts. The last comprises the top 50 customers of the firm. The organization is, therefore, a combination of all three approaches – no segmentation, standard, and custom.

Installing the market-facing organization

Market-facing organizations tend to be relatively straightforward to implement in service organizations. For example, most of the large management consulting firms and auditing firms are now organized around practices, e.g. telecommunications, financial services, etc. Even law firms are now creating vertical market coverage teams. Their challenge is then to mobilize functional specialties effectively across the multiple segments. Market-facing organizations are less easy to install in those product organizations without direct end-user contact. There are two hurdles that must be overcome.

The first is transforming the mindset and skills to fit a market-facing organization. Most product-centric organizations have managers with deep product skills, well-trained in tweaking their products and aggressive in hunting for customers to sell them to. Becoming a market-facing organization requires turning this approach 90 degrees.

Instead of deep product knowledge, the segment manager needs deep customer knowledge, which requires hours of customer interface and careful listening. Instead of aggressively seeking out markets to sell the product to, the market-facing organization aggressively seeks out products and creates services to meet its customers' needs. At its extreme, this changes a company's vision. Alfa Laval's publicly announced mission is "to improve the efficiency of our customers' processes, time and time again," a commitment to seeing their own product embedded in their users' businesses.

To accomplish this without fragmenting the overall business, market-segment managers cannot own products and brands in the same way product managers do. For example, in the 3M example cited above, the Scotch brand and its variants (Scotchgard, Scotch-Brite, Scotchlite, Scotchprint) are shared across all the divisions and manufactured by a common organization. That means all new marketing strategies must be cleared by a central brand council, and changes to product specifications must be co-ordinated with many more people than in a simple product structure.

Some organizations have tried to finesse this by keeping both product and market segment managers in place. However, this seldom works, as the R&D group ends up with two sets of product requirement documents, one written by the product manager and one by the market segment manager. Relatively quickly, one approach or the other wins out.

The second difficulty in creating market-facing organizations comes from the need to define and institute new metrics to measure share and profitability by segment. For example, as credit card companies are more market-facing, they had to stop thinking in terms of share of plastic (cards issued) and learn to think of share of wallet (amount charged on the card as a percentage of total credit used by a consumer). This is a subtle, but nonetheless dramatic, shift.

It also poses a more practical problem. Beginning with financials, but moving increasingly toward product and customer data, complex companies are working to structure their information to let them look at their business along any dimension: product, market, segment, brand, function. However, most are not there yet, and installing market-facing metrics still provides a considerable hurdle.

Metrics are a relatively small problem for strategic planning and budgeting, since planners can create temporary solutions using spreadsheets and one-off analyses. But to really drive the business toward market-facing requires weaving the right measures into the daily fabric of the business, which requires redesigning the complete IT infrastructure. Because of this, a reorganization into market-facing units can take two to three years, twice as long as typical in simpler geographic-functional or functional-product transformation.

Finally, the "right" segmentation often changes as markets evolve and the organization becomes more sophisticated. All organizations require constant fine-tuning, but none more than market-facing. The key signs to look for are new user applications, and processes, signaling the emergence of new segments and opportunities.

Stirring growth

In short, market-facing organizations are increasingly being adopted to stir organic growth and reduce (but not eliminate) internal conflict. It is a tremendously powerful organizational model, but like changing from one type of computer to another, it can require a company to replace its "organizational software," replacing or reskilling managers, instituting new metrics, and embracing a new operating philosophy.

Understanding brand potential

WATTS WACKER

> Brands cannot stand still, they need to develop and grow, while retaining a foundation of authenticity.

Brands have always been viewed in a context of consistency. With the world now being defined by a macro environment of "uncertainty," a brand must, paradoxically, be consistent and inconsistent at the same time. A brand must always be developing, learning, and growing at the same time as much of its bedrock is always seen in a light of consistency. For example, not only is Budweiser the biggest beer brand in the US, Bud Lite is the second largest.

It is also important to reflect on the "rules of branding" and whether or not they are now obsolete. Two critical rules of branding go back to the roots of modern day marketing (1950):

- the concept of a unique selling proposition;
- that a brand can't be "number one in pickles and number one in ketchup" at the same time.

Ted Bates gave us the idea of the unique selling proposition. After 50 years of continual sophistication in marketing and continual sophistication in consumers, unique selling propositions may no longer motivate consumers. For example, "Pringles the potato chip that makes your hands less greasy" is unique, but has no resonance with consumers as far as motivating them to buy the product. Jack Trout and Al Ries, in their marketing treatise *Positioning Battle for the Mind*, put forth the importance of "being first." They also argued that you could not be first in pickles (Heinz) and at the same time be first in ketchup with the same brand name.

My philosophy is that it is more important to identify your core beliefs and "fuse" the core beliefs with the consumer's "take away." Krispy Kreme's promise – creating magic moments – suggests that it should identify all opportunities that reflect a magic moment as potential and fertile areas for franchise extension. For example, if consumer feedback suggests to Krispy Kreme that there are 100 movies produced in the history of Hollywood that are associated with "a moment" of great sharing between two people, then those movies should be thought of as potential areas to explore with the Krispy Kreme brand.

The critical thought here is that if you are perceived as "a wagon master" (as Gateway is), then you should look for every area to which wagon mastering would make sense relative to the emerging needs within individual lives. In the case of Gateway, branding has already shown transference from computer making, to Internet service provisioning, to leasing (never having an obsolete computer) over buying.

Great mistakes

It is interesting to note that most great brands have had a major misstep in their past. Ford almost went out of business. British Airways once stood for "Bloody Awful." IBM was yet another major brand that demonstrated how easy it is to become vulnerable.

This susceptibility to public display of one's shortcomings has a very humanizing effect on brands. What is critical is not that these shortcomings or failures happen, but what transpires immediately afterward. As Miles Davis once said: "When you hit a wrong note it's the next note that makes it good or bad." Great brands that have let down their consumers actually may create even greater opportunities based on how they respond to the specific circumstance. Brands may be well served by "being wrong and fixing it" instead of striving to be perfect.

... and great concepts

While great brands have a tendency to be viewed as having functional superiority (in a blind taste test Coke is not preferred to Pepsi, but does come out on top when identified as Coke), they see themselves in a larger context than just functionality. Chevrolet did not talk about engineering excellence, it talked about "seeing the USA."

It is also important to remember that the people who work on a brand become sensitized to it much more than their customers. Many marketing managers have become bored with their strategies and tactics well before these have reached a level of burnout with their customers. Solarcaine once had some of the world's best advertising ("Mommy, I'm sunburned and feel like a French fry"). Although the spot only ran 20 times in a period of three years, the marketing department was exhausted by having been exposed to it for many thousands of impressions. As a result, Schering-Plough let go of a great concept way too early.

Authenticity

Great brands tend to be referred to by their customers and even their competitors as being genuine and authentic. Whenever authenticity is associated with a brand, the brand tends to have reached a level of involvement in its consuming universe that is of mythological proportions. Anything that causes a "disconnect" between that authenticity and the actions taken by the brand will result in an immediate and severe consumer response.

For example, lite beer was built for 35-year-old ex-jocks. As the brand's marketplace began to reach saturation, Miller's response to the desire for continued growth was to "contemporize" the brand and go after a younger market. Suddenly, the 35-year-old ex-jocks felt like this beer no longer fitted them. And the younger group never felt like it was designed for them in the first place.

This problem is to do with the issue of "cohort brands" versus "life stage brands." Cohort brands are those that become attached to a group of people and travel over time with them. (The word cohort comes from the Latin for the Roman legionnaire, who went into the legion and remained with the same group of people.) Life stage brands are used at specific stages of life. For example, mothers use Coppertone on their young children and then slather themselves with the same product. The children themselves grow into the next life stage brand (like Hawaiian Tropic and Tropical Blend), then grow into another life stage and use Bain de Soleil. When they get married and have kids, they come back to using Coppertone.

The importance of understanding life stage versus cohort is also reflected in the ups and downs of Nike. Whether this was to do with the brand itself or athletic shoes in general, at a certain point the target audience for Nike sneakers (teens and young adults) no longer wanted to wear a shoe that was so ubiquitous their parents were wearing the same brand. Levi's underwent similar circumstances when it went from being work clothing to a fashion item.

Another good learning perspective for understanding a brand's potential comes from the experience of Barbie. Great brands reach the level of having iconographic transfer. But nature abhors a vacuum; if you don't define yourself, the *zeitgeist* defines you. Barbie began to be featured in songs and advertisements for other companies (the Nissan GI-Joe/Barbie commercial) in a light that made Mattel feel uncomfortable. More to the point, Body Shop put ads in its window with Barbie's head on a Rubensesque plastic doll, with copy that said, "there are three billion women in the world, only six of them are super-models." Because Barbie was not defining herself in a relevant context, she was being defined by the *zeitgeist* itself.

In the past three (or so) years there has been ever greater uncertainty, bi-polar living and manifestations of different approaches to life and lifestyles. Through all of this branding just gets more and more important. Going forward, great brands will pay even more attention to what is often called their "essence" relative to their efficacy.

Of course great brands have to "do" what they say they will quite well but they also have to "be" something of relevance beyond their product attributes and benefits. The first oracle of Delphi is ... *know thyself*. And as the bard so aptly put forth, once you know who you are you have to be true to yourself. Great brands are true to themselves in a very consistent way. For example, Dell computer has no R&D department while it would be suicidal for Hewlett-Packard to even consider such a move. I was recently told how VH-1 once planned its annual awards show with featured artists who had never had their videos even aired on the network. Way too often brands present a mixed message because consumers (us!!) don't see the connection between what we've experienced of the brand versus what is currently being presented as a brand's direction.

Does it really make sense for a Swatch car to be built by Mercedes? Why did United Airlines stay with "fly the friendly skies" when we all recognized that flying was not friendly any more?

The "be" of a brand has to speak to the largest "issues" in life. There are 12 archetypal "lessons," seven plots, five passions in world art and six great ideas. My bet is there are two handfuls of global metaphors ... like the blues and the Energizer Bunny (it keeps going and going). All of the above speak to *all* the people in the world ... both sexes ... every race, creed, color ... and of any age.

Great brands align to these "lessons" and values, whether it be "courage" or "goodness." Great brands stand the test of time because of their "be-ness" not their "do-ness." Actually great brands usually don't "do" what they did to make them great in the first place ... just ask Nokia or BMW or GE or even Coke. But what they stand for doesn't vary.

RESOURCES

Gad, Thomas, *4D-Branding*, FT Prentice Hall, 2000.
Wacker, Watts, *The 500 Year Delta*, Capstone, 1997.
Wacker, Watts, *The Visionary's Handbook*, Capstone, 2000.

Global marketing

H. DAVID HENNESSEY

[In the future the opportunities will be very different for global marketers compared to the 1990s. The basic tenets of marketing will stay the same – satisfying consumers' needs and creating value – but the actual process of marketing will be radically different.]

The Internet has reduced the size of the world to two or three clicks from any company to any consumer or buying organization.[33] The web allows consumers and companies to search, compare, and buy almost any product or service from anywhere around the globe. This can be done in point-to-point transactions or in marketplaces with multiple buyers and sellers.

While the halo of the Internet slipped as the bubble burst, the immense functionality continues to offer executives the opportunity to reduce costs and increase value for their customers. Whether it is components for an airplane, polyethylene resin for a milk container, or a rare book, the search, selection, and ultimate transaction will be less costly, more accurate, and more efficient than previous exchanges.

For example, Aeroxchange, founded by 13 airlines in 2000, now has 33 airline users and 400 parts vendors in 30 countries. The exchange will reduce transaction costs, inventory, number of suppliers, and therefore total costs. Industry trading exchanges have been established for oil companies, automotive manufacturers, chemical companies, auto component manufacturers, food retailers, personal computer manufacturers, and many other industries. Most companies will be either selling and/or buying through an industry trading marketplace.

It is important for companies to develop Internet capabilities and establish or join the appropriate trading marketplaces. First and second movers will most likely develop favorable positions in these new market systems that "latecomers" will find difficult to usurp. Jack Welch, then chief executive of GE, told shareholders at the annual meeting in 2000: "Any company, old or new that does not see this technology as literally as important as breathing could be on its last breath."

Price transparency

As the digital world facilitates product and price transparency, companies with regional or global brands will be able to afford the cost of continual innovation to differentiate their products to consumers. As the cost of research and innovation is spread over the global marketplace, it will be a larger total investment than local brands can afford, but it will be less for global products on a per-unit-sold basis.

At first, the price transparency may make it hard for consumers to differentiate products or services. Therefore, E*Trade, Ameritrade, National Discount Brokers, and other online brokers could become commodities. However, consumers will still look for the best value (perceived benefit received minus price, including time). In many cases, consumers will rely on brand image to help decide, but will also be looking for value-added services such as shipment tracking, quality certification, superior logistics, etc. to choose between similar offerings.

While price transparency will tend to encourage price competition or parity, executives must look for ways to use the new technology and the information to provide increased value. For example, Schwab has attracted higher net worth customers with higher average balances than other brokers through the use of personalized advice and portfolio tracking. These value-added services along with a trusted brand have reduced Schwab's customer acquisition cost and increased its average trading revenue over other online brokers.

John Chambers, CEO of Cisco systems, spends 50 percent of his time with customers, first to understand their evolving needs, and second to set a clear example that customers are number one at Cisco. Chambers openly admits that he did not do this in his former positions at IBM and Wang, and that the companies lost market position. His advice to executives is: when you think you have the winning formula, it's time to hire more people from other industries, because the rules of the game are changing so fast.

Point-to-point transactions

The Internet will allow easy point-to-point transactions, which in some industries will eliminate the need for distributors, wholesalers, agents, and retailers. Because of this disintermediation, travel agents, insurance agents, computer retailers, and other channel members will be marginalized unless they can add value to the process. For example, 11 European airlines, including British Airways, Air France, KLM, SAS, and others, have announced the formation of a joint database to reduce distribution and ticketing costs. This has displaced travel agents.

In the personal computer industry, value-added resellers, distributors, and computer retailers were previously the channels used by IBM and HP. This approach required extensive inventory in the channel, manufacturers had to take back equipment that did not sell, and the extra profit margin required by the channel members had to be included in the total costs. Dell has developed a competitively priced direct model that delivers individually configured computers with software loaded on the machine before delivery. The Dell approach requires 7–10 days of inventory compared to 60–65 days for traditional hardware manufacturers. The difficulty that IBM and others face is their legacy sales and distribution systems. Executives will need to examine closely new business models being offered and in many cases make difficult short-term painful decisions to be competitive in the longer term.

Point-to-point communications between buyers and sellers will allow global marketers to gain a better understanding of the needs of each customer and become more customer focussed. Using the latest information, sellers can tailor their offering to specific needs. For example, booksellers can feature recent books on horses in information sent to the equestrian enthusiast, and recent global strategy books to the business executive who has bought similar books in the past.

Specialized industry websites allow marketers to advertise directly to their target audience. For example, the Fish Info Service (http://fis.com) is used by fishermen, processors, and traders to keep up to date with fish stocks and prices, making this the perfect place to speak directly to this audience. VerticalNet offers over 50 different business-to-business trade communities, which appeal directly to specialized markets such as fiber-optics, water supply, dentistry, and semiconductors. Advertising is a major revenue source for VerticalNet.

Through e-mail, many customers can be contacted directly with high-quality, tailored communications. For example, Germany's Mittelstand companies, large private firms in the engineering field, have used the Internet to focus communications with selected customers and suppliers and develop a deep partnership, rather than a mass-market approach.

Global markets

The Internet, the euro, and the interdependence of major world economies are all fostering companies' opportunities to serve the global marketplace. Large and small companies can serve customers around the globe.

Given that any customer can reach a company in two to three clicks, it will become common to sell books, art, travel, market information, music, shares of stock, hardware, machinery, planes, trains, automobile, and many other items over the net. Along with reduced trade and geographic barriers for many products, there will be few limits to the type of products and services that can be sold globally in this way.

- The net eliminates time zone restrictions and speeds up information exchange.
- The net allows for two-way interaction, so each business can receive components only when required (JIT), eliminating inventory, warehousing, and obsolete stock. Of course, low-value physical products will not be shipped around the globe, but many items will benefit from the efficient worldwide delivery and shipping services now available through DHL, FedEx, UPS, Maersk, and others.

Given the large volume of Internet sites and trading marketplaces, a key role of global marketers will be to attract and keep customers at their site. This will require agreements and alliances with search engines and non-competitive sites that serve the customer base. Through search engines and links you will be able to get customers to your site, but that site's quality and perceived value will determine how long a customer stays on it or how many times they return.

Providing product information, negotiating prices, and tracking shipments may be better handled by technology than by a traditional salesperson. In some industries where the salesperson's primary role was to facilitate transactions, they will no longer be required. In other industries, the salesperson's role will be to monitor the customer's industry and work face to face with the customer to add value. This will require salespeople with new skills to assimilate industry information and identify new ways to add value for customers. In business-to-business selling, the salesperson will work closely with marketing to identify and create innovative, value-added products and services.

The challenge of global marketing

The new world of global marketing will require significant e-commerce skills. At first, these skills involve using the electronic point-to-point capability of the Internet to reduce costs and improve customer value. This will require major changes in pricing, product development, advertising, and sales. The digital world provides an amazing variety of new ways to serve customers.

Second, global marketers will be faced with the challenge of co-operation. Companies will be working directly with competitors in trading marketplaces to reduce purchase costs. For example, 64 of the world's leading retailers belong to the Worldwide Retail Exchange, a business-to-business online exchange, established in 2000 to buy, sell, or auction goods and services. This group includes Casino and Auchan of France, Safeway and K-Mart of the US and Kingfisher and Marks & Spencer of the UK. The Worldwide Retail Exchange connects its members to suppliers, for example members can connect to 138,000 suppliers in Asia. The exchange reports that they have saved their members over $900 million over three years through auctions and other online transactions.

It is expected that governments may question some of these new arrangements, which is why in many cases the exchanges are operated by a separate company. For example, a computer component exchange including HP, Gateway, Hitachi, NEC, Advanced Micro Devices, and others will be operated by an independent company yet to be named.

The future of global marketing is difficult to predict in the wired world. Barriers to trade will continue to fall, currency risk and currency conversion costs will decline, and geographic borders will become less important, all leading to an increase in world trade. The winning companies will be those that have the vision and can switch to the new approach without being burdened by legacy systems and methods. Most major firms will need to restructure and redefine themselves. There will be winners and losers. Hold on tight, it should be a great ride.

RESOURCES

Hennessey, H. David and Jeannet, J.P., *Global Marketing Strategies*, Houghton Mifflin, 6th edition, 2000.

Peppers, Don and Rogers, Martha, *The One-to-One Field Book*, Capstone, 1999.

Capturing growth through lifetime customer value

SANDRA VANDERMERWE

[The successful modern enterprise sees every customer as an investment. And, like any other investment, each of these customers has a lifetime value. How much share of lifetime value an enterprise captures is the real measure of its success.]

The idea of the lifetime value of customers rests on a very different logic from conventional theory and practice. The traditional view was based on an era of "things" where money was made by product and service companies according to volumes, market share, and margins. The new logic acknowledges that strategies based on these "things," no matter how good or innovative they may be, can never be sustainable because they are too easy to copy, leading to a no-win situation on a diminishing returns treadmill.

"Things" diminish in value as competitors move in – as they invariably do – whereas the value of customers increases over time.

Here lies the key to growth and prosperity in the new economy: enterprises must get customers to "lock on." This means that customers want the firm or institution as their sole or dominant choice on an on-going basis. They do so because they get superior value at low delivered cost, not either superior value or low cost, as traditional theory led us to believe.[34] Customers stay with an enterprise because they have good and sufficient reason to do so, so lock-on becomes self-reiterating over time, which contrasts with the transactional model based on specification and price at a moment in time (see Figure 5.3).[35]

Figure 5.3: *Customer lock-on*

In other words, the more a company does business with a particular customer, the better the relationship: the more knowledge and information they share; the more proactive and precise is the offering. And the more business done together, the lower the cost, thanks to technology and the fact that the knowledge collected – *the* key resource in the value-creating process – can be reused. This creates a reinforcing loop that improves the depth and quality of the relationship, the amount and quality of the information and knowledge shared, lowering the cost, and therefore intensifying the lock-on, and so on.

The ability to trigger and sustain this customer lock-on loop becomes the only realistic barrier to competitive entry. So, rather than trying to get economies of scale on the supply side from units churned out of product or service factories and then moving these goods down channels to meet market share goals, the new objective is to get a critical mass of individual customers who "lock-on" to the enterprise, who will provide for and receive from the enterprise as much value as possible, over as long a period as possible. In other words, in the new economy, economies of scale stem from demand and not from supply.

And since it is individuals rather than markets that lock on, success depends on an enterprise's ability to satisfy individual customers in a highly personalized way by continually giving them the results or outcome they want (or sometimes may not have imagined possible) and then continuously adapt to their changing needs. When aggregated, this outcome becomes the "market space," a descriptive term for the "playing field" or "customer activity arena." It is here that the modern enterprise operates and seeks to dominate in order to maximize share of customer spend over time, rather than maximizing market share in static product categories at a moment in time, in a transactional fashion.

Beyond conventional marketing

Customer relationship management (CRM), customer retention, customer loyalty, and one-to-one marketing – all terms sometimes used interchangeably – have paved the way for thinking about the lifetime value of customers as the competitive paradigm for the new economy. They are made easier to accomplish because of new technologies. However, if we examine these notions, we see that most have stemmed from product thinking, with the focus on using tools – ranging from loyalty cards to the Internet – to bring customers back again and again to buy and do what they were buying and doing anyway. All of this inevitably leads to commodity behavior and zero gain for everyone, including customers.

We can see this in the results of CRM and associated programs, which top management believed in sincerely and paid for dearly. They have come nowhere near to bringing the promised returns. In a startling contradiction, during the first four years of the new millennium, banks, for instance, spent fortunes on these programs but failed to achieve even a single loyal customer group – in fact, overall satisfaction rates dropped.[36]

As for retention it focusses the enterprise on how many customers it is losing: "how much the bucket is leaking" to quote Frederick Reichheld, which often leads to short term "fixing" measures without really making the true transformations needed to get the customer lock-on that achieves lasting growth.[37]

Here the emphasis is on doing different things to stretch customer relationships further. The aim is to become more involved with the customer's experience in the chosen market space and so increasing amounts of customer spend over time. Take Unilever: instead of just using techniques to induce repurchase and sell more and more detergents and home-cleaning items, or using data gathered through technology on buying patterns to continue to make incremental changes to existing products or distribution systems, it developed myhome.co.uk, which provided cleaning services in the *home and fabric cleaning* market space.

Unilever decided, after 18 months, to sell myhome to the Chores Group (heading for a £20 million goal by 2005), while still retaining a share. Using its well-known cosmetic brand names, the Anglo-Dutch giant has nonetheless used its experience and knowledge and has gone into beauty clinics in Spain and in emerging countries like India where it is said more woman are working and have more money to spend on themselves.[38]

Crossing product and industry boundaries

From the customer's point of view, artificial product and industry separations make no sense. They couldn't care less about how companies are organized, who reports to whom, or who owns what. So defining and dominating market spaces requires spilling over product and industry boundaries.

Take financial services: customers start out as wealth aspirers, borrowing at the onset of adulthood, requiring loans for education or to start businesses (see Figure 5.4). Many banks try to attract students with cheap loans, hoping to hold on to them afterwards, but because such people are seen as a non-money-making proposition, the services given are poor and the strategy tends to backfire.

Then customers become wealth builders: they get married, have children, move around the world, and may build professional practices or businesses. At this stage they become wealth creators – savers and investors – seeking to maintain and enhance their lifestyles and grow their wealth. Once retired, people become wealth protectors: they dis-save, spending their money to sustain and protect their lifestyles. And then wealth passes to the next generation – the wealth inheritors – so continuing the cycle.

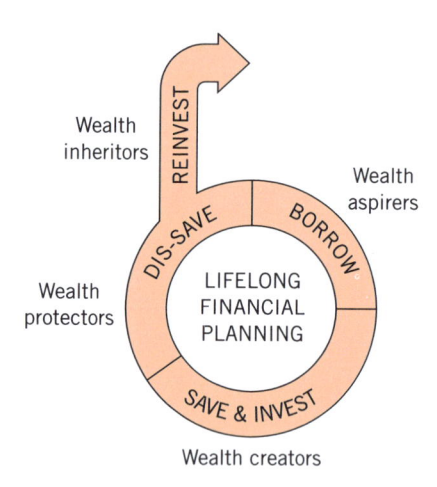

Figure 5.4: *A lifetime customer approach to financial services*

Virgin Banking in the UK is an example of a young brand which aims to cover all these periods of a customer's lifetime financial needs, irrespective of what industry or product "silo" they happen to be in. In their different ways, and geared toward different kinds of markets, it assesses the needs that occur at each critical life stage its customers go through and provides whatever is necessary at that point. And, claim Virgin's executives, over 25 years a customer with an income of £50,000 and a mortgage of £100,000 could gain as much as £125,000, largely by avoiding the inefficiencies and costs in time, effort, and money of having to deal with different institutions and industries to get the various services they need and obtain the results they want in the event cash management market space – cash when, where, and how they need it, whether it be insurance, loans, mortgages, or stocks.

Merrill Lynch, one of the leading US and international stockbrokers, decided that customers, especially the growing numbers of baby boomers, were not only interested in wealth accumulation but also in its preservation for day- to-day use, because as they live longer and are more healthy they are desperately trying to maintain their living standards. As part of its total financial management plan for its customers, the stockbroker offers what it calls "Beyond Banking," which merges the artificially separated buckets of stockbroking and banking and ties them together as part of ongoing, lifetime liquidity management in a single point of customer contact.

Offering the total customer experience

The modern enterprise fills gaps to provide the total customer experience because it knows that if it doesn't someone else will, and that someone will probably be from outside the industry or even a newcomer who emerges from nowhere to take customers and new growth opportunities. It is only by catering to the total customer experience that an enterprise can achieve the outcome for customers, locking them on and competitors out.

Take Direct Line, which entered and revolutionized the automobile insurance industry in 1985 – "we're just a phone call away" – is outperforming its peers, and is soon expected to be the largest personal lines motor insurer in the UK. Having captivated and captured customers by helping them get and manage their insurance differently, it moved to offering advice on cars and financing, and then into breakdown and emergency services, for which it is now the largest provider in the UK, superseding the Royal Automobile Club (RAC) and the Automobile Association (AA), both of which have remained primarily focussed on emergency services.

Adding value through services

The modern enterprise concentrates on achieving the outcome for customers which is encapsulated in the defined market space. Often this can mean selling fewer of their core items (half of IBM's revenues today come from services) or accepting that these are commodities, and concentrating on giving and getting value in ways other than pushing to sell more and more of the "things." In IBM's language, it's not the next big technology it is after to sell, so much as how it will work for customers.

Take an example: most health insurers today concentrate on how to sell more health insurance policies and process claims. International Health Insurance (IHI), based in Denmark with policyholders in over 150 countries, has taken a different route: it is offering the total customer experience. From the starting point of its recognition that customers regard health insurance as a necessary cost they would much rather eliminate, IHI's CEO Per Bay Jorgenson saw that the outcome its target customers – individuals living, working, or retired abroad, as well as corporations with employees overseas – really wanted was lifetime health and personal safety. He then set about directing strategy and resources to ensure that IHI offered all the value added services needed to provide that outcome. By reshaping the company to produce wellness instead of simply covering expenses during illness, IHI has managed to grow year for year even as others in the industry fell on hard times post-millennium.

Being well was redefined by IHI to include health, as well as being and feeling safe while traveling and living abroad. For example, when it comes to companies relocating their employees abroad, IHI examined the entire customer experience. It discovered a series of value adds including better matching of individuals to countries based on their health and comfort profiles; better health regimes suited to a particular country with personalized health plans emphasizing prevention, what diseases to watch out for, and early warning signals; family education on the new cultural environment; the dangers both to the expatriate executive and the family, ranging from earthquakes to terror, allergies to corruption, and what to do; and then, if someone does fall ill, knowing what medicines to take in what countries; where to go if things do go wrong; and how to rehabilitate and prevent a repeat problem.

The end result is that employees feel and stay well and safe as they progress through life and their careers, and thus are more productive on the job; the corporate client saves in total health costs; and IHI not only earns sources of new revenue, but also saves by not having to process unnecessary claims.

Using partners to connect up the customer experience

Modern companies intent on truly capturing lifetime customer value typically acknowledge early on that it is more risky to leave gaping holes for someone else to fill in the customer experience than to try to fill them either themselves or with partners. They also realize that equally risky is to just stick to their core business because it will never give the growth through customers they need to prosper and thrive.

The reasons modern enterprises take a partner is to fill gaps in the total customer experience, because they don't have the adequate or appropriate infrastructure, knowledge, or skills to offer but someone else does, or someone is able to do it better, more quickly, or more cheaply. Partners can do jointly for customers what neither can do individually. IHI will call in an international expert in security to give a corporate customer complex advice on how to protect employees from potentially dangerous situations in foreign countries, for instance.

One of the reasons Amazon.com has grown is because it is filling in the value gaps left by others, using partners whenever necessary. Early on Jeff Bezos saw the disconnects, the innumerable opportunities to put value in and eliminate the many non-value-added activities which manifested in wasted time, hassles, and costs including a customer having to get to the store (sometimes several), searching to find a book (they may not even know which one), trying to get assistance, ordering the book if it is not in stock, queuing to pay and, if unlucky, having to return and start the process all over again!

When Amazon.com uses a courier or postal service to deliver its goods around the world, they partner with the US Postal Service, or the Royal Mail, or DHL. However, because the retailer understands that the delivery service can be as important to the outcome as the choice of the book or CD or DVD itself, and since this is the only "real" contact the customer has in the entire experience, any default could seriously reflect on the Amazon brand. Amazon counters this by insisting that if something does go wrong it is to Amazon that the customer makes recourse, and Amazon is the one which takes on the responsibility of rectifying the situation, therefore retaining the customer "lock-on."

Setting clear standards and having one vision of the customer goal is crucial to this partnering arrangement. Direct Line has over 300 independent shops that do the emergency repairs, yet they are all integrated under the Direct Line brand. Whenever customers have a road problem, they call Direct Line; the car (and customer) is picked up, fixed, returned, and automatically charged through the customer's bank card. Claims are made to the insurer by phone. Direct Line "owns" both the brand and the customer experience. To maintain quality it sets standards – common, consistent, and acceptable service levels – ensuring that all players integral to customer experience work as one value-creating delivery system. Examples include its 24-hour recovery service; 24-hour collection and delivery to and from the customer's home; contacting the customer within 30 minutes of a call for help; and recovering the stranded vehicle within an hour.

Connecting the various parts that make up the customer's experience through partnering cross-product and industry is facilitated by new technology. Simply and at low cost, the new enterprise can gain from networking and from the knowledge, expertise, and resources of linked partners delivering highly personalized superior offerings.

Through its "FordDirect" website, Ford connects customers to a series of dealer partners to create the fully integrated experience, while Ford continues to manage and thus "own" the customer experience. For instance, customers can see what car model all the linked local dealers have in stock instead of having to walk around and ask. The automobile is then delivered to their homes for a test drive. Those interested in used cars can track vehicle ownership and service records to make their assessment. Or, by using the site, potential purchasers can also "build" their ideal vehicle in terms of comparing base models, and choosing colors and options. They can request quotes from a local dealer, and get insurance and financing. Maintenance schedules can be accessed and they can book a service, pay automatically, phone in for help to call centers and, if they want a car for special occasions, get special rental deals from Hertz, also part of Ford. A clearing house of franchised dealers covers emergency breakdowns on a 24-hour basis, and a network of partners enables digital voice-activated phone service for emergency roadside assistance as well as for personalized information such as news, e-mail delivery, and stock quotes, together with 100 channels of digital music and other programs.

Partners may be competitors as firms go multi-brand, recognizing that no single brand can satisfy customers in their various roles, let alone over their lifetime. The new strategy of Ford US is not just for the Ford brand, but also across its family of brands like Aston Martin, Jaguar, Land Rover, Volvo, Lincoln, Mercury, and Mazda. Renault goes further in its carevia.com initiative, the first multi-make information and transaction site for used cars by a single manufacturer.

Stretching horizons further

Once lock-on has been accomplished, the second-round opportunity for the enterprise is to go for adjacent growth. Which means the new enterprise can move into other market spaces, thus extracting even more spend. Chores, now in customers' homes, and so having learned about their needs and preferences, is able to offer a whole range of activities to liberate these customers from their domestic chores: gardening, car cleaning, dog walking, meal delivery, and security – all the unpleasant tasks for people who want value for time, not just value for money, and a better work/life balance. Meanwhile, Direct Line, having firmly established itself as a vehicle insurer, easily moved into home insurance as well as into a range of other financial services, such as lending, savings, and mortgages.

This is the route many of the younger brands, now icons, have taken. For example: Amazon.com (from books into CDs, games, software, and even toiletries, healthcare, and gourmet food among others) or Virgin stretching its wings across the globe (from retailing into airlines, rail services, financial services, and web-based car dealerships, among other things).

Changing the financial algorithm

The formula for lifetime customer value differs from the conventional model in very significant ways. Most obvious is that what is key is not the profitability of each unit, product, segment, or even country at a moment in time, but the profitability of the customer – over time. The new enterprise knows how to calculate the present value of the future revenue streams obtained from customer lock-on and factor this into resource allocation and investment decisions.[39]

It is also aware that a risk factor for customer loss has to be built into these equations over a hoped-for contemplated period. How far it dares estimate into the future is likely to be more about the spirit and aspirations of the enterprise rather than its size, or the intricacies of some sophisticated mathematical formula.

Conventional accounting and reporting standards can program priorities and behavior that can work against customer lock-on. In particular, reliance on old practice perpetuates old product silo thinking and structures, causing disconnects in the customer experience, with enterprises reluctant to do anything that is not regarded as "profitable," even if it makes a vital component of the customer experience. For example, Marks & Spencer used to refuse to accept credit cards because it thought this too costly. The result was a greater cost to the UK firm: customers purchased a fraction of what they might have, although brand loyalty and retention rates were probably high. Not to mention the fact that many customers probably migrated elsewhere for this and other reasons related to their experience, with a consequent loss in their lifetime value to M&S, and the resulting near demise of the legendary retailer.

In the 1990s, Baxter Healthcare in North America created and managed a stockless inventory system (which included non-Baxter goods) for hospitals by ordering, delivering, and receiving inventory directly to wards, just-in-time (JIT). The associated service charges to hospitals were more than offset by the superior value they received. Although Baxter lost individual items to competitors when its product was not ideal or too expensive, it did grow its share of a greater customer spend (governments awarded more funding to these hospitals because they were more efficient). But, because the independent service unit was not making a "profit" in the traditional sense of the word, it was dropped.

When an enterprise uses the lifetime value of the customer, it drives a different set of priorities and behavior. It also employs different success criteria to mere market share. For example, Baxter Renal UK invested and excelled early on in home care services, making it *the* expert on personalized services in the home, although that unit was not "profitable." It began with delivering renal bags, but now the company is able to offer a host of services in the patient's home, such as monitoring prescriptions and blood toxin levels to maximize the efficacy of its treatment. And the company supplies associated drugs for heart disease or diabetes, as well as the competitive treatment in the home that had previously been done only in hospitals.

All of Baxter's R&D product and service activities were geared to extending the life and well-being of the renal patient, not maximizing margins on renal bags. In fact, the margins on the bags dropped, but the lifetime value of the customer went up. And the success indicators used went beyond market share of bags to include the number of people choosing Baxter's therapy; how long they stayed on that therapy; and the amount of high-level services as a percentage of Baxter sales – all of which have increased. In other words, although margins went down, Baxter achieved much more of customer spend, over a much longer period of time.

Capturing lifetime customer value provides many benefits, not yet formalized in traditional accounting. These include revenue going up thanks to:

- *longevity of spend* – spend over longer periods of time, even a lifetime. Or, when working with corporations, "contracts in perpetuity," with an exit clause or understanding of when who will withdraw and why, rather than having to renew contracts annually;
- *breadth of spend* – all the extra revenues the enterprise gets by offering value this adds to deliver a fuller, more total experience in its defined market space;
- *depth of spend* – more share of wallet in traditional areas;
- *diversity of spend* – spend when customers are taken into completely new market spaces.

As well, costs are saved by:

- eliminating protracted and expensive negotiations around renewal costs, tendering, and bidding – a benefit for both suppliers and customers;
- amortizing the huge set-up investment costs required in building the customer relationship;
- low/no acquisition or marginal costs of producing and or delivering extra value-added products and services;
- decreased costs of managing customers, as systems are joined and familiarity and trust set in;
- barriers to reaching influencers shrink, giving access to higher levels of decision makers;
- increased take-up of new innovations, extensions, and opportunities for joint ventures;
- sharing of resources, knowledge, and information, as well as forecasting;
- selling high-level new services like consulting and project management;
- cash flow quality going up – it is more predictable, and could lower the cost of capital;
- leveraging from expertise and knowledge gained, which can be taken to other customers and wider markets at great speed;
- updating and reusing knowledge on customers to deliver on-going value at low marginal costs;
- joint risk taking – all parties have a vested interest in the outcome;
- work done by customers and advice given by customers, such as the reviews Amazon.com's customers provide on its site.

New approaches to cost and pricing

As firms move from a product to a lifetime customer model, top management will have to accept that all of the investment costs cannot be recovered in the initial period, as was typically required in the past when expenses and revenues were squeezed into the same short time frame.

Upfront investment in money, time, and energy will have an impact on cash flow in the short term, but enhance it in the long term – and do so exponentially.[40] Also, not just revenue inflow but combining cash flow *and* investments (i.e. the P&L and balance sheet), which accounts for "free cash flow," is what is needed to ensure success in the new economy.[41]

Pricing strategies may also have to change, as they will no longer be based on the "thing" – the car, the renal bag, the health policy – but could well become based on charges made on the outcome per patient, or on the use of a car when and where customers need it, or on the productivity gained from employee well-being. This will require new ways of thinking and accounting.

Customers also have to change the way they look at pricing and prices. They often want to minimize spend up front, which to some extent can be offset by charging customers for use or subscription rather than for owning the "things."

To get on-demand computing off the ground, IBM has customers pay only when they turn it on. Using computing without buying the machines is part of IBM's story, which dovetails nicely with turning computing power into a utility, available at the lowest possible cost, where people have automatic access to exactly what they need when they need it, but paying only for what they use, in line with an overall need in the marketplace to cut unnecessary costs.

But it will also mean quantifying the result of less than optimal buying inherited form the "things" era, behavior that can lead to higher costs later on for customers. IHI knows, for instance, that 70 percent of the time health problems can be predicted and obviated, with health care costs (both direct and hidden) saved by as much as 50 percent[42] with preventative services.

However, to get customer lock-on means being able to demonstrate that this, or an agreed outcome, has indeed been achieved. Therefore a good deal of effort must go into building a "before" set of baseline data, and then into the "after" data to show corporations what the investment has yielded. The capability to measure these results for customers becomes as essential in obtaining the new customer currency, as working out the costs to make and deliver products and services was in the "things" era.

Getting it – and doing it

The time has come for enterprises to recognize the need to understand and implement a new business model based on customers, rather than on products or services. All firms know what their products or services are worth over time. But few fully appreciate the value of customers over time or how to improve it.

Partly the problem is that they have more confidence in the product figures and columns because they believe these are more reliable and predictable. Ironic, given that the time lag twixt launch and being copied is getting ominously shorter, as are first mover advantages.

E-technology will facilitate this new business model based on lasting customer value, but it is not a substitute. Top management's responsibility is to empower people who understand what has to be done – and let them get on and do it. Success will be determined by the ability to lock customers on and capitalize on customer lifetime value in the future – a future yet to be defined, which they themselves can proactively help create.

RESOURCES

Vandermerwe, Sandra, *Customer Capitalism: Increasing Returns in New Market Spaces*, Nicholas Brealey, 1999, (Colin Whurr, 2001).

Vandermerwe, Sandra, *Breaking Through: Implementing Customer Focus In Enterprises*, Palgrave Macmillan, 2004.

❝Interview❞: Chris Zook

Chris Zook, who heads the worldwide strategy practice for $1 billion global consulting firm Bain & Co, talks about the secrets of sustainable corporate growth.

***How would you define the main premise of your book* Profit From the Core?**

The main idea was that a large number of companies that seem to have all the pieces in place for sustained profitable growth somewhere along the way lose sight of their core, misdefine their core, or prematurely abandon their core in search of new growth.

But *Profit From the Core* actually had several main strands. First, we wanted to compile some basic data on the odds of managing sustained profitable growth. We were writing at a time when companies had extremely aggressive growth targets, both in terms of revenue and earnings. However, we defined our threshold growth at the relatively modest level of 5.5 percent in real terms for both revenues and profits, and earning back the cost of capital on average over five years. Most businesses aspire to do that. They certainly did at that time. Even then, we found that only 13 percent of companies worldwide achieved this average level of performance over a 10-year period.

Then we looked at the companies which had achieved this and asked what was unique or distinguishing about them. We looked at the companies from a lot of different dimensions and discovered a number of interesting things that proved to be jumping off points for our later work.

There was not a disproportionate number of technology companies, despite the fact that the book was written at the end of 2000. Eighty percent of the companies were in basic industries. The distinguishing factor was that they had a leadership position or very strong core. The companies tended to be market leaders or have a strong niche position in one core business or two at the very most. They were companies like Tesco or UPS. Conglomerates or multi-industry companies were disproportionately underrepresented.

Over 80 percent of companies that achieved good growth levels over 10 years grew in a pattern that resembled the emanating rings of a tree. They grew in their core business, possibly gaining a slight amount of market share, but they also pushed out the boundaries of their core businesses to somewhat new areas.

The third thing that came out of the book was a framework that we now use throughout Bain & Co. When we go into a company and work with the client on growth we usually begin by focussing on four questions. These are prescriptive and very diagnostic in terms of understanding growth situations. The four questions may sound trivial, but I think they form the building blocks of growth strategy. They are: What exactly is your core? How close are you to full potential for profitable growth within your core? What are the most attractive adjacent moves that surround your core business – that both reinforce it and draw upon your strengths – which ones should you pursue, in what order, and can the core support that kind of growth? And finally, in certain industries it is very important to ask whether the core is in the process of being redefined or fundamentally changed in terms of the rules of the game.

How does a company define its "core"?

Defining your core involves a combination of judgement and pure analytics. The starting premise is to ask where I am, should be, or will be vis-à-vis my competitors, and am I earning returns equal to or superior to my competitors? Also, in which customer segments do I have uniquely loyal customers who value me more highly than they value my competitors?

Start with the answer to those two questions. Then drill down a layer and ask what exactly is it that allows me to earn differential returns and have more loyal customers. It might be a unique product, a unique insight about customer behavior, or even an entire business system as in the case of Dell Computer. It could be two or three competencies combined in a unique way in a business.

Could you give an example? Take Intel. What would its core be?

Above all I would say it begins with the microprocessor and IA-32 architecture and the embellishments of that. Add to that low-cost manufacturing capabilities with very low error and failure rates, something that is extremely hard for competitors to mimic. Plus, you would add into the core the Intel brand and what it stands for. So, at the center of the business and the reason they have so much market share is the microprocessor architecture, low-cost manufacturing with the lowest error rates and the highest quality, and then the brand.

What do you believe constitutes good growth?

We have a strict definition of good growth. It's market share growth or adjacency growth around a strong core, which earns more than its cost of capital and therefore creates value. We are very skeptical of growth that is pure diversification unless the company has a unique skill that allows it to buy a business and uniquely add value to it. Equally, we are skeptical of revenue growth without profit growth, and also of the sustainability of profit growth without any accompanying revenue growth. Companies frequently make precipitous moves because of the enormous pressure imposed by the equity markets and market analysts to do something in the name of growth.

From your research, which growth path is most often advocated by executives from companies with solid growth? Plus this term you use – "adjacency" – what exactly does it mean?

When you ask executives from companies which have sustained good growth, the number one way was to take the strongest core business and to move into new areas around the core but that leverage the core. So we define that form of growth as "adjacencies." Our research identified six types. These all have three things in common: they are fundamentally strategic in nature as opposed to tactical; they entail a higher level of risk than the average growth move because they are pushing out into the unknown; and they are typically a decision that the executives at the most senior level, CEO or President, get involved in.

You can think of the six most simple types as atoms that can be assembled into molecules. So for example, Nike's growth strategy isn't any one of these but rather a combination of several.

The six types are: geographic adjacencies – Vodafone purchasing Mannesmann to go into Germany for example; product or service adjacency – a totally new product or service but leveraging your current customer service base or leveraging other assets you have; going into a new channel; new customer segments; more rarely done, and more rarely successful, are significant moves up or down the value chain, so forward integration, a manufacturer going into retail, or backward integrating into supply; and finally a company that feels it has a core capability, so to speak, that can be transferred to a totally different arena and the fields of business around it – this is also rare.

So those are what we call adjacencies. We did a lot of analysis with the data of moves closer and further from the core. Eventually we developed a measure for the number of steps away from the core, so adjacent moves could be up to five steps away depending on how far they departed from what was considered central to the core. We discovered that for growth moves more than one and a half to two steps away from the core, the odds of success declined dramatically. Amazingly, the average adjacent move had a failure rate of 75 percent.

What is a good example of a company that moved too far from its core?

In 1998, Mattel purchased the Learning Company Inc. based on the premise that both companies sold to children, and that the plastic toys Mattel sold were vulnerable to being replaced by digital products and software. So Mattel figured it needed to make this move to survive. But it paid $3 billion, enormous in proportion to the size of the Learning Company. Plus, the Learning Company was on the east coast of the US when Mattel was on the west coast. And if you read the press clippings about Mattel at that time it sounded as if the two businesses were more related than it ultimately turned out. In fact it was different customers, different channels, different products, different infrastructure, different competitors, and different brands. It didn't leverage anything of Mattel's. It was fundamentally four or five steps away from the core. Mattel ultimately sold the Learning Company in 2000.

If you had a message for practicing managers, not necessarily senior managers, but middle managers as well, what would the message be?

It would be a very hopeful message. The best growth ideas do not usually come from exotic mental gymnastics, investment bankers, gurus, the pressure to find the next hot market, or invent the next technology. In at least 85 percent of the companies we profiled, the best growth initiatives came from drilling down in more detail into the customer base in one of several ways: taking a customer and mapping out all their life cycle purchases in detail; understanding the customers in so much detail that they can develop new customer segments; sending teams of engineers onto the site and mapping out the customer economics in detail in order to find new product ideas and ways of improving productivity.

So I think the hopeful message for managers is that they may, more than they think, hold the keys to growth. It may come through something as relatively straightforward as drilling down into the customer base, as opposed to something as disorienting and fundamentally risky as searching for the next big idea.

Interview with Des Dearlove

Eleven misconceptions about customer relationship management

PETER C. VERHOEF AND FRED LANGERAK

[Although popular, the performance of customer relationship management (CRM) programs is often disappointing. One reason for this is that managers labor under a number of fundamental misconceptions about CRM and customer behavior. Understanding these misconceptions will enable managers to make better CRM-related decisions and raise the success rate of CRM projects.]

Marketing managers have traditionally been trained to acquire new customers with established marketing instruments such as price, promotions, and mass advertising. They are now shifting their attention to customer retention and customer relationship development. The aim is to maximize customer lifetime value instead of maximizing profits from discrete transactions with customers. In order to do this they have turned to customer relationship management.

CRM is not a totally new concept in marketing. It is based on three aspects of marketing management: customer orientation, relationship marketing, and database marketing (see Figure 5.5). CRM is a managerial process that focusses on the development and maintenance of relationships with individual customers in such a way that value is created for both the customer and the firm using customer databases, statistical decision-support tools, and interactive communication techniques. This definition integrates both the marketing-related and the technology-related cornerstones of CRM. Furthermore, it emphasizes that CRM is a process that makes a trade-off between value delivery to the customer and value creation for the firm.

Despite its roots in marketing, CRM is often associated with the use of software. Survey results show 65 percent of large companies in the US and Europe are aware of CRM technology, 28 percent are developing it, and 12 percent are now using CRM applications. Despite the increasing use of CRM software, however, there is an ongoing debate about the effectiveness of CRM. The success rate of CRM projects reportedly varies between 30 percent and 70 percent. Not surprisingly, a majority of managers are dissatisfied with their CRM performance.

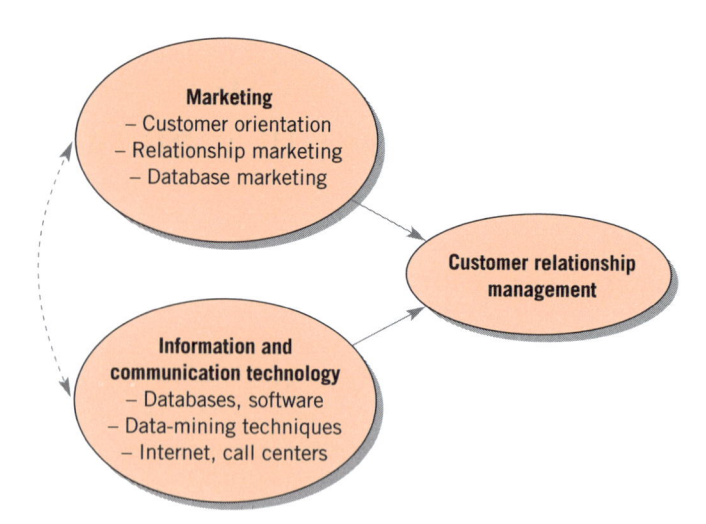

Figure 5.5: *The essence of CRM*

Much of this dissatisfaction is in fact the result of managerial misconceptions about the use of CRM software, the premises underlying CRM, and customer behavior (see Table 5.1).

Table 5.1: *Eleven misconceptions about CRM*

1. CRM software alone will enhance business performance.
2. Firms should focus only on customer relationship development.
3. Customer acquisition and CRM are two unrelated activities.
4. Customers want to have relationships with companies.
5. Long-lasting relationships with customers are always more profitable.
6. Satisfied customers are always more loyal.
7. Firms should focus their marketing efforts on their most profitable customers.
8. The customer pyramid is a good segmentation scheme.
9. Loyalty programs always improve customer loyalty.
10. The lifetime value of individual customers is predictable.
11. The Internet is the most suitable tool to enhance customer loyalty.

Misconception 1: CRM software alone will enhance business performance

CRM is often equated with the implementation of software programs and many managers believe that using such software will directly improve their marketing performance. There are three reasons why this belief is often not fulfilled.

First, CRM is about much more than installing and using software. CRM starts with an acknowledgement throughout the organization that creating value for customers is the driving business philosophy. This requires a real commitment from top management. Moreover, it requires an organization structured around customers with a customer-oriented culture in which different departments and employees jointly focus on creating superior value for customers. CRM software, without consideration of the cultural and organizational aspects of CRM, will at best decrease operating costs and improve the efficiency of marketing operations.

Another reason CRM does not always live up to the expectations is that the successful use of CRM software and decision-support tools is affected by the interplay of information technology, analytical capabilities, marketing data, and marketing. This interplay implies that analytical tools will perform well only if the marketing data used as input is of high quality. A good fit between the CRM support system and the rest of the marketing environment is critical for successful CRM systems. For example, in some CRM software, new statistical techniques such as genetic algorithms and neural networks are used. Many marketing managers do not understand these techniques. As a consequence they are reluctant to use them, although they can probably outperform more traditional techniques.

Adopting CRM software can also disappoint because, despite CRM's emphasis on building long-term relationships with customers, most CRM software focusses on optimizing the short-run response of customers. Applying these models implies that only customers with the highest response probability are targetted. As a result, the same customers are selected repeatedly and bombarded with e-mails, phone calls, and/or direct mailings. At the same time, these attractive (i.e. high-income) customers also receive offers from competitors using the same models and techniques. As a result they may well become irritated and inclined to switch toward less obtrusive suppliers. Most leading firms now have rules on the maximum number of mailings a customer receives in a given time period. Another solution to this problem might be permission marketing, in which the customer directs the content of the offer, the timing, and the type of direct communication method used.

Misconception 2: Firms should focus only on customer relationship development

A focus on managing customer relationships might lead firms to pay little attention (i.e. devote few resources) to customer acquisition. The underlying assumption is that it is more expensive to acquire new customers than to keep current ones. However, does this mean that firms should concentrate their marketing efforts solely on managing relationships with current customers? This is problematic for two reasons.

First, despite every effort to retain customers there will always be some that drop out of the customer base. Therefore, every firm needs to acquire new customers if only to replenish this outflow. Otherwise the customer base will shrink, with damaging consequences for a firm's long-term competitive position. For example, the management of the Dutch newspaper *Trouw* knew that it kept its readers because of the paper's editorial policy, which was based on Christian values and norms. However, this editorial policy did not fit with the growing secularization of society. As a result the customer base was not being replenished. Given the fact that existing subscribers slowly dropped out of the customer base, this development threatened the long-term existence of the newspaper. The management recognized this threat in time and changed the newspaper's editorial policy. *Trouw* is now one of the few newspapers in the Netherlands showing a substantial increase in readership.

Second, in markets with relatively low retention rates a focus on relationship development can cause a firm's downfall. In such markets focussing on maintaining relationships with customers is often hardly worth the trouble since the gains from building such relationships are very limited. Some consumer durables, for example vacuum cleaners and refrigerators, have purchase cycles of 10–15 years. Retention rates in these markets are affected by a number of uncontrollable factors and the buying processes for these goods are often very elaborate. Therefore, most consumer durables manufacturers do not strive to build strong relationships with customers but concentrate their marketing efforts on customer acquisition.

Firms introducing new products or selling existing products in underdeveloped markets should initially also pay more attention to customer acquisition than to CRM. A good example is the marketing strategy of mobile phone service operators. In the early phases of the market lifecycle operators invested millions of dollars in customer acquisition by giving away mobile phones to sell network subscriptions. Now that the market has matured, customer retention has become the buzzword. Thus, firms should carefully spread their efforts over customer acquisition and customer relationship development.

Misconception 3: Customer acquisition and CRM are two unrelated activities

Customer acquisition and CRM are often considered as separate activities. This is reflected by the existence of separate functions or departments for customer acquisition and CRM. However, considering the two as separate activities severely reduces the effectiveness of CRM strategies. They need to be managed simultaneously because customer acquisition strategy impacts customer relationship development.

For example, the insurance industry commonly uses price discounts to attract new customers. Once a prospect has become a customer, companies apply various cross-selling instruments, such as loyalty programs and direct mailings, to develop the relationship. However, this strategy may not always be successful since offering discounts often attracts price-sensitive customers who are more inclined to switch, less liable to buy additional higher-priced products, and are thus less profitable. Another example relates to the marketing channels used to attract new customers. Different channels may attract customers with different profitability levels. Again within the insurance industry, customers attracted via direct-response advertisements in newspapers were more inclined to switch after one year than customers acquired through other marketing channels.

In general it holds that with more selective acquisition strategies the lifetime value of individual customers can be maximized. However, being too selective will hamper customer acquisition and lead to lower profitability levels. Although this trade-off is difficult to manage, it becomes easier when customer acquisition and CRM activities are looked upon as two interrelated activities that must be carried out in harmony and close co-operation.

Misconception 4: Customers want to have relationships with companies

From an economic perspective, customer relationships are often defined as a series of repeated transactions between a customer and a supplier. From a social perspective, customer relationships also include repeated social interactions between a customer and a supplier. As early as the 1960s firms acknowledged the importance of repeated transactions with customers but it was only from the 1980s that they accepted the social dimension of such relationships.

Social interaction is considered important because it shapes customers' commitment to the relationship. As a result, firms use marketing instruments that focus on the social dimension of customer relationships. For example, insurance companies send customers magazines with general information about healthy and pleasant aspects of life. Another example is the Dutch retailer Albert Heijn, which uses a magazine called *Allerhande* to enhance the shopping experience in its stores.

However, the effect of all this is negligible in most consumer markets because social interactions do not add much value to the product or service that is delivered. This is because in most instances customers do not want a personal or one-to-one relationship with a supplier. This is especially true for low-involvement products and utilitarian goods and services. With these products repeat purchase is often based on inertia and/or switching costs. In the insurance industry, for example, customers' affective feelings toward a firm explain only a very small part of customer loyalty.

For high-involvement and/or hedonistic products, on the other hand, relationships might provide customers with highly valued social benefits. For example, the marketing and community programs of brands such as Jeep, Harley Davidson, and Manchester United provide important benefits for both the customer and the firm. Social aspects in customer relationships might also be important in face-to-face contacts in small, often specialized neighborhood stores and service providers.

In other words, depending on the type of product and their shopping behavior, customers may well not *want* to have a relationship with suppliers. Knowing this beforehand saves marketing resources and prevents customers from perceiving suppliers as obtrusive and aggressive.

Misconception 5: Long-lasting relationships with customers are always more profitable

Another assumption underlying the focus on building long-term relationships with customers is the idea that long-life customers are more profitable. The arguments underlying this claim are that customers with long-lasting relationships are less price sensitive and therefore price premiums can be asked; the costs of servicing these customers are lower; the revenues per customer are higher; and loyal customers generate customer referrals.

Although there is some anecdotal evidence for this claim, empirical research has shown that it is a gross simplification to equate loyal customers with higher profits. An explanation might be that the assumptions underlying the positive association between relationship length and customer profitability are wrong. The assumption that customers with long-lasting relationships are willing to pay a price premium is not true. These customers have more experience with the company and a better understanding of the value that it provides. Therefore, long-tenure customers are often *more* price sensitive.

The empirical evidence of lower operating costs for long-lasting customers is also rather scarce because no substantial differences have been found between customers with long and short tenure concerning their promotion costs. Empirical research has, however, found that customers with long-tenure relationships are less inclined to switch.

In summary, it seems that focussing solely on higher retention rates is not a good marketing strategy. Managers should instead try to exploit cross-selling and up-selling possibilities. CRM should focus more on relationship development rather than relationship continuance.

Misconception 6: Satisfied customers are always more loyal

Having satisfied customers is one of the main objectives of customer-driven organizations. Satisfied customers are assumed to be more loyal. Drawing on this assumption, many firms have invested heavily in total quality programs to improve customer satisfaction. Despite these investments, managers frequently report that it is hard to find a positive link between customer satisfaction and loyalty.

There are three reasons for this. First, the link between satisfaction and loyalty is often non-linear. A reversed S-shaped relationship (see Figure 5.6), for example, implies that only customers with a very low or high satisfaction score have a substantial higher probability of becoming more loyal. Therefore, the focus should be on delighting customers instead of creating moderately satisfied customers.

A second problem with customer satisfaction is that it measures today's status quo. It does not capture unfulfilled needs. That is why many academics advocate focussing on the creation of superior value for customers instead of customer satisfaction. The bias of customer satisfaction measurement toward the status quo also implies that it does not capture future developments in the relationship and the market environment. Not surprisingly, only differences in customers' individual satisfaction scores explain why and how the relationship develops.

Instead of a cross-sectional measurement of customer satisfaction, firms should therefore monitor the satisfaction level of their individual customers over time. This is more informative than monitoring the absolute satisfaction level of all customers at one point in time.

A third reason why managers often do not see any link between satisfaction and loyalty is because of customer heterogeneity. The loyalty of some customers is primarily driven by satisfaction while for others it is switching costs, habitual buying behavior, or variety-seeking behavior.

Moreover, the effect of satisfaction on customer loyalty is influenced by customer experience. This has important implications for CRM strategies. In some segments it

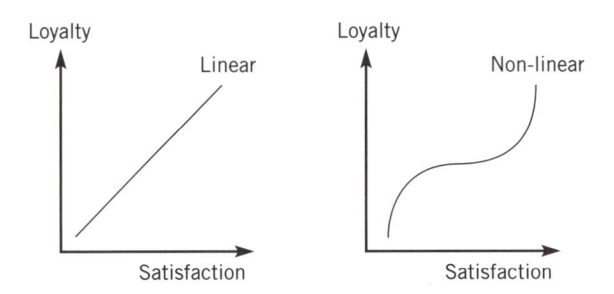

Figure 5.6: *Non-linear relationships between satisfaction and customer loyalty*

is sensible to invest in creating higher levels of customer satisfaction while in others investing in satisfaction does not pay off.

Managers should focus on delighting customers, adopt a more dynamic view of customer satisfaction, and implement programs to improve customer satisfaction only in customer segments in which loyalty is indeed affected by customer satisfaction. In other words, the assumption that improving customer satisfaction always enhances customer loyalty is too simple.

Misconception 7: Firms should focus their marketing efforts on their most profitable customers

It is a rule of thumb that approximately 20 percent of customers are responsible for approximately 80 percent of turnover or profits. These customers are often identified via the customer pyramid (see Figure 5.7). Losing top customers has a strong negative effect on a firm's profitability. Therefore, a key recommendation is that firms should aim their marketing efforts on their most loyal and profitable customers and hence allocate a substantial part of their marketing budget toward these customers.

Bank One is a good example of a firm that focusses its marketing efforts on establishing relationships with its most profitable customers, who are given access to additional services and often receive financial rewards for their loyalty. These reward programs are developed in such a way that the most profitable customers receive the maximum amount of rewards. However, the question is whether these investments are really needed to prevent these customers from switching to competitors.

Empirical research shows that customer loyalty is often primarily driven by inertia, which is independent of any loyalty program. This means that the majority of loyal customers will remain loyal in the future. Thus additional investments in the

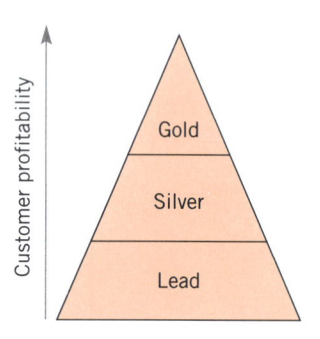

Figure 5.7: *The customer pyramid*

This is based on Zeithaml, V.A., Rust. R.T., and Lemon, K.N. 'The Customer Pyramid: Creating and Serving Profitable Customers,' *California Management Review*, 42 (4), 2001, pp. 118–142.

		Current profitability:	
		Low	High
Potential value:	High	Relationship extension	Relationship treatment
	Low	Relationship harvesting	Relationship continuance

Figure 5.8: *Extending the customer profitability segmentation*

loyalty of profitable customers are a waste of marketing resources. Allocating a large part of the marketing budget to the most profitable customers also implies that less resources are available to up-sell potentially very profitable customers in lower tiers of the pyramid. Thus focussing marketing efforts solely on the most profitable customers harms the long-term profitability of a firm. Companies should therefore not focus exclusively on their most profitable customers but also on customers who have a high future potential value. The resulting segmentation scheme is shown in Figure 5.8.

Misconception 8: The customer pyramid is a good segmentation scheme

One of the key analytical tools within CRM is the customer pyramid (see above and Figure 5.7). This pyramid classifies customers into different tiers according to their profitability. Despite the attractiveness and often-reported usefulness of this segmentation, the customer pyramid has some inherent limitations beyond the exclusive allocation of marketing resources to the most profitable customers.

An important problem with the customer pyramid is that it is often difficult to calculate customer profitability. This is usually calculated by summing the contribution margins of the products and/or services sold to individual customers. These profitability measures are customer-specific only with respect to purchase behavior. Customer-specific costs are often not included. For example, customers with high service costs (i.e. many phone calls, personal service needs, and so on) are valued equally with customers with little or no service costs. Equally, the customer pyramid does not consider non-purchase-related behaviors such as customer referrals. Moreover, the contribution margins considered in the pyramid can be sensitive to the number of products and/or services sold because the margins often increase

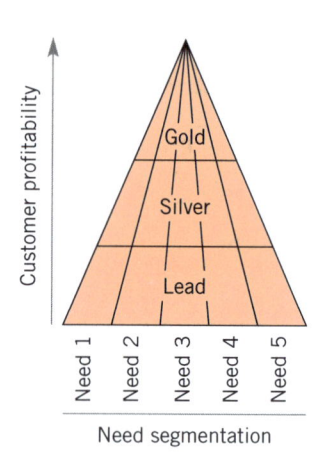

Figure 5.9: *From customer profitability segmentation to customer profitability and customer need segmentation*

when the number of products and/or services sold increases. This is especially true when fixed costs are a substantial part of the costs allocated to a product or service.

Another drawback of using the customer pyramid as a segmentation scheme is that it considers only customers' monetary value. For example, mutual-fund giant Fidelity classifies its customers into segments based on profitability and then uses that information to tailor its offering to the various segments. As a result, managers may be inclined to focus solely on the monetary results of customers' behavior, thereby forgetting latent customer needs. It is therefore not surprising that many firms find it hard to build relationships with customers. In order to overcome this problem firms should aim to capture customer needs in their customer pyramid (see Figure 5.9).

A good example is the approach of Robeco Direct, a capital investment company. It has segmented its customer base into 10 different customer groups based on their attitude toward money, which Robeco identified through questions on life objectives, preferences with respect to financial situation, and the actual financial situation. Two examples of these customer groups are the "safety seekers" and the "self-made man." This need segmentation is subsequently combined with a profitability segmentation. For each need/profitability segment Robeco has developed different customized marketing programs and service systems. Both customers' needs and their expected monetary value direct the content of these programs and systems.

An additional implication of the customer pyramid is that it encourages marketers to drop less profitable customers. Having fewer customers and lower turnover might, however, reduce the contribution margin of each product and/or service sold due to the dependence between the contribution margin and the number of products or services sold. This implies that customers that are currently profitable might become unprofitable when other customers are dropped and they themselves are then subsequently also dropped. This self-fulfilling prophecy is called the customer profitability trap. Dropping customers might also have other negative consequences, in particular when the size of the customer base is an important quality signal for potential customers.

Finally, when using the customer pyramid as a segmentation scheme firms should be aware of how customers perceive differentiated treatment of the various tiers of the pyramid. In markets in which equality is an important social value, a differentiated treatment of customers may harm a firm's reputation. Ethical considerations are even more important when customers receiving an inferior treatment are also the "dropouts" in society. In short, there are some important reasons why firms should be careful in adopting the customer pyramid as a segmentation scheme and following the managerial implications that the pyramid provides.

Misconception 9: Loyalty programs always improve customer loyalty

A loyalty program is the marketing instrument most closely associated with CRM. Although simple loyalty programs have been around for years, technological developments have enhanced the use of these programs. The objective of loyalty programs, often using loyalty cards, is to improve retention rates and to enhance cross-selling. Most loyalty programs provide customers with monetary rewards. These rewards can be either immediate or delayed. For example, loyalty programs in financial services often provide annual financial rewards. Some programs also aim to provide social benefits. For example, in the travel industry (airlines, hotels, and car rentals) members of loyalty programs often receive a preferential treatment through the provision of additional services free of charge.

The implementation of such loyalty programs is costly. Moreover, once a loyalty program has been implemented most firms are very reluctant to stop it because of the negative responses from customers. For example, in the 1980s Shell ended its loyalty program in the Netherlands, followed by a large group of customers boycotting the company. This caused a lot of negative publicity and forced Shell to restart the program, incurring high costs and unfavorable word-of-mouth publicity.

Loyalty programs are often based not on a thorough cost–benefit analysis but rather on managerial intuition and/or the advice of loyalty consultants. For the management of a European holiday resort, for example, the rationale for starting a loyalty program was the success of similar programs in the airline industry. The lack of thorough research might result in a program in which the costs outweigh the benefits. Even when this becomes known, managers are reluctant to stop the program because of the expected negative response from customers. The decision to discontinue a loyalty program becomes even more complex and more difficult if such programs are a well-accepted standard in the market.

There is little empirical evidence about the positive effect of loyalty programs because most firms are unwilling to share data. The evidence that is available reveals that in many established, competitive markets purchasing patterns are so well established that it is difficult to increase customer loyalty above the market norm with an easy-to-replicate loyalty program.

There is, for example, little evidence of a positive effect for loyalty programs in retailing. Anecdotal evidence from retailers in the Netherlands supports this finding. Retailers with loyalty programs were not able to increase their market share while one retailer without a loyalty program was able to do so. In contrast, however, research shows that in the financial service industry loyalty programs have a positive effect on customer loyalty, though the effect is rather small and the costs may still outweigh the benefits.

Firms should therefore be very careful before implementing a loyalty program and make a thorough cost–benefit analysis before making a final decision. Note that the benefits considered should also encompass non-monetary gains resulting from increased customer loyalty. For example, the implementation of a loyalty program may provide retailers with valuable customer information, which can be used to target promotions, forecast sales, and negotiate with manufacturers.

In short, loyalty programs do not always improve customer loyalty. Moreover, in most programs the costs outweigh the benefits. This becomes especially problematic when the loyalty program cannot be discontinued because of expected negative responses from customers.

Misconception 10: The lifetime value of individual customers is predictable

Customer lifetime value (CLV) is one of the most important performance measures within CRM. CLV is best described as the net present value of all future earnings from an individual customer. If a firm knows a customer's net present value, all marketing efforts can be focussed on those customers with the highest expected value. To accurately forecast the lifetime value of each individual customer, managers need information on individual retention and cross-buying probabilities.

Despite the availability of large databases, many firms compare the prediction of CLV with the search for the Holy Grail. Another problem is that CLV is affected by a number of other factors, such as customer satisfaction, competitive actions, and legislation, which are often not stored in the database. This makes it difficult accurately to predict CLV.

Despite the difficulties associated with the estimating CLV, it is still a useful concept for two reasons.

First, using CLV as a performance measure forces managers to adopt a long-term view in their marketing decision making. Instead of focussing on short-term measures, such as market share and sales, they are forced to focus on their future earnings. Second, there are good and relatively simple models available that can be used to predict CLV at the aggregate or group level. The resulting forecast can be used to allocate a budget to customer acquisition and customer development strategies for specific market segments. For example, if the expected value of a newly acquired customer is $200, the maximum customer acquisition costs per customer should be $200.

Misconception 11: The Internet is the most suitable tool to enhance customer loyalty

Although the Internet hype is over, it is still believed that the Internet is the ultimate channel to build customer relationships, especially because of the customization opportunities it offers. The truth might be different, however, because an important consequence of the Internet is that the cost transparency of the market increases. The Internet allows customers to compare prices, for example by means of price comparison sites, and easily switch to other suppliers because traditional switching barriers, such as distance to a store, are not present. Thus the loyalty of customers is likely to decrease on the Internet.

The objective of firms operating on the Internet should therefore be to lock in customers through the provision of customized services. These customized services do not have to be limited to the Internet. For example, home delivery of food products can be adjusted to a customer's personal wishes and constraints using customer profiles built on Internet shopping behavior data.

A potential threat for the Internet as a loyalty-creating medium is the actual use of it by firms. An important advantage is the cost efficiency of the Internet as a marketing channel. Not surprisingly, many firms are eager to move customers from costly traditional channels, such as call centers, to the Internet. To encourage channel switching, firms often reduce the service level in traditional channels. This strategy is rather dangerous because customers may highly value some of these services. One solution is that a firm asks permission from customers to reduce the quality of services in traditional channels by pointing out that the high-quality service is available through the Internet.

For example, Rabobank has introduced a sophisticated e-banking service. Users were approached by letter and a response form in which they could indicate whether they still wanted to receive their bank statements weekly. Thus, the reduction of individual service costs is achieved with the permission of customers. This reduces the chance of customers becoming dissatisfied and switching to competitors. In brief, the Internet is a suitable tool to enhance customer loyalty only when customers voluntarily switch toward the new channel and customers can be locked in through customized offerings.

If managers keep these 11 misconceptions in mind they will have more realistic expectations of what CRM has to offer. Moreover, they will be more careful and selective before investing in CRM projects because they are aware of the fact that successful adoption of CRM requires them to formulate and implement a comprehensive customer-driven CRM strategy.

RESOURCES

Blattberg, R.C., Getz, G., and Thomas, J. S., *Customer Equity: Building and Managing Relationships as Valuable Assets*, Harvard Business School Press, 2001.

Godin, Seth, *Permission Marketing: Turning Strangers into Friends, and Friends into Customers*, Simon and Schuster, 1999.

Peppers, Don and Rogers, Martha, *Enterprise One-to-One: Tools for Competing in the Interactive Age*, Doubleday, 1999.

Roberts, M.C. and Berger, P.D., *Direct Marketing Management*, Prentice Hall, 1999.

Rust, R.T., Zeithaml, V.A., and Lemon, K.N., *Driving Customer Equity: How Customer Lifetime Value is Reshaping Corporate Strategy*, The Free Press, 2000.

Wind, J. and Rangaswamy, A., 'Customerization: The Next Revolution in Mass Customization,' *Journal of Interactive Marketing*, 15 (Winter), 13–32, 2001.

This article previously appeared in *Business Strategy Review*, Volume 13, Issue 4, Winter 2002.

Seven of the best

TONY CRAM

> The way a brand is delivered is the key success factor for service brands. Managers need to be aware of best practice.

Service brands now deliver greater growth than product brands. Leisure, tourism, outsourcing, financial planning, retailing, and telecommunications account for a greater proportion of consumer and business expenditure. Where adjectives encapsulate product brands, service brands are often better described by the way a service is performed. These are frequently adverbs. For example, the distinctive character of an HMV store selling CDs, DVDs, and computer games is probably that the service is delivered *knowledgeably*. Delivering consistent service adverbs is a far more challenging prospect than producing product adjectives.

The value propositions of a product brand and a service brand can be contrasted. The concept of the value proposition (first propounded by Michael J. Lanning and developed in his book, *Delivering Profitable Value*) describes value as a deliberate combination of precise benefits and price that is targetted to a specific group.[43]

Where the product proposition delivers pre-manufactured benefits, the service brand must reproduce the same benefits for each customer in real time. Where the product brand has a price list, the service brand may offer prices that vary by time of day, time of year, or time of booking. Where the product brand can imply in advertising that it has glamorous users, the service brand users can often see other users at the point of consumption. So how does the service brand deliver its consistency in this challenging environment?

Value is created in the mind of the customer. The service brand must focus on this. The service value proposition needs to include its unique behavioral adverb. Thus a service value proposition is a deliberate combination of precise benefits and price targetted at a specific group and delivered in a particular manner. The brand then focusses on consistently conveying this to users at every touch point.

Success in service brands is less about advertising and more about actual behavior. It comes from placing the same picture in the mind of the customer on every occasion. There are seven best practices involved in achieving this.

Best practice 1: Staff retention through internal service quality

People are the platform for the service brand. The basis for service delivery commences with creating the conditions whereby employees (and contractors) are best able and motivated to deliver service quality. In "Breaking the Cycle of Failure in Services," Schlesinger and Heskett identified the critical nature of employee retention to create capability to deliver excellent service.[44] A couple of years ago I learnt that Marriott International had made an award for excellence to the Swansea Marriott Hotel. Shortly afterwards I visited this hotel. The General Manager modestly placed the credit for this accolade on the knowledge and skills of the "associates" (as Marriott terms employees), and commented that her staff turnover was 19 percent per year. Contrast this with the 100–120 percent turnover found in rival hotels and there is an explanation for the excellence of her hotel service.

It is the premise of Heskett *et al.* in the article "Putting the Service Profit Chain to Work" that profit and growth derive primarily from customer loyalty, which is a result of customer satisfaction.[45] This satisfaction is largely influenced by the customer's perception of good value, which is created by satisfied, loyal, and productive employees. Such a workforce is a result of internal quality embracing workplace and job design, employee selection and development, rewards and recognition, and the provision of the right tools for the job.

Of course, in tough times there is the commercial reality of cost cutting and restructuring. In a service business these threaten morale and performance. Barkin, Nahirny, and van Metre of McKinsey & Company offer practical advice on how to take out the right costs, reinforce the focus on customer service, and build a sense of urgency in their article "Why are Service Turnarounds so Tough."[46]

In good and bad times, essential best practice is to create the platform. Attend first to internal service quality in order to achieve the satisfied, productive, and loyal workforce. The secret ingredient is to measure and compare operational management on staff turnover. Improvement will follow and management will naturally find creative ways of enhancing internal quality.

Best practice 2: Choosing your way to outperform

A brand comes to life through its focus on one or two key dimensions. It cannot be number one on every attribute. This best practice is about choosing where a service brand wants to outperform all others. What particular way will you choose to deliver good service? This must, of course, draw from customer needs, and involves selecting one attribute for primary focus. The essence is the adverb you choose to inform all customer contact.

Kwik-Fit, the leading automotive service operator with 2300 service points across Europe, focusses on behaving *reassuringly*. Historically the reputation of the automotive after-market has been tarnished by back-street mechanics exploiting the ignorance of motorists. Kwik-Fit has worked ceaselessly to counter this by developing and training staff to deliver absolute reliability in an open and transparent manner.[47] Pret a Manger, the leading sandwich retailer, focusses on behaving *naturally*. The ingredients are natural and so is the service approach. Employees are trained to close any customer encounter in a natural way, by looking the customer in the eye and making a personal farewell. Staff choose their own words and match them to the customer and occasion so the effect is natural not scripted. McDonald's never uses the word "clean" in advertising, but cleanliness is a strong subconscious need of the parents whose children enjoy visiting McDonald's. Judging from the attention staff pay to mopping floors and wiping tables in McDonald's restaurants around the world, perhaps "*hygienically*" might be their adverb. Marriott behave *hospitably* to their guests – customers are always referred to as guests, and treated as such. Each of these organizations has its interpretation or definition of what "good service" means. Ken Blanchard, in his parable-like book, *Raving Fans – a Revolutionary Approach to Customer Service*, explores this concept further.[48]

Therefore best practice 2 is to choose your definition of good service in terms of the style to which you will operate. The secret ingredient is to seek creative ways to extend this style to every aspect of the customer contact.

Best practice 3: Selecting brand ambassadors

Recruiting and selecting the right type of people is the next best practice to investigate. When each employee is seen as a brand ambassador, it is essential that recruitment be handled with great care. This means that specific ideal characteristics are sought and developed. These derive from the previous best practice.

Personality characteristics are more important than existing technical skill. It is significant that the organizations recognized as great service providers rarely recruit staff from rivals in the same industry. First Direct, the UK telephone bank, makes a practice of recruiting staff with appropriate attitudes from outside the financial services industry. It then trains them in the necessary skills. South West Airlines, the US-based originator of no-frills flying, finds its staff from anywhere but its airline competitors. It looks for staff with empathy, and its selection process involves group activities culminating in each potential employee making a speech about why they should be recruited. The human resources staff watch the other candidates for demonstrations of empathetic behavior rather than listening to the specific presentations. Who is nodding, smiling, and encouraging? These are the kind of people who will make passengers genuinely welcome on board or on the phone. The candidate polishing his notes for his presentation while another speaks is unlikely to be a supportive colleague.

A brand value of international delivery firm UPS is speed. Reportedly (and perhaps tongue in cheek), the company heroes are those who can make a delivery to a building while their van is at a red stop light, returning before the lights change to green. You can imagine that a candidate trudging slowly into an interview would depress their chances of employment! The key lesson is that you recruit staff who actually live the brand values in their behavior. Brands must practice what they preach says Frederick Reichheld, Bain & Co director, who recommends careful recruitment as one of his six principles.[49]

Of course, a side benefit of recruiting the right-minded people is that it ensures a flow of suitable people for senior roles. According to Pret a Manger, 60 percent of its shop managers began as team members.

Best practice 4: Train hard, don't over-communicate

Training and on-going communications naturally follow selection. Ritz-Carlton is seen to offer best practice in training for its upscale hotels around the world. It has a Learning Institute which offers employee training seminars to other industries. Induction training is a vital moment for new recruits. For example, on day one new recruits in the training room are ordered to say "no" loudly and repeat it. It is the last time they will say no in the hotel. Ritz-Carlton aims to respond *positively* to every guest. The response may be in another form from the request, or cost a little more, or take longer, but you cannot make a guest feel good by saying no. (For more insight into how induction training and early job experiences are handled by Ritz-Carlton see "My week as a room service waiter at the Ritz" by Paul Hemp.[50])

Best practice in employee communications can be surprising. A lesson from Colin Mitchell's article "Selling the brand inside" is that organizations frequently inundate employees with briefings.[51] Staff soon learn to ignore over-communication. Mitchell's research recommends that you must choose your moment. A turning point such as a new strategy, merger, new senior executive, or an external crisis will link interest and a readiness to listen. He also recommends that internal brand messages be handled using the skills of marketing communications rather than by the human resource department.

Disney discovered that it is more effective to show rather than to tell, and requires "cast members" (employees) to spend one week a year experiencing being "on-stage" or in front of the theme park visitors. They may sell tickets, retrieve litter, or dress as a character in order to see the way Disney delivers its service ... *magically*.

Best practice 5: Behavioral science says good service happens in the customer's mind

Most service thinking involves a logical left-brain approach – call analysis, speed of response measurement, conversion ratios. Yet good service experiences happen in the customer's perception, which is strongly influenced by right-brain associations. We need to understand what actions, words, and signals trigger the impression we want to place in the customer's mind.

Behavioral science tells us that customers remember an experience not in the manner of a video recording but rather as a series of snapshots of highs and lows. The overall perception is built by the quality and sequence of these snapshots. For example, spending a day at a horse race will feel better if your losses come early in the day and your wins later in the day, better still if you win on the final race. Perceptually, the ending is crucial.

This research is described in the article "Want to perfect your company's service? Use behavioral science" by Chase and Dasu, who make it clear that a strong finish is vital in a service encounter.[52] This sounds self-evident, yet we observe airlines which dazzle with highly trained check-in staff and warm friendly cabin crews but leave passengers alone in the luggage hall to search for bags. Websites offer attractive home pages but, as you explore further into the site, the standard decays. A better example is the humble waiter who knows that a strong finish – like a touch on the shoulder as he asks if you need coffee, a smile delivered crouching at the table to meet the customer's eye level, or a chocolate with the bill – increases the chance of a good tip five fold.

The secret ingredient is to experience the service as a customer yourself to understand the emotions. Ask customers to create a *moodogram* (Figure 5.10) of their emotions during the service encounter. Using this approach a major NHS Trust in the UK is boosting patient opinion of their stay in hospital by delivering the best possible discharge arrangement.

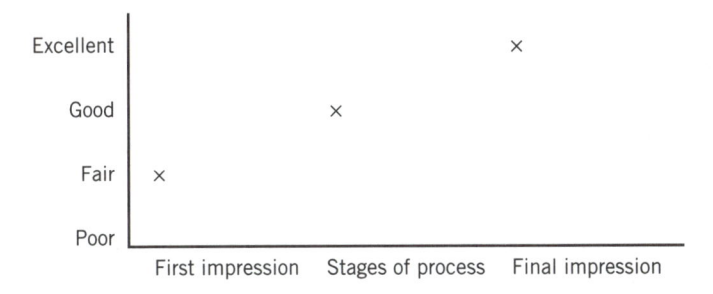

Figure 5.10: *A moodogram*

Best practice 6: Remember the impact of other users

People make the service experience, and this goes beyond employees to include the other customers. Part of a positive service encounter is the atmosphere created by other users. Rowdy fellow diners can ruin an evening in a restaurant. Few service providers consider the impact of other guests. Niche service businesses now take pains to target and select their customers and exclude the non-harmonious. Mass market operators are considering how best to educate their customers in mutual consideration. As patrons take their seats at Cineworld, they see a cartoon with a Lara Croft look-alike who deals drastically with noisy talkers, smokers, and users of mobile phones in order to teach people to make the experience pleasant for other movie goers.

Best practice 7: Make measurement easy

Measurement is the surest way to reinforce positive behaviors or change negative ones. Kwik-Fit follows up customer visits to its automotive centers with a phone survey, funded by insurance sales made to satisfied customers. Pret a Manger uses mystery shoppers who give motivational bonuses to shops providing high-standard service. (For ideas on service metrics and measurement see *Managing the Customer Experience* by Smith and Wheeler and *Building Great Customer Experiences* by Shaw and Ivens.)[53, 54]

To be impactful, it must be easy for customers to respond and the results must be evident to employees and management. I had occasion to call at the Rothersthorpe Motorway Services on the M1 motorway. The toilets were astonishingly clean – they sparkled and I wondered how this could be. On the wall as I left the toilets there were cartoon faces. If you found the toilets dirty you pressed the unhappy face. I pressed the smiley face and a recorded voice thanked me.

Finally

Service brands face demanding customers. Giving highly rated service is difficult because this perception happens in the customer's mind. Yet a marketplace challenge is worth achieving because competitors will find it harder to replicate.

Success comes from placing the same picture in the mind of the customer on every occasion. There are seven best practices involved in achieving this. Begin inside the company with a platform of internal service quality and a clear choice on how to outperform. Follow up with recruiting staff for personal attributes and communicating what success looks like. Learn the lessons of behavioral science and consider the impact of fellow users. Finally make measurement easy.

RESOURCES

Cram, Tony, *Customers That Count. How to Build Living Relationships With Your Most Valuable Customers*, FT Prentice Hall, 2001.

Smith, Shaun and Wheeler, Jo, *Managing the Customer Experience*, FT Prentice Hall, 2002.

Shaw, Colin and Ivens, John, *Building Great Customer Experiences*, Palgrave Macmillan, 2002.

Reicheld, Frederick, *Loyalty Rules!*, Harvard Business School Press, 2001.

Connecting brand equity, brand economics, and brand value

DAVID HAIGH

[Evidence suggests that brands will be important drivers of corporate value in the 21st century. So how do brands add value?]

In financial terms a brand represents the pact between a consumer and a supplier, promising a secure flow of future revenues and profits to the supplier. Ultimately, what gives a brand its value is that it is a specifically defensible piece of legal property with an incremental stream of revenue attached to it.

The supplier's earnings are secure because strong brands create both functional and emotional barriers to competition for the consumer's loyalty. On the functional side, brands simplify recognition and selection; they facilitate split-second purchase decisions at point-of-purchase. Brands provide a guarantee of origin and quality; reliable consumer choices can be made in safety. On the emotional side, brands provide reassurance: "I am a good mother because I use Pampers." Brands satisfy associative desires: "I am one of the in-crowd because I wear Versace." They are aspirational: "I am an up-and-coming executive because I drive a BMW." Finally, they fulfill self-expressive needs: "I am manly because I smoke Marlboro." And so on.

An important additional benefit of strong brands is their ability to transfer established consumer loyalty to new market areas and product categories. In order for brand stretching to be effective, it is necessary that the brand attributes are as appropriate to the new extension area as to the original product or service category. This generally means that core brand attributes must be more to do with image and emotion than with function and rationality. For example, Virgin represents innovative, exciting, youthful, friendly, uncomplicated, good value, whatever category it is extended into; if the Virgin brand had based its appeal exclusively on functional and rational attributes it would still be stuck in the record retailing category.

That strong "brand equity" does translate into better financial performance can be seen in the cola market. In blind tests Pepsi Cola consistently outperforms Coca-Cola in terms of consumer taste preference. But when Coke branded packaging is revealed, stated preference completely reverses. When otherwise identical cars, made in the same factory, are branded either VW or SEAT, the price and residual value profiles differ dramatically. When still tap water is branded Highland Spring, the price shoots up. Branding persuades consumers to behave irrationally, adding value to otherwise functionally identical products and services.

Brand economics

Strong brands with high "brand equity" possess the ability to persuade people to make economic decisions based on emotional rather than rational criteria. They consequently have a profound economic impact and economic value. Brand Finance plc first developed the concept of brand economics in 1999 when it began empirically researching brand-related economic phenomena.

Interestingly, it is sometimes argued that branding is a way for companies to "rip off" consumers, but the following simple example demonstrates that in a free market brands create a virtuous circle of lower prices, higher profits, and higher surplus "consumer utility." Branding consequently has a hugely beneficial effect on individual consumers, individual companies, and the economy as a whole.

Brands favorably affect both the revenue and cost curves of a business. Figure 5.11 shows the average revenue and cost curves of a simple commodity business. Figure 5.12 demonstrates the absolute amount of profit made in that commodity business at a unit sale price of, say, $150. At a price of $150 the volume of demand is 22 units, implying total revenue of $3,300. It will be seen that the average unit cost declines as volume grows; this is because fixed costs are spread over a larger volume of production. The average cost at volume of 22 is approximately $100. Total cost is therefore $2,200, creating a profit of $1,100.

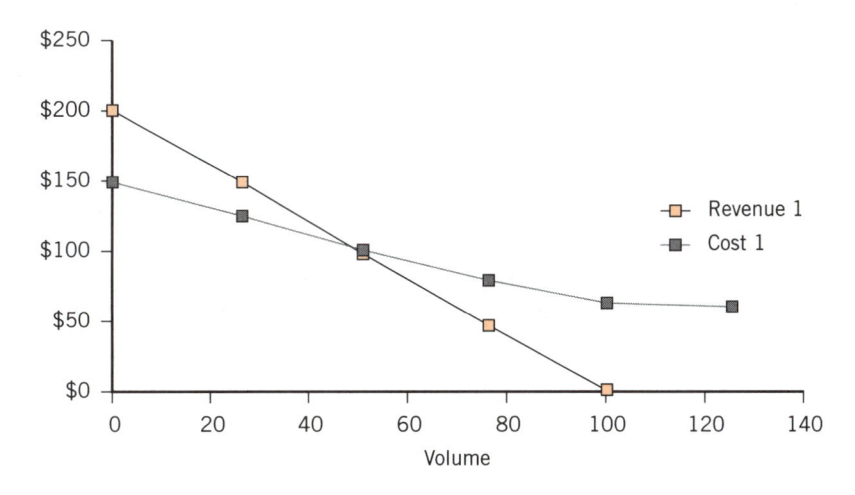

Figure 5.11: *Economic model for commodity product (i)*

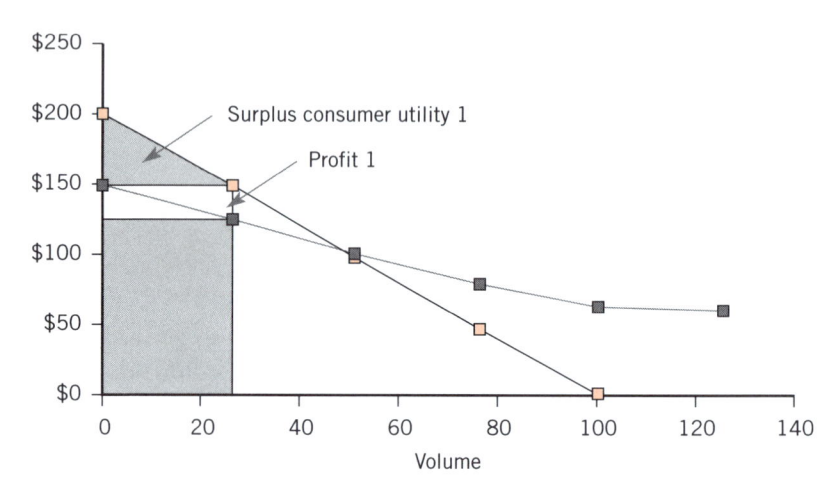

Figure 5.12: *Economic model for commodity product (ii)*

It can be seen in this simplified example that most consumers paying $150 would have been willing to pay a price somewhere above $150. Some would have been willing to pay as much as $200, and the average additional amount they would have been willing to pay is $25. The extent to which the actual price charged is below the price a consumer would have been willing to pay represents a benefit to the consumer, a surplus of "consumer utility." The value of total surplus consumer utility can be calculated in this case at $550, based on 22 units at an average consumer utility value of $25. By contrast, a deficit of consumer utility arises if the price charged is higher than the price an individual would be happy to pay, as representing good value for money. This situation usually arises in monopoly situations or distorted supply situations.

As shown in Figure 5.13, if products are well branded, and have acquired strong brand equity, the demand line moves out to the right because consumers are quite willing to pay more. At a given price more consumers will buy the product, or at a higher price the same number will buy. There are various effects at work causing this phenomenon: higher trial of the category and the brand, higher repeat rates, lower lapse rates, longer customer lifetimes with the product, greater share of requirements, a willingness to pay a premium, the ready acceptance of cross selling and up selling.

Equally importantly, strong brand equity drives down the average cost curve, as noted in Figure 5.14. Strong brands are more willingly distributed and stocked by the trade, resulting in lower commissions, discounts, and stocking fees. Staff are more willing to work at lower average salaries, stay longer, and feel more motivated to work efficiently. Suppliers and providers of capital are willing to accept finer margins and less favorable terms. There are also significant production economies of scale.

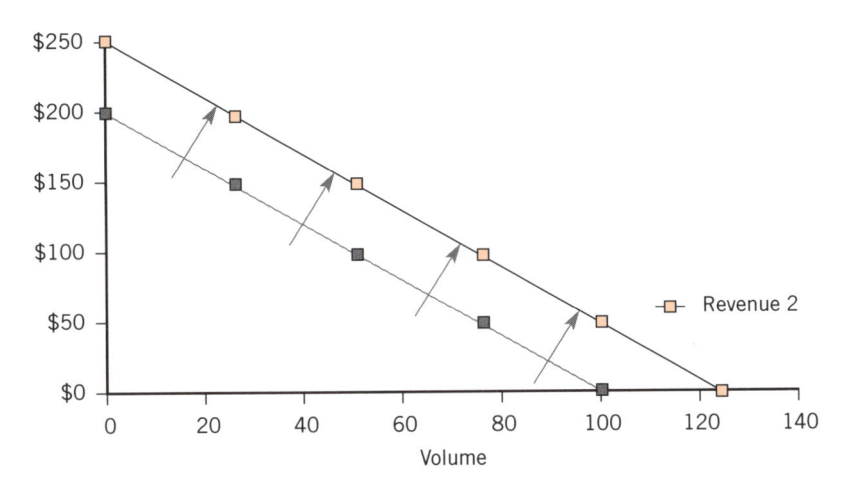

Connecting brand equity, brand economics, and brand value   411

Figure 5.13: Strong brand equity shifts the demand curve

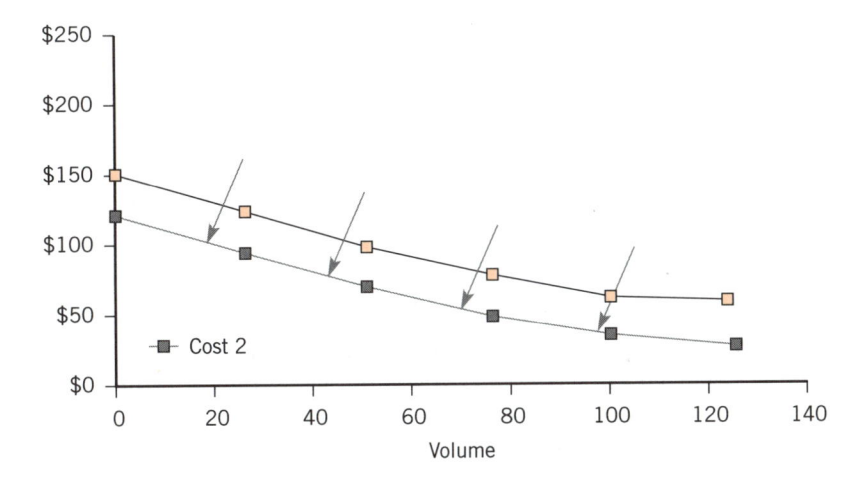

Figure 5.14: Strong brand equity shifts the cost

The net result, shown in Figure 5.15, is a transformation of the commodity economic model to a branded one, with the revenue curve pushed upwards and the cost curve downwards. If the company maintained its unit sales price at $150 it would now achieve unit sales of 45, revenues of $6,750, costs of $3,375 (45 units at an average cost of $75, down from $100 in the commodity example), and profits of $3,375 – 310 percent of the commodity scenario. It will also produce surplus "consumer utility" of $2,250 (45 units at an average consumer utility of $50) – 410 percent of the commodity scenario. Average surplus consumer utility has doubled because preference for the brand expressed in financial terms has increased significantly. Some consumers would now be willing to pay $250 rather than the earlier maximum of $200. Holding the price at $150 provides greater consumer satisfaction or surplus "consumer utility" to all consumers.

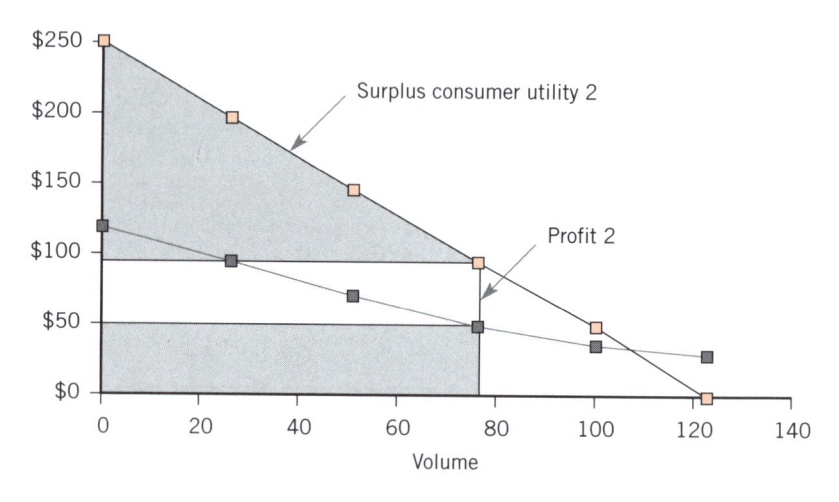

Figure 5.15: *Economic model for power brand*

Some brand owners would be happy to leave the model at that, satisfied that they had achieved higher sales, profits, and consumer utility at the original price point.

Brand economics' impact on corporate strategy

However, a number of interesting strategic options become available under a strongly branded business model. In a commodity business an increase in price quite rationally leads to a proportionate decrease in demand, and vice versa. Volume of demand is negatively correlated to changes in price. If the correlation is perfect then the price elasticity co-efficient is minus 1 – a perfect negative correlation. For every unit increase in price there is a unit decrease in volume demanded. The demand curve in our simplified model is a straight line of this kind.

However, in a branded business, demand varies in irrational ways. Demand curves are often asymmetrical and elasticity co-efficients are seldom a perfect minus 1. As price rises, the volume of demand from brand-loyal consumers often decreases less than proportionately with the increase in price. In other words demand is inelastic with a co-efficient of less than minus 1. As price falls, the volume of demand from loyal consumers may increase more than proportionately because consumers seek to consume or stockpile their favorite brand at what is seen to be a highly favorable price. In this case the elasticity co-efficient may be more than minus 1. The shape of a branded demand curve is often "S" shaped: flattened at both ends.

In some instances brand demand curves vary in apparently irrational ways. For example, in luxury goods, demand often rises rather than falls as price rises. In extreme cases there may even be a positive rather than a negative correlation between volume of demand and price. Perfect positive correlation of plus 1 implies that for every unit increase in price there will be a unit increase in demand volume. With Bulgari jewels or Versace clothes, as prices rise demand also rises; as prices fall demand also falls. Some people are prepared to pay a premium for exclusivity. Buying the psychological benefits of being one of the elite is more important than the functional benefits of owning high-quality, luxury goods.

The shape of a brand's demand curve, and the exact elasticity co-efficients, need to be carefully investigated before deciding on the optimal brand strategy. In the simplified example shown in Figure 5.15 demand increases proportionately with price decreases – there is a perfect negative correlation of minus 1 between price and volume of demand. In the real world this is unlikely to happen for the reasons noted above. If the brand is a strong one, the demand line often flattens and extends as prices fall. However, the example clearly demonstrates the virtuous circle created by brands like Swatch, Mars, or McDonald's.

If in Figure 5.15 the original price is reduced by 33 percent to $100, volume of demand rises from 45 to 75 units, giving total revenue of $7,500 – 230 percent of Figure 5.11 revenues. However, at this volume of demand average unit costs decline from $75 to $50 per unit. Total costs are therefore only $3,750, giving a profit of $3,750 – 350 percent of Figure 5.11 profits. Meanwhile, surplus consumer utility has increased to $5,625 (calculated as average consumer utility of $75 times 75 units) – 1070 percent of Figure 5.11 surplus consumer utility.

In other words the brand owner is working harder to provide more branded product to more consumers. The brand owner is making more profit but simultaneously creating greater consumer satisfaction and utility. Given these numbers it actually looks as though consumers receive greater incremental benefit than brand owners from the model. This is why branding in a free enterprise economy is far from being a consumer rip-off. If it were, consumers would simply stop buying branded products.

The simplified economic model noted above is the model adopted by Swatch when it revolutionized the wristwatch market and has been adopted by many other enlightened brand owners. By building strong brands they kill several birds with one stone, achieving greater turnover and profit, more competitive pricing to keep out competition, and significantly more satisfied, loyal consumers.

Understanding how brand equity drives brand economics

"Equity" is a financial term that has been adopted by marketing people to reflect the fact that the brands they manage are financial assets, which create significant shareholder value. It reflects a growing recognition that responsibility for brands must be shared between the finance and marketing functions. The marketing department will always have responsibility for the creative aspects of brand building, maintenance, and support. But as brands grow in importance, measuring, monitoring, and maximizing brand economics effects and returns on brand investment are increasingly a shared responsibility with the finance function.

However, while brand equity is often talked about, it is seldom clearly defined. How it works to impact on brand economics is not clearly understood. Tim Ambler, of London Business School, defines brand equity as a marketing asset "between the ears" of consumers, trade customers, staff, and other stakeholders, which stimulates long-term demand, cash flow, and value.

He uses the analogy of a reservoir that needs to be topped up if the outflow of water is to be maintained at a constant or increasing rate. If the brand equity reservoir is depleted, revenues and cash flows may remain strong for a period, but eventually the reservoir empties and cash flows dry up. A great visual analogy, but we need to really understand the flow process.

Paul Feldwick, Planning Director of advertising agency, BMP, points out that the term brand equity is often used indiscriminately to describe different points along the stream:

- *Consumer images, associations, and beliefs.* These are high up the flow toward the source. A brand may be described as "young," "green," or "exciting." It is possible to measure and report how such brand images, associations, and beliefs vary from consumer group to consumer group, how they change from time to time, and how they affect purchase decisions. This provides great diagnostic insight into the consumer segments around which a financial brand valuation is structured.

- *Consumer brand strength or loyalty.* These intermediate outputs may be measured in terms of attitudes or awareness, price elasticity, demand volume, purchase frequency. There are many different ways of tracking "brand strength." Econometric modeling of empirical data, experimental trade-off analysis, and "share of category requirements" analysis are just a few of the techniques available. Such measures help forecast future cash flows used in a financial brand valuation.

- *Financial brand value.* Brand valuations are a snapshot of future brand earnings taken at a point in time. They reflect the sustainable outflow and put a firm financial value on it. They depend on an accurate prediction of future brand health because they are based on forecast cash flows generated by the brand. They rely on an accurate estimate of the future flow, which the reservoir has yet to produce. The flow rate may be falling or rising depending on the amount of brand equity left in the reservoir.

Brand finance definition of brand equity

Brand equity measures "the propensity of specific audiences to express preferences which are financially favorable to the brand." Brand equity measurement systems isolate and analyze the attributes that explain changes in this propensity and predict future financial behavior. Brand equity helps explain the shape of demand and cost curves in a brand economics study.

Figure 5.16 illustrates how the flow referred to by Tim Ambler works in practice and how the measures referred to by Paul Feldwick fit together in determining the rate of that flow.

In determining the brand's value at a point in time we consider the current and future financial performance, the expected flow rate from the reservoir. The output measure that allows us to value the brand is ultimately the volume and value of sales generated by the brand. Volumes and values can be explained and predicted by consumer behavioral measures such as trial and repeat purchase rates, or willingness to pay a price premium. These are determined by brand preference.

Moving back up the flow, we see that brand preference is driven by a mixture of functional attributes (such as perceived product quality, value for money, or convenience of distribution) and by image attributes (such as status, ethics, or association with the brand). Brand preference is affected to different degrees by different attributes. We typically use conjoint or trade-off analysis to understand the weight of these attributes on preference and brand choice. These intermediate measures are really the predictive heart of a brand equity measurement framework and allow us to measure and understand how the flow rate will change in the future.

For example, in the case of a retail fuel client we have correlated a balanced scorecard of individual perceptual attribute measures, together with stated brand

INPUTS	INTERMEDIATE MEASURES		OUTPUTS	
ACTIONS	ATTRIBUTES	BEHAVIOR	PERFORMANCE	FINANCIALS
Product	Quality	Trial	Share	Volume
Pricing	Value	Repeat	Growth	Value
Service	Helpful	Frequency	Premium	
Training	Simplicity	Loyalty		
Distribution	Convenient	Recommend		
Advertising	Friendly			
Sponsorship	Sexy			
CRM	Status			
PR	Ethical			

(Awareness) (Preference)

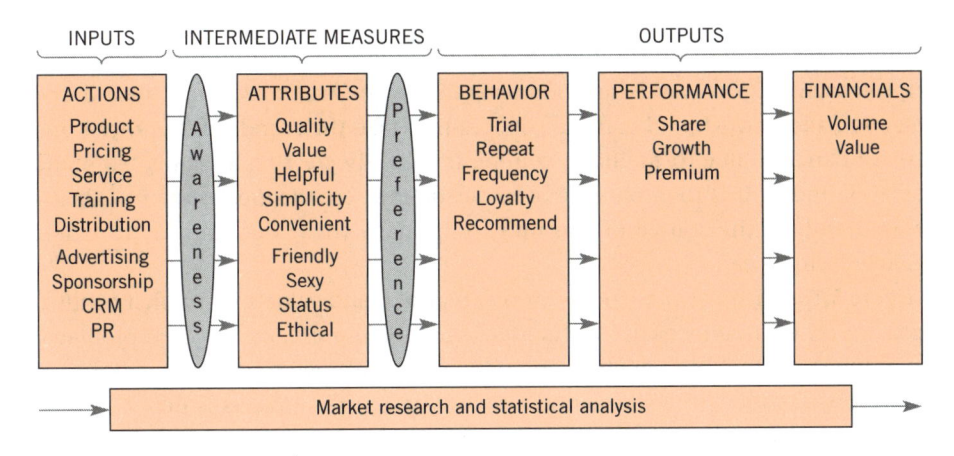

Market research and statistical analysis

Figure 5.16: *Linking brand equity to value drivers*

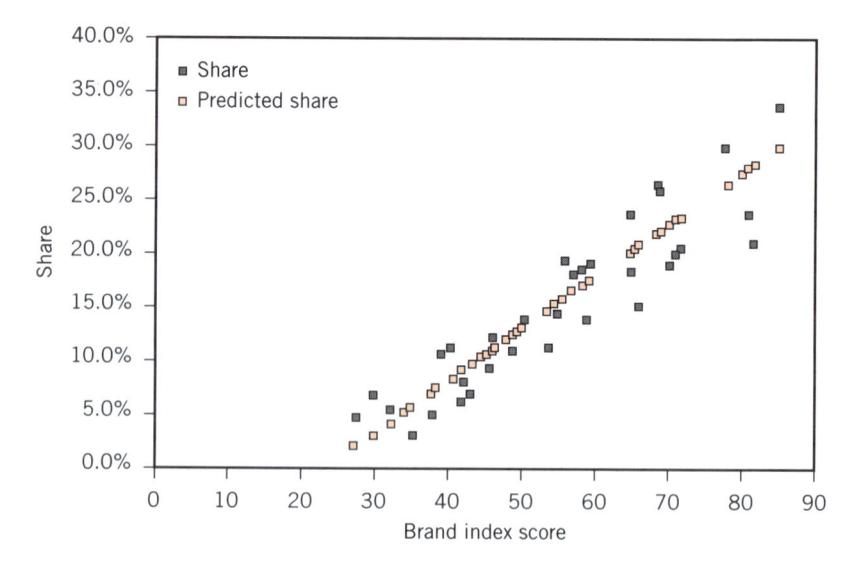

Figure 5.17: *Brand equity index versus volume share*

preference, against relative volume share in over 100 countries. Changes in the composite brand index scores are closely correlated with changes in volume share, as shown in Figure 5.17. This curve can be used for predicting likely volume share changes as marketing actions are taken to improve or deteriorate individual brand attributes and brand preference – making it a very powerful planning tool.

At the source of the brand equity flow are the inputs or direct actions which can be taken by brand owners to affect the perceptions and preferences further downstream. By understanding which perceptual attributes affect brand preference most, and by understanding which actions have the greatest impact on the perceptual attributes, the brand owner is able to decide where to allocate resources to impact the brand economics curves and to maximize brand value.

Should resources be applied to functional changes, like service or product improvement? Or to marketing communications, shifting image attributes? Brand valuation allows the brand management team to take the brand equity process and give a financial value to the flows coming from it. By creating a segmented brand valuation model it is then possible to understand where the greatest value is being created and, at the source of the flow, help make those decisions as to where resources will be best deployed.

Figure 5.18 illustrates the framework of a typical brand valuation. We first conduct a market review to understand all the trends driving the size, growth, and profitability of the market within which the brand operates. We review the competitors and conduct brand strength assessments. A critical part of this process is understanding how brand equity affects the brand economics and we ensure that we fully understand the shape of the demand curves in each of the segments. Critically the

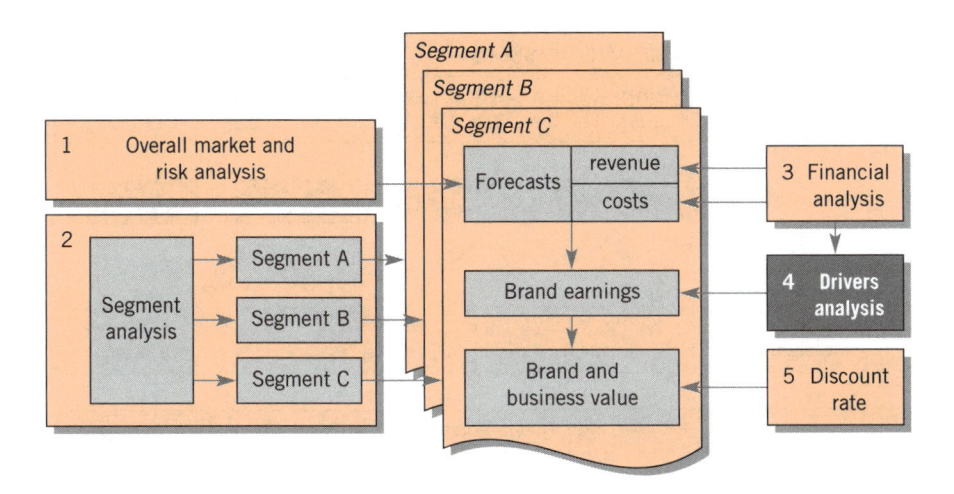

Figure 5.18: *Brand valuation framework*

valuation is segmented into discrete pieces to allow an understanding of the brand contribution by segment. This reflects the fact that demand conditions vary significantly from one geographic or consumer segment to another.

We review the internal landscape, understanding current and forecast cost structures, including how the brand affects the shape and direction of the costs curve. So a brand valuation provides a framework for valuing the brand into segments (by geography, product, channel, or consumer demographic) which matches with the analysis of brand equity and underlying brand economics. By understanding brand equity in aggregate and for the individual segments we are able to better diagnose how and where future value can be maximized.

Figure 5.19 illustrates how the flows described can be turned into a brand scorecard. The purpose of a brand scorecard is to record the input, the intermediate, and the output measures along the flow. They allow managers to measure and report actions taken, perceptual attribute changes, developments on awareness and preference, behavioral measures, their impact on volumes and values, and finally the financial value that all this implies. If this is reported regularly to the management and the board it provides a framework for decision making and corrective action.

Figure 5.20 provides an example of a typical scorecard picking out some key measures for management reporting. Such a scorecard is provided for each key brand and segment or market in which the key brands operate. It is a summary and behind the headlines there is usually a wealth of data kept in a relational database for enquiry once a problem or opportunity has been spotted.

There is no simple measure of brand equity but rather several measures which, taken together, inform management decision making. What major companies are beginning to realize is that all of the measures available need to be gathered, reviewed, and prioritized in a structured brand audit and considered as a whole in

418 Marketing

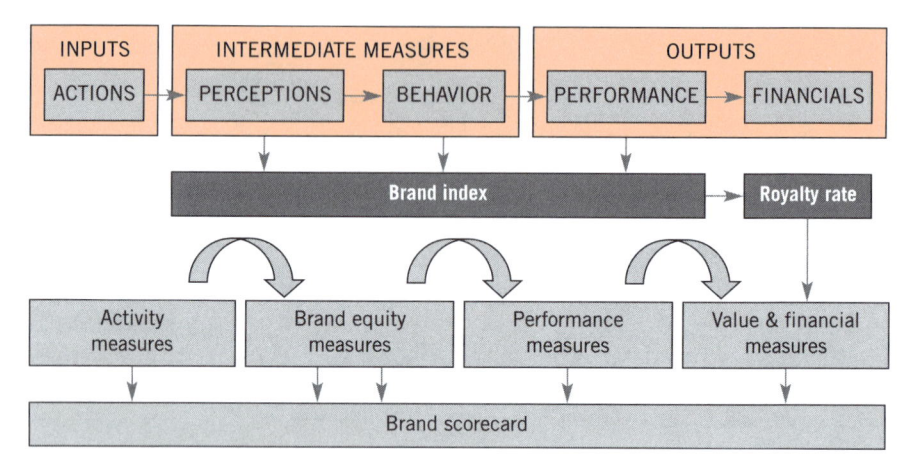

Figure 5.19: *Building a brand scorecard*

Perceptual measures (brand health)

	Actual	vs PY
Awareness	95%	
Customer share of preference	25%	
Customer satisfaction	55%	
Loyalty/favorability	30%	
Perception of technical expertise	25%	

Performance measures

	Actual	vs PY
Market share	20%	
Sales growth	5%	
Points of presence	65%	

Customer measures

	Actual	vs PY
Core customers	60%	
Churn rate	15%	
Customer profitability	20%	

Value measures

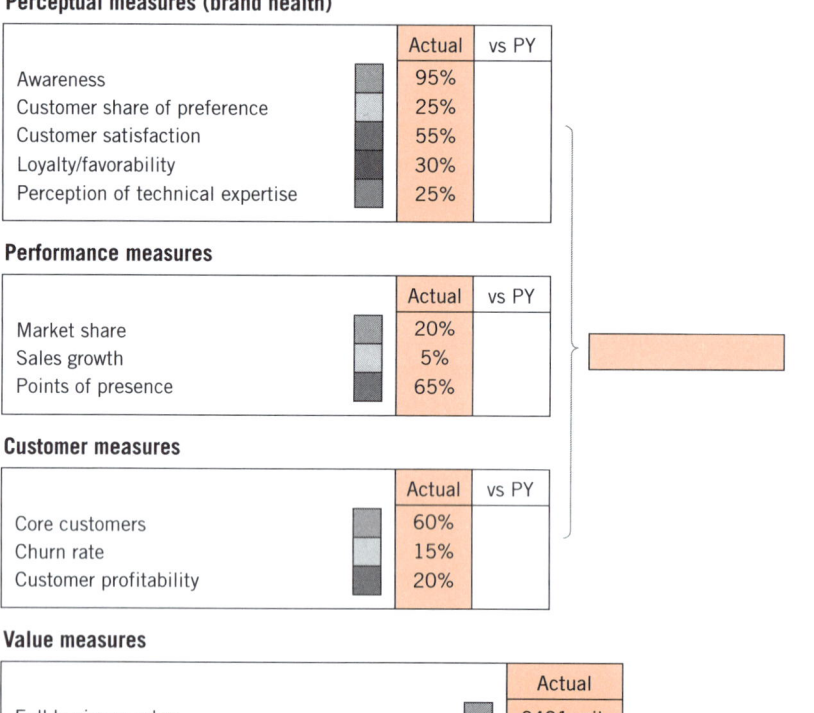

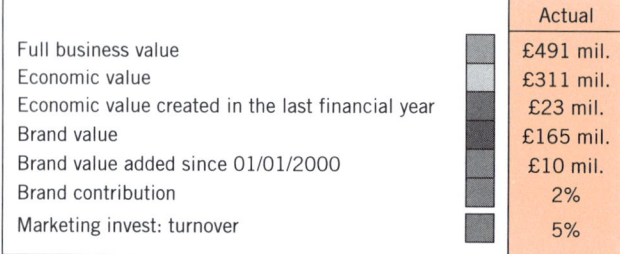

	Actual
Full business value	£491 mil.
Economic value	£311 mil.
Economic value created in the last financial year	£23 mil.
Brand value	£165 mil.
Brand value added since 01/01/2000	£10 mil.
Brand contribution	2%
Marketing invest: turnover	5%

Figure 5.20: *Perceptual measures (brand health)*

the brand evaluation process. Ideally data should be statistically analyzed to find persuasive if not definitive relationships which can be tested empirically.

To this end more and more companies are building brand monitoring and forecasting systems with large volumes of detailed research and financial data incorporating brand equity and brand value measures.

Tracking the brand

Brands will be major drivers of corporate value in the 21st century. Investors and business leaders have recognized this. Financial managers and planners are increasingly using brand equity tracking models to facilitate business planning. They should go one step further. Investors need and want greater disclosure of brand values and marketing performance. They want to understand the brand economics of individual brands to better understand the future performance and value of companies they are investing in. Financial managers should play a lead role in ensuring that such information is adequately communicated to investors, rather than waiting for statutory disclosure requirements to catch up with reality.

Having detailed information on the brand, not just a brand value in financial terms, including information on perceptual, performance, and customer measures, can aid the investor relations function. By utilizing detailed brand equity and brand economics trackers it is possible to show the investment community the contribution of the brand as well as its actual value.

Other key areas in which a greater understanding of brand equity and brand economics aids company performance includes the setting of marketing budgets, resource allocation, internal communication, and brand performance tracking.

Many organizations suffer from a surplus rather than a lack of market and consumer information. Unfortunately, much of this is gathered and stored in isolation. The old functional boundaries of a bygone era still prevent the effective flow and integration of information. Even if brand tracking data makes it onto the intranet or a shared directory, it tends to remain in "research speak" and generally is not used by financial and strategic planners.

What marketers and brand owners need to ensure is that adequate data is collected centrally and regularly, that relationships between the data variables are understood, that the financial value of the brand is understood, and that it is monitored. It is now best practice to have a brand equity, brand economics, and brand value reporting system of this kind and demands for such reporting systems will be further driven by the financial and investment communities in the coming years.

Corporate religion

JESPER KUNDE

> A new definition of corporate management is required for the 21st century, based not on organization but on brand values.

In the old economy the product played the central role, and companies were organized in order to develop, manufacture, and sell new products. Now there is a shift to disparate modes of thinking. Within this the web has been a unique media, in that it allows companies to interact and communicate with their customers rapidly, globally, and individually. But the web only accelerated a development that has been imminent for quite a while: the transition from a product-oriented economy to a value-based economy.

In the true new economy it is essential to be unique, because singularity translates into value for your customers. And in the future value will be everything. We therefore need new definitions of corporate management, definitions which are based on an understanding of brand values.

Brand thinking

Brand thinking is the simplest way of defining and expressing a set of values. I believe the most important management task is being able to put one's company into words, so that everyone inside the company – and outside in the market – shares a common concept of the future. Don't forget: in the future the company becomes the brand. Moreover, employees and consumers will demand a far more comprehensive understanding of the company behind the brand than they have today.

The first step toward achieving this mutual understanding between a company, its employees, and its customers is a corporate religion (CR). The CR is the "sticky stuff" between company and market, allowing the company to manage both enterprise and market wholeheartedly. In psychology, personality is all about perception and is seen from three perspectives:

- What is the world's perception of our company?
- How do we see ourselves?

- How would we like the world to think of us?

The CR expresses the company's soul and personality – and if these are strong enough, they will penetrate the market in a positive way.

Strong companies break through to the market by creating a singular connected force within the corporation that moves into the market and consistently provide the company with a strong market position. It is of utmost importance to focus on building that powerful link between the internal culture inside the company and the brand position you wish to create in the market.

Everything begins with you

It all begins with the top managers. They need to define who they are and where they want to go. "Why?" they will say. "We are already designing strategies and running the company according to solid principles of good management." Wrong. In the new economy where value and the ability to communicate it are all important, you need a whole new set of skills to succeed. In the new economy, everything is constantly changing. Companies built to last become companies built to flip – forcing top managements to pay close attention to what goes on in and around their markets, continuously supplying correct interpretations and adaptive actions.

When everything is changing rapidly, it will no longer be the product that is the glue that makes ends meet in your company. Brand values become the most important point of departure in the future. And remember: no amount of harmless, nice-for-all values will do the job. Only a mission statement that expounds the corporate promise to the market makes it happen. A genuine mission statement describes what the company wants to do better for its customers – and what exactly it is that makes it a unique company in the market.

The mission statement is just the beginning. The next task is to define and phrase the brand values that will link the internal organization with the external position the company wants to conquer.

Precision in formulation adds efficiency to the company. Finding the appropriate words is no easy task and it takes time, but it is worth pursuing. Once the wording is in place and there is consensus, invest heavily in communicating your corporate brand internally and externally.

Believe or leave

In my experience with international concept development, top managers find it very difficult to formulate their company's brand values and generally don't devote resources to this task. They're still chiefly occupied with budgets and organizational structures.

In the new economy, you'd do best to forget about all those budgets and assorted quantities. The great task ahead is figuring out how you transfer your brand values from the old to the new economy. After all, you are never more than the position you own in the heads of your customers.

When everything can change at the drop of a hat, it is important to improve your corporate ability to continuously formulate what your company is about. In other words, strengthen your capability to revise your company at least once a year. Revision is decisive to success and forms an efficient link between management, employees, and customers. Remember: the future calls for incessant fuel injections.

Future top managers need to be on the frontline deciphering what is happening for the good of their companies – rephrasing their corporate brands in the process – and communicating the news for all to seize.

Top managers of the future will remain ahead because they know more and consequently demand more of their employees. Corporate religion is about consensus, about uniting many minds in a common purpose. It's crucial for success that everyone has the same attitudes – and goes along the same shared path to create more value. A company which is governed by a corporate religion only has jobs for believers.

RESOURCES

Kunde, Jesper, *Corporate Religion*, FT Prentice Hall, London, 2000.

Essentials

MARKETING

Affiliate marketing

Affiliate marketing was one of the first marketing models rolled out on the Internet. Amazon.com, for example, is one of its most well-known adherents. What Internet user hasn't come across the omnipresent Amazon banner while surfing some special interest site?

It works like this. Let's say an e-tailer sets up a site selling Persian Rugs – magicarpetz.com. Magicarpetz then contacts other sites, an interior design portal possibly, or a home furnishings e-store, where prospective rug purchasers may be loitering, and persuades the other company to carry a magicarpetz ad banner on its site.

The site affiliate in return receives a reward for allowing magicarpetz to place the banner. This reward could be linked to the number of surfers clicking through the banner ad. Or it might be linked to the number of leads produced. Alternatively, it may be linked to actual sales made in the form of a paid commission.

The beauty of the model is that magicarpetz can build an extensive advertising network in prime positions for no upfront costs. In turn the affiliate gets money for nothing other than giving over an unused space on its site to a magicarpetz banner.

Affiliate marketing is not an entirely failsafe marketing technique. There are several potential pitfalls. If a fictional e-tailer, magicarpetz, signed up too many affiliates without checking the quality of their websites, it could easily damage its brand image. There are few surfers who have not winced at a homepage piled to the rafters with affiliate links. And then there are the disputes over site traffic. What if the affiliates claim they sent x number of people to magicarpetz, whereas magicarpetz reckons it's more like y. Then again it could be such a roaring success that the rugs fly out of the warehouse – but too much time is then spent managing the affiliate program that can't be automated and customer service may suffer as a result.

This is why a number of companies have sprung up offering to manage, to a lesser or greater extent, the affiliate marketing process. The affiliate networks, that include companies such as BeFree, LinkShare, and Click Trade, take a lot of the hassle out of setting up an affiliate program. They can plug a would-be affiliate marketer straight into their own ready-made network of affiliates numbering anywhere between 50,000 and 250,000. It's not a free service, however.

Affiliate network companies make their money, in the main, by charging commission on affiliate earnings – usually around the 30 percent mark.

Four Ps of marketing

In 1960, E. Jerome McCarthy introduced a new concept to the world of business theory. McCarthy took the marketing mix (defined by marketing's *éminence grise*, Philip Kotler, as "the set of marketing tools that the firm uses to pursue its marketing objectives in the target market") and identified its critical ingredients as product, price, place, and promotion. This became known as the Four Ps of marketing. It is a formula that has stood the test of time, and is still recited by students and known by virtually everyone in business.

At the time of their inception, the Four Ps encapsulated the essence of traditional marketing. A company that successfully focussed its attention on all of the Four Ps could develop a soundly based marketing strategy. A company that failed to do so – or that allowed its focus to shift – was unlikely to excel at marketing.

Examining the four categories, first there is the *product* (or the service) being offered. Kotler provided a definition of a product as "a bundle of physical, services, and symbolic particulars expected to yield satisfaction or benefits to the buyer." (This has since been distilled down to "a product is something that is viewed as capable of satisfying a want.")

Next comes the issue of *pricing*. In recent years this has become ever more complex, with an array of pricing strategies covering everything from premium pricing to seasonal or even daily pricing.

The other two elements, place and promotion, are more wide ranging. *Place* embraces how and where the company makes the product accessible to potential customers. This includes, therefore, distribution and logistics – and, increasingly, cyberspace. Finally comes *promotion*. This hides a multitude of activities, all of which have enjoyed an explosion of growth over the last 20 or so years. These include communication, personal selling, advertising, direct marketing, sales promotion, and public relations.

The Four Ps were a useful summary of the dominant parts of the marketing mix in the 1960s when mass industrial marketing was the order of the day. However, the nature of business has changed. No longer is the emphasis on volumes, but on customer delight. No longer does a company blindly start with the product and then attempt to find a market; the customer is the starting point.

The nature of marketing has also fundamentally changed. The divisions between the Four Ps are increasingly blurred, sometimes non-existent. For example, the Four Ps are of limited value if you are marketing and selling your products over the Internet. However, despite great technological leaps forward, product, price, place, and promotion are still important. The trouble is that defining their exact meaning, role, and potential is more and more difficult.

Kotler, Philip

While championing the role of marketing over 30 years, Philip Kotler (born 1931) has coined phrases such as "mega marketing," "demarketing," and "social marketing." His numerous books include the definitive textbook on the subject, *Marketing Management* (now in its eighth edition).

Kotler has a penchant for useful definitions. "When I am asked to define marketing in the briefest possible way I say marketing is meeting needs profitably. A lot of us meet needs – but businesses are set up to do it profitably. Marketing is the homework that you do to hit the mark that satisfies those needs exactly. When you do that job, there isn't much selling work to do because the word gets out from delighted customers that this is a wonderful solution to our problems."[55]

Kotler also provides a useful definition of a product as "anything that can be offered to a market for attention, acquisition, use, or consumption that might satisfy a want or need." He says that a product has five levels: the core benefit ("marketers must see themselves as benefit providers"); the generic product; the expected product (the normal expectations the customer has of the product); the augmented product (the additional services or benefits added to the product); and, finally, the potential product ("all of the augmentations and transformations that this product might ultimately undergo in the future").

The central shift that Kotler has described is from "transaction-oriented" marketing to "relationship marketing." "Good customers are an asset which, when well managed and served, will return a handsome lifetime income stream to the company. In the intensely competitive marketplace, the company's first order of business is to retain customer loyalty through continually satisfying their needs in a superior way," says Kotler.

Kotler regards marketing as the essence of business and more. "Good companies will meet needs; great companies will create markets," he writes. "Market leadership is gained by envisioning new products, services, lifestyles, and ways to raise living standards. There is a vast difference between companies that offer me-too products and those that create new product and service values not even imagined by the marketplace. Ultimately, marketing at its best is about value creation and raising the world's living standards."

Levitt, Ted

The July–August 1960 issue of the *Harvard Business Review* launched the career of American academic Ted Levitt (born 1925). It included his article entitled "Marketing myopia," which, totally unexpectedly, brought marketing back on to the corporate agenda. "Marketing myopia" has sold over 500,000 reprints and has entered a select group of articles that have genuinely changed perceptions.[56]

In "Marketing myopia," Levitt argued that the central preoccupation of corporations should be with satisfying customers rather than simply producing goods. Companies should be marketing led rather than production led and the lead must come from the chief executive and senior management: "Management must think of itself not as producing products but as providing customer-creating value satisfactions." (In his ability to coin new management jargon, as well as his thinking, Levitt was ahead of his time.)

At the time of Levitt's article, the fact that companies were production led was not open to question. Henry Ford's success in mass production had fueled the belief that low-cost production was the key to business success.

Levitt observed that production-led thinking inevitably led to narrow perspectives. He argued that companies must broaden their view of the nature of their business. Otherwise, their customers will soon be forgotten. "The railroads are in trouble today not because the need was filled by others ... but because it was not filled by the railroads themselves," wrote Levitt. "They let others take customers away from them because they assumed themselves to be in the railroad business rather than in the transportation business. The reason they defined their industry wrong was because they were railroad-oriented instead of transportation-oriented; they were product-oriented instead of customer oriented." The railroad business was constrained, in Levitt's view, by a lack of willingness to expand its horizons.

In "Marketing myopia," Levitt also made a telling distinction between the tasks of selling and marketing. "Selling concerns itself with the tricks and techniques of getting people to exchange their cash for your product. It is not concerned with the values that the exchange is all about. And it does not, as marketing invariably does, view the entire business process as consisting of a tightly integrated effort to discover, create, arouse, and satisfy customer needs," he wrote.

Levitt's other main insight was into the emergence of globalization. In the same way as he had done with "Marketing myopia," he signaled the emergence of a major movement and then withdrew to watch it ignite. "The world is becoming a common marketplace in which people – no matter where they live – desire the same products and lifestyles. Global companies must forget the idiosyncratic differences between countries and cultures and instead concentrate on satisfying universal drives," he said.

Permission marketing

It was Seth Godin, the former president of Yoyodyne Entertainment and VP of Direct Marketing at Yahoo!, who first came up with the term permission marketing. The idea was to improve on what Godin termed "interruption marketing." Initially the marketer needs to interrupt the viewer's activity in order to grab their attention. So, for example, on the Internet an interstitial will be a break in the flow of the viewer's experience. Wouldn't it be better, thought Godin, if at least after the first interruption the marketer obtained the "permission" of the consumer to market *with* them rather than *at* them.

The premise is that consumers will willingly give up valuable personal information and grant permission for marketers to send them product information so long as they are given sufficient incentive. This then is the challenge for the permission marketer: finding the right incentive to persuade the consumer to grant permission.

Godin rolled out several variations of permission marketing campaigns during his stint at Yoyodyne. E-mail and web promotions were built around competitions, gameshows, and sweepstakes. For example, the company ran a "Get Rich Quick" campaign where a prize of $100,000 was enough to tempt 250,000 players to the clients' site. Following on from this initial contact sponsors were able to build relationships with the customers through e-mail messages that led to the next level of the game. This information was given in return for permission to pitch products.

Godin offers four simple guidelines for permission marketers to remember:

1. People are selfish – they care about themselves, not the permission marketer.
2. Never rent or sell permission to a third party.
3. Permission can be revoked – it is not given for ever.
4. Permission is not static – unlike buying an address.

Permission marketers have to be careful not to abuse their permission. They also have to manage the relationship if permission is revoked, and also if the permission has lapsed. It's a fine line between e-mailing product information under permission, and spamming.

Relationship marketing

Relationship marketing refers to the benefits that on-going relationships with key customers can bring to an organization. The idea behind it goes back to the earliest trading times, but the term entered the vocabulary of management during the 1980s. At that time, management writers observed it at work within the high-tech business community of California's Silicon Valley.

In 1985, marketing guru Regis McKenna wrote the first book devoted to the marketing of high-technology companies, *The Regis Touch*. "Many of the small, highly innovative Silicon Valley companies didn't market new products to the larger computer companies on an individual basis in the traditional way," he observed. Instead, they sought to establish strategic relationships that allowed the smaller company to work almost as part of the customer's organization.

In a very fast-moving industry, the closeness of these relationships was critical to the ability of smaller firms to develop solutions that met the needs of their customers. It became apparent that their success often depended on personal relationships that had developed into close friendships. Rather than attend to the marketing of products or projects through traditional means, these smaller companies worked extra hard at maintaining on-going relationships.

Relationship Marketing, McKenna's third book, focussed on the interactive relationships vital to market acceptance in the "age of the customer," and drew wider attention to the concept of relationship marketing.

The logic of relationship marketing is simple: rather than communicate intermittently with key customers, it makes more sense to develop a relationship of mutual trust so that the dialog is continuous. Everyone in business has been told that success is all about attracting and retaining customers. But once companies have attracted customers, they often overlook the second half of the equation.

Failing to concentrate on retaining as well as attracting customers costs businesses huge amounts of money every year. It has been estimated that the average company loses between 10 and 30 percent of its customers annually. Organizations are now beginning to wake up to these lost opportunities and calculate the financial implications. Research in the US found that a 5 percent decrease in the number of defecting customers led to profit increases of between 25 and 85 percent.

The route to customer retention is relationship marketing, nurturing relationships with customers that create loyalty. Relationship-building programs now cover a multitude of activities, from customer magazines to vouchers and gifts. In essence, they aim to persuade a person to use a preferred vendor in order to take advantage of the benefits on offer, whether it is a trip to Acapulco or a price-reduction voucher for a calorie-controlled canned drink. Skeptics will say there is nothing new in this. Indeed, businesses have been giving long-standing customers discounts and inducements since time immemorial. What is now different is the highly organized way in which companies are attempting to build relationships and customer loyalty.

The idea is that if you are continually aware of what your customers or partners require and keep them informed of developments within your own organization, the customer–supplier link becomes almost a seamless web. In relationship marketing, the details of the products and services become subservient to the trust that has been established. After all, why would a customer go elsewhere if you are always monitoring and adjusting what you are doing to meet their needs now and in the future? The advantage of such an arrangement is that problems can be averted before they become a crisis. The only reason for losing the customer is if the relationship breaks down.

Technology is likely to have a marked effect on relationship marketing. On the one hand, the emergence of the Internet as a global marketplace means that customers are likely to become increasingly promiscuous, able to flirt with suppliers all over the world. At the same time, technology also allows relationship marketing programs to become ever more sophisticated. When it comes to creating loyal customers, the database is king. Databases mean that companies can target audiences more effectively.

REFERENCES

1. Wind, Yoram (Jerry) and Crook, Colin, *The Power of Impossible Thinking: Transforming the Business of Your Life and the Life of Your Business*, Wharton School Publishing, 2004.
2. Bannister, Roger, *The Four-Minute Mile*, Guildford: The Lyons Press, 1981.
3. Freeman, Walter J., *Societies of Brains: A Study in the Neuroscience of Love and Hate*, Lawrence Erlbaum Associates, 1995.
4. Posnock, Susan, 'Power Play: IT Can Control Madison Avenue,' *American Demographics*, February 2004.
5. Wells, Melanie, 'Kid Nabbing,' *Forbes*, February 2, 2004.
6. Wind, Yoram (Jerry) and Mahajan, Vijay, *Convergence Marketing: Strategies for Reaching the New Hybrid Consumer*, FT Prentice Hall, 2003.
7. Simons, Daniel J. and Chabris, Christopher F., 'Gorillas in Our Midst: Sustained Blindness for Dynamic Events,' *Perception*, Vol. 28 (1999), pp. 1059–1074.
8. CIM Research.
9. CIM Research quoted in: Wood, A., 'Board-level basics,' *Financial Times Creative Business*, August 12, p. 5, 2003.
10. CIM Research (the one mentioned is Elizabeth J. Comstock, CMO and corporate VP marketing, General Electric).
11. From speech given to the Worshipful Company of Marketors reported in: Marsden, A., 'Shareholder value creation,' *Brand Strategy*, June 9, p. 13, 2003.
12. By business metrics we mean business measurements, such as judging product and service quality, rating customer relationships, and measuring employee satisfaction and commitment, that align with the board-level strategy and are seen as critical to improving the bottom line.
13. Crainer, S. and Dearlove, D., *Business, the Universe and Everything*, John Wiley, 2003.
14. E-mail from Don Peppers, August 2003.
15. Browne, J., '*Marketing and trust*,' speech to the Marketing Society, London, March 10, 2003.
16. Benady, D., 'Dead wood,' *Marketing Week*, May 15, pp. 25–27, 2003.
17. Moeller, L.H., Mathur, S.K., and Rothenberg, R., 'The better half: The artful science of ROI marketing,' *Strategy + Business*, Spring, 2003.
18. A recent study of loyalty programs in four firms, for example, found that long-term customers were not cheaper to serve or maintain, but as expensive or more expensive than non-loyal customers. Reinartz, W. and Kumar, V., 'The mismanagement of customer loyalty,' *Harvard Business Review*, July, pp. 86–94, 2002.
19. The importance of satisfying multiple stakeholders (Chakravarthy, B.S., 'Measuring strategic performance,' *Strategic Management Journal*, Vol. 7, pp. 437–458, 1986).
20. Shaw, R. and Mazur, L., *Marketing accountability: Improving business performance*, London, FT Managements Reports, 1997.
21. Schultz, D.E., 'Determine outcomes first to measure efforts,' *Marketing News*, September 1, p. 7, 2003.
22. Haspeslagh, P., Noda, T., and Boulos, F., 'It's not just about the numbers,' *Harvard Business Review*, July–August, pp. 65–73, 2001.
23. Bloomberg.com, Siemens' Neubuerger says recovery hasn't taken hold. August 5, 2003.

24. CIM Research, Insights interview, September 2003.
25. Pitman, B., 'Leading for value,' *Harvard Business Review*, April, pp. 41–46, 2003.
26. Collins, J.C. and Porras, J., *Built to Last: Successful habits of visionary companies*, Century, 1994.
27. Perla, M., 'Do your metrics measure up?' June 10, 2003. Available from www.marketingprofs.com (accessed September 24, 2003).
28. Haspeslagh, P., Noda, T., and Boulos, F., *op. cit.*
29. Malcolm, R., '100 percent marketing,' London, The Brands Lecture, June 17, 2003.
30. Browne, J., *op. cit.*
31. Silver, S., 'Bring on the super-CMO,' *Strategy + Business*, Summer, 2003.
32. Haspeslagh, P., Noda, T., and Boulos, F. *op. cit.*
33. Throughout, reference to consumers includes both consumers and organizations.
34. This traditional view was expounded in the famous Porter, M., *Competitive Strategy*, Macmillan, 1980.
35. For more on customer lock-on, see Vandermerwe, S., *Customer Capitalism: Increasing Returns in New Market Spaces*, Nicholas Brealey, 1999 (Colin Whurr Publishers, 2000).
36. For the failure of loyalty and other CRM programs in the banking sector, see Cicutti, N., 'Account Holders Have No Loyalty to Banks,' *Financial Times*, April 30, 2002 and Molineux, P., 'CRM: What Went Wrong?' *Financial Services*, July 1, 2002. For other, general studies on this point, see Reinartz, W. and Kumar, V., 'The Mismanagement of Customer Loyalty,' *Harvard Business Review*, July 2002; Rigby, D. and Reichheld, F., 'Avoid the Four Perils of CRM,' *Harvard Business Review*, July/August 2000.
37. Reichheld, F., 'The One Number You Need to Grow,' *Harvard Business Review*, December 2003.
38. Prysty, C., 'Marketing – Unilever Raises its India Game: Squeezed by Growing Competition from Foreign and Domestic rivals, Anglo-Dutch Multinational Unilever is Diversifying from just Mass-producing Consumer Goods to Direct Sales and Value-Added Services,' *Far Eastern Economic Review*, October 30, 2003.
39. For calculating the present value of future revenue streams, see among others Blattberg, R., Getz, G., and Thomas, J., *Customer Equity: Building and Managing Relationships as Valuable Assets*, Harvard Business School Press, Cambridge, 2001 and Ofek, E., 'Customer Profitability and Lifetime Value,' *Harvard Business School Note*, August 7, 2002.
40. For more on this new algorithm, see Vandermerwe, S., 'How Increasing Value to Customers Improves Business Results,' *MIT Sloan Management Review*, Fall 2000.
41. Free cash flow in this context is discussed by Mauboussin, M. and Hiler, B. in 'Cashflow.com,' *Frontiers of Finance*, Vol. 9 (Credit Suisse First Boston, February 1999).
42. Statistics on health problems that can be predicted and prevented 70 percent of the time and health care costs decreased by 50 percent from 'Haelen Group Interview with CEO Julie Meek,' in *USA Today*, January 21, 2001.
43. Lanning, Michael J., *Delivering Profitable Value: A Revolutionary Framework to Accelerate Growth, Generate Wealth, and Rediscover the Heart of Business*, Capstone, 1998.
44. Schlesinger, Leonard A. and Heskett, James L., 'Breaking the Cycle of Failure in Services,' *Sloan Management Review*, Spring 1991.

45. Heskett, James L., Jones, Thomas O., Loveman, Gary W., Sasser, W. Earl, and Schlesinger, Leonard A., 'Putting the Service Profit Chain to Work,' *Harvard Business Review*, March–April 1994.
46. Barkin, Nahirny and van Metre, 'Why are Service Turnarounds so Tough?,' *McKinsey Quarterly*, No. 1, 1998.
47. Cram, Tony, *Customers That Count – how to build living relationships with your most valuable customers*, Prentice Hall, 2001.
48. Blanchard, Ken and Bowles, Sheldon, *Raving Fans – a Revolutionary Approach to Customer Service*, HarperCollins Business, 1998.
49. Reichheld, Frederick, *Loyalty Rules!: How today's leaders build lasting relationships*, Harvard Business School Press, 2001.
50. Hemp, Paul, 'My week as a room service waiter at the Ritz,' *Harvard Business Review*, June 2002.
51. Mitchell, Colin, 'Selling the brand inside – you tell customers what makes you great, do your employees know?' *Harvard Business Review*, January 2002.
52. Chase, Richard B. and Dasu, Sriram, 'Want to perfect your company's service? Use behavioral science,' *Harvard Business Review*, June 2001.
53. Smith, Shaun and Wheeler, Joe, *Managing the Customer Experience*, FT Prentice Hall, 2002
54. Shaw, Colin and Ivens, John, *Building Great Customer Experiences*, Palgrave MacMillan, 2002.
55. Mazur, Laura, 'Silent satisfaction,' source unknown.
56. Other career-enhancing HBR articles include Robert Hayes and William Abernathy's 'Managing our way to economic decline', Frederick Herzberg's 'One more time, how do you motivate employees?', Hamel and Prahalad's 'The core competence of the corporation.'

– CHAPTER 6 –

Finance

"Finance is the art of passing currency from hand to hand until it finally disappears."

Robert Sarnoff

"Annual income twenty pounds, annual expenditure nineteen six, result happiness. Annual income twenty pounds, annual expenditure twenty pounds nought and six, result misery."

Charles Dickens

"Capitalism without bankruptcy is like Christianity without hell."

Frank Borman

Better pricing processes for higher profits

HERMANN SIMON, STEPHAN A. BUTSCHER
AND KARL-HEINZ SEBASTIAN

[*Reducing costs may be the instinctive response in an economic downturn, but it is not always the best one. Management should focus on the revenue side. A close examination of the pricing process is one way of doing this.*]

Top management is always looking for new ways to increase shareholder value. To improve profits, they focus primarily on costs. However, reducing costs further is becoming increasingly difficult and managers must now turn their attention to the revenue side, in particular to changing their pricing processes. Improving pricing processes has three clear advantages versus cost cutting (see Figure 6.1).

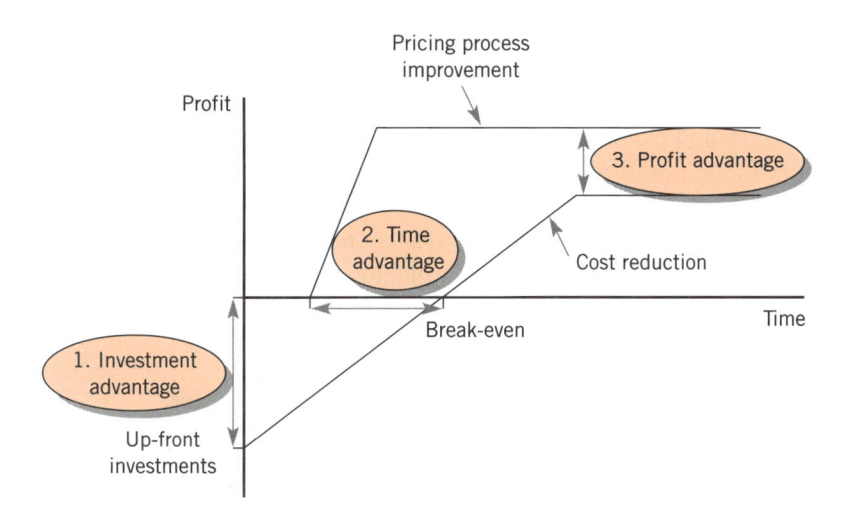

Figure 6.1: *Quick wins: pricing process improvement versus cost cutting*

First, it brings an investment advantage. Costly severance packages or plant closures are not necessary. Second, pricing process improvements have an immediate positive impact on profit and cash flow while the real effects of cost cutting usually don't emerge for several quarters. Third, our experience shows a clear profit advantage. Improvements to pricing processes often have a substantially higher impact on return on sales (ROS) than cost cutting.

The average after-tax profit margin of large European companies is slightly above 2 percent – a catastrophic situation. Increasing prices by just 1 percent would improve profit margins by about 50 percent. How does one enact such measures?

Forget about simply hiking list prices across the board or commanding the sales force to push through higher prices. Such blunt measures are bound to fail. The proper way is the total restructuring of the pricing process itself. This represents a fundamental strategic challenge that strikes at the core of each economic transaction (see Figure 6.2).

Most companies are good or even very good at *value delivery* but fall short in *value extraction* from their customers. Simply put, they fail to harvest the full value of their products. How else can one explain that even innovative, market-leading firms achieve a profit margin of only 1 or 2 percent despite massive cost reductions over the last few years?

One very innovative US-based electronics supplier makes no money precisely because it prices its new products on a cost-plus basis. It even lets its customers examine its cost structure. The company does not fully understand the value of its innovations to customers. As a result it cannot set appropriate prices to charge customers for the benefits it delivers. What should this business do? It should restructure its pricing processes completely. Strictly speaking, it has to introduce a systematic process of value extraction, something it has never had before.

Understanding the value you provide to your direct customers is only one aspect. Ideally, you would explore in great detail how service providers, retailers, and end customers perceive and reward value. The manufacturer Gore, for example, could conceivably treat its main product, Gore-Tex (laminated PTFE used in waterproof clothing), as a commodity, which the physical product essentially is. However, Gore understands and influences the added value for the garment makers, the retailers,

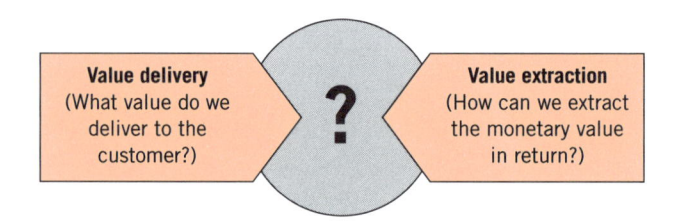

Figure 6.2: *Value delivery and value extraction*

and through to the end customers. This allows Gore-Tex to command much higher prices than comparable products. The brand Gore-Tex plays a central role for value delivery as well as for value extraction.

The pricing process defined

A pricing process is a set of rules and procedures that helps a company to determine and implement prices. It involves:

- information, models, methodologies, rules, responsibilities, incentives, and timing;
- phases (analysis, decision, implementation, and monitoring);
- subjective components (for example, estimates and experience) and objective components (for example, market and competitor data).

Surprisingly, the pricing process is a relatively new topic. This can be attributed to a number of things.

First, those responsible for setting prices have traditionally relied on gut feeling and instinct. Few companies – exceptions include leaders in the pharmaceutical and automotive industries – have succeeded in putting the process idea into practice. Second, hardly any academic research on pricing processes exists. Third, pricing processes are very specific to industries and even individual companies. Finally, these processes are very secret. One automotive supplier will not let its preoccupation with the subject be publicly known under any circumstances.

Pricing processes become particularly vital when a business sells many different products or when prices for each transaction are individually determined, for example through negotiation. In such cases, a company cannot afford to invest too much time and effort in each individual pricing decision. Instead, it needs clearly defined processes in order to extract value successfully and earn appropriate returns.

Higher returns

Our experience shows that companies can increase their ROS by up to two percentage points by making their pricing processes more effective. Given the currently thin returns at most companies, this is revolutionary. Table 6.1 shows that companies of all sizes and industries can make substantial improvement in their return on sales.

Table 6.1: *Overview of ROS improvement through better pricing processes*

Industry	Revenue category	Critical aspects of pricing process improvement	Increase in ROS in percentage points
Engineering	£3.5bn–£6.5bn	Systematic quantification of value-to-customer More comprehensive and reliable competitive to intelligence	approx. 1% points
Supplier	£5bn–£10bn	For innovations: using value-pricing instead of cost-plus Better forecasting of cost developments for long-term contracts	1.2% points
Tourism	£5bn–£10bn	More strongly diferentiated price structure Indicator-supported identification of opportunities with profit potential	1.6% points
Wholesaler	£0.5bn–£3.5bn	Classifying customer- and product groups based on price elasticities Anti-discount incentives for the sales force	2.0% points
Software solutions	£0.1bn–£0.4bn	Reconfiguration of the selling process and guidelines Stronger centralization	8.0% points (−3.0 to +5.0%)
Express services	£3.5bn–£6.5bn	Systematic recognition and elimination of loss-making business International price discipline, controlling, and monitoring	1.5% points
Retail banking	£0.5bn–£3.5bn	Far-reaching extraction of brand value Raising the pricing competence of the customer representatives	1.6% points
Speciality chemicals	£0.3bn–£0.7bn	More through analysis of multi-stage customer value chain New price-decision hierarchy and use of key account management	1.1% points
Machinery	£0.1bn–£0.4bn	Reduction of over-engineering through target valuing/target costing Standardization of processes, especially for limited/small-run series	1.5% points

These higher returns could not have been achieved through straightforward price increases. Each company's specific problems required a more far-reaching and intelligent course of action. The goal is not to fine-tune within an existing structure. Rather, the company must undergo a reorientation of its competencies in order to maximize value extraction and thus increase returns. This insight sounds simple, yet it is crucial for success. The close attention and involvement of top management throughout this reorientation is indispensable.

The pricing process in practice

Consider some examples.

A decision every 3.3 seconds. The product managers of a passenger transportation company had eight days to make 1 million pricing decisions; this is the equivalent to 3.3 seconds per decision. Basic data and information had always been available but had never been distributed and processed in a way that would facilitate optimal pricing. A reorientation increased ROS by 1.6 percentage points by accomplishing three things: limiting detailed pricing work to critical decisions, which an automated system helped identify; restructuring the data to make it available at the right time and in the right format; and differentiating prices more sharply by using airports, utilization rates, and the type of traveler as additional differentiation criteria. Nearly all functional areas – marketing/sales, purchasing, controlling, finance, and IT – participated in the restructuring of the pricing process.

Managing unprofitable accounts. A freight company offers its services in more than 100 countries. Local managers enjoyed pricing authority. Our analysis showed that they abused this authority in order to manage volumes and capacity utilization. This created extreme price differences between customers for the same services, both within a country and across countries. These, in turn, resulted in a large share of unprofitable business. Prices could have even collapsed if they had become more transparent to customers. The company raised its returns by 1.5 percentage points by systematically eliminating the unprofitable business and making the pricing authority more centralized through the setting of target and minimum prices.

Managing price changes. The prices for a chemical commodity fluctuate according to supply and demand. The manufacturer tended to react too late when prices rose and too quickly when prices declined. This company increased its return on sales by almost one percentage point by introducing better forecasting, which allowed it to time the signing of contracts to its advantage as prices rose or fell. The new forecasting model combines objective market data with the sales force's estimates of how prices will develop in the short and medium term.

Depending on discounts. The sales team of an industrial goods company with a range of more than 40,000 articles needed – and got – considerable leeway in making pricing decisions. The sales force was compensated based on revenue but the pressure to reach the revenue targets and fend off competitors led the sales force to depend heavily on discounts. Returns had fallen by half in the previous five years. The company introduced a new bonus system that rewarded the sales force partly on their ability to maintain and defend certain target price levels, which were set by central sales management differentiated by customer type. They reduced the average discount from 16 percent to 14 percent without a loss of customers. The ROS increased from 4.5 percent to 6.5 percent.

Pricing structure. A provider of standard software for the financial services industry priced its software as a conventional product, with one single payment. It charged an hourly rate for maintenance services. Thorough analysis revealed that it would earn more money by scrapping product-based pricing and replacing it with a subscription model. The monthly subscription includes software, maintenance, and updates. Above all, it makes it very difficult for customers to compare the company's prices to its competitors', who still use product-based pricing. The company feels that a margin increase from 10 percent to 15 percent is realistic.

Eighty percent "exceptions." At a speciality chemicals company, marketing determined the price positioning of each product. Sales could go below marketing's price limits only after consulting with sales management and providing a detailed documentation of the individual customers' situation. In practice, the limits were too high. More than 80 percent of all cases were "exceptions" that required internal negotiation between marketing and sales. These constant discussions wasted considerable time. The company instituted a framework of rules and regulations that improved the quality, efficiency, and speed of the pricing decision. The framework called for different price steps and the definition of segment-specific target, limit, and minimum prices. Profits rose by 20 percent.

Value to customer. The US-based electronics supplier mentioned earlier realized that the starting point for rebuilding its pricing process lay in gaining a better understanding of value to customer along the entire value chain. For each important innovation, the pricing team now works out a comprehensive quantification of this value – without having any idea of the actual product costs. This value quantification process starts long before the product launch in order to ensure a secure basis for value extraction. Two leading US pharmaceutical companies served as benchmarks and role models for the new process. Finally, the company now denies customers access to its cost data. The company expects its margins to increase by between 1.5 and 2.5 percentage points.

Increased cross-selling. For the private banking business of a large financial institution, the way to higher revenues lay in a more targetted differentiation of the client groups. The bank discovered that a certain regular customer group reacted strongly to a change in conditions while another segment – as well as most new customers – showed no reaction to the same measures. The improved co-ordination of pricing, segmentation, and communication strategies has made marketing and pricing much more efficient. The bundling of specific services and prices to packages plays a central role, especially for cross-selling. Bottom-line improvement reached approximately two percentage points.

These examples show that achieving higher profits is not a simple matter of raising or lowering prices. The parameters to improve – such as information, knowledge, competencies, price structures, multidimensional or non-linear prices, price bundling, multiperson pricing, differentiation, responsibilities, and incentives – are considerably more complex. In the end, success derives not from bluntly raising a company's prices but rather from raising its pricing IQ.

Four essential phases

A pricing process typically comprises four phases: analysis, decision, implementation, and monitoring. Pricing and price optimization is hard work and strongly driven by data analysis. Optimizing the analysis phase means looking at questions such as:

- Is the data available in the right format, quality, and quantity?
- Do the right people have access to this data and do decision makers have access to the right data?
- What data should we have that we don't and where can this data be obtained in the right format?
- Are clear goals and deliverables defined for the analysis (key indexes, segmentation, level of aggregation, and so on)?
- Do the right people get the results at the right time in the right format?

The decision phase will bog down unless a company has the right rules and guidelines in place to allow it to draw insights from the analyses and act on them. Decision makers need a framework that helps them decide what can be done and what must be done to set prices, differentiate prices, and so on.

The implementation phase is the key test every pricing process will have to face. Pricing decisions and optimization efforts are only as good as their implementation. Managers need to communicate clearly the rules and guidelines defined in the decision phase to the sales force – pricing's frontline. Furthermore, implementation will work only if bonus and incentive systems adequately reflect pricing decisions and support the overall strategic goals of the company. In a recent project for a consumer technology manufacturer, we found that country managers had profit-based incentives while the sales organization had revenue-based ones. The resulting internal conflicts undermined the original price and discounting goals the company had so carefully worked out.

The final phase is monitoring. The right systems and analytical tools must be in place to detect any variations from the pricing and discounting goals and guidelines. These systems must also include appropriate measures and sanctions to ensure that such mistakes are corrected and future ones prevented.

In a recent project for a logistics company, the comparison of actual realized prices with the target prices set out in the clear discounting and pricing policy revealed that more than half of all parcels were shipped at prices below the maximum discount thresholds. What's worse, some 20 percent of all shipments were sold at prices discounted more than 50 percent below the maximum discount thresholds. Such terrible pricing discipline had cost this firm tens of millions of dollars over the years. After reviewing and altering its pricing process, the company now informs sales reps and account managers once a month on all accounts that received too high a discount. A new IT system allowed the company to automate this analysis fully and thus implement it with very low running costs. The company asked the reps to renegotiate prices with all affected customers, starting with those who received the most excessive discounts.

The market reaction was interesting. Many customers not only accepted higher prices but also expressed surprise that the company had taken so long to approach them on this matter. Only a small percentage of customers switched to the competition. By gradually improving discipline and removing the biggest discounting traps over two years, the company improved its bottom-line significantly.

A challenge for management

Using pricing processes to make value extraction more effective – and thus increase profits – is a challenge for top management. The case studies show that this challenge involves many functional areas. It often requires substantial changes in the organization, backed by the appropriate power and commitment from above. Top managers have to be personally involved in the effort to increase profit on the market side, just as they have long done on the cost side.

Companies have begun to acknowledge this trend and organize themselves accordingly. The US-based Professional Pricing Society already has 1,000 members, whom one could call "value extraction managers." General Electric introduced high-level positions for pricing managers, who report directly to divisional CEOs. Many companies have begun to adopt this model after seeing GE's improvement in pricing competence, discipline, and processes. The redesign of the pricing processes requires a very systematic approach and takes three to nine months, depending on the complexity. During this time, some improvements can be implemented immediately.

Instead of reflexively focussing only on cost control and cost reduction, top managers should see the value-extraction side as an equally attractive and viable way to achieve sustainable profit gains. No company should ignore this opportunity.

RESOURCES

Simon, Hermann, *Power Pricing*, Free Press, 1996.

Simon, Hermann, Bilstein, Frank and Luby, Frank, *Profit Renaissance*, Harvard Business School Press, 2004.

This article previously appeared in *Business Strategy Review*, Volume 14, Issue 2, Summer 2003.

Forecasting financials

MARK WHITTINGTON AND KEN BATES

[Past earnings and growth isn't always an accurate indicator of future performance. To get a more reliable picture some financial forecasting know-how is necessary.]

We all know that you buy what a product or service will do for you, not what it has done or where it might have been before. Shares are no different. We buy them for future potential – dividends and share price growth. Impressive earnings records and past revenue growth may have led to impressive management bonuses, excellent dividends, and a rising share price, but they do not necessarily signal more of the same – we need further evidence. Indeed, expectations rise and an ever greater level of success in the future seems to be necessary if the share price is to keep rising.

The rear-view mirror – use it, but don't over-use it!

Would you feel safe driving your car with most of the windscreen blocked by a rear-view mirror? Probably not, but investors, analysts, and company managers seem to spend much more time analyzing the financial history of a company than they spend forecasting its future. However accurate the historical figures, a good estimate of future financials is what we really need. Any self-respecting accountant would admit that meaningful financial statements are more the result of reasoned judgement than scientific precision. Forecasting future financials will be even less scientific and very subjective, yet systematic approaches are likely to produce the most useful and justifiable results; good quality data sources and a sound methodology are essential to meaningful forecasting.

Published financial statements are a primary source of data but we must recognize that they reveal only a narrow spectrum of management performance. They are designed to give a shareholder perspective and hence concentrate on explaining how well the company has performed and may not address the key question for a creditor, i.e. is the company solvent? In the past some countries have developed creditor-based accounting as befits their earlier economic development, but the increasing take-up of international accounting standards is resulting in the overriding shareholder focus becoming global.

As we look at the financial history of a company we must also recall that the accounts have a particular time focus. Not only does the slicing of the business into annual reporting periods not fit the economic activity of some companies, but the judgements on accounting policies are based on a medium-term view. The reality of cash is purposely distorted by recognized accounting methods to give a smoothed view of performance, for example by spreading the cost of investments over their expected useful lives and allowing companies to build stock and have slow debtor collection without any profit and loss penalty. Published accounts are useful but they have their limitations and hence the intelligent user must understand the "terms and conditions" that apply to them.

Why forecast?

Investors will want to forecast dividends and share price increases. Indeed, a company with a shareholder focus will want to prepare its own forecast to understand how satisfied its shareholders are likely to be. There are a variety of other groups of people, firms, and institutions that may be interested in forecasting the future performance of a company or group of companies and they may each have different reasons for embarking on the process. While these differences will affect what they do with the information they glean, the overall objective will be the same – an assessment of the future prospects for the company and the knock-on implications for them. In modern management speak, this means focussing on value.

Can we use the past to predict the future?

Yes and no. We can certainly interpret the company's recent financial performance in the light of its chosen strategy using the CORE (Context, Overview, Ratios, Evaluation) strategic financial appraisal model outlined by Bates and Moon in *CORE Analysis in Strategic Performance Appraisal*. This model first requires the user to fully consider the external context (the global economic and political environment) that impacts on the company's industrial sector, which in turn will impact on the company itself and be a key factor in the determination of the company's strategy. Next, the model reflects on the company's capabilities and other aspects of its internal context which must be set in tune with the environment through the company's chosen vision and strategy. Then it is advisable to gain an overview of the company's performance by inspecting key figures and trends and noting key events that may have a significant impact on financial performance. Armed with a full understanding of the context, all those tedious ratios become illuminating rather than confusing and we can explain the key movements in ratios in the light of our understanding of the company's environment and its chosen strategy.

Forecasting financials

- Company's financial performance
- Company's strategy and vision
- Company's internal context
- Industry/external context
- Global environment

The past and present → The future

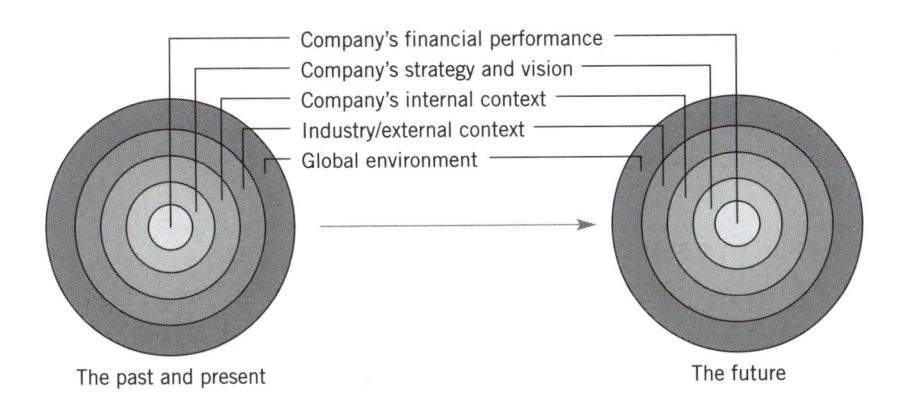

Figure 6.3: *Assessing the past and present and the future*

This will enable us to assess the current relationships (e.g. how sales growth is linked to investment in assets) and here we start to focus on the *drivers* of performance. If there were absolutely no changes on the horizon, we could easily produce a forecast from this information.

Of course there will inevitably be many changes, the company will constantly be reviewing its performance against budget, and if it is going off course action will be taken. In some circumstances the economic conditions will have changed so dramatically that a quick steering adjustment will not be enough to stay on the road and there may need to be a bigger feedback loop and a change to the strategy itself. In either case there will be altered relationships and we must estimate the effects on the key drivers of future performance and feed this new information into the preparation of our forecast.

In summary, we first need to assess the past and present environment and the associated company strategy and financial performance, and then form a view as to the likely future environment, and the effect that changes will have on strategy and future financial performance – as shown by Figure 6.3.

It is only by doing this that we give ourselves any hope of a sensible (and hence useful) forecast.

Mind over spreadsheet

It is no accident that analysts are sector specialists. The best forecasts come from those in the know. Insider dealing may be illegal, but that doesn't mean you should be completely uninformed. While there are plenty of readily available information sources, immersing yourself in an industry takes time and commitment as the knowledge domains may be more diverse than at first realized.

Steps in forecasting

Having given an overview of our recommended approach to forecasting let us get down to the detail and break the process down into a series of steps.

1. The objective of the forecast – why am I doing this?

We already mentioned that a current or potential shareholder investor and the market analyst may need the forecast in order to assess whether the value of the company is fully reflected in the current share price. The objective may be to decide whether to buy, sell, or hold the shares. The company's directors/management team will obviously be interested in investor and analysts' opinions and will want to undertake their own analysis for comparison. However, the managers are in a privileged position in terms of both the availability of information and having the opportunity to react to the findings. If the current share price is lower than predicted by their own forecast, perhaps the market does not have the "perfect information" that academic theories tend to assume and management may need to feed out relevant information. Alternatively management might need to face up to the nature of their rose-tinted spectacles.

Keeping the market abreast of recent strategic changes and developments is an art in itself – being illuminating without revealing and in particular not advantaging one group of shareholders over others. If the management forecast shows the current share price to be a little high there may be a need for urgent action to "change the future" and lend credence to the seemingly misplaced market optimism or an urgent need to "manage expectations."

A further reason for a forecast would be to identify acquisition or merger targets. Assuming we have sufficient access to information, we might need two or three separate forecasts. First we would prepare a forecast for the acquisition target on the assumption that it remains in its present ownership, as this will give an indication of the base value, perhaps the starting point for negotiations on price. This may well be close to the current share price, unless the company is already "in play." Working through this stage gives us a good understanding of current market expectations and provides the foundation for the assessment of alternative opportunities.

We then need to assess the value of this company to us and the safest way to do that is to value our own business "without" the acquisition (we might already have done this!) and then value it "with" the acquisition. The difference is the value (to us) of the target company, taking into account the synergies that can be achieved. If the difference is negative we should go no further, but if it is positive, and more than the value of the acquisition target in its current ownership, it will give us the top limit on our price. Persuading current shareholders to sell always requires the offering of a premium, so the positive gain in value needs to be greater than the 20 or 30 percent mark-up often needed to clinch the deal. Directors need to be careful to pay less than this "value to the acquirer," otherwise they would in effect be paying for the synergies that they have yet to create. The alternative valuations give the bandwidth within which to negotiate.

Competitors and those in trading relationships with the company also need to assess value and future prospects. Trading with winners is an obvious part of sensible strategy. Growing by 10 percent by having customers that are all growing at 10 percent is far more achievable than finding 10 percent more customers each year. Suppliers that make sufficient money to reinvest in themselves offer stable relationships. Value-creating competitors need to be watched carefully and learned from!

This list could be extended further to include, among others, trade unions assessing tactics on pay bargaining and government departments considering future employment prospects.

2. The environmental context

A detailed review of the past and future political and economic environment is an essential precursor to any review of past performance and any forecast of future results. To accomplish this requires wise use of inclusive models such as STEP (Sociological, Technical, Economic, and Political) and Porter's Five Forces Framework. This may seem like a tall order, but in many cases it will already have been done (e.g. in preparation for the last strategy away day) and only needs updating, and there are plenty of sources of information that may be accessed, such as *The Economist* and *FT* sector reports. This falls into two linked reviews – that of the wider environment and that of the specific industry being considered.

The annual reports of the major players in the market are an excellent source of data for this stage, so long as we remember the cautions noted at the start of this chapter. For example, to undertake a meaningful analysis of the car retailer Pendragon Plc, one would have to get a feel for the trading conditions for motor retailers in the UK, the US, and in Germany as these are the three main geographical locations of this company's dealerships. The annual report includes some analysis of the general economic climate in these three countries and its impact on motor trading. We may not agree fully with the analysis but it is a starting point for our research. We may also be informed about the company's reactions to its environment and we can feed this information into our predictions for future performance, e.g. the fact that there is little sign of improvement in the German market has led Pendragon to reduce the level of overheads in its six German dealerships, to counter the negative effects of falling sales volumes. Clearly our forecast will need to reflect lower sales and squeezed margins in Germany and we need to form a judgement about how long these adverse conditions are likely to last.

Independent assessments must be viewed alongside company statements as the "true" statements may not be "fair" in terms of balance or inclusiveness. Note that

US-based companies, and others which need to produce an American version of their accounts, are forced to give a more detailed market and risk assessment, making them much more useful for this purpose.

Getting into the closer external context in more detail requires us to move to the next circle in the diagram and look specifically at the industry and its key players to get a detailed understanding of the competitive environment faced by our company. We should analyze the market structure (where is it on the continuum from monopoly through oligopoly and monopolistic competition to perfect competition?) and consider the market concentration. For example, we can establish that more than 70 percent of the UK food retail market is accounted for by the four big players (recently reduced from five with the acquisition of Safeway by William Morrison), and we would want to explore how this affected the competitive intensity of the marketplace.

We need then to consider the different strategies of these key players and answer key questions, such as the following:

- Do they compete on similar lines or (more likely) do they have ways of differentiating themselves?
- How well are the alternative strategies working?
- Is there a market leader who sets the price?
- Who competes on a low-cost basis and who competes at the quality/value-added end of the market?

We must not forget to investigate important suppliers and customers and bear in mind that our definition of the market may be inadequate. For example, recent acquisitions by Tesco bring it into the convenience store sector with a 6 percent market share. The aim is to understand the situation well enough to be able to extrapolate likely events and scenarios into the future and hence value the businesses concerned.

3. The internal context

Having fully considered the external political and economic environment and its impact on the industry we need now to focus on the company itself and its internal context. Relevant factors will include its size and its relative market position, whether it is a key player which may have a major impact on the market itself, or whether it is merely small fry – competing at the edges and searching for a niche. The past and current level of profitability and the soundness of the company's financial structure will be important to future investment levels and its potential for growth. Ownership structure may be important too, not least in terms of the ease of access to financial markets. There are of course factors that cannot be gleaned from the financial statements – they may contain statements about vision and strategy, but what about the abilities of the management team, and the level of skill and knowledge of the company's workforce? Downsizing and cost-base reduction may enhance margins short term but what tacit knowledge is lost and is there a danger of weakening core capabilities?

We have stressed the need to examine the external environment, but we do not wish to underestimate the importance of gaining an understanding of the company's internal competencies. Throughout the 1990s there was a rebalancing of emphasis among strategy theorists, and in particular Hamel and Prahalad argued that "core competencies" are found within the company and that these can lead to competitive advantage. A view of strategy that starts and finishes with the outside world is unlikely to be adequate in either seeking out future success or weighing up the options and opportunities facing another business. Some insights into specific features or skills within the firm may be essential to understanding it now and in the future. However, Koch makes the point that finding such "nuggets" within your own company can be just wishful thinking. Perhaps the key to competitive advantage is the fit between the inside of the organization and its environment, hence a need to consider the quality of this fit by assessing the internal alongside the external.

4. The company's history and trends

It is important not to rush to calculate performance ratios, as in doing this too soon there is a danger of not being able to see the wood for the trees and hence finding it difficult to explain the ratios. We therefore need to get an overview by examining the recent trends in key figures (such as turnover, Ebit, net assets, Ebitda). This should give us "a feel" for what is going on, for example: an investment phase, rapid expansion, or declining profits. We can also list key facts or major events that may be relevant to our interpretation of the figures. Major acquisitions or disposals spring to mind, new contracts, new products, and new markets, refinancing plans, and changes in key personnel even.[1]

Changes in accounting policies may also be worth consideration and in fact where comparisons are being made from company to company we may need to adjust for different accounting policies – accounting standard harmonization will help a little here, but probably not as much as some seem to hope. One obvious example would be the recent high-profile disclosures that the new UK standard on pensions has caused – it would clearly be naive to ignore pensions.

5. Assessing financial performance in this context

Now we have an understanding of the situation as it has developed and some views as to what may happen next, we can choose appropriate financial ratios and interpret them in this context. There are many introductory texts to accounting that do a good job of explaining ratios and their meaning, e.g. *Accounting for Non-accounting Students* by J.R. Dyson. For a more thorough and developed approach, see *Interpreting Company Reports and Accounts* by Holmes, Sugden, and Gee.

If we are to forecast movements in profit, Ebitda, and value creation, we need to come up with parameters for factors such as sales margin (how many pence in each £ of sales gets right through to profit?) and asset utilization (how many £s of sales can be generated from each £ of assets?). Ratios produced from the last set of accounts are unlikely to give us the exact relationships that we should use going forward, but they form the base for a discussion on what the future values of key drivers may be. Establishing trends over a number of years would also show the direction and pace of change for a ratio and this, in the light of our analysis of the internal and external context and changes in strategy, will enable us to estimate the likely future values.

A word of caution – we should never take the existence of the long term for granted. It is always necessary to consider the possibility of the company running out of cash and being declared insolvent. A five-year forecast for a company on the brink of bankruptcy may be unduly optimistic.

6. Forming the model

We now need to pull together all the qualitative and quantitative information that we have gathered and building a spreadsheet model is likely to be the way forward. At this point a clear understanding of what drives performance and value is necessary for the linkages (formulae) to be derived. Rappaport came up with a system of seven drivers of value:

1. How long a company is likely to continue growing.
2. By how much each year are sales likely to grow?
3. The expected operating profit margin.
4. The expected corporation tax rate.
5. The need for investment in working capital (stock, etc.).
6. The need for investment in fixed assets (land, buildings, and equipment).
7. The rate at which the company needs to allow for the diminishing value of money over time as investors wait for their cash return (the cost of capital).

These are only the starting point. Rappaport himself refers to these as "macro drivers" which, in type, are common to all companies but are each made up of "micro drivers" that are business specific. For example, operating profit margin will be influenced by factors such as rising labor costs and the changing level of competitive forces. And note the links between drivers – the pace of sales growth will undoubtedly be influenced by investment in fixed assets and working capital, and vice versa. Managing the split between the fixed and variable costs – operational gearing – would be seen by some to be a further macro driver.

7. Building the model

The aim is to forecast the financials for the company. At this point spreadsheet skills come to the fore and a friendly accountant may well be a key member of the team. The drivers can be used to construct a year-by-year model of future financials – revenue, operating profit, Ebitda, and cash flows. However, we cannot simply add together the cash flows from future years to derive a present-day valuation for the company.

You are probably well aware of the costs for investors in waiting to receive an income stream from an investment – often referred to as the cost of capital (Rappaport's seventh driver). The key point behind this is that investors (like everyone else) would prefer cash now and need to be rewarded with more cash if they are made to wait. The amount of compensation they need is based on a number of factors. Generally the most important are thought to be the return on the lowest-possible-risk investment – usually lending to the government – and the relative risk of the firm's activities compared with the economy as a whole. Hence each year's cash flows are "discounted" at this rate – the further into the future, the more the present value of the cash flow is reduced.

A second difficulty in working out value is the forecasting horizon, which Rappaport referred to as the "value growth duration" period – the first driver in the list. A company may have been growing for four years at 20 percent per annum and it might be expected to do so for the next four years, but there has to come a point at which growth needs to slow down, probably to the rate of growth of the economy as a whole. To assume otherwise would be to assume that the firm could eventually be bigger than the global economy. This leaves us with a further problem – what to do with all the years beyond the growth horizon. The normal response is to have a "terminal year," a final year that is representative of all future years and then mathematically adjust the year to enable it to reflect the value of all future years beyond the growth horizon. This is shown diagrammatically in Figure 6.4 with the growth horizon assumed to be four years. The summed discounted cash flows give us an estimated corporate value of the firm.

8. Testing the model

Once the model has been designed and forecast driver values are inserted, one test is to see whether the value created, when adjusted for outstanding debt and divided by the number of shares in issue, resembles the current share price. The share price represents the views of the market about the future of the firm and its potential. Unless there are rumors of a takeover, reasonable forecast parameters should yield a result close to the current price – assuming the stock is actively traded. If so this is reassuring as it is a test of the "reasonableness" of the model and its assumptions. Alternatively a difference may be explained by the application of expert or inside knowledge (which the market does not possess) in the preparation of the forecast.

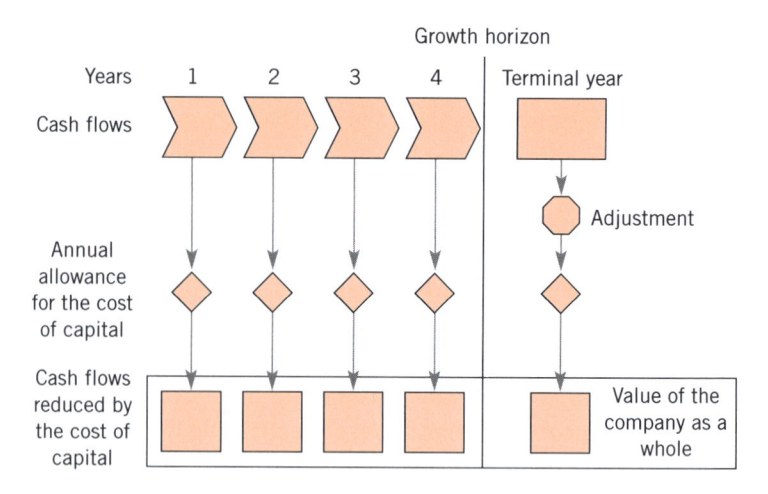

Figure 6.4: *Beyond the growth horizon*

9. Scenarios

Having a satisfactory model allows us to value the effect of alternative futures for the company under analysis. For example, what if we:

- Stop future capital investment, have lower growth, but potentially higher cash flows in earlier years – does this lead to a higher present value?
- Reduce margins, increase sales, and investment?
- Are faced with a major new competitor stealing a major slice of sales?

We can learn a great deal about a company's opportunities and the potential of it being run with a different strategy – as long as we have sufficient industry background to be able to think through the effects on the business of each change. Note however that we must not consider the effect of changes *we* might make in isolation of the likely reaction of *our competitors* and the other players in the industry – at least a previous industry analysis will prepare us to have a good attempt at this.

Keeping one step ahead

The future is never under control, but management can be negligent of their duties if they don't perform thorough research into their environment and formulate their plans and strategies using all the information available.

The changing environment needs to be reviewed often. One criticism of Porter's Five Forces Framework is that it is a static depiction of a dynamic situation. We must always look for what has changed and what will change in the future. Continuous monitoring of the situation is the best solution, but has significant cost. Building a database of relevant information, both hard and soft, and keeping it regularly updated is the sensible way to keep abreast of the effects of today's dynamic business environment.

For operational control reasons, the annual budgeting exercise may still be necessary, but there is a risk that this yearly exercise may just reduce flexibility and lengthen response times to environmental change – forecasts will need to be reviewed as often as the pace of change dictates. Such change is inevitable, management has a duty to predict it and react quickly and effectively. Managers never want to have to say "with the benefit of hindsight we see that we should have acted differently." With a comprehensive and scientific approach to forecasting they should provide themselves with the foresight to act appropriately – before it is too late.

Put another way, being one step behind is a recipe for disaster.

RESOURCES

Bates, K. and Whittington, M., 'Intense Competition, Revised Strategies and Financial Performance in the UK Food Retailing Sector,' in Jerker Nilsson and Gert van Dijk (eds), *Strategies and Structures in the Agro-food Industries*, Van Gorcum, 1996.

Dyson, J.R., *Accounting for Non-Accounting Students* (6th edition), FT Prentice Hall, 2003.

Hamel, G. and Prahalad, C.K., *Competing for the future*, Harvard Business School Press, 1994.

Holmes, G., Sugden, A. and Gee, P., *Intrepreting company reports and accounts* (8th edition), FT Prentice Hall, 2002.

Koch, R., *The Financial Times Guide to Strategy*, FT Prentice Hall, 2000.

Moon, P. and Bates, K., 'CORE Analysis in Strategic Performance Appraisal' *Management Accounting Research* 4:(2), June 1993.

Porter, M., *Competitive Advantage*, The Free Press, 1980.

Rappaport, A., *Creating Shareholder Value*, The Free Press, 1998.

Commentary

The rise of the Chief Risk Officer

The need for robust risk management processes is dramatically underlined by recent events. The war with Iraq and the increased threat of terrorist attack are just the most visible manifestations of the growing exposure to risk in the business world. Other factors include the rising tide of corporate failures and downgrades in credit ratings, volatility in equity markets, and tighter financial regulation in the wake of Enron and other corporate scandals.

Risk management is now a major concern in the boardroom. Over the last decade the challenges companies face in this area have increased significantly. This has prompted the creation of a new executive role – the Chief Risk Officer (CRO) – to co-ordinate risk management across organizations.

For many companies, the appointment of a CRO is the logical response. Richard Sharman, director of KPMG's Enterprise Risk Management Practice in the UK, confirms that there is a clear trend toward appointing someone with overall responsibility for risk management. "The catalyst for creating a head of risk or CRO is that organizations increasingly see the importance of risk management for managing a durable business," he says. "It is not a fad or fashion, but an increasingly vital part of managing a modern business."

There are estimated to be between 200 and 300 CROs worldwide, a figure predicted to rise to 1,000 by 2005. The origins of the role go back to the early 1990s when the first CROs began appearing on the organizational charts of US financial services companies.

Underpinning the CRO role is the idea of integrated risk management (IRM) – also called enterprise risk management. IRM involves managing risk across an organization's activities to manage the total exposure rather than treating different areas of risk in isolation. The CRO provides a central co-ordinator or champion.

The man credited with creating the role is James Lam, who was appointed CRO at GE Capital in 1993, and subsequently held the post at the mutual fund company Fidelity Investments before co-founding ERisk, a New York-based consulting firm. The job title was inspired by the rise of chief information officers (CIOs) at that time.

"I saw a parallel between IT and risk," Lam explains. "The CRO role has responsibility for integrating all forms of risk within a firm – including credit risk, market risk, and operational risk – and evaluating the awareness and understanding of these risks to the board level."

Today, the CRO role is most prevalent among banks and insurance companies. In a survey of 45 financial institutions across Europe and North America by consultants Oliver, Wyman & Company, for example, two-thirds endorsed the need for the CRO role. According to Tom Garside, managing director of the finance and risk practice at Oliver Wyman & Co., the job of the CRO is "to ensure that key risks, both financial and non-financial, are effectively identified, quantified, and mitigated wherever they occur across the company."

In the financial community, the CRO role is now well-established. "The majority of financial institutions in the UK, and across the developed world, have now appointed a chief risk officer," says Sally Rowley-Williams, who leads the global wealth management division of headhunter Korn-Ferry. "The position has largely arisen within the past five years in response to increased regulation and an increasingly complex world in general."

The CRO role or equivalent is now spreading across all industries, according to Richard Sharman. "They may or may not be called the CRO, but increasingly there is someone responsible for co-ordinating risk management across all areas of the organization," he says. "Other titles are director of risk management, or global head of risk management. The key thing is that someone is now looking at risk across the organization – not just at insurable risk, health and safety issues, or business continuity, but right across all these areas."

He says that where a CRO is formally appointed the individual is typically part of the executive management team, just below board level. In other cases, the role may be fulfilled by someone who still reports to the CFO or finance director. The experience required for the job depends on the situation. "To work on the management team, a CRO needs a strong background in business, not necessarily a background in risk management," says Sharman. "There will be a structure below with heads of risk management reporting to them." But if they are lower down, reporting to a CFO, he says, the role is more likely to be filled by someone with a background in risk management.

Heightened awareness of risk in UK boardrooms is likely to accelerate the trend. Research indicates that companies see a rise in their exposure to risk in the current environment. In a November 2002 survey of financial directors and other directors in FTSE 500 companies by the Institute of Chartered Accountants of England and Wales and the Risk Advisory Group, the majority reported the risks to their businesses had increased significantly in the past 12 months.

Directors saw risk rising across a range of areas, including accounting issues such as financial misstatement, non-compliance with laws and regulations, and terrorist and criminal acts. Reputation was seen as the most important risk, but the largest perceived increase came from the economic and political environment.

Commentary (continued)

Yet despite these concerns, the survey found that there is room for improvement in board-level monitoring.

One in four boards (26 percent) reviews such risks formally only once every six months or less. A half (47 percent) review risk at every board meeting and the remainder (27 percent) review risks once a quarter. Even among the largest companies in the sample (those with a turnover of £1 billion or more), one in six (17 percent) conducts formal reviews only once every six months or less. Appointing a CRO would seem to be a logical step to plug this gap.

"The CEO is ultimately the chief risk officer in any organization. I don't think anyone would disagree with that," says KPMG's Richard Sharman. "But the CEO hasn't got time to do that on a daily basis so the CRO does it for them. But to do the job properly, the CRO needs sufficient authority to put risk management on the organizational agenda and drive through them".

Financial literacy: understanding the numbers

ROMESH VAITILINGAM

[Everything we do in business has some effect on the "numbers" – whether they're costs, gearing, profits, return on investment, or sales. For those who are unwilling, or unable, to attain a basic grasp of the financial implications of their actions, managing effectively becomes difficult, rising to the top almost impossible.]

It is true there may have been a time when financial literacy was not quite so essential. In the highly functionalized and hierarchical organizations common in the past, perhaps some successful managers could proceed through their entire careers with only a limited knowledge of finance. But not now. In the flatter organizations of the modern world, where responsibility is typically devolved to business units, managers need a far broader range of expertise and the ability to qualify virtually all their decisions in financial terms.

There's no doubt that the people who do really well in business these days have a sophisticated knowledge of finance. And the reason is clear: as you rise through an organization, so many things relate to the numbers. To be taken seriously by the FDs, the MBAs, and accountancy-trained colleagues, to construct budgets and win the internal battles for resources, you must be able to talk the language of finance. Money and authority inevitably go to the most trusted people in an organization and they will be the ones who can explain convincingly the impact of their projects on the bottom-line.

But becoming finance-savvy is not just about ambition. It's also about taking responsibility for the investment your employer is making in you. In the first few years of your career, it's almost certainly right to focus on your primary task – whether it's selling in huge numbers, designing inspired marketing plans, or inventing great new products. But to take responsibility for a team, a department, or a business unit, you have to take financial responsibility. You must get used to being chased repeatedly for your numbers – whatever the indicators are by which your boss will measure your performance.

Taking responsibility for financial outcomes applies equally if you plan to go out on your own further down the road. Whether you intend to be an individual entrepreneur or a rising star within a large corporation, you'll need resources. That means taking responsibility for the money you're being given by the bank, by a venture capitalist, or by your employer. And you can do that only by becoming financially literate – not just numerate but also able to understand what the numbers really mean.

Figuring it out

So what exactly do you need to know? First, there are the three main financial statements of company life: the profit and loss account (P&L), the balance sheet, and the cash flow statement. Most managers are familiar with the first of these and its relatively straightforward formula that profits (for a company, a division, a business unit, or even a single product line) equals sales minus direct costs and expenses. Fewer people understand the balance sheet, which indicates the real health of the business: how much it owes and how much it is owed. And fewer still grasp the vital importance of cash flow, how much money is coming in and out of the business.

From these three statements come the key ratios that can be used to manage the business. These include gearing (the extent to which the company relies on other people's money – debt), return on investment (profits as a percentage of the capital employed to earn them), and gross and net profit margins (profits before and after deducting expenses as a percentage of sales).

At a more local level, financial literacy demands the ability to create a departmental budget – to lay out your plans for the coming year in terms of projected sales, production costs, selling and distribution costs, and expenses. It also demands the ability to make a case for new projects through the process of investment appraisal. To get the resources to implement your latest great idea, you must be able to analyze the costs and benefits of the project, its future path of profit and cash flow, and its risks. Most importantly, you need to understand the time value of money – that because of uncertainty, money expected in the future is worth less than money in the bank today.

Finally, aspiring managers must get to grips with the big-picture financial issues that are specific to their companies and then understand what that means for the appropriate focus of their business units. These will vary according to what senior managers and shareholders care about and the key drivers of business success in the industry. In retailing, for example, where profit margins are incredibly thin, the primary goal is to protect those margins through fierce cost control and rapid stock-turn. In contrast, in management consultancy, where expenses are huge but so are margins, business managers tend to be most concerned about increasing sales or "top line" growth.

Improving financial competence

That's the basic syllabus. But how should you go about improving your knowledge of finance? The ideal way is to do it internally by finding a mentor, someone who understands the company's finances and is willing to help you learn. Make friends with the FD or business manager for your division: they will appreciate your enthusiastic interest and as powerful players in any company, once they trust you and your burgeoning financial literacy, you will have a great ally. And as your competence with the numbers grows, demand more information from your senior colleagues: how profitable is my division and my product? And more broadly, what do the shareholders want in terms of financial performance?

An alternative or additional strategy is to go on a course. It's hard to beat the potential impact on your career development of a week's intensive training in "finance for the boardroom" or "finance for non-financial managers." The finance components of distance learning or part-time MBAs from one of the top business schools are also worth looking at.

Finally, you can teach yourself via books and the web. There are plenty of useful paperback introductions out there, including *The Penguin Guide to Finance* by former Financial Times journalist Hugo Dixon, and *Smart Things to Know About Business Finance* by Ken Langdon and Alan Bonham.

Online, the choice is vast. Many of the best guides to finance online come at it from the perspective of investing in the stock market. But the principles of company valuation they describe all fit neatly together with the principles of business finance you'll want to understand. If you can appreciate what shareholders are looking for, you'll begin to see how those aims cascade down through an organization to the things you'll increasingly be hoping to manage: budgets, new project appraisal, and the overall financial performance of your business unit.

In terms of training products aimed directly at improving professional management skills, including financial expertise, Capstone Publishing's Express Exec is a promising example. And Pearson's Financial Minds site is an excellent starting point for a range of educational material available both online and in print – and takes you from the basics of financial literacy right through to stuff you may need when you've reached the very top.

RESOURCES

Bonham, Alan and Langdon, Ken, *Smart Things to Know About Business Finance*, Capstone, 1999.
Dixon, Hugo, *The Penguin Guide to Finance*, Penguin Books, 2000.

www.financialminds.com

The real Warren Buffett

JAMES O'LOUGHLIN

[Warren Buffett, the greatest investor of our times, is hailed for his investment wisdom. But his real wisdom lies in acting like a CEO, an owner rather than an investor.]

"We're only responsible for two functions ... First, it's our job to keep able people who are already rich motivated to keep working ... Secondly, we have to allocate capital."

Warren Buffett[2]

Warren Buffett is chairman and chief executive of Berkshire Hathaway, an enormously diverse company with interests that stretch from the insurance industry to shoe manufacturing and from the production of flight simulators to vacuum cleaners. It generates revenues in excess of $42 billion, employs over 45,000 people, and measured by its market capitalization of $137 billion is the 12th largest company in the US. Remarkably, along with his partner, Charlie Munger, Buffett manages this undertaking with a staff of just 12 other people. Yet during his 38 years at the helm, Buffett has grown the stock market value of Berkshire Hathaway at a compound growth rate of over 23 percent per year. That means anyone who had the foresight to invest $10,000 in Berkshire Hathaway 38 years ago when Buffett took charge of the company would have seen the value of this stake grow to a colossal $42 million. By comparison, $10,000 invested in the S&P 500 in 1965 would today be worth the pygmy sum of less than $500,000.

The surprise for most people is that Warren Buffett has not delivered this performance by being a stock picker, the activity in which he famously excels. Instead, he has done it by being a CEO. He has resolved the conflict that exists between managers and shareholders by acting like an owner; taking corporate governance to a higher level. He has elicited levels of compliance from his senior managers that disciples of command-and-control would not dream of, paradoxically, by setting his managers free from control. And he has engineered a mandate that gives him freedom to allocate capital where, when, and at the pace he sees fit that has proven vital to Buffett's ability to shape-shift Berkshire through nearly four decades of change. Warren Buffett has achieved all this by managing capital and leading people.

Managing capital and leading people

"We've been deploying capital since I was 11. That's our business."

Warren Buffett[3]

"He has a way of motivating you. He trusts you so much that you just want to perform."

Bill Child, R.C. Willey Home Furnishings[4]

Buffett bought his initial stake in Berkshire Hathaway, a New England manufacturer of textiles, in 1962, seven years after forming a partnership to invest in the stock market. On closer inspection Buffett recognized that Berkshire was over investing in an inherently low-return business, thereby squandering the opportunity to invest in areas of higher return. Subsequently, he took the unusual step for a fund manager of acquiring a controlling interest in the company and installing himself as chairman.

Buffett's training as an investor taught him that "the investment shown by the discounted-flows-of-cash calculation to be the cheapest is the one that the investor should purchase."[5] This conveyed upon Buffett a perspective on the role of the corporate manager that other managers lacked: as allocator of capital. "The heads of many companies are not skilled in capital allocation," comments Buffett. "Most bosses rise to the top because they have excelled in some area such as marketing, production, engineering, [or] administration … Once they become CEOs, they face new responsibilities. They must now make capital allocation decisions, a critical job that they never have tackled and that is not easily mastered."[6]

Uniquely for a CEO, Buffett came to conceive himself as a fragment of a capital market, the job of which is to direct resources to where they can be most efficiently utilized within the economy. Indeed, within Berkshire Buffett became a one-man capital market, allocating capital to its point of best use within his circle of competence, be this in the insurance industry, candy manufacturing or any other business that he intuitively understands, is able to forecast and can value. He therefore rationed Berkshire's use of capital and funneled the excess into investments that would yield permanently higher returns. Since it gave him discretion over a company's cash flow, Buffett's preference was (is) for outright ownership rather than fractional ownership via the stock market – hence Berkshire's conglomerate structure.

Saving for shareholders

"Although our form is corporate, our attitude is partnership. Charlie Munger and I think of our shareholders as owner-partners, and as ourselves as managing partners."

Warren Buffett[7]

As a major shareholder in Berkshire, Buffett's motive for pursuing this strategy was self-interested – but not selfish. The ethos that underpins Buffett's role as allocator of capital also originated from his previous career. Just as he husbanded his partners" savings as an investor, he resolved that his job as a manager would also be to save, this time on behalf of his shareholders. This is what it is to act like an owner in the management of an enterprise.

Accordingly, Buffett came to describe Berkshire Hathaway not as an insurance company or conglomerate but as a "corporate saver."[8] Berkshire "saves for its shareholders," says Buffett "by retaining all earnings, thereafter using these savings to purchase businesses and securities."[9] The assurance he gives his shareholders in doing so is this: "We will only do with your money what we would do with our own, weighing fully the values you can obtain by diversifying through direct purchases in the stock market."[10] Naturally, this means Buffett fixes his gaze firmly on the long term: after all, he is part owner of a business that he "expects to stay with indefinitely."[11] And, since he has "always preferred a lumpy 15 percent return to a smooth 12 percent," he cares not a fig for short term results, as long as he has a rational expectation of ultimately delivering returns to his shareholders above those available to them from a diversified portfolio of investments.[12]

Occupying the high ground in the allocation of capital, Buffett's principle of acting like an owner is also the instrument of his leadership. Buffett rejects the Jack Welch school of authoritarian management, which speaks of a distrust of that part of human nature that will attend to its own interests if allowed – "setting stretch goals, and relentlessly following up on people to make sure things get done."[13] Buffett opts instead for a model that is founded on that immutable tenet of human behavior that informs him that the trust and fairness with which the treats managers will be reciprocated with compliance and effort.

That is why Buffett sets his managers – whom he chooses with extreme care – free from control. Buffett's is a leadership model that taps into the most powerful motivational force that humans know: the intrinsic motivation that comes from within, which, in this case, tells his managers that acting like an owner is the right way to behave. Professing that his managers "are truly in charge,"[14] Buffett's only request of them is that they "run their companies as if these are the sole asset of their families and will remain so for the next century."[15] In doing this, he assures them that there will be no "show-and-tell presentations in Omaha, no budgets to be approved by headquarters, no dictums issued about capital expenditures."[16]

Buffett's hidden police officer is the remuneration policy that he puts in place at Berkshire, which is designed to reinforce the intrinsic motivation of his managers by rewarding the behaviors that underpin the principle of acting like an owner and discouraging those that threaten to undermine it. Buffett charges his managers for the use of Berkshire's capital; bonuses are premised on return on capital rather than size or growth and are put at risk; managers are only paid for results that are within their own bailiwick (which gets them to take the inner responsibility for their behavior that Buffett craves and which psychologists recommend), and most importantly, via the architecture of their bonus structure, managers are incentivized to send excess capital to Buffett so that he, the one-man capital market, gets to allocate it rather than them.

The results are impressive. The return on equity in most of Berkshire's subsidiaries is extraordinarily high and a river of cash flows to Omaha. During the 15 years of his tenure, for example, Ralph Schey, CEO of Scott Fetzer, one of Berkshire's largest subsidiaries, sent $1,030 million to Buffett against a net purchase price for the business of $230 million.[17] Similarly, Chuck Huggins at See's Candies put up earnings of $857 million pre-tax by 1999, on a purchase price of $25 million in 1972, absorbing very little additional capital in the process.[18] Crucially, those managers who have run out of opportunities to deploy capital at required returns have been content – contrary to normal managerial instinct – to see their domains shrink. And yet, in his 2002 letter to Berkshire's shareholders, Buffett could boast that, in 38 years, he has never had a single CEO of a subsidiary elect leave Berkshire to work elsewhere. This is compliance of the highest order.

Evolutionary robustness

> "We do have a few advantages, perhaps the greatest being that we don't have a strategic plan."
>
> Warren Buffett[19]

Buffett needs such compliance. He wants to allocate Berkshire's capital, not micro manage its affairs, and he needs capital to allocate. It's his talent for managing in this sense that largely explains Berkshire's superior returns. Alarmingly, however, Buffett does so without a strategy. "To earn 15 percent annually will require a few big ideas," he tells his shareholders. "Charlie Munger ... and I do not have any such ideas at present, but our experience has been that they pop up occasionally. (How's that for a strategic plan?)"[20]

Buffett has two reasons for ditching the strategic plan. First, he does not believe that the economy lends itself to forecasting. "We have no view of the future that dictates what business or industries we will enter ... [and] we will continue to ignore political and economic forecasts, which are an expensive distraction for many investors and businessmen," he says.[21] Second, Buffett recognizes that strategic plans incline managements to the cardinal sin of polarizing around them to the exclusion of other possible uses of capital and normally, since this is where their self-interest is found, to pursue growth.

Managing without a plan, Buffett is able to attest: "We're not in any business, per se. We're big in insurance, but we're not committed to it. We don't have a mindset that says you have to go down this road. So we can take capital and move it into businesses that make sense."[22] That explains why he and Munger "feel no need to proceed in an ordained direction ... but can instead simply decide what makes sense for our owners."[23] In doing that, Buffett always compares any move with dozens of other opportunities open to him: "a discipline that managers focussed simply on expansion seldom use."[24]

Berkshire's cornerstone insurance businesses grant Buffett a particular advantage in this regard. In a way that most industries do not allow, Buffett can operate these at quarter-speed when pricing is poor and turn on the volume through an unimpaired distribution network when pricing is attractive.[25] Notwithstanding this edge, Buffett has shaped Berkshire Hathaway to the shifting contours of an unpredictable environment, inexorably migrating capital from areas of diminishing return toward manifestations of higher return. Tomorrow he will do the same, and Berkshire will change shape once more, possibly to something resembling a prior form, or, since its scope "is not circumscribed by history, structure, or concept,"[26] most likely into a novel configuration. Berkshire Hathaway is thus a product of the irregular environment in which it operates, not an imposition of Warren Buffett's will upon it. And it is the evolutionarily robustness that Buffett has engineered into Berkshire that both explains Buffett's longevity at its helm (against the eight-year average tenure of a CEO) and the startling returns he has delivered to its shareholders.

To act like an owner

> "CEO's don't need 'independent' directors, oversight committees or auditors absolutely free of conflicts of interest. They simply need to do what's right."
>
> Warren Buffett[27]

> "We receive our rewards as owners, not managers ... We look at the business as to how much we're worth, not the stock price – because the stock price doesn't mean a thing to us."
>
> Warren Buffett[28]

In spite of widespread evidence of failure, the accepted method of encouraging managers to act like owners is regulatory in nature. Boards of directors exist to represent the interests of shareholders and to keep managers in check. Stock markets are there to vote daily on managerial performance. Warren Buffett needs neither. He acts like an owner because *he thinks like an owner*, and his standards of corporate governance are assured by the practical alternative he has embraced: personal integrity combined with an alignment between his interests and those of his shareholders.

Current practice has it that managers wishing for such alignment should pursue it through the use of share ownership. Buffett is skeptical of this arrangement. Many managers "start with the assumption, all too common," says Buffett "that their job at all times is to encourage the highest stock price possible."[29] His concern is that managers who have both eyes fixed on the stock market cease to focus on managing the business and proceed to manage the expectations upon which stock prices are set; a dance with "investors" that can become a compulsive embrace. "A significant and growing number of otherwise high-grade managers … have come to the view that it's okay to manipulate earnings to satisfy what they believe are Wall Street's desires," observes Buffett. "Indeed, many CEOs think this kind of manipulation is not only okay but actually their *duty*."[30] All too often this leads to chicanery. "Charlie and I have observed many instances in which CEOs engaged in uneconomic operating maneuvers so that they could meet earnings targets they had announced," attests Buffett.[31] And, as CEO behavior corrodes, uneconomic maneuvers often transcend into the accounting fixes that Buffett likens to heroin addiction[32] – with results that should be predictable.

Achieving true alignment

> "We do not want to maximize the price at which Berkshire shares trade. We wish instead for them to trade in a narrow range centered at intrinsic business value."
>
> Warren Buffett[33]

Buffett's revelationary insight into aligning his interests with those of his shareholders is to strive for market efficiency in Berkshire's stock price, not maximization. That way Buffett can concentrate on managing the business *and* measure his wealth by how well the business is performing, free from distractions and contrary motives.

In pursuit of market efficiency, Buffett recognizes that "management cannot determine market prices" but that it can, "by its disclosures and policies, encourage rational behavior by market participants."[34] Accordingly, Buffett reports fully and fairly the data that helps investors answer three key questions: "(1) Approximately how much is this company worth? (2) What is the likelihood that it can meet its future obligations? And (3) How good a job are its managers doing, given the hand they have been dealt?"[35]

In doing this Buffett *tells it like it is*. He does not dress up Berkshire's results for consumption. "Many managements view GAAP not as a standard to be met but as an obstacle to overcome."[36] He publicly warns his shareholders when he believes Berkshire's stock is mispriced. And he is at pains to put current results into long-term perspective. "We may have years when we exceed 15 percent," he tells them by way of example "but we will most certainly have other years when we fall far short of that – including years showing negative returns."[37]

An essential element in Buffett's pursuit of alignment is to attract the right kind of shareholders to Berkshire Hathaway. If the turnover in Berkshire shares approximated that of the average listed company, which exceeds 100 percent, its shareholders would not be saving with Buffett; they would be speculating via him. In this case his mandate would *not* be to act like an owner; it would be to act like the CEOs that are the source of his skepticism. Buffett recognizes therefore that in order to pursue his vision he has to attract investors who also think like owners.

"To obtain quality shareholders is no cinch,"[38] observes Buffett, but "we feel that high-quality ownership can be attracted and maintained if we consistently communicate our business and ownership philosophy – *along with no other conflicting messages* – and then let self-selection follow its course. We try to attract investors who will understand our operations, attitudes, and expectations ... fully as important, we try to dissuade those who won't. We want those who think of themselves as business owners and invest in companies with the intention of staying a long time."[39]

Serendipitously, Berkshire's shareholders, "if properly informed," says Buffett, "can handle unusual volatility in profits so long as the swings carry with them the prospect of superior long-term results." Since he wants his managers "to think about what counts, not how it will be counted," this means that he can tell them "they should not let any of their decisions be affected even slightly by accounting considerations."[40] In addition, Buffett can instruct his managers to "manage for maximum long-term value, rather than for next quarter's earnings."[41] By contrast, he argues "very few CEOs of public companies operate under a similar mandate, mainly because they have owners who focus on short-term prospects and reported earnings."[42]

Buffett's strategy works. "Over the long term," he says, "there has been a more consistent relationship between Berkshire's market value and business value than has existed for any other publicly-traded equity with which I am familiar,"[43] and he maintains "we are almost certainly the leader in the degree to which our shareholders think and act like owners."[44]

So saying, Buffett achieves the Holy Grail of aligning his interests with those of his shareholders. He secures their mandate to manage Berkshire according to his strengths and, *sans* strategy, unusual style. He acts like the owner he wants to be. He carries his managers with him as he does so. And, by design, he delivers.

*The quotes taken from Warren Buffett's letters to his shareholders are by kind permission of Mr Buffett.

RESOURCES

O'Loughlin, J., *The Real Warren Buffett*, Nicholas Brealey, 2002.

www.ragm.com
www.lens.com
www.fortuneinvestor.com

www.bigcharts.com
www.yardeni.com

Marketing: the trouble with finance

TIM AMBLER

[*Top executives are reassured by financial measurements. But that may not always be the best way to plan and measure the effectiveness of the marketing effort.*]

Just as in ages past alchemists sought the philosopher's stone, so 21st-century executives try to express important concepts in single financial numbers. "That's a great idea," they say, "but what will be the effect on shareholder value?" Consequently, in our research, we routinely found top-flight managers who were unable to understand brand equity as being anything but its financial valuation. If this level of simplification made any sense, management would be child's play.

Managing for value has become a dominant philosophy in many modern companies. Strategic options are analyzed to provide their forecast shareholder value and determined accordingly. Costs are reduced and assets are squeezed. The question is whether this approach assists or damages the generation of inward cash flow, i.e. marketing. We should not be surprised if any new managerial panacea, such as this, turns out to have hidden dangers.

Four centuries intervened between Sir Walter Raleigh's promotion of tobacco in Europe and our recognition of its damage to health. In moderation, the mind-altering effects of alcohol are benign; damage results only from excess. Financial analysis is both essential for modern business and, in moderation, beneficial, but addiction may cost your company dearly.

Maximizing the ROI on marketing

Calls for marketers to achieve more with less money have been growing. Other executives harbor the suspicion that marketing is an extravagance and should be put through the same financial wringer as other functions. The call goes up to maximize the ROI on marketing. They do not, of course, mean marketing in the broad sense. That would be like asking for the ROI on eating: if you do not do it, you die. A firm that suspended marketing in the broad sense (generating cash flow) would soon be bankrupted. The challenge is to promotional expenditure and, especially, advertising.

In principle, ROI is a useful way to choose the preferred option for the marketing mix when the total budget is fixed. But ROI can be seriously misleading when it is used more broadly. In the first place, those using ROI in marketing usually just compare a year's revenue with a year's investment. They forget that the year's revenue is the result of investment in previous years and, likewise, this year's investment will build brand equity for the future.

If the net profit – that is, the return – is positive, the firm should do more of it until the returns turn south. Figure 6.5 illustrates the point: the high point of the profit line maximizes the return. On the other hand, the maximum ROI, which divides the profit by the "investment," is well short of that – a sub-optimal choice.

ROI makes more sense when, as may be the case for advertising or a new brand launch, it is truly an investment – that is, the payback comes in later years. But here too it fails. Accountants have long since, and rightly, moved to the concept of present value, discounted cash flow (DCF) less the cost of the investment. "Payback" – how long it will take to recover the cost of the investment – is the crude alternative and is often a useful rule of thumb.

When people talk of the ROI from marketing they usually mean the profit return after deducting the cost of the campaign: it is return *minus* investment, not return *divided by* investment. And of course we are considering discretionary marketing activities (the budget), not marketing as a whole. When making this point, one response has been that the ratio is still useful for comparing alternative uses, in marketing or in other areas, of the same budget. In fact, if the I is constant, then R–I peaks at the same point R/I does, so the ratio is still redundant at best and possibly misleading. The immediate reaction to a high ratio is the expectation that more should be spent which means that the I is no longer constant and the logic is disappearing up its own nadir.

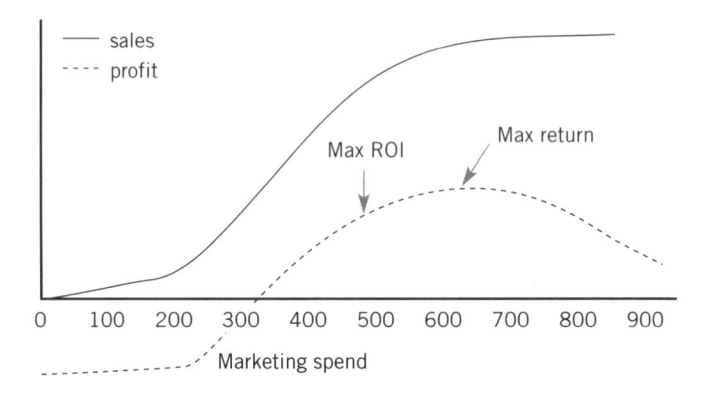

Figure 6.5: *Marketing returns*

Marketing: the trouble with finance   467

Furthermore, the ROI approach was devised for assessing capital projects where the investment is made once and the returns flow during the following years. Marketers like to flatter themselves that marketing is an "investment" in much the same way that politicians refer to any expenditure favored by them as investments but this is misuse of language. Marketing expenditure is continuous and, mostly, maintains the brand and the bottom line. Some of it may be investment for the future, or disinvestments if brand equity is being drained. In any case it is not all investment and it is misleading to treat it as such.

Thus DCF is a sound tool for comparing alternative ways to spend a firm's discretionary cash but ROI is not. A more reliable process is to establish what levels of expenditure seem to be needed to achieve goals and then fine-tune the plan to achieve the same, or at least acceptable, goals for less cost.

In short, ROI is never a useful ratio in marketing because it uses division where there should be subtraction. DCF and payback are, however, valid methodologies. If the comparison is just within a single year, then the net profit returns are enough. In all cases, allowance should be made for any significant change in brand equity and talk of the return from marketing rather than the ROI or ROME (Return On Marketing Expenditure).

The dangers of brand valuation

As an example of best practice, Figure 6.6, developed by Adrian Joseph and colleagues at AT Kearney and Ogilvy, shows a strong (0.7) relationship between the

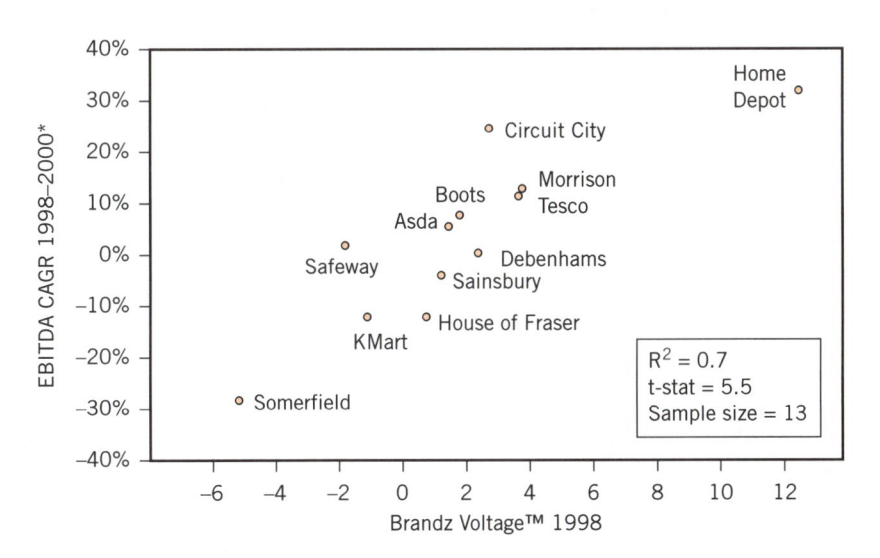

Figure 6.6: *Brand equity drives future profits*

Source: AT Kearney, 2002, Brandz Voltage™ from Millward Brown.
* Compound annual growth rate of earnings before interest, taxes, depreciation, and amortization (June 1998–June 2000)

Millward Brown index of brand strength (Brandz Voltage) and the two subsequent years' profits for selected US and UK retailers. The vertical axis is "earnings before interest, tax, depreciation, and amortization compound annual growth rate." The selection of retailers in this analysis was based on the availability of data and it is possible that some bias may thereby have been inadvertently created. Nevertheless, such technicalities do not detract from the successful use of brand equity as a predictor of future profits.

Figure 6.6 differs from the oft-made comparison of brand valuation and market capitalization. One usually finds a decent correlation and the claim is then made that brand equity drives the share price. This is bogus. Most brand valuations are based on the forecasts of future cash flow less the hypothetical cash flows from an equivalent but unbranded product. Since the cash flow from a non-existent product is difficult to estimate, some judgement is made of the branding effect in year one and the cash flows thereafter follow similar trajectories.

Market capitalization is also, at least in perfect markets theory, a projection of cash flows from the same firm. Accordingly, all three cash flows are broadly the same. One would not expect correlation to be faultless since markets are not perfect and different people make the projections, but they should be strong. This has nothing to do with brands driving anything; they are just different projections of the same artificial data. If I chose to call the present value of this cash flow a turnip, then a turnip would be an excellent predictor of market value. Indeed, turnips may even be driving market capitalization.

Brand valuation is being used internally and its great attraction is the first impact on top executives made by its financial size. Brand valuation gets the marketing foot in the executive door if it is not already there. Thereafter the benefits prove elusive and companies either widen the market metrics they review or give up brand valuation. Some are more determined.

A senior manager at a leading UK bank told us: "What we couldn't do was take that [brand valuation] and turn it into any kind of tangible measure and equate it to business decisions. There would be strange things, like we sell more product and make more money for shareholders, but the brand value would go down. There were a lot of peculiar things you just couldn't make sense of. The only thing we could equate it to was just the fact that it didn't take account of some of the financial management tools that we have to use in this market. And when other people's businesses shrank their brand value went up."

Companies using brand valuation as part of marketing performance assessment may well be right to do so if it is one of a range of metrics. It should not be used as a sole indicator of brand equity. Specialist brand valuation companies agree that the process of marketing analysis that leads to the valuation is important not the number itself.

In all of this, the question of brands on the balance sheet has been a distraction. No country allows the value of brands to be placed on balance sheets although the UK allows the *cost* of certain acquired brands to be included. The cost has to be shown to exceed current (internal) valuations but, unless the value has fallen seriously, it is the original purchase price that appears, not the current value. Internally, the financial value of the brand is unlikely to provide useful information beyond an appreciation of scale.

The reality is that valuation based on projections of cash flow is flawed both behaviorally (forecasting is inherently unreliable) and conceptually (because those forecasts include the results of future marketing).

Customer lifetime value in theory and practice

Faced by these difficulties, attention has moved from the brand to the customer with the recognition that customer retention typically provides a better financial return than seeking new customers. Within that, firms are recommended to analyze their customer base according to the profitability of each segment and allocate resources accordingly.

The theory is based on customer loyalty. The late Professor Peter Doyle, for example, suggested that "for most companies, customer loyalty is the single most important determinant of long-term growth and profit margins." Frederick Reichheld instigated the movement and asserted that a customer loyal over, say, seven years contributes six or seven times more than a new customer in his or her first year. This arises from:

- increasing expenditure over time as loyalty breeds increased demand;
- reduced operating costs as the company and customer become familiar with each other;
- referrals as loyal customers increasingly recommend the company to others;
- price premium as longstanding customers become progressively less price sensitive.

Plausible as they may seem, and each is true sometimes, all four claims are dubious. None has been supported empirically. Professor Robert East and colleagues have challenged the increasing gain from referrals. They looked at recommendation rates in four types of services compared with the length of time that the respondents had been customers (tenure). In three out of four cases, recommendation declined over time.

They concluded that the relationship between referrals and tenure was context (sector) dependent. In most cases, initial enthusiasm can be something of a honeymoon effect. The exception was car servicing, which is both complex and an experience that extends over several years. In these circumstances, compared with their other three services (current account banking, credit cards, and car insurance), the views of long-term users would be increasingly sought and given credence. East and colleagues had previously found decreasing recommendations with tenure for hairdressing and supermarkets.

Very similar conclusions were drawn in a larger US study by Professors Werner Reinartz and V. Kumar, who do not pull their punches: "Much of the common wisdom about customer retention is bunk." Like East they found that longer-term customers were not "necessarily cheaper to serve, less price sensitive, or particularly effective at bringing in new business." They also cast doubt on Reichheld's second and fourth points (cost to serve and price sensitivity). My colleague, Professor Kathy Hammond, is working on the first claim and her evidence so far does not support the Reichheld hypothesis.

Nevertheless, the prevailing advice remains to analyze customers into segments but not to assume that they will automatically become more profitable with time. They will become more or less profitable according to their future needs and how you tailor your market to fit.

Even Reichheld could not have imagined that the relationship between the value of the customer and tenure was linear because, sooner or later, all customers die. This is not as trite a point as it may seem because it is the key distinction between working at the individual and segment levels. Even where customers are companies, they will, sooner or later disappear. So let us assume it looks something like Figure 6.7.

In the first year, due to acquisition costs, the company makes a loss. Business expands quite fast up to year five and then more slowly until decline sets in and, ultimately, death brings down the curtain. Customer lifetime value (CLV) is defined to be the net present value of the customer but here is where the fudge comes in. In practice, very few firms do, or could do, this calculation for each customer. In their place, customer segments are used. It could be a cohort that would march through time like a customer, and ultimately die. But far more often, segments are defined in fixed socio-economic or behavioral ways so individuals move through segments. For example, the segment containing pregnant mothers is forever pregnant.

If you plot the customer (segment) value over time, it will be fairly flat in a stable business. It will look nothing like Figure 6.7. The number of customers in that segment may also be constant because acquisitions are offsetting customer losses. In

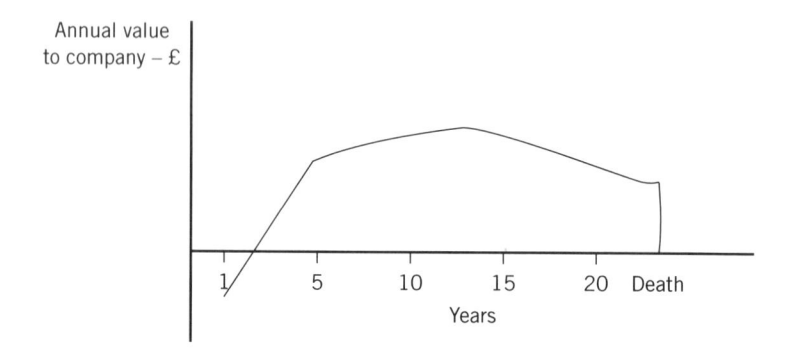

Figure 6.7: *Customer lifetime value*

other words, the whole logic of the single-customer life cycle is lost when customers are replaced by segments.

Of course, it is good practice to allocate marketing budgets to segments according to the probable cash flow consequences. But this is not to say that, as CLV enthusiasts often do, most resources should be allocated to the most valuable customers.

Retail banks in the UK all adopted this idea around 2000. They identified a "wealth" segment whose members each had about £750,000 or more in spare cash. This segment was age-linked as they were mostly heirs to recently dead parents who had left them the family home in addition to the one they already had. We are talking about people in their 50s who have little or no mortgage commitment or money problems. This is quite a good piece of segmentation as it is age-related and one can empathize with the needs of these customers as a group. The banks soon discovered, as many have before, that the wealthy are often still wealthy because they are reluctant to part with their money. The banks were gently let down as this segment was also reluctant to move their accounts.

Lower down the age scale, banks have long targetted college students, unprofitable as they are in the short term. They increase usage as they develop their careers and retention rates are high.

The moral, of course, is that it is not necessarily sound policy to allocate marketing resources to those customers who have the most money. Retention may not be increasingly more profitable than acquisition and it may not be best to prioritize the most valuable segment, which may already be spending as much as it ever will.

CLV, like most financial analysis, does have its place but we should note that the fallacies lie in giving cash flow forecasts more credence than they deserve and in regarding customers as assets. Customers are not owned by their suppliers and they are not there to be milked. The idea that the objective of marketing has changed from creating value for the customer to creating shareholder value, as suggested by Doyle, goes too far. Of course he was simplifying in order to get the shareholder into the mind of the marketer, but we need to remember which comes first.

For both conceptual and behavioral reasons, anticipating the future in assessing the marketing performance to date brings huge problems. So let us turn to shareholder value.

Shareholder value analysis

The root of the fixation with shareholder value lies in the perception that the main objective of any company is to maximize the shareholders" return on their equity. This is not a new idea but the formalization was developed in the 1980s thanks to Rappaport and various firms of consultants.

In essence we are dealing with DCF just as we were with brand valuation and customer lifetime value. The technical adjustments for debt, risk, and the costs of capital are important but not relevant here. The dangers, and perhaps fallacies, are once again both conceptual and behavioral. Shareholder value analysis has been over-promoted from a useful tool for resource allocation to a universal framework for decision making. The first set of problems below are conceptual.

Conceptual

- In theory, shareholder value gives a long-term view by forecasting the future. But look more closely and you will find the future looks remarkably like today. By projecting the present into the future, without adequate allowance for external changes, management is condemned to relive *Groundhog Day*, a movie where the hero is awakened by his alarm clock every morning to discover it is the same day over again. The long term is an illusion; we are just looking at today repeated with minor variations.
- The focus is internal and on concepts than can be expressed in money terms. More important, but non-financial, drivers are excluded.
- Excessive emphasis on shareholder value leads to seeing customers and employees as merely means to the achievement of what the CEO really cares about: profits and share prices. It will not take long for customers and employees to get the feeling they are being used.
- The allocation of costs may give top management a false picture. Applying shareholder value analysis to business units, for example, requires central costs to be spread on some arbitrary basis that is probably false to the extent that the units do not directly give rise to these costs.

Behavioral

- Value analysis is a means to compare existing alternatives. In practice, the eyes-down nature of this analysis prevents managers looking for better alternatives; they just battle for the one they want against whatever alternative has been put up by their counterparts.
- Similarly, the complications enable marketers, who soon develop the technical skills, to apply their creativity to manipulating the numbers as distinct from implementing the best marketing program.
- Conversely, marketing investments with outcomes that are hard to express in financial terms are more likely to be put on the back burner. Radical innovation leads to performance well nigh impossible to forecast; yet many firms owe their continuing existence to these leaps of faith. Using a higher discount rate to allow for increased risk is no solution – subtracting an arbitrary number from a wrong number can only make it right by chance. So the things that might transform the business are abandoned in favor of more cuts to the status quo.

All the financial systems discussed rely on projecting the present into the future and then believing that future to be realistic. If nothing much changes – not customers, not competitors, not the environment – then the future will indeed look much like the present but, in a rapidly changing world, that is exceedingly unlikely. Shareholder value analysis is a valuable technique for identifying the assets and costs, including marketing costs that can be squeezed. It is a useful internal discipline but it tells us nothing about the marketplace, even though it may incorporate some market data, or about the sources of cash flow or how they can be increased.

Although models of shareholder value do recognize, just about, that cash comes from customers, they are limited to what they can measure in financial terms. So while the company's capabilities, for example, are recognized as drivers of shareholder value, when it gets to the model presented to management, capabilities have dropped out because the accountants cannot put a price on them.

A major problem with long-term planning systems, including shareholder value analysis, is tunnel vision. Jack Welch closed down the central planning system when he became CEO at General Electric because he recognized that it closed out the search for what he called "white space." Whatever instructions were given, in practice managers projected the businesses from the status quo. As a result, smaller, more lively firms beat them to the draw in new countries and new product categories that they had not really thought about. In an empirical study with the Boston Consulting Group, we found that new product development, or at least radical new products, entered the planning process only after they had already been launched. If success requires circumventing the system, then the system is flawed.

The research was exploratory and the sample was 11 cases from nine packaged goods multinationals. BCG consultants familiar with the cases and respondents gathered the data through interviews. Although only one respondent explicitly used the term "brand equity," that appeared to be the key driver along with a generic need to enhance net cash flow. Considerations included rejuvenating the brand, protecting its image, and leveraging the brand. Concerns were not to dilute the brand and the extent to which the new product fitted the brand. In all cases the extensions had to clear a predetermined financial hurdle. Where management was keen on the project, this did not prove a problem.

When a large drinks multinational introduced value-based management in the early 1990s, the marketers were aghast but they soon learned to live with it. After a crash course in the methodology and language, Excel sheets became a key feature in marketing plans. The technicalities of shareholder management, and especially the residual values for the cash flows 10 years out, were used to justify the budget approvals they would have sought in any case. As anyone versed in large corporate life will appreciate, budget approval owes more to politics than to mathematics. Securing the appropriate budgets is good for the business, but value analysis was contributing little to the process; it was simply a new means to the pre-ordained solution.

Perhaps the most surprising source for the observation that big new revenue-generating ideas flow from vision and drive, not DCF, is the economist John Maynard Keynes. Keynes saw animal spirits as the "spontaneous urge to action rather than inaction, and not as the outcome of a weighted average of quantitative benefits multiplied by quantitative probabilities." The term "animal spirits" was adopted from Descartes and brings together the emotional, ideological, and determination characteristics of human nature.

Animal spirits may seem an archaic, albeit graphic, term but Stanford researchers Professors James Collins and Jerry Porras reached much the same conclusion in their study of 200 large companies. Their bottom line was that success was not driven by shareholder value but through "let's try a lot of stuff and keep what works." Successful companies had vision and a core ideology that differentiated them from others. Maximizing shareholder value was only one objective among many.

Marketing is the means of achieving shareholder satisfaction through first achieving the goals of customers and employees. None of these groups is necessarily more important than the others, any more than salt is more important than pepper. The point is the logic of the sequence: employees have to get cash from customers before the shareholders can have some. This is precisely why market metrics should be considered before shareholder value.

The last problem area may seem trivial in comparison but is a regular feature of executive committee debate. In a large company, shareholder value is used to evaluate the performance of the various brands or business units. Those that provide above-average returns are presented as drivers and those below average as destroyers of value. No one would quarrel with the need to get low performers to do better but the discussion usually turns to selling them off or closing them down.

It may be obvious that doing so will result in the overheads being reallocated over a smaller number of brands or business units, thereby presenting a new list of value destroyers. In the heat of the discussion, executives tend to forget that they are actually reducing the sources of cash flow when the discussion should be about reducing overheads. As in so much of the practical application of value-based management, the pseudo-science diverts attention from the marketplace.

In summary, shareholder value analysis, or managing for value, is a useful discipline for squeezing assets and costs and reviewing investment choices; it is dangerous only in excess. As a dominant philosophy it damages innovation, customer, and employee relationships, crimps imagination and leads to downward spirals of cost cutting. It tells the company nothing about the sources of cash flow or how they can be made more productive and still less about new sources of cash flow.

Using financial techniques in marketing

So, how can financial analysis be best used to assist marketing performance?

The basic issue is balance. Non-financial metrics will give a better picture of the market than the financial and yet financial tools should still be used to explore the likely impacts of alternative marketing strategies and actions. But in moderation.

The second balance requires more attention to be given to a scientific analysis of the facts today rather than hypothetical lifetime values. However, historical data, bought-in data (for example, for simulated test markets), and proven tools can improve the predictive qualities of those forecasts.

Today's reality can be measured but the future can only be guessed or estimated. I am not suggesting the elimination of forecasting nor of financial tools but only the importance of focussing on measurable facts (metrics). Get the decisions and actions right today and the future will be as good as it can be. In other words, we need to look more closely for the present indicators of future consequences and spend less time fantasizing with Excel spreadsheets.

This now versus the future issue requires more attention. The moral of *Groundhog Day* was that the future is merely a repetition of today unless changes are made today. Looking to the future does not drive future cash flow, but the actions we take today do. The competitive edge arises from applying different imagination to the same market facts.

Integrating information

Large companies have pockets of market data throughout the organization. They are commissioned by different people for different reasons and cover different time periods. The commissioners believe they "own" the data and do not necessarily want to share it with colleagues. This is part of the argument for market metrics being consolidated under the CFO, but only a minority of large firms agrees with that.

Francis Bacon suggested 400 years ago that knowledge, or perhaps information, is power and it would not have been a new idea then. The financial perspective, and consequentially value analysis, is strengthened by accounting information and responsibilities being closely integrated. That is not usually true for market information. Most, if not all, of the potentially important indicators need to be brought together. The UK leading supermarket chain, Tesco, recognized this in 1994 and appointed a small specialist company, dunnhumby, to manage its customer database. The objectives were to achieve better understanding of customers and strengthen loyalty by making customers feel that their needs were receiving more personalized attention. Today, dunnhumby takes care of 14 million customer records for Tesco and offers similar services to large retail organizations in the UK and US.

Of course, databases of this type are driven by transactions, usually at point of sale, and personal information provided by customers when they sign up for their loyalty card. There are large blocks of important market information they exclude – competitive data for example.

Segmentation

A principal attraction of databases of this type is segmentation. Groups of customers with similar characteristics can be deduced from what they buy. The next step is to lead them to what, on the evidence from other members of their group, they might buy. These should be called "affinity groups" rather than segments because even large corporations cannot have separate marketing programs for each group. But what they can, and do, achieve is effective development of their business with each customer through merchandizing and direct mail individualized to fit each affinity group.

Now we can estimate the value of each customer and affinity group. More importantly, we can realistically estimate their unfulfilled profit potential. Notice how this analysis is rooted in market data before it gets to financial valuation.

Relatively few companies outside financial services and chain retailing have the resource, or the need, to conduct sophisticated segmentation in this way. Indeed, Professor Andrew Ehrenberg has challenged the whole concept of segmentation. When he analyzed packaged goods purchases by the usual demographic classifications, he found no significant differences. Clearly the issue is category-specific: poor people rarely buy premium cars.

But whether segmentation is worthwhile is a side issue. The key is to use all available market information to establish a firm base for any forecasts. This is not just the base for year one. Quite often, year one is simply projected without any specific attention to changes in the environment, competition, and the company itself. Yet it is possible to draw inferences about these matters from current and historical information and these inferences should be used.

Using prediction to decide the best courses of marketing action

Finally we come to the main use for financial analysis – evaluating alternative strategies. One cannot evaluate every option but, as Wharton's Professor George Day points out, it is crucial to avoid rushing into financial evaluation before *all* the feasible strategies have been assembled and the less attractive eliminated through competitive assessment. Understanding how the marketplace will, or could, react to each strategy needs to precede value analysis.

The attraction of comparative assessment is that many of the future estimates, for example interest rates, are less critical than for single assessments, for example brand valuation, because they are the same for both. In other words, they may be wrong but they net out. The extent to which the comparisons are affected to future estimates can be determined by sensitivity analysis. Once the Excel spreadsheet is prepared, it can be copied to other pages and run with higher and lower future interest rates, for example. The future does not matter, only the comparison that is being made now.

In a perfect world, shareholder value analysis and monitoring brand equity would provide the same financial numbers. The future cash flows from today's brand equity would equal the forecasts in the value analysis. Either concept would inspire the same decision. In practice, both are needed in decisions such as line extensions. A quick way to gain new sales and distribution in the market, line extensions may come at the expense of later sales of the original products and of brand equity; in other words they are short-termist. Too often, a line extension can be merely the shortest distance between two profit forecasts.

On the other hand, leveraging the existing brand (extension) is between five and ten times cheaper than launching a new brand. An analysis of 130 US consumer companies between 1993 and 1997 showed that the more leveraged brands generated, on average, 5 percent more return than less leveraged counterparts.

Paradoxical as it may seem, shareholder value is best served by not giving it too much attention. In essence, marketing maximizes shareholder value through first attending to the aspirations and needs of customers and employees. This difficult three-way balancing act is not helped by worrying, at least at this stage, about other stakeholders such as suppliers and the wider community. So the advice is regularly to compare brand equity metrics with shareholder value analysis and to see the extent to which previous brand equity metrics predict current changes in shareholder value – and the extent to which shareholder value predictions were accurate. Once a year is enough for this type of comparison.

Where both forms of prediction are accurate, then, obviously, it does not much matter which is used. Differences are more interesting. If shareholder value predictions are proving more reliable, the finance enthusiasts will claim victory but they would be wrong. We are looking at something more serious: the firm's business model is false. Its own selection of market metrics is giving it misleading readings. Where shareholder value differs from brand equity analysis, then either the brand equity is right or the metrics need to be changed. In neither case should shareholder value analysis be preferred; it is merely a check on the firm's most valuable asset.

RESOURCES

Ambler, Tim, *Marketing and the Bottom Line*, FT Prentice Hall, 2nd Edition, 2003.

Ambler, Tim, 'Brand development versus new product development: toward a process model of extension decisions,' *Marketing Intelligence and Planning*, 1996.

Ambler, Tim and Barwise, Patrick, 'The trouble with brand valuation,' *Journal of Brand Management*, 5, 1998.

Barth, Mary E., Clement, Michael, Foster, George, and Kaszkik, Ron, "Brand values and capital market valuation,' *Review of Accounting Studies*, 3, 1998.

Day, George, *Market Driven Strategy*, The Free Press, 1990.

East, Robert, Wendy Lomax, and Narain, Radhika, 'Customer tenure, recommendation and switching,' *Journal of Consumer Satisfaction, Dissatisfaction and Complaining Behavior*, 14, 2001.

East, Robert, Lomax, Wendy, and Freeman, Ed, 'Lip service: variables associated with recommendation,' *Proceedings of the Academy of Marketing*, July, 2002.

Ehrenberg, Andrew and Kennedy, Rachel, 'There is no brand segmentation,' *Marketing Research*, 13, 2001.

Reichheld, Frederick, *The Loyalty Effect: The Hidden Force Behind Growth, Profits, and Lasting Value*, Harvard Business School Press, 1996.

Reinartz, Werner and Kumar, V. 'The mismanagement of customer loyalty,' *Harvard Business Review*, July, 2002.

Rust, Roland T., Zeithaml, Valarie, A., and Lemon, Katherine N., *Driving Customer Equity: How Customer Lifetime Value is Reshaping Corporate Strategy*, The Free Press, 2000.

Earnings – its role in assessing performance and value

MIKE CAHILL

[There are many measures of corporate performance. Among the most popular are those that revolve around earnings. But just how helpful are these measures and what are the challenges of using them?]

The trend in earnings per share (EPS) is often regarded as a key measure of a company's performance. Much stock market attention is focussed on the projected earnings of a company. As the number the company reports net of charges, it is a shorthand way of reflecting the trend in the price, volume, and cost drivers of the business. Analysis of corporate results invariably revolves around an assessment of earnings compared with expectations. Whether this focus is correct is highly debatable – we will explore the problems later. Nonetheless, the growth in EPS is deemed a critical guide to how well a company is doing and will drive the share price.

Earnings definition

The calculation of earnings per share is, in principal, very straightforward. You take the profit left after tax that belongs ("attributable") to ordinary shareholders. The earnings per share figure is then derived by dividing the attributable profit by the number of ordinary shares in issue.

A fictional UK brake-unit manufacturer Full Stop had operating profits of £7.5 million in 2003. Interest costs were £2.5 million, so deducting that from the operating profits gives a pre-tax profit of £5 million. If a tax rate of 30 percent is applied, post-tax profits, called earnings, are £3.5 million.

If there are 30 million shares in issue, the earnings per share number is 3.45m/30m or 11.5p per share.

The numerator (earnings or attributable profit) must belong to ordinary shareholders. Therefore, any preference dividends must be deducted. Similarly, any minority charges must also be subtracted. Minority charges relate to the outside shareholder's claim on the profits of the company – again they are not attributable to the ordinary shareholders. So if an outside company has a 25 percent investment in the company (or a subsidiary), it is entitled to 25 percent of the earnings of that company.

To ensure accuracy of the EPS number, the correct number of shares needs to be established. In particular, allowance must be made for the impact of any convertible shares or outstanding share options in issue. This is referred to as the "fully diluted" number of shares.

What earnings are we using?

There is an abundance of earnings numbers and potential confusion when different definitions are used. It is crucial to be clear as possible and define carefully:

1. the time period to which the earnings relate;
2. the accounting definitions used.

Prospective versus historic

Historic earnings refer to the earnings reported in the last fiscal year. However, investment is a forward-looking business. The market will focus on future earnings and will look to the management for guidance. There is clearly risk in doing this (the forecast may prove far from accurate), but again this is an integral component of investment – the confidence in the forecast is a key factor in valuation. The forecast is very useful when examining the earnings growth delivered by the company and how it compares to the company's sector and the stock market overall.

Pre-exceptional, pre-amortization earnings versus stated earnings

The simplest and easiest way to compare earnings on a standardized basis is to use pre-exceptional, pre-amortization numbers. The rationale for using this definition is that exceptional charges are by nature one-off, and amortization is a non-cash cost – neither should be allowed to distort the underlying trend in the business.

Exceptional items

Exceptionals can come from a variety of sources. For example, it could be the costs associated with closing a factory, or writing down the value of an asset. These items would appear as a negative in the P&L. Exceptional credits might derive from the disposal of an investment or property.

What should be deemed exceptional?

It is very important to differentiate between "operating" and "non-operating" exceptional items. Operating debits relate to the core business. Non-operating charges relate to financial or capital transactions such as the disposal of a property asset or business. The broad rule is that if the items relate to "capital" items, they are legitimate exceptionals, whereas if they relate to the core business, they are not. Operating charges and the reasons behind them need to be carefully examined. Companies may be tempted to include (usually large) items that are in fact normal costs of doing business. This will inevitably prompt cynicism and mistrust among investors. In particular a real danger sign is if these charges occur year in year out – so they are hardly an exceptional occurrence.

An interesting example is the UK food retailer Sainsbury's. It had an exceptional debit of £20 million in the 2002 R&A debited from the UK stores performance, down from £37 million in 2001. The reason for this charge is cited as follows: "The costs in Sainsbury's Supermarkets relate to the business transformation program which involves upgrading its IT systems, supply chain, and store portfolio. These costs are exceptional due to the *scale, scope and pace of the transformation program*. These costs primarily relate to the closure of depots and stores and associated reorganisation costs" (page 24 of the 2002 accounts).

Are these charges really exceptional? On a strict definition no – they relate to the core business and have occurred in successive years. These costs are deemed exceptional due to the scale of the action needed to upgrade the "IT systems, supply chain, and store portfolio." However, consistent spending on these areas is crucial to maintain the company's competitiveness. One interpretation of the scale of this upgrade is that the company failed to invest on a consistent basis and hence the need to "catch up." The company has seen a progressive erosion of its market share and this may well reflect this lack of investment. On this basis, it seems inappropriate to treat this item as exceptional.

Exceptionals and earnings comparisons

Exceptional items distort performance comparisons. A competitor that consistently invested in these crucial areas would have incurred costs and depressed its operating margins – but is in a much more competitive position. Similarly, treating the restructuring charge as exceptional means that the operating margin (calculated on a pre-exceptional basis) does not suffer.

Performance comparisons can be distorted if a company makes a major restructuring provision and elects to "kitchen sink" the numbers, making them as large and as "exceptional" as possible. This will flatter future performance as the use of provisions will reduce costs. A company that consistently kept costs low and incurred redundancy costs as a regular feature would not have the advantage of this large-scale provisioning. However, its continuing focus on low costs would be a much more competitive approach.

So what has started out as a simple issue has become complicated by the issue of exceptionals. Just because a company reports an exceptional item does not mean investors will agree with its treatment. Indeed a company's frequent use of exceptionals will be investigated to ensure it does not reflect an over-inflated cost base that is finally being treated or reflect a systematic under-investment in the business.

Amortization

This refers to the writing off of "goodwill" a company is obliged to do when it acquires another company at a premium to assets. The premium to book value is called "goodwill" and reflects the value of the group's brand names, etc. Some businesses, most notably service-related businesses, have little by way of assets, so goodwill can be considerable. This goodwill is then "written off" over the course of its "economic life." So far a business with £20 million of assets purchased for £100 million, the goodwill is £80 million. If this is written down over 10 years it generates an £8 million annual charge to the P&L. It should be stressed that this charge to the P&L does not involve an outflow of cash (and is referred to as a non-cash item).

Quality of earnings

While the headlines focus on whether earnings are hitting targets and the growth rate, it is crucial to establish the quality as well as the quantity of earnings. The quality of earnings is a vital component in valuation. In addition, the less volatile the earnings stream, the lower the cost of capital. When assessing earnings quality, the following should be considered:

1. The use of very straight and conservative accounting policies – the earnings number is a true reflection of the company's performance.
2. The profits are being generated by the core business and not from one-off benefits.

3. The sustainability and visibility of earnings – how easy is it to predict the earnings?
4. What does management have control over and what can it influence?
5. The earnings convert into cash flow very efficiently.
6. The earnings growth is not at the expense of investment returns/value-added.

The first two are clearly related. The more a company engages in accounting manipulation to "hit" earnings targets, the poorer the quality of its earnings. Critically, to the extent that earnings are benefiting from manipulation, the less sustainable its performance – at some stage the trading reality will assert itself.

Achieving earnings targets through manipulating accounts or one-off benefits, while the performance of the underlying business disappoints, will ultimately be detected. As the "benefits" drop out, earnings will be dependent on the underlying performance of the business. It should also be stressed that decisions to cut discretionary expenditures such as advertising and promotion to hit an earnings target will not be received favorably – such a measure will be seen as an unsustainable boost to numbers and will potentially undermine the competitive position of the company.

Another important aspect for earnings quality is what management can influence. In commodity-based businesses, for example, earnings will be volatile. A timber trading company will be subject to the vagaries of price movements and the impact of currency movements in determining its profits. Both of these are very difficult to predict and lie outside management's control. If the business benefits from sharp price rises, how much of the improved performance is attributable to good management?

Earnings and cash flow relationship

The ability to generate cash is crucial to a company's health and wealth. It is also the ultimate driver of value. Therefore, it is important that earnings growth translates into cash generation.

There are a number of ways that the earnings growth can be registered (on top of accounting duplicity) without cash flowing into the company. One of the most important is earnings growth achieved through an associate or related company. This is where the company has an investment of over 20 percent but below 50 percent. The company "equity accounts" its investment, i.e. it books its share of that company's profits. If the associate is growing rapidly, the company's P&L will reflect this. If it accounts for all the growth, investors will question the performance of the core business.

Critically, the impact on cash flow is very different. The cash received will be only the dividends paid out – something management may not be able to influence. If the investment is growing rapidly there may be no dividend at all – the cash will be reinvested in the business.

Another key area is provisions and cash flow. If earnings growth is being achieved through aggressive (exceptional) write-offs, cash will be going out on redundancy payments or other costs associated with the provisions. This can be particularly true for highly acquisitive companies.

Earnings and added value

What the focus on earnings growth may not be picking up is whether this growth is "adding value" for shareholders – i.e. generating a return that exceeds the cost of capital. (As with cash flow this is a crucial driver of value.) The deals carried out at the height of the stock market boom demonstrate that management's desire to grow can destroy value on a large scale.

Not all earnings growth is created equal

Therefore, when looking at earnings it is important to focus on both quantity and quality. The source of earnings growth is crucial to valuation. Earnings growth achieved by a one-off gain, currency movements, or an asset disposal (if not deemed exceptional) will be valued very lowly. Meeting expectations through a disposal will see the share price fall and question marks raised over earnings quality.

The same reservations might apply to reduction in costs, albeit these are critical to the competitiveness of the company. The problem is that they may provide a one-off boost to earnings but not growth (though the lower cost base may enable extra market share to be won). US retailer Home Depot's Q3 2002 figures indicated that, while the company's earnings met market expectations, the shares fell 13 percent. This was because the target was met entirely through cost cutting. Market disappointment revolved around the overall performance of the business. Despite numbers in line with expectations, the "top line" or revenue performance suggested the company might be losing ground to its competitors. It is wrong to focus solely on earnings – all the performance metrics will be scrutinized. Growth achieved through volume and price growth, if sustainable, is indicative of a company performing well on a broad front while cash and returns are key drivers of value.

Another sensitive area is earnings growth following provisions. This might occur after an acquisition or a major restructuring. A large exceptional charge will see shareholders' funds written down sharply, reducing the net asset value. In addition, there is likely to be a cash outflow to pay for this earnings growth. In the case of acquisition-related provisions there will be problems when the provisions run out. This may lead to the company pursuing another acquisition to maintain momentum – something the market is increasingly nervous and cynical about.

Earnings from acquisition growth will be valued far more lowly than that generated organically. The risks attaching to growth through this route are much higher. Earnings growth can be easily achieved via acquisition while failing to add value. Growth being achieved at the expense of economic returns or through an increase in the risk profile will not be viewed favorably.

Therefore while investors will monitor earnings and how they relate to expectations, what has been driving earnings will also be taken into account. In particular the relationship with cash flow and economic returns are crucial in considering the overall performance of the business. The make-up of earnings will be a key influence on how the shares are valued. This leads us to consider how earnings are valued through the P/E ratio.

Price/earnings ratio

This is a simple and very effective way of establishing value. The P/E ratio is simply the share price divided by the earnings per share (EPS). The P/E is often referred to as the stock's "multiple" or "rating." In essence the P/E is driven by a combination of:

1. the growth of earnings;
2. the quality of earnings.

It is wrong to focus on one of these in isolation. Growth needs to be generated by the performance of the underlying business (strong volumes and prices and a close attention to cost control) if it is to command a high valuation.

On the face of it a low P/E is going to be more attractive than a high P/E; however, this may not always be the case. A low P/E may not mean a share is attractive but reflect a combination of:

- uncertainty over a company's prospects;
- a highly cyclical sector;
- company serving volatile markets;
- a sector with over-capacity and weak pricing power;
- a sector or company with consistently low returns (operating profit margins, ROIC, and value-added);
- a mature sector;
- a company which is ex-growth;
- poor management;
- no convincing strategy for growth;
- poor cash generation;
- weak balance sheet.

The first four factors mean it is difficult to forecast earnings with any accuracy – they are low quality. This volatility suggests a low P/E. If earnings are revised down, the shares become a lot more expensive. Indeed the low P/E may be "discounting" or anticipating just such a downgrade.

These factors are clearly interrelated. A poor profits outlook due to weak pricing would lead to weak returns – low margins and returns on capital employed. This in turn leads to weak cash generation and a poor financial position, putting pressure on the company's investment plans. This "vicious circle" obviously makes it extremely difficult for the company, and hence the shares, to make money.

A company dominating its market with excellent margins but with no clear strategy may be "ex-growth." Again this leads to a low P/E. If there is no convincing strategy, there will be pressure on the management to distribute cash to shareholders. The shares may then be attractive on yield grounds – but the lack of growth suggests a low P/E.

Conversely, a high P/E may not mean the shares are expensive but instead may reflect:

- an excellent growth record and prospects for growth;
- a high growth sector;
- confidence in the company's forecasts;
- predictable/stable revenues;
- strong market share;
- pricing power;
- high barriers to entry;
- high margins, returns on investment which "add value";
- strong cash generation;
- excellent growth strategy.

The first two factors mean the company is seen as a growth investment leading to a high P/E. The confidence in forecasts and the predictability of revenues suggest good quality earnings – again implying a higher rating.

Characteristics such as high market share, strong barriers to entry, and pricing power will translate into high returns on sales and capital. A good management track record suggests an efficient cost base and clear focus on the needs of the market – characteristics deserving a higher valuation.

As mentioned with the "vicious circle," these factors are interrelated. A "virtuous circle" of growth and high returns will lead to strong cash generation. Invested properly, this cash flow will generate even higher growth in the long term.

Re-rating and de-ratings

If the P/E is too low given the outlook for, and quality of, earnings, then management must consider why the market is being so negative. The valuation reveals the balance of the market's views. While management may feel the market is wrong, it should respect the market's view (it is very often right). Establishing the concerns of the market is crucial to understand what may act as a catalyst to generate a re-rating.

Factors that might trigger a reassessment of the company's valuation might include:

- results beating market expectations;
- the company gains market share;
- a disposal of a business that has been holding back the main business;
- a disposal or deal which transforms the balance sheet;
- the cash flow profile is far more attractive than originally thought;
- a new CEO or management team with a convincing strategy;
- takeover and consolidation activity among similar companies;
- improved industry pricing as a result of consolidation.

While there may well be a very good case for a re-rating, without a catalyst the shares may continue to languish (often referred to as a "value trap"). Furthermore, it may require better performance being delivered over a period of time to get the market to change its mind.

Conversely, shares that disappoint expectations undergo a severe de-rating. If the expectations that justify the high rating are not fulfilled, the P/E will fall dramatically. As well as disappointing growth, the downgrade is likely to flag up risks and issues not previously considered.

Factors that cause earnings to disappoint and growth assumptions to be questioned include:

- a new entrant takes market share;
- competition from a new product or service;
- pricing disappoints;
- demand proves susceptible to economic slowdowns when previously thought to be recession proof;
- costs go out of control;
- a poor acquisition or strategic decision is made.

The last factor is more a case of management disappointing rather than weak growth. Nonetheless, it can be an important trigger for a de-rating.

The advantages and disadvantages of using P/Es

The case for using P/Es is linked to the analysis of earnings as a performance number, though accounting issues, the manipulation of earnings, and the relationship between earnings and cash/returns are real concerns. However, by focussing on the quality of earnings, we can try to sidestep some of these problems.

Advantages of using P/Es

- easy to compute.
- conventionally and widely used.
- considerable focus on "consensus earnings" as a performance measure.
- takes into account forecasts and relative growth rates.
- earnings is a measure of what is generated for shareholders.

Given its widespread use, it is vital to appreciate the pros and cons of the P/E as a valuation measure. Though it has genuine attractions, it is important to be aware of the potential pitfalls.

The disadvantages of using P/Es

The two main problems with the P/E as a valuation tool are:

- it does not take debt/financial structure into account; and
- it does not take investment returns into account.

For example, companies that make acquisitions financed entirely by debt will see earnings grow rapidly due to the impact of the deal and the tax advantages of using debt financing. However, the company may not be "adding value," i.e. generating a return exceeding the cost of capital. This highlights the conflict that exists between growth and returns. This is at the heart of many corporate governance disputes – growth benefits management in terms of status and remuneration rather than shareholders.

The use of debt benefits earnings as it is tax deductible. Therefore, on a P/E basis the highly indebted company appears cheaper. However, a highly indebted company may have a higher risk profile and a higher cost of capital than a better financed peer. (Other valuation techniques such as enterprise value will tell a different story as it takes debt structure into account.)

Other factors which suggest caution when using the P/E include:

- comparisons undermined by different accounting policies across companies and countries (depreciation, amortization, tax, etc.);

- earnings are particularly prone to manipulation;
- targetting earnings may lead to decisions that disadvantage the business;
- it cannot be used to value loss-making early-stage growth or cyclical businesses;
- it does not take cash generation into account;
- difficulties in assessing quality of earnings.

Many of these problems revolve around the conflict between companies looking to generate growth but this having a detrimental impact on the business or returns. This suggests that while the P/E is a useful and widely used measure of value, it should not be considered in isolation. In particular, the company's debt structure and ability to add value must be factored into any assessment.

Assess earnings carefully

The use of earnings is a widespread and useful way of assessing corporate performance and valuation. However, defining earnings can be problematic, especially when it comes to the treatment of exceptional charges. Operating exceptionals need to be scrutinized and carefully considered to assess their legitimacy. A close examination may reveal a lot about the company's competitive position. The emphasis and targetting of earnings can lead to management manipulating accounting policies. Decisions may be taken to enable a target to be hit but at the long-term expense of the company's competitive position. This will engender cynicism and mistrust from investors (especially if remuneration is linked with earnings).

Furthermore, targetting earnings growth aggressively may be at the expense of value-added – shareholders not being compensated for the risks involved. This is especially relevant in mergers and acquisitions, where value added is often a casualty. As with all performance measures, focussing on one variable will deliver a very partial story – and not necessarily the most relevant one. Earnings may not correlate with other drivers of value, in particular cash flow and value added. Importantly, shareholders are being far more vocal about this disconnect between growth and value.

Fools, gold, and greed

GERRY GRIFFIN AND CIARAN PARKER

> Always look a gift horse in the mouth.

There is a proverbial *schadenfreude* felt by observers when they see someone lose a lot of money: "A fool and his money are soon parted.' They may have made this through the sweat of their brows, or inherited it. Maybe they felt that this pile of loot made them more important than they really were. But they lose it through their folly. It's not as if they were robbed. They have only themselves to blame.

It has always been fairly hard to make money, but relatively easy to lose it. This hasn't changed over the centuries. Money shouldn't be worshipped, but it should be treated with respect. It is as useful now as it ever has been. One of the best pieces of advice for any investor is to be cautious. This does not mean adopting a sheepish and timid attitude to life or being pathologically risk-averse. Streets have to be crossed so as to get to the other side, but it is always best to keep your eyes open. When it comes to matters financial we all learn by our mistakes – rather we all *should* learn by our mistakes and the errors of others. And herein lies the trouble: some of us just cannot. It is not because we're stupid. It is because we fall victim to irrational and often childish emotions that cloud and obscure our vision of the world.

Throughout history people with money have been fooled. Some have been systematically targetted by conmen. The form of the deception varies, but it has a common theme. What you have now is nothing to what you can have in the future. The deception is nearly always based around a scheme that offers fantastic returns, the promise of ever augmenting wealth.

The prospects of such financial snowballs have always been extremely unlikely. It is theoretically implausible. History hasn't been kind either. Wherever and whenever such a scheme or bubble appears it inevitably bursts, leaving a few lucky (and usually criminal) people very rich (and absent), but for the majority of dupes it ends in big losses. They have been deluded by a specter that appeals to their greed. This overthrows their reason.

Financial misfortunes have three central elements: greed, speculation, and delusion. These three unlikely brothers sometimes act together. At other times one of them takes the leading part, while the other two supply the necessary back-up.

Greed is bad

Of the three, greed is by far the oldest. He is a misunderstood figure who has for years and years suffered a bad reputation. He feels that he has been blamed for the mistakes and excesses of others. Rather than attracting reproach he feels he deserves a bit of overdue gratitude. In the real world most people are uneasy about greed. It is true that in the 1980s there were people like Ivan Boesky who proclaimed that greed was good.

In reality, greed can never be good. We don't say this standing on some ethical high ground. Furthermore it's not our fault. Greed is not a scientific phenomenon. If anything it is the product of a value judgement. The fact is, and it is a fact verified by history, that greed has always been viewed negatively. It has never been defined precisely or mathematically; it cannot be. It is related to notions of excess, but excess is related in turn to the concept of going beyond what is needed for health and happiness. But this is a moving goalpost. No one can say truthfully when the environment of greed has been entered. There is usually a big difference between the objective and subjective notions of what having "enough" entails. To misquote a cliché, one man's vichyssoise is another man's dishwater. Even if you are very rich there is usually someone else who is richer, so keeping up with the Rockefellers is a constant, and expensive, chore.

We might say that human beings are greedy. This would make a lot of us unhappy. "Me greedy?" we would protest. We strive after what we hope will give us satisfaction. We've always been like this. Our very remote ancestors had to struggle to survive. If they were hungry they had to go out and hunt for some food. Later on they grew it, or got someone else to grow it for them. They also had desires, or better said, needs for warmth, security, and comfort. These had to be acquired. We have inherited their acquisitive instincts, even though we no longer have to strive physically after their satisfaction. We are all motivated by a desire to acquire. That's evolution.

One of the objects of greed has been money. There are many who are greedy for non-financial assets. They want power, influence, and yes, food. These often come at a high price, so you need money to get them. But even if power falls into your lap it is an unwritten rule (maybe a golden rule?) that the more power you have, the more wealth you have, or potentially can have.

For all its allure, money has had a very bad reputation for a very long time. Admittedly those who denounced it, such as the Christian church, said that it was man that made money evil. On its own it was harmless. This was just as well as in the Middle Ages the church had more of the stuff than anyone else. But while it was neutral it seemed to breed a desire for more. Those who had money were able to make it grow into larger amounts. How was this done? Not for the first time those who couldn't do it condemned it. Money could be made by lending it and charging interest. At first such practices were denounced as sinful and wicked, but the hostility was eventually relaxed.

At about the time that printing was discovered (c. 1450), and the Old World realized that there was a New World beyond the waves full of riches waiting to be exploited, a further discovery was made. Money wasn't bad after all. It wasn't wrong to lend it at interest, and making a profit wasn't a bad thing either. Money came out of the closet. It was also a good idea to try to get as much of the stuff as you could because there wasn't much you could do without it. Money worked and it could work miracles, almost. It could change the way people looked at you, not to mention your status in the world. But how could you get it, and if you already had some, how could you get more?

Speculate to accumulate

Speculation is probably the most ostentatious and flashy of the three brothers. He too suffered a bad reputation but that's all past now. He likes to be in the center of things. He enjoys the bright lights and a fast life style. He's a bit shallow. Some have said he's selfish, but others have always seen him as the most straightforward of the three.

For a long time Europe was gripped by a delusion called alchemy. It taught that stones could be turned into gold. That's all it could teach. Huge amounts of money were spent trying to find the means to do it, but without success. We can laugh at it now, but in its heyday even the greatest scientists, such as Isaac Newton, took an active interest.

A lot of new wealth was discovered in the Americas, but money, like manure, has to be spread around to do any good. The wheels of commerce needed oiling by capital, and these needs were met in an institutionalized way by stock markets. This was still a risky business. From the beginning of the 18th century schemes began to appear offering huge, no-risk returns on investment. But they inevitably crashed, and those who had been poor before were usually still poor, if not a little poorer.

But the genie had been let out of the bottle. True, in the aftermath of a crash there was a feeling of dejection, a bit like a hangover following a high-octane booze session. The last thing any of those suffering from it wanted to hear was talk about drink. But this inevitably passed. People liked to speculate because they had a desire to acquire money. But they wanted to do it as quickly and painlessly as possible. This was not greed.

Gambling can be seen as a form of speculation, though dedicated partisans of both activities would react angrily to the comparison. Both the stockbroker and the gambler in the bookie's shop don't willfully throw away their money. There are factors that influence their decisions, not the least of which is the probability of a positive return. This is a reward that would take a certain amount of time and effort to make in a more traditional way. The fact that neither the stockbroker nor the punter want to do this does not make them greedy. So speculation is a neutral, value-free activity.

But speculation, again like gambling, has suffered because of its lack of visibility and apparent effortlessness. If a gambler backs the winning horse, and if a speculator invests in an equity or future which appreciates, money is made, but for what? Where is the effort that a manual worker or a craftsman expends in return for wages? Also, where is the product of such effort? For this reason successful speculation was seen for a long time as money for nothing, and this was the worst kind.

This is a very old prejudice, going back at least to the Middle Ages. It still persists in some areas, especially in the revulsion felt by some Christian sects toward gambling. It also informs an unspoken but nevertheless real feeling of unease about the financial services sector. There is a certain aura of carelessness and frivolous insensitivity attached to the term "speculator." An investor on the other hand has more solidity. The investor is viewed as making a more long-term commitment. It is as if the investor is a loyal spouse in a financial relationship; the speculator is the serial philanderer.

The illusion of delusion

The last of the three brothers is probably the most dangerous. He appears to be in another world. Sometimes it is hard to see him at all as he is surrounded by a sort of fog. He is a great storyteller, and in his way is the most persuasive of the three, but he should never be given much credence.

Delusions are part of being human too. They generally stem from a desire for the world to be different, even for a moment. Anyone who, on a wet winter afternoon, day dreams about sun-kissed beaches and pina coladas is temporarily in a delusional state. It never does them any harm: it probably helps them to stay human, so it is a very benign form of delusion. Others hope for a positive outcome, even in the face of overwhelming odds to the contrary. They are told that a wonder stock is going to keep appreciating in value, that it is never going to go down in price, that it will always leapfrog inflation, and that they can be rich. There are people who advise caution and who point out the historical precedents; who warn that these things always end in tears. But they are ignored and reviled as party poopers.

The deluded souls who are dancing on a precipice of financial ruin probably need to believe in some good news. They yearn, no doubt secretly, for when they were kids, and everything was black and white – usually white. But it would be unjust to describe these people as lost in their own idiocy. Apart from daydreaming, delusions are never passive affairs. There has to be an active, external agent – someone who does the deluding. There are occasions when we agree to be deluded. We participate in the ruse. An example would be anyone who attends a magician's performance. We gasp in amazement at the tricks. We just cannot rationalize how the rabbit gets into the hat. But we realize on calmer and more sober reflection that there is an explanation, albeit one known only to members of the Magic Circle.

But then there are the people who are more dedicated delusion artists, the ones who sing to high heaven the virtues of certain types of stocks. They seldom work on their own, and may have a small army of helpers, many of whom are also in the dark. They are masters of hype. The information age has spawned a deluge of news sources, but it must be remembered that just because something is in a newspaper or on the Internet does not make it accurate.

Must this madness continue? Will people keep being stung? The answer must be a heavy-hearted yes. It is because we are human beings that we want more, and it is because we were once children that we look for the silver lining and the cloudless sky. All is not lost. More people now realize the importance of caution and the wisdom of asking the right questions. There is also greater confidence in personal ability to do this. This goes hand in hand with a healthy skepticism of "the experts." Although there is a surfeit of information out there, not all of it is bogus. Ponzi schemes, and other get rich quick schemes, still occur, but they usually break out in regions of the world where knowledge of economics is poor, as poor as the people themselves. It is people who already have little who lose most.

RESOURCES

Griffin, Gerry and Parker, Ciaran, *Fools Gold*, Work Foundation, 2004.

Essentials

FINANCE

Activity-based costing

Activity-based costing (ABC) aims to provide a dynamic and realistic means of calculating the true cost of doing business. It precisely allocates direct and indirect costs to particular products or customer segments. ABC emerged from Harvard and, in particular, the work of Robert Kaplan (perhaps best known for his work on developing the balanced scorecard, a strategic management and measurement system).

ABC is, in some ways, a financial version of reengineering. The company identifies core processes and analyzes the costs at each stage within the process. This enables it to know how much an activity, such as R&D, costs the business and how much R&D expenditure should be built into the costs of a particular product or service. Properly applied, ABC allows companies to better understand and streamline their cost structures. The drawback is that it requires careful examination of what is actually going on in the business.

According to consulting firm Booz Allen Hamilton, companies typically spend 20–25 percent of sales with third-party suppliers for goods and services not directly related to the end product or services of the business. These costs sometimes exceed those spent directly on the end product.

So why don't companies manage their indirect costs better? The simple answer is that you can save money only if you actually know how much you spend in the first place and where you spend it. That's where activity-based costing comes in. If it is to be produced, a product or service – "cost object" in the language of ABC – requires the input of certain "activities." Activities include the traditional business functions (marketing, R&D, production, marketing, etc.) as well as indirect costs such as maintenance, storage, and administration. Taken together, these activities are the processes that form the business. There are a number of factors influencing the costs of a particular activity, such as whether it is premium quality. In ABC-speak these are "cost drivers."

In addition there are "activity drivers" – measures of the demand placed on certain activities by particular cost objects. One product may, for example, require greater marketing expenditure than another. Clearly, activities require resources: people and machines. "Resource drivers" are measures of the demands placed on resources by activities.

ABC does nothing, in itself, to reduce costs. But the better understood the relationship between resources, activities, and processes, the more likely it is that the most cost-effective resources will be channeled to the right activities at the right time in the process. This is the underlying logic of ABC.

Discounted cash flow

Discounted cash flow (DCF) refers to a method of valuing a company used by private company investors and venture capitalists to determine the size of their investments in projects.

Discounted cash flow analysis takes into account all benefits (cash flow, tax credits, net sale proceeds, paper losses), not just cash flow. The aim is to assess a projected stream of economic benefits and calculate the maximum equity contribution that an investor should be willing to make. It also enables an analyst to compare an equity amount with a stream of benefits and calculate an overall rate of return. The investor's minimum rate of return is called the discount rate, the rate at which the investor will discount benefits promised in the future. The discount rate converts benefits promised in the future into an equivalent value today, called present value.

Despite its complexity, discounted cash flow analysis is based on a simple idea – that cash today is worth more than cash promised in the future. It assumes that any investment should yield a return over and above current cash value. It makes no sense, for example, to invest $100 today for the promise of only the same amount in the future. If you invest $100 today, you should receive more than that amount back at a later date.

There are a number of factors involved. The first is the risk incurred. An investor in a property development, for example, is looking for cash flow and appreciation, but neither is guaranteed. The investor bears significant market risk, and risk demands some compensation. Part of the return on investment is compensation for taking risk. (The greater the risk, the higher the rate of return demanded by investors.)

Second, inflation reduces the value of money. An investor needs some return just to preserve the value of the capital. If inflation is proceeding at 4 percent a year, an investor needs a 4 percent after-tax return just to get back what they have invested. The other justification of return on investment, then, is compensation for inflation.

Third is the opportunity cost of the investment. When an investor places money in an investment, they give up the right to use it for anything else – alternative investments or consumption. Economists call this "opportunity cost." So, the third part of return on investment is compensation for opportunity cost.

An investor's perception of these three factors – risk, inflation, and opportunity cost – determines their desired rate of return, the minimum return required for a particular investment.

For the purposes of venture capitalists, discounted cash flow assumes that the future value of a company can be estimated by forecasting future performance and measuring the surplus cash flow generated by the company. The surplus cash flows and cash flow shortfalls are then related back to a present value using a discounting factor and added together to arrive at an overall valuation. The discount factor used is adjusted for the financial risk of investing in the company. The mechanics of the method focus investors on the internal operations of the company and its future.

Like any other valuation method, discounted cash flow has its shortcomings. It ignores outside factors that affect company value, such as price-earnings ratios. It also ignores asset values and other internal factors that can reduce or increase company value. Since the method is based on forecasts, a good understanding of the business, its market, and its past operations is essential.

Shareholder value

Shareholder value arrived with the sort of trumpeting that usually accompanies a big idea. Yet it really didn't say anything new. Shareholder value simply contends that a company should aim to maximize its value to shareholders. Indeed, this should be its *raison d'être*. The concept gave rise to value-based management, which suggested that generating profits was not enough, and that share price performance in particular should be viewed as a key indicator of corporate competence.

This exposes two very different views about the role of companies. It suggests that shareholders are the only ones that count. This overlooks the responsibility to employees and the wider community. But to large organizations, this perspective can be attractive for a number of reasons. First, it articulates the reasons for a company's existence with commendable clarity. There is none of the vagueness of making *reasonable* profits and pleasing all the company's stakeholders. It sounds both laudable and achievable – and shareholders are duty bound to like the idea. Second (with some adjustments), it fits with the entire idea of the stakeholder corporation. Shareholders are stakeholders and their numbers are increasingly likely to include other stakeholders, such as employees. Clearly, adding value to the investments of shareholders can have widespread benefits inside and outside an organization.

Advocates of shareholder value claim that it encourages a longer-term view of corporate performance. Instead of desperately seeking to boost quarterly results, executives can channel their energies into creating long-term value growth for shareholders. Institutional investors like the long view and this element was vital in the development of the concept.

Critics voice doubts about whether long-term perspectives are indeed encouraged. After all, they argue, downsizing was popular among shareholders who, perversely, often saw the value of their investments go up when a company announced it was downsizing.

While such arguments are difficult to prove either way, what can be said is that value-based management seeks to bridge the gap between the aims of executives and employees and those of shareholders. In the past, companies tended to measure success solely in terms of profits. If profits increased year on year, executives felt they were doing a good job. If, at the same time, the share price underperformed, they offered reassurance to institutional investors, but little else. In contrast, value-based management is as interested in cash and capital invested as in calculations about profitability. "Cash is a fact, profit is an opinion," argues one of the creators of the concept, Alfred Rappaport of Northwestern University's Kellogg School of Management.

While skeptics suggest that shareholder value is simply yet another consulting invention, its popularity among companies like Lloyds-TSB Group and top US conglomerates suggests it is a robust tool to, at least, monitor performance. And, for global businesses, perhaps the greatest advantage of shareholder value is that it provides universally consistent corporate results rather than ones produced to the dictates of local accounting rules.

REFERENCES

1. At the time, the report on bonfire night 1991 that Robert Maxwell was 'lost at sea' may have been considered relevant to any analysis of the financial performance of Maxwell Communication Corporation Plc.
2. The Outstanding Investor Digest (1998) Volume XIII Numbers 3 & 4, September 24.
3. The Outstanding Investor Digest (2000) Volume XVI, Numbers 4 & 5, Year End Edition.
4. Bill Child: R.C. Willey Home Furnishings in Robert P. Miles, *The Warren Buffett CEO: Secrets from the Berkshire Hathaway Managers*, p. 192, Wiley, 2002.
5. Letter to the shareholders, Berkshire Hathaway Annual Report, 1992.
6. Letter to the shareholders, Berkshire Hathaway Annual Report, 1987.
7. Letter to the shareholders, Berkshire Hathaway Annual Report, 1983.
8. Letter to the shareholders, Berkshire Hathaway Annual Report, 1997.
9. Letter to the shareholders, Berkshire Hathaway Annual Report, 1997.
10. Letter to the shareholders, Berkshire Hathaway Annual Report, 1983.
11. Letter to the shareholders, Berkshire Hathaway Annual Report, 1996.
12. Letter to the shareholders: Berkshire Hathaway Annual Report, 1986.
13. Welch, Jack and Byrne, John A., *Jack: What I've Learned Leading a Great Company and Great People*, Headline, p. 4, 2001.
14. Letter to the shareholders, Berkshire Hathaway Annual Report, 1999.
15. Letter to the shareholders, Berkshire Hathaway Annual Report, 1999.
16. Letter to the shareholders, Berkshire Hathaway Annual Report, 1999.
17. Letter to the shareholders, Berkshire Hathaway Annual Report, 2000.
18. Letter to the shareholders, Berkshire Hathaway Annual Report, 1999.
19. Letter to the shareholders, Berkshire Hathaway Annual Report, 1995.
20. Letter to the shareholders, Berkshire Hathaway Annual Report, 1984.
21. Letter to the shareholders, Berkshire Hathaway Annual Report, 1994 and letter to the shareholders, Berkshire Hathaway Annual Report.
22. Lowe, Janet, *Warren Buffett Speaks: Wit and Wisdom from the World's Greatest Investor*, Wiley, p. 80, 1997.
23. Letter to the shareholders, Berkshire Hathaway Annual Report, 1995.
24. Letter to the shareholders, Berkshire Hathaway Annual Report, 1995.
25. Letter to the shareholders, Berkshire Hathaway Annual Report, 1987.
26. Letter to the shareholders, Berkshire Hathaway Annual Report, 1985.
27. Buffett, E. Warren, 'Who Really Cooks the Books?' *The New York Times*, July 25, 2002.
28. Letter to the shareholders, Berkshire Hathaway Annual Report, 1984 and *The Outstanding Investor Digest*, Volume XV, Numbers 3 & 4, December 18, 2000.
29. Letter to the shareholders, Berkshire Hathaway Annual Report, 1998.
30. Letter to the shareholders, Berkshire Hathaway Annual Report, 1998.
31. Letter to the shareholders, Berkshire Hathaway Annual Report, 2000.
32. Berkshire Hathaway annual general meeting, 2003.
33. Letter to the shareholders, Berkshire Hathaway Annual Report, 1988.

34 Letter to the shareholders, Berkshire Hathaway Annual Report, 1985.
35 Letter to the shareholders, Berkshire Hathaway Annual Report, 1998.
36 Letter to the shareholders, Berkshire Hathaway Annual Report, 1988.
37 Letter to the shareholders, Berkshire Hathaway Annual Report, 1998.
38 Letter to the shareholders, Berkshire Hathaway Annual Report, 1983.
39 Letter to the shareholders, Berkshire Hathaway Annual Report, 1983.
40 Letter to the shareholders, Berkshire Hathaway Annual Report, 1998.
41 Letter to the shareholders: Berkshire Hathaway Annual Report, 1986.
42 Letter to the shareholders, Berkshire Hathaway Annual Report, 1998.
43 *The Outstanding Investor Digest,* Volume XIII, Numbers 3 & 4, September 24, 1998.
44 Letter to the shareholders, Berkshire Hathaway Annual Report, 1983.

CHAPTER 7

Organization

"The living organization is reality. The real metaphor is the mechanistic view of organizations."

Richard Pascale

"In a knowledge-dependent company, leaders must be thinking about creating space and freedom in their organizations – the antithesis of control and predetermined outcomes."

Arie de Geus

"Once an organization loses its spirit of pioneering and rests on its early work, its progress stops."

Thomas J. Watson

"The company is an economic vehicle invented by society. It has no rights to survive. But value systems and philosophies survive. People take it with them."

Edgar H. Schein

"A group of people get together and exist as an institution that we call a company so they are able to accomplish something collectively that they could not accomplish separately."

David Packard

The secrets of success

STUART CRAINER AND DES DEARLOVE

[*What makes a successful business? Trawl through the thoughts of the great business practitioners and thinkers and there is actually some consensus on the answer to this question. But how many of us have the time to discover what it is? So, for the time-poor, here is the condensed version.*]

There are hundreds of business books published each year and a profusion of journals and magazines. Cricket has been described as five minutes of excitement spread over five days and a similar rule applies to business wisdom. A book shelf of business books may contain a single nugget which could change your business.

So, to save you from the need to devour the contents of Harvard Business School's library, here is the business wisdom it contains distilled into 10 secrets of success. (Ten, of course, is a neat but random number.)

The first secret is that successful companies are not in business solely for the money. Companies which are geared to making money at all costs tend not, in the long run, to be successful. Henry Ford remarked that a company which only makes money is no sort of company at all. He was right. For successful companies money is a by-product of doing the right things.

Secret number two is the corollary of secret number one: companies which succeed have a broader notion of why they are in business. They have values. They know what they stand for, what is important, and this is reflected in their expectations of their employees.

Third, success is about culture. Companies which succeed have strong cultures. The same rule applies in sports. The best teams do not necessarily have the best players. Over the last decade, Manchester United have won many games in the final minutes sustained by their culture of success as much as by their ability.

This does not mean that the cultures are all enlightened and people-friendly. Successful companies sometimes have cultures which are, in some ways, unpleasant and unbalanced. They may, for example, encourage employees to work all the hours of the day or travel incessantly. Cultures come in all shapes and forms, but they encourage people to commit to the organization and its goals.

Customer facing

The fourth habit of highly successful companies is that they know their customers. They don't just have a vague idea what goes on in the minds of consumers; they intimately understand their needs, aspirations, and behavior. This is hardly earth shattering. But the instances of bad service are as frequent now as they ever were.

For all the talk of customer relationship management and customer loyalty, things haven't improved. Pop into one of the few remaining local banks and there is a long queue. The chances are there is an equally long queue at the post office – a post office which doesn't accept debit cards for some reason. The list of dismal service experiences is lengthy and lengthening. Knowing your customers and, as a result, being able to give them what they want remains an exception rather than the rule.

Secret number five is that successful companies are persistent and powerful communicators. Corporate politics kills communication. People keep information and bright ideas to themselves or communicate with a select few. In the best companies information and ideas are shared naturally and continually. Scott McNealy of Sun Microsystems has a favorite formula: 0.6L. Every time information passes a layer in the organization, only 60 percent gets through. This quickly adds up, especially in hierarchical firms. So the onus is on constantly communicating to ensure that the message gets through.

Secret number six is that great companies minimize the rules. Some organizations have recreated themselves as nanny states, such is the size of their corporate rule books. Rules stifle. Companies with strong cultures and a clear sense of values do not need a behavioral bible inspired by Stalin. How people behave is understood. Unencumbered by rules, people tend to get on with the job.

Of course, the most famous example of a company without rules was Enron. The greatest corporate failure of modern times hid its misbehavior behind the façade of being a freeflowing entrepreneurial company which gave executives the freedom to express themselves. This is laudable but, as Enron proved, it has to be backed by a strong sense of values and integrity. Enron had neither.

Simply the best

The seventh secret is not a secret at all: simplicity. Great companies, great leaders, and great entrepreneurs delight in simplicity. They run businesses simply. They cut back needless waste and hierarchy. They focus minds on the things that matter.

Keeping it simple is harder than it seems. It is easy to become distracted, to be taken in, to become carried away. Keeping faith in simple practices and principles is the preserve of the chosen few. Think of Warren Buffett. The master investor was unimpressed by the dot-com boom. He seemed out of step with the times. But he was right. Buffett has stayed resolutely faithful to his deceptively simply investment theories for decades. It works, so why elaborate?

Successful companies often explain what they do with persuasive simplicity. At Disney the sugary vision is to "make people happy" and at Motorola it is "Wireless." 3M focusses on "solving unsolved problems." AT&T talks about IM&M – "information movement and management."

Not only do they keep it simple, but successful companies never, ever rest on their laurels – no matter how impressive their laurels might be. They never sit still. Whether things succeed or fail, they learn from it and move on. Look at Microsoft. It is restlessly creative. It invents, launches, and then goes back to the beginning. It is in a perennial state of reinvention. Bill Gates is too curious to engage in self-congratulation.

Success is also about leadership. Successful companies have leaders who live the values of the company and continually set the culture. The role of the CEO is not to charm investment analysts or to seek out ever bigger acquisitions. The job of the CEO is to keep the culture and values of the company on track.

This is the link between leaders as diverse as Lord Weinstock, Richard Branson, and Herb Kelleher of Southwest Airlines. They set the tone. It doesn't matter how they do it. When Alan Jones was group managing director of TNT Express, he set the tone of the company by constantly writing personal notes to people. It showed that he knew that they had done well (or not); it showed that he was on the case; and it showed that he cared. If you receive a personal note from the MD you are likely to pay attention – and tell other people about it.

The final characteristic of highly successful companies is that they make a lot of money. Money is the happy result of the first nine habits. But if it doesn't turn out that way, please don't blame us; that's business.

RESOURCES

Boyatzis, Richard E., *The Competent Manager: a model for effective performance*, John Wiley, 1982.
Collins, James and Porras, Jerry, *Built to Last*, Harper Business, 1994.
Covey, Stephen, *The Seven Habits of Highly Effective People*, Running Press, 2000.
Dearlove, Des and Coomber, Stephen, *Heart & Soul*, Blessing White, 1998.
Handy, Charles, *The Future of Work*, Blackwell, 1984.
Mintzberg, Henry, *The Nature of Managerial Work*, McGraw Hill, 1973.
Schwartz, Peter, *The Art of the Long View*, Doubleday, 1991.

The new boy network

GEORGINA PETERS

[Clubs have always been an important part of doing business, places where power brokers thrashed out corporate deals. Today the marbled pillars and leather chairs of the gentlemen's club are making way for the technology-enabled power networks of cyberspace.]

The Reform Club on London's prestigious Pall Mall is not a place normally associated with business models. It is a gentlemen's club and one in which gentlemen are expected to wear ties. Founded in 1836, the Reform Club has no need for a plaque or sign outside. Members know where to find it. Inside, the Club is full of pillars, testament to the classical pretensions of its architects. It has the air of having witnessed better days. From here Jules Verne's fictional hero Phileas Fogg set off to travel the world in 80 days.

"Think of this as the emergent business model. The club. What could be simpler?" says Leif Edvinsson, a highly networked Swede best known for his championing of the concept of intellectual capital. "Think of the psychology of belonging, the ability to share knowledge with like-minded people, the prestige." To Edvinsson the club is not a leftover from P.G. Wodehouse, but a vibrant entrepreneurial engine of value and ideas. "The club is part of the emerging new theory of the firm, a model in which everybody is in charge," he says.

Increasingly, Edvinsson's enthusiastic endorsement of the club model is borne out by events. The entrepreneurial ferment of Silicon Valley was stirred by the activities of the Churchill Club and the Valley Association of Software Entrepreneurs. Established business clubs, such as the Conference Board, also remain robustly healthy even in a downturn.

The club concept suits the times. Businesses are increasingly seen as communities of people serving client communities. The onus is on relationships rather than processes – and if clubs are about anything they are about relationships. Today's network-obsessed business world has spawned a new generation of elite business clubs. Every businessperson knows the importance of networking; the more exclusive the club, the more cachet for members. "The more time you spend with distinguished people, the more distinguished you become," one club insider observes.

A club may be defined as an association of people with shared interests meeting in a specified place (even if the space is now as likely to be cyberspace as Fifth Avenue). In the past clubs tended to be social, charitable, political, artistic, or philosophical. Now people are brought together by and for business. In addition, clubs are no longer the preserve of individuals. Corporate membership is encouraged.

Of course, not all clubs label themselves as such. Words such as network and institute are popularly substituted, though the effect and the intent are often the same. Equally, other organizations which proclaim themselves to be clubs are little more than management portals attempting to sell every known business service.

While clubs are increasingly business-centered and run like businesses, their attractions remain universal and timeless. Clubs imbue their members with a collective identity, a sense of belonging to something larger than just themselves. In a world of ambiguity and alienation, clubs offer certainty and a sense of solidarity. Their enduring appeal is that they neatly fulfill a number of business and social functions. Clubs offer a range of benefits that are unmatched by other organizational forms.

The power of the network

The most obvious attraction is the network effect. For new members the club provides instant access to a professional network.

The club was a natural habitat for the networking-obsessed entrepreneurs and venture capitalists of the new economy who realized that value increases in correlation with the numbers of connections made. Loose networks became clubs and then businesses. Take First Tuesday, a meeting place and market for Internet start-ups, which began life in October 1998 at the Alphabet Bar in London's Soho. The club eventually had 100,000 members worldwide. In 2001 it was sold to a network of First Tuesday cities comprising a majority of the city licensees and a group of private investors.

Club purists may cavil at the inclusion of First Tuesday. Exclusivity is central to the *modus operandi* of many clubs. Every club wants to be the natural home of the new power elite. Networks are one thing; exclusive networks quite another.

In recent years the idea of privileged access has been taken to new heights. Consider the Global Business Network (GBN). Founded by scenario-planning guru Peter Schwartz and four friends in 1987, GBN emerged around a pool table in a Berkeley, California, basement. The five co-founders – Schwartz, Yale professor Jay Ogilvy, writer and futurist Stewart Brand, media executive Lawrence Wilkinson, and former Royal Dutch/Shell executive Napier Collyns – envisioned a worldwide learning community of organizations and individuals.

When they conceived GBN the founders had a definite metaphor in mind, says Peter Schwartz. "It was a British metaphor – the high table at Queens College,

Oxford, where we were all sitting not too many years before. The level of conversation of the people seated at the table was what we had in mind with GBN. It was more that than the traditional gentlemen's club you find in St James in London."

Indeed, GBN is based in Emeryville, CA, in a former tractor factory, and is now part of the consulting firm Monitor, after being bought in December 2000 for a seven-digit figure. GBN's corporate members include the likes of Coca-Cola, IBM, General Motors, Shell, and Unilever, which pay upwards of $35,000 annually to belong. The government of Singapore is also a member.

Key to GBN's success are its individual network members – the so-called "remarkable people." Individual members are invited to join only if they can "contribute remarkable insights, original ideas, and deep experience to our understanding of the forces transforming the present and shaping the future." Originally 60-strong, the number of remarkable people has now doubled.

Leading GBN members and advisers include the management luminaries Gary Hamel, Esther Dyson, Arie de Geus, and Michael Porter (founder of Monitor). Bill Joy, co-founder of Sun Microsystems, is another GBN member, as is John Kao, author of *Jamming* and founder of The Idea Factory. Kevin Kelly of *Wired* magazine, and artists including Brian Eno, Peter Gabriel, and the novelist Douglas Coupland, are also GBN members or advisory members. The author Bruce Sterling, a GBN member, has reflected that "it's like a Masonic group. It is a lot like the masons, but free masons."

"We made some good choices at the beginning," says Peter Schwartz. "Most fundamentally we saw the power of networking. That you could really amplify your business model and connection and create much more value through a network model – and it worked. We were among the first to see that."

GBN has three main activities: first, its Worldview membership services include regular meetings – with their famed learning journeys – recommended books, and a steady flow of publications and essays on topical issues. Second, it offers training courses, mainly on scenario planning. Third, corporate members can choose to contract GBN's strategic consulting services. Peter Schwartz believes it is a model that suits the times. "Lots of people have tried to create the model where you get people to feel that they belong to your community, whether it is airline miles or the idea that I can go to a grocery store and get a discount because I'm a member of the loyalty program. So, the notion of making people feel they belong to something that delivers value, and then in turn building platforms of service and products on top of that is a strong model."

Publisher Richard Stagg, of Pearson Education, attended a three-day GBN event in New York. He confirms the appeal. "It was one of the most stimulating experiences I've ever had in business. At one point I found myself in a discussion group with the head of a Texas oil company, a film maker, a professor, and someone who worked with the CIA."

Offering diverse perspectives is a GBN hallmark. Stagg also experienced a GBN learning journey, involving a tour of downtown NYC. "I spent the afternoon teamed up with a teenager in a public school in South Bronx. He told me that he used to do all his learning through the web but he'd just discovered books. As a publisher that really makes you stop and think. If I was a company I would definitely join a network like that. I would send along maybe my marketing director and my brightest young thing in the strategy department."

Members only

If one of the great attractions of clubs is that they allow members to rub shoulders with the great and the good, another is that they allow them to do so in an informal way. There is no need to make an appointment when with a minimum of planning you can simply bump into the person you want to talk at a club event. Clubs, then, offer another important advantage: they provide long-term relationships.

In business, the boundaries of most relationships are well defined. They are prescribed by a contract, an assignment, or a transaction. Opportunities to meet with potential clients and suppliers without a formal agenda are rare. Moreover, continuity of relationship depends on an ongoing stream of work.

The club is different. Continuity of relationships is provided by membership of the club. Members continue to associate over many years regardless of their formal business ties. The doors are always open. For the club as business model continuity has serious attractions. It allows the club organizer to generate revenue simply by maintaining and servicing the membership. Consider the Strategos Institute, part of Strategos, the consulting operation founded by strategy guru Gary Hamel. The Strategos Institute is a club in all but name. It offers two levels of membership – general or full partner level. General members can participate in two of the four research streams the Institute is pursuing, while partners can participate in all four. Partnership has its privileges – a one-day workshop with Gary Hamel designed expressly for the company. "Partner-level membership brings your company into an elite circle of leading-edge organizations that truly form a knowledge-creating community," says Strategos.

Strategos has used the club model to create a new twist to conventional consulting. The beauty of its approach is that customer loyalty is built in. In traditional consulting, lines of communication go cold and billing ends between assignments. The club model offers a continuous stream of revenue. To its members it also offers cachet in abundance.

GBN's consulting business is also self-perpetuating. "The highest value business you can get is repeat business," says Peter Schwartz. "The cost of acquisition is so much lower and therefore so much more profitable that that has an enormously high value and I think people have come to recognize that."

Communities of mutual interest

All clubs are based on common interests. Whether members share a vocation, a hobby, or simply a desire to be rich and famous, they are bound by common threads. They have a reason to hang out together. The Groucho Club which opened its doors to London's literati in 1984, for example, was meant to be a club for non-clubby media and arty types. Taking its name from Groucho Marx's quip "I don't care to belong to any club that would accept me as a member," the Groucho has thrived. In 2001 it was bought for £11.7 million by a consortium including Matthew Freud (a relative of Sigmund and also Rupert Murdoch's son-in-law).

Today, communities of mutual interests offer new possibilities. The club as marketplace or commercial match-making agency becomes an attractive proposition. Companies such as Garage.com built a business out of providing a marketplace for investors and entrepreneurs to come together with a view to pursuing mutual interests. Clubs can fulfill a similar role.

The reach and potential of clubs is growing. Membership can forge new contacts in distant places or help span disparate groups. Today, an increasingly global economy demands increasingly global clubs. Clubs that reach across national borders can provide access and instant introductions around the world.

The Internet is also spawning a new club model – the virtual club. It is no longer necessary to go to the club house; the club can come to you. One man pushing the concept is Dr Eddie Obeng, founder of Pentacle, the Virtual Business School. Obeng, previously a b-school lecturer, set up Pentacle in 1994. Today, it has two full-time employees, a network of management trainers, and a turnover of over $1.5 million. Obeng's latest venture is a series of cyber clubs, dubbed New World Pioneer Clubs. Obeng believes the days of the fusty club house are numbered. "The traditional business club is heading the way of the dinosaurs," he says. "People can't spare the time to go to meetings, to seek out people with similar backgrounds, and listen to the outdated philosophy of a management spin-doctor."

The first of the Pentacle cyberclubs, allchange.com, was launched in September 2000. The idea, to provide a "fun and interactive place to learn, swap ideas, play, teach, shop, and explore." It now has over 600 members. The cost of membership ranges from £450 ($675) to £5,000 ($7,500) a year.

"The great thing about a club is that it has a barrier to entry," Obeng explains. "The people inside want to be there and if the barrier to entry is a particular competency or expertise, this ensures that club members have quality conversations. Once our love affair with massive corporations comes to an end, clubs will be the way in which people interact. In the short term, people are going to have to become smarter about how they market themselves during a downturn. Clubs offer one possible solution of getting to a very targeted audience in a positive environment."

In a business world of ambiguity and alienation, clubs offer certainty and a sense of belonging. That isn't going to change. If you can't beat them, better have your check book at the ready.

> ### Napier Collyns and the GBN network
>
> Founded in 1987, GBN owes much of its appeal to the elite list of individual members, thanks in no small part to co-founder Napier Collyns. Described as a networker extraordinaire, Collyns was one of the original scenario planning team at Shell under Pierre Wack in the 1960s, and quickly gravitated to his natural role as a network co-ordinator. When GBN was mooted he was able to populate its elite membership almost single-handedly from his personal network. Today, he travels constantly, tirelessly communicating with the network and adding new names, from fields as diverse as rock music, computer science, and management, to his contacts book.
>
> The link between these people appears elusive, but is actually close to hand: Collyns collects interesting people. In Collyns' world everyone (everyone who matters at least) is connected; it is just a question of identifying the link. Collyns describes GBN as "an intellectual elite in a business context." "We instinctively knew this was going to be a networked world even before the Internet was established. We happened to invent a model that worked. We never tried to sell it. We didn't have to. When anyone heard about GBN they wanted to join."
>
> Membership, says Collyns, can be rewarding both intellectually and financially. "Like all clubs it's a group of friends who then select their own friends. We set out with 400 names and selected 60 original members. It's an elite club. It's like being a member of an Oxford or Cambridge college; once you're in you are always a member."
>
> With GBN's co-founders, Collyns grasped early on that electronic communication would have an important influence on the future of global business. "It is not a coincidence that GBN was born as a network at a time when the networking idea was growing," he says. "GBN was always an online network, from the mid-1980s on, long before the Internet proper." In those days, members used Shell's internal IT network and the Well, an open communication channel established by GBN co-founder Stewart Brand. "That gave us – all the members of GBN – instant communication."
>
> GBN quickly became a force to be reckoned with in the global economy. It is an image it has cultivated. A 1994 article about GBN in *Wired* magazine, for example, was headlined "Conspiracy of Heretics." "It's very difficult to have an elite group of people that outsiders don't think is a conspiracy," Collyns says.

Napier Collyns and the GBN network (continued)

Exclusivity, he knows, is a key factor in GBN's success. In return for their corporate membership cards, thrusting executives get the chance to hob-nob with each other and GBN's remarkable people at seminars and conferences, picking up fresh ideas and perspectives on the way. "People join GBN to hear ideas about the future and share their own ideas. Belonging allows them to talk to people they couldn't otherwise get access to," says Napier Collyns.

Harking back to Churchill

Silicon Valley's prosperity is built on a heady cocktail of brains and contacts. Among the organizations bringing the two together is the Churchill Club, based in Campbell, CA. Founded in 1985 as a non-profit organization, it now boasts over 5,000 members and has a staff of seven.

The club, which was founded by Rich Karlgaard, publisher of *Forbes* magazine, and Anthony Perkins, chairman and editor-in-chief of Red Herring Communications, prides itself on being a place where "important people say important things." The club invites speakers and gives members an opportunity to network and rub shoulders with the digerati and others. Over the years it has hosted many of the brightest stars in the high-tech firmament, including Marc Andreesen, Steve Ballmer, John Chambers, Jim Clark, Larry Ellison, Andy Grove, Meg Whitman, and a certain William Henry Gates III. George W. Bush's visit on April 30, 2002 was the first time a sitting president had addressed the Churchill Club.

As its name suggests, the Churchill doffs its cap in the general direction of the UK. "The original mission of the club was more political," explains executive director Kim Moeller. "The two founders thought of Jefferson and Lincoln but wanted to be non-partisan. Churchill was non-partisan and also had a wealth of other interests apart from politics. Over the years our focus has shifted to business, technology, and entrepreneurialism."

So, why do people join? "First, we present a broad range of topics so it is a good place to get information on your industry and other industries. People also like to hear from people who started their own companies. In addition, some of our programs give very specific advice, such as a recent one on doing business in Europe," says Kim Moeller. "The second reason is to network. Members appreciate the diversity of people they meet. They're not all from the same industry.

Harking back to Churchill (continued)

"For corporations often it's a question of visibility. When companies – big or small – are interested in increasing their visibility in Silicon Valley, they join. Corporations also benefit from the networking opportunities, especially at the higher level of membership."

Kim Moeller believes that the Churchill benefits from having panels of speakers rather than individuals running through their standard speech. "That way you get people to say things they wouldn't normally say. We want it to be Churchillian in nature – solid information, contrarian thinking, combined with wit."

RESOURCES

de Geus, Arie, *The Living Company*, Harvard Business School Press, 1998.

Watson, Thomas, Jr, *A Business and its Beliefs*, McGraw Hill, 1963.

Whyte, William, *The Organization Man*, Simon & Schuster, 1956.

The integrated organization

FONS TROMPENAARS AND PETER WOOLIAMS

> Gradually it is becoming clear that a purely financial view is much too limited to capture the quality of an organization. Return on investment has been shown to be too one-sided. It follows in a long line of failed attempts to pin down organizational success.

Scientific Management once dominated organization theory. But it was not humane enough. A human organization is more than a collection of rational robots that need to operate in a most efficient way. By the 1960s, the human relations school was lecturing organizations on how to motivate their workers through the subtle use of carrots and the not so subtle use of sticks. Subsequently, attention moved outside the organization as the importance of customers became apparent. Suddenly, customer satisfaction – and even delight – became the number one priority for organizations.

Less than 10 years ago the focus shifted again. Shareholders, who had been all but forgotten in the stampede to delight customers, were reinstated on the organizational throne. The tunnel-vision era of shareholder value began. Organizations scrambled to create value for people who never share. In the era of shareholder value, employees are judged on their contribution to corporate profit. This monolithic model now looks to have burned itself out.

After the eras of the "homo efficientis," the "homo socialis," the "homo clienteles," and the "homo economicus," what is next? The time has come for an organizational mindset that can integrate opposites: the "homo reconciliens." This is the organizational model where opposites, dilemmas, and trilemmas can be reconciled on higher levels.

Toward the integrated organization

A company's stock price is completely dominated by financial and, therefore, historic factors. In combination with expectations, these determine the share price. Recent corporate scandals mean, however, that there is growing distrust of numbers alone. We need to find more reliable indices. (Personally, we have always questioned why the value of an organization made up of employees, suppliers, clients, and shareholders should be determined by a relatively small group of stock market traders.)

But what is the alternative way of determining value? Very much in line with the criteria of good individual leadership we need to fundamentally redefine and recalibrate the criteria for the quality of the collective organization. Many traditional methods for determining leadership qualities are based on a number of criteria, where the extremes of the scales are often mutually exclusive. The ISTJ (introvert, sensitive, thinking, and judging) score, for example, is the most popular type of successful manager in the Myers Briggs typology. With Shell managers it was the more analytical and realistic manager with helicopter quality that prevailed. But all of these qualities exclude their mirror images.

It is not that the extrovert, emotional, and perceiving manager, or the creative, imaginative, and grounded manager should get more chances. It is simply that these characteristics can, if handled well, be useful qualities. They are useful to the organization so it is a question of integration. To ascertain the essential qualities of a leader we need to judge how well an individual integrates opposites. The effective leader uses emotions to increase his or her power of thinking. They use analysis in order to test the larger whole; and they use imagination to make realistic decisions. The same applies to organizations in which these leaders operate.

In the course of our consulting work we have encountered many tensions and dilemmas that are common within organizations. From these we have identified 12 golden dilemmas that recur again and again. We then carried out some experiments with 10 blue chip organizations. We researched whether we could map the value of an organization in an alternative way by the degree to which these organizations integrated the tensions. From this we derived our Return on Reconciliation (ROR) Index. Our hope was that the average score would give us a much better insight than pure financial and technical analysis.

Some of the examples speak for themselves. They suggest that the value of an organization is affected by its capacity to reconcile a number of tensions. So, for example, the reconciliation of the dilemma between efficiency of the internal organization and the development of the employees is of prime importance in determining the value of an organization. Here the homo efficientis meets the homo socialis. On the field of tension between financial short-term results and investments for the long term the homo economicus meets the homo clienteles. The development of technology needs to reconcile itself with the demand of the market in such a way that the market helps decide which technologies to push. On the other hand, the push of technology helps determine the markets one wants to be pulled by.

The need for consistencies in the global organization needs to be fine-tuned with the need for local flexibility and sensitivity. In other words, the homo clienteles needs to be integrated with the homo efficientis. The last example relates to a simultaneous high score on both specialization in supply and the value added of the organization by a broad assortment of products.

In our research so far, employees were asked to fill in the 12 "reconciliation scoreboards" to produce the ROR-index. The next stage is to ask clients, suppliers, and financial analysts to provide their opinions and score the organization on the 12 golden dilemmas. In time, this may provide an alternative ROR-index that will eventually augment or even replace financial-technical analyses. With our approach, historical indices are enriched by a measure of future potential. Return on investment (ROI), we hope, will eventually be replaced by the much more illuminating return on reconciliation (ROR).

Twelve golden dilemmas

The last five years of research has given us the opportunity to look at the dilemmas that were raised by our clients. We have asked all participants to our workshops to fill in what we call our "webcue." In preparing for the workshop, they are asked about the issues, challenges, and problems they are facing in their business. They are asked to phrase their challenge as "on the one hand ... on the other." In this way, we have encouraged the participants to see their issues as a dilemma.

Our analysis of the results found dilemmas in all stakeholder areas, in particular with shareholders.

For the efficiency of the internal organization, the results highlighted 12 recurrent dilemmas (see Figure 7.1). The first eight are discussed below.

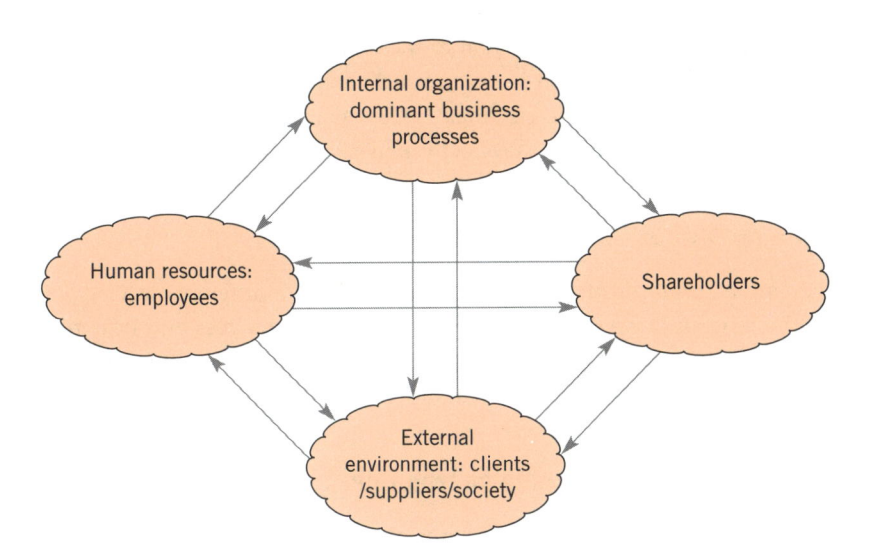

Figure 7.1: *Four basic organizational dimensions*

1. Internal organization versus external organization/client/supplier/society

All dilemmas raised related to how the internal organization prepared itself to be more effective for its environment. One of the most frequently discussed tensions, for example, is on the one hand, the need for (global) consistency and (central) standards, and on the other hand, the need for (local) flexibility and (decentralization) customization to serve local customers better. The question here is whether the systems, the processes, and the leadership in the central organization serve the decentralized operations optimally. Conversely, the challenge is whether the local best practices are taken seriously to best serve the larger organization.

2. External organization versus internal organization

The second major dilemma concerns the co-ordination between societal demands and organizational goals. The question here is whether the internal allocation of resources is in line with the long-term demands of society. Obviously the sustainable organization is the reconciliation of this issue with the need to make a profit.

3. Internal organization versus human resources

Similarly we found some interesting dilemmas in the people area. The first dilemma concerns the tension between the efficiency of business processes and the motivation of employees. Most recently, the issue of cost reduction versus development of people has become more significant. Traditionally one is done at the cost of the other. Manpower reduction is often detrimental to the motivation of employees. Conversely, highly motivated people are often less concerned about the efficiency of the organization. All dilemmas however were essentially focussed around the tension between the efficiency of the organization and the effectiveness of its human resources.

4. Human resources versus internal organization

This dilemma is similar to the second dilemma but has a different starting point. It is about the tension between the effectiveness of the employees and how they can help the organization to become more efficient. One example here that was raised is how the values held by the employees can be reconciled with corporate strategy.

5. Internal organization versus shareholders

The importance of this dilemma is perhaps one of the most underestimated ones. The separation of ownership and management gives rise to many dilemmas. These center on the tension between a fair return in the short term and an even better return in the long term. Our findings suggest that in many cases employees feel that the quality of the internal organization is too often sacrificed for the quarterly returns of the shareholder. Therefore the fifth major dilemma is the famous tension between the long-term needs of investments for sustainable growth within the organization and the often short-term needs to pay a reasonable return to the shareholders.

6. Shareholders versus internal organization

A growing challenge is to convince shareholders that they have a responsibility for the effectiveness of the organization. Several dilemmas were raised here. Many were related to the corporate governance issues. On one hand there is a feeling that shareholders should participate in the decision-making process. On the other, however, there seems to be a need for freedom and independence of management and employees to come to the right business decisions.

7. Human resources versus shareholders

This tension has not been raised often in our database of dilemmas. That does not mean it is not an issue. The seventh dilemma concerns the relationship between employees and shareholders. If too much decision-making power resides with the employees, then shareholder interests suffer. Conversely, once shareholders get too much to say, employees are often underpaid and feel too much dependent on the whims of investors; for example, their desire to cut costs through headcount. Obviously reconciliation lies in a form of co-determination or partnership such as stock options.

8. Human resources versus external organization

This tension relates to the challenges employees face in relating to the outside world, i.e. their clients and suppliers. The major issue at stake is to connect the internally controlled culture, and, in particular, technology push, with the externally controlled world of market pull. The dilemma lies in the fact that reconciling these two tensions is central to a culture of inventiveness. A consumer electronics company like Philips, for example, has great knowledge and inventiveness in specific technologies. Its marketing function is also very strong. The problem facing the company is that the two major functional areas don't communicate effectively. The success of Philips and any organization depends on the integration of both areas.

This perfectly illustrates the importance – and value-enhancing properties – of reconciliation. It is only by gaining a better understanding of, and finding creative ways to manage and measure, the impact of such tensions that the true potential of organizations can be assessed. It is only by embracing and integrating the inherent tensions of organizational life that organizations and the people who populate them can truly thrive.

RESOURCES

Trompenaars, Fons and Wooliams, Peter, *Business Across Cultures*, Capstone Publishing, 2003.

Commentary

Piling on the pounds

In recent years, managers have applied the corporate equivalent of liposuction to their organizations. Companies have been transformed into lean, mean commercial machines. But the latest thinking suggests it may be time to put some fat back.

A 2003 report by the Economist Intelligence Unit indicated that cost control is now the number one priority for CEOs. But there is growing evidence that organizations that focus exclusively on cost can become dangerously anorexic. The issue is especially relevant in the light of tragedies such as the Columbus space shuttle disaster.

Management research is increasingly focussing on the trade-off between cost efficiency and reliability. Some experts believe that the key to the next generation of organizations lies with so-called high-reliability organizations (HROs). First identified in the 1980s, HROs are defined as "mission-critical organizations that have operated high-hazard, low-risk technologies at very high levels of reliability over a long period of time." They include air traffic control, nuclear power plants, and aircraft carriers which manage in such a way that they almost never experience a high impact failure.

Among those researching the topic are three academics from Cranfield University. Professor David Tranfield, Dr David Denyer, and Javier Marcos, from the Advanced Management Research Center, argue that the HRO model is increasingly relevant both in the private and public sector. "We are reaching the limits of taking a singular focus on 'lean' as the key guiding principle of management thinking and organization design," says Professor Tranfield. "It has brought many benefits over the last 20 years or so. But where this mindset allows mission delivery to become jeopardized, it can result in corporate failure, or worse still in safety-critical functions, in disaster."

To understand HROs, say the Cranfield academics, you first have to understand how and why failure occurs. Research into large-scale catastrophes suggests that accidents rarely occur spontaneously. Most have lengthy incubation periods.

Over time, the imperative for cost efficiency can reduce the tolerance for unexpected events and create organizational systems that are fragile. "Without a sympathetic appreciation of mission-critical factors, constant across-the-board cheeseparing turns lean into anorexic," says Professor Tranfield.

One study of the 1986 Challenger space shuttle disaster, by William H. Starbuck and Frances J. Milliken of New York University, concluded that "fine-tuning reduces the possibilities of success ... until a serious failure occurs."

Commentary (continued)

The Cranfield research focusses on transferring the lessons of HROs to other organizations. "Although the original work was done in high-hazard–low-risk environments, the ideas can be used in all organizations," says Professor Tranfield. "All organizations have mission-critical aspects, and it is here that HRO principles should be applied."

In particular, Professor Tranfield and his colleagues believe that HRO ideas are relevant to the construction sector in the context of the Private Finance Initiative (PFI) and Public Private Partnerships (PPP), where project timescales are longer – up to 25 years – and failure-free service is vital to profitability.

So what are the management lessons of HROs? The Cranfield trio identify eight dimensions, or mechanisms, that contribute to high reliability. First, is a strong organizational culture of reliability, with a low or zero tolerance for errors. Second, HROs create reserve capacity and back-ups to cope with unexpected circumstances.

Third, HROs' cultures emphasize continuous learning. Recognizing that learning by trial and error is not an option, they train staff to follow standard operating procedures, and identify potential sources of failure. The fourth factor is effective and varied patterns of communication: HROs create information-rich environments by measuring processes and making the data widely available internally. Fifth, HROs recognize the importance of psychosocial factors such as staff commitment, satisfaction, and motivation. Sixth, HROs have an adaptable approach to decision making. They also exhibit high collective responsibility. The buck stops everywhere.

Flexibility is the seventh characteristic. HROs demonstrate an ability to shift between three modes of operation: bureaucratic, high tempo, and emergency. Although hierarchical, they are able to switch to a flatter structure when danger threatens. Finally, HROs have a distinctive approach to technology. Equipment may not be state-of-the-art but it is maintained to exceptionally high standards. They also avoid adding new technology that adds unnecessary complexity.

High reliability, the Cranfield researchers argue, is not about any single one of these characteristics, but about finding the right balance between them. In practice, argue Professor Tranfield, Dr Denyer, and Mr Marcos, the challenge will be to integrate the best elements of the lean and high-reliability models. "The need is not to lose hard-won efficiencies but to focus on efficiency and reliability as key objectives in creating high-performing organizations. We need to go beyond lean."

Carrying some fat can be costly. But the costs of not doing so can be far higher. The Air France Concorde accident killed 109 people and led to compensation claims of £150 million. The total cost of the meltdown of the Chernobyl nuclear plant is estimated at $235 billion.

Organizational democracy and organizational politics

DAVID BUTCHER AND MARTIN CLARKE

[*Democracy may be the preferred model for the governing of nations but it is yet to become the corporate organizational model of choice. Should democracy have more of a role in the workplace?*]

The democratization of organizations has advanced considerably in the past 20 years. Substantial changes in economic structure have forced enterprises to rethink the internal distribution of organizational power. However, despite these developments there is increasing evidence that employees do not always see themselves as beneficiaries of such changes. Surveys and reports regularly highlight unacceptable levels of employee cynicism, disillusionment, and alienation. Thus it would seem that attempts to instill democratic principles in organizations are at odds with the acceptance of democratic values in society at large.

The values that underpin democracy have created a convergence of the political order worldwide, permeating both parliamentary systems and institutions across many societies. But the idea that organizations, too, can be viewed as democratically governable political systems has usually been confined to "interesting experiments," as with such notable successes as the Spanish Mondragon Cooperative, or simply dismissed as inimical to rational management and unitary organizational purpose.

But experiments aside, there is ever less dispute that organizations are inherently pluralistic in terms of their goals, that this diversity of view must be given voice, and thus that managers should and certainly do exercise power in pursuit of conflicting objectives. This raises two fundamental questions: how is that power to be used, and to achieve whose objectives?

The principles of democracy, of course, stipulate clear answers to both these questions in terms of a supporting political system. But if the use of politics is itself illegitimate, or even inadmissible, then what is the basis for an appropriate organizational democratic process? Does the acceptability of organizational democracy depend on the legitimization of organizational politics?

Organizational democracy in the workplace

The move to redistribute workplace influence has a long history. It can be traced from European feudalism, through the industrial revolution, the many attempts to introduce participation schemes and co-operative enterprises over the past 100 years, to the more recent emphasis on delayering and empowerment. Today democratization is center stage.

While there are divergent views about the nature and form of democratized organizations, there is some agreement that they are likely to share the following principles:

- devolved power and responsibility for many more organizational decisions, leading to smaller, self-organizing units;
- acceptance of diverse internal and external interests based on power as a function of successful relationships rather than structure;
- high levels of psychological ownership of organizational activities that depend on individual contribution, knowledge, and leadership.

However, instances where these principles are to be found in practice do not arise simply as a result of the well-intentioned application of democratic values. Rather they are a response to very real business imperatives. Technological advancement, innovation, globalization, and an increasing concern for business ethics are forcing management to reconsider its approach to this issue.

The drivers of organizational democracy

- The need for continual innovation and improvement has led to the recognition that individual knowledge is a valuable organizational asset that necessitates acceptance of the power of the possessor.
- The recognition that customer satisfaction is critical to organizational success has facilitated the idea of employee empowerment and delayering. For example, in AT&T Universal Card Services front-line staff are trusted to handle 95 percent of requests on the first call, even credit extensions.
- The benefits of managing knowledge and reducing hierarchy are realized through attracting, retaining, and developing key talent. In the words of Charles Handy, employees are increasingly treated as "members of voluntary clubs" rather than organizational assets, or human resources.
- As organizations align ever more closely with the needs of specific customer groups, individual business units become more specialized. The resulting

> fragmentation of organizational structures transfers power away from the corporate center in the service of particular customer needs.
>
> - The interdependence of organizations with their suppliers and customers has led to increasing acceptance that external stakeholders influence decision making and ultimately, competitive advantage. Democratization, therefore, is also being driven by the need for organizational boundaries to be permeable and at times altogether removed.
>
> - The need to secure greater levels of employee commitment has led organizations to democratize their approach to rewards and ownership. Stock ownership plans are now commonplace, and in some organizations, such as the UK-based John Lewis Partnership, include all employees as owners.
>
> - At an institutional level, the democratization process has also been influenced on a global scale by growing legislation in the areas of employee protection, participation, and communication. For example in Europe, an EU directive will, in due course, force organizations with more than 50 employees to consult staff about decisions that may lead to substantial changes in work organization.

All of these trends reflect the increasing importance of many voices in the management of contemporary organizations. They act incrementally on society at national and global levels, edging organizations closer to accepting the need to reconcile different aims as the basis for managing. Yet there remains a question as to the real impact these changes are having. Newspapers and management journals regularly report on surveys highlighting worrying levels of employee dissatisfaction and stress, often fueled by issues such as poor communication, race and gender discrimination, and organizational injustices such as harsh lay-offs. Even in areas where progress has supposedly been made there is considerable evidence that change has been patchy at best. The benefits of autonomous work teams, for example, have been known since Pehr Gyllenhammer's experiments at Volvo over 40 years ago, yet this organizing principle has never been widely adopted. Or consider the move toward empowerment. As Chris Argyris points out: "Like the emperor's new clothes, we praise it loudly in public and ask ourselves privately why we can't see it. There has been no transformation in the workforce, and there has been no sweeping metamorphosis."[1]

Furthermore, this gap between public praise and reality devalues the efforts of management to democratize organizations and worse, creates cynicism. A survey by Gallup revealed that 80 percent of employees in the UK are not engaged at work, that is, they are not psychologically bonded to their organization even though they may be productive.

It is not hard to find reasons for this in the everyday experience of managers. For example, enlightened management's efforts to treat employees as corporate citizens by enhancing their employability falls into disrepute when training and development budgets are slashed in the face of poor trading performance. Much the same tension arises when "independent" business units are subject to top-down budgeting processes. Examples are legion because they are routine. Evidently something beyond good intentions and the changing business environment is required to effect a fundamental redistribution of organizational power.

The rational organization

There are of course well-rehearsed explanations for this continuing disconnection: management simply does not want to relinquish power; most employees do not want power, because with it comes responsibility. No doubt the arguments around these positions will continue. But let us consider an altogether more powerful reason for the discontinuity between the desire for democratization and organizational practices – the *rational mindset*.

Mindsets are the particular ways that individuals come to think about everyday experience, saturating attention to the exclusion of all else. They are driven by values that are created and reinforced at an institutional level, and define what is appropriate and inappropriate in specific contexts. In the context of "rational organization," the mindset is governed by values about rationality, creating a deeply held belief system that governs what is assumed about organizations as they are worked in each and every day.

Thus despite their self-evident diversity of goals and need for dispersed power, organizations implicitly remain places of unity where employees work with consistent strategies toward clear corporate goals. Top management continue to provide direction through vision and value statements that reflect prescriptions about desired behaviors. Key to these behaviors is still the need for employees to appreciate the logic of working collaboratively in order to share effort and knowledge in the wider interests of the enterprise.

Yet these principles of rational organization are not in themselves in opposition to those of democracy. Indeed, the argument in support of organizational democracy is persuasive, particularly because of its emphasis on combining the best of both value systems. But in practice, the rational mindset implicitly undermines the democratization process.

Consider the first principle of the democratized organization we highlighted earlier – the idea that power must be hierarchically devolved. This of course does not obviate the need for hierarchy. Rather, it ensures that decisions are made by those best placed to take them. In rational terms it promotes efficiency and effectiveness. Yet there are countless examples of management embarking on empowerment strategies only to wrest decision-making control again in times of economic downturn. Significantly, one recent longitudinal research program led by Frank Heller, designed to assess the devolution of power at work, concludes "that organizational influence sharing appears to have made only limited progress during the last 50 years."[2]

The second principle of democratized organizations, the reconciliation of diverse interests, is also accommodated within the rational model in theory, but not necessarily in practice. Stakeholders, particularly employees, can be satisfied through a range of motivational devices and management tools that "balance" potentially clashing demands. The "business scorecard" concept does just that. Likewise, the separate and often conflicting interests of business units, projects, product lines, and even brands can be managed as an in-house market democracy. Businesses like 3M, Apple Computer Inc., and MCI have done it successfully for years. Yet the intention to meet this diversity of interests is easily submerged in the pursuit of corporate goals. Not surprisingly, research has consistently shown that employees tend to surface act espoused corporate goals rather than wholeheartedly embrace them, raising the question of whether congruity of interests is the means to a corporate goal or an end in itself.

This priority of corporate vision and values also serves to undermine the establishment of the "psychological ownership" principle. Even small organizations can be sufficiently complex and fragmented such that corporate goals and values become disconnected from the *raison d'être* of constituent business units, or become too generic to provide meaningful ownership. Yet there is solid research evidence that employees attach greater psychological ownership to local issues having a direct impact on them than they do to distant corporate business agendas. This simple understanding underpins the massively devolved structures of successful companies like engineering giant ABB, and WPP, the global marketing services company. Consider, for example, the energy often invested by front-line workers in recommending improvements within their sphere of activities. Consider also how easily this commitment can be extinguished by management inaction born of desire for corporate neatness. Again, the concept of local identification does not itself contradict the principle of organizational unity. But in practice, psychological ownership of organizational activities that depends on individual contribution, leadership, and knowledge is limited by the rational mindset.

Progressive politics

If rational thinking undermines the practice rather than the principles of organizational democracy, it can only be because the mindset has failed to evolve beyond a conception of organizations that did not need to legitimize diversity of goals and agendas. In society at large the means of achieving such democratic reconciliation is not at issue. We call it the political system. But rather than recognize the possibility of systematizing the administration of diverse agendas, the rational mindset has the closed-loop effect of associating "organizational politics" with misuse of power, secrecy, and backroom deals. That this may sometimes be the case further obscures the conception of politics as a constructive organizational mechanism for resolving partisan agendas.

Certainly, the use of power to promote partisan interests is open to abuse. In the context of governing through the political system, this process is judged principled so long as a cause is just. But if a just cause is at times an elusive concept in government, it is doubly so in organizations. There, one person's just cause may be another's slashed budget, leading, as in government, to the question of who decides what is in the best interests of who. However, political interest is institutionalized in democratic systems, as are the mechanisms for reconciling just causes. As political theorists have shown, these mechanisms are both formal and informal (as with "behind the scenes" lobbying). Those with formal power (elected members of an administration) have the great responsibility of both representing the interests of the (theoretical) majority and preserving the integrity of a system that represents the interests of all. The organizational parallel lies in the role of top management – often now argued to be one of stewardship and grand social design, achieved through the mediation of many strong interests internal and external to their organization.

Organizations, of course, do not have the same constitutions as governments, nor can they fully emulate the principles of democracies. For one thing, most organizations do not elect their managers, and for another, managerial agendas are not usually associated with great social causes. Furthermore, unlike organizations, government itself does not have corporate goals. Rather, it is the institution through which the corporate goals of consecutive administrations are realized. Nevertheless, the principles of democracy, representing as they now widely do the ideal of constructive politics, arguably contain the model for organizational democracy. They do this in two key respects.

- Constructive politics, in this general sense, represent the *logical process* by which diverse interests and stakeholders may be reconciled in organizations. Given that it is in the nature of organizations for powerful interest groups to form, more than ever in today's decentralized corporations, how else can this reconciliation be achieved? Not through hierarchical control – the evidence for that is overwhelmingly clear. Indeed, within the model of constructive politics, significant interest groups check the power invested in formal hierarchy. Thus, far from being an irrational organizational response, therefore, the political system, as with institutional government, is the only judicious way of managing inevitable differences.

- In recognizing the multi-goal nature of organizations, the political organizational model explicitly values diversity. Generic corporate goals (that is, survival, growth, or profit) become an umbrella under which (competing) top management visions and disparate local interests can be balanced. The democratic management of these differences is thus a primary component of organizational working, and many examples are to be found. Some are well-documented experiments in democracy such as St Luke's, the UK advertising agency, a collective in which all employees become shareholders. No job descriptions exist, and employees work in "citizen cells" of no more than 35 people which have complete control over their budgets and income streams, and can question their own direction at any time. But there are many unsung, yet nonetheless successful examples. Such organizations have one noticeable feature in common – diversity is considered both desirable and essential.

Toward democracy

In the light of the above discussion, the problem of how to accelerate the process of organizational democratization is better cast as one of how to hasten the legitimization of organizational politics. However, it is a daunting prospect given the values underlying the rational mindset run as deep as those of democracy. After all, the language of rationality applies alike to military organizations, churches, universities, and Wal-Mart. So how might politics gain a rightful place as an organizing principle?

Executive development seems an obvious answer until we remind ourselves that this activity does not exist independently of the rational mindset. Consider corporate university programs. These have become a prevalent means of ensuring that managers live the organizational values that align behaviors to the mission and strategy. The values of rationality that lie behind such interventions remain deeply embedded, even though much of this effort appears to have little long-term impact, if the persistence of alternative agendas is any guide. Part of the problem lies in what is meant by executive development. Many activities so described are not in practice developmental, in that they do not enable managers to consider their own values and beliefs, and how these influence behavior. Yet it is those personal values that managers must consider before alternative models of organizing can be explored.

In contrast, the business schools should provide the independent intellectual critique required to address alternative organizational models. In practice, however, they too are caught in the same rational mindset trap as their client world. Indeed, the academic communities of North America and Europe have played a substantial role in articulating and encouraging the use of the rational mindset. In any case, b-schools are also businesses and, like most businesses, not given to alienating their clients with unpalatable messages. Furthermore, development is not often on the curriculum because the intellectual heritage of many b-school faculty members leads them to emphasize the cerebral rather than the emotional domain of learning. Case studies, models, and research findings tend to be the established currency, not in-depth personal development.

While there are pockets of academics who critique the institutionalized values and processes of executive development, it seems unlikely that there will be any rapid alteration of existing priorities. This is likely to come only with a societal-level shift that influences education as a whole, a process of transformation almost certainly measurable in decades rather than years. However, this does not mean that the individual in a given organization has to wait for sea changes in society. The ability of individuals to promote alternatives is, after all, the cornerstone of democracy, and in the context of a single organization, it is this notion that probably provides the most realistic way of accelerating the process of democratization.

In any one business it may be the determination of individuals and groups to promote their alternative organizational agendas, to act on principled causes, which serves to dislodge the rational mindset. In other words, within the context of any one organization, constructive political action may legitimize itself. Consider how progress toward democratization has been made in particular enterprises, of the impression made by champions of organizational innovation such as Percy Barnevik, the former CEO of ABB, Andy Grove of Intel, or Richard Branson of Virgin. They and others like them impact, not just on their own organizations but on popular consciousness as well. While their businesses, like all businesses, enjoy mixed fortunes over the long term, this does not eclipse their greater contribution – they create organizations that become models for other organizations. Moreover, in terms of the power of individual action they are but the tip of the iceberg, for in many corporate businesses it is possible to find champions of constructive politics who have won widespread respect and admiration for their opposition to ill-conceived corporate policies. Those organizations, or pockets of good practice within them, provide glimpses of how truly democratized large-scale organizations might be managed.

Similarly, many smaller organizations experiment with radical approaches to managing. For example, at Acer, the personal computer company, Stan Shih, co-founder of the group, has built a federation of self-managing firms held together by mutual interest rather than legal ownership. Some companies are R&D centers, others marketing organizations. Its management and home country investors jointly own each one, with (usually) only a small minority ownership stake held by Acer. At Oticon, an international hearing aid manufacturer, they have gone one step further still in ushering democratization into the process of management.

> ### Oticon
>
> The Danish company Oticon is a world leader in the manufacture of hearing aids. It has received widespread attention for its enlightened working practices. These are defined by a number of features. First, there is an underlying assumption that all employees are responsible adults who come to work to do their best. They are also considered to be unique individuals with diverse interests and ways of working. This means that work is established on an internal market; while project managers pursue the people they would like on their projects, individuals are free to work on any project that will accept them or to propose their own initiative. In effect, employees design their own jobs, but everyone must find projects in which they can take roles outside of their own core expertise in order to encourage a broad perspective.
>
> Employees are developed by "mentors," whose responsibility is to support their pupils' professional development, review performance, and co-ordinate salary adjustments. The allocation of time and attention to different tasks is not controlled by central authority but arises out of a negotiation process. The resolution of conflicts is left to mutual agreement between employees, project leaders, and mentors. Strategic priorities are discussed with all employees by a development group which also co-ordinates the overall process, evaluates project initiatives, and allocates financial resources. William Demant, the holding company for Oticon, was named European Company of the Year 2003.

These are organizations where action by leaders at the top makes it possible for the values of democracy to flourish. But not that many organizations are led by enlightened entrepreneurs or radical corporate visionaries, so what are the possibilities for individual or group action working from less favorable organizational starting points?

Pursuing an agenda that competes with the agendas of others happens only because individuals or groups see it as worthwhile. The risks are too great otherwise, above all when that agenda runs counter to the corporate interest. The exception is political activity for its own sake, but this can be dismissed, and usually is, as game playing – that is to say, as aberrant behavior.

Political action is not an end in itself but a means to an end, and most individuals engage in politics only when there is a gain to be had. For political action to be constructive, any gain must be in the service of others, not just self-seeking. Worthy causes are thus the key, and that these appear to be abundant in any organization. They are to be found in the ambitions of deeply committed project teams, the frustrated values of true professionals, the enterprising attitudes of front-line entrepreneurs. They are implicit in the "wish lists" produced in "off-site" management workshops, the unrealized actions from appraisal processes, the unheeded agendas of career development discussions.

The rightful question is whether there is a willingness to pursue worthy causes, and that is a matter of responsibility. It places the emphasis on individuals and groups to go beyond talking of their agendas – enthusing, deliberating, protesting, whinging – and on those (managers) well placed to encourage action to do so.

While individual and isolated group agendas appear insignificant, in the context of one organization they provide a point of departure in legitimizing politics. Progress toward democracy is made by exploiting the loopholes and contradictions of the rational mindset from within, since the benefit of constructive political behavior appears to be best appreciated when experienced in practice. But in terms of creating a wholesale shift in organizational democratization it is a gradual process. That said, it is important to remember that the rational model of organizing has guided managerial values for at least two centuries, if not much longer, yet in the last 20 years there has been a significant unfreezing of organizing principles.

Contemporary organizational forms and management models allow greater scope for individual agendas to be voiced. On a more optimistic note, then, true organizational democratization, built on principles of constructive politics, may be closer than its painstakingly slow emergence suggests.

RESOURCES

Butcher, D. and Clarke M., *Smart Management, using politics in organizations*, Palgrave, 2001.

Gratton, Lynda, *The Democratic Exercise: Liberating Your Business with Individual Freedom and Shared Purpose*, FT Prentice Hall, 2003.

Law, Andy, *Open Minds, 21st Century Business Lessons and Innovations from St Lukes*, Orion Business Books, 1998.

Lipman-Blumen, J. and Leavitt, H., *Hot Groups – feeding them, seeding them and using them to ignite your organization*, Oxford University Press, 2001.

Mintzberg, Henry, *The Structuring of Organizations*, Prentice Hall, 1979.

Mintzberg, Henry, *Power In and Around Organizations*, Prentice Hall, 1983.

Mintzberg, Henry, *Mintzberg on Management: Inside Our Strange World of Organizations*, The Free Press, 1989.

Capitalizing in on corporate competencies

JONAS RIDDERSTRÅLE

[We are in the midst of a revolution at least as important as the industrial one. But companies are proving slow to respond in terms of restructuring themselves to use, rather than abuse, knowledge. Here is one way to get it right.]

The balance sheet is probably the only 500-year-old supermodel still capable of arousing a few people. But despite its long-lasting allure, it often captures only 20–25 percent of the real value of many modern companies. Research by the economist Jonathan Kendrick shows that the overall ratio of intangible to tangible resources has shifted from 30/70 in 1929 to a current 63/37. Competition used to be a question of brawn. Now it boils down to brains.

Though there is growing recognition and awareness of the power of knowledge, actually managing things differently and imaginatively has proved beyond many managers and organizations. Most organizations are still using measurement systems that were originally meant for shareholders and tax authorities. Instead of preemptive medicine, they are practicing business autopsy. Organizational solutions still favor the exploitation of givens, rather than the creation of novelty. The true irony is perhaps that as intelligence and intangibles replace raw materials and capital as the true sources of competitive advantage, many executives start asking for the advice of lawyers instead of accountants. They replace one breed not exactly world famous for its creative abilities with another.

So what is new, some of you may say – has not knowledge always been important? Certainly, but because of the current trends of digitization, deregulation, and globalization, the economic value of knowledge is becoming much greater. First, individuals and organizations with unique talent and capabilities, respectively, have almost unlimited opportunities to leverage these assets across geographical borders.

Second, a product offering is merely frozen creativity. The successful offering of the past was a combination of a lot of stuff and a little knowledge. In contrast, many of the new winners offer consumers a lot of knowledge combined with a little stuff. Or put differently, the *density* of successful product offerings is decreasing. Just consider a typical GM car. In the early 21st century, material costs accounts for only 16 percent of total costs. Or take a look at the PC on your desk. In 1984, hardware accounted for 80 percent and software for 20 percent of the costs; today the situation is reversed.

Often, bits are replacing atoms; for instance, the production and distribution costs per copy of *Encyclopedia Britannica* in the form of atoms in a book are in the area of $250. For bits on a CD-ROM we are talking about $1.50 (on the web approaching zero). In fact, in 1999 a dollar's worth of imports or exports weighed on average 30 percent of what it did 30 years ago. Our economy is increasingly weightless. Competences are up whereas commodities are down. The average commodity is now worth one fifth of what it was 150 years ago.

As a result, companies must design and implement an organizational architecture that enables them to unleash the full potential of their knowledge networks.

To describe the nature of a firm's knowledge system and how it relates to competitiveness, the four partly interrelated dimensions of space, scope, skills, and speed are useful. The strategic actions taken by a company will shape its position in all these dimensions and thus have an impact on its current and future potential. In all these respects many companies have also undergone transformations of seismic proportions during the last few decades. My research suggests that the kinds of knowledge systems that modern firms need to utilize are simultaneously becoming more dispersed and diverse. These systems are also marked by an increasing depth, and the economic durability of knowledge is often decreasing.

The new knowledge landscape: competence complexity

The firm of the past was active in times when creation of cutting-edge know-how, by renowned universities, aggressive companies, and other competence-producing organizations, was primarily restricted to the West. The pool of technologies to combine in new ways was also more limited than it is today and only a relatively small number of individuals had a degree in engineering or business administration. On markets, demand mostly exceeded supply and the rate of change and proliferation of customer preferences was not as great as is currently the case. Henry Ford's (in)famous comment that people could get the Model-T in any color as long as it was black is symptomatic of those days.

The archetypal firm of the early and mid-20th century, such as Pilkington, DeBeers, or Xerox, often had as much as 20–30 years to globally exploit its competitive advantages. These companies could use an incremental and sequential internationalization process, gradually adding nation after nation. However, if exploitation was global, creation was mostly local. The great majority of companies developed competitive advantages at home and their products were often limited in technological scope (within the confines of the respective divisions of the firm). The typical bureaucracy also relied heavily on a few highly educated and professional top managers to captain the boat. That was then. This is now.

Globalization increases knowledge dispersion. The recent wave of deregulation, internationalization, and global integration already affects most organizations, and not only traditional business organizations. In a 1999 Premier League game in football between Chelsea and Southampton, the Chelsea squad did not include a single Englishman.

As for globalization of business, the average level of tariffs in the industrial countries is now less than 10 percent of the level before the First World War. The cost of shipping a ton of goods from the US to Japan has dropped by more than 70 percent in the last 40 years. The total stock of foreign direct investment has increased by 1,600 percent in the last 15 years. The turnover of the world's foreign exchange market has risen 50-fold in the past 20 years and during the last 40 years, international trade has increased by 1,500 percent. In industry after industry competition has become truly transnational. Still, we have probably not seen anything yet. A recent McKinsey study shows that as of today some 20 percent of world output is open to global competition. In 30 years' time, the forecast suggests that the equivalent figure will be 80 percent. Knowledge is now more evenly spread across the globe. No wonder that in a recent interview John Chambers of Cisco Systems said that he will put his jobs anywhere in the world where the right infrastructure is, with the right educated workforce, and with the right supportive government.

The "dispersion challenge" facing multinational firms comprises five elements. First, in efforts to use the comparative strengths of different subsidiaries, especially acquisition-generated companies have strategic product mandates with global responsibilities scattered throughout the world.

Second, the internationalization of business functions that mostly started with sales and marketing and later included manufacturing have in many cases also come to encompass strategic research and development activities. Globalization used to be a question of ensuring output. Now, it is also a game played to gain valuable input.

Third, in the age of outsourcing most modern multinational companies rely heavily on supplier networks that span the globe. A company such as IBM recently had to wire no less than 12,000 suppliers throughout the world to its system.

Fourth, particularly organizations combining knowledge from many different fields of expertise are beginning to realize that sophisticated demand and supply are not always co-located. A majority of the most advanced trendsetters in the world do not live in the vicinity of Helsinki. This situation constitutes a true challenge for Nokia, the Finnish mobile phone company. The firm has to send its people to Kings Road in London or Venice Beach in LA to pick up the latest signals.

Fifth and finally, although large multinational companies dominate the world economy, many of these firms are heavily reliant on a small number of people. Even Bill Gates once admitted that if 30 people were to leave Microsoft, the company would risk bankruptcy. Such "core competents" are omnipresent. In a study by the Corporate Leadership Council, a "computer" firm recognized 100 core competents out of 16,000 employees; a "software" company had 10 out of 11,000; and a "transportation" group deemed 20 of its 33,000 employees as really critical. In other words, the percentage of core competents varied between 0.6 percent and 0.06 percent. "Core competents" are so rare that you rarely find them in one location. And you certainly cannot command the "Jagger and Richards" of the corporate world to move. Talent is not under your thumb.

Conversion increases knowledge diversity. Creation of novelty requires combination in one or several ways. Knowledge must be integrated. From this perspective, modern customer offerings are becoming more complex. First, it is increasingly difficult to separate products from services. Often, the product as such is becoming a mere platform for delivering services. Some people even claim that it is better to talk about "provices" and "serducts." In the automotive industry, developing and launching a competitive customer offering requires mixing mechanics with electronics, design, PR, and finance skills. A single firm may of course not have to control all these competencies, but the process still needs to be co-ordinated.

Second, we also see more customer offerings being turned into purely multi-technology products. SonyEricsson's P800 mobile phone/camera/Internet device and Casio's Exilim digital camera, including also an MP3 player, are just two recent examples. Third, combine these two trends and the result often equals increasing industry convergence. Just consider the intersection of IT and biotech.

Fourth, the use of a simple process of either technology push or market pull is being challenged by genuinely cross-functional efforts in which technological and market knowledge is combined. Stories of parallel "rugby" development projects and concurrent engineering, especially in Japan, are widely spread.

Finally, increased conversion is not limited to atoms and bits, technologies, industries, and the need for cross-functional collaboration, but also encompasses the people possessing these skills. In Silicon Valley companies, for example, traditional "corporate minority groups" such as women, immigrants, and people below 35 are dramatically over-represented compared within traditional US firms. Remember that in 1998, one-third (2,775) of all Silicon Valley CEOs were either Indians or Chinese.

Education increases knowledge depth. Knowledge develops cumulatively. Bearing this in mind we can conclude that never before has so much knowledge existed. And the last few decades mark a veritable explosion in competence development. The US Patent & Trademark Office hands out 195 percent more patents than it did a mere two decades ago. Or, consider this. Since the early 1960s, the number of MBAs graduated in the US has increased by 1,500 percent. Even in former communist country Hungary there are now 14 different MBA programs.

Also, spending on executive education is skyrocketing. Motorola employees get at least 40 hours of training per year. Companies such as Apple and Intel have instituted sabbaticals for some of their top people. To keep up, the typical firm is forced to change its definition of learning into something that is life-long and more personal. In addition, the internal distribution of competence is no longer as concentrated to a few people at the top. Currently, knowledge workers may be found on every level of many firms. At FedEx, front-line employees and second-level managers must attend 10–11 weeks of mandatory training in the first year. The boss no longer always knows best. "I am completely ignorant about three-quarters of the stuff that goes on. And my colleagues on the senior management team? They are 98 percent ignorant," Michael Gillman, Senior VP of research at Biogen, told *Fast Company*.

Acceleration decreases knowledge durability. Continuous innovation, revolutionary and evolutionary, is a necessity, possibly an evil one but even so a fact of life in most industries. The innovation–imitation–commoditization cycle is picking up speed. As competition accelerates, knowledge becomes a perishable. Bill Joy, chief scientist at Sun Microsystems, estimates that as much as 20 percent of the company's technical knowledge becomes obsolete each year. Companies are forced to cut development time and increase the frequency of new product introductions. They just cannot wait. Organizations are forced to accelerate. It is not only product life cycles that are becoming shorter; the pressure to continuously develop new routines, systems, and procedures, allowing firms to move faster into the future, is also reaching boiling point.

By use of new software allowing it to run tests directly on the computer, Ford Motor Company has cut its average product development cycle from 55 to 32 months. Now the company is pushing for 24. Spanish clothing retailer Zara takes a fashion idea from the drawing board to the store shelf in 10–15 days. The third largest cement company in the world, Mexican CEMEX, has invested $200 million in a customer information system that allows it to meet a 20-minute delivery window with 98 percent accuracy. In 1998, the company had a 35 percent profit margin compared with an industry average of 21 percent. Learning and unlearning capabilities appear to be of utmost importance to just about any firm in the new economic landscape evolving in front of our eyes.

My discussion so far of the drivers forcing firms to change the characteristics of their knowledge systems is summarized in Table 7.1.

Table 7.1: *Forces shaping the nature of modern knowledge systems*

Dimension	Space	Scope	Skill	Speed
Driver	Globalization	Conversion	Education	Acceleration
Consequence	Dispersion	Diversity	Depth	Durability

Organizational responses: the modular model

The traditional hallmark of the large and complex firm of the 20th century is the pervasiveness of the hierarchical organizational model. But while the balance sheet is being wheeled into the ward for long-term patients, the hierarchical supermodel is now on its way to the morgue. Hierarchy builds on a number of important underlying assumptions and key organizing principles that are completely at odds with the new strategic requirements. In short, hierarchical design assumes that the sources underlying competitiveness are given, eternal, and kept internally. The principal challenge is one of finding an organizational form that will efficiently exploit this specific combination of knowledge by minimizing interaction among people and units.

Consider the following. For how many contemporary companies is the creation of novelty optional? Name five firms living as Lone Rangers! We also know that new customer offerings are often the result of processes where knowledge has been combined and recombined across geographical, organizational, technological, and possibly also institutional borders – at the speed of light. Picture this. A recent Philips DVD recorder development team spanned three operating divisions: semiconductors, optimal systems, and consumer electronics. On top of that, underlying technological collaboration was carried out with five rivals, including Sony, Rico, and Yamaha.

As a result, the development of a competitive knowledge system is only the first step. To speed up the knowing–doing circle, firms also have to be prepared to develop a new organizational architecture that utilizes corporate creativity to its fullest potential. Under these new circumstances, the challenge is one of designing and implementing an architecture based on the principle of recomposition rather than decomposition. Another response to knowledge complexity is of course to externalize parts of it by outsourcing a number of non-core activities. In doing so, internal complexity of competencies certainly decreases but on a network level the difficulties still need to be handled. Let me therefore elaborate on seven organizational principles making up the cornerstones of an architecture for the kind of company that is indeed capable of recomposition – innovation by combination – a future firm that is *multiplicational* rather than multidivisional; the modular model.

People

While the traditional hierarchical firm is heavily dependent on a few individuals who plan, co-ordinate, command, and control operations (and a large pool of disposable workers to carry out repetitive tasks), the modular organization must draw in enough talent to ensure renewal. Getting great people on board is contingent on (a) having a *tale* to tell talent, and (b) ensuring talent *transfusion* by increasing individualization.

Attraction of human capital becomes more important than allocation of financial capital when the scarcest resource is no longer investment but imagination. And competition for talent is truly global. Talent is free to know, go, do, and be. Core competents have a global passport. These men and women can select themselves in and out of countries and organizations – and they do. Forget about organization man. Enter opportunistic man (and woman). So, all organizations need to ask themselves one critical question: do we have a seductive story that will make talent fall flat on its face? Talent and tales go together like love and marriage. And a story they have whether they like it or not.

Markets are conversations, and with the advent of the Net, these are increasingly global conversations. Everyone who has ever interacted with a company is telling their story. Prospective employees will communicate with present employees. The guy who was fired last week will not keep his mouth shut. And remember that stories are sticky, for better and for worse. Organizations either try to prevent the inevitable from happening or choose to contribute to the conversation. Proactive companies will even provide platforms for such conversations. Doing so not only enables them to better control the process, but also opens up the opportunity to use the information as a valuable input for improvements.

One additional advantage of having a strong story is that it will attract talent wanting to piggy-back on the organizational "brain-brand" to build their own brand called Me, Myself, and I. Consider the case of McKinsey & Company. Many people regard this as the most prestigious management-consulting firm in the world. It can charge among the highest fees in its industry, not only for its senior consultants but also for its new recruits. Freshly baked MBAs know that the simple fact that they were once recruited by McKinsey and can put that in their résumés will greatly enhance their chances of later landing a top job somewhere else. The McKinsey alumni, headed by Lou Gerstner of IBM, are spreading like a forest fire throughout the business community.

Not only that, the brain-brand also helps to retain good people. For most McKinsey consultants, with a few notable exceptions such as management guru Tom Peters, even if you are among the best of the best, leaving the company would not necessarily enable you to charge higher fees as a free agent. You would have to do business without the legitimacy of the McKinsey brand stamped on your forehead (and invoices). Brands are uncertainty reducers, and quite often in the consulting business customers are willing to pay a hefty premium for what is perceived as the "best" corporate comforter around. (I suspect few executives ever got fired for following the advice of a McKinsey report.)

Increased calls for individualization, in turn, rest on the simple assumption that talented individuals are not bulk goods. People differ, especially generation I. Gen I is international, informed, informal, impatient, intense, and extremely individualistic. And since from a demographic point of view it is clear that soon most Western industrialized countries will experience a white-haired revolution, more and more companies will have to do with this pool of young me, me, me men and women. Also note that a talent deficit will only result in an "idiocracy."

Personalization and individualization imply flexibility. At the innovative Brazilian company Semco, for instance, there are 11 different ways to get paid, ranging from a fixed salary to stock options, royalties, and bonus schemes, all of which can be combined in various ways. As little as Posh or Becks will settle for anything the slightest bit normal or average will corporate stars put up with what is merely mediocre. It used to be XM (extra medium). Now it must be XMe. Recall what JFK once said: conformity is the jailer of freedom and the enemy of growth. Today, it is curiosity over conformity. Talent wants voice and choice. So, corporate leaders must ask themselves whether they are really prepared to surrender their own egos to the talent of core competents.

Since companies with complex knowledge systems are internationally and individually diverse, personalization also implies being sensitive to cultural differences. Unfortunately, the typical multinational corporation is still pretty parochial. Before reconciliation there needs to be respect, but too often foreigners are just regarded as strange. Letting managers with such attitudes interact with a group of competents from another country is like inviting an elephant to dance in a china shop. Also note that most talented individuals do not leave companies – they leave managers.

Perspective

Variation, of a cultural as well as a competence kind, is innate in an organization with a complex web of competencies. Diversity can be constructive or destructive – melting pot or powder keg – but it is always disruptive. For firms doing business in a non-linear world this disruptive nature of systems with built-in variation is a source of opportunities in that it opens up venues, enabling them to depart from the road traveled in the past. But diversity in principle does not always translate into practice. The talent pool of the company may be diverse, but the dominant group within the firm could still be very homogeneous. I have seen (too) many examples of organizations recruiting deviants and outsiders just to place them in corporate quarantine or ship them off to the Siberian subsidiary. To gain the perspective so critical to innovation, companies simultaneously need to ensure (a) the *inclusion and participation* of talent in the strategic decision-making process, and (b) the *decentralization* of power moving decisions closer to where talent resides.

As Richard Pascale (author of *Surfing the Edge of Chaos*) observes, survival in nature is dependent on a sufficient degree of mutation and variation. You never know in advance exactly what set of genes will be most apt to survive. Variety in turn is ensured by sexual reproduction. You mix two beings into a new and fundamentally different one. The alternative, parthenogenesis (cloning), does not result in any mutation or variety at all. Still, at many companies the clones are in charge – *Star Wars II* reincarnated – or, as Pascale call them, "the enemies of sex."

One, if not the, main objective of a recomposable regime is to create novelty. So, in order to ensure action, the diversity of the organizational members must be reflected also in the composition of top management teams. From research we know that corporate OD – zero diversity – kills creativity. Still, and particularly at the senior-executive level, many organizations continue to be incredibly inbred. The implications of most recent studies on careers support my observation by suggesting that if you really want to make it, there is only one (almost) safe bet. Be born as a white male and get a partner who stays at home to take care of the kids (alternatively, be gay but for God's sake do not tell anyone). At the time of writing only 3 percent of the top corporate officers of Fortune 500 companies are female. And things are not better in Europe. A mere 2 percent of the executive directors in FTSE 350 companies are female. Just four companies have a female chief executive and only 6 percent of the non-executive directors are women. Individualization and competence-based competition imply the fall of the homo organization and the rise of hetero corporations. Otherwise group-think, constipation, and decline is the inevitable result.

Having a perspective on things also means relying more on the periphery – being on the edge. In a company with a complex knowledge system, rapid decisions need to be taken closely to where critical, in-depth knowledge resides, geographically as well as organizationally. The time from problem detection to solution implementation must be reduced. In a disruptive world, self-renewal is dependent on anticipation rather than prediction. To boost the anticipatory capabilities, power needs to be located where the action goes on, and as noted by former US Vice President Al Gore, most organizations encounter change at their edges, not at their centers. Other measures than centralized planning are necessary to cope with the challenges raised by competence complexity. A more decentralized and delayered architecture is required. Sensing and making sense can and should no longer be the preserve of a few managers at headquarters.

Purpose

Control and co-ordination in the bureaucratic organization is based on legal authority and formalization. In a firm with a complex knowledge system, integration cannot be handled in such a manner. The conditions change so fast that formalized procedures become too rigid and static. Experts in various fields need to know about the general direction from those in charge but often they will control the skills necessary to come up with the answers required to initiate the proper actions. As the knowledge system increases in complexity, companies must rely on an organizational purpose providing direction by delineating a shared (a) *idea*, (b) *identity*, and *incentives* that shape behavior. In other words, socialization, rather than formalization or standardization, becomes the preferred mode of co-ordination. These few mutual principles must secure co-ordination while still allowing for flexibility. They provide the minimum critical specifications so critical for enabling self-organization.

All organizations need a shared idea of why they exist, who they are, and where to go, but those with complex competencies even more so. A shared idea channels and focusses the disruptive forces of the system. The idea should inspire commitment and be continually communicated. Scott McNealy of Sun Microsystems has a favorite formula: 0.6L. Every time information passes a layer in the organization, only 60 percent gets through. Essentially, the idea distills the company's direction into the most potent capsule. Great ideas are not only shared but in many cases also quite simple. At Disney the vision is to "make people happy" and at Motorola it is "Wireless." 3M focusses on "solving unsolved problems." AT&T talks about IM&M – "information movement and management." These statements are simple enough to be shared by all employees, and they are clear in saying what the companies should *not* be doing. Try showing up at Motorola with a wire and see what happens.

The modular firm relies heavily on personalization to attract talent. But people are not only individualistic creatures; we also want to belong. Firms with a future will use this fact to their advantage. To prevent Cacophony Inc. from becoming Chaos Inc., they will build an organizational community or tribe where people share a common identity. More than 10 years ago in a *Harvard Business Review* article Jack Welch of GE pointed out: "The new psychological contract is that jobs at GE are the best in the world for people who are willing to compete, we have the best training and development resources, and an environment committed to providing opportunities for personal and professional growth." Since the easiest way to get people to share your values is to hire those that already do, we see more and more organizations recruiting people with the right attitude and then training them in skills. Look at Hell's Angels or Southwest Airlines. Just imagine Hell's Angels hiring for skills! These organizations simply do not believe in the idea of bringing in smart people and then brainwashing them at training camps. One, because the half-life of knowledge is coming down so fast that if you recruit someone with relevant knowledge today, three months down the road these skills may be obsolete. And two, since for most of us it is easier to change our skills than our basic values.

To ensure behavior in accordance with the purpose, new rewards and incentives promoting recomposition and innovation are called for. Companies must give talented individuals incentives for sharing rather than keeping. To build a collectively intelligent corporation capable of recomposition, organizations must start rewarding not only the individual exploitation of knowledge but also the internal exports of competencies – the transfer of knowledge to other parts of the firm. One of the companies that I have studied even had a scheme to reward "human exports." Headquarters basically subsidized the (temporary) transfer of local stars to other parts of the network. Rewards must also capture the rate of renewal. A laudable first measure that is now quite commonplace among companies is to base bonuses not only on sales but also on sales generated by new products.

At many companies, rewarding recomposition also implies strengthening the role of project managers vis-à-vis the line management. Far too many teams where creative work is carried out suffer from having lightweight project leaders so that critical decisions are still taken by senior executives in the positional structure. And if project leaders are of the real stuff, they are often promoted away from the projects into (apparently) more important positions. Projects are no solution if you cripple them into operational impotency. Instead of lightweights, projects, and particularly international ventures, should be run by organizational equivalents of *sumo wrestlers*. Real projects, rather than committees, must have considerably more power than is generally the case in most contemporary companies. To get results, we must give up rewarding exploitation while merely praying for creation.

Process-platform

To drive recombination, companies need tools and arenas where such processes can occur. No dialog – no development. Successful transfer, assimilation, transformation, and even destruction of knowledge are all contingent on the organization developing a platform made up of four components: (a) a system-wide *knowledge map*, (b) a shared *language*, (c) a sophisticated *info-structure*, and (d) socialization ensuring *know-who*.

Information and information flows increasingly define what an organization is and is not. But unless the company knows what it knows, the organization is doomed to be a place with pockets of individual creativity rather than a collectively intelligent corporation. In the bureaucracy, the general manager or chief executive officer is supposed to know who knows who, who knows what, who knows how, and who knows where. The firm with a complex knowledge system needs a more holographic design where more or less everybody knows who, what, how, and where – where the whole is reflected in all parts.

Expansion, particularly in space, also increases the probability that problems and solutions may be permanently decoupled. With rising complexity it becomes more difficult to keep track of, and update, the map of organizational knowledge. This reasoning is also valid as for the awareness of resources located outside the legal boundaries of the firm, such as knowledge controlled by customers and suppliers. Due to increased complexity, these processes of expanding knowledge awareness must be more actively managed. Successful companies therefore use a systemic approach for handling their most vital resources. A knowledge map should include a detailed inventory of core competencies and competents. By actively collecting, codifying, and communicating the knowledge of core competents to the rest of the organization, the firm builds a platform that enables the different parts of the company to utilize the entire body of organizational knowledge.

To share knowledge people also need to speak a common language. International communities such as Jews, overseas Chinese, gypsies, the Catholic Church, medical doctors, or more recent ones such as hip-hoppers, have all relied on or still rely on a shared language to act as a force of integration. For most modern companies this means making sure that all individuals with strategic roles speak English. For some nationalities this procedure may be a bitter pill to swallow, but then remember that even the French are following suit. Cement giant Lafarge expects all managers to speak English and therefore offers language classes. But for most complex organizations, the language issue extends beyond the Tower of Babel issue. People in different divisions and departments also need to be able to communicate. Recomposition requires a shared definition and understanding key concepts and words, whether these are CRM, TQM, Six Sigma, or more specific technical terms, bridging the different parts of the company (possibly including actors also in the inter-organizational domain).

A vital part of the process platform should also be a pull-oriented "info-structure" that enables the parts to inform themselves on a need-to-find-out basis. For companies with complex knowledge systems, a traditional push-logic, where the top of the positional structure is responsible for informing the rest of the organization on a need-to-know basis, just will not suffice. With more open intranets and Internets, old lines of communication and authority can be short-circuited as information does not have to travel via the top of the hierarchy any more. Actions are carried out within the realms provided by the company purpose.

The criticality of face-to-face communication should not be downplayed, however. Know-who is critical in that it helps talent both to locate carriers of competencies and to judge the relevance and quality of information provided by these. Rather, the two types of communication are complementary. By having people working in teams, spending time together after work, attending corporate training programs, etc., over time, such groups develop tacit knowledge. The members of the team will know things that they cannot tell. Instead, they will be able to communicate without words. And increasingly tacit knowledge is what companies are left to compete with. As soon as something can be articulated it can also be imitated. Tacit knowledge is sticky and does not diffuse with the same speed.

The existence of tacit knowledge also carries a bonus advantage in that it makes it trickier for people to walk out the door with their skill sets intact. Part of the body of knowledge of a specific knowledge nomad will be nested in an inter-personal network of relationships with existing colleagues. Anyone threatening to leave can thus only bring the intra-personal skills with him or her. Socialization increases tacit knowledge that in turn works as knowledge handcuffs. This fact not only transforms human capital into structural capital but also increases the likelihood that people will stay with the firm for longer periods of time, something which appears more critical for companies competing on recomposition.

Partnership

Adam Smith pointed out that as the size of a market increases, so should the degree of specialization. Over the last few decades, many multinationals have indeed become both narrower and hollower. As a consequence, to dominate their industries they need to rely more on partners. The network, rather than the single firm, is becoming the relevant unit of analysis and action. In the hierarchical solution with a more vertical logic, however, there is little room for suppliers and customers – they sit outside the firm. Partnerships must cover two key areas: (a) ensuring *input* of an exploitative or creative nature, and (b) securing *output* by engaging in system-wide efforts to establish standards.

Since not all assets can be kept internally, companies must co-operate with customers, suppliers, *and* competitors. It is one network/supply chain against the other. Arrangements to gain input of an exploitative nature by outsourcing manufacturing of standardized components or even entire products are now common place. Nike has struck gold by not applying its slogan. Instead of just doing it – the company just does not do it. Many successful firms no longer make what they sell. Timberland, for instance, is a shoeless shoe company.

Ensuring creative input is more demanding. Recomposition across institutional borders requires the firm to move beyond standardization and planning and co-ordinate activities by mutual adjustment. Strong relationships need to be established not only at the top management level; differences in the respective organizational architectures also need to be aligned, at least on a project level. Accordingly, we find most examples of successful creative combination in cases where the two firms share a history of co-operation. Experience has resulted in routines for leveraging knowledge and a climate of trust minimizing secrecy and cheating.

But gaining valuable input is often not enough. It is also increasingly difficult for a single firm to dominate an entire market alone. More and more companies have been forced to realize that if you cannot beat them, join them. Alternately, have them join you. Sony's experience with the Betamax video format is a well-known example. Or as a former Apple top executive once put it in a *Business Week* interview: "Apple had an ice cube in the desert and everybody wanted it. They could have licensed it to anybody. Now all they've got is wet sand." On the contrary, a company such as Nokia states that it "firmly believes that open standards are vital to the future success of the communications industry. The substantial effort and resources the company puts into GSM standardization has contributed to its success and this philosophy continues for 3G." The company therefore has a substantial presence in most standardization bodies. Standards not only simplify co-ordination of joint development but also secure market acceptance for new products and solutions.

Persistence

Business life has, until now, been built around spurts of creation and extended periods of exploitation. Companies exploited natural resources, exploited technologies, and exploited people. We are good at exploitation because we have hundreds, not to say thousands, of years of experience. In contrast, we are not very good at creation. Our organizations are not designed for it. And most people are not trained for it.

Still, all organizations must uphold a fruitful balance between the exploitation of givens and the creation of novelty. Two main forces, however, counteract the possibilities to maintain such a balance. First, there is a built-in resistance in most organizations to the unknown and uncertain. And acts of creation are indeed less certain and obvious, and the consequences more remote in time than is the case with activities of exploitation. Second, research by Stanford Professor James March and others suggest that organizations learn from experience how to allocate resources between the two types of activities. This distribution, in term, has short-term as well as long-term effects. Since the feedback loops of exploitation consequences tend to be quicker and more precise, adaptive processes generally improve exploitation more rapidly than creation. Over time, activities of creation will therefore crowd out acts of creation.

In the light of this, we should not be surprised that history is littered with companies that failed because they got trapped in their own success as exploiters of a particular competence combo. In fact, this very argument is brought forth by Harvard academic Clay Christensen in *The Innovator's Dilemma*. "... good management was the most powerful reason they failed to stay atop their industries," writes Professor Christensen. To secure durance and countervail the forces crowding out creation, companies need to develop (a) *experimentation* routines, and (b) greater *tolerance* for failure.

While search in the hierarchical organization is essentially a question of strengthening the core to maximize return on investments in the short run, the recomposing firm must operate distinctively different. The prime task of talent is not to perfect the known but to look for novelty. So, the organization must use a more long-run perspective, or perhaps sometimes even a no-run outlook. Successful combinations often arise as the result of search beyond what is currently rational. Goals must therefore take on a more multi-rational nature rather than a purely economic one.

Routine is also a question of time. And innovation certainly takes time. Slack is a prerequisite for innovation. It may be true that today you are either fast or forgotten, but innovative companies also work hard to construct corporate speed bumps. Truly creative organizations give people time without knowing exactly what results will emerge. 3M does just that with its 15 percent policy – researchers can spend up to 15 percent of their time on their own projects. The 15 percent policy is called, among other things, "the bootleg policy." It may also be called a competitive advantage because it has helped foster and nurture so many good ideas, most notably the Post-it Note. Since we cannot tell in advance exactly what combinations will be successful, the aim should be the creation of a bubbling ferment of ideas. "The object is to spur as many ideas as possible because perhaps 1 in 1,000 will turn out to fit," says Post-it developer Art Fry.

Innovation requires experimentation. Experiments are risky. We can succeed or fail. In effect, an innovative environment must have an exceptionally high tolerance for mistakes. And so must leaders of innovative organizations. We have got to fail faster to learn quicker and succeed sooner. The trouble is that the typical company is not the most forgiving of environments. In many firms, failure carries the corporate equivalent of the death penalty. This sends a signal to the corporate system that failure is punished. Killing people who fail not only stops people from failing, however, it also stops them from trying. It leads to the building of systems that act against innovation rather than ones that nurture innovation.

True innovators are prepared to fail in pursuit of unknown territories – *terra incognita* instead of *terra firma*. Traditionalists should remember that the only way not to fail is not to try. And try we must. No failures; no development. Philosopher Ludwig Wittgenstein even argued: "If people never did silly things, nothing intelligent would ever happen." To become successful recomposers, companies must first become breeding grounds of risk takers. I am not saying that leaders should promote risk taking *per se*. Rather, it is a question of making it less risky to take risk. Perhaps as suggested by management author Thomas Stewart, in addition to mission statements companies need *permission* statements.

Passion

The future does not lie only in front of companies successfully applying the modular model. It must also rest within them – in the heads and hearts of the people. To get to the future first, companies need speed. Velocity is a function of mass and energy; the greater the energy and the lower the mass, the higher the velocity. In the corporate world, the 1980s and 1990s were largely devoted to processes of "demassification" – downsizing, outsourcing, etc. Managers were told to focus on core competencies and create a knowledge-based organization where IQ could flourish. Meritocracies replaced bureaucracies. So far, however, most companies have by and large neglected the other variable in the function. While tomorrow's winners may well be "empires of the mind" that Sir Winston Churchill once talked about, they still need a sense of spirit – *energy* through *emotion*.

In an economy where talent has more or less endless choice, success is increasingly a question of capturing the emotional human being – not the rational one. The time has come to stop re-engineering and start "re-energizing" our organizations. Ensuring and enabling change in a brain-based organization is not a question of rearranging the boxes and arrows. Steve Ballmer of Microsoft recently pointed out that the company had probably gone through too many reorganizations. Now the challenge was one of re-missioning people rather than reorganizing them.

Competition in the high-end niche of the job market used to be a question of security and salary. Then we swapped security for stock options. Now, we are in the business of having to create an emotional experience for talented individuals. Companies used to be consumers of competence. Now, they must be both co-creators of competence *and* providers of personality. Once it was money for mastery; now, it must also be meaning for membership. The relationship between employer and employee becomes both transactional and relational. In the future firm, people have a calling as much as a career. Here, the true benchmarks are non-for-profit organizations such as the Red Cross and Amnesty International. Talent wants money and meaning, value and values. To thrive, companies must learn how to combine skill and soul.

Extraordinary achievements depend on passion. Certainly, successful companies have core capabilities that determine what they can do. Most organizations also have core opportunities reflecting what is possible to do. But more important than anything else are the core compassions, what people in organizations actually care about doing, because you see without passion no energy, and without energy no performance. Know-how and know-who are small things compared with know-why.

In fact, most important relationships in our lives are characterized by love. We love Manchester United or Arsenal. We love our hobbies. We love our spouses (at least in the beginning). We love our pets. Today, how many people are dedicated enough to tattoo the corporate logo on their bicep (or elsewhere)?

The main organizing principles guiding a company applying the modular model are summarized in Table 7.2.

Table 7.2: *Organizing principles behind the modular model*

Principles	Features	Objectives
People	Tales	Draw
	Transfusion	
Perspective	Participation	Disruption
	Decentralization	
Purpose	Idea	Direction
	Identity	
	Incentives	
Process-platform	Memory	Dialog
	Language	
	Info-structure	
	Socialization	
Partnership	Input	Dominance
	Output	
Persistence	Experimentation	Durance
	Toleration	
	Trust	
Passion	Energy	Dedication
	Emotion	

Toward a networked economy: Seven management lessons from Microsoft

JAMIE ANDERSON AND ROBIN WOOD

[The most successful company of our times has been examined from almost every angle. But, managerially, what makes Microsoft tick?]

Since its inception in the mid-1970s, Microsoft has consistently been underestimated by its competitors. Giants like AOL/Time Warner, Palm, and Sony have each had a run at Microsoft and failed. And companies like Nokia, Apple, Novell, Borland, WordPerfect, Lotus Development, Sun, IBM, Netscape, Oracle, and SAP either disappeared or have lost market share in their battles with Microsoft. In order to understand why Microsoft is so successful, there is no point in hiding behind accusations that it pursues monopolistic practices. To understand why Microsoft is so successful, we need to look elsewhere: at the new rules for the experience economy, and at where the new "high ground" for business models in this experience economy is.

Let us start with the high ground, which defines the strategic position from which a company and its value web can capture the maximum share of value and customer spend from users for the least effort and resources. In the experience economy, customers value products and services which can enhance the quality of their life experience. Due to the glut of stuff and information people are bombarded with every day, they are motivated to simplify their lives through easy-to-use, quality services, interfaces, and appropriate content. The majority of customers just do not care about technological infrastructure or the nature of the devices and software these services, information, and content are offered on, as long as they work and are user-friendly.

So, what are the different routes to the high ground? As illustrated in Figure 7.2, the high ground integrates digital infrastructure, products, and services into experiences, delivered via appliances and interfaces to communities of users. Each of the companies which has attempted to claim this high ground has done so from its strengths in one or more of these seven areas. Each has underestimated the difficulty of making that integration work successfully.

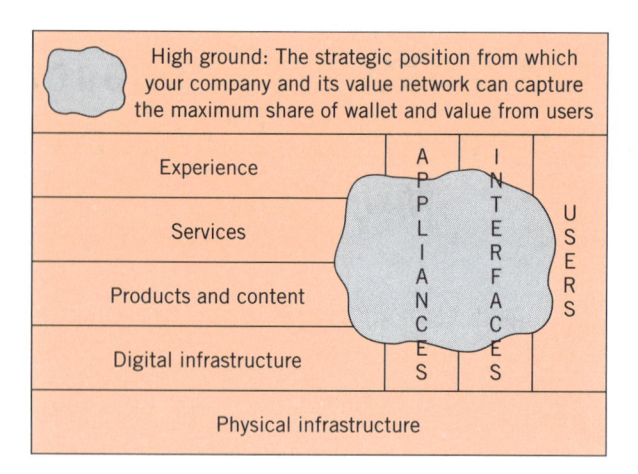

Figure 7.2: *The high ground in the convergence zone between the information, communications, and entertainment arenas*

For example, AOL has been quite successful in building online communities with tens of millions of users in North America, and to a lesser extent Europe. It has tried with limited success to translate this franchise into a dominant position on the user interface and in the content business through the merger with Time Warner. Nokia, Symbian, and Sony/Ericsson have come at the high ground from their positions of strength in making fashionable, user-friendly electronic appliances for communications, entertainment, gaming, and personal productivity, attempting to create a dominant position through open mobile and broadband architectures, and building a value network around themselves to create the experiences users want. These companies have bumped hard into the Microsoft swarm of products and services centered around the .Net open software framework and the PocketPC, Smartphone, and X-Box.

So, what are the seven key lessons we can learn from Microsoft?

1. Thrive on co-evolution and head for the nodal position in your value web: think "business ecosystems"

In the experience economy, every marketplace is a complicated web of interconnecting relationships, where business models are defined by the totality of relationships between the various players. Business ecosystems are continuously evolving based on the changing relationships between organizations and business models, where competition is for the richest, most connected position within the ecosystem – the "nodal" position, where your company will have some strategic advantages and the ability to appropriate real value. The ability to "turn your company outside in" through partnering becomes essential, as network technologies allow customers, employees, and partners to mingle under the same electronic tent. Yahoo!, for example, partnered liberally with outside players, built connections so successful that other companies paid to establish links, and created the flexibility to constantly add new functions. Companies that truly bank on this sort of networking understand that outsourcing and joint ventures are long-term skills, not just techniques.

Microsoft has built the world's largest business ecosystem, made up of 6 million developers, tens of thousands of companies generating trillions of dollars of revenue, together with Intel and the makers of personal computer hardware. By controlling the evolution of its software through application programming interfaces, Microsoft is able to protect its intellectual property while still enabling others to collaborate with it and develop according to relatively open standards. It now also gets instant feedback on software performance through automated error reports delivered over the web any time there has been a program error on any Windows XP application, so the customer feedback loop is now part of the ecosystem, as well as feedback from developers and makers of information appliances.

2. Innovate at the right pace or die

Palm, creator of the world's first truly successful PDA product, is struggling. Just a few years ago electronic organizers running Palm's operating system owned 75 percent of the handheld computer market. Today, Palm's share has dropped below 50 percent. Microsoft's initial move into the market, Windows CE, was considered technologically inferior. But after reworking and relaunching the product as Pocket PC, Microsoft now holds over a third of the market, with analysts projecting that it may control roughly 50 percent by 2005. How did it happen? Palm violated a basic rule for surviving Microsoft: innovate or die. Its initial success blinded it to the need to add new features. Palm's early goal was to make a simple product at a cheap price. Yet as microchips, screens, and batteries improved, it made sense to pack handhelds with new applications like those for playing music and video. Palm mostly sat still. Meanwhile, Pocket PC-based machines, like Compaq's Ipaq, were steadily improving, with faster processors and more memory – and getting cheaper.

3. Innovation creates value, good business models capture value

Competitive dynamics in the 21st century are not about technology, but business design. What wins or loses the competitive game is an organization's ability to create different levels of value through adaptive re-combinations of the components of a business model. Understanding how to identify and select new options for creating and capturing value, using the new tools, business models, and markets emerging in the connected economy is key. Because information courses through every artery of business these days, companies need adaptive business processes to keep pace with ever-increasing customer demands. Where the Internet opens new opportunities – whether it's a way for car designers to collaborate with their parts suppliers, or a web marketplace for bidding on office supplies – businesses can't be afraid to forge new processes around them. Innovating your business model demands reinvention of the organization.

The most innovative models alter the structure of their industries, the way Dell Computer's build-to-order PCs pushed the entire computer business to change its ways. Companies must view their process as a product, too. Ensure that your current and new business ideas align with or can shape the trends in and around your industry, and protect/enhance the value which you are able to create through your business design. Business models based upon complexity principles are, however, much more likely to generate money and above-average market capitalization relative to revenues.

Microsoft has exploited increasing returns in its business model by continuing to earn increasing returns on its dominant position on the desktop in operating systems, browsers, and applications. It is now working on extending this to the palmtop and the mobile telephone.

4. Be an early adapter, not an early adopter

If we ask "who gets the value from innovation," it's usually not the innovator. People download and re-engineer. In the high-technology business the biggest risk is of a new product failing in the early market. New products have to pass through what is known as a chasm in order to reach the point at which they can take off. This phenomenon used to be limited to technology companies. Now, for all businesses in this fast-moving world, the ability to launch successful new services and experiences becomes critical.

But new products can go through a "chasm" where they often perish, before they find a "beachhead" where they can safely grow. Once a company has been through the chasm and found the beachhead, they can often experience the tornado of growth, where scalability and process become critical. Microsoft has been very successful at scanning for better ways of doing things, and then pouncing when it sees a way to assist a company or technology across the chasm.

5. Community and commerce make content king

The first rule of information states that as the technologies for the codification of information advance, the amount of information available rises dramatically and the cost of much information approaches zero. Huge quantities of free or incredibly cheap data swamp our senses every day. Because our current digital infrastructure and physical infrastructure lack the intelligence to make sense of all of this noise for us, we interpret much of this data as noise rather than useful information. We are the first generation to have the novel experience of searching for content using a search engine on the Internet, only to be overwhelmed with predominantly irrelevant information.

In this content-saturated world, content-driven business models fueled by advertising revenues have in-built limits, constrained by the amount of information and advertising people are able to pay attention to. A whole new generation of content management, campaign generation, knowledge management, customer relationship management, and "customer process"-driven software is now aiming to ensure that we ask people for their attention only when it is appropriate to their needs or wants at a particular time. This requires businesses to:

- redefine both their business designs and their business and management processes in order to evolve to a customer process-driven operation;
- invest in intelligent digital infrastructure which can drive the customer-directed value chains and networks required to deliver the winning value propositions of the networked economy.

The latest versions of Microsoft's products and its focus on services via the .Net frameworks mean that it will soon be at the forefront of new service creation and enablement in the experience economy. Community and commerce will then lie at the heart of the user experience, making relevant content available just when, how, and where the user needs it.

6. Use network effects to create and harness embedded intelligence

The value of a network is potentially greater than the square of the number of nodes in the network. Because the nodes in an industrial network communicate seldom or at all with each other, the value of the network remains low as the connections between the nodes are both silent and unintelligent. In the knowledge economy, however, the connections between the nodes are capable of being made intelligent using a wide variety of technologies, enabling value-adding communication, scheduling, and co-ordination to occur. When this happens in a linear fashion up and down a value chain, significant cost reductions and revenue enhancement are possible.

In collaborative value networks, such as are springing up in travel, telecommunications, retailing, manufacturing and distribution, and financial services, much greater economic returns are possible, due to the increasing returns which such networks can deliver to customers and participants. This also causes the value of the network to rise dramatically in proportion to:

- the level of intelligence installed between the nodes of the network; and
- the value of the functionality such intelligence offers users.

In the experience economy the economics of increasing returns plays a critical role in determining the winners and losers in every industry. One of the most attractive features of network effects which emerge from digital infrastructures is that we can use them without having to think too much or even at all. Microsoft is actively aiming to build intelligence into every device through the .Net framework, and to enhance the bandwidth available to such devices through broadband networks such as Teledesic. While Sun, HP, IBM, and others, with Java, Unix, and other technologies, have been able to see this vision, they have not had the business models or the market positions to embed their technology platforms into enough devices to create ubiquitous network effects like Microsoft.

7. Adapt and learn real-time

New waves of technology create complexity which needs to be mastered to build and deploy new value-adding capabilities. Market opportunities must be envisioned and seized – incremental movement will be too slow. Organizational intelligence generates foresight and insight into opportunities. Many asset-based positions will be arbitraged away by global capital markets. Knowledge assets need to be created and deployed for value across the world. Products must be developed in close partnerships with all constituents. Real-time information is critical to efficiently manage across all partnerships and geographies. The transformation of business and management processes is often a prerequisite to develop the characteristics required to compete effectively in the experience economy.

Microsoft cultivates a culture where employees are treated as equals, and encouraged to question everything. Though this can be harsh at times on those who are not able to assertively defend their positions, this meritocracy encourages everyone to look carefully at their assumptions, and to embrace new ideas and thinking rapidly if they are proven to work better than current approaches. In a business where innovation is critical, the ability to recognize new patterns in the environment, and then to rapidly build and change mental models to reflect what is going on out there and anticipate future developments, is a crucial survival skill.

The Microsoft way

Many of the old competitive strategy rules still apply in determining whether a business can create real value for its stakeholders: market share, quality of management, segmentation for lifetime customer value, competing on distinctive capabilities, and building barriers to entry still apply to make an economic return. But in an increasingly networked world of evolving ecosystems and value webs, concepts such as nodal positions, network effects, the impact of dominant standards, and community building must be understood by managers should they wish to create significant value for their organizations and shareholders.

Table 7.3: *Financial highlights (in millions, except earnings per share)*

Year Ended June 30	1999 $	2000 $	2001[2] $	2002[3] $	2003[4] $
Revenue	19,747	22,956	25,296	28,365	32,187
Operating income	10,010	11,006	11,720	11,910	13,217
Income before accounting change	7,785	9,421	7,721	7,829	9,993
Net income	7,785	9,421	7,346	7,829	9,993
Diluted earnings per share before accounting change[1]	0.71	0.85	0.69	0.70	0.92
Diluted earnings per share[1]	0.71	0.85	0.66	0.70	0.92
Cash dividends per share	–	–	–	–	0.08
Cash and short-term investments	17,236	23,798	31,600	38,652	49,048
Total assets	38,321	51,694	58,830	67,646	79,571
Stockholders' equity	28,438	41,368	47,289	52,180	61,020

(1) Earnings per share have been restated to reflect a two-for-one stock split in February 2003.
(2) Fiscal year 2001 includes an unfavorable cumulative effect of accounting change of $375 million or $0.03 per diluted share, reflecting the adoption of SFAS No. 133, and $4.80 billion (pre-tax) in impairments of certain investments, primarily cable and telecommunication investments.
(3) Fiscal year 2002 includes $4.32 billion (pre-tax) in impairments of certain investments, primarily related to our AT&T investment and further declines in the fair values of European cable and telecommunications holdings, and a $1.25 billion (pre-tax) gain on the sale of Expedia, Inc.
(4) Fiscal year 2003 includes $1.15 billion (pre-tax) in impairments of certain investments.

Microsoft understands and integrates these concepts as part of its broader strategy development, and has been able to build and consolidate an extremely strong base for success in the future networked economy. Of course, it is unclear whether Microsoft knows exactly how this future world will emerge. But whatever the range of possible futures, it has built a portfolio of options to take it there.

This article previously appeared in *Business Strategy Review*, Volume 13, Issue 3, Autumn 2002.

Commentary

What companies do wrong

Books on how to get rich, or turn a company into a world beater in a matter of minutes, continue to fly off the bookshelves. But instead of dreaming of effortless profits and making one brilliant decision after another, managers might be better advised to contemplate the nightmare scenario: how companies fail.

Focussing on failure rather than success is not as stupid as it initially appears. First, most success stories are embellished by twenty-twenty hindsight. No one gets it right all of the time. Remember that Enron was widely touted as a business exemplar and written about in reverential terms. Second, if you avoid some of the common business mistakes you are more likely to succeed.

Learning from failure is also fashionable theory. Entrepreneurs are repeatedly told that failure is no disgrace. If you haven't failed, you haven't taken enough risks. Big corporations now work hard at encouraging a risk-taking culture. When he took over as CEO at Eli Lilly in the 1990s, Randall Tobias surprised managers at an annual awards ceremony by introducing awards for the best failures. Failure is acceptable – though success is still preferable.

Personal and corporate failure is the subject of a book by Sydney Finkelstein of the American business school Tuck. In *Why Smart Executives Fail*, Finkelstein helpfully identifies "seven habits of spectacularly unsuccessful people" and looks at what links corporate mistakes. "The literature and business schools are dominated by best practice – the best way to do things, how to get things right, how to be successful. Very seldom do we look explicitly at the other side, even though intuitively we always say we learn from mistakes," says Professor Finkelstein.

As an example he points to General Motors and its investment of nearly $45 billion in automation under CEO Roger Smith in the 1980s. Smith believed that robots would enable GM to cut labor costs and to compete with the Japanese. It became an obsession. Despite the massive investment, the company's market share fell from 48 percent to 36 percent.

According to Finkelstein, high-risk situations for companies occur when they try to start new businesses (beware of corporate spin-offs like Motorola's Iridium); when they are faced with the need for innovation and change; when they enter into mergers and acquisitions (think of AOL Time Warner and a host of others); and when they face new competition.

Indeed, there is surprising consistency in what companies habitually do wrong. The most obvious failure factor is complacency. Corporate smugness is manifest in a variety of ways. These include blind faith that things will be alright despite plummeting sales or over-confident disregard for upstart competitors.

Commentary (continued)

The corollary of complacency is distance from the consumer. Companies which fail tend to be estranged from the people who use and consume their products. Because of this they can't offer consumers what they want. Some treat their customers with something approaching contempt – witness Gerald Ratner's comments about his customers and his company's speedy demise – or simply overlook them.

Companies under-estimate consumer power at their peril. In 1974 Schlitz was America's second most popular beer. Then the brewers introduced a revolutionary new process – "accelerated batch fermentation." This saved time and money and the beer tasted the same. The trouble was that drinkers believed the beer was below the standard they had come to expect – it tasted the same, but customers *believed* it wasn't the same. Schlitz's market share fell to less than a single percentage mark and the value of its name declined from in excess of $1 billion in 1974 to around $75 million in 1980.

Linked to this is self-awareness. Companies which fail tend not to be well informed about their customers, their markets, the competition, or, indeed, themselves. What they are good at remains a closely guarded secret until, eventually, it is forgotten. "Companies are often unclear on which factors they compete on," reflects Renée Mauborgne of Insead. "That is a large part of the reason organizations are overtired and lacking in creative momentum. Because companies often lack a clear, compelling strategy that everyone understands and that sets the company apart, projects are often undertaken that pull the organization in different directions." If you don't know what you are good at and where you are going, oblivion beckons.

Attitudes to money are also at the heart of failure. We all know that managing money is important, but how companies think about money is also central. If money is the *raison d'être* of a business, it is likely to encounter trouble. Money is the happy by-product of success. If the entire culture of a company is geared to making money at all costs, the costs can be high. Sydney Finkelstein points to the example of WorldCom where "customers, employees, and shareholders were all pawns in the game of making money."

The final failure factor is fear. Businesses know what to do but don't do it. "If you ask a group of CEOs how to make their organizations more innovative, you will get a huge laundry list of ideas on how to do it – allow experiments, reward new ideas, do not punish mistakes, and so on. The problem is not that they don't know how to do it but that it doesn't happen," says London Business School's Costas Markides. "Senior executives know what they can do to promote innovation. But the personal risks are simply too high. Innovation carries a huge personal risk, so how many people would actually do it?" Failure begins at the top.

RESOURCES

Finkelstein, Sydney, *Why Smart Executives Fail*, Viking, 2003.

'Interview': Charles Handy

Management commentator turned social philosopher, Charles Handy discusses the changing corporate world and what that means for society and for individuals.

You define a company as a community and you say the workers are, in effect, "citizens" of the company.

If businesses no longer "own" the people they employ, it follows that they have to have a different kind of relationship with them. That relationship is like that of a country and its citizens. Citizens have certain rights: residence, justice, free speech, a share in the wealth of society, and some kind of say in how it is governed. Translated into corporate terms, a citizen's right to residence means some guarantee of employment. That doesn't mean a job for life any more, but I can envisage employees making contracts that will last for an agreed period of time, rather as members of the British armed forces bind themselves to three- and five-year contracts for service.

How can organizations work more efficiently?

I'm not sure if we can use the term "efficiency" in the new economy, by which I don't mean e-business and certainly not dot coms, though of course e-business is a factor that we can't ignore. Speed, flexibility, and transparency of communications have had the effect of dividing the business world into what I call "elephants" and "fleas." As opposed to old-style corporations, fleas are small, agile, creative, unpredictable, and above all adaptable. Examples are the growing numbers of contractors, freelancers, independent consultants, and small specialized suppliers on which the elephants increasingly depend. What matters is that they should deliver on time, to cost, and to specification. They are effective rather than efficient. It's not doing things right, but doing right things that matters.

What does that mean for management?

What I think you are asking is how the flea model operates and how it can be managed effectively. Well, look at the film business. There are no big studios any more, just a few elephants – a director, producers, and money men – who get an idea, assemble a team of fleas – actors and technicians – make the film, collect the money from distributors, and then dissolve the team. Woody Allen's film company and Steven Spielberg's Dreamworks are examples of this type of enterprise: without permanent, money-draining investment in people and plant, such a company thrives in good times and bad.

A crucial skill will be to find where the fleas are and assemble the right team of fleas for the job. They will often be working remotely, from home or from some office of their own, so trust is a key part of the relationship. But how can we trust people we don't see and who aren't around? Communication helps, and you can hardly have too much of it. At the same time business travel is continuing to increase alongside the varieties of electronic communication. So are conferences in which leaders from all sections of business and the community can meet and share their ideas.

Has the new economy changed the way companies need to manage people?

The relationship has changed. In the old loyalty- and job security-based organization, employees were prepared to hand over the ownership of their ideas unconditionally, but that is no longer the case. They know that the assets of the organization are largely made up of what is in the heads of the people they employ. So the fleas are striking up new bargains with the elephants. We can find one sign of it in the film world. When the titles roll at the end, what we are seeing is the fleas visibly being given credit for their contribution. That is what makes them employable in the next job that comes up. They will also expect a much greater share in the fruits of success than the arbitrary reward structure of the old-economy organization allocated to them. A reflection of that is the huge sums of money that go to the stars who bring in the audiences.

You claim that the classical organization concept will not be valid any more. What's coming?

I believe that the organization of the future will be federal. Federalism is a means of linking independent bodies together in a common cause. There are already examples of this – ABB, Unilever, and Nike to mention some examples. They operate what are in effect independent companies; Unilever doesn't even have any brands under its name. In federal companies there is a center but not a headquarters. The center does not direct or command but co-ordinates and operates on the basis of subsidiarity, which is that responsibility and decisions should be pushed as far out and down the organization as possible. Federal firms bring their brains together from around the world to agree strategy and aims. They do not issue edicts from the top.

How does capitalism affect society?

One effect that capitalism is having is to widen the gap between those at the top and those at the bottom. In some US companies the CEO is earning 500 times more than the lowest-paid worker. That is creating ghettos of resentment and poverty which I think capitalism will have to address because society – and hence customers

– are beginning to demand it. There is a growing demand for companies to behave in a socially acceptable way: look what happened to Shell in Germany over the protests of the company's policy in Nigeria. I think we are moving toward a new, more complex bottom line in which profit, environmental concern, and social responsibility will have to be in balance. Those are the forces that will shape the new society.

This requires a new mindset from corporations, but there are benefits in that for them. Take the effect of the Internet. It poses a real threat to traditional organizations. All kinds of intermediaries are disappearing from the screen as their role is questioned. How do you create value when so many goods and services are commoditized? One way to do that is to turn to new markets or to think about markets in a new way. A case in point is Lever Hindustan. It has found a profitable Asian market for cosmetics in sachets costing a few cents and distributed through village traders, whereas its customers were unable to afford a couple of dollars for the same stuff in a bottle. The new economy needs a new, flea-like mindset. That is why big elephant companies are developing activities as venture capitalists and business incubators to keep the fleas who come up with the ideas. The new model of growth is to create business opportunities in which the fleas can flourish and develop their management skills.

Are people's lives thus becoming harder?

Yes, but they can make choices, especially the young, between freedom and commitment, time, and money. That's why there's so much interest now in the idea of the work/life balance.

If balance is important, what about selfishness?

The big danger in the new relationships between people and corporations is that it leads to the creation of a very selfish society in which nobody feels any obligation toward anybody else. We are already seeing the results of this in the crime-ridden streets of prosperous European cities. I don't believe that business can flourish outside the moral order. Selfishness, or at any rate self-interest, is a natural human condition, but it ought to be what I have called "proper selfishness," a realization that pure selfishness, in which every man is out for himself, is counter-productive in that it destroys the society which makes the enjoyment of life possible.

Essentials

ORGANIZATION

Adhocracy

Coined by the leadership expert Warren Bennis in the 1960s, and popularized by futurist Alvin Toffler, adhocracy is basically the opposite of bureaucracy. An adhocracy is an organization that disregards the classical principles of management where everyone has a defined and permanent role, in favor of a more fluid organization where individuals are free to deploy their talents as required.

Essentially, the concept was an attempt to answer the question of how companies should create an appropriate organizational model for the future. It addresses the nature of managerial work and the strategy formation process, as well as social issues. (From a historical perspective, the organizational form can be seen as an evolution from Simple Structure, to Machine Bureaucracy, to Divisionalized Form, to Adhocracy.)

The concept was explored by Alvin Toffler in his 1970 book *Future Shock*. An adhocracy is a non-bureaucratic networked organization. "This form is already common in organizations such as law firms, consulting companies, and research universities. Such organizations and institutions must continually readjust to a changing array of projects, each requiring somewhat different combinations of skills and other resources. These organizations depend on many rapidly shifting project teams and much lateral communication among these relatively autonomous, entrepreneurial groups," notes Toffler.

Toffler has gone on to assert that the social and cultural institutions that currently exist have become unwieldy and outdated. The problem, he claims, is a lack of flexibility. "Why is it that all our institutions seem to be going through a simultaneous crisis?" he asks. "The answer is that we have sets of institutions that were designed either for agrarian life ... as parliaments were, or ... the Industrial Age, but no longer meet the requirements of today." What is needed, Toffler suggests, is a wholesale move to adhocracy.

The concept was further developed by strategy theorist Henry Mintzberg. Mintzberg's adhocracy represents smaller-scale, fluid, often temporary structures. Typically, a group of line managers, staff, and operating experts come together in small product, customer, or project-focussed teams. Informal behavior and high job specialization are typical characteristics of these adhocracies. Teams have their terms of reference (decentralization) provided by more senior management and a team's scope for action and membership may run counter to the command structure of the rest of the organization.

Mintzberg distinguishes between two types of adhocracies. The *operating adhocracy* works on behalf of its clients (for example a creative advertising agency or consulting firm), while an *administrative adhocracy* serves itself (and offers a model for a wide range of companies).

Along with the benefits of a more fluid organizational form, Mintzberg observes, are some potential drawbacks. One problem, he notes, is that managers in an adhocracy may spend too little time on making strategy. They may be sucked into just responding to problems rather than proactive analysis and formulation of radical, corrective programs. An effective adhocracy, he says, must balance the need for action in the short term with the need to take a longer-term view of changes occurring within its environment.

Agility

Like adhocracy, the concept of corporate agility is a response to the need for companies to be more adaptive to changing market conditions. It recognizes that speed of response to market opportunity and threats and flexibility are what distinguishes many successful companies from their lumbering rivals.

Sometimes linked with the emergence of virtual organizations, a number of writers and academics have written about agility. Tom Peters and Richard Pascale are among those who have propounded it in recent years. But if the movement has a principal architect, it is Roger N. Nagel, an expert on competitiveness.

Nagel focusses on agile manufacturing and agile competition, and co-authored the 1995 book *Agile Competitors and Virtual Organizations* with Steven L. Goldman and Kenneth Preiss. The book defined agility at the organizational and individual level: "For a company, to be agile is to be capable of operating profitably in a competitive environment of continually and unpredictably changing customer opportunities. For an individual, to be agile is to be capable of contributing to the bottom line of a company that is constantly reorganizing its human and technological resources in response to unpredictably changing customer opportunities."

Nagel, Goldman, and Preiss present agile competition as a system, with four strategic dimensions:

1. Organizing to master change and uncertainty: an agile company is organized in a way that allows it to thrive on change and uncertainty. (There is no single right structure or size, it can support multiple configurations.)

2. Leveraging the impact of people and information: in an agile company, management nurtures an entrepreneurial company culture that leverages the impact of people and information. People are seen as an investment in future prosperity.

3. Co-operating to enhance competitiveness: co-operation – internally and with other companies – is an agile competitor's operational strategy of first choice.
4. Enriching the customer: an agile company is one that is perceived by its customers as enriching them (and not only itself) in a significant way.

Agility allows companies to migrate from one business to another. In Nagel's view, agility is more than simply speed of action; the ability to adapt and make lateral moves is more important.

Barnard, Chester

Chester Barnard (1886–1961) was a rarity: a management theorist who was also a successful practitioner. Barnard won an economics scholarship to Harvard, but before finishing his degree he joined American Telephone and Telegraph to begin work as a statistician. He spent his entire working life with the company, eventually becoming President of New Jersey Bell in 1927.

Although he was the archetypal corporate man, Barnard's interests were varied, and he also found time to lecture on the subject of management. His best-known book, *The Functions of the Executive*, collected together his lectures. The language is dated, the approach ornate but comprehensive. Much of what Barnard argued strikes a chord with contemporary management thinking. For example, he highlighted the need for communication so that every single person could be tied into the organization's objectives. He also advocated lines of communication that were short and direct.

To Barnard, the chief executive was not a dictatorial figure geared to simple short-term achievements. Instead, part of his responsibility was to nurture the values and goals of the organization. For all his contemporary-sounding ideas, Barnard was a man of his times – advocating corporate domination of the individual and regarding loyalty to the organization as paramount.

Even so, Barnard proposed a moral dimension to the world of work. "The distinguishing mark of the executive responsibility is that it requires not merely conformance to a complex code of morals but also the creation of moral codes for others," wrote Barnard. In arguing that there was a morality to management, Barnard played an important part in broadening the managerial role from one simply of measurement, control, and supervision to one also concerned with more elusive, abstract notions, such as values.

Core competencies

Instead of identifying what business they are in, the core competencies approach calls on companies to identify the distinctive and differentiating competencies that lie at their heart. Identifying core competencies allows an organization to nurture and build from its strengths rather than pursuing red herrings for which it does not possess appropriate skills. A clear understanding of core competencies can also help a company decide which areas of its business are non-core and better outsourced, and which are so vital to its competitive position that they must be maintained at all costs.

While there are clear drawbacks to religious adherence to the tenets of core competencies, the concept marks an important development. Once, differentiation was regarded as being solely concerned with products. Companies sought to develop their products to compete. Now, differentiation is increasingly identified with the skills, knowledge, and aspirations of the organization. Differentiation comes from the "soft" areas of branding, organizational innovation, and service. As a result, differentiation is more human and harder to achieve than ever before.

Actually identifying what a company's core competencies are is fraught with difficulty. The champions of the concept of core competencies have been the American academics Gary Hamel and C.K. Prahalad, authors of *Competing for the Future*. They suggest that a core competence should provide potential access to a wide variety of markets, make a significant contribution to the perceived customer benefits of the end products, and be difficult for competitors to imitate. In practice, these are highly demanding tests. As a result, what tends to emerge is a wish list of what the company would like to be good at, a compendium of vague aspirations.

Part of the problem is that there is confusion between personal competencies and corporate competencies. The temptation for companies when they set out in pursuit of competencies is to start with the personal. These are relatively easy to establish. Companies can then synthesize the skills of their people into generic competencies that apply to the firm as a whole. This is not what Hamel and Prahalad intended. The end result of the bottom-up approach may be personally beneficial but, from a corporate viewpoint, is usually confusing. Instead, Hamel and Prahalad advocate that companies take a much broader view, seeking out links between activities and skill areas.

For those organizations able to determine a persuasive and useful list of their core competencies comes the next stage: developing strategies that are driven by those competencies. Herein lies what some consider the greatest danger of the neat theory. If a company seeks out markets, mergers, and acquisitions in areas where its core competencies would be most advantageous, it may well be entering markets about which it knows nothing.

In effect, the concept of core competencies encourages companies to diversify. They need to go where their competencies would be put to the most effective and profitable use. Unfortunately, corporate history is littered with unhappy experiences of diversification.

Another weakness to the core competence argument is that a business's critical competencies and insights often reside among a small coterie of people, not necessarily senior managers. In a knowledge- and information-intensive age, this is increasingly the case. If the people depart, so, too, do the competencies.

Geneen, Harold

A formidable mythology has built up around the career and management style of Harold Geneen (1910–97). Born in Bournemouth on England's genteel south coast, Geneen became the archetypal bullish American executive, a remorselessly driven workaholic who believed that analytical rigor could – and surely would – conquer all.

Harold Geneen qualified as an accountant after studying at night schools. He then began climbing the executive career ladder, working at American Can, Bell & Howell, Jones & Laughlin, and finally Raytheon, which was taken over by ITT. He joined the board of ITT in 1959 and set about turning the company into the world's greatest conglomerate.

Geneen's basic organizational strategy was that diversification was a source of strength. By 1970, ITT was composed of 400 separate companies operating in 70 countries. Keeping the growing array of companies in check was a complex series of financial checks and targets. Geneen managed them with intense vigor and a unique single-mindedness. As part of his formula, every month over 50 executives flew to Brussels to spend four days poring over the figures. "I want no surprises," he announced. He hoped to make people "as predictable and controllable as the capital resources they must manage." While others would have watched as the deck of cards fell to the ground, Geneen kept adding more cards, while managing to know the pressures and stresses that each was under.

Facts were the lifeblood of the expanding ITT – and executives sweated blood in their pursuit. "The highest art of professional management requires the literal ability to *smell* a *real fact* from all others – and, moreover, to have the temerity, intellectual curiosity, guts, and/or plain impoliteness, if necessary, to be sure that what you do have is indeed what we will call an *unshakeable fact*," said Geneen.

By sheer force of personality, Geneen's approach worked. Between 1959 and 1977, ITT's sales went from $765 million to nearly $28 billion.

ITT rapidly disintegrated following Geneen's departure in 1979. His followers were unable to sustain his uniquely driven working style. The underside of ITT was exposed – it had worked with the CIA in Chile and been involved in offering bribes. The deck of cards tumbled to the floor.

Handy, Charles

Charles Handy (born 1932) is a bestselling writer and broadcaster. His work is accessible and popular. Because of this it is dismissed by some. Yet Handy has brought major questions about the future of work and of society on to the corporate and personal agenda.

Irish born, Charles Handy worked for Shell until 1972 when he left to teach at London Business School. He spent time at MIT, where he came into contact with many of the leading lights in the human relations school of thinking, including Ed Schein.

Handy's early academic career was conventional. His first book, *Understanding Organizations* (1976), gives little hint of the wide-ranging, social and philosophical nature of his later work. It was in 1989 with the publication of *The Age of Unreason* that Handy's thinking made a great leap forward. The age of unreason that he predicts is "a time when what we used to take for granted may no longer hold true, when the future, in so many areas, is there to be shaped, by us and for us; a time when the only prediction that will hold true is that no predictions will hold. A time, therefore, for bold imaginings in private life as well as public, for thinking the unlikely and doing the unreasonable."

In practice, Handy believes that certain forms of organization will become dominant. These are the types of organization most readily associated with service industries. First and most famously is what he calls "the shamrock organization" – "a form of organization based around a core of essential executives and workers supported by outside contractors and part-time help." The consequence of such an organizational form is that organizations in the future are likely to resemble the way consultancy firms, advertising agencies, and professional partnerships are currently structured.

The second emergent structure identified by Handy is the federal one. It is not, he points out, another word for decentralization. He provides a blueprint for federal organizations in which the central function co-ordinates, influences, advises, and suggests. It does not dictate terms or short-term decisions. The center is, however, concerned with long-term strategy. It is "at the middle of things and is not a polite word for the top or even for head office."

The third type of organization Handy anticipates is what he calls "the Triple I." The three "Is" are Information, Intelligence, and Ideas. In such organizations, the demands on personnel management are large. Handy explains: "The wise organization already knows that their smart people are not to be easily defined as workers or as managers but as individuals, as specialist, as professional or executives, or as leader (the older terms of manager and worker are dropping out of use), and that they and it need also to be obsessed with the pursuit of learning if they are going to keep up with the pace of change."

As organizations change in the age of unreason so, Handy predicts, will other aspects of our lives. Less time will be spent at work – 50,000 hours in a lifetime rather than the present figure of around 100,000. Handy does not predict, as people did in the 1970s, an enlightened age of leisure. Instead, he challenges people to spend more time thinking about what they want to do. Time will not simply be divided between work and play – there could be "portfolios" that split time between fee work (where you sell time), gift work (for neighbors or charities), study (keeping up to date with your work), homework, and leisure.

Handy has reached his own conclusions. He says he has made his last speech to a large audience. He now sets a limit of 12 to his audiences, reflecting that "enough is enough." Handy has become a one-man case study of the new world of work on which he so successfully and humanely commentates. At a personal level, he appears to have the answers. Whether these can be translated into answers for others remains the question and the challenge.

Matrix model

An organizational structure adopted by many multinational companies, the matrix model is an attempt to deal with the complexities of managing large organizations across different national markets. It was developed by the electronics company Philips after the Second World War, and represents a compromise between centralization and decentralization.

Under a simple matrix management system, a marketing manager in, say, Germany reports ultimately to a boss in that country, but also to the head of the marketing function back in the company's home country. The two reporting lines (more complicated matrix structures have multiple reporting lines) are the two sides to the matrix, which has a geographical and a functional axis.

As a theoretical model, the matrix is a neat solution to the complexity of large companies. However, in reality power cannot be evenly balanced, and conflicts inevitably arise. When you add in additional complexity such as cross-functional reporting lines in project teams or start-up operations, manager can find themselves trying to please several different bosses at the same time.

Many multinationals continue to operate as matrix management structures simply because they haven't come up with a better model. In the beginning, organizations were neat, hierarchical, and linear, with simple chains of command. Worker A reported to manager B, who reported to senior manager C, who reported to board member D, who reported to the managing director or CEO. Corporate life was relatively simple, understandable, and clear-cut.

As companies became bigger, they began to organize themselves differently. In the 1920s, the American company DuPont championed federal decentralization. This gave the headquarters responsibility for core central functions such as finance and marketing. Business units were granted greater autonomy and responsibility for their own performance. This approach was championed by Alfred P. Sloan at General Motors, and later emulated by the likes of General Electric and Shell.

Federal decentralization brought professional rigor to management. However, its fundamental flaws were that one central function tended to emerge as the dominant one; it did little to share value, information, and knowledge between units; and it helped create an entire layer of headquarters-based middle managers whose value-adding role was increasingly difficult to determine.

The inevitable rebuff to decentralization is centralization, taking power back to the corporate center. The trouble is that this involves a degree of dictatorship and commitment that few senior managers can carry through for any length of time.

Matrix management is a middle way. It is a hybrid of decentralization and centralization. A matrix organization is arranged in such a way that each unit has at least two bosses. Instead of being based around a linear chain of command, the matrix is multidimensional – depending on how many dimensions are deemed to be useful or practically possible. An organization may include regional managers, functional managers, country or continental managers, and business sector managers.

Herein lies the problem. The mythical matrix boss is seven headed. Matrix management is complex, ambiguous, and confusing – little wonder that it has generally had a bad press. In *In Search of Excellence*, Tom Peters and Robert Waterman were dismissive of matrix organization as "a logistical mess," arguing that "it automatically dilutes priorities" and that structure should be kept as simple as possible. The hackneyed criticism is that a matrix organization is "an organization in which nobody can make any decision on his or her own, but anybody on his own can stop a decision being made."

While these criticisms are generally justified, the matrix organization may be, in fact, a more realistic delineation and description of responsibilities and hierarchies. Built around a network of responsibilities, it fosters broader perspectives. Managers don't view matters within the narrow perspectives of their unit, their function, or their fiefdom. Instead, they have to view them from a variety of perspectives – local, corporate, national, international, global, functional.

Matrix management can be made to work – some large European multinationals have done so. At its heart, however, lies an element of ambiguity and uncertainty with which managers remain uncomfortable. The trouble is that management theorists and researchers are virtually all agreed that ambiguity and uncertainty are the new facts of corporate life. Matrix management – in one form or another – may be the most appropriate means of making organizational sense of these disturbing realities.

Shamrock organization

In recent years, the organizational structure most appropriate for the future has been widely discussed. British management thinker Charles Handy has been one of the most considered participants in this debate. He anticipated that certain models of organization would become dominant. These were the type of organization most readily associated with service industries.

First and most famously came Handy's shamrock organization.[3] This describes a type of organizational structure with three parts, or leaves – "a form of organization based around a core of essential executives and workers supported by outside contractors and part-time help."

The consequence of such an organizational form is that organizations in the future are likely to resemble the way consultancy firms, advertising agencies, and professional partnerships are currently structured.

This model, or variations of it, is often used to explain the move to outsourcing non-core functions. In Handy's analogy, the first leaf of the shamrock represents the organization's core staff. These people are likely to be highly trained professionals who make up the senior management. The second leaf consists of the contractual fringe – either individuals or other organizations – and may include people who once worked for the organization but now provide it with services. These individuals operate within the broad framework set down by the core, but have a high level of discretionary decision-making power to complete projects or deliver contacts.

The third leaf includes the flexible labor force. More than simply hired hands, in Handy's model, these workers have to be sufficiently close to the organization to feel a sense of commitment ensuring that their work, although part-time or intermittent, is carried out to a high standard.

The second emergent structure identified by Handy was the *federal organization* – not, he pointed out, another word for decentralization. He provided a blueprint for federal organizations in which the central function co-ordinates, influences, advises, and suggests. It does not dictate terms or short-term decisions. The center is, however, concerned with long-term strategy. It is "at the middle of things and is not a polite word for the top or even for head office."

The third type of organization Handy anticipated is what he called "the Triple I" – Information, Intelligence, and Ideas. In such organizations the demands on personnel management are large. Handy explained: "The wise organization already knows that their smart people are not to be easily defined as workers or as managers but as individuals, as specialist, as professional or executive, or as leader (the older terms of manager and worker are dropping out of use), and that they and it need also to be obsessed with the pursuit of learning if they are going to keep up with the pace of change."

More recently, Handy has suggested that successful organizations of the future will be what he calls "membership communities." His logic is that in order to hold people to an organization that can no longer promise them a job for life, companies have to offer some other form of continuity and sense of belonging. To do this, he suggests, they have to imbue their members with certain rights.

What Handy is advocating in fact is some notion of the federal organization, built on the principle of subsidiarity. This places a large degree of trust in core professionals and other knowledge workers. Under Handy's membership community model, the center is kept small and its primary purpose is to be "in charge of the future." Only if the organization is severely threatened does decision-making power revert to the center. This allows the company to react quickly in a crisis. The rest of the time, decision making is highly decentralized.

The virtual organization

Much beloved of management theorists, the notion of the virtual organization has more than one interpretation. To some people, the virtual concept refers simply to the ability of companies to use IT to allow people in different locations, and even on different continents, to work together effectively. For others it goes further, describing an amorphous organization, made up of project teams that form to fulfill a specific purpose and disband at a moment's notice.

From the traditional images of machinery, the organization has become an elusive, ever-changing ameba. Describing the organization of the future, American writers William Davidow and Michael Malone say: "To the outside observer, it will appear almost edgeless, with permeable and continuously changing interfaces among company, supplier, and customers. From inside the firm, the view will be no less amorphous with traditional offices, departments, and operating divisions constantly re-forming according to need." The end result is the virtual organization.

The theory on which the concept is built is perfectly sensible. Technology enables companies to dismantle their cumbersome headquarters buildings, the costly bricks and mortar of the conventional business. Employees can work at home or occasionally in satellite offices when required. Linked by networks of computers, communicating by e-mail and modems, people become more productive if freed from the burdens of commuting and the regularity of office life. With no expensive tower blocks to support, organizations make massive cuts in operating costs. The virtual organization is life and profit enhancing.

The ability of employees to communicate and share information also means that the patterns of decision making are fundamentally altered, with no necessity for co-ordination from the center. If we think of individual workers as dots on the organizational map, then one justification for traditional structures was to provide a framework to direct their efforts. But as soon as you can connect each dot – or computer terminal – to any other, the need for a formal structure disappears. If we go a step further and think of those dots as light bulbs connected with the power of communication, then, theoretically at least, a virtual organization can instantly light up any pattern or configuration of skills required, and can switch it off just as quickly.

The virtual organization is well understood and a logical extension of technology. But virtual organizations are, as yet, notable by their absence. There are organizations that appear virtual to customers, but are not truly virtual in reality. Internet banking seems more virtual than the bank down the road, but even e-banking companies have their conventional headquarters buildings. Companies may relocate to cheaper alternatives, but they are still choosing to invest in reassuring concrete. If the arguments for the virtual organization are so persuasive, why are so few decision makers persuaded?

First, virtual organizations are off-puttingly fashionable. They remain terminally associated with smart and creative companies. Ad agencies, design companies, and software houses are thought to be candidates for virtuality, not less esoteric manufacturers. This is a limit of perception rather than reality. A manufacturer in Dudley can benefit from organizing itself in a virtual way as much as one in Palo Alto.

The second stumbling block is that the virtual organization requires a quantum leap rather than steady evolution. Making it work requires more than short-term enthusiasm on the part of senior managers. It demands some understanding of the technical possibilities, as well as a harmonious and respectful relationship with corporate IT specialists.

This brings us to the third obstacle. The virtual organization uses IT as a primary corporate resource. The trouble is that many organizations continue to regard IT as a function rather than a dynamic organizational tool.

This list could be supplemented by the crucial fact that people, and managers in particular, remain wedded to their offices. With its social rituals, human interest, and politics, office life retains a strong attraction.

Given the apparent difficulties in creating truly virtual organizations, the way forward may rest with compromise solutions, such as hot-desking or the use of virtual teams, groups that are accountable for the achievement of transient or short-term objectives. For most companies, true virtual working is still some way off.

Weber, Max

The German sociologist Max Weber (1864–1920) was the original champion of the bureaucratic model of organizations. In terms of management theorizing he has become something of a *bête noir*, the sociological twin of Frederick Taylor, the king of scientific rationality.

Weber observed emerging organizations in the fledgling industrial world. He argued that the most efficient form of organization resembled a machine. It was characterized by strict rules, controls, and hierarchies, and driven by bureaucracy. This Weber termed the "rational-legal model."

At the opposite extreme was the "charismatic" model where a single dominant figure ran the organization. Weber dismissed this as a long-term solution – once again, he was the first to discuss this phenomenon and examine its ramifications. No matter what Peters and Waterman say, history bears Weber out – an organization built around a single charismatic figure is unsustainable in the long term.

The final organizational form that Weber identified was the traditional model where things were done as they always have been, such as in family firms in which power is passed down from one generation to the next.

If it was pure efficiency you required, there was, said Weber, only one choice: "Experience tends universally to show that the purely bureaucratic type of administrative organization – that is, the monocratic variety of bureaucracy –

is, from a purely technical point of view, capable of attaining the highest degree of efficiency and is in this sense formally the most rational known means of carrying our imperative control over human beings," Weber wrote.

In *The Theory of Social and Economic Organization*, he outlined the "structure of authority" around seven points:

1. A continuous organization of official functions bound by rules.
2. A specified sphere of competence.
3. The organization of offices follows the principle of hierarchy.
4. The rules which regulate the conduct of an office may be technical rules or norms. In both cases, if their application is to be fully traditional, specialized training is necessary.
5. In the rational type it is a matter of principle that the members of the administrative staff should be completely separated from the ownership of the means of production or administration.
6. In the rational type case, there is also a complete absence of appropriation of his official position by the incumbent.
7. Administrative acts, decisions, and rules are formulated and recorded in writing, even in cases where oral discussion is the rule or is even mandatory.

Modern commentators usually cannot resist the urge to scoff at Weber's insights. It was an undoubtedly narrow way of doing things and one that seems out of step with our times. Yet, in the early part of the 20th century, it was a plausible and effective means of doing business. Like all great insights, it worked, for a while at least.

REFERENCES

1 Argyris, C. 'Empowerment: The Emporor's New Clothes,' *Harvard Business Review*, May–June, 1998.
2 Heller, F. 'Influence at Work: A 25 Year Program of Research,' *Human Relations*, Vol. 51, No. 12, 1425, 1998.
3 Handy, Charles, *The Age of Unreason*, Century Business Books, 1989.

– CHAPTER 8 –

Ideas, information, and knowledge

"When you invest in raw materials, like a mine or an oil field, there is only one thing that you can be absolutely, 100 percent sure about: Sooner or later, you are going to run out of that stuff. But when you invest in human imagination – feelings and fantasy – the sky is the limit. There is no end. And so, limitless leverage is possible."

Jonas Ridderstråle

"Thought, not money, is the real business capital."

Harvey Firestone

"Just as energy is the basis of life itself, and ideas the source of innovation, so is innovation the vital spark of all human change, improvement and progress."

Theodore Levitt

"Management means, in the last analysis, the substitution of thought for brawn and muscle, of knowledge for folklore and superstition, and of co-operation for force."

Peter Drucker

"What information consumes is rather obvious: it consumes the attention of its recipients. Hence, a wealth of information creates a poverty of attention and a need to allocate that attention efficiently among the over-abundance of information sources that might consume it."

Herbert Simon

Open innovation

HENRY CHESBROUGH

[The *closed innovation* model, characterized by an internal R&D focus, has been consigned to history. Organizations increasingly embrace *open innovation* in the continuing quest for creative new ideas.]

Vertical integration was the dominant business logic of the last century. Explained by Alfred Chandler and practiced by General Motors, Standard Oil, DuPont and many others, it emphasized corporate centralization and integration. Underlying the logic was the belief that valuable knowledge was fundamentally scarce. As a result, companies sought to develop a knowledge advantage that others could not match.

This corporate world view brought with it a number of working assumptions:

- The company which gets an innovation to market first, will win.
- If you create the most, and the best ideas in the industry, you will win.
- The smart people in our field work for us. Companies competed for the best and the brightest graduates and offered these recruits the best salaries and equipment.
- If we discover it ourselves, we will get it to market first. Internal R&D was seen as a barrier against smaller competitors.
- To profit from R&D, we must discover it, develop it, and ship it ourselves. The rise of companies like DuPont, General Electric, General Motors, IBM, Xerox, Merck, and Procter & Gamble was fueled by sustained investment in internal R&D. A by-product of this emphasis was "Not Invented Here" syndrome, where companies rejected any technology that had come from outside.
- We should control our intellectual property, so that our competitors don't profit from our ideas.

For most of the 1900s, this closed innovation model worked. We can thank it for a whole range of inventions and developments. It enabled Thomas Edison to invent the phonograph and the electric light bulb among other things. In the chemicals industry, companies like DuPont established central research labs to identify and commercialize an amazing variety of new products such as the synthetic fibers nylon, Kevlar and Lycra. And Bell Laboratories researchers discovered groundbreaking physical phenomena and harnessed those discoveries to create a host of revolutionary products, including transistors and lasers.

The innovation shift

Over the past two decades things have fundamentally changed. It is still true that no company can grow and prosper without new ideas. It is also clear that the changing needs of customers, increasing competitive pressure, and the evolving abilities of suppliers necessitate continual creative thinking for a company to stay ahead of the pack.

The challenge is that the distribution of this critical knowledge has shifted. This has important implications for how every company thinks about growth and innovation.

The reasons behind this basic change are many and varied. In the United States one factor was the success of the GI Bill which increased college numbers in the post-war years. Other factors include the rise in the amount and quality of university research, the increased mobility of skilled personnel between companies, and the growth in venture capital and private equity that created a pool of risk capital to fund the development of new ventures.

The result was an erosion of the carefully created and nurtured knowledge monopolies inside leading industrial corporations. Instead of being retained within corporate walls, knowledge streamed out of centralized R&D to suppliers, customers, start-ups, and spin-offs. A new generation of companies arose, including Microsoft, Cisco, Dell, Pfizer, and Schwab, which innovated with ideas brought in from outside. Of course, they added to this knowledge base, and crafted innovative business models around that knowledge. But they did little internal R&D on their own, relying instead on licensing, acquiring, and copying external technology.

We have moved from closed innovation to a new logic of innovation: *open innovation*. This new logic builds upon the recognition that useful knowledge is widely distributed across society, in organizations of all sizes and purposes, including nonprofits, universities, and government entities. Rather than reinvent the wheel, the new logic employs the wheel to move forward faster.

The limits of closed innovation

By way of illustration, compare Lucent, which inherited the lion's share of Bell Laboratories after the break-up of AT&T, with Cisco. Bell Labs was perhaps the premier industrial research organization of the last century. On the surface at least this heritage should have been a decisive strategic weapon for Lucent in the telecommunications equipment market. Yet, Cisco, without the deep internal R&D capabilities of Bell Labs, has consistently managed to stay abreast of Lucent, occasionally beating it to market.

This can be explained. The two organizations were simply not innovating in the same manner. Lucent devoted enormous resources to exploring the world of new materials and state-of-the-art components and systems, seeking fundamental discoveries that could fuel future generations of products and services.

In contrast, Cisco deployed a very different strategy. Whatever technology the company needed, it acquired from the outside, usually by partnering or investing in promising start-ups (some, ironically, founded by ex-Lucent veterans). In this way, Cisco was able to keep up with the R&D output of perhaps the finest industrial R&D organization in the world, all without doing much internal research of its own.

The story of Lucent and Cisco is hardly an isolated instance. IBM's research prowess in computing provided little protection against Intel and Microsoft in the personal computer business. Similarly, Motorola, Siemens, and other industrial titans watched helplessly as Nokia catapulted itself to the forefront of wireless telephony in just 20 years, building on its industrial experience from earlier decades in the low-tech industries of wood pulp and rubber boots. And pharmaceutical giants like Merck and Pfizer have watched as a number of upstarts, including Genentech, Amgen, and Genzyme, have parlayed the research discoveries of others to become major players in the biotechnology industry.

The new assumptions

Not surprisingly, the assumptions underlying open innovation are radically different from those which lie behind closed innovation.

Not all the smart people work for us. Consider the dramatic rise of Nokia in wireless communications. The company's success has been due, in part, to its taking a strong lead in establishing the Global System for Mobile Communication (GSM) technology as a standard for cellular phones. Accomplishing that required working closely with a number of other companies, as well as the governments of many European countries. Specifically, Nokia research helped define the now-accepted standards for moving GSM from a narrow to broad bandwidth spectrum, and the company pushed hard to establish that technology: it willingly licensed the research to others and partnered with companies (including competitors) to develop the chipsets necessary for implementing the standard.[1] Those efforts have helped Nokia to become the world's dominant supplier of wireless-phone handsets, controlling nearly 40 percent of the global market.

Or look at Procter & Gamble which has an illustrious history of creating superior consumer products through the application of advanced science and technology to the needs of people in their daily lives. P&G's leaders realized several years ago that it had perhaps 8,600 scientists and engineers on its payroll, while there were more than 1.5 million such people working outside the company. It made little business sense to ignore that enormous pool of external talent, even for a company of P&G's size. In order to gain better knowledge of and access to this huge pool of external brainpower, P&G created a group of corporate scouts it called *technology entrepreneurs*. Over its nearly five-year history, the group has grown to include about 50 scouts. As Nabil Sakkab, senior vice president of R&D in P&G's Fabric & Home Care division, wrote in *Research-Technology Management*: "One of our technology entrepreneurs has made several important connections to new ways to achieve a discontinuity in cleaning performance ... [Activities like this] illustrate the unprecedented opportunity we all have to enrich our innovation portfolios."

External R&D can help create value; internal R&D is needed to capture a portion of that value. Intel competes in the technologically advanced semiconductor industry. Much of the internal R&D it undertakes, though, is done to connect the company to external research in its supply chain (through its Components Research Lab) or to its customers and developers (through its Intel Architecture Labs). Intel also spends more than $100 million annually in funding university research, seeking new ideas that it can bring into its business. Intel does not own these ideas; it does, however, gain early access to them. To capture value from these ideas, Intel uses its internal labs. Most of Intel's internal research is concentrated in its Microprocessor Research Lab, which focusses on new-generation Pentium technologies and architectures.

Says Sun-Lin Chou, director of Intel's Components Research Laboratory: "You have to ask yourself, where is the next big idea, such as the next transistor, the next IC, the next successor to silicon going to come from? If you believe it will come from directed discovery, then you are well advised to invest in focussed internal research activities to increase your chances of finding it. If, however, you believe that the next big idea is likely to come from any one of a large number of areas, then you're better advised to structure yourself to be able to monitor a variety of research sources, and to respond quickly to research discoveries when and if they arise."

We don't have to originate the research to profit from it. IBM is perhaps the leading corporate supporter of both Linux and Java software, devoting thousands of its own staff to advance these languages. Yet IBM neither invented nor "owns" either. It provides such extensive support to Linux and Java because they help IBM connect its own products together, and integrate them with other companies" hardware and software.

Similarly, P&G has tremendous expertise in building brands, and enjoys enormous influence with consumer goods retailers. These assets mean that P&G can generate real value from ideas that come from outside of P&G. For example, P&G acquired the Spinbrush electric toothbrush from a team of four entrepreneurs. The product went to market in 2001, and in the first year after the acquisition, P&G generated more than $200 million in sales from Spinbrush.

Building a better business model is better than getting to market first. In 1987, before IBM embraced open innovation, the company introduced the MicroChannel bus to increase the speed of personal computers" add-on boards. However, it was a proprietary device, and most PC manufacturers resisted adopting it. In 1990 Intel contacted Dell Computer and other companies to craft an alternative bus, the Peripheral Component Interconnect (PCI) bus, which was not proprietary. Within a few years, IBM's MicroChannel faded into history, and every PC today uses Intel's PCI bus design instead. Dave Carson, manager of the PCI initiative, says: "PCI set the tone for other Intel initiatives. When we set out to do so, we can move the industry in a useful direction."

Today, Intel is trying to do so again with its Centrino chip, which builds in support for wireless communications technologies such as WiFi. Centrino is late to this market, competing with designs from Atmel, Broadcom, TI, and many others. Intel is trying to move the industry toward its Centrino approach by creating "pull" from public spaces. Intel has already persuaded leading hoteliers like Starwood to incorporate its Centrino WiFi standard into "hotspots" that automatically connect WiFi laptops to a network in their hotels. If Centrino overcomes its late start, it will be due to the business model Intel is building around it.

If you make the best use of external and internal technology, you will win. Intuit, which sells personal financial software products, such as the popular Quicken program, has become very adept at identifying and adapting outside technologies. In this way, the company has consistently been able to profit from innovations it did not discover. For example, it acquired two of its popular products – TurboTax (a tax-preparation program) and QuickBooks (small-business accounting software) – from the outside, and enhanced each in order to meet customers' needs.

Intel has seldom, if ever, had the fastest processor, the most technologically advanced processor, or the cheapest processor. Yet its processor sales are more than four times that of its nearest competitor, and have been so for many years. The reason is that Intel's technology is supported by more people in more companies than any other processor. Some of these "fellow travelers" are working on processes for making Intel's chips, while others are developing new hardware and software that consume vast amounts of processing power. Collectively, they greatly increase the demand for the Intel architecture.

We should profit from others' use of our ideas, and we should buy others' IP whenever it fits our business model. IBM has embraced this aspect of open innovation. The company reported royalties of $1.7 billion in 2001, about 15 percent of its operating income that year. It received these royalties in payment for licensing its technology for other companies to use in their businesses.

P&G is also an active participant in the marketplace for externally generated ideas. It determined that, in 2001, about 10 percent of its pipeline of new products came from external sources. It decided that in order to meet its growth objectives, the percentage of external ideas should rise to 50 percent over the next five years. P&G also set a policy in place that, if a patented technology had not been picked up by at least one P&G business within three years, that technology would be made available to outsiders – even competitors. P&G rightly assumes that its technology is perishable, and that keeping it on the shelf only dissipates any potential value from the technology. If P&G is not going to use it, it is better to let others do so and profit thereby.

Open to a point

But this is not to argue that all industries have migrated or will migrate to open innovation.

For example, the nuclear-reactor industry depends mainly on internal ideas and has low labor mobility, little venture capital, few (and weak) start-ups and relatively little research being conducted at universities. Whether this industry will ever migrate toward open innovation is questionable.

At the other extreme, some industries have been open for some time now. Consider Hollywood, which for decades has innovated through a network of partnerships and alliances between production studios, directors, talent agencies, actors, scriptwriters, independent producers and specialized subcontractors such as the suppliers of special effects. And the mobility of this workforce is legendary: every waitress is a budding actress; every parking attendant has a screenplay he is working on.

Many industries – including copiers, computers, disk drives, semiconductors, telecommunications equipment, pharmaceuticals, biotechnology, and even military weapons and communications systems – are currently undergoing a transition from closed to open. For such businesses, a number of critically important innovations have emerged from seemingly unlikely sources. Indeed, the locus of innovation in these industries has migrated past the confines of the central R&D laboratories of the largest companies and is now situated among various start-ups, universities, research consortia, and other outsiders. And the trend goes well beyond high technology. Other industries such as automotive, health care, banking, insurance, and consumer package goods have also been leaning toward open innovation.

Their realization is that, in a world of abundant knowledge, hoarding technology is a self-limiting strategy. No organization, even the largest, can afford any longer to ignore the tremendous external pools of knowledge that exist.

RESOURCES

Chesbrough, Henry, *Open Innovation: The New Imperative for Creating and Profiting from Technology*, Harvard Business School Press, 2003.

Cohan, Peter, *The Technology Leaders: How America's Most Profitable High-Tech Companies Innovate Their Way to Success*, Jossey-Bass, 1997.

Utterback, J., *Mastering the Dynamics of Innovation*, Harvard Business School Press, 1994.

von Hippel, E., *The Sources of Innovation*, Cambridge University Press, 1988.

The 21st-century CIO

MARK POLANSKY WITH TARUN INUGANTI AND SIMON WIGGINS

[The information technology leadership role has transformed significantly in the 15 years since the title Chief Information Officer was initially coined. As the intrinsic economic value of information rises, the CIO's portfolio of responsibilities evolves to keep pace. The on-going process of rapid change and wrenching transformation is unlikely to end soon.]

Our analysis is based on interviews with CIOs at leading global organizations. One overarching truth emerges: the CIO's position in the corporate structure is rising steadily and inexorably from the tactical/operational level to the strategic/management level.

"The CIO of tomorrow wants to help the business achieve its business objectives," says Boeing CIO Scott Griffin. "We will not chase technology for technology's sake." The CIO's projected rise in stature and visibility will offer significant benefits, both to the CIO and to the organization he or she serves. There are also significant downsides, the most obvious being that as the weight of responsibility increases, speed and flexibility tend to decrease.

As a result, the 21st-century CIO will be required to master the analytic and forecasting capabilities necessary to plan and successfully manage a complex portfolio of IT investments. The CIO will also be required to possess the skills and means for tracking the business impact of technology investments throughout the organization with a far greater degree of precision than the CIO of today. "The position of CIO will increasingly be recognized as a core executive business position," says Carl Wilson, CIO at Marriott International. "This will be driven by companies realizing that information technology capabilities are not only critical to supporting their business strategies, but that they are also necessary to competitively shape their business strategies."

The 21st-century CIO will be expected to enhance the value of information at multiple points along the value chain. The CIO's responsibilities will extend far beyond the traditional boundaries of the IT department. Indeed, the CIO will be required to exercise leadership across the width and breadth of the enterprise.

Accenture CIO Frank Modruson summarized the situation succinctly: "If you look at the role of a CIO over the past 15 years, it has changed as dramatically as the technology has. Technology has in essence gone from supporting point solutions to supporting most day-to-day activities, underpinning all individual and corporate processes. In this period, the role of the CIO has evolved to providing technology that supports the entire strategy of the company and becomes an integral part of daily operations."

There is a common thread of insights, concerns, and expectations. We have distilled them into a 10-point IT leadership agenda:

1. IT strategy – the CIOs agree that for the foreseeable future, the fundamental task of every IT department will be to align its goals and objectives with the business goals and objectives of the enterprise. The primary job of the CIO is to achieve this alignment by developing an IT strategy that focusses on building solid business cases based on projected returns on investment.

2. IT governance – faced with limited resources and increased pressure to measure results objectively, CIOs will be forced to implement robust processes to monitor and evaluate the performance of systems. IT portfolio management will be essential to the survival of the enterprise. Review processes for project funding, standardized performance metrics, and project management will become the norm. IT spending will be regarded from an investment perspective, accelerating the transformation of the IT department from a cost-center to a profit-center.

3. IT organization and staffing – the organization and staffing of the IT function will be considered from an enterprise perspective instead of a departmental perspective. Decisions about whether to implement centralized or decentralized organization models will be made on the basis of enterprise need, rather than departmental need. The same logic will hold for decisions regarding shared services, reporting relationships, staff augmentation, on/near/off-shore outsourcing, capabilities, maturity, training, and other human capital management issues.

4. Technology and architecture – here again, decisions about adopting a bleeding edge, leading edge, or trailing edge approach to new technologies will be made from the enterprise perspective. Technology investment issues (such as build or buy; suite or best-of-breed; insourced or outsourced) will be considered on the basis of likely outcomes at the enterprise level, or more specifically, on how they will affect net income and earnings per share.

5. Technology awareness – the 21st-century CIO will own the responsibility of developing, articulating, and selling an enterprise-wide vision of technology at every level of the organization, from the boardroom to the mail-room. At many organizations, the CIO will be responsible for communicating a clear technology vision that will extend the supply chain to include outside contractors, vendors, distributors, value-added resellers, retailers, and end-users.

6. Corporate governance – regulatory initiatives have radically altered the business landscape and forever changed the roles of information managers. Corporate governance, financial accountability, and greater transparency are no longer ideals – they are now law. Ready or not, the CIO has been saddled with a host of new burdens including regulatory compliance, reporting, business continuity, security, privacy, and intellectual property protection.

7. Business intelligence – the traditional IT department furnishes decision makers with historical data. The 21st-century CIO will be expected to serve up actionable business intelligence. This will require significantly larger systems for collecting, managing, and analyzing data. Unified data warehouses will replace loosely connected databases. Powerful analytic tools will sift through mountains of data to spot emerging trends and patterns. Over the next few years, the CIO will evolve rapidly from a supplier of information to a provider of insight driving business value.

8. ERP/business transformation – led by the CIO, the IT department will be expected to deliver competitive advantage, speed, productivity, and agility to the enterprise. The CIO will increasingly assume a leadership role in guiding business integration and transformation initiatives, process improvement strategies, activity-based costing, value chain management, Six Sigma, and other quality programs.

9. Customer care – customer service responsibilities often pose the greatest challenges for IT. This reality is unlikely to change. Nonetheless, the CIO will be expected to deliver customer relationship management (CRM) programs, contact center operations, customer portals, and other externally-oriented initiatives that will provide the enterprise with distinct competitive advantages. The ability to develop, implement, assess, and manage customer-facing systems will become a critical skill for all CIOs.

10. Internet and e-business – the Internet is now another channel, with its own set of business issues. Despite (or perhaps because of) its wide-spread acceptance, the Internet will continue posing challenges for IT departments. Additionally, the CIO will be held responsible for creating, implementing, and managing e-business strategies, as well as for developing and implementing practical web-enabled applications, employee portals, and telecommunications alternatives such as internet-based voice communications (VoIP).

"CIOs will be more focussed on standardizing, simplifying, and consolidating all aspects of IT to meet enterprise needs," says Kathy Lane, Senior VP and CIO of the Gillette Company, in summarizing the 21st-century CIO's leadership agenda. "We will drive performance and an organizational culture that recognizes and rewards achievements. CIOs of tomorrow will serve an increased value-added function which is a fully integrated partner with our business counterparts." Boeing CIO Scott Griffin put it this way: "It's all about transforming the enterprise."

From reactive to proactive

The CIOs we interviewed uniformly embraced change as essential to survival. They were refreshingly optimistic about their capability to stay in synch with the changing business environment. Important points of agreement include the following:

- The role of the Chief Information Officer is moving from one of technical implementation to strategic planning and from reactive support of business needs to driving innovation and competitive advantage.
- The CIO increasingly reports to the top general management position in the enterprise or business unit, and has a place on the executive leadership team.
- The ideal qualifications for the CIO are changing as the IT function becomes more central to business planning and operations.
- Leading the transformation of the CIO role and capturing its increased value potential is an important human resource challenge for companies.

Far from being pessimistic about the future, the CIOs shared a vision of virtually limitless potential, tempered only by experience and business savvy. "While the tech bubble may have burst, fundamentally technology will continue to be a business imperative," says Rajan Nagarajan, CIO of Philips Medical Systems. "We have not even scratched the surface in terms of driving its capability through the value chain."

More than hardware

Unlike their earlier counterparts, today's CIOs do not see themselves as "techies." Their worldview is increasingly strategic. They dismiss the parochial image of the IT department as a maintenance shop for digital hardware. "It's not about running the computers any more," says Doreen Wright, CIO of the Campbell Soup Company. "It's about using IT to enable and innovate. There's no part of your company that can run without IT – so value it and get everything you can out of it."

Furthermore, it is the job of the CIO to create a long-term strategic plan for their business and gain buy-in of their strategy from the CEO. "CIOs need to create a shared IT vision for the company with their CEO," said Alan Boehme, CIO of Best Software. "But it can't be a 12-month vision. IT is not transaction oriented. You need to play three years out into the future at a minimum."

The CIOs we interviewed also foresee the creation of a new operating charter for the information technology function. This new IT charter will consist of:

- strategic focus;
- governance of it;
- management of composite resources.

They expect that their success will be defined by their ability to constitute and manage a portfolio of hardware and software vendors, service providers, and staffing alternatives. The ability to create and drive technology-based value across the enterprise will be critical.

The CIOs also agreed that the IT leadership role title has reached a logical plateau. The true Chief Information Officer, reporting to a CEO, has arrived at the ultimate organizational rank. "The CIO position should be a counselor to, and partner with the CEO and other business executives," says Jeff Spar, SVP and CIO at The Readers Digest Association. "The CIO must be broadly involved in all facets of the business, operating IT based on general management disciplines with a technology orientation."

Spar also offers a valuable insight about the CIO's relationship with other C-level executives: "The CFO and CIO should be partners and peers, each with complementary business driven agendas. The days of the CIO reporting to the CFO are gone at companies who truly value the impact IT can deliver. The CFO focus is on generating value through cost management and financial processes, while the CIO delivers value by leveraging IT against the company's 'sweet spots' to generate value. Both should work directly for the CEO, to maximize shareholder value and business impact."

Further, as the typical CIO becomes more strategic – with better business education, deeper background and wider corporate experience – more CIOs will break through the glass ceiling into general management. There was less agreement as to when CIOs would be considered natural candidates for top corporate posts such as CEO. The CIOs we interviewed agreed that more work is needed to set the stage for this progression.

It seems likely that with the creation of technical oversight committees at board level, more CIOs will be sought after and elected to boards – at their own companies as well as those of other companies. Mostafa Mehrabani, CIO of the McGraw-Hill companies, offers this advice to upwardly mobile CIOs: "Think business first. Build credibility with the senior team and the board. Deliver on commitments – every time. Hire and maintain top talent. Communicate."

Looking ahead

The CIOs paint a vivid picture of a rapidly changing business universe with IT as a pervasive component. They anticipate having more responsibility, not less, as technologies evolve and improve. As a group, they are not overly concerned by the threat of outsourcing. "I predict that wholesale outsourcing will become less popular," says Graham

Gillespie, CIO at Rexam. "More businesses will insource their information technology due to lack of perceived value and/or poor service from outsource service providers. You can't beat loyal employees and the most loyal ones are the ones on your payroll."

Many, however, expressed concern over regulations requiring higher levels of financial accountability and transparency. Richard Ross, the CIO of Amerada Hess, summed up the challenge neatly: "This is something totally new and it will radically change the role of the CIO. For example, it has always been okay for businesses to say that they did not want to implement something, even if it made great architectural sense and would improve the flow of information in the company. That is no longer the case. If I can go to jail for bad information flows in a business, you can bet those flows are going to get changed, pronto. This will force investments in data architectures and middleware that would not have likely happened, and will put the CIO in the position of explaining why they are so important. We will become the guardians of the corporate data processes."

The future, as seen through the eyes of the CIOs, looks like this:

- Expect CIO responsibilities to continue shifting from technical/operational to strategic/management. This will result in a steady elevation of the CIO role in relationship to other C-level executives.
- CIO success will be redefined to encompass strategic, enterprise-wide business goals and objectives.
- The mission of IT and the focus of the CIO will be redirected away from internal customers to external customers, partners, service providers, and other links in the extended value chain.
- Human capital management (e.g. recruiting, motivation, retention, evaluation, promotion, compensation, and diversity) will become a key CIO responsibility.
- IT portfolio management, IT investment management, and risk assessment will become key CIO responsibilities.
- Business continuity and disaster recovery will continue to be seen as primary CIO responsibilities.
- Actionable business intelligence will become a standard deliverable from IT. Balanced scorecards, executive dashboards, and other highly visual presentation formats will become ubiquitous in the decision-making process.
- Regulatory compliance issues will require the CIO to develop a deeper understanding and more intuitive grasp of corporate finance and accounting processes.
- CIOs will assume leadership roles in shaping and creating a world economy fueled by information.

Carl Wilson, CIO of Marriott International, concludes: "At Marriott, there are no purely technology projects. Instead, we have business projects with technology components."

Whose ideas are they anyway?

STUART CRAINER AND DES DEARLOVE

> The world of thought leadership is a battlefield of ideas where consulting firms, academics, gurus, and a host of others vie for pole position. The creator of tomorrow's fashionable management concept stands to make a fortune. But in the cut-throat arena of thought leadership it is often the originators of the best ideas that are ignored, forgotten, or shouldered aside.

Here is what happened with one of the brightest business concepts of the last five years. The idea was originated by an unknown academic. A company then adopted elements of his model and proclaimed it as its own. One of its executives began writing a book. A professional writer was approached to help and decided it was such a good idea he'd write a book himself. An unseemly rush to publish followed. Before long there were three books on the subject all with the same title – not to mention a host of related consulting packages, seminars, and business school programs. None was written by the idea's originator who continues to plow his intellectual furrow in relative obscurity.

It is not an isolated case. "Thought leaders usually do not get the credit. Thought mass marketers get it," observes Richard D'Aveni of the Tuck School of Business, at Dartmouth College. "Many ideas that are common knowledge within academia and that have been talked about for years get summarized in the *Harvard Business Review*. The authors become the gurus, *certified* in some way by Harvard."

Management is particularly prone to the mass marketing phenomena. It is a magpie science, drawing inspiration from a broad range of subjects – economics, psychology, biology, chaos theory. Today's obscure model in a dry academic publication is tomorrow's snappy guru presentation. Originality is in the eye of the beholder.

The harsh truth is that most management ideas are far more original. "Most great ideas have already been discovered, they are just continually rediscovered, and re-stated in a new and compelling way," observes Sam Hill of Helios Consulting and co-author of *Radical Marketing*. "Basically re-engineering was similar in substance and technique to an old practice from the fifties called *brown papering*, a process previously discovered by Frederick Taylor and later rediscovered in Benson Shapiro's article 'Staple yourself to an order,' then rediscovered yet again by Champy and Hammer. Stalk's competing against time was very similar to an old consulting product called short interval scheduling. Geoff Moore's tornado and chaos were basically riffs on the industry life cycle argument. Seth Godin's permission marketing at the end of the day smells an awful lot like the arguments behind sweepstakes, and my new book owes a lot to the system theory arguments of the sixties. They rediscover and package ideas in new ways. Geoff Moore restated the life cycle in a way managers could get a handle on it, with new relevance and new support for a new generation of practitioners."

Some are honest enough to admit the initial source of their inspiration. Michael Porter cites the influence of his mentor, the economist Richard Caves. Harvard's Porter developed the model still regarded as essential reading for strategy. His genius has lain in producing brilliantly researched and cogent models of competitiveness at a corporate, industry-wide, and national level. But the seeds of his Five Forces Framework lay in an industrial economics framework – the Structure-conduct performance paradigm (SCP) – buried in academic literature. What Porter did, and did brilliantly, was translate it into the context of business strategy.

The originators

Richard D'Aveni argues that behind every great idea there is usually a "leading indicator" – someone who pushes the idea before it goes public. "The originator of a really novel idea is often very controversial – and forgotten when the idea moves to the mainstream. It was George Bernard Shaw who said that every great idea starts as a blasphemy," says D'Aveni. "At least in scientific fields, the originator ultimately gets recognized by a Nobel Prize."

The originators are people like John Nash, John Harsanyi, and Reinhard Selten who received the Nobel Prize in 1994 for their work in the development of Game Theory. They remained largely unacknowledged outside the world of economics. Then two business school academics, Barry Nalebuff and Adam Brandenburger, took the concept and gave it a makeover in their book, *Co-opetition.* An economic theory unknown to most managers was given a spin and was, briefly, the latest big idea.

And people like Reg Revans. Revans was a former Olympic athlete who worked at the Cavendish Laboratories at Cambridge University and for the UK's National Coal Board. These experiences led him to develop the concept of "action learning" – basically that managers learn best when they work on real issues in a group, rather than in the traditional classroom. According to Revans: "Action learning harnesses the power of groups to accomplish meaningful tasks while learning."

Revans died in 2002 and his career remains largely uncelebrated, yet his idea has worked in countries as far apart as Belgium and South Africa, and been embraced by corporations – the Work-out program introduced by GE's Jack Welch included a form of action learning. Business schools, too, have embraced the idea and action learning is now much in vogue in the executive education world.

Other originators get lucky. Lauded in Japan, ignored in his homeland, W. Edwards Deming was destined to life as an obscure statistics academic until he featured on an NBC program on the Japanese economic revival. The rest of his life was spent in a desperate whirlwind as he sought to communicate his quality gospel to as many people as possible.

Many more originators remain untouched by fame and fortune. Undeniably, some are bitter and feel that their ideas have been hijacked, given a fresh gloss in the name of management science. They may bridle but unless an act of outright plagiarism occurs, intellectual theft is difficult to prove. We know of no example of an aggrieved party taking legal action or seeking other recompense. Most are surprisingly sanguine. Academia and management consulting are dog-eat-dog worlds. Different rules apply. Managerial ideas tend to be broad, catch-all concepts – such as re-engineering – rather than being precisely tied down and defined. They are open to reinterpretation, enhancement, and customization. Interestingly, the rise of the Internet has precipitated wider discussion of intellectual property rights which may, eventually, have an impact on management ideas.

So where should you look for original ideas? Here are some leading indicators:

First, established gurus are constantly searching for new ideas. So, ask them who they are reading. (Recent favorite answers to this are Malcolm Gladwell's *The Tipping Point*, Manuel Castells, author of *The Rise of the Network Society*, and anything do with biology.)

Second, tracking the business thinkers. Keep abreast of the latest management literature and you will develop a keen sense of which thinkers have a handle on what is going on in the real world. (Digests are available of most management magazines and, despite the profusion of titles, you can quickly narrow essential reading down to a maximum of six publications a month.) Occasionally, a theorist or two will be relevant – though many are doing little more useful than counting the number of angels that fit on the head of a pin. If you find someone whose work is useful, keep up-to-date with their latest research and developing ideas; volunteer your company as a potential example; ask for their insights on other useful thinkers; do everything in your power to extract free consultancy from them and, if that fails, offer them money. (A more Machiavellian route is to approach the acolytes, associates, or assistants of the thinkers. Often they know just as much, have access to the same material, and charge much less.)

Tracking ideas: very few ideas truly burst onto the business scene from nowhere. It is useful to look at the acknowledgements in business books. Often the writer's inspirations and influences are mentioned in passing – look out for PhD supervisors and older mentors who may actually be the true inspirations. Also, check the social sciences index for references to the topic that a current guru is talking about. They may have coined a new buzz-phrase to describe an old idea that recurs over and over. In private, some academic insiders claim that at least three well-known strategy models are variations of the same thing.

Don Tapscott, co-author of *Digital Capital* and other books, cites the influence of Nobel laureate, Ronald Coase, whose work he was introduced to in 1993. "A firm will tend to expand until the costs of organizing an extra transaction within the firm become equal to the costs of carrying out the same transaction on the open market," Coase wrote. And this forms the basis for Don Tapscott's current theorizing – "Coase defined transaction costs broadly including the cost of co-ordination, collaboration, of finding the right people. We have been systematically extending his ideas to the New Economy," he explains. "All the things Coase wrote about are being built right into the Net whether it is auction tools, payment systems, or collaboration tools like Lotus Notes. As the Internet is a public infrastructure, you can deconstruct the firm and then reconstruct it on the web as a business web."

The story of the seven Ss

In other cases, the origination of concepts becomes blurred in the synthesis of ideas. This can then be compounded by the race to publish. The story of the Seven S framework, for example, is linked to two of the most influential business books of the past two decades. Developed at the beginning of the 1980s, the framework provides a useful alliterative checklist for identifying the characteristics of a business – strategy, structure, systems, style, skills, staff, and shared values.

The roots of the framework go back to the summer of 1978 when the McKinsey consultant Robert Waterman asked Richard Pascale, from Stanford, and Anthony Athos, from Harvard, to help him out. Waterman and his McKinsey colleague, Tom Peters, were trying to make sense of some research they had done on the characteristics of successful companies, and which would eventually form the basis of the best-selling *In Search of Excellence*. They were struggling to establish the crucial links. It was agreed that the four would spend five days in a small room discovering what they knew and didn't know about organizations.

Concerned that the hyperactive Peters would hijack the proceedings, Athos suggested that an agenda for the five days was essential. He recalled an approach used by one of his colleagues, Cyrus (Chuck) Gibson, which would provide a useful framework for the discussions. Gibson had a scheme – strategy, structure, and systems – which he had developed for Harvard's Program for Management Development which Gibson and Athos ran. Athos suggested they use this as the framework for their discussions. To this he added his own themes of "guiding concepts," which he re-named "superordinate goals," and "shared values." Pascale added "style."

From these and subsequent discussions involving Julien Phillips, another McKinsey man, the Seven S Framework emerged. It first saw the light of day in published form in June 1980 when Waterman, Peters, and Phillips put together an article, "Structure is not organization," for a relatively obscure academic journal.

Meanwhile Pascale and Athos were working on what was to become *The Art of Japanese Management,* published in 1981. They decided to use the Seven S model in the book. This introduced it to a mass audience. Peters and Waterman also featured the framework in *In Search of Excellence* when it was published a year later. So, whose idea was the Seven S framework? Depending on your perspective it could be said to be Chuck Gibson's or any one or all of Waterman, Peters, Pascale, and Athos.

Back to basics

Of course, not all great ideas emerge from great minds. What is perplexing about the process by which business concepts reach the mass market is that the most reliable source of ideas may well be closer at hand than the book store or the guru-led conference. "The best place to get new ideas is from thoughtful practitioners – leading CEOs and people of high intellect, not necessarily those who then commercialize them," says Danny Samson, author of *Patterns of Business Excellence*. "Most new management fads fail, or mostly fail, and they cost companies many millions in consulting fees and wasted effort. Excellent companies apply sound fundamentals, not so much new ideas. They do things like strategy, leadership, human resource management, motivation, change implementation, etc. exceptionally well."

The message is that discovering – or rediscovering – the basics is the best route to the ideas that are of most use to your business. And the basics are practiced day in, day out on the factory floor, in the humdrum office suites. The solutions are the same; the questions different. "The basic ideas and solutions are always there, but the problems and their manifestations are cyclical. When a problem works its way back up the agenda, like the loss of organizational know-how, people either rediscover or dust off old ideas and reform them in a way that the current generation of managers (many of them not yet born the last time people were talking about this problem) finds useful. The germs of ideas come not from academia or consultants, but from managers wrestling with the ideas on the factory floor or sales office," says Sam Hill, before going on to outline the downside. "Practitioners seldom escape the three traps of self-congratulation, anecdote in lieu of analysis, and narrow-minded dogmatism. Academics insist on rooting their work in a grand-theory-of-the-universe, but seldom pull it off, and end up with obscure, hard to implement stuff. They're trained to be descriptive not prescriptive. Having someone who's never had a chance to observe try to create insight is a bit like hiring a priest to write a sex manual. Consultants often write prose that is unreadable. So I think it boils down to the individual. Some have the knack of picking up old ideas, seeing how they are relevant to today's generation of managers, and rephrasing them in a useful way, and some don't."

Not everyone buys the argument that the best ideas are inevitably rooted in best practice. "Most management thinking consists of identifying companies that are better than average, studying what they do, and then trying to generalize – the archetypal example being *In Search of Excellence*," says Don Sull of London Business School. "In many cases a single company provides the basis for best practices – such as, Noel Tichy's work on General Electric under Jack Welch. While this approach can produce some extremely useful and insightful findings and recommendations – both the Peters and Waterman and Tichy's work is outstanding – I am not sure it is the source of enduring insights. These, I think, tend to come from theory. Porter's work on strategy draws on a well-established body of literature in industrial organization economics, Drucker's work on management depends heavily (although he is less explicit in acknowledging his intellectual sources than Porter was) on a school of economists known as the 'Austrian School,' which includes some obscure economists like Carl Menger and Ludwig von Mises as well as well-known economists like Hayek and Schumpeter. I am increasingly convinced that enduring management insights are built on the firm foundation of well-developed theory rather than the shifting sands of current management practice – even best practice."

And there is one final problem. "In my experience ideas are easy. If you sit down with a group of managers to discuss new business ideas you can fill the flip chart in no time. It is the same with ideas for improving performance or strategy," says Andrew Campbell of the Ashridge Strategic Management Center in London. "The problem is how to figure out which are the good ideas. This is particularly tough because the best ones are usually counter intuitive. So trial and error proves to be the best way. It is expensive, but it is better than any other way yet developed. Which is why the market economy is so much better at coming up with good new ideas – more trial and error."

"Of course, there is one final problem. Implementation. The best ideas in the world are worthless if you can't make them work." While there may be nothing so practical as a neat theory, you still have to find the right theory.

Originality be damned

The current trend is to extract managerial lessons from historical figures. Shakespeare, Elizabeth I, Jesus Christ, Robert E Lee, and Moses are among those whose relevance to modern-day managers has been explored in recent books. Machiavelli and Sun-Tzu are also long-time stalwarts of management theorists. One attraction is that there are no copyright problems. A neat matrix based on Moses' human resource management techniques is unlikely to lead to legal action.

While such diversions provide entertainment, their usefulness is highly questionable. Indeed, some see such books as evidence of the superficiality of much management thinking. "There is a lack of a real intellectual basis for much of what you see," says the economist and author John Kay, former head of Oxford University's Said Business School. "History is picked up somewhat bizarrely – the management secrets of Attila the Hun, management tips from the Garden of Eden, and that sort of thing. People have to find gimmicks and they like to give the appearance of intellectual seriousness and pretension. If the story is derived from something historical, they can write seven tips on destroying the enemy in 30 minutes so that it appears to give a basis in scholarship and erudition. Sometimes it's like the study of economics 200 years ago, physics 500 years ago, or medicine 100 years ago. People know a lot but don't have the structure to make sense of it. One hundred years ago your success as a doctor depended on the confidence you exuded. Today's CEOs and management gurus are very much like that."

As yet, there are no signs that originality rather than confidence is set to become the key measure of a thinker's merit.

RESOURCES

Crainer, Stuart, *Key Management Ideas*, FT Prentice Hall, 2000.
Dearlove, Des, *The Ultimate Book of Business Thinking*, Capstone/Wiley, 2002.

www.thinkers50.com

The strategic potential of a firm's knowledge portfolio

DAVID BIRCHALL AND GEORGE TOVSTIGA

[Knowledge, not capital assets, is increasingly the source of wealth in today's global economy. Better understanding of a company's knowledge portfolio is key to understanding its competitive position.]

Astonishingly, despite the wide consensus on the importance of knowledge to today's organizations, many firms still do not have at their disposal even the most rudimentary tools or methodologies for assessing the breadth and depth of their capabilities-embedded knowledge portfolio.

Knowledge maps that capture, identify, and lay open the firm's knowledge in its various forms are a first step toward managing knowledge in the firm. Knowledge manifests itself primarily in the firm's competencies and capabilities, and it is the tacit knowledge content of competencies and capabilities – rather than the explicit form of knowledge – that underlies the firm's real basis of competitive advantage.

A truly key or core capability – one that provides a clear basis for competitive differentiation – will substantially consist of knowledge in a highly tacit form. Unlike explicit knowledge, which is captured in manuals, procedures, working papers, minutes of meetings, process flow charts, and the like, this tacit knowledge rests in the minds of employees and teams. This feature of a capability carries a number of important implications for competitive differentiation. One of these has to do with the ease with which a capability can be replicated, transferred, or lost to a competitor.

Our premise is that a high degree of tacitness is an effective barrier to diffusion of knowledge. From the external perspective, this represents a protective mechanism; for internal operations, it represents a challenge to be overcome.

A firm's portfolio of knowledge-driven capabilities is a dynamic entity. Clearly, it must be managed in the context of the firm's rapidly changing environment. Any analysis of this type must therefore focus on the current as well as the future competitiveness of the firm. The methodology (Figure 8.1) begins with mapping any one of the firm's business processes from a value-creation p erspective.

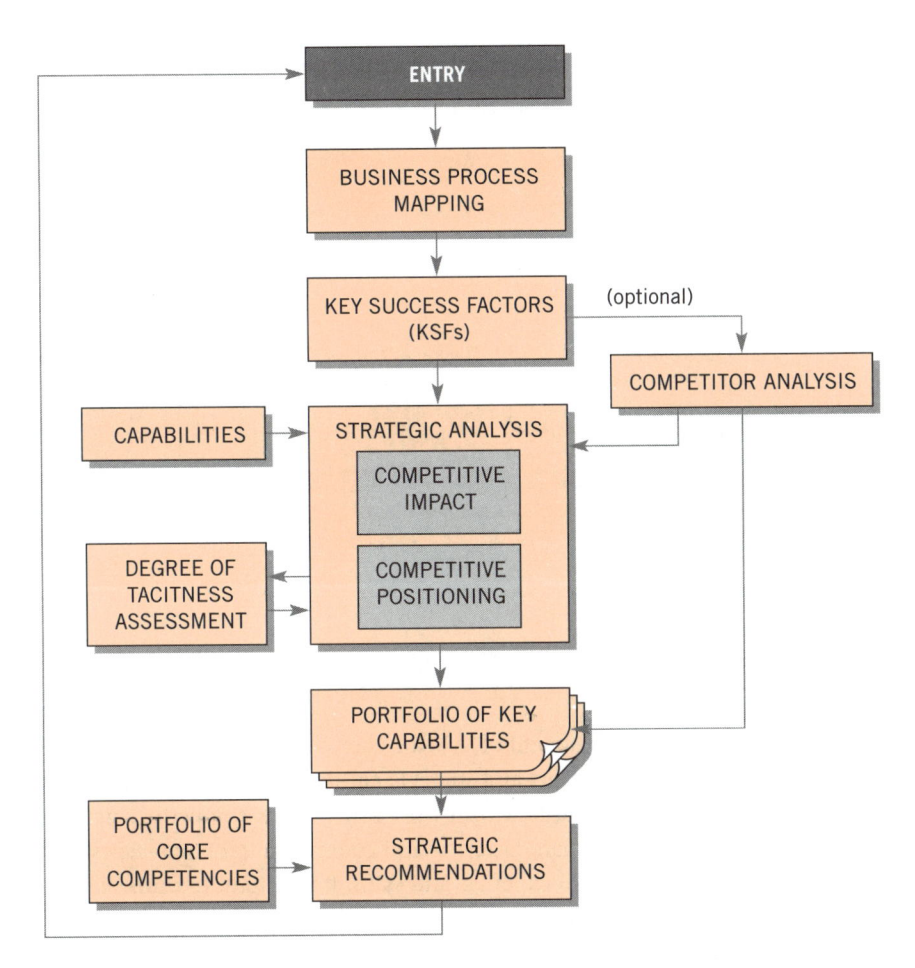

Figure 8.1: *Schematic overview of methodology*

Business process mapping

The first stage of the methodology focusses on breaking down the firm's business activities in terms of its business process chain. A business process is understood to be any activity or group of activities that takes an input, adds value to it, and provides an output to an internal or external customer.

It is a useful exercise at this stage to think about how individual subprocesses contribute to the value generated by the overall business process chain. Clearly, some of the subprocesses will contribute more to the fulfillment of customers' needs (value generated) than others will. It is these important subprocesses on which we want to focus. An example is shown in Figure 8.2.

Figure 8.2

BUSINESS PROCESS VALUE CHAIN

CUSTOMER NEED IDENTIFIED → Identify Needs → Win Work → Prepare Work → Perform Work → Closeout Work → CUSTOMER NEED SATISFIED

STRATEGIC ACTIVITIES:

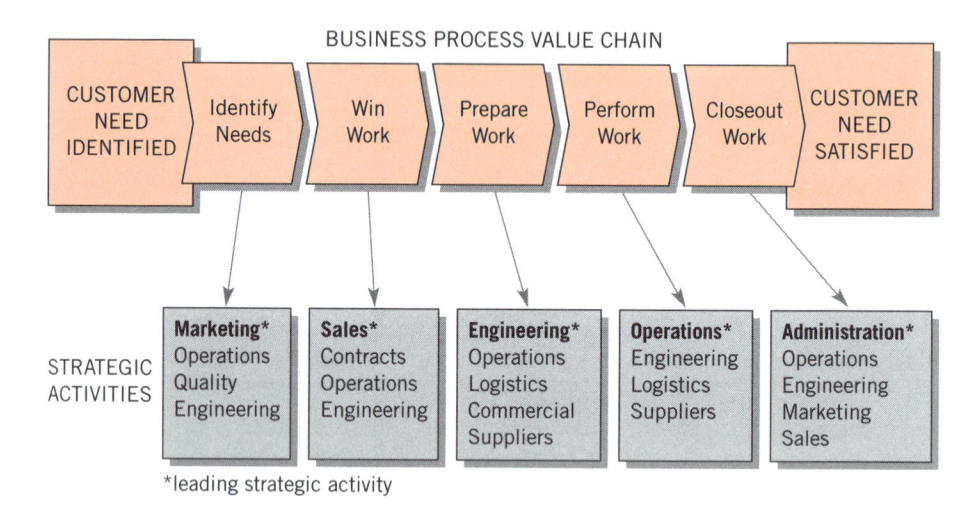

- **Marketing*** — Operations, Quality, Engineering
- **Sales*** — Contracts, Operations, Engineering
- **Engineering*** — Operations, Logistics, Commercial, Suppliers
- **Operations*** — Engineering, Logistics, Suppliers
- **Administration*** — Operations, Engineering, Marketing, Sales

*leading strategic activity

Figure 8.2: *Business process value chain*[2]

Key success factors

These strategic variables can be thought of as being common to the firm's industry. They are just as relevant to its competitors and strategic partners. That is, key success factors are characteristic of the marketplace within which the firm is competing, such as an ability to carry out competitive manufacturing and commercial process reviews, and to attract employees with the critical expertise and skills. It is helpful to think about current and future developments in the industry's timeframe and scope, stakeholder profiles, and the general macro environment when selecting key success factors.

Identification of capabilities

The challenge in implementing a competitive strategy lies in identifying and developing those capabilities that constitute the critical building blocks of the firm's core competencies. These, in turn, will have an impact on the most important key success factors of the firm's industry. The capabilities are drawn from the large and diverse array of fundamentally knowledge-based discrete activities, skill, and disciplines embedded in the organization.

Capabilities may be broadly broken down into different categories, such as:

- market-interface capabilities, including selling, advertising, consulting, technical service;

- infrastructure capabilities, focussing on internal operations such as management information systems or internal training;
- technological capabilities, directly providing support to the firm's product or service portfolio.

Competitive impact and positioning of capabilities

Capabilities – based on competitive impact – can be classified as *emerging* (has not yet demonstrated potential for changing the basis of competition), *pacing* (has demonstrated its potential), *key* (already has major impact on value-added stream: cost, performance, quality), or *base* (necessary, but confers only a minor impact on value-added streams).

Similarly, a firm's degree of control (relative competitive position) over its capabilities relates to its ability to exploit its current portfolio of capabilities. The firm's degree of control can be *high*, *neutral*, or *weak*. For example, a capability may be controlled by a supplier if it is embedded in a bought-in component, or it may be controlled by a partner, as in the case of distribution by an intermediary. A decision tree approach to classifying the degree of control is presented in Figure 8.3.

The results of the knowledge-by-knowledge classification can be used to construct the firm's capability portfolio, as illustrated in Figure 8.4. Capability C^1_{int} is a strategically important capability for the firm and one over which it has considerable control. C^2_{int}, on the other hand, is a capability that has become commoditized and

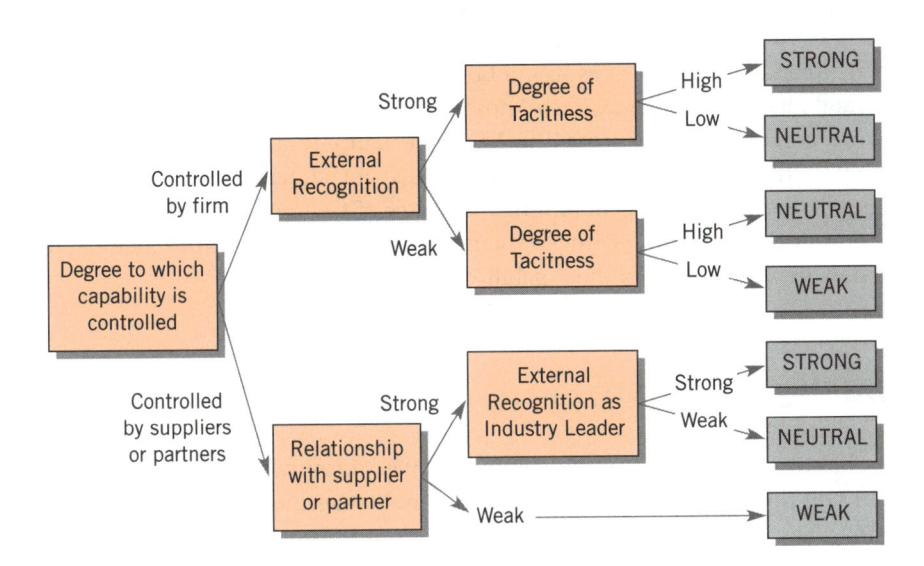

Figure 8.3: *Assessment of degree of the firm's control over capability*

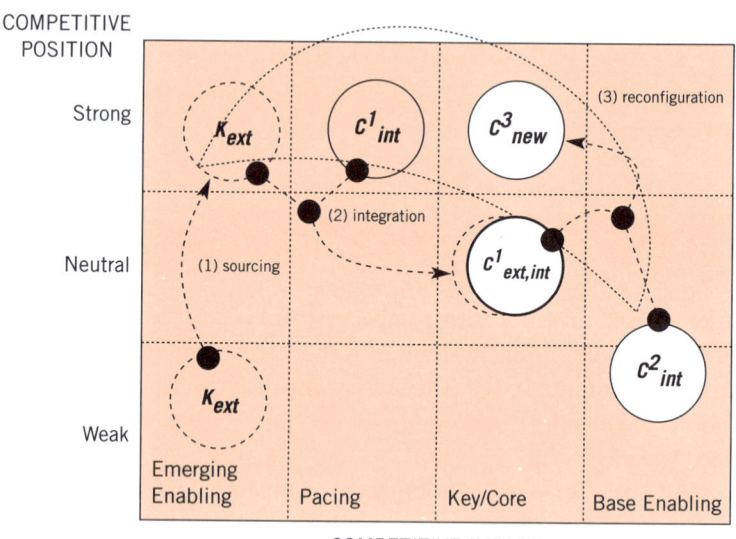

Figure 8.4: *Capabilities portfolio*

therefore is readily replicated by other firms. K_{ext}, in contrast, is a knowledge domain that is emerging and is likely to have an impact on the products or services offered by the firm. It is an area where mastery is expected to become important and therefore greater control is desirable. The potential offered for integration with existing capabilities for recombinations addressing new market needs is shown in Figure 8.4, where C^3_{new} represents a capability over which the firm has secured a high degree of control.

Tacit knowledge in capabilities is invariably embodied in "soft," accumulated experiential knowledge such as would be found in troubleshooting, "process tweaking," and relational networks. Tacit knowledge embodied in capabilities can exist to varying degrees, ranging from the barely perceptible, subconscious awareness (highly tacit), to just barely codifiable (low degree of tacitness).

An ordering scheme for determining the degree of tacitness is shown in Figure 8.5. The greater the degree of tacitness, the greater the difficulty even in identification and then in classification of the capability.

Strategic analysis

The objective of this stage of the methodology is to formulate strategic recommendations on the basis of the capabilities portfolio. Management action could focus on the following:

- *Scanning.* Recognizing that capabilities can originate from a very diverse set of sources. It further involves developing and nurturing environmental

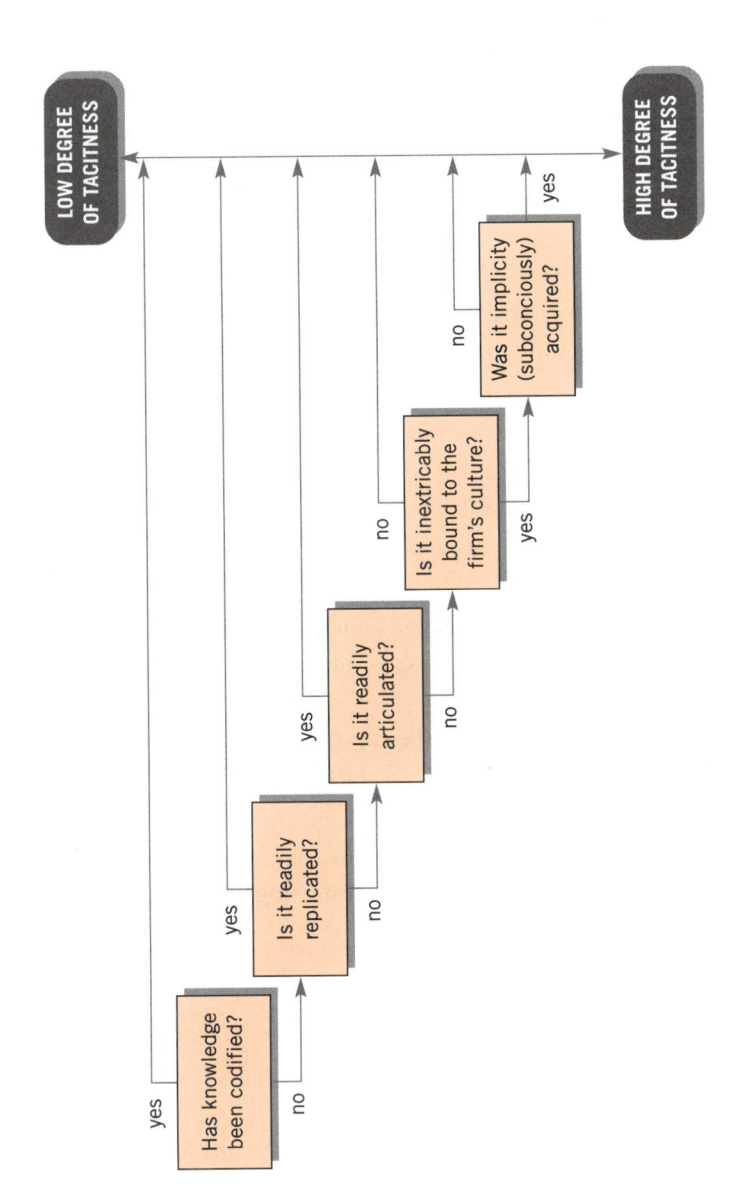

The strategic potential of a firm's knowledge portfolio 599

Figure 8.5: *Ordering scheme for assessing degree of tacitness of capability – embodied knowledge*

scanning capabilities to detect strong or weak signals, indicating both threats and opportunities.

- *Protecting.* Protecting against any eventuality, whether external (competitive factors) or internal (mismanagement of knowledge resources), that threatens the integrity of the capability portfolio – in either an active or a passive way.
- *Enriching.* Nurturing the business environment most conducive for growth of current capabilities, via in-house capability building, formation of strategic alliances, or acquisitions.
- *Optimizing.* Continually seeking to improve and refine existing capability assets toward better addressing current needs, thereby increasing the degree of control over strategically critical knowledge capabilities.
- *Disposing of.* Disposing of all or parts of a current knowledge capability/asset that is contributing little to the firm's longer-term direction.

This process can be quite involving and complex. Critical assumptions are made throughout; these need to be scrutinized and challenged at each of the stages. It is well worth the effort to review the outcome of the strategic assessment at the end of the process using the following guidelines:

- Does the final outcome (strategic positioning matrix) make sense? Is the resulting portfolio of capabilities plausible?
- What are the critical assumptions on which the analysis is based? How valid are they; how sensitive to variation are they? How would the outcome change if you were to modify these assumptions?
- How, if at all, might the outcome be expected to be different if another group, representing different functional backgrounds in the firm, had carried out the same exercise?

Ideally, of course, this is undertaken as a multidisciplinary exercise – and, depending on the time framework of your industry, on an on-going basis.

RESOURCES

Chiesa, V. and Barbeschi, M., 'Technology Strategy in Competence-based Competition,' *Competence-Based Competition* (G. Hamel and A. Heene, eds), John Wiley, 1994.

Teece, D. and Pisano, G., 'The Dynamic Capabilities of Firms: an Introduction,' in *Technology, Organization and Competitiveness* (Dosi, Teece and Chytry, eds), Oxford University Press, 1998.

Segmenting and destroying knowledge

KEVIN C. DESOUZA

[An organization's knowledge resource is the key determinant for differentiation and strategic advantages. But two key capabilities often get overlooked when managing knowledge: *segmentation* of knowledge and *destruction* of knowledge.]

When organizations first became aware of the importance of managing knowledge the major issue was simply getting people to contribute their knowledge. Now, organizations face the opposite problem: getting people to contribute only what is *truly knowledge*. Most organizations have an all-embracing approach to knowledge management, valuing everything from how to fix a broken copier to how to win the next consulting engagement. This practice leads to the Wild West syndrome, where an organization is overloaded with so-called knowledge, and efforts to manage it cannot be productive.

To overcome this, managers need to ask: what comprises organizational knowledge? They must adopt a resource-based view, asking: is this knowledge object rare, non-substitutable, non-imitable, and valuable? Most knowledge objects will meet the conditions of valuable. But only a select group of an organization's knowledge resources will meet the requirement of rarity.

Consider a software engineering firm. While every piece of code written has some value, is it unique? Probably not. Moreover, the knowledge processed by each software engineer is also valuable, though only a small portion is truly rare because most personnel knowledge is complementary and overlapping. While almost all knowledge can be argued to provide value, it does so in an operational sense – aiding in getting routine tasks complete. In contrast, knowledge objects that meet the condition of uniqueness can contribute to strategic goals.

The conditions of non-imitation and non-substitutability are critical here. Knowledge that cannot be imitated easily by members of the organization, or by other external organizations, is truly valuable because it is not easily subject to acts of substitution. It is this kind of knowledge that forms the basis for competitive advantage.

Segmenting knowledge objects in the organization leads to a better-focussed management agenda. The knowledge objects that do not meet any of the conditions should not be the focus of management efforts. Those that meet the basic condition of being valuable should be managed in a limited fashion, as the return on those assets is minimal. Critical organizational resources are those that cannot be imitated or substituted with ease. These must be the focus of knowledge management efforts, as they have the potential to truly deliver corporate value.

Segmenting knowledge helps address the cost–benefit issue as it enables resources to be focussed on the most critical knowledge assets. Organizations may want to dedicate a group (or individual) as knowledge gatekeepers. These gatekeepers will evaluate knowledge contributions and decide which characteristics of a resource they meet. Based on this evaluation they can be given the appropriate management attention. Moreover, they can also be housed on different knowledge management systems depending on their significance to operational and strategic goals of the organization.

Destruction capabilities

Led by the fallacy that more is better, most organizations pay attention only to the mass generation and storage of knowledge. While more may be better for traditional resources like land, labor, and capital, it is not necessarily true for knowledge. Excessive knowledge on products, processes, and practices can actually have negative consequences. Problems can occur in terms of knowledge overload, where there are multiple versions of the same knowledge on aspects of products and services. Excessive knowledge also leads to poor search and seek times when knowledge retrieval is conducted.

Unless old knowledge is purged in a timely fashion, organizational change becomes difficult. Routines and practices are institutionalized, which makes any efforts for future change and thinking creatively impossible. As such, the organization will make only incremental and minor improvements on this past knowledge without much hope for seeing and seizing the future of the marketplace. This consequence has been evident in the past with companies such as Polaroid, which lost ground in the advent of digital imaging, and Swiss watchmakers who lost ground to leaner and more agile Japanese competitors. Extensive reliance on the past stifles one's motivation to think creatively.

Individuals in organizations frequently try to answer questions based on the knowledge resources they have. As a result, problem definition is based solely on the solutions at hand. In most cases, past knowledge has limited value for future organizational efforts. Organizations operate in a dynamic and fiercely competitive environment. Their knowledge, much like computer hardware, has a high rate of depreciation. Important lessons learned from past endeavors need to be qualified.

But macro lessons suffice rather than micro detail. While helpful in an operational sense, much of yesterday's knowledge has little if any bearing on designing the future. Designing or charting the future will call for new, uninhibited creativity. Unless the old is purged or challenged, no one will question its existence. Hence, myths become corporate knowledge because no one questions their relevance.

Systematic destruction of knowledge must be a component of knowledge management efforts in organizations. Knowledge managers must institutionalize destruction capabilities. The term *destruction* is not used casually. While most organizations have capabilities to purge old and outdated knowledge, they do not engage in destruction. As such, while the old knowledge artefacts may not exist, practices based on those knowledge assets continue to prevail. An organization's destruction capability must include both purging explicit knowledge and modifying or updating practices and procedures based on tacit knowledge. Personnel can be designated to review knowledge in systems and purge or archive old knowledge in a timely fashion. The use of automated technologies can also be used to conduct such activities. Training and development programs are also vital aspects of the destruction capability, as they infuse the organization with new knowledge.

RESOURCES

Edvinsson, Leif, *Corporate Longitude*: Discover Your True Position in the Knowledge Economy, FT Prentice Hall, 2002.

Stewart, Thomas, *Intellectual Capital*, Nicholas Brealey, 1997.

Stewart, Thomas, *The Wealth of Knowledge*, Nicholas Brealey, 2001.

'Interview': Sumantra Ghoshal

Sumantra Ghosal, one of the most gifted business academics of his generation, died in March 2004. In one of his last interviews the Robert P. Bauman Chair in Strategic Leadership at the London Business School he talked about the power of knowledge in the marketplace.

Critics have suggested that knowledge management (KM) was a big idea that failed to deliver.

To say knowledge management hasn't delivered the goods is an exaggeration. But overall, organizations haven't reaped the benefits predicted. Many companies initially saw knowledge management as a technical task and handed it over to their IT people, who went away and created sophisticated IT systems. But it's really a social, not technological, issue. Where it has been effective it is because much more attention was put on the human dimension – the social, emotional, and relational contexts.

You're saying that KM goes beyond codifying and compiling?

In the first rush of enthusiasm for KM, many organizations largely missed the point that a substantial amount of knowledge in any organization is tacit and cannot be written down. Even when knowledge can be codified, there is no guarantee that useful knowledge will be identified and exploited. An example involving British Telecommunications highlights the difficulties of practicing knowledge management. It came to light that for 14 years BT had been sitting on a US patent covering hyperlinks, one of the key building blocks of the worldwide web. Despite KM initiatives, the patent, which was potentially worth millions, remained buried in a filing cabinet in the company's vaults along with thousands of other global patents.

How do you find tacit knowledge?

Companies must address human capital at a more profound level. Often we make the mistake of thinking of human capital as just knowledge. A second important aspect is social capital – networks and relationships. The third dimension is emotional capital – the ability and willingness to act.

Knowledge, relationships, and the willingness to act may call for dramatic cultural changes in many organizations. Correct?

There is no solution other than a trust-based culture. It's not so much "I have this knowledge which I give to you," it's more "how do you shape questioning and frame learning?" Those are cultural considerations. At BP, for example, a quarter of the knowledge management budget is spent on coaching people. If you look at Skandia, it is trying to institutionalize questioning. What is special about the company is not the tools it uses but its attempts to embed curiosity in the culture.

Why curiosity?

Most companies have only scratched the surface of this bigger issue. The new source of competitive advantage is dreams and ambitions. Today we are in the world of the volunteer employee. People choose to invest their human capital in companies to get the best returns. They are mobile investors. The real challenge for KM lies in creating the context in which people will want to invest themselves and their knowledge in the company. That will require senior management to demonstrate its ability to obtain a good return for the individual.

This focus on the individual, and the uniquely human components of the organization, certainly calls organization structure and strategy into question.

William Whyte's *Organization Man* of the 1950s is still the model organizational citizen for too many companies. But the philosophy of that day suggested that if strategy, structure, and related organizational systems were well defined, the rest – namely the individuals – were not important. That model is obsolete. It is necessary to change the focus from the organization to the individual. That is a fundamental and necessary shift.

Is this part of a "managerial revolution" of the 21st century?

That is an attractive way of exaggerating the issue. In the 20th century there were great innovations in management. The greatest one, without any doubt, was Alfred Sloan's organization of General Motors. Until the 1980s and 1990s all corporations were organized functionally – Sloan's vision. That was what was meant by "organization" and "corporation." But now it is clear that the model has reached its limits. The 21st century is a whole new ball game than Sloan's time.

Sloan's ideas were awfully effective.

That is very true. Let's go back in history, so that we can understand what Sloan did and what is now done. In the 1920s and 1930s the big corporations were full of complicated problems – they were too big and terribly complex. That's when Sloan invented the "multi-division structure," which was not only a structure, it was also a new management philosophy. That made possible the diversifying of products and businesses, and globalization. All the big corporations that survived till today are children of Sloan's invention. In the 1980s, in my opinion, they peaked, and a new innovation became necessary. Enter Percy Barnevik of ABB and Jack Welch of General Electric. The modern Sloan and DuPont.

If "structure follows strategy" is not the correct blueprint for success, what is?

All those polemics surrounding structure and strategy are children and grandchildren of the same model created by Sloan that we have talked about. They are two faces of the same coin. It is time to override this contradiction. We now need to view the successful corporation as defined by its aims, by its processes, and by its people. Let's end that old debate about strategy–structure and vice versa. "Strategy" needs to inspire creativity and individual initiative. That is fundamental in today's corporation. Organizational processes need to facilitate the innovation and renovation necessary to permanently reshape companies. People and processes are part of the same strategic effort.

Is this a "strategic revolution," in the sense that we've read about in many books?

I am suggesting changing the conditions, the ambience, the environment, the "smell of the place" so that revolutionary strategy may emerge.

In this new organization, is there a place for middle managers or are they condemned to death?

In no way is that position in peril! It would be completely wrong, a catastrophe. Many corporations made that mistake in the last decades marked by downsizing frenzy. Managers are actors at three levels, all necessary: in the front line (as entrepreneurs), in the middle (as facilitators and integrators), and at the top (as strategists). The middle role is vital; it is like a glue. There is no death but a redefinition of roles.

Do you think that Europe will be producing examples of this new corporate model, introducing the emergence of a new group of European thinkers with world importance?

History will tell. But there are several examples that come to mind immediately: ABB, Siemens-Nixdorf, Ericsson. Or look at what IKEA had done in the furniture business, or ISS in the cleaning area. So I think the answer is yes.

Making big or "revolutionary" changes is tough for a small company, and tougher for a large organization.

No doubt about that. So the process needs to be done incrementally. The necessary steps include starting by rationalizing and creating an entrepreneurial spirit (a giant task in itself), fostering and rewarding the new behaviors, and then working to revitalize the organization, changing the processes, and developing synergy that actually creates an auto-renovation dynamic.

So, with some work, paraphrasing Rosabeth Moss Kanter, an elephant really can learn the change dance?

Consider one final example: the transmission and distribution division of Westinghouse, purchased by ABB in 1989. A radical transformation occurred with exactly the same management team, but with a new philosophy and a new enthusiasm. I believe in this: the essential problem is not to change people, the real problem is to create a new atmosphere, what we call "the smell of the place." What ABB did in that Westinghouse division was to create a new smell, instead of behaving like an invasion army. It did not follow the classical trend in the takeover, and the results speak for themselves.

Securing information: governance issues

JEAN-NOËL EZINGEARD AND DAVID BIRCHALL

[Scarcely a week goes by without a worrying press report about corporate boards lacking good management information, leaks, and damaging computer viruses. Today, information security is fast becoming a strategic issue.]

Information security is usually defined as maintaining the confidentiality, integrity, and availability of the information that is the lifeblood of the business (this is also often referred to under the broader umbrella term of information assurance).

Although information security should be implemented at a functional level, it is imperative that the protection of an asset as valuable and critical as information is subjected to board-level leadership, management, and control. If organizations are to go beyond merely managing the risk associated with information security, to capture the opportunities for competitive advantage, then a strategic, multi-disciplinary approach is needed.

Why is information security a board issue?

There are essentially three reasons why information security is now a board issue. First, boards are responsible, in many countries legally, for their organization's risk management system and internal control. In the UK, the Turnbull and Higgs Reports highlight the board's responsibilities in ensuring that adequate control mechanisms are in place, with the key objective of reducing financial risk. The objective is not zero risk – as Nigel Turnbull pointed out in 1999, "profits are, in part, the reward for successful risk-taking ... the purpose of internal control is to help manage and control risk appropriately rather than to eliminate it."

Furthermore, institutional investors pay increasingly close attention to the governance practices of the companies in which they invest – or avoid – seeking out companies with good governance practices as a positive indication of a shareholder-value focus. In practice, this means that boards need to take an interest in what information is needed to ensure that these controls work – and to make sure that no unmanageable risks are taken through poor information security.

Second, good information security can be a source of competitive advantage. For example, companies that are known to have good security standards can build superior reputation among consumers. It has also been shown that investors are increasingly concerned about business continuity and information security risks in general and that published security glitches could have an impact on an organization's share price. Also, a good information security environment can lead to greater returns from investments in technology (enabling less to be spent to remain compliant for instance), better management information, and greater confidence of trading partners.

Third, greater board involvement in information security will affect the success of an organization's information security initiatives. Board-level commitment is necessary with initiatives that have a wide-ranging impact on business processes and the behaviors of employees. Information security is one of these initiatives.

Five key trade-offs

Research carried out at Henley Management College suggests that information security policy making should be informed by attempting to identify a firm's position with regards to five key trade-offs.

Procedures versus creativity. Most people associate security with control, and this is the same for information security. Good information security often requires precise procedures to be established, followed, and monitored. This often starts with access control to buildings, documents, and electronic information. Yet we all know that rules can get in the way. In particular, an excess of rules and regulations can discourage innovation, not only by annoying creative staff but also by slowing down the pace of creative developments. In talking to board members and senior managers in companies across the world, we have come across organizations that had made a conscious decision to "innovate first – think of the information security consequences later." This may not be a panacea for all organizations, but illustrates that a trade-off between procedural controls and security needs to be managed.

Furthermore, the trade-off may be more complex than it seems, as creativity is not necessarily the enemy of security. In some situations it will be necessary for an organization's security experts to react swiftly and creatively to a breach. It might be necessary for a media relations team to "break some rules" to salvage a difficult security situation. Most organizations will therefore want to find the right balance between the two sides of the trade-off. Strategies we have come across at leading organizations include:

- Ensuring that appropriately qualified committees review creative business decisions for their information security risks on a regular basis (but not necessarily before the decision is implemented), and that the committees' views are used as input to the development of new business initiatives;
- Ensuring that the business's performance management system is balanced and encourages adherence to business rules but also rewards open communication;
- Ensuring that staff are trained to handle unusual emergency situations and that adequate resources can be put in place to deal with the situation swiftly.

Top-down control versus trust. When looking at ensuring the confidentiality and integrity of its information, an organization will often need to find the right balance between top-down control and trust. An over-controlling environment may encourage irresponsible behaviors among some staff if they feel they are not trusted. When looking at the security of its information, should an organization exercise a high degree of top-down control, strictly limiting access to information with clear rules and penalties, thus increasing security, or, conversely, should the company develop a culture where employees are given a wide range of information and expected to behave ethically?

Top management involvement is particularly important in order to ensure that strong and sustainable information security practices are developed. Controls that are too tight, however, can be very demotivating. The two sides of the trade-off are however not necessarily incompatible:

- We know organizations that rely successfully on very prescriptive, top-down information security policies, but where few actual checks on their implementation were made and trust played a substantial role.
- The culture of trust may vary significantly between different parts of an organization. Technical specialists may have a tendency to over-emphasize security risks, while customer-facing staff may emphasize trust a lot more. A right balance can often be found when decisions are made by teams with a good mix between "people coming from the business route" and "people coming from the IT route."

Exposure versus ease of doing business. Should a company expose its information systems globally, for instance via the Internet, in order to allow customers and suppliers to undertake business with them easily or should the company increase security by minimizing this exposure? As pointed out by a senior manager at Smile, the only bank in the UK to be accredited for information security under ISO 17799, "We believe that it is possible to make our systems virtually fraud proof. However, they would be almost impractical for ordinary people to use."

It is clear that because all business transactions, whether internal or external, involve exchanging information, they are potentially a source of risk. All parties in the transaction have an interest in keeping the level of risk low but will, at the same time, wish to keep information flowing.

Two methods can be envisaged to achieving a resolution of the trade-off:

- Simplicity of interface – although customers demand adequate security, especially when financial details are involved, they also require an interface which they feel comfortable with and can use easily. Trading partners might be more tolerant to cumbersome security measures if the rest of the system is easy to use and navigate.
- Education of trading partners – in our research we came across an organization that saw its customers' "carelessness" with their password as its biggest security headache. Educating trading partners will never totally eliminate risks but may mitigate them down to a level where they are manageable. Customer education, however, can prove costly and, if it is too complicated, the customer may not understand it, or it may even frighten them unnecessarily.

Insourcing versus outsourcing. Any form of process outsourcing will be a source of information security risk. Even if the organization that takes charge of the process has very secure systems and procedures, as well as the right culture in place to ensure that the confidentiality of the outsourced information is never compromised, questions of availability and integrity still need to be addressed.

Information security itself is a process that some organizations may choose to outsource, but should organizations seek high levels of control by using their own IT department to establish and implement security technology and procedures or should they use the expertise and experience of a firm outside the company? Outsourcing can provide a company with much-needed expertise, including leading-edge or tailor-made security systems. It can provide the board with the reassurance that they will get a world-class information security environment since too much would be at stake for the supplier of the outsourced services if they failed to deliver a secure environment.

In taking decisions about outsourcing, creative methods of dealing with the dilemmas discussed above can be devised. For instance:

- Periodic reviews of outsourcing agreements of any business process that are designed to include a review of the information security implications of the arrangements;
- A comprehensive review of all outsourcing procedures and contracts to "build in" security in the provision of all services;
- The use of different outsourcing policies across the world perhaps, to take into account the local risk environments and the need for agility in the business development cycle.

Reputation versus the bottom line. A breach in security will have an impact on a company's reputation. Consequently, is an organization willing to make large investments in order to increase security to enhance its reputation? Business reputation can be influenced by a number of factors, including organizational culture (e.g. sharing information can expedite customer service), the simplicity of the customer user interface, business processes (e.g. complex business processes can reduce efficiency and effectiveness for customers), customer education, innovation, organizational work effectiveness, and the empowerment of employees. High information security can have an impact on these factors. For example, if information is not shared throughout the company, innovation, work effectiveness, and employee empowerment may be reduced. These may result in a decline in customer service and education, which will have a severe impact on the organization's reputation.

On the other hand, a breach in security can obviously influence reputation and brand value is often intimately linked to reputation. Some organizations, in banking for instance, ensure that their information security achievements are well published, arguing that it is an important driver of customer purchase decisions. Furthermore, an organization enjoying a good reputation with its customers or suppliers may find it easier to attract new trading partners into a potentially risky venture or new product.

There is also a trade-off between reputation and expenditure. Long-term security measures may be budgeted from the capital expenditure account, whereas the cost of repairing any security damage may come from the revenue budget. This, of course, will affect the company's bottom line.

Organizations that are capable of managing perceptions about their information security environment, both internally and externally, will undoubtedly benefit greatly. This could help reduce the cost of security provision, reduce the threats placed on the organization, and ease recovery from incidents. Placing too much emphasis on reputation may however be a risky strategy. Two strategies may be used to help manage the trade-off:

- The recognition that not all information security risks carry heavy reputational risks will lead some organizations to prioritize where information security efforts should be focussed;
- In some situations, the ability to demonstrate effective problem handling "after the event" may be as important as the ability to manage perceptions about the defenses of the organization.

Twenty questions

In order to assist in deciding what importance should be given to each of the trade-off dimensions (as illustrated in Figure 8.6), and how to resolve these trade-offs creatively, 20 key questions can be asked to facilitate reflection. These are shown in Table 8.1.

Securing information: governance issues **613**

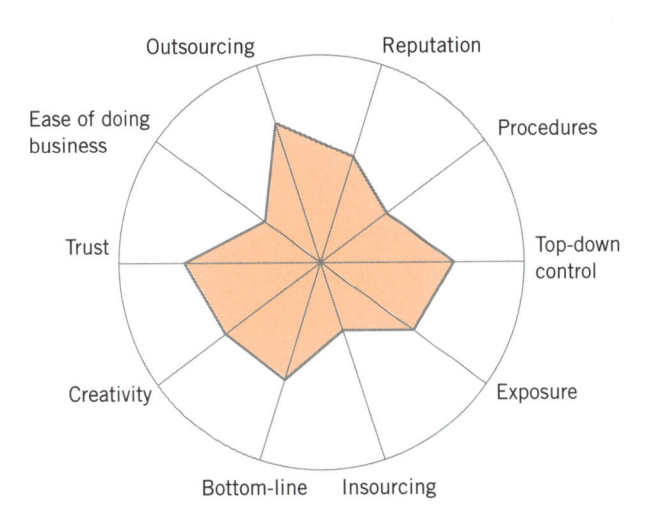

Figure 8.6: *Information security trade-offs and desired profile*

Table 8.1: *Twenty questions to help manage the information security trade-offs*

Procedures and creativity

1. What information (and sharing mechanisms) drive our ability to innovate?
2. What information security measures would not hinder creativity?
3. How can we ensure that the information security impact of product innovations is discussed at an early stage?
4. What need is there for creative responses to information security threats in our business?

Trust and top-down control

1. How can an appropriate balance between top-down control and bottom-up self-regulation be achieved?
2. What information security risks can we not leave to trust?
3. How do "messages" intended to tighten information security impact on employee perceptions of the organization and their behavior?
4. How can the information security culture be developed easily and inexpensively?

Exposure and ease of doing business

1. What are the expectations of the market in terms of information security?
2. What are the market conditions? Is there a lot of competition? How do our competitors interface with their customers? What types of security measures do our competitors have?
3. How can our trading partners (customers and suppliers) be educated in good information security practices?

4. How can interfaces be simplified to make information security easier?

Outsourcing or insourcing

1. What would the cost–benefit equation look like if we chose to change existing arrangements?
2. What "crown jewels" would we risk giving away if we outsourced the handling, storing, or protection of proprietary information?
3. How can the risks of outsourcing be mitigated?
4. What strategic benefits would be gained or lost?

Reputation and the bottom line

1. What risks would an information security problem place on our reputational capital?
2. How can we mitigate information security risks by managing perceptions and expectations?
3. How would accreditation (for instance ISO 17799/BS7799) help us manage perceptions?
4. What competitive advantage would be created by publishing our information security strengths widely?

Management implications

Even if most managers may only be at the receiving end of an information security policy, it is important to remember that the five information security trade-offs we present here will influence most day-to-day projects. It is only by understanding how these trade-offs are seen at a corporate level that good alignment between what is implemented operationally and corporate objectives can be achieved. Managers may also be called upon to justify taking (or not taking) certain security measures as part of their day-to-day management decisions. Presenting these decisions in terms that highlight the choices they have made in attempting to reconcile trade-offs may help build a balanced case.

RESOURCES

Birchall, D., Ezingeard, J.-N. and McFadzean, E., *Information Security: Setting the Boardroom Agenda*, GRIST, London, 2003.

Boyce, J.G. and Jennings, D.W., *Information Assurance: Managing Organizational IT Security Risks*, Butterworth Heinemann, 2002.

www.iaac.org.uk   UK Information Assurance Advisory Council
www.isaca.org   US Information Systems Audit and Control Association

Essentials

IDEAS, INFORMATION AND KNOWLEDGE

Disintermediation

Disintermediation is all about cutting out middle men. Using the Internet as a sales channel is a great way of cutting down the supply chain. The traditional model is that of a manufacturer selling to a wholesaler who in turn sells to the retailer, before finally passing on the goods to the customer. Each link in the chain between the manufacturer and customer (intermediaries or middlemen) adds to the final cost price of the goods to the consumer.

The ubiquitous Internet smashes the traditional supply chain model. Manufacturers can sell directly to the customer, cutting out the intermediary and passing on the cost saving to the purchaser. This process is called disintermediation and is exemplified by Dell Direct, the online computer company.

Yet despite the opportunity to cut out the middleman the Internet affords, reports of the intermediary's demise have been greatly exaggerated. Consumers are still distrustful of buying direct from manufacturers. Increasingly sophisticated consumers require price comparison and competing product information before making a purchasing decision. A whole host of websites have sprung up to offer these kinds of services, services like mySimon.com that use intelligent agents to determine the best possible price, for example. The new middlemen still require revenue to survive, whether through advertising or commissions, and this is likely to impact on the purchase price of the product in an indirect way.

Dynamic pricing

At first, e-commerce on the Internet was a reflection of its non-virtual counterpart. Business models were simply cut and pasted from the world of bricks and mortar onto the Internet. Now, however, companies are beginning to push the envelope and use the qualities of the Internet to be truly innovative.

One such innovation is dynamic pricing. Why should every customer pay the same price for a product or service? The reason fixed pricing was the model of choice, certainly for the last century or so, is that the necessary information to make dynamic pricing decisions was not available. Neither were the complex mechanisms required to deliver it.

Internet technology is bringing dynamic pricing closer all the time.

Research by MIT Media Lab under Professor Patti Maes and other tech companies is likely to bring us a world where most prices on the Internet are flexible to a degree. But if you're worried about your ability to haggle online, don't be. Dynamic pricing will be carried out by bots – intelligent automated software. Despatch your shopping bot and it will haggle for you, obtaining prices from other websites" pricing bots. Meanwhile, you'll be able to enjoy a cup of coffee and plan what to do with the money you save.

E-commerce

Generally associated with doing business over the Internet, "e-commerce is any commercial activity that takes place by means of connected computers." But despite the current hype surrounding the new web technology, e-commerce is no magic bullet. With a few exceptions, most companies are still struggling to create profitable business models based on the Internet.

Jeffrey Rayport of Harvard Business School provides a framework for understanding the development of different e-business models. First, there was "the content business" – "People who supplied content to online services ... got credit for helping keep users online."[3] Next along was the advertising model, driven by measuring the volume of traffic. More volume meant more sets of eyeballs viewing the content and a better selling proposition to advertisers. The trouble with this model was that a few sites dominated – search engines including Yahoo! and the like, and stars such as Amazon.com and CDnow.

The third business model was selling things over the Internet. The enticing logic of this was that companies could be virtual, with dramatically lower overheads than their conventional competitors. The most celebrated example of this is Amazon.com.

This evolves naturally into the fourth e-commerce model: "never making a profit selling real products for real money." This in essence means establishing a base of customers and then converting their loyalty into money somewhere down the line. One example of this is Free-PC – this company gives customers a PC in return for information and a long-term relationship.

For all the talk about e-commerce, surprisingly little has been written about how to manage the move from a traditional business to Internet-based business. For some, it will happen. It will not be by luck, but by effective management. There are lessons to be learned from the implementation of IT in the 1980s. The companies that used IT to best effect then were those that approached it with a clear idea of what they wanted to achieve.

As Adrian Slywotzky[4] has pointed out, the question that enlightened organizations asked in the 1980s was "What business are we in?" In the early 1990s, that changed as companies such as Dell began asking, "What is the best business model?" The question is now changing yet again. Today, it is "How digital is your company?" The key question in the future will be "What can e-commerce do for the customer?"

In reality, it is all about applying the new technology to the right part of the business. It is no good simply creating e-channels for the sake of it. Digital technology is most effective when it is linked to a specific strategic goal.

So, for example, when Intel invested $300 million in CAD/CAM technology in 1986, it did so to achieve a clear objective. CAD/CAM was the digital answer to a purely competitive question: How could Intel create a two-year lead over its competitors? Becoming more digital in the design and production of microchips was key to improving competitive advantage.

Other companies are making investments today that will create competitive advantage in the future. The hard part is figuring out where the new technology can make the most difference. The same rigor should be applied to e-channels. According to Booz Allen Hamilton consultants Steven Wheeler and Evan Hirsh,[5] e-channels can be leveraged by companies at three different levels:

- as an information platform;
- as a transaction platform;
- as a tool to build and manage the customer relationship.

The impact on the business increases as you move up the levels. Currently, most companies primarily use e-channels as an information platform, although increasingly they are experimenting with innovative ways to use them as transaction platforms and to build more sophisticated customer relationships. The most effective e-channels involve an evolution from low-value to high-value platforms.

Level 1: informational platform: e-channels are already used widely as informational platforms to provide customers with instant information on product specifications and features. They also allow the customer to customize features and options – even colors – to make a personalized purchase decision. For example, Dell and Gateway both have websites that allow the customer to build a PC to their own specification, from a list of off-the-shelf components. The site automatically adjusts the price. In future, smart interfaces – which reconfigure to meet individual customer requirements – and higher Internet speeds will make this increasingly powerful.

Level 2: transactional platform: at the second level, e-channels provide additional information and a mechanism for making transactions. Already, such systems are used to provide quotations, place orders, check availability, and to access additional services, such as applying for finance or insurance. The stumbling block here remains the security of payment. However, this is unlikely to present a serious problem for the future development of e-channels.

Level 3: a platform for managing customer relationships: it is here that e-channels have the most potential impact. By creating an on-going dialog with customers, theoretically they offer a way to market to segments of one. To date, however, the practice is a long way behind the theory. Some companies are experimenting at this level through interactive entertainment, special offers targetted at customer segments, and even tie-ins with other products. So, for example, Internet service providers and magazines use information push technology to deliver regular updates and advance information via e-mail. Over time, this will become more widespread.

The key attribute of the e-channel is its ability to push as well as pull information. But push too much information at the customer and they will become irritated and pull the plug.

The Internet is an exciting new frontier. It opens up new business The Internet is a fascinating new vista. But it would be foolhardy to assume it is an easy option – far from it.

Incubator

Incubators are a fairly recent phenomenon. They are partly a response to the lack of finance and know-how available to young Internet entrepreneurs.

One of the key differences between incubators and other kinds of financing for start-ups is the extent of back-up provided. Office space, technological know-how, legal and financial advice, web design; all these services are offered by the average incubator. In return incubators take a slice of the equity. And this may be a large slice of the pie as incubators are effectively another mouth at the trough. Most incubators will have access to venture capital (VC) funding through an associated or partner company. But the VCs will usually want their share as well.

If you can get by without needing an incubator's help and go straight to the VC, it will probably mean giving away less equity. If, however, you have a really compelling idea but lack the infrastructure to convert that idea into a successful company, an incubator may be invaluable.

Well-known incubators include Idealab in the US and Brainspark in the UK. Management consultancies have also got in on the act – McKinsey & Company has its own accelerators and Bain & Co. has its Bainlabs, for example. In another interesting development, some business schools, such as the Haas School of Business at Berkeley in the US and Cranfield School of Management in the UK, have begun to develop an incubator-like environment for their MBA students.

Intellectual capital

Capital used to be viewed in purely physical terms – factories, machinery, and money. Now, the quest is on for greater understanding of the most intangible, elusive, mobile, and important assets of all: intellectual capital.

Intellectual capital can be crudely described as the collective brain power of an organization. The switch from physical assets to intellectual assets – brawn to brain – as the source of wealth creation has been under way in the developed economies for some time. In his (1997) book *Intellectual Capital: The New Wealth of Organizations*, Thomas A. Stewart (a leading commentator on the subject) claims that the changes taking place are as significant as the industrial revolution. "Knowledge has become the most important factor in economic life.

It is the chief ingredient of what we buy and sell, the raw material with which we work. Intellectual capital – not natural resources, machinery, or even financial capital – has become the one indispensable asset of corporations," he says.

Intellectual capital is irrevocably bound up with the notion of the knowledge worker and knowledge management. Their root, as with so many other ideas, lies in the work of Peter Drucker. His 1969 book *The Age of Discontinuity* introduced the term knowledge worker, to describe the highly trained, intelligent managerial professional who realizes his or her own worth and contribution to the organization. The knowledge worker was the antidote to the previous model, corporate man and woman.

Drucker recognized this new breed, but key to his contribution was the realization that knowledge is both power *and* ownership. Intellectual capital is power. If knowledge, rather than labor, is the new measure of economic society, then the fabric of capitalist society must change.

The information age places a premium on intellectual work. There is growing realization that recruiting, retaining, and nurturing talented people is crucial to competitiveness. Intellectual capital is the height of corporate fashion. But converting knowledge into intellectual capital is a new and elusive form of corporate alchemy. "Intelligence becomes an asset when some useful order is created out of free-floating brainpower," notes Stewart. "Organizational intellect becomes intellectual capital only when it can be deployed to do something that could not be done if it remained scattered around like so many coins in a gutter."

Intellectual capital is useful knowledge that is packaged for others. In this way, a mailing list, a database, or a process can be turned into intellectual capital if someone inside the organization decides to describe, share, and exploit what's unique and powerful about the way the company operates.

Intellectual capital is often divided into three categories:

1. human capital;
2. customer capital;
3. structural capital.

Human capital is implicit knowledge; what's inside employees" heads. Customer capital involves recognizing the value of relationships that exist between the company and its customers. But structural capital is knowledge that is retained within the organization and can be passed on to new employees. According to Stewart: "Structural capital is knowledge that doesn't go home at night." It includes all sorts of elements, including processes, systems, and policies that represent the accumulation of the organization's experience over its lifetime.

According to Stewart the knowledge economy also augurs the end of management as we know it. Today's knowledge workers carry the tools of their trade with them between their ears. It is they and not their managers who are the experts and must decide how to best deploy their know-how. As a result, what they do has more in common with work carried out by people in the professions and must be assessed not by the tasks performed but by the results achieved.

From this, he says, it follows that the professional model of organizational design should supersede the bureaucratic. So where does this leave managers? The answer, Stewart suggests, is that the only legitimate role for managers is around the task of leadership – although they don't yet have a proper understanding of what's involved. He says: "If 'values' and 'vision' and 'empowerment' and 'teamwork' and 'facilitating' and 'coaching' sometimes sound like so much mush-mouthed mish-mash – which they sometimes are – that's a reflection of the fact that managers are groping toward a language and a means for managing knowledge, knowledge work, and knowledge-intensive companies."

Intellectual property

Intellectual property has become a critical issue in e-commerce, particularly in the area of domain names and proprietary technology. Lawsuits over the infringement of intellectual property rights are becoming increasingly commonplace, especially in the US.

Legal disputes about intellectual property issues on the Internet tend to fall into one of three categories: copyright, trademark, and patent. The following definitions are a guide to the meaning of these terms:

- Copyright is the exclusive right given to the author of a work – words, music, video, sound, picture, architecture, and so on – to reproduce, distribute, display, license, or perform their work. So, for example, the *New York Times* sued Amazon for reproducing a list from the *Times* on the Amazon website. Amazon agreed to change the presentation and the dispute was settled out of court.

- A trademark is a distinctive word, picture, or symbol that is used to distinguish and identify the origin of a product. Trademark disputes are likely to become increasingly common as domain names are registered and trademarked.

- A patent means the inventor of a piece of intellectual property is able to prevent others using the patented design for a limited period. This covers hardware and software. The problem with patents is that it may take only minor differences in design to negate the protection afforded by the patent. Examples of this kind usually involve media technologies like streaming media, or in the case of Amazon, its patented 1-Click express ordering system.

Knowledge management

Knowledge management (KM) is one of the most influential new concepts in business today. A logical follow-on from intellectual capital, knowledge management is based on the idea that companies should make better use of their existing knowledge – everything from licenses and patents, to internal processes and information about customers. The concept has been steadily gaining ground since the early 1990s.

In a now famous statement, Lew Platt, former Hewlett-Packard CEO, is attributed with saying, "If HP knew what it knows, we'd be three times as profitable." This sums up the challenge facing firms that want to create value from the knowledge that exists, in fragmented forms, inside their organizations. The logic is that in an accelerated business world, a company's knowledge base is really its only sustainable competitive advantage.

In their efforts to corral know-how and expertise, some companies have even created the new post of chief knowledge officer (CKO). Those attempting to capture and exploit their hitherto hidden know-how include Unilever, BP, Xerox, General Electric, and Motorola. Behind their efforts is the idea that they are sitting on a treasure trove of knowledge that could improve their business operations if only it were captured and made available to everyone in the organization. "To make knowledge work productive is the great management task of this century, just as to make manual work productive was the great management task of the last century," Peter Drucker has observed. Managing something as ethereal as know-how, however, is problematic.

Research suggests that many knowledge management initiatives have failed to make a significant contribution to corporate effectiveness. In part, the problem seems to lie with the corporate mindset, and more specifically with overzealous IT departments. Technology has its uses, of course, but it is diverting attention from the human dimension of knowledge creation.

In particular, there seems to be some confusion about what constitutes knowledge and what is merely data. Many knowledge management initiatives have involved the creation of large-scale repositories of information in databases or intranet sites. To some extent, this misses the point by simply collecting data without the understanding of its significance or usefulness.

Knowledge is not simply an agglomeration of information; it is the ability of the individual or the company to act meaningfully on the basis of that information. Information is not knowledge until it has been processed by the human mind. Technology may be the conduit, but the rubber hits the tarmac at the point where the human brain and the technology meet.

Modern technology makes transmitting information easy, but companies have to create the right environment and incentives to persuade individuals to share what they know. The trouble is that "knowledge," as the old adage tells us, "is power." One of the greatest barriers to effective knowledge management lies in the basic insecurity and fear that prevail in many companies.

The real issue for companies is: how do you persuade individuals to hand over their know-how when it is the source of their power – and the only guarantee of their continuing employment? Until companies address this, knowledge management will remain a pipe dream for most.

Toffler, Alvin

American futurologist Alvin Toffler (born 1928) is, along with John Naisbitt, the world's best-known purveyor of trends, scenarios, and predictions. His work has often been prophetic and is always interesting.

Toffler's first high-impact work was *Future Shock* (1970). "*Future Shock* suggested that businesses were going to restructure themselves repeatedly," says Toffler. "That they would have to reduce hierarchy and [adopt] what we termed adhocracy. This sounded sensational to many readers."[6] It also sounded laughable to many others. In 1970, corporate America was at the height of its powers. The oil crisis of the 1970s was yet to happen; corporate giants appeared to have achieved immortality; economists mapped what would happen decades into the future with apparent confidence. At a time of security and arrogance, Toffler preached insecurity and humility.

Toffler differed from mainstream thought in a number of other ways. First, he was not taken in by the burgeoning overconfidence of the time. His starting point was that things needed to change dramatically. Second, he had a keen awareness of the technological potential. The future he envisaged was driven by technology and knowledge. These two themes are constant throughout his work.

While others looked at the impact of technology or of increased amounts of information, Toffler sought out a panoramic view. In his book *Third Wave* (1980), he wrote: "Humanity faces a quantum leap forward. It faces the deepest social upheaval and creative restructuring of all time. Without clearly recognizing it, we are engaged in building a remarkable new civilization from the ground up. This is the meaning of the Third Wave."

Toffler ushered in the new technological era and bade farewell to the Second Wave of industrialization. "The death of industrialism and the rise of a new civilization" meant mass customization rather than mass production. "The essence of Second Wave manufacture was the long 'run' of millions of identical standardized products. By contrast, the essence of Third Wave manufacture is the short run of partially or completely customized products," he wrote. This notion of mass customization has since been picked up by a wide variety of thinkers and, in some areas, is already in existence.

From a technological perspective, Toffler has been amazingly accurate in his predictions. In 1980, for example, he had to explain what a wordprocessor was. Just a few years later it was reality for many in the industrialized world (or de-industrialized world, according to his perspective).

The company of the future, he predicts, will be a "multipurpose institution," driven to redefine itself through five forces:

- changes in the physical environment: companies are

having to undertake greater responsibility for the effect of their operations on the environment;
- changes in the "line-up of social forces": the actions of companies now have greater impact on those of other organizations such as schools, universities, civil groups, and political lobbies;
- changes in the role of information: "as information becomes central to production, as 'information managers' proliferate in industry, the corporation, by necessity, impacts on the informational environment exactly as it impacts on the physical and social environment," he writes;
- changes in government organization: the profusion of government bodies means that the business and political worlds interact to a far greater degree than ever before;
- changes in morality: the ethics and values of organizations are becoming more closely linked to those of society. "Behavior once accepted as normal is suddenly reinterpreted as corrupt, immoral, or scandalous," says Toffler. "The corporation is increasingly seen as a producer of moral effects."

The organization of the future, Toffler envisages, will be concerned with ecological, moral, political, racial, sexual, and social problems, as well as traditional commercial ones.

His perspective became even broader with the 1990 book *Powershift*. In this, he accurately predicted the growth of regionalism and the profusion of local media. The bomb underneath the Western world continues to tick. "The emerging third-wave civilization is going to collide head-on with the old first and second civilizations. One of the things we ought to learn from history is that when waves of change collide they create countercurrents. When the first and the second wave collided we had civil wars, upheavals, political revolutions, forced migrations. The master conflict of the 21st century will not be between cultures but between the three supercivilizations – between agrarianism, industrialism, and post-industrialism."[7]

REFERENCES

1 See Haikiö, M., *Nokia – The Inside Story*, Pearson Education, 2002 for an account of Nokia's R&D approach to GSM.
2 Kaplan, Robert S. and Norton, David P., *The Balanced Scorecard*, Harvard Business School Press, 1996.
3 Rayport, Jeffrey F., 'The truth about Internet business models,' *Strategy & Business*. Third Quarter, 1999.
4 Slywotzky, Adrian, 'How digital is your company?', *Fast Company*, February, 1999.
5 Hirsh, Evan and Wheeler, Steven, *Channel champions: The rise & fall of product-based differentiation*, Jossey Bass, 1999.
6 Gibson, Rowan (ed.), *Rethinking the Future*, Nicholas Brealey, London, 1997.
7 Schwartz, Peter, 'Shock wave (anti) warrior,' *Wired*, 1993.

– CHAPTER 9 –
Entrepreneurship

"Entrepreneurial profit is the expression of the value of what the entrepreneur contributes to production."

Joseph Schumpeter

"Innovation is the specific tool of entrepreneurs, the means by which they exploit change as an opportunity for a different business or a different service. It is capable of being presented as a discipline, capable of being learned, capable of being practiced. Entrepreneurs need to search purposefully for the sources of innovation, the changes, and their symptoms that indicate opportunities for successful innovation. And they need to know and to apply the principles of successful innovation."

Peter Drucker

"In embracing change, entrepreneurs ensure social and economic stability."

George Gilder

"Entrepreneurs are simply those who understand that there is little difference between obstacle and opportunity and are able to turn both to their advantage."

Niccolo Machiavelli

The entrepreneur

STUART CRAINER AND DES DEARLOVE

> There is no blueprint for the perfect entrepreneur, but research and experience suggests that entrepreneurs share a number of common characteristics.

There is a profusion of wish lists of the traits required by entrepreneurs. Tim Waterstone, founder of the eponymous book chain and a successful entrepreneur, observes that great entrepreneurs share the following characteristics. They:

- are inspirational leaders;
- believe their vision is right and don't falter in their belief;
- derive energy from being the underdog;
- are driven by a strong desire to beat the competition – to defeat the enemy;
- combine enormous energy with fortitude and tenacity;
- demonstrate courage – by taking risks;
- have a deep respect for the people in their team, and value team building;
- understand how money works – not necessarily in a technical way, but in an intuitive way.

Research by the Hay Group identified nine competencies essential to entrepreneurial success:

- integrity
- initiative
- commitment
- drive and determination
- directiveness
- confidence
- self-direction
- selling
- leadership.

There are a host of other lists, rankings, and profiles. Distill down their essence and the following seven attributes appear essential.

Energy and enthusiasm

Entrepreneurs are dynamic, restless creators. They buzz. "I always run through the office," says Amazon's Jeff Bezos. "I mean physically I'm a little bit hyperkinetic. That's why I like this environment."

High energy levels are vital for entrepreneurial success. There aren't many lazy success stories out there. Energy is a prerequisite for the job. But there is a difference between possessing energy and being a seriously hard worker. Maximizing entrepreneurial energy is more than running fast or working harder. Anyone can work 16 hours a day. For entrepreneurs, how they spend their time, how they enthuse others is more important than the hours they work. "Entrepreneurs are particularly strong in their ability to align their own needs and priorities with the needs of the business, and generally put the business before their personal and family concerns," says Chris Dyson, director of the Hay Group.

The energy characteristic of entrepreneurs leads them to question what others assume. Their belief and desire to change things give them energy and inspire others. They discover energy from the mundane, from the routine. They extract ideas to generate enthusiasm. They invent different approaches and try new things. They generate energy from themselves and stimulate energy out of those they work with. They attract people with energy.

More than money

To top off energy, entrepreneurs are natural enthusiasts. Not for nothing does a major US auto manufacturer carry out training in enthusiasm. "Some people think enthusiasm at work is childish. We reject that notion. Emotion, enthusiasm, energy, passion, whatever you call it, is the lifeblood of entrepreneurial activity," say Matt Kingdon, Dave Allan, Kris Murrin, and Daz Rudkin, the founders of the innovation consultancy ?What If!. "Too many managers have erected barriers to protect themselves from these very emotions. We believe that in time, creative revolutionaries will swarm over this barricade. They will demand to know why emotions are excluded from a large proportion of people's lives. They will throw off the chains traditional managers have shackled themselves and others with. Yes, we are passionate about this."

For entrepreneurs the job itself provides a reservoir of motivation. Their motivation is rarely purely financial. In the Hay Group research, Robin Saxby of ARM Holdings observes: "Although many of us at ARM have now achieved a position of personal financial security, it is the non-financial achievements that are most motivating and satisfying."

Entrepreneurs who succeed rarely start off with the sole intention of making money. They want to change the world, solve a problem, or maximize the potential of their brilliant idea. Money is a welcome by-product of success.

Communicating the essence

The next characteristic of entrepreneurs is an ability to focus energy and thinking on the issues, trends, and people that really matter. They channel energy into the essence of what is important.

The ability to cut out the dross, the distracting stuff, has never been more important. Choice and complexity can overwhelm. The supply of information and opinions business leaders receive is incredibly complex. Despite the flood of calls, the letters, faxes, and e-mails, entrepreneurs make sense of it and extract the important details from the vast bulk of paper and input from a wide variety of sources. No matter what, they keep communication as simple as possible.

Entrepreneurs understand the importance of precise communication. "Say you have a meeting and someone goes home at night and the next day there's a 10-page memo that's crisp in evaluating the ideas – that's a smart piece of work. In software, it's not like ditch-digging where the best is two or three times faster than the average. The best software writer is the one who can make the program small, make it clever," says Bill Gates. At one company executives giving presentations are restricted to no more than three overheads.

The need for considered brevity also applies to entrepreneurs at the earliest stages of their business. Their presentation must cover the length of an elevator journey. David Ishag, of the Internet investment firm Idealab, says: "Plans have to be light as a feather. You have to be able to make your case in an elevator – and I'm talking about an elevator in a very low building."

Entrepreneurs communicate, distill, communicate, and then distill some more.

Maximizing technology

When it comes to new technology entrepreneurs get it in a way most big companies can only dream of. "The nerds have won," management guru Tom Peters proclaimed when the market valuation of Microsoft exceeded that of General Motors. Nerds – geeks – techies – we've invented labels for them, but the reality is that increasingly, they are the people who call the tune.

Many in business still regard technology with suspicion. It is powerful but prone to gimmickry; it has potential but they're not sure for what. (At the other extreme there are those who see it as the cure for all known organizational ills.) Entrepreneurs regard technology as a tool. It is a tool to make money, have a better quality of life, and a tool to enjoy yourself. They see technology in an entirely practical light.

Failing persistently

Failure is increasingly recognized as an essential part of personal and professional development because, simply, it provides learning. "Because many professionals are almost always successful at what they do, they rarely experience failure. And because they have rarely failed, they have never learned how to learn from failure," says Harvard Business School's Chris Argyris. Entrepreneurs have mastered the art of failing. They fail, then fail again. Along the way they learn.

Failure is inextricably linked to risk. "Share, understand, and confront – then risks, even if they fail, can become learning," advise leadership theorists Randall White and Philip Hodgson, authors of *Relax, It's Only Uncertainty* (2001). "Fear of failure has to give way to respect for failure and learning from failure. Executives need to toughen up. They are going to be tested and tested again in ways they never previously contemplated. This takes humility and bravura. Building from failure tests executive resilience. Our work with derailed executives found, not surprisingly, that all executives make mistakes. At senior levels these mistakes could be costly, capital-intensive ones. The crucial thing was that when the successful executives made mistakes they acknowledged and accepted them. The derailed, however, rejected them, often blaming others. The resilient executive takes in experiences, particularly failures, and incorporates them into a structure of concepts that is used to evaluate future experience and guide future actions. Resilient executives learn from experiences, both good and bad."

Entrepreneurs recognize that, though painful, failure is good for you. When life gives you lemons, make lemonade.

Constant learning

More than ever before, education equals money. In the new economy, it pays to have an education. Where once entrepreneurs pooh-poohed a formal business education, they are now trained to the max. Business schools are falling over themselves to prepare entrepreneurs rather than corporate administrators. From being a peripheral subject, entrepreneurialism is moving to the heart of the world's MBA programs.

Like other schools, INSEAD, the international b-school based just outside Paris, has beefed up its entrepreneurial courses in recent years. This is a clear response to student demand. "Thirty years ago MBA students dreamed of running General

Motors; ten years ago they dreamed of working at Goldman Sachs; five years ago it was McKinsey. Now they dream about running their own company," observed Antonio Borges, when dean of the school.

Many students go to b-school with the express intention of starting a business. Between 30 percent and 40 percent of Harvard MBAs do something entrepreneurial at some point in their careers. But since the mid-1990s there has been a significant change: students now start companies within four to six years of graduation, rather than the 10–15 years previously. More than one third of INSEAD MBAs end up running their own company five to ten years after graduating. The problem is that the world is hardly awash with academics with specialist e-commerce or entrepreneurial knowledge.

The human touch

The final important element in entrepreneurial DNA is that they value the human dimension. They ooze empathy, easily and effortlessly. Previous generations just paid lip-service to the idea. Entrepreneurs know that people make the difference. Their greatest commitment is to their immediate colleagues and staff. Entrepreneurs are people people.

RESOURCES

Crainer, Stuart and Dearlove, Des, *Generation Entrepreneur*, FT Prentice Hall, 2000.

Commentary

Pitching and catching

Executives live with constant pressure. They work every hour under the corporate sun to deliver results. Not a minute is wasted. Their diaries are planned out to the minute. And yet, when they communicate, countless hours are wasted. Pithy, to-the-point communication is unusual in the world of business. How many snappy presentations have you been to? How many terse memos or e-mails do you receive? Probably not many.

When it comes to communication, managers appear to believe that more is inevitably better. And so, their PowerPoint presentations look at every possible angle, business plans expand to fill volumes, and even executive summaries suffer from the literary equivalent of urban sprawl. The motivation for such communicative excess is simple: fear. A 100-page business plan can be all things to all men. It is far easier to say nothing in 100 pages than it is to distill a business proposition down to a paragraph or two.

The business pay-offs of being able to pithily communicate an important message or piece of information are immense. Think of the time saved and consider how much more persuasive a few lines can be compared with a weighty report. Indeed, being able to distill complex ideas and a mass of information lies at the heart of the modern executive's role. "At a time of unrelenting complexity, leaders simplify," says Phil Hodgson of the business school Ashridge, who is an expert on the skills required of modern leaders. "Being able to communicate effectively and powerfully without wasting time is paramount. Messages from business leaders must be distilled and must resonate with people – inside and outside the organization."

In search of inspiration in communicating directly and effectively, managers should cast their eyes in the direction of Hollywood. Nowhere is the art of distillation more refined than in the world's movie capital – somewhat ironic given the same place's enthusiasm for sprawling pointless epics of all sorts. Distillation is at its purest at the pitch, the face-to-face sales presentation, the much mythologized moment at the inception of businesses, movies, advertising campaigns, and much more. The pitch is the intense but short period – 20 minutes on average in Hollywood – when the hopeful pitcher has the opportunity to persuade others to back his or her idea. The pitch is so important in Hollywood that there are hosts of bodies offering advice on how to make an effective pitch and also festivals which allow hundreds of movie hopefuls to pitch their ideas at movie makers. There is even a Worldwide Pitch Festival which uses the Internet to enable global pitchers to communicate their big idea.

Commentary (continued)

Some pitches take brevity to its limits. The pitch for the movie *Twins* was reputedly: Danny de Vito + Arnold Schwarzenegger = Twins. Similarly, the movie *Speed* was sold as "*Die Hard* on a bus." At their best, pitches are poetical shorthand; gloriously accessible *haikas* in a world of *Middlemarches*.

Pitches are a fact of business life whether you are in tinsel town or an entrepreneur in a room of venture capitalists. We all live by selling something. Yet surprisingly little research has been done into the dynamics at work in pitches. This is a pity because the issues raised in pitches are potentially very important. After all, pitches are where vital decisions are made for the future of organizations and individuals.

Previous research is limited, if not rustic – one piece of research involved students evaluating the creativity of people described in hypothetical letters of recommendation. More convincingly, research by Kimberly Elsbach, an associate professor of management at the University of California, and Roderick Kramer, William Kimball professor of organizational behavior at Stanford University, draws on Hollywood pitch meetings over a lengthy period (1996–2001) and interviews participants on both sides – the pitchers and the catchers, the industry executives in search of the next movie blockbuster or situation comedy hit.

Their first conclusion is that catchers tend to fit pitchers into convenient stereotypes which they identify as the artist, the storyteller, the showrunner, the neophyte, the journeyman, the dealmaker, and the non-writer. The latter is the kiss of death and is characterized by "displaying jaded attitudes or a lack of passion for one's ideas; appearing formulaic in their pitching; seeming too 'slick' or appearing desperate." It might be worth remembering this list next time you have to give a presentation so that you are suitably passionate, original, unpracticed rather than slick, and as un-desperate as is possible when your job is on the line.

Going against stereotype, the catchers are surprisingly indulgent when they come across pitchers they categorize as artists. "Sometimes the more dull a writer is in a room, the better you think their writing is because you assume they have an internal world they're in, and that's what they do," says an understanding producer.

The second conclusion of Professors Elsbach and Kramer is that catchers are highly aware of their own reactions to the pitch and use these reactions to evaluate the pitch's merit. The catchers are looking for signs that they are personally engaged with the pitch. If they think of themselves as involved in the pitch in a mode of creative collaboration, they are more likely to look positively upon the pitcher. The logic is that if the pitcher can turn the catchers into creatives, he or she is almost certainly highly creative. Conversely, if the catchers are not engaged in the pitch, they are quick to categorize the pitcher as uncreative.

Professors Elsbach and Kramer conclude that their research suggests that the dynamics of assessing creative potential are highly complex. For pitchers the lessons are that engaging the catchers is everything. Never underestimate the suits – even if the fine art of distillation is beyond them.

❝Interview❞: Liam Black

The CEO of the groundbreaking Furniture Resource Center discusses the power and practise of social entrepreneurship.

How big is the Furniture Resource Centre in business terms?

Sales will be £7 million this year so I hope it keeps going that way. We made a £650,000 net profit last year. Because of the nature of the organization, that money stays here, to refurbish here, to develop new products, and give ourselves outrageous pay rises!

How many people do you employ?

Last financial year we had 150 people in employment during the course of the year. At any one time we have 110 or 120. Forty of those people are here on a year-long training program. Some of them we will take on as we grow but most will go to other companies.

So these are long-term unemployed people who are coming through who you're giving a platform to?

If they're in logistics they get a driving license for heavy goods vehicles and can drive a fork lift truck. If they're in upholstery they get various qualifications. But the most important thing they get – and this is what we've learned from working with long-term unemployed people – is not the qualifications but the experience of getting up in the morning, having to be here at seven o'clock, because if they're not here customers don't get their furniture, we don't make a profit, and everyone's unhappy. At the end of the year, we write a reference and can say they've got this qualification and that they turned up on time and were reliable and if we had a vacancy we'd take them on and that helps us to get a very high rate of people into jobs when they're through here.

It feels like it's a normal business. What's the difference between what you're doing and what private sector business is doing?

The people here. We actually go out of our way to recruit people with low skills, low self-esteem, people who've been to prison recently. That's what we're for. Part of what we're for is to open the door for people like that. We will take people on who we have to work very, very hard with to make them productive workers. But that's part of our business – to get you to become a productive worker for us so you are employable with anybody. So, on the labor side, that's the big difference.

With regard to the core business of furnishing places, there are private companies which have come into the market we've created. They're not really interested in the tenant. But we are interested in the asylum seeker, the mum with kids. The sale to the local authority is very important but that's the means to the end. The end is you as a vulnerably housed single mum or dad getting furniture. The purposes are the difference. The means are as good as the best you would see in the private sector.

There's been a lot of talk about social enterprise and there are a lot of definitions. How do you understand it?

A social business is an organization which invents commercially viable trading activity in order to achieve its social purpose.

What's the double bottom line? Can you explain it?

One of the bottom lines is that you want to do things that are profitable so you are bringing in more cash than you're spending. The second bottom line is we also want to get long-term unemployed people off the dole and back into meaningful work. So we can quantify that by the number of qualifications we give, the number of people we take on, the number who go into work after they've left us, what they get paid in their next job. That's another bottom line – the actual numbers of people we're supporting and helping.

There is a third bottom line – our environmental impact. Some of our business is actually picking up rubbish, bulky household furniture, so we can say the amount of stuff we actually do – how many wardrobes and fridges aren't being dumped in Liverpool but are collected properly and refurbished. All the business we do has an impact on the environment – the packaging, the diesel – how we can minimize that so that when we're doing all our work which makes a profit and helps all of those people we're minimizing our impact on the environment, so that my kids and other people's kids will inherit a world which is not full of poison and plastic.

A lot of this is going on in Liverpool. Why is it happening?

Some of it is strategy. The city council has had a policy over the years to try to help the social economy. They realize that money from the private sector isn't going to be enough given the amount of jobs that are needed. They have been lucky that there have been people with the desire and with the entrepreneurial flair to do things and that there is money available because it's regeneration land and there are start-up grants. It's a mixture of all that – luck and planning.

Is this a new form of capitalism?

I think it might be. The bringing together of how you run a successful business. We spend a lot of time learning from the private sector but we want to learn these techniques not simply to make profits, the capitalist way – and there's nothing wrong with that – but in order to bring a social return, changing society. For us that's about furniture and it's about long-term unemployed people. For others in this area it's about the environment, making the urban environment look better, or working with young black people who are excluded. Social purposes vary, but you try to learn from the capitalist way of inventing products and services which people are willing to buy, marketing those effectively, supporting the customer, all of that we try to learn from. It is a mutant form of capitalism in a way, but very benign.

Is it an evolution or a revolution?

If you look around great cities like Liverpool, what is going to regenerate them? What is going to offer opportunity to people who are ignored? Incoming private investment will do some of that, but the guys we hire won't get jobs in call centers or jobs in IT or web companies unless we say to hell with them, you're a 30-, 40-, 50-year-old man who hasn't worked for a long time and who isn't going to be taken on, that's who we're after.

We're part of the mix. We're not saying social enterprise can or should replace private enterprise. Of course it won't. There is a role social business will play in reaching those parts the private sector is unwilling or unable to reach. That's where we thrive, in that gap. If you picture a kind of crossroads between the public, private, and voluntary sectors that's where social business does its job. It's like the private sector in the sense that it feels like it, looks like it, and promotes itself like it. It's doing work with the public sector so there's that sense of civil society, that sense of it's our city, our community, and we want to change it. And I hope there's also the best of the vision, passion, and aspiration of the community sector, in getting alongside people who are our neighbors and who are excluded. We're trying to bring the best of those three sectors together to achieve our purpose.

Will the social dimension become a competitive weapon so that the private sector behaves more like social enterprise?

That's a very big question, isn't it? All I can say is that with the private companies we deal with – our suppliers and people on our board – they're very interested in how they can continue to make money and expand their business but also how they can open the door to long-term unemployed people and to look at their long-term environmental impact. I can have more effect on Littlewoods or the small SME who makes wardrobes for us in addressing their impact on the world much better than walking up and down outside with a banner saying they're all bastards and capitalist pigs who we want to shut down. There's a role for protest and I get a lot of what anti-globalization is about, but that's not what we do. We're trying to come up with sustainable, alternative ways of growing the economy here for those who are excluded from it.

Social entrepreneurship: The emerging landscape

ALEX NICHOLLS

[The term social entrepreneurship has become part of the lexicon of international social and business commentary, as well as an academic hot topic. Why is there such a growing interest in the subject?]

Today, social entrepreneurship – entrepreneurial initiatives with a social mission – is the subject of intense consideration by policy makers, non-government organizations, business academics, managers, and others. There are three main reasons for this.

First, it is a global phenomenon that is growing fast. The 1990s saw an explosion in the number of citizens groups registered around the world, with many countries showing a growth of 60 percent, including Canada (to a total over 200,000), Brazil (to over 1 million), and the US (to over 2 million). In France 700,000 new groups emerged during this same period. Similarly, a study of the rates of employment in the social sector of eight leading developed countries demonstrated that they outstripped those in the overall economy by a factor of two and a half to one. One analysis of the voluntary sector suggests that it now accounts for over 7 percent of all employment in the UK. In the US the growth rate in new not-for-profit companies has been more than double that of traditional businesses. Social entrepreneurs are also now reaching large numbers of people: by late 2002, the Grameen Bank in Bangladesh was offering empowering micro-credit to over 2.4 million borrowers.

Second, social entrepreneurship is engaging support from a broad base of influential stakeholders, as the range of institutions linked to the sector has broadened dramatically in the last 10 years. For example, there has been a marked increase in the financial support for social entrepreneurship. In the US this amounted to $200 billion in 2002. Funding was derived through the emergence of dedicated philanthropic foundations, such as the Roberts Enterprise Development Fund and Skoll Foundation (set up by Jeff Skoll, the co-founder of eBay), individual donors, and government support. Furthermore, new "venture philanthropy" firms such as the Acumen Fund have also come into being.

At a global level, the World Economic Forum has engaged with the social entrepreneurship agenda via the Schwab Foundation, inviting leaders in the sector to its annual Davos meeting. Similarly, the World Business Council on Sustainable Development promotes environmental and social objectives via a heavyweight membership of major, multinational corporations, including ICI, BP, Vodafone, DuPont, General Motors, and Hewlett-Packard.

In the UK, no fewer than seven major initiatives have started since 1997, including the School for Social Entrepreneurs, the Community Action Network, and the Social Enterprise Unit within the Department of Trade and Industry. The Blair government has offered significant legal and institutional support to the sector, including the provision of the Community Interest Company (CIC) Bill in the 2003 Queen's Speech and the establishment of "UnLtd," a funding body launched in 2003 by the Millennium Commission with a £100 million endowment to distribute to individual social entrepreneurs.

Over the same period, new academic institutions focussed on social entrepreneurship have also been emerging rapidly. In the United States, for example, major academic centers in social entrepreneurship have been established at Harvard Business School (Initiative on Social Enterprise), Stanford (Center for Social Innovation), and the Fuqua Business School at Duke University (Center for the Advancement of Social Entrepreneurship).

In the UK, research and teaching in social entrepreneurship has been developing at, among others, the London School of Economics, Bath University, the Judge Institute at Cambridge, and London Business School. In 2003, a major new academic hub was also announced at the Said Business School in Oxford: the Skoll Center in Social Entrepreneurship. This latter will offer a unique MBA in social entrepreneurship that will be supported by five fully funded scholarships to encourage applications from established social sector candidates.

A number of other important institutions have also emerged creating new, global networks that transmit knowledge and expertise and offer best-practice frameworks that are replicable across cultures. The most ambitious of these has been Ashoka in the US (founded by an ex-McKinsey consultant, William Drayton). Since 1982, the Ashoka network has identified and provided support to over 1,300 outstanding social entrepreneurs in 44 countries.

Network effects are also evident across the social sector in the growth of international knowledge networks and hubs offering academic programs and other training to develop social entrepreneurs. Similarly, online discussion sites such as Social Edge bring together the international community to develop ideas and exchange experiences and expertise.

Third, and, perhaps, most importantly, social entrepreneurship is pioneering extraordinary changes in the social fabric of many communities. These successes indicate that social entrepreneurship offers a sustainable platform to really benefit people's lives. The positive social impact of such activities offers both a pragmatic and morally convincing argument for putting social entrepreneurship at the heart of the current, embryonic interface between business and social development.

Social entrepreneurship creates quantifiable benefits through the generation of social capital, improved and more efficient provision of public goods, and via the establishment of new "hybrid" business forms that will ultimately open up the markets of the future through new models of trade and credit. In doing so, they will also redefine the role of enterprise within the social sector.

Thus, social entrepreneurship would appear to articulate much of the emerging zeitgeist of the 21st century. It represents a sea change both in the way in which the social sector operates, and in turn, in how business views the social sector.

The meaning of social entrepreneurship

A single definition of social entrepreneurship remains elusive. Despite widespread agreement among community activists, NGOs, policy makers, the media, international institutions, leading thinkers, and commercial managers on the impressive growth in social entrepreneurship globally, the precise meaning of the term is a matter of debate. Thus, the title "social entrepreneurship" has been applied to a startling range of organizations and activities. Everything from grass-roots campaigns to the "social" actions of multinational corporations has been branded as social entrepreneurship.

Central to this debate is the issue of funding and, particularly, the nature of "social enterprise." While social enterprise and social entrepreneurship are sometimes used as synonyms (particularly in the US), the former is, in fact, a subset of the latter. The primary distinction lies in which funding model is adopted with respect to achieving a social objective, namely social enterprises look to move away from grant-dependency toward self-sufficiency via the creation of income streams. Furthermore, they are unlike traditional not-for-profits, being more results driven and striving for accountability via social impact metrics and audit mechanisms.

The landscape of social entrepreneurship can, therefore, best be conceptualized as a continuum, with non-profit voluntary activism at one end and corporate social responsibility at the other (see Figure 9.1). Lying along the continuum are four broad groupings:

- First, a range of not-for-profit organizations that are socially driven. These range from fully grant funded to those that are partially self-sufficient, having developed some internal sources of income.
- Second, organizations that are partially self-sufficient, having developed some internal sources of income in addition to grant funding.

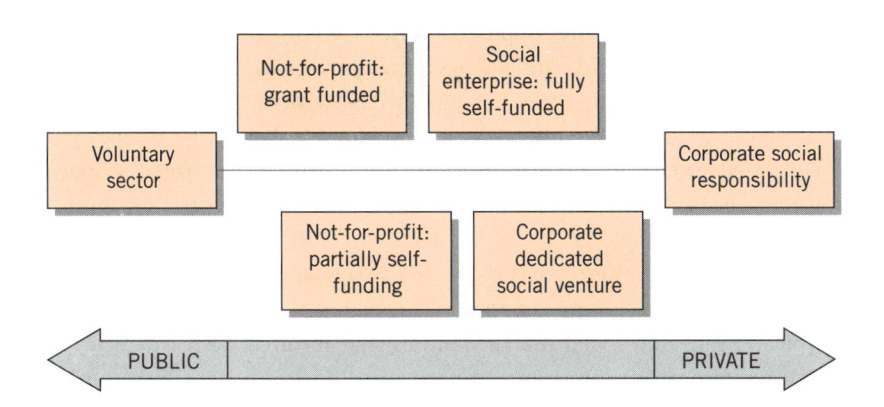

Figure 9.1: *Dimensions of social entrepreneurship*

- Next come social enterprises that are fully self-sufficient (or moving toward self-sufficiency) either through exploiting profit opportunities in their core activities or through developing distinct businesses through which the social mission may be funded.
- Finally, there are corporate divisions or discrete projects within conventional companies that, while usually remaining profitable, also aim at a social objective.

In summary, social entrepreneurs engage with a wide range of business and organizational models, both non- and for-profit, but the success of their activities are measured first and foremost by their social impact. The sector is chiefly not-for-profit, but not always non-profit. What is not in dispute, however, is the primacy of the social mission to any conception of social entrepreneurship.

Social entrepreneurship may, therefore, be defined as a professional, innovative, and sustainable approach to systemic change that resolves social market failures and grasps opportunities.

The rise of social entrepreneurship

Social entrepreneurship may be a newly coined term, but it is not a new concept. While a number of authors have traced social entrepreneurship back over the past 150 years in the activities of public innovators such as Florence Nightingale, Susan B. Anthony, and Mahatma Ghandi, the roots of the modern social entrepreneurship culture lie in both supply and demand side issues over the last 40 years.

On the supply side, since the 1960s, the number of potential social entrepreneurs has increased dramatically. The key drivers have been the widespread growth in GDP per capita (averaging 5 percent per annum in developed countries) and rising education levels (average adult literacy rates improved from 43 percent to 60 percent of the population in the developing world), and an emerging middle class in developing countries. Broadly speaking, there are now more people with the time, financial independence, and understanding to engage with social issues than ever before. Furthermore, as has been mentioned above, there has been a whole spectrum of new institutional actors entering the social field, from network and support organizations to new foundations and policy initiatives.

On the demand side, there has also been a huge increase in the social sector of both developed and developing economies. In the former, the rise of social entrepreneurs typically reflected social market failures that resulted from the retreat of the state from welfare provision: namely, gaps in provision for social issues such as health care, education, sustainable development, and community regeneration. In many cases, the commercial market put little value on these social goods and, consequently, gaps in provision inevitably appeared (and continue to do so). These gaps were often filled by small-scale, local activity focussed around generating social, rather than commercial, capital. The nature of this grassroots activism differed across countries, according to the differences in state provision of social goods, but was primarily aligned with social activists and NGOs.

In developing economies, demand was typically driven by environmental and social problems that emerged in tandem with global industrialization and the drive toward multinational trade. These include the HIV/AIDS crisis in sub-Saharan Africa, environmental degradation in many newly industrialized areas, and the challenges of ensuring sustainability in the agriculture of developing economies. Huge advances in the dissemination speed and accessibility of global information have also contributed, as digital technology has made citizens in developed countries more aware of, and connected with, global issues.

Apart from the demand- and supply-side factors that acted as catalysts for the expansion of the social sector, there are other drivers behind the particular phenomenon of social entrepreneurship. There had been an explosion in the number of civic groups, with the result that the market for funding has become increasingly crowded and competitive. Furthermore, the financial market crash of the late 1990s significantly reduced the available support from foundations and individual donors, making them more demanding of those who applied for their support. The result of these changes was to force third-sector groups to become more businesslike and professional and to look to improve and demonstrate the efficiency with which they used resources. At the same time, the notion of self-sufficiency through the social enterprise model became more attractive. The increasing public policy focus on the sector as superior providers of public goods, noted above, also contributed strongly.

Implications for business

The social entrepreneurship revolution is redefining the relationship between business and the social sector. Consequently, there are a number of important implications for today's business managers in the rise of social entrepreneurship. With the growth of the social sector, many new opportunities for commercially successful partnerships exist. Whether these are public–private initiatives, such as have been encouraged by the UK government, or collaborations with emergent social enterprises, there are clear opportunities for new business initiatives.

Just as social entrepreneurs have learned professionalism, innovation, and the need for accountability from business, so business can increasingly learn lateral thinking and innovative risk taking from social entrepreneurs. However, in order to achieve this, managers need to reconfigure the traditional definition of value. One such model that is now well understood in management analysis is "triple bottom line" accounting, that broadens the definition of a company's performance beyond merely a financial profit figure to include environmental and social measures of success. More recently, Emerson's "Blended Value" proposition – a construct that aims to integrate social and economic returns more fully – has further developed this idea by highlighting a range of linked investment and return issues across a variety of activities of primary social impact.

At its simplest level, businesses can benefit from developing more effective and strategic uses of corporate philanthropy to maximize both social and economic value. New tools and metrics are emerging in this area.

Social return on investment (SROI) measures that attempt to track the non-financial returns generated by a venture or investment of capital can be used to assess the former. However, these metrics for social impact are still being developed and remain highly contested. Much of the commercial value of social actions has typically been measured through their PR and marketing impact of positive social actions, either as proactive or reactive acts of corporate social responsibility that enhance brand value. However, for the far-sighted company, the business opportunities in the social sector range wider than this. Most attractive are the opportunities to enfranchise new consumers for goods and services through contributing innovative approaches to social issues in developing markets. Expanding the provision of micro-credit in developing countries provides a good example.

Thus, socially entrepreneurial business behavior (either in partnership with the social sector or alone) offers the opportunity of first-mover advantage in new areas with high growth potential, often away from saturated developed markets. While two-thirds of the world's population earns less than $2,000 a year, as a group these consumers represent a significant market running into billions of dollars. Similarly, business is beginning to realize that investment in a social good such as education can help produce better trained staff and that helping lower unemployment in a community increases the number of consumers. At the other end of the supply chain, the rapid growth of fair trade demonstrates the commercial value in connecting producers and consumers across the globe in a new transactional paradigm that combines both enterprise and social good.

Finally, as commercial managers increasingly recognize that social problems are also economic problems, engagement in tackling social issues can encourage lateral thinking and innovative uses of resources across a corporation. Collaboration with the social sector can seem risky, but also offers opportunities to try out news ideas and technologies and develop new strategies to problem solving that are unavailable in more traditional business contexts. Increasingly, truly innovative firms will be looking to add social value to markets in such a way that their own productivity and success is also enhanced. While it is clearly not the case that social entrepreneurship and business will always be effective partners, it is unquestionable that each can benefit greatly from a dialog.

Future challenges

As social entrepreneurship continues to evolve, there are a number of key issues confronting the sector. Perhaps, the most pressing of these is the development of a market for social investments. Currently, social entrepreneurs have four main external sources of funding open to them: social venture funds or venture philanthropy, strategic philanthropy funds within larger institutional funds, foundations and individual donors, and government grants. In the US this funding amounted to $200 million in 2001, of which the majority (65 percent) came from individual donors. However, this investment in social and environmental activities, outside the public sector, that do not attract a direct financial return accounted for only roughly 1 percent of total investment.

Generally speaking, social entrepreneurs have little access to mainstream capital markets, due to their high-risk profile, lack of established and transparent performance metrics, and long time frames by which success or failure must be assessed (for example in health, education, or offender rehabilitation programs). Consequently, the "social" capital market has a number of significant problems that inhibit the further development of social entrepreneurship. These are characterized by the striking lack of appropriate financial instruments and the frequent failure to reflect organizational performance in capital allocation.

Similarly, on the supply side the lack of an organized and accessible social capital market often results in potential investors encountering frustration and confusion as they look to fund social projects. While there are a number of such markets under development, there is no clear evidence on how easy it will be to create a properly functioning marketplace for the social sector. Participating in such a market offers another opportunity for enterprising businesses to raise the bar and create differentiation within the growing market for socially responsible investments (that accounted for more than 12 percent of the investment market in the US in 2002).

Social entrepreneurship is a phenomenon of our time, but one that is continually looking forward toward innovative solutions to social problems. Bringing together the growing army of social entrepreneurs across the globe with the intellectual, financial, and physical resources that are needed to achieve sustainable and effective change is a significant challenge. This challenge will be met only when business, the social sector, and civil society all engage together to transform lives across both the developed and the developing worlds.

RESOURCES

Alter, S., *Social Enterprise: A Typology of the Field Contextualized in Latin America*, IDB, 2003.

Austin, J., *The Collaboration Challenge: How Non-Profits and Businesses Succeed Through Strategic Alliances*, Jossey-Bass, 2000.

Bornstein, D., *How To Change The World: Social Entrepreneurs and the Power of New Ideas*, Oxford University Press, 2004.

Boschee, J., *The Social Enterprise Sourcebook*, Northland Institute, 2001.

Dees, J.G., "The Meaning of Social Entrepreneurship, 1998. Available at http://faculty.fuqua.duke.edu/centers/case/files/dees-SE.pdf

Dees, J.G., 'Enterprising Nonprofits,' *Harvard Business Review*, January–February, 1998.

Dees, J.G., Emerson, J. and Economy, P., *Enterprising Non-profits: A Toolkit for Social Entrepreneurs*, Wiley, 2001.

Dees, J.G., Emerson, J. and Economy, P., *Strategic Tools for Social Entrepreneurs: Enhancing the Performance of Your Enterprising Non-profit*, Wiley, 2002.

Emerson, J., *The Blended Value Map*, 2003. Available at www.blendedvalue.org

Kanter, R., 'From Spare Change to Real Change. The Social Sector as Beta Site for Business Innovation,' *Harvard Business Review*, May–June, 1999.

Leadbeater, C., *The Rise of the Social Entrepreneur*, Demos, 1997.

Martin, R., 'The Virtue Matrix: Calculating the Return on Corporate Social Responsibility,' *Harvard Business Review*, March, 2002.

Osbourne, D. and Gaebler, T., *Reinventing Government*, Addison-Wesley, 1992.

Putnam, R., *Bowling Alone*, Simon and Schuster, 2001.

Salamon, L. and Anheier, H., *The Emerging Sector Revisited*, Johns Hopkins University, 1999.

www.skollfoundation.org/socialedge/index.asp
www.ashoka.org
www.dti.gov.uk/socialenterprise
www.sse.org.uk
www.socialent.org
www.sbs.ox.ac.uk/html/faculty_skoll_about.asp

Commentary

The best of the fringe

Think of a creatively managed brand and you might think of Virgin. A lean business model? That'll be Dell. An e-commerce master? Inevitably Amazon.com.

In the business world the usual names crop up again and again. Finding exceptional unknowns is far from easy. You have to dig diligently into the corporate detritus. But seek and you will eventually find exceptional management and leadership lurking undetected and unacknowledged on the corporate fringes. The peripheral can be exceptional.

Searching through the fringe throws up some unlikely stars. Think of the gloriously named Tipton, PA-based New Pig Corporation and its brilliantly imaginative branding; France's Formule 1 hotel chain which rethought the hotel experience and came up with a highly successful no-frills experience; or ?What If! a wacky London-based innovation consultancy, which puts 1 percent of its profits into a "cash crisis pot" to help out employees if times are tough, and which also helped the airline easyJet reduce the average turnaround time of its planes from 50 to 33 minutes.

Or listen to the story of the furniture manufacturer Stokke which has built an international reputation for its innovative designs despite being based in the small Norwegian town of Skodje (population 3,500). In the mid-1980s, Stokke employed 40 people. Now the family-owned business employs over 500 people in 14 European countries, Japan, and the US where it opened a subsidiary in Atlanta, Georgia in 2000.

Stokke's most successful product is the Tripp Trapp (named the KinderZeat in some countries), a wooden chair for babies and young children. Designed by Peter Opsvik, the chair's height can be altered as children grow. It also encourages children to sit naturally rather than in an unhealthily slumped position. It is stylish, simple, easily cleaned, and robust. Stokke's marketing includes giving Tripp Trapps to children's nurseries and kindergartens free of charge. Parents see the chairs being used and abused. This often proves persuasive enough for them to buy one.

One of the reasons Stokke has succeeded is a keen awareness of the market segments it is aiming for. Stokke's other products – ergonomically designed furniture – attract a different audience. These can basically be categorized as "free agents," freelance professionals. The company sometimes refers to them as "people who buy Apple Macs." The trouble with this group is that it is disparate, with a wide range of ages, occupations, and needs. Stokke's approach is to let the group come to them. Having decided that face-to-face interaction was important, it established Stokke Centers in major cities. These centers host regular parties for specific groups such as physiotherapists and musicians to introduce them to the company's products.

Another star of the fringes is the London-based de Baer which designs and manufactures staff uniforms. The company started life in 1984 with as many staff as clients: one. Now it has 70 staff and can produce 10,000 garments a day. De Baer has four professed values: fun, integrity, openness, and learning. "If the senior managers don't live the values, then no one else will," says the company's founder Jacqueline de Baer. De Baer practices what she preaches. Every new manager has a benchmarking telephone interview to identify their values before being asked to the first formal interview. The aim is to weed out applicants who don't share the values before they reach interview stage. At other levels within the organization, questions aimed at identifying values are incorporated into the first interview.

Of course, corporations do not have a monopoly on managerial best practice. The futurist Watts Wacker, author of *The 500 Year Delta* among other books, let us into a secret. In search of the next cool thing, he visits museums and reckons on visiting around 50 every year. He is not alone. Executives from Rubbermaid, routinely celebrated as one of America's most innovative companies, have been known to visit the British Museum and come out with ideas for new kitchen products.

"Going to museums is the greatest out-of-house activity in the world. A good futurist is usually a better historian," Wacker explains. "I'm intrigued by different types of museum. Going to museums is the cornerstone of learning about different cultures. One of the first things I always do when I visit somewhere is to see what the new museums are." (Wacker's recommendations include New York's Tenement Museum, the Voodoo Museum in New Orleans, the PT Barnum Museum in Bridgeport, Connecticut, and Houston's Menil Collection.)

The business lessons? Old things can be packaged, presented, and sold in new ways. Making a pile of old bones a riveting experience is quite a challenge. Good museums pull it off. Second, involvement is all important. If staff believe they have some involvement in what is happening they are liable to contribute to the experience. Likewise, if the experience is built around customers rather than being built to thwart customers, it will inform, entertain, and educate more successfully.

Look for inspiration and you will find it in unusual places. You can even find spicy inspiration in an Indian restaurant. In the UK there are over 10,000 Indian restaurants. The Indian food industry is the single largest sector of the UK restaurant industry; the fastest growing retail food sector; predicted to be worth around £3.5 billion in 2002. Indian restaurants now employ more people than the coal mining, shipbuilding, and steel-making industries combined.

Commentary (continued)

Again there are business lessons. The Indian restaurant industry actually embodies many now fashionable management theories. The restaurants are small businesses which utilize networks among the Indian, Pakistani, and Bangladeshi communities. They are strongly independent and are run as partnerships or by families. This strength has enabled them to see off any threats from interlopers wishing to create a single restaurant brand. There is not, as yet, a Colonel Sanders of the Indian restaurant world.

Indian restaurants have also proved highly adept at adapting their products and services to local taste. The most popular dish in Indian restaurants in the UK is chicken tikka masala which was invented in Glasgow, Scotland rather than Delhi. This is a recipe specially devised to appeal to British taste buds. Indian restaurants are not only adaptable in their products, their service is also notably flexible compared with the competition.

The message from this pot-pourri of examples is that if you actively seek out alternative inspirations you will find them, but they are unlikely to be where you expect them to be.

‘Interview’: Jeff Skoll

Jeff Skoll, co-founder of eBay and philanthropist, talks about why he is so passionate about social entrepreneurship.

Did eBay have a social mission from the very start?

Absolutely. Always, from the very start, the success of the community was the success of the company. One of the things that we were proudest of was that there were people who were buying and selling on eBay who were able to improve their lives substantially. It was because they had access to a level playing field, something that they had never had before. So single mothers were able to stay at home with their kids and make a living, disabled folks were able to make a living. Seniors, who couldn't get around too well, were able to make a living, and they were also able to communicate with a lot of other people.

Because of the nature of how eBay started there was a lot of collector-oriented material being sold on the site. A lot of times the seniors might be experts in a particular field. All of a sudden, rather than being isolated in their homes and unable to see many people, they are able to share their knowledge online with other people who really appreciate that.

So there was a very good combination of heart and wallet from the start. In the genes of the company was a recognition of the importance of giving back to the community as the company grew. That led to the eBay Foundation which was unique at the time. It was the first foundation created with pre-IPO stock. It took a little bit of work to make happen, but once we did that it became a model that other companies have followed since.

Was there a turning point where you thought it was time to do something instead of eBay?

Yes, I think so. The turning point for me came probably came about two, two and a half years after eBay had gone public in 1998. The company had reached the point where I felt comfortable that the management team could handle the company without me being there. Because of my involvement in the genesis of the company, until that point there was always something, some value or some knowledge that I had of the way that this all worked. So I was very reluctant to let go. But once I felt that the values had been infused in the management team (and it is a superb group of senior managers, much more experienced than I was), once I felt that they had grasped the incredible importance of that community–company synergy and the values that held it together, at that point I felt comfortable moving on to start pursue the dream I had of making a difference in the equation of inequities.

What do you understand the term social entrepreneur to mean?

At the Skoll Foundation we call social entrepreneurs society's change agents: the pioneers of innovation for the social sector. I think there is a lot of overlap between social entrepreneurs and business entrepreneurs. Both see and act on what others miss, the opportunities to improve systems, to create solutions, to invent new approaches. Like business entrepreneurs these folks are also intensely focussed, self-driven, and very, very determined in pursuit of their vision. The biggest difference though is that whereas business entrepreneurs are going after a problem from purely an economic viewpoint, social entrepreneurs usually have a vision of something that they would like to solve in the social sector. They are not necessarily in it for materialistic or monetary remuneration for themselves.

I'll leave it at that for the definition, but I firmly believe that there is a groundswell. The concept of social entrepreneurship has been around for a very long time. The last 10 years though have brought an awareness of, and in infusion of people into, the field of social entrepreneurship. It's important. The traditional approaches that we've had in society to address problems have been primarily through government or business, even technology, and the advancement of technology. But a lot of people are realizing and recognizing that the social ills around the world are not going away, and that the traditional approaches are not going to work. I think social entrepreneurs recognize this, and they are dedicating their time and their talents to solving these social ills. I think their success will make or break how well we advance as a species over the next century.

Is this groundswell a significant movement, or is it a fad?

I'm definitely in the camp that we are at the beginning of a massive, massive movement. I think our best hope for the future is this group of dedicated people who are working to solve many of the social problems, the ills around the world. I think of the parallel to 100 years ago when the field of business was starting to take root. Back then it was kind of a groundswell, a lot of activity, but nobody was formally examining the principles and underpinnings of what was going on. It was right around that time that we began to see business schools and academic institutions take an interest in that field.

Look at the research done by Bill Drayton, a leading social entrepreneur who founded the firm Ashoka. He's done some studies and it seems that the non-profit world has been the fastest-growing sector of employment all over the world. In the US, for example, the number of non-profits has doubled over the last 10 years from 500,000 to 1 million. Even in the developing world, in a country like Brazil, it has gone from about 1,000 non-profits to 1 million over a 20-year span. So the growth is huge and I think that people are starting to notice this. I really don't think it is a fad.

Can you teach social entrepreneurship or is it something that they have in them?

I think that there are examples of great social entrepreneurs who have come from the grassroots, not from study, and who have not tried to develop the tools and the knowledge structures with which they could improve their effectiveness. But I would say that those are few and far between. Many of the most successful social entrepreneurs that I've seen in my travels have had at least some level of study in some area that has contributed to their later success with their social enterprise. This program at Said will, I think, be the first program that is really directly targetted at these people and their mission in life, and at providing them with the tools to go ahead and pursue that.

So what do you look for at the Skoll Foundation when you are deciding to make a contribution to a social entrepreneur?

We are quite analytical when looking at the people who approach us, regarding their plans, or their next stage of evolution. We look at four qualities. First is the entrepreneurial quality of the idea. How innovative it is it? How much of a breakthrough is it? Is it designed to effect systemic change? Then we look for traction. Generally we do not fund early-stage social entrepreneurs but social entrepreneurs who have already demonstrated that they have a viable program which is on its way to effecting systemic change.

The third quality is capacity. Nothing happens without individuals, but nothing lasts without institutions. We look at how the social entrepreneurs are building the capacity to drive that their innovation forward. Because innovation without a base of resources, the right people, etc., behind it probably won't go as far as it could otherwise. And then the fourth quality that we look for is integrity; that the social entrepreneur just rings true; that these are people that really walk their talk; that they are absolutely dedicated and that they have the power of their convictions, and also know how to mobilize and inspire other people to join them.

So on the one hand we have a 100-points scale and we weigh different criteria, and we are very rigorous about that. But on the other we have what I would call the ping test – do they ring true? In nearly every case it is very clear whether a person is a social entrepreneur or whether they are an effective non-profit leader, but probably not a social entrepreneur. A social entrepreneur is very driven toward measurable impact. For example, someone like Roshaneh Zafar, founder of the Kashf Foundation, is working in Pakistan and actually opening micro-finance institutions, opening thousands of them. She is very aware of what the metrical progression is for her work to get to a scale where she is really transforming the economic possibilities for the women of Pakistan.

Which project are you most passionate about?

I'm passionate about a few of them. It's kind of like which of your children do you love most. I'll say this. I've been spending time with a few projects more than others. Most recently, this year I spent a fair bit of time with a fellow by the name of Bill Strickland. He is an educator out of the inner-city in Pittsburgh, Pennsylvania, who created a center there that really transformed the inner-city. Now he is building these centers in other cities around the US. His program in Pittsburgh is called the Manchester Craftsman's Guild. He takes about 2,000 at-risk high school students and young adults into his programs for training in arts and technology primarily. His philosophy is that if you treat poor people incredibly well they will respond. He has had a really profound effect around that city, and now in other parts of the country.

Where do good ideas come from?

JOHN W. MULLINS

[Failure is endemic in entrepreneurial ventures. But that doesn't stop millions of people trying. So, how can you ensure your business idea is a good one?]

Right now there are 2 million entrepreneurs in the UK actively engaged in starting a new business. Many of their ventures will never get off the ground. Of those that do, the majority will fail. There are more than 15 million entrepreneurs in the US doing the same thing. Most of their ventures will fail too. Less than 1 percent of those who submit business plans to business angels, venture capitalists, or similar sources of funding will be successful in raising the money they seek.

This picture of entrepreneurship is not an attractive one. The odds are daunting, the road long and difficult. Why, then, are a stunning one in every 19 adults in the UK – and one in 10 in the US – actively pursuing entrepreneurial dreams? In a word: opportunity. Opportunity to develop an idea that seems, at least to its originator, a sure-fire success. Opportunity to be one's own master – no more office politics, no more downsizing, no more working for others. Opportunity for change. Opportunity to experience the thrill, excitement, challenge, and just plain fun inherent in the pursuit of entrepreneurial adventures. As a former entrepreneur, I know, because I've been there.

But there's a problem. *Most opportunities are not what they appear to be, as the business failure statistics demonstrate*. Most of them have at least one fatal flaw that renders them vulnerable to all sorts of difficulties that can send a precarious, cash-starved new venture to the scrap heap in a heartbeat. An abundance of research makes it clear that the vast majority of new ventures fail for opportunity-related reasons:

- Market reasons: perhaps the target market is too small or simply won't buy.
- Industry reasons: it's too easy for competition to steal your emerging market.
- Entrepreneurial team reasons: the team may lack what it takes to cope with the wide array of forces that conspire to bring fledgling entrepreneurial ventures to their knees.

As long-time venture capitalist William Egan notes: "You may have capital and a talented management team, but if you are fundamentally in a lousy business, you won't get the kind of results you would in a good business. All businesses aren't created equal."

I have developed a framework for assessing just how attractive an idea for a new venture really is. It addresses a question that's important for aspiring entrepreneurs and investors alike: "Is your idea really an opportunity that's worth investing the time and effort to develop a business plan – and perhaps ultimately worth pursuing – or is it among the majority of ideas that simply won't fly?" But such a framework begs a more fundamental question, that of finding an attractive opportunity in the first place.

Great opportunities: where do they come from?

Everyone who aspires to be an entrepreneur has ideas. For some, ideas arise on a daily basis. The real challenge, though, is to find *good* ideas, ideas that are more than just ideas – they're opportunities! Where do great opportunities come from? How are they born?

History tells us that there are four common sources of opportunities – opportunities that are more than mere ideas – that any would-be entrepreneur can use to find his or her opportunity:

- opportunities created by macro trends in society;
- opportunities found by living and experiencing the customer problem;
- opportunities created through scientific research;
- opportunities proven elsewhere that you can pursue *here*.

Opportunities created by macro trends

We live in a changing world. Trends of all kinds are swirling around us each and every day. Studying these trends and anticipating their impact on the lives we live, on the industries where we work, and on the markets we serve is a rich source of opportunities. The business world abounds with successful companies built on the back of such trends.

In India, in the early 1980s, Brijmohan Lall Munjal saw the growing but still modest buying power – a demographic trend – that would fuel a growing need for motorized two-wheeled transportation in India. His company, Hero-Honda, now sells more than 1 million motorcycles each year.

In the US at about the same time, John Mackey identified the sociocultural trend toward health and nutrition that would spur rising demand for natural and organic foods. The result: Whole Foods, his rapidly growing chain of natural foods supermarkets.

In California's Silicon Valley, Jeff Hawkins of Palm Computing saw what pen-based computing technology might bring about. His response to this technological trend led to the development of the PDA that's probably in your pocket right now.

Whether the trends are demographic, sociocultural, economic, technological, regulatory, or natural – such as global warming – there's nothing more prolific for the creation of opportunities just waiting to be discovered by entrepreneurs. In management guru Peter Drucker's words: "The overwhelming majority of successful innovations exploit change." According to Drucker, identifying opportunities is about "a systematic examination of the areas of change that typically offer opportunities." And it's aspiring entrepreneurs who often spot them. If you want to find a good opportunity, systematically study today's trends, as Drucker suggests, and ask yourself how those trends will influence the life you and others lead, the markets you serve, or the industry where you work.

Living and experiencing the customer's pain

Phil Knight and Bill Bowerman, Nike's founders, had lived the customer problem and felt the pain – literally. As distance runners themselves, they had subjected their bodies to mile after mile of feet meeting ground, suffering shin splints and sprained ankles that better shoes might have eliminated. Equally important, they had sometimes been edged out at the finish line, wondering whether lighter shoes might have given them a competitive edge.

Knight and Bowerman knew first hand of these customer problems and were well placed to solve them. Their now legendary invention of the waffle sole – created initially with some latex and the Bowerman family's waffle iron – ultimately revolutionized the athletic footwear industry.

If we think about it, most of us can also recognize opportunities where something can be improved – products, services, processes, or whatever – in the lives we lead or the work we do. Fixing what is inadequate or broken is another rich source of opportunities for watchful entrepreneurs.

The fertile ground of scientific research

In many institutional settings – university research labs, industrial R&D groups, and so on – extensive efforts are under way to create new knowledge that can, intentionally or otherwise, spawn commercially viable new products.

That was the case for EMI, the UK company (better known today for recording The Beatles and the Rolling Stones than for its technological prowess) where Godfrey Hounsfield's research in the 1970s led to the medical technology breakthrough that made CAT scanning possible and won a Nobel prize in 1979.

The key that can unlock the challenge of turning basic scientific research into viable new ventures is linking the promise of scientific discovery with genuine customer needs – sometimes latent ones – so that real customer problems are solved.

Unfortunately for consumers, research scientists often lack the market and industry understanding to identify the commercial applications that may be present in their science and their principal interests sometimes lie more in the knowledge itself than in its commercial application. If you are – or have access to – a cutting-edge scientific researcher, give some attention to how this research might solve some customers' problem.

It works in Italy: Let's try it here

Starbucks' Howard Schultz didn't invent the espresso machine or the coffee bar. The Italians did more than a century ago. Schultz was, however, alert enough to see the coffee bar culture in Italy and its social role, and insightful enough to believe that it might translate well to American shores. Many opportunities, especially those of the niche variety, arise because an entrepreneur sees something new in one place and brings it home. Italian coffee bars were replicated in Seattle. European fashions found their way to Los Angeles. Cable television crossed the Atlantic from the US to Europe. QXL mimicked America's eBay in online auctions.

In a study of the fastest-growing companies in the US, Amar Bhidé found that most of the founders simply replicated or modified an idea they encountered through previous employment or by accident. Looking for opportunities in one place and bringing them home can be a great source of opportunities that are already market tested. And they're a great excuse for taking a holiday away.

RESOURCES

Mullins, John W., *The New Business Road Test: What Entrepreneurs and Executives Should Do* Before *Writing a Business Plan*, FT Prentice Hall, 2003.

Making corporate venturing work

JULIAN BIRKINSHAW

[Corporate venturing seeks to inculcate large organizations with entrepreneurial zeal. But with a variety of approaches to venturing on offer, making it work requires that companies select the most appropriate.]

At the height of the dot-com boom, many large companies turned to corporate venturing as a way of promoting innovation, investing in business opportunities beyond their borders, and retaining their entrepreneurially minded employees. Taking their cue from the model developed by the venture capital industry, companies as wide ranging as Nokia, Royal Sun Alliance, Diageo, and Marks & Spencer created small stand-alone "venture units" and charged them with the job of investing in and gaining a return from a portfolio of start-up businesses.

At the time of writing, four years later, corporate venture investments levels have fallen by 75 percent; many venture units have closed down, including those of Royal Sun Alliance, Marks & Spencer, and Ericsson; and most of those that remain are struggling to justify their existence. A survey by management consultancy Bain & Company rated corporate venturing 23rd most popular out of 25 management tools in 2002.

What went wrong? Part of the problem was simply the boom–bust in valuations during this period. Large companies arrived late at the party. Their venture units invested in start-up businesses at the peak of the market, most of which subsequently lost much of their paper value. Rather than give their venture units time to recoup their losses, it was often easier just to close them down.

But this sorry state of affairs can also be blamed on a lack of understanding of the corporate venturing model. The reality is that corporate venturing takes many different forms, and that by using the wrong approach, or by flitting from one approach to the next, the chances of success drop dramatically.

Success strategies

So what should be done? Research conducted at London Business School and Ashridge Strategic Management Centre has looked at both failed venture units and successful cases such as Intel, Johnson & Johnson, and Nokia. It suggests the following pieces of advice.

Choose your venture model carefully. Four distinct models fall under the corporate venturing umbrella, each with its own unique objectives.

- "Venture harvesting" involves setting up a separate unit to turn spare internal resources into cash. Its primary purpose is to spin out new businesses. For example, BT established a venture unit called Brightstar to harvest value from the 14,000 patents and 2,500 unique inventions it holds in its research labs.

- "Ecosystem venturing" involves investing in companies that are complementary to existing businesses. They may be suppliers or customers, or, as at Intel Capital, companies making related products or software. The objective is to create a more vibrant environment in which these businesses can operate. For example, Intel Capital's primary purpose is to increase demand for its core microprocessor business.

- "Venture innovation" involves using venturing techniques to stimulate entrepreneurial activity within an existing function of an existing business. For example, Shell created a program called Gamechanger in 1996 to increase innovation in its exploration business. Ten percent of the technical budget was set aside and used to fund promising but non-traditional ideas through a staged funding process similar to that used by venture capitalists.

- "Corporate private equity" involves setting up a stand-alone unit to compete in the private equity industry. For example, Nokia Venture Partners was set up in 1998 to make investments in start-up companies in the wireless Internet industry. It operates exactly like a VC company, and its success is measured purely in financial returns, rather than in terms of any particular benefits to Nokia Corporation. As one of the partners explains: "We do not do strategic investments [for Nokia] but the reason we exist is strategic for Nokia."

The single biggest cause of failure in corporate venturing occurs when managers fail to make a clear choice among these four models. Without a decisive choice, strategic and financial objectives are typically ambiguous, structure and staffing decisions are out of alignment, and the unit's managers find themselves being pulled in several directions at once.

By contrast, Nokia Ventures Organization (NVO) recognized the risk of blurred goals and created three distinct units, each with its own highly specific goals and dedicated employees. New Growth Business is a venture innovation unit that aims to complement Nokia's existing R&D activities. Nokia Venture Partners, as mentioned above, is a corporate private equity unit that invests in wireless Internet start-ups. And Nokia Early Stage Technology invests in promising technologies, most of which will end up being spun out of the company – a venture harvesting operation.

Build specialized capabilities. Venture capitalists often view corporate venture units as poor relations – they see them as short-term funds with blurred objectives, typically managed by corporate executives who lack the networks, experience, or discipline to build new businesses. While this is gradually changing, the reality is that corporate venturing requires distinct capabilities that can only be built up through experience. Such capabilities include a system for identifying and judging new ideas, a network from which to recruit team members, and a disciplined approach to funding that kills off unpromising ventures quickly.

Separate, separate, separate. Rule number one in structuring a venture unit is to give it freedom, through such vehicles as a separate fund, a high level of decision-making autonomy, strong links to the venture capital community, and incentives based on the equity value of the business portfolio. Research suggests a strong correlation between various measures of autonomy and venture unit performance, particularly for units that are just getting established.

Build links to the rest of the company when the unit is established. It is rare for a venture unit to be successful purely as a stand-alone entity. For the parent company to realize the wider strategic benefits it must create operational links with the unit. These can take many forms – staff from the business unit might help with due diligence, or executives take board seats on portfolio companies, or there might be explicit partner agreements between portfolio companies and the parent company. But there is also an issue of timing. In the early stages of development, complete separation is necessary. Only when the venture unit has established itself – with some proven winners and a positive return on investment – should it begin to cultivate links back to the parent company.

High-level sponsorship and critical mass. Venture units are by definition misfits. And misfits are always the first things to be killed off whenever high-level strategic changes are made, or whenever problems arise. To survive these periodic culls, the venture unit needs commitment from the highest levels – preferably the chief executive or president of the company.

Critical mass is also important. Corporate venturing is all about managing a portfolio, on the basis that a few big winners will make up for the many underperformers and outright losers. So for venture units to be successful in the long term they should probably be looking at a portfolio of at least 30 companies.

Corporate venturing should not be seen as a standalone activity, but as one element in a wider corporate strategy, along with acquisition, strategic investment, and alliances. Venturing is appropriate for certain forms of business development, and highly inappropriate for others. If the company takes an integrated approach to corporate strategy, investment or development "vehicles" can be matched directly with opportunities. This is easily said, but it requires a high level of co-ordination to work, which is hard to maintain while also giving autonomy to the venture unit.

Ultimately, corporate venturing should not be viewed as a permanent solution. Established companies need to develop a capability for "business creation." Corporate venturing can help, but it is not the only approach, and indeed it is probably not as effective as getting people throughout the company to act on new business opportunities as they arise. The venture unit can therefore be seen either as a "second-best" solution in corporations that feel they will never be able to win over the masses, or it can be seen as an "agent of change" whose role is to build specialized capabilities in venturing, and proselytize to the rest of the organization. Several venture units, such as those at BAT and Roche, have successfully evolved their own roles to reflect this broader agenda.

In sum, the underlying problem with corporate venturing is that it is fragile, risky, and non-core. But if you know what you are trying to get out of it, and you follow these rules of thumb, it can become a valuable capability for any company.

RESOURCES

Birkinshaw, Julian, Buckland, Andrew and Hatcher, Andrew, *Inventuring: Why Big Companies Must Think Small*, McGraw Hill, 2003.

Campbell, Andrew, Birkinshaw, Julian and Batenburg, Robert, 'The Future of Corporate Venturing', *Sloan Management Review*, 45(1), 2003.

– CHAPTER 10 –

Ethics

"What is wrong is that profit is becoming the only value around which people are organizing. The only other value I see out there is speed. Put them together, and one sees company after company trying to do just one thing: make money, fast. That combination is dangerous."

Meg Wheatley

"I recommend a test: what values would you continue to hold even if the market, your industry, customers, and the media penalized you for holding them? Only such values are truly core."

Jim Collins

"The man who is admired for the ingenuity of his larceny is almost always rediscovering some earlier form of fraud. The basic forms are all known, have all been practiced. The manners of capitalism improve. The morals may not."

J.K. Galbraith

"The market is a mechanism for sorting the efficient from the inefficient, it is not a substitute for responsibility."

Charles Handy

"Just being honest is not enough. The essential ingredient is executive integrity."

Philip Crosby

"One of the great paradoxes of the workplace and marketplace today is that technology is hastening a return to traditional values in business."

Thomas Petzinger, Jr.

Do principles count?

ELEANOR R.E. O'HIGGINS

[Principles-based systems are useless without principled practitioners at management levels.]

Observers of corporate life claim that the very nature of everyday routine in contemporary business organizations fosters a disregard for the ethical dimension of decisions. The bureaucratic principle by which modern corporations are supposedly organized espouses impersonality in decision making. This can lead to automaton-like behavior, devoid of ethical considerations.

Dennis Gioia, a management scholar who was a Ford Motor Company executive, associated with the failure to recall the Pinto car model after its faulty fuel tank design had been blamed for fatal fires, describes automatic behavior as due to "script processing." Basically, we have routines of behavior in given situations, founded on unquestioned assumptions. For example, we would have a fairly complex script of how to behave in a fancy restaurant, even if we don't think about it while we do it. This unthinking playing out the script may cause the actor to filter out and ignore information inconsistent with the plot. Thus, ethical considerations may be filtered out in the interests of efficiency. This tendency to avoid considering the potential negative human impact of an unethical act is compounded by the requirement that emotions be controlled in business situations.[1]

Management educators point out the mundane nature of much unethical behavior by executives.[2] Drawing on parallels between management behavior during the Holocaust and contemporary practices, we see how modern managerialist techniques can have a dehumanizing effect. These are:

- quantification and distantiation – representing people in quantitative terms and diminished feelings of responsibility for individuals – employees, customers, and suppliers – with whom we do not deal on a face-to-face basis and who are removed from us in space;
- categorization – the representation of people as objects in technical and ethically neutral terms, e.g. human resources;
- exclusion – the exclusion of certain groups from ethical consideration.

Basically, these dehumanizing processes result in a moral intensity deficit, so that the ethical significance is dissipated, even of the most heinous deeds. "The total dehumanization of the Jews was achieved through a process of categorization and stigmatization, not entirely dissimilar to the construction of labor as an expense."[3]

The responsibility for misdeeds in large organizations is not easily pinpointed thanks to the fragmentation of work. Specialization means that no one may take overall responsibility for a questionable train of events. For example, blame for the sale of a defective product that caused harm may be laid at the door of the product designers, material suppliers, manufacturing, over-zealous salesmen, unclear usage instructions, or even misuse by the customer. People evade personal responsibility for decisions made in groups where things have gone wrong. Agility in avoiding blame is a critical skill in corporate life. At upper levels of the hierarchy, managers have the power to push details and accountability downwards. Meanwhile, credit for success is pulled upwards, usually appropriated at the highest level possible. Subordinates whose ideas have been appropriated are not expected to complain, since this would violate an unspoken rule against making the boss lose face.

The social-political world of managers

The pursuit of self-advancement by managers can also induce moral lapses. Hierarchies mean that some people have power over others, and that there is competition to seize and use power. Essentially, having power is the ability to get one's own way, to impose one's will over the direction of the organization, and to arrange things to one's own advantage. Robert Jackall, an observer of organizational life and its moral hazards, describes the jockeying for power that occurs in organizations as "social contexts that breed alliances, fealty relationships, networks, coteries, or cliques." In fact, Jackall claims that managerial circles can best be described as "gangs."[4]

While bureaucratic structures espouse impartiality, with promotion based on merit measured by objective criteria, the facts are otherwise. Authority is experienced in personal terms, and advancement is dictated by particular relationships with patrons and power brokers in the hierarchy. Moreover, the closer one gets to the top, the less concrete and the more uncertain and capricious are the criteria for advancement. Thus, managers experience ambiguity about what precisely are the criteria for promotion. The savvy ones are aware that pleasing their superiors is essential. Often, this may mean negating one's own opinions, desires, and moral impulses, consciously or unconsciously. Indeed, managers in this position may have adopted mental models that preclude any questioning of their superiors' actions, and just behave obediently in an automatic way, hoping to be in the driving position themselves some day.

Certainly, in many organizations and units, especially highly politicized ones, power can and does corrupt. Jackall shows how organizations possess institutionalized inequities, since quality and excellence are not valued as highly as the "exchange of personal favors and the dispensation of patronage" to seal alliances. Moreover, those in power use that very power to argue their own "legitimacy," and "by pervasive secrecy, called confidentiality, … cordon off the knowledge of deals already made." This secrecy reinforces the political means and accompanying non-transparency of how people advance, ultimately resulting in mediocrity. "In such a world, notions of fairness or equity that managers might privately hold, like measures of gauging the worth of their own work, become merely quaint." In a culture of mediocrity, advancement is not to be found in collective achievement. Instead, much energy is expended in working the system to make oneself look good.

An executive who has engaged in cutting ethical corners on his way to the top is then in no position to adopt a culture of high-minded values, since he may then expose his patrons and himself. He is essentially trapped by his own past misdeeds into repeating and, perhaps, amplifying them. In that sense, it is interesting to refer to Dante's *Inferno*, whereby Dante proves that "we are not punished for our sins, because our sins are our own punishment. They deform our lives in the here and now." Among the sins listed are those common in the business world – hypocrisy, flattery, bribery, stealing, lying, etc.[5]

Who gets ahead in today's organizations? According to writer Maurice Punch, "it is very simply that those personality characteristics which take people to the top and establish them as all-powerful decision makers tend to include the very nastiest of human traits – extremes of egocentricity, insincerity, dishonesty, corruptibility, cynicism, and on occasions ruthless murderous hostility toward anyone who threatens their position. Even worse, if that is possible, than the traits which take them to the top, are those which they acquire upon arrival – pomposity, paranoia, and megalomaniac delusions of grandeur."[6]

The following ballad excerpt sums up promotion prospects in today's companies:

The Executive Commandments[7]
There are three things
That executives do
Which the boss tells me
I must now eschew;
I must not speak before I'm told
Or interrupt, or be too bold.

So I went on a course
Interpersonal skills,
For executives who
Have obtrusive wills
I learned how never to aver
And how politely to demur.

The important thing
In the corporate race
'S not to self-destruct
But to self-efface
And he who does not get frustrated
Will be highly compensated.

There's a final thing
In this crazy song
I must not suggest
That the boss is wrong!
For when my boss is underground
I'll be the only boss around.

Pressure and principles

Principles can easily fall by the wayside under pressure. Pressure can emanate from outside forces, like competition or regulation, or from within the organization itself. Often both go hand in hand, when an organization tries to deal with failing performance by cutting ethical corners and covering up, as happened with Enron. In these circumstances, individuals may be coerced to behave contrary to their personal principles. The problem is that once such behavior becomes commonplace in an organization, it assumes a taken-for-granted quality, an embedded part of the culture. Those who do not adopt it find themselves out in the cold.

While no organization is exempt from temptation, some enterprises are more prone to ethical breaches than others. Some of the signals of vulnerability include the following:

- *Highly visible competitive environments.* These environments are like a war zone. Winning becomes all-important and assumes a life-and-death quality. In fact, not being seen to lose may become an obsession that can lead to ill-considered decisions – not only unwise in business terms, but morally dubious. All sense of moral balance is lost in a state of desperation. The competitive arena can be price wars for market share, or for acquisitions, or the securing of a lucrative contract or client.

  So, what is the wrong in paying a bribe to clinch that all-important deal? For bribery to occur to procure business contracts, of course, money does not have to change hands. It can assume other forms, such as sympathetic articles in publications in return for advertising, junkets for government officials and procurement officers, improper use of old boys' networks, or conspiracy to cover up wrongdoing in exchange for favorable treatment. An example was Andersen's collusion with Enron, a client it was billing about $1 million monthly in auditing and consulting fees. A particularly pernicious form of corruption during the heyday of the late 1990s/early 2000s bull market was the misleadingly optimistic "buy" recommendations by analysts, touting shares of companies that were clients of the analysts' own firms" investment banks. In one notorious case, Jack Grubman, a telecom analyst with Citigroup, upgraded his recommendation for AT&T shares from "neutral" to "buy" after being asked by Sanford Weill, chairman of Citigroup to "take a fresh look" at AT&T. Mr Grubman had been hoping to get his twin daughters into a prestigious nursery school with the help of Mr Weill. Shortly after the upgrade, Citigroup won some lucrative AT&T contracts, and simultaneously donated $1 million to the nursery school, where the Grubman twins were subsequently admitted.

Indeed, if you can't beat your competitors, join them – collude – as happened when Sotheby's and Christie's agreed to fix commissions and share client lists. This scheme cost their customers hundreds of millions of dollars. Some of the principals involved served time in prison or have been given immunity in return for co-operating with the authorities. However, Sir Anthony Tennant, former chairman of Christie's, continues to elude the US legal system and refuses to answer criminal charges made against him in relation to the scandal. Interestingly, it was Sir Anthony who replaced Ernest Saunders as chief executive of Guinness in 1987 to try to restore credibility to the company after the insider trading scandals in the Guinness takeover battle for Distillers.

- *Highly diversified, complex organizations with far-flung geographical operations.* In these companies it is harder to control business units and subsidiaries which are subject to different industry and political, social and cultural environments, and competitive pressures. How can a company, often with hundreds of subsidiaries, know what is happening on the ground, especially with the trend to shrink headquarters? The scandal in Dutch supermarket Ahold's operations in South America is an example of this phenomenon. Accountability can sometimes be opaque in these circumstances. It is easy for a rogue business unit manager to obfuscate his activities, especially when his superiors do not really understand what he is doing. Just one out-of-control subsidiary can have a devastating effect, especially in a relatively small company without the depth of management at headquarters to monitor and control risk.

Even when stringent management control systems can be imposed in highly diversified organizations, on their own they are unlikely to suffice in preventing moral hazards. They must be underpinned by enterprise-wide values and beliefs in doing what is right. However, that is the very issue of diversification – how to effect a unified values system in the face of diverse business situations and subcultures.

- *Businesses that rely on government contracts.* This vulnerability relates to domestic and foreign contracts. It is no surprise that many corrupt industries are in large infrastructure construction contracts and arms/defense industry, according to Transparency International, the Berlin-based corruption watchdog. These happen to be industries where governments are big buyers. For example, the chief executive of Boeing, Phil Condit, was forced to resign after the company was involved in blatant conflicts of interest in trying to secure a lucrative Pentagon contract.

- *Competing for high stakes.* Companies that emphasize profits above all build a culture where everything is measured by its effect on the bottom line. Thus, employees who are seen to be boosting profits become the stars and heroes, and reap commensurate rewards with their celebrity status. This approach is one where the ends justify the means. The temptation to do whatever it takes to feed the profit machine is irresistible. Such situations reached their apotheosis in the hectic trading rooms of the 1990s/early 2000s. Trading rooms were the ultimate venues for fear and greed, the twins that are indicative of exaggerated stakes, when rewards and punishments are out of all proportion to performance. Fear of failure, of not making the big numbers, of being deemed a loser (and literally losing one's job) went hand in hand with ambition to be seen as master of the universe and all the prizes that went with it. This is what gave us Joseph Jett at Kidder Peabody Bank and Nick Leeson at Barings in the 1990s, and a rogue trader at National Australia Bank in 2004. The Jett scandal is especially interesting because Kidder Peabody was a subsidiary of General Electric at the time. Bear in mind that the parent company aims to be Number One or Two in every business it owns or it will dispose of that business. It is a diversified conglomerate controlling its varied businesses largely through its tough profit target reward system. Jack Welch, GE's then Chairman and CEO, pronounced that companies should cull the bottom 10 percent of their staff every year to ensure successful performance. One can imagine the pressure on employees who want to keep their jobs, and the jockeying for position among those who want to look good in the GE regime.

There is a growing tendency in business circles to justify ethical behavior for material gain, rather than because it is an intrinsic value in its own right. Behaving ethically for the sake of enhancing reputation or to preserve confidence in financial markets is not really being ethical at all. In that case, once the benefits of unethical behavior outweigh any reputation or market malfunction costs, unethical behavior will prevail. This is because this way of thinking, i.e. prevailing financial-economic theory, views ethics as a constraint on wealth maximization, rather than an intrinsic good. This logic about the relationship between ethics and profits is illustrated by the results of an annual survey of CEOs around the world, carried out by PricewaterhouseCoopers in conjunction with the FT, to identify the world's most respected companies and business leaders. Companies that make it to the top are usually those that are seen to be profitable, rather than ethically worthy. Even in 2004, Bill Gates and Jack Welch are among the most respected business leaders. This is notwithstanding the alleged abuse of monopoly power by Bill Gates' Microsoft, and the fact that Jack Welch is almost two years retired from General Electric. Respect for him is undiminished among executives worldwide, despite his greedy image after his retirement package and perks were revealed in his high-profile divorce proceedings from his second wife.

- *Weak corporate governance structures and processes.* Ineffectual company boards may fail to safeguard the stakes of investors and the long-term sustainability of the company. Often this reflects a board's impotence when faced with a dominant chief executive or senior management team, with non-executive directors who are not truly independent. In such cases, we may find non-executive directors who have ostensible direct conflicts of interest with the company, i.e. supplying goods or services to the company. A blatant example was Lord Wakeham (Margaret Thatcher's former cabinet minister), who was a member of the Audit Committee of Enron. In addition to his $50,000 annual director's fees, Wakeham collected $6,000 monthly in "consulting" payments.

  However, lack of real independence can be altogether more subtle and pernicious. It may happen when non-executives are beholden to the management for their lucrative directorships, and when cronyism pervades boardrooms. This situation is usually reinforced when business and social circles intertwine in an "old boys" network, and "clubbiness" prevails. At minimum, the damage caused may be seen in stereotyped decision making. When executives are allowed to get away with dubious practices, because non-executives do not dare to challenge their buddies, probity falls by the wayside. Where were the non-executive directors of WorldCom when Bernie Ebbers, its flamboyant CEO, was lent more than $400 million to meet margin calls and stop him from dumping WorldCom stock? Submissive boards, compromised non-executive directors, and docile institutional investors can be a lethal combination.

Principled people, especially leaders, really count – but can be hard to find

On a less dramatic note, research conducted in the US demonstrated that the capacity for ethical reasoning and moral action in major public accounting firms increases in staff and supervisory levels and decreases in manager and partner ranks.[8] While this may reflect who gets ahead, it also has resonances about socialization practices. The following ballad, entitled "Creative Accounting," might explain how this comes about:[9]

> *When I was wet behind the ears*
> *And innocent in former years*
> *Not really knowing – what you credit –*
> *My trial balance from my debit*
> *I held the simple-minded view*
> *That one and one were always two,*
> *And what was basic to accounting*
> *Was truth, and aptitude for counting.*
> *But nothing, I now know, encumbers*
> *The poor accountant more than numbers*
> *Since sentiment among some clients*
> *Made budgets more an art than science,*
> *Or what they call, with losses mounting*
> *"Creative" methods of accounting,*
> *Which means in euphemistic diction*
> *Accounts with elements of fiction.*

The verse illustrates how unethical behavior becomes embedded through habits developed under pressure to conform to corrupted norms. Abstract principles of right and wrong can become reality only when they are grounded in everyday action by principled people, starting at the top.

War and the corporation

ERIC W. ORTS

> Efforts to construct the social institutions required to achieve and maintain world peace must include business corporations. Corporations and those who manage them must therefore be seen as having moral and political constraints and duties as well as economic responsibilities.

The theories of war advanced by Carl von Clausewitz, Sun Tzu, and Machiavelli remain popular not only in military thinking but also in business strategy. Presciently, Clausewitz described war "as a kind of business competition on a great scale." In Clausewitz's time business firms – to the extent that they were beginning to come into existence in the 19th century – were considered instruments of the nation-states in which they were based. The size of business firms relative to nation-states was negligible. For much of the 20th century the subordinate relationship of business corporations to the nation-states that were seen to create them continued.

Today, business corporations can no longer be so easily compartmentalized – and neither can the problem of war. Increasingly, business corporations act internationally and transnationally as citizens of the world rather than any particular nation-state. According to United Nations statistics, from 1969 to 1990, the number of multinational firms more than tripled – from 7,000 to 24,000. By 2000, the number of multinational firms had more than doubled again to 60,000, with 800,000 foreign subsidiaries. Multinational business now accounts for approximately one-quarter of world economic output.

Although the number of cross-border mergers and acquisitions fell by about 50 percent in 2001, especially after the events of September 11, the slowdown followed a three-year surge in international linkages, and most observers believe the trend toward global companies is likely to resume. Two US-based companies exemplify this changing reality of global corporate governance. General Electric today classifies more than 35 percent of its assets as foreign (up from only 13.5 percent in 1994), and IBM now has more than half of its total assets located overseas. The German-US hybrid DaimlerChrysler also illustrates this trend. Its recent advertising features a single flag sewing together the smaller flags of different states and boasts that the company calls over 200 different countries "home." The concept of global "corporate citizenship" has entered the business lexicon, even if what this idea really means is not yet clearly determined.

Many large multinational corporations have indeed become much larger – in terms of overall economic wealth and political influence – than many nation-states. Although comparing the economic size and political muscle of business corporations and countries is to compare apples with oranges, one can say nevertheless that the *relative* size and influence of business corporations has increased dramatically in recent years compared with nation-states.

According to Noreena Hertz in *Silent Takeover: The Rise of Corporate Power and the Death of Democracy*, 51 of the 100 largest integrated economic entities in the world today are business corporations; the remaining 49 are nation-states. This comparison is somewhat overstated, but the fact remains that in terms of raw and simple measurements of economic size and power, large corporations have become at least equal to many of the smaller nation-states.

Economic, political, and cultural forces of globalization have created what the theorist Jürgen Habermas calls a "new postnational constellation." Globalization is best understood as "a process" that "characterizes the increasing scope and intensity of commercial, communicative, and exchange relations beyond national borders." It involves expanding networks of "satellite technology, air travel, and digital communications." One might even say that the process of globalization has reached the status of "a condition – a globality, a world economy in which the traditional and familiar boundaries are being surmounted or made irrelevant."

Mark Duffield describes these emerging patterns as "paradoxes of globalization." The changing competence of the nation-state, according to Duffield, results in a shift from a reliance on hierarchical national governments to "wider and more polyarchal networks, contracts, and partnerships of governance." Globalization raises problems of political accountability and democratic legitimacy. Considerations of economics become elevated over politics in many areas. In addition, globalization seems to occur in tandem with an increase in "cultural, ethnic, linguistic, [and] religious separatisms and demands for local and regional autonomy."

Globalization of this kind transforms the nature of war. According to historian Martin van Creveld: "The state, which since the middle of the 17th century has been the most important and most characteristic of all modern institutions, is in decline. From Western Europe to Africa, many existing states are either combining into larger communities or falling apart ... Globally speaking, the international system is moving away from an assembly of distinct, territorial, sovereign, legally equal states toward different, more hierarchical, and in many ways more complicated structures."

The nature of war

In a globalized society, simplified versions of Clausewitz no longer apply. Nation-states are losing their grip on their monopolies of violence. Global society may be returning to a world characterized by complex struggles. If so, we may well expect the return to prominence of mercenaries and private armies such as those that characterized the period of the Reformation and the Thirty Years War in Europe.

Perhaps the leading contemporary theorist of war, John Keegan, agrees with the premises of this diagnosis. According to Keegan, war has become too expensive for modern rich states to wage against each other in its "full potentiality," but it has also "become, paradoxically, a cheap and deadly undertaking for poor states, for enemies of the state idea, and for factions in states falling apart." Rather than states, we therefore face new kinds of enemies. "The rogue ruler, the terrorist, and the fundamentalist movement, the ethnic or religious faction," Keegan writes, "are all enemies as serious as any, in an age of junk weapons, as civilization has ever faced."

In other words, new technologies and the political challenges of war in a modern, globalized world have changed significantly. Limited rather than unlimited war has become the rule rather than the exception.

Important implications for a contemporary moral perspective on war follow from its new globalized and more complex character. War changes over time. "Like a disease," again according to Keegan, "it exhibits the capacity to mutate, and mutates fastest in the face of efforts to control or eliminate it." Keegan defines war broadly as "collective killing for some collective purpose." It retains a "scourge-like nature ... to threaten the very survival of civilization itself."

War Inc.

From the perspective of the business corporation, this account of the modern, globalized nature of war raises a number of important issues. First, business corporations have increasingly become detached from nation-states in their operations. The driving force of this process of globalization is fundamentally economic rather than political. "Nation-states do not trade with one another," writers Michael Almond and Scott Syfert argued recently with only some overstatement: "enterprises do." Because business corporations are fundamental to the globalization process, they are also the key to understanding the changed nature of the disease of modern war and its possible remedies.

Second, the central role of business enterprises in globalization means that they cannot avoid becoming implicated in global issues of war and peace. If not to the same extent as the nation-states that field great armies, business corporations often have occasion to ally with states in using force and even to hire military help independently of states. If nation-states cannot protect business, then business will seek ways to protect itself. Take contemporary Russia, where hiring a private security agency is counted as a norm of doing business. Indeed, the rise of private security companies is a global growth industry that seems to illustrate both a decline of the protective powers of political states and an increase in business responses to social insecurity.

Third, the decline of the relative influence of nation-states means that the "new enemies" of international society – including terrorists as well as organized crime – may misuse corporate and other business organizational forms for illicit ends. A chilling example is the virtually "corporate" organization of the Al Qaeda terrorist network. International channels and methods of business may be employed for illegal political and economic purposes; new organizational responses to these threats are required.

Fourth, the nature of modern war highlights the fact that business corporations are not just abstract economic entities but also social institutions. As organizations composed of human beings, they have moral and political as well as economic responsibilities. Like states, business corporations must therefore develop their own foreign and domestic policies, either implicitly and unconsciously or, much better, explicitly and with awareness. This does not mean that large global corporations need to appoint new vice presidents for war or defense; but it does require corporate leaders to take the larger global issues of war and peace seriously from a moral as well as an economic perspective. In a "postnational" world business corporations can no longer simply rely on nation-states to take on problems of international security – if, indeed, they ever could.

What are corporations for?

Milton Friedman has memorably expressed one common understanding of the nature and purposes of the modern business corporation. In general, according to Friedman, corporate executives have the responsibility "to make as much money as possible while conforming to the basic rules of the society, both those embodied in law and those embodied in ethical custom." Unpacking this approach into a more formal analytical framework, the American Law Institute's *Principles of Corporate Governance* states that the "objective" of a corporation is "the conduct of business activities with a view to enhancing corporate profits and shareholder gain" and that legal and ethical considerations qualify this economic objective.

Specifically, there are at least three qualifications propounded by the American Law Institute. First, "even if corporate profit and shareholder gain are not thereby enhanced, the corporation, in the conduct of its business … is obliged, to the same extent as a natural person, to act within the boundaries of the law." Second, a corporation "may take into account ethical obligations that are reasonably regarded as appropriate to the responsible conduct of business." And third, a corporation may "devote a reasonable amount of resources to public welfare, humanitarian, educational, and philanthropic purposes."

Modern war raises concerns on all three levels related to the corporate objective. These are economic, legal, and ethical. On the purely economic dimension, private corporations may seek to make profits and enhance shareholder value by engaging in the business of war – manufacturing and selling weapons, munitions, and military services. There is much money still to be made in war and business corporations act as primary vehicles for the purpose. News of the September 11 attacks sent military stocks upwards for good reason.

Special issues of law and ethics arise in military contracting. Billion-dollar contracts create great temptations for corporate executives or other employees to fudge the rules on political lobbying and fair economic competition. The regulation of government procurement contracts has therefore traditionally been very detailed, again for very good reasons.

Another important issue involves the regulation of financial contributions to political campaigns. Although it is not illegal for business corporations to contribute to the political process, the question arises whether a military contractor should, as a matter of policy, have significant influence in choosing political leaders. At least arguably, the economic objective should not allow corporations in the business of war to support candidates who have especially aggressive foreign policy agendas.

Another troubling trend raises the issue of whether business corporations should sometimes be banned from engaging in at least some kinds of military profit-making: the recent increase in what have been called "private military companies" (PMCs). For example, Military Professional Resources Inc. claims "the greatest corporate assemblage of military expertise in the world," including 17 retired US generals as well as hundreds of former US Special Forces personnel. Vinnell, a subsidiary of TRW in Virginia in the US, employs approximately 1,000 former US military personnel in training 65,000 members of the Saudi National Guard, the personal security contingent protecting the Saudi royal family. Executive Outcomes (EO) was a South African company that until it was closed for business in 1999 fielded thousands of combat soldiers in sub-Saharan Africa. EO's air capabilities included a fleet of helicopters and MIG fighter jets.

The existence and use of PMCs raises a central question with respect to the economic objective of corporate law. Unlike informal or ad hoc networks of mercenary armies in the past, PMCs today have developed a distinct corporate nature that includes a public relations dimension. But are corporate "soldiers of fortune" to be accepted as just another way of doing business?

Probably not. A primary aspect of the claim to legitimacy by political states involves an assumed monopoly on military force. PMCs threaten to erode this monopoly. The economic objective of maximizing shareholder value does not compare favorably with theories of political democracy as a legitimate basis for the use of military force. Another policy problem concerns the competitive disadvantage that nation-states may begin to face as the best military leaders decide to accept jobs with more lucrative compensation in PMCs rather than to remain in government military careers. A good argument can be made, therefore, for working toward an international agreement to ban PMCs, though the social forces of globalization may make such an agreement difficult to achieve.

Law and the war business

Contrary to what one might assume from a strict shareholders-only view of the business corporation, the accepted general rule in the US is that a corporation has an obligation, in the words of the American Law Institute (ALI), to follow the law "to the same extent as a natural person." Official commentary on this requirement makes clear that cost-benefit analysis, though it may have an appropriate role in government determinations about the adoption of legal rules, should not apply to a corporation's own decision whether or not to comply with the law. Because "the resulting legal rule normally represents a community decision that the conduct is wrongful as such," then "cost-benefit analysis whether to obey the rule is out of place."

This requirement to follow the law even if it is economically inconvenient is mandatory, in contrast to the two permissively formulated ethical and philanthropic qualifications to the economic objective of business corporations. The ALI's Principles of Corporate Law recognizes, however, that the requirement to follow the law finds its own justification in the "moral norm of obedience to law." The legitimacy of this norm derives in turn from the democratic legitimacy of governments that enact the law.

However, several complications arise. First, in a global environment, corporations will often find themselves subject to inconsistent regulations. One may say, as Lockheed Martin does in its code of ethics and business conduct, that a corporation will "obey all the laws of the countries in which we do business." But this promise does not account for hard choices that have to be made when laws of different countries conflict. In the case of a major government contractor such as Lockheed Martin, one assumes that loyalty to its "home country" (the US) outweighs conflicting laws of other countries. But this choice requires a moral judgement. It is not merely a technical question of conflicts of laws.

Second, even with respect to following one set of national laws, complex regulations may mean that it is practically impossible to comply with all regulations all of the time. Third, the question of obeying the law "to the same extent as a natural person" raises the question of the scope of the comparison. Many examples in this category are trivial but "natural persons" certainly often do not follow the law, and decide instead to accept the risks that if they get caught they will pay the fine or penalty. Arguably, at least, business corporations should enjoy a similar freedom of action in at least some circumstances.

Lastly, the moral obligation to obey the law does not always trump other more basic moral obligations. Potential conflicts between the obligations of law and morality are large. Suffice it to say that a corporation engaged in the business of war may sometimes face serious moral considerations that require abstention from following a law or even affirmative civil disobedience of an unjust law or a tyrannical government. To take one example, corporations doing business within Nazi Germany cannot claim simply to have been "following the law" to justify war profits. Similarly, corporations today must make judgements about the morality of doing business with various nation-states and other actors. Following the law is not a sufficient reason to act immorally. This principle applies more strongly to fundamental problems of war and peace than in other circumstances where the stakes for human beings and their fundamental rights may be smaller.

Acknowledging the moral imperative

In addition to following the law, both Milton Friedman and the American Law Institute's *Principles of Corporate Governance* recognize ethical constraints on business beyond formal legal requirements. Ethical business practices do not begin and end with the law.

The *Principles of Corporate Governance* does not exhaust the analysis required of corporate managers, especially high-level executives. It recognizes "ethical obligations that are reasonably regarded as appropriate to the responsible conduct of business," which echoes Friedman's allowance for "ethical custom." But notice the logical circularity in both of these formulations – someone must make the ethical decisions that eventually become "reasonably regarded" by the business community as "ethical customs."

Much moral ground remains to be tilled to determine the appropriate ethical conduct for transnational business in situations involving war. Answers to tough moral problems in business ethics cannot be given solely by reference to the experience of previous generations or entrenched customs. Previous moral answers have their source in reasons and principles and new moral situations require fresh reasoning, if not new principles, to resolve them. Following the crowd is not an ethical strategy.

The third and last exception in the ALI's discussion of the economic objective permits corporations to "devote a reasonable amount of resources [that is, donate] to public welfare, humanitarian, educational, and philanthropic purposes." This exception is recognized in so-called charitable contribution statutes in almost all US states. Commentators have added the limitation of "reasonableness," presumably to curtail corporations from acting too lovingly, especially when the love for someone is expressed by giving away other people's money. One relevant example of this ethical permissiveness appears in the wave of charitable giving to victims of the

September 11 attacks. To what extent, however, may corporations also decide to contribute directly to the American-led "war against terror"? The answer is not immediately obvious and bears careful thought.

In many situations, moral philosophers argue that it is worse to commit a serious wrong than to avoid doing a good act. In philosophical terms: other things being equal, directly causing harm is very often worse than allowing harm to occur. A common example discussed in philosophy is the difference between killing and letting die. Both are usually bad, but intentional killing is usually thought to be worse than various inactions that fail to save lives.

To apply this idea to the context of war and corporate governance it seems worse to contribute weapons of war to a tyrannical regime that then has the consequence of the unjustified deaths of many people than to fail to make charitable contributions to good social causes (including causes that would save many lives through medical aid or economic development programs). The philosophical complications in this area are considerable and require references to specific situations to work out correctly. The world is morally complicated. Therefore, it makes sense to identify clear moral constraints as opposed to moral permissions. The former, of course, should be taken much more seriously when a person (or corporation) faces a choice of action.

Still, one worries about the fact that ALI's *Principles of Corporate Governance* refers to moral constraints themselves only as "permissive." One might interpret this approach to allow for quite evil corporate acts as long as they are legal. Only a cursory reflection on the problems of war crimes, genocide, and other major human rights violations should be sufficient to dispel this notion. Probably, the ALI should recognize that at least some moral requirements are imperative, not merely "permissive" or "voluntary." The *Principles of Corporate Governance* err on the side of caution by avoiding a straightforward statement that corporations must adhere to ethical as well as legal constraints. But this strategy seems dangerous given that some business corporations inevitably face great ethical responsibilities in matters of war and peace. At the least, corporate lawyers (and academics) should make clear that following the law – or following the crowd – does not permit a corporation to transgress foundational moral boundaries.

Building a framework for peace

Even the most hard-bitten economic analyst must admit that the stark moral choices posed by war should constrain business enterprises. In modern societies, a business corporation may have a primary objective of "enhancing corporate profit and shareholder gain," but this objective is grounded in an implicit assumption of relative peace. In other words, the profit-seeking objective of a corporation finds its limits in the political will of democratic states as expressed in positive law. When the peaceful legal framework is shattered by war, then even the limits of law are insufficient. Doing business with pirates, slave traders, or terrorists cannot be morally justified, even if international law cannot yet reach these wrongs. Co-operating with Nazis or Al Qaeda cannot be morally condoned even if legally permitted.

In addition, corporate decisions to participate in and profit from war – even for a just cause – carry moral as well as legal responsibility. Wars and corporate participation in them must have a higher moral and political justification than economic profit and shareholder gain. Contemplation of the truth of modern war – and the participation of business corporations in it – reveal that some higher moral values must play a significant role in contemporary corporate law and governance when matters of war and peace are at stake. Business corporations, as well as nation-states and individual citizens, cannot avoid confronting important moral issues of responsibility when they participate actively in war.

Finally, to conclude on a potentially positive note, the institutions of business – including business corporations and the competition of organized markets – may also contribute to a social and psychological solution to the long-standing problem of war in human society.

On one hand, modern business corporations supply the means of modern war. They may profit from war and this fact raises a very difficult political issue of isolating the business interests of "the military industrial complex" from political decision making about war and peace. On the other hand, business competition may help to provide what the philosopher William James called "the moral equivalent of war" needed for the permanent institution of peace. Like sports, business competition may provide a social-psychological substitute for aggressive instincts.

Business corporations have often been instruments of war, but they can also serve the cause of "the invention of peace." In a globalizing and increasingly interdependent world, there is a strong argument for what Umberto Eco has described as "an intellectual duty to proclaim the inconceivability of war." To only make proclamations, however, does not itself advance the practical conditions of peace. Building institutions of peace will require the effective outlawing of acts of war between civilized peoples. New and improved structures of international law will be required. In addition, a peaceful civilization will need large business corporations not only for their economic performance but also for their role in promoting the rule of law and ethical practices. Then, perhaps, we can at last hope to establish – or at least establish improved probabilities for – a reign of peace.

Sadly and tragically, peace will not come without the collective monopolization of force that makes war possible. Business corporations, therefore, have an essential role to play in the enterprise of peace, even as they contribute to the modern armories of war. Corporations – and the social and political institutions that regulate them – must take their responsibilities seriously and with the proper ethical gravity. War is not merely a game for business to play for profits. If war is a game, it is a deadly serious one that requires ethical restraint and legal regulation – as well as economic calculation.

RESOURCES

American Law Institute, *Principles of Corporate Governance: Analysis and Recommendations*, 2 vols, 1994.

Eco, Umberto, *Five Moral Pieces* (Alastair McEwen trans.) 2001.

Habermas, Jürgen, *The Postnational Constellation: Political Essays* (Max Pensky trans.), 2001.

Hertz, Noreena, *Silent Takeover: The Rise of Corporate Power and the Death of Democracy*, Crown Business, 2002.

Howard, Michael, *The Invention of Peace: Reflections on War and the International Order*, Yale University Press, 2001.

Jay, Anthony, *Management and Machiavelli: Discovering a New Science of Management in the Timeless Principles of Statecraft*, FT Prentice Hall, 1994.

Keegan, John, *War and Our World*, Hutchinson, 1998.

McAlpine, Alistair (ed.), *The Ruthless Leader: Three Classics of Strategy and Power*, Wiley, 2000.

McNeilly, Mark R., *Sun Tzu and the Art of Business: Six Strategic Principles for Managers*, Oxford University Press, 2000.

van Creveld, Martin L., *The Transformation of War*, The Free Press, 1991.

von Ghyczy, Tiha, Bassford, Christopher and von Oetinger, Bolko (eds), *Clausewitz on Strategy: Inspiration and Insight from a Master Strategist*, Harcourt Inc., 2001.

For an extended version of some of the ideas expressed here and additional references to sources, see Eric W. Orts, 'War and the Business Corporation', *Vanderbilt Journal of Transnational Law*, vol. 25, pp. 549–84 (2002).

This article previously appeared in *Business Strategy Review*, Volume 13, Issue 3, Autumn 2002.

Commentary

Is corporate responsibility worth it?

Once the preserve of socially progressive companies, it seems that every company is jumping on the corporate social responsibility (CSR) bandwagon. For many companies embracing CSR is not entirely altruistic. Instead they realize that adopting a CSR agenda can offer several benefits.

Some economists, notably Milton Friedman, have argued that social responsibility has no place within the corporation. The role of the corporation, they maintain, is to make profits and deliver value to shareholders. Friedman famously asserted that social responsibility was a "fundamentally subversive doctrine," saying: "There is one and only one social responsibility of business – to use its resources and engage in activities designed to increase its profits."

These economists appear to have overlooked or at least discounted the possibility that a company can focus on its core business, make profits, deliver value to shareholders, and still behave in a socially responsible manner. Russell Sparkes, a director of the UK Social Investment Forum and author of *Socially Responsible Investment – A Global Revolution* (2002), defines CSR as the situation when companies are judged "not just by the products and profits they make, but also by how those profits are made." CSR is not the same as corporate philanthropy.

A number of drivers are involved in the rush to adopt socially responsible business practices. CSR can play an important role in risk management. Companies that have experienced a crisis or been embroiled in a scandal often turn to CSR as part of a risk management program.

Closely allied to risk management is another driver: reputation management. In a brand-conscious world a company must protect the value of its brand. Interbrand's 2003 annual ranking of 100 of the best global brands values the McDonald's brand at $24 billion, Nike is worth $8.1 billion, BP $3.5 billion. No wonder that these companies are looking for strategies to safeguard that value.

The drive toward CSR isn't always internal. CSR can be forced upon a corporation by external pressures. Stakeholders, like communities and shareholders, or regulatory bodies, can steer companies toward CSR. Equally, companies hope that by displaying an interest in CSR, however superficial, they will avoid further regulation.

The rise of socially responsible investment (SRI) is another important factor. In the US, SRI funds account for over $2 trillion worth of investment. With that level of investment interest no company wants to risk the stigma of being removed from the list of acceptable investments.

Commentary (continued)

While corporations attempt to convince the world of their socially responsible credentials, cynics remain unimpressed. CSR is frequently dismissed as style over substance, a public relations exercise, naked self-interest. No matter how hard some companies try, and how genuinely they take their corporate responsibilities, many commentators remain skeptical. It seems a little unfair that companies like McDonald's, Nike, and Starbucks, for example, which operate many socially responsible programs, do not receive much kudos for their actions. As some activists argue, surely it is better that they, and all other companies, adopt some socially responsible practices, rather than none at all. Whatever the motives.

Wanted: Boardroom coach

SUSAN BLOCH

[Recent corporate scandals have led to exhortations for non-executive directors to be both more vigilant and more proactive. This reflects an important development in boardroom culture. What is increasingly clear is that good board governance cannot be built on legislation alone.]

Centuries ago, Plato argued for a society run by perfect guardians. Juvenal is said to have replied, "And who will guard the guardians?" Now, centuries later, that has often been the dilemma facing regulatory bodies. If indeed "good-governance" regulation on its own does not produce good boards, the answer must lie in the social system of the directors. "How we work together" becomes a critical success factor in building effective boards who live up to the expectations of good governance.

It may seem curious that no one, until recently, fretted if a chief executive or chairman stacked his or her board with friends. There are many high-profile examples. The Disney board once included Michael Eisner's lawyer, his architect, and the principal of his kids' school. With this type of supervision, CEOs could do no wrong. In 2001 Dennis Kozlowski, former CEO of Tyco, demanded a contract (before his supposed crimes came to light) that guaranteed his severance payment, even if he committed a felony. The Tyco directors might have reasonably asked whether he was plotting to "commit a crime." Instead, they agreed to his demand.

In the meltdown of what were once considered great companies, such as Enron, Marconi, and Equitable Life, attention was again focussed on boards. In the majority of instances, these boards followed most of the accepted standards of governance practices. These practices were, however, mainly concerned with rules and procedures. Audit and remuneration committees were in place, members attended meetings, and codes of ethics were agreed. The boxes were ticked. Yet, clearly, this did not prevent the excesses that later came to light.

At the time of these crises, we probably needed to ask some additional and uncomfortable questions: "Were some of the directors aware of irregularities? Did they actually benefit, or would they have benefitted financially? Were they just too naive? Were they asleep at the wheel? Or were they just incompetent?"

Boards should act as boards

In the panic that followed it has became clear that a fundamental review of how boards should operate and be evaluated is needed. It has also become evident that mere laws, new regulations, and even the threat of prison sentences on their own are not sufficient. In fact, many good and bad companies alike have already adopted most of these practices. Boxes continue to be ticked. But now more than ever, shareholders, investors, executive, and non-executive directors are being asked to ensure that this problem does not recur.

The trouble is that new rules are not the solution. The spirit of governance rather than the letter of the law offers the best insurance against future scandals. What are needed are new behaviors and attitudes rather than more boxes to tick.

It is easy to accept that boards need to operate in a climate of transparency and openness, with strong interpersonal cohesion. All recent reports recommend that directors need to be encouraged to learn how to engage in constructive professional debate. Importantly, we know that a board's performance should be evaluated annually to provide feedback both to individuals and to the board as a whole group. After all, almost everyone else in a business has some kind of performance evaluation. But on its own this is not enough. Plans should then be put in place to address the outcomes of the board audit, enhancing the capability of individuals in the boardroom as well as of the board as a whole.

There are four key things that need to happen to ensure that boards become and stay effective:

- the board must ensure it receives adequate information and on time;
- board members need to develop mutual respect and trust;
- they should challenge one another's assumptions and suggestions, using inquiry rather than advocacy. Taboos should be aired;
- they should make robust decisions without feeling the pressure of groupthink.

Ultimately, it is the chair who needs to create the atmosphere for all these things to happen – and set a tone for the team to be robust and open. What goes on behind closed doors should be more transparent to key stakeholders; all the *unsaids* need to be *said*.

To make the boardroom a place of candid discussion and personal accountability, the next generation of non-executive and executive board members requires developmental support. Coaching offers a way forward. The alternative is that we continue with the old ways whereby new board members, who had little or no training, were inducted into the existing culture.

Two case studies illustrate the point.

Bringing Alex onboard

Imagine for a moment the excitement and nervousness that Alex felt when he was offered a role in a FTSE 200 company as CFO, a main board position. After carefully considering his career options, he decided that it was time for a change. He was now 41 and after six years as the finance director of a subsidiary board in the construction industry, it was time to move on. Jobs were scarce in 2001. It was an opportunity to move into a new league, be an executive for the first time, and play with the big boys. He also felt that travel would be more exciting than construction. A 30 percent pay rise with hefty stock options were also enticing. However, he was nervous as to how he would work with his new boss. He had heard that the CEO was rather distant and could at times be extremely domineering. He also worried as to how accurate the accounts really were.

Ambition strongly dominated his final decision to join. Excitement took over his anxiety, and two months later he walked into his new office, feeling energetic as he swung in his new leather chair behind the desk. Along with a steaming cup of coffee, his new assistant cautiously gave him the board papers for the meeting to be held three days later and he wondered when he would find time to read them. His diary had been filled with induction meetings, so he would need to burn the midnight oil.

He found the first board meeting difficult, as he struggled to follow some of the discussion in depth, but fortunately did not attempt to join much of the debate. What he did realize was that most of the non-executive directors didn't join in either. This seemed to be a performance, carefully orchestrated by the chairman, and dominated by the CEO. Overwhelmed, he decided he needed some help. Two days later, he decided to contact an executive coach he had worked with three years previously to help him manage his former transition. What became quite clear to him in their first meeting was that he had underestimated the challenge of the boardroom dynamics. Rather naively he had assumed that strong governance knowledge about structure, processes, and audit was enough.

Together with his coach he reviewed the assessment they had completed three years previously. It had been evident then that he possessed strong strategic and analytic skills, was highly ambitious and determined, and was a good planner and organizer. He was weaker in areas of communication skills, empathy, and sensitivity. His strong intellectual capability made him seem rather arrogant and disrespectful of those who could not keep up with his fast thinking. What he needed more than ever was to work on his interpersonal skills, and map out relationship management strategy. Importantly, he needed to begin to connect with all the board members, including the five non-executive directors, key investors, and the management team.

Assuming the mantle

With his coach, Alex began to build his personal development plan which included the following:

1. Reviewing the strategy and structure

Alex tried to make sense of whether the company's current structure and capability was appropriate for implementing its chosen strategies. He reviewed the threats and opportunities in the external environment, and was quickly up to speed by reading four previous board minutes. Contingency plans were discussed with his senior finance team as corporate and financial strategic options were debated. Risk was evaluated.

PROBLEMS: He began to have concerns about the strength of the business in the Pacific Basin. Despite increased investment last year, the cost base seemed too high. He could not fathom out how the profit margins were ever going to improve, unless logistics were reviewed and payroll cut. Restructuring seemed to be the only option.

2. Connecting with mission, values, and objectives

Meetings with the chairman and non-executives, as well as the CEO, helped him to assimilate the company's vision and mission. In light of political and economic turmoil, he was able to integrate the business objectives conceptually, and understand how they would impact on profit margins.

He was determined to review the values and norms in his own team, and create a culture of transparency.

PROBLEMS: The ever constant terrorist threat seemed at times to create a fog of ambiguity in the boardroom. Travel was so negatively affected; construction in the UK barely. This made it difficult for Alex to understand where the company really wanted to go. In fact, when comparing the notes after his conversations he found little agreement between two of the non-executives and the executives. "How," he wondered, "could he align his team up with something that wasn't there?"

3. Monitoring, controlling, and implementing the strategy

Performance management processes needed to be reviewed. Internal control procedures were examined to ensure they were providing reliable and valid information for monitoring operations and performance. Review processes were to be examined to monitor policies, legal, and fiduciary obligations and risk.

PROBLEMS: Performance management processes had previously been introduced but implemented only on an ad hoc basis. The successes and failures of senior management were difficult to communicate accurately. "I trust him to deliver ... we have worked together for 15 years," was a common comment by management. As measures and systems of measurement were not made clear at the outset, Alex struggled to get managers to begin to set these standards of performance. Their mindset was quite "anti" the whole concept.

4. Developing and maintaining relationships with investors and shareholders

Communication strategy was reviewed and investor relations given more prominence. Ensuring that relationships with the city were to be nurtured, regular briefing meetings were set up. Journalists needed to be treated with respect.

PROBLEMS: Bad press over a year ago as a result of health scares on cruise liners had impacted badly on the business. The CEO then decided that there should be no communication whatsoever with journalists, who were constantly maligned. The city, too, had become nervous that "something was going on" as communication was so tight-lipped.

Like many other senior managers who move into board roles for the first time, Alex was not prepared for the life in the boardroom. Commonly, executives believe that expertise around the legal and accounting aspects of governance, combined with strong functional and technical expertise, are enough to ensure that they can play a significant role in running the business. Naively, insufficient attention is paid to leadership style, interpersonal skills, decision making, communication style, impact, and influence. To top it all, many executive directors have little or no contact with their non-executives.

In fact, a survey by the Change Partnership, part of the Whitehead Mann Group, showed that 20 percent of top management had no contact with the non-executives in their business. A report by the Leeds University Business School and the Judge Institute of Management at Cambridge concluded that "the work of the non-executive is almost completely invisible to all but fellow board members. It is perhaps for this reason that investors, working at a distance, have focussed on issues of board structure and composition, as proxies for board effectiveness."

Danielle in the lion's den

A pan-European telecoms company with UK headquarters was delighted to raise its diversity profile when it recruited a woman non-executive director onto the board. Danielle was the CFO of a British electronics company and demonstrated all the right competencies for the role. Along with the company secretary and her coach, she carefully planned her induction, ensuring that she met with the heads of business units, visited some of the operational sites, and met with other board members on an informal basis. She was sufficiently self-aware to recognize that the multi-cultural composition of the telecoms board was complex, but nothing could have prepared her for her first board meeting. She was astonished to see how differently this meeting was chaired when compared to home base.

"We started about 20 minutes late, and one non-executive bragged over coffee to me that he had not really had a chance to read all the papers. He carried on saying that nothing much happened anyway and that the meetings were quite boring. He even laughed and suggested I take another coffee to keep awake." The meeting lasted five hours, and it became quite clear that little strategic debate was going to take place. Operational heads had been invited to present their results over the last quarter and they were encouraged by some of the members to talk about the problems they had experienced during this time. It was quite clear they were being pushed to cut costs, but without any conceptual link to the future strategy of the business.

By the end of the meeting, Danielle noted that two of the six non-executives had barely participated in the debate at all. In fact, one had even nodded off from time to time. Not surprising when he had taken the red eye in from New York that morning.

At the end of the meeting, the chairman asked Danielle if she could spare a few minutes. She was surprised when he asked for her feedback on the meeting. She found herself in a difficult position given it was the first meeting, and realized she didn't have much positive feedback. She was faced with a real ethical dilemma: "If I give the open feedback I believe I should, will I be fired from my very first and really important non-executive role?"

Danielle took a deep breath, and decided not to be critical, but to try to listen to his concerns. During the discussion he said that he was aware that some of the non-executives were not contributing as they should to quality debate, but was unsure how to address this. She was surprised to learn that none had ever been given feedback. He was also concerned as to how this might be done. On the one hand, one director in charge of the P&L for Central and Eastern Europe was still stuck in an operational mindset. Despite being 3.5 percent ahead of budget, he struggled to sit down and discuss strategy. The chairman felt quite rightly that his contribution in the boardroom was weak, but certainly didn't want to demotivate him by giving him negative feedback. On the other hand, one of the non-executives was seen as too hands on. Besides this role he was the CEO of a logistics business in the Benelux area, and struggled to stand back and critique. He and the chairman had been at university together and they still mixed in the same social circles. Their daughters were best friends. "I don't know how to tell him that he is still behaving like a chief executive. It is one thing to challenge," he said, "and another thing to be a nuisance. He hasn't realized that he is not in charge of making decisions over here!'

Danielle was sensitive enough to realize that he was asking for help, but smart enough to recognize that she was probably the wrong person to give it to him. She did, however, know someone who could. She recommended she contacted an outfit which had conducted a board effectiveness review for the electronics company where she held a director role. She explained how the process worked for them.

"We had a really intensive diagnostic process. All directors were interviewed individually. We also all completed a peer feedback questionnaire. We were then observed during one of the meetings. We then received one-to-one feedback on our peer reviews as well as observed behavior in the board meeting. The whole board then took half a day to go through the collective feedback from the coach to help us understand how we operated both in and out of the boardroom; how we made decisions. Not only did we get to realize how the group norms and behaviors were impacting on our effectiveness, but we also acknowledged that we struggled to communicate with the management team below. Importantly, it gave our chairman the courage to have formal appraisals with all the non-executives. You would be surprised," she added, "to know that it worked wonders. We all began to share more and become less defensive."

Taboos can derail board effectiveness

The audit for the telecoms board was completed in May last year, and presented to the board at a special meeting just before the summer. A courageous non-executive raised an extremely sensitive issue during the context interview, and initially was extremely reluctant to discuss this with the other members. Apparently, it was no secret among senior management that the CFO was having an affair with the sales director for Northern Europe. The fact that no one had told the chairman (and he seemed to be the only person who didn't know) seemed to suck the oxygen out of the room at board meetings; no wonder the energy level seemed so low.

It is too soon to say whether all the issues and taboos that were raised in the debrief have been adequately acknowledged, but the chairman has begun to have meaningful conversations with all the board members on a regular basis. Danielle's proactive challenge and support for the audit has certainly acted as a catalyst for a more robust discussion.

If openness and trust are the basis of good working relationships on which the effectiveness of the company depends, consider the importance of strong role models in the boardroom. Decisions made at the top which are influenced by a reluctance to challenge some of the behaviors, values, and style of fellow board members will inevitably be viewed critically. Where directors and management teams then have to implement these decisions, the "elephant will always be dancing in the room."

Demystifying the board

Despite efforts to ensure that boards are structured in line with governance suggestions, the business community had yet another loud wake-up call at the end of 2003, when irregularities were revealed in the Parmalat affair. Surely this once again highlights the need for directors to be responsible and accountable for good-governance regulation. This must also depend on the social system that operates between board members. The leadership style and conduct of the chairman in board audits that we have conducted are the key in creating a climate for non-executives to be effective. An effective chair needs to develop strong and open relationships with all board members, and build a climate where all members are encouraged to do the same with one another. This do not mean that positive challenge and professional conflict do not exist in debate; on the contrary, without respect and trust, people tend to hold things back and be defensive.

Investors' curiosity about what happens behind the boardroom door needs to be satisfied. It is not enough to say "I did not know" and get away with it. Surely it is every board member's duty to demystify what the board is and demonstrate a transparency to key stakeholders.

RESOURCES

McNulty, T., Roberts, John and Stiles, Philip, *Creating Accountability Within the Board*, The Boardroom and Leadership Debate: January 2004.

Commentary

Profiting from corporate philanthropy

Corporate giving is an important business, an activity that nearly every major corporation indulges in. Yet despite the benefits for the recipients, and the possible benefits for the corporations, charitable contributions appear to be on the wane. As a percentage of profits, corporate giving has fallen by 50 percent over a period of 15 years.

Harvard Business School's Michael Porter has explored the subject in the *Harvard Business Review* article "The Competitive Advantage of Corporate Philanthropy" (2002, co-written with Mark Kramer). Porter questions some of the assumptions underpinning Friedman's statement, notably that corporate and social ends are separate and distinct. This is not necessarily so. As Porter points out, philanthropy can be a means by which companies improve the quality of the business environment in which they operate. Something Porter calls "strategic philanthropy."

An example of this type of strategic philanthropy would be where a company set up a program aimed to reduce unemployment. The program would educate people in the locality within which the company operates, equipping them with skills that meet any skills shortages within the company. With this scheme both the participants on the program and the company stand to benefit. Other types of strategic philanthropy might include charitable giving that improves the quality of life in the local area; or giving to bodies that aim to improve corporate transparency and business ethics; or giving that promotes the growth of industry clusters. Such context-related philanthropy would advocate giving only in situations where corporate and social interests coincide. Care must always be taken to ensure that giving remains within the legal definitions of charitable giving.

Critics could argue that context-related corporate giving also benefits competitors. But if it does, Porter asserts, it is not to the same extent that it benefits the philanthropic company. For example, it is unlikely that all the competitors will reside in the same location. Also, the more tailored a philanthropic program is, the less likely it is to benefit other companies. Companies that lead the way with philanthropic initiatives often gain a greater advantage; through forging closer relationships with other institutions for example.

Achieving a competitive advantage while doing social good requires the corporation to select the grantees carefully. Only the best grantees must be selected and promoted; the corporation can use its expertise to improve the efficiency of the grantee. The corporation can also act as a catalyst for innovation within the grantee.

Commentary (continued)

One longstanding difficulty in justifying corporate philanthropy is that even though the measures are designed to maximize the benefits to both corporation and grantees, it is still difficult to measure the contribution to the bottom line in any meaningful way. Some companies are making progress on this front, however. For example, Johnson & Johnson uses measurement techniques designed to measure the manufacturing quality of products to measure the effectiveness of corporate philanthropy. However, until reliable measurement of the return on corporate philanthropy is possible, the effectiveness of corporate philanthropy remains open to debate.

Pathways to commitment: Values-driven performance

MATTHEW MAY

[Corporate values can prove the difference between average and high performance. Yet while widely acknowledged as important, dynamically applying values to all corporate activities is achieved by a select few.]

Conventional wisdom says that core values are a must-have for organizational success. Indeed, there are probably few companies that don't have some formal statement of guiding principles up on the walls, usually in a strategic location sure to be frequented by customers and visitors. But the truth is, beyond the initial exercise of wordsmithing lofty and aspirational platitudes and the occasional executive mention in company communiqués, true values-based action is quite rare. Given that values can be one of the most powerful ways to guide, inspire, and bring meaning to the work of both the individual and organization, the question simply becomes: *why?*

Two reasons seem evident:

- First, values are not well understood – we're told we need them, but we're not sure why, or how they actually work to elevate us. Individuals themselves do not spend enough time clarifying what matters most to them.
- Second, we don't know how to practically align and leverage well the power of values – little attention is spent on individual and team values.

My work and research with the global Toyota organization has made one thing clear: overall employee commitment is highest when clarity around personal values exists, and those personal values are aligned with those of the team and broader organization. Clarity around company values alone yields little. This destroys the relevance of the traditional corporate practice centered on simply having and communicating company core values.

> ### Common ground: the key is in the connection
>
> Most companies focus their core values efforts on ensuring clarity around the company core values. This chart shows the power of bifocal clarity as it relates to employee commitment, defined by various factors such as engagement, satisfaction, loyalty, performance, and productivity. Commitment is highest when both personal and company values are well understood and are in alignment.
>
> *Key Strategy: Ensure your employees understand their own values and how they connect and contribute to those of the organization.*
>
> (*Source*: Aevitas Learning; University of Toyota)
>
> **Figure 10.1:** *Associate commitment*
> (Axes: Understand Toyota values / Understand my values)

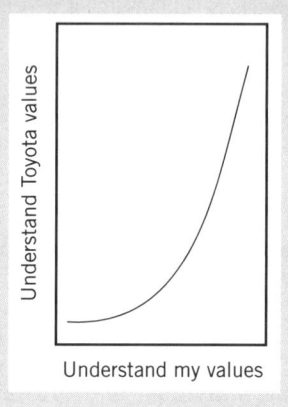

Toyota has a monumental goal of becoming the most respected and successful car company in the world. Toyota's executive leadership team knows that unless every employee walks through the door each day ready to engage fully, that kind of primacy will remain elusive. They know that when individual values are in play, their associates have access to their best personal resources, strengths, and abilities. They know that without any kind of deeper purpose or meaning, people simply won't pay attention to the corporate mission. They know that when employees are absolutely clear on their personal values, they are able to make choices based on principles. These principle-centered decisions bring significance and elevate the status of the work. They also set the foundation to move beyond narrow self-interests, to serve a greater good, and to establish a wide range of productive and meaningful relationships.

Dynamics of values

To tackle the values challenge, we need to understand how values work, how to create value-based alignment, and how to leverage the various levels of values. The concept of values is not a difficult one to grasp: *values are positive qualities held to be most inherently worthwhile and important by the holder.* No justification is required.

Values represent a wide spectrum of work and personal priorities, and provide the meaning we assign to the choices we make. Whenever we make important decisions, we rely on our most deeply held values. It's not a matter of whether or not values enter into the equation – they do.

Some of our values are inborn (e.g. "I have this great need for stability in my life"), some are acquired through experience or are influenced by others (e.g. "My dad always encouraged us to do our best"), and others still are chosen (e.g. "Valuing the diversity of others is the most important thing we can do in our organization").

Our values are unique to us, and we cannot assume others share our values. Within teams and organizations, a diversity of values exists. So, to work better as a team and make decisions that lead to commitment and action, it is first necessary to recognize the range of values that can influence decision making. While our values are dynamic and can change over time (this is true of individuals, groups, organizations, and, ultimately, society, both because the environment in which we live and work is always changing and because we are always developing our values), our most deeply held values tend to be rather stable, and stay clustered around a core theme.

Table 10.1: *Personal value themes*

MEANING	MASTERY	IMPACT	DUTY
Ethics	Progress	Results	Security
Authenticity	Vision	Adventure	Equity
Service	Excellence	Action	Standards
Unity	Competence	Variety	Order
Advocacy	Challenge	Play	Authority
Growth	Ideas	Exploration	Consistency
Causes	Influence	Autonomy	Dependability
Diplomacy	Logic	Achievement	Tradition
Inspiration	Ingenuity	Spontaneity	Community

Clarity and connection

The simple values definition offered goes far in explaining why, in a personal relationship, imposing our values on others generally leads to conflict. The same is true of corporate values. If what matters most to the individual competes in any way with what is most important to the company, conflict is inevitable. The typical executive edict related to values usually ends up backfiring – not for lack of good intention but for the lack of savvy or experience in properly executing a values-driven approach. The sad fact is that most people feel that they do not "belong" in their organizations in some way. While a sobering reality, it is one of the truths about working in organizations – to some degree we feel like we're outsiders.

This lack of connection creates a mental distance – the proverbial "disconnect" – between the person and the organization that can in turn foster feelings of detachment. The resulting huge impact on the organization manifests itself in the individual investing only a part of their available discretionary energy in their work. For the leader of any organization aiming for higher performance, the loss in potential productivity is staggering.

This brings us to the very real need to know how best to actively build the right kinds of connections at every level.

Table 10.2 is a simple matrix that shows the broader framework against which a values-centered approach can be applied. The logic behind it is simple. Values need to move from the organizational level down to the individual level (where the real power resides). They also need to move from being understood to being fully leveraged, as insight without action breeds cynicism.

Table 10.2: *The broader framework against which a values-centered approach can be applied*

	Understand	**Align**	**Leverage**
Organization	What are our overarching values?	Are our overall values evolving in response to market realities?	Are values part of the leadership agenda?
Teams	What are the values that are central to the work of the team?	Are our team values aligned to the organization's?	Are values part of the daily work of teams and business units?
Individuals	What do I stand for – what matters most?	Are my values fully aligned to the team values?	Do I feel empowered to act on my values?

Most organizations stop at the box in the upper-left corner (see matrix diagram), leaving the real strength of a values-driven approach untapped. Only when all of these questions can be answered will the true power inherent in the individuals and teams – and thus the organization as a whole – be fully realized.

The discovery process

The most common mistake made is in the activities surrounding the development of some kind of statement of values. Executive teams huddling in offsite meetings designed to produce a document miss the power of values entirely. The goal is not a deliverable, and the objective is not to post a set of values; rather, the focus should be to dig deep into the history and heritage of a company's strength and success to discover the true drivers.

When Toyota set out to codify "The Toyota Way," they spent months sifting through stories and speeches and significant events. The deeper they dug, the broader and more nebulous the critical success factors became. It went far beyond the vaunted Toyota Production System, far deeper than their widely studied quality methods. Finally, they arrived at two (yes, only two) core values: *continuous improvement* and *respect for people*. Every system, every product, every decision, every success the organization has ever had could be traced to these two deep and vague principles. In Toyota's world, the more vague and deep, the better, because it enables every individual to engage in discussions centered on interpreting the meaning of these values in their own way. The task became one of pursuing the nine boxes in the values matrix, and their efforts can be cited as a template for action.

Critical to the overall success of Toyota's values-based approach was the realization that the goal was not to induce adherence to a creed but to encourage a forum for dialog, discussion, and discovery of how each person's values can be met in the workplace – the end result of which would be a profound connection to the mission. Small workshops were conducted at all levels of the organization, centered first on putting every associate in touch with their own values, then showing how their values had contributed to Toyota's success, and finally how their personal values align to Toyota's. These discussions concluded with uniquely personal commitments to furthering The Toyota Way. In effect, each person became a keeper of the flame.

Over time, pursuing values in this manner creates the strong connections that not only help to create the context for higher levels of employee commitment and engagement but also counter the sometimes stressful forces of organizational life. In the end, values will always set the agenda. Understanding, aligning, and leveraging values – at the individual, team, and company levels – provides a true pathway for higher performance.

RESOURCES

May, Matthew, *Absolute Impact: The Drive for Personal Leadership*, Peloton Publishing, 2003.

The changing role of business

LANCE MOIR

[The issue of business responsibility to society has been present for many years, but is increasingly evident in the face of more demanding customers and a growing number of factors questioning the fundamental role of business.]

Corporate social responsibility (CSR) has become a hot topic, particularly for multinationals. There have been many instances over the past few years where firms have come under pressure for "irresponsible" actions – Shell's attempt to dump the Brent Spar oil rig in the North Sea, Nike's reported use of child labor, Nestlé's marketing of infant milk formula in the developing world, Premier Oil's decision to operate in Myanmar and then to sell its interests.

There are a number of factors at work here. First, consumers, and other stakeholders, are becoming more demanding. Second, there is greater visibility of business via the Internet and non-governmental organizations (NGOs) and lobby groups such as Amnesty International and Greenpeace. The use of the Internet has led to greater scrutiny and the impacts of globalization bring new pressures on the supply chain. A third factor is that investors now take a growing interest. Socially responsible investing, together with the launch of indices such as FTSE4Good and the Dow Jones Sustainability Group Index, is a big growth area.

In this changing environment, the social expectations of business mean that business has to pay more attention to its relationships with society and multiple stakeholders, rather than focus narrowly on maximizing shareholder value. The area defined by advocates of CSR increasingly covers a wide range of issues such as plant closures, employee relations, human rights, corporate ethics, community relations, and the environment. In this context, managers will have to manage the firm on behalf of all stakeholders, including the shareholder. As such, many directors will recognize this natural juggling act. In this environment the key issue is whether business is there just to make money for its owners, or whether business exists to meet broader social expectations, of which economic success is a part.

This perspective on business means that companies should not just focus solely on shareholder value, but also recognize that business is part of society and has responsibilities to society that go beyond the economic. This is essentially an issue of what John Elkington, one of the world's leading authorities on sustainable development, has described as the Triple Bottom Line, a requirement for business to pay attention to its impact not just economically but also on the environment and on society; this is also termed by Robert Rubenstein, founder and CEO of the Triple P Performance Center (a competence and training center for triple bottom line investing), as "people, profits, and planet."

Some firms, such as Johnson & Johnson, have taken this position for many decades. "The company's responsibilities are to be fair and honest, trustworthy, and respectful, in dealing with all our constituents," says J&J. Similarly, Volkswagen adopts a position which builds both shareholder value and workholder value in order to deliver "sustainable growth for the future." It defines CSR as "the ability of a company to incorporate its responsibility to society to develop solutions for economic and social problems." Indeed this is the goal of the EU, which aims to build the most dynamic economy, while maintaining social cohesion and sustainability.

Managing in a CSR environment

But do firms respond to this changing business environment and, if so, how? Proponents of CSR claim that it is in the enlightened self-interest of business to undertake various forms of CSR. The forms of business benefit that might accrue would include enhanced reputation and greater employee loyalty and retention. Simon Zadek, in *The Civil Corporation*, observes that there are four ways in which firms respond to CSR pressures:

- A defensive approach – to alleviate pain. Firms will do what they have to do to avoid pressure that makes them incur costs.
- A traditional cost–benefit approach – thus firms will undertake activities they can identify as a direct benefit.
- A strategic approach – thus firms will recognize the changing environment and engage with CSR as part of a deliberate emergent strategy.
- As an approach to innovation and learning – an active engagement with CSR will provide new opportunities to understand the marketplace and will enhance organizational learning and thus provide competitive advantage. This is the form of the new economy.

Zadek represents these approaches as fitting together to form a composite business case for CSR, as in Figure 10.2. Thus, the business case can be built up from a number of angles and there may be multiple reasons that fit together.

Firms are still largely at a reactive stage, where reputation and risk management are the key issues. Very few firms are engaging with CSR in a proactive manner. Part of the problem in moving toward this proactive approach could be to do with the competitive mindset. A number of commentators in the field of CSR have

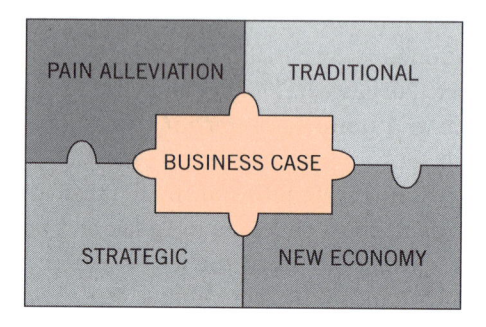

Figure 10.2: *The business case for CSR*

Source: Zadek, *The Civil Corporation* (2001)

observed that a necessary condition is to enter into trust-based relationships with stakeholders.

In this environment, firms will need to think of themselves as being part of a network in which value is created and where co-operation is more important. A way to think about the case for business for CSR is to move away from a purely business focus toward one that explores the impact and value on society, which then impacts further on business. Thus firms should not think narrowly about creating value for their shareholders and examine CSR initiatives in a pure instrumental manner where they think about "the business case for CSR" but move to a "case for business for CSR."

If business recognizes that it is part of society and is there to create value *for* society, it will be able to consider the value that is created both for the firm and for society by recognizing the impacts that business and society have on each other (see Figure 10.3).

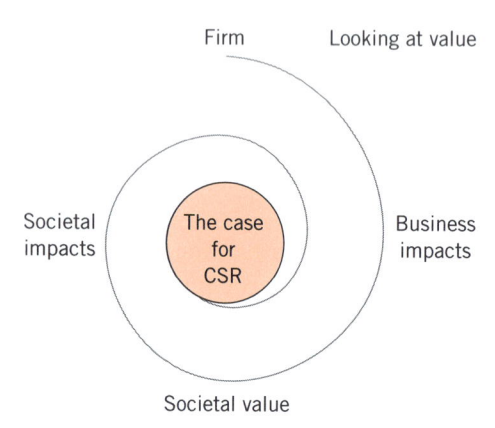

Figure 10.3: *How business and society impact on each other*

Some commentators suggest that all decisions can be mediated via the market mechanism and assessed against the impact on firm value. However, this does not match the reality of how managers actually manage.

It's all very well to say "maximize value," but for a manager confronted with a profitability target, sweatshop labor, and active NGOs, what does he or she actually do? In order to address this question, it is necessary to go back to the trust-based view of the firm's relationships with its stakeholders – almost a sense of social capital. In these types of situations, what is also needed is a set of guiding principles within which business operates. There are some standards, such as SA8000 on labor or more broadly the United Nations Global Compact. These help frame issues that some might regard as purely economic, such as the decision to move production to a low-cost area, only to find themselves confronted with new issues such as child labor.

Called to account

Companies are subject to increasing scrutiny and the environment within which they operate is changing, which is causing managers to re-examine the purpose of their firm within a wider society. This does not mean removing the need to be profitable and provide a return to shareholders, but it does mean having to think about business impacts on wider society and focussing on a wider range of objectives.

For some companies this may be true, for others it could be a learning exercise to lead to new business opportunities. Some firms may need to change their business focus, particularly if they intend to be around for a long time. For others, CSR becomes part of their business – for example, in the UK the Co-operative Bank has acknowledged that while its lending policies may mean lost business, they have become part of its strategy.

The pressures to be more accountable are growing. Larger firms are already reporting and those that do not may find that a push from European legislation will force them to report or else a pull from investors will make them pay attention. At the same time, press and NGO scrutiny brings pressures from different and unexpected angles. For some firms this will be a bolt-on activity; for others it will provide new strategic and learning opportunities. The issue appears to be not one of whether there is anything to do but one of how to integrate CSR issues into business practice.

RESOURCES

Beaumont, J., Pedersen, L.M. and Whitaker, B.D., *Managing the Environment*, Butterworth Heinemann, 1994.

Burrough, B. and Helyar, J., *Barbarians at the Gate*, Arrow, 1990.

Campbell, A. and Tawadey, K., *Mission and Business Philosophy*, Heinemann, 1990.

Cannon, Tom, *Corporate Responsibility*, FT Pitman, 1993.

Dearlove, Des and Coomber, Stephen, *Heart & Soul*, Blessing/White, 1998.

Demb, A. and Neubauer, F.F., *The Corporate Board*, Oxford University Press, 1993.

Donaldson, T., *The Ethics of International Business*, Oxford University Press, 1989.

Kanter, Rosabeth Moss, *Common Interest, Common Good: Creating Value Through Business and Social Sector Partnerships* (with Shirley Sagawa and Eli Segal), Harvard Business School Press, 1999.

Stewart, J.B., *Den of Thieves*, Simon & Schuster, 1991.

Zadek, Simon, *The Civil Corporation*, Earthscan, 2001.

REFERENCES

1. Trevino, L.K. and Nelson, K.A., *Managing Business Ethics – Straight talk about how to do it right* (3rd edition), Wiley, 2004.
2. McPhail, K., 'The other objective of ethics education: Re-humanizing the accounting profession – A study of ethics education in law, engineering, medicine and accountancy,' *Journal of Business Ethics*, 34: 279–298, 2001.
3. Ibid., p. 88.
4. Jackall, R., *Moral Mazes: The World of Corporate Managers*, New York: Oxford University Press, 1988.
5. Koehn, D., 'Traversing the inferno: A new direction for business ethics,' *Business Ethics Quarterly*, 10: 255–268, 2000.
6. Quotation in Punch, M., *Dirty Business: Exploring Corporate Misconduct*, London: Sage Publications, 1996.
7. Ramsbottom, B., *The Bottom Line: A Book of Business Ballads*, London: Century Publishing, 1985.
8. Ponemon, L.A., 'Ethical judgments in accounting: A cognitive developmental perspective,' *Critical Perspectives in Accounting*, 1: 191–215, 1990.
9. Ramsbottom, op. cit.

'Interview': Robert A.G. Monks

The founder of leading corporate governance consulting firm Institutional Shareholder Services on the abuse of power and reinventing the corporation for the future.

You don't fit the stereotype of an anti-capitalist protestor.

I would describe myself as a corporate reformer rather than anti-capitalist. My views are radical but I am not preaching revolution. Instead, what I am talking about is making the system work more efficiently and more fairly.

You have described the President as the ultimate CEO. Is this a good thing?

Not at all, it is a bad thing in the context of the United States. Since the Declaration of Independence one of our founding principles has been the distribution of accountable power. Our constitution disperses power.

Now we see that other sources of power have emerged – think of *The Oprah Winfrey Show*, for example. So what has happened is that the political model has been supplanted by an economic system in which authority is exercised along the lines of a totalitarian system. So we now have a President behaving in the autocratic and unaccountable way characteristic of CEOs and contrary to our best traditions. Corporatism has won. Corporate priorities are now routinely accepted as national priorities.

A CEO can go to war, but a political leader needs to be a lot more careful, getting the support of the public and other constituencies. It is messy and troublesome but it minimizes the risk of power being used stupidly. The CEO is the closest thing we now have to an absolute dictator.

There is no attempt to understand or explain where corporations fit in. Instead, there is morass of misunderstanding. I believe there can be no "philosophy" of corporations. They are legal creations, pure and simple. They are amoral, impersonal, and profit maximizing.

Hasn't the corporation long wielded power?

It's true that increasing corporate power and presence has been evident on many fronts. The influence of interest groups, for example, is nothing new in US politics. But what is new is the scale, how blatant it now is with the highest officials weaving between directorships and CEO jobs and high appointed and elected office. The reality is that the failure of leadership from those from whom it should be expected combined with government entropy has created a political crisis, a crisis of power filled by big corporations.

If you were to trace this back, when do you think the nature of CEOs began to change?

I would go back to the creation of the Business Roundtable in the 1970s. At the time the business community was having a miserable time having to deal with foreign competition, unions, regulators, and so on. Then John Connelly, the former governor of Texas, came up with the idea of the roundtable. The Business Roundtable didn't have a big Washington presence. There was no staff, just CEOs from large companies who were there by invitation only. The executive committee assigned projects to CEOs and then the CEOs went back to their companies and their staffs worked on the projects. So public issues were addressed using the best-paid executive resources.

The Business Roundtable was very effective. The CEOs argued as a group purportedly for their companies but also, effectively, for themselves. CEOs used it to bully the accounting profession so they withdrew their objections to options being issued without reflection on the profit and loss statement. As a result, CEOs gained a lot of money.

You think CEOs are overpaid?

Twenty years ago, CEOs were happy to receive salaries which were 30 to 40 times those of entry-level employees. Now a 1,000 times multiplier is common. This is simply the result of exercising power and is a reflection of the all-dominant corporatist ethic.

How will – or should – things change?

It is difficult to see how things will change. You can't really regulate a company from outside. If a government gets chesty about a corporation, the corporation will simply move outside the country. Look at the number of German automakers making cars in the US. Look at Scandinavian companies moving to the UK. So, as it is difficult to regulate, the limitation on power must come from within.

From the board of directors?

No, in the US boards are essentially cosmetic to forestall concerns about the absolute power of CEOs. They give the impression of acting like monitors. But boards are basically fig leaves. Look at the pattern of CEOs acting as presiding officers of the board. It doesn't matter who they are, it is impossible for someone to monitor their own conduct.

The real owners of corporate America are the institutions which represent 100 million mutual fund holders and pensioners and who own most of the voting equity in publicly held companies. They have an obligation to act as owners, to preserve and enhance value. They have been ignored, but increasingly they are activist owners. Now that's a real legitimate lever. After all, the owners aren't beholden to anyone.

However, they are financial conglomerates with many other business relationships with companies. Conflict of interest is the cancer which has immobilized the real owners of corporations. As a result, CEOs have become more powerful along the way and CEOs have destroyed teamwork in companies. It is the American way to ignore something, then ignore it some more.

Don't shareholders already have a forum?

The annual meeting is when companies have to listen to their owners. Indeed, it is the only time they are required to do so.

I attended the ExxonMobil annual general meeting and was given four minutes to speak. This was timed. After four minutes that was it. Considering my family have a few million dollars invested in the company I thought that was a bit much. I was very polite but referred to the CEO as an emperor – it seems to me CEOs have empires and entourages so are deserving of the title. They're not bad people (though some are) but a Darwinian species.

Would changing the title from CEO to an alternative be useful?

Semantics are very important. You hear intelligent people talking about things that are simply wrong. They talk, for example, of directors being elected. That's simply not true. If they are elected it is in elections akin to those in Eastern Europe in the Cold War years. Then we have leaders from some of the world's most respected institutions who simply don't and won't lead and a government which doesn't enforce laws.

Independent directors are an oxymoron because they are a group of self-selecting people. Having the status of a director is important to people. They are loyal to the rules of the club rather than to the shareholders. If an independent director is bumptious or truly independent they won't get work.

Doesn't decreasing CEO tenure suggest that the tide is turning?

Not necessarily. Amid the abuse of compensation one of the pieces is the arrangement by which people can leave early with huge benefits. We've actually provided a counter incentive to achieving long-term results.

So, change is required led by shareholders.

Yes, there are three areas where progress can, and needs to be, made. First, majority shareholders must persuade managers that effective accountability is essential to maintaining a corporate system. Second, government must recognize that getting more involvement from owners in the governance of public companies is critical. Third, the courts must recognize that viewing corporations as "persons" and offering them protection on that basis is wrong.

PART THREE

Management skills

– CHAPTER 1 –

Managing globally

"Tough domestic rivalry breeds international success."

Michael Porter

"There will be two kinds of CEOs who will exist in the next five years: those who think globally and those who are unemployed."

Peter Drucker

"International life will be seen increasingly as a competition not between rival ideologies – since most economically successful states will be organized along similar lines – but between different cultures."

Francis Fukuyama

"Think globally, act locally, think tribally, act universally."

John Naisbitt

Doing business the American way

ALLYSON STEWART-ALLEN

[The best way to successfully work with American business partners is to think like them. That means understanding and accepting their values and in particular their addiction to planning of all kinds.]

To understand a business culture requires an understanding of its values. Americans in business are a straightforward and direct group, especially helpful when trying to gain insights into what makes them tick. True to the national constitution, there are three things held dear in pursuit of the almighty business deal: life (read: having fun at work); liberty (read: having control and freedom over the work we do); and the pursuit of happiness (read: money).

Everyone knows that "time is money," everyone knows that you've got to "speculate to accumulate," and everyone knows that "the early bird gets the worm." Everyone also knows, too, that what enables these activities and business achievements to be had by anyone is the value we place on equality, freedom, and meritocratic distribution of the fruits of our labors.

What is astounding is the constancy of the business values in the US today – stable for the past several decades – which have so quickly flavored and integrated with the national values and cultures brought with the waves of immigrants starting their new lives. Those values are as follows.

Competition. There is a shared understanding that competition raises the stakes of the game and that winning brings sweet rewards. It is akin to playing tennis with a better player because you know you rise to their level. Our business language often looks to competitive sports for its inspiration: slam-dunk, home run, left field. The love of rankings is an indicator, too, of our love of competition: the *Fortune* 100; the 100 best companies to work for in America; the best bosses; the best business schools.

Win/win. This is one of the best and most productive approaches to most business opportunities since it works on the basis that both parties to a business deal emerge victorious. The rules of the US business game are clear: make as much money as you can, as fast as you can. This game theory approach perhaps comes from the economics of abundance rather than the economics of scarcity and invasions, so well-known in Asia and Europe. It's apparent in the language of business negotiations with phrases such as "how can we both make this work?" and "we're really excited about working with you on this." The downside of this approach, however, is the assumption by Americans in business that cash is the universal motivator and language of business. An appreciation that in most business cultures with which Americans work, winning is measured in more rounded ways (such as social inclusion, access to exclusive information) is often lacking.

Anything is possible. Americans believe that if you really want to pursue a business idea it's possible to make it happen and it's even possible you'll make good money trying. How will you recognize this? Because no matter how ludicrous an idea you present to your American boss or colleagues, it'll be given time and treated with respect. And we know from the history of business successes in the US (look at the success of pet rocks about 15 years ago and 3M's Post-It notes), some of the wackiest ideas really make it to the big time. The downside of this positive and optimistic outlook, however, is that those who raise concerns or reservations are usually viewed as negative, destructive, unhelpful, and launching personal attacks. Tact and well-structured objective arguments against will go a long way toward avoiding this perception.

Information is free. Phone any US company for your market research exercise and they'll not only usually answer your questions but also route you to additional information sources. It's unlikely you'll be asked why you want to know and you won't be grilled about who you are and any ulterior motives. Most American companies know that if *they* don't tell you the information about themselves you'll find the information elsewhere – such as via the Internet – and at least if you've gained the information from them, they are controlling the messages and the content. This openness and lack of suspicion come from a belief that it's not what you know or who you know, it's how you've used what you know. In Europe, on the other hand, companies are highly suspicious of the motives of any researcher or enquirer (and even customer) since power is derived by what you know and who you know it from.

Liberty and justice for all. This phrase, recited daily in American classrooms as part of the "pledge of allegiance," reflects the meritocratic, "all men are created equal" ethos that runs through the business culture. The classless society has proven that even those from the most humble beginnings can (and do) become business success stories. This belief in rags-to-riches is reinforced regularly in the stories about such people in *The New York Times, Wall Street Journal, Fortune* and *Business Week*. Which is in part why everyone's ideas and opinions count – because you don't know from where the next "killer app" might come. Calling the boss by his or her first name, wearing the same "smart casual" attire as the mailroom boy, cleaning out your own coffee cup regardless of your job title, not putting a list of academic qualifications on business cards, are all indications of the value placed on equality at work and the desire for equal treatment. It's even possible your boss is significantly younger than everyone else in the company (Steve Jobs at Apple, Jeff Bezos at Amazon, Bill Gates at Microsoft, for example).

Insular. In part because the number of weeks allowed for annual vacations is low in the US relative to other countries, true insights, empathy, and understanding of other national and business cultures is very weak. The negotiating power and confidence of non-Americans when striking a deal with a US partner is underpinned by the simple fact that Americans will know less about your country and business culture than you already know about theirs through the pervasive distribution of American TV, movies, and books (remember Michael Douglas' character, Gordon Gecko, in the film *Wall Street*?). The attitude toward non-American ways of doing business is generally intolerant: "that's different, so that's wrong." Speaking languages for business other than English and possibly Spanish is extremely rare and most Americans in business who do venture to foreign climes seek out local and familiar destinations: US hotel and car rental chains and US food chains. It's based on the belief that anything you could possibly want materially is already found in America so why look elsewhere? A tip for your next US meeting: bring a map of your region and show your colleagues where your London and other offices are, explaining that the region is not like a United States of Europe but rather richer for its histories and cultures.

Welcoming. Despite the insularity of Americans in business, the openness, informality, optimism, humor, curiosity, and friendliness instantly put most people at ease. This is especially helpful when coming from business cultures with steep class hierarchies and formal rituals. Humor is a tool subconsciously used to relax the mood and build an atmosphere of friendliness and informality. Because of the belief that anything *is* possible in American business, this optimism carries over to your relationship too: the glass will be half full rather than half empty. Don't be surprised if your American opposite number suggests that the "problems" you foresee are actually "opportunities."

Transactions rule. Doing the deal is more important than building relationships and getting to know the other parties to the deal. This is apparent when beginning negotiations with your American colleagues, who may forget to offer you tea or coffee since the transaction is dominant in their minds – which might explain why so many bring their own Starbucks coffees along with them. (I advise my own clients not to take this single-minded focus too personally.) The small-talk that comes with relationship building is usually saved for the end of the negotiations. After all, "time is money" and transactions not only give more immediate rewards (a high return on time) but also deliver short-term positive commercial results at a faster pace than do relationships. Which *is* at odds with the usual American focus on all things to do with the future.

Live to work. Generally, your occupation defines who you are in the US and gives you a branding and positioning despite your best efforts. Renowned for the 60-hour week, Americans in the world of business relish the satisfaction that comes from a good day's work – a sort of cleansing of the spirit, answering that Puritan calling. One way you can recognize this tendency toward overachievement is by the display of trophies, diplomas, sports medals, and awards in the office, demonstrating the love of work and reinforcing the ethos that hard work pays off. Another clue is a statistic from a survey by consultants Accenture in 2000 that 83 percent of US office workers who went on a summer vacation for a week or more stayed in touch with their offices while away, usually by phone or e-mail.

The urge to plan

But what's the context of these values? In what types of corporate situations will you be exposed to them? The likeliest and earliest experience you'll probably encounter is planning, one of our most fundamental business needs. The strength and depth of this urge is probably most closely linked to our heritage: the immigrants who left behind their economies of scarcity. By planning, you could plot your way to having a share of the scarce resources such as food, shelter, education, and jobs. Recent trends give added importance to planning and the need to blueprint our futures, such as the disappearance of the job for life, the receding social security nets to look after employees in their golden years, and, of course, unpredictable acts of terrorism. Where a few decades ago the optimism of US business was that life would still get even better, we now live in a more sober era of downsizing, restructuring, and unpredictability.

Our perception is that if you're not first in the race to conquer your environment, to stake your claim in the "manifest destiny" then it's not worth doing. The pace of commerce is fast and our frontier spirit is alive and well. Mastering one's destiny is a shared cultural view, an insight into our deterministic culture. We believe we *do* control most (if not all) of our environment and that through planning of any kind we can master the elements in our environment. Fatalism is the old world; determinism is the new.

Why we plan

According to the cross-cultural commentator Richard Lewis in his book *When Cultures Collide*, the American business philosophy is plain: to make as much money as fast as you can. And one of the best ways of doing so is through lots of very good planning. Everything in our culture is goal-oriented and action-oriented with a perceived meritocratic pay-off of results-based rewards.

The construction of plans is a valued behavior in our culture; it's not that *not* planning is destructive but not planning is viewed as being poorly organized and a signal that winning the race is not that important to you.

Another driver of planning in US companies is the linkage of personal performance to organizational performance – a management practice known as "performance management." By ensuring company goals (a by-product of the planning process) and individual goals are interdependent, US enterprises try to ensure individual acknowledgement and rewards stay merit-based. For some companies, planning for performance is about planning for fun. In an interview in *Fast* magazine Mona Cabler, director of fun at telecoms company Sprint, asserted that "fun and work are mutually reinforcing," adding "when [US] companies say they're employee centered, they usually mean centered on helping employees achieve the company's goals. We emphasize helping individuals achieve their personal goals."

Accelerating decision making is one of our favorite past-times since this fuels our need to take action, to *do* things. Sports company Nike's long-serving strapline "Just Do It" is evidence of this strong need, communicated very well.

Other motives for our planning include avoidance of the accusation that we're following a "seat-of-the-pants" strategy – an irresponsible, profligate, unfocussed, unmethodical set of steps toward pursuing the Holy Grail of business: profits. In order to responsibly allocate our corporate resources, be they human, cash, or intellectual property, planning helps us believe we've done so in a considerate way. The planning process also helps us believe we'll minimize our risk of becoming just another statistic in the graveyard of failed corporate missions – our "plan or die" ethos must prevail.

The prioritizations that result from planning – making and communicating choices – are ingrained in Americans in business from an early age. We're taught these skills early in life and to believe decisiveness means proactiveness, that indecision brings loss of control. With decisiveness comes a perception of self-reliance and independence. "The buck stops here" religion reveals the importance we attach to making independent decisions, whether for business or private life.

We also plan – alone or with a team – in order to construct the business case that lets us win budgets, increased territory, authority and recognition from our peers. He who crafts the plan usually controls the resource purse.

Types of planning

The variety of categories of plan in use reveal the pervasiveness of the practice. Strategic, operational, contingency, business, and financial planning add fuel to the driver of the idea, the entrepreneur (the patron saint of US business). It permeates every aspect of our life at work and at home. When not planning what to do for lunch, we'll plan our holidays, our investment strategies, our careers, our parties, and even our life. As if further evidence is needed, an entire industry, "life planning," has emerged in the US over the last seven years with counselors helping busy workers to juggle the demands of home and work, to prioritize life's demands for a happier, healthier, shinier, longer existence.

There's a relatively new category posited by US calendar manufacturer Franklin Covey called the "personal productivity planner," which allows you to plan gift-giving occasions using its online reminder service. Franklin Covey, one of the leading personal desktop calendar manufacturers, conducted research in the last few years to better understand how Americans plan. It found that over 50 percent use a calendar, 30 percent notebook-style organizers, and that over 80 percent make lists. Nearly 75 percent say they "always or frequently" know what they want to accomplish in life, nearly 40 percent have written financial goals, and about 33 percent have written career goals.

The vocabulary of battle is often prevalent when Americans engage in planning. They get armed or equipped; lead or defend; attack competitors; win customers; slaughter the competition; win the war. Whatever strategy is employed, clear winners and losers are likely to emerge. There's also the planning acronyms: MBO (management by objectives), SWOT (strengths/weaknesses/opportunities/threats), and STEP analysis (sociocultural/technological/economic/political).

Another phrase that's successfully taken root, thanks to the long best-selling Stephen Covey book *Seven Habits of Highly Effective People*, is that we should "begin with the end in mind" – a plea to visualize the prize that comes with good planning. But to seize the prize, a well-constructed "business case" – an often-heard phrase – shows how the ROI (return on investment) can be achieved.

Who does all this planning?

Planning is typically an event, a project usually done in purposefully formed teams whose prime source of cohesion is the need to complete the planning task at hand. There's no real need to get to know one another, just to collaborate on the planning event to produce a lucid series of arguments to support the business case. If true friendship results, then this is a fantastic bonus.

Usually junior-level management and above, across all functional departments and SBUs (strategic business units) participate on a planning team of one sort or another. Often the group is managed like a sports team, which can alienate women members not familiar with locker-room pep talks or sports analogies.

It is often an impersonal, routine, and regular activity, usually quarterly – borne out of our cultural needs for independence and objectivity – which often hinders the creation of true teamwork. The schism between self-reliant, independent professionalism, and wanting to be popular with the planning team is often a challenge, as task-leaders and emotional-leaders hardly ever exist within the same individual.

Even the best laid plans…

… do go wrong. Especially when it comes to US companies trying to grow in overseas territories. Despite our intense hunger for "factoids" (thanks to CNN for this word), figures, and almanac trivia, doing in-country research abroad is an often-neglected part of the planning activities. It's often unlikely that anyone employed by a US company physically sited within the 50 states speaks that local language or profoundly understands that local culture. It's very often just too difficult to plan for more substantive information gathering since no one locally understands such far-flung places.

The marketing graveyard of misnaming (Chevrolet's "Nova" automobiles became "doesn't go" in Spanish-speaking markets), slogan mistranslations (Kentucky Fried Chicken's long-term strapline "Finger lickin' good" became "So good you'll suck your fingers off" in Chinese) and other international blunders are proof of such planning omissions.

Thus, the American company will often assume it must be a lot like America and will enter and grow that market accordingly. These frequent approaches are what keep the business consultants, accountants, and lawyers a very happy group of guides.

Decision making

Planning the "attack" on the market is the front-end of the business cycle; selling it internally with decision-making colleagues is the critical, implementation part of the planning process that allows us to demonstrate our acute "action" skills. This hunting/gathering view of business planning encourages the masculine, macho behaviors often seen during this cycle of business activity.

According to some keen observations put forward in a *Harvard Business Review* article ("What you don't know about decision making" by David Garvin and Michael Roberto, September 2001), most US business professionals see planning as an event, a contest rather than a collaborative problem-solving process – with team discussions serving as a platform for demonstrating skills in persuasion and lobbying.

The team members charged with taking the decisions about a plan typically play the role of spokesmen, advocating a clear position, aiming to convert the rest of the organization, defending their collective point of view, and playing down any weaknesses in their arguments. While minority views are tolerated, they're usually discouraged or dismissed. The result: clearly identifiable winners and losers emerge as a result of the decision as opposed to a cadre of winners who share collective ownership. Because planning is a one-off event, it minimizes the *quality* of decision making by ensuring it is not an on-going, iterative process. Instead, the event, with its finite start/stop, can take on a significance, drama, and status all its own.

The resistance to overt conflict means decisions are often the least well informed of all possible routes, scenarios, or options, which do not get debated by the team. Once a decision is made, rarely is it re-examined during the fiscal year since this could imply possible mistakes or omissions and loss of face and embarrassment for those who took the decision. After all, there are reputations to uphold.

Our view as a culture that dissent is destructive means that there's a bias in favor of those who support a team decision and advocate it. Members who question a decision and the assumptions it is built upon are viewed as negative, unhelpful, politically motivated, subjective, and are often unpopular as future team members.

Might this be one of the less attractive values that allows dysfunctional cultures such as Enron, Tyco, and WorldCom to exist? Quite possibly. But it's also the force that *quickly* mobilizes teams and implements plans. Let's not forget, after all, one of our fundamental values: "time is money."

RESOURCES

Stewart-Allen, Allyson and Denslow, Lanie, *Working with Americans*, FT Prentice Hall, 2002.

Trompenaars, Fons and Hampden-Turner, Charles, *Riding the Waves of Culture*, Nicholas Brealey, 1997.

Commentary

The art of Swedish leadership

No less an expert than Jack Welch has observed that "pound for pound, Sweden probably has more good managers than any other country." And management Swedish-style is profoundly different from that practiced elsewhere in the world. So what can the Swedes teach the rest of us?

For a start they are informal. They were turning up for work in polo shirts and chinos long before the inhabitants of Silicon Valley – though they tend to have more protective layers to keep out the cold.

Getting hold of the CEO of any decent-sized US corporation isn't easy. There is a secretary or PA to get past. They will try to send you elsewhere. Eventually, you might get to speak with the CEO, but it usually takes persistence and patience. In Sweden CEOs are likely to answer their own phones. They then talk as if they have time to spare.

The media presentation of business leaders is also notably different in Sweden. While American CEOs become corporate touchstones, icons, their Swedish counterparts like Kurt Hellström of Ericsson or Leif Johansson of Volvo remain studiously anonymous. The Swedes like their heroes unheralded. The adulation heaped on ABB's Percy Barnevik ("Europe's Jack Welch") in the 1990s or on SAS's Jan Carlzon in the 1980s made them slightly uncomfortable. The media hype was altogether un-Swedish.

The lack of managerial layers, the informal air of professionalism, and the air of sophisticated affluence, gives the foreign visitor the distinct impression that Sweden is a can-do culture. Not so fast. While the Swedes have the systems and the attitudes in place to allow them to do things with reckless, risk-defying speed, they choose not to. "Just do it" does not quite work in Sweden. The typical Swedish edict is "See what you can do about it" rather than Nike's call to arms.

Swedish leadership is about consensus and empowering people. It is about harmony. Swedes hate conflict – witness their historical role as peace-makers and arbiters. In their desire for harmony there are parallels with the Japanese. The two cultures share a belief in the importance of the group or the team ahead of the individual. Sweden is, after all, a solidly social democratic nation. Even its hugely successful vodka brand Absolut is state-owned.

Contrast this with the US or the UK where there is a highly individualistic culture, where kids learn from a young age to stand up for themselves, to seek out attention, and to compete with their peers. In Sweden, the reverse is true. Kids are expected to be average (though the Swedish word *lagom* sounds a lot better than average), and the school system dampens down any naturally competitive instincts. In Sweden there is a joke about a clothing size called "extra medium" which is supposed to fit the entire nation.

And clothing is important to Swedes. They like to dress in black but it has to be the right shade of black. For a nation that venerates engineers – "Being a 50-year-old engineer is something we dream of!" one bright young thing said – the Swedes are highly fashion conscious. They love technological wizardry. Sweden has been labeled the most "future ready" country in the world. Seventy percent of people have Internet access. Mobile telephone penetration is close to 100 percent.

In addition, Sweden punches above its weight in the worlds of design and entertainment. It is a creative economy. Among other things, the Swede Max Martin is responsible for penning Britney Spears' hits.

To this cultural mix, you can add the Swedes' high level of *tolerance of uncertainty* – the ability to ride the rollercoaster of life without fear of crashing or falling off. Swedes are less resistant to change, more able to accommodate new ways of thinking, and more tolerant of foreigners. This final factor has proved crucial. Rather than exporting their way of doing things wholesale, the Swedes have a knack of fitting in. In a world of would-be globalists, Swedes are the genuine article.

When it comes to producing cosmopolitan companies, Sweden is remarkably successful – the only worthwhile European comparisons are with Switzerland and the Netherlands. Swedish companies transcend boundaries in ways few others can manage. Internationalization is in the Swedish genes. Exports account for 40 percent of Sweden's GDP. Transfers to foreign subsidiaries have long been regarded as important learning opportunities rather than demotions. Many Swedes end up spending decades overseas, though most return home sooner or later.

Thanks to this apparently random mix of global perspectives, informality, a yearning for consensus, fashion consciousness, and a generally low-key approach, Sweden has more large companies per head of population than any other country in the world. Many of them are still independent world leaders in their chosen sectors – Ericsson in mobile infrastructure, Sandvik in tooling, Electrolux in white goods. Swedish management and leadership, in other words, offers something both undeniably different and effective. And the bottom-line is simple: it works.

Global account management

H. DAVID HENNESSEY

> Global Account Management was introduced by professional service firms over 20 years ago, as accounting, advertising, and consulting firms saw a major benefit in co-ordinating the sales and service effort for large global customers. With customers and organizations becoming more global, new organizational structures to service global customers have emerged. The most common new structure is the global account management program.

As more and more companies attempt to adopt a global account management organizational structure, the limitations and shortcomings become clearer. Global account management (GAM) has been shown to be very successful in certain situations. But it is difficult and expensive to implement.

Much has been written about the experience of companies using global account management. This knowledge has been augmented by a number of studies on global account management. The outcome of these writings has been the development of a set of key success factors (KSFs) for global account management. These are accepted by most experts and practitioners. They include:

- the process of selecting global accounts;
- the need for a global information technology system;
- the process of selecting global account managers;
- the need for appropriate compensation and metrics;
- the global account management process; and
- the need for high-level executive support of a global account management system.

In one survey of the executives who manage their companies' global account management programs, we found that these KSFs were acknowledged and supported by leading practitioners. However, when looking at the process of creating value through global account management, we found that there were other factors, which were not widely known.

Global account management is an organizational structure designed to better serve global customers. Underlying this objective, the global account management system must create new value for the global accounts. This paper reviews the KSFs of global account management and focusses on the underlying or hidden factors which contribute to the creation of real value.

Senior management commitment

A global account management program needs senior management commitment for three reasons. First, global customers expect to meet with senior managers from their key vendors on a regular basis. Second, to allocate the appropriate people and resources to global account management, the program needs senior management support. This will often require moving key people and resources from countries and regions to a global account unit which may be geographically located near their global account headquarters.

Finally, the place where senior management commitment adds the most value is in the indirect support of the global account manager. The global account manager can be a person, a portion of a person, or a team of people, often located in the country where the customer is headquartered. For the global account manager to create value for the global account, this executive must co-ordinate activities across geographic and business units. The ability to accomplish these tasks is a direct function of senior management commitment. Without this management commitment, the global account manager will not have sufficient clout to co-ordinate and direct activities across the traditional division and geographic organizational structures.

For example, Reuters' global account management program was driven by senior management. All team members involved in the global account management program reported directly to a senior vice president. At Xerox, at the end of a quarter, lead sales representatives may want to see a few additional units at a discounted price to a global account but everyone knows the commitment the company has to global accounts, and therefore resists the temptation.

Selecting global accounts

Global customers with major operations in three or more continents are important because of their sales volume. These customers will often ask to be treated globally especially regarding pricing, which they want to be low. However, companies with global account programs have found that not all global customers make good global accounts. The potential global accounts need to meet a minimum revenue level, so the relationship can afford the overhead of global account management. Marriott International requires potential global accounts purchase over $25 million annually from hotels. While customers often desire to become a global account to reduce prices, vendors anticipate a global account program will differentiate a vendor and result in increased sales volume. Most companies tend to have 20 to 30 global accounts; however, Xerox and IBM both have over 100. The primary reason to limit the number of global accounts is to maintain the necessary focus.

The really critical factor in account selection is to select accounts where the relationship is strategically important to both parties. For example, does the vendor have over 50 of the customer's sales in product category, and is the product somehow important to the customer. The critical issue is that the vendor and customer must be willing to share business issues, and potential product development efforts, so that there is an opportunity to create real value. The talk about partnership and strategic relationship is everywhere, but not all companies are willing to open up, so real value can be created.

Information technology infrastructure

A KSF for global account management is the need for a robust information technology system which may include a global customer relationship management system. Of course a sophisticated global IT system is needed to track progress of a global account in terms of orders, back orders, shipments, accounts payable, complaints, returns, etc. The people serving the global account need this information to manage the account. These same people also need a sophisticated system to record what is happening within different parts of the global account. Finally, the people working on the account need to be able to communicate with each other. At DSM Engineering Plastics, global customers often comment that the DSM global account manager knew more about what was happening at the company than the global purchasing people knew about their own firm.

However, the real importance of the robust IT system comes from the way it creates value for the customer. For example, at Marriott International which serves IBM, the global account manager was able to track globally the conference cancellations of IBM. The cancellations cost IBM over $1 million. The Marriott International account manager was able to create an internal electronic bulletin board for IBM employees to purchase canceled space, therefore reducing IBM cancellation fees.

Selection of global account managers

The successful global account management program will always have high quality global account managers. Therefore, it is not surprising that companies report the selection of global account managers to be one of the KSFs for global account management. Global account managers need to be able to build relationships with

CEOs, COOs, and senior executives. The global account manager also needs to be perceived as a respected senior manager within their own organization, so they can co-ordinate and direct activities of others who may not be under the global account manager's authority. As global account managers will interact with individuals from both the customer and vendor from multiple cultures, it is expected they will be able to build and maintain trusted relationships across diverging cultures, geographies, and economies.

The biggest mistake in selecting global account managers is the assumption that all good national account managers can be good global account managers. This is not the case. Many national account managers do not have the cross-cultural skills and the broader business skills to be a successful global account manager.

The really critical skill needed by global account managers is the ability to analyze an industry, understand competitive strategies, and identify scenarios where a vendor can contribute to a customer's strategy. The skills of a global account manager may be more closely aligned with a general manager than with a senior salesperson.

Measurement, metrics, and rewards

The sales function has always included some form of measurement, metrics, and rewards tied to sales, profit, or market share. Therefore, it is not surprising that measurement, metrics, and rewards are a KSF for global account management. Marriott International, Xerox, Steelcase, and IBM all have some measurement system to track the sales of the global account and the implied result of the global account management effort. Of course, this may cause some tension between the global account manager and the regional or local manager, unless the vendor has some form of double counting. A number of vendors also track market share, completion of identified projects, and customer satisfaction.

All of these metrics attempt to measure the success of the vendor with the global customer. However, the underlying success of any global account management system is the impact it has on the customer's strategy and profitability. Only through understanding the customer's industry, the customer's strategy, and the vendor's role in supporting the strategy, will real value be measured.

Global account planning process

The global account planning process is acknowledged as a KSF for global account management. The global account planning process sets clear objectives for the global account and aligns the necessary resources to implement the plan. Given that the account is global, the account planning process also allows vendor sales from around the world to interact and identify additional ways to serve the global account. Often, the sales managers within the countries where the customer operates are included in the global account planning process, so their country plans and goals are aligned with the global account plan.

The global account planning process is critical to understanding the global account and determining how to add value. To maximize the global account planning process, it is very important that the customer be involved in the process. Maersk Sealand holds a global sales meeting, which includes the customer in setting goals and action plans for the year.

A weakness of many account plans is that they focus on projects and volumes. The result is a set of actions based on how the vendor can get a larger share of the potential volume of the account through improved technical service or improved customer service. This is not the best approach. The real value creation comes from understanding the customer's industry, the customer's strategy within the industry, and the opportunity for the vendor to contribute to the strategy.

For example, a global coating supplier sold a sophisticated coating used on extruded products. The product needed to be coated as soon as it was extruded to enhance the product's capability. Manufacturing lines were extremely expensive and proprietary. When the coating manufacturer studied the industry which the extruded product was used in, it determined it was a high-growth industry, where its customer had a high price and high quality, but capacity was limited. As the coating manufacturer understood the industry, it realized it could speed up the application of the coating on the extruded product and therefore increase the extruder's capacity and its customer profitability.

Global account management is a new organizational form designed to better serve global customers. While there are some similarities with national account management programs, the real value comes from understanding the customer from a global perspective. When DSM Engineering Plastics found its largest customer was losing its share to lower quality parts made in China, they were able to understand how the industry was changing. Within a year both DSM and the customer had built facilities in China. DSM has also developed a specific color additive which cannot be replicated by other manufacturers, therefore eliminating the threat of lower quality copied products.

RESOURCES

Hennessey, H. David and Jeannet, J.P., *Global Marketing Strategies*, Houghton Mifflin, 2004.

Hennessey, H. David and Jeannet, J.P., *Global Account Management: Creating Value*, Wiley, 2003.

❝ Interview ❞: John Micklethwait and Adrian Wooldridge

The authors of Future Perfect discuss the reality of globalization.

Gathering together the disparate strands of globalization has proved beyond many others. Is globalization simply too complex and chaotic to be fully understood?

JM: There is some truth in this. The things that push globalization are especially chaotic. Small things matter extraordinarily. But that does not mean that globalization is spinning out of control. Too often that is used by politicians as an excuse for doing nothing. Without political will, globalization runs into trouble.

AW: There are a number of myths which surround globalization. The first is that globalization is driven by giant companies and international institutions conspiring together to run the world. Not so. The other myths are that globalization is ushering in an age of global products; that it has ended the traditional business cycle; that globalization is a zero-sum game (in which some people have to lose so that others can win); and that it means that geography does not matter. Beyond the mythology, globalization is about individuals making decisions. Globalization is, and has to be, driven by men and women in the street.

Isn't globalization concentrating power in the hands of a global elite?

AW: We talk of the rise of a class of cosmocrats – perhaps 20 million people worldwide. This class is in the process of forming. It is made up of people who have similar global lifestyles and who possess the ideas, connections, and sheer chutzpah to master the international economy. It is a formally meritocratic class produced by Western education systems and companies. Yet, while there is a great feeling among Western educated people that their values are universal, their institutions are not very good at reaching out to the developing world. Western educational institution and companies should be reaching out to recruit the talented people from developing countries.

JM: We expect the number of cosmocrats to approximately double by 2010. Within the Western world the numbers of people expected to be international is growing. The increase in technology will clearly also contribute. The next significant factor is that huge populous nations such as China, India, and Brazil will begin producing their own cosmocrats.

Does managing globalization require new, highly complex management tools and techniques?

AW: Back to basics is not a bad slogan in the dot-com world and the same applies to the globalized world. If companies ignore basic principles they can be doomed. Even so, globalization is incredibly difficult to manage and, for most managers, it is usually more a source of fear than of excitement. First, global management has to be multicultural. Second, it involves mixing and matching skills and ideas from different parts of the world. What will drive companies to be global will be their ability to take the best skills and ideas from wherever they are in the world.

JM: If something doesn't make sense under national management it will be a disaster globally. Companies sometimes fail to export their domestic best practice – for example, Sony should have applied the same managerial standards outside Japan as it did inside Japan. The more you look at how companies operate globally you see that being small and nimble works very well. Technology makes this readily available. One company which has handled globalization particularly well is GE. It has worked very hard at it. Yet, if you look around GE headquarters nearly all the people are American. Over the next 20 years an entire generation of cosmocrats will shape companies like GE. The change will be dramatic.

Is the business world generally in favor of globalization?

AW: Business people are never in favor of open markets and competition; they are in favor of monopolies! At an individual level, business people can be suspicious of globalization. But, on the whole, business people know that market competition and globalization is the way to go.

JM: It is a fragile coalition. In general most people are pro-free trade and globalization – but not in their specific industry.

You are particularly critical of Silicon Valley. How come?

JM: Silicon Valley needs to be measured against the standards of industrial clusters. If you look at history, clusters often disappear. Some, like Hollywood, survive. Many have also been unpleasant places – look at Detroit in the 1970s. There are industrial reasons why Silicon Valley will lose ground. The Valley has a fascination with cool ideas rather than products. And, over time, more suits will move in. Some elements of the social divide in Silicon Valley are not acknowledged. There are also infrastructure problems which will not be solved by the next cool idea.

AW: While Silicon Valley is good at creating wealth, it is less good at doing something with this wealth. One of the great aims of the book is to issue a wake-up call to techno-determinists who believe technology is doing everything.

Is globalization a force for good?

JM: It can be. Globalization exaggerates weaknesses and strengths. It hands power to individuals but it also increases inequality. While some people are left behind, millions more leap ahead. The winners hugely outnumber the losers. It can make bad government worse, but the onus should be on crafting better government, rather than blaming globalization. While it curtails some of the power of nation-states, they remain the fundamental unit of modern politics. Globalization is not destroying geography, merely enhancing it.

❛ Interview ❜: Fons Trompenaars

The consultant and expert on cross-cultural issues focusses on how to deal with the complexities of managing across cultures.

You speak frequently about "cultural reconciliation." What does this mean?

Simply put, it refers to the necessity of reconciling the host of cultural differences between employees; or, for that matter, citizens of a country. Reconciled cultures have created a culture of their own by enriching the cultures of the partners involved. Organizations and societies that can reconcile cultural differences better are better at creating wealth. It's as simple as that.

That sounds reasonable. Why is it so difficult to accomplish?

Culture is a series of rules and methods that a society has evolved to deal with the recurring problems it faces. They have become so basic that, like breathing, we no longer think about how we approach or resolve them. Every country and every organization faces dilemmas in relationships with people, dilemmas in relationship to time, and dilemmas in relationships between people and the natural environment. Mix and match people from different cultures, who interpret such issues diversely, and you have organizational chaos that has to be managed differently than other organization issues.

Cultural mixing is an everyday feature of organizational life, especially in these times of huge corporate acquisitions, mergers, and alliances. Relational aspects like cultural differences and lack of trust are responsible for 70 percent of alliance failures. This is even more striking when we realize that building trust is a cultural challenge in itself. Lack of trust is often caused by different views of what constitutes a trustworthy partner. In addition, intercultural alliances involve differences in corporate cultures as well as national cultures. Perceptions of these, as well as of more-or-less "objective" cultural variations, can lead to big problems.

Is there a way to predict typical sorts of clashes that might arise in a large alliance or merger?

There are seven continua that characterize the predictable dilemmas in need of reconciliation. Universalism-Particularism is the battle over standardized rules versus flexibility; Individualism-Communitarianism is the question of what the organization most promotes: individualism or group cohesiveness; Neutral-Affective is the question of emotional control versus emotional display; Specific-Diffuse asks how personally involved in business the employee is; Achievement-Ascription is the organization's stance on status based on merit as opposed to other factors, such as age or family background; Sequential-Synchronic refers to time orientation – whether employees deal with time (and projects) sequentially or in parallel, juggling multiple projects simultaneously; and Internal-External Control is a question of motivation – whether it tends to come from within or outside of the person.

In the case of a merger or alliance, when faced with cultural differences, how should the organizations respond?

One effective approach is to compare the two profiles to identify where the major differences originate. In practice, the major origin of cultural differences between your organization and the new partner may lie in the most dominant one or two cultural dimensions. By reconciling the dilemmas deriving from the differences on the dimensions, organizations can begin to reconcile their cultural orientations.

Your ideas suggest a radical redesign of the manager's job, especially international managers.

Absolutely! How international managers reconcile differences is the very essence of their job. The international manager needs to go beyond awareness of cultural differences. He or she needs to respect these differences and take advantage of diversity through reconciling cross-cultural dilemmas.

For example?

Consider the fundamental differences between the universalist and the particularist. Universalists (including Americans, Canadians, Australians, and the Swiss) advocate "one best way," a set of rules that applies in any setting. Particularists (South Koreans, Chinese, and Malaysians) focus on the peculiar nature of any given situation. Universalists doing business with particularists should, for example, be prepared for meandering or irrelevancies that do not seem to be going anywhere; moreover, they should not take "get to know you chatter" as small talk. It is important to particularists.

Particularists doing business with universalists should be prepared for straightforward, no-nonsense, rational and professional arguments and presentations. We need a certain amount of humility and a sense of humor to discover cultures other than our own, a readiness to enter a room in the dark and stumble over unfamiliar furniture until the pain in our shins reminds us of where things are. Most managers, it seems, are more intent on protecting their shins than blundering through darkened rooms.

Do any success stories come to mind?

Executives like Jim Morgan of Applied Materials, Karel Vuursteen from Heineken, Acer's Stan Shih, Anders Knutsen of Bang and Olufsen, and Club Med's Philippe Bourguignon have typically resolved three or more of these dilemmas. A great example is McDonald's. Its recent success has been built through globalizing local learning. During the Asian crisis it found it couldn't import potatoes into Malaysia so it re-introduced rice on to the menu. This was a great success so it tried it out elsewhere in the world. It worked.

All of your examples are men.

We did have difficulty finding women leaders for the leadership book. First of all, there aren't that many female senior executives, and the first 25 we approached to be interviewed all said that they were too busy. Men said the same but usually relented. The women did not. Our conclusion is that they are less vain. Too bad because they seem to be better reconcilers than men.

How can an alliance predict intercultural dilemmas?

Our team has developed a methodology that we call Cultural Due Diligence. This provides an operational framework intended to be facilitated by the HR directorate to make these cultural differences tangible so that their consequences can be made explicit and thereby reconciled to ensure benefit delivery. It is based on the three Rs: recognition, respect, and reconciliation.

Recognition, respect, and reconciliation refer, essentially, to what?

The first task for human resources is to help all players recognize that there are cultural differences, their importance, and how they impact organizational life. The second task is to demonstrate to organizational members that different cultural orientations and views of the world are not right or wrong – they are just different. And the third task is to demonstrate the growing conviction that wealth is created in alliances (including mergers and acquisitions) by reconciling values. This is a new contribution to the debate on alliances and mergers in business. Cultural due diligence is the means to bring about reconciliation of these seemingly opposing views.

The human resources professional, then, plays a central role in the success of any corporate alliance?

It is a pre-requisite that HR professionals are engaged in the integration process as early as possible. Unfortunately, in many situations their expected contribution often is limited to developing an early retirement scheme for those people who become redundant because of the expected economies of scale of the integration. In our experience HR professionals can play a crucial role in the facilitation of a successful reconciliation of cultures. They need to become "culture coaches" facilitating the basic processes of post- and pre-merger integration. They are in the best position in the organization to link HR activities to the inherent and overt strategy of the alliance or merger.

For the manager, then, cultural due diligence accomplishes what?

This approach will inform managers how to guide the social side of alliances of any kind. It has a logic that integrates differences. It is a series of behaviors that enables effective interaction with those of contrasting value systems. It reveals a propensity to share understanding of others' positions in the expectation of reciprocity and requires a new way of thinking that is initially difficult for Westerners. Put differently, international success in alliances depends upon discovering special veins of excellence within different cultures. Just because people speak English does not mean they think alike. That no two cultures are the same is what brings richness and complexity to multi-nationalism. Cultural due diligence gives the manager that understanding. And with it, the manager stands a reasonable chance of reconciling the cultural dilemmas that so often derail the best laid alliance plans.

RESOURCES

Bartlett, C. and Ghoshal, S., *Managing Across Borders*, Century Business, 1989.

Hofstede, Geert, *Cultures and Organizations*, McGraw-Hill, 1991.

Kotter, J.P. and Heskett, J.L., *Corporate Culture and Performance*, Free Press, 1992.

Trompenaars, Fons, *Riding the Waves of Culture*, Nicholas Brealey, 1993.

Trompenaars, Fons, *The Seven Cultures of Capitalism* (with Charles Hampden-Turner), Piatkus, 1994.

Trompenaars, Fons, *21 Leaders for the 21st Century: How Innovative Leaders Manage in the Digital Age* (with Charles Hampden-Turner), McGraw-Hill, 2001.

Trompenaars, Fons, *Building Cross-Cultural Competence: How to Create Wealth from Conflicting Values* (with Charles Hampden-Turner), Yale University Press, 2000.

Commentary

Things to do in airports

It's 7.30 am and you're sitting in an airport lounge. You have read the newspaper and drunk a coffee. You still feel the heavy weight of sleep on your eyelids and in your limbs. Your briefcase sits heavily on the floor. Now is the moment of truth. Do you open the briefcase? Do you open your laptop and work on those spreadsheets?

Modern business life is filled with such dilemmas. Most executives take the easy option. They begin work on the spreadsheets. The world's airport lounges are filled with executives crouched uncomfortably over laptops.

They would argue that such work can be immensely productive. Perhaps.

The reality is more likely to be that working in public places on laptops is highly inefficient. If it was the peak of efficiency, the al fresco office would have arrived.

So, what should executives waiting for planes do with their time? Some ideas:

1. Plan their careers, lives, futures – airports are happily anonymous places. Thanks to check-in times you have an hour of emptiness (or an hour of spreadsheets). You can sit and daydream. You can stare into the distance. No one will stop you. Take advantage of the freedom to think of where you are going, what you are doing, what you would like to do, and where you would like to be. It is highly therapeutic as well as being stimulating.

2. Read about where you are going – an astonishing number of highly intelligent business people travel with their eyes shut. If it's Tuesday it must be another Four Seasons in another country. They rarely explore beyond the heavily carpeted confines of their hotels. They exist in a business comfort zone. Why not prepare to spend an hour or two sightseeing on arrival?

3. Good housekeeping – you are unlikely to be highly inspired or efficient when there are 300 other people in the room. Rather than preparing intricately argued reports it is better to spend time tidying up the detritus of executive living – sort out expenses, organize your growing collection of business cards, put some new batteries in the powerless calculator which has been at the bottom of the briefcase for two months.

4. Turn your their mobile off – how many times do you hear people at airports talking into their phone, saying things like: "I'm now at the

airport, are there any messages for me?" Why bother? Most calls on mobiles from airports are a means of wasting some time before the flight is called. Try turning it off and doing something useful.

5. Have a conversation – high risk, we know, but it is amazing how much you can find out in a casual chance conversation. (It is also amazing how many professional secrets executives can divulge in a single conversation, but that's another story.)

6. Listen – listening is a much under-valued skill in life as well as business. How about listening to music or a recorded book? Entertaining, improving, relaxing, and effortless.

7. Mental gymnastics – in the age of intellectual capital, our brains are our competitive weapons. The only trouble is that we do little to ensure that our competitive armory is in good working order. So, as the seconds tick away, try a mental workout. As a start, try remembering the titles in the bookshop or the timings on the flight information board. Your inability to do so may drive you immediately back to the spreadsheets, but the more the brain is exercised the better you will become. Once you have mastered the art of memorizing the entire bestseller list, make sure you travel with someone likely to be impressed by such a feat.

8. Talk to a colleague – traveling with a colleague or client can prove highly important in developing a relationship built on mutual understanding. Sitting next to someone for five hours gives you a great opportunity to learn more about their views, aspirations, and personality. If this person is your boss, it also gives you five hours to impress or make yourself redundant. So, as you sit in the airport lounge, you may like to think about who you should take your next trip with.

9. Do something else, anything else, not related to business – if you are traveling to a meeting you should have done your preparation before arriving at the airport. You need to be intellectually fresh when you arrive. Cramming the preparation into a few hours in the airport lounge or on the plane between cups of indifferent coffee is not advised. The best advice is to think about something entirely different.

10. Make lists – this is mental gymnastics for the anally retentive. Two senior managers we know often travel together. They wile away the time by issuing challenges. Name every one of Shakespeare's plays. How many American states begin with the letter "M"? Name the locations of the last 10 Olympic Games. Who were the last seven heavyweight champions of the world? Foolproof. Before you know it, your flight is being called and you are desperately trying to remember Leon Spinks' name.

Commentary

Traveling light

Passports, tickets, money and ... what else? Every business traveler finishes the ritual checklist with their own personal essential ingredient for a successful trip. For some it is the portable PC or electronic organizer. Others cannot have a satisfactory flight without their personal stereo and favorite opera. The list is long and totally individual. Some feel naked without a copy of the latest business blockbuster, others bring their own personally tailored ear plugs, face masks, and atomizers. And some travel with as little as possible.

A frequent-flyer consultant describes his modest hand baggage as "a raincoat, a book, and a pair of overshoes I was given many years ago." "I travel light but always take a pair of slippers with acupressure nodules and ylang-ylang, which is an aromatherapy essence of oil," says Alan Briskin, author of *The Stirring of Soul in the Workplace*.

Others have a more extensive list of essentials. Peter Fisk, CEO of the Chartered Institute of Marketing, lists his essential items as: "My handheld computer, which contains everything I used to take my laptop for, but fits in the pocket and only takes seconds to fire up. Other essentials would include my running gear if it's more than a day trip, mobile phone unless it's the US, and a photo of my wife and baby daughter."

Business travelers may be at 30,000 feet, but there is no need to leave the office behind. "I travel so much that I have to take work with me," says Randall White, co-author of one of the business blockbusters, *Relax, It's Only Uncertainty*. "So, on a trip I take my in-box. If I'm going to be away for four or more days I'll take my laptop which has my calendar and phone organizer. There are also magazines and journals to read, correspondence, and any briefing materials I need to prepare for the client I am visiting. It adds up to a heavy briefcase and a fully laden computer carrying case."

The spectacularly itinerant Mark McCormack routinely traveled over 200,000 miles a year and always took two briefcases on board. These contained yellow pads with details of restaurants, shops, art galleries, as well as lists of addresses of friends. He carefully prepared a folder for each appointment he had scheduled, with copies of the relevant papers. "Some business people throw the entire filing cabinet into their briefcases on the just-in-case theory. The smart business traveler plans more carefully," warned McCormack. "Decide what you will have time to do on your trip and plan when to do it."

David Coles, managing director of the express freight company DHL International (UK), suggests that the best solution is to regard travel as "mobile work time. This makes you productive and reduces stress. I keep a file in my office of things to do/read when traveling. Also keep your mobile in your briefcase – you will forget it at security otherwise."

The in-flight office is now common practice. The big question is whether to work or to lay back and enjoy the distance from the office. "I usually do not work, except when I have a meeting planned shortly after landing in which case I simply read my notes for that meeting. Otherwise, I just read non-work related books or magazines," says Solon Ardittis, CEO of Tradeyoursite.com.

"Use plane time wisely," advises the American consultant Bruce Tulgan. "Sleep, read, sort receipts, sort business cards. I try not to do 'serious' work that requires concentration on the plane because I find I am about half as effective as normal."

Simply reading a good book is sometimes difficult for work-obsessed senior managers. "For many talented and successful managers the idea of having idle time is anathema," says business psychologist Robert Sharrock of YSC. 'Often they value the enforced space of a flight. It is uninterrupted time, an opportunity to really focus on work." And, of course, to catch up with all the things you should have done – "I go through all the correspondence I haven't replied to," confesses Eddie Obeng, founder of Pentacle, The Virtual Business School. "On the return trip I type up details of the meeting and write a thank you letter. I come prepared with a laptop, mobile phone, wallet, and credit cards."

Key to getting things done is the laptop computer which is almost obligatory for the traveling executive, but be warned – "The only time I ever used one, the passenger next to me talked for over an hour on the relative merits of other laptops and introduced me to a few functions I didn't know existed," recalls a publisher.

The variations are endless. One executive always ends up with an empty cup in his briefcase – he likes to finish his morning coffee in the taxi to the airport. Another mysteriously explained his sole traveling companion was a pocket compass.

Dominic Swords of Henley Management College identifies two essentials: "Chocolate biscuits – even the same brand is never quite the same in different countries – and a screw driver to change the plug of my electric razor." Henley's communications director, Michael Pitfield, always takes a dual-time backlit watch (for night-time long-haul flights), a really good book, Handspring Visor (instead of a heavy laptop), a camera, and a small torch.

It is a good idea to keep your eyes and ears open (though many travelers identify ear plugs as necessary). Fellow passengers can sometimes be extremely helpful. "It's always worth having a look when the person next to you takes out some work," says one consultant. "On one flight the person next to me was from the company I was going to meet. His reading material included a memo which was relevant to my meeting. Remember that you don't know who's sitting next to you or who you are divulging your innermost corporate strategies to."

Commentary (continued)

It is a point emphasized by Neville Thrower, an international projects director. "Confidentiality is a real issue," he says. "I have heard real horror stories about travelers giving away secrets to a neighboring passenger who finds your work more interesting than his own and indeed might be a competitor."

But, before retreating into watchful silence, remember the value of networking – one aspect of work which definitely requires no extra luggage. Indeed, some would say that traveling offers a huge networking opportunity. Sitting next to a complete stranger there is none of the usual social distractions and complications. "The power dynamics are completely different," observes Gerry Griffin, author of *The Power Game*. "There is none of the fear and nervousness you can experience during ordinary social situations. You are there, in your seat, and that is where you will be for a few hours. In some respects it is constraining. After all, you may not want to speak to the person next to you. But it is mostly liberating, an opportunity to talk in a completely different situation."

Some business leaders actually use traveling time as a means of getting to know the people who work with them. One CEO always travels along with a younger colleague. Usually there is a good reason for this, but sometimes he just brings them along for the ride. He finds that five or six hours talking with someone is usually long enough to gauge the person's abilities, attitude, and aspirations, as well as finding out about how the CEO and the company are perceived. It is work, but not as we usually think of it.

– CHAPTER 2 –

Leading

"The only real training for leadership is leadership."

Anthony Jay

"Leadership is practiced not so much in words as in attitude and in actions."

Harold Geneen

"Leadership is the capacity to translate vision into reality."

Warren G. Bennis

"I start with the premise that the function of leadership is to produce more leaders, not more followers."

Ralph Nader

"Lead, follow, or get the hell out of the way."

Ted Turner

"Our prevailing leadership myths are still captured by the image of the captain of the cavalry leading the charge to rescue the settlers from the attacking Indians. So long as such myths prevail, they reinforce a focus on short-term events and charismatic heroes rather than on systemic forces and collective learning."

Peter Senge

"A leader is a dealer in hope."

Napoleon Bonaparte

Leadership for the future

DES DEARLOVE

[People have been debating for centuries what makes great leaders – certainly as far back as the Ancient Greeks. More than 2,000 books on leadership are published every year. We are still searching for definitive answers. The latest leadership thinking suggests we may have been looking in the wrong places.]

Heroic leadership is out of favor with the theorists. The idea that one person is responsible for the success of an entire nation or a multinational company, they argue, is absurd. Yet most leadership texts still come with a list of larger-than-life exemplars. Experts may pour scorn on the heroic leadership model but they still reach for heroes. Winston Churchill, Ghandi, and Napoleon are popular. In the business arena, former GE boss Jack Welch, Virgin's Richard Branson, and Michael Dell of Dell Computers are routinely trotted out as leadership role models.

"Most attempts to study leadership – in an era in which everyone says we need more leaders and better leadership and the problem is a lack of leadership – deal with individual character, drive, experiences, and personality or they deal with actions – what do leaders do, how do you create a vision, mobilize a team, and so forth," says Harvard Business School's Rosabeth Moss Kanter. "But there's another element which needs to be examined in greater depth, and that is the third side of the triangle. If there's character and there are actions, there are also circumstances and conditions. And so this means some organizations produce more leaders, empower more people who are able to take initiative, engage in acts of leadership, find those inner characteristics, and use them."

Professor Kanter points to New York's mayor Rudy Giuliani as an example of a leader who rose to the occasion when circumstances made it possible for him to exhibit a level of leadership that was thought of as exemplary.

The latest crop of leadership literature ranges from the frivolous to the profound. But what links it is the suggestion that we should widen the search for role models. Sporting stars are now pressed into service as leadership exemplars, as are figures from history. In their book *How Did They Manage? Leadership Secrets of History*, Daniel

Diehl and Mark Donnelly, two television documentary makers, offer an entertaining cocktail of leadership wisdom drawn from historical figures, including Shakespeare, Solomon, Moses, Confucius, and Elizabeth I. The leadership basics, the book suggests, are timeless.

One leadership thinker whose work has stood the test of time is Warren Bennis. The American academic has done more to debunk the heroic leadership myth than just about any other business thinker. Leaders, he argues, are made not born. Usually ordinary – or apparently ordinary – people rather than charismatic or talismanic stereotypes, the heroic view of the leader, he believes, is now outdated and inappropriate. "The new leader is one who commits people to action, who converts followers into leaders, and who can convert leaders into agents of change," says Bennis.

From his base at the University of Southern California where he is founder of the University's Leadership Institute, in Los Angeles, Bennis has produced a steady stream of books, including the bestselling *Leaders* and *Geeks and Geezers*, which compares leaders under 35 ("geeks") with those over 70 ("geezers").

Bennis' research suggests that "crucibles," powerful, life-changing experiences, play a vital role in the development of leaders. "I think what the geeks haven't experienced are the crucibles like the Second World War and the Depression. They have had formative years of almost uninterrupted prosperity, growth, and success. They are often children of affluence. So September 11 was the first collective shock to the world view they grew up with," says Bennis.

He believes that we encounter potential crucibles all the time. "Having to fire people, being fired, being shipped to an office you don't like, thinking that you have been demoted when maybe you haven't. My concern is how we use such everyday crucibles which we're not sometimes conscious of. We all experience crucibles, but what do we do at the back end of them? Do we learn from them? Do we extract wisdom from them? It isn't a question of how we create them; they happen, and happen almost all the time. But do we think of them as a dream so that when we wake up and brush our teeth it vaporizes, or do we think about the dream and learn from that?"

Other commentators challenge the entire notion of leadership being timeless. Peter Fisk, CEO of the UK's Chartered Institute of Marketing, argues that the traditional leadership model is outdated. He points to the rising failure rate among CEOs and suggests it is time to reinvent leadership for the challenges of the 21st century. "The old models of leadership are creaking under the strain of modern business life," says Fisk. "Leaders are struggling with complexity and the sheer speed of today's economy. Leadership itself is in a state of flux."

The new business environment, Fisk says, requires digital leaders. "Digital is shorthand for a new approach to business. It reflects the growing complexity of the business environment. Digital is a state of mind as much as it is a technological phenomenon. For traditional leaders, the business environment can seem chaotic, uncertain, and ambiguous. But digital leadership embraces complexity – it is a different way of being a leader."

In the past, leaders have been admired for their certainty, for sticking to their guns. Digital leadership focusses attention on another dimension – the ability to change direction and even perform U-turns. Bill Gates, for example, is a digital leader because he is able to assimilate huge amounts of complex and often contradictory data and change direction. Gates was a relatively late convert to the Internet, for example, but his personal epiphany transformed Microsoft to meet the new challenge. "What Gates has demonstrated again and again is the ability to transform his own perspective and to mobilize the organization," says Fisk.

Whatever it is that great leaders do, at least we know a great leader when we see one. Or so we thought. But even that is now being challenged. Recent research suggests that the business world has been celebrating the wrong leaders.

In his book *Good to Great*, Jim Collins examines how a good company becomes an exceptional company. The book introduces a new term to the leadership lexicon – Level 5 leadership. Level 5 refers to the highest level in a hierarchy of executive capabilities. Leaders at the other four levels may be successful, but they are unable to elevate companies from mediocrity to sustained excellence. Level 5 leadership challenges the assumption that transforming companies from good to great requires larger-than-life-leaders. The leaders who came out on top in Collins' five-year study were relatively unknown outside their industries. The findings appear to signal a shift of emphasis away from the hero to the anti-hero.

The late Darwin E. Smith, for example, was the CEO of the paper company Kimberly-Clark for 20 years. He was described as shy, unpretentious, and even awkward. With his heavy, black-rimmed glasses and unfashionable suits, Smith looked more like a small-town hick than a corporate titan. Yet under his quiet rule, Kimberly-Clark outperformed not just competitors like Procter & Gamble but also GE, Hewlett-Packard, Coca-Cola, and 3M, and every other star of corporate America.

According to Collins, humility is a key ingredient of Level 5 leadership. His simple formula is Humility + Will = Level 5. "Level 5 leaders are a study in duality," notes Collins, "modest and wilful, shy and fearless."

So are we entering the era of the unheroic leader? Not quite. Even Collins can't resist the heroic role model. Abraham Lincoln, he says, was a Level 5 leader. Some heroes never change.

RESOURCES

Bennis, Warren, *Leaders: The Strategies for Taking Charge* (with Burt Nanus), Harper & Row, 1985.

Bennis, Warren, *On Becoming a Leader*, Addison-Wesley, 1989.

Bennis, Warren, *Why Leaders Can't Lead*, Jossey-Bass, 1989.

Bennis, Warren, *An Invented Life: Reflections on Leadership and Change*, Addison-Wesley, 1993.

Bennis, Warren, *Old Dogs, New Tricks* (with Ken Shelton), Executive Excellence, 1999.

Bennis, Warren, *Geeks and Geezers* (with Robert J. Thomas), Harvard Business School Press, 2002.

Collins, Jim, *Good to Great: Why Some Companies Make The Leap ... and Others Don't*, HarperBusiness, 2001.

Diehl, Daniel and Donnelly, Mark, *How Did They Manage? Leadership Secrets of History*, Penguin, 2003.

Kotter, John, *The Leadership Factor*, Free Press, 1988.

Kotter, John, *Leading Change*, Harvard Business School Press, 1996.

Kotter, John, *Matsushita Leadership*, Free Press, 1996.

Kotter, John, *What Leaders Really Do*, Harvard Business School Press, 1999.

Commentary

What do CEOS really do?

Most jobs come with a job description, a lengthy list of the exact parameters of responsibility. But when you reach the top, the job descriptions come to an end. You are Chief Executive Officer, a phrase as empty of meaning as it is resonant with corporate status. You are left alone to make it up as you go along.

The loneliness can be oppressive. Not knowing what it is you should do, or when, or with who, offers more freedom than most executives have usually experienced in the corporate cocoon. In their previous incarnations executives have often been purveyors of certainty; as CEOs they find that uncertainty rules.

It can bewilder even the best prepared. "The CEO faces uncertainty outside the organization in the form of expectations about organizational performance, direction, and, if appropriate, stock price, but also faces uncertainty inside the organization in the form of managerial performance, operational effectiveness, and realization of human potential," says Phil Hodgson, co-author of *Relax: It's Only Uncertainty*. "The role of the CEO is therefore to choose the areas of uncertainty where the strategic challenges will be met externally, and support the areas of learning where the managerial challenges will be met internally."

Easier said than done. There is a profusion of differing opinions on the CEO's job. To some, the job is all about strategy. To others, depending on their prejudices, the CEO is really the Chief Marketing Officer or the Chief Financial Officer. Their performance can be measured by the price of a company's stock or on sales or on profits or on brand value or on intellectual capital. Take your pick.

Research into how CEOs spend their time is notoriously unhelpful. Most famously, the strategy guru Henry Mintzberg spent time analyzing senior executives at work. Mintzberg found that managers were slaves to the moment, moving from task to task with every move dogged by another diversion, another telephone call. The median time spent on any one issue was a mere nine minutes. (As Mintzberg's work was published in 1973 it would be safe to conclude that this figure has probably been significantly reduced thanks to e-mail, mobile phones, and much more.)

"I think the CEO has three jobs/roles," says Barry Gibbons, former chairman and CEO of Burger King and now an author and consultant. "First, to have 'The Dream' (this is *not* a mission, or a mission statement). It is Bill Gates seeing a PC on every table. Second, the CEO is all about *how* you do business, less about what you do. The style factors. What do you stand for? What do you stand by? What are the imperatives? What's the balance of the company?

Are you responsive or deaf? Backbone or invertebrate? Third, the CEO is the leader figure – and watched by a whole range of audiences. This is not about style versus substance, it's about understanding how you *personally* can best impact the first two roles. What are the key audiences – Wall Street? Consumers? Lobby groups? Your employees? Unions? Get involved personally and show them what you and the company stand for."

A similar threefold role is outlined by Bruce Tulgan, author of *Winning the Talent Wars* and founder of RainmakerThinking: "Number one: thinking. Number two: what they should be thinking about: Vision, mission, leadership. That means the CEO must always be thinking about the big, big picture, and revising/adjusting what the company is; what it should be; and how to bring it from what it is to what it should be, considering the facts of that big, big picture. The *how* is always going to come down to people – that is, people who can get all the work done. Getting the work done, I think, is a far more meaningful way to talk about what most people call 'execution.' The real trick of leadership is getting the vision/mission all the way down to the front lines. If that doesn't happen, the CEO fails – nothing else matters. So number three is communicating the vision/mission to one and all, and clarifying all the time, what it means for people throughout the ranks – so that each person can figure out for themselves what they should be focussing time and energy on all day long."

The job of CEO is increasingly seen as being about communicating the things that really matter – or the things they *think* really matter – in a personal and inspirational way. "CEOs often fail not because of lack of strategic thinking but a lack of coherent thought about implementation and mobilizing the organization," says Gurnek Bains, managing director of the business psychology consultancy YSC. "It really is about people. Before being CEOs, managers usually understand this intellectually, but only when they actually do the job do they tend to understand it emotionally. Typically CEOs spend 40 to 50 percent of their time communicating with people. They also spend a surprising amount of time thinking about the top talent in the company, building teams, and attracting talented people."

Some descriptions of the role of the CEO are colorful. "Talk to most CEOs and I think that their top job is to try to describe the opening in the fence to a flock of sheep determined not to go through it," says Richard Nissen, former CEO of the Virtual Office. "The best ones succeed in getting most of the sheep to get it and then manage to get most of the flock into the next field where there is enough grass to feed them and thereby most stay alive to fight another day. The CEO may be the shepherd who leads but he certainly never gets to have a sheep dog."

Commentary (continued)

Most agree that leadership is key to the CEO's job. "Successful CEOs simply lead, or better, they make sure a leadership climate is fostered and maintained. They succeed by sharing leadership. They no longer command; they coach. The special duty of the CEO is to ensure that a climate of leadership exists everywhere in the organization. The modern CEO inspires," says Laurence Lyons, senior vice president of the Executive Coaching Network. "In practice the CEO often excels simply by doing the things that no one else in the company would ever think of doing." It is as simple and as complex as that.

Old-style CEOs would struggle to cope with the profusion of stakeholders and vested interests they now have to consider. "The CEO has multiple roles and constituencies, from Wall Street to customers," says leadership expert Randall White. "The role is difficult and fragmented. There is little time to do everything well and so he/she faces a continuing series of trade-offs of time, energy, and focus."

Given all this it is, perhaps, little wonder that CEOs tend not to hang around. A survey, carried out by academics from Cranfield School of Management on behalf of venture capital group 3i and headhunters Sanders & Sidney, found that, in the top 100 quoted companies in the UK, CEOs last just over four years, with 72 percent in the role for less than five years; only 7 percent of CEOs in the top 100 quoted companies have survived over 10 years.

The survey confirmed that it is increasingly tough at the top. Regardless of sector, CEOs say that their role is becoming increasingly difficult and challenging. Key factors behind this include pressure from financial institutions to meet performance expectations; increasing complexity and competitiveness of business as a result of globalization; restructuring and managing change; increasingly demanding customers; difficulties in finding good people; and technological change, particularly the use of information technology.

Faced with such challenges, above all CEOs need to be wise. Gurnek Bains concludes: "The key thing CEOs do is exercise wise judgement around priorities, what's really important. Judgement calls on these issues are where CEOs add value rather than all the analysis and strategic plans in the world."

❛ Interview ❜ : Paul C. Reilly

Korn/Ferry CEO Paul C. Reilly surveys life at the top and the state of the executive job market.

How long should a CEO remain in the job?

It depends on the company, what's required, and the CEO's ability to transform themselves along with the business and keep ahead. Effectiveness depends on the skills the company needs at that time. Different sized companies need people with different scale experiences. Then there are specific situations, such as turnarounds, which require specific abilities. But for every rule there are people like Bill Gates or John Chambers who have taken a start-up and turned it into one of the world's biggest companies.

When it comes to changing CEOs, sometimes it is simply time for a change. There's an observation about political leaders that they get too much credit when things go well and too much blame when things go wrong and I think that also applies to CEOs.

What do you regard as the key performance measures for a CEO?

There is a lot of focus on the short-term numbers. I look at market numbers and at developing a strategy which is long-term. I could do a lot of things to improve short-term performance, but are they strategic and sustainable? The key is to execute effectively in the short term while creating a long-term strategy and setting targets. There needs to be a balanced scorecard.

What about the relationship between the CEO and the board?

The board's job is ever more crucial. Managing the board wasn't a challenge for me because in a professional services mindset you share information. Everything is shared with the board. Meetings are very open.

There's a lot of debate about non-executive chairmen and so on. All have their pros and cons. Having a separate chair is technically superior, but sometimes they simply don't get on, different personalities. I am chairman and CEO and I am comfortable with that dual role. But our board is very active. Their job is not to run the company, it's to provide oversight. At the same time, debate is good.

Is there too great an emphasis on short-term performance?

In some cases the markets are too short-term, but part of the CEO's job is clearly to delivery short-term results. There are no time-outs in business so there is a bias to the short term. The important thing is to know that everything you do you have to live with.

Do you feel that over recent years CEOs have been unfairly maligned?

Well, I think you can say that the last couple of years have been pretty tough on all employees, CEOs notwithstanding. In the media it can appear that every CEO is a crook or entirely self-serving. There is lots of coverage of Enron, Parmalat, and the like, but when all that was happening some CEOs were taking salary cuts and dealing with low morale, with pay freezes, and so on. CEOs worked harder and got less recognition.

It's true also that some CEOs were over-glorified when they were simply riding on the back of market forces. The reality is that most employees trust their CEOs.

Yet there is still a feeling that CEOs are over-paid.

There remains a sense that CEO compensation is out of step and that the spread between the pay of the average worker and the CEO is out of whack. Again, the reality is that CEO compensation was down last year. It does actually follow the market. If you look around – in merchant banking, for example, and elsewhere – there are many people who earn a lot more money than CEOs.

CEO compensation should be tied to performance. But it is a capitalist system. Shareholders didn't complain when times were good. While shareholder activism and greater transparency are probably good things, their impact will lessen as the economy improves.

In the end, the CEO still does a *job*. In the 1990s there was a period of the superstar CEO when CEOs were glorified, but that has gone away. People expect the CEO to be strategic, to bring a team together, and then to get things done. It is about integrity and implementation, knowing the business and getting the job done.

I think that while the money is obviously nice, CEOs are in the job because they want to make a difference. If the pay was less, people would still want to do it.

Is there really a global market in CEOs?

There is a globalizing trend. Go back a few years and all CEOs were local. In industries which have globalized, like financial services, this is no longer the case. Changes are happening. Look at the American executives at Deutsche Bank; Jim Schiro, CEO of the insurance company, Zurich; or the American co-CEO at Credit Suisse.

In the global market, talent is everything, so the global market for CEOs is evolving. The challenge for executives who aspire to CEO roles is to have experience around the world. At the same time you have to be realistic and accept that boards have to judge character when they hire a CEO. They are likely to be more comfortable with local candidates. They will understand the nuances.

The hardest thing for global CEOs is the job. It is 24 hours a day. You are always traveling. There is a non-stop cycle which is very demanding. It is a day and night job.

How do you spend your time?

Initially I spent more time at head office getting to know things. Then it became a question of getting the right team in place, placing people internally into the right positions. Now I perhaps spend some 20 percent of my time internally, the rest is about pushing the strategy into the organization and the marketplace. CEOs now are more market facing, out with their customers and their people.

There is a transformation stage and then a driving stage. There is not necessarily a maintenance stage any more. Put simply, if you're always a transformation person you die.

The job changes all the time. Some people are naturally curious. They can't help but learn. No matter how many times you run a company you learn new things and acquire new skills. A lot of people grow up in business as technical experts and then move into management. If you're not intellectually curious, your knowledge becomes outdated. It's not about age.

What are the attributes you bring to the CEO's job?

I am strategically oriented in terms of vision but also I am an implementer and bring people along. I am curious and have always developed successors.

How much time do you spend on succession issues?

I think about succession every day. I worry about developing people because it is what companies are worst at. They talk about being a people business, but often they keep people in their jobs and end up with a group of people with limited experience who have stayed in their jobs too long. Of course, it is hard to tell people they need to move, but some companies manage to do it exceptionally well.

What about the executive recruitment market? What does the future hold?

The demographics are very good for us. There is little or no growth in the workforce demographically. Also, more people will be retiring – 10 percent of the US workforce was retired at the start of the decade, by the end it will be 19 percent. There will be a shortage of managerial talent.

The second thing is that we're now in an improving economy with people investing. Therefore, there will be more demand for people.

Third is what I call velocity. According to a recent executive survey, 58 percent of executives plan to change jobs in the next year. They won't all do so, of course, but they want new horizons. There will be more velocity in the marketplace.

So all this makes for higher demand all round. That's why I moved into the business. I felt we were in a new industry while I had previously worked in a mature industry. There are only a handful of global human resource companies, so there is a chance to globalize in a unique way. Finally, our industry has traditionally been a single-product business. We are evolving to a human capital solutions business with a broader range of services.

Leadership roles and role models

RANDALL P. WHITE AND PHIL HODGSON

[Leadership role models come in a variety of shapes and sizes. Some are more durable and far-reaching in their behavioral implications for leaders.]

For the past 15 years we have been exploring the role of leaders and leadership in an uncertain world. During this time we have seen any number of situations that call into question the effectiveness – even usefulness – of leaders. Accounting scandals, presidential affairs, insider trading, and other stock market manipulations all contribute to this unease. And, as is the case in every era, a highly effective leader has emerged, who is able to manipulate followers to take action that the majority of the Western world finds offensive. Yet we must admit that Osama Bin Laden has had a far greater impact on western thought, action, and living than many others. Don't believe us? Have you stood in a security queue at an airport lately?

We now find ourselves clinging to the ideal that leaders and leadership make a difference. Not in a world of certainty – leadership has probably never been about operating in a world of certainty – but in a world of uncertainty, confusion, and turbulence. Real leaders, we would argue, make a difference in a world seeking definition, understanding, and the next big (new) idea. We also see leadership evolving so that there are three equally compelling ways for leaders (and followers – remember you can't have leaders without followers) to approach the world:[1]

- command and control
- empowerment
- learning.

There are two broad categories of people who operate as role models for leaders facing high levels of uncertainty: children and travelers.

Why these two groups? Because children are playful, experimental, don't worry about mistakes, and by and large don't fear failure. For children, learning is linked directly to their experience of the world. Experienced travelers and explorers are prepared to go where others don't; are not afraid to take a different path when their original one is blocked. When they can't get through one way, they persevere by finding another way, and they are resilient and self-confident enough to believe that they will get there eventually. Experienced travelers boldly seek out the new and novel, and they are always focussed on the outcome of the journey.

These attributes of children and travelers have led us to research, identify, and document eight positive attributes of leaders who thrive in an uncertain world – where learning is the key to successful leadership.

A lesson in change

In preparing our book on how leaders face ambiguity and uncertainty, we wrote a draft introduction talking about the new aspects of business life and saying that things were changing at an unprecedented rate.[2] One of our editors challenged our view of leadership and change: "It's not new," he said. "That's all I've ever known, it's ordinary." He was interested in what things were going to be like in the next 10–20 years. He was aged 31 – we felt a hundred years older.

Our editor was helping us understand an important point that became even more clear when we talked to people in organizations like Cisco, Yahoo, and Hewlett-Packard. Having a brief history means that you don't have a past that tells you something can't be done now because it couldn't be done before. When we expressed surprise at how quickly Cisco could close its books at the end of a financial period, one of our contacts replied: "An organization of our size, but with a longer history than we have, would know that a one-day close was impossible. But we started that way, so we didn't have to unlearn anything. Even so, we are constantly under pressure to improve."

What leadership used to mean

For those of us who have been around a bit longer than our editor and our Cisco contact, it can seem that the change in our view of what leadership is and what leaders do that has occurred in the last four or five decades is startling. It was only 40 years ago that we had a series of contingency theories, of which perhaps the Situational Model of Leadership was the best known. Drawing from the Ohio State Studies, leaders were seen to use two types of behaviors: task and relationship. At their root, such contingency theories really required the leader to know what had to be done and additionally to have a pretty good idea of how to do it. Situational Leadership and other models like it required the leader to be able to step in if the follower's output wasn't what was wanted. In short, there was a "right" and a "wrong" way to do many of the things that needed to be done. The effective leader was the expert and was in control.

Later we learned of empowerment. We invited people to reach for a vision. It was often a charismatic or at least an emotional process. We managed while we wandered about, we took on hairy, audacious goals, and if we really had let go of the need to control, we acknowledged that while we still knew *what* we wanted to achieve (the vision), neither we nor anyone else knew *how* to achieve it (see Table 2.1). Nor could anyone achieve it entirely on their own. So the effective leader empowered others. She knew what task she wanted to accomplish but couldn't get there alone.

Table 2.1: *Different styles of leadership*

Leadership style	Control	Empower	Learn
Leadership knows *what* to do	yes	yes	no
Leadership knows *how* to do it	yes	no	no

The current situation

It would be simple if leaders always knew what to do and at least sometimes knew how to do it. But our research over the last 15 years has shown that uncertainty has a habit of creeping into every kind of circumstance. Who – apart from a small group of fanatics or an incredibly prescient intelligence service – would have predicted the events of September 11, 2001?

Our political leaders, our community leaders, and our business leaders are facing great levels of uncertainty. The true meaning of "things can never be the same again" is that we as followers or as leaders have learned something irrevocable. But perhaps we have also learned that learning itself is the key to future survival, freedom, and prosperity – and whatever we choose to define as success.

The modern leader needs to have all the skills that leaders of the past acquired over painful years, plus they need an extra dimension of skill. They sponsor learning. At a conference held a few years ago at Cornell University's Johnson School of Business in Ithaca, New York, a number of senior executives gathered to discuss how organizations could become more dynamic. Two of the conference contributors stood out as they discussed how they sponsored learning in their organization's quest to become more agile.

Corning, a company of 150 years' standing that grew its name and reputation in the field of glass cookware and television tubes, now supplies technologies like fiber optics and flat-panel displays and has become "the information revolution's prime contractor." Its then CEO John Loose said: "It is so easy for a company that has been so successful for so long to become a prisoner of processes of the past. We needed to accept ideas from outside – we acquired $10 billion of companies in the previous five years. But the whole transition has been accomplished by execs who have mainly worked in the Corning Company. Transformation is not a project – it is a mindset."

Marty Coyne, then President of Commercial Group, Kodak, on the power and importance of speed, risk, and personal growth – a heady learning formula indeed: "You can never move fast enough, even though it seemed as if you were going too fast at the time. If you make a mistake, the world won't come to an end. If you think of delaying, ask what you'd really learn in the next few months – just move. Everything is a development opportunity, even finance meetings. I have yet to find a personal development plan that is too aggressive."

Why do leaders create these tough and demanding learning opportunities and challenges? Precisely because leaders of today sometimes find themselves in the positions of not knowing *what* needs to be done and not knowing exactly *how* to do it.

Because the things Loose and Coyne refer to are difficult to learn and at the same time valuable to the organization, they can lead to some form of sustainable competitive advantage and to value creation for the organization. By taking on what we call *difficult learning*, organizations hope that their competitors are unable or unwilling to follow them along such a steep, demanding, and risky learning curve. But leaders who promote this approach recognize that the route to difficult learning is not to head toward things they and their organizations know a lot about. Instead, it is to head toward the things they know least about – the areas of uncertainty and ambiguity. Interestingly, these are conditions that young children and experienced travelers live with every day.

The child as role model

In a world where uncertainty reigns, we all have to escape the safety net of interpreted experience. We must move beyond. We must attain a beginner's mind and come to terms with the "foreignness" of people and situations. We have to unleash *childlikeness* on the challenges we now face.

The leader as child? The child as leader? It flies in the face of all traditional concepts of leadership roles and role models. Leaders, by convention, are supermen and superwomen, larger than life, strong, indomitable, and all knowing. But think about how much uncertainty children face just in the process of growing up. Discovering the world around them, their strengths and weaknesses, and infinitely more playfulness.

The skills and perspectives of supermen and superwomen are ill matched against uncertainty. Childlikeness makes business sense. Work can equal play without the bottom line being forgotten. Microsoft, for example, has proved particularly adept at harnessing the learning capabilities and energy we find in children. It may now be a huge corporation, but it retains the atmosphere and the behaviors of a precocious upstart. It outwitted the field through its naive smartness and seems determined to hang on to it. Typically, its corporate headquarters at Redmond, near Seattle, is nicknamed "the campus." Consciously or unconsciously, Microsoft seeks to utilize the freewheeling, flexible, stay-up-all-night, ideas-driven atmosphere of a college campus. The dividing lines between work and play are blurred to the point of not existing.

Interestingly, movie makers are attracted to the idea of letting a childlike mind loose in the grown-up world of business or anywhere else bedeviled by orthodoxy. Peter Sellers' *Being There* featured Sellers as an innocent gardener whose homespun wisdom won him political acclaim. Tom Hanks in *Big* was a corporate executive with a childlike passion for toys. The message was humorous, but underneath there is a more important point. We realize that children can see things as they really are. They can strip away the jargon, the complexity we have loaded onto something, and get to its heart. They ask awkward questions and are not saddled with preconceptions. They live with uncertainty all the time, but are able to cope, grow, develop, and learn.

Practically, what lessons can children teach us? Children can handle, cope with, and grow from uncertainty for a number of reasons.

Creativity

Children are naturally and instinctively creative. Contrast this with organizations, which naturally and instinctively distrust creativity. In the traditional company, creative elements are cordoned off. It is risky to do the new and different. The nerds and geeks inhabit a world of their own, set apart from the mainstream; difficult to manage, organizations choose not to manage them. The stereotype suggests that though they may have bright ideas, they have no grasp of commercial reality. Compartmentalized they can be controlled, and the pernicious effects of their offbeat creativity won't infiltrate the rest of the organization.

Absorbing stimuli

Children move easily from one activity to another. One minute they are happily contemplating a jigsaw, the next they are painting. They take in different stimuli effortlessly. They move on quickly without letting go of what they have just learned.

As we have seen, executives also jump from one job to another, phone call to video conference, sales call to board meeting. The trouble is that while they are adept at taking in stimuli, they are poor at learning from it so it can be used at a later date. They go through a wide range of experiences and emotions every day of the week and then go home to start afresh on the next day. They are continually letting go of what they have just learned and experienced.

Accepting no right way

Children do not know there is a right way to do anything. This is a positive advantage – for children and for corporations (though not necessarily for parents). They seek out different methods, however unusual or different. They are not handicapped by the way things have always been done, the way something should be done, or the way used by a particular individual.

Learning

There is a famous observation that it is the mouse and not the mother cat that teaches the kitten how to catch mice.[3] As the mice become tougher to catch, so the kitten learns how to catch tougher mice. The point is that children, or kittens, progressively learn by playing and play by learning. The lessons for corporations are that when learning is play, it is highly effective – look at Microsoft. When learning is work it is ineffective – look at all the executives "forced" to go on training courses. The learning that sticks has a joy of discovery, playfulness. Many executives have been to brainstorming seminars where an atmosphere of deliberate playfulness often stimulates high levels of executive learning for an hour or so. Corporations of the future are going to need to find ways to extend that hour to cover the entire working day.

Adaptability

Children are good at dealing with the unknown and unexpected. If something unusual occurs, they attempt to make sense of it, to understand. Somewhere along the line we have lost this precious curiosity. "When you're a kid and you're learning, it's okay because a lot of things are confusing and you persevere with it," says Bill Gates.[4] Children persist at learning in a way that is difficult to achieve in an organization full of truculent and ambitious adults ready to make you seem a fool if you've failed or come up with a crazy idea. After all, getting it wrong may cost you your job.

Leaders as travelers

True leaders are also like experienced travelers.

Travelers are romantic figures. We are attracted to the idea of the quest, struggling against the odds, overcoming the might of nature. *In Search of Excellence* was a great title because it suggested a quest; in fact, a more proper description of the book might have been "Here is our current view of excellence."

We like the idea of the quest so much that we send managers on outdoor training exercises. We want to turn them into explorers and adventurers, often without thinking why.

Of course, the managers of our times are travelers, skipping from one airport to another, time zone to time zone. They travel, but are they true travelers? Too often, they are mere passengers. And, in the new reality, who wants passengers? As you become more adventurous it is notable that excitement and uncertainty increases. But what is it that experienced travelers do that we are seeking to emulate?

Focus on the quest

They combine focus on their particular quest with a pragmatic realization that there are a multitude of ways of getting there. They take the obscure byways and are entertained and educated by diversions, without losing sight of why they are there in the first place.

Experienced travelers combine focus on given objectives with a flexibility to explore the unexpected byways. Competitive advantage comes from going off the beaten track and moving to an area of uncertainty.

Pragmatically interpreting your corporate and personal quest has important implications for corporate missions. Instead of being fixed and unvarying "solutions," leaders regard missions as continually evolving.

Take risks to learn and achieve

To reach their destination, especially one they have never traveled to before, the best travelers are open to new experiences – their own and those of others – and can adapt to unforeseen circumstances.

Planes, trains, and automobiles are often delayed and sometimes take you where you don't want to go. Experienced travelers shrug their shoulders and change their behavior and expectations to meet the new demands of the situation. Remember the movie, *Planes, Trains, and Automobiles* with John Candy and Steve Martin? The perennially unsuccessful and apparently clueless John Candy character was a far better traveler than the suave and sophisticated character played by Steve Martin because he was flexible and able to play the system.

Understand and play the system

Some people move through the system effortlessly, others get gridlocked and struggle with the constraints and distractions. Travelers take it for granted that they can, and do, move through the organization easily and swiftly. Achieving agreement from people or getting clearance for projects, are minor hindrances rather than weighty obstacles to reaching their goals.

This is often an unconscious skill. Travelers do it so well that they often don't realize what they are doing. It is akin to a hurdler reaching his or her peak –

automatically they take the right number of strides between hurdles. They don't need to think or alter their stride pattern; it is natural and effective.

By talking to people, approaching allies in the right way at the right time, knowing how the system works, travelers are able to work around a great deal of delaying bureaucracy and corporate politics to concentrate on action. They seem at ease in the corporate waters and, additionally, are acutely aware of which environment – which waters – they operate most effectively in.

Respect cultural differences

Travelers realize that if we were all the same – clones of each other – the world would be a boring, uncreative place. But difference also produces difficulty because we do not all think, act, and react the same way to the same stimuli. Difference, then, needs to be encouraged and understood.

Thrive on discovery

They are prepared to go where others haven't gone before. Travelers seek out challenges and use a combination of hard, factual data and inner sense. They use maps, compass, timetables, but also have an inner sense of where to go, what to do, and how to behave. When all other sources of information fail, travelers trust their instinct to know what to do.

Enrich perspectives through experiences

They learn through each and every experience. No matter how many times an experienced traveler has traveled a particular route, they are always on the look-out for the new or unexpected.

Future personal styles

The conclusion? Children and experienced travelers share a number of things in common. Both are adaptable and flexible. Most importantly, however, they are constantly learning. For them, everything is an opportunity for learning, whether it is a new country, a different paintbrush, or meeting new people.

If we are to move toward uncertainty, leveraging learning is a corporate and personal imperative, no matter what your business, no matter what your aspirations, no matter what your status or skills. Learning is the driving force behind future leaders and the organizations of the future. And learning is the gateway to the eight broad strands of behavior that seem to help people cope with ambiguity. We call the skills "enablers," and we have characterized them as different personal styles, which are listed in Table 2.2.

Table 2.2: *Different personal styles or "enablers"*

1.	Mystery Seekers	. . . are curious people who are attracted to areas that are unknown and to problems that appear to have no obvious solution.
2.	Risk Tolerators	. . . can make decisions when necessary despite incomplete information and will tolerate the risk of failure. They are not hampered by insufficient or ambiguous data.
3.	Future Scanners	. . . have the ability to question deeply and make links between apparently different pieces of information, while being constantly on the look-out for even the faintest signals of what the future might hold.
4.	Tenacious Challengers	. . . resolutely pursue difficult and challenging issues and problems. This skill is most often seen in inventors and start-up artists and is sometimes seen as the entrepreneurial part of entrepreneurs. They are at home with conflict.
5.	Exciters	. . . create excitement and energy at work not just for themselves but for others around them also.
6.	Flexible Adjusters	. . . have the ability to make adjustments in the face of problems and to be able to sell those adjustments to others.
7.	Simplifiers	. . . are able to get to the essence of something and be able to communicate it to others in such a way that they not only understand it but become enthused and committed to it.
8.	Focusers	. . . know what are the few most important things to do or keep a watchful eye on, no matter what else may be going on and however many options beckon.

Facing the future

Facing high levels of uncertainty and ambiguity used to be entirely the province of senior executives, those termed leaders. They were the only ones who had all the available data, assembled painstakingly by their loyal support staff. Very often they were the only ones aware how incomplete (and confusing) all the available data really were.

Now with ever more data that can be brought to bear on any decision, leaders can so easily be paralyzed by the sheer tonnage of material and knowledge that they can invoke. Combined with worries about corporate governance, executives can be straitjacketed in their search for appropriate actions which will guarantee the future success of their organizations.

We find that executives need to be nimble and able to move among the various perspectives on leadership-controlling. Controlling here, empowering there, and embracing uncertainty for the sake of organizational growth. The problem is, there is no right way to be, and thus no instruction manual can be issued to those who become our leaders. What we have observed is that children and intrepid travelers possess behavior that when utilized in the executive suite propels leaders toward sources of future competitive advantage.

RESOURCES

Hodgson, Phil and White, Randall P., *Relax, It's Only Uncertainty*, FT Prentice Hall, 2001.

Hodgson, Phil, White, Randall P. and Crainer, Stuart, *The Future of Leadership*, FT Prentice Hall, 1996.

The mantle of authority

ROB GOFFEE AND GARETH JONES

[Leadership cannot be faked. All the self-help books in the world won't confer a leader with the mantle of authority.]

Each leader is unique, and it is that difference that others follow. There is no golden rule for top managers but the best have some traits in common. There is one question guaranteed to bring a stunned silence to the boardroom or business school lecture theatre: "Why should anyone be led by you?"

In this age of empowerment, it is difficult to do anything in organizations without followers – and they are becoming harder to find. Increasingly, executives need to know more than just how to manage; they need to understand what it takes to lead effectively – to inspire and win commitment.

Most executives admit they need help with this issue. If anything though there is too much advice. Bookshops are full of self-help manuals, autobiographical accounts and recipes for success, leading many to believe that replicating someone else's style will make leadership easy. Nothing could be further from the truth: leadership has much more to do with personal authenticity than an easily learned formula. The real challenge for aspiring leaders is to be true to themselves, not to emulate the habits of some other leader. For some, of course, this means recognizing that they have certain fundamental flaws that will always limit their leadership capability. Without doubt the final truth about leadership will never be written. However, there seems to be agreement that leaders need energy, a strong sense of direction, and a clear vision. Our work suggests that the most effective leaders also share four rather unexpected characteristics.

Strength in weakness

The first of these is that leaders reveal their weakness, but let us be clear what this means. We are not encouraging new finance directors to admit that they have problems with discounted cash-flow analysis, or operations directors to confess a limited understanding of supply chain management. Weaknesses like these are so central that they would constitute a fatal flaw.

Rather, what we mean is that leaders should reveal their human foibles – perhaps they are irritable on Monday mornings, rather shy with new people, or a little disorganized. Such admissions reveal their humanity and send out an implicit message; "I am like you – imperfect."

In effect, this confirms that the leader is a person, not merely a role holder. But there are other benefits. In revealing weakness, leaders show how others can help them and this builds good teamwork. It is also undeniable that followers can feel better if they are offered something to complain about. In effect it can become the psychological equivalent of the Wailing Wall. Finally, by sharing at least some of their weaknesses, leaders can protect themselves against others inventing potentially more damaging problems. In many workplaces, of course, the reality is that a manager's weaknesses are often exposed by others. This is rarely a positive experience and can cause feelings of inadequacy and defensiveness. Further, large organizations can be regarded, rather bleakly, as machines for the production of conformity. The pressure to bureaucratize, to standardize, to make more predictable, to surround with rules, is enormous. In this environment it becomes harder to reveal one's weaknesses. Ironically, the current fashion for strong culture in large companies may reinforce this pressure to conform.

Rigid performance targets also encourage rule following rather than a willingness to think creatively. Those at the top might have the confidence to challenge orthodox practices, but for those on the way up it may seem a risky strategy. Finally, the management development industry tends to distract from the development of leaders in its pursuit of technical perfection. The endless polishing of competencies may produce managerial ability but has little to do with leadership qualities.

Leadership rests upon more than mature appreciation of strengths. Great leaders acknowledge their incompetencies – they may even make it work for them.

Sensing the situation

Good leaders rely extensively on their ability to read situations. They *sense* an environment, picking up and interpreting soft data without having it spelt out for them. They know when team morale is shaky or when complacency needs challenging. Often they seem to collect this information almost through osmosis.

There are three levels of situation sensing, each of which has its own distinctive skills. First consider individuals. Effective leaders are continually learning about the motives, attributes, and skills of their important subordinates. They also know the best place to pick up such knowledge. For example, many executives say that they learn the most about people when traveling with them. Second, leaders read teams. They analyze the balance between members, the tension between the tasks and processes, and how the team builds its capabilities.

Finally, they are concerned with decoding the cultural characteristics of organizations and are aware of subtle shifts in organizational climate. Even those who are not great at situation sensing will at least realize the importance of gathering this kind of information and will find trusted colleagues to do it for them. For example, Ray van Schaik, former CEO of Heineken, was always able to read the unspoken signals of Freddie Heineken, the person who was "always there without being there," and translate them into clear messages for his colleagues on the executive committee. His ability was based upon many years' experience of working with Heineken and a finely tuned ability to read people.

Is situation sensing a natural instinct, or can it be learned? We suspect it is both. Some individuals seem to have a natural ability – think of a gifted salesperson who can judge a sales project on the back of a handshake and eye contact. On the other hand, many executives have clearly improved their situation sensing through systematic training in interpersonal skills. But this skill can be learned through experience as well as training. Franz Humer, chairman of Roche, for example, attributes his situation-sensing abilities to early student experience as a tour guide. Relying on tips he soon became skilled at identifying where he would earn his money among large groups.

Situation sensing is a critical leadership attribute, but it carries certain dangers too. Imagine a radio that picks up a range of signals, many of which are weak and distorted. Situation sensing can be similar – messages can be obscured by the static. Leaders must continually test their instincts against reality. The skillful leader may have sensed from other colleagues that moral is low in the finance team but they must always check whether that perception is accurate before acting.

Concern is paramount

Sadly it has become almost platitudinous to say that leaders care for their people. And there is nothing more likely to prompt cynicism in the workforce than seeing a manager return from the latest people-skills training course with apparent concern for others. Effective leaders don't need a training program to convince their employees that they really care. They empathize with the people they lead and they care intensely about their work.

Executives often see the word care as a synonym for softness or weakness. But genuine care, is of course, very difficult because it always involves personal risk – showing some part of yourself and your most strongly held values about work and how it should be carried out.

For example, Alain Levy, chief executive of EMI Music, passionately communicates his views on album track selections to his colleagues and subordinates, often in colorful language. In many businesses this might be considered obtrusive and unwarranted, yet Levy's passion for the music business echoes the obsessive concerns of his younger executives.

The general point is that when people care strongly about something, they are more likely to reveal their true selves. In doing so they communicate authenticity – they show others that they are doing more than simply playing a role.

Genuine care typically balances respect for individuals against the requirements of the task the organization is addressing. Maintaining this balance is not always easy. It should not be assumed, for instance, that caring always translates into standing shoulder to shoulder with your staff. It may take some detachment – the ability to stand back, see the whole picture, and sometimes take tough decisions. Leadership is not a popularity contest.

Stress the difference

Early social scientific theories of leadership attempted to measure universal traits that uniquely characterize good leadership. Various leaders were weighed, measured, and subjected to a battery of psychological tests. But the attempt to identify common characteristics ended in failure. Trait theory, as it was called, found only a set of weak links where causal relationships were difficult to determine. Was personal confidence, for example, a cause or consequence of gradual exposure to leadership experiences?

Effective leaders use their differences, whatever they might be. In one way, leaders might express their differences in dress style or physical appearance. More importantly though they move on to distinguish themselves through personal qualities such as sincerity, creativity, expertise, resilience, or loyalty.

How do leaders know which differences to use? Typically this is a learning process. For example, Jan Timmer, former president of Philips, learned to use his physical presence as a leadership asset. His broad shoulders and bull neck topped by his bald dome dominated situations for him.

Leaders can also use their powerful and distinctive motives as leadership assets. Examples include a desire for power – "you know me, I like to run things" – or wanting to develop a satisfying relationship – "I like to build string teams around me."

The particular skills they have acquired over the years are also useful. These could be technical skills – superior marketing knowledge or mathematical wizardry – or social skills such as listening or coaching.

Finally, passions – overriding goals, compelling missions, and deeply held beliefs – can differentiate leaders. Think of Anita Roddick's passion for a different kind of world, which proved a great asset to her leadership at The Body Shop.

Leaders get to know which of their attributes are most powerful mainly through experience and interaction with others. In the world of leadership development courses, conventional wisdom holds that leaders should interact with as many different types of leaders as possible; hence the current drive to encourage executives to seek new experiences in prisons, charities, or even zoos.

Yet learning through experience and interaction can really work only when leaders have time to reflect. In fact, many report that they are too busy to adequately exploit their experiences for insight. In some cases, women and members of minority groups may feel that stereotypical differences are attributed to them, which are not necessarily the ones that they would choose. They then use a number of strategies to cope with this – not always successfully. Some women, for example, dress conservatively to keep a low profile and avoid stereotyping; others attempt to turn stereotypes such as helper, nurturer, or seductress to personal advantage. There are costs in both strategies. The former prevents women from revealing their true differences and the latter results in the persistence of potentially harmful stereotypes.

Using one's differences is a critical leadership skill. But as always there is a danger; leaders can over-differentiate. The determination to express separateness leads some to lose contact with their followers, and they find themselves moving phantom armies around the board. Too much distance makes it impossible to sense situations properly or to communicate effectively.

Be yourself with skill

All of these qualities are necessary for effective leadership, but they can not be used formulaically. This is why leadership recipe books often fail. The challenge facing all those who aspire to be leaders is to be themselves but with more skill. Awareness of these qualities can help individuals develop a unique style that works for them. If you want to be a leader, you have to discover and express your authenticity. This is easier said than done.

Leadership myths

In teaching and writing about leadership, we have often seen executives profoundly misunderstand what makes an inspirational leader. Here are four of the most common myths.

1. *Everyone can be a leader.* Not true. Many executives don't have the self-knowledge or the authenticity for leadership. At the same time, self-knowledge and authenticity are necessary but not sufficient conditions for leadership. Individuals must also want to be leaders, and many perfectly talented employees are not interested in shouldering that responsibility. Others prefer to devote more time to their private lives than to their work. After all, there is more to life than work, and more to work than being the leader.

2. *Leaders deliver business results.* Not always. Some well-led businesses do not necessarily produce short-term results, while some businesses with successful results are not necessarily well led. If results were always a matter of good leadership, picking leaders would be easy. In every case, the best strategy would be to go after people in companies with the best business results. But clearly, things are not that easy.

3. *People who get to the top are leaders.* Not necessarily. One of the most persistent misperceptions is that people in leadership positions are leaders. But people who make it to the top may have done so because of political acumen, not necessarily true leadership quality. What's more, real leaders are found all over the organization, from the executive suite to the shop floor. By definition, leaders are simply people who have followers – and rank doesn't have much to do with that. Effective military organizations have long realized the importance of developing leaders at many levels.

4. *Leaders are great coaches.* Rarely. A whole cottage industry has grown up around the idea that good leaders ought to be good coaches. But this belief rests on the assumption that a single person can both inspire the troops and impart technical skills. Of course, it is possible that great leaders may also be great coaches, but we see that only very occasionally.

RESOURCES

Goffee, Rob and Jones, Gareth, *The Character of the Corporation*, Profile, 2002.

Commentary

Wrinkles and the leader

Think of a leader. The likelihood is that, unless David Beckham comes to mind, your leader is at least 50 years old. Leadership is the preserve of the mature and wise. The young aren't leaders – too immature, too inexperienced, too naive, well, too young. In politics we require that our leaders have a few grey hairs. Elsewhere, our military leaders are burdened with the heavy weight of their medals and the worry lines acquired through years on the parade ground, in the mess, and on the bridge. Leaders have wrinkles.

In the business world this is even more apparent. CEOs are not pimply youngsters but grizzled veterans of corporate warfare who have risen manfully through the Machiavellian ranks. The dot-com bubble brought a few bright young things to leadership roles. Unfortunately, this proved a case of premature elevation. The adolescent CEOs disappeared with the bubble, leaving the field clear for the old executive hands once again. Look at any collection of big company CEOs and you will see a collection of middle-aged men with the very occasional woman (only 11 women lead Fortune 1000 companies) and the odd young man (usually a whizz with technology).

To some extent it appears obvious that the senior-most jobs require more experience. Taking over as a first-time CEO is challenging, but slightly less so if you have an extra 10 years of experience under your belt. Mike Day is CEO of Indicater, which provides information and software for the catering industry. This is his second CEO job. He vividly recalls his initial experience. "It was daunting. I had 450 staff, a £7 million turnover, and 65 locations. But it is only when I became a CEO for the second time that I began to realize how I became a CEO in the first place and the mistakes I made. You don't necessarily get it right first time. By the second time, hopefully, you have become softer and more effective."

The danger of youthful CEOs is that a wisdom gap can develop, warns Peter Knight, CEO of CEO Circle, a discussion forum for CEOs. "CEOs are getting younger – the average age is now 50 – so there is the danger of wisdom being undervalued. The reality is that wisdom can be worked on but experience only comes with time. The majority of CEO appointments come from within the organization, so CEOs still have to serve their time within the organization so they really understand its values and culture. Being a CEO is all about knowing the business and knowing the best thing to do."

So is age a prerequisite for any leadership role? "Only in situations where the followers expect it – because of culture, or because they have been conditioned by the past success of previous leaders," says Phil Hodgson, director of leadership programs at the business school Ashridge. "If we could isolate the task

Commentary (continued)

of leadership from the cultural context then I think we would find a number of new traits that younger leaders find relatively easy to do, that older leaders have difficulty in replicating. Among other things, younger people seem more able to multi-task, are comfortable with fuzzy tasks and objectives, and are not dependent on location to do their work.

"Older leaders need to work very hard not to let their decision making and their understanding of a situation be dominated by their past experience of success and failure. It is very hard to accept that what worked before may not, probably will not, work as well again. Equally, what failed last time, does not necessarily define what will fail this time. The successful older leader stays successful by reinventing themselves so that they employ the learning without deploying the methods gleaned from yesteryear."

The issue of age is also occupying the mind of Warren Bennis, one of the most insightful thinkers on leadership over the last 50 years. Now in his late seventies, Bennis has grey hairs in abundance. As well as thinking about leadership, Bennis is a leader. In the Second World War, he was the youngest infantry officer in the US Army in Europe. "It shaped me so much and pulled from me things I may never have experienced," Bennis recalls. "I was very shy and felt that I was a boring human being and then, in the course of being in the Army, I felt that I was more interesting to myself. It was a coming of age – though I still didn't feel as though I was a leader."

For Bennis the war was what he calls a "crucible" – "utterly transforming events or tests that individuals must pass through and make meaning from in order to learn, grow, and lead." The trouble for youthful leaders is that crucibles are rare and cannot be artificially reproduced. You can't recreate Nelson Mandela's Robben Island.

Bennis' book *Geeks and Geezers* (co-authored with Robert Thomas) examines a selection of "geeks," leaders between the ages of 21 and 35, and "geezers," men and women between the ages of 70 and 93. For many of the older leaders, the war and the Depression were crucibles in which their values were formed. "The geezers were brought up in survival mode," Bennis explains. "Often they grew up in some poverty, with limited financial aspirations. They thought that earning $10,000 a year would have been enough. Compare that to the geeks, some of whom made a lot of money when they were young. They are operating out of a different context. If the geeks were broke they would be more concerned with making a living than making history."

The message for would-be leaders is that leadership is founded on deeply felt experiences early in life. Youth may not be an obstacle to becoming a leader, but only if you have been through a crucible and emerged unscathed on the other side.

Leading the way

ROBERT P. GANDOSSY AND MARC EFFRON

[Leadership is about more than individuals. Developing a strong leadership team may be the best means of setting your organization apart from the competition.]

Surveying the crowd at the first meeting of IBM's Senior Leadership Group in 1996, Lou Gerstner, the blunt-talking chief executive charged with saving Big Blue from the brink, issued an edict: Go back to school! The directive must have surprised and likely angered more than a few of the 300 senior executives – including Gerstner's own direct reports – many of whom had been with the tech giant for decades.

But Gerstner hadn't been recruited from R.J.R. Nabisco to make friends. His immediate challenge was to save an institution that had quite literally been placed on a 24-hour deathwatch. Those in the room that day understood they had been hand selected because they were critical to IBM's recovery. So, when Gerstner told them they would be participating in a program focussed on developing their leadership capabilities, they knew they'd better listen.

That's not to say that everyone had confidence in Gerstner's ability to breathe new life into IBM. A downward spiral had taken the company's $6 billion profit in 1990 and quickly turned it into an $8.1 billion loss by 1993. In an industry that was expanding rapidly, IBM had lost half of its market share since 1985. It ranked 11th in customer satisfaction among companies in the computer industry, trailing several companies that no longer existed. IBM's stock price stood at an all-time low, and competitors like Hewlett-Packard and EMC clawed at its market share. On April 1, 1993, the day Gerstner took charge, IBM's stock had dropped from a high of $43 per share in 1987 to $13 per share.

The organization that had long held court as America's most admired company was forced to abandon its guarantee of lifetime employment, sending tens of thousands of workers in search of new jobs. Many of those workers found employment within the legions of new dot-coms and undoubtedly snickered at IBM as a soon-to-be-extinct dinosaur. However, it wouldn't be the dot-com millionaires but Big Blue that would ultimately have the last laugh.

Just as Wall Street was preparing to throw the first shovel full of dirt onto IBM's casket, something miraculous happened: the giant rose from the dead. In 2001, profits reached over $8 billion on revenues of $83 billion, and shares hit an all-time high. The company once credited by *The Washington Post* for inventing the computer industry was back – with a vengeance. And, in an instance of ultimate irony, *Business Week* declared IBM the largest dot-com in the world. Gerstner and his team had pulled off the turnaround of the century, leading IBM back to profitability – without chopping up the company into separate operating units, a plan that had been in the works when he took over as chief executive.

While Gerstner himself has been given much of the credit for IBM's amazing turnaround, Big Blue's boss clearly recognized that the company's leadership strength extended far beyond his office. On his watch, a comprehensive approach to building great leaders was crafted, including careful selection, development, and rewards for IBM's best talent. Leaders were held accountable for growing leaders and good leadership was viewed as a critical asset to be carefully managed for the best possible return.

Gerstner's mandate accomplished much more than saving IBM. It positioned the company for the future by building a deep bench to ensure that Big Blue's dramatic turnaround wasn't just a passing phase. The fact that the transition from Gerstner to new CEO Sam Palmisano in 2002 was flawless in the eyes of the hypersensitive stock market and critical business press drives that point home. And with IBM facing likely retirement of as much as 75 percent of its senior management team by the year 2007, Gerstner's investment in a powerful leadership development and succession management process will prove to be an absolute necessity if IBM is to retain its regained crown and Gerstner's turnaround legacy is to last.

Reaching the boiling point

As Gerstner's story demonstrates, it is the development of a strong leadership team, rather than the actions of a single individual, that sets one organization apart from the rest. The facts are indisputable: great leadership teams build trust and confidence among their people. They motivate and inspire. They anticipate challenges and redirect the enterprise in timely and appropriate ways, unifying the workforce behind a single cause and driving the kind of performance that allowed a Southwest Airlines to soar or an IBM to reboot itself. Simply put, they deliver better business results. The opposite is true as well: an incompetent leadership team wreaks serious damage and creates inflexible bureaucracies, often destroying shareholder value and dooming the organization to failure. The corporate landscape is littered with hundreds of overly managed, poorly led institutions.

Tales of leadership successes and failures have served as juicy fodder for the likes of the *Wall Street Journal*, CNN, and Fox News. They've put leadership on the map, awakening many sleeping corporate giants in the process. It's clear now that there is a cause and effect – great returns for those organizations that invest in leaders and failure for those that do not. After decades of largely paying lip service to building great leaders, executives everywhere have begun to think more seriously about their own leadership processes.

This new awareness arrives at the right moment as daunting demographic trends loom. Those trends will forcefully challenge how companies develop their leadership talent. In the 1970s, 1980s, and 1990s, companies became spoiled by the enormous Baby Boomer generation – the pig moving through the python – which provided millions of talented, dedicated workers. While efforts were made to increase the capabilities of this group, the mindset that you could "buy" a leader when needed became ingrained in many firms. Revenue at executive search firms nearly tripled in the seven-year period from 1993 to 2000 as companies tried to find outside what they could not or did not develop inside.[5] "Twenty years ago," says Jeff Sonnenfeld, Associate Dean at Yale's School of Organization and Management, "only 7 percent of major firms hired CEOs from the outside. Now it's over 50 percent."

In the late 1980s, one Fortune 50 company was so concerned about the inability to grow leadership talent and the shortage of qualified leaders inside the company that it began to identify and track executives outside the company. The CEO and Senior Vice President of Human Resources undertook a confidential but rigorous process to review exceptional executives from other firms – they even developed tracking mechanisms on their growth and development. They went so far as to structure forums – industry task forces, board presentations, golf outings – to observe targets firsthand.

The shortage will worsen. Aging Boomers are beginning to trade the workforce for the golf course, trading corner offices for porch rocking chairs, company cars for golf carts. As this Boomer bubble bursts, we will see a 15 percent drop in the number of men and women of "key leader age" – those in the 35–44-year-old range. Since peaking in the late 1990s, the numbers for this group have decreased markedly and will continue falling until approximately 2015 when they will once again begin a slow upward climb. It is a fundamental economic principle that, when supply of a product decreases, its price increases. Companies looking to pay the "market price" for an executive may soon find the quality they want is not in their range.

But that's not all. Boards of directors and shareholders have increasingly less patience with leadership teams that do not produce results. In 2001, a record number of 555 CEO departures was recorded.[6] In 2002, nearly 100 CEOs of the world's largest 2,500 companies were replaced for performance reasons, almost four times the number asked to leave in 1995.[7] The challenges of running complex, global enterprises are immense. Modern leaders must carefully manage organizations with large cultural differences, be able to draw out multiple perspective, and lead diverse teams. Leaders who can do all these things effectively will be a rare, valuable commodity through the "Boomer trough."

Focussing on the facts

The combination of demographics and economic challenges means that companies no longer have the luxury of taking a trial-and-error approach – or of having no approach at all – to building leadership quality and depth. They want fact-based, tested methods and tools that fit with their organization's culture and support their business goals. They need clear guidance on how to build a diverse, highly qualified leadership team today and how to plant the seeds for great leadership tomorrow. Unfortunately, many companies find that fact-based, clear guidance is in short supply.

The answers are elusive. Our research discovered that narrowly focussed studies on topics like succession planning, executive education, and performance management were widely available, but no study looked broadly and systematically at the combined factors that enable companies like GE, IBM, or Colgate to be so successful in growing great leaders. And that combination of factors seems to offer the best possible explanation for the consistent stream of great leaders at top firms. After all, it was more than great leadership development programs that produced GE's three CEOs in waiting.

We started our research in 2002 by surveying CEOs and human resources executives at 240 of the world's top 500 multinational companies, posing questions about a broad variety of topics that would influence how leadership strength is built. We conducted hundreds of in-depth interviews with leaders at more than 50 companies. In 2003, we added a global perspective, surveying not only 320 US companies but hundreds in Europe and Asia as well.

To avoid one pitfall of previous studies, we maintained the basic premise that there had to be a relationship between great leadership and superior financial results. So we passed all data through a financial screen. In our 2003 study, we used the five-year compounded growth rate of earnings before income and taxes (EBIT) as this screen. Those that failed to perform at or above their industry median over a five-year period from the study date were eliminated, surprisingly knocking out many well-known firms with reputations for strong leadership programs.

In the second phase of our study, we went back to the top companies and interviewed nearly 100 senior executives and high-potentials, including a number of CEOs, to better understand, from their perspective, what makes the difference in companies that build great leaders. These in-depth interviews provide the nuance and subtlety that separate one company's programs from another's and reinforced what we heard in the survey process.

We learned a great deal. Many of our preconceived notions about leadership were challenged. There are no silver bullets. No formulas or prescriptions. No best practices to steal and embed in your organizations. There are patterns, however, and the patterns are what we were after. The top companies share a combination of beliefs and values and results-oriented practices for identifying, nurturing, and rewarding future leaders. These elements form the cornerstone of their programs and set them apart from the vast majority of organizations today.

The three fundamental truths of building great leaders

These elements aren't "best practices," but they capture what we call a leadership "truth." A "truth" can be thought of as an inviolable rule of building leaders – a foundation element of top companies. We believe that all three truths must be in place for a company to consistently build leadership quality and depth.

Leadership truth 1: CEOs and board of directors at top companies provide leadership and inspiration

Without the passionate and visible commitment of the CEO, developing great leaders is not possible. It seems intuitive that CEO involvement would be a critical success factor. After all, the support of senior management has proven to be critical for a wealth of corporate initiatives to succeed. But "top-down support" has become such a catch-phrase in recent years; the real impact and meaning have grown fuzzy. "Involvement" takes on an entirely new meaning in the realm of growing great leaders.

It is imperative that chief executives not only support the program but also actively participate in it, communicate frequently about it, and provide the inspiration, passion, and the necessary resources. It must have their stamp, their imprint. For example, CEOs at the top companies are intimately involved in their talent-review processes – reviewing top candidates, ensuring their teams conduct thorough, fair reviews of their direct reports, and that the process is used to fill key roles with top people. Fred Smith, founder and CEO of FedEx, literally wrote a book on leadership at FedEx and he continues to rewrite and update it every year. When we met with Bob Nardelli, CEO at The Home Depot, he was preparing to visit every division for several days each for business and talent reviews. Leadership development workshops in many companies have a "guest appearance" by the CEO – at top companies, CEOs are not only present much of the time teaching, learning, engaging, and observing, they believe it is their forum. They own it.

This is not head-nodding, passive support. It is often a passionate, "in your gut" belief that it is one of the single most important roles for the top executive. And it is the way to better results. For CEOs of the top companies, that means spending at least a quarter of their time and, in some cases, over half their time devoted to leadership. They spend the time because they know there is a direct link to results; running the business is building leadership capability.

What's more, the financial consequences are compelling: when a CEO is actively involved in leadership development, the organization averages a 22 percent return to shareholders over a three-year period. Without direct leadership from the top, the numbers drop to an astonishing negative 4 percent. Even in down times, these companies consistently outperform the market by 1–2 percent. Although that may not sound like much, when you look at market capitalization, it equates to billions of dollars.

Perhaps that's why board members are so dedicated to leadership development at the top companies. And you can bet boards will be even more active in the future, coming on the heels of legislative and regulatory reform and shareholder pressure. Highlighting a key difference between the top companies and others, fully 90 percent of the boards are involved in the process at these firms, meeting with high-potential leaders, getting to know them both personally and professionally, and learning to understand their career direction and how they think. This enables members to come to the next board meeting and honestly say, "I have a better understanding of the quality and depth of the leadership talent in this organization." Getting the board involved not only gives high-potential people better coaching, it also keeps pressure on the CEO to continue doing the same.

Each year, Dick Antoine, Global Human Resources Officer at P&G, and A.G. Lafley, CEO, review the top 150 people at P&G with its board. "They get exposed to our top talent in a lot of ways," says Lafley. "They not only see them make presentations to the board and in social situations, but also see them in action in their category and country businesses, and even reviewing innovation programs at their technical centers." Scott Cook, for example, CEO of Intuit and a P&G alum, arrives a day early for board meetings so he can spend time with P&G's highest-potential employees. He wants to get to know them, see how they think, how they behave.

Board members also spend time visiting P&G's global operations – understanding its markets, competitors, and its people, observing the business firsthand, not through PowerPoint. At a P&G board meeting in Geneva, members arrived midweek and Lafley divided them into teams and they fanned out across Europe to visit P&G facilities in the UK, Frankfurt, Warsaw, and Prague. They spent time with the region's leadership, key customers, and the company's best talent. They reconvened in Geneva on Saturday armed with fresh insights into P&G's operations, its customers, and its people. It is important to Lafley and his leadership team that the board be involved in key decisions at P&G and to do that they have to know the company and its key talent. Board members Norman Augustine, Meg Whitman, and Scott Cook routinely teach at P&G's leadership development programs as well.

Leadership truth 2: top companies have a maniacal focus on the best talent

It begins with a strong talent pipeline. Many of these companies have built a respected marketplace image, reputations for developing talent, and innovative and selective recruiting processes, ensuring a full and powerful pipeline. Southwest Airlines receives over 200,000 unsolicited applicants per year; it may hire only 5,000 – 2 percent of those that apply.[8] Procter & Gamble brings in hundreds of interns every summer from leading business schools and hires 1,200 new graduates globally each year. And it has done this for decades. The Home Depot receives several hundred thousand applications a year. It has the ability to screen applicants online or at computer kiosks in its stores and determine whether to interview the candidate even before they leave the premises. GE sells careers – not jobs – and its reputation as a leadership factory ensures a strong talent pool to select several thousand recent graduates annually and hundreds more from competitors, consulting firms, and the military.

These companies are not recruiting and not hiring the best and the brightest "out there," but they are hiring the best for them and they spend time and care doing so. Once hired, they spend the same time and care identifying and developing the best.

Learning that top companies focus on developing their high-potential talent should not be, in and of itself, particularly surprising. But they not only spend considerable time identifying and evaluating their high-potential people, they also focus heavily on matching leaders with jobs, providing cross-functional experiences, and global or regional assignments that promote strong development. They invest in discovering what matters in preparing people for certain roles. IBM, for instance, not only understands the critical experiences needed for developing candidates for key jobs, it understands the sequence in which these experiences should occur.

Sometimes when we explain these developmental moves to others, people get the wrong impression. Make no mistake – these are tough, challenging assignments with difficult goals. These companies intentionally take leaders out of their comfort zone and stretch them to test their capabilities and their capacity to grow. And while support is provided – unlike the Darwinian sink-or-swim models we see in some companies – there is tremendous challenge and pressure to succeed. Being high-potential in the top companies often means you're held to a higher standard.

Top companies also recognize the immense value these people bring to the organization. Studies have consistently shown that top performers produce in value at least 100–150 percent more than average performers in similar jobs. People who fall into this category should have compensation opportunities significantly above their lesser-performing peers. If they see only 5 percent pay increases, it isn't particularly motivating. In fact, a recent Hewitt study showed the average differentiation for high performers was a relatively insignificant 10 percent. Better compensation isn't an option – no pun intended – it's critical. All of the top companies differentiate pay between high-potentials and average performers in the same role. This frequently entails at least 75th-percentile pay and perhaps even as high as 90th-percentile pay. While that may sound excessive, it's still quite a bargain when you consider the value that these star performers bring to the table.

Leadership truth 3: top companies put in place the right programs, done right

Many firms can build a good leadership development program. However, even the most soundly designed leadership practices can be undermined by inconsistent implementation or lack of integration with other leadership processes. What sets the best firms apart from the rest is not just careful design of the right process but a relentless dedication to executing these flawlessly. And that means ensuring what they do is integral to the business.

GE's performance and succession planning process, known as Session C, has been a model for companies throughout the world. A fact little known outside of GE, it was invented by former CEO Ralph Cordiner in the 1950s, not Jack Welch. But Welch revolutionized it and made it a critical process for running GE. Session C provides a forum for leaders to discuss GE's talent and the opportunities to strengthen it, but as importantly, it provides a place for candor and debate, for calibration of standards and business priorities, and the reinforcement of cultural norms and values.

The process begins every January with hundreds of thousands of GE employees completing an online self-assessment, listing their accomplishments, adherence to GE's values, developmental goals, and career aspirations. At the same time, they update their internal résumés – jobs they've held and educational experiences – used for GE's global internal posting system. Supervisors and managers then complete a similar evaluation on each employee before meeting for an open discussion.

These individual evaluations flow upward, in a reverse cascade, through every department, function, geography, and business unit. Managers and leaders of departments meet and discuss unit by unit the talent they have and the talent they need. In May of each year, CEO Jeff Immelt visits each of GE's 13 business units for full-day Session C meetings, starting in the early morning and ending late into the night. The dialog is rich and open. Talent discussions on GE's top 500 positions are intertwined with business challenges, needs, and key initiatives like Six Sigma, digitalization, or the commercial or marketing side of GE. These strategic priorities are inseparable from the discussion of talent.

But the focus is clearly on the development of leaders to meet the business challenges ahead. Immelt probes and questions as every top executive is discussed. "Do people like working for her?" he will ask. "Who has she brought along? What does he want to do next?" If the executive is ready for a move, Bill Conaty, GE's vice president of human resources, and Susan Peters, vice president of executive development, facilitate cross-business assignments.

In July, Immelt and Conaty conduct a video conference with heads of the business units and their HR leaders to gauge progress on the May decisions. The public review and visibility is no accident. Follow-up and accountability are part of the DNA of high-performing companies and GE has been a charter member of that club for decades. Progress is checked again in the fall during operating review sessions.

The process is an integral part of running GE's $130 billion business. The discussion of talent throughout GE follows strategic reviews of each business and the key strategic initiatives shared with top management at GE's annual meeting in January, held in Boca Raton, Florida, for the top 600 executives. Following Boca, Peters and Conaty develop the agenda for Session C discussions to be held in the business units in the coming months. "Think about half the session focussing on the review of talent, the other half on the talent and organizational capability needed for the key business issues flowing out of Boca," said Peters. Strategy, talent, and operations are all intertwined, connected.

GE's formula for winning the war for talent is not that complicated, but few have achieved and sustained what they have for so long. Its building blocks are simple: hire outstanding talent, create an intense performance culture, and rigorously assess performance and promotability. Words to many. But at GE, they back it up. They continuously evaluate performance, formally and informally, and ensure differentiation in pay and opportunities between the best and the least effective. They "sell" careers and they have the infrastructure, and the discipline, to do what they say.

For other companies like IBM, Honeywell, and The Home Depot as well, talent assessments, development, and succession planning are intertwined with discussions of strategy and operations. It's no tangential exercise.

In our book, *Human Resources for the 21st Century*, several contributors posited that the future value of HR – indeed the very viability of the function – rests on its ability to integrate its activities more directly into the heart of the business, much like supply chain management, technology, and customer relationship management have done.[9] Each of these critical processes is a reinvention of predecessor functions that were necessary but of marginal value. Over the last decade, using technology and revamping tired, disconnected systems, they have become core to the modern enterprise.

At top companies, managing and developing talent is running the business. Strategy – where the company is headed, the products and services offered, and markets served – and operations – how decisions are made, the infrastructure, systems, and processes to support the strategy – are inseparable from the talent needed to do both. In top companies, HR builds the systems and processes, but the line drives it.

"One of the real differences between Colgate and other companies is that the whole leadership development program is facilitated by HR but driven by the line," says Colgate-Palmolive's chief operating officer Lois Juliber. "I think that's very important … the line owns leadership development, we work with HR to get all the tools, and they put in place the mechanisms. But if the line doesn't own it, it's not going to happen."

The result is a company with a reputation as a place where leaders want to work – a "leadership brand," that will ultimately separate the winners from the losers in the battle for leadership talent. The fact is, for the best talent, it's always a seller's market, and they can pick and choose from the best available opportunities. Those organizations that have cultivated a strong leadership brand will be far better positioned to attract and retain top leadership talent.

The three truths are important, but they don't quite capture all of it. There's more. There are a number of subtleties, nuances, an intensity, and pervasiveness of feeling, small patterns that account for some substantial differences between top companies and those below them. Leadership truth 1 emphasizes the importance of the CEO and the board in developing great leaders, but it goes well beyond them – everywhere you turn, the importance of finding and developing talent permeates the organization. It is a way of operating. Leaders and managers willingly to "give up" their best people to grow the organization, to build capability. They regularly take calculated risks, individually and organizationally, to move people out of their comfort zones to test new skills, strengthen others, and build the confidence needed for senior executive roles. This movement of talent across businesses, functions, and geographies creates a powerful web, a network that facilitates learning, a connectivity that fuels speed and communications, and a pride in the larger whole, not its parts. Individuals develop strong ties and a desire to give back to the organization and to the people that helped them, took the time to coach, support, and provide opportunities for them.

As we look to the future, the challenges are daunting and the opportunities are great. Top companies are well on their way to preparing themselves, and their people, to meet these challenges head on. They are a step ahead of the rest and they are not complacent. No executive we met felt they had it nailed. None has checked "developing leaders" off their priority list. That is yet one more differentiator for the best companies and the best leaders – they are less cynical, less complacent, always uncomfortable, and always aware that there is more work to be done.

This chapter was modified from *Leading the Way: Three Truths From the Top Companies for Leaders*, John Wiley, 2004.

'Interview': Michael Critelli

The chairman and CEO of mail and document management company Pitney Bowes talks about the role of the CEO and how to turn transformation into a reality.

You lead a company in a relatively unfashionable industry and in a mature market. What challenges does that provide?

I would take issue with us being in a mature market. We were in a mature market and had we not set out to reshape the market that would still have been a very accurate characterization. The communications marketplaces that we participate in, both mail and document management, are very large markets. We believe that the parts we can address with our competencies would be about $250 billion and are going through massive change – regulatory, technological, and competitive change. Wherever there is massive change there is an opportunity for growth. Customers want help trying to navigate their way through change.

You are known for emphasizing the role of values in your organization. Most major companies have a list of values. Are they still meaningful and practical, or just another form of PR?

Certain values are extremely critical to our brand and our success in the marketplace. One of our brand attributes is that we rank very highly on being trustworthy and reliable. We handle worldwide well over $15 billion, probably closer to $20 billion, of other people's money. We even own a bank in the United States, so having the attribute that we are honest, trustworthy, and reliable is not only a nice thing to have from a standpoint of commercial success but is critical to our value proposition.

The other attribute which has served us well is that we have always valued the opinion of our employees. We have always tried to create a work environment in which employees of different genders, origins, ages, and points of view can be successful and can tell senior leadership what it needs to hear.

The third is a sense of mission beyond making money. People need to believe they are doing well by doing good. I think that employees need to feel proud of the quality of their work and the mission to which their work is contributing. We are also known, justifiably I think, as a company which gives value back to the community. Our community activity is integral to the company's brand.

You emphasize R&D and innovation but that is something normally associated with Silicon Valley and high technology.

There are different ways to be inventive. You can invent a physical product which is completely new, but you can also invent a new market, or find innovative ways for technologies to work together which permit activities to be done in new ways.

So our innovation comes from studying problems and figuring out where there are opportunities as opposed to becoming enamored with the technology itself. If you think about Silicon Valley, a lot of those people are inventing tools rather than applications. We are an applications inventor for a specific set of marketplaces.

How long can you be effective as CEO over a sustained period?

Ten to thirteen years for our size company is optimal. If I was running General Electric then 20 years may be optimal. You keep the succession pipeline fresh. One of the risks of staying in the job for 20 years is that talented people who are a little younger and aspire to my job would leave. If they can have a reasonable tenure, I can keep them engaged and have a stronger team behind me. There is a benefit to having an orderly succession process and not staying until the board of directors forces you to leave. Beyond a certain length of time you get to believe that you can't be replaced so it is best to leave when you are still on top and still fresh.

A friend of mine told me that during the first three years on the job you're basically trying to get acclimatized. During the next five or six years you are a change agent, you put in place your programs and vision for the company, and in the last four years you are focussed on succession planning, ensuring the talent is there for the next generation. It has worked out that way for me. Between 2001 and probably 2005 or 2006 is my sweet spot to be a change agent. Partially overlapping that, even today I am actively working on the succession process.

How do you create a talent pool?

The most important thing to do in any succession process is to figure out what the world might look like in five to ten years. The second thing is what kind of skills and competencies that world will require. From there you use a variety of tools and techniques to make people ready and to test out whether they will have those skills and competencies.

Obviously at this senior level, it is most important that executives get exposure to areas outside their direct responsibilities. They need external experiences to develop skills and competencies. We have changed people's job accountabilities and given them more scope and wherever I can I work with them to give them coaching and advice. We provide them with 360-degree feedback supplemented with coaches. We have very frequent interaction with the board of directors. What is different today from the process by which I was selected is that boards of directors are much more active in the selection process. They want to get to know the candidates much earlier. We create a variety of mechanisms so that the next generation of executives can interact with the board of directors. I also work in partnership with the board in them assessing me and assessing the talent which reports to me.

What do you think are your key competencies as a CEO?

I am a change agent. Why I am the way I am I don't know, but I have always been a person who comes at problems in a different way. Then I ask, why isn't it this way?

I have a knack of seeing the world differently and then I try to relentlessly move toward the things which make that world a reality. I started out as a trial lawyer and I did a wide range of cases. I had to learn complex subject areas quickly and to master what the experts would tell me. I learned not to be intimidated by experts and specialists. I tell them that I need to be able to understand what they are saying in simple language. If I can't understand them, they are probably not thinking clearly. As a trial lawyer I had very limited windows of time to get the attention of judges with very limited patience. They would make us do quick pitches. I learned how to do that and I learned how to force people to think clearly, simply, and explain things that way.

The other thing I bring to business is a sense of thinking about it in terms of economics rather than accounting. I know accounting but a lot of people confuse accounting profits with economic profits. I tend to look at what makes economic sense.

There are two other characteristics which have helped me. One is I have a very good understanding of the value of time and speed. Having charged for my time as an attorney, I intuitively convert time to money and make economic decisions which take into account the money value of time. The other attribute is that I tend to be very driven by getting results as opposed to worrying which budget or cost center is affected. Tom Peters talks about a professional services mindset where you assemble a team to get a job done and then they move on. He uses the example of the film industry. I have always thought that way. Some people tend to get too fixated on their status in the organization and the way the organization is currently structured.

How do you divide your time?

Probably 5 percent of my time is spent on board and corporate governance matters. The next 25–30 percent is spent on meetings – individually with people who work with me, staff meetings, and a lot of one-on-ones. I have around 150 of those a year with people who don't work directly for me from all levels of the organization. I like to get directly to the source of information. I spend another 5–10 percent of my time meeting with postal officials, politicians, and other regulators. The next 10–15 percent of my time I spend in some form of interaction with customers. Then there are maybe a few days a year talking to shareholders, analysts, and the rating agencies – probably five days a year. The remaining time is spent on a variety of outside activities which somehow relate to my job.

How do you measure your personal performance as CEO?

There are certain things I want to accomplish over time at Pitney Bowes. But my own measure of success is probably whether I have reshaped the culture and direction of the company. There are a handful of ways I would measure that. One is whether I have leveraged the full power of the company behind a single unified brand. When I took over this was a very decentralized company which didn't really have everyone working together. So my first measure of success is whether we are behaving as one company.

Second, are we behaving with confidence and competence in shaping the world we live in rather than reacting to it? As a person I am highly driven by the desire for security. But the only way you can be secure in the world is to be at the table when the decisions are made about the rules of engagement. If you shape the rules you have a lot more security. You can't be secure by escaping conflict.

The third measure of my success is making us a global company. I am very excited that we are in many markets today where English is not the only language spoken. I want us to be confident and comfortable dealing across the globe.

Fourth, are we being very solutions and customer-driven rather than simply providing tools and assuming customers will know best how to use those tools? There are a couple of other things obviously. Every leader has to have a financially strong company that is stronger than the one he or she inherited. The other thing is that the company has the strength in depth of talent.

Implicit across all this are values. We have always been a company that people are proud to work for. Obviously I want to make sure that that doesn't change. In that respect I am not a change agent. I want to preserve the traditions and values we are known for.

You can't be a dictator or, at the other extreme, someone who listens to everyone. You have to balance stakeholders and make independent judgements. People put you in the job to represent the collective will of the organization, not to respond to every fad and fashion of the moment.

People often bemoan the dearth of leaders in the business world. Is this a fair observation?

To an extent, but there are many more leaders of good quality than people realize. The expectations of what leaders can do are wildly unrealistic. The politicians and regulators keep imposing more and more obligations on leaders without regard to the other things they already have to do. Having been in the job for many years, I have the capacity to absorb some of the additional things the new laws and regulations require, but I think we are slowly creating a situation where it will become impossible for leaders to balance all of the different responsibilities they have.

Value leadership: The principles driving corporate value

PETER S. COHAN

[Business and effective leadership depend on trust – creating it, preserving it, and, above all, valuing it.]

In the post-Enron years, the litany of problems facing equity capitalism has been well aired. The simple reality is that the misbehavior of a small number of rogue executives, analysts, and bankers has made life much harder for the majority who are honest, hardworking, and eager to enrich their shareholders, employees, customers, and communities. What executives need now is a way to rethink their businesses that will inspire people and revive corporate performance.

First the good news. There are companies that planted the seeds of their greatness in the midst of economic gloom by responding effectively to scarcity and challenge. These companies have followed a fundamental axiom of business that has eluded rogue executives: business depends on trust – creating it, preserving it, and, above all, valuing it. When trust is absent, business suffers in the long run. Trust is about relationships, in which people's actions correspond with their words; and the relationships that matter in business are with stakeholders – customers, investors, employees, suppliers, communities, and others.

Conversely, when this simple truth is appreciated – and held up as a corporate creed – people within an organization tend to find it inspiring. We must address the problems in our corporate cultures by inspiring people to act in the right way, not simply because it is right but because they and their organizations will be better off as a result.

The importance of building relationships on trust, and of inspiring behavior that serves those relationships, is central to the concept of "value leadership." Moreover, companies' adoption of the value leadership concept is so closely tied to their superior financial performance that value leadership pays.

According to John Bachmann, managing director of Edward Jones, the privately held securities broker based in St Louis, this imperative helped him transform the company when it was perched on the brink of extinction 33 years ago. In 1970, the brokerage industry was in the doldrums. The Dow was down 50 percent and the equivalent of the NASDAQ had plunged 75 percent. Edward Jones, which had grown to over 100 offices from its founding in the 1920s, was suffering badly. And it had only $1million worth of capital left to its name. Furthermore, the industry was about to get worse as the government deregulated fixed commissions for trading securities.

Bachmann, who was running the firm's Columbia office, and Ted Jones, the founder's son, made a crucial decision at the time that has propelled Edward Jones to an enviable position in 2003. The company now has 8,700 offices, over 25,000 employees, and $2.2 billion in revenue. It has sustained double-digit growth in revenues and profits for two decades while the industry as a whole has seen its fortunes plunge. Edward Jones topped *Fortune*'s survey of the 100 Best Companies to Work For in 2002 and 2003. And it has won other awards, including a number-one ranking in the J.D. Power & Associates customer service survey.

The crucial decision that Bachmann and Jones made over 30 years ago was simple but profound. With dwindling capital, they decided that Edward Jones's survival would depend on focussing on just one type of customer: the long-term individual investor. This decision caused Edward Jones to quit its activities targetted at the institutional investor – such as commodities trading – because the firm lacked the capital and resources to compete for institutional trading business.

For Bachmann and Jones, the focus of Edward Jones would be "the Mrs Ballews" of the world. Mrs Ballew was the proprietor of a local funeral home and over the years Edward Jones had advised her on how to invest the cash that her business generated.

Finding and serving the Mrs Ballews of the world was Edward Jones's version of the search for the Holy Grail. Jones had an interest in agriculture and told his father that he did not want to spend his career in St Louis. Instead he went out into the countryside knocking on doors, meeting small business people and farmers, building trust with them, and advising them on long-term investments. In such small communities, word would get around if a customer was not treated well.

Jones's values fitted well with the needs of the market. Since he had no children, he decided not to sell the business as he grew older. Instead, he took on partners, giving up his ownership so others could act as stewards of Edward Jones. And a crucial element of this stewardship was that every investment representative who joined Edward Jones would have to engage in their own search for the Holy Grail by spending the first three to four months of their careers personally meeting with 25 potential customers a day – creating relationships.

Edward Jones is a life-support system for people willing to undertake this quest. Its values are based on respect – for external customers, for long-term relationships, for contributions to the organization, and for generating results. It sells only stocks, bonds, and other investment products that appeal to long-term investors. It provides its customers with statements that aggregate in one place all their accounts, from investments to mutual funds, credit cards, bank accounts, and more.

Edward Jones invests an unusual amount of effort in hiring and developing its people. Of the 15,000 job inquiries it receives each month, the firm hires only 200.

It looks for high achievers with a sense of purpose. Interestingly, it discourages people from talking about their honesty and integrity. According to Bachmann, his mother warned him: "Be careful John, you could break your arm patting yourself on the back."

Once investment representatives are hired, Edward Jones invests in training them to pass their Series 7 exam, the general securities representative license. And if these investment reps take responsibility for their work, demonstrate an aptitude for inventing growth opportunities consistent with the firm's values, and earn the respect of their peers while achieving success, they are offered shares in the firm's partnership.

What Edward Jones chooses *not* to do is as important as what it does. Each investment representative is a profit center. Edward Jones does not create separate profit centers for each product. Everyone at Edward Jones works together to help the investor – they don't compete with each other. The company reinforces this value by paying its bonuses based mostly on the firm's overall performance above a minimum threshold. Rather than offering incentive travel to, say, the top 10 percent of its investment reps, it offers such travel to anyone who achieves a predetermined level of success. In 2002, 3,500 out of 9,000 total investment reps earned such awards.

Since, at the time of writing, many industries have limited pricing power and very little access to capital, they need to learn how to deal with scarcity in a way that makes them operate more effectively. Bachmann's advice to these companies is timeless:

- decide who your customer is
- know how your company creates unique value for that customer
- choose not to perform activities that do not create value for that customer
- align all your company's activities to create that value
- recognize that meaningful change takes time, so take the long view.

Fixing the problem by changing corporate behavior, not regulation

This example is intended to highlight an important conclusion – government cannot rebuild confidence in American capitalism. Looking for government to solve the problem is tantamount to expecting a new manager to turn a poor soccer team into a World Cup contender. The place to look for guidance is a concept that has helped create value for companies like Edward Jones during good times and bad.

The notion that made the difference for Edward Jones was a novel approach to value itself. Value traditionally refers to purchasing something – whether shares of a company or a product – at below market price. But Edward Jones's successful turnaround hinged on extending the concept of value across many different dimensions of its business. Edward Jones decided to create superior value for its *owners* by narrowing the focus of its scarce capital (excluding institutional investors and targetting long-term individual investors) to increase its likely partnership profits.

It created a better deal for its existing employees by carefully screening new employees for their fit with its core beliefs and for their ability to add profitable new clients while preserving its reputation. Its employees created a better future for its clients by selling products that yielded long-term investment value. And by creating a better deal for carefully selected employees and customers, Edward Jones enriches the communities in which it operates.

Edward Jones's success is due to its belief in a powerful new concept of value – value leadership. This is based on very specific notions of value and leadership. It recognizes that a company cannot survive without the participation of others – employees, customers, investors, and communities.

The "value" in value leadership alludes to the nature of the relationship between the company and these others. These relationships have value if both the company and the others are better off as a result of forming and sustaining the relationship.

The "leadership" in value leadership suggests a connection between how well a company creates value in its relationships relative to its peers and the relative rate of return that the company offers its investors. Companies battle to create competitively superior value for the "best" employees, customers, investors, and communities. Winning these battles yields competitively superior returns for investors because the best people, co-ordinated effectively, generate the most effective and efficient solutions to customer problems. Through profit sharing and/or stock ownership, employees and investors share in the gains from these solutions.

Value leadership means giving a company's employees, customers, investors, and communities a better deal than competitors. Value leadership depends on providing competitively superior value to individual groups such as customers and employees as well as on orchestrating the relationships among these groups to create a self-sustaining system of value creation.

Value leadership's seven principles

Value leadership depends on seven management principles that have been tested in periods of economic expansion and contraction. These principles are:

- value human relationships: treating people with respect so they achieve their full potential;
- foster teamwork: getting people in different functions to advance corporate interests;
- experiment frugally: harnessing happy accidents to create value for customers and partners;

- fulfil your commitments: saying what you intend to do and doing what you said;
- fight complacency: maintaining a health paranoia that drives companies to keep improving;
- win through multiple means: outperforming competitors in conducting activities to create value for customers;
- give to your community: using corporate resources to inspire employees and enhance the community.

Measuring and managing value leadership

In my view, the passion that CEOs have for winning propels them to follow these seven principles. To help executives in their quest, I have developed the concept of the value quotient (VQ). The VQ is based on the idea that in order to translate these seven principles into action, companies must perform activities in a new way.

Based on analysis of case studies comparing how value leaders (see below) and their peers realize the principles, I have identified 24 specific activities on which the VQ depends. For example, the four activities supporting the principle experiment frugally are:

- grow organically: build new lines of business in markets that are large and growing in which competitive success depends on capabilities that your company can perform better than incumbents;
- manage development risk: break down new product development projects into small pieces with numerous go/no-go decision points. If a project does not achieve specific predefined goals at these decision points then the people and money dedicated to these projects can be reallocated to higher-potential projects;
- partner internally: when developing new products or processes, form internal teams that include all the business functions that will be affected by the new product or process. These teams can help the company to identify and resolve potential problems early in the development process, thus lowering the cost of product development, cutting the time to market, and increasing the product's market acceptance;
- partner externally: similarly, when companies develop new products that may affect the entire industry, such as those involving product standards, companies should work closely with their peers in order to address and resolve differences so that the final product will satisfy customer needs.

The VQ measures how well companies perform these 24 activities relative to the value leaders. Companies should conduct interviews with key stakeholders such as employees, customers, communities, and regulators to gather meaningful data. Then they can compare how well they perform these activities to the companies in the value leadership database that my firm maintains.

The value leadership database is an electronic catalog of VQs along with the specific rationale behind the scores. For each company, the value leadership database includes its score on each of the 24 activities along with a description of its approach to the activity. The value leadership database serves two purposes. It offers a way for managers to calibrate their VQs by comparing the way they approach activities with that of the companies in the value leadership database. While there is always an element of judgement involved in assigning activity scores, the value leadership database helps increase the objectivity of the scoring process. Second, the value leadership database contains a rich array of best practices. These can be particularly useful for companies which calculate their VQ and are looking for ways to improve the way they perform specific activities for which they received weak scores. As the value leadership database adds more companies, it will become an even richer source of best practices within specific industries, specific countries, and globally.

For managers and investors, the VQ is a particularly powerful tool because it correlates so well with long-term shareholder returns. In plotting value leaders" 10-year shareholder returns relative to the market averages against their VQs, the correlation is unmistakable. In short, the higher the VQ, the higher the long-run shareholder returns.

The VQs are developed through a four-step process:

- Score each company on how well it performs the activities within each of the seven principles. The scores for each activity range from 5, excellent, to 1, poor.
- Total the scores for each activity and multiply the sum by a weight that enables each principle to contribute equally to the overall score. For principles with four activities, the multiplier is three; for principles with three activities, the multiplier is four. As a result, the maximum possible score for each principle is 60.
- Sum the weighted scores for each of the seven principles.
- Divide the result by the maximum possible score of 420.

Value leadership and economic cycles

Value leadership is intended to help executives address different challenges at different stages of an economic cycle. It offers concepts and methods that can help executives restore faith in their companies during a period when the excesses of the previous boom are being worked out. In future periods of economic contraction, the principles of value leadership are intended to be equally useful.

During periods of rapid economic growth and optimism, value leadership can help executives from straying too far from the values that produced the success. Human nature suggests that during the periods of greatest success, executives risk becoming arrogant and insulated from the values that led to that success. Conversely, during periods of economic contraction, executives proclaim their willingness to conform to tight management discipline. Because value leadership analyzes companies that have sustained superior performance through good times and bad, its principles serve executives throughout the full amplitude of an economic cycle.

Most of all, value leadership pays. By screening 1,500 companies via 11 criteria tightly linked with the seven principles, I found eight US companies that follow the principles more closely than their peers. These "value leaders" – Synopsys, Wal-Mart, Goldman Sachs, MBNA, Johnson & Johnson, J. M. Smucker, Southwest Airlines, and Microsoft – grew revenues 35 percent faster, earned 109 percent higher profit margins, and increased shareholder value at five times the rate of their peers between June 1992 and June 2002.

So, what's your VQ?

Value leadership represents an enormous business opportunity for managers with the vision and ambition to seize it. Value leaders" superior financial performance and shareholder returns hint at its magnitude. The first step is to find out how much your company embodies value leadership. By calculating your company's VQ, you can assess how your company stacks up against the value leaders. More importantly, knowing your VQ can help you identify which improvement initiatives will be most valuable. Your shareholders, employees, customers, and communities demand no less.

RESOURCES

Cohan, Peter, *Value Leadership: The 7 Principles that Drive Corporate Value in any Economy*, Jossey Bass, 2003.

Welcome to the real world – eight essential perspectives for the new top leader

PHIL HODGSON

[After a career of striving, you eventually reach the corporate summit. But what's next?]

"Congratulations, you've just been appointed as the new CEO." Great news, isn't it? So, what do you do next? We've been researching the practicalities of how people survived and grew as managers and leaders when they took on a top leader role. We called it the Top Leader Journey.[10] Our definition of the top leader's role is simple: it is where the buck stops. You feel the responsibility, you probably take it home with you, and you understand in some way that it is on your shoulders that matters now press.

"You are met with this overwhelming need to deliver which exists in any role, but suddenly the buck very definitely stops with you," one leader told us. "I don't think that was a surprise, but there is a pressure there that becomes all apparent, and if you're performing well, and your team is performing well, it's not an issue, it's a big buzz. If you're not performing well, or the business isn't performing well, that's where the pressure comes in and I think that's something you expect, but it's not until you come into the role that you realize the level of the pressure."

Leading at the top has never had guaranteed success. The various estimates for the duration of tenure in the CEO's role vary from five years[11] to 6.5 years for European CEOs and 9.5 years for CEOs from the US.[12] In one report, 50 percent of the company's reputation is seen as attributable to the CEO.[13] The pressures, the politics, the need to achieve while being compared with a previous leader's performance build a significant challenge to the new top leader.

But what is new in this tough and rarefied world? Leadership was never a matter of simply following some rules, but at least in the past there were lots of examples of people who, apparently at least, did it well.[14,15,16] However, in the few years surrounding the transition from the second to the third millennium, so much changed in the style in which leadership was accomplished and so many famous leadership role models turned out to be less perfect than expected. Think of the Internet bubble, Enron, fat-cat rewards for failure, the collapse of stock market prices. Since the late 1990s this well-documented fall from grace of so many leaders and their organizations has left present-day leaders and those aspiring to such roles with few proven and trustworthy examples of how to behave.[17,18]

We wanted to know how this millennium's leaders are coping. What is most important now? Are there some timeless approaches to leadership that they still value? What is the current leadership agenda? From our research we identified eight perspectives on that agenda that seemed to be the tools and approaches that the people we researched found most useful.

Credibility is a currency

Top leaders need credibility: no surprise there.[19] But the idea of credibility seems to be supplanting power and influencing. It includes both. Although few of the people we researched used the term directly, most of them were very aware that in order to get things done and to use their power and influence effectively, they had to have credibility with the right people at the right time. We saw credibility being earned, spent, risked, wasted. In some ways it was like money, so we defined it as follows: "Credibility is like a kind of currency, it's based on others" beliefs or perceptions that you can perform and deliver. It can be increased, lost, spent, loaned, and stolen."

We also noticed that credibility had a connection with those other two staples of the leadership diet, confidence and courage. In the activities of these modern leaders we saw confidence being "a combination of a leader's own perception of their capability to do something, plus their assessment of other people's credibility in them."

Courage – often an important element in leadership – can now be understood in terms of credibility: "To knowingly risk the loss of credibility or a personally damaging outcome, in order to achieve a desired goal, often in the face of adversity."

Top team

The new top leader would be like an air guitar player unless he or she has the skills and capability to do the job well. Hopefully, the previous years will have furnished them with the requisite skills. But even the most skillful player will reach a very small audience unless they have decent amplification. The top team is the amplifier. If the new top leader doesn't get at least some people around them who are in tune with their thinking and style, then no matter how energetic the leader, the effect of the leader will be small. If the top team is perceived by followers not to be in line with the leader, it's even worse, because that team will act as a damper and diffuser to the leader's efforts.

Focus of attention

Many of our respondents had thought hard about taking on the new job before they arrived. It fascinated us to discover that the areas into which they put most energy in the first few days and weeks of their job (what we called their focus of attention) seemed to be driven as much by their history and previous competence as by any particular organizational need. A person with a financial background would spend most time on the finances; a sales person focussed on market. It seemed as if the expertise a person brought with them into the new job in some way took precedence over the situation and defined that area of expertise as the most significant area for them to focus on.

We would suggest that effective top leaders will often need to step outside their favorite competences so that they can pay more attention to areas which need their attention, even though their previous experience may not have equipped them with the necessary knowledge or skills. Sometimes it is even an opportunity to use that lack of knowledge as a way to help the organization develop. Here is a new CEO with a background in marketing, who was trying to get to grips with logistics in her furniture retailer company. "The first thing was that I had never worked in logistics or supply chain so there was a huge gap … My background was sales and marketing. I knew nothing about warehousing, delivery, etc. So I went to the senior management who had been in the business for 10 to 12 years and I told them that I didn't know anything about it. I went into a room and pinned up brown paper all around the walls. I said I know nothing about this. Treat me as a customer. Imagine I've come in and bought my furniture. Now what happens? So I had accounts, buying, and supply chain there. Each of them stood up and told me what they did and the process was captured on the brown paper wall.

"They thought that I was completely bonkers to begin with, as they had never been asked to sit in a room together, and when I described the process as a relay race they thought it was rather odd. They didn't know when to let go of the baton and to pass it on to someone else. They discovered in an hour and a half that there were all sorts of cross-functional activities which were going on which were historical and not logical. By late afternoon they were running the supply chain and I wasn't. They were going up to the brown paper and questioning why this function was done by this department and not another."

By admitting her lack of knowledge, but by not letting that get in the way, this new CEO gained a lot of credibility with senior members of the organization.

Emotional and intellectual support mechanisms

Modern leaders seem to understand that while the job is still lonely, they don't have to struggle on bearing the weight of responsibility alone. It did not seem to be regarded as a sign of weakness to expect to have support. In our sample we found a variety of ways that people coped with the "loneliness" of a top job.

Many of the people we talked to had taken active steps to build personal support mechanisms that they called on as the pressures of the job had their effect. Coaching particularly seemed to be of significance to many, where for the most part the coach was found outside the organization's walls. Many of these leaders were instrumental in arranging coaching for their own staff and seemed content that these conversations would occur as their own conversations did, i.e. with total confidentiality between coach and leader.

Learning as if your life depended on it

It was noticeable that although the CEOs whom we interviewed had status within their organization and often in their industry, they didn't think of themselves as much different from anyone else. They thought of themselves as ordinary people called upon to do extraordinary things and recognized that they would have to become extraordinary in the process. One CEO said: "During the week I'm chauffeured around by the company, at the weekend I am the chauffeur for my children, and I'm still the same person."

The world of the top leader is a continual balancing act, knowledge against possibility, information against intuition, risk against certainty. In some ways, nothing exactly prepares you for what you have to deal with today, and today may not prepare you for tomorrow. Not at least unless you work at it. What screams at us from the data is the way so many leaders were continuously learning and continuously developing. They often didn't talk of it in those terms, but it was clear that they expected that they and their organizations had to develop on a continuing basis if they wanted to survive.

Yet we wonder how many organizations are set up to encourage new and prospective top leaders to understand how fundamental continuous learning will be to their development and their ability to take on bigger and bigger roles? Is top-level learning and development just a cliché that is mouthed and forgotten? Independent evidence suggests that companies identified as highly effective on a long-term basis share a practical emphasis on developing learning in all its forms at all levels in the organization.[20]

Spotting and developing potential

It is not enough for top leaders to be learners. Many top leaders take a deep and personal interest in spotting and developing talent across the organization. For some it seemed to be almost a reflex action. Wherever they were, in offices, shops, factories, whenever they were talking with their staff, they would be assessing and looking out for signs in people of a readiness to improve.

But spotting wasn't enough for many top leaders. They would put some of their personal time and energy into giving high-potential people opportunities to use their talents in bigger, different, or more productive ways.

Inspiration and energy

Effective leaders need energy for themselves, that has long been known. But these leaders that are going to empower their followers to take on and succeed will need their own source of energy. Effective leaders also need to inspire energy in their followers. Yet although many of the people we researched were fluent and able to convey their ideas easily, few of them thought of themselves as directly inspiring.

So to try to understand how their minds worked on this topic, we asked what inspired them, and got answers that ranged from "my mum," through, "a previous boss," to "my friend who achieves amazing things despite being haemophilic." In many cases they had borrowed something from the style of the person who had inspired them. We found that there were very few famous business leaders offered to us as sources of inspiration, however charismatic those people were in their jobs. It suggested that the modern top leader looks closer to home for inspiration and not on the front pages of the business press for their sources of inspirational energy. Charisma is probably still there, but it is of a different kind. Not the sort that ordinarily gains headlines, more the day-to-day sort that simply gains genuine admirers.

Managing upwards and outwards

Top leaders are seldom completely alone. They have chairmen, presidents, ministers, family owners, non-executives, managing committees, and boards, as well as a host of observers and analysts. Sometimes, a significant part of the top leader's role is to establish and make those relationships work. Where a particularly close working relationship was anticipated, many found it useful to establish early on how that working relationship should operate. How, for instance, they would expect the other to behave when things were going well and when things were going badly.

Whatever the situation, the skill of managing relationships with key stakeholders and building credibility with them was a frequent theme.

At the top in the real world

It's a tough job, but then it is often a tough world. Our findings suggest that the top leader of today and tomorrow is first and foremost oriented toward learning. They operate in an atmosphere where stimulation and transition are the norm. It can be a great ride – new CEOs can probably develop faster than they have ever done before. But it can also have serious downs – that same CEO a few months later can sink faster into disaster and oblivion than they ever believed was possible.

Is there a formula for success? We doubt it. Organizations and their environments are both very complex systems. It is probably never possible to know all that it would be necessary to know in order to make by pure logic the decisions that top leaders are called on to make daily. Do they guess? Not too often, we hope. However, our evidence suggests that they use many of the eight perspectives we have identified which help them – if not to guarantee success – at least to increase its probability.

RESOURCES

Hodgson, Phil and White, Randall, P., *Relax, It's Only Uncertainty*, FT Prentice Hall, 2001.

Hodgson, Phil and Crainer, Stuart, *What Do High Performance Managers Really Do?*, FT Pitman, 1993.

If Colin Powell had commanded Enron: The hidden foundation of leadership

OREN HARARI AND LYNN BREWER

[The leadership principles and actions of Colin Powell, US Secretary of State, are in direct contrast to those of the executives of the failed energy giant Enron. Oren Harari and Lynn Brewer analyze the differences and draw lessons for how leadership should be developed and exercised.]

This article is not about Colin Powell, the person, but rather the leadership he espouses. The attributes of leadership that Powell has demonstrated throughout his 40-year career are ones that managers in all industries would be wise to demonstrate, especially in today's market environment, which seems to be spiked daily by yet another disappointing day on the stock exchanges of the world, another government investigation, another investor-backed lawsuit, another bankruptcy announcement, another wave of earnings restatements, and another criminal indictment of a high-profile executive.

The proven leadership that Colin Powell has shown as a military officer, National Security Advisor, Chairman of the Joint Chiefs, and head of the State Department is in stark contrast to the leadership that marked the acme of corporate malfeasance and shareholder decline: Enron.

We highlight Enron for two reasons. First, there is Enron's obvious notoriety. From 1997 to 2001 Enron and its managers catapulted into "rock stardom" in the business world. Heralded as the "corporation of the new millennium," Enron was the darling of analysts, investors, professors, and journalists. Its stock value ascended to a dizzying $90.56 per share in August 2000 (boasting a 700 percent return over the prior decade) as its revenue explosion elevated its status to the fifth-largest company in the US. The company was showered with countless awards and accolades.

The second reason for our choice is that one could argue that in terms of reflecting executive greed, strategic distortion, and market damage, Enron had "first-mover" advantage in our current cycle of corporate corruption.

Yet just as this is not a history of Powell, it is not a critique of Enron. Our interest is in contrasting the behaviors of former leaders of Enron with the leadership principles of Powell in order to develop a new perspective of leadership, appropriate for the realities of today's marketplace.

Beginning with an odd conclusion

If you consider the advice of many acclaimed leadership "gurus" about what constitutes effective leadership in organizations, you might come to an odd conclusion: the senior managers at Enron were actually superb leaders worth emulating. Did they have a bold, market-leading vision for Enron? *Yes.* Were they able to inspire "the troops" to buy into and carry out this vision? *Yes, again.* Were they able to create a fast-paced, highly innovative, change-oriented, entrepreneurial culture to execute this vision? *Yes, a third time.* Were they able to attract the best and brightest and provide a culture where these hard-chargers were empowered to perform and were highly rewarded for their accomplishments? *On all accounts – affirmative.*

The conventional criteria for good leadership outlined above are attributes that senior Enron people such as Chairman Kenneth Lay, CEO Jeffrey Skilling, CFO Andrew Fastow, Chief Accounting Officer Richard Causey, Chief Risk Officer Richard Buy, and the entire Enron board of directors had in spades – attributes that are both valid and necessary. But for genuine leaders, they represent only half the story. The other half of the story turns out to be the less flashy, below-the-surface *foundation* of leadership.

The hidden foundation of leadership: seven tenets

1. Keep looking below surface appearances. Don't shrink from doing so just because you might not like what you find.

Colin Powell argues that good leaders are not easily misled by superficial analysis, surface truths, or "spin." Further, they continually probe for data, follow up on their hunches, and tenaciously dig below the surface, always asking: "What are we doing, right or wrong? How can it be improved? What needs to be changed?"

Authentic leaders have enough integrity and self-confidence to ask the toughest, most disruptive, and most uncomfortable questions. That's how they uncover problems and inspire change. Throughout his career, Powell has lived this principle, which is why, for example, he came to painfully reassess the military's "flabby thinking" (Powell's words) in Vietnam in the 1960s and its unqualified support of the Shah of Iran, who was ultimately overthrown in the 1970s.

Now let's consider Enron's leadership, where top managers did a 180-degree turn on this principle. They systematically pushed unjustifiable decisions and developments below the surface via deliberately opaque accounting and financial reporting and sneered at outsiders who questioned Enron's strategies or financials.

When Richard Grubman, a Boston hedge fund manager, attempted to keep looking below surface appearances, by pointing out that Enron was the only company of its kind that failed to present its balance sheet with the release of its earnings, CEO Jeffrey Skilling attempted to publicly shame him into submission by calling him an "asshole." This, of course, from a company whose official values statement called for "respect" and stated that "ruthlessness, callousness, and arrogance don't belong here."

The board of directors played along. In 1999–2000, the board's audit committee, headed by Robert Jaedicke, heard several reports from Arthur Andersen that Enron was a "maximum risk" client whose accounting practices were "at the edge." The board asked and did nothing. In 2001, the board would receive a presentation that demonstrated that between 2000 and 2001 there had been a 300 percent increase in "whistleblowing" reports to the Office of the Chairman from executives inside the company. Of the reports received, 75 percent were reports of fraud.

Today, the fact that the directors whine they "didn't know" because they were "misled by management" really begs the question: why were board members willing to look the other way?

The guilty plea of CFO Andrew Fastow, as well as former finance executive Michael Kopper, to fraud and money laundering suggests that what was going on below the surface was even more serious than many outsiders imagined. The *New York Times* cited legal experts who concluded that Enron's entire strategy "… has lost its veneer of a business idea and taken on the air of little more than a financial fraud in which only a small number of insiders knew the truth."

Had the outside world been willing to look at the foundation of Enron's leadership they too would have found it was shaky. In Enron's 2000 Annual Report to shareholders, Jeff Skilling proclaimed: "The company's net income reached a record $1.3 billion in 2000." However, a closer inspection would have revealed that the company's net income was only $979 according to its *audited* financials located only a few pages behind the hyperbole.

Conclusion: Great leaders don't construct a veneer; they take the initiative to crush it in their quest to know the truth. Powell argues: "Untidy truth is better than smooth lies that unravel in the end anyway." Powell argues that "it is best to get the facts out as soon as possible, even when new facts contradict the old," even when the "truth" challenges leaders' own decisions and actions.

2. The day soldiers stop bringing you their problems is the day you have stopped leading them. They have either lost confidence that you can help them or concluded that you do not care. Either case is a failure of leadership.

A corporate culture with integrity encourages what Powell calls "a noisy system" filled with "the clash of ideas" where even contrarians who challenge sacred cows are encouraged and protected. It all begins with leadership that *lives* accessibility and listening to the troops.

Powell's career has been based on this principle. When he visits foreign outposts, he surprises country desk officers by dropping in unannounced. Often during official tours, he will carve out a segment of his daily calendar for private conversations with front-line people. From Powell's perspective, good leaders have a finely tuned capacity to listen to all hands, to accept insights and advice from any source when the facts warrant it, and to create a climate where the "clash of ideas" is genuine and far reaching. Only then, argues Powell, can you have a *sustainable* environment of mutual trust, open communication, and creative problem solving.

At Enron, not only was it the case that leaders themselves didn't dig under the surface for the truth, it was clear to the "soldiers" in the organization that top management didn't want them to dig either. Top management had no interest in listening to bottom-up straight talk about shady accounting or flaky investments. Yet according to many employees, red flags were everywhere.

On 29 August, 2001, for example, Margaret Ceconi, a manager with Enron Energy Services (EES), sent an e-mail to the head of Enron's human resources, requesting it be forwarded to the board of directors, stating: "EES has knowingly misrepresented EES' earnings." The e-mail was never forwarded. Likewise, when vice-president Sherron Watkins, Enron's famed whistleblower, provided evidence of potential accounting scandals, Chairman Kenneth Lay, in essence, dismissed her claims while CFO Andrew Fastow seized her computer and attempted to fire her. Meanwhile, when the board learned of Watkins' memo, not a single member made any further inquiry, even though the memo pointedly addressed private partnerships, which were subject to review by the finance committee chaired by Herbert "Pug" Winokur.

Ironically, for a company heralded as innovative, Enron was remarkably rigid in terms of exacting conformity to the party line. While individual innovation in spearheading new trading initiatives was rewarded, employees operated in a quasi-totalitarian climate when it came to challenging (or, more appropriately, not challenging) the prevailing wisdom.

The semi-annual 360-degree performance review process reinforced this climate. The review process, which aimed to weed out the 5 percent poorest performers, also served to oust another 10 percent of employees who ruffled feathers and challenged the process by asking "inappropriate" questions. Apart from fomenting distrust and backstabbing among the "troops," the performance review process allowed leadership to continue its attitude of supremacy.

Conclusion: Great leaders create cultures marked by an unfettered clash of ideas, candid communication, and unfiltered dialog – all aimed at solving problems in extraordinary ways. The opposite culture, marked by Enron, dramatically contributed to its implosion. To use Powell's terminology, Enron employees stopped bringing their problems to management because they lost confidence that managers would help them or they concluded that they did not care.

3. Never neglect details

For Powell, vigilance in details is essential for strategic preparation and execution. Powell doesn't buy into the concept of the leader who stays perched on a lofty pedestal having "delegated" to others the details of his or her "grand vision." Good leaders are not micro-managers, nor are they obsessive-compulsives. They delegate liberally. But at the same time, they are intensely committed toward being "in the know" and they refuse to lose connection with the people and activities they are supposed to be leading.

The transcripts of the military commanders' meetings before and during the 1990 Gulf War against Iraq revealed how carefully Powell and Norman Schwarzkopf, the most senior executives of the command, paid attention to a constant flow of details to keep themselves in the loop as well as to minimize unpleasant surprises, accelerate urgency, continually shift people's attention to the right places, and generate contingency plans on a rolling basis.

When leaders remove themselves from the details they lose touch. And when they lose touch, their decisions are increasingly made in a self-serving, undisciplined vacuum. This is precisely what happened at Enron. The former top executives and board members of Enron (and of its partners Arthur Andersen and law firm Vinson and Elkins) are falling over themselves in trying to win the "who knew less?" contest. It seems that nobody in a position of power knew anything.

Either these people are simply lying, or they blatantly violated a basic principle of responsible leadership – they failed to know; they failed to stay in touch.

To assume that underlings at Enron could pull off the scam of the century without top management's knowledge is on the surface ludicrous, but if true, clearly demonstrates how being "out of touch" can rock the foundation of an organization that is not built on solid leadership principles. "If you don't know what information is flowing through your organization," warns Powell, "you don't know what's going on in your organization."

Conclusion: No leader can or should be aware of all details, but great leaders make it a point to stay in the loop with the important details. In the case of Enron, the 2,300 subsidiaries and off-balance sheet partnerships, the concealment of hundreds of millions of dollars of debt, the gross inflation of earnings, and the collapse of sizeable investments in the trading of non-energy commodities like water and broadband should have been foremost in the details considered important by Enron's leadership.

4. If the troops are cold, you're cold. Corporate leaders ought to learn that. Too often those at high levels don't quite understand the sacrifices and hardships of those at the bottom.

For Powell, the principle of "shared sacrifice" is a critical attribute of leadership and not simply because it represents ethics and decency. As Powell argues, in order to galvanize shared direction, innovation, and *esprit de corps* on a sustained basis, "they (employees, soldiers) must believe that they are part of a team – a joint team – that fights together to win." For genuine teamwork and togetherness to occur, a leader must *care* about the welfare of his troops.

If there is one thing that impartial observers can agree upon, it's that senior managers at Enron violated this principle thoroughly and convincingly, especially as the stock descended. Even as they were assuring nervous employees and institutional investors that Enron was sound, 29 Enron officials sold off nearly $1.2 billion of company shares, while rank-and-file employees were often legally barred from doing so. Top managers pocketed $680 million in 2001 alone. Lay, himself, sold off $70 million of stock between February and October 2001.

While all these events were happening, of course, ordinary Enron employees got crushed, as did millions of outside investors, as the stock dropped from $79.00 to 50 cents in a year.

For leaders like Powell, such self-serving actions are incomprehensible, especially in an environment where teamwork, collaboration, and mutual trust become increasingly important.

Conclusion: Trust is essential for a leader's influence and credibility. While many factors affect trust, the traits which Powell labels as "selflessness, sacrifice, and empathy" are high on the list. Great leaders are happy to share the wealth with team members when times are good and, unlike at Enron, they do so generously and with grace. But the true mettle of leadership occurs when times are bad. Great leaders share financial pain. In contrast, too often we read about a faltering corporation whose employees face layoffs and salary cuts even as their executives keep their huge compensation packages and golden parachutes.

5. Never let your ego get so close to your position that when your position goes, your ego goes with it.

Good leaders have very healthy egos. But when they wed their egos to the status quo, problems begin, because the status quo inevitably changes. Rather than focussing organizational resources to protect their current positions – a sign of strategic myopia and personal insecurity – great leaders apply their healthy egos toward capitalizing on the changes around them.

By the late 1980s, for example, Powell saw mammoth changes emerging in his environment. The Soviet Union collapsed, the Warsaw Pact imploded, the Berlin Wall fell, and the ideologies of Marxism and Leninism sank into disrepute. "In the military, to put it in corporate terms," said Powell, "our product line was now out of date. I saw it as my main mission to move the armed forces onto a new course, one paralleling what was happening in the world today, not one chained to the previous 40 years."

Powell began shaping a vision that revolved around a leaner, nimbler, more mobile, technologically "smarter" military that could anticipate and put out fires from multiple sources around the world. Certainly, in the current war against a global terrorist network, his thinking proved prescient.

On one level, the innovation at Enron was praiseworthy. It was originally aimed at transforming the company from a bricks-and-mortar energy provider to a financial powerhouse that could trade any commodity and reinvent value chains in any industry. On another level, however, as the company grew, it became apparent that the financial returns were spurious and the business model itself was unsustainable. It was at this point that senior executives at Enron allowed their egos to get too close to a position (the new, virtual, web- and derivatives-based Enron) that was sexy and exciting on the surface but hollow on the inside.

As in so many companies which struggle to tread water with a flawed strategic approach, desperation became synonymous with innovation. The obsession became two-fold: do whatever it takes – however "creatively" – to prop up the business model, and do so by doing whatever it takes to raise stock value.

Hence, the business model became sacrosanct, even as it became more of a charade. Since the great fear was that if anyone peered through the curtains, the house of cards – along with executives" egos, careers, reputations, and compensation – would collapse, enormous amounts of energy were devoted to propping it all up. Increasingly, the innovation and entrepreneurship revolved around creative accounting and financial sleight of hand.

Conclusion: When a leader's primary strategy is to disregard market warnings and "circle the wagons" to protect existing business designs, strategies, and products, the end is in sight, both ethically and competitively. Great leaders balance their strong egos with humility, which allows them to continually press for new positions in light of external changes and reality checks. As Powell has advised others throughout his career: "Dig deep and rip out that old mission and fill it immediately with a new mission and then start training for it. You cannot tolerate a vacuum!"

6. It is more important to do what is right than to do what is personally beneficial. Whatever the cost, do what is right.

For Powell, "doing what is right" is at the core of courage and character, both of which are paramount for leadership. Doing what is "right" means standing for an honorable value or deal even in the face of adversity. It means holding the banner for personal excellence, setting the right example, walking the talk, and, most important, being straight and honest. Ethical and integrity-based leadership are critical parts of great leadership.

In the public sector, Powell has always operated with this principle in mind. Even though he concedes that they are "corny," he argues that values matter. Honesty matters. Duty matters. Integrity and honor matter. These intangibles are hard to operationalize, but people know when leaders exhibit them, just as they know when leaders exhibit opposing behaviors of expediency, opportunism, evasiveness, self-aggrandisement, or outright dishonesty.

From employees' perspective, it was clear which path top managers chose at Enron, which is not to say that Enron did not have a "code of ethics" or a "values statement." Both existed. But for Powell, the "do the right thing" admonition emphasizes "do" as much as it does "the right thing." Powell has often said that "setting an example" is the single most important role of the leader – "The leader sets an example. Whether in the army or in civilian life, the other people in the organization take their cue from the leader – not from what the leader says but what the leader does."

A leader's behavior ensures that organizational value pronouncements can go in one of three paths: one path is where they are "lived" and "owned" in every decision and action, every day; the second is where value pronouncements are, in practice, simply irrelevant when it comes to important strategic, operational, or budgetary decisions; and the third is where values are used strictly as window-dressing and propaganda statements.

Enron's leaders "wrote the book" on the second and third paths. Enron's public values of *respect, integrity, communication,* and *excellence* were often used for little more than image promotion. Repeatedly, senior leaders at Enron said one thing and did another. Even as lies and deceit became endemic in the workplace, an internal film introducing Enron's new Vision and Values campaign would show Ken Lay saying: "At Enron, we stand by our word. We mean what we say, and we say what we mean." Meanwhile, Jeff Skilling added: "It's a very competitive world out there and there probably are times that there's a desire to cut corners. We can't have that at Enron."

Like many executives today, Skilling and his cohorts saw "building shareholder value" as equivalent to doing "what is right." Building shareholder value is both a necessary and desirable goal for any corporate leader but it is a consequence – a scorecard – of doing the right things strategically and operationally. On its own, "building shareholder value" says nothing about the worth of an organization's underlying values or, for that matter, the worth of its strategy.

Small wonder that Enron's employees and investors lost faith in the company's leadership, based upon the mismatch of word and deed they observed. Yet paradoxically, even as they lost faith, they began to emulate their superiors in order to reap short-term corporate accolades and rewards. Since doing what is personally beneficial trumped doing what is right, it should not be surprising that a "me first" and "get mine" attitude began to fester. Nor should it be surprising that as Enron's stock began to plummet, so did employees' fragile loyalty to the company. Employees, whose conscience had been hedged with inflated Enron stock, began leaking information to the press about their leaders. And in a final act of characterless behavior, the leaders themselves became, and remain, enmeshed in legal subterfuge, finger pointing, and charges of betrayal.

Conclusion: Doing the right thing is the mark of character, integrity, and courage. It is a necessary ingredient for sustained leadership credibility and performance excellence. When leaders fail to do what is right, followers become cynical. When cynicism reigns, the leaders' credibility plummets, while followers' loyalty, commitment, collaboration, and *espirit de corps* suffers greatly.

7. Leadership is not rank, privilege, titles, or money. It is responsibility

Powell often points out that the final responsibility for the success or failure of a mission rests with the leader. Real leaders embrace that responsibility. They recognize that they are ultimately responsible for the organization's mission and strategy, the culture and values that exist in it, the key decisions and behaviors of its members, and the organization's progress – or lack thereof.

At the end of the day, after a leader has listened, collaborated, delegated, and empowered, it's time for him or her to step up – to set the right course of action, inspire hope and confidence, bless the right initiatives, anoint the right people, articulate the right standards, and define the right metrics. During the Enron heyday, the leaders of Enron were certainly willing to enjoy the perks and privileges of their positions. Today, ex-chairman Kenneth Lay complains that he really didn't understand what was going on, it wasn't his fault, he was kept in the dark, others betrayed him. Great leaders blend their responsibility to their mission and their people. Yes, they take ownership of company-wide setbacks and errors and constructively mobilize their people's efforts at fixing them. And on the flip side, they let their people own the triumphs.

After the Gulf War victory in 1991, the editors of *US News & World Report* wanted Powell on the magazine's cover. To their surprise, Powell tried to convince them to feature Schwarzkopf, the field commander of Desert Storm, instead. At Enron, a perfect mirror image occurred: top executives took credit for the victories and now blame their people for defeats.

Conclusion: Great leaders not only accept, but also seek, final responsibility, fully and unequivocally. They don't make excuses after the fact. Responsible leaders take joy in success, making sure to let team members share the glory and rewards. Likewise, responsible leaders take public ownership of setbacks and errors and then constructively focus on solving problems and capitalizing on new opportunities. They truly lead by the old adage that "the buck stops here."

A new model of leadership

Figure 2.1 illustrates the leadership dynamics highlighted by our Powell–Enron contrast.

The tip of the leadership iceberg

ABOVE THE WATERLINE

- Create a bold, inspiring vision
- Empower people who are committed to the vision
- Develop a fast-paced, innovative culture
- Attract the best and brightest

waterline

The hidden foundation of leadership

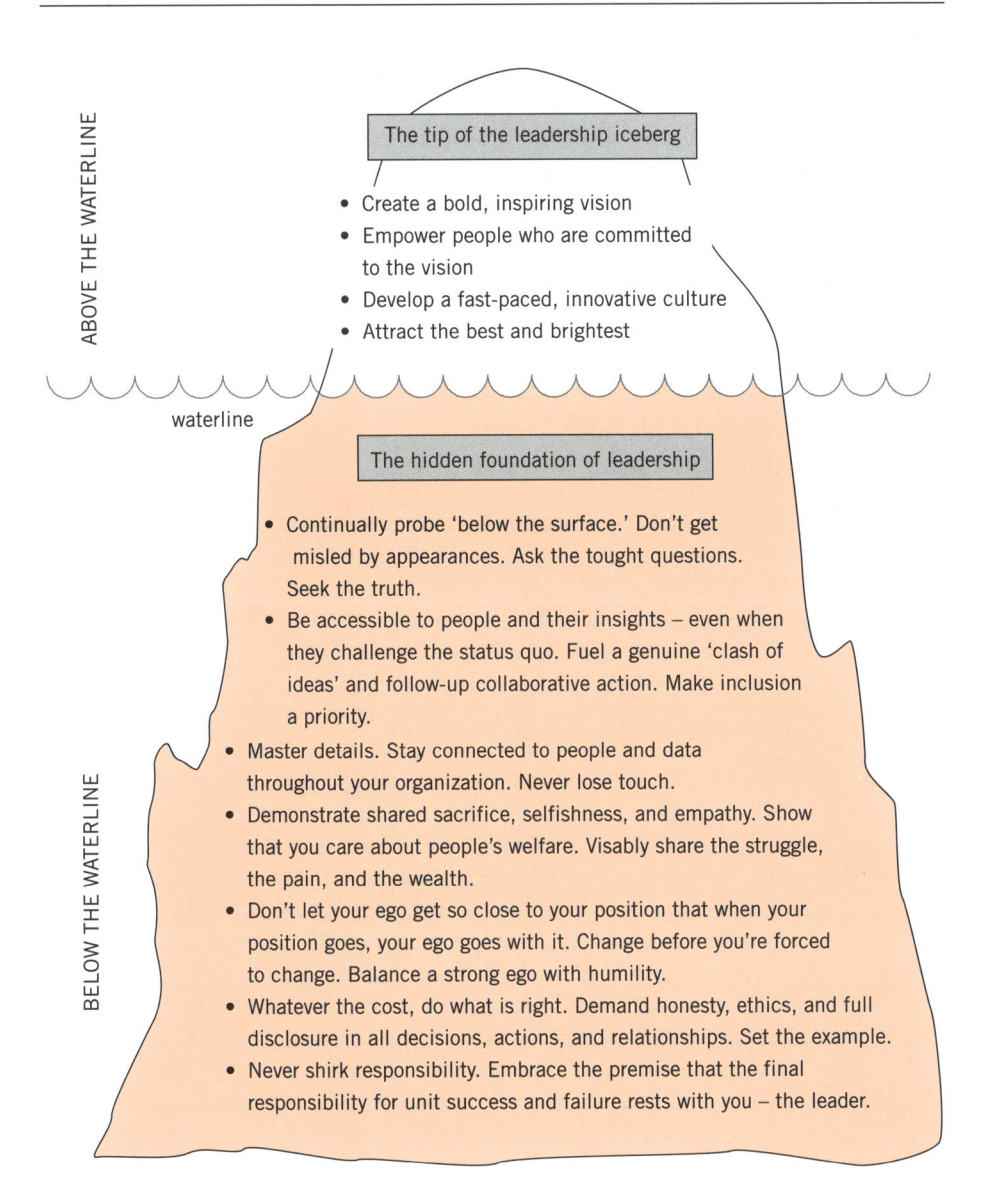

BELOW THE WATERLINE

- Continually probe 'below the surface.' Don't get misled by appearances. Ask the tough questions. Seek the truth.
- Be accessible to people and their insights – even when they challenge the status quo. Fuel a genuine 'clash of ideas' and follow-up collaborative action. Make inclusion a priority.
- Master details. Stay connected to people and data throughout your organization. Never lose touch.
- Demonstrate shared sacrifice, selfishness, and empathy. Show that you care about people's welfare. Visably share the struggle, the pain, and the wealth.
- Don't let your ego get so close to your position that when your position goes, your ego goes with it. Change before you're forced to change. Balance a strong ego with humility.
- Whatever the cost, do what is right. Demand honesty, ethics, and full disclosure in all decisions, actions, and relationships. Set the example.
- Never shirk responsibility. Embrace the premise that the final responsibility for unit success and failure rests with you – the leader.

Figure 2.1: *A new model of leadership*

Like an iceberg, what's underneath the waterline is far bigger and weightier than what is above. The tip of the iceberg reflects today's conventional wisdom about leadership. The attributes and behaviors listed in the tip are important and necessary, but in today's world they are no longer sufficient. The hidden foundation of leadership lies below the surface and like the bottom part of an iceberg it's *big*, as is its impact on unit goals and performance excellence. It is so big, in fact, that it can literally "make or break" an organization.

It's time to move our attention to the traits below the surface. And when we do, we will find deeper challenges for any would-be leader, because the submerged traits require *courage*. Powell is very specific that leadership requires "moral, physical, mental, and spiritual courage." Can that courage be taught? Can it be learned by anyone? What sorts of action steps can be extrapolated from these traits? And what will the long-term effect be if we fail to recognize their importance? These are the questions that researchers and practitioners should begin urgently to address.

RESOURCES

Harari, Owen, *The Powell Principle: 24 Lessons from Colin Powell a Legendary Leader*, McGraw Hill, 2002.

This article previously appeared in *Business Strategy Review*, Volume 15, Issue 2, Summer 2004.

❛Interview❜: Warren Bennis

The distinguished academic and acknowledged authority on leadership discusses the traits required of tomorrow's leaders.

Do you see yourself as a romantic?

If a romantic is someone who believes in possibilities and who is optimistic then that is probably an accurate description. I think that every person has to make a genuine contribution in life, and the institution of work is one of the main vehicles to achieving this. I'm more and more convinced that individual leaders can create a human community that will, in the long run, lead to the best organizations.

Do great groups require great leaders?

Greatness starts with superb people. Great groups don't exist without great leaders, but they give the lie to the persistent notion that successful institutions are the lengthened shadow of a great woman or man. It's not clear that life was ever so simple that individuals, acting alone, solved most significant problems. None of us is as smart as all of us.

So, the John Wayne type of hero is of the past?

Yes, the Lone Ranger is dead. Instead of the individual problem solver we have a new model for creative achievement. People like Steve Jobs or Walt Disney headed groups and found their own greatness in them. The new leader is a pragmatic dreamer, a person with an original but attainable vision. Ironically, the leader is able to realize his or her dream only if the others are free to do exceptional work. Typically, the leader is the one who recruits the others, by making the vision so palpable and seductive that they see it, too, and eagerly sign up.

Inevitably, the leader has to invent a leadership style that suits the group. The standard models, especially command and control, simply don't work. The heads of groups have to act decisively, but never arbitrarily. They have to make decisions without limiting the perceived autonomy of the other participants. Devising and maintaining an atmosphere in which others can put a dent in the universe is the leader's creative act.

But isn't this somewhat unrealistic?

True. Most organizations are dull, and working life is mundane. There is no getting away from that. So, these groups could be an inspiration. A great group is more than a collection of first-rate minds. It's a miracle. I have unwarranted optimism. By looking at the possibilities we can all improve.

What will it take for future leaders to be effective?

The post-bureaucratic organization requires a new kind of alliance between leaders and the led. Today's organizations are evolving into federations, networks, clusters, cross-functional teams, temporary systems, ad hoc task forces, lattices, modules, matrices – almost anything but pyramids with their obsolete top-down leadership. The new leader will encourage healthy dissent and values those followers courageous enough to say no.

This does not mark the end of leadership – rather the need for a new, far more subtle and indirect form of influence for leaders to be effective. The new reality is that intellectual capital (brain power, know-how, and human imagination) has supplanted capital as the critical success factor; and leaders will have to learn an entirely new set of skills that are not understood, not taught in our business schools, and, for all of those reasons, rarely practiced. Four competencies will determine the success of new leadership.

What's first?

The new leader understands and practices the power of appreciation. They are connoisseurs of talent, more curators than creators. The leader is rarely the best or the brightest in the new organizations. The new leader has a smell for talent, an imaginative Rolodex, is unafraid of hiring people better than they are. In my research into great groups I found that in most cases the leader was rarely the cleverest or the sharpest. Peter Schneider, president of Disney's colossally successful Feature Animation studio, leads a group of 1,200 animators. He can't draw to save his life. Bob Taylor, former head of the Palo Alto Research Center, where the first commercial PC was invented, wasn't a computer scientist. Max DePree put it best when he said that good leaders "abandon their ego to the talents of others."

Then, second, the new leader keeps reminding people of what's important. Organizations drift into entropy and the bureaucratization of imagination when they forget what's important. Simple to say, but that one sentence is one of the few pieces of advice I suggest to leaders: remind your people of what's important. A powerful enough vision can transform what would otherwise be routine and drudgery into collectively focussed energy. Witness the Manhattan Project. The US Army had recruited talented engineers from all over the United States for special duty on the project. They were assigned to work on the primitive computers of the period (1943–45), doing energy calculations and other tedious jobs. But the Army, obsessed with security, refused to tell them anything specific about the project. They didn't know that they were building a weapon that could end the war or even what their calculations meant. They were simply expected to do the work, which they did slowly and not very well. Richard Feynman, who supervised the technicians, prevailed on his superiors to tell the recruits what they were doing and why. Permission was granted to lift the veil of secrecy, and Robert Oppenheimer gave them a special lecture on the nature of the project and their own contribution.

"Complete transformation," Feynman recalled. "They began to invent ways of doing it better. They improved the scheme. They worked at night. They didn't need supervising in the night; they didn't need anything. They understood everything; they invented several of the programs we used." Feynman calculated that the work was done "nearly 10 times as fast" after it had meaning.

Charles Handy has it right in his book *The Hungry Spirit*. We are all hungry spirits craving purpose and meaning at work, to contribute something beyond ourselves, and leaders must never forget to remind people of what's important.

What else does a new leader strive for?

The new leader generates and sustains trust. We're all aware that the terms of the new social contract of work have changed. No one can depend on life-long loyalty or commitment to any organization. Since 1985, 25 percent of the American workforce has been laid off at least once. At a time when the new social contract makes the ties between organizations and their knowledge workers tenuous, trust becomes the emotional glue that can bond people to an organization.

Trust is a small word with powerful connotations and is a hugely complex factor. The ingredients are a combination of competencies, constancy, caring, fairness, candor, and authenticity – most of all, the latter. And that is achieved by the new leaders when they can balance successfully the tripod of forces working on and in most of us: ambition, competence, and integrity.

And lastly?

The new leader and the led are intimate allies. The power of Steven Spielberg's *Schindler's List* lies in the transformation of Schindler from a sleazy, down-at-the-heels, small-time con man who moves to Poland in order to harness cheap Jewish labor to make munitions which he can then sell to the Germans at low cost. His transformation comes over a period of time in which Schindler interacts with his Jewish workers, most of all the accountant, Levin, but also frequent and achingly painful moments where he confronts the evil of the war, of the Holocaust. In the penultimate scene, when the war is over and the Nazis have evacuated the factory, but before the American troops arrive, the prisoners give him a ring, made for him, from the precious metals used by the workers. As he tries to put the ring on, he begins crying, "Why, why are you doing this? With this metal, we could have saved three, maybe four, maybe five more Jews." And he drives off in tears.

It is hard to be objective about this scene, but though this was a unique, singular event, it portrays what new leadership is all about: that great leaders are made by great groups and by organizations that create the social architecture of respect and dignity. These new leaders will not have the loudest voice, but the most attentive ear. Instead of pyramids, these post-bureaucratic organizations will be structures built of energy and ideas, led by people who find their joy in the task at hand, while embracing each other – and not worrying about leaving monuments behind.

If you go into a company, what's the most important question you ask?

On a scale from 1 to 10, 10 meaning 100 percent and 1 meaning close to zero, how much of your talents are being deployed in your job? And why?

What question would you like to ask the managers of the world?

How do you learn?

Essentials

LEADING

Bennis, Warren

Warren Bennis (born 1925) has had a lengthy career that has involved him in education, writing, consulting, and administration. Along the way he has made a contribution to an array of subjects and produced a steady stream of books, including the bestselling *Leaders* and most recently *Organizing Genius: The Secrets of Creative Collaboration*. He is now based at the University of Southern California where he is founder of the University's Leadership Institute in Los Angeles.

From being an early student of group dynamics in the 1950s, Bennis became a futurologist in the 1960s. His work – particularly *The Temporary Society* (1968) – explored new organizational forms. Bennis envisaged organizations as *adhocracies* – roughly the direct opposite of bureaucracies – freed from the shackles of hierarchy and meaningless paperwork.

Despite his varied career and life, Bennis remains inextricably linked with leadership. With the torrent of publications and executive programs on the subject, it is easy to forget that leadership had been largely forgotten as a topic worthy of serious academic interest until it was revived by Bennis and others in the 1980s. Bennis's work stands as a humane counter to much of the military-based hero worship that dogs the subject. He argues that leadership is not a rare skill; leaders are made rather than born; leaders are usually ordinary – or apparently ordinary – people, rather than charismatic; leadership is not solely the preserve of those at the top of the organization – it is relevant at all levels; and, finally, leadership is not about control, direction, and manipulation.

Bennis's best-known leadership research involved 90 of America's leaders. From these, four common abilities were identified. The first was management of attention. This, said Bennis, is a question of vision. Successful leaders have a vision that other people believe in and treat as their own. The second skill shared by Bennis's selection of leaders is management of meaning – communications. A vision is of limited practical use if it is encased in 400 pages of wordy text or mumbled from behind a paper-packed desk. Bennis believes that effective communication relies on use of analogy, metaphor, and vivid illustration as well as emotion, trust, optimism, and hope.

The third aspect of leadership Bennis identified is trust, which he describes as "the emotional glue that binds followers and leaders together." Leaders have to be seen to be consistent. The final common bond between the 90 leaders Bennis studied is "deployment of self." The leaders do not glibly present charisma or time management as the essence of their success. Instead, the emphasis is on persistence and self-knowledge, taking risks, commitment, and challenge but, above all, learning. "The learning person looks forward to failure or mistakes," says Bennis. "The worst problem in leadership is basically early success. There's no opportunity to learn from adversity and problems."

Most recently, Bennis has switched his attention to the dynamics of group working. The relationship between groups and their leaders is clearly of fundamental interest to Bennis. "Greatness starts with superb people. Great groups don't exist without great leaders, but they give the lie to the persistent notion that successful institutions are the lengthened shadow of a great woman or man."

Indeed, the heroic view of the leader as the indomitable individual is now outdated and inappropriate. Bennis says: "He or she is a pragmatic dreamer, a person with an original but attainable vision. Ironically, the leader is able to realize his or her dream only if the others are free to do exceptional work."

There is a rich strand of idealism that runs through Bennis's work. He is a humanist with high hopes for humanity. To accusations of romanticism, he puts up a resolute and spirited defense:

"I think that every person has to make a genuine contribution in their lives and the institution of work is one of the main vehicles to achieving this. I'm more and more convinced that individual leaders can create a human community that will, in the long run, lead to the best organizations."

Employability

The concept of employability is meant to provide the basis for a new psychological contract between workers and employers. With companies no longer able to guarantee long-term job security, employability represents a shift to a new deal whereby employers offer shorter job tenure with an undertaking to provide skills development and training that will make staff more employable later on.

Employability grew out of the delayering and downsizing exercises that occurred at the end of the 1980s and early 1990s. As a global recession began to bite, many companies set about restructuring and reengineering, a process that shocked a workforce accustomed to the concept of "a job for life." Downsizing and delayering revoked the unspoken, unwritten contract between corporate man and woman and the company. The bond of trust between employee and employer was irredeemably broken.

In the face of change, HR departments were forced to rethink what the company was able to offer in return for a degree of loyalty. The new message from organizations is: "We can't offer you a job for life, but we will add to your employability." Typically, this involves a move away from the traditional paternalistic approach to career development toward one where the employee is expected to manage their own career prospects. Today, loyalty can no longer be taken for granted – on either side.

Some commentators argue that the next step down this road is to move to explicit employability contracts. This would involve replacing traditional employment contracts, based on on-going employment, with renewable fixed-term contracts whereby employees negotiate pay and development opportunities on an individual basis.

But not everyone buys into employability as a concept. One of its most vociferous critics is the influential business commentator Richard Pascale, formerly of Stanford Business School. "A new social contract based on 'employability' is the sound of one hand clapping," he has observed. "Its impetus is wishful thinking masquerading as a concept – a lived-happily-ever-after ending to replace the broken psychological contract of the past. The hard truth is, there is no painless remedy. In fact, the death of job security, like any death, means that we have to learn to relate to the pain, not escape from it."[21]

Employability, says Pascale, is a simplistic attempt to shore up rents in the social fabric. "There is a fundamental flaw with this convenient new arrangement: philosophically, employability is a slick palliative that sidesteps the need to confront our essential humanness."

There are, he says, three interlocking elements to the problem. First, job loss and employment insecurity are inherently painful experiences that trigger a loss of self-esteem and social identity. Second, corporations and those who work for them cannot resolve these issues by themselves. Third, a new social context is needed to legitimize and deal with the grief associated with the experiences of loss and betrayal in our working lives.

Employability may turn out to be something of a Pandora's box. Having opened the lid on the loyalty issue, most companies have yet fully to come to terms with the wider implications. In the coming years, with skills shortages predicted, they are likely to reap the whirlwind. Having made it abundantly clear that they are prepared to dump employees when times are tough, organizations shouldn't be at all surprised if the most talented employees feel no sense of loyalty to them when times are good.

The Peter Principle

There is precious little to laugh about in the work and thoughts of management thinkers. The few exceptions, therefore, stand out as eccentric beacons of hope.

Laurence J. Peter (1919–90) was a Canadian academic who targetted the absurdities of the corporation and management hierarchies. He observed incompetence everywhere he looked. The result was the Peter Principle, which said that managers in an organization rise to their level of incompetence through being promoted until they fail to do well in their current job. "For each individual, for you, for me, the final promotion is from a level of competence to a level of incompetence," wrote Peter.

Peter's greatness lay in the fact that his humor is grounded solidly in corporate reality. Anyone who has ever worked for an organization can identify with his observations – "There are two kinds of failures: those who thought and never did, and those who did and never thought"; "Fortune knocks once, but misfortune has much more patience"; or "If you don't know where you are going, you will probably end up somewhere else."

Peter's book, *The Peter Principle* (co-authored with Raymond Hull), was an antidote to the many hundreds of books celebrating corporate success stories. Around his basic joke, Peter weaved a mass of aphorisms and *bon mots*. These included: "An economist is an expert who will know tomorrow why the things he predicted yesterday didn't happen"; and "Originality is the fine art of remembering what you hear but forgetting where you heard it." We all know that farce and failure dog our lives. Peter simply reminded us of this.

Townsend, Robert

Robert Townsend (1920–98) did all the right things to become corporate man. He was highly educated – at Princeton and Columbia – and held a number of important executive positions. But in 1970 he transformed himself into a witty commentator on the excesses of corporate life. His bestseller *Up the Organization* (1970) was subtitled "How to stop the corporation from stifling people and strangling profits" and was hilariously funny. Its sequel was *Further Up the Organization* (1984). Most recently, Townsend wrote *The B2 Chronicles* (1997), which recounts the story of a company called QuoVadoTron and includes characters such as Crunch, Dooley, and Archibald.

Townsend's genius lay in debunking the modern organization for its excess, stupidity, and absurdity. He was the ultimate skeptic. Those with power, or who think they have power, are dangerous beings. He was, by turn, playful, indignant, critical, and practical. "A personnel man with his arm around an employee is like a treasurer with his hand in the till," he noted. His quip on consultants: "They are the people who borrow your watch to tell you what time it is and then walk off with it" remains one of the most quoted putdowns of an entire industry.

Townsend had no time for the adornments of executive office and his list of "no-nos" included reserved parking spaces, special-quality stationery for the boss and his elite, Muzak, bells and buzzers, company shrinks, outside directorships and trusteeships for the chief executive, and the company plane. He was, in fact, preaching a brand of empowerment and participation 20 years ahead of its time. Amusing it may have been, but, as with all great humor, there was a serious undercurrent.[11]

REFERENCES

1. Kelley, R., *The Power of Followership*, Doubleday, 1992.
2. Hodgson, Phil and White, Randall P., *Relax, It's Only Uncertainty: Lead the Way When the Way is Changing*, Financial Times Prentice Hall, 2001.
3. Observed by the early cybernetician W. Ross Ashby and more recently developed by Christopher Bartlett.
4. Quoted in White, L., 'Net prophet,' *Sunday Times*, November 12 1995.
5. Reginald, Jennifer, 'Headhunting 2000,' *BusinessWeek*, p. 74, May 17, 1999.
6. Challenger Gray and Christmas, 'CEO Departures Increase, Survey Says,' *East Bay Business Times*, July 1, 2002.
7. 'Study Finds Number of Chiefs Forced to Leave Jobs Is Up,' *The New York Times*, p. C2, May 12, 2003.
8. Southwest Airlines, A Stock for Mom; Selena Maranjian, May 2001; http://www.fool.com/specials/2001/sp010508b.htm
9. See, for example, Davis, Stan, 'Is This the End of HR?' in Effron, Marc, Gandossy, Robert and Goldsmith, Marshall (eds), *Human Resources in the 21st Century*, John Wiley, 2003.
10. Hodgson, Phil, Briner, Wendy, Hollingsworth, Julie, *Top Leader Journey Report*, Ashridge, UK, February 2004.
11. Carey, Dennis and von Weichs, Marie-Caroline, *How to Run a Company: Lessons from Top Leaders of the CEO Academy*, Crown Business, 2003.
12. Report from Booz Allen Hamilton Inc., *Business Week*, December 2, 2002.
13. Burson-Marstellar, quote by Frances Cairncross in *The Economist* survey of Corporate Leadership, October 25, 2003.
14. Hodgson, Phil and Crainer, Stuart, *What Do High Performance Managers Really Do?*, FT Pitman, 1993.
15. White, Randall P., Hodgson, Phil and Crainer, Stuart, *The Future of Leadership*, FT Pitman, 1996.
16. Hodgson, Phil and White, Randall P., *Relax Its Only Uncertainity*, FT Pearson, 2001.
17. Mintzberg, Henry, *Beyond Selfishness* and *The World Gone Mad*, Mintzberg.com.
18. Cassidy, John, *Dot.Con: The Greatest Story Ever Sold*, HarperCollins, 2002.
19. Kouzes, James M. and Posner, Barry Z., *The Leadership Challenge*, Jossey-Bass, 2002.
20. Collins, Jim, *Good to Great*, Random House, 2001.
21. Pascale, Richard, 'The False Security of Employability,' *Fast Company*, April 1996.

– CHAPTER 3 –

Managing change

"I believe that if you repeat the restructuring process more than two or three times, what happens in the end is not only do you cut some fat, but you also start losing muscle. Corporate anorexia develops, leading to total weakness."

C.K. Prahalad

"Things change, and they need to change, and change is driven by technology and knowledge. But change comes at a cost, sometimes a very high cost."

Alvin Toffler

"Changing the direction of a large company is like trying to turn an aircraft carrier. It takes a mile before anything happens. And if it was a wrong turn, getting back on course takes even longer."

Al Ries

"To meet the demands of the fast-changing competitive scene, we must simply learn to love change as much as we have hated it in the past."

Tom Peters

The reality of transformation

TONY ECCLES

[Managers are told that they must transform their companies – and themselves. Radical change is their only hope it appears – risky and prone to failure as it is. Yet how far is this useful, or even relevant, advice? We need to know when transformation is, and isn't, sensible.]

Imagine you are running a chain of branded, up-market hotels. It could be Hilton, Inter-Continental, Shangri La, Four Seasons, Meridien, Ritz-Carlton, or Kempinski. Your city hotels are typically in elegant areas, close to good shops, theaters, museums and galleries, restaurants, business districts, and parks. You might be located on the Reforma in Mexico City, Park Lane in London, or Union Square in San Francisco.

One of your executives has a bright idea. Let us be radical and transform what we do, he declaims. Our present hotels are built on very costly and constrained land; labor isn't plentiful or local. Let us reduce our cost base by building in a slum area, where land is cheap so that we can have space and easy parking. There is endless unemployed labor, admittedly unskilled, but we can train them and pay low wages. Of course, there are no local facilities that our guests might want, but at least the sound of gunfire is only intermittent. Security might be a problem, but we'll still save on costs. He rests his case. It is certainly different, transformational even. But would you get any guests?

Equally, many products do not change that much. Take the features of a good, large, long-established hotel and think how it was 40 years ago. Every present-day function would have been there. It would have had bedrooms with an integral bathroom, a telephone, a radio, and a TV set. There would be an elevator, a lobby, reception desk, concierge, and restaurant. Today, of course, there would be more information technology behind the scenes and in the bedrooms; the elevators would be faster, and the guest wouldn't have to open and close the elevator doors manually; the restaurant menu would be more eclectic – but nothing fundamental would have altered.

Similarly, if you looked at the early automobile mass production outputs and viewed the specification of, say, a late 1930s Buick car, and compared it with a 2002 Buick Park Avenue, I would defy you to show a single fundamental functionality that is not present in both. The 1930s car would have pneumatic tyres on its four wheels, each wheel fitted with brakes. There would be a spare wheel (in 60 years we haven't overcome the effect of punctures). It would have a multi-cylinder internal combustion engine driving an axle through a multi-speed transmission. There would be several forward-facing leather seats, opening doors with opening glass windows, a steering wheel, speedometer, horn, electric headlights, and a boot or trunk. It would have a heater and a radio, probably an early Motorola.

Naturally, there would be differences to note. Many of the manual functions would now be operated electrically or electronically; today's vehicle would be more luxurious, less prone to faults, easily maintained, safer, and waterproof. The heater would have become an air-conditioning unit. The radio would now be a stereo system. Many of the 1930s features would be much improved. But allowing for those, and with the possible example of hatchbacks and SUVs, what new features are we left with? Door mirrors, Satnav, a moon roof, and cup holders. It is not much to show for 60 years of endeavor.

This is not to jeer. Huge changes have occurred in the automobile industry, and in the refinement of its products. It is just to point out that many things remain reassuringly and productively appropriate. We need to take care when absorbing the reification of transformation as being the only true route to organizational salvation. There are industries and circumstances where it is fruitful to be different, but not radically so. There are others when it is sensible to be all but similar, to emulate what others are doing, with only minor divergences in case those alienate the customers, many of whom value the reassurance of predictability and the comfort of familiarity. This similar strategic logic and positioning can be the best place to stay, even if several competitors occupy the same ground.

Some product and service progress occurs at a stately, if not glacial, pace. It took 100 years from the invention of the telephone before we got around to telephone banking. It took 46 years from the creation of canned food before we invented the can opener. (Cans were opened by hammer and chisel until then, in case you are wondering.) The pop-up toaster was invented 75 years ago and we are still trying to get it to do what we want.

The other element where care is needed is in our focus on markets themselves. Which of them are exploding, which are pulsating, and which are close to stagnation or even decline? Highly dynamic markets are being called "exponential," though that description has limited accuracy. We are all familiar with the test of how many times you can fold a sheet of paper in two before it becomes as thick as a telephone directory. It is 10 times at best. Take it to 20 times and the result would be 80 feet thick; 50 times and it would reach to the sun. There are few markets of any size which double many times over. Rapidly expanding markets are better described as "tornado" markets, in which there is a sudden, violent change in demand, followed by relative calm and perhaps the collapse of fresh demand – just as has been happening for dot-com IPOs and for the telecom industry.

The Hush Puppy effect

There are also what have been described as "contagious" markets (see Malcolm Gladwell's book *The Tipping Point*), where a sudden change in fashion (Hush Puppies) or the utility of a new technology (fax machines, i-mode phones, text messaging, e-mails) transforms a market, perhaps for years, perhaps as a temporary fashion. These are all marvelous markets to be in – provided that your timing is right, that you have the robust ability to scale up fast, and that you know when and how to cut back or change again if demand falls, competition becomes excessive, or a yet newer innovation from a competitor looks likely to take off.

Then there are the "superior" markets, in which growth, although not mercurial, usually outstrips the growth in the economy because the superior markets are supercharged and do not grow hand in hand with overall economic growth. It doesn't take more than a few years of 7 percent annual economic growth in India to double or triple the size of its middle class, with consequential effects on the markets for middle-class purchases. Nor are superior markets necessarily highly price sensitive. Burgeoning demand is rarely a sign of a price-driven market.

Many financial services markets across the world have been in this superior, not too cost-sensitive state. No sooner has an employee ceased to be paid in cash and is reimbursed via a bank checking account, than he or she will be prone to acquiring a deposit account, a credit card, a debit card, perhaps foreign exchange, and an insurance product. There is a multiplier effect, sometimes in markets that are typically forecast to stagnate.

Despite the example of two- and three-car households, it is worth recalling that the television set market was forecast to become solely a replacement market once almost all households had one set. In practice, it is not difficult to find households with as many sets as inhabitants – sometimes more. Similarly, most dual-income families now have multiple telephone lines and many have more than one home computer. In each case, the products have moved from semi-luxury to unexceptional purchase, as costs and prices have fallen.

Naturally, not all market growth is of a tornado or superior kind. Some is just "linear" and rises – or falls – in line with the economy, be it the domestic, regional, or world economy. Other markets decline, or are hit by substitute products, even in growing economies. Storage heaters, glass drinks containers, and transatlantic passenger ships are in this category. Some serious reinvention will be required if their recovery, let alone their transformation, is to take place.

The key requirement for sensible strategic analysis is to locate the nature of the product markets, be they tornado, contagious, superior, or linear, and their likely trends, and so reach a better understanding of what strategic logic the organization needs, instead of endlessly repeating the mantra about the necessity and inevitability of the transformation of organizations. We need a mapping process.

	Strategic Logic		
	Emulation	Difference	Transformation
Exponential, Tornado, Contagious		The Toy/Fad, Personal Computers	Wireless Networking
Superior	Branch Banking	Sentient Technologies	e-financial Services
Linear	Milk, Coal	Boutique & Townhouse Hotels	Mini Steel Mills

(Market Growth — vertical axis)

Figure 3.1: *Market growth and strategic logic*

Figure 3.1 sets out some dimensions of strategic logic and market growth in order to help this mapping process. The logic behind the grid is an assumption that emulation and imitation are likely to be the driving forces in stable, linear markets, as competing firms converge on a similar, sustainable strategy. They all reside in the bottom-left corner of the grid. For example, it is hard to spot the differences between different brands of large, chain hotels, or between the branch outlets of different banks. Yet chains of hotels have been persistently, and profitably, expanding their networks in the face of what has been significant market growth. Differentiation can happen, as with hotel chains moving into boutique and townhouse hotels, or banks disguising their branches as coffee shops, but it is usually at the margin and does not affect most of what they do and how they do it.

The upper-right corner of the grid is inhabited by firms pursuing nascent technologies and markets, where the potential for explosive growth in a tornado market all but forces transformational activities on both existing firms and new ventures. It is a risky place to be by its very nature. Outright failure is habitual, and for success, timing is often the key. Radical new products and markets wax and wane like tornados. The technologies and processes, and sometimes the business models, disrupt existing limits on what is produced and how it is used. Cisco, Lucent, Nortel, Marconi, and Spirent have all been there, and hope to stay there yet. Ballard's long struggle with fuel-cell technology may yet propel it into that grid position.

We can all argue about where particular industries or sub-industries should be placed on the grid. It is also clear that, wherever you place an industry, its trends may be driving it elsewhere, as in Figure 3.2, and its sub-sets may be in different places. For example, e-financial services may well move up into the tornado area since, as has rightly been predicted, the real wealth creation of the Internet is yet to come. Once the question of online security has been answered, the prospects for explosive growth in e-financial services will be enticing. Sentient technologies, in the shape of telematics in cars and homes, as well as interpretive medical monitoring devices, are already

	Strategic Logic		
	Emulation	Difference	Transformation
Exponential, Tornado, Contagious		Personal Computers	Wireless Networking
Superior	Branch Banking	Sentient Technologies	e-financial Services
Linear		Boutique & Townhouse Hotels	

Market Growth

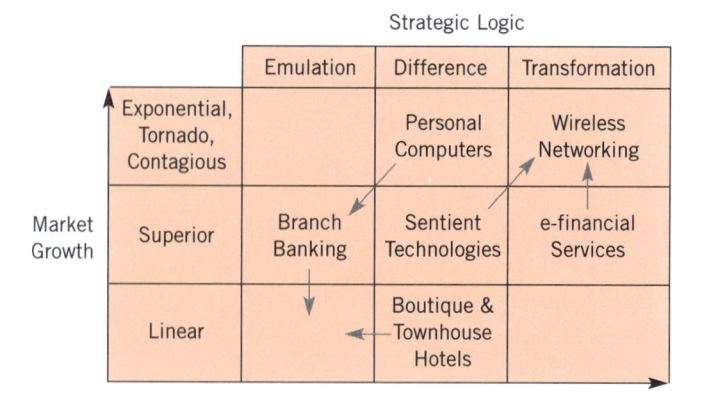

Figure 3.2: *Market growth and strategic logic trends?*

well into the rapid growth area, though whether they will transform the strategic logic of the firms involved is less certain.

In contrast, branch banking may be sinking into the linear area. Personal computer makers are also converging toward just being badges of reputation on virtually indistinguishable boxes of products offering similar performance (with the possible exception of the niche maker, Apple) as market growth slows, the ubiquity of Microsoft Windows continues, and other makers emulate Dell by moving into direct sales. Tornado markets include the short-lived fashion markets, such as Beanie Babies, Pokemon cards, Destiny's Child and Pashmina shawls. Yet fashion markets are often supplied not by upstarts but by stable, long-established companies which do not need to transform themselves in order to cope. We should not simply accept the fallacious view that innovations come only from new firms and from sources outside an industry. Transforming innovations are alleged not to come from incumbent firms. Well, sometimes they do. The record of AT&T's Bell Laboratories has been hugely impressive over many decades. The float process for making flat glass was invented and developed by Pilkington, one of the world's leading glass companies. Well-established firms have coped well in transforming the music industry.

Time often favors well-established incumbents, as upstarts exhaust themselves in the quest to gain a sustainable foothold in a new market. If we reflect on the main suppliers of video recorders and disposable nappies, we might recall the names of the pioneers – Ampex and Chux – and wonder whatever became of them once the Japanese electronics firms, and Procter & Gamble respectively, had used their reputation, their operational, logistical, and marketing skills to capture these markets.

The top-left corner of the grid has the combination of tornado markets and stable, emulating firms. This mixture may have few obvious candidates, but it can be occupied, if only temporarily. An example might be the upsurge in demand for Filofax products, followed by its deflation as it was superseded by the wave of demand for the much different and innovative Psion Organiser, and then the Palm Pilot, and now the Treo and its like. This corner of the grid is typically occupied by traditional firms which occasionally find themselves caught up in a sudden resurgence of fashion for their long-established products. But it is not a great place to be for an ambitious firm. Relying on the vagaries of fashion is only for the brave and talented.

The bottom-right corner can be inhabited by firms utilizing new, disruptive processes, operating in a linear market – such as mini steel mills – in which the new venture supersedes old technologies in a stable market. The center of the grid will be colonized by firms and industries offering fresh products in superior markets where, for example, one or more of the players may suffer a relapse or, alternatively, explode into a tornado market, as is happening with Bluetooth and WiFi.

It is true that every firm, no matter which type of market it occupies, should be constantly looking out for innovations, be these of product, service, distribution, process, or organization, for while many markets have elements of outstanding stability and continued relevance (standard life insurance, property, and casualty insurance), these are often mixed in with recent innovations (mortgage protection, health and employment insurance). Active scanning for trends, new technologies, and fresh markets should be the perennial habit of all competing organizations. Exploring new ideas is a normal requirement, for only by initiating trials and experiments will a successful new venture be likely to emerge. Yet such new ventures do not have to be radical. They may be simply improvements in well-established products and services.

We are tempted by the prospect of radical innovation because it is exciting, novel, and appealing, even though business history is littered with the debris of failed innovations, be they the Sinclair C5, WebVan, Just2clicks, or the Iridium global phone system. The seductive allure of transformation has been based on the fallacy that, because there are tumultuous industries and also examples of successful transformation of industries and markets, the rest of the world is like that too, or shortly will be. Since the winners write history, and the failures sink from view and bias our memories, we need to be endlessly alert in gauging which of our existing products and processes should be cherished and which should be transformed, so that we are not besotted with the very notion of novelty itself, to the point of it threatening our existing and successful strategies.

One inference could be that the norm for companies is to inhabit linear, or preferably superior, markets from which they intermittently grasp for tornado possibilities, while perpetually claiming to be "transforming" themselves and convincing themselves of the truth that they are. It is a process that evidently persuades them of their radicalism, but which leaves them looking much as before to the outsider. Apart from their e-banking efforts, have you noticed any serious changes so far in the "transforming" financial services firms?

Another inference might be that tornado markets subside into superior markets and superior markets decay into linear markets. Yet reverse movement occurs, even with stable technologies. Stimulating growth in a linear or declining market can be as fruitful, and potentially less risky, than grasping at a tornado market that may not exist, or which can be ephemeral.

We are told that innovation in products and markets is to be praised as a general virtue because the small proportion of companies' new products introduced into new markets is responsible for a major part of those companies' profits. That may well be true, but so what? If we could, or did, count in the earlier costs of all those new products which failed in new markets to the extent of never making any sales, let alone profits, would the return on radical investment look so enticing?

The lesson of all this is not to ignore the prospects for innovation; indeed it is the opposite in requiring constant care in searching out fresh possibilities. As Andy Grove of Intel put it: "Only the paranoid survive." However, the easy assumption that everything needs to be transformed is countered by the evidence. Procter & Gamble is still making soaps; Kelloggs is still producing cereals; Unilever and Nestlé continue to offer us processed foods; Rolls-Royce is still making aero engines. Indeed, if you stripped out the transformations in the worlds of communication/entertainment and chemical/medical/surgical advances, would the rest of the world seem so transformational? Of course, the industries of farming, housing, tourism, and shipping have each adapted over the generations, but they would still be largely recognizable to previous generations.

To say that "we are transforming our business" is immensely flattering and ennobling to a manager, and offers justification and great satisfaction to those involved in that endeavor. Yet the seductive mantra of transformation should be treated with considerable caution, in case it is simply inappropriate for the particular situation and, if adopted too readily and taken too literally, will lead only to disappointment.

To show the misuse of the revolutionary mantra, it is worth recalling the reaction of a senior executive in the Distillers alcoholic spirit company (now part of Diageo) who, in response to the appointment of the very first chief executive who had not come from the dominant whisky side of the business, gasped: "This is revolutionary. He has spent all his career in gin."

RESOURCES

Bennis, Warren, *The Planning of Change* (with Benne, K.D. and Chin, R., 2nd edition), Holt, Rinehart & Winston, 1970.
Eccles, Tony, *Succeeding with Change*, McGraw-Hill, 1996.
Gladwell, Malcolm, *The Tipping Point*, Brown and Co., 2000.
Kanter, Rosabeth Moss, *The Change Masters*, Simon & Schuster, 1983.
Kanter, Rosabeth Moss, *The Challenge of Organizational Change* (with Stein, B. and Jick, T.D.), Free Press, 1992.
Kotter, John, *A Force for Change*, Free Press, 1990.

This article previously appeared in *Business Strategy Review*, Volume 13, Issue 2, Summer 2002.

Commentary

Tipping over the edge

The notion of the tipping point entered public consciousness thanks to Malcolm Gladwell's influential book, *The Tipping Point*. Gladwell, a former science writer for *The Washington Post*, observed how fashions take hold. He found parallels with the spread of infections and the science of epidemiology. Rather than the measured process that had previously been thought to be at work, he noticed that "ideas and products and messages and behaviors spread just like viruses do." In particular he noted that it takes only one or two people acting as carriers to spread the cultural infection. Once it takes hold, it shows up as a dramatic upward curve. The point at which the curve hits critical mass is the "tipping point."

Technology magnifies the effect via e-mail and websites. Viral marketing – word of mouse – is a potent marketing tool. Viral marketing had been around for a while but found expression on the Internet with Hotmail, the first universally accessible e-mail service. Following the launch of Hotmail in July 1996, the subscriber base grew at an astronomical rate, faster in fact than any company in history. Part of the reason for the success was the way the product was marketed. Every e-mail sent through Hotmail contained a hyperlink to sign up for the service, so the product spread like a virus. Microsoft bought Hotmail at the end of 1997 for around $400 million.

Little wonder then that the tipping point is increasingly applied to the business world. "The tipping point exists in all complex systems. The problem is that it can never be predicted," observes the Swedish entrepreneur and author Alexander Bard. According to Bard, the true hero of the tipping point concept in business is the humble manager who avoids all temptations to predict exactly where the tipping point is, but is constantly aware of its crucial role in the complex systems which now constitute a business. "If you believe in your message, whether you try to convince your customers or clients or colleagues, go for it, eventually you reach the tipping point, and then the walls of Jericho come tumbling down," Bard prophesizes.

The notion of the tipping point was further developed by W. Chan Kim and Renée Mauborgne, professors at the leading French business school Insead. Their article in the April 2003 issue of the *Harvard Business Review* was entitled "Tipping point leadership." Kim and Mauborgne point to the work of Los Angeles police chief William Bratton as an example of tipping point leadership. Working in New York in the mid-1990s Bratton cut felonies by 39 percent, murders by 50 percent, and theft by 35 percent in two years. Bratton's

Commentary (continued)

track record also includes successful stints at the New York Transit Police, Boston Metropolitan Police, Massachusetts Bay Transit Authority, and Boston Police District Four. In all he brought about significant change.

Bratton's leadership is built around four elements – the cognitive (communicating and ensuring managers are in touch with the problems), politics (keeping internal foes quiet and isolating external ones), resources (initially concentrating on trouble areas), and motivation (matching messages to various levels within the organization).

According to Kim and Mauborgne, Bratton's change management skills can be replicated – and, indeed, need to be if the momentum of true change is to be created and maintained. "In any organization, once the beliefs and energies of a critical mass of people are engaged, conversion to a new idea will spread like an epidemic, bringing about fundamental change very quickly," they say.

Of course, there is an irony to the tipping point becoming hot property. "The tipping point is an incredibly compelling concept which has almost magically benefited from the very phenomenon which it describes," observes Peter Cohan, author of *Value Leadership*. "Unfortunately, the tipping point is a concept whose effect is far easier to trace in retrospect than it is to manage prospectively."

At the core of using the tipping point for business is the challenge of identifying and influencing three groups of people described by Malcolm Gladwell as *mavens*, *connectors*, and *sales people*. Easier said than done. There are no databases or mailing lists containing the names and contact information of these individuals. Even if such a database existed, in order to be useful it would need to be somewhat different for every new product and idea that companies sought to market. "Perhaps the biggest challenge facing such tipping point managers is to devise and execute strategies to influence these three groups of individuals to get excited about their product, service, or concept in the right sequence," reflects Peter Cohan. "What I find intriguing is that the tipping point's value to business would decline as its adoption spread. If managers began to figure out how to manage the tipping point for business ends, the skills needed to do so would spread to more and more companies. This leveling of the corporate playing field would ultimately nullify the competitive advantage enjoyed by a company which mastered these skills."

Before we get carried away, a word of caution from Jonas Ridderstråle, co-author of *Funky Business* and *Karaoke Capitalism*. "The true challenge in achieving change is not concerned with the science of efficiency and re-engineering but with re-energizing people. Efficiency is given. If you bet on efficiency, you are betting on the incompetence of your competitors," he says. "It is easy to underestimate the fact that beyond the tipping point you need leadership skills."

'Interview': James Champy

One of the leading authorities on business reengineering outlines what makes a reengineering effort successful and where the reengineering movement is now making the most difference.

Reengineering is often seen as ambition gone haywire, especially by the general public.

That is because the reengineer's motivations are too often simply assumed. As change agents, we don't have to talk openly about our ambition, but we should examine it carefully. We should look at the quality of our ambition – for what purpose do we strive, is there a "greater" purpose in what we do beyond just generating profits? Too often we experience the ambition of others as overreaching and failure. Most people talk and write about ambition in that way. Sometimes well-intended people get to a point where they believe themselves infallible – like a Bill Clinton – and they do foolish things. That's what we see. We don't see the really good ambitions of Bob Shapiro, the former CEO of Monsanto, who wanted to figure out how to feed the world.

Has the reengineering movement been positive?

I think that the balance is very positive. In global terms, I think that we have only reached 10 or 20 percent of what we intended, so there is still a lot to be done. In this moment there is a very real reaction to reengineering that comes from people who do not understand the concept. Many consider it very similar to the downsizing trend. Others have not yet understood the need for a fundamental change in the way in which corporations work. Reengineering is exactly that – it is a radical change in the way people perform their work in corporations. The basic idea of reengineering is now a global phenomenon. More than a management fad and a buzzword, it is really a genuine need.

Which sectors of the economy had the best results?

I am not sure that there is a clear answer to your question. I can name those industries that, in my opinion, should urgently start reengineering projects. In the first place are the industries linked with technologies, the telecommunications and media enterprises. Your business (press), for example, is a strong candidate for reengineering because your industries are making a revolution in the history of information and of publications. In the second place are the financial services, the banks in particular, whose reengineering isn't done yet. Then there are the health services. In the US, maybe more than in Europe, the health system is suffering important changes. It is also important to note the public utilities that live in a phase of deregulation and privatization around the world. Last are the transport industries, which stand to reap great benefits from reengineering that presently are being lost.

Were there reengineering differences between Europe, the United States, and Asia?

In cultural terms, I think that North American managers are better prepared to be radical and to cut with the past. In Europe generally, managers are more conservative. Some countries, such as France, are heavily influenced by socialist traditions. But in Germany, there is recognition of the necessity of applying reengineering. Germany is one of the better markets nowadays to apply the concept. Although the Germans are conservative, they are very much aware of the need for change, particularly in the automobile sector. In Asia, I have seen reengineering in locations like South Korea, Japan, and Hong Kong. Of these, the Japanese are the ones who show more willingness to try to do things differently.

Why the Japanese?

The Japanese are facing a great challenge because they are not moving as fast as their competitors in the management of change. That is one of the motivations for Japanese corporations to build new plants outside of Japan. Change is easier to implement because the culture is less resistant. With the Koreans the situation is different. They are more open to foreign ideas and ways of thinking. The Chinese, on the other side, still do not have reengineering infrastructures in place because their businesses are like collections of small operations. In spite of everything, they seem to be facing the change well.

How will the dramatic changes you talk about manage to take place?

Without being ironic, I think that each corporation needs a shrink. My work is to persuade the manager to see the market in a different way, to understand the level of change that is adequate, and to agree about the necessity of making changes in how work is done. That is without any doubt the most difficult part. I think that the techniques related to process redesign are easy to understand and implement. Those linked with great cultural changes are more complicated. That is due to the fact that the managers still have, in my opinion, a traditional way of thinking. The change I talk about is radical and discontinuous, not incremental, contrary to what we are used to daily.

Are consultants **required** *to implement reengineering?*

Companies will probably learn to do it by themselves, but, in my opinion, not with the greatest change efforts. Companies still do not know how to change strategy, the processes, the technology, and the culture simultaneously, without external help. It will still take 10 years until the muscle of management will be capable to do it. The reengineering movement still has to go through all the steps that strategy has already passed. Ten years ago, the best consultant companies that specialized in strategy were growing at a good pace – McKinsey, Boston Consulting Group, Bain and Monitor, Michael Porter. On a large scale that business decreased due to the fact that managers have learned to develop that discipline. Nowadays people know that the way to a good performance doesn't lie only in having a brilliant idea or strategy, but also in looking at the processes. I think that the consulting firms still have about five to ten good years of reengineering work. After that, it is probable that there will be a new phase of accommodation.

How long is a reengineering journey?

In my opinion, the complete journey takes two to three years. But there should exist concrete results in the first 12 or 18 months, otherwise the resistance to reengineering will certainly grow.

And to counter that resistance?

Many people don't understand the subtleties of managing. They believe that a manager must be decisive, that the world is black and white. In fact, a good bit of the business world today is gray; you may not know immediately what to do. It's okay to think for a while. There is a lot of intellectual work to management, but that counters the macho approach that managers often adopt to maintain power. Operating only through control diminishes your power to lead people. It suggests that you really don't know what's going on.

When two companies become one

ANDREAS HINTERHUBER

[Mergers and acquisitions are an accepted part of corporate strategy. Yet despite their enduring popularity, their success rate is surprisingly low. This article shows how M&As can be made to work.]

As frenetic as merger and acquisition (M&A) activity in recent years, so heated are debates questioning and defending its potential to add value. On the one hand, CEOs are usually enthusiastic and quick to affirm that broader reach, increased efficiency, and a more comprehensive product portfolio will allow to significantly enhance shareholder value. Stock markets, on the other hand, are more cautious. Within our own research on Best Practices in M&A, we compared the stock-market performance of the largest mergers and acquisitions completed in 1999 with the development of the S&P 500 index. The results were surprisingly disappointing. Merged companies, including Vodafone, Exxon, Astra Zeneca, Honeywell, and SBC, not only significantly underperformed the S&P 500 index but have to date failed to create any significant value at all.

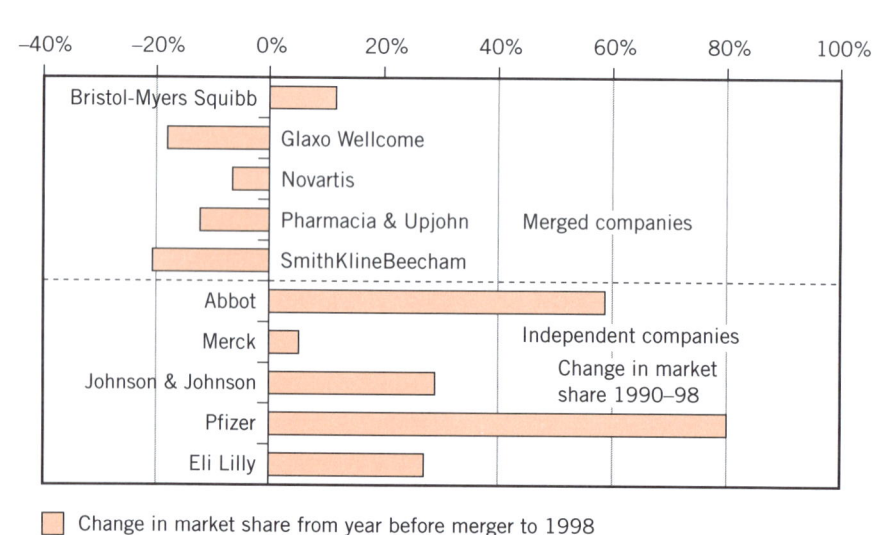

Figure 3.3: *Market share of merged companies: the case of the pharmaceutical industry*

Broader research (summarized in Table 3.1) also suggests that the average merger is doomed to fail.

The stock market is not the only place where mergers are won or lost. Equally important is the marketplace. An analysis of the market share development of pharmaceutical companies reveals that the market share of merged companies usually declines strongly in the period following a merger. On the other hand, significant growth in market share is usually realized by independent companies (see Figure 3.3).

Finally, as job losses accompany most mergers, employees are usually the least enthusiastic constituency – recent empirical research shows that employee productivity can decline up to 80 percent in a merger phase. In this context it is clear that

Table 3.1: *Merger research*

Source	Scope of study	Period studied	Main findings
A.T. Kearney	115 mergers and acquisitions	1993–1996	58 percent do not create positive shareholder returns
Mercer Management Consulting	All mergers from 1990–1996	1990–1996	48 percent destroy shareholder value
Pricewaterhouse Coopers	97 mergers and acquisitions	1994–1997	Over 40 percent fail to create shareholder value
Booz-Allen & Hamilton	117 mergers and acquisitions	1994–1996	Over 50 percent underperform relative to industry peers
KPMG	700 mergers and acquisitions	1996–1998	53 percent of deals reduce shareholder value; 82 percent of CEOs view transaction as succesful
Boston Consulting Group	277 mergers and acquisitions	1985–2000	56 percent of mergers destroy shareholder value
McKinsey & Company	193 mergers and acquisitions	1990–1997	89 percent of companies fail to increase revenues after merger

companies planning to merge face a steep uphill battle, despite all promises of future growth, reduced costs, and rising profits.

Our research into M&As produced two main findings. First, most mergers fail because managers apply a set of apparently common-sense rules. Second, outstanding "integrators" are able to create extraordinary growth in shareholder value, and employee and customer satisfaction by applying a set of apparently counterintuitive measures in M&A integration.

Common assumptions in M&A integration

Most executives implicitly follow a set of commonly held assumptions when merging or integrating two companies. The most widely spread assumptions are:

In depth planning as key requirement for success

The prevailing opinion is that an over-investment in planning pays off in the integration and long-term performance of the two companies. Therefore, the average deal is "closed" 8–12 months after announcement, in order to allow for enough time to hammer out the details of the deal. A VP of Siemens summed up the prevailing wisdom in the following way: "Speed is not enough, planning is more important than speed."

Synergy realization as primary goal once deal is closed

There is no doubt that the ultimate goal of mergers is an increase in profit beyond what each company individually would have been able to do. Thus, in the first year after a merger, synergy realization is generally seen as the single most important task of management in relation to ensuring merger success.

"Early wins" in integration – pick low hanging fruit first

It is common wisdom, that early wins in the integration stage build the necessary trust and commitment to attack more complex issues at a later stage. As Nelson and Lagges, two principals with management consultancy A.T. Kearney, say: "During the first year, it is important to combine two cultures and organizations, but it is fatal to get bogged down in heave operations integration. Start out by picking the low-hanging fruit" (Nelson and Lagges 1993).

> **Integration managers are appointed for monitoring and implementation of synergies**
>
> In nearly all of the companies we studied, integration managers at various levels of the organization were specifically nominated to monitor the implementation of synergies. The globally identified synergies are broken down by year, business line, and region, with integration managers monitoring progress in synergy realization. Objective is to ensure that reported synergies are also auditable by external or internal auditors.
>
> **Financial yardsticks are best instrument to monitor progress of integration activities**
>
> Finally, most companies studied have strong controlling instruments in place to benchmark the progress realized in the integration process. Consultant companies have developed a broad array of tools, such as the ERI (Ensuring Rapid Implementation) tool by BCG in this area, aimed at ensuring that the targetted synergies are also reflected in the P&L statement of the merged company.

These practices appear commonsensical. Yet our research indicates that they lead many companies dangerously astray. Though apparently focussed on the integration process, they ultimately distract companies from the grounds where the real battle for integration success is fought – the *marketplace*. This is the main reason why most mergers fail.

Outstanding M&A integrators

When we started to study the integration practices of some companies with immense acquisition experience such as GE, Thermo Electron, Citigroup, and others, a set of counterintuitive patterns began to emerge. Similar patterns surfaced when we studied the rare cases of successful mergers, such as Aventis. The implicit assumptions of managers responsible for integration within these companies were radically different in critical ways.

First, the focus of all integration activities was the creation of an immensely competitive organization, rather than beating analysts' estimates of expected synergy levels. Second, managers in these companies realized that the creation of a common mindset was the most important prerequisite for achieving this objective.

The key lessons from outstanding integrators can be summarized in the following way:

The window of opportunity is small – if after 3–6 months integration is not complete, it will never occur

The best integrators recognize the need for urgency, rather than planning, in integration. Less focussed on producing detailed business plans with the next three-year sales and earning developments, they know that the window of opportunity in integration is open for only a very limited period of time. A distinctive feature of outstanding integrators is speed. They start very early in pre-merger assessment and move very quickly in integration.

Success is determined largely by how quickly a common mindset is created

The creation of a common mindset calls for the perpetuation of strong values and a performance-oriented corporate culture attentive to signaling effects.

Strong values and a strong corporate culture are necessary to give the employees joining the new organization a powerful sense of what the organization will stand for. These values are a combination of external market requirements, the unique strengths of both organizations, and the envisioned future of the new organization. They should also carry the organization toward a point in the future that is never quite reached yet is powerful enough to guide day-to-day decisions.

While most organizations pay at least some attention to values and corporate culture, only outstanding organizations realize the strong signaling effects that all actions implicitly have on the enforcement of corporate culture. In a merger, these effects are particularly important in two instances: commitment to start at the top with synergies, and commitment to let top performers go if needed.

The outstanding integrators in our sample realize that synergies implemented at the executive floor send a strong signal to the rest of the organization about top management commitment to synergies. By contrast, weak integrators, in their reluctance to let senior executives go, frequently move these people to staff positions deliberately created, thereby implicitly communicating to the organization that complacency is more important than performance, that history matters more than the future. With this, middle managers are tacitly encouraged to be softer than the requirements of the external marketplace, making it impossible for the company to realize any significant cost savings beyond what each organization would have been able to do individually.

Signaling effects are also important in decisions regarding top performers violating company values. In weak organizations, high performance confers the license to do everything not prohibited by law. Outstanding integrators know that top management commitment to company values is credible only when adherence to values is put above performance, which means to let high-performing individuals go on occasion. These considerations apply especially during the integration phase, where

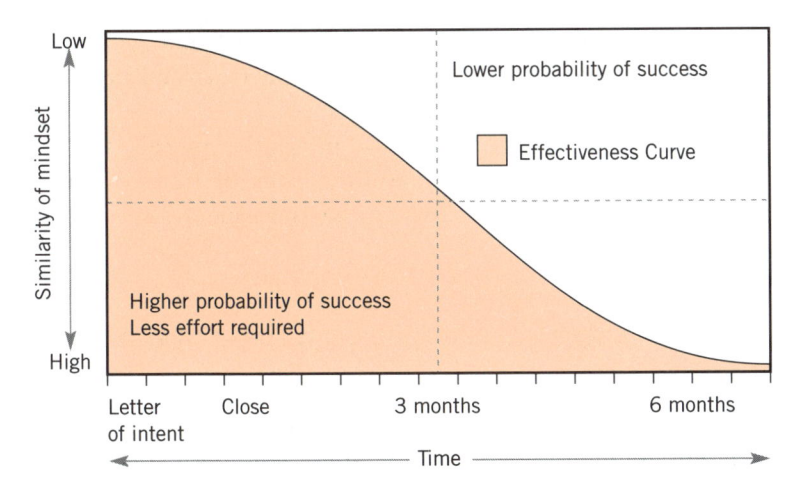

Figure 3.4: *Performance measurement in integration – success is dependent on how quickly a common mindset is realized*

middle and senior management not only need to adhere to specific values but also have to facilitate the creation of a unified body of new values (Figure 3.4).

The vision of creating an immensely competitive organization drives all integration activities

Outstanding integrators realize that the only vision worth pursuing in the disruptive phase following a merger is the vision of creating an organization focussed on being extremely competitive in the marketplace. Several steps are involved.

First, an audit of the competitive profile of the two companies is conducted by an independent party to assess strengths and weaknesses of the two companies *in the eyes of key customers*. This view is then confronted with the perception of executives about strengths and weaknesses of their own and of the merged or acquired company. Second, an *ideal competitive profile* is drafted, taking into account the requirements of a competitive marketplace, company aspirations, and existing strengths and weaknesses.

Third, in light of usually considerable gaps between current customer perceptions of the company's strengths, management perception of actual strengths, and the competitive profile required in the future, action plans – frequently requiring drastic changes in operating logic, staffing, and strategy – are laid out, discussed, and implemented.

Finally, the company has to be energized toward achieving the desired goal of competitiveness from the very beginning of the integration process. Training, lectures, and so on are usually helpful but, in the end, frequently only drastic changes in the way people perceive themselves, the company, and competition are able to produce the required changes. In addition to sometimes demanding implementation skills, outstanding integrators have the skills to deeply touch and affect people's minds and hearts.

The energy level generated during this kind of integration process is in no way comparable to the lackluster atmosphere resulting from the fruitless attempt to motivate employees to achieve abstract synergy goals, frequently encountered in mediocre integrators.

Start with radical changes – manage the easier parts later on in the process

In contrast to cautious changes and multiple rounds of reorganization typical of inexperienced integrators, we found outstanding integrators reorganize aggressively from the start. The desired competitive profile, discussed above, is the blueprint for reorganization at this stage. In the experience of outstanding integrators, which we amply support, it is far preferable to reorganize heavily and drastically at the beginning of the integration process – but only then. Afterwards, the organization is given the time and the psychological reassurance to establish its own identity and internal cohesion.

Compare this to the erratic rounds of reorganization observed in the vast majority of mergers. At the beginning, fearful of provoking conflict with the other party, only minor adjustments are made to company structure; later, in a second round of reorganization, the resulting inefficiencies are eliminated until, in a further round of restructuring, changes in the marketplace can be addressed. During this process, employee morale goes from bad to worse while the executive management is unable, even if it were willing, to provide any direction to the company.

Integration managers focus on the competitive profiling of the new organization

It follows naturally that integration managers will not be held responsible for synergy planning and implementation. Experienced integrators, although aware that synergies are followed by financial analysts on Wall Street, know that synergy realization can never be the ultimate aim of a merger or acquisition; they also know that a highly competitive organization will produce earnings and cash flow consistently above expectations.

This, in turn, defines the role of the integration managers. Concurrently with business line, functional, or country heads, they ensure that the competitive profile of the merged company is consistent with the overall aspirations. The strategic impact resulting from this task usually far exceeds the rather mundane surveillance of headcount reductions. Here, external critical success factors, customer requirements, and the position of leading competitors are monitored periodically – at least twice per year. The vision of a strongly competitive company is then translated into action-items following current customer perceptions and market demands.

In some organizations, the observed impact of this periodic feedback loop with the market are huge: organizations, happy with delivering products in the past, integrated their supply chains with key customers and redesigned key attributes of some of their products in order to consistently exceed customer specifications. In another case, a "middle-of-the-road" profile shortly after the merger (no specific weaknesses but also no significant strengths) evolved gradually into a competitive profile extremely focussed on lowest costs and superior delivery reliability.

Performance along *external* critical success factors is the primary instrument for assessing integration progress

Outstanding integrators recognize that integration success means that a common mindset creates an immensely competitive company. For this to occur, this common mindset – shared values and cultural identity – is established quickly. Second, the integration progress is measured by comparing the performance along external, customer-defined, critical success factors against the targetted competitive profile outlined in the previous section (see Figure 3.5).

Alongside, indicators for internal efficiency are spread throughout the organization – some of the outstanding integrators created a "library of best practices" on working capital efficiency and other internal benchmarks that was then cascaded through the organization. Again, this permanent focus on the requirements of the competitive marketplace provides a much clearer orientation for employees at all levels than less inspiring calls for quicker implementation of synergies.

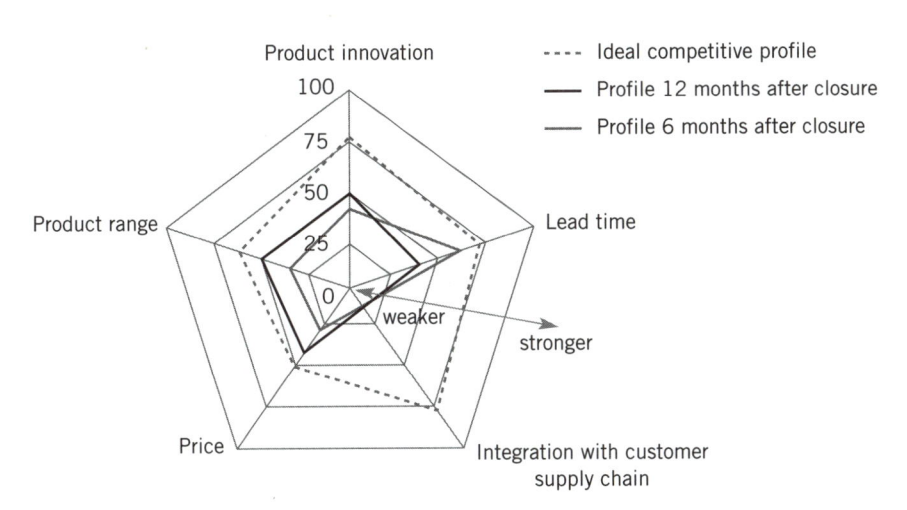

Figure 3.5: *Performance measurement in integration – actual competitive profile is periodically monitored against ideal*

The rules of outstanding integrators

1. The window of opportunity is small – if after 3–6 months integration is not complete, it will never occur.

2. Success is determined largely by how quickly a common mindset is created.

3. The vision of creating an immensely competitive organization drives all integration activities.

4. Start with radical changes – manage the easier parts later on in the process.

5. Integration managers focus on the competitive profiling of the new organization.

6. Performance along external critical success factors is the primary instrument for assessing integration progress.

Integration distilled

In the end, the unconventional wisdom of the world's best integrators boils down to a few essential rules. Whereas most companies get caught up in internal struggles and start to concentrate far too much upon themselves, outstanding integrators focus on the vision of competitiveness during the whole merger process – the demands of the external market take precedence over self-contemplation.

By the same token, soft issues are treated as the real hard issues. The creation of a common mindset, linking people's values with company culture, is seen as the single most important requirement for a successful merger by successful integrators. For this to be achieved, the organization is energized with a set of values derived from the demands of the marketplace, future aspirations, and current strengths of the merging companies.

Finally, speed takes clear precedence over accuracy. Today's mediocre integrators fail to see that the competition eagerly and happily waits for any slowdown accompanying the typical search for a detailed pre-merger plan. By contrast, the world's best integrators are *fast*: internally, in creating a common mindset, and externally, in becoming very competitive very quickly.

RESOURCES

Carey, D., 'Lessons from Master Acquirers – A CEO Roundtable on Making Mergers Succeed,' *Harvard Business Review*, 78 (3), 2000.

Huff, Anne S., *John Reed and James March on Management Research and Practice*, Academy of Management Executive, 14 (1), 2000.

Nelson, C.A. and Lagges, J.G., 'Corporate Boards and Mergers,' *Corporate Board*, 3, 12–16, 1993.

Slater, R., *Jack Welch and the GE Way – Management Insights and Leadership Secrets of the Legendary CEO*, McGraw Hill, 1998.

This article previously appeared in *Business Strategy Review*, Volume 13, Issue 3, Autumn 2002.

The myths of change management

MICHAEL JARRETT

> When it comes to change, organizational resistance is grossly underestimated. Change agents believe that change can be managed and these assumptions lead to faulty interventions. But if the dynamics of change cannot be predicted with certainty or controlled, then the advocates of change must manage themselves to ride the crest of changes' fortunes – for that is the only thing that can be managed.

Lou Gerstner, Sandy Weill, and Jack Welch are lauded and envied by the corporate world. IBM was hemorrhaging $4.97 billion in 1992 before Gerstner turned it around. Citicorp's Weill and his executive team successfully managed a complex integration of companies to become the global leader in financial services and the most profitable bank in history. GE's "Work Out" methodology became the mantra for change. The successes suggested that the alchemy of change was within easy reach.

However, these corporate successes of transformational change are the exceptions rather than the rule. They have become the mythical purveyors of change and have unintentionally perpetuated a myth that change is "easy" providing you follow the recipe.

Experience with executives suggests these approaches do not work for most companies. Why? There appears to be a series of myths and half-truths about change that have become the basis of failed organizational interventions. Perhaps we need a different approach to understand change. In using the term "change" in this article we are interested in strategic or "transformational" change as opposed to operational or incremental change. Thus, we are concerned with changes in strategy, culture, leadership and authority, structures, and systems.

The first myth to explode is that change always creates value.

Myth 1: Organizational change management creates value

The ugly truth about organizational change is that it is exceedingly difficult. The research on change management does not make compelling reading. In fact, in most cases of cultural and organizational change the expected benefits are not realized.

The academic literature suggests that as many as 70 percent of change management programs fail and that transformational change occurs only about 30 percent of the time. A comparative study of change initiatives concluded that cultural and people factors were among the key determinants undermining change.

It is understandable why the myth persists. The slogan of "change or die" reflects the dynamic and changing environment that surrounds us. This is not to suggest that organizations should not change. Change is absolutely necessary in a shifting environment. We simply need to get better at it. However, it seems that "change" is just poorly understood, based on misinformed assumptions, poorly executed, or all of these.

The rest of this article aims to explain why change fails. It draws on the theories of "punctuated equilibrium" and complexity as alternative approaches and focusses on three inter-related areas:

- the nature and purpose of resistance;
- the implications regarding the assumptions of change management programs;
- the nature of interventions, including the role of the proponents of change.

Myth 2: Resistance can be overcome

"Strategies for overcoming resistance" misunderstand its nature, purpose, and depth. It remains latent in the form of inertia or, if confronted, resurfaces later.

The popular expression regarding the prospects for change is represented in management consulting by the "change equation." It suggests that change happens if $Ch = f(D \times V \times P) > Co$.

Change (Ch) takes place if the Dissatisfaction (D) with the status quo, multiplied by a Vision (V) of the future, multiplied by agreed Processes (P) that remove obstacles blocking access to the desired state, is greater than the Cost (Co) of change. The multiplicative nature of the variables means that if any is zero then change will not occur.

However, it seems that the popular explanation as to why change succeeds or fails has understated an important factor implicit in the work of Kurt Lewin who inspired the above understanding – the role of competing social dynamics and the forces of resistance. He refers to this as a state of "quasi-stationary equilibria," where resistance is the current state and to tackle it head on tends to create an immediate counterforce to maintain the equilibrium.

Thus the equation should be rewritten: $Ch = f(D \times V \times P \times R) > Co$, where R is resistance.

There are a number of implications if this additional dimension holds. First, given the implied direction of resistance to be negative, it means that change is always operating with the brakes on. It is unlikely that resistance would be zero. Second, it also implies that "resistance" is part of the deep, embedded structure of the organization. If you push, it will push back. Finally, we could reframe and understand the purpose of resistance as providing a useful function of continuity and equilibrium for the current state.

There is considerable discussion to suggest that the roots of resistance can be found in fear and survival and it operates at several levels to protect social systems from painful experiences of loss, distress, chaos, and the emotions associated with change.

- *Personal defenses.* Individuals set up personal ego and psychological defenses to deny the reality of change and the pain that goes with it.
- *Group conflicts.* The nature and dysfunctional dynamics of leadership groups, inter-group conflict, and differences also prevent change.
- *Organizational and political.* The management of different interests maintains the status quo and inertia.
- *Institutional dynamics.* Networks of customers and markets make it difficult to do things differently and these can be traced back to history, context, and environment.

These essentially lead to inertia. Where change is tried then unintended consequences may also take place. Thus, resistance first needs to be understood and reinterpreted. It is the "shadow" side of the organization that cannot be ignored or easily overcome. Misunderstanding this basic tenet leads to flawed change initiatives.

British Airways – the Bob Ayling years

In 1996, when Bob Ayling was appointed chief executive of British Airways, the company announced pre-tax profits of £474 million. Nevertheless, BA was losing business to other airlines. One of the strategies Ayling implemented was the intention to cut costs by £1 billion within three years.

There was considerable "resistance" by fellow executives, the organization, and the contextual and institutional relations, including customers. Management also became embroiled in two disputes in 1997. The first was in an attempt to restructure the pay system and overtime allowances of cabin staff. The second was with the catering staff when Ayling tried promoting the idea of the "virtual" airline, employing the minimum number of staff to reduce overheads.

In both of these disputes the management took a tough and confrontational stance. There were warnings of dismissal, loss of promotion, and the withdrawal of benefits. An unintended consequence was that these tactics turned moderate staff against management.

> In July 1997, 300 cabin crew went on strike for three days and another 2,000 went on sick leave (approximately four times higher than normal for that period), causing longer-term disruptions. The cost of the strike was estimated at £125 million.
>
> Low morale at BA is often attributed to the effects of the strike, with Ayling the target of ill feeling among staff. Passengers deserted to rival airlines such as Virgin and United and many were never to return. The image of BA as a bullyboy employer is said to have lingered in the memories of many potential travelers.
>
> BA's shares consistently underperformed the market and in 2000 it suffered a loss of approximately £200 million. Ayling resigned in March 2000.
>
> *Sources*: BBC News on-line, IRRU, Warwick Business School.

There are a number of implicit assumptions that appear to go hand in hand with "constructivist rational" approaches to change that are dominant in the literature. Challenging these can help to explain some of the variance between expectations and experience. In particular, we need to look at three further beliefs and propose a different paradigm to understand change. These are:

- change is constant;
- change can be managed;
- the "change agent" knows best.

Myth 3: Change is constant

"Change is constant" is a cry often heard within organizations. The subjective reality is not to be denied. However, this claim can be reframed in a number of ways.

First, it is helpful to distinguish between transformational change as it is defined in this article and incremental change/continuous improvement. Thus, while there may be constant noise in the background due to incremental change or fine-tuning, it should not be confused with "transformational change." As a senior manager of a UK development agency put it: "Yes, I can see the difference between the 'big push' at the beginning and then the constant settling in and smaller initiatives."

Second, empirically, studies suggest that large-scale change within organizations tends, on average, to be low and take place infrequently. Far from constant, change is infrequent.

Finally, the theory of "punctuated equilibrium" also helps understand this apparent difference between experience and reality. It suggests that systems evolve through the alternation of periods of equilibrium and periods of revolution. The deep structures discussed above provide relatively long periods of stability (equilibrium) but are punctuated by compact periods of radical change. Thus, organizational systems can accommodate the gradual addition of stress in small incremental change until a certain threshold is crossed, after which a catastrophic reordering takes place.

Studies by Tushman and Romanelli (1985) and Romanelli and Tushman (1994) strongly suggest that:

- change does seem to systematically follow the dynamics presented by punctuated equilibrium where there are long periods of stability interrupted by rapid and relatively shorter periods of change that lead to strategic reorientations and change in culture and leadership;
- transformational change is rapid and large and the corollary suggests that change by a series of incremental steps is less likely to happen;
- these changes tend to be also associated with changes in the external environment (impacts on a secondary effect of poor performance) and the intentions of the senior executives.

This perspective on change also helps to explain the role and purpose of resistance. It describes "resistance" as a network of "deep structures" of organizational culture, leadership, and organization. These provide continuity and stability to the system, which can then tolerate incremental change.

In addition, punctuated equilibrium suggests that far from change being constant, it is more a protracted series of discontinuous leaps with the dynamics driven by factors outside of the change process and that timing is critically important.

Thus, successful change is time dependent and context driven, though it has been argued that these variables are rarely featured in our models of change and represent a gap in our understanding of organizational change. In addition, "change" is rare but often traumatic as it takes people out of their "comfort zone" and can lead them into defensive strategies as an attempt to manage it, which in term reinforces the dilemma.

Myth 4: Change can be managed

The theory of punctuated equilibrium also forces us to rethink our assumptions on "change management." Original concepts of planned change management and its assumptions were based on linear, rationalistic thinking, humanistic ideals, and equilibrium conditions. These provided useful tools at the time but implied that change could be managed.

The theory of punctuated equilibrium implies that the rapid development of change and its divergent antecedents means that change is not something that can be managed with certainty. Outcomes can be both divergent and unexpected. This shares many of the principles of complexity theory, which captures the core tension most organizations or social systems in disequilibrium face seeking stability. However, without periods of instability, inertia and complacency may leave them as victims unable to adapt when the environment changes.

Complex adaptive systems surf on the edge of chaos when provoked by a complex task. Organizations and other social and complex systems experience the same journey. These outcomes are a feature of the rapid span within which change takes place. But they are also informed by the reworking of the "deep" and "embedded" structure as power and authority relations are renegotiated and institutional and organizational dynamics play a part.

The proponents of change can stimulate the change or even steer through it. But it cannot be managed.

Myth 5: The change agent knows best

It is a fair assumption that most agents of change are well intentioned. However, the assumptions that inform traditional approaches of change present difficulties, both externally and internally. It follows that where outcomes are both uncontrollable and unpredictable, it is difficult for the proponent of change to know best.

Complexity theory suggests that during periods of "bounded chaos," emergent processes take place, leading to self-organizing sub-systems influencing the final outcome of change. We see these self-organizing systems in the BA case. Thus, contrary to the change agent knowing best, it is the informal systems that channel the energy, or wind of change, for good or for ill.

Second, the change agent is also hampered by a lack of awareness of his or her own internal resistance. The recipe model of change provides familiarity and a secure base for the consultant/agent, but it is also a trap. It can stop thinking, creativity, and managing the unknown elements of change that are mediated through multiple agents and institutional dynamics. Their "knowing" can reinforce the resistance and undermine the very change they aim to release. Thus the change agent is unable to direct the system; they can only disturb it. They can become a catalyst, but the system works out the result. They have to become skilled sailors where the wind is determined and they have to work with it.

The proponents of change must accept that they are not omniscient. They have to "let a thousand flowers bloom" through the facilitation and support of self-organizing systems. This means a different role for both proponents of change and the intervention strategies they employ.

If the assumptions about change management are dubious, then so must be the interventions that follow. The final two myths are comments about the implications for interventions for successful organizational change.

Myth 6: Accepted wisdom is to follow the steps

The change management literature tends to be characterized by normative principles on how to make change happen. These will often have a variety of key steps for success. The most influential of these is John Kotter, who suggests that there are eight steps to change. Other writers in this tradition also identify a series of often iterative steps that change requires.

The Six Pack Model (Figure 3.6) distils these essential ingredients for successful change management:

- create the change imperative or sense of urgency;
- agree strategic leadership;
- create a sense of shared direction, both about the what and the how;
- implement the changes;
- score some early victories;
- sustain the game for culture change.

This model has great appeal. It provides a framework for understanding the change process. However, executives and clients often had different experiences that were not fully accounted for in this approach. Transformational change is an iterative and dynamic process. As one executive from a retail bank put it: "It's an imperfect jigsaw rather than a series of steps."

This notion that managing change is not a series of predictable steps concurs with the theoretical propositions in this article. The actual process of change is rapid and great. Thus, making a difference through manageable steps does not always follow and it is considerably more messy, uncertain, and chaotic.

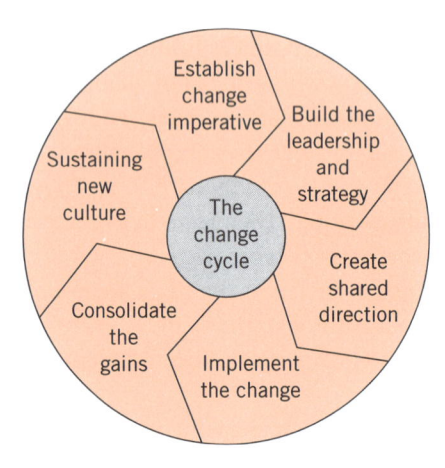

Figure 3.6: *The Six Pack Model*

This requires us to rethink the dynamics of change, managing these different elements or levers of change more interactively and making quick judgements during its rapid phase rather than using a magic recipe that bears no relationship to the timing or environment. Thus, it is not that the components of change are wrong; it is more the relationship between them. They are more interactive with each other all of the time rather than in a serial, linear fashion. We need to jump outside the straitjacket of this thinking.

Thus, the model of change is a dynamic, interactive flow of key elements that is driven by context and time-dependent factors. It is supplemented internally by self-organizing sub-systems and the intentionality of the leadership. But the outcome is unpredictable. It is more like sailing a racing yacht and using the winds and waves of change; you have to tack, take cover, anchor, and even change course to realize your intentions. This is in sharp contrast to the ocean liner that takes several miles just to stop, let alone turn around. The "step-wise" model does not match the rapidly changing and chaotic dynamics of change where a more flexible and resilient approach is required.

Myth 7: Big changes require big changes

Transformational programs were once introduced as huge events. Mercury, BA when privatized, and Whitbread were among those that launched such programs in the 1980s and 1990s.

One of the contradictions about the dynamics of change is that little things can produce great outcomes. In change management it was once known as identifying the "critical mass" for change: the minority of people who were willing and able to influence and implement the changes, thus causing a cascade effect. Malcolm Gladwell has described it more forcefully as the "tipping point." He demonstrates, using several cases ranging from the revival of Hush Puppy shoes to stemming crime in New York, how small interventions can create huge impact. Three factors are identified as common:

- the context of contagiousness, where the timing, environment, or seeds of a good idea are just ripe for the moment and they spread, almost like a virus, to infect others – by the 1990s New York was ready for an anti-crime drive;

- little causes can have big effects – the snowball effect of text messaging took the telecom operators by surprise and created an unexpected new market;

- these changes take place in a dramatic moment and thus things happen very quickly.

Complexity theory mirrors these ideas and they are consistent with the timing, context, and rapidity of change discussed earlier.

Thus, in stimulating change, you do not need to change everything all at once or on a big scale. It does, however, take a little thought, co-ordination, and judgement. It is like pulling the mainsheet and jib when tacking to a change in the wind.

Here are some examples of playing the elements of change.

Infect a sense of urgency by identifying the "critical number." Sir Brian Pitman of Lloyds-TSB talked of doubling shareholder value every three years. It provided a rallying point, helped the two banks to go forward on a common agenda, and created the energy for change. The sense of intentionality and reasons to give up those zones of deep structure and comfort are both present in this scenario. Without them, we wait for time and changes in the environment like a ship without a rudder.

Develop the strategic coalition. It is critical that the top management group is aligned on the changes. These are the minimum boundary conditions for change. The outcome can be disaster if they are not met. A financial service business group saw its cross-market opportunities slip away as the top team could not agree to work their business units together and thus lost many of the advantages of their own internal convergence.

Create the shared direction. Use communication, communication, communication. When two national retail organizations merged they had to harmonize compensation and benefits. The result was that most employees received enhanced conditions up to 10 percent of salary. If I gave you a check for 10 percent of your salary, would you be pleased? Not in this newly merged company. When questioned about it they replied: "Even the way the pay rise was communicated was a shambles. I blame those people at the top." Good news that is poorly communicated can damage a change program very quickly.

Implement small things quickly. Test the boundary conditions and gain quick wins. Start small and focus.

Reward the right behaviors. Tube Investments, once an engineering company, spent considerable energy, time, and money getting teams to work better. They had names like Alpha, Omega, and the like to engender the edge of a high-performance team. However, the initiative unexpectedly ran aground. Deeper analysis identified that they continued to reward people on their individual performance and so the rewards did not match the behaviors they desired.

Cultivate and embed the new changes. After a highly charged period of rapid change, the new embedded structures sit with the old. This is the period of renewed equilibrium, of incremental and fine-tuning changes. These elements are constantly interacting and being directed by the intentionality of the people advocating change and their personal mastery. The latter means the ability to manage the only real factor under their control, themselves.

The challenge of change requires a paradigm shift

This article has argued that one of the reasons that helps explain the failure of most organizational change initiatives is that they are based on a number of prevailing myths and assumptions about its nature. These are constructed on rationalist ideas that lead to linear or tunnel thinking as well as a series of planned interventions.

It proposes a paradigm shift in thinking about change that draws upon the theory of punctuated equilibrium and complexity. These provide additional insights and implications for the role and interventions of change advocates. It challenges the myths of change and suggests some initial propositions for further study.

- Change is misunderstood and thus the value it can create is lost. The dynamics of transformational change are better understood using systemic thinking and theories of complexity and disequilibrium rather than convergent rationalist models in a rapidly changing environment.
- Resistance is embedded into the deep structure of organizations at several levels. It provides continuity and stability but also inertia. It cannot be pushed; otherwise defensive routines will be remobilized.
- Transformation is infrequent but rapid, leading to traumatic change as most resist or at best remain unprepared. This short review suggests that change depends more on timing, the environment, and the advocacy of the CEO. Thus, watching the winds of change through environmental scanning, influence, and understanding timing are all critical capabilities for change advocates.
- Change cannot be managed. It may be possible to stimulate, steer, or tack with the winds of change. Change advocates need to have personal mastery and emotional intelligence in order to manage the uncertainty, flexibility, and resilience that it requires.
- Change advocates need to be able to work with uncertainty and "not knowing." They appear to work effectively when they are able to tap the informal and self-organizing sub-systems as the real levers for change.
- The elements of change form a framework of constant adjustment, flexibility, and alertness that needs to be applied in the micro-moments of rapid change.
- Big pushes can increase resistance. Small interventions can lead to large impacts.

It also seems to suggest that in order to seize the full potential of change, leaders and change advocates need to be attuned to emergent and opportunistic strategies since they may precede change.

The implications for engaging with change are that leaders and change advocates have to have emotional resilience and personal mastery. Their actions may appear as counter-intuitive using this different paradigm and it also suggests that in some instances waiting and doing nothing may also be useful, as it accepts that one cannot always work alone against the tide.

Learning is change

In conclusion, this approach to understanding transformational change of complex adaptive systems helps to critically review current assumptions as well as rethink and reorder some basic strategies. It appears that change programs need a different set of working assumptions and to be sensitive to timing, the environment, and the dynamics of leadership.

It also leads to the uncomfortable but not surprising conclusion that much of the transformational agenda is often outside organizational control. However, the important factor that affects successful transitions is how it is dealt with internally – and that appears to make a difference.

This article also offers some tentative propositions for change advocacy that need further discussion, systematic research, and more rigorous testing. However, there is one point many will agree upon and that is that there will always be change of this order and being unable to respond will lead to atrophy.

Perhaps one way we can think about change programs is that they build internal capability for organizational learning and further change, so that during the "pause" they can take advantage of the next opportunity. Too often, though, it seems as if organizations are too traumatized to take the lessons from the last change. However, they need to stop, reflect, and start to make sense of their experience rather than be drawn by the tendency to act out defensive routines that naturally occur when you disturb long-standing embedded structures of organizations.

RESOURCES

Bennis, W.G., Benne, K.D. and Chin, R., *The Planning of Change* (4th edition), London, Holt, Rinehart and Winston, 1985.

Bion, W.R., *Experiences in Groups and Other Papers*, Tavistock Publications, 1961.

Feldman, M.L. and Spratt, M.F., *Five Frogs on a Log: A CEO's Field Guide to Accelerating the Transition in Mergers, Acquisitions, and Gut Wrenching Change*, HarperCollins, 1999.

Freud, A., *The Ego and the Mechanisms of Defense*, International Universities Press, 1966.

Gladwell, Malcolm, *The Tipping Point*, Little, Brown and Company, 2000.

Kotter, John P., 'Leading change: why transformation efforts fail,' *Harvard Business Review*, March/April, pp. 59–67, 1995.

Pascale, R., 'Leading from a different place,' in *The Leaders Change Handbook*, Jossey-Bass, 1998.

Romanelli, E. and Tushman, M.L., 'Organizational transformation as punctuated equilibrium: an empirical test,' *Academy of Management Journal*, Vol. 37, No. 5, pp. 1141–1166, 1994.

Tushman, M.L. and Romanelli, E., 'Organizational evolution: a metamorphosis model of convergence and reorientation,' in L.L. Cummings and B.M. Shaw (eds), *Research in Organizational Behavior*, Vol. 17, JAI Press, 1985.

This article previously appeared in *Business Strategy Review*, Volume 14, Issue 4, Winter 2003.

'Interview': Rosabeth Moss Kanter

The Harvard Business School professor and founder of the consulting firm Goodmeasure talks about the influences and aspirations that lie behind her work.

Is there a strand that links your work together?

Every five or six years I've had a major theme and a major book. Each, I hope, has broken new ground. But always I have stressed innovation: how to create new value, how to unleash new ideas and bring them to market, how to solve complex problems, how to make organizations – and the world – better places.

One thread is that organizations have cultures and they affect the behavior and performance of people in the company. My first book, *Commitment and Community*, defined a theory of organizational arrangements which promoted commitment. It was one of the first discussions of corporate culture. The corporate culture boom came a full 10 years later. I am very interested in system dynamics and cultures which arise from that, the roles and norms and how they influence people's behavior. That explains why some people succeed and others fail, some companies grow and others do not.

Culture is not fuzzy attitudes; it includes all the pieces of the organizational structure and the culture of innovation. Innovation partnerships, alliances, and global connections are also major themes in my work. They come together in the subject of culture.

Then there is the theme of change, the processes by which things happen, how we get things done. Once you understand the pattern, the dynamics of the system, you can set about changing things. How to make things change includes the necessary leadership skills, the steps in the process, and whether you have a culture which allows for change.

Another theme is empowerment. When more people are involved and making a contribution, then performance increases. Ideas and competencies too often lie buried within organizations.

Are you an idealist?

I am a very realistic idealist. The ideas I have put forward work. The ideas are useful and effective. We sometimes think of idealists as setting out a utopian vision, but my work is very empirically grounded. It is based on research, not on an artificial model. I believe that things can get better. We can strive for higher degrees of excellence. We don't have to settle for grim and boring workplaces or products which aren't of the highest quality.

Do you have any sense that things are improving?

Yes, organizations have improved, though it is easy to slip. Workplaces have improved all over the world. Organizations are now faster and more diverse. Most have professionally trained managers and more women. There is much more emphasis on leadership.

We have been going through 20 years of striving for new organizational models which move us away from machine-like bureaucracy. There is still sweatshop-type labor in which people have no chance to think, but in the global information age the mental component of every job has become bigger and more important.

New organizational models are now accepted. There is, for example, less hierarchy, more emphasis on alliances and partnerships, and encouragement of innovation. Even so, lots of companies have policies which look and sound right – like flexible working – but which don't actually happen. Managers are often not very good at motivating people or treating them well. There is a lot of lip service.

There are a lot of concepts which have been proven in practice yet are not used. Look at gain sharing, for example. This is where the cost savings which result from employee ideas are shared among employees. Every organization which has used gain sharing has found that performance has improved. So, why doesn't everyone do it?

Have you got an answer?

There is a still a tendency to hold onto power at the top of organizations. There are a lot of turf battles and the like. People cling to their old behavior. To some extent it is human behavior, but it is also encouraged by corporate cultures.

If organizations have been changing for 20 years, to what event or date do you look back as a turning point?

The new wave was starting in terms of practice in the late 1970s. There was a big productivity crisis in the early 1970s; global competition became a factor in the late 1970s; and then we had the first of the new consumer-oriented IT companies. The microprocessor was born in 1973 and Apple in 1977. My 1977 book, *Men and Women of the Corporation*, was about the old-fashioned machine bureaucracy in which people's performance was inhibited because there was no opportunity for growth or access to power.

At that time, my consulting company Goodmeasure got a contract with General Motors which was then working on quality of working life programs and wanted to develop the diversity of its workforce. I got insights into a giant corporation trying to change. I also worked with a major computing firm which wanted to increase its productivity. It was very different, younger, more interested in new ideas. It was an alternative model.

So I would date the modern corporation to around 1980 when the giant corporation first started to realize that a new type of company was beginning to emerge.

But large corporations didn't suddenly embrace the new ways of working outlined in your 1983 book, Change Masters?

No. Companies looked at *Change Masters* and said its ideas were unrealistic. Five years later they were practicing them.

What was the next stage in this organizational process of change?

The opening of the World Wide Web in the early 1990s accelerated the process, made the new model more important, and added a few twists.

Would it be correct to see your new model as compassionate capitalism?

It is capitalism with a human face. Back in 1996, when there were newspaper headlines announcing that capitalism had won, I warned that if the business community wasn't attentive the headlines would be soon announcing that socialism is back. Now there is a huge backlash. This was reflected in my book, *World Class*, which is very much an activist's book and which looked at the need among companies, communities, and regions to create an infrastructure for collaboration.

There are strong social responsibility themes in my work. At the same time I believe that globalization can bring positive benefits if investments are made locally. I believe that government matters, public policy matters, and can effect the creation of entrepreneurial organizations.

What needs to be done to make capitalism effective and popular?

To save capitalism it needs to be inclusive and to pay attention to people at all levels. The global economy needs to work locally.

How is your take different on what is happening in the corporate world?

What distinguishes my work is that it's not flashy. It tends to be grounded. One of the reasons I continue to be based at a university – though I consult and am involved in other things – is that base in research. Some people whose ideas have become popular produce work which is based less and less on deep research. A university reminds you of the need for depth.

Who were your mentors?

I didn't really have mentors as such. As a woman in this field I was generally the first and only. I didn't have deep guidance, though people like Warren Bennis, Peter Drucker, and numerous colleagues, including my business partner and husband, Barry Stein, helped me along the way.

What would you regard as your skills?

I think I am good at synthesizing a great deal of information and seeing patterns, their significance, and defining the patterns. You have to be able to cut through the clutter and the data to say what's important.

What is the key question you ask when you go into a company?

What are you trying to accomplish – and what's standing in your way? I want to find out about goals and decisions at the corporate and individual level, what really drives people. Sometimes it's very clear. People point to missions, but sometimes these missions don't link to what's happening. Then the next question is: *What strengths do you have to help you get there?*

If you had one question for the managers of the world, what would it be?

What worries you the most – what keeps you awake at night? I always want to know about problems, trends, what's emerging, what's bothering people: what Peter Drucker calls "discontinuities." What doesn't fit?

CHAPTER 4

Communicating

"Today, communication itself is the problem. We have become the world's first overcommunicated society. Each year we send more and receive less."

Al Ries

"Think like a wise man but communicate in the language of the people."

William Butler Yeats

"In the last analysis, what we are communicates far more eloquently than anything we say or do."

Stephen Covey

"Words are tools which automatically carve concepts out of experience."

Julian Huxley

Creating Strategic Dialog

DAN YANKELOVICH AND STEVE ROSELL

[Strategy creation is a corporate imperative. Yet the optimal way to formulate strategy has proved elusive. A growing number of companies are discovering the power of strategic dialog.]

For more than 40 years the largest corporations have been experimenting with strategic planning, searching for the most effective way to carry out this indispensable corporate function. In the early phases of experimentation, companies developed strategic planning departments, only to disband them when they turned out to be the wrong way to do strategy. Other companies flocked to the big consulting firms for help on strategy, but this avenue too proved less than optimal.

More recently, companies have assigned responsibility for strategy to the operating executives responsible for each business, based on the sound insight that "that's what we pay them for!" While responsibility for strategy has now been assigned where it truly belongs, there is a problem of implementation. Developing strategy is a special skill and most companies still lack specialized techniques to enable their executives to carry out that responsibility most effectively. Instead they rely on business as usual approaches that fall short when companies have to deal with important changes outside the usual comfort zone.

Strategic Dialog is a specialized technique for companies which wish to rely on their own executives to develop strategies that address important trends or changes in the business environment and the society at large.

What is Strategic Dialog?

The purpose of Strategic Dialog is to work through the consequences for a company of one or more major trends or changes. While identifying a trend or change is relatively easy, it is far more difficult to determine its consequences – the strategic challenges and opportunities it creates – and what to do about it.

This specialized form of dialog fills an important hidden gap in business decision making. The gap occurs when companies must respond to changes that move it outside its comfort zone (e.g. a crisis of confidence or mistrust, or a threatening shift in the economy, or technology). This gap goes unrecognized because of the widely held assumption that while special methods may be needed to *identify* important changes, no special methods are needed to figure out the best response to them.

Unfortunately, this assumption is not valid for changes that challenge normal ways of operating, basic assumptions, or culture. When change falls outside a company's comfort zone, business as usual decision making can lead to the worst possible blunders. Consider the following, for example:

- American Airlines, facing bankruptcy if employees prove unwilling to make wage concessions, secretly favors executives with special incentives to remain with the company. Result: the company placed in greater jeopardy; the CEO forced to resign.
- Monsanto, investing heavily in genetically modified products, relies on industry insiders and fails to anticipate the tremendous international opposition that follows. Result: the company in jeopardy and reorganized; CEO leaves.
- The Red Cross, reallocating donations received for 9/11 to other needs in accordance with its usual procedure, fails to be responsive to public expectations. Result: tremendous public criticism and loss of credibility; CEO forced out.

In responding to changes outside the comfort zone, companies need special methods to:

- identify key certainties and uncertainties;
- make sure they fully understand the change and its implications;
- question familiar and comfortable responses;
- expand the range of available options;
- weigh the potential intensity of emotional reaction to the company's decisions on the part of a wide range of stakeholders;
- bring a wide diversity of points of view to bear;
- create a strong sense of ownership for the decisions the company adopts;
- do all of this quickly.

Strategic Dialog is a method to accomplish these tasks with the company's own executives, and without relying on outside consultants. This is a point of critical importance. When companies turn to outside consultants, it is the consultants who do most of the learning. Too often this produces "solutions" that are not owned by key executives, are limited by the consultants' repertoire, cannot be implemented quickly or effectively, and may not be sustainable.

When facing challenges that demand genuine innovations, companies need a systematic way to engage key employees and stakeholders in working through the critical choices. An effective Strategic Dialog program is designed to do just that, providing companies with the tools that enable them to create their own solutions.

How Strategic Dialog works

To be effective, a Strategic Dialog program should be customized to a company's particular requirements, drawing on a portfolio of techniques. These include the following:

- Formulating special *micro-scenarios for action*. Each scenario elaborates one possible response to the change, and one set of choices the company might make, spelling out the scenario's key elements and pros and cons.
- *Structured dialogs* with a wider range of key company employees, other important stakeholders, and selected outside experts. These dialogs are designed to:
    - *expand the range of options* by including a wider array of participants in the dialog, especially those who bring to bear the perspective of knowledgeable and objective outsiders;
    - *uncover the "archeology of assumptions"* – a process for bringing layers of hidden assumptions into the open and critically examining them;
    - ensure that *relevant factual information* is brought to bear on decisions and given its proper weight;
    - *probe for unintended consequences* – digging deeply into how decisions are likely to play out in reality, in spite of good intentions;
    - build *commitment to implementation* of the decisions that will be taken.
- Briefings for senior decision makers in a specialized format that enables them to *crystallize the insights* gained through the dialogs and their implications for the decisions at hand.

Applying Strategic Dialog

One recent Strategic Dialog program for a Fortune 500 company included the following basic steps:

1. Determining the focal issue (the change or trend(s) to be examined) with the relevant top executives.
2. Reviewing data on the change or trends already collected by the company or available from other sources.

3. Interviewing top executives on how they see the change and the strategic challenges or opportunities it creates for the company, to ensure their thinking informs the subsequent dialogs.
4. Designing the dialogs and the facilitator's guide.
5. Preparing a workbook to be used in the dialogs with company executives. This workbook is a critical element in the strategic dialog process allowing executives to work through a very complex subject in a relatively brief time. The workbook presents the key data on the change or trends, and a structured dialog process for working through the consequences of those trends.

    The structured dialog process includes:
    - examining trend data and the different ways in which trends can interact and converge;
    - identifying key certainties and uncertainties;
    - further developing and assessing different scenarios of the situation the company would face if trends converge one way or another;
    - working through the consequences for the company under each scenario (including the consequences for existing and new products, competitive position, customers and consumers, employees, marketing and distribution);
    - defining a preliminary agenda of action steps to deal with those consequences.
6. Conducting one or more day-long dialogs with company executives. Generally each dialog includes no more than 25 executives. In some cases, depending on the subject, strategic partners or other stakeholders may be included.
7. A briefing for top executives on the findings of the dialogs designed to highlight the consequences identified and the action steps recommended, and to enable executives to focus and crystallize the insights gained through the dialogs.

Benefits

Strategic Dialog enables companies to tap their own executives more effectively to find better responses to changes outside the usual comfort zone. Examples include:
- a major change in technology or markets that affects the nature of the business;
- dealing with a crisis of confidence or mistrust with outside stakeholders;

- significant revisions in the unwritten social contract within the company (e.g. in pension or health benefits);
- making a major merger, acquisition, or strategic partnership work.

Wrestling with hard choices for action, and examining them from differing viewpoints, is the best way to develop the genuine innovations required. It also enables key players within the company to "own" those innovations so they can be implemented more quickly and effectively.

In this way, Strategic Dialog can make a valuable contribution to the strategy creation process. Most importantly, it combines an internal and external perspective to help create a strategy that is both meaningful to the company and relevant to its context.

RESOURCES

www.ViewpointLearning.com

The write stuff

STUART CRAINER AND DES DEARLOVE

> Instead of being consigned to history, writing is an increasingly important executive skill.

It is a truth universally acknowledged that great business leaders are great communicators. And, in an age of e-mails, cell phones, text messaging, instant messaging, web pages, web-logs, satellite link-ups and the rest, they have never had so many ways to communicate.

Amid all the excitement about the new communication channels it is easy to forget that, though it may be a digital world, the written word remains the fundamental tool of communication. With message overload an increasing problem, good writing is more important than ever.

While the corporate communications or PR department is on call to help draft public documents for external audiences, executives have to rely on their own literary devices for the multitude of internal documents that are increasingly grist to the management mill. Being able to write effectively and persuasively – whether creating an e-mail, business plan, report, appraisal, or positioning statement – is a core executive skill.

The decline in secretarial support also means that the person who once corrected their grammar or tweaked their punctuation, is largely gone. Be it purple or otherwise, the full glory of an executive's prose is likely to be exposed to the organization. If they can barely string a sentence together let alone construct a pithy argument, their subordinates will know.

"There's a growing misconception that the proliferation of multi-media technology has diminished the need for strong writing skills – and this is just plain false," says Don Spetner, senior vice president for global marketing at recruitment firm Korn/Ferry International. "At the core of all communications is content, which is a fancy word for good old fashioned story telling, or straightforward, concise writing. We take a very critical eye toward a candidate's ability to write, whether it's in their résumé, their cover letter, or the various samples of work product that reflect the quality of their skills."

The reality is that executives spend increasing amounts of time writing in one form or another. Consider the ultimate modern written medium, e-mail. Literary purists may regard e-mail as writing's poor cousin, but its influence is undeniable. In the pre-e-mail age, executives reached for the telephone. Now, e-mail is the dominant form of corporate communication. The 2003 *E-Mail Rules, Policies and Practices Survey* from the American Management Association, Clearswift, and the ePolicy Institute, found that the average employee in the US spends about 1 hour 45 minutes a day dealing with e-mail.

Academics at the Goizueta Business School in Atlanta put this even higher. Research among 1,200 executives by Professor Deborah Valentine at the Goizueta Business Writing Center, and Ruth Pagell, executive director of Goizueta's Center for Business Information (CBI), found that more than half spent at least two hours per day answering e-mail at work and 30 percent spent an additional hour or more at home. That's about four months per year dealing with e-mails.

As Jeff Skoll, co-founder of eBay and now CEO of the Skoll Foundation, told us: "It's funny, that in an age when e-mail has become such a dominant form of communication, people are writing more than they ever have. They spend so much time in front of the computer these days with written communication, and yet it seems that the art of that communication has declined over the same time."

Of course, it is not just e-mail. Techno-savvy executives may have their own weblogs, *blogs*. Blogdex.net, part of a research project run by the Massachusetts Institute of Technology, estimates there are now more than 1 million blogs and rising. Instant messaging (IM), once associated with teenagers and chat rooms, is also rapidly finding its way into corporations. Forrester Research estimates penetration of IM in corporations at 45 percent. With companies like Microsoft and IBM both adopting and pushing the technology, it is likely to become ubiquitous.

The power of the pen

The style of business writing is also changing. The rise of e-mail and other electronic channels has coincided with a growing need for executives to ensure that their communication is more direct – more personal. Flatter management structures mean that executives can no longer rely on their hierarchical power to get things done. Issuing an edict is not an option. Instead, managers must increasingly rely on persuasion – and inspiration. This requires a more sophisticated style of communication, one that is directed at the individual and imbued with emotional context as well as content.

One survey of 60 executives found that the messages that get attention are those where the message is personalized, evokes an emotional response, comes from a trustworthy or respected sender, and is concise.

Of course, great leaders have long been aware of this. They realize that while speeches can be inspirational, they are transient. At best they are absorbed into an organization's oral history. But written communications, whether they spur employees to greater productivity, boost morale, announce triumphs, – or disasters, endure.

"Great business leaders, and those who aspire to the status, succeed in communicating well what is important. Their writing stands out from the whirl of information. It memorably expresses the values, focusses, and thrusts necessary for their companies to prosper. It summarizes and reinforces the message of all their forms of communication," says Peter Knight, CEO of The CEO Circle, a network for chief executives.

Jack Welch habitually wrote handwritten notes which he sent to workers at all levels – from part-time staff to senior executives. Some even framed his notes, as a tangible proof of their leader's appreciation.

From the hand-written to the homespun, Warren Buffett, CEO of Berkshire Hathaway, is another exponent of the corporate missive. Each year, the Sage of Omaha pens a letter that has become an annual media event, summarized in *Fortune* magazine, and dissected by stock analysts everywhere. Buffett's annual letter to the Berkshire Hathaway shareholders can move markets and make fortunes.

But it's not just the old guard that appreciates the power of writing. According to Jeff Skoll, writing laid the foundation of the eBay culture. When eBay first started, many of its employees, in customer service for example, were highly dispersed around the world. Communication was invariably by e-mail. "How do you build an organization, how do you build a culture, when your primary means of communication is written?" Skoll muses. "I guess the answer is you have to be very thoughtful, and you have to be clear in your writing style. Both Pierre [Omidyar] and I put a lot of effort into getting our points across in writing."

The new language of business

While executives may recognize the importance of their writing skills, time pressures often conspire against quality. The language used in a great deal of business writing would offend literary purists. Jargon, obfuscation, poor punctuation, garbled syntax, and tortured grammar are facts of business life.

Sam Hill, author of *Radical Marketing*, founder of Helios Consulting (and now a published novelist), taught business writing skills to fellow consultants at his former employer, consulting firm Booz Allen, and occasionally at Northwestern University. Does he think business writing is getting worse?

"No, I think it's always been terrible. But I do think tools like Powerpoint and e-mail, coupled with the organizational downsizing of secretaries, has given illiterate business people the ability to send babble out unedited, and this has increased visibility of the problem."

E-mail hasn't improved things. Paradoxically, the medium which has done more than any other to elevate executive writing's importance is often characterized by literary sloppiness and inattention to detail.

There are several reasons for this. Dealing with e-mails is time-consuming. So executives take shortcuts. The language becomes compressed. Please becomes pls. Such linguistic contortions become trendy and are adopted as a sign of belonging. E-mails, too, are more informal than letters. So less thought is given to the construction of the message.

If e-mail has corrupted the English language, then the rise of instant messaging suggests worse is to come. Most instant messages involve little preparation or considered thought. Together with texting (SMS and MMS messages), which is still a largely European phenomenon, it is the most casual of increasingly casual modes of communication.

"Most of us relax the rules of grammar, punctuation, and spelling, when participating in a chat or instant messaging situation because the speed of this type of communication makes formatting difficult," observes Goizueta's Professor Deborah Valentine.

But, despite the havoc wreaked on the conventions of writing, the use of the lower case personal pronoun i, the wholesale omission of vowels, the mass abbreviation, does any of it really matter? Is this new writing, bad writing?

John Patrick is president of Attitude LLC and former vice president of Internet technology at IBM, where he worked for 34 years. Patrick, whose blog patrickweb.com offers a commentary on technology and its impact on business and society, believes effective writing is a critical skill for the future – as it always has been. But we shouldn't blame the medium if the message is poorly constructed.

Says Patrick: "E-mail is a form of writing. Like with pen and paper, some people are good at it and some are not. Well written e-mail is powerful and has numerous other positive attributes including its ability to be sorted, archived, indexed, and so on. I also think blogging is grossly underestimated by just about everyone."

The return of the punctuators

A panda goes into a bar and orders some food. After finishing his meal the panda produces a pistol and shoots into the ceiling before heading to the door. The barman catches up with the panda outside and asks why he behaved in such a way. "A panda eats, shoots and leaves," the panda replies, thereby illustrating the power of the humble comma.

There is a burgeoning back to basics movement. As we write, *Eats, Shoots and Leaves: The Zero Tolerance Approach to Punctuation* by Lynne Truss is rising up the UK bestseller lists. The book sold 50,000 copies in the 10 days after publication and US rights were sold for a six-figure sum. Punctuation is bizarrely fashionable.

Good writing, it seems, is reasserting itself. One of Professor Valentine's key findings is that 60 percent of the executives surveyed prefer standard usage in business English. This is, she suggests, because traditional grammar and punctuation has developed over many centuries – and for a good reason – to guide the reader. "Paragraphs provide a visual break, and punctuation slows, or stops, the reader at the appropriate place," she notes.

Professor Valentine suggests there are three important reasons why the shortcuts used in e-mail and instant messaging have little place in executive level communication. First, not every executive will understand the acronyms and abbreviations. Savvy executives, she says, will write with the needs of their audience in mind.

Second, clarity is essential and the shortcuts can obscure meaning. (Warren Buffett for one has opined that if he doesn't understand something, he assumes that someone is trying to fool him.) Finally, careless e-mails can prove costly – as brokerage firm Merrill Lynch found out. The firm made a multi-million dollar settlement with New York State Attorney General Eliot Spitzer after e-mails revealed the firm's analysts disparaging stocks they talked up in public. It is best to remember, Valentine advises, that e-mail is for ever. Bad writing habits, however, needn't be.

The opportunity

For literally challenged executives, help is at hand. Increasing recognition among executives of the importance of good writing is manifest in the growth in business writing tuition. Executives and consultants increasingly turn to communications experts, including journalists, for help. Effective business writing courses help managers raise their communication game.

Says Peter Knight: "The whole purpose of The CEO Circle is to assist CEOs to improve their performance, to achieve greater success. To find better ways of expressing this was why I attended a writing workshop, and it certainly helped me. All I write is colored by my belief that well written communication of what really matters helps produce the performance that makes companies and leaders great."

There is a profusion of writing coaches, classes, and ghostwriters ready to make sure the message is finely phrased. "Our clients – senior executives at technology and financial services firms – understand the increasing importance of clear, persuasive writing in internal and external communications. The explosion of electronic information distribution over the Internet provides enormous opportunity and an enormous amount of content to be digested," says Lynn Kearney, co-founder of The Write Effect (writeEffect.com), who has consulted on communications and organizational issues with private and public institutions for more than 20 years.

"In years past, we have worked with corporate training and development managers to create business writing courses. We now get calls directly from senior business unit managers with specific requests for highly customized programs that include not just content but also guidance on how to package ideas that grab readers' attention. Increased competition for readers – clients – has alerted managers to the need for improved writing quality as a means to build and maintain client relationships."

Our own experience training executives and MBA students in effective business writing confirms that many managers and fledgling managers recognize their deficiencies in this area. Many have similar issues. For example, we are often asked about how to create effective messages for different audiences – for example, internal and external stakeholders; and how to structure and present information in the most compelling way. Other requests include how to overcome blank page syndrome or first paragraph hell. Writers' block, we helpfully tell course participants, is a luxury executives cannot afford.

With limited time on their hands, executives tend to accept poor writing as a fact of business life. Yet, improving the quality of writing is actually much easier than people imagine. The good news is that most executives recognize the difference between good and bad writing. Unfortunately, they often don't apply that knowledge to their own writing. If they begin to bear in mind what constitutes good writing and apply it as a quality standard to their own written words, they can make a substantial improvement. Similarly, acknowledging the importance of writing and becoming more aware of the role it plays in your work is likely to make a difference.

"Great writing is a state of mind as much as anything," says Gerry Griffin of the London-based Business Communication Forum, a media training organization. "Once I was reminded of the basic characteristics of good and bad writing, my own writing improved. Instead of taking it for granted, I began to think about writing more carefully, to think about my audience and so on."

Self-awareness about writing makes a significant difference to the quality of written output – and, potentially, your career. "Good writing is a wonderful way to differentiate yourself inside a company," says Sam Hill. "Back when I was competing with all those other aggressive young associates at Booz Allen, all of us in the same charcoal gray Jos. A Banks suits and faux Hermes ties, I used the ability to express myself clearly to get myself noticed. I used to work for hours at home secretly writing and rewriting reports until they were logical and stylistic masterpieces. The next afternoon, I'd drop them on my partner's desk casually and do my best to create the implication that I'd just dashed them off – and hopefully create the impression in his mind that I was effortlessly brilliant. It must have worked, I made partner." The write stuff works.

The good, the bad, and the ugly

Business writing is riddled with literary nightmares. Take this job ad:

> The Senior Business Analyst will have primary responsibility to elicit, analyze, validate, specify, verify, and manage the real needs of the project stakeholders, including customers and end users. He/she will take the role of functional area manager, where he/she is the primary conduit between the customer community (the functional areas) and the software development and implementation team through which requirements flow.

The classic writing by committee approach tends to produce lists of verbs to cover every eventuality and to introduce buzz words such as stakeholders, customer community, and implementation at every opportunity.

Jargon is endemic and can render statements completely meaningless. One organization pronounced:

> We continually exist to synergistically supply value-added deliverables such that we may continue to proactively maintain enterprise-wide data to stay competitive in tomorrow's world.

Beware of synergy in its many guises and value in its confusing array of valueless forms.

Another common mistake is to completely overlook the audience. An annual report from a food company contained the following paragraph:

> With the continued growth of hand-held foods, the commercialization of our patented sauce filling cold forming extrusion technology has attracted industry-wide interest for appetizer, hand-held and center-of-plate applications.

Unfortunately, the audience for the company's annual report – investors, analysts, reporters, and so on – were unlikely to be knowledgeable about extrusion technology.

Luckily, there are examples of good business writing. Consider the opening from Gary Hamel and C.K. Prahalad's bestseller *Competing for the Future*:

> Look around your company. Look at the high-profile initiatives that have been launched recently. Look at the issues that are preoccupying senior management. Look at the criteria and benchmarks by which progress is being measured. Look at the track record of new business creation. Look into the faces of your colleagues and consider their dreams and fears. Look toward the future and ponder your company's ability to shape that future and regenerate success again and again in the years and decades to come.

The good, the bad, and the ugly (continued)

This, remember, is a book about strategy. Despite their unpromising subject matter, Hamel and Prahalad manage to write clearly, concisely, and effectively. Note the short sentences, the direct, personal tone, and the accessible language.

Or think of some corporate slogans which manage to motivate and drive entire organizations with a few well-chosen words – such as Microsoft's visionary call to arms, "A computer on every desk in every home.'

The quintessence of effective business writing comes in advertising. Whether it is IBM's *Think* or Budweiser's *King of Beers*, great advertising slogans manage to distil complex messages down to a few well chosen words. Indeed, the addition of a single word – *New* – before a product routinely boosts sales. Written words are powerful tools. Handle them with care.

The power of words

The wrong words in the wrong place can prove costly. In 1983 computer manufacturer Coleco wiped $35 million off the balance sheet in one quarter. How? Customers swamped the company with returns of a new product line. The manuals were unreadable. The firm went bust.

In another example, a major oil company sank hundreds of thousands of dollars of R&D into developing a new pesticide only to find that one of its own employees had discovered the same product some time ago. Why did no one know? Because the report the discovery was written up in was such heavy going, no one had bothered to read it all the way through.

One study of military personnel researchers noted that officers took up to 23 percent less time to read clearly written documents. The researchers concluded that the Navy alone could save over $30 million in wasted man hours if documents were written in a plain, easy to understand style.

RESOURCES

Truss, Lynne, *Eats, Shoots and Leaves*, Profile Books, 2003.

Commentary

Silence can be golden

The best run companies in the world tend not to measure their success by column inches. They are often undemonstrative, quietly and efficiently mining their markets. Their CEOs tend not to have corporate jets nor seek out cover stories in *Fortune*. For them silence is golden.

One of the best examples of this unassuming, but very successful, breed is the American corporation Pitney Bowes which has over 2 million customers, more than 3,500 active patents, and a turnover in excess of $4 billion. Indeed, the company was identified by management author Jim Collins in his bestseller *Good to Great* as one of his corporate paragons.

So what are the lessons you can learn from quiet over-achievers?

First, there is leadership. This is not leadership according to the gung-ho, up-and-at-em military model. Nor is it the populist leader-as-loudmouth approach. Silent giants tend to be led by ego-free team players with a long view. They are intent on being effective rather than eye-catching. They are patient but persistent.

The second characteristic of the quiet firm is that they know their business inside out. Think of Pitney Bowes which is in the unsexy, old fashioned mail and document management industry. It knows the technology because it invented a great deal of it and it knows the customers.

Third is the question of culture. Silent giants live by a code of values. Pitney Bowes CEO Michael Critelli bridles when it is suggested that values statements tend to be anodyne. "Certain values are extremely critical to our brand and our success in the marketplace. We handle worldwide well over $15 billion, probably closer to $20 billion, of other people's money. We even own a bank in the United States so having the attribute that we are honest, trustworthy, and reliable is not only a nice thing to have from a standpoint of commercial success but it is critical to our value proposition."

For quiet over-achievers, values aren't mere abstracts or fashionable statements of intent, but daily reality. The trouble is that succeeding by actually treating people decently and responsibly is not a great news story. Being nice tends to be corny and ridden with clichés.

Take Yum! Brands which owns Kentucky Fried Chicken, Pizza Hut, Taco Bell, and the Long John Silver seafood chain. It has 850,000 employees worldwide in 100 nations. Its aim is, obviously enough, to put a *yum* on everyone's face.

A lot of the company's energy has been directed into recognizing exceptional work. When people engage in behavior Yum!'s chief executive, David Novak, wants to see, he hands out floppy chickens with the person's name on it and what they've done. Every manager at the company now has to have some form of personal recognition. When one of the company's top franchisees died, he was buried with his floppy chicken.

"Good guys do win," says Randall Tobias, former CEO of the pharmaceutical giant Eli Lilly. "I've done business in countries all over the world and I have applied the same standards. Is it the right thing to do? If you can't do business according to those standards we won't do business. There may be a short-term advantage in bribing or cheating but in the long term you can't point to any company which has sustained success through anything other than high ethical standards. They do the right thing."

The next characteristic of this type of company is that they invest in the future in everything they do. For quiet giants the future influences decisions made every day. It may not be in Silicon Valley or in a fashionable high-tech industry, but Pitney Bowes emphasizes innovation at every turn. It knows that coming up with solutions for the customers of the future is the best way to safeguard its future.

Finally, quiet giants have clear ideas on what constitutes success. To them success is about more than money. "My first measure of success is whether we are behaving as one company," says Michael Critelli. "Second, are we behaving with confidence and competence in shaping the world we live in rather than reacting to it. Third, I want us to be confident and comfortable dealing across the globe. The final attribute is being very solutions and customer-driven rather than providing tools and letting customers decide how to use those tools. In other words, making customers successful and being recognized for making customers successful as opposed to just providing a tool like a franking machine that gives them the ability to be successful but we leave it to them how they're going to use it. If someone said he has done those four things before I retire that would be an accomplishment."

Communicating in the age of consent

MARK STUART

[In an age of information overload, it is still imperative that communications connect with consumers. That is the conclusion of an Agenda Paper produced by the UK's Chartered Institute of Marketing (CIM).]

The modern consumer is under siege. From the moment we wake up to the moment our heads hit the pillow, we are bombarded with unsolicited marketing messages.

Breakfast is served with on pack promotions, and a barrage of radio and TV ads. The postman comes with unwanted junk mail. The once unpartisan taxi or bus to work is branded with a sponsor's livery. At home or the office, e-mail inboxes bulge with unasked for, and often unsavory, spam. Even our mobile telephones brandish branded text messages.

The result: information overload; marketing which fails to connect.

Consider this:

- The average consumer is exposed to around 1,500 advertising messages every day.
- A third of all direct mail is thrown away without being opened, and nearly 60 percent is thrown away without being read.[1]
- In America, experts believe the spam epidemic is now interfering with the country's productivity, as workers waste their employers' time deleting unsolicited e-mails.
- Microsoft blocks around 2.4 billion junk e-mails a day, some 80 percent of the messages that hit MSN servers. BT Openworld estimates that, of the 25 million e-mails that it monitors, 41 percent is spam.[2]

Message fatigue

So how did we reach a situation in which marketing communication is a pointless deluge rather than a targetted stream?

The most obvious cause is media proliferation. For both the consumer and the marketer the choice of satellite, cable, or terrestrial channels is overwhelming. New media have added to the noise. The Internet and mobile phones, for example, began purely as communication tools, but have been hijacked by lazy, rogue marketers. Banner ads, pop-up ads, unsolicited e-mails, and SMS text advertising are now the norm.

Media proliferation has been accompanied by audience fragmentation. As media choice expands and usage patterns evolve, marketers have to work harder and harder for a share of consumer attention. What worked in the past no longer presses the right consumer buttons – witness the declining impact of TV advertising. In the quest for attention, advertisers have to become ever more inventive, finding new ways to reach their audience – adverts on petrol pumps, talking posters in pub toilets, tattoos on students' foreheads, and so on.[3]

Yet none of this alters the fundamental fact: interruption has become intrusion. Customers increasingly resent the intrusion and ignore the marketing messages. Even worse, many customers are being put off brands by inappropriate and unwanted communications.

In the United States some 54 million people have already signed up to a national "do not call" register. In one survey, 25 percent of people said they were using e-mail less because there was so much junk.[4]

Technology is increasingly being used by consumers as a shield to protect their privacy from unwanted incursions. An arms race is developing as consumers discover new ways of blocking the noise out. Already, PVRs (personal video recorders, such as TiVO), enable consumers to cut out TV adverts.

And governments are now putting their weight behind customer privacy with new legislation. As of December 11, 2003, the Privacy and Electronic Communications Regulations Act (PECR) means that UK marketers require consumer opt-in to send unsolicited electronic messages. In the US a similar trend is emerging. In November 2003, for example, AT&T was fined $780,000 for bothering householders on the company's own "do not call" register.[5] AT&T is the first company to fall foul of a ban on calling Americans who've specifically asked to be left in peace.

All this has massive implications for business. Indeed, marketing as traditionally practiced is becoming increasingly illegal.

For the un-reconstituted (or unrepentant), a communications crisis looms. By 2006, it is predicted that more than 20 billion spam messages will be sent daily worldwide – leading to communications gridlock.[6]

Less is more

"Human beings ... are finally rebelling!" says Cathy Ace, a consultant on marketing communications at the University of British Columbia. "We are used to perceiving and filtering millions of pieces of information each day. But we have never before been bombarded in the way we are now. How do we get our messages to the right audiences in a timely manner that cuts through the clutter? That's the challenge."[7]

By 2010, companies will be able to communicate with far fewer people and collect much less information on individuals than they currently can. Data protection laws will become more onerous. We are moving from a communications free-for-all to an age of consent.

Managing consent is the new imperative. The concept of permission marketing is well known and passively accepted, but inertia and habit mean that *interruption marketing* is still the norm. It's easy to design a pop-up advert; it's cheap to send unsolicited e-mails. Direct mail and cold calling are still done by companies because they've always done it. We need to enter the age of consent across the media spectrum. This will involve a shift from a model of intrusion to one of communicating and building relationships through collaboration.

High-impact collaboration

The new collaborative model has a number of characteristics. It is:

- customer initiated;
- based on consensual relationships (trust-driven and permissive);
- maintained through appropriate dialog (two-way and on-going);
- built on mutual value;
- neutral across media;
- cost effective (aimed at improving efficiency).

In traditional communications, marketers intrude on the time and consciousness of their target audience. In the new model, enlightened marketers collaborate with customers to build a dialog that creates value for both parties.

The key to this is consent – doing things on customers' terms, when they want it, where they want it, and how they want it.

The new model also has profound implications for media planning. It requires a neutral approach to the media mix which eschews formulaic ways to use media to create a campaign. Instead, the new model takes an objective view on the most effective media to deliver marketing messages that are relevant, timely, and welcome. This requires new ways of working among marketers and the creative agencies. Here, too, collaboration will be critical.

The idea that firms will collaborate with customers – and vice versa – is already gaining currency both theoretically and practically.

"We are moving to a new form of value creation, when value is not created by the firm and exchanged with the customer, but when value is co-created by the consumers and the company. So the first question is: how do you go from a unilateral view of value creation by the company, to co-creation of value by consumers?" says C.K. Prahalad, co-author of *Competing for the Future*. "Co-creation of value is a very different thing from being consumer oriented. This is not the firm targetting consumers and being more sensitive to them. It is about enabling consumers to be an equal problem solver, so that collectively they create value, and collectively they extract value. So that the consumer is helping the company to create value and also taking value away by extracting value through either explicit or implicit bargains."[8]

At a practical level, according to Graham Lancaster of the Communications Agencies Federation (CAF), if a brand can engage with its customers, "then the customer may collude with the brand, be receptive, and even seek out its messages and conspicuously wear/display its brands." Consumer collaboration can thereby leverage a brand to a level that is intangibly higher than competitors'.

And because consumers do not view active collaboration as advertising – they see it as news or current affairs – they do not screen it out or reject it; the message gets through.

Making the move

How do you turn this into reality? The CIM Insights Team has identified five key ways to move from intrusion to collaboration:

- self-segmentation;
- open planning;
- creating messages that matter;
- managing legal boundaries;
- measuring return on communications.

1. Self-segmentation

Malcolm McDonald, from the UK's Cranfield School of Management, believes that the biggest problem facing marketers "is the same as it always has been – pointless, wasted, profligate communications."[9] McDonald asserts that CRM (customer relationship management) views the communication challenge the wrong way round. "It should be CMR (customer managed relationships) encouraging the customers in a particular segment to communicate with us using the channels preferred *by them*."

This is the heart of the issue. Putting customers in charge offers a route to *self segmentation*. Customers will identify the segments they belong to, providing a far richer supply of personal data than could ever be possible using traditional segmentation techniques.

Intrusion model	*Collaborative model*
■ Scattergun	Consent-based dialog
■ Seller benefits	Mutual benefits
■ Media constrained	Media transparent
■ Invasion of privacy	Respect for privacy
■ Poor innovation	Radical innovation
■ Impact unknown	Return on communications known

Engaging the customer's consent and respecting privacy leads to successful communications with a high rate of return – Figure 4.1 shows why this is the case.

Each ring represents a level of customer intimacy or consent. Like personal space, each level can only be accessed if the consumer gives his or her consent.

The outer rings represent unsolicited messages – billboards, radio advertising, etc. They equate to public places – channels unlikely to be affected by privacy legislation or technology filters. Their effectiveness is also limited. The consumer is aware of them, but does not act on them and is not consciously aware of them having any effect.

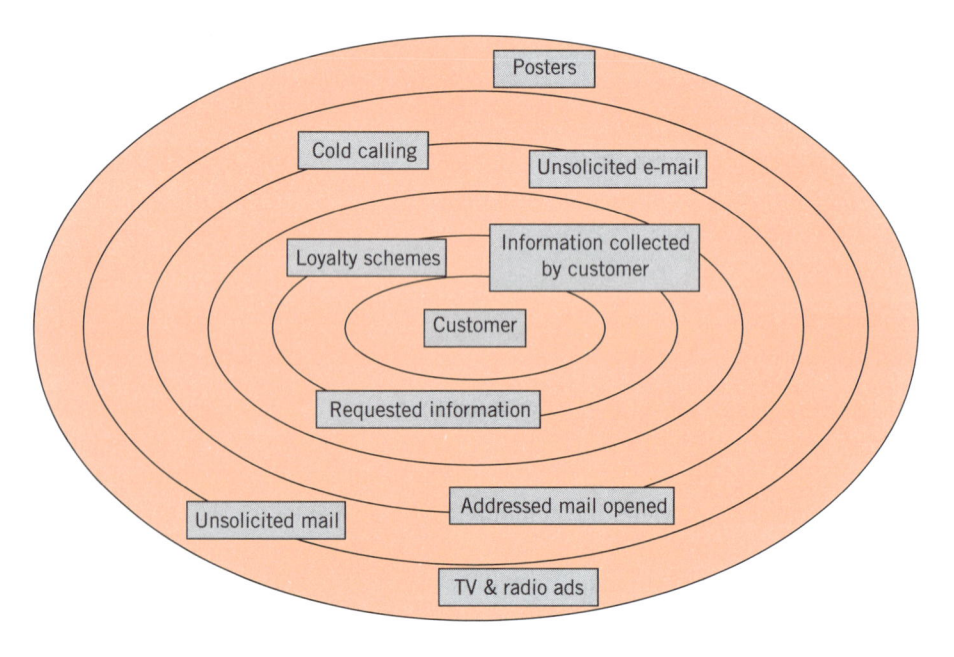

Figure 4.1: *Rings of consent*

The middle rings represent marketing that the customer has acted on – direct mail they've responded to, loyalty schemes or store cards they have signed up to, for example.

The inner layer represents messages, or information, *requested* by the customer. The customer embraces this information and does not consciously regard it to be marketing; it is part of a collaborative, consensual relationship. This is the layer that the marketer of the future will aim for.

This model emphasizes the customer at the *center* of communications – not as a target at the *end* of a process. By considering the customer as the pivot, he or she can be encouraged to trust, embrace, and welcome the messages being received. If such trust cannot be created, the cost of any communications will outweigh the benefits, as the customer refuses to listen to any more fragmented pieces of information.

The corollary of this is that companies need to find new, more accurate, and more collaborative ways of gathering data. In the future, companies will increasingly buy personal data from customers, either in exchange for benefits – or even for money. Such transactions will be one way to persuade customers to self-segment. However, they will be no more than an opening move in a long courtship – akin to buying a potential partner a drink, with a view to getting to know them better.

Long-term success will be built on mutual interests and values rather than bribes. In Sweden, for example, a mobile phone company offers customers free call time if they listen to an advertisement. This is only effective if the message is meaningful to the customer. Similar incentives could be offered to consumers willing to share their personal data.

Alternatively, the first move could be initiated by the customer. Where a customer has a strong affinity for a brand, they may welcome an opportunity to self-segment. Companies which create effective channels to allow customers to inform them of their preferences will benefit from this process. So, for example, a customer might register interest in receiving information on all new product launches.

Such *self-segmentation* is one of the keys to communicating in the age of consent. While consent is passive, self-segmentation is active. Self-segmenting customers actively listen, and want to be involved. They can also co-create value.

Take organic food, for example. Supermarkets are currently unclear about whether customers want it, how much they want it – and how much of a premium they're prepared to pay for it. It remains largely guesswork. Self-segmenting customers could clarify the situation for supermarkets.

In recognizing the customer as the owner of his or her data, a significant step has been made toward the customer *allowing* the marketer to engage. This is fundamental to creating a consensual relationship. The self-segmenting customer controls the flow of information and increasingly will be protected by legislation.

2. Open planning

Collaborative communication also requires media to be used in new ways to achieve business objectives. The aim must be to utilize the most effective and appropriate mix of media to transmit the message rather than remaining wedded to a particular media for historical reasons. This has been labeled Media Neutral Planning (MNP).

Professor Angus Jenkinson and the Center for Integrated Marketing – working in conjunction with the CIM – suggest an approach which they call *Open Planning*. This begins with developing *Open Customers*. Open customers are those "self-segmenting" customers willing to receive communication, with communication then aiming to create open customers with open wallets. MNP puts the customer at the center of the process, providing a consumer – brand – discipline – media dynamic to create guidelines for the creative output, not the other way round.[10]

The notion of Open Customers is central to this approach. It recognizes that only communication that has value to the recipient actually benefits the brand. The value may be entertainment, a good idea, helpful information, or social equity, but without being appreciated or winning approval it won't build brand or customer equity, indeed it may even destroy it. MNP begins with the person to whom communication is going to develop appropriate content, style, and media; including how and when communication is delivered.

Open Planning applies to all stakeholder groups, including, for example, employees, journalists, and influencers, with the same truth operating: unwelcome means not working.

Open Planning then requires *Open Thinking* and develops through eight action areas – see Figure 4.2.

Open Thinking may seem an obvious requirement but it turns out to be neither obvious nor easy. Most senior marketers on both brand and agency sides believe in integrated or media neutral communication. Huge effort is being put into achieving this, yet large problems remain – for example in optimizing and evaluating the communications mix.

Open Thinking | **Open Planning** | Open Disciplines / Open Media / Open Channels / Open Process / Open Structure / Open Relationships / Open Results / Open Tools | Open Customers with open wallets

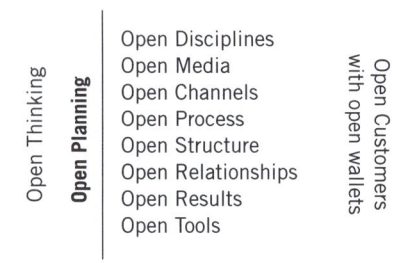

Figure 4.2: *Open Planning*

This is because most attempts to solve the problem operate at the same level as the problem itself. Many popular assumptions about marketing communications on closer examination are dubious or constraining, and yet these are redeployed in many attempted solutions. Solving the problem requires thinking at a different level to the problem itself, and this requires an open mind.

Open Disciplines and Open Media reflect findings about the marketing communication disciplines, including advertising, direct marketing, PR, design, selling, and so on. Closer examination shows that many of the rules of thumb used in selecting disciplines and media for a communication project don't stand up. Examples of this include: "advertising is for awareness"; "above the line" and "below the line"; "mail closes the sale"; "rational and emotional media"; and "each discipline needs its own objectives."

Open Media proposes that any medium can be used by all disciplines, in almost any mix. That means you can advertise in the mail, the Internet, and product packaging, as well as on radio and TV. You can even use salespeople to advertise. MNP widens the conventional understanding of media to include anything that conveys a message to a recipient. Any brand-stakeholder interface implies a medium. That means that all contact or touch points should be included in the mix and taken into account for effectiveness and preference.

Leading media agencies and consultancies already recognize this, as when Mother recommended to Costa Coffee that it spend its money on redesigning the store rather than TV ads; or when Michaelides and Bednash recommended that BHS spend money on in-store shopping assistants to keep customers buying, rather than TV to attract them there.

Open Results means developing a common currency for marketing communications. It also means developing goals that really matter, rather than just following convenient measures. Take for example the dominance of awareness as a measure and goal of much marketing communication. Some 45 percent of pay by results schemes currently use advertising awareness as the basis for assessing performance, despite the weakness of correlation between awareness and market share.[11]

3. Creating messages that matter

Messages aren't getting through to the consumer because there are too many messages. Better planning and self segmentation can help. But, in addition, moving beyond imprecise, impersonal targetting requires innovative messaging.

Good messages are memic; catchy and viral. The extension of permission marketing is viral marketing – turn customers into advocates, and they will do your marketing for you.

Guerrilla marketing works because it legally breaks the rules. But as Chris Clarke, creative director at digital advertising agency Abel & Baker, says: "Once you've done it, you've done it – you have to move on."[12] Collaborative communication can never become a matter of routine.

Consider iCoupon, which creates mobile marketing technology that companies can use to text electronic coupons to customers on their database. In our media saturated world, text messaging is potentially just another irritation. But what if the way in which you use it is truly innovative?

Marc Lewis is the company's founder and CEO. "Imagine it's a hot sunny day. At 9.00 am, very hot, sweaty commuters emerge from a packed Tube. Then a little message pops up offering them a free drink or ice cream at a nearby café.

"This kind of message could work. You'll get the customer in, and you can track the information because the redeeming of the electronic 'coupon' works the same way as normal coupons – the required customer data can be tracked. You get a wider cross-section of people because the coupons approach does not just attract time-rich, penny-watching pensioners, as paper coupons tend to do."

4. Managing legal boundaries

If marketers don't self-legislate, governments will. Privacy and anti-junk legislation is rapidly becoming more stringent in clamping down on intrusive marketing.

In Sweden, for example, marketing to children on television has been illegal for over a decade. Greece too has legislation against targetting children. And in the US, a lawsuit has been taken out against Heineken, Bacardi, and five other drinks producers by parents who claim that their advertising is targetting teenagers.[13]

Companies are taking note. Coca-Cola has recently announced that it will no longer advertise to children under the age of 12. In practice, this means none of its brands will be shown during the hours of children's TV broadcasts.[14]

As new legal barriers are erected, the immediate marketing response is to try to think of ways of getting round the legislation; to think of other ways of invading; to enter an arms race with the legislators. Examples include spammers inserting literary words to convince the spam filters that the messages are not junk; or breaking up typical spam words to fool the filters (e.g. "en.hance your attra.ctiveness"). But this is ultimately unsustainable and will lead to dissatisfaction on both sides. Consumers will still be unhappy with the logjam of messages and unwanted information, and marketers will be unhappy because they will find the messages do not get a response.

So what can marketers do? Some charities, such as Cancer Research UK, ask the question "How often do you want to hear from us?" Simple – but the charity saves costs and the messages are more likely to reach their intended destination. This idea has been around for a dozen years or so – but has not yet been adopted by many firms. If the less is more principle were adopted by all companies, the pile of junk mail on the doormat each morning could be dramatically reduced.

In the age of consent, the consumer determines the model. Invading consumers' private space is no longer acceptable – or effective. Instead, companies must seek their active consent to participate in dialog with their target audience. Let customers be in charge – let them sell to you or share with you, what information they want to, and ask them when they want to hear from you.

For instance, consider the advantages and disadvantages of abandoning cold calling. At present, having got hold of a phone number, marketers ring consumers at times they are likely to be in – say between 6 and 7.30 pm. In the distant past this technique had a proven success rate – small, but throw enough mud and some sticks. However, as customers become more aware of their right to privacy, the willingness to talk to cold callers declines. While a response rate of 5 percent might be seen as a success in a campaign, the quantities of people for whom it creates a strong negative impression of the company can outweigh the benefits brought by the 5 percent who respond.

Cold calling continues because the hits directly scored by the campaign – however slim – can be measured. The number of people who are driven away from the company as a direct result of the cold calling – however great – cannot be measured.

Some companies are recognizing the importance of a comprehensive, legally compliant policy on customer privacy. A survey carried out by CSO magazine (a US security publication) found that 12 percent of companies in the US currently have a Chief Privacy Officer.

While the legislation and the need to gain permission might seem like hard work, it actually presents a distinct opportunity for the shrewd marketer. Those who seize the initiative will create a much better relationship with the customer – one in which customers are enabled to say what they want, and when and how they want it.

The advantages are obvious. Until now, marketers have gamely battled with unwieldy concepts like CRM. Such theories essentially recognize that the customer is resistant, because customers aren't spontaneously receptive to what is on offer. Imagine how different things could be if customers *became* spontaneously receptive. Consensual marketing could take us there.

5. Measuring return on communications

It is estimated that £100 billion is spent on advertising globally every year. Remarkably, much of this investment is not subjected to rigorous ROI measures. "We have really lousy ways to try and measure any type of integrated program or activity," says Professor Don Schultz of Northwestern University. "Most are based on some type of outbound, communication-driven program ... from the 1960s – i.e. recognition, awareness, etc. Clearly, today the consumer operates in an interactive, networked, global communication-driven workplace where inbound communication is as important as outbound. Yet, we're still using the tools that attempt to measure each communication activity separately and independently."

Marketers use these measures because they've always used them. Professor Schultz believes these measures are less and less relevant. Nike, for instance, doesn't measure outputs (e.g. communications awareness or response levels), but outcomes (e.g. how many people take up sport) – this then enables the company to concentrate on innovation. If you discover that the numbers of people playing basketball are increasing, then that becomes the sport you want to look at when innovating.

Measuring effectiveness is about more than the efficiency of operations execution. Intangible returns can be as important as the tangible ones.

It has been estimated, for example, that media neutral planning could reduce marketing communications spend by as much as 30 percent.[15] Improved database software will reduce the wasted amounts spent on mailing deceased people or defunct addresses. And self segmentation will reduce the vast amounts spent on advertising that does not reach its target and close a sale, but merely gains awareness.

All together now

Privacy and consent will increasingly impact on successful communications. Legislation will increase; consumers will become more and more frustrated by unwanted messages.

The challenge is simply explained by Seth Godin (author of *Permission Marketing*): "Talk to people who want to be talked to, in a way that they want to be talked to. The idea that marketers are in charge and can demand attention whenever they want it is totally over. It's not about you. It's about me. You don't invade my privacy if I *ask* you to talk to me. And the only way I'm going to ask is if you offer me something of great value, or create a product that's remarkable."[16]

In the old days, the door was open unless the consumer said it was closed. Today, the door is closed unless the consumer says it is open. So, unless today's marketer sends messages with consent and with respect for privacy, the communication won't be received. Marketers who do this first, will have an advantage. Good communication is about being two-way and interactive.

Customer collaboration means putting the customer at the center of the communications; making sure you have their permission before you communicate with them; ensuring all your media are fully integrated and focussed; and that there is genuine creativity.

Commentary

We're blogging it

Until recently the traditional media – television, radio, newspapers, and magazines – was always the automatic choice for obtaining news and entertainment. Today, however, the Internet is challenging the position of the traditional media. In the 2002 Pew Internet and American Life survey a sample of predominately techno-literate Americans were asked which form of media they would find the hardest to give up. Newspapers and magazines came bottom of the list. Well behind the Internet.

Over the last decade the media landscape has changed dramatically. Barely over a decade ago there were only a few TV or radio channels, now there are hundreds. Specialist print publications reach out to an increasingly niche readership. People watch movies on mobile phones. Not to mention the Internet. Modern media grows more fragmented by the second.

Take the blog as an example. Blog is short for web-log: a web-page published in the form of a regularly updated online diary containing a combination of news and opinion. Although they date back to the mid-1990s the number of blogs on the Internet has exploded in the last couple of years – estimates put the total at anywhere from several hundred thousand to millions.

While predominately an amateur undertaking, traditional media should not underestimate the threat from blogs. Blogs have several characteristics that make them attractive information sources. They are timely, picking up news via the Internet and disseminating it before the traditional media has had time to process the same news through its editorial system. Also blogs are personal. They are often written by people with specialist knowledge and infused with passion. They may even report directly on breaking events.

One significant obstacle to the bloggers' assault on the mainstream press was their low profile. Scattered across the web in their thousands, finding a blog with the information you wanted was like tracking down the phone number for Mr Smith; a waste of time without an address. But now there are aggregators and keyword search engines that unify the diverse range of blogs, creating a powerful information source. Through the profusion of links to other blogs and websites, bloggers have created their own news network.

An example of the power of the blog is Salam Pax. Pax, who blogs under a pseudonym, is better known as the Baghdad Blogger. During much of the war in Iraq, he gave an on-the-battleground, Baghdad resident's perspective of the invasion. Forced off the ether when the allies entered Baghdad, he was soon back giving a front-line account of the reconstruction of Iraq.

Commentary (continued)

Blogs have some way to go before they usurp conventional media – or the Big Media as bloggers like to write. Blogs may provide comment and opinion, but their owners do not have an army of reporters doing the newsgathering. Instead they tend to rely on secondary, rather than primary, news sources. Also the traditional media is adept at dealing with competition; ruthlessly in many cases. It may not be possible, or convenient, to buy out the bloggers, but the media giants can adopt a number of defensive strategies including assimilating blogs into their own product, imitating the blogs, and clearly differentiating their product from blogs.

Still, traditional news media should heed the words of Matt Drudge, the legendary Internet underground reporter who broke the Monica Lewinsky story. In a 1998 speech to the National Press Club, Drudge said: "We have entered an era vibrating with the din of small voices. Every citizen can be a reporter, can take on the powers that be. The net gives as much voice to a 13-year-old computer geek like me as to a CEO or Speaker of the House. We all become equal. And you would be amazed what the ordinary guy knows."

REFERENCES

1. WARC, *Marketing Pocket Book*, p. 173, 2004.
2. Anon, Junk mail, *VNU*, 2003. Available from *http://www.vnunet.com/Specials/1141452* [accessed December 18, 2003].
3. In 2003, 100 students featuring the CNX logo went walkabout in five UK cities over two days. Parmar, A., 'Maximum exposure: advertisers use bodies as billboards to up brand visibility,' *Marketing News*, p. 6, 2003.
4. Fallows, D., *Spam: how it is hurting email and degrading life on the Internet*, Pew Internet, 2003. Available from *http:www.pewinternet.org* [accessed December 18, 2003].
5. Anon, Business, *Economist*, November, 8–15, p. 9, 2003.
6. According to the market analyst IDC.
7. Correspondence with Insights, October 2003.
8. Interview with Des Dearlove, November 2003.
9. Correspondence with Insights, October 2003.
10. Kaye, T., 'Ideas in Media Neutral Planning: just today's buzz word or a genuine new world order?' 2003. Available from *http://www.marketing-society.org.uk/downloads/MEDIA-NEUTRAL-PLANNING.pdf* [accessed December 18, 2003].
11. ARC, Paying for advertising, *ISBA/ARC*, 2000. Available from *http://www.isba.org.uk/publications/PFA3-qa.pdf* [accessed December 18, 2003].
12. Murphy, D., 'Hip, cool, and against the law,' *Marketing Business*, October, pp. 26–27, 2003.
13. ARC, op. cit.
14. Klienman, M., 'Coke halts advertising to under-12s,' *Marketing*, November 20, p. 1, 2003.
15. Jenkinson, A. and Bishop, K., 'Communications Optimisation: The Role and Practice of MNP,' CIM/The Center for Integrated Marketing, p. 1, 2003.
16. Correspondence with Insights, October 2003.

– CHAPTER 5 –

Managing yourself and your career

"Only those who will risk going too far can possibly find out how far one can go."

T.S. Eliot

"The first essential in a boy's career is to find out what he's fitted for, what he's most capable of doing, and doing with a relish."

Charles M. Schwab

"The secret of long life is double careers. One to about age sixty, then another for the next thirty years."

David Ogilvy

"The raising of wages leads to overwork among the workers. The more they want to earn, the more they must sacrifice their time and perform slave labor in which their freedom is totally alienated ... In so doing they shorten their lives ... Thus, even in the state of society which is the most favorable to the worker, the inevitable result for the worker is overwork and premature death, reduction to a machine, enslavement to capital."

Karl Marx

Who are you?

GEORGINA PETERS

[*When it comes to deciding what career to pursue, or whether it's time for a career change, the first thing to do is to ask some searching questions about yourself – what sort of career are you looking for, and just as importantly, what sort of person are you?*]

When we make consumer choices we buy according to our preferences. Nervous drivers don't tend to buy Ferraris. Given a choice, lovers of peace and quiet prefer not to live in the hurly-burly of the city. When it comes to holidays, thrill seekers will choose sky-diving over lying on a beach in the Caribbean, bungee jumping over a golfing vacation. That is not to say that you can't have an adventure on a golf course. It's a matter of personal taste.

It's no different for careers. The starting point for any career decision is self-awareness. Having a thorough knowledge of likes and dislikes, strengths and weaknesses, values, and other character traits is essential for selecting the right career. The more you understand yourself, the easier it becomes to make career choices, and the better chance you have of matching those choices with your capabilities.

"Self-knowledge is extremely important," says Joyce E. Barrie, career coach and founder and chief fun officer of Joymarc Enterprises. "You have to really know yourself, your strengths and weaknesses, and be able to reinvent yourself on a dime, literally, to be able to advance in life. The world is moving so quickly that it's not a matter of just catching up, but of being in the forefront given all of the competition."

Back in the 1960s, The Beatles memorably sought enlightenment from an Eastern mystic, Maharishi Mahesh Yogi. Whether he provided them with career direction or spiritual clarity is unclear. Most people however, are not afforded such luxury. There is no hirsute guru with all the answers. Only one person can provide the key to career happiness. You.

Asking the right questions

Ask yourself some tough questions and be honest with the answers. It is better to find out now that salary is the most important factor in choosing a career, rather than when you're stuck in a company that pays you peanuts. It's best to discover now that you hate being responsible for others, rather than when your boss tells you that you're in charge of a team of 30 people. If you are a down-to-earth, rational, logical-thinking person, discovering that the career you have chosen requires a creative dreamer will make you miserable and unhappy.

So how do you start on the voyage of self-discovery? One good starting point is to grit your teeth and ask your friends and colleagues what they think of you. Get them to write a list of your five greatest strengths and weaknesses. However, while this exercise may help, and it should certainly be an eye-opener, it is unlikely to reveal the real you. On your own it's difficult to separate out the *how you would like to be* self from the *how you really are* self.

Labels can also get in the way. A publisher found himself out of a job and asked a career adviser friend for help. "Well, what are you good at?" his friend asked him. "I'm a very good publisher," the man replied. "Yes, but what skills do you possess?" the career adviser asked. "Publishing skills," the publisher replied. The conversation went round in circles for a while until the career adviser said he would help him but only if he would agree to a simple condition. The publisher had to ask people who knew him – friends and professional contacts – what he was good at, and come back in a week. A week later, he duly appeared and reported that he had done as asked. "And what did these people say?" his friend enquired. "The funny thing is," he observed, "no one mentioned publishing."

The publisher reeled off a list of useful attributes. He was a good communicator, who could talk to anyone; he had a knack of summarizing the main points of an argument without going into too much detail; he was good at persuading other people to do what he wanted them to do; and was skilled at mirroring the views of the people he was with to make them feel comfortable. Beyond this he was skilled at manipulating and massaging words.

"Ah," said the career adviser, "that is interesting. Have you considered a career in politics?"

The point of the story is simple. You are not defined by your job, your industry, or your preconceptions.

The appliance of science

For those who remain unconvinced that self-discovery is a matter of self-help, scientific help is at hand. When it comes to self-awareness and unbiased, objective help, there's a whole industry out there waiting to provide it. There is a plethora of tools and techniques to help understand the sorts of roles a person is best suited to. Many of these tests were developed by psychologists. They cover four main areas – personality, skills, values, and interests – and provide an objective assessment of each of these aspects.

Most of the tests, or inventories as the psychologists prefer to call them, cost money; however it's worth weighing the cost of the test against a lifetime working in a unsuitable career, There's plenty of research to support the link between dissatisfaction at work and ill-health.[1]

Getting personal

Most personality tests are rooted in the work of the Swiss psychologist Carl Jung (1875–1961). Jung developed a theory of personality based on eight personality types: extroverts, introverts, thinking, feeling, sensing, intuitive, judging, and perceptive.

Jung believed individuals used two basic kinds of function: how they perceived things or took in information, and how they made decisions. These categories were further divided in two. Individuals perceive things via their senses or intuitively. Individuals make decisions objectively or subjectively. Although he believed people used all four functions, Jung also believed they did so to different degrees. One function would be dominant. These functions in turn could be "extraverted" or "introverted." (Jung considered himself an introvert.)[2]

Jung ended up with eight personality types:

1. Extroverted Sensing.
2. Introverted Sensing.
3. Extroverted Intuition.
4. Introverted Intuition.
5. Extroverted Thinking.
6. Introverted Thinking.
7. Extroverted Feeling.
8. Introverted Feeling.

Many personality tests used in career planning are based on Jung's personality types. The most popular of these are the Myers-Briggs Type Indicator and the Keirsey Temperament Sorter.

Myers-Briggs Type Indicator (MBTI)

The MBTI is the mother of all personality inventories used by over 3 million people annually. The initial research on the inventory was conducted by Katherine C. Briggs, around the time of the First World War. Her work built on Jung's theories of personality and was further developed by her daughter, Isabel Briggs Myers, who created the Myers-Briggs Type Indicator in the 1970s.

Briggs Myers concluded that each individual has a principal way of operation with respect to:

- our flow of energy – how we receive our stimulation, internally or externally;
- how we take in information – how do we absorb information, by trusting our senses to take it in or by trusting to our intuition?
- how we make decisions – do we make decisions by utilizing objectivity and thought or do we trust our personal subjective value systems?
- the everyday lifestyle we lead – on a day-to-day basis do we prefer to be structured and organized (judging) or laid back, relaxed, and open (perceiving)?

Individuals are naturally more comfortable with one or other of these modes of operating.

Within each of these categories we prefer to be:

1. **E**xtroverted or **I**ntroverted.
2. **S**ensing or i**N**tuitive.
3. **T**hinking or **F**eeling.
4. **J**udging or **P**erceiving.

Taking the test will result in a score indicated by the four letters denoting the individual's preferences – ESFJ, for example. Numbers next to the letters indicate their weighting. The MBTI instrument is regularly updated to reflect the latest research in type theory. Data for over 4,000 research studies provides a sound empirical foundation for the test.

Keirsey Temperament Sorter

The Keirsey Temperament Sorter is another popular indicator of personality type. The "test," now over 20 years old, was devised and developed by American clinical psychologist David West Keirsey. It is now available online (*www.keirsey.com*). The sorter is intended to indicate temperament. Individuals complete the test and, depending on their responses, are categorized as Artisans, Guardians, Idealists, or Rationals.

According to Keirsey, guardians are "concrete in communicating, operative in implementing goals, and highly skilled in logistics." They tend to be reliable, respectable, and do good deeds. Guardians comprise up to 45 percent of the population. Famous guardians include Mother Theresa, George Bush, F.W. Woolworth, and Thomas Hardy.

Artisans are "concrete in communicating, utilitarian in implementing goals, and can become highly skilled in tactical variation." They can be daring, adaptable, and graceful in action. Artisans comprise up to 40 percent of the population. Famous artisans include Barbra Streisand, Elvis Presley, Ernest Hemingway, and Winston Churchill.

Idealists are "abstract in communicating and co-operative in implementing goals, and can become highly skilled in diplomatic integration." Benevolent, empathetic, and authentic, Idealists make up only about 10 percent of the population. Famous idealists include Plato, Gandhi, James Joyce, and Lenin.

Rationals are "abstract in communicating and utilitarian in implementing goals, and can become highly skilled in strategic analysis." Rationals tend to be competent, autonomous, and strong-willed. Famous rationals include Abraham Lincoln, Albert Einstein, Walt Disney, and Bill Gates.

Highly skilled

Having contemplated who you are, next you should consider what you are good at. You may have spent your whole life harboring a secret desire to be a pilot. But if your hand-eye co-ordination is so bad you have trouble hitting a tennis ball; if your maths barely runs to working out your tax; if you have difficulty navigating your way to the local superstore; then flying is probably not for you.

A skill is the ability to do something. More than that, it is the ability to do something well. For the thousands of bedroom guitarists, competent and incompetent strummers, there are just one or two highly skilled musicians, an Eric Clapton or an Andrés Segovia. For all of the fumbling students in the biology dissection class there will be one person who renders the whole messy process effortless – the next Christiaan Barnard? Not that skills are solely for the supremely gifted. Even the most humble individual has a skill or two tucked away, even though they may not realize it.

Skills can be loosely divided into work or job-specific skills and transferable skills.

Job-specific skills are skills such as the ability to perform complex surgery or read music, to strip an engine or to program a computer, to navigate a cargo ship or to tailor a suit. These are the skills that are essential for carrying out work. They may be acquired through education, on the job, or picked up on life's journey. As people learn what is easy to do and what is difficult, what they enjoy and what they dislike, so they refine their personal suite of work-specific skills accordingly.

Transferable skills are something different. These are non-work-specific skills, which can be carried from one job to the next. Many of these skills are used in everyday life. Problem solving, the ability to communicate, organizing time, researching information, these are transferable skills.

Skills assessment enables a person to determine what skills they possess, what skills they are good at. It is also worth considering what skills are enjoyable. If job satisfaction is important, as it tends to be with most people, then a lifetime of performing a skill you detest, regardless of how good you are at it, is not a recipe for fulfillment. You may be a gifted mathematician, but that doesn't mean that you want to spend a working life crunching numbers.

In the US in 1990 the then Secretary of Labor Lynn Martin set up the Secretary's Commission on Achieving Necessary Skills (SCANS). Its goal was to "define critical skills that everyone needs in order to succeed in the workplace." The commission defined the skills it thought necessary in a high-performance economy and published them in its report "A SCANS Report for America 2000." In the high-performance workplace envisaged by SCANS, basic skills such as computation and literacy form a foundation. On top of this workers need more advanced soft skills such as complex problem solving and the ability to apply this knowledge.

If you are a person who can do all or most of the following then you are well equipped for work in the 21st century. If not, it is time to think about acquiring some of these must-have skills as indicated by SCANS – see Table 5.1.

Table 5.1: *SCANS skills*

Workplace competencies	Foundation skills
Resources	Basic skills
C1 Allocates time	F1 Reading
C2 Allocates money	F2 Writing
C3 Allocates material and facility resources	F3 Arithmetic
C4 Allocates human resources	F4 Mathematics
	F5 Listening
Information	F6 Speaking
C5 Acquires and evaluates information	
C6 Organizes and maintains information	**Thinking Skills**
C7 Interprets and communicates information	F7 Creative thinking
C8 Uses computers to process information	F8 Decision making
	F9 Problem solving
Interpersonal	F10 Seeing things in the mind's eye
C9 Participates as a member of a team	F11 Knowing how to learn
C10 Teaches others	F12 Reasoning
C11 Serves clients/customers	
C12 Exercises leadership	**Personal qualities**
C13 Negotiates to arrive at a decision	F13 Responsibility
C14 Works with cultural diversity	F14 Self-esteem
	F15 Sociability
Systems	F16 Self-management
C15 Understands systems	F17 Integrity/Honesty
C16 Monitors and corrects performance	
	For full details on the competencies
Technology	and skills go to: *www.scans.jhu.edu*
C18 Selects technology	
C19 Applies technology to task	
C20 Maintains and troubleshoots technology	
C17 Improves and designs systems	

Value conscious

What are values? It's a difficult question to answer simply, but one way of understanding the concept of values is to consider them as priorities that relate to an individual's behavior. They are priorities that motivate a person's course of action. Values can be divided into two categories: intrinsic and extrinsic:

- Intrinsic values are about the work you are doing and how it relates to society.
- Extrinsic values are to do with external factors such as salary, location, and work environment.

Various approaches have been developed to better understand values. These include the following.

Hall Tonna Inventory of Values

Psychologist Brian Hall and sociologist Benjamin Tonna conducted research into the nature of values over a 20-year period. They identified 125 cross-disciplinary and cross-cultural values that they appraised as critical and that played a fundamental part in the personal growth and development of an individual.

The conclusions they drew from their research were that:

- values are an expression of concepts (i.e. personal constructs) that represent dynamic clusters of energy;
- values are described by those words in a language that convey significant personal meaning. This meaning carries with it a certain psychological energy that activates a person's behavior;
- values are learned and can be measured.

From the research findings Hall and Tonna developed the Hall Tonna Inventory of Values built on four premises:

1. Values are an important component of human existence and can be identified and measured.
2. Values are described through words.
3. Values are learned and developed through assimilation.
4. Values are modified and shaped by our world-view.

What does this mean for the career seeker? A values inventory, such as that devised by Hall and Tonna, allows you to assess what values are important to you. From this you can ensure that any career you pursue encompasses those values. So if helping others is important to you, a career in public service is likely to be more satisfying than a career in the money markets.

The Minnesota Importance Questionnaire (MIQ)

The Minnesota Importance Questionnaire is another values tool that looks at vocational needs and values. It aims to measure six vocational values (altruism, comfort, safety, autonomy, status, and achievement) and 20 vocational needs derived from those values.

A paper-and-pencil inventory of vocational values and needs. The MIQ comes in two forms. In the paired form pairs of vocational needs statements are listed. The person taking the test selects the most important needs from each pair. The test takes roughly 30 minutes. In the ranked form vocational needs statements are grouped in batches of five. The person taking the test ranks each set of five, according to their importance. The ranked form MIQ is quicker to complete than the paired form taking roughly 15–20 minutes.

Survey of Interpersonal Values (SIV)

The Survey of Interpersonal Values measures six critical values regarding an individual's relationship with others. Those values are:

- benevolence: doing things for others;
- conformity: being accepted; doing what is socially correct;
- independence: making decisions, getting your own way;
- leadership: being in charge; having power and authority;
- recognition: being highly regarded and admired; having status, being important;
- support: being treated with understanding and consideration.

Organizational values

It's not just about finding out your own values either. Values are important to organizations. In their book *Built to Last*, James C. Collins and Jerry I. Porras discovered that one quality of enduring companies is that they establish and cherish a set of corporate values. Values are important for determining whether you are likely to feel comfortable within a particular organization.

Take General Electric, for example. Under its former CEO Jack Welch, GE explicitly linked the performance of its managers to the company's values. Some 5,000 GE employees took part in the debate about the company's values over a three-year period. In 1989, an early draft of the values statement urged staff to embrace the GE values. Those who did not, Welch suggested, might fare better elsewhere. "Individuals whose values do not coincide with these expressed preferences will more likely flourish better outside the General Electric Company," the statement read. It became known as the "flourish off" statement, and caused such an outcry that it was dropped from the final values statement.

During his time at GE Welch carried a laminated card in his pocket bearing the GE values. Failure to live those values was grounds for dismissal. At one meeting Welch surprised his audience saying: "Look around you: there are five fewer officers here than there were last year. One was fired for the numbers, four were fired for (lack of) values."

Love your work

Few people succeed doing something they don't love. People who make a career out of their interests or hobbies seem to have it made, especially when the money is good. But before you can turn an interest into a career, you have to find out what your interests are. For the single-minded this task will be a lot easier than for the more eclectic natured. We may not all be in our ideal career but by increasing the match between work and interests we can fashion a completely fulfilling career from a barely satisfying one. As with values, tests of interest usually come in the form of inventories asking questions designed to elicit your interests.

Strong Interest Inventory (SII)

Developed by celebrated psychologist E.K. Strong at Stanford University in 1927 "the Strong," as it is known, is the most powerful and widely used interest inventory. Since its inception it has been revised and upgraded.

The Strong consists of a questionnaire with 317 items, words or phrases covering a wide range of hobbies, activities, and occupations. The respondent expresses a preference for three response categories for each item. The responses are scored by computer and detailed in a report, usually called a profile.

The information from the test is broken down into five categories. Preferences for work in general are indicated by the scores on the six General Occupational Themes. Next come scores on 25 Basic Interest Scales; these indicate interests or aversions in 25 specific areas. Occupational Scales, 211 of them, demonstrate a similarity or otherwise between the respondent and men and women representing 109 different occupations. Style scales measure a person's preferences for the style in which they like to work, learn, and take risks. Lastly, three administrative indexes weed out unusual or invalid responses.

The Strong assumes that there is a correlation between a particular job and the interests of people in that particular job. By assessing an individual's interests and comparing them to the interests of people in various occupations it seeks to determine the type of occupation most suitable for an individual.

Handy's intelligence profiles

In his book *The Hungry Spirit*, Charles Handy outlines 11 different intelligence profiles, any of which can stimulate self-respect and subsequently become the foundation of a fulfilling career. Consider the following in light of your life and learning experiences:

- Factual intelligence – encyclopedic knowledge.
- Analytic intelligence – reasoning and conceptualizing.
- Numerate intelligence – mathematical skill.
- Linguistic intelligence – verbal and communication skill.
- Spatial Intelligence – an ability to see patterns in things.
- Athletic intelligence – physical co-ordination.
- Intuitive intelligence – aptitude for sensing and seeing what is hidden from most others.
- Emotional intelligence – self-awareness, self-control, persistence, zeal, and self-motivation.
- Practical intelligence – common sense.
- Interpersonal intelligence – social and leadership skills.
- Musical intelligence – the creation, production, or performance of music.

"What matters most," says Handy, "is the message behind the list: these many and varied intelligences or abilities are all resources that we can use to contribute to the world, to earn a living, and to make a difference."

Holland's Self-Directed Search

Another widely used interest inventory is Dr John Holland's self-directed search. Over 20 million people worldwide have used it in their quest for self-awareness. The search is supported by over 500 research studies and translated into 25 different languages.

Holland developed a theory of personality that categorized individuals into one of six types: Realistic, Investigative, Artistic, Social, Enterprising, and Conventional. Furthermore Holland found that occupations and work environments could be similarly categorized. This is a result of the tendency of similar types to associate together and create an atmosphere conducive to that type of person.

People are happiest and most likely to be successful in environments that they feel comfortable in. These environments are likely to be found where there are people of a similar type. So an artistic person is more likely to achieve success in an artistic environment such as a theater or dance studio than in a chemical research laboratory or an accounting firm.

Retracing your steps

"No one has ever learned fully to know themselves," said the poet, novelist, playwright, courtier, natural philosopher, and all-round career adventurer Johann Wolfgang von Goethe. "The final mystery is oneself," wrote dramatist Oscar Wilde.[3] Self-discovery is a quest as old as mankind itself.

For those who have taken one of the many personality, interests, skills, or values tests or inventories available it is an important step on the way to discovering the answer to the question posed by Alice to the White Rabbit: "Who in the world am I?"

Armed with this knowledge it is possible to identify the types of work that are most suited to you. Only then will you be ready to take the next step toward a truly fulfilling career. And remember before you do, self-assessment is an on-going process. What is right for a teenager setting out from college is not necessarily right for the same person 20 years later, even a year later. Remember to return to the tests and inventories at regular intervals along your career journey. That way you can make sure you always stay on track.

RESOURCES

Bougle, C., *The Evolution of Values Studies in Sociology*, August M. Kelly, 1970.

Briggs Myers, Isobel and McCaulley, Mary H., *Manual: A Guide to the Development and Use of the Myers Briggs Type Indicator*, Consulting Psychologists Press, 1992.

Briggs Myers, Isobel, *Gifts Differing*, Consulting Psychologists Press, 1972.

Coomber, Stephen, Crainer, Stuart and Dearlove, Des, *The Career Adventurer's Fieldbook*, Capstone, 2002.

Curtler, Hugh Mercer, *Rediscovering Values: Coming to Terms with Postmodernism*, M.E. Sharpe, Inc., Armonk, 1997.

Holland, John L., *Exploring Career Options*, Self-Directed Search, Psychological Assessment Resources, 1990.

Keirsey, D., *Please Understand Me II*, Prometheus Nemesis Book Co., 1998.

Krebs Hirsh Consulting, *Using the Myers-Briggs Type Indicator in Organizations*, Psychologists Press, 1991.

Rokeach, Milton, *Understanding Human Values: Individual and Societal Individual and Societal*, Free Press, 1979.

Rokeach, Milton, *The Nature of Human Values*, Free Press, 1973.

www.advisorteam.com/user/ktsintro.asp
www.careerinnovation.com/panel/values
www.cedarcreek.org

www.cpp-db.com
www.knowyourtype.com
www.ksu.edu/acic/career/holland/holland.html
www.mbtypeguide.com/Type
www.minessence.net/html/aboutavi.htm
www.personalitypathways.com
www.self-directed-search.com
www.teamtechnology.co.uk
www.valuestech.com

Commentary

Who gets training?

It is increasingly acknowledged that training is key to improving individuals' employment and earnings prospects – and to maintaining competitiveness. While initial education ensures that people enter the labor market equipped for their chosen occupation, acquisition of skills on the job offers the potential to keep up to date with changing technology throughout their working lives. Unless the workforce is continually acquiring new skills, it is difficult to reap the returns from technological progress.

ISER economists Alison Booth and Mark Bryan, together with Wiji Arulampalam of the University of Warwick, have explored who receives training using data from the European Community Household Panel (ECHP) survey. The ECHP has followed representative samples of people in different EU countries since 1994, using a harmonized questionnaire to ensure that the information collected is comparable across countries. This study analyzes the experiences of 10 countries – Austria, Belgium, Britain, Denmark, Finland, France, Ireland, Italy, the Netherlands, and Spain – over a period of six years. It focusses on the training of employees who have completed their initial education and are aged between 25 and 54.

The results reveal wide differences in the annual proportion of workers undertaking formal continuing training: from under 10 percent in Ireland, Italy, and the Netherlands, to over 35 percent in Britain, Denmark, and Finland. But concealed within these variations, there are a number of patterns that show up consistently across countries. In particular, there is no evidence that women are less likely to undertake training than men. Indeed, in Denmark, Finland, Italy and Spain, women are considerably more likely to start a training course than men – by between 10 percent and 60 percent.

The researchers also look at how the likelihood of training varies with age. In other words, is there any evidence of lifelong learning? For women, there is little correlation between the probability of starting formal training and age, and this could be interpreted as evidence in favor of "lifelong learning."

But in nine out of the ten countries (all except Italy), older men are less likely to get trained than younger men. A typical example is Finland, where a man between 50 and 54 years old is predicted to be 10 percentage points less likely to receive training than a comparable 25–29-year-old with the same education level and employment status. So these results provide little evidence of lifelong learning for men.

The results also show that in most countries, training incidence is higher in the public sector, typically by around five percentage points, after taking account of other personal and job characteristics likely to affect training. This effect generally applies to both men and women, but since women are overall more likely to work in the public sector, the impact on women's training is greater.

In most countries, the higher people's educational levels, the more likely they are to undertake a training course. For example, in Spain, both men and women with degrees are five percentage points more likely to receive training than comparable individuals who have completed only the lower level of secondary school. The only country where educational level does not seem to influence training is Belgium.

What's more, even after accounting for these education levels, workers at the bottom of the wage distribution are less likely to receive training, perhaps because of a poor history of previous training and experience. For example, in Britain, both men and women who are in the bottom fifth of the wage distribution are around 10 percentage points less likely to begin training courses.

European countries have adopted widely varying policies on employment protection. In economies where permanent workers have high levels of employment protection, temporary or fixed-term contracts can provide a mechanism for enhancing labor market flexibility, since a firm can adjust its workforce by varying the number of temporary workers. But there might be less training in fixed-term contracts since there is less time for the firm to reap the benefits.

This highlights a potential further indirect outcome of the employment protection legislation: it increases fixed-term contracts and fixed-term contract workers may get less training. On the other hand, in some countries training may be an explicit component of fixed-term probationary contracts.

Consistent with these different possible effects, the researchers find that in about half the countries, fixed-term contracts are associated with a lower likelihood of training (for example, it is reduced by 11–12 percentage points for Danish men and women). In the other countries, there is no significant effect. Where negative effects do exist, they will have a greater impact on women insofar as they are more likely to be covered by fixed-term contracts.

Women are also more likely to be found in part-time work, and once again we might expect training to be less frequent among part-timers as there are fewer working hours in which to capture the benefits. But the results show little evidence of any such effect. Only in Britain and Finland are part-timers less likely to begin a training course than other workers with similar characteristics. For example, British part-time women are 11 percentage points less likely to train than their full-time equivalents.

Overall, the research reveals the range of different factors influencing who gets access to training in Europe, and how these factors vary between men and women. Training differs both because women have different characteristics to men – for example, they are more likely to work in the public sector – and because their characteristics sometimes have different effects – for example, older women do not seem to receive less training, unlike older men.

Generational Shift™

BRUCE TULGAN

[The workplace is a-changing.]

There is a fundamental shift under way in the norms and values of the workplace. That change is driven by a historic macro-economic change: the great forces of history – technology and globalization – have led the larger economy to a new stage of global interconnection, high speed, and complexity. Over the last 10 years, the worldwide business environment has become one of high-risk, erratic markets, and unpredictable resource needs. In order to adjust, organizations of all sizes have tried to become more lean and flexible. After years of downsizing, restructuring, and reengineering, the myth of job security is dead. What is the result? The traditional long-term hierarchical employment relationship has morphed into something new: a short-term transactional relationship.

In an effort to track and understand these profound changes, my organization, RainmakerThinking, Inc.®, has been conducting extensive research on the front lines of the workplace since 1993.

Why do we call this shift a "Generational Shift"? Let me explain. At first, we were investigating the generation gap between older employees and the new Generation X (born 1965–77) employees who were then entering the workforce. Back then, Generation Xers were widely viewed as being less loyal than previous generations, unwilling to pay their dues and climb the proverbial ladder. Gen Xers didn't trust large institutions and were turning away from the traditional career path and its norms of success. All of this was seen as a youthful aberration back then. But over the course of just 10 years, most employees of all ages have lost confidence in the traditional employer–employee relationship. Few employees of any age believe they could pay their dues and climb the corporate ladder and be rewarded with long-term job security and long-term financial payoffs. The Gen X attitude has spread across the workforce among people of all ages – it has become mainstream.

More than 10 years later, we are still investigating these changes. Since 1993, we have interviewed more than 10,000 individuals, studied the management practices of 700 different companies, held dozens of focus groups, polled thousands of respondents, reviewed internal survey data from 300 companies, and led more than 1,000 interactive seminars with hundreds of thousands of participants. While this research continues, we can report six findings.

Finding 1. Work has become more demanding on employees

In just about every industry, in nearly every organization, individuals at all levels are in widespread agreement that work has become more demanding. Over and over again, people tell stories about the growing intensity of the workplace and the increased challenges they face. And they are right.

Productivity improvements are coming, not only from new technology but also from increased human effort and effectiveness. Employees are working harder and facing increasing pressure to work longer, and/or smarter, and/or faster, and/or better. Meanwhile, employers are reducing tolerance for employee error, waste, and inefficiency. This creates a constant imperative to get lots of work done very well very fast all day long.

What is more, employees must routinely learn and utilize new technologies, processes, practices, skills, and knowledge, all the while adjusting to on-going organizational changes which cause growing fear of imminent job loss. At the same time, employees receive less management guidance and support, work in smaller teams with greater requirements, and have less time to rest, recuperate, and prepare. As a result, employees manifest increased physical and psychological stress and related problems (including anger, interpersonal conflict, and "burnout"). As the workplace becomes more demanding, there is a widespread counter-trend, which is a routinely stated desire for greater work–life balance.

Finding 2. Employer–employee relationships have become less hierarchical and more transactional

Traditional sources of authority are being supplanted by new sources. Seniority, age, rank, and rules are diminishing. Organization charts are flatter; layers of management have been removed. Reporting relationships are more temporary; more employees are being managed by short-term project-leaders, instead of "organization-chart" managers. On the rise as sources of authority are more transactional forms such as control of resources, control of rewards, and control of work conditions. At least partly due to these trends, employees nowadays are less likely to define "success" in relation to rank or seniority in an organization chart, and more likely to define success in highly personal terms.

Among the consequences of these changes in organizations are that employees today are more likely to disagree – often privately, sometimes openly – with their employers' stated missions, policies, and decisions. At the same, employees are less obedient to employers' rules and supervisors' instructions, more likely to question or challenge employment conditions and established reward structures, and more likely to make individual requests regarding desired employment conditions and rewards.

It should also be noted that employees are more likely to agree, obey, co-operate, and perform at a higher level when their employers promise a specific quid pro quo. That's right, agreement, obedience, co-operation, and performance can be bought. It is quite possible and may be extremely practical for employers to make short-term deals with employees on a wide range of matters. Employees will put in abeyance their doubts and complaints and, for a price, get the job done, whatever the job may be.

Finding 3. Employers are moving away from long-term employment relationships

One of the basic strategies for achieving organizational flexibility over the last 10 years has been a fundamental change in employment practices, away from long-term stable employment relationships and toward a more efficient supply-chain management approach, known as human capital management. Employers today are more likely to undertake major business changes that eliminate jobs regardless of employees' length of service; such changes include mergers, acquisitions, spin-offs, restructuring, and liquidations. As well, employers are more likely to implement new technologies that eliminate jobs due to reengineering. Meanwhile, there is a strong trend among employers of hiring fewer "employees" (full-time, exclusive workers), while hiring more contingent workers, and employers' staffing strategies for the future reflect this change. As a result, "employees" are diminishing as a percentage of the overall workforce, while the percentage of contingent workers is increasing.

Employers are less likely to award status, prestige, authority, flexibility, and rewards on the basis of seniority, and more likely to award status, prestige, authority, flexibility, and rewards on the basis of short-term measurable goals. As well, employers are reducing long-term fixed pay as a percentage of overall employee compensation, while increasing the percentage of variable performance-based pay. Employers' compensation strategies for the future reflect this change. Part of this new compensation strategy includes a reduction in the percentage of employee "benefits" (paid for by the company for full-time, exclusive workers) in relation to overall compensation. Further, employers are increasing the percentage of "employee services" (paid for by the worker on a pre-tax basis); such services include health insurance and retirement savings. Because of these new realities, employers are now less likely to make formal or informal guarantees about continued employment and job security.

Finding 4. Employees have less confidence in long-term rewards and greater expectations for short-term rewards

While many employees may doubt the sincerity of long-term promises, many more employees worry that their prospects for receiving long-term rewards are vulnerable to a whole range of external and internal forces that might shorten the natural life of the organization employing them. Workers worry openly about events or circumstances that have little or nothing to do with business, such as politics, diplomacy, war, terrorism, and natural disasters. They worry about broad business factors beyond the control of organization leaders, including monetary policy, global market shifts, changes in particular industries, and organizational changes. As well, they are acutely aware that the organization employing them might simply lose out in the fiercely competitive marketplace. Or short of their employer suffering in the marketplace, workers worry about the continued employment of their immediate supervisors and other leaders who know them best, or about their own continued employment.

There are numerous consequences of this diminished confidence among employees. First, employees are investing a lower percentage of savings in long-term vesting retirement plans and pensions, while investing a greater percentage in self-managed cash balance plans. Second, employees are less willing to make immediate sacrifices in return for potential long-term pay-offs. Thus, given the choice, employees are more likely to prefer short-term over long-term incentives. Third, employees are more likely to make specific requests for immediate increases in pay, benefits, and work conditions. Fourth, short-term incentives are more successful than long-term for maintaining high levels of employee productivity, quality, morale, and retention.

Finding 5. Supervisors are now the most important people in the workplace

Employees think of their immediate supervisors as the primary representatives of their employers' missions, policies, systems, and practices. The supervisor is the point of contact, but much more than that, on a daily basis, the supervisor defines the work experience. Every day, the supervisor determines assignments, work conditions, recognition, and rewards. There is a widespread consensus: in study after study, we find that the number one factor in productivity, morale, and retention is the relationship between supervisors and their direct reports.

The supervisor is even more important today than ever before. Everybody is under more pressure. Everything is happening on a shorter timeframe and with higher stakes. Expectations are greater on all sides. Employees are expected to work longer, harder, smarter, faster, and better. And employees are not about to wait around for long-term rewards. They want to know, "What's the deal around here? What do you want from me? And what do I get for my hard work today?"

In this process, employees rely on immediate supervisors more than any other individuals for meeting their basic needs and expectations and dealing with a whole range of day-to-day issues that arise at work. These include the assignment of tasks, resource planning, problem solving, training, scheduling, dispute resolution, guidance, coaching, recognition, promotions, and other rewards. It is the immediate supervisor an employee turns to, whether he/she is seeking a special assignment, obtaining necessary resources, pursuing a special work location, avoiding a certain co-worker, looking for a good performance evaluation, or hoping for a raise.

Finding 6. Supervising employees now requires more time and skill than ever

In operational terms, the key workforce management strategy is to increase worker productivity and quality. That's why, in just about every organization in just about every industry, supervisors are under increasing pressure from senior executives. The marching orders? Get more work and better work out of fewer employees, while utilizing fewer resources.

This puts a tremendous burden on the average supervisory manager. Even while supervisors juggle their own tasks and responsibilities, managerial spans of control (the number of employees officially reporting to each supervisor) are increasing. At the same time, many supervisors are being given more administrative duties and are expected to handle their own recruiting, selection, orientation, training, performance management, and retention. All of this requires the average supervisor to deal with more bureaucratic red tape.

Meanwhile, supervisors must learn to deal with and accommodate the needs and expectations of an increasingly diverse workforce. Employees are more likely to make special requests (or demands) of supervisors regarding assignments, work conditions, benefits, rewards, or other special needs. Employees need, expect, and request more coaching and guidance than they currently receive from supervisors. Most workplaces are severely undermanaged considering today's requirements. Managing people has become a very high-maintenance endeavor. That's why supervisors across the board are so frustrated.

The bad news is that supervisors who spend less time engaged in managing employees spend more time rectifying employee errors, salvaging lost resources, mediating conflicts among co-workers, resolving complaints from vendors and customers, and solving other problems; these supervisors also spend more time on lower-level tasks.

The good news is that supervisors who learn, practice, and implement proven management techniques generate higher productivity, quality, morale, and retention; these supervisors also spend more time on high-level tasks.

According to our research, the most effective managers in today's workplace employ a more transactional approach, which requires more time and skill than traditional management. These managers tend to ignore red tape and bureaucracy over which they have little control and, instead, focus on their own immediate sphere of authority and influence. These managers tend to rely a great deal on the power of interpersonal communication skills, engaging direct reports in on-going coaching dialogs about performance standards, goals, and deadlines. These managers also gain power by positioning themselves as being able to do more for people: they bend over backward to gain control of discretionary resources and then use those resources as day-to-day bargaining chips with employees. Finally, these managers tend to be extremely rigorous about holding employees accountable on a daily basis: setting expectations clearly, correcting performance problems immediately, and quickly removing low performers from the workplace.

The generational shift will continue

The workplace revolution of the last decade has been profound, but now there are powerful demographic forces under way that will cement the Generational Shift. First, those of the Silent Generation (born before 1946) are gradually exiting the workforce; by 2006, two experienced workers will leave the workforce for every one who enters the workforce. So we are losing a great number of our most traditional workers. Second, the Baby Boomers (born 1946–64) are becoming the aging workforce; every day 10,000 Baby Boomers turn 55 years of age. So the workforce is aging quickly. Third, the prime-age workforce will be made up increasingly of Generation X and Generation Y (born 1978–87).

No matter how effective organizations may become at retaining older workers in flexible roles, as Generation X and Generation Y become the dominant players in the prime-age workforce, they will usher out the last vestiges of the old-fashioned workplace values and norms and finish the workplace revolution. Meanwhile, huge cadres of aging workers (often with significant power in organizations) will reach advanced life stages, at which they will need and demand more flexible work conditions (ironically) pushing the "free agent" agenda in their own ways for their own reasons. On top of all that, a new generation of younger workers with no attachment to the old-fashioned career path and work patterns will emerge.

What will this mean?

The revolution in workplace values and norms will continue. The traditional career path and old-fashioned management tactics will finally fade away. The one-size-fits-all approach to employer–employee relations will be dead. In good times and bad alike, the idea of a long-term career in one company will be rare. Employees will come to accept that they must take responsibility for their own success and fend for themselves as best they can. The most successful people will be focussed on learning marketable skills, building relationships with decision makers who can help them, and selling their way into career opportunities.

As most workplaces become less hierarchical and less formal, relationships between employers and employees will become increasingly short-term and transactional. Individual careers will be much more fluid and self-directed. Most communication will be just-in-time oriented, tied to the growing availability of information through easy-to-use technology. The pace of everything will continue to accelerate, while long-term thinking and planning will be much less relevant. Managers will have to discard traditional authority, rules, and red tape, and become highly engaged in one-on-one negotiation and coaching with employees to drive productivity, quality, and innovation.

Business leaders and managers are going to be scrambling for the foreseeable future to get more work and better work out of fewer people, consistently. Having hired like crazy in the frenzied seller's market of the late 1990s, they found themselves downsizing even faster throughout 2001 and 2002. They are not going to make the same mistake again of hiring every warm body in sight. Rather, the pressure will be on to hire the best person for every role at every level and then manage every person aggressively to reach higher levels of productivity. Welcome to the real new economy.

The generation game

Is the workplace revolution really a "Generational Shift"? Since 1993, RainmakerThinking has conducted in-depth interviews to study the attitudes of different generations and the impact of generational differences on workplace issues. Although it is dangerous to make vast generalizations about tens of millions of people, it is clear that there are strong generational trends in norms and values. Each generation comes from a different perspective, is going through different life and career stages, and has different needs and expectations. That's why it can be so powerful to look at the changes in the workplace through this generational lens:

- Silents (born before 1946)   10 percent
- Baby Boomers (born 1946–64)   46 percent
- Gen Xers (born 1965–77)   29 percent
- Gen Yers (born 1978–87)   15 percent

Silent Generation

Born before 1946, roughly 10 percent of the workforce. Years of experience have taught Silents to rely on tried, true, and tested ways of doing things, and many would still agree that if it's not broken, don't fix it. Silents still favor established systems, policies, and procedures. They like the old rules. They have paid their dues and climbed the ladder, and they want to enjoy the fruits of seniority. After years of working under command-and-control management, Silents are experiencing a radical change in the new workplace. Silents respond best to leaders and managers who respectfully assert their authority and demonstrate a clear track record of success.

Baby Boomers

Born 1946–64, roughly 46 percent of the workforce. Boomers generally believe they've paid their dues and climbed the ladder under the old rules and now find themselves operating amidst constant downsizing, restructuring, and reengineering. Boomers still pride themselves on their ability to survive "sink or swim" management, and often they resent the demands of today's young upstarts. Boomer women led the charge for workplace flexibility, and now many Boomers have caught on to the free-agent mindset. Boomers respond best to leaders and managers who listen attentively to their input and include them in decision making, while challenging them to keep growing.

Generation X

Born 1965–77, roughly 29 percent of the workforce. When Generation Xers hit the workforce in the late 1980s, they were typecast as disloyal job-hoppers who didn't want to pay their dues and wanted everything their own way. But by the mid to late 1990s, it was clear that Xers formed the vanguard of the free-agent workforce. Now Xers are growing up and moving into positions of supervisory responsibility and leadership, but they are not settling down. Xers remain cautious, and they know their security rests in staying on the cutting edge. Always in a hurry, Xers will often sidestep rules as they push for results. They're willing to take risks to keep learning and innovating. Gen Xers respond best to leaders and managers who spend time coaching, clarifying the day-to-day bargain at work, and giving credit for results achieved.

Generation Y

Born 1978 and later, roughly 15 percent of the workforce. Gen Yers are the children of Baby Boomers and the optimistic, upbeat, younger siblings of Gen Xers. Like Xers, they have a transactional approach to dealing with employers. But unlike Xers, they have high expectations for established institutions. Gen Yers have been told by parents, teachers, counselors, and churches that they can do anything. And they believe it – they are overflowing with self-esteem. Their facility with information technology makes them would-be experts on everything, and they are mastering a new just-in-time strategic approach to thinking, learning, and communicating. Poised to be the most capable and the most demanding generation in history, Gen Yers respond best to leaders and managers who keep them engaged with speed, customization, and interactivity.

RESOURCES

Tulgan, Bruce, *Hot Management*, HRD Press, 2004.
Tulgan, Bruce, *Winning the Talent Wars*, W.W. Norton, 2001.
Tulgan, Bruce, *Managing Generation X*, W.W. Norton, 2000.

www.rainmakerthinking.com.

❝ Interview ❞ : Alan Briskin

California-based Alan Briskin, author of *The Stirring of Soul in the Workplace* and co-author of *Bringing Your Soul to Work*, talks about work, the soul, and honesty.

How did you come to reject standard corporate operating practice?

My father was an entrepreneur in Manhattan. I rejected the way my father worked all the time. Later I recognized the importance of getting things done with others. I became interested in the unconscious life of groups, how we each take on a psychological role that is in relation to how we see ourselves in the organizational system.

What do you mean by "soul"?

I use the word differently than some. To me it includes the body and the network of relationships that make up our communities. Soul is the relationship between our inner life and the world we participate in. Many of the things written in the business field are very absolute – do this or do that. I am interested in what we do daily; how we listen to our own breath.

Why don't we bring our souls to work?

There's a great deal of fear. People think that if they show who they are, they will make themselves more vulnerable. But people gain so much if they bring themselves to work. And their work also gains. It has to begin with individuals making a commitment to respecting their own inner life and their own health. This is not just for their own benefit but for the benefit of those they work with, their organizations and communities.

But surely it's not very professional to unburden yourself. Aren't managers more interested in budgets than souls?

Professional is a euphemism. It means that people are guarded, not themselves. I talk to people who feel betrayed by their organizations.

Yes, but can they really voice that betrayal? What's people's reaction when you suggest they bring their souls to work?

A few years ago people weren't receptive. In the 1980s there hadn't been a business book with the word "Soul" in the title. Now there are 74 titles under soul and work. There has been a shift toward greater openness. I assume skepticism but usually find openness. The level of discussion is improving. The real issues are about human interaction, power, and how we get things done.

Are companies really changing?

Companies are having to take responsibility for the effects of what they're doing and new economy companies really are different. I talked to a lumber company which had sat down with pressure groups and negotiated a forestry plan. I've talked to a manager who was influenced by the practices of native Americans and a company which talks of having a "shining soul." There is a convergence taking place between the organizational field, collective intelligence, and the wisdom traditions of religions. There is a belief in a larger spiritual calling. This is a movement growing at the edges.

Isn't it still peripheral to what companies actually do and stand for?

It can't be about fluff. Companies are legal shells. As such they are weak. So, it matters a great deal that a company has an identity and values. Of course, having "good" values does not mean that you'll be successful.

This is a pivotal time in which we can see that we are making a difference – in the air, in the environment. It is time to decide what to do. We are stakeholders. If we change our theories of organizations we will change our organizations.

What happens when managers move on to come up with another buzz-word?

There is a pattern beyond the use of a single word. I'm not worried about words replacing the word "soul." We are creating a different expectation of how people work in organizations. Honesty is the next movement, addressing the discrepancy between appearance and reality. That's when people lose hope – hopelessness is a by-product of not telling each other the truth.

Personal agility

ELIZABETH WELDON

[Managers increasingly work in fast-paced, uncertain environments. Today speed and flexibility are needed to react quickly to unexpected events, to adapt rapidly to changing business environments, and to take fast action to shape situations in transition. These managers must be agile to succeed.]

For many managers, eliminating uncertainty is at the heart of their jobs. They take time to define clear, well-specified objectives. They conduct detailed analyses and use formal planning tools to define clear paths to their goals and develop contingency plans to manage disruptions. Once their plans are set, they monitor performance against them, take corrective action to control deviations, and trigger contingency plans when required.

But other managers find that uncertainty cannot be eliminated or planned away. They may be working in a rapidly developing business environment, such as a developing country or newly deregulated industry, or figuring out how to use new technology to create a market. They may be trying to do something new so that known actions, routines, and templates cannot be applied. They may be working in an unstable, emerging environment or in an environment in transition, where events that affect the manager's ability to meet his goals cannot be controlled or anticipated or planned for. For these managers, uncertainty is part of the job, to be accepted and embraced.

To be effective, these managers supplement their repertoire of management behavior and their portfolio of management tools with new ways of thinking and acting that help them to react quickly and effectively. In short, they are agile managers.

Take, for example, the uncertainty that faced three Russian entrepreneurs when they created Frontstep CIS to sell and install enterprise resource planning software systems (ERP) in local companies. Although the founders had experience as software developers, they knew little about information systems for business enterprises. But they felt they could learn quickly enough to modify existing ERP software to meet their customers' needs. They decided to buy ERP software from a French firm, rather than develop a system themselves.

Although many challenges were anticipated, the way to meet them was not always clear – for example, building an effective relationship with their French supplier and understanding their customers' needs. Knowing that they must act quickly, before other companies moved in, they decided to go ahead and figure out solutions as the problems occurred. At the same time, many unforeseeable problems also appeared. When their French supplier went out of business, the managers at Frontstep scrambled to find a new supplier and to convince their customers to accept this new product instead. Then, in the summer of 1998, when the value of the rouble fell dramatically, Frontstep had to respond quickly and creatively to survive. Luckily the founders were agile enough to do so.

Or consider the uncertainty facing the project manager in charge of rocket engine development at Boeing Rocketdyne. After designing the engine for the space shuttle, Boeing Rocketdyne hoped to put that knowledge to commercial use. But success would require radical changes to the design of the engine and the production processes. A commercial rocket engine would have to be much cheaper, faster to produce, and last much longer.

To meet this challenge, Boeing created a strategic alliance with two other firms, and together they recruited a project team. The team would work together virtually – a new experience for all team members – and each member would devote just 15 percent of his time to the task. In addition, although team members were experts in their disciplines, only a few had experience with rocket engine design.

Given the difficulty of the task and the uncertainty involved, Boeing Rocketdyne had a hard time persuading an engineer to lead the project. But finally a team leader was found who felt that he and his team could improvise their way to a new design. While keeping the goals of the project clearly in mind, they tried out new ideas and experimented to see what might work. Each team member freely offered solutions, listened to those proposed by others, and adjusted and massaged their ideas based on what they heard. Using this approach, the team could test design ideas rapidly and learn from their experiments.

The team also improvised a way to work together as a virtual team. Although they began with procedures for using their collaborative communication technology and CAD tool, they set aside procedures that got in the way, and created novel ways of interacting as the need arose. For example, when the team realized that they were generating too much information to be captured in written form, they decided to couple written documentation with oral communication. In preparing for a meeting, team members would post incomplete messages and share the rest during the teleconference. The team also changed their rules about face-to-face discussions among co-located members. Originally the group believed these sorts of discussions should not take place, because others were left out, but later they agreed that spontaneous discussions could be useful, as long as those involved shared the outcome with all team members.

The team's results were spectacular. In 10 months, they created a radically new thrust chamber for the rocket engine that used six parts instead of 1,200, decreased manufacturing cost from $7 million to $0.5 million, and substantially increased reliability. Their strategic improvisation, flexibility, and agility paid off.

Strategic improvisation: the path to agility

When using strategic improvisation, managers attack their task quickly, learn from their actions, and use what they have learned to develop a plan. The cycle of acting, learning, and planning continues, so they develop their plans as they go. This allows them to react quickly to surprises in their work, change direction in response to unexpected events, and adjust plans, goals, and priorities to adapt to and shape a changing situation. By responding spontaneously to the situation as it is, managers can create plans that fit the situation and reduce the risk of taking action that is irrelevant, unproductive, or harmful.

Although agile managers are spontaneous and improvisational, they do not shoot from the hip or adopt a cavalier approach to their work. Rather, their success depends on four key capabilities.

Four capabilities

Spontaneity, quick learning, fast and flexible decision making, and extending one's reach are the four capabilities that my research has shown to provide the skills that agile managers need to use strategic improvisation effectively.

Spontaneity. Being spontaneous allows the agile manager to respond quickly and creatively to a changing situation. In fact, agile managers behave much like improvisational actors, who create a theatrical performance before an audience, spontaneously, in real time. According to Lilly Frances, who teaches improv at the Second City Training Center in Chicago, "Improvisation involves thinking on your feet and responding to the scene as it develops."

To be spontaneous, actors and agile managers are "in the moment." They react to what is happening, not to what they wish would happen or what they thought might happen. They do not get ahead of themselves and the situation, but they have the flexibility to adapt when the scenario takes an unexpected turn. They remain open to possibilities, recognizing that the obvious response is not always the most interesting or useful one. They reconsider, shift position, and change focus to follow the new direction and see what emerges. Agile managers, like improvisational actors, also demonstrate a bias for action – doing nothing is not an option. Instead, they pick an idea and go with it to see what happens. Then they respond accordingly.

Quick learning. The ability to learn quickly is a manager's primary tool to ensure success in unfamiliar circumstances and fast-changing environments. In strategic improvisation, quick learning comes from action and experiments. Agile managers jump in, try things out, assess the situation, and make plans based on what they learn. Quick learners commit to exploration, experimentation, and trial and error to learn quickly by doing quickly.

Agile managers also focus on learning rather than on performance in the early stages of a project. They assess their knowledge by asking these questions: What is known? What could be known? How long would it take us to find out? What cannot be known? What will I have to figure out as I go? And, paradoxically, quick learning can be enhanced by reflection. Agile managers take time, however briefly, to reflect on and evaluate their actions. To become more agile, ask yourself these questions frequently: What happened today? What did I do? What was the result? What did I learn? How should I proceed?

Fast, flexible decision making. Effective strategic improvisation also requires fast, flexible decision making. Agile managers know how fast they need to be. They assess the strategic nature of time to establish the real timeframe for making a decision. They ask: What is the norm in the industry? How fast are our competitors? How important is the new, innovative, or trendy to our customers? How do our customers value speed versus perfection?

Agile managers also establish a clear decision-making process, knowing that uncertainty regarding authority can slow things down. Managers at all levels in the organization should know in advance when they can decide on their own and when it is necessary to consult others. They also need to be sure that everyone else is clear on their roles. Finally, agile managers maintain agility by making early decisions that allow flexibility. One agile manager likened the process to playing chess, a highly strategic game, in which flexibility is especially key in the opening moves. A good player uses opening moves that keep options open while at the same time shaping the trajectory of the game.

Extending one's reach. Agile managers use a broad network of relationships to mobilize the resources they need to move quickly. Although few control all the resources they need to get things done, they can reach out to others for help.

Nimble managers extend their reach in two ways. First, they take an active approach to developing a strong network of relationships. They map their current network, and then build relationships to fill the gaps. Second, they make it easy to connect to those who can help. They keep contact information complete, current, and accessible, and they use collaborative technology to provide quick access to and efficient use of others' expertise. Using this technology allows them to quickly combine their own expertise with that of others, in a reconfigurable network of relationships, to get things done.

The power of strategic improvisation

Using strategic improvisation, agile managers can deliver speed, flexibility, relevance, influence, and opportunity to benefit themselves and their companies. Strategic improvisation allows agile managers to move ahead quickly, making rapid decisions, in real time. It provides flexibility and relevance because plans are created to fit the changing situation and resources are configured to focus on the task. By being in the moment, strategic improvisation helps the agile manager shape the situation as it develops. And by focussing on strategic direction, the agile manager can maneuver quickly to capture relevant opportunities as they arise.

RESOURCES

Baker, W., *Achieving Success Through Social Capital*, Jossey-Bass, 2000.

Crossan, M., Klus, L., Lane, H. and White, R., 'The Improvising Organization: Where Planning Meets Opportunity,' *Organizational Dynamics*, Spring 1996, pp. 20–35.

De Meyer, A., Loch, C. and Pich, M., 'Managing Project Uncertainty: From Variation to Chaos,' MIT, *Sloan Management Review*, Winter 2002, pp. 60–67.

Kepner-Tregoe Business Issues Research Group, December 2000, *Decision Making in the Digital Age: Challenges and Responses*.

Korotov, K., Florent-Treacy, E. and Kets de Vries, M., Frontstep Russia (A & B): High-tech start-up and survival in a new 'time of troubles,' INSEAD, 2002.

Malhotra, A., Majchrzak, A., Carmen, R. and Lott, V., 'Radical Innovation without Collocation: A Case Study at Boeing-Rocketdyne,' *MIS Quarterly*, 25 (2): 229–249, June 2001.

Weldon, E., 'Fast Managers Use Strategic Improvising and Social Capital to Get Things Done,' *Perspectives for Managers*, IMD, #91, August 2002.

Commentary

Beware burnout

In the US, the phenomenon of career burnout has been recognized for many years. Employees who work too hard, for too long, can become demotivated, depressed, and in extreme cases become severely ill. The situation in the US is so bad that almost one-third of the workforce feels overworked or overwhelmed by the amount of work they have to do. Comparative figures are hard to come by, but anecdotal evidence suggests that the problem may be getting worse in the UK.

People talk a great deal about achieving a balance in their lives. Often, however, work takes over. Like the mythical village of Brigadoon, a perfect work–life balance remains an elusive concept, shrouded in a mist of conflicting needs and desires.

One obvious measure of the pressure on employees is the number of hours they work. "I personally work long hours, but not as long as I used to," Bill Gates once observed. "I certainly haven't expected other people to work as hard as I did. Most days I don't work more than 12 hours. On weekends I rarely work more than eight hours. There are weekends I take off and I take vacations." Not much room for a life, then.

When it comes to working hours Americans work the longest hours in the industrialized world. The average American worker clocks up nearly 2,000 hours at work every year. Despite the heady speed of technological innovation, American working hours have actually increased by 4 percent since 1980.[4] America fares badly compared with a wide range of nations. Norwegian workers work an average of 1,399 hours per year, while Japanese workers work nearly two weeks less than their American counterparts. The general trend is downwards. German hours fell from 1,742 to 1,560 between the 1980s and the late 1990s. At the same time as workers in Europe have been working fewer hours, productivity has actually been rising. Indeed, productivity growth of 22 percent in Western Europe since 1980 exceeds that experienced in the United States.

The tendency toward ever increasing hours at work is alarming. There is a well-documented connection between long working hours and ill-health. A five-year tracking study by the UK's Institute of Management and the University of Manchester Institute of Science and Technology found that the work and home life balance was still a pipe dream. Over 80 percent of executives worked more than 40 hours a week and one in ten worked over 60 hours. A depressing 86 percent said that the long hours had an effect on their relationship with their children and 71 percent said that it damaged their health.

"*Feeling Overworked: When Work Becomes Too Much*" is a survey conducted by the non-profit Families and Work Institute, supported by international accountancy firm PricewaterhouseCoopers.[5] Overworked was defined by the authors of the study as "a psychological state that has the potential to affect attitudes, behavior, social relationships, and health both on and off the job."

The study looked at a sample of 1,003 adults who performed paid work for an employer (as opposed to being self-employed). When asked how often they felt overworked and/or overwhelmed by work over a period of three months, over half said that they felt overworked and overwhelmed sometimes and a significant number said they felt that way most of the time.

Restructuring has added to job insecurity, reduced the number of employees, and heaped higher workloads on those who remain. Some workers pay the ultimate price for their loyalty. In Japan, a small number of managers are believed to die from work-related stress each year. The authors of a book on the subject claim that companies can no longer afford to ignore the problem. "Burnout is the outcome of a mismatch between workers and the workplace," say Michael P. Leiter and Christina Maslach, authors of *The Truth About Burnout*. "A critical point about burnout which is often missed is that it is a management problem, not simply an individual one. Too often managers side-step the issue as being either outside of their mandate or impossible to address."

Professor Andrew Kakabadse at the UK's Cranfield School of Management has also investigated the phenomenon of burnout as part of a worldwide study of top executive performance. His data, based on a detailed survey of 6,500 managers from 10 countries, suggests all leaders are prone to burnout, but their organizations are often embarrassed by the phenomenon and don't know what to do about it. "Corporate life requires deadlines to be met and inevitably workloads are unevenly shared, meaning that organizations generate their share of workaholics irrespective of the wishes of the individual," he says. "In addition, organizational chaos is rife, yet most workplaces still implicitly demand employees be 'corporate people,' living and dreaming about attaining success in organizational life."

Serious attention, Professor Kakabadse says, should be given to how burnout happens, how to recognize and cope with it, and how to combat it. The symptoms include:

- increasing fatigue;
- not listening effectively;
- feeling saturated with work;
- feeling unable to participate in routine operational conversations.

Commentary (continued)

What make the tell-tale signs hard to spot, however, is that declining morale and feelings of personal vulnerability usually emerge slowly and insidiously. "Increases in stress, job pressure, competition, higher work complexity, faster pace of life, and the greater likelihood of redundancy all make for an inevitable drip, drip of negativity which leads many top managers to burnout," says Professor Kakabadse.

Some of the causes of burnout can be linked to the removal of middle management tiers in many organizations, with more senior managers being required to undertake a greater volume of repetitive, detailed, and often tedious tasks.

The move to flatter management structures inevitably means that the spans of control are increasing, with managers having direct responsibility for a larger number of employees. In many cases, the traditional reporting spans have altered without sufficient support for managers who have to adapt to the new way of operating.

According to Dr Barrie Brown, a consultant psychologist: "The traditional view was that the optimal span for reporting lines was seven. Older managers – people aged 40 and over – were taught that directing the work of more than seven people makes it very difficult to remain in control. But some companies now have reporting spans of up to 150 people. If you double the number of people a manager is overseeing, then unless the manager delegates authority the workload will automatically double too."

The problem is compounded in companies where a macho "can do" culture means that delegating authority is viewed as a sign of weakness. Ambitious young managers can become obsessed with keeping their plates spinning to the detriment of their health. Flatter organization mean fewer promotions, with people stuck in the same job for longer periods. "Prolonged demotivation leads to an emotional deterioration which is worsened by a realization that to some extent current lifestyle traps us in our jobs," says Professor Kakabadse. "Age, difficulty in matching remuneration packages, and the continuity needed to support family life contribute to a sense of being trapped."

It is often worse for those further down the organization. Evidence suggests that stress is more pronounced among those who are not in control of their own destiny.

Employees who are suffering burnout and feeling overworked and overwhelmed by work are detrimental to an organization. According to the Families and Work Institute study, overworked employees are more likely to:

- make mistakes at work;

- resent their employers for expecting them to do so much;
- resent co-workers who do not work as hard as they do;
- look for a new job.

While these effects are bad for the employers, it gets worse for the employer. The study also found that employees who feel overworked:

- are more likely to suffer from sleep loss;
- are more likely to neglect themselves;
- are less likely to report very good or excellent health;
- feel less successful in personal relationships;
- experience more work–life conflict;
- have higher stress levels;
- are less able to cope with everyday life.

For anyone who recognizes these symptoms, who suffers from significant overwork or feels constantly overwhelmed by work, it's time to start thinking about a change. This doesn't necessarily mean finding a new employer. It might mean negotiating new hours, new workloads, or a different job within the same organization. However, it might also mean it is time for a new employer, or a new career.

"We want to have it all: More money – and more time. More success – a more satisfying family life. More creature comforts – and more sanity. We can work hard, we can find love and have a family, and we can enjoy the fruits of our success." So concluded a survey in *Fast Company* magazine. But for most people, the reality of working life is a far cry from this utopia. Equilibrium remains frustratingly elusive, burnout all too common.

Worked to death

At 8.30 a.m. on October 24, 1988, Satoshi Nagayama, aged 28, climbed out onto the rooftop of the Kawasaki Steel Corp. building in Tokyo, walked over to the edge, and threw himself to his death.

In April of that year Nagayama, a Kawasaki Steel employee with a promising career ahead of him, was asked to take on the development and implementation of an experimental plan. This was a task outside his normal responsibilities. Nagayama worked diligently on his new project. Too diligently. Most days he worked until midnight. He worked weekends. He worked holidays, including public holidays. He

Worked to death (continued)

even stayed at the office overnight. For the month of October 1988 his overtime amounted to 85.5 hours – excluding the overnight periods from midnight to 8.00 a.m. The night before he hurled himself to his death, Nagayama phoned his mother. He was exhausted he told her, and couldn't continue.

As tragic as it was, Nagayama's death wasn't entirely in vain. In a groundbreaking decision his death was found to be of an occupational cause by the Tokyo Central Labor Standards Inspection Offices (LSIO), one of the main local authorities that promote occupational safety and health.

Why did they come to this decision? For three main reasons. 1) He was mentally overstressed because he had almost sole responsibility for completing the planning project. Plus repeated modifications in the plan increased his workload. 2) From July 1988 onwards he exhibited the symptoms typical of reactive depression. The increased workload is believed to have aggravated the depression. 3) There was an absence of other factors that might have caused mental stress; it was therefore concluded that the depression which led to his untimely and tragic death was solely due to significantly heavy mental stress because of work. Nagayama's death and the resulting LSIO decision bought the issue of overwork in Japan into sharp focus.

The Japanese have a word for it: they call it *karoshi* – death by overwork. *Karoshi* became a social problem in the late 1980s. As the country's economic miracle ran out of steam, the number of hours put in by workers increased. As unemployment became a growing concern, the pressures on overworked salarymen intensified. Used to a job for life, the social stigma attached to redundancy means that workers are often unwilling to complain even when their workload has become unbearable. The Japanese government officially recognized *karoshi* as an occupational hazard in 1994.

In June 2000, the Japanese advertising company Dentsu made legal history by admitting responsibility for the *karoshi* of an employee who committed suicide in 1991. Ichori Oshima worked an average of 80 hours a week, on grueling shifts, sometimes toiling from 9.00 a.m. to 6.00 a.m. the following morning. The case against Mr Oshima's employer was pursued by his parents for eight years. The company belatedly demonstrated its remorse to the tune of Y168 million ($1.65 million). Sadly, however, Mr Oshima is not an isolated case.

The inevitable corporate restructuring of recent years has piled more work onto those who survived the job cuts. "Service overtime," or working beyond normal hours without payment, is a growing problem. Government figures show that there were a record 819 claims for compensation in the 2002–2003 period leading to 160 confirmed cases.

RESOURCES

Berglas, Steven, *Reclaiming the Fire: How Successful People Overcome Burnout*, Random House, 2001.

Demarco, Tom, Slack: *Getting Past Burnout, Busywork, and the Myth of Total Efficiency*, Broadway Books, 2001.

Maslach, Christina and Leiter, Michael P., *The Truth About Burnout*, Jossey-Bass, 1997.

Essentials

MANAGING YOURSELF AND YOUR CAREER

Carnegie, Dale

Dale Carnegie (1888–1955) was the first superstar of the self-help genre. Go forth with a smile on your face and a song in your heart and sell, sell, sell. His successors, whether they be Anthony Robbins or Stephen Covey, should occasionally doff their caps in Carnegie's direction.

First, Carnegie presented the "fundamental techniques in handling people" – "don't criticize, condemn, or complain; give honest and sincere appreciation; and arouse in the other person an eager want." To these he added six ways to make people like you – "become genuinely interested in other people; smile; remember that a person's name is to that person the sweetest and most important sound in any language; be a good listener – encourage others to talk about themselves; talk in terms of the other person's interests; make the other person feel important – and do it sincerely."

Born on a Missouri farm, Carnegie began his working life selling bacon, soap, and lard for Armour & Company in south Omaha. He turned his sales territory into the company's national leader, but then went to New York to study at the American Academy of Dramatic Arts. Realizing the limits of his acting potential, Carnegie returned to salesmanship, selling Packard automobiles. It was then that Carnegie persuaded the YMCA schools in New York to allow him to conduct courses in public speaking.

Carnegie's talks became highly successful. So successful, in fact, that he turned them into a string of books: *Public Speaking and Influencing Men in Business*; *How to Stop Worrying and Start Living*; *How to Enjoy Your Life and Your Job*; *How to Develop Self-Confidence and Influence People by Public Speaking*; and his perennial bestseller, *How to Win Friends and Influence People*, which has sold over 15 million copies.

It is easy to sneer at Carnegie's work – it is homespun wisdom adorned with commercial know-how. But it is difficult to sneer at the enduring popularity of his books and his company's training programs. Long after his death, they continue to strike a chord with managers and aspiring managers because they deal with the universal challenge of face-to-face communication.

Machiavelli, Niccolo

Power is a fact of corporate life. And its patron saint is undoubted: the

Florentine diplomat and author Niccolo Machiavelli (1469–1527). Machiavelli's bible on power is *The Prince*. Within it, embedded beneath details of Alexander VI's tribulations, lie a ready supply of aphorisms and insights that are, perhaps sadly, as appropriate to many of today's managers and organizations as they were half a millennium ago.

Machiavelli portrayed a world of cunning and brutal opportunism. "I believe also that he will be successful who directs his actions according to the spirit of the time, and that he whose actions do not accord with the time will not be successful," he wrote.

He gave advice on managing change and sustaining motivation, and even had advice for executives acquiring companies in other countries: "But when states are acquired in a country differing in language, customs, or laws, there are difficulties, and good fortune and great energy are needed to hold them, and one of the greatest and most real helps would be that he who has acquired them should go and reside there ... Because if one is on the spot, disorders are seen as they spring up, and one can quickly remedy them; but if one is not at hand, they are heard of only when they are great, and then one can no longer remedy them." Executives throughout the world will be able to identify with this analysis.

Above all, Machiavelli was the champion of leadership through cunning and intrigue, the triumph of force over reason. An admirer of Borgia, he had a dismal view of human nature. Unfortunately, as he sagely pointed out, history has repeatedly proved that a combination of being armed to the teeth and devious is more likely to allow you to achieve your objectives. It is all very well being good, said Machiavelli, but the leader "should know how to enter into evil when necessity commands."

RESOURCES

Maslach, Christina and Leiter, Michael P., *The Truth About Burnout*, Jossey-Bass, 1997.

REFERENCES

1 Read *Well-Being and the Workplace* by Professor Peter Warr (Chapter 20 in *Well Being: The Foundations of Hedonic Psychology* edited by D. Kahneman, E. Deiner and N. Schwarz. New York: Russell Sage Foundation, 1999).
2 McLynn, Frank, *Carl Gustav Jung*, St Martin's Press, New York, 1997.
3 Wilde, Oscar, *De Profundis: The Complete Text* by Holland, Vyvyan (ed.) New York: Philosophical Library: 1950.
4 Surveys have found that employees believe working continually long hours affects their health. *The Family Friendly Workplace: An investigation into long hours cultures and family friendly employment practices*, London: Austin Knight, 1995. *Breaking the Long Hours Culture* by Kodz, J., Kersley, B., Strebler, M. T. and O'Regan, S., Brighton: IES, 1998.
5 Galinsky, E., Kim, S. and Bond, J., *Feeling Overworked: When Work Becomes Too Much*, Families and Work Institute, 2001.

– CHAPTER 6 –
Making it happen

"Strategy will involve change and change is something that is here to stay. Managers throughout the business and at all levels have got to recognize the management of change (project management) as a core skill and so opportunities as *managers of projects* will become a key building block of experience in most people's careers."

Tony Greener

"For those of you considering being on a project – executive summary: Run Away!! Run Away!!"

Scott Adams

"Any fool can take off in an aircraft, but it takes a pilot to land it safely."

Anon

"To bring out the very best in the very best people, managers must create clarity on an on-going basis around three key questions: Which roles are being played by which people in pursuit of which missions? Where does each employee's responsibility begin and end? And, how and for what will each contributor be held accountable?"

Bruce Tulgan

"Opportunity is missed by most people because it is dressed in overalls and looks like work."

Thomas A. Edison

"Never mistake motion for action."

Ernest Hemingway

"The mad rush to improve performance and to pursue excellence has multiplied the number of demands on executives and managers. These demands come from every part of business and personal life, and they increasingly seem incompatible and impossible."

Rosabeth Moss Kanter

H.O.T. Management™

BRUCE TULGAN

[Making it happen demands that managers are hands-on and transactional.]

Managers in every workplace are engaged in a tug of war. On one side, employers are demanding more work and better work out of people – often out of fewer people, with fewer resources. On the other, employees are feeling pressured, overworked, and in need of some relief in the form of flexible working conditions, or at least some incentives for all their hard work. Stuck in the middle, trying to negotiate these competing needs, is every single person with supervisory authority.

I coined the term H.O.T. Management™ to describe the highly engaged management style of the most effective supervisory managers in today's extremely demanding workplace. H.O.T. is an acronym that stands for hands-on and transactional.

The fundamental principle of H.O.T. Management is that the most successful approach to supervisory management nowadays is to be transactional, rather than hierarchical. That means there is a quid pro quo for everything: if employees want rewards, they simply must perform. The more employees perform, the more rewards they receive. And high performance is the only option. Equally important is the emphasis on being hands-on, rather than hands-off. If managers are going to be transactional, they must be extremely knowledgeable about the work their direct reports are doing, they must spend a lot of time with direct reports spelling out expectations, clarifying standards, and defining goals and deadlines. And they must have the guts to hold employees accountable.

Our research indicates that when managers take this hands-on and transactional approach to managing, they are able to do much more for employees. At the same time, they are able to require much more from employees. This results in much higher productivity, quality, morale, and retention of high performers.

What do you have to do to become a H.O.T. Manager?

1. Become extremely knowledgeable about the tasks and responsibilities of your direct reports.

2. Start spending time with every direct report in daily coaching sessions.
3. Focus your daily coaching sessions on performance standards and concrete assignments – that means talking about clear goals and deadlines.
4. Provide regular direction, guidance, support, and coaching.
5. Start a written tracking system to monitor and measure every individual's performance on a daily basis.
6. Understand, accept, and embrace the new reality that managing people has become a day-to-day negotiation.
7. Decide what your deal breakers are – what's not open to negotiation – and then be prepared to negotiate regularly about everything else.
8. Whenever possible, tie financial rewards (and detriments) to measurable instances of employee performance and nothing else.
9. Be creative and use your discretion and discretionary resources to tie non-financial rewards, incentives, and benefits to measurable instances of employee performance.
10. Look for every employee's needle in a haystack and use those needles to make custom deals with individual performers in exchange for exceptional performance.
11. Have the discipline and guts to enforce every deal you make and don't flinch when it comes to providing the promised rewards and detriments.
12. And remember: You cannot be hands-on without being transactional, and you cannot be transactional without being hands-on.

Being hands-on is not the same as micro-management

There has been so much emphasis on empowerment in recent years that supervisory managers have moved too far away from providing direction. If you want to empower direct reports, you simply must define the terrain in which they have power. That terrain consists of effectively delegated goals, with clear guidelines, and concrete deadlines. It is within this terrain that a direct report has power. I call that terrain the circle of empowerment.

Mastering the articulation of goals, deadlines, and guidelines is mastering the art of effective delegation. That is the hard work of managing people. If you don't do that work, you are not "empowering," but rather, you are negligent. The trick is in figuring out, with each person and each instance of delegation, the following: How large should the goal be? How far out should the deadline be? How many guidelines are necessary? In other words, how big should the circle of empowerment be? Here is the answer: as a direct report demonstrates proficiency and performance, you should enlarge the circle a little bit at a time until you reach the person's appropriate sphere of responsibility. If there is a new project, you should usually shrink the circle. If you need to increase productivity and quality, it often helps to shrink the circle. If there is a performance problem, definitely shrink the circle until the problem is corrected.

Getting started: introduce your team to H.O.T. Management

Before you undertake a major shift in your management style and start implementing H.O.T. Management, you should prepare your team for the changes ahead. You will have to announce this coming change in your management style. How are you going to do that?

First, you should consider holding a meeting with your whole team to announce the change: "More is expected of us all and I want you to know that I am going to try very hard to be a better manager ... Here's what I'm going to do." Be prepared to deal with the fact that a lot of your team members might think this is just the management flavor of the month. So, before you hold your team meeting, you had better be sure, at least in your own mind, that this is something you are going to stick with. Let people know that this is not a fly-by-night idea. This is something you are going to start doing, something that you are going to stick with, and something that is not going to go away.

Don't be surprised if your team meeting turns into an intense discussion about the past, present, and future of your team. Think through all the things you are going to say, the likely questions you are going to face, and how you are going to answer those questions. Don't forget that some questions will be better answered one-on-one between you and a direct report. And also please remember, sometimes the best response is, "I don't know yet. We'll have to see how it goes."

Once you've had your team meeting, your next step will be to have an initial meeting with each individual on your team. Those initial meetings should start out the same way: "More is expected of all of us and I'm going to try to be a better manager ... Here's what I'm going to do." Be prepared: every person is going to want to figure out exactly what H.O.T. Management is going to mean for him/her. Remember that when you are holding these initial meetings, you are presenting good news, not bad news. You are committing yourself and your team to a management relationship that ensures high performance all the time. And you are going to make sure that rewards follow performance, every step of the way.

The centerpiece: regular coaching sessions

The centerpiece and the very most important practice of H.O.T. Management is the daily (or every other day, or at least once a week) coaching session with every person. Why is it so important to have regular coaching sessions?

First, preparing for your regular session will force you and your direct report to remain up to speed and up to date about the key details of your direct reports' tasks and responsibilities. Second, the very act of making time several times a week to discuss expectations is a tremendous source of psychological and actual accountability. When managers and direct reports talk regularly about the details of the work to be done, the relationship takes on a new focus: it becomes a partnership of shared expectations for high performance. Third, the daily coaching session is a chance to check in and make sure there is nothing in the way of performance, nothing in the way of getting lots of work done very well very fast all day long. Fourth, the meeting is also a chance for managers to engage in important reminders, for managers to teach, for managers to test the knowledge and preparedness of direct reports, to make sure direct reports are on board and engaged, and to generate some urgency.

So this is the most important habit to create: schedule and carry out a regular meeting with every direct report every day (or every other day or once a week). You have to make the time. You have to create the habit. Of course, every conversation will be different with every person every time. But there are some basics to every conversation that should remain consistent. Your regular meetings should follow this basic format.

1. Has anything happened since our last meeting that I should know about?
2. Let's review progress from our last meeting. Last time we talked about (some or all of the following):
    – performance standards
    – goals, guidelines, and deadlines
    – specific to-do list
    – resource needs
    – troubleshooting
    – what you need from me
    – anything else.
3. Please give me an update, a report on your progress on each item. OK, here's my evaluation and feedback on (some or all of the following):
    – performance standards
    – goals, guidelines, and deadlines
    – specific to-do list
    – resource needs

- troubleshooting
- what you need from me
- anything else.

4. Here's what I want you to do next on (some or all of the following):
   - performance standards
   - goals, guidelines, and deadlines
   - specific to-do list
   - resource needs
   - troubleshooting
   - what you need from me
   - anything else.

5. Do you understand? Is that fair? Is there anything you need from me?

Remember that every individual is different and work is a moving target. The daily meeting format is just a broad outline. You must take charge and offer clear direction in the form of performance standards, concrete goals, deadlines, guidelines, and parameters, but it is also important to get input from your direct reports throughout the process. Talk through standards, goals, deadlines, and guidelines, and try to reach a mutual agreement about what is reasonable, anticipate problems and resource needs together, strategize together about how to reach ambitious targets, and give your direct reports some ownership and complicity in the goal-setting process. You'll have to be prepared to negotiate every step of the way (at least anything that isn't one of your deal breakers).

The manager's notebook: you need a tracking system

Next to the daily coaching sessions, the most important discipline of H.O.T. Management is documentation. I don't care what you call it: taking notes, a tracking system, keeping a written contemporaneous record, making a paper trail. Whatever you call it, you must make an absolute habit of taking written notes of each coaching session with each direct report. First, written notes will help you keep track of all the details of all the work of all your direct reports. Second, written notes will help you create clarity around expectations for you and your direct report. Third, written notes create psychological and actual accountability. Fourth, written notes create the documentation you'll need in the case of informal or formal disputes, or when you want to justify giving a direct report special rewards.

What should you write down? Just keep a running log of your routine coaching sessions (and any special sessions) with every direct report. We recommend organizing and keeping a "manager's notebook," in which you make all of your running notes about your management relationship with each direct report. Organize the notebook as a tracking system, both chronologically and by person. Then keep track of the essential details of your discussions of the following:

- reminders about overall performance standards;
- goals;
- deadlines;
- guidelines and parameters;
- anticipating and planning for resource needs;
- anticipating and planning to avoid problems;
- questions asked by your direct report;
- requests made by your direct report;
- any quid pro quo you have promised in exchange for specific performance;
- any other special issues that come up.

You should refer your on-going log before every session with a direct report. Make any notes in advance that you need to make in preparation for the coaching session. Then make notes during the conversation as necessary. And you should stop after every discussion, go over your written notes, and make sure that you've noted everything of consequence.

The manager's notebook is not just a paper trail. It is a management tool to help you drive performance, track performance, and stay on top of the details of every direct report's tasks and responsibilities. For that reason, you should keep your manager's notebook in whatever format works best for you. Some people choose to keep their contemporaneous record in electronic form on a computer. Others prefer to keep an old-fashioned written notebook. Once you've decided on whether to keep your notebook in writing or electronic form, you should create a structured form to use. The idea is to create standard fill-in-the-blank pages that makes sense to you and your direct report and that will be easy to use and understand.

Doing more for people: using bargaining chips to drive performance

If you want to be effective as a H.O.T. Manager, you have to be able to put your money (and non-financial rewards) where your mouth is. You have to be able to do more for your direct reports. We all know of managers who do more for their people. Right? They bend over backwards, jump through hoops, and go to bat to get more resources for their team. If you are not one of those managers, what is your problem? Being a manager who can do more for your people is an important source of transactional power.

The real trick, though, is that you have to have the discipline to do more for your direct reports only when they do more for you. That is the art of the quid pro quo. "Here's what I need from you. What do you need from me?"

First, let me offer another reminder: if you are going to commit to performance-based rewards, which is the essence of the bargaining chip approach, you must commit to doing it properly. That means you must give every person the opportunity to succeed against clearly defined expectations and, in return, earn performance-based rewards. You must spell out up-front the performance necessary to earn rewards. You must make sure it is clear every step of the way. You must document the mutual promises you and your direct report make to each other. And you must monitor and measure the performance of the direct report against his/her promises. Then you must make every effort to deliver on your end of the deal.

Whenever I start talking about bargaining chips, managers often tell me that they don't have the power to change the compensation system or they don't have the influence necessary to make custom deals with direct reports. Based on my experience, I can tell you what we've learned: you will never be able to do everything for everybody. But you can almost always do more for almost everyone. You just have to be willing to bend over backward and jump through hoops.

That's why, in your dealings with direct reports, you should always make clear what is within your sphere of authority and influence and what may not be. Sometimes you can say, "I can do that." Sometimes you must say, "I'll try to do that." Sometimes you have to say, "I can't do that, but I can do this." If you are managing a cashier in retail, for example, you probably won't be able to let that person be a telecommuter, but you might be able to offer more scheduling flexibility. And so on. In some cases, a requested reward is simply out of proportion to the performance in question: You might say, "Can you work late?" And the direct report might say, "Only for $1,000." And you might have to say, "Come on, that's ridiculous." Remember, the negotiation is always on. There are still other times when you might think that a direct report's request is reasonable and appropriate, but you are just not sure you can make it happen. That's a good time to say, "I don't know if I can do it. But I will promise you this: I will go to bat for you." Even if you cannot make something happen for a direct report, sometimes it can be a valuable reward just knowing that you, the supervisor, are willing to go to bat for your people when they work hard for you.

By uncovering a whole menu of things to offer in return for high performance, you will open up the terrain of possibilities for motivating your team. The more bargaining chips you have at your disposal, the more leverage you have to drive smarter, faster, better performance. Here's the process we recommend:

- *Step one.* Evaluate all the resources at your disposal under the current system. Often you will find there are opportunities to position rewards in exchange for performance under the system as it is.

- *Step two.* Brainstorm ways to get discretionary resources in your control.

Think about what you've done in the past. Think about what your colleagues have done. Think about what those managers who do more for their people are doing.

- *Step three*. In all of your dealings with direct reports, try to position all rewards in exchange for performance. All requests made by direct reports should be considered only in relation to a quid pro quo of specific performance requirements. The same goes for any reward you consider giving to a direct report. And you should always consider offering a special reward when you are asking for performance above and beyond the norm. You must get in the habit of saying, "You want this? OK. Here's what I need from you. If you deliver for me, I'll do my best to deliver for you."

If you want to take the bargaining chip approach one step further, you are ready to make custom deals with your high performers. How? By finding and using needles in a haystack, one person at a time, one day at a time. Needles in a haystack are those unique needs and wants of individual direct reports. Sometimes they can be granted, sometimes not. Just take the bargaining chip transactional approach one step further. When a direct report makes a special request or when you want to make a special request of a direct report, think about what that person wants/needs and determine whether you can offer a win–win transaction. "I'll do this for you, if you do x,y,z for me." Remember, granting a direct report a custom deal is an exceptional reward, so you should require exceptional performance in exchange. And it must be 100 percent clear that the deal is always on the table, contingent on continued high performance.

High performance is the only option: dealing with performance problems

What do you do when, despite your regular coaching, a direct report fails to meet your regularly stated performance standards and the daily goals and deadlines that you agree on together? As soon as a person's performance starts to slip, you need to take action right away.

Here is our six-step approach to dealing with performance problems:

- *Step one*. Be even more hands-on for a while. Step up your schedule of coaching sessions and meet every day or twice a day if necessary. Set smaller goals with shorter deadlines. Be even more explicit about your expectations and make sure the direct report in question understands.
- *Step two*. If the problem persists, diagnose the problem in terms of ability, skill, and/or will. If the problem is ability, then your direct report's natural strengths are not a good match with some or all of the tasks and

responsibilities in his/her current role. If the problem is skill, then the employee needs additional training. If the problem is will, then either the problem is internal and requires outside help, or the problem is external and the employee requires stronger incentives to perform.

- *Step three.* Prepare to engage the direct report in a performance improvement intervention. This means you must review all of your notes and documentation, clarify what's wrong, and be prepared with specific examples, as well as an approach to solving the problem.
- *Step four.* Consult your allies in HR and discuss the matter to make sure you are following all the proper procedures.
- *Step five.* Create a script for your performance improvement conversation, rehearse the script, and then carry out the conversation.
- *Step six.* After the conversation, follow up aggressively and try to turn the downward spiral into an upward spiral. You'll have to meet with this direct report for frequent coaching sessions until the employee demonstrates improved performance and starts consistently meeting goals and deadlines with all the guidelines and parameters.

What if, despite your best efforts to turn around the performance problem of a direct report, the problem continues? I believe, as strongly as I believe anything, that if you cannot help an employee improve, you simply must remove that person from your team. There are four reasons to remove stubborn low performers ASAP. First, low performers get paid. Second, low performers cause problems that high performers have to fix. Third, high performers hate to work with low performers. Fourth, low performers send a terrible message to the rest of the team, your vendors, and your customers: "Low performance is an option around here." Don't let them send that message. Instead, send another message: "High performance is the only option around here."

Of course, there will be obstacles to H.O.T. Management. This is the real world. Be honest with yourself about which ones are truly out of your control. Those things that are truly out of your control are simply not your concern any more. Why should they be? You cannot control them. First, focus on what you can control. Be thorough and courageous and tackle those obstacles. Second, it is my experience that there are no 100 percent obstacles. So be honest with yourself about that too. Recognize that of course you won't be able to implement H.O.T. Management 100 percent. So what? Deal with the obstacles. Work around them. What if you can only implement H.O.T. Management 20 percent or 30 percent or 40 percent or 50 percent or 60 percent or 70 percent or 80 percent or 90 percent? There are no 100 percent solutions to anything. So, do as much as you can today. And try to do even more tomorrow.

RESOURCES

Tulgan, Bruce, *H.O.T. Management*, HRD Press 2004.

Decision making: risk and escalation

HELGA DRUMMOND

> Making a wrong decision is bad enough, throwing good money after bad by persisting with the wrong course of action is worse. It's a phenomenon called escalation and, surprisingly, it's something many managers do. However, it can be avoided.

Almost all decisions involving uncertainty have some unintended consequences. Sometimes, however, the results are the very opposite of what was hoped for.

When it becomes obvious that a venture is failing, managers may be faced with a choice between cutting their losses or persisting in the hope of eventually succeeding though at the risk of making matters worse. History is rich in examples of managers choosing to carry on to the bitter end. For example, US film studio United Artists continued making *Heaven's Gate* even though it knew that the venture might put the studio out of business – as indeed it did. Barings continued posting millions of pounds in collateral to support Nick Leeson's trading even though the financial markets in the Far East were ablaze with rumors suggesting that Barings was close to collapse.

Why do experienced and sophisticated managers behave in such an apparently irrational way? The issue is important because although market forces eventually curb non-viable ventures, they are frequently slow to act. By the time such forces play themselves out the damage is usually well and truly done. Meanwhile organizations may incur needless losses that are ultimately passed on to society in higher prices, diminished pension funds, and other losses.

Over-optimistic

Part of the problem is that we know a lot more about how to galvanize organizations into action than we do about how to stop them if they start to move in the wrong direction. That said, research by social scientists offers some clues. For example, the most dangerous time in a new venture is usually at an early stage. Enthusiasm and confidence tend to be high. Almost anything appears possible, so much so that ventures can appear more important than they really are. It is also a time when decisions are taken that can subsequently return to haunt the takers.

United Artists, for example, was ecstatic when it succeeded in contracting the hugely successful Michael Cimino to produce *Heaven's Gate*. Believing that it could not fail with Cimino in charge, United Artists agreed to all his conditions, including complete artistic freedom, absolute control over the making of the film, and other onerous terms.

Technically, a decision fails if expectations are not met. In order to gain support a prospective venture has to promise much. The trouble is that managers frequently create problems for themselves by promising too much at the outset only to discover that they are unable to deliver. Eurotunnel, for example, assured prospective investors that constructing the Channel Tunnel would be a fairly easy task and even if there were problems the venture would still yield fabulous profits.

In theory, managers can protect themselves against making rash promises by taking an analytical approach to decision making. In practice, planning can actually produce myopic vision.

Planning involves envisaging something that does not yet exist. It is basically dreaming with discipline. What can happen is that the plans are made to fit the dream. Estimates of costs are pared down, projected revenues are scaled up, and timescales shortened until the venture makes economic sense. For example, when planners say that Manchester's new tramline extension will carry 45 million passengers a year, how do they know? What they really mean is that it *had better* carry that number of passengers if the venture is to be financially viable. What is really frightening, however, is that decisions can be authorized even though the figures are absurd. For example, the attendance estimates for the Canadian Expo 86 trade fair assumed that every man, woman, and child in Canada would visit the fair at least once.

It is easy to say we would never allow such things to happen. But research suggests that as human beings we are more sensitive to the relative magnitude of change than the absolute magnitude. This means that managers can easily lose sight of the totality of tinkering and fine-tuning that may lie behind best-laid plans. In addition, research suggests that the very existence of a plan (especially if it is supported with copious information) can make managers overconfident. Indeed, business plans can be made to sound so convincing that it is easy to forget that they are only guesswork.

Unreasonable behavior

Few things are achieved without will and determination. Yet we can become so obsessed in the pursuit of an ambition that it becomes an obsession. Although the cliché states that something is worth what someone is willing to pay for it, that does not always turn out to be true.

The auction of the UK's third-generation (3G) mobile phone licenses may turn out to be a case in point. Analysts forecast that the winning contenders might end up paying as much as £3 billion. In fact, the auction raised over £20 billion, the real winner being the government. The *Financial Times* called it "the most expensive poker game in history" and "a gamble of heroic proportions" by companies desperate for additional spectrum but which "were bidding without knowing what the services will look like, or how many people will be prepared to pay a premium for them. In effect, they are buying an option that may never come into the money."

Perceived need may not have been the only factor fueling an auction. Our determination to succeed is not always driven by reason. To illustrate the point to MBA students I sometimes auction a textbook that will be useful to them on the course. There is no reserve price on the book so in theory an impecunious student could acquire it for as little as one pence compared with a cover price of £20. There is a catch, however, in that the second-highest bidder must also pay the bid price. Students typically start bidding and racking up the stakes for fun but inevitably two parties become trapped in an ascending spiral. The book almost always sells for at least double the cover price, though bids of £70 (with £50 as the second-highest bid) have been achieved. When students are questioned afterwards about what drives them to make such extravagant bids, they frequently report that they would rather pay money than lose face.

Just how many dangerous price wars between newspapers, airlines, and supermarkets have been perpetuated for the same reason? Did Motorola really say it would rather throw its prestigious Startac telephones in the dustbin than bring down the price to a level that ordinary consumers could afford?

Research suggests that our unwillingness to appear foolish in front of other people in scenarios like the book auction may mean that bidding becomes driven by the desire for revenge. When someone humiliates us they damage our self-esteem. Revenge is sweet because it restores it. Since self-esteem may be worth more than money, no price may be too high if it enables us to achieve restoration. Business is by nature competitive and competition creates winners and losers. Just how many ill-advised mergers and acquisitions, for example, have actually been motivated by a desire for revenge?

Taking a reality check

The reckoning comes when plans and reality meet. The sequence is like a medieval cart piled high with pottery setting out along a rutted road. The result may be a chain reaction as one bad decision forces another.

The London Stock Exchange learned this lesson when it agreed with the financial establishment's demand that Project Taurus, which began in 1986, an £80 million computer system aimed at enabling paperless share trading, would be completed in 18 months – a ridiculously ambitious timescale for such a huge infrastructure project.

Having committed itself, the Stock Exchange then decided that the only way to meet the deadline was to buy a software package known as Vista to drive the system. Vista is a good package but it was never designed for the uniquely complex UK stock market. A rule of thumb in software engineering is that if alterations to a package are likely to exceed 50 percent, it is better to build from scratch. Once it had started on the task, however, there was no question of abandoning the Vista package, despite the near insuperable difficulties of adapting it. The budget for reengineering Vista was £4 million. When the Stock Exchange canceled the project three years later the cost had risen to over three times that and the task was still far from complete.

It is not the inevitable breakages that do the damage, however, so much as managers' slowness to acknowledge failure, especially if they are liable to be held personally responsible for it. Instead they tend to go into denial, seizing on any information that seems to support their preconceived views, even if it means clutching at straws, while downplaying or even ignoring potentially ominous news. Since this process occurs unconsciously, managers can end up living in a fool's paradise while matters go from bad to worse. Managers may even develop a bunker mentality, cutting themselves off mentally and physically. In consequence they soon lose sight of reality altogether, just as Hitler retreated to his bunker only to end up issuing orders to an army and air force that no longer existed.

Chasing your losses

Experiments by psychologists have shown that people may go to extraordinary lengths to avoid loss, even if it means behaving recklessly. To be more precise, research has shown that faced with a choice between accepting a definite loss and the possibility of incurring a much greater loss later on, we tend to become *risk seeking*. To be risk seeking is to take a bigger gamble than objective conditions warrant – like betting on a long shot. Interestingly, most betting on long shots takes place during the last race as race-goers try to recoup earlier losses. By definition, gambling against heavy odds seldom pays off.

Taurus could have been canceled 18 months earlier. The Stock Exchange and, indeed, the financial community had so much invested in the project, however, that they decided to press on despite deepening unease. This compounded the waste of time and money. Likewise, officials' unwillingness to slaughter a few thousand cattle as a precaution when BSE was first diagnosed in the UK led to the destruction of millions of healthy cattle later on.

The experience of loss can affect us in other ways. Research by psychologists suggests that loss has more impact than gain. For example, the pain of losing a £20 note is much greater than the pleasure experienced in finding the same amount. In the context of business strategy, managers may react irrationally to losing market share or part of the business by engaging in an all-out effort to win it back. It is not the initial loss that does the damage but the opportunity cost of expending resources in a futile quest.

It is not only monetary loss that we dislike. Flagship ventures can absorb huge resources and create huge opportunity costs for little strategic value. Yet organizations cling to them, fearing the loss of prestige. Barclays Bank should have disposed of its merchant-banking acquisition BZW when it became obvious that the merger had failed. Instead, Barclays clung to the dream of becoming a global investment bank for over a decade only to end up, according to analysts, virtually paying Credit Suisse First Boston to take BZW off its hands.

More recently, the London-based restaurant chain Chez Gerard has suffered severely thanks to a failed ambition for expansion into the provinces. If it had closed the loss-making restaurants and accepted the loss of prestige it might have avoided the possible humiliation of a takeover bid.

Generally speaking, it becomes more difficult to terminate a failing course of action as time passes. Outside investors may have a stake in the outcome. Sponsors expect to see results. Staff may be recruited and whole departments created to support the venture. What manager wants to rock the boat? Eventually the venture may acquire a taken-for-granted status. That is, it survives because no one dares to question it.

Some projects, however, are retained because they are too expensive to close. When Chicago's new sewer system was finally completed it was so poor that it was inevitably described as money down the drain by the media. Yet there was no possibility of starting again – it was just too expensive. A more recent white elephant is Sheffield's "super tram" system. The trams have never carried anywhere near the number of passengers originally forecast but the sheer cost of ripping up the tracks means that it would be unthinkable to abandon the project.

So-called long-haul projects that require huge investment and yield no revenues until the work is finished are particularly fraught because time equals risk. Concorde was planned when aviation fuel was cheap. By the time the plane entered service, however, that situation no longer applied – one reason why the development costs have never been recouped. How will the market for mobile telephones have changed by the time 3G applications become available?

Ironically it is the managers with the most successful track records who are most prone to making the kind of misjudgements that lead to escalation. This is because as human beings we interpret success as confirming our competence even if it is due entirely to luck. Repeated success can be dangerous because it makes us feel infallible and therefore encourages us to take bigger and bigger risks. Research into gambling behavior has shown that players who experience early wins in games of chance tend to bet more than their less successful counterparts. Repeated success can undermine a manager's decision-making ability because it leads to complacency. For example, repeated success may tempt a manager to dispense with market research and rely upon hunches because he or she has always been right in the past. The trouble is that the reason they were successful was because they took the trouble to conduct careful market research. Inevitably there comes a reckoning.

Although the precise links between escalation and perceived self-efficacy are unclear, managers with successful track records are more likely to persist in the face of failure because their self-confidence tells them they will win through in the end. It can be very hard for those unaccustomed to failure to recognize the limits of their powers. Sometimes it takes a severe shock, such as a profits warning, to force them to recognize reality. By then, however, it may be too late.

Managing escalation

First, ask: What might you be getting into? The Chinese proverb "he who rides a tiger can never dismount" suggests that it is easier to get into something than it is to get out of it. It is important to think through the implications of embarking on a course of action that may seem to involve little risk and can easily be broken off if it fails. The decision by fast-food chain McDonald's to sue environmental campaigners John Morris and Helen Steel for libel was a public relations disaster. Yet McDonald's did not begin by issuing writs, it merely sought an apology.

As human beings we tend to be more aware of why we are doing something rather than what we may be doing. The trick is to consider the significance and possible long-term consequences of embarking upon a particular course of action. Although decision making is surrounded by doubt, there are also some certainties. A decision is like a bridge – it separates us from some future state. A question that should always be asked before crossing that bridge is: "If I do X, what will definitely follow?" For example, anyone who enters my book auction risks becoming trapped in a bidding war. Yet few students think about what they might be getting into and what a few moments of fun might end up costing them. The wisest students in my book auction are those who never bid.

In theory, withdrawal is always an option. Yet it may be wiser to assume the opposite and then consider whether a decision still makes sense. Quite simply, once you invest resources in a venture, you are committed and therefore bound to deliver, come what may. This applies particularly to long-haul projects. In the words of the aviation industry, managers should always remember that although take-off is optional, landing is compulsory.

Begin with doubts. It was Francis Bacon who said that it is better to begin with doubts than certainty. All decisions involving uncertainty run the risk of failing to turn out as expected, no matter how rock solid they may appear. For example, McDonald's had good reason to believe that an apology would be forthcoming because of its experience of similar cases. To McDonald's surprise and consternation, however, Steel and Morris refused to apologize.

It can be difficult for managers to resist becoming caught up in a tidal wave of enthusiasm that may accompany a prospective new venture. The best way of countering myopic vision is to confront the risks and the possible downside of a venture in addition to conducting a conventional cost/benefit analysis. No one can make a decision without guessing what the future is likely to hold. Ultimately managers can only play their cards and take their chances. The point is that they must remember that they are doing precisely that.

What are you trying to achieve? Almost all ventures are a means to an end but they can become an end in themselves. Managers can become so absorbed in a particular venture that they develop tunnel vision. Completing the project becomes all-important at the expense of considering whether the project makes sense any more and whether there might be better or easier ways of reaching a particular goal. The solution is to stand back from things periodically and consider what you are trying to achieve.

Insist on facts, not optimism. The next question is how you can be sure of achieving the goal. This is where mental rigor and determination really count, as it is essential to pin others down to facts and figures. Managers also need to pay proper attention to what their information is telling them and resist the urge to escape into wishful thinking.

Winner's curse. As the saying goes, "you can have anything you want provided you are prepared to pay too much for it." Managers should set limits on their involvement and pull out once those limits are reached. This applies particularly to auctions, as emotions can run high and once the gavel falls you are committed. Besides, all auctions are a trap. This is because logically the true worth of an item is the second-highest bid, hence the aphorism "winner's curse."

Alternatives are power. It is easier to let go of a cherished ambition if there is something to take its place. Alternatives are a source of power. Managers who possess alternatives are much less likely to become caught up in an escalatory spiral or pay too high a price for something because the possession of alternatives increases their freedom of action and enables them to view competition with detachment.

Alternatives may not always be obvious but they can always be found provided managers are willing to expend time and effort looking for them. Indeed, the search for alternatives can be highly rewarding because it can generate possibilities that competitors miss in their relentless pursuit of a strategic imperative.

A becomes B by avoiding B. A fiasco does not just happen, it is created. Although management may involve the application of common sense, common sense can be wrong and managers need to develop an eye for a potentially destructive paradox. For example, our efforts to prevent something can create the very situation that we are trying to avoid. McDonald's sued in order to protect its reputation but did infinitely more damage than if it had simply ignored the protest. It never stopped to think whether the cure might be worse than the disease.

Another dangerous scenario is when people interfere with a project. Interference is often prompted by good intentions but ends up paving the road to hell because the venture effectively becomes something else. For example, what may have started as a simple project using tried-and-tested technology becomes more and more complicated and, therefore, more risky. It is like planning to build a tanker and ending up with a super-tanker. The result is not just a bigger ship but also a vessel with profoundly different handling characteristics.

Don't be afraid to hear the worst. It was Winston Churchill who said that in war truth is so precious that it must be guarded with a tissue of lies. The same can apply to failing ventures. It can be difficult for managers to discover the true state of affairs because politically adroit subordinates are only too aware of what can happen to messengers bringing bad news. The only way to counter such caution is to demonstrate, by deed, that you are equal to hearing the worst. Failing that, the best people to ask for information are junior staff working at the coal face. They may respond bluntly but that is because they are being honest.

Can the project be modified? Technically a venture fails when expectations cannot be met. A venture only really fails, however, when it no longer commands the support of people in the organization. It may be possible to restore support for a failing venture by redesigning it or by dividing it into smaller, less risky ventures. In order to do this it may be necessary to change the project manager and other key personnel. Dedicated and committed staff can become a liability if their passion descends into monomania.

Does the project still make sense? One way of resisting the temptation to engage in risk-seeking behavior is by acting on reality and thereby changing it. More specifically, we tend to become risk seeking when we see the situation as a choice between losses – either a definite loss at time A or a possible bigger loss at time B. The way out of this mental trap is to forget all about losses and simply to ask whether continuance represents the best return on investment or whether alternative courses of action might be more rewarding. Incidentally, this can mean terminating a successful venture if better opportunities become available.

It is not what has been done that managers should consider in making decisions about whether to quit or continue but what remains to be done. It is also important to bear in mind in any reassessment of a project that six months and £5 million could easily become 12 months and £10 million. The golden rule in poker is that no matter how much money you have invested, if the odds are against you – quit. It is good advice for managers too.

A good decision maker has no ego

In theory, ego is easily subtracted from the equation because it is within the control of the individual. In practice, subtracting ego can be very difficult, though not impossible. One possibility is to consider what ego-defensiveness is going to cost. Another technique is to imagine how a detached outsider might weigh up the situation. For example, the *Financial Times* Lex column might say: "The offer for the company may be less than so and so would like but they should accept."

Although escalation is a trap, nothing need be inevitable. Setting one's ego aside can be the key to liberation. Significantly the word risk derives from the early-Italian *risicare*, meaning "to dare." It requires daring to persist against ever-widening odds just as it requires daring to say "stop." The point is that the notion to dare implies that escalation is not a fate but a choice.

RESOURCES

Bernstein, P.L., *Against the Gods*, Wiley, 1998.

Drummond, H., *Escalation in Decision Making: The Tragedy of Taurus*, Oxford University Press, 1996.

Drummond, H., *The Art of Decision Making*, Wiley, 2001.

Kahneman, D. and Tversky, A., 'The psychology of preferences,' *Scientific American*, 246, 162–170, 1982.

Staw, B.M., 'Escalation research: An update and appraisal,' in Z. Shapira (ed.), *Organizational Decision Making*, Cambridge, Cambridge University Press, 1996.

Taylor, S.E., *Positive Illusions*, Basic Books, 1980.

Teger, A.I., *Too Much Invested to Quit*, Pergamon, 1980.

This article previously appeared in *Business Strategy Review*, Volume 14, Issue 1, Spring 2003.

Measuring and managing the right things

MIKE KENNERLEY AND ANDY NEELY

[Focussing executive attention in the right places can boost individual and personal performance.]

It is an often quoted adage that what gets measured gets done. There can be little doubt that measuring performance significantly influences people's behavior and the results that they achieve. Unfortunately the media is littered with examples of the perverse behavior of people attempting to achieve performance targets or improve their position in league tables.

Used effectively measurement can help improve the effectiveness of executives by focussing their attention on the important issues in the achievement of strategy. Measurement can help managers clarify and communicate an organization's strategy as well as ensure that it is being executed effectively.

Clearly, however, to realize these benefits of measurement executives must ensure that they are measuring the right things and using the measures to make the right decisions and ensure the right actions are taken. While frameworks such as the balanced scorecard and performance prism can help executives identify appropriate measures, there is no universal answer that can be applied "off the shelf." Using the right tools and processes can ensure that a performance measurement system can be developed that will help to drive the organization toward achieving its strategic objectives.

Measuring the right things

Organizations have always measured performance. Historically this has been done through financial accounts. While traditional financial measures tell us the bottom-line score, they give little indication of how that score was achieved. Traditional financial measurement systems are criticized for being historical in nature, providing little indication of future performance, encouraging short termism, being internally rather than externally focussed with little regard for competitors or customers, lacking strategic focus, and often inhibiting innovation.

In their 1992 *Harvard Business Review* article, Bob Kaplan and David Norton introduced a measurement system designed to resolve the problems with traditional measurement systems – the balanced scorecard.[1] The balanced scorecard has become by far the most well known and accepted performance measurement framework. Research studies suggest that somewhere between 40 and 60 percent of organizations have implemented a balanced scorecard.

But what is a balanced scorecard?

Originally the balanced scorecard prompted users to identify an equal number of measures in each of four perspectives:

- financial perspective;
- customer perspective;
- internal perspective;
- innovation and learning perspective.

This demonstrated the need to balance financial and non-financial measures, internal and external measures, leading and lagging measures, and short- and long-term measures. The approach ensures that managers don't take a narrow view of performance based on too few measures.

Balanced scorecard has become common terminology among executives; however since its introduction the concept has evolved. With each of Kaplan and Norton's books on the subject (in 1996,[2] 2001,[3] and 2004[4]), less emphasis has been placed on the exact balance of measures and more on the need to explicitly link desired performance outcomes to the drivers that enable achievement of those outcomes.

Having balance in the number of measures is no longer considered strictly necessary. In fact Art Schneiderman, who developed the first scorecard while at US circuit manufacturer Analog Devices, argues that balance is actually harmful and that *"good scorecards will be unbalanced; containing mostly non-financial, internal, leading, short-term measures."*[5] As long as we understand how they contribute to the ultimate objective we will not be taking our eye off the ball.

Kaplan and Norton propose the use of strategy maps (sometimes referred to as success maps) to understand how the drivers of performance affect the top level objectives. Strategy or success maps explicitly link performance outcomes to the drivers of those outcomes. Figure 6.1 is an example of a success map which explicitly shows how non-financial, internal, leading, short-term measures such as employee development or employee satisfaction affect financial, external, lagging, long-term measures such as return on capital employed or profit growth. The success or strategy map provides a model of the performance of the organization which tells the story of the organization's strategy that can be presented on a single piece of paper. When

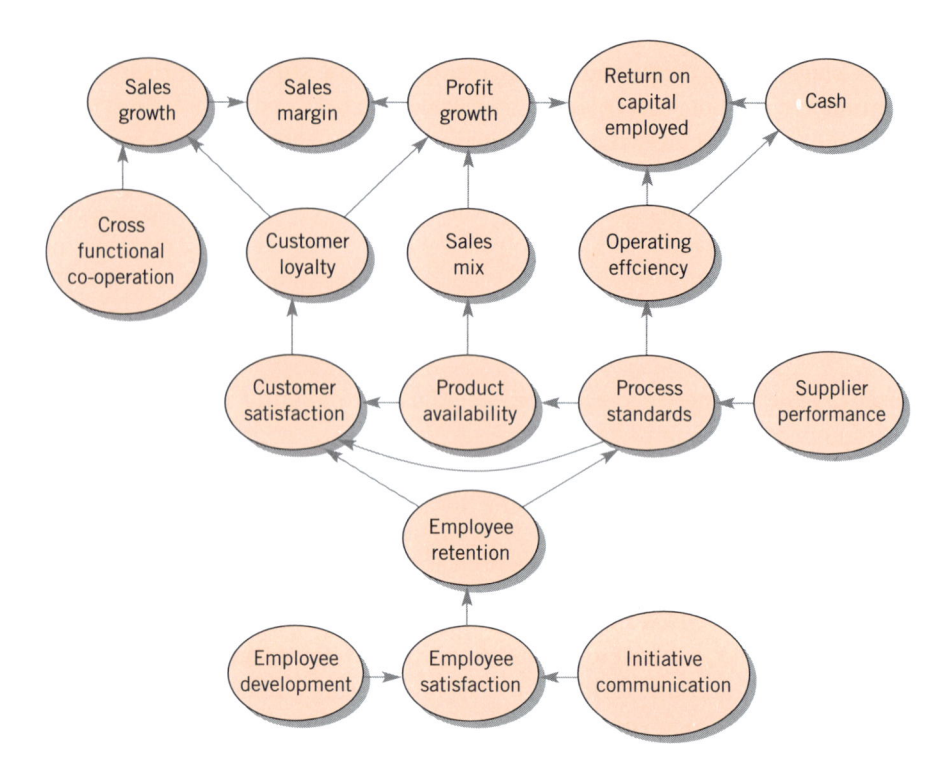

Figure 6.1: *An example of a success map*

Schneiderman talks about a "good scorecard" it is a strategy or success map to which he refers regardless of whether the balanced scorecard, performance prism, or other measurement framework has been used to develop it.

Designing performance measurement systems is all about deciding which measures to select, and just as importantly, which measures to ignore. The principle behind the balanced scorecard and performance prism is that the number of measures should be limited to give clarity to what the organization is trying to achieve. Therefore developing the right performance measures is all about selecting the key objectives that the organization needs to improve and designing appropriate measures to track this improvement.

When management teams do this together it clarifies their thinking on what is important. Having a debate refines their views and makes explicit the mental models each holds in their heads about how they believe the organization works. Our experience shows that this process in itself is highly beneficial. It can help the top team to clarify and agree strategy even if the measurement process does not progress further.

The success map should show all the key objectives the organization is trying to achieve over the coming period on a single sheet of paper. They are linked showing the main cause-and-effect relationships between the objectives. This is an extremely good communication tool both within the management team and for communicating the objectives by demonstrating how the actions of employees throughout the organization contribute to its overall objectives.

Having identified the key objectives and drivers of performance it is necessary to design the performance measures to assess these objectives and drivers. Measures drive behavior, so it is important to translate the objectives into appropriate performance measures, paying attention to precisely how they are calculated; it is not sufficient to just identify the title of the measure and the formula to calculate it. The performance measurement record sheet (Table 6.1) shows all of the details that need to be defined if a measure is to be effective and meaningful.

Table 6.1: *Performance measurement record sheet*

Measure	Title of the measure
Purpose	Why do you want to measure this?
Relates	To which of the business's objectives does this measure relate?
Target	What level of performance are you targetting?
Formula	How will you calculate this measure?
Frequency	How often will you measure this?
Who	Who will measure this?
Source of data	From where will they get the necessary data?
Who acts?	Who will act on this measure?
What do they do?	What will they do?
Notes	Any other notes and/or comments?

Once measures have been identified and designed to reflect the organization's strategy and drivers of performance, the final stage is to assess whether they are going to deliver the change in behavior required. Table 6.2 presents 10 tests to assess whether a good measure has been designed. Checking each measure against these criteria will ensure not only that the numbers reported suggest objectives are being achieved but also that behaviors are in line with objectives. Furthermore, satisfaction of these tests over a sustained period of time is necessary to ensure that measures continue to support and deliver the desired behavior.

As measurement systems are designed to support the achievement of the organization's strategy it is important that when the organization's strategy changes so do the measures used to assess whether it is being executed. So regardless of the framework used to develop the original measures, over time these should change to reflect the organization's changing circumstances and hence measurement system should always be bespoke to reflect the strategy being pursued.

Table 6.2: *The 10 measure design test*

Truth test	Is the measure definitely measuring what it's meant to measure?
Focus test	Is the measure only measuring what it's meant to measure?
Relevance test	Is the measure definitely the right measure?
Consistency test	Is the measure consistent whenever or whoever measures?
Access test	Can the data be readily communicated and easily understood?
Clarity test	Is any ambiguity possible in interpretation of the results?
So what test	Can, and will, the data be acted upon?
Timeliness test	Can the data be analyzed soon enough so action can be taken?
Cost test	Is it going to be worth the cost of collecting and analyzing data?
Gaming test	Will the measure encourage any undesirable behaviors?

Managing the right things

Designing and implementing the right measures is all well and good, but without an effective decision-making and action-planning process it is a waste of effort. Furthermore, research by Ernst & Young on the "measures that matter" found that investors find strategy execution the most important factor when valuating companies, more important than the quality of the strategy being implemented. Despite this, relatively few organizations give significant consideration to the way in which performance in relation to strategy execution is monitored. It is common to see performance reports used by executives which consist of tables of data or limited visualizations of data which provide little insight into the actual performance situation or action that is required to improve.

If the skills and knowledge of executives is to be fully exploited, the performance review process should focus their attention on discussing the issues raised by the performance measures and the actions necessary to meet organizational objectives, rather than trying to interpret what the measures actually say. This can be achieved by focussing on reporting insights to executives rather than performance data by following a number of key steps:[6]

- Restructuring meetings based on the objectives of the organization.
- Focussing the agenda on the key performance outcomes represented on the organization's strategy map. The agenda should be a series of key questions for each of the key objectives, i.e. "Is the objective being achieved?" and "If not, why not?"
- Analysis and interpretation of data should be dealt with by specialists in these tasks (the role of "performance analysts") who identify what insights performance data provides.
- Performance analysts should be responsible for analyzing performance measurement data, presenting to executives the answers to the questions (backed up by analyzed data) rather than providing the raw data itself. Analysis includes identification of the root causes of performance issues and

analysts are encouraged to propose possible future actions based on their analysis. This enables the executives to focus their attention on discussing the issues raised and the actions necessary to meet organizational objectives.

- Communities of practice should be established to enable analysts to learn from each other, enabling improvement of analysis skills. They allow learning about best ways of communicating to the key decision makers, visualization of messages, and telling the story of the organization's performance.

- Meetings should change from discussing performance data to identifying and agreeing future actions. Because this is a more effective use of time, board meetings can be more efficient. They should be supported by an issues management process that ensures actions are prioritized based on importance and that actions are completed as and when necessary.

- Following these steps moves the focus performance management from review of past performance to the discussion of how strategy is executed to deliver future performance objectives. This focusses executive attention on the issues facing the organization in the future and the achievement of strategic objectives.

Using measurement to challenge strategy – double loop learning

A systematic process for using performance measurement to check whether strategy is being implemented and whether performance is improving in line with strategic objectives as described represents a process of single-loop strategic learning.[7] In addition it is possible to use performance measures to challenge whether the approach being applied is appropriate. Organizations such as Sears,[8] and the anonymous company in the study by the Institute of Employment Studies, have used statistical analysis of performance measurement data to challenge whether the strategy being followed is leading to the desired outcomes. This enables double-loop strategic learning to be applied by challenging the assumptions that underpin the strategy of the organization. The strategy map forms a hypothesis of the drivers of performance. Gathering and analyzing performance measurement data enables testing of this hypothesis, allowing executives to make informed decisions about whether the assumptions underpinning the strategy are valid and whether the strategy needs to be changed.

If designed and used appropriately, performance measurement systems can significantly change the way in which an organization is managed and change the behavior of employees, aligning actions to the strategic objectives of the organization. At the heart of performance measurement is the premise that measures and measurement systems must reflect the strategies of the organization implementing them. The efficiency and effectiveness of performance management activities can be enhanced by applying a systematic approach to the use of performance measures which aligns the performance review process with the organization's measures and strategy. Such an approach can enable organizations to clarify their strategy, communicate their strategy, check whether strategy is being implemented, and challenge whether the strategy is appropriate. Furthermore, used appropriately performance measures can facilitate both single-loop and double-loop learning to improve strategy formulation and achievement.

RESOURCES

Kaplan, Robert and Cooper, Robin, *Cost and Effect: Using integrated cost systems to drive profitability and performance*, Harvard Business School Press, 1998.

Kaplan, Robert and Norton, David, *The Strategy-Focussed Organization: How Balanced Scorecard Companies Thrive in the New Business Environment*, Harvard Business School Press, 2000.

Neely, A., Adams, C. and Kennerley, M., *The Performance Prism: The Scorecard for Measuring and Managing Business Success*, FT Prentice Hall, 2002.

Valuing the business – the use of enterprise value

MIKE CAHILL

[Enterprise value is a term often encountered in corporate valuation and used to assess a firm's total liabilities. But what, exactly, does it mean and how is it calculated?]

The recent debates over who has responsibility for pension deficits, the importance of health care liabilities, and the use of off-balance sheet vehicles has focussed attention on the liability side of the equation in corporate valuation. This has been reinforced by the increasing use of debt to fund the business given its cost advantage relative to equity and the focus on balance sheet efficiency. The total liabilities of a business are reflected in its enterprise value (EV). Despite the frequent use of this term, its calculation is often not as comprehensive or detailed as it should be.

The most useful way of thinking about EV is that it is the sum of the liabilities required to purchase 100 percent of a company's cash flow. Its great advantage is that it takes debt, and other debt-like liabilities, into account in the valuation process. This overcomes one of the major deficiencies of using equity-based valuations, such as the P/E, which do not take the company's funding structure into account.

EV is especially useful when comparing companies that may have different corporate structures, accounting, or tax regimes. This is critical in an increasingly cross-border/global investment environment; indeed it evolved as a valuation technique to enable pan-European comparisons. Many European countries have a history of cross shareholdings and significant minority holdings. Accordingly a company will not enjoy 100 percent of the cash flows of its associate or majority-owned holdings.

The other important aspect of EV is its focus on valuing the "core" business. Stripping away the effect of cross shareholdings, associates, and minorities enables the core business to be valued on a "clean" basis. Critically, this allows comparisons with peer groups to be conducted on a like-for-like basis.

Calculating EV

Reflecting these considerations, the formula used for calculating EV is:

Market Cap + Average Debt + Buy out of minorities + Provisions − Peripheral Assets

The equity component consists of the number of shares outstanding multiplied by the share price. All classes of equity need to be taken into account as well as any outstanding options and warrants.

Average debt and provisions

When calculating the debt component, the average level of debt provides a much fairer view of the company's indebtedness. Debt may swing markedly during the course of the year for seasonal trading reasons. In addition, a company will often make sure it manages its working capital aggressively toward its year-end to minimize debt.

It is also crucial to ensure that the market value of any outstanding preference or convertible bonds is reflected in the debt number and hence the EV. Similarly, to get a comprehensive view, off-balance sheet debt and finance leases need to be taken into account. Recent accounting scandals and the aggressive use of off-balance sheet vehicles, or related party transactions, focus attention on the need for vigilance.

Investors and, more critically, the debt-rating agencies are taking a much broader view of liabilities. Provisions for pension, health care, and environmental liabilities must be taken into account. Long-term liabilities which are discounted back to a present value gives them debt-like characteristics.

In particular, pension fund deficits (where benefits have been guaranteed by the company) and, in the US, health care liabilities have added considerably to gearing levels. Many companies have had their debt downgraded due to pension fund deficits. The $14 billion bond issue by General Motors early in 2003, which was injected into its pension fund, crystallized the extent to which this liability had debt characteristics (albeit that accounting issues remain surrounding its assumptions of capital growth for the funds subsequently invested). Its health care liabilities to both current and past employees are also a significant factor when assessing its overall liabilities. Again assumptions about the inflation of health care costs have a marked impact on operating performance numbers. Therefore it can be seen these liabilities affect both earnings and cash flow – and must therefore affect valuation.

Buy-out of minorities

The other potential outlay to secure 100 percent of the cash flow is the buy-out of minorities. The minority holders may not wish this to happen, making it very difficult to assess what the cost might be. Where a substantial minority exists it can be a long-winded and costly exercise to buy out the minority. Again many companies have found difficulty executing deals in Europe where a large minority player has been reluctant to agree.

Peripheral assets

With the objective of valuing the "core" business, the market value of non-core assets needs to be subtracted. These may be property holdings, investments in other companies (associates), or other assets. If associates are treated as a non-core asset, care must be taken to strip out the contribution to profits and earnings. That is why ratios using EV tend to refer to "operating" income or assets, precisely to exclude the non-operating income from associates or investments. Valuing these non-core assets can be very subjective.

While complex, the need to assess EV comprehensively is a crucial part of valuation. As it is based on the company's entire capital/liability structure, it can be used to value those performance numbers such as Ebitda and sales which are generated by all classes of capital.

This leads us to consider two widely used performance numbers, Ebitda and sales, and the way in which they are valued.

Defining Ebitda

The Ebitda is derived from adding back non-cash costs of the business, depreciation, and amortization to the operating profit (which is struck before interest charges). Table 6.3 details the components of Ebitda, and the make-up of enterprise value for a fictional engineering company. It operates in a highly cyclical business with overcapacity and constant price pressure. In addition a few dominant customers account for a significant proportion of turnover.

The next step is to divide the EV by the Ebitda. This is normally expressed, again like a P/E, as a multiple. The average EV/Ebitda for companies in the stock market is normally between 8× and 10×. The lower it is, the cheaper the share is looking, although bear in mind all the issues surrounding the quality of the company and the volatility of its trading performance – all the issues surrounding the quality of earnings apply with equal force to Ebitda. The multiple is also affected by the capital intensity of the business.

Table 6.3: *Engineering Co: Ebitda and enterprise value*

Engineering Co	
	Year 1
Forecast operating profit	£22.5 m
Depreciation	£20 m
Amortization	£2 m
Ebitda calculation (in millions)	22.5 + 20 + 2
Ebitda	£44.5 m
Market capitalization	
138 m shares × 100p	£138 m
Liabilities	
Debt	£30 m
Preference shares	£20m
Environmental liabilities	£10 m
Pension fund deficit	£30m
EV calculation (in millions)	138 + 30 + 20 + 10 + 30
EV	£228 m

For Engineering Co the EV/Ebitda calculation is 228/44.5 which gives a multiple of 5.1×. As we might expect, this makes the share look "cheap." However, with overcapacity and pricing pressure and the intrinsic cyclicality of the company's earnings, the dangers of a downgrade to profit expectations is highly likely. Accordingly it is on a significant discount to the market.

Ebitda as a performance measure

Ebitda has become an increasingly controversial measure of performance. Many commentators have expressed skepticism and investment guru Warren Buffett has even referred to its use as often being "fraudulent."

Ebitda developed as a performance number partly because it strips out the effect of different accounting, depreciation, and amortization policies. As institutions invest on a pan-European or global basis, and companies from different countries are increasingly being compared, it is important to avoid the distortions of different accounting policies. For example, some countries' tax regimes may encourage the accelerated depreciation of assets. This would lead to a very high depreciation charge (because it is tax efficient) but correspondingly depress earnings. Therefore comparing across countries is invalid at the earnings level. Companies in the same country and indeed the same sector might have different depreciation policies, making comparisons difficult.

Ebitda is struck before exceptional items, avoiding another potential accounting distortion to comparisons. Whether this is an advantage is debatable, especially when "operating" exceptionals are concerned. Underperforming companies with uncompetitive cost structures may engage in frequent restructurings which necessitate "exceptional" charges. These need to be treated with caution and have generated cynicism toward Ebitda, leading to its alternative description as "earnings before the bad stuff."

The other reason for its use is that it serves as an approximation for cash flow. Depreciation and amortization are non-cash costs, i.e. while deducted before arriving at profits, no cash goes out of the company. Accordingly it gives an indication of gross cash flow. This can be especially useful for management buy-outs or other leveraged transactions where the debt servicing capacity of the business is crucial.

The other key advantage of using Ebitda is that it takes different capital structures into account. There are advantages to using debt over equity – it's cheaper and tax deductible. In the 1990s, companies looking to minimize their cost of capital increasingly used debt finance. Given the gearing advantages of the higher debt on earnings, comparisons can be more effectively assessed by using EV/Ebitda ratios. An interesting comparison here is between Allied Domecq and Diageo. Allied Domecq has used debt to fund its acquisitions of wine assets. The tax deductibility of the debt enables the deals to be earnings enhancing, though work is needed to ensure they add value, illustrating the difference between growth and returns. On a P/E basis, therefore, Allied looks considerably cheaper than Diageo. However, when the debt funding of these deals is incorporated into the EV/Ebitda ratio, Allied no longer looks cheap.

Ebitda is also used as a performance measure by companies with no earnings. A company at an early stage of development, yet to generate a profit, will reassure investors if it can generate a positive Ebitda. It might be that a major program of capital expenditure has been completed to get the business under way. These assets will be depreciated so the business is generating cash though not earnings. However, Ebitda measure of performance excludes the financing costs of this investment – interest which must be paid. The risk is of course that the investment does not generate the returns to service this debt, let alone compensate shareholders for the risks they are running.

As with other multiple-based measures, EV/Ebitda depends on the growth and quality (the visibility of the earnings combined with conservative accounting policies) of the number. It also depends on the capital intensity of the business – the more capital you need, the lower the multiple. As with all ratios driven by growth and quality, and one of Buffett's main concerns, the question is whether this growth is actually generating value for investors (i.e. returns exceeding the cost of capital). This is particularly relevant where growth is driven by an aggressive acquisition policy that is failing to add value.

A key drawback of Ebitda, and another of Buffett's principal objections, is that depreciation is a very real cost of doing business and it is wrong to ignore this cost. It is crucial for the company to protect its competitive position – a key driver of value – and maintenance capital expenditure is critical in this regard. This, combined with the need for working capital and movements in provisions, prevents Ebitda from being an effective proxy for cash flow.

Ebitda has fallen into disrepute in the post-bubble years. Many companies, especially in the US, that championed it as a performance metric ran into serious financial trouble. The use of Ebitda often reflected the fact that all other performance measures were disappointing, especially for young, high-growth companies requiring heavy investment. In many cases this led to over-investment and returns were decimated as growth failed to materialize. Growth was being achieved as a result of aggressive investment and acquisition policies and even more aggressive accounting. While this affected all performance measures, the use of Ebitda arguably encouraged this growth at the expense of balance sheets and shareholder value.

Summarizing the pros and cons of this valuation technique we can say that the advantages of Ebitda are:

- it takes the whole funding structure into account (unlike P/Es);
- it allows comparisons between companies with different accounting policies toward depreciation and amortization;
- it ignores exceptional charges, again allowing comparison;
- it is a cash flow-based measure;
- it can be used for growth companies incurring start-up losses.

The disadvantages of Ebitda as a performance number are as follows:

- Is Ebitda being used when all other measures are disappointing?

- Maintenance capex is a key cost and working capital requirements – so not a true measure of cash flow?
- What does it measure ... neither cash nor profitability?
- Earnings can still be manipulated.
- Earnings before the bad stuff ... missing the crucial story of what is happening further down the P&L.
- Investment can grow Ebitda (ebit, depreciation and amortization) but what is the rate of return on that investment compared with the cost of capital?
- It is used in capital-intensive, high-growth industries where no profits/EPS are generated ... but over-investment and low returns.
- Variations in tax charges may mean a different outcome for shareholders.

Valuing sales

Another way to measure the value of shares is to consider the sales of a company – valuing the "top line" of the profit and loss account. Sales are made up of the prices and volumes of the company's goods and services. As this drives everything else further down the P&L it is a logical performance number to value. The trend in sales is an indication of the company's growth and its competitive performance.

When compared with its enterprise value this effectively shows how much you are paying for a £ of sales. So assuming sales are £60 million and the EV is £120 million, the calculation is 120/60 which gives EV/sales equaling 2× or 200 percent. This effectively means that you are paying £2 for each £1 of the company's sales. Conversely, if sales were £240 million then you would be paying 50p per £ of sales.

Some commentators use market capitalization to sales ratios as a valuation technique. EV/sales is more comprehensive and takes into account the fact that sales are generated by all the liabilities that make up the capital structure, not just equity (which drives the market capitalization).

Accounting for sales

Historically it was felt that sales were one of the few numbers not subject to widespread accounting manipulation. However, as a number tends to become popular as a valuation measure there is an incentive to manipulate it. Many recent accounting scandals have tended to revolve around sales manipulation. Indeed in 2000 70 percent of SEC accounting and audit enforcement cases were problems of revenue recognition (reported in the *FT* on June 6, 2002). This reflected either recognizing future revenues too early or recording revenues that did not exist at all.

Sales recognition is a particular area of concern where there are long-term contracts involved such as building projects or software contracts. The photocopier company Xerox was forced to restate its sales and profits to a significant extent. The SEC alleged that it had inflated revenues by over $3 billion and earnings by $1.5 billion over a four-year period. Revenues were being booked well before sales actually took place.

At the height of the stock market bubble, the manipulation of sales was also a feature of the technology and telecommunications sector. "Hollow swaps" (where telecoms companies sold capacity to each other and booked it as revenues) and related party transactions were undertaken to boost the sales figure – the sales did not generate earnings or cash, they were purely cosmetic. This was to give the appearance of high growth and also reflected the fact that sales was increasingly featuring as a valuation driver. This manipulation of sales tends to boost profits as there is a "mismatch" – the costs related to those sales are invariably not recognized until they are incurred at a much later date.

Drivers of sales value

The valuation of sales is obviously dependent on the profitability of those sales – a higher margin sale is clearly more desirable than a lower margin one (subject to how much capital is needed to generate that turnover). Operating margins depend on the capital intensity of the business. In theory, higher capital intensity should lead to higher margins. Of course, higher operating margins are essential to ensure that an appropriate return on capital is generated. Conversely, where relatively little capital is needed, e.g. a distribution business, margins will tend to be lower and the EV/sales ratio will correspondingly be lower. Therefore, comparing the EV/sales of two diverse activities, with differing capital intensity, would tell you little of value.

As with other valuation metrics, the quality (predictability or visibility) of sales as well as the projected growth rate determines the multiple. Clearly the extent to which prices or volumes are volatile will undermine the quality of sales. In particular, where a company has a high proportion of fixed costs (high operational gearing), a small reduction in prices can cause a sharp reduction in operating profits and hence operating margins. Take a company with turnover of, say, £3 billion, in a highly price-competitive market making a 10 percent operating margin, producing £300 million of operating profit. A 5 percent reduction in prices would see £150 million reduction in turnover. This would all come off the bottom line and cause operating profits to fall to £150 million – a halving of operating profit. This would of course see operating margins halve – margins fall to 5 percent – and this would clearly lead to a significant downward revision to the value attaching to those sales.

This highlights that sales quality (especially the stability of margins) will be greater to the extent that the company has pricing power due to a strong product offering, high market share, and through operating in a consolidated market. Another aspect influencing visibility of sales may be the frequency of repeat business or a long-term contract. If sales can be forecast out for many years due to the nature of the contract (for example, maintenance in a PFI hospital), it will be valued highly by investors.

Another way of using the EV/sales ratio is when considering turnaround and takeover situations. Here one can assess the scope for cost savings and/or synergy benefits to get a sense of what operating margins the business could deliver if run more efficiently. This gives a sense of what the company could be worth. If one can buy those sales at a significant discount to this, the deal clearly has potential. So if the EV/sales ratio is reflecting a business generating operating margins of 4 percent (say it is trading at 35 percent of sales) and through better management could be delivering 10 percent, there is significant upside. Even paying a 30 percent premium, 45 percent of sales, would leave considerable upside potential. If the sales can indeed deliver double-digit margins, the value would be nearer 100 percent of sales.

The EV/sales ratio therefore is related to:

- the operating margins the company generates;
- the confidence in those margins being sustained;
- the growth rate of the company's sales;
- the quality or visibility of those sales.

As a rule of thumb, a company with operating margins of around 10 percent, generating sales growth of around 5 percent, would trade on around 100 percent or $1 \times$ sales.

The food retailing sector, for example, has a ratio of around 0.5× and margins for the individual companies do indeed tend to be in the region of 4–6 percent. These companies have relatively little capital employed as the working capital tends to be financed by suppliers. As a result this low ratio is not a problem because the companies generate very good returns on invested capital. Automobiles and parts are trading around 0.4×. Margins due to competitive pressures and the purchasing power of the big car makers also tend to be very low. Unfortunately, unlike the food retailers, these companies tend to employ significant amounts of capital. As a result returns on invested capital tend to be low and not cover their cost of capital. This is why care is needed when comparing EV/sales ratios across sectors – capital intensity and the type of capital needed may vary enormously.

EV – a critical measure

Establishing the total liabilities of a company in terms of its enterprise value is a crucial element of the valuation process. This is especially true given the increasing focus on pension fund and health care liabilities to which companies may be exposed and which have debt-like characteristics. This covers the inadequacy of the P/E, a long-standing valuation technique but one which does not take into account a company's liability structure. Using enterprise value then allows performance numbers toward the top of the P&L such as Ebitda and sales (generated by all the resources at the company's disposal not just equity) to be assessed. Crucially this helps avoid the dangers of using just one valuation number or one performance metric when assessing the value of a company.

There are strengths and weaknesses with all the main valuation techniques and care and scrutiny is required. Examining the answers generated by a range of different valuation methods will provide a more detailed and comprehensive picture.

Making projects fly

STEPHEN CARVER

[Projects are now the centerpiece of corporate strategy. Yet research shows that most projects fail. It doesn't have to be this way.]

Choosing and implementing the correct strategy is rightly seen as the key to success in a rapidly changing world. Strategy formulation is considered one of the most important business skills, and organizations worldwide devote huge amounts of time, money, and intellectual effort to getting it right. Yet once the strategy is selected, very few organizations take the time to properly set up – or control – the resultant projects. The consequence is that most fail, bringing down much of the strategy, and often people's careers, with them.

Research, confirms that most projects fail. If they arrive at all, they arrive late and over-budget. Of those that are completed, many fail to deliver the benefits they promised. In short, if projects were civil aircraft we would be living in a world where jumbo jets regularly fall out of the skies. Airport runways would be strewn with wreckage and passengers waiting endlessly in lounges would be rightly terrified at the prospect of boarding the plane.

So why is it that so many projects fail? And more importantly, what can organizations do about it?

The flying analogy

There are, of course, a variety of complex project management models, processes, and frameworks to choose from. Yet in my experience, a simple analogy is the most effective way to get senior management to grasp the importance of project management execution. Often mainstream project management techniques such as P.E.R.T. (Performance Enhancement and Response Team) and W.B.S. (Work Breakdown Structure) are feared and avoided by busy people in organizations, whereas this analogy seems to "click" and be put into practical use.

Put simply, managing projects is rather like flying commercial passenger airplanes, and program management is akin to air traffic control. Some of the analogies include:

Pilot	Project manager
Cabin crew	Project team
Passengers	Stakeholders
Air traffic controller	Steering group
Air traffic control	Program management
Flight plan	Project plan
Fuel	Project budget
Flight time	Project timeline
Airspace	Project environment/culture
Aircraft type	Project complexity/size/risk
Flight instruments	Project status reports
Pre-flight checks	Feasibility study
Takeoff	Project launch
Landing	Project handover
Flying rules	Project systems/methodologies
Weather	Project risk
Flight log	Post-project review

Let's lay down some ground rules. First, like all analogies, taken too far this comparison can start to lose validity; second, this article provides only an overview; and third, I am not a commercial pilot so please forgive any aero-technical errors.

The selection of commercial aircraft (as opposed to military) is deliberate. Fighter pilots are trained for war, the most extreme form of crisis. Most company projects are hopefully not war zones. Their aim is to launch (and then successfully land) the right projects on time and in budget, such that the key stakeholders are satisfied. This process should ideally be continuous, professionally managed, safe, and largely uneventful. Like projects, most people prefer their flights to be uneventful.

Using the flying analogies it is possible to construct a model of project management within an organization.

The pilot

No one would let an untrained pilot fly an aircraft full of passengers. Yet in many companies the selection and training of suitable project managers is an arbitrary process. A good commercial airline pilot is a total professional, whose entire focus is to ensure that the flight is as well planned and executed as possible. Like professional project managers, they go to great lengths to ensure that the flight goes smoothly.

Pilots do not take off without doing the necessary preparation: planning (flight plan), check lists (pre-flight checks), risk management (weather), and constant monitoring and control. They instill confidence in others by always appearing calm and in control and communicate clearly and factually. Their training is to plan and then have a plan to back up the plan. They enhance their skills in flight simulators (project risk/contingency planning).

Like project managers, pilots are acutely aware that if the flight ends in disaster they will "arrive at the scene of the air accident first." (Unlike fighter aircraft there is no ejector seat.) Pilots also have to sign off aircraft before take off (project launch/project charter) knowing that some systems may not be fully functional. In extremis, they can refuse to sign if they think that the level of risk is too high. In many organizations, project managers are not given any choice in the matter and are sometimes misled about the status of the project that they are expected to fly. Small wonder then that in such cultures "smart people avoid projects."

Airspace

Airspace is the environment in which projects fly and it is divided into two types.

- *Controlled*. Here all flights fly within strict air corridors controlled by air traffic control (think of project procedures and steering committees). In the real airline world it is known as IFR (instrument flight rules) and pilots are carefully tracked and monitored by controllers on the ground to ensure that flights are correctly prioritized and collisions are avoided. An added advantage of IFR is that the pilots can "fly blind" through clouds or at night relying on the controllers to keep them safe.

    In our project analogy these flights will be flown according to "rules" which, in organizations, are the project procedures, and methodologies and program management processes. These rules ensure that projects are controlled in a standardized way such that whole project programs can safely be co-ordinated.

- *Uncontrolled*. Here the pilots are largely free to fly as they like but have to ensure their own safety by basically "looking out the windows." In the real world this is known as VFR (visual flight rules) and as long as they steer clear of the air lanes controlled by IFR they may largely make their own decisions as to how and where to fly.

In our project analogy these tend to be smaller projects (often run within a single department) where air traffic is light and complex tracking and co-ordination systems are not required. It should be emphasized that the pilots (project managers) have to assess the risks for themselves and that flying blind is extremely hazardous! In the real world it is usual for pilots to submit a VFR flight plan that outlines their intended flight time, course, and destination. If they fail to arrive, their hope is that someone will come out to look for them.

The aircraft

Projects, like aircraft, come in many shapes and sizes.

- *Concorde.* Usually to be found flying IFR between major airports, these are high-profile, high-flying, unique, and fast. Often they are sponsored by CEOs and as such they "must not fail" and despite being seen as high risk very few actually come to harm due to the care, priority, and attention lavished on them. The aircraft analogy type is the Concorde, which although sadly no longer flying is a good example of such a project type. These projects are often symbolically important and as such the costs are largely unimportant and emotion can often overrule the head. Pilots loved flying Concorde due to its elite status and the fact that it involved very high levels of flying skills. These projects are vital as they are organizational flagships and act as role models to aspiring managers.

- *747.* Usually to be found flying IFR between major airports, these are often large, costly, but high-benefit projects that are similar to other projects undertaken previously by the organization. They are not as fast or as high-prestige as Concordes but long term, they deliver high returns and the consequences of failure are high. The aircraft analogy type is the 747 jumbo jet which (although perhaps lumbering and ugly) is the practical and profitable mainstay of most fleets. Again, good pilots are needed to fly them and, while the kudos is not as great as Concorde, they are given high priority (management attention) due to their large size and high payload.

- *737.* Again, usually to be found flying IFR between smaller and/or major airports, these are smaller projects that run so numerously and frequently in organizations that they almost become taken for granted. The payload and range is far less than 747's but they often feed the 747 "hubs" and as such are vital to the overall operations. The aircraft analogy here is something like a

737 – nimble, flexible, and where most pilots start their careers. It is interesting to note these pilots are often the "best" (in terms of flying skills) as they do more take-offs and landings than other types, despite the lower kudos and priority given to them. In organizations, the best project managers are often those who manage smaller 737 projects and who are used to dealing flexibly with the everyday issues of low prioritization and lack of senior management support.

- *Light aircraft.* These projects are very different from the above types. They are usually to be found flying VFR and seldom from major airports. They are generally the "light aircraft" of the project world and carry few passengers – and usually only within individual departments. These projects are vital to the organization in that their freedom to fly virtually anywhere (at their own risk) means that they often "discover" new destinations to fly to – new markets/ways of doing things. These destinations can then often be developed into new airports for the organization to capitalize on and they then lay in new air corridors under IFR and hence get the large aircraft projects to fly in.

Air traffic control

With all the project/aircraft types flying around the organization it is vital to prioritize and control them, so that accidents or collisions do not occur. This is the role of air traffic control/steering groups. They will ensure that projects are allowed to take off only if the runway is clear (resources are available), and that they have a place to land (handover and deliver benefits). Air traffic controllers are not required to be pilots; rather their task is to establish and control air corridors, where projects can be tracked, given guidance, and prioritized for take-off and landings – an IFR system. It is interesting to note that sometimes air traffic controllers look after several flights at once and similarly some managers will find themselves members of several steering groups. The world's air traffic control is made up from many integrated national systems, and likewise divisional/global organizations should have a common project system/language that allows interdivisional programs of projects to be undertaken successfully.

Weather

One of the greatest concerns of pilots is the weather – in project terms "risk." They typically go to considerable trouble to study forecasts and when flying will often use radar or visual information to avoid turbulence, or thunderstorms that could make the flight "eventful." Likewise project managers should use weather (risk) forecasting methods to ensure that risks are identified, avoided, or controlled – thus ensuring as smooth a flight as possible.

While forecasts and a weather eye can help avoid the worst weather conditions, there is always the possibility of clear air turbulence (CAT) – in project terms "the unexpected" – and good pilots must be capable of sometimes dealing with events that were neither planned nor forecast. Like the pilot they can achieve this only if they have the rest of the systems under control and correctly trimmed. Severe weather often leads commercial pilots to fly longer routes (using more valuable fuel) to ensure a smooth flight. Project managers do likewise, but sometimes budget or time constraints mean that the flight has to fly through turbulence – projects can be very stressful to individuals.

Application to organizations

This has been only an overview of the flying analogy for project and program management. There has been little time to mention the crew (project team), or perhaps the most important, the passengers (stakeholders), without whom the flight would have no objective.

In my experience, few companies take the training, development, and audit of their pilots and steering groups as seriously as they should. As a result, there are far too many project near-misses and sometimes, sadly, major disasters. The level of effort and commitment required is obviously dependent on the number (and speed) of projects flying around the organization and this is obviously a decision to be made by senior management.

Like most high-reliability systems run by professionals, piloting and controlling projects can become largely invisible and perhaps taken for granted. Just because there are no air accidents for a while it doesn't mean you should stop pilot training and close down air traffic control. It is important therefore to build a project-supportive culture where smooth flights are recognized as a sign of professionalism and where projects are seen as an opportunity to enhance careers and develop the organization.

Companies that want their projects to fly should fill out the following pre-flight checklist on behalf of their organization:

- Do you have properly trained project flight crews?
- Is there an integrated air traffic control system?
- Do you know the flying status of all your projects?
- Are there adequate project flying procedures and checklists?
- Are your sponsors/steering groups trained in air traffic control?

If the answer to any of the above is negative, the chances are that the organization is flying its projects by the seat of its pants. In such an organization it is not a question of if, but rather when, a major project air accident will occur.

The rise and fall of the COO

STUART CRAINER AND DES DEARLOVE

[Heirs apparent or masters of the nitty gritty? The jury is out on the role of Chief Operating Officers.]

In recent years, COOs have seemed more like heirs apparent than benchwarmers. Richard Parsons at AOL Time Warner, Hector de Ruiz at Advanced Micro Devices, Samuel Palmisano at IBM, David Brown at Owens Corning, and Keith Rattie at Questar have each made the leap from chief operating officer to chief executive officer.

The advancement of COOs is potent proof that they are now an important feature of the corporate landscape. Yet as the spotlight on the CEO's job grows ever brighter, the No. 2 slot remains consigned to the shadows. Just how important is the COO role in a modern corporation? Is it largely decorative, or vital to corporate performance?

Step into the shadows, and you quickly discover that not all COOs are created equal. For some companies, the role is indeed a stepping-stone to the top job. Others interpret it as a purely operational position. What research has been done on COOs also suggests that the jury is still out on the contribution they make to corporate performance. Intrigued, we set out to find out more.

First, we got a history lesson. The job title itself can be traced back to the great railroad era of the 19th century, though it really took off in the corporate world in the 1970s. In the mid 1980s, CEOs began to acquire shadows as surely as cacti in the desert. A Princeton University study of 433 large US corporations found that in 1964, not one of the companies had a COO. By 1994, more than two-thirds did. Today, the COO is an institution in major corporations. "The CEO is the outside voice of the company, and the COO is the internal voice," observes Chuck Wardell, a managing director at headhunter Korn/Ferry International. "In many cases, the COO will be the informal sounding board up and down the organization. He or she serves as a buffer and broker to the CEO."

Someone to actually run things

But what prompted the creation and rapid spread of this new executive role? In part, believes Princeton researcher Frank Dobbin, the spread of COOs was driven by corporate fashion. "David Rockefeller appointed a COO at Chase Manhattan in 1975, and this clearly influenced a number of other firms," he says. "In the 1970s, it was mostly very profitable firms that appointed COOs, and they did so because they had the luxury of creating another costly executive position that could take some of the pressure off the CEO. In those years, CEOs were expected to focus on acquisitions and long-term planning. Once a group of high-profile, highly profitable firms had COOs, investors came to associate them with success and came to expect any forward-looking, successful firm to have a COO."

The gradual development of the role, however, suggests that the COO title is more than a passing fad. What had begun as a luxury became a necessity. One reason is that appointing a COO has become an accepted part of a company's development. Sunlight brings shadows. As firms grow, the size and scope of the executive function expands. Once companies reach annual sales of around $50 million, the introduction of a COO tends to be justified by the complexity of the revenue streams. Bringing in a COO is a means of keeping the growth of the executive function in check and reining in growing complexity.

More broadly, the rise in COO numbers is attributed to the growing demands placed on CEOs. In particular, as the top job has become more finance-dominated in many companies, operational responsibilities are more likely to be delegated. This was particularly the case during the dot-com boom, when CEOs had to increasingly focus on managing analysts, Wall Street, and venture capitalists. They needed someone to handle the day-to-day running of the business. Enter the COO.

"It was almost a return to the railroads, with huge capital requirements and operational complexity, and often the technology is so sophisticated the CEO couldn't comprehend it," says COO researcher Donald Hambrick of Penn State's Smeal College of Business Administration. "Some of today's capital-intensive industries or technologically complex industries might be seen as modern counterparts to the early railroad." The presence of COOs in the boardrooms of many high-achieving high-tech companies also gave the position a degree of glamor that it hadn't previously enjoyed.

Another reason for the growth in COOs is that it enables organizations to split the senior executive roles. The operational role allows other executives – usually the CEO and chairman – to focus their attention on more strategic issues.

What do COOs actually do?

This has produced the stereotype of the COO as a safe pair of executive hands dealing with the nitty-gritty of the business while the CEO ponders the grander things in corporate life and manages the increasing demands of the media and investment communities. Like most stereotypes, this possesses a kernel of truth.

Dobbin believes the role has changed over time. "Early COOs were responsible for day-to-day operations," he says, "leaving CEOs free to do long-range planning and to raise funds for acquisitions. Increasingly, however, as investors came to favor firms with a clear focus over highly diversified firms, the CEO took back the reins of production and sales decisions."

Felipe J. Alvarez, COO of Con Edison Communications, likens the role to executive maintenance. "The most basic explanation of the COO's job is taking care of all of the day-to-day running of the company," he says. "You turn up service for the customer and keep it up and running. It's an operational job, so I sometimes describe myself as someone running around a factory floor with an oil can in my hand."

Alvarez is typical of the new breed. A 42-year-old MBA graduate with a sales-and-marketing background, he knows the company's business inside out, having been one of the initial trio involved in its inception. For Con Edison Communications, the need for a COO emerged through the sheer complexity of rolling out a fiber-optic network in New York City. Alvarez took on the role at the beginning of 2000. He describes himself as the organization's lightning rod.

Alvarez and Peter Rust, Con Edison Communications' president and CEO, divide their roles fairly conventionally. "Peter and I have always been clear about the different disciplines of the respective jobs. The CEO focusses on external things such as managing the investment community, as well as long-term strategy, where we're going, looking at mergers and acquisitions, opportunities, overall vision, and leadership, how we're positioned," Alvarez explains. "That doesn't mean I don't do external things, but most of the external things I deal with are customer-facing: helping closing a sale or working with customers who've had a problem."

He regards the COO's role as making the company's vision operational, but warns of the dangers of becoming mired in the complexities of delivery: "It can be very internally focussed if you allow it."

Managing the studio

The COO works in an uncomfortable corporate hinterland. This is reflected in the array of different job titles for much the same role. One company's COO is another's chief administrative officer, chief of staff, or executive vice chairman. Normally, if someone has the title president and no other title, he is probably operating as a COO. Whatever the semantics, the COO works at the point where corporate strategy is delivered. While the title suggests a focus on operations, the reality is that the COO slot requires a variety of managerial, political, and motivational skills. They have to be diplomats in dealing with angry customers or with CEOs wholly committed to their vision. They have to manage large amounts of detail. They must be able to communicate at a board level as well as with customers and a variety of others in the organization.

"If I had to describe the COO's role, it would be as a gatekeeper or as someone who has to connect all operations in the company," says Jerome Artigliere, COO of

Palm Beach-based Applied Digital Solutions, a leader in biosensor technology. "At the corporate level, the question is always: How do you run the company when there's operations, marketing, accounting, R&D, and so on? All those items need to come together at some place, so that information can be compiled and things put together. So that's my role."

On a day-to-day level, Artigliere believes that coaching is one of the key requirements. "You have to be a coach. You have people with different agendas and different motivations. You have to understand the business as a whole as well as dealing with some pretty detailed stuff, especially in the accounting function. Putting out fires is also part of the job."

If CEOs are the artists, with occasional artistic excesses, COOs are the studio managers who ensure that the master's ideas are acted upon.

COO today, CEO tomorrow

Donald Hambrick suggests that there are two basic kinds of COO. One is the heir apparent, the next in line to be CEO; the other is a plain-vanilla COO who is slated to remain in the No. 2 slot. In companies with COOs, the two roles tend to occur in similar proportions.

"The people who are chosen as pure COOs – as opposed to CEO heirs apparent – usually don't have the skills set, the orientation, or the aspiration to become CEO," Hambrick says. "In the same vein, COOs tend not to move from company to company. There isn't a fluid market in COOs, because a lot of the value added is very firm-specific. To do it well, you have to understand the firm – you can't just parachute in."

The COO as heir appears increasingly accepted. In 2002, for example, Paul S. Otellini was appointed Intel's president and COO in anticipation of his taking over when CEO Craig Barrett retires by 2005. Otellini had already run Intel's microprocessor-products division, which, according to some Wall Street analysts, generates 80 percent of the company's sales. Barrett himself was president and COO before succeeding Andy Grove in 1998.

Though the jobs of CEO and COO are quite different, being a COO is a sound building base. It provides a stepping-stone from a purely functional job to the more generalist role of CEO. The COO needs to know everything and everyone – what is really going on. As Hambrick points out, there is an irony in using the COO role as preparation for being CEO. The CEO-in-waiting spends more time on external matters than would normally be the case with a COO. External matters form the bulk of the CEO's job but are often the area in which most would-be CEOs have the least experience. The person employed to keep an eye on the innermost workings of the organization is likely to have his attention focussed outside the organization for significant periods.

Having a COO can be seen as a constant CEO backup, a vice-presidential role. Corporate boards are under pressure to have a carefully managed succession just in case; there's a need to have an heir apparent even if the designated person never becomes CEO. A COO may not have supreme authority, but he typically attends every board meeting and sits in on analysts' briefings. With access to all the company's issues and problems, he develops a wide range of knowledge about the company. If an unforeseen situation arises – and in a period of startling accusations and revelations, who knows? – he's a clear choice to serve as interim CEO until the board decides whether to look outside or anoint him.

Sometimes it takes two

In other cases, the COO role is seen as an integral part of a leadership duo, the old one-two. When Herb Kelleher, Southwest Airlines' colorful and longstanding leader, stood down in June 2001, he was succeeded by a leadership double act. Colleen Barrett, a 30-year Southwest stalwart and formerly corporate secretary and executive VP for customers, became president and COO; vice chairman James Parker, a former VP and general counsel, took on the CEO mantle. Kelleher remained as chairman.

According to Korn/Ferry's Chuck Wardell, CEOs drive the majority of COO appointments. "In most cases, it is a very personal appointment by the CEO," he says. "They generally pick someone who is strong in areas where they are either not strong or not interested. The CEO chooses a No. 2 to pick up the slack in certain functions, or in lesser markets. For example, a CEO may decide that he will win or lose in North America and needs to put his full attention on that market, but if the company has operations overseas, he may bring in a COO who can go to those markets and make decisions."

In the 1970s and 1980s, say Frank Dobbin and his Princeton co-researchers, CEOs of fast-growing companies appointed COOs "because they had the luxury of doing so." Over time, in an era when many companies pursued a strategy of diversification, the role became a necessity to manage a sprawling portfolio of businesses. By the mid-1980s, however, as firms shifted their strategic focus from diversification strategies to core competencies, the spread of COOs slowed, and CEOs became more inclined to hire and work closely with chief financial officers. This supports the notion that the functional orientation of the second-in-command is heavily influenced by the shifting ground that CEOs are expected to occupy, or by the gaps in an incoming CEO's knowledge.

Some companies explicitly recognize that a good COO can provide a counterbalance for the CEO. Cary Blair of Ohio-based Westfield Group, a financial-services company, has held the top job for 11 years and has been planning his succession for the past four. Blair believes that intelligent succession planning should factor the

No. 2 role into the equation. Westfield Group has a record of mixing and matching the skills at the top of the company: operational specialists are balanced by financiers, and vice versa.

How much difference does he make?

The bottom line must be whether having a COO actually helps a company's performance. Here, there are mixed messages. Logically and anecdotally, it appears commonsensical that having another experienced senior executive taking care of specific aspects of a company's business should be a help.

Champions of the role point to increasing numbers of COOs becoming CEOs and cases of COOs improving performance. Probably the best-known example is that of Bob Herbold, a Procter & Gamble marketer whom Microsoft brought in as COO in 1994. The software giant was struggling to reconcile its huge size and related pressures to deliver with its collegiate corporate culture. In the next seven years, revenues quadrupled, profitability multiplied by seven, and expenses, as a percentage of revenues, fell from 51 to 40 percent. Insiders credited Herbold with keeping the ship on an even keel. Yet the small number of academics who have examined the COO phenomenon tend to be skeptical of the impact that COOs have on corporate performance.

Penn State's Donald Hambrick was intrigued to learn that in companies that had COOs, the CEO often had some difficulty describing their exact role. This prompted him to undertake a specific study to look into the effect of the COO. After adjusting for industry and other factors, his research showed that firms with COOs actually have inferior performance than those without.

Hambrick offers two possible explanations, both debatable. First, having a CEO/COO duo is an inherently flawed design that attempts to separate formulation from implementation. Second, a COO is often a proxy for a weak CEO. "While other CEOs take on the full spectrum of CEO responsibilities, the CEO with a COO tends not to be comfortable with the full spectrum and is particularly not interested or comfortable with running the company itself. These are CEOs who don't do plant visits."

Princeton's Frank Dobbin agrees that delegating operations is likely to be viewed negatively. "The stock market doesn't like hands-off CEOs these days," he says, "so I doubt we'll see more CEOs turning over operations to others." While that may be true in some cases, the counter-argument is that it takes a strong CEO to admit that he needs to delegate part of the job.

Whether taking on the COO role is necessarily a good career move is also a contentious issue. "It takes a certain personality, someone who is willing to play a strong supporting role as a COO," agrees Chuck Wardell. "Often the COO's fortunes will rise or fall with those of the CEO. If the CEO bombs, the COO can't really say he or she didn't know what was going on."

Potential COOs should take note. Life in the shadows may leave you permanently in the dark.

Commentary

Garageland

Businesses start with a bright idea, a glimpse of a gap in the market, a once-in-a-lifetime opportunity. And then what? Well, then you have to make it happen. But where? For some, the answer is a cupboard under the stairs, or the spare bedroom. For others the answer is the garage.

Garages loom large in corporate history – though, admittedly, not as large as over-weaning ambition, greed, and the willingness to work 24 hours every day. Garage start-ups have launched a thousand businesses. Some have conquered the world. Others have remained where they begun, constrained by location and inspiration as surely as others have found garageland an inspiration.

Garages have been called America's secret weapon. There are plenty to choose from – 97 percent of new American houses have attached garages, and the trend over recent years has been to two- or three-car garages. Starting a business in a three-car garage is rather like learning to drive in an automatic car; the result is the same, but the experience quite different.

While it is true that some of the biggest businesses which began life in garages have been American – Hewlett-Packard, Apple, Ford, and many more – garages are universal. A garage in Korea is as viable a corporate HQ as one in Madrid or Cleveland. Alongside the American corporate titans is a host of other global garage success stories.

Garages come in different shapes and sizes. One man's garage is another's warehouse. They are, essentially, small, empty spaces with a minimum of accoutrements and creature comforts. Poor lighting and a complete lack of heating or ventilation are also vital ingredients in the entrepreneurial mix.

Whether some companies can be considered true garage businesses is a matter of debate. Sony began life in 1946 in the garage-like surroundings of a bombed-out Tokyo department store, but cannot be designated a genuine garage start-up due to the space it had available. Boeing's first plane was constructed in a boathouse which is, for garage afficionados, almost permissible.

The English spin on the garage start-up is the garden shed housing the brilliant but ever so slightly eccentric inventor. This is laudable but different from the authentic garage experience. Inventors tend to be loners. Part of the joy of garage start-ups is that a number of people are crowded into a confined space to create the genuine entrepreneurial aroma. The garden shed is bucolic; the garage, concrete and urban.

For budding entrepreneurs (not to mention rock stars), the allure of garages is simple. First, they are there. Free, available space is highly attractive for the

Commentary (continued)

aspiring start-up. It is better to labor amid the detritus of family living – the children's toys, garden tools, dust-gathering sports equipment, old tires and exhausts – than it is to hand over large sums of money to a landlord.

But the second attraction is psychological. Businesses which begin in garages – or other constrained domestic situations – feel as though they are underdogs. They have something to prove. They are at the bottom of the commercial pile. The fatal flaw of the dot-com bubble was that people began businesses with superiority complexes. Armed with a business plan, venture capital, and office space they assumed they were onto a winner. Garages businesses assume nothing. Garages are accompanied by natural feelings of inferiority and insignificance.

"On one hand, it is fun, a bit of a game, pretending you're an established business though you are sitting in your dressing gown in a cupboard under the stairs," reflects Barnaby Moffat, founder of Foresite, a four-year-old Internet solutions company which now employs 12 people. "It is also a struggle, but it allows the business to start. Without the cupboard under the stairs, this business wouldn't have happened. There comes a time when you have to move out – six months in our case."

Perhaps the most famous garage is that once used by Bill Hewlett and David Packard. They began their company, Hewlett-Packard, in 1937 with a mere $538 in a rented garage at 367 Addison Avenue, Palo Alto, California. "We thought we would have a job for ourselves. That's all we thought about in the beginning," said Packard. "We hadn't the slightest idea of building a big company." The garage was the birthplace of Silicon Valley. The Hewlett-Packard garage still exerts an influence over the company. It has been featured in a recent ad campaign and was actually bought back by the company for $1.7 million – a price reflecting the fact that garages usually come with a house.

Another among the pantheon of garage greats is the birthplace of the hardy publishing perennial the *Reader's Digest* which began life in a garage in Pleasantville, New York. As the name suggests, this is not a garage in the oily sense of the word, more of a *pied à terre*, from which DeWitt and Lila Wallace launched their easily digestible and incredibly successful take on the world.

The high point of the garage start-up was, not surprisingly, the rise of the motor car industry. At the end of the 19th century a plethora of mechanically minded obsessives were at work in their garages. Among them was Henry Ford who should perhaps be identified as the father of the garage. Ford's first prototype was the Quadricycle which he built in a coal shed. Unfortunately, his building work led him to overlook some fundamental practicalities. When the prototype was complete, it could be removed only by partly dismantling the building.

Walt Disney's Uncle Robert's wooden garage in North Hollywood was the unostentatious base for Walt Disney when he arrived in California in 1923. He paid $1 a week for the garage which has now been moved en masse to a museum. Disney has moved on to generate annual revenues of $25,402 million.

Garage miracles are still happening. Roger Keenan, a British engineer, started Eyretel in his garage in 1991. He became a multi-millionaire when the business was floated in Spring 2000. Amazon.com is also a hero of garageland. The business began at Jeff Bezos' rented home in a Seattle suburb. Crucial to the operation was the garage, which was also the warehouse and working area. The prototype of the PalmPilot was created when Jeff Hawkins disappeared into his garage with some mahogany and plywood. As part of the design process, Hawkins then carried the low-tech model with him, in his shirt pocket, taking it out from time to time and pretending to look up an address or phone number on it.

Perhaps the most famous modern entrants into the garage hall of fame are Apple founders Steve Jobs and Steve "Woz" Wozniak. Then in their twenties, Jobs and Wozniak turned the Jobs family garage into a workshop and set out to build a personal computer. Jobs sold his Volkswagen. Woz ditched his prized scientific calculator. After a year of garage toil the Apple I was born. Jobs remains with Apple, which made a profit of $786 million in 2000 on sales of $7.98 billion.

The Apple remains the technology of choice for the garage start-up. The magazine *Red Herring* began life in a converted garage with a single Apple computer, a telephone, and a filing cabinet. Garage start-ups hope that the magic of the original Apple garage will somehow rub off.

While the Apple duo knew what they wanted to achieve, other garage start-ups are marked by a kind of desperate flexibility. They will do anything. Hewlett-Packard did not churn out printers from day one. Its early products included everything from a shock machine which was supposed to help people lose weight, to an automatic urinal flusher. Similarly, when Mattel began life in another Californian garage – quite a substantial one actually – it made picture frames rather than Barbie dolls. It then moved onto furniture for dolls' houses, and musical toys (including the "Uke-A Doodle").

There is of course, no formula to succeeding with a garage start-up – though there is, inevitably, a book on the subject, *Build Your Own Garage*. Some garages work and grow; other businesses remain firmly based in the garage where they belong. While there are garages, there is always entrepreneurial hope.

Essentials

MAKING IT HAPPEN

Decision theory

An entire academic discipline, decision science, is devoted to understanding management decision making. Much of it is built on the foundations set down by early business thinkers, who believed that under a given set of circumstances human behavior was logical and therefore predictable. The fundamental belief of the likes of computer pioneer Charles Babbage and scientific management founder Frederick Taylor was that the decision process (and many other things) could be rationalized and systematized. Based on this premise, models emerged to explain the workings of commerce which, it was thought, could be extended to the way in which decisions were made.

In general, management literature defines two different types of decisions:

1. *Operational decisions* are concerned with the day-to-day running of the business. Typical operational decisions might involve setting production levels, the decision to recruit additional employees, or to close a particular factory.
2. *Strategic decisions* are those concerned with organizational policy and direction over a longer time period. So, a strategic decision might involve determining whether to enter a new market, acquire a competitor, or exit from an industry altogether.

Madan G. Singh, chair of information engineering at Manchester Institute of Science and Technology, prefers an alternative breakdown of decision levels, which recognizes some of the changes taking place within companies. He divides the decisions in an organization into three levels:

- day-to-day decisions
- tactical decisions
- strategic decisions.

Day-to-day decisions, he says, are those made by front-line staff. Collectively, they make thousands of decisions daily, most of them in a short timeframe and on the basis of concrete information: answering a customer's request for information about a product, for example. Their decisions usually have a narrow scope and influence a small range of activities.

Tactical and strategic decisions, on the other hand, are both longer-term decisions. The data needed to make them is much broader, extending outside the organization, and the information derived from that data is less precise, less current, and subject to more error. Tactical decisions cover a few weeks to a few months, and include decisions such as the pricing of goods and services, and deciding advertising and marketing expenditures. Strategic decisions are those with the longest time horizon – 1–5 years or longer. They generally concern expanding or contracting the business or entering new geographic or product markets.

To help managers cope with all these decisions, there are numerous models, frameworks, tools, techniques, and software programs. Decision-making models assume that the distilled mass of experience will enable people to make accurate decisions. They enable you to learn from other people's experiences. The danger is in concluding that the solution provided by a software package is *the* answer.

Decision theorizing suggests that effective decision making involves a number of logical stages. This is referred to as the "rational model of decision making" or the "synoptic model." The latter involves a series of steps: identifying the problem, clarifying the problem, prioritizing goals, generating options, evaluating options (using appropriate analysis), comparing predicted outcomes of each option with the goals, and choosing the option that best matches the goals.

Such models rely on a number of assumptions about the way in which people will behave when confronted with a set of circumstances. These assumptions allow mathematicians to derive formulae based on probability theory. These decision-making tools include such elements as cost/benefit analysis, which aims to help managers evaluate different options.

Alluring though they are, the trouble with such theories is that reality is often more confused and messy than a neat model can allow for. Underpinning the mathematical approach are a number of flawed assumptions, such as that decision making is consistent, based on accurate information, free from emotion or prejudice, and rational. Another obvious drawback to any decision-making model is that identifying what you need to make a decision about is often more important than the actual decision itself. If a decision seeks to solve a problem, it may be the right decision but the wrong problem.

The reality is that managers make decisions based on a combination of intuition, experience, and analysis. Despite the growing body of evidence that many of the best business decisions are not strictly rational, the belief in "decision theory" persists. This is a very Western view. Eastern cultures take a variety of different approaches. The Japanese, for example, have traditionally relied on a consensus-building process – *ringi* – rather than a decision-making formula. Under this system, any changes in procedures and routines, tactics, and even strategies are originated by those who are directly concerned with those changes. The final decision is made at the top level after an elaborate examination of the proposal through successively higher levels in the management hierarchy. The acceptance or rejection of a decision is the result of consensus at every echelon.

In the West, the emphasis is on finding the right answer and moving on to implementation as speedily as possible. The Japanese, in contrast, tend to place the emphasis on defining the right question. They are especially good at managing a process by which they reach a consensus on the need to make a decision about a particular issue. Once that consensus has been reached, it is possible to move quickly because there is broad agreement that a decision is needed.

REFERENCES

1 Kaplan, R.S. and Norton, D.P., 'The Balanced Scorecard – Measures that Drive Performance,' *Harvard Business Review*, January–February, pp. 71–79, 1992.
2 Kaplan, R.S. and Norton, D.P., *The Balanced Scorecard – Translating Strategy into Action*, Harvard Business School Press, 1996.
3 Kaplan, R.S. and Norton, D.P., *The Strategy-Focussed Organization: How Balanced Scorecard Companies Thrive in the New Business Environment*, Harvard Business School Press, 2000.
4 Kaplan, R.S. and Norton, D.P., *Strategy Maps: Converting Intangible Assets into Tangible Outcomes*, Harvard Business School Press, 2004.
5 Schneiderman, A.M., 'Time to Unbalance Your Scorecard,' *Strategy + Business*, Issue 24, pp. 3–4, 2003.
6 For a case example of this approach see Neely, A., Adams, C. and Kennerley, M., *The Performance Prism: The Scorecard for Measuring and Managing Business Success*, Financial Times Prentice Hall, 2002.
7 Argyris, C. and Schon, D.A., *Organizational Learning II: Theory, Method, and Practice*, Addison-Wesley Publishing, Reading, MA, 1996.
8 Rucci, A., Kirn, S., and Quinn, R., 'The Employee–Customer Profit Chain at Sears,' *Harvard Business Review*, January–February, pp. 83–97, 1996.

– CHAPTER 7 –

Developing and learning

"Management education should be based on experience. Managers cannot be made in vitro."

Henry Mintzberg

"In the simplest sense, a learning organization is a group of people who are continually enhancing their capability to create their own future. The traditional meaning of the word learning is much deeper than just taking information in. It is about changing individuals so that they produce results they care about – accomplish things that are important to them."

Peter Senge

"Just-in-time training is in sync with the learning needs of individuals in today's information environment because it allows learners to select immediately the precise information they require to fill skill and knowledge gaps as they occur."

Bruce Tulgan

"Failure is success if we learn from it."

Malcolm Forbes

Executive coaching

LAURENCE S. LYONS

> Executive coaching has emerged as the modern way of revitalizing people in organizations. Frequently regarded only as a tool to assist personal development, coaching has far more to offer – for example, as the central component for managing risk in a large-scale change program, to dramatic effect.

In common with many truly powerful management tools, coaching defies easy definition. Ambiguity has as yet failed to curtail explosive uptake of this new management art.

In its basic form, executive coaching involves a series of development conversations between two people, a coach and a client. The coach will assume that the client is vocationally competent. Executive coaching is certainly not training; its techniques cannot help a bad accountant become better at accounting. With its focus fixed firmly on *behavioral* development, executive coaching is in essence a modern form of process consulting, acted out in the workplace.

Today's external coaching practitioners are drawn from a rainbow of specialist disciplines. We can find the behavioral psychologist, career counselor, and business consultant all freshly rebranded as executive coach. Looking outside the management arena, popular comparisons with the more familiar sports coach abound, and carry varying degrees of validity. Then again, a new breed of life coach has emerged to further blur the broader definition.

Better business people

Variety in both style and approach is a healthy sign in any personal development interaction, as the world is full of people with differing needs. While each facet of coaching practice may indeed have something useful on offer, there is only one type sure to gain approval in the boardroom. Quite clearly, in the organizational setting executive coaching exists solely to produce better business people. The ultimate value of executive coaching lies in its ability to help better business people go on to produce better business results.

One individual will become a better business person by expanding his/her repertoire of inter-personal skills. Another will sharpen his/her strategic thinking. Yet others will want to learn how to become better team players or hone political savvy. Executive coaching offers each person a custom-built learning mechanism to grow their own healthy business behavior in whatever way is meaningful to them within their organization.

Headlines of an action plan, agreed between a coach and a client, will call out specific areas for personal change. A global or local change management agenda can be immensely helpful when building such a plan. This remains true even when the coach uses a purely non-directive approach, always insisting that the decision to select personal development areas remains squarely with the client.

Business people strive to get good value. Coaching offers most value when its dialog is "leading somewhere," provided that the destination represents a good place to be and the journey is worth the effort. When coach and client together contract to prioritize development areas – in the light of an organizational change agenda – coaching will extend its impact to become a powerful tool of strategic intervention.

The management of change

Change management initiatives emerge from an organizational will or ambition to become something different. Post-merger integration, product improvement, channel innovation, industry change, or new customer demands are typical events that will have set the stage for these major change initiatives. Their large-scale delivery programs require careful design, and are best orchestrated as the co-development of the organization together with its populace.

Change involves risk. Risk is simply the probability of program failure. It is important to remember that any vision of a future "changed" organization must be founded upon certain beliefs, so we are always dealing with a transformation that must necessarily contain untested assumptions. Risk ideally vanishes once a change program has achieved total success; in the meantime it is practically safe to assume that change management *is* risk management. Management of risk is the key to success in any change program. Risk will be well managed when the program properly engages both the process and social dimensions within the organization.

One ever-present assumption is that the organization itself has the skill and capacity for transformation, especially if it is to continue "business as normal" while doing so. Of course, corporate visionaries can never be fully informed by the personal reality of those who are to experience the change: this is because their new experience has yet to happen. To be effective, change architects must find ways to continually keep a two-way dialog flowing between vision in boardroom and reality as experienced by individuals on the ground. The efficiency of this conduit is a good proxy for measuring execution risk in any change program.

Achilles' heel

Those involved in the design and implementation of change programs have long felt that something important is missing in the management toolbox – an effective method for putting strategy into practice.

The crucial moment comes at the point of implementation. Once corporate direction has been established and hearts and minds won over, a well-designed change program will call into play dedicated components for anchoring the vision and remodeling behavior throughout the organization. So, at least, goes the theory. In practice, however, this critical stage of change management, where personal drive needs to pick up the baton from corporate intellect, has long been recognized as the weakest link in the whole change management chain. Until now.

A marriage made in heaven

When combined, change management and executive coaching offer the organizational designer a marriage made in heaven. The "top-down" voice of the organization from the former system provides broad direction to the latter. In return, we have at our disposal a behavioral mechanism for locally validating and instilling change in each team, group, and individual. The difference that can be made in the attitude of those individuals who are being asked to change can be remarkable once this connection is made. Change is no longer perceived only as an externally imposed command. An integrated approach allows for a win–win combination in which individuals can graft their personal development onto the corporate agenda. The new connection makes change relevant and desirable to all.

Integrated change management and executive coaching designs can provide the foundations of a cascading values-based change system, as depicted in Figure 7.1. This integrated model has now been used successfully in several organizations. Pages 976 to 978 briefly describe one recent intervention in Aventis that is based on this design philosophy.

Proper application of tools taken from the newly enhanced leadership toolbox makes it possible to construct a system of symbiotic organizational and personal change. Executive coaching can make the designer's dream come true: practical interventions now continuously link corporate intent all the way through to individual behavioral change; effectively, rapidly, and with much reduced execution risk.

Executive coaching 975

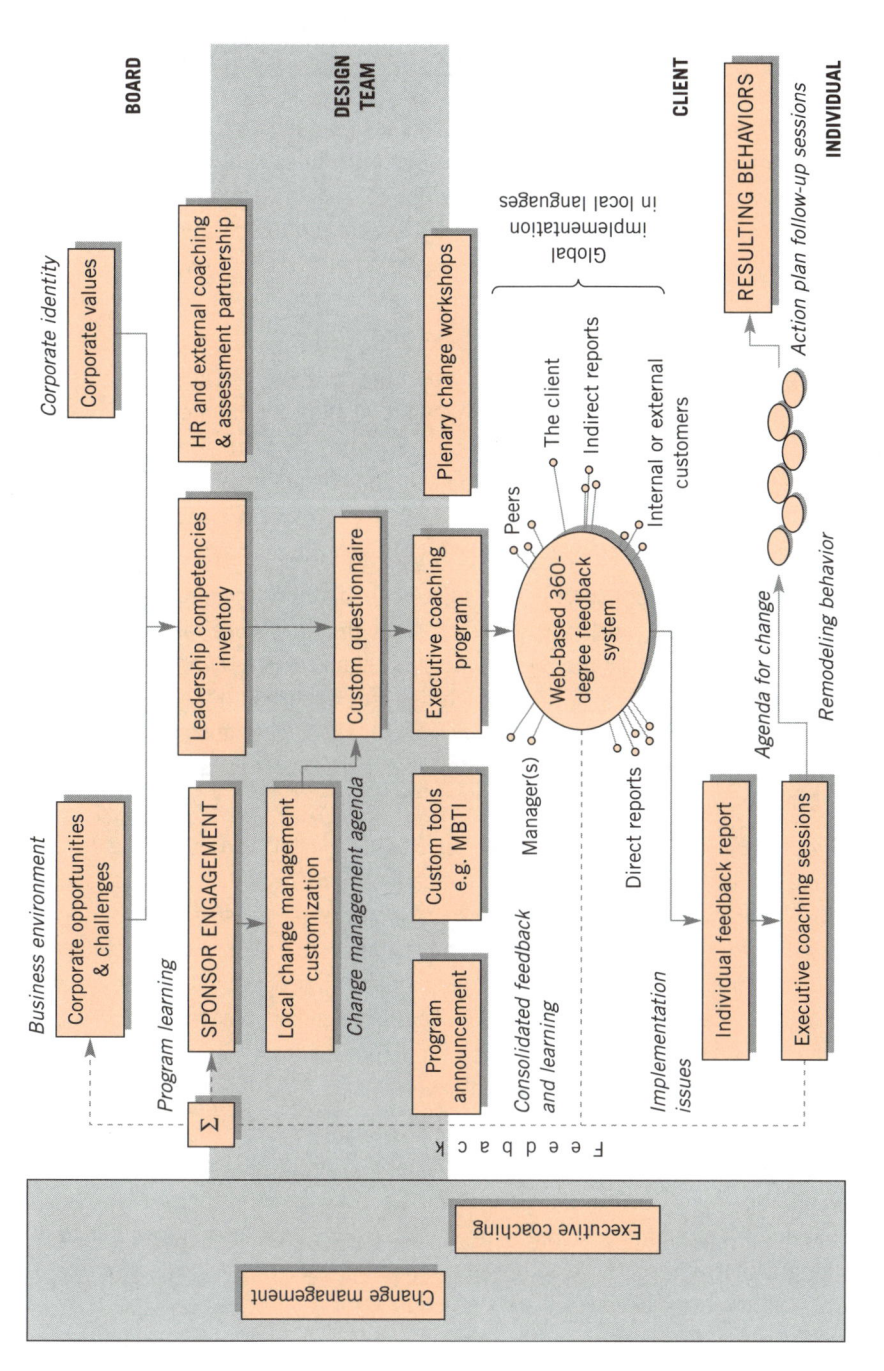

Figure 7.1: *From sponsor engagement to resulting behaviors: key process elements in an integrated system*

Aventis industrial operations coaching for change

Aventis, the major global pharmaceutical company renowned for its prescription drugs and human vaccines, reported core business sales of €17.6 billion in 2002. Industrial Operations is responsible for 50 manufacturing sites around the world employing some 19,000 people – over a quarter of the company's worldwide workforce. This case study demonstrates how executive coaching can be a driving force within a change management intervention, powerfully stimulating both individual and organizational change.

There are two distinct "clients" – one group and one team. Each is a quite separate global function supported by members of the same human resources organization. Leverage of the excellent relationship enjoyed by HR in each management function was to become extremely valuable in projecting a sense of credibility and program value in the mind of each client, inspiring their confidence, commitment, and support.

The Finance Controlling Group holds total responsibility for manufacturing accounting through a group of worldwide site controllers. Those taking part in this program come from across Europe, the US, Latin America, and Asia Pacific. All site controllers perform a broadly similar job, each holding a supremely pivotal role in an increasingly empowered and complex organizational structure. Aventis views the leadership development of site controllers as a critical success factor for its business.

The Process Development Management Team is responsible for an organization of around 600 employees working in four locations across Germany, France, and the US. The key role of process development is to create robust manufacturing processes, taking new chemical formulations from research and development laboratories through to full-scale global production. In a recent reorganization a top layer of management had effectively been removed so it became important that the two sub-functions – Chemistry and Biotechnology – work together effectively with minimal top management involvement.

From the outset HR intended to create more business value than would be achieved from simply providing personal coaching. As these two independent programs ran in parallel, the design team seized every opportunity to cross-fertilize knowledge and best practice in areas of change management and coaching effectiveness. This achieved economy of scale and cost-effective service from the external coaches and consultants.

Working in partnership with the external providers, HR's first action was to assemble a design team that included functional sponsors. The purpose of the

Aventis industrial operations coaching for change (continued)

first design workshop was to share opportunities and challenges being presented by the business context, and also to assess the full potential of available tools and approaches.

In reality, the ideas of linking coaching to organizational change were developed through this consultation process into a credible implementation plan which was large-scale in scope and change-management in nature. As a large-scale endeavor it required comprehensive planning, adequate financial investment, and demonstrable results. As a change intervention, significant importance had to be attached to positioning the programs in the mind of the clients, and in ensuring that the specific business process and contexts were well understood at an early stage of design.

The Aventis board has already signed off an inventory of company-wide leadership competencies. Much prior work had been done to ensure that the inventory was grounded in agreed corporate values and informed by the strategic challenges facing the company. These competencies are expressed in an Internet-powered, 360-degree feedback questionnaire that is being used for coaching senior managers throughout the business. By adding a customized subset to the inventory and using feedback from the questionnaire as the basis of individual coaching dialogs, value-based executive coaching was incorporated as a key change component into both programs. Given the global reach of the intervention, data entry, reporting, and personal coaching were made available in a variety of local languages.

The site controllers' program was based on a new role specification that had been developed in a recent conference. This put significantly more emphasis on strategic support, leadership, and the need to challenge, benchmark, and network. Some 19 role-specific competencies were compared to those on the standard corporate inventory which was then extended as necessary.

With its primary focus on inter-personal behavior and the improvement of teamworking, the process development program used a standard competence inventory together with the Myers-Briggs Type Indicator. To consolidate learning and behavior, a team workshop was incorporated at the end of this program.

Design work continued until the team was confident that individual coaching would relate clearly to the business organizational development objectives. Once this point was reached, HR formally made proposals for senior management approval, including the negotiation of costs and the implementation timetable.

Aventis industrial operations coaching for change (continued)

The Site Controllers group launched their program as part of a worldwide conference. The process development team utilized a regular management meeting to introduce their program. Customized assessment tools were used in both cases, as were face-to-face and telephone coaching. Importantly, each program incorporated follow-up coaching and a specifically designed questionnaire to assess impact.

Implementation went to plan. One difficulty did occur when some feedback reports were delayed due to late submission. But this was easily resolved through prompt action of the service providers. This demonstrates the importance of service in the supply of assessment tools; we were fortunate to have had a flexible and responsive supplier.

Participant confidentiality was maintained at all times while the structure of the exercise ensured that valuable aggregated information could be obtained to support the business objectives.

As always with qualitative endeavors, it is hard to measure success. We do know that the programs provided clear evidence of both intent to improve personal performance and the increasing use of personal development plans. At a business level, the process development management team has certainly functioned more effectively. The site controllers are today recognized as providing a new and higher level of support – in line with expectations in their role specification.

Bertrand Cordier, head of industrial operations controlling, reflects: "This program was definitely a vital component in changing the culture, values, focus and behaviors of the Controlling organization."

Describing the program as an "interesting and rewarding experience," Dr Manfred Worm, Aventis vice president process development chemistry, said that the program "provided us with a unique insight into our working preferences and the ways in which others perceive us. It has provided awareness of how we can communicate with others in a manner that they would feel most comfortable."

The HR team and senior management firmly believe in the value of the design team workshops and our investment in the "contracting" stage. Had these been omitted, the personal assessments would probably have gone ahead but with far less enthusiasm on the part of the participants and definitely less impact on the organizational change objectives. Indeed, we believe the full potential of the exercises would never have been achieved if not for the partnership relationship with the coaching consultants and the integrated systems approach.

Risky business

This is not to say good program design will always eliminate risk in a change program. Instead, an integrated system shifts the locus of risk from local execution back toward original corporate intent and the environment. This has to be good news. In the extreme, if a change program has to fail it is better it should do so because the corporate ambition was unattainable, rather than that the execution was inadequate.

Our over-pinning guidelines for program success are clear, if all too infrequently stated. We want good initiatives to materialize. We want locally unworkable issues to surface quickly and signal we have found a problem that needs to be addressed. We are prepared to learn and adjust while in transition. The world may not turn out as we expected. Our failure to sensibly orchestrate our own resources is the outcome to avoid at all costs. Environmental risk may be unavoidable; business risk may be countenanced; execution risk is unacceptable.

The benefits of an integrated system can be summarized by simple rules of risk reduction. Integrated design reduces execution risk: feedback dialog reduces business risk. Programs that consciously set out to satisfy these rules by flexibly linking the necessary social building blocks are poised to succeed.

Agent of change

Organizations engage outside suppliers for their ability to do essential things that otherwise would not be possible. From their wide experience in other organizations, external consultants may bring with them knowledge of tried and tested techniques. Often an organization is perfectly capable with its own resources to perform certain tasks, yet brings in external suppliers purely to reduce or help manage risk.

In change management work the general skill the coach-consultant must bring to the table is an ability to orchestrate feedback. Such orchestration ensures that feedback surfaces in whatever forum needs its particular message. This is a very wide requirement as recipients of feedback may include individual executives, a local sponsor, or the main board.

In order to orchestrate feedback, new communications channels may need to be opened up within the organization. This can be a sensitive activity. It is an area demanding strong role clarity whenever external agents are engaged in a change program, and is best carried out in partnership with the design team or sponsor.

The desired end point is not simply to deliver feedback, as this is but one step in a broader process of fostering a wider dialog. The goal is to create a process through which people in organizations can find pathways for change. Where this dialog may lead is purely a matter for the client organization to determine. It is always the client who knows their business. It is the client who must own any business decisions. The main job for the agent of change is to ensure that channels are open so that meaningful dialogs can take place.

Feedback

Coaching is founded in feedback. The collective experience of managers, direct reports, peers, and customers all provide raw feedback that must first be validated in a personal coaching session before incorporating into each client's action plan.

Validation takes on special meaning when used in a coaching context. It is a process through which raw data gets transformed into the self-insight on which a personal action plan will rest. There are many ways in which feedback might be inadequate, contaminated, or biassed. The need to validate arises because feedback is a product of many factors which include the general organizational climate, specific local, team, or personal issues that were prevalent when the feedback was collected, the time that the client has been in post, events that may have occurred after feedback was collected.

As an example, many senior executives today take on a number of roles, so it is not uncommon for their teams to report a feeling of alienation. In this case, the executive is less likely to be a poor communicator than a person who has insufficient hours in a day. Validation has to tease out the underlying cause. The validation process allows a client to address genuine skill development areas instead of trying to fix current gripes and merely tinker with apparent symptoms.

While validation tests the feedback, *challenge* tests the client's beliefs and assumptions. A good coach will always point out to the client those clear instances where overwhelming feedback is at variance with their personal view of reality. Without relaxing the pressure to challenge the client, a good coach will ensure that each individual's feedback gets validated at an early stage in their coaching relationship. Validating, challenging, and selecting personal development areas are part and parcel of the art of coaching.

The popularity of personal feedback in coaching goes hand in hand with our growing general awareness of the importance of feedback in organizations. This, too, is a good thing. Feedback is an essential component that change designers tend to forget. Often feedback is the only factor that will make a change design come alive in practice. Seasoned change practitioners notice it is invariably the dotted feedback lines of execution plans that turn out to be most important when sleeves get rolled up at implementation time. In the same way that coaches use feedback to benefit individual executives in developing behaviors, change agents should use feedback to squeeze out risk from organizational change programs. An easy way for consultants to achieve this is to simply treat the collective "organization" as another coaching client.

Providing feedback in an organizational setting, however flat, always involves personal risk when top-level intentions give rise to unforeseen obstacles elsewhere. It may be difficult for an individual to speak up, and for as long as this persists, the organization is really shouldering a hidden risk. Any gap between the sponsor's current expectation of program outcome and what may be believed to be workable locally represents a key source of execution risk. Fortunately, such risk is manageable. Execution risk can be handled through program feedback contained in a dialog orchestrated by the coach.

Orchestrating feedback

A fundamental role of an external agent, whether coach or consultant, is to orchestrate dialog. For this to happen smoothly, rules of best practice have to be in place. Before opening up any new dialog, the consultant will want to ensure that it is based on validated feedback that has been grounded in reality. In addition to this technical need, social rules of *etiquette* must create a context within which good practice can occur and where people feel comfortable to exchange candid views. Etiquette covers matters such as the treatment of confidential personal information and the use of consolidated data for program feedback.

An individual's action plan may follow one of two basic paths. The normal route is for the corporate values, ambition, and consolidated feedback to become manifest in a plan to develop personal behaviors. Another possible outcome, not much discussed in standard coaching texts, occurs when an individual believes the corporate ambition may not be workable.

A coach may observe a recurrent issue is being voiced by several executives in the same program and come to believe that there may indeed be a serious obstacle in the way of the change program objectives. This places the coach in a unique position. The coach is the only person in the system having this collective knowledge. The coach (or coaching team in larger programs) has clear sight of consolidated program feedback which is also a proxy for the cultural climate in which the program is set. Until this vital information, presently known only to the coach, finds its way to the design team for validation – and possibly to senior management to trigger a program adjustment – the business is carrying a dangerous risk.

One world

At first sight it might seem that executive coaching and large-scale organizational change programs are worlds apart. On closer inspection we find more than a good fit – each has something important to offer the other. By linking organizational development to personal change, integrated programs become increasingly attractive to the very people involved in change. With thoughtful design it becomes easy to create and manage the social paths so vital to the healthy development of an organization and the people within it.

Real life executive coaching and organization programs are of course far more complex than a single article could hope to cover. The underlying concept of risk has been introduced as a method of unifying some key ideas. The intention has been only to provide a glimpse of what may be achieved with the leadership tools change architects now have at their disposal. Rather than being worlds apart, we may, indeed, have found opportunities to build a better world.

Acknowledgements

Thanks to Helen Frost, Aventis HR Program Support, Frankfurt, for the case study material used in this chapter.

Myers-Briggs Type Indicator and MBTI are registered trademarks of Consulting Psychologists Press, Inc.

RESOURCES

Coulson-Thomas, Colin, *Creating Excellence in the Boardroom*, McGraw-Hill, 1993.

Coulson-Thomas, Colin, *Developing Directors: Building an Effective Boardroom Team*, McGraw-Hill, 1993.

Lyons, Laurence S., 'Coaching at the Heart of Strategy,' in Marshall Goldsmith, Laurence Lyons and Alyssa Freas, *Coaching for Leadership: How the world's greatest coaches help leaders learn*, Chapter 1, Jossey-Bass/Pfeiffer, 2000.

Marquardt, M. and Reynolds, A., *The Global Learning Organization: Gaining Competitive Advantage through Continuous Learning*, Irwin, 1994.

Senge, Peter, *The Fifth Discipline: The Art and Practice of the Learning Organization*, Doubleday, 1990.

Senge, Peter, *The Fifth Discipline Fieldbook: Strategies and Tools for Building a Learning Organization* (with Roberts, C., Ross, R., Smith, B. and Kleiner, A.), Nicholas Brealey, 1994.

Senge, Peter, *The Dance of Change* (Senge et. al.), Doubleday, 1999.

Senge, Peter, *Schools That Learn* (with Nelda H. Cambron-McCabe, Timothy Lucas, Bryan Smith, Janis Dutton and Art Kleiner), Doubleday, 2000.

Improving on success

MARSHALL GOLDSMITH

[Success may breed success yet it can also be dissipated by an inability to make necessary changes in behavior. But executive coaching – and the help of colleagues – can make it happen. Here's how.]

In my role as an executive coach, I am asked to work with extremely successful people who want to get even better. They are usually key executives in major corporations. They are almost always very intelligent, dedicated, and persistent. They are committed to the success of their companies. They have high personal integrity. Many are financially independent. They are not working because they *have* to. They are working because they *want* to. Intellectually, they realize that the leadership behavior that was associated with yesterday's results may not be the behavior that is needed to achieve tomorrow's innovation.

Most of us can easily see the need to change the behavior of others. This is one of the great challenges in leadership. We wonder why it is so difficult for them to change. Yet we often have difficulty in changing even small aspects of our own behavior. As we become more successful, it seems even harder to change. As Charles Handy has pointed out, the "paradox of success" occurs because we need to change before we have to change. However, "when things are going well we feel no reason to change."

I have reviewed research related to the topic of helping successful people change their behavior. Most research on behavioral change has focussed on dysfunctional behavior with clear physiological consequences (for example, alcoholism, drug addiction, eating disorders, or smoking). A substantial amount has been written on why successful people succeed. Not surprisingly, very little has been written on the unique challenges involved in helping successful people to change. The entire concept is somewhat counter-intuitive.

My assumption is that you, the reader, are a successful person. You may not be a key executive in a major corporation. However, I would guess that you are successful by most socio-economic standards. My second assumption is that you are working with other successful people. I am also going to assume that many of the people you work with are knowledge workers. In most cases your most valued co-workers are also there because they want to be there, not because they have to be. You frequently have the challenge of helping yourself and helping them make the changes that will take your team to the "next level."

What have I learned about helping people like you and your colleagues change?

In almost all cases, even the most successful leaders can increase their effectiveness by changing certain elements of their behavior. (The same is true for us as spouses, partners, friends, parents, and children.) By becoming aware of how we can improve, we can almost always get better. I have also learned that the key beliefs that can help us succeed can become challenges when it is time to change.

Four key beliefs of successful people

There are a variety of reasons why successful people succeed. Some factors can be changed and some cannot. Every person does not have the potential to succeed in every activity. For example, a poor athlete may become better through practice. However, physical limitations may prohibit his or her chance of ever becoming a professional. As Howard Gardner has pointed out, different individuals have different "intelligences" that can dramatically impact their potential in different fields.

My review of research focussed on the beliefs individuals hold that tend to differentiate more successful people from their peers (who may have similar potential to achieve). Successful people tend to have four underlying beliefs:

- I choose to succeed.
- I can succeed.
- I will succeed.
- I have succeeded.

Each of these beliefs can be labeled differently (self-determination, self-efficacy, optimism, and so on). But each increases the likelihood of achieving success. All of the beliefs are inter-related and positively correlated with each other. Each belief will be discussed in terms of why it generally leads to success and how it can inhibit change.

I choose to succeed. Successful people believe that they are doing what they choose to do because they choose to do it. Successful people have a high need for self-determination. The more successful a person is, the more likely this is to be true. Successful people have a unique distaste for feeling controlled or manipulated. In my work, I have accepted the fact that I cannot *make* executives change; I can only help them get better at what they choose to change. One of the great challenges of coaching (or teaching or parenting) is to realize that the ultimate motivation for change has to come from the person being coached, not the coach.

Having the belief "I choose to succeed" does not imply that successful people are selfish; many successful people are great team players. But it does mean that successful people need to feel a personal commitment to what they are doing. They need a sense of ownership. When leaders have a personal commitment to a mission, they will be much more likely to achieve results. They will lead with their hearts as well as their minds. They will also be effective in attracting and developing fellow "believers" who want to get the job done.

"I choose to succeed" is a belief that is highly correlated with achievement. Adding "and I choose to change" can be a very difficult transition.

Successful people's personal commitment can make it hard for them to change. The more we believe that our behavior is a result of our own choices and commitments, the less likely we are to want to change our behavior.

One of the best-researched principles in psychology is cognitive dissonance. The underlying theory is simple: the more we are committed to believing that something is true, the less likely we are to be willing to change our beliefs (even in the face of clear evidence that shows we are wrong). Cognitive dissonance works in favor of successful people in most situations. Their commitment encourages them to stay the course and to not give up when the going gets tough. But this same principle can work against successful people when they should change course.

Japan is a macro-level example of this phenomenon. In the 1980s Japanese managers were widely praised as role models for leadership behavior. The country's economic growth was one of the greatest success stories in business history. Books were written and benchmarking trips organized so that leaders from around the world could learn from Japan's success. This attainment had a deep impact on many leaders. Business success went beyond financial results and was transformed into national pride about "Japanese management." Leaders were not just proud of what they had achieved, they were proud of how they achieved it.

Unfortunately, the style that worked in the 1980s did not work in the 1990s. Rapid changes in technology, the economy, the role of manufacturing, and the workforce made the Japanese management approach far less desirable. It has taken a decade for many leaders in Japan to admit that their previous approach was no longer working. Many leaders denied it for years before accepting the fact that change was needed. The same commitment that had brought a huge success in the 1980s led to a mammoth challenge by the turn of the century. The leaders who have had the wisdom and courage to let go of the past are the ones who are succeeding in the new Japanese economy.

I can succeed. Successful people believe that they have the internal capacity to make desirable things happen. This is the definition of self-efficacy. It is perhaps the most central belief shown to drive individual success. People who believe they can succeed see opportunities where others see threats. This comfort with ambiguity leads people with high self-efficacy to take greater risks and achieve greater returns. To put it simply, they try more different things.

Successful people tend to have a high internal locus of control. In other words, they do not feel like victims of fate. They believe that they have the motivation and ability to change their world. They see success for themselves and others as largely a function of this motivation and ability, not luck, random chance, or external factors. (This explains why a state-run lottery is in effect a "regressive" tax.)

There is a very positive (and not surprising) relationship between the need for self-determination and internal locus of control. If people believe that the world is largely out of their control and that they are merely cogs in the wheel of life, they will not feel as bad about being controlled or manipulated. (After all, that's just the way it is.) If people feel that they can change their world and make it better, they will find external control and manipulation much more distasteful.

While the "I can succeed" belief is generally associated with success, it can (when combined with optimism) lead to what is called "superstitious behavior." This superstition can lead to difficulty in changing behavior even when others see this behavior as obviously dysfunctional.

Successful people often confuse correlation with causality. They often do not realize that they are successful because of some behaviors and in spite of others. Any human (in fact, any animal) will tend to repeat behavior that is followed by positive reinforcement. The more successful people are, the more positive reinforcement they tend to receive. One of the greatest mistakes of successful people is the assumption: "I am successful; I behave this way. Therefore, I must be successful *because* I behave this way."

Superstitious behavior is merely the confusion of correlation and causality. Many leaders get positive reinforcement for the results that occur. They then assume that their behavior is what helped lead to these results. Just as successful athletes believe in lucky numbers or perform rituals before a contest, successful business leaders tend to repeat behaviors that are followed by rewards. They may fear that changing any behavior will break their string of success.

One financial services chief executive was viewed as an outstanding leader but was also seen as incredibly weak in providing coaching to his direct reports. (This is fairly common for top executives.) He had developed an elaborate rationalization as to why coaching "at my level" was not important, was a waste of his time, how he had "made it this far" without providing coaching, and how he had never received much coaching himself and it obviously had not hurt his career.

Fortunately, this executive had some highly respected direct reports who were both courageous and assertive. He decided to accept their wishes and "give coaching a try." After achieving very positive success, he finally admitted that this had been a personal weakness for years. He realized he had been successful in spite of his lack of coaching, not because of it.

I will succeed. An unflappable sense of optimism is one of the most important characteristics of successful people. Successful people not only believe that they can achieve, they believe that they will achieve. This belief goes beyond any one task. Successful leaders tend to communicate with an overall sense of self-confidence. In a study with the consultancy firm Accenture involving over 200 high-potential leaders (from 120 companies around the world), self-confidence ranked as one of the top 10 elements of effective leadership for leaders in the past, the present, and the future.

Successful leaders not only believe that they will achieve, they assume that the people they respect will also achieve. As stated earlier, they see success as a function of people's motivation and ability. If they believe that their people have the motivation and ability, they communicate this contagious sense of optimism and self-confidence to others.

Successful people tend to pursue opportunities. If they set a goal, write down the goal, and publicly announce the goal, they will tend to do whatever it takes to achieve the goal.

While this sense of optimism is generally associated with success, it can easily lead to overload if it is not controlled.

Successful people tend to be extremely busy and face the danger of over-commitment. It can be difficult for an ambitious person with an "I will succeed" attitude to say no to opportunities. The huge majority of executives I work with feel as busy (or busier) today than they have ever felt in their lives. In North America, this perception was consistent for the last four years of the 1990s, a decade that featured one of the longest economic expansions in history. Most of these executives were not over-committed because they were trying to save a sinking ship; they were over-committed because they were drowning in a sea of opportunity.

Successful people achieve a lot and they often believe that they can do more than they can. My favorite European client was the executive director of one of the world's leading human services organizations. His mission was to help the world's most vulnerable people. Unfortunately (for all of us), his business was booming. His biggest challenge, by far, as a leader was avoiding over-commitment. Without externally imposed discipline, he had a tendency to promise more than even the most dedicated staff could deliver. Unchecked, this "we will succeed" attitude could lead to staff burnout, high turnover, and ultimately less capability to help those in need.

One of my clients recently completed a study of graduates of her company's executive development program. As part of the program each graduate was expected to focus on behavioral change. They were all instructed in a simple process to help them achieve this change. At the end of the program over 95 percent of the participants said (in a confidential survey) that they would follow the steps in the process. One year later about 70 percent had done so. This group showed huge improvement in effectively changing behavior. Approximately 30 percent did nothing. This group showed no more improvement than a control group. When they were asked why they hadn't implemented the behavioral change as promised, by far the most common response was "I was over-committed and just did not get to it."

I have succeeded. Successful people tend to have a positive interpretation of their past performance. High achievers not only believe that they have achieved results, they tend to believe that they were instrumental in helping the results get achieved. This tends to be true even if the positive outcomes were caused by external events that they did not control. So, in a positive way, successful people are "delusional." They tend to see their previous history as a validation of who they are and what they have done. This positive interpretation of the past leads to increased optimism toward the future and increases the likelihood of future success.

While the belief "I have been successful" has many positive benefits, it can cause difficulty when it is time to change behavior.

Successful people's positive view of their performance can make it hard to hear disconfirming information from others. Successful people consistently overrate their performance relative to their professional peers. I have personally asked over 10,000 successful professionals to rate themselves relative to their professional peers. Eighty percent to 85 percent of all successful professionals rated themselves in the "top 20 percent" of their peer group (who were, by the way the exercise was defined, statistically as successful as they were). Professions with higher perceived social status (for example, doctors, pilots, investment bankers) tend to have even higher self-assessments relative to their (equally prestigious) peers.

A classic example of this characteristic occurred with a group of medical doctors. I told the group that I had done extensive research that had proved that exactly half of all medical doctors had graduated in the bottom half of their medical school class. Two of the doctors insisted that this was impossible.

In trying to help successful people change, it is important to help them separate the message from the messenger.

Successful people tend to deny the importance of disconfirming input for three common reasons: the input is being delivered by someone they do not see as an "equal" in terms of success and therefore it "doesn't count'; they assume input that is inconsistent with their self-image is "incorrect" and the other person is "confused"; or they agree with the input but assume that the behavior must not be that important since they are successful.

Helping successful people change

In our work with leaders, my firm focusses on helping successful people achieve a positive, measurable, long-term change in behavior. To measure impact, we have completed before-and-after studies with tens of thousands of participants. The steps in the behavioral change process have been developed to work with successful executives. However, these steps can be used to help any successful person change their interpersonal behavior.

Have the successful person receive input on important, self-selected behaviors as perceived by important, self-selected raters. It is hard to measure effectiveness in changing behavior unless there is a clear agreement on what desired behavior is. Successful people have a high need for self-determination. Ultimately, the ownership of the behavioral change process will have to come from the people who are changing their behavior, not from an internal or external coach.

One reason that successful people tend to deny the validity of behavioral input is that they were not involved in determining the desired behavior for a person in their position. The more they are involved in determining what this desired behavior is, the more likely they are to buy in to the validity of demonstrating this behavior. Successful people are very responsive to help in achieving goals that they have set. They tend to resist changes that make them feel judged or manipulated.

Successful people also have a desire for internal consistency. If leaders publicly state that certain behavior is important, they will be more likely to strive to be a positive role model in demonstrating that behavior.

From my experience in developing leadership profiles I have found that almost all executives will develop a great profile of their desired behaviors. In most cases, understanding what behaviors are desired will not be their major challenge. Their major challenge will be demonstrating these behaviors.

An example of the value of involving leaders in developing their own profile occurred with a chief executive client several years ago. When he received feedback from his co-workers (on his own behavior), he looked skeptically at one of the lower-scoring items and asked: "Who wanted to include that item?" I replied: "You." He then remembered why he wanted to include it and also began to face the fact that the real problem was his behavior, not the wording of an item.

The first reason that people deny the validity of behavioral input is "wrong behaviors." The second reason is "wrong raters." If successful people select the raters, they will be much more likely to accept the validity of the ratings. Most executives respect the opinion of almost all of their key colleagues. By letting the successful person pick the raters, you can avoid a potential reaction like "why should a winner like me listen to a loser like him?"

One argument against letting people pick their own raters is that they will choose their friends and the input will not be representative. I have not found this to be true for two reasons.

First, almost all of the executives I have met end up selecting raters that are similar to the group I would select anyway. The only time they do not want to include someone is if the person is about to leave the company or they have a deep disrespect for a person. In my experience, I have never had an executive want to exclude more than two raters. Second, when 360-degree feedback is used for developmental purposes, the "items for improvement" that emerge from self-selected raters are quite similar to the items that come from other-selected raters.

Bev Kaye, Ken Shelton, and I asked more than 50 thought leaders and teachers to describe a time when they learned something that made a key difference in their lives. This led to our book *Learning Journeys*. More than half of the respondents described a situation in which they had received feedback or a challenge from someone they deeply respected. Interestingly enough, most agreed that the same message would not have had much impact if a different person had delivered it. This made us realize that the source of feedback and suggestions can be as important as their content. If successful people respect the source of information, they will be much more likely to learn and change.

Successful people will almost always respond constructively to advice and input when they are involved in selecting the behaviors and selecting the advisers. It is hard to deny the validity of items that we say are important as evaluated by raters that we respect.

After receiving input, have the person select one to two important areas for behavioral improvement. I used to suggest that executives pick one to three areas for behavioral change. After doing before-and-after interviews (one year after receiving input), most executives have let me know that three is too many. As mentioned earlier, a main reason that people do not stick with their change plan is over-commitment. They don't need another laundry list of goals. I now suggest that two should be the maximum number of behaviors to change. Changing one high-leverage (that makes the most impact) behavior can create a very positive difference.

You also need to challenge the people you are coaching to work on only those behaviors that can make a real difference. I was asked to review the 360-degree summary report of one of the world's most successful "new economy" chief executives. After receiving his confidential feedback, he considered his lowest item (listening) and asked himself: "If I become a better listener, will this make our company a better company? I am busy. Is working to become a better listener the most effective use of my time?" Before he began to work on changing his behavior, he checked it out with the board and with people he respected. He then decided that this change was indeed worth his effort.

I was greatly impressed with his thoughtfulness and maturity in dealing with this type of information. He had a clear mission and did not want to be distracted by dealing with behavioral change that was not relevant to the achievement of that mission.

If successful people see the connection between their behavioral change goals and their personal goals, they will be much more likely to change. They need to understand the difference between "because of" and "in spite of" behaviors. Some interesting research indicates that the desire to achieve the skills associated with success is more highly correlated with achievement than the desire for success itself. If the successful people you are coaching see the connection between changing behavior, achieving their vision, and living their values, they will be much more committed to doing what it takes to achieve lasting change.

Have the person involve respected colleagues in the behavioral change process. On-going involvement from supportive colleagues is almost always associated with positive behavioral change. Colleagues are much more likely to help if they feel that they are respected and that their advice is requested (as opposed to expected).

In involving key colleagues, we teach successful leaders to have brief conversations with each colleague during which they:

- thank each colleague for his/her feedback and express gratitude for the positive recognition that was received;
- let each colleague know the one or two areas for improvement that have been selected and why they are important;
- ask each colleague to help them by providing constructive, future-oriented suggestions that may help the leader achieve positive, measurable change;
- recruit respected colleagues to provide on-going supportive coaching to help them improve.

Findings on the usefulness of this process are very clear. Positive measurable change is much more likely to occur when successful people write down goals, announce these goals to respected colleagues, and involve them (in a supportive way) in helping achieve the improvement.

Teach the successful person's colleagues to be helpful coaches, not critics or judges. Unlike some forms of achievement (for example, academic achievement), behavioral change is dependent on an interpersonal relationship that involves more than one person. If successful people feel that they are being encouraged and supported by the people around them, they will be much more likely to stick with it and achieve positive, long-term behavioral change. If they feel they are being judged or manipulated, they will tend to become hostile to the process and stop trying.

Years ago, I had an experience of this "turn-off" effect with the chief financial officer of a major computer company. He was perceived as being aloof and arrogant. He saw himself as introverted and somewhat shy. (It is not uncommon for introverted high-level executives to be perceived as arrogant.) One suggestion from employees was that he "get off the top floor" and spend more time with the finance staff. On his first visit, he was greeted with sarcastic comments like "what's the matter, is the air conditioning broken up there?" and "what are you doing down here, slumming it?" He found the experience negative and embarrassing.

I later discussed this with one of his employees. The employee thought this was "funny" and did not realize that he was sabotaging his manager's efforts to meet his own request for behavioral change.

In our coaching process, we work not only with the executive but with the people around him or her. We do not get paid unless positive, measurable change occurs (after at least one year). The executive does not define whether he or she achieved positive, measurable change; the people around the executive determine that.

We help these co-workers help the executive by asking them to do the following:

- *Let go of the past and focus on the future.* Successful people are much more likely to change by envisioning a positive future than by reliving a humiliating past. Proving that a successful person was "wrong" is often a counter-productive waste of time. Successful people respond well to getting ideas and suggestions for the future that are aimed at helping them achieve their goals. The analogy used by racing drivers is "focus on the road, not on the wall." The executive should not be expected to do everything that their colleagues suggest. Leadership is not a popularity contest. However, well-intended and constructive suggestions for the future are almost always useful.

- *Be a supportive coach, not a cynic.* Successful people attribute more validity to the sincere recognition of progress than to the sincere acknowledgement of failure. Behavioral change is almost always "non-linear." Almost all adults will have setbacks when attempting to change behavior. Co-workers need to realize that this is a natural part of the process and not give up on the executive. We all have a tendency to revert to behaviors that were correlated with success in the past. The more successful we are, the easier it is to rationalize this return to past behavior.

    If the executive is encouraged to move beyond setbacks and colleagues do not dwell on them, the odds for long-term change improve greatly. The colleagues' goal should be to help the executive feel like a "winner" as they participate in the process of change.

- *Develop a follow-up process that provides an opportunity for on-going dialog.* Our research on follow-up has clearly shown that leaders are much more likely to achieve a positive, measurable change in behavior if they consistently involve selected colleagues (through follow-up dialogs) in the change process. These follow-up dialogs are very focussed and need take only a few minutes. They can be done by phone or in person.

    In one study (involving 8,000 respondents in a Fortune 100 corporation), only 18 percent of all leaders who received 360-degree input but did no follow-up were rated as a +2 or +3 on increased effectiveness in one year (on a −3 to +3 scale). This was no better than a control group who had received no training and no input. On the other hand, 86 percent of leaders who did consistent (or periodic) follow-up received top ratings on increased effectiveness.

    When co-workers are trained to be supportive coaches, the follow-up process provides an on-going opportunity for constructive suggestions and recognition. It reinforces the individual's public commitment to change. On-going dialog creates a process in which both parties are focussed on improving the relationship, not on judging each other.

    Mini-surveys can be a simple and efficient way to measure behavioral change. Mini-surveys are usually very short and focus only on the behaviors that have been selected by the person being coached. They are designed so that the raters evaluate behavior that occurs only during the coaching period. They focus on the rater's perception of improvement. If the executive agrees upon the desired behaviors for change, selects highly respected co-workers as raters, takes the process seriously, and follows up, positive change will almost always occur. After receiving the mini-survey results the executive thanks the raters, involves them in future change, and continues the process. This is almost always a positive experience for the executive and for the co-workers.

In summary, helping successful people change behavior is both an opportunity and a challenge. Our before-and-after research has taught us a great lesson – successful people will not change behavior because they go on a course; they will get better because of their own efforts and the efforts of respected colleagues. By understanding the unique issues involved in helping successful people change, organizations can get a huge return on investment from their development efforts.

The marginal gain for helping a highly successful person move from the top five percent to the top one percent may be greater (to the organization) than the gain from helping the average performer move from the top 50 percent to the top 20 percent. This is especially true with high-potential leaders who represent one of the greatest sources of value for the organization of the future.

RESOURCES

Goldsmith, Marshall, Kaye, Beverly L., and Shelton, Ken, *Learning Journeys*, Davies-Black Publishing, 2000.

Goldsmith, Marshall, Lyons, Laurence and Freas, Alyssa, *Coaching for Leadership: How the world's greatest coaches help leaders learn*, Jossey-Bass/Pfeiffer, 2000.

So you think you want to be coached?

MICK COPE

[Executive coaches are increasingly seen as an effective way to improve management performance or overcome leadership deficiencies. But there are a number of questions to ask yourself before approaching a coach.]

The potential power of coaching as a tool for personal development is self-evident. Examples of its use can be seen increasingly in the corporate world and in the sporting context (where coaches are becoming almost as famous as their clients). Coaching is also the tool of choice in areas as diverse as dieting, personal fitness, and teaching. The notion of someone who is there just for you – in a role that is designed to help you help yourself – has an obvious appeal. Little wonder, then, that coaching is rapidly becoming the dominant tool used by personal development experts.

Yet coaching has its limitations. One of the problems with coaching can be in the implicit transfer of the problem from client to coach. When people have a problem it is too easy to go to the coach in the expectation that they will wave a magic wand and solve the problem. The trouble is that the coach has no miracle cure. All they have is a process to help you make sense of the problem yourself. Coaching is simply about *helping people to help themselves*. Helping themselves is the definitive part of the statement.

Since this is the case, it makes sense to try to help yourself before you see the coach. Coaching is a collaborative relationship. You get out what you put in. If you are serious about it then get serious about undertaking the necessary preparatory work. That way when you meet the coach they will be more inclined to take you seriously and invest the necessary time and energy to resolve your issue.

People who believe they can benefit from coaching should first embark on a short journey of self-discovery. In this journey they will ask a number of questions of themselves in relation to coaching and draw a number of conclusions they might not have previously considered.

The 7Cs coaching framework outlined below offers a robust and well-used model that can help build a set of questions to both challenge and educate the client.[1]

What follows is a brief overview of the seven-stage model and some of the questions you might choose to consider before meeting your coach.

Coaching problems

Let's first consider the seven factors that can cause coaching to be ineffective. The typical problems that are often seen, but less commonly considered are as follows:

- The client is not sufficiently challenged in the opening stage to ensure they really understand their current position and test the seriousness of their intent to take action. The result is they embark on the coaching journey only to find that they don't really want to make the necessary sacrifices when placed under pressure.
- There is a failure to really clarify what root issues caused the present situation. The consequence is that solutions are generated that resolve surface symptoms but don't touch the root cause.
- Imported or ill-thought-out solutions are created that do not resolve the problem. This often occurs when coaches or clients think they have already made solutions that "worked elsewhere." The trouble is that all solutions are context dependent and can rarely be transported without some form of modification.
- Clients are not helped to work through the pain of change and to let go of the old way of thinking, feeling, and behaving. The client might be prepared to take on board a new way of working while the coach is around to act as an external prop, but if the change feels uncomfortable there will be a natural tendency to revert to the old ways.
- There is a failure to accurately measure and confirm that the change has delivered the desired outcome. This is often the hard part; actually confirming that the desired change has taken place. The important thing here is that it is easy enough to measure the extrinsic factors to demonstrate that the change has been successful, but unless the intrinsic factors are measured then any change may well be a short-term fix.
- Once the client's eye is off the ball and focussed on new ideas, they don't continue to operate in a new way. They then revert to their comfort zone. It is easy to stay on the diet when you are at the slimming club, but what happens when you are out on your own and get confronted by a large chocolate cake? Unless the coach has really embedded a sense of self-reliance and inner security, the old urges will take over and destroy all the good work.

- The change is not properly closed down and the end of the engagement just drifts. When this happens it can leave both the client and consultant with a sense of frustration and uncertainty where neither is really sure whether they have added value to the engagement.

Once the issues that cause change to fail are understood, it is a relatively simple process to create a series of steps and actions that need to be considered to help deliver a sustainable outcome.

The collaborative coaching framework

The collaborative coaching framework (Figure 7.2) offers a simple but robust framework for both the coach and client to follow.[2] The main benefit of using such a framework is that both coach and client work together in a collaborative relationship and avoid many of the power problems that arise in the coach/client relationship. The seven stages that the coach will seek to help the client consider can be broadly described as follows:

1. *Client* – this is about understanding the person and their problem. The first stage is to seek to understand the patterns and habits used in the way they feel, think, and behave. Second is to understand the problem to be addressed and what the perfect picture will look like.

2. *Clarify* – at this point the goal is to delve into the topic to understand what is really going on, to initially climb inside the roots of the situation, including issues that the client is happy to discuss and those issues they are less willing to share. Then consider what (if any) limiting beliefs the client might have that prevent them from moving forward.

3. *Create* – in this stage the optimum solution is generated. First of all define what could be done to resolve the situation and then finally what should be done, i.e. what is the best solution from the range of options. An important issue here is to challenge the assumptions that underpin each of the potential solutions. Second, assure that the choice is robust and will be carried through by the client.

4. *Change* – This is about mobilization, taking action, and delivering the desired outcome. The coach will first help the client consider what sacrifices and trade-offs are involved as a consequence of this action, i.e. just how difficult it will be for the client to let go of the old and accept the new. Second, to agree with the client what level of control the coach can and should exert to help mobilize action and ensure they will deliver on the agreed action plan.

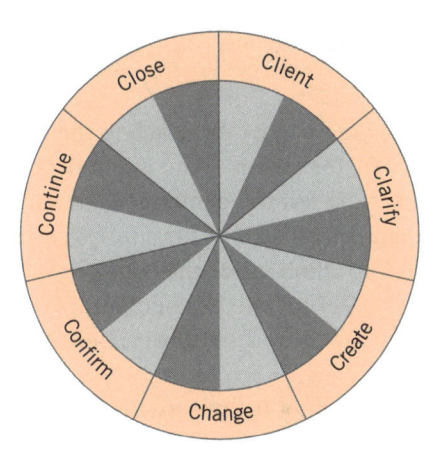

Figure 7.2: *Collaborative coaching framework*

5. *Confirm* – this is when the measurement takes place to see whether the desired outcome has been achieved. The key thing is to appreciate that the measurement stage can be the hardest because it is the point when the truth comes out and as a consequence it is the point when truth games are played. Second, to help the client develop an intrinsic measurement system so that they can self-determine when things are going right and wrong and any necessary corrective action.
6. *Continue* – continuance is about ensuring that the change will last – asking what will happen once the engagement is over and the client is left to be self-sufficient. In this case the coach must help the client consider what are the things that will cause the client to revert to old habits. Second, to ensure that the client is not deceiving themselves that big or complex problems can be solved by simple solutions.
7. *Close* – this is the point where the added value is noted and the client looks forward to their next developmental stage. The first point is to shift the client from looking just at the change and look at the value of the change. Second, to let go of the current topic and look forward to future developmental actions.

Over the life of the coaching partnership the journey will touch upon all seven stages in the framework. Importantly, the idea is not that it will start at the client stage, move to clarify, and move progressively round to the close stage. In a perfect world this might happen, but we don't live in a perfect world and as such coaches need to adapt and respond to the changing dynamics in the coaching relationship. Hence the coach will go to whatever stage is necessary, based upon the situation context, content, and client needs.

The client questions

The pre-coaching questions are given by the coach to the client before agreeing to a new coaching partnership. So, for example, you might decide that you need help in gaining promotion because your last three interviews haven't worked out very well. In this case the coach might spend a short time with you to understand the background, but would not seek to climb inside the issue or consider how to resolve the problem. Once they have a feel for the problem and what you wish to achieve, then you may be asked to take away a set of questions to consider ready for the next meeting.

Table 7.1 sets out the basic form of the pre-coaching question. Although there are variations, they give the basic backbone of the questions that you should seek to address before engaging fully with the coach.

Table 7.1: *The basic form of the pre-coaching question*

	Questions	Explanation
CLIENT	1a Why do I want coaching, why now, and why with this coach – what can the coach do that I can't already do for myself?	Are you really serious about addressing the issue or is the need for a coach simply a way to transfer the problem onto someone else's shoulders? What specific value do you want the coach to give – if you don't know, then how will they?
	1b What is the change I want to make and how will it deliver value for me?	If you can't be specific about the outcome you want then you will enter the coaching session looking woolly and vague. Hence much of the time will be spent going round in circles trying to understand exactly what you want to achieve.

	Questions	Explanation
CLARIFY	2a What is stopping me from doing this already?	Most coaching sessions are about helping the person take their foot off the brake rather than putting their foot on the accelerator. People generally have all the resources they need to achieve what they want – they just don't know or believe it.
	2b Can I be sure that my assumptions about the issue are not biased or clouded?	We all have maps of the world that are clouded and corrupted. Clouded by laziness and a unwillingness to look beyond the horizon. Corrupted because we believe the stories that our friends, newspapers, and television tell us. Much of the coaching process is about stripping away these false horizons and getting a clear and focussed picture of what is going on.
CREATE	3a – Do I have a hidden solution already in mind, and am I really prepared to look at alternate options?	Many people meet the coach with a predefined solution in mind. They might not voice it at the first meeting, but it is there. An example of this might be I am unhappy (the answer is a villa in Spain) or I am overweight (the answer is a diet).
	3b – Have I thought through the criteria for a successful solution?	Too often solution generation takes place without understanding the criteria for a good solution. It always pays to consider Time (when do I need it by?), Cost (can I afford it?), and Quality (how perfect does it need to be?).

	Questions	Explanation
CHANGE	4b What might I find difficult about making the change?	All change is about letting go of the old and accepting a new way of thinking, feeling, and behaving. However, as human beings we tend not to like this and prefer to stay in the same old slippers or comfy chair. This seeks to question just what difficulties will surface with the letting go and whether you are prepared to deal with them.
	5a How might the coach help me through any difficult stages?	At some point when preparing for your first marathon you may not want to get out of bed. Does the coach get you out (and so begin the addiction of dependency) or do they let you stay in bed and deal with the problem on your own (with a risk that you might give up altogether)? The level and type of intervention that you want and need must be considered.
CONFIRM	5a How do I "know" there is a problem – what evidence do I have?	It is easy to go to the coach and give vague outlines of a problem, but you need evidence. This evidence helps convince the coach that you are serious and gives a baseline to know when you have resolved the problem. The difficulty is that since most coaching problems are intrinsic rather than extrinsic, you need to look inside for evidence. Something that we are not really encouraged or trained to do.
	5b How will I "know" when it is resolved?	Coaching is a finite activity – if you don't have a clear end point, the risk is that you go on and on – never quite graduating and closing down the engagement.

	Questions	Explanation
CONTINUE	6a Have I tried this before (unsuccessfully)? If so, why did it not stick?	So often coaching has little to do with the activity under consideration. In many cases it is about someone's inability to stick with change (note the huge failure of diets to stick). If you have a habit of not sticking with change, then be honest and tell the coach about it. That way it can be considered as part of the coaching cycle.
	6b What are the triggers that might cause me to revert to old habits?	Triggers are external factors that cause slippage and reversion to old habits. Think about the things that have historically caused you to slip and share them. You can then prepare a plan to deal with them before the coaching partnership is closed.
CLOSE	7a When complete, how will things be different for me?	Coaching that focusses on the change itself will struggle to stick. Coaching that can focus on the end value has more chance of lasting. Don't think about giving up smoking – because all you will picture in your mind is the cigarette and the associated pleasure that is being lost. Instead define how life will be richer at the end and hold on to this as a future anchor.
	7b What problems might I have in maintaining the change once the partnership is closed?	One day the coach will leave. Think about any difficulties you might have when this happens and deal with them while the coach is around – don't leave it to the last minute to panic and start calling them for help.

By considering these questions before meeting with the coach you can signal how serious you are about delivering a sustainable change. By doing so, you signal that you are not just looking for a quick-fix miracle solution. Be serious about yourself and the coach will be as well.

However, it is important to understand what can often happen when the client is asked to undertake work prior to the first session. Three of the more common outcomes include the following:

- You smile enthusiastically and agree to do this, but never quite find the time to look at the questions. This is often an indication that you did not really want to be coached, and maybe just wanted cuddles and a simple solution provided on a plate. As such it is a good outcome because it has saved wasting both players' time.
- You take the questions away, begin to consider them, and find that you don't actually need the coach after all because your answer has surfaced in undertaking the investigation. This is coaching in its purest form – where the coach has helped the client with a minimum of effort and cost on both sides.
- In working on the questions you can answer half of them but really struggle with the other half. This is great because it helps both you and the client understand where to focus most of the energy.

Hopefully you will fall into the latter two options. But if you find that the first has happened, you will have saved yourself a great deal of time and possible embarrassment.

Reaping the anticipated benefits

Although some people might view these questions as potentially off-putting and painful, they should be viewed in the same way as the mock exams. This pre-test process serves a number of purposes. Clearly the major one is to help filter out those who "will" from those who "won't" or "can't." But they also have other additional benefits. They help grow confidence in your ability to deliver, they take a lot of the fear away from the process, and they help to identify areas where improvement can be taken prior to the real event. All of which in a coaching context can add real value for the coach and client. Coaching is a very expensive personal development option and anything that helps limit the level of pain and cost for both players must add value.

Possibly one of the most important aspects of the pre-coaching questions is that they help begin the transfer of ownership. The soft underbelly of coaching is the idea of power distribution. It is far too easy for the client to end up in a subordinate role, where the coach is viewed as a god, guru, or genius, someone who has the wisdom and power to solve all your problems. This leads to a huge array of issues, one of which is the notion of dependency. As with any cult leader, once the leader dies or disappears, the cult will wither and fade because the people are in most cases overly dependent on the leader. This can also happen (and often happens in the sporting world) when the client ends up in a subordinate role. Once the coaching is over, old habits return and all the good work fades because the coach is no longer around to prop up the good work.

Use of the pre-questioning process helps reduce the chance of this happening because from the outset the coach is saying to the client "you own this," "you must do the work," and "you must own the solutions." As a consequence the questions help move the coach's role from that of content expert to process guide and as such one they can withdraw more easily.

Honest coaching

However, as with all things, there is a cost – and this cost falls to you as the person who wants to be coached. So if you do think you want to be coached, you must be prepared to commit time and energy to the necessary pre-work. In most cases this pre-work isn't of an extrinsic nature where you have to carry out research or write papers. It is significantly harder than that. It is the world where you need to look inside and be honest with yourself, because often all the great coach is doing is asking you to look in the mirror – and asking you why you don't do certain things. As a client, are you really willing to allow the coach to shine a light into dark caves that you might be happier to bypass? This can involve emotions, which both parties need to recognize is OK as part of learning.

Arthur C. Clarke suggested that "the best measure of a man's honesty isn't his income tax return. It's the zero adjust on his bathroom scale." In answering the pre-questions it is easy to fake it and not tell yourself or the coach the truth. But the only person who is wasting their time is you. Honest use of the questions will help you really address many of the issues that have prevented peak performance in the past. In surfacing issues that you have suppressed or not bothered to look at, the coach can really help turn poor performance into peak performance – something you both wish to achieve from the coaching partnership.

So, if you do think that you want be coached, take time out to consider the pre-coaching questions and start the process now – rather than waiting for the coach to push the start button.

RESOURCES

Argyris, Chris and Schon, Donald, *Organizational Learning: A Theory of Action Perspective*, Addison-Wesley, 1978.

Argyris, Chris, *On Organizational Learning*, Blackwell, 1993.

Argyris, Chris, *Knowledge for Action*, Jossey-Bass, 1993.

Argyris, Chris, *Flawed Advice and the Management Trap*, Oxford University Press, 2000.

Cope, Mick, *The 7Cs of Coaching: The Practical Guide to Collaborative Coaching for Optimum Results*, FT Prentice Hall, 2004.

Cope, Mick, *Lead Yourself: Be Where Others Will Follow*, Momentum, 2001.

Training and development – new approaches for changing needs

DAVID BIRCHALL AND MATTY SMITH

[
E-learning has been hailed as a means for delivering more effective training and development at lower cost. But will the reality live up to the expectation? What are the implications for managers? How can managers take advantage of the new opportunities?
]

Many factors are combining to put pressure on organizations to increase their levels of training and development. The expanding reach of automation resulting in the shift to knowledge work, the rapid uptake of new technologies, the drive to improve effectiveness to combat increasing global competition, the shortage of key skills, the rising expectations of the workforce are just some of the forces for change. Managers find themselves confronted not only by the demands of the organization for better resource utilization but also by staff for improved opportunities for professional development. In addition, managers themselves need to manage their personal development in order to ensure the currency of their capabilities and also act as a strong role model for others.

The term e-learning has become widely used but, as with many new terms, there is no one standard definition. This definition from the European Commission gives a comprehensive picture:

> E-learning is the acquisition and use of knowledge distributed and facilitated primarily by electronic means. This form of learning currently depends on networks and computers but will likely evolve into systems consisting of a variety of channels (e.g. wireless, satellite) and technologies (e.g. cellular phones, PDAs) as they are developed and adopted. E-learning can take the form of courses as well as modules and smaller learning objects. E-learning may incorporate synchronous (real-time) or asynchronous (any-time) access and may be distributed geographically with varied limits of time.

So e-learning systems offer a flexible range of approaches capable of adaptation to many different training and development needs. The learner can be freed from time and place constraints. Short learning opportunities in the form of learning objects can be accessed on a just-in-time basis at the workplace to support everyday problem solving, the demands of new situations, or novel project work. Longer programs can be designed to lead to formal qualifications.

In the early stages of e-learning emphasis was placed on the electronic delivery of course-ware, the knowledge to be passed on to the learner. But many systems now provide much more than just basic knowledge for self-study. Electronic diagnostic tools provide competence reviews and assessment of learning needs to help in deciding an appropriate route for learning. Electronic tutoring, progress monitoring, and assessment are being built into comprehensive e-learning offerings. Many systems act as a gateway (a learning portal) to learning resources from a variety of sources distributed across the net. Learning solutions can thus be tailored to each individual learner's particular needs. The technology of mass customization makes this possible at a reasonable cost. As the supply industry is becoming more sophisticated, new quality standards are being introduced to ensure uniformity in basic standards underpinning development and inter-operability.

The e in practice

In leading-edge companies with high numbers of knowledge workers e-learning is just one element in the support of these workers. Knowledge management systems are coming together with e-learning to ensure that new knowledge is effectively captured and made available in learning resources. Communities of practice are becoming commonplace, set up to accelerate knowledge generation and sharing. The infrastructure has been put in place to encourage and support learning not only of individuals but of groups and organizations as well. Efforts are being taken to develop a learning culture, including systems of mentoring to motivate learners and to assist with the embedding of the learning.

A 2003 study at Henley Management College found that e-learning within organizations was being used to meet a multiplicity of needs. It seems particularly effective where consistency of training approach and content is sought across the organization (best practice transfer, improvements in the consistency in the use of IT systems) and where rapid rollout of new systems has to be supported by wide-scale training (software training to remote locations, training of mobile technicians in the maintenance of new hardware). It is also effective in providing "micro training": short training inputs not worth leaving the workplace to participate in.

E-learning is now beyond the honeymoon phase and expectations of the benefits are more realistically positioned. While the scale of adoption is less than original forecasts, it is widely recognized that much can be done to improve on early e-learning offerings. With new approaches being developed, there is now less emphasis on the application, or functionality of the technology and more focus on its application, with an increased attention being paid to how learners learn and their learning needs. E-learning is increasingly being seen as a support to learners, but only as part of an effective learning process. "Blended learning" – a combination of e-learning and face-to-face activities possibly supported by electronic interaction among learners and with tutors – is seen as offering a better solution to the development needs of organization-based learners.

E-learning and management development

Management is clearly a complex process which does not lend itself to decomposition. While many popular competency models attempt to fragment overall competency into subcompetencies, these frameworks offer little in the way of explanation of high performance. Given this complexity, the design of management development programs is a mix of science and art.

Experienced managers often find it difficult to explain just how they carry out their job. This is because they have considerable knowledge of which they are not specifically aware. This has been described as *tacit knowledge* – that which we know but can't tell. It has been suggested that the role of the management developer/educator is to help learners understand the larger role that tacit knowledge plays in their lives and to help them avoid believing that they are acting more rationally that they actually are. By making tacit knowledge explicit in propositional form managers can better understand the conditions under which it is most appropriately used.

This process of making tacit knowledge explicit, learning how to value it, and finding ways of making it available in propositional form is a huge challenge for the management developer regardless of approach and medium for delivery. In their classic work in the 1970s, Chris Argyris and Donald Schön distinguish between *espoused theories* and *theories in use*. They suggest that managers are intellectually and emotionally committed to espoused theories which describe the world as they would like it to be but which don't accurately describe their own actions. They see what they anticipate seeing and thus get self-confirmation of their actions, which in turn leads them to develop more poorly founded theories about their actions. This self-confirmatory learning they define as *single-loop learning* as opposed to *double-loop learning*. Double-loop learning is the result of openness to feedback and self-analysis, a much more challenging and often painful process.

Managers who are seeking to achieve double-loop learning respond well to situations which enable "learning from doing," i.e. activity-based learning. Kolb (1974 and 1984) presents a four-stage model for experiential learning:

1. Planning and deciding to take action (active experimentation).
2. Implementing and experiencing the consequences (concrete experience).

3. Observing outcomes and considering them against expectations, intentions, and beliefs (reflective observation).
4. Concluding and relating to other experiences (abstract conceptualization).

The cycle starts over again.

Working with others jointly tackling problems in learning sets can be particularly fruitful if the team members set out to maximize personal learning. It is now nearly 50 years since Reg Revans proposed *action learning* based on groups of colleagues working together on real work-based problems. Motivation is likely to be high since solutions to problems can clearly impact directly in the workplace. Also the managers can see the results of their analysis, planning, and implementation. Working in teams enriches the process since members will each have their own perspective on issues and questioning leads to modification of espoused theories and hence double-loop learning.

Given the impact on the learning process of a focus on solving authentic problems and of interacting with challenging peers and others, is there a role for e-learning?

The importance to the manager of basic knowledge and understanding should not be underestimated. Areas such as budgeting, project planning, employment legislation, appraisal systems, marketing management, business analysis all have an underpinning knowledge component which can be made readily accessible through an e-learning system. Also basic tests of understanding are available. E-learning systems can provide access to knowledge nuggets on an as-needed, just-in-time basis which offers clear advantages over having to wait for scheduled courses.

Through the loops

Earlier we stressed the importance of double-loop learning which is developed through exposure to challenge, particularly through testing this declarative knowledge in practice. E-learning can make a contribution to this. First, e-learning formats can be configured to help learners organize their arguments and to develop a case for action. Through membership of an electronically based learning network these ideas can be exposed to challenge by others. Learning also takes place through the active engagement of other participants in the learning network. This process may develop naturally from interactions at work, e.g. in task groups or special working parties, but it is likely to benefit from the support of an experienced facilitator.

E-learning systems can also link into the company's human resource system. This may include competence frameworks which enable personal review and the identification of specific needs. A catalog of development opportunities offered by the business can be made available through the learning platform. A record of achievement can be maintained electronically.

Any well-devised e-learning system will be subject to regular review. This gives learners the opportunity to express opinions, critique personal benefits, and suggest means for improvement and areas for development not currently catered for. This process of reflection on the learning experience is clearly invaluable to those responsible for training and development, but it can also help individual learners in taking personal stock.

Management development is clearly being enriched by the addition of e-learning. But as we pointed out earlier, blended solutions have more to offer than e-learning on its own. When putting together a personal development strategy, blended learning offers managers a richer array of approaches to choose from, ranging from attendance on more traditional courses to e-learning, combining off-the-job learning with formal study, informal learning any time, any place, mentoring or coaching, individual and team-based, activity-based and action learning, accredited and non-assessed. E-learning can be used as either central to the approach or as additional support.

One of the most significant benefits of e-learning to the learner is the opportunity it affords to take personal control of one's own development. It can be seen to democratize the learning process.

Managers and e-learning

New approaches to training inevitably bring about new challenges. Faced with increasing competitive pressures many organizations are seeking to become more effective as learning organizations. This implies encouraging all staff to actively engage in a process not only of personal development but also of contributing to the improvement of organizational understanding and capability. But a marked change which has taken place over the last decade is the shift in thinking about who is actually responsible for managing personal development. Governments as well as employers are promoting the concept of individuals taking personal responsibility for their training and development – planning, undertaking, and reviewing. There is also increased emphasis on achieving external recognition for achievement, not only as a motivating factor but also as a means for securing future employment in a rapidly changing labor market.

What is the manager's role in building a culture of self-managed development and where might e-learning sit? In the Henley report the authors note: "In many organizations there is not a culture where workplace learning is recognized as legitimate, even where courses being undertaken by employees will directly impact on their job performance." This may well reflect managerial philosophies and approaches. Unless managers actively support and encourage staff they are unlikely to see the value to the organization of their personal development. But possibly of greater importance is the emphasis placed on ensuring that opportunities exist, wherever possible, for the application of the newly acquired knowledge and skills. Clearly regular reviews will contribute significantly to the development of new knowledge and skills. Specific steps that may be taken include special but business-relevant projects, assignment to working parties, task groups, or work shadowing.

It is in the interests of management to ensure that personal development sponsored by the employer fits with the needs of the organization, both short and long term. Managers have an important role to play as internal customers of training and development departments and working with these specialists in ensuring the sound specification of development needs and then ensuring that the training offered meets specification. The processes underpinning the design of e-learning courses draw on a wide range of skills but depend for success on sound specification and continuous dialog with customers to receive early feedback on effectiveness.

Learner motivation is one issue which is of particular concern and actions by managers can make a difference. We earlier referred to the move away from pure e-learning with its emphasis on self-directed study to a more blended approach. In part this has been done to address the issue of poor course completion rates and limited learner achievement. The importance of social interaction in the learning process has been reaffirmed. This interaction may be with tutors or trainers, but, possibly more importantly, it is between peers. It may be in a virtual environment, at the workplace, or in the training room, or a combination. It serves a number of purposes. It reduces feelings of isolation; it gives support in overcoming difficulties of understanding; it tests learner understanding; it gives an opportunity to discuss application at the workplace and compare and contrast different situations, hence strengthening understanding. Management has a role to play in ensuring that the learning system is adequately meeting learner needs, that learners have the space to learn, and that line managers show support and encouragement.

Mentoring, particularly for high-level skills development, is being recognized as a useful component in the support of the blended learning process. Ideally mentors are not directly involved with the operational work of the learners. Their role is very much one of encouragement and support, with a particular emphasis on learner self-reflection. For the manager carrying out the mentor role outside the immediate area of responsibility, it can help develop a personal understanding of issues and problems confronting learners.

Managers have a key part to play in ensuring that appraisal and performance review systems are effective in identifying development needs, plans are agreed, and follow-ups are effective. The diversity of learning styles has long been recognized. So ideally a choice of study modes should be available to meet the training needs identified. However, e-learning should not be seen as the choice of last resort. Its unique benefits make it the most appropriate route for many learning interventions. Systems need to be in place to offer choices and assist learners in making a reasoned choice.

There is an increasing recognition of the manager's role in developing the organization as a learning community. Many aspects already covered demonstrate the potential contribution. One final element is that of passing on management know-how to others. Managers can themselves take on a tutoring role with blended learning delivery. Where learners are distributed, particularly across divisional or national boundaries, this can be of particular benefit to learners but also enriching for the manager concerned.

Commentary

Mentoring

When Odysseus, King of Ithaca, left for the Trojan Wars (circa 800 BC) he instructed Mentor, his trusted companion, to assume the role of father figure, adviser, counselor, tutor, and role model to Odysseus' son Telemachus. Jump from the writings of Homer to the present day and the word "mentor" has become part of everyday language, signifying a wise and trusted counselor, a sagacious adviser, a tutor.

For some time now mentoring has been recognized as beneficial for managers. In a survey of 1,200 top managers of the largest US corporations in the 1980s, for example, over two-thirds had been mentored.[3] In a later study of Fortune 500 CEOs, when asked what factors had contributed to their success, many CEOs referred to effective mentoring as a key factor.[4] Women have found mentoring particularly effective as a means of smashing the glass ceiling. In a survey conducted in 1996, of the female executives interviewed 99 percent had been mentored.[5]

Modern definitions of the term include that of Linda Phillips-Jones, one of the leading experts on mentoring, who describes mentors as "skilled people who go out of their way to help you clarify your personal goals and take steps toward reaching them." In her book *Mentors and Protégés* she describes some characteristics of mentors and the mentoring relationship:[6]

- Mentors are usually older than their protégés.
- Mentors frequently – but not always – initiate the relationship.
- Mentor–protégé relationships do not need to be particularly close.
- It is possible to have more than one mentor at a time.
- There are patterns and cycles in mentor–protégé relationships.
- Mentoring should benefit both partners equally.

In an organizational setting mentoring may cover the following areas: appropriate dress, conflict resolution, communication, company protocol and culture, ethical practice, leadership, networking, office politics, presentation, project management, time management, work–life balance.

What can a mentor do for you?

Today mentoring is recognized as a very important adjunct to career development and many companies offer mentoring relationships. Here's how a mentoring relationship can help. A good mentor can:

- expand horizons and perspectives;
- help build confidence and give moral support;
- provide a professional role model;
- improve skills levels and emotional and intellectual development;
- provide professional connections, and acquaintance with industry-specific values and customs;
- provide objective feedback on a performance;
- help enter into and advance within a chosen career.

Mentors can be very useful in relieving one of the most significant factors in determining job satisfaction: stress. According to Linda Hill, consultant and Harvard Business School academic, even the most experienced managers often report feelings of conflict, ambiguity, and isolation. "The myriad challenges encountered when one becomes a manager are difficult to shoulder alone," she says. Unfortunately, new managers can be reluctant to ask for help; it doesn't fit their conception of the boss as expert."[7]

A good mentoring relationship is a win–win situation. Possible benefits to the mentor include:

- satisfaction from passing on knowledge and experience;
- a sense of know-how;
- increased sense of self-worth;
- credibility and prestige through the success of the protégé;
- greater power;
- financial rewards;
- extra resources for professional assistance on work projects;
- refined interpersonal skills;
- enhanced status in the organization;
- creative input;
- revitalized career.

Possible benefits to the mentor include:

- increased confidence;
- greater self-worth;
- improved opportunities for advancement;
- avoiding mistakes made through lack of experience;
- increased sense of authority;

> **Commentary (continued)**
>
> - productivity and ratings higher than for non-mentees;
> - better pay;
> - increased career satisfaction;
> - improved skills and knowledge;
> - faster attainment of executive status.

The mentor's role

The mentor's role varies according to a variety of factors, including the quality of the relationship between mentors and the mentee, the level of skills and knowledge of both parties, time available, and organizational culture.

With an experienced mentor and relatively inexperienced mentee the mentor may take on the role of tutor, counselor, encourager, life coach, and if both parties are located close to one another they may, over time, develop a strong friendship. For a more experienced mentee, the mentor's role may be closer to sponsor and facilitator. They may provide a sounding board, someone to discuss and explore ideas and experiences.

In the various literature on mentoring a number of specific roles associated with mentors have been identified, including the following:

- *Acceptor*: in acceptor role, a mentor provides unconditional support and encouragement for their mentee. This encourages the mentee to take risks and push themselves beyond their normal boundaries without fear of failure. Good mentors are fans of their mentees. They visualize how through their efforts the mentee will be improved to fulfill their full potential. In return the mentor receives affirmation of their own qualities through the respect and trust and admiration of the mentee.

- *Counselor*: the mentor can help the mentee with their personal problems. Ethical issues, such as the balance between maintaining personal integrity and values and career advancement or the struggle to maintain a work-life balance, can be discussed. If the mentor can empathize with the mentee, personal internal conflict can be worked through and resolved. If left undealt with, this internal conflict can cause withdrawal, interfere with career satisfaction, and adversely affect the quality of work and quality of life.

- *Coach*: the role of coach is one of the most important that a mentor can play. As coach the mentor may provide crucial information about an organization's mission, vision, and goals. They can suggest appropriate strategies for completing tasks as well as providing critical feedback. Linda Hill acknowledges the role of mentor as coach, saying: "Given the complexities of their new responsibilities and all that they have to learn, new managers, no matter how gifted, still need coaching." Without a mentor to coach them a new recruit will be at a distinct disadvantage, lacking critical information and insight about the organization.

- *Challenger*: by pushing the mentee through the assignment of difficult and challenging tasks the mentor prepares the mentee for promotion and greater responsibility. Mentees must be prepared to work outside their comfort zone; the mentor can help break the barrier. People who do not have access to challenging assignments will lose skills over time.
- *Friend*: the mentor as a friend may provide a different generational perspective. They can teach the mentee to be more comfortable in the company of senior figures. In turn the mentor may be re-energized by the friendship of someone younger than themselves and gain a renewed sense of vitality.
- *Listener*: another essential and important role of the mentor is that of listener. Non-judgemental listening is a rare skill. Listening may sound easy but try out some of your friends and acquaintances and see how well they listen, and whether they judge or are critical.
- *Inquisitor*: the mentor as inquisitor adopts the methods of some of the great mentors of all time such as Buddha, Confucius, and Moses. Like the great philosopher Socrates they teach by asking questions. The Greek philosophers called it Socratic dialog. It involves the mentor leading the mentee on a path to wisdom, through effective and provocative questioning. When Fortune 500 CEOs were asked what made their mentors so effective, the most common answer was "they asked great questions."
- *Protector*: In this role the mentor prevents the mentee from taking unnecessary risks. In certain circumstances the mentor may shield the mentee from blame. The mentor must be careful not to overprotect their charge, however, as they risk inhibiting the professional and personal growth of the mentee.
- *Sponsor*: The mentor as sponsor acts as an advocate for their mentee both within and outside the organization. With only a single mentor acting as sponsor, the fortunes of the mentee are very closely linked to those of the mentor. If the mentor leaves the organization, or falls from grace, the career of the mentee is likely to suffer. It is better, and safer, for the mentee to obtain more than one sponsor if possible.

Commentary (continued)

The perfect mentor, someone who can assume all of the roles above, probably does not exist. Rather than pursuing a fruitless quest to find the perfect mentor you would be better advised to assess which type will be most valuable to you, and then look for a mentor who embodies those qualities. It also pays to learn how to become a perfect mentee, so that mentors will want to take you on. Realistically assess whether you are an attractive proposition to a mentor. Are you ambitious, willing to confide in others, willing to learn? If you're not, then why should a mentor give up their valuable time to help you?

What type of mentoring program do you need?

Some organizations, including large international corporations such as Federal Express, Johnson & Johnson, the IRS, and the US Army, have constructed formal mentoring programs. One reason for this was that informal mentoring was taking place in insufficient numbers. These organizations found that a more productive mentoring experience could be obtained for a greater number of people through a structured program. This allows for the formal training of mentors to prepare them for the task. It also ensures that employees who were less likely to attract a mentor, if left to their own devices, could obtain one.

Yet informal mentoring has its own supporters. They maintain that the "chemistry" in an informal mentoring relationship is a vital ingredient for its success, and one often lacking in formal mentoring. The reason for this is that in informal mentoring relationships, there is no obligation on either party to undertake the relationship in the initial stages. Instead there is normally attraction/admiration/respect underpinning the initial contact. It is possible, and the proponents of informal mentoring would probably agree, that a stronger bond is likely to be formed in an informal mentoring situation. Fans of formal mentoring programs counter that the chemistry is unnecessary and the point is developing a professional relationship rather than one of "best buddies."

Ultimately individuals will have to decide which style of program best suits them. This will depend on their personal objectives as well as those of their company. If someone already has a mentor and their company wishes to enroll them on a formal mentoring program, they will have to make a difficult decision. It is not always easy to have two mentors and devote sufficient time to making both relationships work. However, for those who can strike the right balance, this arrangement can be very rewarding.

Finding a mentor

For those people who work for a company that does not have a formal mentoring program, the onus is on them to find a mentor, in or outside the workplace.

Leading mentoring consultant, practitioner, and author Dr Shirley Peddy suggests four keys to a perfect mentor match:[8]

- The ability to communicate. Both mentor and mentee need to be able to communicate. Otherwise mentor sessions become difficult and awkward, and a daunting and unwelcome prospect for both parties.
- Commitment to a two-way process. "A relationship that is not mutually rewarding won't last," says Peddy.
- Honesty. Both parties need to be honest and true to each other, and unafraid to share their successes and failures.
- A willingness to participate. If either party is forced into the mentor relationship, it is unlikely to be a success. "Nobody should be dragged kicking and screaming into the relationship, and neither should be asked to give beyond what they desire," Peddy explains.

Pitfalls

Things don't and won't always go smoothly in a mentoring relationship. We are talking about two human beings after all – it is hard enough to form and maintain relationships in life generally, let alone within a formal work-oriented framework. Take all a person's foibles and quirks, combine them with all those of their mentor and it is clear that there is potential for the relationship to break down.

To avoid this it helps to spot danger signs early. Warning signals include:

- poor training and poor follow-up;
- reluctance of mentor to take on changing difficult issues;
- passive behavior and an unwillingness to participate;
- poor communication;
- inappropriate behavior – mentor is too autocratic/judgemental;
- forced participation – fruitful mentoring is unlikely to rise from forced participation;
- unwillingness to commit time.

Commentary (continued)

Formal mentoring programs should always be voluntary. Just because an individual has the requisite experience or seniority doesn't mean that they will make or want to be a mentor. Voluntary programs avoid the resentment from being forced into a mentoring relationship.

Finally, beware envy. The reason to enter into a mentoring relationship is career advancement and personal improvement. As a result, the mentee may be promoted, and will hopefully achieve great things in their career. Hopefully when they tell their mentor of their achievements the mentor will be both proud and pleased. Sadly, envy and jealousy are all too common human traits. Both mentor and mentee would do well to remember this.

Equally they should be aware of the feelings of peers, co-workers, and family. They may be jealous of the close mentoring relationship. Sensitivity toward the needs of your co-workers and family are important, as is discussing the mentoring honestly and openly so as to avoid any negative sentiments or misunderstandings.

Occasionally mentoring relationships fail. To cover this situation, it is wise to include a no-fault escape clause so that either party can unilaterally walk away from the relationship if it is clear that is not working; part without blame and recrimination. If it is a formal mentoring relationship it may be possible for the organization to interview both parties to see whether the relationship is salvageable. In the case of informal mentoring be clear from the outset on how both parties should approach breaking the relationship off if they wish to. This prevents embarrassment and bad feeling later.

RESOURCES

Caldwell, B.J. and Carter, E.M.A., *The principles and practice of mentoring, The return of the mentor: Strategies for workplace learning,* Falmer Press, 1993.

Clutterbuck, David and Megginson, David, *Mentoring Executives and Directors,* Butterworth-Heinemann, 1999.

Kram, K.E., *Mentoring at work: Developmental relationships in organizational life,* University Press, 1988.

Phillips-Jones L., *Mentors and Protégés,* Arbor House, 1982.

Zachary, Lois J., *The Mentor's Guide: Facilitating Effective Learning Relationships,* Jossey-Bass, 2000.

Essentials

DEVELOPING AND LEARNING

Action learning

Invented by British management thinker Reg Revans (1907–2003), action learning is a deceptively simple idea. So simple, in fact, that its power was overlooked for years. The basic idea is that managers learn best when they work on real issues in a group, rather than in the traditional classroom. According to Revans: "Action learning harnesses the power of groups to accomplish meaningful tasks while learning."

Revans was a former Olympic athlete who worked at the Cavendish Laboratories and for the National Coal Board. He developed his approach in the 1940s, but it was his 1971 book *Developing Effective Managers* that sparked international interest in the concept.

Although largely ignored in Britain, Revans is highly regarded in countries as far apart as Belgium and South Africa. Fans of action learning include Jack Welch, General Electric's celebrated CEO, whose Workout program is a form of action learning, and Herb Kelleher, head of Southwest Airlines, another US company that has been a trailblazer for the concept.

To explain action learning, Revans created a simple equation: $L = P + Q$. Learning (L), he says, occurs through a combination of programd knowledge (P) and the ability to ask insightful questions (Q). In essence, action learning is based around releasing and re-interpreting the accumulated experiences of the people in a group. Working in a group of equals (rather than a committee headed by the chief executive or a teacher), managers work on key issues in real time. The emphasis is on being supportive and challenging, on asking questions rather than making statements.

While programmed knowledge is one-dimensional and rigid, the ability to ask questions opens up other dimensions and is free flowing. The process is a continuous one of confirmation and expansion. The structure linking the two elements of knowledge and questions is the small team or set, defined by Revans as a "small group of comrades in adversity, striving to learn with and from each other as they confess failures and expand on victories."

Asking questions and listening to answers is an increasingly important managerial skill. Action learning encourages both. The potential benefits of action learning, however, cannot disguise the challenge it presents. Action learning is no quick fix. It requires a fundamental change in thinking.

All action learning shares a number of features. It:

- uses a genuine current problem or issue as a learning vehicle (not a past case study);
- takes a group approach (peers working together provide support and different perspectives);
- accepts that there are no experts (naive questions illuminate the issues);
- requires commitment from the sponsoring organization and management;
- focusses on asking questions rather than providing solutions.

Argyris, Chris

Chris Argyris (born 1923) is a formidable thinker, even by the lofty standards of his employer, Harvard Business School. Argyris was brought up in the New York suburbs and spent some time in Greece with his grandparents. Prior to joining Harvard he was Professor of Administrative Science at Yale. His qualifications embrace psychology, economics, and organizational behavior.

Argyris's early work concentrated on the then highly innovative field of behavioral science. Indeed, his 1957 book *Personality and Organization* has become one of the subject's classic texts. Argyris argued that organizations depend fundamentally on people and that personal development is and can be related to work. The problem in many organizations, he believed, is that the organization itself stands in the way of people fulfilling their potential.

Central to Argyris's work has been the entire concept of learning. He has examined learning processes, both in individual and corporate terms, in huge depth. His most influential work was carried out with Donald Schön (most importantly in their 1974 book, *Theory in Practice*, and their 1978 book, *Organizational Learning*).

Argyris and Schön originated two basic organizational models. In Model 1 managers concentrate on establishing individual goals. They keep to themselves and don't voice concerns or disagreements. Model 1 managers are prepared to inflict change on others, but resist any attempt to change their own thinking and working practices. Model 1 organizations are characterized by what Argyris and Schön labeled "single-loop learning" ("when the detection and correction of organizational error permits the organization to carry on its present policies and achieve its current objectives").

In contrast, Model 2 organizations emphasized "double-loop learning," which Argyris and Schön described as "when organizational error is detected and corrected in ways that involve the modification of underlying norms, policies, and objectives." In Model 2 organizations, managers act on information. They debate issues and respond to, and are prepared to, change. A virtuous circle emerges of learning and understanding. "Most organizations do quite well in single-loop learning but have great difficulties in double-loop learning," they concluded.

Corporate fashions have moved Argyris's way. With the return of learning to the corporate agenda in the early 1990s, his work became slightly more fashionable.

The learning organization

The work of Peter Senge at MIT's Sloan School of Business has been influential in convincing companies that the ability to learn is a key success factor. Senge has undoubtedly done much to develop and popularize the concept of the learning organization. However, the term was first used by Harvard Business School's Chris Argyris to mean a firm that learns as it goes along, adjusting its way of doing business very responsively.

Closely involved in and greatly influenced by the human relations school of the late 1950s, Argyris has examined learning processes, both in individual and corporate terms, in depth. "Most people define learning too narrowly as mere *problem solving*, so they focus on identifying and correcting errors in the external environment. Solving problems is important, but if learning is to persist, managers and employees must also look inward. They need to reflect critically on their own behavior," he says.[9] Problems with learning, as Argyris has revealed, are not restricted to a particular social or professional group. Indeed, it is the very people we expect to be good at learning – teachers, consultants, and other "professionals" – who often prove the most inadequate at actually doing so.

The entire concept of learning was brought back onto the agenda with the publication and success of Peter Senge's 1990 book, *The Fifth Discipline*. This brought the learning organization concept to a mass audience. It was the result of extensive research by Senge and his team at the Center for Organizational Learning at MIT's Sloan School of Management. Senge argued that learning from the past is vital for success in the future: "In the simplest sense, a learning organization is a group of people who are continually enhancing their capability to create their future. The traditional meaning of the word *learning* is much deeper than just *taking information in*. It is about changing individuals so that they produce results they care about, accomplish things that are important to them."

The organizations that thrive, Senge claimed, would be those that discovered how to tap their people's commitment and capacity to learn at every level in the company. This involved encouraging managers and other employees to experiment with new ideas and feed the results back to the wider organization. The book looked at how firms and other organizations can develop adaptive capabilities in a world of increasing complexity and rapid change. Senge argues that vision, purpose, alignment, and systems thinking are essential for organizations. He gave managers tools and conceptual archetypes to help them understand the structures and dynamics underlying their organizations' problems. "As the world becomes more interconnected and business becomes more complex and dynamic, work must become more *learningful*," he wrote.

For the traditional company, the shift to becoming a learning organization poses huge challenges. In the learning organization, managers are researchers and designers rather than controllers and overseers. Senge argues that managers should encourage employees to be open to new ideas, communicate frankly with each other, understand thoroughly how their companies operate, form a collective vision, and work together to achieve their goal. "The world we live in presents unprecedented challenges for which our institutions are ill prepared," says Senge.[10] Whatever the official line, it is the underlying culture of the organization that sets the tone. Senior managers can talk about learning organizations until they are blue in the face, for all the good it will do if those behaviors are not supported by the culture.

In particular, managers are unlikely voluntarily to shoulder additional responsibilities if the message from the organization's culture is that the most likely outcome of putting their heads above the parapet is having them shot off.

One of the clearest indications of an organization's decision-making culture is how tolerant it is of mistakes. To a large extent, this will determine how willing managers are to take risks. It is also an important factor in whether the organization has the ability to learn. Soichiro Honda, the founder of Honda Motor Corporation, once said: "Many people dream of success. To me success can only be achieved through repeated failure and introspection. In fact, success represents the 1 percent of your work which results only from the 99 percent that is called failure."

Despite current thinking, which suggests that experimentation is vital for companies to remain vigorous, in many corporate cultures there is very low tolerance of mistakes, and individuals' career prospects can be severely damaged if a creative decision goes wrong. Creating learning organizations has proved difficult in practice, not least because companies are set in their ways.

Lewin, Kurt

Kurt Lewin (1890–1947) was a German-born psychologist who fled from the Nazis to America. Prior to his death, he worked at MIT, founding a research center for group dynamics.

In 1946, Lewin was called into a troubled area of Connecticut to help create better relations between the Black and Jewish communities. Here it was found that bringing together groups of people was a very powerful means of exposing areas of conflict. The groups were christened T-Groups (the T stood for training).

The theory underlying T-Groups and the Lewin model of change was that behavior patterns need to be "unfrozen" before they can be changed and then "refrozen." T-Groups were a means of making this happen.

Keen to take the idea forward, Lewin began making plans to establish a "cultural island" where T-Groups could be examined more closely. A suitable location was identified shortly before Lewin's premature death, which robbed the human relations movement of its central figure. The National Training Laboratories for Group Dynamics were established in Bethel Maine and proved highly influential to an entire generation of human relations specialists, including Warren Bennis, Douglas McGregor, Robert Blake, Chris Argyris, and Ed Schein.

Thought leadership

The term "thought leadership" was coined in the early 1990s by the then editor of the *Harvard Business Review*, Joel Kurtzman. In an economy increasingly driven by ideas and concepts, Kurtzman observed, the ability to plant an intellectual flagpole in new territory was a potent source of competitive advantage. In key sectors, especially the consulting industry and business school sector, thought leadership conferred first-mover advantage to the originator.

Kurtzman subsequently wrote a book called *Thought Leaders* (1998) in which he interviewed the leading business thinkers. The term is now generic, and denotes what has become a battleground among the leading consulting firms and the growing ranks of management gurus. The power of thought leadership is that it is a more effective way to brand and market intellectual horsepower than traditional advertising.

The term may be new, but as a strategy the origins of thought leadership go back much further. The traditional leader in this field is McKinsey & Company. McKinsey does not advertise. Instead, it relies on its intellectual prowess to carry the brand. It has long been the intellectual benchmark for consulting firms and, largely, continues to be so. "The Firm," as it is affectionately known by McKinsey insiders, bolsters its brand through the *McKinsey Quarterly*, a serious, heavyweight publication that has been around for 35 years and that sometimes makes the *Harvard Business Review* appear frivolous by comparison. Intellectual vigor exudes from every page, which is exactly what McKinsey wants readers to think and experience.

McKinsey flexes its intellectual muscles in a number of other ways. In 1990, it set up the McKinsey Global Institute, the objectives of which are characteristically bold. It aims, according to the firm, "[to] help business leaders understand the evolution of the global economy, improve the performance and competitiveness of their corporations, and provide a fact base for sound public policy making at the national and international level." In addition, since the McKinsey-authored *In Search of Excellence* rolled off the presses in 1982, the firm's consultants have been churning out books with admirable dedication.

More recently, the creation of consulting businesses by the Big Five accountancy and auditing firms has increased competition in this area. The need to differentiate themselves from each other has raised the stakes in the thought leadership arena. The top consulting firms now invest millions of dollars in thought leadership as a brand-building strategy.

The battle for thought leadership lacks the glamor of image advertising, but it is incredibly intense. *McKinsey Quarterly* imitators have been launched by rival consulting firms. Booz-Allen & Hamilton, for example, publishes its own heavyweight journal, *Strategy & Business*. Consulting firms have also been busy turning out business books that they hope will position them as thought leaders on the important emerging ideas.

Inevitably, however, the success of the thought leadership strategy depends on the quality and take-up of the ideas that are generated. The whole concept feeds on its ability to generate more and better business concepts. It is a sign that consulting firms have started to believe their own propaganda.

REFERENCES

1. See Cope, Mick, *The 7Cs of Consulting*, FT Prentice Hall/1999.
2. See Cope, Mick, *Collaborative Coaching*, Pearson Education, 2004.
3. Zey, M.G., 'A mentor for all', *Personnel Journal*, p. 46, January 1988.
4. Bell, Chip R., *Managers As Mentors: Building Partnerships for Learning*, Berrett-Koehler 1996.
5. Shaw, E., *Mentoring goes modern*, The Arizona Republic, July 7, 1998.
6. Phillips-Jones, Linda, *Mentors and Protégés*, Arbor House, New York, 1982
7. Hill, L.A., 'Developing the star performer,' in F. Hesselbein (ed.-in-chief), *Leader to leader: San Francisco*, Drucker Foundation, No. 8 (pp. 30–37), Spring 1998.
8. Peddy, Dr Shirley, *The Art of Mentoring: Lead, Follow and Get Out of the Way*, Bullion Books, 1998.
9. Argyris, Chris, 'Teaching smart people how to learn,' *Harvard Business Review*, May–June, 1991.
10. Senge, Peter, 'A growing wave of interest and openness,' Applewood Internet site, 1997.

PART FOUR

Resources

50 great management decisions

Management is one of the great triumphs of our age. In the 20th century, humanity discovered management as a discipline, as a profession, and sometimes as a calling. Of course, management is nothing new. Napoleon was exercising management when he deployed his forces. The Ancient Egyptians practiced management when they built the pyramids.

The more you look for great management decisions, the more you see. None of the great monuments of history would exist if it weren't for management. The Italian painters of the Renaissance may have been artistic geniuses but they were also shrewd managers able to take advantage of delegation. The teams of laborers who helped build London's St Paul's Cathedral did not gather spontaneously – they were recruited and managed.

The somewhat daunting reality is that virtually all decisions we make are managerial in nature. Decisions usually concern people (human resources), money (budgeting), buying and selling (marketing), how to do things (operations), or how to do things in the future (strategy and planning).

While management is a truly human science, it is interesting that people-related decisions are generally not the ones which remain strongly imprinted in people's minds. Indeed, the most cited great decision makers are Henry Ford and Bill Gates – two managers not exactly renowned for their people management skills. Instead, people remember decisions which change businesses, industries, and history.

Curiously, while management is eternal and all embracing, debates continue to rage about what actually constitutes management. The host of definitions now available cannot cloud the central fact that management is about decision making. Decisions are the essence of management. Management without decision making is a vacuum. Of course, that does not mean that every decision a manager makes is important or that they always make the right decisions. The vast majority of decisions made by managers are completely unimportant. And often the decisions they make are the wrong ones. Managers are not perfect, but who ever said that management was about perfection? The reality is that management is about a combination of following inexplicable hunches, getting lucky, working hard, and taking risks. Often managers fall on their faces. That's part of the job. For every great decision there are hundreds which didn't quite work out.

The truly great decisions just happen. They are spur-of-the-moment phone calls. Crazy ideas tried when you are desperate. Things that emerge out of the corporate ether. Forget about strategy. Even the strategy gurus are all too ready to admit that strategy is fatally flawed by the messiness of reality. "I am a professor of strategy and often times I am ashamed to admit it," confesses Gary Hamel, co-author of

Competing for the Future, "because there is a dirty secret: we know a great strategy when we see one. In business schools we teach them and pin them to the wall. They are specimens. Most of our smart students raise their hands and say, wait a minute, was that luck or foresight? They're partly right. We don't have a theory of strategy creation. There is no foundation beneath the multi-billion-dollar strategy industry. Strategy is lucky foresight. It comes from a serendipitous cocktail."

At their moment of triumph – as the serendipity kicks in and everything turns rosy – it is unlikely that managers shout Eureka! Managers tend not to celebrate when decisions are gloriously justified. Why? Because usually they do not even realize they have got it right. It is one of the great disappointments of life that perfect decisions are usually perfect only in retrospect. Henry Ford did not sprint around Detroit announcing the arrival of mass production. Queen Isabella of Spain did not immediately proclaim her wisdom when she sponsored Columbus to sail off into the distance.

The greatest decisions change things. Here is a list of 50 of them, great management decisions drawn from throughout the ages and from around the world. It is an eclectic and eccentric selection as you would expect. It is also an intriguing insight into management through the ages.

The 50 decisions

1. After failing to convince Montgomery Ward to move into retailing, Robert E. Wood was hired by Sears, Roebuck in 1924. Julius Rosenwald liked the idea; Sears opened its first retail store in 1925 and became the world's largest general merchandiser.

2. After the death of the company founder, the two offices of consulting firm McKinsey & Co went their separate ways in 1939. A.T. Kearney in Chicago launched his own firm. Marvin Bower in New York kept the McKinsey name, deciding, correctly, that using his name, would only lead clients to expect his involvement in every assignment. McKinsey became The Firm.

3. Apple's decision to chase the prize of the first saleable PC created an industry. The Apple I led to Apple II then VisiCalc and finally the Mac, first shipped in 1984. (It also drew a veil over Xerox's decision not to go ahead with development after its PARC team had made a vital breakthrough.)

4. Around 59 BC Julius Caesar kept people up to date with handwritten sheets which were distributed in Rome as well as, it is suspected, using fly posters around the city. The greatness of leaders has been partly measured ever since by their ability to communicate.

5. During Fall 1943, Paul Garrett of General Motors rang a young Austrian teacher and writer, Peter Drucker. Garrett invited Drucker to study the company; the career of the century's foremost management thinker was launched.
6. During the 1920s, Matsushita was a struggling young business and its latest product, a bicycle light, was initially unsuccessful. Then Konosuke Matsushita ordered salesmen to leave a working light in each store. Seeing the light work changed perceptions. Sales took off – and so, too, did the company.
7. During the 1970s Japanese giant Matsushita developed VHS video and made the decision to license the technology. Sony developed the immeasurably better Betamax but failed to license it. The world standard is VHS and Betamax is consigned to history.
8. During the mid 13th century a number of cities in Northern Germany entered into an association to promote their commercial interests. The Hanseatic League eventually had around 40 members with representatives throughout Europe.
9. During the Second World War, Robert Woodruff, president of Coca-Cola, committed to selling bottles of Coke to members of the armed services for a nickel a bottle. Customer loyalty never came cheaper.
10. Eighteenth-century English inventor Richard Arkwright, one of the founding fathers of the Industrial Revolution, licensed his technology, confident that he could innovate to stay ahead. His decision brought in the then fantastic sum of £200,000.
11. Henry Ford's decision to start his own company in 1903 led to the first mass production line, created a mass market in automobiles, launched a corporate giant, changed perceptions of travel, led to the establishing of a variety of other industries, and provided a blueprint for industrial production.
12. Henry Luce's creation of *Fortune* in 1929 spawned the *Fortune 500* which provided the corporate benchmark for the 20th century – as well as being a clever marketing gimmick for the magazine.
13. Honda arrived in the US in 1959 to launch its big motorbikes. Customers weren't keen on the problematical performance of the big bikes, but admired the little Supercub bikes Honda's managers used. Honda bravely switched direction and changed the motorbike business virtually overnight.
14. Ignoring market research, Ted Turner launched the Cable News Network in 1980. No one thought a 24-hour news network would work. It did.
15. In 1072–73 the Italian cities of Venice and Genoa entered into partnership to fund commercial voyages. The joint venture was born.

16. In 1798 the US government decided to give a contract to Eli Whitney to make 10,000 guns. It was supposed to take two years but eventually took eight. Along the way, Whitney developed the basic techniques of mass production.

17. In 1850 Julius Reuter used carrier pigeons to communicate share prices between the end of the Belgian telegraph line in Brussels to the end of the German line in Aachen. It was the beginning of a news and information business.

18. In 1892 Henry Heinz of the H.J. Heinz food company decided the company needed a slogan. He came up with "57 varieties" to describe the foods sold by the company. This was one of the few cases of successful under-selling – Heinz produced 60 products at the time – but one which has stood the test of time.

19. In 1905 Sears, Roebuck opened its Chicago mail-order plant. The Sears catalog made goods available to an entirely new audience. The Sears operation was also a model for mass production.

20. In 1914 Henry Ford paid his workers $5 a day. It was a great leap forward for human resource management, but it was not a benevolent decision – Ford effectively created the market for his own product.

21. In 1924 Thomas Watson Sr changed the name of the Computing Tabulating Recording Company to International Business Machines – the company had no international operations, but it was a bold statement of ambitions.

22. In 1930 Messrs Eugene Ltd of Dover Street, London decided to use closed-circuit television to advertise their permanent waving technique at the Hairdressing Fair of Fashion. The TV ad was born.

23. In 1931 Procter & Gamble introduced its brand management system which elevated brands to center stage and provided a blueprint for its management, followed ever since.

24. In 1950 Frank McNamara found himself in a restaurant with no money and came up with the idea of the Diners Club Card. The credit card changed buying and selling throughout the world.

25. In 1961 Jean Nidetch was put on a diet by the Obesity Clinic at the New York Department of Health. She invited six dieting friends to meet in her Queens apartment every week. The decision created Weight Watchers and the slimming industry.

26. In 1970 Spencer Sylver of 3M invented the Post-it Note. But it took Arthur Fry to recognize the opportunity in 1979. The Post-it remains a ubiquitous money-spinner.

27. In 1977 Ben & Jerry decided to do a $5 correspondence course in ice cream making. They now make a lot more ice cream than they ever thought possible.
28. In 1981 Bill Gates decided to license MS/DOS to IBM while IBM ceded control of the license for all non-IBM PCs. This laid the foundation for Microsoft's huge success and IBM's fall from grace.
29. In 1982 Johnson & Johnson pulled Tylenol from store shelves. It put customer safety before corporate profit and Johnson & Johnson CEO Jim Burke provided a lesson in media openness.
30. In 1989 Coca-Cola was involved in one of the corporate debacles: the new recipe coke. This was truly ill advised. The great decision was to quickly go back to the older recipe. Many would have been tempted to stick with the decision and weather the storm.
31. In April 1978, McKinsey's John Larson asked colleague Tom Peters to step in at the last minute to do a presentation on some research he'd done. The presentation led to *In Search of Excellence* which changed the business book market and created the management guru industry.
32. In desolate post-war Japan, Toyota listened to an obscure American statistician, W. Edwards Deming, who arrived unheralded in 1947. Deming introduced Toyota to quality techniques; it conquered the world.
33. In the 1930s Motorola was performing indifferently. CEO Paul Galvin was encouraged to misrepresent how well the company was performing. He refused. "Tell them the truth, first because it is the right thing to do and second they'll find out anyway."
34. In Thebes in 1000 BC someone lost their slave called Shem. They decided to post an advertisement offering "a whole gold coin" for the slave's return. This is the oldest existing ad and the precursor of the modern advertising merry-go-round.
35. Michael Dell's decision to sell PCs direct and build to order. Now everybody in the industry is trying to imitate Dell's strategy. Too late.
36. Nineteenth-century businessman Cyrus McCormick is best known for developing the mechanical harvester. But fierce competition in the 1850s led to his decision to develop some of the fundamentals of marketing, such as deferred payments and guarantees.
37. On November 27, 1948 there was a demonstration of the world's first instant camera, the Polaroid Land Camera Model 95. The brave management decision was to price it at $89.75 against Kodak's Baby Brownie priced at $2.75. The entire initial stock of 56 was sold in the first day and Polaroid was launched.

38. Pierre du Pont decided that the DuPont company needed financial management. During his time with the company (1902–40), he developed modern corporate accounting including concepts such as double entry accounting, financial forecasting, and return on capital invested.
39. Publisher P.T. Barnum decided to promote a woman who claimed to be George Washington's nurse in the late 1830s. Barnum became a master of promotion, sowing the seeds for the growth of popular entertainment as well as promotional skills.
40. Queen Isabella of Spain's decision to sponsor Columbus's voyage to the New World. The ultimate in R&D.
41. Ray Kroc liked Mac and Dick McDonald's stand in San Benardino, California selling hamburgers, fries, and milkshakes so much that he decided to buy the rights and then franchised them, creating a huge global company and a vast market for fast food.
42. Sony chief Akito Morita noticed that young people liked listening to music wherever they went. He put two and two together and the company developed what became the Walkman, first made in 1980. There was no need for market research. "The public does not know what is possible, we do," said Morita.
43. The 1962 decision by IBM's Thomas Watson Jr to develop the System/360 family of computers cost the company $5 billion – more than the development costs of the atomic bomb. The result was the first mainframe computer even though IBM's market research suggested it would sell only two units worldwide.
44. The decision of the Wilsons of Memphis to go on a motoring vacation was initially unsuccessful. It was not a great deal of fun staying in expensive or poor motels. So, Kemmons Wilson built his own: the first Holiday Inn was opened in Memphis in 1952.
45. The far-sighted recognition by William Hoover that cars would soon kill his business (which made leather accessories for horse-drawn carriages) led to the 1908 creation of the Electric Suction Sweeper Company which created the mass-market vacuum cleaner and provided a (largely ignored) blueprint of moving with the times.
46. The founding of the Society of Jesus (the Jesuits) in 1540 by Ignatius de Loyola provided an organizational model with an emphasis on practical work rather than contemplation. It became, according to Peter Drucker, "the most successful staff organization in the world."
47. The *Grateful Dead* established immense customer loyalty during the 1980s by allowing fans to tape concerts. The result? In 1996, sales of merchandise were around $50 million and 100,000 people visit the group's Internet site every day.

48. The second Vatican Council (1962–65) called by Pope John XXIII launched one of the biggest change management programs in history. It altered the shape of the Catholic Church – a decentralized, low-hierarchy management model which has stood the test of time.
49. Walt Disney listened to his wife, Lillian, and decided to call his cartoon mouse Mickey rather than Mortimer. Entertainment was never the same again after Mickey and Minnie debuted in *Steamboat Willie* in 1928.
50. While William Durant created General Motors, Alfred P. Sloan created a means by which it could be managed. Durant initially rejected his ideas. When Pierre du Pont took control in 1920, he decided to follow Sloan's planned reorganization: the dominant corporate form of our times ("federal decentralization") emerged.

80 books all managers should read

The last two decades have seen an explosion of interest in business and management books. They routinely feature in bestseller lists, arouse controversy, and earn some of their authors large amounts of money. Along the way, usually through a process of osmosis rather than dramatic conversion, they also alter the ways in which managers manage.

In the instant, action-oriented, pressurized world of business, books change things. They change perceptions. They change behavior. They alter expectations and aspirations. They inform. "In no other profession [besides business], not excepting the ministry and the law, is the need for wide information, broad sympathies, and directed imagination so great," reflected Owen D. Young, then chairman of Radio Corporation and General Electric in 1929.[1] And never has the need been greater than the present.

In no other field do books now hold such a central role in the dissemination of best practice and new concepts. Helped by the fact that business is increasingly global and the skills of management often universal, books make their way round the world, shaping the management of the future.

Since 1945 we have witnessed the inexorable "professionalization" of management (indeed, some have argued that we have witnessed the professionalization of almost every occupation). In the past, the quest for knowledge – new tools, techniques, and ideas – was part of the process of professionalization. Now, it is the route to survival.

If knowledge means survival, managers cannot be criticized for their relentless search for new skills and new approaches. But too often these resemble an indecent race to find the latest bright idea, the single-stop answer to all their business problems. Managers are addicted to the newest and brightest ideas. They buy the fashionable books of the moment and then within months, perhaps weeks, move on to the next fashion. This is good news for publishers.

For managers it means a relentless and largely impossible quest to keep up to date with the latest thinking. Books and articles are devoured and pored over. It is a losing battle, but one they must endeavor to fight. "The only thing worse than slavishly following management theory is ignoring it completely," observes *The Economist*.[2]

Richard Pascale, author of *Managing on the Edge*, is a vehement critic of the managerial enthusiasm for fads and instant solutions. In *Managing on the Edge* he charts the rise and rise of fads since the 1950s. He calculates that over two dozen techniques have come and gone during this period, with a dozen arriving during the period 1985 to 1990 alone. Pascale believes that this trend is likely to continue.

Much of what is written is indigestible. Economist John Kay describes the formula for an article in the *Harvard Business Review*: "One idea per article, although it will not be taken seriously if expressed in less than 3,000 words. Assume no prior knowledge of anything ... definitely no jokes – our audience has no sense of humor – but frequent references to exchanges with senior executives such as John Harvey-Jones and Akito Morita."[3]

The skeptics are right to question the practical usefulness of much that is published. "You can be very bold as a theoretician. Good theories are like good art. A practitioner has to compromise," says Warren Bennis.[4] Even so, the canon of management literature is full of ideas which have been implemented and which have affected the lives and performance of millions of managers. "All the great business builders we know of – from the Medici of Renaissance Florence and the founders of the Bank of England in the late 17th century down to IBM's Thomas Watson in our day – had a clear theory of the business which informed all their actions and decisions," observes Peter Drucker in *Management*.[5] Cut through the dross and there is a broad swathe of carefully researched, well-written, insightful books on what makes managers and their organizations tick.

The *Harvard Business Review* may be lacking in humor and brevity, but a great deal of the material it includes is perceptive and practically useful. There are business books which stand the tests of time and usefulness. They are not placebos but vibrant cures.

And, lest it be forgotten, books and the research behind them do change things. Look at the part played by W. Edwards Deming in the renaissance of Japan. Think of the impact of Michael Porter's work on the value chain which has been taken up by companies throughout the world, as well as his work on national competitiveness which has altered the economic perspectives of entire countries. Porter has been called in by countries as far apart as Portugal and Colombia to shed light on their competitiveness. Who thought customer service was a key competitive weapon before Peters and Waterman? In the business world, books are more than ornamental shelf-fillers. The influence of best management practice and leading-edge thinking is increasingly all pervasive. Ignore it at your peril.

The books

Pre 1900

500 BC Sun Tzu: *The Art of War*
1500 Niccolo Machiavelli: *The Prince*
1776 Adam Smith: *The Wealth of Nations*
1831 Karl von Clausewitz: *On War*
1832 Charles Babbage: *On the Economy of Machinery & Manufactures*

1900–1929

1911 Frank Gilbreth: *Motion Study*
1911 Frederick W. Taylor: *The Principles of Scientific Management*
1916 Henri Fayol: *General and Industrial Management*
1923 Henry Ford: *My Life and Work*

1930–49

1931 James Mooney and Alan Reiley: *Onward Industry*
1933 Elton Mayo: *The Human Problems of an Industrial Civilization*
1937 Dale Carnegie: *How to Win Friends and Influence People*
1938 Chester Barnard: *The Functions of the Executive*
1941 Mary Parker Follett: *Dynamic Administration*
1947 Max Weber: *Theory of Social and Economic Organization*

1950–59

1951 Elliot Jacques: *The Changing Culture of a Factory*
1954 Abraham Maslow: *Motivation and Personality*
1954 Peter F. Drucker: *The Practice of Management*
1956 William Whyte: *The Organization Man*
1958 C.N. Parkinson: *Parkinson's Law*
1959 Frederick Herzberg: *The Motivation to Work*

1960–69

1960 Douglas McGregor: *The Human Side of Enterprise*
1961 Rensis Likert: *New Patterns of Management*
1962 Alfred Chandler: *Strategy and Structure*
1962 Ted Levitt: *Innovation in Marketing*
1963 Alfred P. Sloan: *My Years with General Motors*
1963 Robert Cyert and James March: *A Behavioral Theory of the Firm*
1963 Thomas Watson Jr: *A Business and its Beliefs*
1964 Robert Blake and Jane Mouton: *The Managerial Grid*
1965 Igor Ansoff: *Corporate Strategy*
1966 Marvin Bower: *The Will to Manage*
1967 Philip Kotler: *Marketing Management*
1969 Laurence Peter: *The Peter Principle*
1969 Peter F. Drucker: *The Age of Discontinuity*

1970–79

1970 Robert Townsend: *Up the Organization*
1973 Henry Mintzberg: *The Nature of Managerial Work*
1978 Chris Argyris and Donald Schön: *Organizational Learning*
1978 James MacGregor Burns: *Leadership*
1978 Taiichi Ohno: *Toyota Production System*
1979 Reg Revans: *Action Learning*

1980–89

1980 Alvin Toffler: *The Third Wave*
1980 Michael Porter: *Competitive Strategy*
1981 Richard Pascale and Anthony Athos: *The Art of Japanese Management*
1982 John Naisbitt: *Megatrends*
1982 Kenichi Ohmae: *The Mind of the Strategist*
1982 Tom Peters and Robert Waterman: *In Search of Excellence*
1982 W. Edwards Deming: *Out of the Crisis*
1983 Rosabeth Moss Kanter: *Change Masters*
1984 Meredith Belbin: *Management Teams*
1985 Edgar Schein: *Organizational Culture and Leadership*
1985 Harold Geneen: *Managing*
1985 Warren Bennis and Burt Nanus: *Leaders*
1986 Akio Morita: *Made in Japan*
1987 Jan Carlzon: *Moments of Truth*
1988 Joseph M. Juran: *Planning for Quality*
1988 Konosuke Matsushita: *Quest for Prosperity*
1989 Charles Handy: *The Age of Unreason*
1989 Christopher Bartlett and Sumantra Ghoshal: *Managing Across Borders*
1989 Stephen Covey: *The Seven Habits of Highly Effective People*

1990–99

1990 Kenichi Ohmae: *The Borderless World*
1990 Michael Porter: *The Competitive Advantage of Nations*
1990 Peter Senge: *The Fifth Discipline*
1990 Richard Pascale: *Managing on the Edge*
1992 Tom Peters: *Liberation Management*
1993 Fons Trompenaars: *Riding the Waves of Culture*
1993 James Champy and Michael Hammer: *Reengineering the Corporation*
1993 Ricardo Semler: *Maverick!*
1994 Gary Hamel and C.K. Prahalad: *Competing for the Future*

1994 Henry Mintzberg: *The Rise and Fall of Strategic Planning*
1994 James Collins and Jerry Porras: *Built to Last*
1994 Michael Goold, Andrew Campbell and Marcus Alexander: *Corporate-Level Strategy*
1995 Daniel Goleman: *Emotional Intelligence*
1995 David Packard: *The H-P Way*
1996 Frederick Reichheld: *The Loyalty Effect*
1996 John Kotter: *Leading Change*
1996 Robert Kaplan and David Norton: *The Balanced Scorecard*
1997 Arie de Geus: *The Living Company*
1997 Stan Davis and Christopher Meyer: *Blur*
1997 Thomas Stewart: *Intellectual Capital*
1998 Patricia Seybold: *Customers.com*

REFERENCES

1. *Time*, January 6, 1930.
2. *The Economist*, February 26, 1994.
3. Kay, John, 'Handy guide to corporate life,' *Financial Times*, August 17, 1995.
4. Crainer, Stuart, 'Doing the right thing,' *The Director*, October 1988.
5. Drucker, Peter F., *Management*, Harper & Row, New York, 1973.

50 concepts all managers should be familiar with

A steady flow of new ideas is redefining what managers should be doing, how they should be doing it, and critically what their performance is evaluated against. For this reason alone, it is important to stay abreast of the latest thinking. Today's theory is tomorrow's task.

Today, a growing number of managers have been to one of the many business schools around the world. For these people, schooled in management theory, the power of concepts is understood. But those who did their management training in the school of hard knocks may ask, why bother? They might argue, with some justification, that management is fundamentally a hands-on activity, and has little relation to the grandiose or ethereal theories of management gurus. They have a case, but only up to a point. Think about how the job of the manager has changed in the past few decades.

What is needed in today's business world, it is almost universally agreed, is a lighter touch on the reins, a more intelligent use of human resources. Today, the manager is seen as a leader and facilitator rather than controller and policeman. At the same time, the sort of environment and organization in which managers operate is changing to fit new conceptions of what a business should look like. Even the fundamental understanding or psychological contract between the manager and the organization is being transformed by redefinitions of the employee–employer relationship. Where do such notions come from? From the management literature, of course. From the thousands of business books, articles, case studies, and models that are produced each year. These have a constant drip, drip, drip effect on the consciousness of managers everywhere.

Most enduring concepts have some of the following characteristics:

- *Timeliness*. They meet an immediate need, or anticipate one that is not yet recognized.
- *Self-containment*. Even though they are built on earlier ideas, the best concepts stand on their own. They can be understood in isolation from what came before.
- *Real-world credibility* – either from extensive research or experience at the sharp end of business, and preferably both.
- *Intellectual rigor*. The quality of thought and insight is another distinguishing feature of ideas that last. Some ideas are deliberately vague to allow universal application. Great concepts are razor sharp; they have their own internal logic. They are consistent, and provide useful definitions.

- *Simplicity*. The best concepts are derived from basic and universal principles. They are intuitive. They help us make sense of the world around us.
- *Practicality*. Perhaps the real difference between fads and ideas that last is their usefulness to managers – their practical application.

Against these criteria, certain thinkers have an impressively high batting average. They seem to have a knack of anticipating – and even shaping – the future. Scratch the surface of many of the concepts and you find the same names just beneath. People like Peter Drucker and Douglas McGregor have had a profound and lasting influence on the way managers, and other management thinkers, understand the world. Go back even further and the names of Henri Fayol, Mary Parker Follett, and even Frederick Taylor echo down the years.

A good idea is no guarantee of success of course. Most are poorly implemented. But for all that, the ideas below will continue to have a fundamental impact on what real managers do. It's not simply that business process re-engineering or downsizing are likely to put them out of a job; there is a more subtle process at work. Just as the best theory is (or should be) derived from the real world, so the real world is changed by the promulgation of the theory. The great business school and consulting concepts are theory created out of practice, which is then presented back into the workplace as best practice. Concepts cannot be ignored.

The concepts

1. Action learning
2. Activity-based costing
3. Adhocracy
4. Balanced scorecard
5. Benchmarking
6. Boston Matrix
7. Branding
8. Broadbanding
9. Channel management
10. Core competencies
11. Core values
12. Crisis management
13. Decision theory
14. Discounted cash flow
15. Downsizing

16. Emotional intelligence
17. Employability
18. Empowerment
19. Four Ps of marketing
20. Game Theory
21. Intellectual capital
22. Interim management
23. Just-in-time
24. Knowledge management
25. Leadership theory
26. Lean production
27. Learning organization
28. Managerial grid
29. Maslow's Hierarchy of Needs
30. Matrix Model
31. Mentoring
32. Outsourcing
33. Porter's Five Forces
34. Psychological contract
35. Re-engineering
36. Relationship marketing
37. Scenario planning
38. Scientific management
39. Seven S Framework
40. Shareholder value
41. Strategic management
42. Succession planning
43. Supply chain management
44. Theories X, Y (and Z)
45. Thought leadership
46. 360-degree feedback
47. Time-based competition
48. TQM
49. Transnational corporation
50. Value innovation

Six classic cases

JULIAN BIRKINSHAW

[Case studies still form the backbone of business education. Learning from best practice as well as corporate failure can prove educational and inspirational.]

Diageo in high spirits

The background

Diageo was formed in 1997 through the merger of Guinness and Grand Metropolitan. Both companies were themselves products of earlier mergers – Guinness had famously acquired Distillers in 1986, while Grand Metropolitan had diversified from its origins as a hotel chain into spirits (IDV), food (Pillsbury), restaurants (Burger King), and pubs.

As with most mergers, the initial changes were relatively superficial. Executives argued for the synergies between the various businesses, but the only real integration occurred between the spirits businesses of the two companies. Fairly quickly, however, a more focussed strategy emerged. When Seagrams announced the sale of its spirits and wine business, Diageo quickly moved in to pick up as many brands as it could (competition rules prevented a complete acquisition). Pillsbury and Burger King were sold off, and the Guinness business was integrated into the global spirits organization.

The premium drinks strategy

The purpose of all these changes was to make Diageo the world's leading premium drink company. During the post-merger integration, CEO John McGrath and his executive team had homed in on their real strength: the ability to build a premium consumer brand, and leverage it on a global basis. They built a sophisticated methodology – the "Diageo Way of Brand Building" – based around insights into their consumers' need states. They identified a set of global priority brands (e.g. Smirnoff, Baileys) for managing on a worldwide basis. And they developed a unique organization structure in which country operations were organized not by geographical region but according to their expertise and potential. There were four "lead" markets (UK, US, Ireland, Spain) that were expected to take leadership roles in developing new brands, 14 "key" markets where Diageo already had a strong position, and then a larger group of "venture" markets, in which there was a "tight focus on fewer brands, using a more flexible model." The theory was that brands would be developed in the lead markets and then rolled out quickly on a global basis through the key and venture markets.

The enormous success of Smirnoff Ice has validated the Diageo model. Under new CEO Paul Walsh, Diageo has invested heavily in "ready to drink" (RTD) brands including Smirnoff Ice. These were initially aimed at the female pub-goer who did not like beer but increasingly targetted toward male drinkers. Smirnoff Ice was launched in 1998 in the UK, and once it was proven there it was rolled out over the next two years to a further 15 countries, with total sales so far in excess of 1.5 billion bottles. And not only is Smirnoff Ice a big seller in its own right, it also has two very attractive side-benefits: it helps to invigorate the core Smirnoff brand, and it takes market share away from beer. For the global beer companies like Heineken and Interbrew, Diageo is suddenly a serious threat.

The lesson

Diageo provides a clear example of a company that understands and leverages its core competence. Rather than pursue multiple strategic thrusts back at the time of the merger, the company put its faith in its ability to build global drinks brands, and it created an organization that allowed it to extract value from that ability. In a difficult market, Diageo still managed 9 percent organic growth over the last 12 months, and it looks well set for further growth as it launches new RTD products such as J&B Twist.

Ford's venture into consumer services

The background

Jac Nasser became CEO of Ford Motor Company in 1998, with a reputation as a problem solver, cost cutter, and agent of change. One of his key initiatives was to enter the world of automotive consumer services, which covers such things as car financing, insurance, maintenance, repair, parts, and recycling. These services were estimated to account for 60 percent of the total value of the automobile industry, and most of it was far higher margin business than Ford's core business. Nasser wanted Ford to become a major player in this downstream part of the business system.

Building an auto services group

Nasser hired Michael D. Jordan to create Ford's "Automotive Consumer Services Group." Their first significant move in 1999 was to buy Kwik-Fit, the UK-based exhaust repair company owned by Sir Tom Farmer, for £1 billion. A number of smaller acquisitions followed, in the areas of car servicing, collision, and recycling. The strategy was to buy operations across this fragmented sector and to create the first consolidated automotive services group. Nasser and Jordan saw enormous opportunities for gaining synergies between the various parts by cross-selling services, transferring best practices, and building a complete set of consumer-oriented services.

Emerging problems

But while the strategy looked good on paper, it proved difficult to implement. Apart from Kwik-Fit, which had a well-known brand and operations in five countries, there were very few companies of significant size worth buying, so it took a long time to make progress. And from the perspective of Ford as a whole, with 2001 sales of $131 billion, even Kwik-Fit was a relatively small acquisition.

But the real issue ended up being problems elsewhere. Ford reported weak results in 1999 and 2000, thanks to a declining performance across the whole industry as well as problems of its own in Europe. Buying Volvo and Range Rover used up much of the company's cash reserves. Then, in 2000, the Firestone tire problem hit, and Ford was thrust into a public relations nightmare, leading to extensive product recalls and large write-offs. In early 2002, Chairman Bill Ford, the great-grandson of the founder, had had enough. He ousted Nasser and took the job of chief executive himself. With the company now in a very weak financial position, and with its reputation tarnished, Bill Ford announced a back-to-basics strategy – 35,000 jobs were cut, along with five factories and four product lines, and the automotive consumer services group, which was a non-core activity as well as being clearly associated with departed CEO Jac Nasser, was quickly axed. In 2002, Kwik-Fit was sold to UK private equity group CVC for £330 million.

The lesson

Ford fell into the classic value trap in building new businesses. It saw a logical extension of its business by building on its existing consumer base, and finding new services that those consumers could buy. But by moving down this route, Ford found itself in unfamiliar territory – a fragmented, service-intensive, local industry rather than the globally consolidated, capital-intensive world of car engineering and manufacturing. It was by no means impossible for Ford to traverse this gap, but it needed to develop a new set of capabilities, and overcome the inertial resistance to the new strategy. And ultimately, Bill Ford never completely bought into the idea.

He was a "car guy," and for him (and his family) this meant designing, building, and selling cars. The jump into automotive services was a big one, and Nasser did not have either the time or the good fortune to pull it off.

Fitting it together with Lego

The background

Founded in 1932 by a Danish entrepreneur, Ole Kirk Kristiansen, Lego became an international success story in the post-war years. Its famous plastic bricks were first sold in Denmark in 1947 and then quickly rolled out across Europe and North America. Gradually the basic bricks gave way to more complex model sets, then a range of related products including Duplo, Lego Technics, and Lego figures for girls. By the late 1980s, Lego was one of the biggest toy brands in the world.

Lego remained family-owned and was built around four core values: creativity, play, learning, and development. The word Lego was formed from the Danish words *leg godt* (play well).

The threat

In the early 1990s the toy market changed dramatically with the introduction of Nintendo's N64/Game Boy and Sony's Playstation. Children were no longer content with self-guided play. They quickly embraced the interactive offerings from the electronics industry. And rather than playing for the sake of playing, they began playing for the sake of winning. Traditional toys were still selling but the growth was in the electronics segment.

Lego's response

Lego's initial reaction to the threat of electronic toys was to do nothing. Game consoles were anathema to the values of the company – they were not creative and they did not help the child develop. Lego had also experimented with combining bricks with electronics (Lego Dacta) in the 1980s without much success.

But faced with the continuing growth of electronic toys, in 1996 Kjeld Kristiansen, CEO and grandson of the founder, created a new division, Lego Media, to develop software, music, and videos. Three interactive software products were developed on CD-ROM: Lego Creator, Lego Chess, and Lego Loco. A new programmable "intelligent brick" product called Mindstorms was launched at the top end of the market. And Lego developed its online offerings with a range of games, kids' clubs, and merchandising opportunities.

But despite (or because of) all this, Lego found itself in difficulties. It posted its first-ever loss in 1998. The following year was profitable, largely because of its enormously successful *Star Wars* product range. In 2000 there was a deeper loss.

The lesson

Why the bad results? Lego suffered all the classic problems companies face when entering new markets. Nintendo and Sony were established competitors and were not prepared to give up ground to Lego without a fight. The multimedia industry was immature and all players, including Lego, struggled to make money out of it. In addition, Lego moved beyond its proven areas of capability. As Paul Plougman, executive vice president, said in 2000: "We lost focus. We will now refocus on our core business, which is materials for open-ended play for children." Lego has now scaled back many of its multimedia operations and is focussing on those that fit with its core values and capabilities, including a themed product line called Bionicle. With cost-cutting measures in place, 2001 was once again profitable.

The underlying lesson is important – it is not enough just to follow your customers into new product areas, you also need the capabilities to deliver on their new demands. Lego could not hope to compete head on with Sony and Nintendo. Instead it had to rethink its product range to combine its core values and skills with what today's children are looking for.

Mike Harris and the creation of Egg

The background

In 1995 Peter Davis became CEO of Prudential Insurance, which at the time was seen as a rather slow-moving and old-fashioned company in an industry undergoing rapid change.

Davis made a number of acquisitions to take the company into new areas of insurance and investment, but his central thrust was what became Egg – a business designed to offer banking, mortgages, and other financial services via the telephone and cut out expensive branch networks and commission-hungry independent financial advisers.

The creation of Egg

To lead the Prudential's foray into telephone banking, Davis approached Mike Harris, who had made his name in UK business circles by leading the creation of First Direct bank when he was at Midland (now HSBC). Davis knew Harris quite well, and quickly convinced him to take the job. And Harris, like Davis, felt that the time was ripe for a new class of customer-focussed intermediaries to compete with the lumbering, vertically integrated incumbents in banking, cards, and insurance.

During 1997 the business plan for Egg took shape. It would be established as a completely separate company, financed and owned by Prudential but with its own buildings, its own culture, and its own brand. Consumer research had established that while people liked the concept, they could not square it with the Prudential's traditional image. So Harris and his team chose Egg, which evoked many of the values they were looking for. The name "proved to be a very hard sell to the board," but with Davis's backing it was accepted.

Harris and his team invested heavily in customer research to try to understand how people *really* wanted to interact with their bank. His team followed 1,000 people for a year, and Harris personally took part in customer feedback sessions on a weekly basis. The original concept was for a telephone-only bank, but as the potential of the Internet became apparent, they developed an online offering as well. Their timing was fortuitous: UK Internet usage boomed during 1998, largely thanks to the launch of free ISPs like Freeserve, so Egg became de facto the first Internet bank in the country.

The result

Egg was a spectacular success. Within days of launching the business, Egg had to more than double the size of its call center operation to cope with customer demand. Thanks to its separate business model, it managed to get the new capacity up and running within four days. In contrast, Davis observed, "the Prudential would not have found the forms in four days."

Launched in 1998 after a spend of £80 million, Egg reached its initial five-year target of 500,000 customers and £5 billion deposits in six months. It then developed its product line to become a financial services supermarket, offering loans, insurance, mortgages, credit cards, and funds as well as banking. After an IPO in 2000 – to "institutionalize its independence," according to Harris – Egg broke into profit in the fourth quarter of 2001 and reported pre-tax profits of £9.4 million on revenues of £79.6 million in the third quarter of 2002. With 2.4 million customers, Egg's market value at the end of 2002 was £1.1 billion, and it was set for expansion into France.

The lesson

While there were many contributors to Egg's success, two factors were key. First, the complete separation of Egg from the rest of Prudential gave Harris the freedom to move quickly into a new area, unencumbered by tradition or bureaucracy. Second, Harris and his team were obsessive about consumer research: they did not just repeat the First Direct model he launched at Midland bank, they started with a clean sheet of paper to find out what consumers really wanted.

The destruction of Marconi

The background

General Electric Company (GEC), the British company with no relation to America's GE, grew rapidly in the 1960s under Arnold Weinstock's domineering but effective leadership. Like its US counterpart, GEC became a conglomerate, with interests in such diverse businesses as white goods, defense electronics, telecoms, and power systems. While there was no real logic underlying this array of businesses, Weinstock held the company together through a combination of his imposing personality and a strict system of financial controls. At its peak GEC had sales of £11 billion and a cash pile of £2 billion.

Simpson's masterplan

Lord Weinstock retired in 1996 and was replaced by George Simpson, a former executive at Rover. Over the course of the next five years, Simpson and his Finance Director, John Mayo, masterminded a complete rethinking of GEC's corporate strategy. He decided to focus the company on the fast-growing telecoms equipment industry. He bought two mid-sized US competitors (Reltec for $2.1 billion and Fore for $4.5 billion) and invested in developing a range of new products to compete with industry leaders Cisco and Nortel. To pay for this growth, most other businesses, including defense electronics, white goods, and power systems, were sold off. To reflect this change of strategy, GEC was renamed Marconi.

The denouement

Marconi's share price peaked in August 2000 at £12. Then things started to go badly wrong. The dot-com bubble burst, and demand for new telecom equipment dried up. Lucent, Cisco, and Nortel all announced profit warnings. Marconi's share price dropped, even though it denied that its sales had been hit. Then, when the profit warning finally came, angry investors dumped the stock. The downturn was far more severe than anyone anticipated, and with large and mounting debts Marconi was facing bankruptcy, its shares worth less than 1 percent of their peak value. George Simpson and John Mayo were forced out. A new executive team was brought in, but by then £37 billion of market value had been destroyed in just a year and a half.

The lesson

Marconi's story is a classic tale of an over-ambitious growth strategy and subsequent collapse. But the lesson to take away is that despite their ultimate failure, Simpson and Mayo did some important things right.

First, they correctly reasoned that if Marconi was going to become a major player in telecoms it would have to grow aggressively and it would need a strong US position. Hence its acquisitions of Fore and Reltec. This approach worked for Cisco. Where Marconi went wrong was that it paid cash, partly because it had plenty of it, and partly because it did not have a full listing in the US (so its paper was not an attractive currency). So rule one – if you are going to overpay for an acquisition, better to overpay with your own overpriced shares. The cash drain from these acquisitions is what ultimately killed Marconi.

Second, Marconi's decision to major on one business, and sell the rest, is exactly what the markets were asking for. Conglomerates were OK in the 1970s and 1980s, but the trend during the 1990s was toward highly focussed corporations. Indeed, Simpson was lauded for his courage in breaking up and focussing the company he took over from Lord Weinstock.

But Marconi's failure underlines how risky this sort of refocussing can be. Simpson put all his eggs in one basket, but it was a relatively untested and new basket at that. Such dramatic changes in corporate strategy can work. For example, Spirent made a successful transition from industrial conglomerate to fast-growing telecoms company during the late 1990s. But more often than not major changes in strategy take the company into new areas that it does not really understand, and the results end up being disastrous – as the shareholders of Vivendi and Enron will confirm.

Volkswagen strikes back

The background

Volkswagen began importing the Beetle in the early 1950s. The Big Three (GM, Ford, Chrysler) did not take it seriously. One executive called it "a personal insult." It was noisy, cramped, air-cooled, and it had its engine "where the trunk was meant to be." But it was enormously successful, with sales growing to a peak of 570,000 in 1970. This was partly due to the Beetle's unique positioning as a small, affordable car ("Ugly is only skin deep" stated one famous ad). But more importantly it achieved cult status among the hippies and beatniks of the 1960s anti-establishment movement.

Success continued into the 1970s. The Beetle was replaced with the Rabbit (Golf in Europe), but it never reached the same level of popularity. Quality problems started to appear. New competitors, particularly Honda and Toyota, arrived in the US for the first time. And the decision in 1978 to start manufacturing in the US proved to be a fateful one for Volkswagen, because the cars lost their distinctive European styling and handling.

Close to exit

Through the 1980s, Volkswagen's US market share declined. The brand's unique positioning disappeared, and the product quality was not up to the standard of Japanese competitors. The manufacturing plant was closed in 1987. By 1993 Volkswagen was selling only 49,500 in the US, and thought to be losing significant amounts of money. Industry observers were predicting that the company would soon follow the lead of Peugeot, Fiat, and Rover, and exit the US market.

But Volkswagen's new CEO Ferdinand Piech refused to give up on the world's largest and most competitive car market. And he oversaw a remarkable turnaround, from a low of 49,000 units in 1993 to the most recent figures of 356,000 in 2001.

Secrets of a turnaround

How did Volkswagen do it? There were four key elements to the turnaround. First, it sorted out manufacturing quality. The turning point came in 1992 when Bill Young, President of the US operation, refused to accept any of the new Golfs and Jettas from the Mexican plant because of quality problems. This was a gutsy decision because it meant the dealers had no cars to sell for six months, but it proved he was serious. The Mexican plant got its act together, and quality standards improved markedly.

Second, the brand image was revived. Volkswagen had become famous for its offbeat advertising, but it lost its direction during the 1980s. In 1992 the US company replaced its long-standing agency DDB Needham with a small Boston agency called Arnold, which managed to recapture the values and spirit of the earlier campaigns. Its tagline: On the road of life there are passengers and there are drivers … Drivers Wanted.

Third, a new management team was put in place, led by Clive Warrilow, formerly head of Volkswagen Canada. He faced a disillusioned workforce and angry dealers, but through a strong focus on empowerment, trust-building, and partnership he was able to win them around.

Fourth, and by no means least, was the New Beetle, a product that was conceived, designed, and built in North America. If anything symbolized the return to glory of Volkswagen in the US, this was it – a throwback to the company's heyday in the 1960s, but at the same time a thoroughly modern product built on the same platform as the Golf. The turnaround was already in place before the New Beetle was launched, but this proved to the skeptical US public that Volkswagen was truly back.

CONTRIBUTORS

Allyson Stewart-Allen (*allyson@intermarketingonline.com*) is an American international marketing consultant who has been based in London for the last 15 years. She is the founder of the consultancy International Marketing Partners and co-author of *Working with Americans: How to Build Profitable Business Relationships* (2002).

Tim Ambler is Senior Fellow at London Business School. His books include *Marketing and the Bottom Line: The marketing metrics to pump up cash flow* (2nd Edition, 2003), *Doing Business in China* (2000), *The SILK Road to International Marketing* (2000), and *Marketing from Advertising to Zen* (1996). He is a chartered accountant and was previously joint managing director of International Distillers and Vintners, now part of Diageo.

Jamie Anderson is a program director and lecturer within the Centre for Management Development, London Business School. His research interests include business strategy, technology-based innovation, and value chain evolution. Jamie previously held research and teaching positions at the University of Melbourne and Monash Mt. Eliza Business School, Australia. He can be contacted at *janderson@london.edu*.

Ken Bates lectured at Coventry University before joining Warwick Business School in 1990 where he now lectures financial and management accounting, on undergraduate, postgraduate, and executive courses, and is the Academic Director for the Distance Learning MBA (DLMBA). He is the course organizer and study note author for the DLMBA Management Accounting module and also contributes to the Financial Accounting study notes. His research interests include financial analysis, strategic management accounting, performance measurement and cost management systems in both service and manufacturing sectors, and accounting education.

David W. Birchall is director of the Centre for Business in the Digital Economy at Henley Management College. He has research interests in the areas of innovation practices in organizations and organizational implications of IT. He is the author of a number of books, including *Creating Tomorrow's Organization – Unlocking the Benefits of Future Work* (1995), *The New Flexi Manager* (1996), and *Future Proofing* (2002).

Julian Birkinshaw is associate professor of strategic and international management at London Business School. Julian is the author of *Inventuring: Why Big Companies Must Think Small*, with William Buckland and Andrew Hatcher (2003), and *Leadership the Sven-Goran Eriksson Way* (with Stuart Crainer, 2002). He previously worked at the Stockholm School of Economics.

Susan Bloch is global head of professional services at the Change Partnership, part of Whitehead Mann, where she leads thought leadership and board effectiveness reviews.

Alan Braithwaite is the chairman and founder of LCP Consulting, a specialist consultancy in supply chain management and logistics. He is also a visiting lecturer at Cranfield School of Management. At LCP, he has pioneered the development of innovative supply chain analysis and modeling techniques.

Lynn Brewer (*lynn@TheIntegrityInstitute.org*) is President of The Integrity Institute, Inc., and a former Enron executive and author of *Confessions of an Enron Executive: A Whistleblower's Story* (1st Books Publishing, 2004).

Peter J. Brews is a professor of management at Kenan-Flagler Business School, the University of North Carolina at Chapel Hill.

Thomas L. Brown is a champion of vanguard thinking about leadership. A progressive thinker and social commentator, he is also the author of over 400 published articles. Tom wrote the first online book on leadership: *The Anatomy Of Fire: Sparking A New Spirit Of Enterprise*, which explores the look and feel of leadership in the 21st century. You can track his most recent works on *www.thomaslbrown.com*.

David Butcher is director of executive development at the Cranfield School of Management. David trained originally as a psychologist, and worked for DuPont and Courtaulds before embarking on a career in management development. He focusses on developing top teams and leadership capability at senior management level. His books include *Smart Management: Using Politics in Organisations* (2001).

Stephan A. Butscher is a partner at Simon-Kucher and managing director of the London office.

Michael Cahill writes on investment and provides bespoke financial training. His highly acclaimed book *Analyzing Companies & Valuing Shares*, was published in June 2003. Prior to this he spent 10 years at leading investment bank UBS Warburg in the number one-rated research team covering the building materials and construction sector.

Stephen Carver is a director of the MBA personal communications course and a lecturer in project management at Cranfield School of Management. He is also the founder of a specialist project management consultancy, and his clients include many blue-chip companies around the world. Prior to his work as a consultant and lecturer he was head of strategic programs at a large multinational corporation.

Martin Clarke is a program director of the Cranfield general management program at Cranfield School of Management. He works as a management development consultant to a broad range of international companies and is co-author of *Smart Management: Using Politics in Organisations* (2001).

Henry Chesbrough is executive director of the Center for Technology Strategy and Management at the Haas School of Business. Previously, he was an assistant professor of business administration, and the Class of 1961 Fellow at Harvard Business School. His research focusses on managing technology and innovation, a subject on which he is a world-renowned authority. His books include *Open Innovation: The New Imperative for Creating and Profiting from Technology* (2003).

Dr Jong Chow is a partner at Chicago-based Helios Consulting Group. Previously, he was a consultant at Booz Allen Hamilton and held position at Innovate@, a venture capital partnership between Booz Allen and Lehman Brothers. Dr Chow holds a PhD in Operations Research from Cornell University.

Peter S. Cohan is president of Peter S. Cohan & Associates (*www.petercohan.com*), a management consulting and venture capital firm. He is the author of seven books, including *Value Leadership: The 7 Principles That Drive Corporate Value in Any Economy* (2003).

David L. Collinson is FME Professor of Strategic Learning and Leadership at Lancaster University Management School. He has published six books and over 50 articles and chapters that develop a critical approach to organizational studies. His current research focusses on the development of critical approaches to leadership and learning.

Steve Coomber is a business writer and co-author of *Architects of the Business Revolution* (2000) and the *Career Adventurer's Fieldbook* (2002).

Mick Cope is a coach, consultant, and MD of WizOz, a training and consultancy company. He is the author of a number of books, including *Lead Yourself* (2002), *Personal Networking* (2003), *The 7Cs of Consultancy* (2003), and *The 7Cs of Collaborative Coaching* (2004).

Stuart Crainer is joint editor of the *Financial Times Handbook of Management*. He is author of numerous books. These include *The Management Century, Generation Entrepreneur* (with Des Dearlove), *MBA Planet* (with Des Dearlove), *Key Management Ideas*, a biography of the management guru Tom Peters, and *The Ultimate Business Library*. His work appears in magazines and newspapers worldwide. Stuart is one of the founders of the training and consulting company Suntop Media.

Tony Cram is a fellow of the Chartered Institute of Marketing and a program director at Ashridge Business School focussing on business strategy and market innovation, with a particular interest in long-term customer relationships. He also works with the Swedish Institute of Management and is the author of *Customers that Count – How to build living relationships with your most valuable customers* (2001).

Des Dearlove is joint editor of the *Financial Times Handbook of Management*. He is a contributing editor to *Strategy & Business*, a long-time columnist for *The (London) Times*, co-founder of Suntop Media, and author of a number of books. Des's books include *Gravy Training* (with Stuart Crainer), *The Ultimate Book of Business Thinking, Key Management Decisions, MBA Planet*, and *The Ultimate Book of Business Brands* (both with Stuart Crainer).

Kevin C. Desouza of the University of Illinois at Chicago has served as a consultant to numerous corporations in the areas of knowledge management and strategic management of information. He is the author of *Managing Knowledge with Artificial Intelligence* and is an associate editor of the *Journal of Information Science and Technology*. His research interests include knowledge management, national security, and military intelligence.

Tony Eccles is Visiting Professor of Strategic Management at Cranfield School of Management. He has also been Professor of Strategic Management at London Business School for over 10 years, where he runs senior management programs for CUES, BG Group, and Aviva. Private clients include Rolls-Royce and Smith & Nephew. His recent book on strategy implementation, *Succeeding with Change: Implementing Action-driven Strategies* (McGraw Hill), was reprinted in 2002. He is also author of *Under New Management* and co-editor of *European Cases in Strategic Management*.

Deborah Doane is an Associate of the New Economics Foundation, a London-based not-for-profit think-tank aiming to construct a new economy centered on people and the environment.

Helga Drummond is Professor of Decision Sciences at the University of Liverpool Management School. Professor Drummond is known internationally for her research into risk and decision making, and has advised public and private corporations on risk management.

Leif Edvinsson was appointed the world's first corporate director of intellectual capital in 1991 at the Swedish financial services company Skandia. He is co-author of *Intellectual Capital* (with Michael Malone, 1997), *Accounting for Minds* (with Gottfried Grafström, 1998), and author of *Corporate Longitude* (2002).

Marc Effron is the global leader for Hewitt Associates' Leadership Consulting Practice. He helps the world's leading corporations develop their leadership quality and depth. He is co-author with Robert Gandossy of *Leading the Way: Three Truths from the Top Companies for Leaders*. He is a frequent speaker at business and HR conferences globally, and widely quoted on the topic of leadership.

Jean-Noël Ezingeard is a member of faculty at Henley Management College. His research interests are focussed in the area of business processes management. He is a regular speaker on information systems and information management, both in the UK and abroad. His report *Information Security: Setting the Boardroom Agenda*, co-authored with Monica Bowen-Schrire and David Birchall, was published in 2003.

Peter Fisk recently stepped down as chief executive of the Chartered Institute of Marketing in the UK. He previously led the worldwide marketing consulting team of PA Consulting Group, where he developed market strategies and solutions for a wide range of business and consumer-based brands. Most recently he has focussed on value-based marketing, making the hard connections between marketing activities and the creation of long-term shareholder value. He is co-author of *The Complete CEO* (2004).

Robert Gandossy is a global leader for Hewitt Associates' Talent and Organization consulting practice. He has written over 40 articles and five books on a variety of subjects, including HR strategy, M&A, change management, innovation, and business ethics. He is the co-editor (with Marc Effron and Marshall Goldsmith) of *Human Resources in the 21st Century* (2003), co-author with Marc Effron of *Leading the Way: Three Truths From the Top Companies for Leaders* (2004), and co-editor with Jeff Sonnenfeld of the forthcoming book *Leadership and Governance From the Inside Out*.

Marshall Goldsmith has been named by the American Management Association as one of 50 great thinkers and leaders who have impacted the field of management over the past 80 years. He has worked personally with over 70 major CEOs. His 18 books include *Global Leadership: The Next Generation* and *Coaching for Leadership*. Goldsmith's coaching methodology is now being used by Hewitt Associates, the largest executive coaching firm in the world. His article was adapted from "Helping successful people change" in *Leading for Innovation* (2002).

Rob Goffee is deputy dean and Professor of Organisational Behaviour at London Business School. He has held positions in a number of other universities, most recently as Visiting Professor at the Australian Graduate School of Management, University of New South Wales. He was Director of the Accelerated Development Programme from 1989–91 and has been a member of the Governing Body. He is currently director of the Innovation Exchange of London Business School. His research and publications are on the subjects of entrepreneurship, business formation and growth, and managerial careers. He has published seven books including *Entrepreneurship in Europe, Women in Charge, Reluctant Managers, Corporate Realities* and *The Character of a Corporation* (with Gareth Jones, 1998).

Lynda Gratton is associate professor of organizational behavior at London Business School. After extensive experience working in industry, she has established herself as one of the world's premier HR thinkers. She is the author of *Living Strategy* (2000) and *The Democratic Enterprise* (2003).

Gerry Griffin is founder of the Business Communication Forum. Gerry was formerly European director of training at Burson Marsteller and director of communications at London Business School. He is the author of *The Power Game, .Con, Reputation Management, Games Companies Play* (with Ciaran Parker), and *Fool's Gold* (with Ciaran Parker). Gerry is also director of business strategy at Internet broadcaster Joose.TV and is a frequent lecturer at London Business School.

David Haigh is the founder of consultants Brand Finance. Prior to this he worked at Interbrand as director of brand valuation in its London-based global brand valuation practice. A fellow of the UK Chartered Institute of Marketing, he is author of *Brand Valuation* (FT – Retail and Consumer Publishing, 1998), *Brand Valuation – a review of current practice* (IPA, 1996), and *Strategic Control of Marketing Finance* (FT/Pitman Publishing 1994).

Oren Harari (*harario@usfca.edu*) is professor of management at the Graduate School of Business and Management, University of San Francisco, and author of *The Leadership Secrets of Colin Powell* (McGraw-Hill, 2002).

H. David Hennessey is Professor of Marketing and International Business at Babson College, Wellesley, Massachusetts, and an associate of Ashridge Management College. He is co-author of *Global Marketing: Strategy and Cases* (6th Edition, 2004) and *Global Account Management: Creating Value* (2003).

Sam Hill is co-founder of Helios Consulting which focusses on growth and marketing issues and has offices in New York and Chicago. Before that, he was vice chairman and chief strategy officer of DMB&B, and partner and chief marketing officer at Booz Allen

Hamilton. He began his career at Kraft General Foods as an engineer. He has an engineering degree from the University of Georgia and an MBA from the University of Chicago. He is the co-author of a number of books including *Radical Marketing* (1999), *Brand Chemistry* (2000), and *The Infinite Asset: Managing Brands to Build New Value* (2001), and author of *Sixty Trends In Sixty Minutes* (2002).

Andreas Hinterhuber is vice president of Hinterhuber & Partners, a strategy consulting company headquartered in Innsbruck, Austria. As manager at Aventis, he has steered the integration process in the Region Asia-Pacific.

Phil Hodgson is director of leadership programs at the business school Ashridge and on the visiting faculty at Duke Corporate Education, Cornell's Johnson Business School, the European School of Management and Technology, and the Cabinet Office. He has published numerous books and articles including *What Do High Performance Managers Really Do?*, *The Future of Leadership*, *Relax, It's Only Uncertainty*, and *The Top Leader Journey*.

Tarun Inuganti is a Korn/Ferry client partner in Los Angeles and a member of the firm's Global Advanced Technology and Information Technology Practices.

Dr Michael Jarrett is Adjunct Associate Professor at London Business School and the Managing Partner of a niche change management consultancy.

Gareth Jones is a Visiting Professor at INSEAD. His career has spanned both the academic and business worlds. He has taught at the London Business School and Henley Management College, and also worked as Senior Vice President for Polygram's global human resources and as Director of Human Resources and Internal Communications at the BBC. He is the author of several books, including the recent *The Character of a Corporation: How Your Culture Can Make or Break Your Business*, co-authored with Rob Goffee.

Andrew Kakabadse is Professor of Management Development and deputy director of Cranfield School of Management. He is Honorary Professional Fellow at the Curtin University of Technology, Perth, Australia, and Visiting Professor of the Hangzhou University, China. His areas of interest focus on improving the performance of top executives and top executive teams, excellence in consultancy practice, and the politics of decision making. He has published 20 books including *The Politics of Management*, *Working in Organizations*, and *The Wealth Creators*.

John Kay (www.johnkay.com) is the founder of the consulting firm London Economics, former director of the Said School of Business at Oxford University, and one of Britain's leading economists. His interests focus on the relationships between economics and business. He writes a column in the *Financial Times* and his books include *The Truth About Markets* (2003).

Dr Mike Kennerley is a Research Fellow in the Centre for Business Performance at Cranfield School of Management. He has been working in the field of performance measurement and management for 10 years undertaking academically rigorous and practically relevant research. Prior to joining Cranfield he held positions at the University of Cambridge and UMIST. He also co-authored the book *The Performance Prism: The Scorecard for Measuring and Managing Business Success* published by Financial Times Prentice Hall in May 2002.

W. Chan Kim is the Boston Consulting Group Bruce D. Henderson Chair Professor of International Management at INSEAD, France.

Charles H. King is managing director and head of global board services at leading executive recruiting firm Korn/Ferry International.

Fred Langerak is Associate Professor of Strategic Marketing Management at the Rotterdam School of Management, Erasmus University.

Eleanor O'Higgins is on the faculty of the business school at University College Dublin in Ireland where she specializes in the areas of strategic management, business ethics, corporate social responsibility, and corporate governance. She chairs the International Theme Committee of the US Academy of Management and is a member of the United Nations Global Compact Learning Forum, and of the Business Ethics Faculty Group of the Community of European Management Schools (CEMS). She is also on the Board of Management of The Institute of Director's Centre for Corporate Governance at University College Dublin.

James O'Loughlin is Head of Investment Process at the Co-operative Insurance Society (CIS), a leading socially responsible investor that, along with The Co-operative Bank, is part of Co-operative Financial Services (CFS). James is the author of *The Real Warren Buffett: Managing Capital, Leading People*.

Laurence S. Lyons (*www.lslyons.com*) is director of the Metacorp Group, a coaching and change management consultancy. He is also European practice director for the Global Alliance for Strategic Leadership (*A4SL*) based in San Diego. A former technical director at Digital Equipment Corporation, he is a member of the associate faculty at Henley Management College and founding director of research of the Future Work Forum.

Costas Markides is Professor of Strategic and International Management and holds the Robert P. Bauman Chair of Strategic Leadership at the London Business School. He is the author of a number of books including *All the Right Moves: A Guide to Crafting Breakthrough Strategy* (Harvard Business School Press, 1999), *Strategic Thinking for the Next Economy* (Jossey-Bass, 2001), and more recently *Fast to be Second: From Creating to Conquering New Markets* (2004). He is also associate editor of the *European Management Journal* and on the editorial board of the *Strategic Management Journal* and the *Sloan Management Review*.

Renée Mauborgne is the INSEAD Distinguished Fellow and a professor of strategy and management in INSEAD in Fontainebleau, France.

Matthew May is director of Los Angeles-based Aevitas Learning, a senior adviser to the University of Toyota, and the author of *Absolute Impact: The Drive for Personal Leadership*.

Lance Moir is Senior Lecturer in Finance and Accounting at Cranfield University School of Management having previously held a number of senior financial positions in industry over 20 years. He is a fellow and member of the Council of the Association of Corporate Treasurers and chair of the academic board of the European Academy of Business in Society. He is the author of *Managing Liquidity* (1997).

Karl Moore is a professor in the faculty of management, McGill University, and an associate fellow at Templeton College, Oxford University. He has taught on executive programs at LBS, Duke, USC, the Drucker School of Management, and the Rotterdam School of Management.

John W. Mullins is Associate Professor of Management Practice and Chair of the Entrepreneurship group at the London Business School. He is co-author of *Marketing Management: A Strategic Decision Making Approach*, 5th Edition, and *Marketing Strategy: A Decision Focussed Approach*, 4th Edition, and author of *The New Business Road Test: What Entrepreneurs and Executives Should Do Before Writing a Business Plan* (2003). His research has won national and international awards from the Marketing Science Institute, the American Marketing Association, and the Richard D. Irwin Foundation.

Caroline W. Nahas is Korn/Ferry International's Managing Director/Southwest Region and a member of the Board Practice. Korn/Ferry International has conducted director searches for ExxonMobil, Lincoln National, Goodyear, The Southern Company, Aramark, and many other prominent corporations.

Andy Neely is chairman of the Centre for Business Performance at Cranfield School of Management (*www.cranfield.ac.uk/som/cbp*), deputy director of AIM Research (*www.aimresearch.org*), and managing partner of The Performance Practice, a consultancy specializing in performance measurement and management. His books include *Measuring Business Performance* (1998) and *The Performance Prism* (2002).

David Newkirk is a senior vice president of Booz Allen Hamilton, where he works with global companies on issues of strategy and organization. During his time with the firm, he has served as head of its strategy practice and director of European Operations. He held a series of marketing and management roles with American Express in the US, Asia, and Europe. He holds degrees in Mathematics and Philosophy from Carleton College and Oxford University.

Alex Nicholls is Lecturer in Social Entrepreneurship at Said Business School, Oxford. He has written a number of refereed articles and presented several international conference papers and is currently co-authoring a major research book on Fair Trade for Sage Publishers (due November 2004). A Fellow of the Academy of Marketing Science and Member of the Institute of Learning and Teaching, he also sits on the regional social enterprise expert group for the South East of England Development Agency.

Sebastian Nokes is a management consultant who specializes in valuation and the measurement of value creation by IT spend. Before joining his current firm Project Value Associates, he worked for IBM, Credit Suisse First Boston, and the RAF. He is the author or co-author of a number of management and finance books including *The Definitive Guide to Project Management: The Fast Track to Getting the Job Done on Time and on Budget* (2003).

Kjell A. Nordström is based at the Institute of International Business at the Stockholm School of Economics and is on the board of various companies. He is the co-author of *Funky Business* (2000) and *Karaoke Capitalism* (2004).

Anne-Valérie Ohlsson is a Research Associate at IMD. Her work focusses mainly on trajectory management, strategy, and marketing. Prior to IMD she worked for Pfizer and the IOC. Her cases have won awards and have been published in leading management textbooks.

Eric W. Orts is the Guardsmark Professor of legal studies and management at The Wharton School, University of Pennsylvania.

Ciaran Parker is a writer, researcher, translator, and reviewer. Ciaran holds a doctorate in history from Trinity College, Dublin and has written extensively on Ireland both past and present. Ciaran is co-author of *Games Companies Play* (with Gerry Griffin).

Helen Peck is a Senior Research Fellow in Marketing Logistics in the Centre for Logistics and Supply Chain Management (CLSCM) at Cranfield University. She is project manager for CLSCM's on-going program of government-funded research into supply chain resilience. As well as writing for a variety of publications she is an award-winning writer of management case studies. Her material is used extensively on marketing and logistics programs at Cranfield and by other teaching institutions around the world.

Georgina Peters is a business writer. She is a regular contributor to magazines worldwide including *Business Life* and the American Management Association's *MWorld*.

Mark Polansky is a Senior Client Partner in New York for Korn/Ferry International. He serves as the firm's Information Technology Practice Leader for North America.

Roger Pudney is a tutor in international strategic management at Ashridge. He teaches and consults extensively in the area of creating competitive advantage from strategic collaborations and the integration of mergers and acquisitions.

Jonas Ridderstråle of the Center for Advanced Studies in Leadership at the Stockholm School of Economics is on the board of several Internet-related companies. He is co-author of *Funky Business* (2000) and *Karaoke Capitalism* (2004).

Jorge Nascimento Rodrigues is the editor of www.gurusonline.tv and the editor of the *Portuguese and Brazilian Management Review*. He is the co-author of *Business Minds* (2002).

Dennis A. Rondinelli is the Glaxo Distinguished International Professor of Management at the Kenan-Flagler Business School, University of North Carolina at Chapel Hill.

Steven Rosell is co-founder and President of Viewpoint Learning Inc., a firm that develops specialized applications of dialog for business and public policy. He acts as an adviser to governments, international agencies, and major firms, and is the author of numerous articles and four books on governance, leadership, and learning, including: *Renewing Governance: Governing by Learning in the Information Age* (Oxford University Press, 1999), and *Changing Frames*, now available online at www.viewpointlearning.com/leadership.html.

Henri J. Ruff has spent much of his 30 years working life in financial services, in Europe and the US, reflecting on the underlying principles that shape or dictate management behavior. Trained as an economist, his entry into banking involved negotiating third-world debt lending and debt rescheduling, before gaining experience as a lobbyist in Washington DC. More recently, as economic adviser at Visa International, his extensive experience working in Central Europe and the Middle-East on formulating the future of card payment systems has sensitized him to the foundations of cross-cultural differences in managing the future.

Karl-Heinz Sebastian is a senior partner at Simon-Kucher.

Hermann Simon is chairman of Simon-Kucher & Partners Marketing & Strategy Consultants and co-author of *Power Pricing* (1996) and *Profit Renaissance* (2004).

Jonathan Story is Professor of International Political Economy at INSEAD, in France, dealing with comparative business systems in a global context. As the Shell Fellow in Economic Transformation, he specializes in global transformation. He is the author of a number of books including *The Frontiers of Fortune: Predicting capital prospects and casualties in the markets of the future* (1999) and *China: The Race to Market* (2003).

Paul Strebel is the Sandoz Family Foundation Professor of Management and Director of the Breakthrough Program for Senior Executives at IMD. His main area of activity is trajectory management, especially the anticipation of industry break points, the assessment of business reality, and the design and implementation of change processes. Paul is author of *The Change Pact: Building Commitment to Ongoing Change* and *Breakpoints: How Managers Exploit Radical Business Change*.

Mark Stuart is an editor at the Chartered Institute of Marketing where he leads the editorial side of the Institute's Insights program of white papers.

Donald N. Sull is Assistant Professor of Entrepreneurial Management at the Harvard Business School. He was formerly at London Business School and prior to that was vice president, corporate planning at Uniroyal-Goodrich/Clayton & Dubilier and a consultant with McKinsey & Company. He is the author of *Revival of the Fittest: Why Good Companies Go Bad and How Great Managers Remake Them* (2003).

George Tovstiga is Associate Professor of Technology and Innovation Management at TSM Business School, University of Twente, in the Netherlands.

Fons Trompenaars is founding principal of Trompenaars Hampden-Turner InterCultural Management Consulting and of the Centre for International Business Studies (Amsterdam) and author of *Riding the Waves of Culture*.

Bruce Tulgan is widely recognized as a leading expert on workplace issues and a leading authority on generational differences in the workplace. He is an adviser to business leaders all over the world and the founder of the management training firm RainmakerThinking Inc. (*www.rainmakerthinking.com*), based in New Haven, Connecticut. Tulgan has written numerous books, including *HOT MANAGEMENT* (2004), *Winning the Talent Wars* (2001), and *Managing Generation X* (1995).

Romesh Vaitilingam is the author of numerous articles and several successful books in economics, finance, management, and public policy, including *The Financial Times Guide to Using the Financial Pages*. As a specialist in translating economic, financial, and other social science concepts into everyday language, he has advised a number of top management consultancies and investment managers as well as various UK government agencies. His work also involves media consultancy for the international social science research community. In 2003 he was awarded an MBE for services to economic and social science.

Sandra Vandermerwe holds the Chair in Management at The Management School, Imperial College, University of London. Previously, she spent a decade as Professor of Marketing and International Services at IMD, Switzerland. She is the author of several books, including *Breaking Through: Implementing Customer Focus in Enterprises* (Palgrave Macmillan, 2004), *Customer Capitalism: Getting Increasing Returns in New Market Spaces* (1999, 2001), *The 11th Commandment: Transforming to 'Own' Customers* (1996), and *From Tin Soldiers to Russian Dolls: Creating Added Value through Services* (1993).

Peter C. Verhoef is Associate Professor at the Rotterdam School of Economics, Erasmus University Rotterdam in the Netherlands.

Watts Wacker is a lecturer, author, commentator, and social critic. He is CEO of First Matter and previously was the futurist at SRI International, the Menlo Park think-tank, and spent 10 years with the social research organization, Yankelovich Partners. He is the co-author of *The 500 Year Delta*, *The Visionary's Handbook* and *The Deviant's Advantage: How Fringe Ideas Create Mass Markets* (2002).

Elizabeth Weldon is Professor of Organization Behavior at the International Institute for Management Development (IMD) in Lausanne, Switzerland. Her research, teaching, and consulting activities focus on strategy execution, leadership development in Western and Chinese companies and high-speed organizations. Her latest book is *Strategic Improvisation: How to Become a Nimble Manager* (2004).

Randall P. White is co-author of *Relax, It's Only Uncertainty*, *The Future of Leadership*, and *Breaking the Glass Ceiling*. While at the Center for Creative Leadership in Greensboro, North Carolina, he was a key member of the research team for the groundbreaking study on learning, growth, and change. Now a principal of the Executive Development Group in Greensboro, North Carolina, and Leadership

Forum Inc. in Hillsborough, North Carolina, he specializes in executive coaching and teaches leadership courses in the executive education group at the Fuqua School of Business, Duke University. He currently serves on the board of Division 13 (Society of Consulting Psychology) of the American Psychological Association.

Mark Whittington worked in a variety of roles in the accounting function at British Steel (now Corus Group) before taking up a management training role within the company. He has been at Warwick Business School for over 10 years where he lectures MBAs on accounting and financial management, management accounting, and financial analysis. He is the course organizer and study note author for the DLMBA Financial Accounting module and also contributes to the Management Accounting notes.

Simon Wiggins is a Korn/Ferry Client Partner in London and leads the firm's European Information Technology Practice.

Richard Wilding is a senior lecturer in Logistics and Supply Chain Management at Cranfield School of Management. His research into chaos and complexity in the supply chain and inventory policies in times of uncertainty has received international media coverage.

Jerry Wind is The Lauder Professor and Professor of Marketing at the Wharton School of the University of Pennsylvania. He is the founding director of the Wharton think-tank, The SEI Center for Advanced Studies in Management. His recent books include *Convergence Marketing: Strategies for Reaching the New Hybrid Consumer* (Financial Times/Prentice Hall 2002), and *The Power of Impossible Thinking: How Changing Your Mental Models Will Transform the Business of Your Life and the Life of Your Business*, with Colin Crook and Robert Gunther (Wharton School Publishing, 2004). He also serves as an adviser to many Fortune 500 firms and a number of non-US multinationals.

Robin Wood is a Fellow of the Centre for Management Development at London Business School, where he graduated with a Doctorate in Business Administration in 1995. He has been working intensively in the telecommunications industry and mobile space for the past decade. His recent research has focussed on the principles of complexity science to develop theories and models on how companies can adapt and prosper in the complex and turbulent business environment that globalization and the connected economy has brought about.

Peter Woolliams is Professor of International Business at the Ashcroft Business School, APU, and is also a partner/owner in Trompenaars Hampden-Turner Consulting.

Daniel Yankelovich is founder and chairman of Viewpoint Learning Inc. (a firm that advances dialog-based learning as a core skill in newer forms of leadership), DYG, Inc. (a market research firm tracking social trends), and Public Agenda (a public education not-for-profit). He is the author of 10 books, including *Coming to Public Judgment* (1991) and *The Magic of Dialogue* (1999).

Top lists

The top 20 business schools

#	Business school	#	Business school
1.	University of Pennsylvania: Wharton USA	11.	Northwestern University Kellogg
2.	Harvard Business School USA	12.	IMD Switzerland
3.	Columbia Business School USA	13.	Yale School of Management USA
4.	London Business School UK	14.	Iese Business School Spain
5.	INSEAD France	15.	Instituto de Empresa Spain
6.	University of Chicago GSB USA	16.	Cornell University: Johnson USA
7.	Stanford University GSB USA	17.	University of North Carolina: Kenan-Flagler USA
8.	New York University: Stern USA	18.	Georgetown University: McDonough USA
9.	MIT: Sloan USA		
10.	Dartmouth College: Tuck USA	19.	University of Virginia: Darden USA
		20.	Duke University: Fuqua USA

Source: FT Global business school rankings, 2004

The top 50 business gurus

#	Guru	#	Guru
1.	Peter DRUCKER	16.	Stephen COVEY
2.	Michael PORTER	17.	Edgar H SCHEIN
3.	Tom PETERS	18.	Chris ARGYRIS
4.	Gary HAMEL	19.	Kenichi OHMAE
5.	Charles HANDY	20.	Bill GATES
6.	Philip KOTLER	21.	Kjell NORDSTRÖM and Jonas RIDDERSTRÅLE
7.	Henry MINTZBERG		
8.	Jack WELCH	22.	Clayton CHRISTENSEN
9.	Rosabeth MOSS KANTER	23.	John KOTTER
10.	Jim COLLINS	24.	Nicholas NEGROPONTE
11.	Sumantra GHOSHAL	25.	Jim CHAMPY
12.	C.K. PRAHALAD	26.	Andy GROVE
13.	Warren BENNIS	27.	Scott ADAMS
14.	Peter SENGE	28.	Richard PASCALE
15.	Robert KAPLAN and David NORTON	29.	Daniel GOLEMAN

30. Naomi KLEIN
31. Chan KIM and Renée MAUBORGNE
32. Don TAPSCOTT
33. Michael DELL
34. Richard BRANSON
35. Edward DE BONO
36. Ricardo SEMLER
37. Thomas A. STEWART
38. Geoffrey MOORE
39. Jeff BEZOS
40. Paul KRUGMAN
41. Lynda GRATTON
42. Alan GREENSPAN
43. Manfred KETS DE VRIES
44. Robert WATERMAN
45. Watts WACKER
46. Patrick DIXON
47. Geert HOFSTEDE
48. DON PEPPERS
49. Stan DAVIS
50. Fons TROMPENAARS

Source: www.Thinkers50.com
Suntop Media

The top 10 global brands

#	Brand
1.	Google
2.	Apple
3.	Mini
4.	Coca-Cola
5.	Samsung
6.	IKEA
7.	Nokia
8.	Nike
9.	Sony
10.	Starbucks

Source: The Global Brand of the Year 2003
www.brandchannel.com
Interbrand

The 10 most valuable brands

#	Brand	Brand value $ millions
1.	Coca-Cola	70,453
2.	Microsoft	65,174
3.	IBM	51,767
4.	GE	42,340
5.	Intel	31,112
6.	Nokia	29,440
7.	Disney	28,036
8.	McDonald's	24,699
9.	Marlboro	22,183
10.	Mercedes	21,371

Source: Interbrand's Annual Ranking of 10 of the Best Global Brands, 2003

The 20 largest family firms

	Company	Revenues	Employees	Country
1.	Wal-Mart Stores	$244.5 billion	1.4 million	US
2.	Ford Motor Co.	$163.4 billion	350,321	US
3.	Samsung	$98.7 billion	175,000	South Korea
4.	LG Group	$81 billion	130,000	South Korea
5.	Carrefour Group	$72.035 billion	396,662	France
6.	Fiat Group	$61.014 billion	186,492	Italy
7.	Ifi Istituto Finanziario Industriale S.p.A.	$59.239 billion	198,764	Italy
8.	PSA Peugeot Citroën S.A.	$57.054 billion	198,600	France
9.	Cargill Inc	$50.8 billion	97,000	US
10.	BMW	$44.315 billion	101,395	Germany
11.	Hyundai Motor	$40.111 billion	49,855	South Korea
12.	Koch Industries	$40 billion	11,000	US
13.	Robert Bosch GmbH	$36.659 billion	224,341	Germany
14.	SCH (Banco Santander Central Hispano S.A.)	$32.524 billion	114,927	Spain
15.	ALDI Group	$30 billion	--------------	Germany
16.	Auchan Group	$28.888 billion	143,000	France
17.	Pinault-Printemps Redoute	$28.692 billion	113,453	France
18.	Ito-Yokado	$28.436 billion	125,400	Japan
19.	Tengelmann Group	$28.227 billion	183,396	Germany
20.	J Sainsbury	$27.433 billion	174,500	UK

Source: Family business magazine – www.familybusinessmagazine.com

The largest US bankruptcies 1980–2003

#	Company	Bankruptcy date	Total assets pre-bankruptcy
1.	Worldcom, Inc.	07/21/02	$103,914,000,000
2.	Enron Corp.*	12/2/01	$63,392,000,000
3.	Conseco, Inc.	12/18/02	$61,392,000,000
4.	Texaco, Inc.	4/12/1987	$35,892,000,000
5.	Financial Corp. of America	9/9/1988	$33,864,000,000
6.	Global Crossing Ltd.	1/28/2002	$30,185,000,000
7.	UAL Corp.	12/9/2002	$25,197,000,000
8.	Adelphia Communications	6/25/2002	$21,499,000,000
9.	Pacific Gas and Electric Co.	4/6/2001	$21,470,000,000
10.	MCorp	3/31/1989	$20,228,000,000
11.	Mirant Corporation	7/14/2003	$19,415,000,000
12.	First Executive Corp.	5/13/1991	$15,193,000,000
13.	Gibraltar Financial Corp.	2/8/1990	$15,011,000,000
14.	Kmart Corp.	1/22/2002	$14,600,000,000
15.	FINOVA Group, Inc., (The)	3/7/2001	$14,050,000,000
16.	HomeFed Corp.	10/22/1992	$13,885,000,000
17.	Southeast Banking Corporation	9/20/1991	$13,390,000,000
18.	NTL, Inc.	5/8/2002	$13,003,000,000
19.	Reliance Group Holdings, Inc.	6/12/2001	$12,598,000,000
20.	Imperial Corp. of America	2/28/1990	$12,263,000,000
21.	Federal-Mogul Corp.	10/1/2001	$10,150,000,000
22.	First City Bancorp.of Texas	10/31/1992	$9,943,000,000
23.	First Capital Holdings	5/30/1991	$9,675,000,000
24.	Baldwin-United	9/26/1983	$9,383,000,000

Source: BankruptcyData.com/New Generation Research, Inc. Boston, MA
* The Enron assets were taken from the 10-Q filed on 11/19/2001.

Best selling *Harvard Business Review* articles

#	Article
1.	One More Time: How Do You Motivate Employees? Frederick Herzberg / Jan-Feb 68
2.	Management Time: Who's Got the Monkey? William Oncken and Donald Wass / Nov-Dec 74
3.	How to Choose a Leadership Pattern. Robert Tannenbaum and Warren H. Schmidt / Mar-Apr 58
4.	Pygmalion in Management. J.Sterling Livingstone / Jul-Aug 69
5.	The Management Process in 3-D. Alec MacKenzie / Nov-Dec 69
6.	Marketing Myopia. Theodore Levitt / Jul-Aug 60
7.	Barriers and Gateways to Communication. Carl R. Rogers and F.J. Roethlisberger / Jul-Aug 52

Source: "The 100 best-selling Articles" HBR published at the time of HBR's 75th anniversary in 1997.

Where are they now: the fate of original Dow 12

The company	Its fate
American Cotton Oil	Distant ancestor of Bestfoods
American Sugar	Evolved into Amstar Holdings
American Tobacco	Broken up in 1911 antitrust action
Chicago Gas	Absorbed by Peoples Gas, 1897
Distilling & Cattle Feeding	Whiskey trust evolved into Millennium Chemical
General Electric	Still in the DJIA
Laclede Gas	Trading, removed from DJIA in 1899
National Lead	Now NL Industries, removed from DJIA in 1916
North American	Broken up in 1940s
Tennessee Coal & Iron	Absorbed by US Steel in 1907
US Leather (preferred)	Dissolved in 1952
US Rubber	Became Uniroyal, today part of Michelin

The top American companies of 1929

#	Company	Assets ($ million)
1.	US Steel	2,286
2.	Standard Oil (NJ)	1,767
3.	General Motors	1,131
4.	Standard Oil (Ind)	850
5.	Bethlehem Steel	802
6.	Ford Motor	761
7.	Mobil Oil	708
8.	Anaconda	681
9.	Texaco	610
10.	Standard Oil (Calif)	605
11.	General Electric	516
12.	Du Pont	497
13.	Shell Oil	486
14.	Armour	452
15.	Gulf Oil	431

Source: Kaplan, ADH, *Big Enterprise in a Competitive System*, 1964

Index

360-degree feedback 977, 989–90
3G mobile phone licenses 930–1
3M 21, 273, 359, 360, 504, 525, 540, 544
100 Day Plans 69
Abernathy, Bill 293–4
ABI, CSR guidelines 122
Ace, Cathy 867–8
Acer 528
Across The Board 26
action learning 588, 1008, **1019–20**
activity drivers 495
activity-based costing **495–6**
Acumen Fund 636
added value 484
adhocracy **561–2**
advertising 151, 332, 339, 875
  see also marketing
Aeroxchange 366
affiliate marketing **423–4**
agility **562–3**, 905–9
Ahold's 663
airports, things to do 728–9
Alessi, Alberto 268
Alfa Laval 360
Allan, Dave 627
Allen, Louis 177
  Professional Management 177
alliances, cultural differences 724–7
Almond, Michael 669
Alvarez, Felipe J. 961
Amazon.com 162, 163, 376, 378, 423, 616, 620, 967
Ambler, Tim 414, 415
Amelio, Gil 207
American Airlines 852
American Law Institute, *Principles of Corporate Governance* 670–2, 673, 674
American Management Association, *E–Mail Rules, Policies and Practices Survey* 857

Amoco 67
amortization 482
annual reports 445
Ansoff, Igor 100
  Corporate Strategy **100**
Antoine, Dick 768
AOL 548
Apple 207, 268, 332, 525, 534, 967
appraisal 244–5
Ardittis, Solon 731
Argentina 120, 121
Argyris, Chris 8, 629, 1007, **1020–1**, 1021, 1023
  Personality and Organization 1020
Argyris, Chris and Schön, Donald
  Organizational Learning 1020
  Theory in Practice 1020
Arthur Andersen 663, 792, 794
Arthur, Brian 19
Artigliere 961–2
Arulampalam, Wiji 892
Asea Brown Boveri (ABB) 528, 568, 605, 607
Ashoka 637
Ashridge Strategic Management Centre 12, 654
Astra-Zeneca 69
AT&T 42, 64, 344, 504, 522, 540, 867
Athos, Anthony 108, 113, 295, 590, 591
Augustine, Norman 768
Austrian School 592
autonomous work teams 523
Aventis 827, 976–8
Ayling, Bob 836–7

Babbage, Charles 968
Bachmann, John 777–9
Bailey, Julia 277
Bain & Co 618
Bains, Gurnek 207, 740

balanced scorecard **101**, 260, 347, 938, 939–42
Ballmer, Steve 545
Bangladesh 120
Bangle, Chris 269
Bank of America 276
Bank One 50
banking 470–1, 610
   on-line 399–400, 1049
   telephone 1048–50
Barclays Bank 933
Bard, Alexander 819
Barings 664
Barnard, Chester **563**
   The Functions of the Executive 563
Barnevik, Percy 163, 528, 605
Barrett, Colleen 207, 963
Barrett, Craig 962
Barrie, Joyce E. 880
Barrow, Kevin 277
Barsoux, Jean-Louis 213
Bartlett, Christopher 163, 167–9
Bartlett, Christopher and Ghoshal, Sumantra
   Managing Across Borders 167, 168
   The Individualized Corporation 168–9
Bates, K. and Moon, P., *CORE Analysis in Strategic Performance Appraisal* 442
Bates, Ted 362
Baxter Healthcare 379
behavioral development 972
behavioral event interviewing 182
Belgium 143
Bell Laboratories 575–6
benchmarking **309–10**
Bennis, Warren 204, 205, 257, 561, 735, 762, 801–4, ***805–6***, 1023, 1037
   Leaders 735, 805
   Organizing Genius: The Secrets of Creative Collaboration 805
   The Temporary Society 805
Bennis, Warren and Thomas, Robert, *Geeks and Geezers* 735, 762
Berkshire Hathaway 458–64
best demonstrated practice 309
best related practice 309
Bezos, Jeff 376, 627, 967
Bhidé, Amar 653
BHP 69
Bijur, Peter 311

Billiton 69
Bishop, Michael 311
Black, Liam 633–5
Blair, Cary 208–9, 963–4
Blake, Robert 232–3, 1023
Blake, Robert and McCanse, Anne Adams, *Leadership Dilemmas – Grid Solutions* 233
Blanchard, Ken, *Raving Fans – a Revolutionary Approach to Customer Service* 403
Blank, Arthur 206
blended learning 1007
Blessing/White, *Heart and Soul* 11
blogs 857, 877–8
Bloomberg 96, 98
BMW 269
board members, recruitment and selection 217–20
Body Shop 759
Boehme, Alan 584
Boeing Rocketdyne 906–7
books managers should read 1037–40
Booth, Alison 892
Booz Allen Hamilton 495, 617, 1024
   Strategy & Business 1024
Boston Consulting Group 102, 106, 321, 473
Boston Matrix **101–3** (f6) 106
Bowerman, Bill 652
Bowes, Pitney 773
Boyatzis, Richard 181
BP 67, 193–4, 195, 197, 198, 199, 200, 202, 225, 338, 348, 604, 621, 677
Brainspark 618
brainstorming 222
brand economics 409–15 (f11–f15) 419
brand equity 408, 409, 410, 411 (f13, f14), 413–19 (f16, f17) 477
Brand Finance plc 344, 409
brand management organizations 355, 356
Brand Scorecard 417, 418 (f19, f20)
Brand, Stewart 506
brand tracking 419
brand valuation 342, 408–19 (f18), 467–9 (f6) 477, 677
Brandenburger, Adam 588
branding 331, 362–5, 408–19
Branson, Richard 242, 504, 528
Bratton, William 819–20
bribery 662–3
Briggs, Katherine C. 882

Briskin, Alan 730, 903–4
British Airways 363, 836–7, 841
British Midland 311
British Telecom (BT) 198, 201, 202, 604
broadbanding 225
Brookings Research Institute 21
Brown, Barrie 912
brown papering 587
Browne, John 193–4, 197, 200, 338, 348
Brundtland, Gro Harlem 155
Bryan, Mark 892
Bryce, David 318
Buffett, Warren 458–64, 503–4, 858
bullying 210
Burgelman, Robert, *Strategy is Destiny* 88, 89
burnout 910–15
business continuity issues 304
business drivers, and conditions 57–62 (f1, f3)
business ecosystems 548–9
business intelligence 583
business process mapping 595
business process reengineering *see* reengineering
business schools 5–6, 8, 527–8
business scorecard 525
Business for Social Responsibility 155
business travel 730–2
Byham, William 205
BZW 933

Cabler, Mona 710
CAD/CAM 274
Cadbury Schweppes 344, 348, 349
cafeteria benefits 229
Callaway Golf 97
Campbell, Andrew 12, 592
Canada 143, 145
Canon 52, 73, 83
capabilities 45–6, 596–7
capabilities-based strategy 594–600 (f1–f5)
capability managers 202, 203
capital allocation 459
capital flight 121
capitalism 17, 559–600
Carnegie, Dale **916**
Carrefour 138
Castells, Manuel 17
Caterpillar 74

Caves, Richard 588
CDnow 616
Ceconi, Margaret 793
Cementos Mexicanos (CEMEX) 73–4, 83
centralization 568
Centre for Integrated Marketing 872–3
Chabris, Christopher 335
Chambers, John 367, 533
Champy, James 319, 821–3
    Reengineering Management 320
Champy, James and Hammer, M.,
    Reengineering the Corporation 319, 587
Chandler, Alfred 86–90, 575
    Strategy and Structure 44, 86, 87, 88
    The Visible Hand 87
change, resistance 231, 835–7, 843
change management 811–49, 973–82 (f1)
change masters 231
channel management **310**
chaos 14
Chase, Richard B. 405
Chase, Rodney 195, 197, 200
Chez Gerard 933
Chicago 933
chief executive officers 699–701, 738–40, 741–4, 959
chief information officers 581–6
chief knowledge officers 621
chief operating officers 959–64
chief risk officer 452–4
child labor – abolition 151
China 94, 127–40, 353
    ACFTU 137
    business risk – approach to 131–2
    corporate integration 138
    corruption 133–4
    financial system 132
    franchising 139
    holding companies 139
    impact of recent political history 127–8
    labor costs 1236
    management of human resources 136–7
    management of production 137–8
    market entry 134–6 (f2)
    marketing 138
    private enterprises 133, 136
    public opinion and the party–state 133–4
    role of CCP 132
    urban working class 133

choice 16, 17, 196, 197–8, 202–3
Chou, Sun-Lin 578
Christensen, Clay, *The Innovator's Dilemma*
    544
Christie's 663
Chrysler 63
Churchill Club 511–12
Churchill, Winston 936
Cisco Systems 63, 66, 367, 533, 576–7
Citibank 357
CitiGroup 123, 663, 827
citizenship 147–9
Clarke, Chris 873–4
Clausewitz, Carl von 667
climate change 120
club concept 505–12
Co-operative Bank 697
coaching 921, 923–4
Coase, Ronald 590
Coca-Cola 153, 154–5, 204, 205, 353, 874
cognitive dissonance 985
Cohan, Peter, *Value Leadership* 820
cold calling 875
Coleco 863
Coles, David 263, 730–1
Colgate–Palmolive 771
collaboration 868–76
collaborative coaching framework 996–7 (f2)
collaborative value networks 552
collective bargaining 151
collectivism 17
Collins, David 12
Collins, James 474
Collins, Jim, *Good to Great* 12, 736, 864
Collins, Jim and Porras, Jerry, *Built to Last* 12, 13, 346, 887
Collyns, Napier 510–12
communication 404, 542, 563, 570, 631–2, 739, 850–78, 979
    consent 866–76
    electronic 190
    mergers and acquisitions 68–9
    strategic dialog 851–5
    written 856–63
Company-Wide Quality Management (CWQM) 314
Compaq 63, 66
competencies 17, 531–46
competition, Five Forces Model 76, 110–11,
    445, 451, 588
competitive advantage 44–6, 162, 266–75,
    609, 751
competitive profiling 830–1
complexity theory 14, 839, 841
computer industry 547–54
computers, handheld 549
Conaty, Bill 770, 771
concepts managers should know 1041–4
Concorde 933
Conran, Sir Terence 268
consent, and communication 866–76
consultants, external 186
consumer's surplus 337
contestable market 44
Convergys 277
copyright 620
Cordier, Bertrand 978
Cordiner, Ralph 770
core activities 185, 186, 188
CORE analysis 442
core competencies 45, **563**–5
Corning 747–8
corporate citizenship 147–59
    definition 148
corporate governance 583, 665
Corporate Leadership Council 533
corporate loyalty 9–11, 563
corporate mortality 12–13
corporate parents, role 12
corporate private equity 655
corporate religion 420–2
corporate social responsibility 122–23, 157, 352, 677–8, 694–8 (f2, f3)
corporate strategy, impact of brand economics 412–13
corporate venturing 654–7
corruption 150, 664, 790
cost
    of capital 449
    law of lowest total 251, 253
    social and environmental impacts 124–5
cost drivers 495
Costco 332
counter intuition, law of 252, 257
Covey, Stephen, *Seven Habits of Highly Effective People* 711
Coyne, Martin 748
Cranfield School of Management 618, 740

Crawford-Mason, Clare 292, 293
creative capabilities of organization 191
Creveld, Martin van 668
crisis, definition 311
crisis management **310–11**
Critelli, Michael 205, 773–6, 864, 865
critical success factors 191
Crosby, Philip 323
cross-selling 438
cultural diversity 169–70
Cultural Due Diligence 726
cultural integration, mergers and acquisitions 66–7
cultural reconciliation 724–7
culture 142, 143
  corporate 240–1, 831, 832
currency transactions 125
customer capital 619
customer managers 202
customer pyramid 394–7 (f7, f9)
customer relationship management 330, 339, 350–1, 372, 387–400 (f5–f9 t1) 583
customer service 401–7
customer-managed relationships 330
customers
  acquisition 390–1
  care 583
  database 428, 475–6
  lifetime value 371–82, 398–9, 469–71 (f7)
  loyalty 339, 372, 391, 393–5 (f6) 397–8, 399–400, 414, 469, 616
  retention 372
  satisfaction 393–4 (f6) 406, 513
  segmentation 358–9, 395–7 (f9) 470–1
customization 202
Cutler, Lloyd 21

DaimlerChrysler 63, 667
danwei 132
Dasu, Sriram 405
data mining 197
Datamonitor 23
D'Aveni, Richard 587, 588
Davidow, William and Malone, Michael 570
Davis, Bryan 22
Davis, Miles 363
Davis, Peter 1048–9
Day, George 476–7
Day, Mike 761

de Baer 645
de Geus, Arie, *The Living Company* 12, 13, 113
decision making 929–37
  models 969
decision theory **968–9**
decisions, 50 great management decisions 1029–35
delayering 226, 806
delegation 921
Dell Computers 7, 368, 550, 615, 617
Dell, Michael 7
demand curves, brands 412–3 (f15) 415
Deming, W. Edwards 255, 292–3, 297–8, 299, **312–13**, 316, 317, 588–9, 1037
democracy 521–30
democratic enterprises, leading 193–203
Denyer, David 519, 520
DePree, Max 802
deregulation 91
design 268–75
Development Dimensions International 205
DHL UK 263
Diageo 345, 348, 1044–5
Diehl, Daniel and Donnelly, Mark, *How Did They Manage? Leadership Secrets of History* 734–5
differentiation 266–75, 278, 564
dilemmas 515–17
diminishing returns 19
Direct Line 375, 377, 378
directors, boardroom coaching 679–86
discounted cash flow 467, 471, **496–7**
disintermediation **615**
Disney 404, 504, 540, 679
Disney, Walt 967
distance learning 188
distinctive strategic position 52
diversity 144–5, 538
division of labor 20
Dobbin, Frank 959–61, 963, 964
double-loop learning 943, 944, 1007–8, 1020
Dow Chemical 348
Dow Jones Sustainability Group Index 694
downsizing 9, **225–6**, 227, 239, 320, 806
Doyle, Peter 469
Doz, Yves 12, 160–3
Doz, Yves and Santos, José, *From Global to Multinational ...* 163

Drayton, Bill 648
Drucker, Peter 7–8, **30–2**, 592, 621, 652, 849
  Management: Tasks, Responsibilities, Practices 5, 30, 31, 1037
  The Age of Discontinuity 619
  The Concept of the Corporation 30
  The Practice of Management 27, 30, 31
DSM Engineering Plastics 720
Duffield, Mark 668
DuPont 567, 575
dynamic pricing **615–16**
Dyson, Chris 627

e-commerce 366–70, 583, 615, **616–18**
e-learning 1005–11
e-mail 69, 368, 856–7, 858–9, 860, 866, 867
earnings 479–89
earnings per share 479–81
East, Robert 469
eBay 332, 647, 857, 858
Ebbers, Bernie 665
Ebitda 947–50
Eco, Umberto 675
economic instability 120
economic rent 44, 45
economic value 337, 337–8, 343
economic value added 44
ecosystem venturing 655
education *see* executive coaching; learning; training
Edvinsson, Leif 505
efficiency 20, 558
Egan, William 650–1
Egg 1048–50
Ehrenberg, Andrew 476
Electrolux 715
Elkington, John 694–5
Elsbach, Kimberly 632
emerging markets 91, 93–4
Emerson, J. 641
EMI 652, 758
employability **806–7**
employee manager 202–3
employees
  commitment 523, 689, 690 (f1)
  communications 404
  confidence 897
  dissatisfaction and stress 523
  insight 201
  recruitment and selections 403–4
  relationships 199
employer–employee relationships 895–6
empowerment 185, **226–8**, 846, 921
Enron 663, 665, 790–800
enterprise value 945–52
entrepreneurs 18, 626–30, 626–57, 965–7
environment 54–5, 120
environmental management systems 151
ERI tool 827
Ericsson 138, 139, 715
Ernst & Young 942
espoused theories 1007
ethics 658–701
euro 368
Eustace, Clark 21
exceptional items 481–2
executive coaching 972–82 (f1) 984–5, 994–1004
executive development 527
Executive Outcomes 671
experience curve 43, 106
Exxon 311
Eyretel 967

failure 555–6, 629
fair process 98
Families and Work Institute 911
fast tracking 242
Fastow, Andrew 792, 793
Fayol, Henri **32**
  Industrial and General Administration 176
federal decentralization 567
Federal Express 535, 1016
federal organization 569
feedback
  360-degree 977, 989–90
  executive coaching 980–1
Feldwick, Paul 414, 415
Feynman, Richard 803
Fidelity 396
financial literacy 455–7
financial ratios 456, 465–78 (f5–f7)
financial services, lifetime customer approach 373–4 (f4)
Finkelstein, Sydney, *Why Smart Executives Fail* 555, 556
Finland 143
First Direct 403

First Tuesday 506
Fish Info Service 368
Fisk, Peter 730, 735–6
fit 53–4, 55
Five Forces Model 76, 110–11, 445, 451, 588
flexibility 54, 896
flexible employment contracts 187
flexible working 10
Florida Power & Light 299
Follett, Mary Parker 226, **228**, 232
Foot and Mouth disease 300, 306–7
forced labor 151
Ford, Bill 1046
Ford, Henry 17, 20, 34, 89, **313–14**, 322, 426, 966
Ford Motor Company 123, 269, 299, 363, 377, 535, 659, 1045–7
forecasting financials 441–51 (f3, f4)
foreign aid 147, 149–50, 155, 156, 158
foreign direct investment 121
France 145, 157, 822
Frances, Lilly 907
franchising 139
Frank, Reuven 292
Franklin Covey 710–11
Free–PC 616
freedom of association 151
Freeman, Walter 328
Friedman, Milton 670, 673, 677
Friedman, Stephen 195
Frontstep CIS 905–6
Fry, Art 544
FTSE4Good 122, 694
Fulmer, Robert 8
fun days 213
functional organizations 355, 356
Furniture Resource Center 633–5

gambling 492–3
Game Theory **103–4**
Gandossy, Robert P. and Effron, Marc, *Human Resources for the 21st Century* 771
garage start-ups 965–7
Gardner, Howard 984
Garside, Tom 453
Gates, Bill 17, 150, 153, 242, 504, 533, 628, 665, 736, 750
Gateway 617
gearing 456

Geneen, Harold **565**
General Electric Company 1050
General Electric (GE) 7, 10, 58–62, 63, 169, 206, 336, 366, 440, 473, 540, 567, 588, 592, 605, 621, 664, 667, 769, 770–1, 827, 834, 887–8, 1019
General Motors (GM) 8, 89, 123, 555, 567, 575, 605, 628, 946
"generational shift"™ 894–902
generic strategies 111
geographic organizations 354, 355–6
Germany 142, 290, 822
Gerstner, Louis 207, 537, 763, 764, 834
Ghoshal, Sumantra 9, 163, 167–9, 604–7
  see also Bartlett, Christopher and Ghoshal, Sumantra
Gibbons, Barry 738–9
Gibson, Cyrus 590
Gillespie, Graham 585–6
Gilman, Michael 535
Gioia, Dennis 659
Giuliani, Rudy 734
Glacier Metal Company 230–1
Gladwell, Malcolm, *The Tipping Point* 814, 819, 820, 841
Glaxo Wellcome 67, 225
global account management 716–20
Global Business Network 506–7, 508, 510–12
global firm 167–8
global managers 141–6
global marketing 366–70
Global Reporting Initiative 125, 157
global warming 152
globalization 112, 117–72, 186–7, 321, 426, 533, 667–8, 669, 721–3, 848
goals 200, 524, 525, 544
Godin, Seth **426–7**, 587–8, 876
Goizueta Business School 857
Goldman Sachs 194–5, 199
Goldsmith, Marshall, Kaye, Ben, and Shelton, Ken, *Learning Journeys* 990
goodwill, writing off 482
Gore 434–5
grammar 859–60
Grand Metropolitan 1044
greed 490, 491–2
Greener, Sir Anthony 953
Griffin, Gerry 861
  The Power Game 10, 732

Griffin, Scott 581, 584
Grobe, Andy 89
Groucho Club 509
groupware 190
Grove, Andy 114, 142, 528, 818, 962
  Only the Paranoid Survive 114
Grubman, Jack 663
Grubman, Richard 792
GSM technology 162, 577
Gucci 270
Guinness 1044
Gulick, Luther 176
Gupta, Rajat 194, 196
Gyllenhammar, Pehr 523

Haas School of Business 618
Haberman, Jürgen 668
Haigh, David 344–5
Hal, Brian 886
Hall Tonna Inventory of Values 886
Hambrick, Donald 960, 962, 964
Hamel, Gary 48, 87, **104–6**, 313, 508, 1029–30
Hamel, Gary & Prahalad, C.K., *Competing for the Future* 45, 91, 93, 105, 447, 564, 862–3
Hammer, M. *see* Champy, James and Hammer, M.
Hammond, Kathy 470
Hampden-Turner, Charles 170
Handy, Charles 44, 187, 522, 558–60, **565–7**, 568–70, 889, 983
  The Age of Unreason 566
  The Hungry Spirit 803, 889
  Understanding Organizations 566
Hanson plc 122
Harley-Davidson 274
Harris, Mike 1048–50
Harsanyi, John 104, 588
Harvard Business Review 1036–7
Harvard Business School 6, 12, 637
Hawkins, Jeff 967
Hawthorne Studies 235
Hay Group 626
Hayes, Robert 268, 293–4
health 375–6
Heijn, Albert 391
Heineken, Freddie 757
Heller, Frank 525

Hellström, Kurt 714
Hemp, Paul 404
Hendersen, Bruce 102, **106**
Henley Management College 191, 609, 1006
Herbold, Bob 964
Hero-Honda 651
Hertz, Noreena, *Silent Takeover: The Rise of Corporate Power and the Death of Democracy* 668
Herzberg, Frederick **228–9**
  The Motivation to Work 229
Heskett, James L. 402
Hewitt Bacon & Woodrow 277
Hewlett, Bill 235, 966
Hewlett–Packard 63, 66, 235–6, 621, 966
Heyden, Karl von der 229–30
hierarchy 535–6
Hierarchy of Needs **233–4**
Higgs Report 608
high reliability organizations 519–20
Hill, Sam 591, 861
  Radical Marketing 587, 858
Hirsh, Evan 617
Hodgson, Phil 631, 761–2
  Relax: It's Only Uncertainty 738
Hofstede, Geert 164
  Culture's Consequences 164
Holland, J. 889
Holland's Self-Directed Search 889
Hollywood 631–2
Home Depot 484
Honda 73, 321
Honda, Soichiro 1022
Hong Kong 822
Hotmail 819
Hounsfield, Godfrey 653
Hubbard, Elbert, *A Message To Garcia* 24–6, 29
Huggins, Chuck 461
human capital 195, 619
human capital management 896
Human Relations philosophy 183–4 (t2)
human resource (HR) function 200–1, 202, 203, 279
human resource management 726
  China 136–7
  scientific management 175, 176
human resources 516, 517
  outsourcing 276–7

Human Resources Model 183–4 (t2)
human rights 150, 151, 156, 157–8
Humana 204
Humer, Franz 757
humor in the workplace 212–16
hygiene factors 228

IBM 7, 8, 114, 207, 225, 276, 277, 348–9, 363, 375, 381, 577, 578–9, 667, 718, 719, 763–4
Ibuka, Masaru 195, 291, 294
ICI 47
iCoupon 874
Ide, Nobuyuki 199
Idealab 618
ideas 587–93, 650–3
identity 16
IKEA 268
Imai, Masaaki 316
Immelt, Jeffrey 10, 206, 770
incubator **618**
India 94
Indian restaurants 645–6
individual autonomy 194
individualism 15–18
industrial action 306
industry analysis 80
information 551, 586, 608–14 (f6, t1)
information technology 190, 196–7, 279, 571, 581–6, 718
innovation 83, 191, 231, 544–5, 549–51, 575–80, 817–18, 938
innovative management 278
Inoue, Bunzaemon 291
INSEAD 12, 629
instant messaging 859
intangible assets 20–2
integrated organization 513–18
integrated risk management 452
Intel 89, 114, 142, 528, 534, 578, 578–9, 617, 818, 962
intellectual capital **618–20**
intellectual property 138, **620**
interim management **229–30**
internal communications 10
International Council on Human Rights Policy 156, 157–8
international firm 158
International Health Insurance 375–6, 381

International Monetary Fund 125
international public policies, and transnational corporations 151–2, 155–7
internationalization 715
internet 22, 23, 162, 190, 351–2, 366–70, 399–400, 423, 509, 550, 560, 583, 615–18, 694, 819, 848, 877–8, 1049
intranet 197
investment, economic multiplier effect 125
Ishag, David 628
Ishikawa, Ichiro 292
ISO 9000 standards 323
ISO 14001 standards 151
ISS 63
ITT 565
Ivester, Douglas 204, 205

Jackall, Robert 660–1
Jaques, Elliott **230–1**
   The Changing Culture of a Factory 231
   The General Theory of Bureaucracy 231
Jaedicke, Robert 792
Japan 108, 110, 142, 145, 165–6, 227, 255, 279, 291–2, 293, 294–6, 312, 313, 314, 315, 316, 317, 322, 822, 913–14, 969, 985
   Federation of Economic Associations 291–2, 298
   Japanese Union of Scientists and Engineers 292, 298
Jenkinson, Angus 872–3
JetBlue 268
job security 142, 186, 894, 911
Jobs, Steve 207, 268, 967
Johansson, Leif 714
John Lewis Partnership 523
Johnson & Johnson 138, 688, 695, 1016
Johnson, H. Thomas 260–1
Jones, Alan 504
Jones, Edward 777–80
Jonson, Ron 268
Jordan, Michael D. 1046
Joseph, Adrian 467
Joy, Bill 535
Juliber, Lois 771
Jung, Carl 882–4
Juran, Joseph 298, 312, **314–15**, 323
   Planning for Quality 314
   Quality Control Handbook 298, 314
   Quality Planning Road Map 298

just-in-time (JIT) 315–16

Kahn, Herman 112
kaizen **316–17**
Kakabadse, Andrew 276, 278–80, 911–12
kanban 315–16
Kanter, Rosabeth Moss 226–7, **231–2**, 734, 846–9
   Change Masters 227, 231, 848
   Commitment and Community 846
   Men and Women of the Corporation 231, 847
   World Class 848
Kaoru, Ishikawa 299
Kaplan, Robert 101, 260–1, 347, 939
Karigaard, Rich 511
karoshi 914
Kato, Takeo 291
Kawasaki Heavy Industries Group 315
Kay, John 593
Kearney, Lynn 860–1
Keegan, John 669
Keenan, Roger 967
Keirsey Temperament Sorter 883–4
Kelleher, Herb 207, 504, 963, 1019
Kendrick, Jonathan 531
Kett, Joseph 664
Keynes, John Maynard 474
KFC 139
Kidder Peabody Bank 664
keiretsu 279
Kiersey, David West 883
Kim, W. Chan 819–20
Kimberly–Clark 736
Kingdon, Matt 627
Klein, Naomi, *No Logo* 123
Kleiner, Art, *The Age of Heretics* 113
Knight, Peter 761, 858, 860
Knight, Phil 652
knowledge 8, 22, 194, 531–6, 539–40, 541–2, 575, 576, 601–3, 618–20, 621
   tacit 594, 597 (f3), 598, 599 (f5) 604, 1007
knowledge economy, strategy 96–9
knowledge management 604–5, 619, **620–2**
knowledge markets 22
knowledge workers 21, 619
Kobayashi, Koji 292
Koch, R. 447
Kodak 299, 318
Kopper, Michael 792

Kotler, Philip 337, 350–3, 424, **425**
   Marketing Management 425
Kotter, John 840
Kozlowski, Dennis 679
Kramer, Roderick 632
Kruger, Barbara 16
Kumar, V. 470
Kurtzman, Joel 1023
   Thought Leaders 1023
Kwik–Fit 403, 406, 1046
Kyoto Protocol 152

labor costs, China 1236
Lacity, Mary 318
Lafarge 137
Lafley, A.G. 768
Lagges, J.G. 826
Lam, James 452
Lan & Spar Bank 50
Lancaster, Graham 869
Landler, Mark 26
Lane, Kathy 583–4
language 541–2
languages, knowledge of 143–5
Lanning, Michael J., *Delivering Profitable Value* 401
Lasorda, Tommy 6
Latin, Dave 197
laughter 212–16
law, and the war business 672–3
Lay, Kenneth 793, 795, 797, 798
leadership 193–203, 733–810
   Colin Powell compared with Enron 790–800
   development programs 770–1
   qualities required 514, 755–60
   recruitment 765, 768–9
   role models 745–54 (t1, t2)
   value leadership 780–3
lean production **317–18**
lean thinking 255
learning 7–8, 13, 750, 752
   blended 1007
learning culture 187
learning curve 106
learning organization 8, 187, **1021–2**
Leeson, Nick 664
Lego 1047–8
Leiter, Michael P. and Maslach, Christina, *The Truth About Burnout* 911

Lev, Baruch 21
Lever Hindustan 560
Levitt, Ted 191, **425–6**
 'Marketing myopia' 425–6
Levy, Alain 758
Lewin, Kurt 835, **1022–3**
Lewis, Marc 874
Lewis, Richard, *When Cultures Collide* 709
life expectancy (corporate) 13
Lloyds–TSB 346, 498, 852
lobby groups 694
lobbying governments 151–2
Loewe, Raymond 275
logic 221
logistical variety and complexity, law of 251, 254 (f2)
logistics 249–50
 Seven Laws of 251–7
 see also supply chain management
Londe, Bernard La 320
London Business School 637, 654
London Stock Exchange 931–2
Loose, John 747–8
loyalty *see* corporate loyalty; customer loyalty
loyalty programs 339, 394, 397–8
Lucent 576–7
Lyons, Laurence 740

MacArthur, General 291
McCarthy, E. Jerome 424
McCormack, Mark 730
McDonald, Malcolm 869
McDonald's 403, 677, 725–6, 934, 935
McGrath, John 345, 1044
McGregor, Douglas 240, 243–4, 1023
 The Human Side of Enterprise 243
Machiavelli, Niccolo **916–17**
McKenna, Christopher, *The World's Newest Profession* 87–8
McKenna, Regis
 Relationship Marketing 428
 The Regis Touch 427
Mackey, John 651–2
McKinsey & Company 200, 533, 537, 618, 1023
McKinsey Global Institute 1023
McKinsey Quarterly 1023
Macnamara, Robert 41
McNealy, Scott 503, 540

macro drivers 448
Maersk Sealand 720
Maes, Patti 616
Magil, W.S. 291
Malcolm, Rob 348
management of production 137–8
management reporting 417
management/managers
 appraisal 244–5
 competencies 181–3 (f1, t1)
 early management theory 175–7
 education/training 6, 189, 1007–8, 1009–11
 empirical studies 177–80
 global 141–6
 Human Resources Model 183–4 (t2)
 impact of organization changes 184–7
 notebook 924–5
 personal development 188, 189
 philosophies 183–4 (t2)
 relationships 199
 rewards 188
 role 6, 107, 180
 as stakeholders in mergers and acquisitions 67–8
 structures 912
 styles, HOT Management™ 920–8
managerial grid **232–3**
Manhattan Project 802–3
March, James 544
Marconi 1050–1
Marcos, Javier 519, 520
Marcus, Barnard 206
market capitalization 468
market growth, and strategic logic grid 814 (f1), 815–17 (f2)
market segmentation 358
market structure, factors determining 43
market-facing organizations 354–61
marketing 326–431, 866–76
 4Ps 327, 328, 353, **424**
 affiliate marketing **423–4**
 China 138
 compared with selling 426
 global 366–70
 hard edged 336–49
 impact of Internet 351–2
 mental models 327–35
 permission marketing **426–7**

marketing (*continued*)
  relationship marketing **427–8**
  return on investment 465–7
  skills required 348–9
  use of financial ratios 465–78 (f5–f7)
  see also advertising
marketing mix 424
Markides, Costas 556
Marks & Spencer 242, 378–9
Marriott International 402, 403, 717, 718, 719
Martin, Lynn 885
Maslow, Abraham
  Hierarchy of Needs **233–4**
  Motivation and Personality 233
matricing 357
Matrix model **567–8**
Matsushita, Konosuke 227
Matsushita, Masaharu 291
Mattel 385–6, 967
Mauborgne, Renée 556, 819–20
Mayo, Andrew, *The Human Value of the Enterprise* 21
Mayo, Elton **234–5**
Mayo, John 1050, 1051
Mazur, Laura 341
MBAs 6, 534, 629–30
MCI 525
measurement, performance *see* performance measurement
Media Neutral Planing 872
Mehrabani, Mostafa 585
mentoring 188, 194–5, 1010, 1012–18
Mercury 841
mergers and acquisitions 63–70, 724–7, 824–33 (f3 – f5, t1)
Merrill Lynch 374
message fatigue 866–7
metanational company, concept of 160–3
metrics 641
Mexican CEMEX 535
Meyer, Aubrey 126
Micklethwait, John 721–3
micro drivers 448
Microsoft 17, 21, 114, 504, 533, 545, 547–54 (f2, f3) 628, 665, 748–9, 819, 863, 964
military contracting 671
Military Professional Resources Inc 671
mindset, common 831, 832

Minnesota Importance Questionnaire (MIQ) 887
Mintzberg, Henry 6, 44, **106–8**, 561–2, 738
  The Nature of Managerial Work 107, 178–9
mission statement 421
MIT 616, 857, 1021
Mitchell, Colin 404
Mitsubishi 123
Modruson, Frank 582
Moeller, Kim 512
Mondragon 16
Monks, Robert A.G. 699–701
Monsanto 329, 852
Montgomery, Cynthia 12
Moore, Geoff 588
Morita, Akio 165, 291, 294–5
Morrison, Jasper 268
motivation 34, 182, 228–9, 232, 235, 243–4, 279, 627, 830, 1008, 1010
Motorola 138–9, 504, 534, 540, 621
Moulton, Jane 232–3
multinationals 118, 167, 567, 667–8
Munger, Charlie 458
Munjal, Brijmohan Lal 651
Murrin, Kris 627
Myers, Isabel Briggs 882–3
Myers–Briggs Type Indicator (MBTI) 882–3, 977
mySimon.com 615

Nagarajan, Rajan 584
Nagayama, Satoshi 913–14
Nagel, Goldman, Steven L. and Preiss, Kenneth, *Agile Competitors and Virtual Organizations* 562–3
Naisbitt, John 622
Nalasone, Robert 204
Nalebuff, Barry 588
Nardelli, Robert 206
Nash, John 104, 588
Nash's Equilibrium 104
Nashua Corporation 299
Nasser, Jac 1045–6
national business system 131
National Health Service, Laughter Clinic 213
National Training Laboratories for Group Dynamics 1023
NBC 292–3, 313
NCR 64

needs, Hierarchy of Needs **233–4**
Neslon, C.A. 826
Nestlé 694
Netherlands 143
networking 189, 505–12, 732
networks 190, 551–2
Neumann, John von 103
New Economics Foundation 125
New York Times 620
Nike 82, 122, 331, 543, 652, 677, 694, 876
Nissen, Richard 739
Nokia 7, 138, 143–4, 150, 157, 161, 267, 268, 272, 533, 543, 548, 577, 655
non-coercive thinking 221–4
non-executive directors, conflicts of interest 665
non-governmental organizations (NGOs) 694
Northern Regional Management Centre 181–2
Norton, David 347, 939
Norton, David & Kaplan, Robert, *The Balanced Scorecard ...* 101
Norway 143
Novak, David 864–5
Nozick, Robert 221–4
  Anarchy, State and Utopia 223
  Invariances: the structure of the objective world 221
  The Nature of Rationality 221

Obeng, Eddie 509, 731
objectives 330, 670–2
OECD, Guidelines on Multinational Enterprise 123
Ogha, Norio 269
Ogilvy, David 334
Ogilvy, Jay 506
Ohio State Studies 746
Ohmae, Kenichi 165–7, 295
  The Mind of the Strategist 296
  Triad Power 167
Ohno, T. 255
Ollila, Jorma 143–4, 267
Omi, Hanzou 291
one-to-one marketing 372
online auctions 23
open planning 872–3
operational decisions 968

operational efficiency 82
opportunities 651–2
Opsvik, Peter 644
organizational culture 612
organizational democracy 521–30
organizational environment 54–5
organizational politics 525–7
organizational structure 565–6, 567
organizational transformation 42
organizational values 887–8
organizations
  brand management 355, 356
  charismatic 571
  federal 559, 566, 569
  functional 355, 356
  geographic 354, 355–6
  market-facing 354–61
  product-focused 355, 356
  rational-legal model 571
  SBU 355, 356
  shamrock organization 566, **568–70**
  structures 354–7
  virtual **570–1**
Oshima, Ichori 914
Otellini, Paul S. 962
Oticon 528–9
Ouchi, William, *Theory Z* 295
Ounch, Maurice 661
outsourcing 14, 185–6, 188, 276–7, 278–80, 305, **318**, 611, 614 (t1)

P&G 578, 579, 768
Packard, David 235, **235–6**, 966
Pagell, Ruth 857
Palm 549
Pareto's Law 254
Parker, James 207, 963
partnering 549
partnership 542–3
Pascale, Richard **108–9**, 113, 562, 590, 807
  Managing on the Edge 108, 1036
  Surfing the Edge of Chaos 538
Pascale, Richard and Athos, Anthony, *The Art of Japanese Management* 108, 113, 295, 591
patent 620
Patrick, John 859
pay 742, 896
payback 467

PDA 652
Peddy, Shirley 1017
Pemberton, Carole, *Strike a New Career Deal* 230
Peng, Li 130
Penrose, Edith 44
Pentacle 509
Peppers, Don 202, 337
PepsiCo Inc 229–30
performance analysis 942–3
Performance Enhancement and Response Team (PERT) 954
performance management 709
  employees 920–8
performance measurement 260–5, 831, 938–44 (f1, t1–t2) 947–50
Performance Measurement Record Sheet 941 (t1)
Performance Planning Value Chain 263
performance prism 938, 940
performance-based rewards 920, 921, 926–7
Perkins, Anthony 511
Perla, Michael 347
permission marketing **426–7**, 587–8
Perrier 311
personality tests 882–4
Peter, Laurence J. 807–8
  The Peter Principle 808
Peter Principle **807–8**
Peters, Susan 770, 771
Peters, Tom 113, **236–8**, 271, 537, 562, 628
  Thriving on Chaos 237
Peters, Tom and Austin, Nancy, *A Passion for Excellence* 237
Peters, Tom and Waterman, Robert, *In Search of Excellence* 108, 113, 236–7, 295, 568, 571, 590, 591, 592, 750, 1023
Pettigrew, Andrew, *The Awakening Giant* 47
philanthropy 687–8
Philip Morris 82–3
Philips 567
Phillips, Julien 590
Phillips-Jones, Linda, *Mentors and Protégés* 1012
Piech, Ferdinand 1052
Pine, Joseph 202
pitches 631–2
Pitfield, Michael 731
Pitman, Brian 346–7, 842

Pitney Bowes 205, 864, 865
planning 81
Platt, Lew 621
point-to-point transactions 367–8
political instability 120
Polkinghorn, Frank 291
Porras, Jerry 474
  see also Collins, Jim and Porras, Jerry
Porter, L.W. and Lawler E.E., *Managerial Attitudes and Performance* 182
Porter, Michael 48, **109–12**, 588, 592, 687, 1037
  Competitive Strategy 43, 110–11
  Five Forces Model 76, 110–11, 445, 451, 588
  generic strategies 111
  The Competitive Advantage of Nations 44, 111–12
portfolio matrix 43
positioning 331
post-entrepreneurial firm 231
Post-it Note 544
postgraduate courses 6
poverty 119–20, 123
Powell, Colin 790–800
Power, J.D. 266
Prahalad, C.K. 12, 91–5, 869
  Future of Competition 93
  see also Hamel, Gary and Prahalad, C.K.
Premier Oil 694
Pret a Manger 403, 404, 406
price transparency 367
price/earnings ratio 485–9
Priceline 332
pricing 331–2, 380–1, 409–13, 433–40 (f1, t1)
principles 659–66
Prisoner's Dilemma 103–4
privacy 867, 875, 876
Privacy and Electronic Communications Regulations Act (UK) 867
Private Finance Initiative 520
private military companies 671–2
Procter & Gamble 276, 332, 355, 577–8, 769
producer's surplus 337
product-focused organizations 355, 356
productivity, maximizing 20
Professional Pricing Society 440
profit margins 456

profits, and ethics 664–5
Project Underground 156
projects 188
  definition 282
  life cycle 284–9
  management 281–9, 953–8
  sourcing 186
  teams 357
  work breakdown structure (WBS) 286–8
Protzman, Charles 291
Prudential Assurance 1048–9
Prudential Financial 277
Prusak, Larry 22
psychological contract **238–9**
psychological ownership 525
Public Private Partnerships 520
public–private initiatives 641
punctuated equilibrium 837–9

quality 297–9, 312
quality circles **316–17**
quality management 315–16
Quanjude 139

R&D
  internal 575
  see also innovation
Rabobank 399
Radcliffe-Brown, A.R. 214–15
RainmakerThinking 894
Rappaport, Alfred 448, 498
rational mindset 524, 527
rational organization 524–5
Ratner, Gerald 215, 556
Rawl, Lawrence 311
Rayport, Jeffrey 616
Reader's Digest 966
RebusUK 277
recomposition 536–46, 540
recruitment
  board members 217–20
  executives 743
Red Cross 852
Red Herring 967
reengineering **319–20**, 587, 821–3, 896
Reform Club 505
Reh, F. John 26
Reichheld, Frederick 373, 404, 469
Reid, David 197

Reilly, Paul C. 741–4
Reinartz, Werner 470
relationship marketing **427–8**
relative cost position 309
remuneration, cafeteria benefits 229
reporting spans 912
reputation 611–12, 614 (t1) 677
resource drivers 495
resource-based analysis 44, 82–3
Responsible Care program 151
restructuring 226, 911, 914
return on equity 346
return on investment 456
  marketing 465–7
Reuters 717
Revans, Reg 588, 1008, 1019
  Developing Effective Managers 1019
Ricardo, David 44
rich/poor gap 119
Richardson, George 44
Ridderstrale, Jonas 11, 820
rightsizing 226
ringi 969
risk 610–11, 629, 973, 979
  China 131–2
  management 452–4, 677, 973
  seeking 932
Robeco Direct 396
Roberts Enterprise Development Fund 636
Roddick, Anita 759
Rogers, Martha 202
Romanelli, 838
Romer, Paul 19, 22–3, 266
Rongji, Zhu 131
Ross, Richard 586
Rotary International 153, 154–5
Rowley-Williams, Sally 453
Royal Bank of Canada 351
Rudkin, Daz 627
Ryanair 329

Sainsbury's 481
St Lukes 527
Sakkab, Nabil 578
sales, valuing 950–2
Samson, Danny, *Patterns of Business Excellence* 591
Sanders & Sidney 740
Sandvik 715

Santos, José 160–3
Sarasohn, Homer 291
Savage, Charles 20
Saxby, Robin 627
SBU organizations 355, 356
Scania 273
SCANS skills 885 (t1)
scenario analysis 222
scenario planning **112–13**
Schaik, Ray van 757
Schein, Ed 239, **239–41**, 1023
  Coercive Persuasion 240
  Organizational Culture and Leadership 240
Schey, Ralph 461
Schiltz 556
Schlesinger, Leonard A. 402
Schlumberger 50
Schneider, Peter 802
Schneiderman, Art 939–40
Schön, Donald 1007, 1020
Schrager, Ian 274
Schultz, Don 342–3, 875–6
Schultz, Howard 653
Schwab 367, 637
Schwartz, Peter 506–7, 508
  The Art of the Long View 113
Schwarzkopf, Norman 794
scientific management 20, 34, 175, 176, 322, 513
Sculley, John 207
Sears 943
Second World War 290–1, 312
secondments 188
self-awareness/self knowledge 194, 195, 880–91
self-confidence 987
self-efficacy 985–6
self-esteem 931
self-regulation 123, 150–1, 155–6
self-segmentation 869–71
selfishness 560
selling, compared with marketing 426
Selten, Reinhard 104, 588
Semco 537
Senge, Peter 7, 8, 1021
  The Fifth Discipline 1021, 1022
September 11th 119
service brands 401–7
service quality 402

Seven S framework 108, **113–14**, 590–1
shamrock organization 566, **568–70**
Shapiro, Benson 587
shared purpose 198
shareholder value 337, 340, 343, 344, 347, **497–8**, 513
shareholder value analysis 471–4, 477
shareholders 516–17
Sharman, Richard 452, 453, 454
Sharrock, Robert 731
Shaw, Robert 341
Sheffield 933
Shell 13, 112–13, 397, 560, 567, 655, 694
Shepard, Barry 273
Shewhart, Walter 290, 291, 312
Shih, Stan 528
short interval scheduling 587
Siemens 74, 83, 290–1, 344
Silicon Valley 162, 505, 534, 722, 966
Silver, Steve 351
Simons, Daniel 335
Simpson, George 1050, 1051
Singapore Institute of Management 180
Singh, Madan G. 968
single-loop learning 943, 944, 1007, 1020
Situational Model of Leadership 746
Six Pack Model 840–1 (f6)
Six Sigma program 58, 59, 60, 61
Skandia 604–5
Skilling, Jeffrey 792, 797
skills 884–5 (t1)
Skoll Foundation 636, 648–9, 857
Skoll, Jeff 647–9, 857
slack 308
Sloan, Alfred 89, 169, 567, 605
Slywotzky, Adrian 616
SMH 98
Smile 610
Smith, Adam **32–4**, 542
  The Wealth of Nations 20, 33–4
  Theory of Moral Sentiments 33
Smith, Darwin E. 736
Smith, Fred 767
Smith, Roger 555
social advertising 151
social enterprise 633–5, 638
social entrepreneurship 636–43 (f1) 647–9
social and environmental issues 150
social investments 158, 642

social responsibility 148–59, 848
social return on investment 641
socially responsible investment (SRI) 677, 694
Sonnenfeld, Jeff 765
Sony 165, 195, 199, 269, 294–5, 543, 548, 722
Soros, George 150
Sotheby's 663
soul 903–4
South Korea 822
Southwest Airlines 207, 213, 403, 768–9, 963, 1019
spam messages 866, 867
Spar, Jeff 585
Sparkes, Russell, *Socially Responsible Investment – A Global Revolution* 677
speculation 490, 492–3
speed, quality and accuracy, law of 251, 255
Spetner, Don 856
Stacey, Ralph, *Complexity and Creativity* 14
Stagg, Richard 507–8
stakeholder mapping 67
stakeholders 337, 340
Stalk, George and Hout, Thomas, *Competing Against Time* 321–2, 587
Standard Oil 575
Starck, Phillipe 268
Steel, Bob 199
Steelcase 719
STEP 445
Stern Stewart 44
Stewart, Rosemary, *Managers and their Jobs* 182
Stewart, Thomas 545
  Intellectual Capital: The New Wealth of Organizations 618–20
STMicroelectronics 161
Stokke 272–3, 644–5
strategic decisions 968, 969
strategic dialog 851–5
strategic improvisation 906–7, 909
strategic inflection point **114–15**
strategic innovation 55–6
strategic logic, and market growth grid 814 (f1), 815–17 (f2)
Strategic Management Journal 44
strategic philanthropy 687
strategic position 49, 50, 53

strategic thinking 295
Strategos Institute 508
strategy 39–116, 606, 851, 943–4, 953
  capabilities-based 594–600 (f1–f5)
  choosing 51–2
  definition 42
  development 51
  distinctive capabilities 45, 46
  fair process 98
  flows identified by Mintzberg 107–8
  as formal planning 75–6, 78, 80–2
  generating ideas 50–1
  Japanese businesses 166
  in knowledge economy 96–9
  as learning 77, 78, 81, 84
  as leverage 77, 78, 82–3
  maps 939, 940 (f1)
  matching capabilities to markets 45–6
  parameters 49
  as positioning 76, 78, 80
  reproducible capabilities 45, 46
  resource-based view 45
  as stretch 77, 78, 79
  and structure 87
  as SWOT 75, 78
  three Cs 166, 296
  value innovation 96–9
stress 523, 911, 912, 913, 914
stretch goals 79
Strickland, Bill 649
Strong, E.K. 888
Strong Interest Inventory (SII) 888
structural capital 619
structure-conduct-performance paradigm 43, 588
Stuart, Spencer 206
study of management 5
subcontracting 186
success 502–4, 1022
  improving on 983–93
  key factors 596
success maps 939, 940 (f1) 941
succession planning 204–9, **241–3**
Sull, Don 592
Sun Microsystems 503, 535, 540
Sunderland, John 348
Sunter, Clem 113
supervisors 897–9

supply chain
  law of asymmetry 251–2, 256–7
  management 249–59, **320–1**
  risk 300–8
  unlocking value 258
  volatility 251, 252–3
Survey of Interpersonal Values (SIV) 887
sustainability 157
sustainable corporate growth 383–6
Sweden 714–15, 874
Switzerland 143
Swords, Dominic 731
SWOT analysis 75, 78
Syfert, Scott 669
Symbian 548
systems thinking 14

T-Groups 1022–3
tactical decisions 968–9
Tapscott, Don 590
Target 268
Taylor, Bob 802
Taylor, Frederick 20, **34**, 175, 322, 587, 968
  Principles of Scientific Management 34, 175, 176
teamworking 977
technology 547–54, 570, 617, 621, 628–9
Teerling, Richard 274
teleworking 10
Tennant, Anthony 663
terrorism 119
Tesco 197, 201, 203, 333, 475
Texaco 311
texting 859
theories in use 1007
Theories X and Y **243–4**
Thermo Electron 827
Thoman, Richard 204
Thompson, Edmund 351
Thornton, John 198–9
Thrower, Neville 732
Tichy, Noel 274, 592
Timberland 543
time span of discretion 231
time-based competition **321–2**
Timmer, Jan 758
tipping point 819–20, 841
tobacco companies 157
Tobias, Randall 555, 865

Tobin, James 125
Tobin tax 125, 126
Toffler, Alvin **622–3**
  Future Shock 561, 622
  Powershift 623
  Third Wave 622
Tonna, Benjamin 886
Topel, Robert 226
Total Quality Management 317, **322–3**
Townsend, Robert **808**
  Further Up the Organization 808
  The B2 Chronicles 808
  Up the Organization 808
Toyoda, Kiichiro 317
Toyota 313, 315, 316, 317–18, 689–90, 693
Toys R Us 204
trademark 620
training 8, 404, 534, 534–5, 750, 892–3
  e-learning 1005–11
  see also executive coaching; learning
trajectory management 57–62 (f1–f3)
Tranfield, David 519, 520
transnational citizenship 148
transnational corporations 147–59, 167–9
  beneficial impacts 153–5
  corporate influence
    counteracting 157–9
  dangers 155–7
  economic power 148
  foreign aid 147, 149–50, 155, 156
  and international public policies 151–2, 155–7
Transparency International 664
transportation risks 304
triple bottom line accounting 641, 695
Triple I organization 566, 569
Trompenaars, Fons 169–71, 724–7
  Riding the Waves of Culture 170
Trompenaars, Fons and Hampden-Turner, Charles, *Mastering the Infinite Game* 170
Trout, Jack and Ries, Al, *Positioning Battle for the Mind* 362
Trouw 390
Truss, Lynne, *Eats, Shoots and Leaves* 859
trust 777, 806
Tube Investments 852
Tuck School, Dartmouth 6
Tucker, Albert 103
Tulgan, Bruce, *Winning the Talent Wars* 739

Turnbull Report 608
Turner, Ted 150
Tushman, 838
Tuvalu 120
Tzu, Sun **115**
   The Art of War 115

Ugarteche, Oscar 121
UN Environment Program 120
UN Global Compact 122, 123, 151, 697
Unilever 150, 152, 339, 355, 373, 621
United Artists 929, 930
UPS 404
USA 95, 142, 290, 292–3
   business philosophy 706–13
   Global Climate Coalition 152
Useem, Michael 318

Valentine, Deborah 857, 859, 860
value 340, 341
   creation 93–4, 346 (f2) 868–9
   destruction 346 (f2)
   enterprise value 945–52
   perceptions of 337
value chain, fragmentation 92
value innovation 96–9
value leadership 780–3
value-based management 344, 345, 348, 473, 497–8
values 9, 11, 563, 689–93 (F1, t1 & t2) 886–8
venture capital 618
venture harvesting 655
venture innovation 655
vertical integration 575
VerticalNet 368
Vicere, Albert 8
Vinnell 671
Vinson and Elkins 794
viral marketing 819
Virgin 528
Virgin Banking 374
virtual organization **570–1**
vision 295, 525, 805
Volkswagen 695, 1051–2
Volvo 523

Wacker, Watts 16
   The 500 Year Delta 645
Wakeham, Lord 665

Wal-Mart 73, 82, 83, 144, 256–7
Walsh, Paul 345, 1045
Walton, Sam 73, 83
war and the corporation 667–76
Wardell, Chuck 959, 963, 964
Warrilow, Clive 1052
Waterman, Robert 113, 590
   see also Peters, Tom and Waterman, Robert
Waterstone, Tim 626
Watkins, Sherron 793
Weber, Max **571–2**
   The Theory of Social and Economic Organization 572
Webvan 333
Weill, Sanford 663, 834
Weinstock, Lord 504
Welch, Jack 7, 10, 11, 13, 58–62, 206, 366, 473, 540, 588, 592, 605, 664, 665, 714, 770, 834, 858, 887–8, 1019
Wellcome 67
Westfield Group 208–9
Westinghouse 169
Wharton School, University of Pennsylvania 5
Wheeler, Steven 617
Wheeler, Steven and Hirsh, Evan, *Channel Champions* 310
Whitbread 841
White, Randall 730, 740
White, Randall and Hodgson, Philip, *Relax, It's Only Uncertainty* 629
Whitley, Richard 131
Whitman, Meg 768
Whole Foods 652
Whyte, William, *Organization Man* 605
Wilkinson, Lawrence 506
Willcocks, Leslie 318
Williams, Mitchell 21
Wilson, Carl 586
Wolf, Gregory 204
women, as corporate officers 539
Wooldridge, Adrian 721–3
Work Breakdown Structure (WBS) 954
work-out program 588
work/life balance 560
working hours 910
workplace violence 210–11
World Business Council on Sustainable Development 637

World Economic Forum 637
World Trade Organization 123, 124, 139
WorldCom 556, 665
Worldwide Retail Exchange 369–70
Worm, Manfred 978
Wozniak, Steve 967
Wright, Doreen 584
written communication 856–63

Xerox 52, 83, 204, 309, 322, 621, 717, 718, 719, 950–1
Xiaoping, Deng 127, 130

Yahoo! 162, 163, 549, 616
Yamaha 321
Young, Owen D. 1036
Yum!Brands 864–5

Zadek, Simon 156
   The Civil Corporation 695
Zafar, Roshaneh 649
Zara 535
Zemin, Jiang 130
Zook, Chris 383–6
   Profit from the Core 383